ISBN: 9781407675152

Published by:
HardPress Publishing
8345 NW 66TH ST #2561
MIAMI FL 33166-2626

Email: info@hardpress.net
Web: http://www.hardpress.net

A DICTIONARY OF
ENGLISH CHURCH HISTORY

EDITED BY

S. L. OLLARD, M.A.

Vice-Principal and Tutor of St. Edmund Hall, Oxford
Examining Chaplain to the Bishop of Worcester
and Hon. Canon of Worcester

ASSISTED BY

GORDON CROSSE, M.A.

New College, Oxford, and of Lincoln's Inn
Barrister-at-Law

WITH TWO MAPS

A. R. MOWBRAY AND CO., Ltd.
LONDON: 28 MARGARET STREET, OXFORD CIRCUS, W.
OXFORD: 9 HIGH STREET
MILWAUKEE, U.S.A.: THE YOUNG CHURCHMAN CO.

PREFACE

If any apology be needed for the publication of a Dictionary of English Church History, it is to be found in the fact that no work of the kind exists in English or in German. Never before probably have English historians been so numerous and so active as in the last thirty years, but the results of their researches are still chiefly contained in biographies, in series, and in isolated monographs. The object of this Dictionary is to embody a synthesis of these results so far as it can be obtained.

Such an object would have been unattainable without the help of many scholars. From the outset the idea of the Dictionary was approved and aided by those English bishops best known as Church historians —the present Bishop of Bristol (Dr. G. F. Browne), the late Bishop of Gibraltar (Dr. W. E. Collins), and the late Bishop of Salisbury (Dr. John Wordsworth). Illness unhappily prevented the Bishop of Bristol and the late Bishop of Gibraltar from contributing articles; while the late Bishop of Salisbury had completed only two of his promised articles when, to the heavy loss of English learning, he was removed by death.

The Dictionary is intended not so much for the scientifically trained historian as for the ordinary member of the English Church who desires to know the best ascertained facts in the history of the society to which he belongs. To attain this result in one volume compression and some omissions have been necessary. Yet, notwithstanding this, it is hoped that the broad features of the story have been covered. Any lack of proportion in treatment is due to the consideration that a subject admittedly obscure, when treated by an expert, demands more generous space than a subject already familiar, for which authorities are easily accessible. In fairness to the contributors, it should be said that many articles have been rigorously compressed owing to exigencies of space. It has not been thought necessary to insist on uniformity in the spelling of proper names as to which scholars of repute differ. References have been appended to most articles, designed not so much to justify the conclusions arrived at, as to direct the reader to fuller and more detailed treatment of the matter discussed.

The scope of the book is strictly that of the English Church, that is to say, the Provinces of Canterbury and York, and no attempt has been made to treat the history of the Church in Ireland and in Scotland and in America.

To one feature of the book attention may be drawn. In the list of the bishops of the various sees each appointment by Papal Provision has been specially marked. No complete list has hitherto been attempted. Dr. Stubbs in his *Registrum Sacrum Anglicanum* (2nd ed., 1897) records such Provisions intermittently, while Fr. Gams, O.S.B., in his *Series Episcoporum Ecclesiae Catholicae* (Ratisbon, 1875), gives a less complete and less accurate list. To Miss Dorothy Garrard, B.A. of the University of Manchester, who has revised the list of each see in this volume, these records owe their exactness.

Of the two maps included in this book that showing the English dioceses as they were until 1836 is a facsimile of the map issued with vol. vi. of the *Valor Ecclesiasticus* in 1834 by the Public Records Commission.

An Index has been added in order that the reader may be directed to the information on persons and subjects not separately treated.

I desire to express my most grateful thanks to the Ven. W. H. Hutton, Archdeacon of Northampton, who originally encouraged me to undertake the editing of this Dictionary, and who taught me my first lessons in English Church history; to the Rev. F. E. Brightman, Fellow of Magdalen College; to Mr. F. Morgan, Tutor of Keble College; to Dr. Darwell Stone, Principal of Pusey House; and to Dr. E. W. Watson, Regius Professor of Ecclesiastical History. To them I have frequently had recourse in the progress of the work, and on their learning I have made large demands. I am bound to mention specially a course of lectures by Dr. Watson on 'The Organisation and Revenue of the English Church' delivered in Hilary Term, 1911, to which this book owes much; while to Mr. Brightman I owe a heavy debt not only for the constant aid of his counsel and erudition, but also for his great kindness in reading and correcting the proof-sheets. These scholars are, however, in no way responsible for the ultimate form of any articles save those which they have signed. I have to thank my former pupil, Mr. Duncan Armytage, for help readily given; and the name of the Assistant Editor would occur before that of any other among these acknowledgments if it were not already printed on the title-page. On him has fallen a heavy share of the work, and without his aid I could not have performed my task.

S. L. OLLARD.

St. Edmund Hall, Oxford,
St. Matthew's Day, 1912.

CONTENTS

LIST OF CONTRIBUTORS

ASSINDER, G. F., M.A., B.C.L. St. John's College, Oxford, and of the Inner Temple.

BARNS, THOMAS, M.A. Keble College, Oxford; Vicar of Hilderstone.

BASKERVILLE, G., M.A., Lecturer, Librarian, and formerly Tutor of Keble College, Oxford.

BEECHING, Very Rev. H. C., D.D., formerly Exhibitioner of Balliol College, Oxford; Hon. D.Litt. Durham; Dean of Norwich.

BLACKIE, E. M., B.A. London; Rector of St. Paul with St. Barnabas, Edinburgh; Hon. Canon of Edinburgh.

BLAXLAND, BRUCE, M.A. Oriel College, Oxford; Vicar of Holy Cross, Shrewsbury.

BRIGHTMAN, F. E., M.A., Fellow and Tutor of Magdalen College, Oxford; Prebendary of Lincoln; Hon. D.Phil. et Litt. Louvain; Examining Chaplain to the Bishop of Oxford.

CAPES, W. W., M.A., Hon. Fellow of Queen's College, Oxford; Canon and Prebendary of Hereford.

CLARKE, C. P. S., M.A., formerly Scholar of Christ Church, Oxford; Vicar of High Wycombe.

CODRINGTON, R. H., D.D., Hon. Fellow of Wadham College, Oxford; Prebendary of Chichester.

CROSSE, GORDON, M.A. New College, Oxford, and of Lincoln's Inn.

DAVIS, A. C., B.A. St. Edmund Hall, Oxford.

DAVIS, H. W. C., M.A., Fellow and Tutor of Balliol College, Oxford; formerly Fellow of All Souls College.

DUDDEN, F. H., D.D., Fellow, Chaplain, and Lecturer of Lincoln College, Oxford; Examining Chaplain to the Bishop of London.

ELLIS, Miss DOROTHY M. B.

FIGGIS, J. N., M.A., Litt.D., Hon. Fellow of St. Catherine's College, Cambridge; of the Community of the Resurrection, Mirfield.

FISHER, J., B.D., formerly Scholar and Exhibitioner of St. David's College, Lampeter; Rector of Cefn, St. Asaph.

FOWLER, J. T., M.A., Hon. D.C.L. Durham; F.S.A., M.R.C.S.; Vice-Principal of Bishop Hatfield's Hall, Durham, and Hon. Canon of Durham.

FRERE, W. H., D.D., formerly Scholar of Trinity College, Cambridge; Superior of the Community of the Resurrection, Mirfield; Examining Chaplain to the Bishop of Winchester.

GAIRDNER, J., C.B., Hon. D.Litt. Oxford; Hon. LL.D. Edinburgh.

GEE, H., D.D. Oxford and Durham; formerly Scholar of Exeter College, Oxford; Hon. D.D. Aberdeen; F.S.A.; Master of University College, Durham; Examining Chaplain to the Bishop of Ripon.

GREEN, E. TYRRELL, M.A., formerly Scholar of St. John's College, Oxford; Professor of Hebrew and Theology, St. David's College, Lampeter.

GREGORY, Miss ELEANOR CHARLOTTE.

HERVEY, LORD FRANCIS, M.A., Senior Fellow of Hertford College, Oxford.

HUNT, W., M.A., D.Litt. Trinity College, Oxford.

HUTTON, Ven. W. H., B.D., Archdeacon of Northampton and Canon of Peterborough; Fellow and formerly Tutor of St. John's College, Oxford; Examining Chaplain to the Bishop of Rochester.

JAMES, M. R., M.A., Litt.D., Provost of King's College, Cambridge; F.S.A.; Fellow of the British Academy; Hon. LL.D. St. Andrews; Hon. Litt.D. Dublin.

JENKINS, CLAUDE, M.A., formerly Exhibitioner of New College, Oxford; Librarian of Lambeth Palace.

LACEY, T. A., M.A., formerly Exhibitioner of Balliol College, Oxford.

LAFFAN, R. G. D., B.A., formerly Scholar of Balliol College, Oxford; Fellow of Queens' College, Cambridge.

LARNER, H. M., M.A., formerly Scholar and Chaplain of Pembroke College, Cambridge; Rector of Busbridge.

LEACH, A. F., M.A., formerly Fellow of All Souls College, Oxford.

MACLEANE, D., M.A., formerly Fellow and Chaplain of Pembroke College, Oxford; Prebendary of Salisbury; Rector of Codford St. Peter.

MARSON, C. L., M.A. University College, Oxford; Vicar of Hambridge.

MONTGOMERY, Rt. Rev. H. H., D.D. Trinity College, Cambridge; Hon. D.D. Oxford; Hon. D.C.L. Durham; Secretary to the Society for the Propagation of the Gospel.

MORGAN, E. M.A., Tutor of Keble College, Oxford.

MORTIMER, E. C., B.A. St. Edmund Hall, Oxford.

OLLARD, S. L., M.A., formerly Scholar of St. John's College; Vice-Principal and Tutor of St. Edmund Hall, Oxford; Hon. Canon of Worcester and Examining Chaplain to the Bishop of Worcester.

OMAN, C. W. C., M.A., Chichele Professor of Modern History and Fellow of All Souls College, Oxford; Hon. LL.D. Edinburgh; Fellow of the British Academy.

ORD, CLEMENT, M.A., formerly Scholar of King's College, Cambridge; Lecturer at University College, Bristol.

PEILE, Ven. J. H. E., M.A., formerly Fellow of University College, Oxford; Archdeacon of Warwick and Rector of Great Comberton.

POOLE, A. L., B.A. Corpus Christi College, Oxford.

POOLE, R. L., M.A., Fellow of Magdalen College, Oxford; Ph.D. Leipzig; Hon. Fellow of the Royal Historical Society; Fellow of the British Academy; Hon. LL.D. Edinburgh; Keeper of the Archives of the University of Oxford.

PORTUS, G. V., B.A., B.Litt. New College, Oxford; formerly Lecturer in the University of Sydney, N.S.W.

PRESCOTT, Ven. J. E., D.D., formerly Fellow of Corpus Christi College, Cambridge; Archdeacon, Chancellor, and Canon of Carlisle.

PULLAN, L. M.A., Fellow and Tutor of St. John's College, Oxford.

RACKHAM, the late R. B., M.A., formerly Exhibitioner of Worcester College, Oxford; of the Community of the Resurrection, Mirfield.

READE, W. H. V., M.A., Tutor and Dean of Keble College, Oxford.

ROMANES, Mrs. G. J., of Pitcalzean.

RUSSELL, Rt. Hon. G. W. E., M.A., formerly Exhibitioner of University College, Oxford; Hon. LL.D. St. Andrews.

SANDERS, F., M.A. New College, Oxford; F.S.A.; Vicar of Hoylake.

SHAW, MARTIN, Director of Music at the Church of St. Mary the Virgin, Primrose Hill, N.W.

SKRINE, Mrs. M. J. H.

STONE, DARWELL, D.D. Merton College; Principal of Pusey House, Oxford.

USHER, R. G., Ph.D., Professor of History in the University of Washington, U.S.A.

WARREN, F. E., B.D. formerly Fellow of St. John's College, Oxford; F.S.A.; Hon. Canon of Ely; Rector of Bardwell.

WATSON, E. W., D.D., Regius Professor of Ecclesiastical History and Canon of Christ Church, Oxford ; Examining Chaplain to the Bishop of Lichfield.

WEBB, C. C. J., M.A., Fellow and Tutor of Magdalen College, Oxford.

WHITNEY, J. P., B.D., formerly Scholar of King's College, Cambridge ; Hon. D.C.L. Trinity College, Toronto, and Bishop's University, Lennoxville ; Professor in Ecclesiastical History, King's College, London.

WOODARD, A. L., B.A. Trinity College, Cambridge.

WORCESTER, Bishop of, Rt. Rev. H. W. Yeatman-Biggs, D.D., Hon. Fellow and formerly Scholar of Emmanuel College, Cambridge ; F.S.A.

WORDSWORTH, C., M.A., formerly Scholar of Trinity College and Fellow of St. Peter's College, Cambridge ; Prebendary of Salisbury ; Examining Chaplain to the Bishop of Salisbury ; Master of St. Nicholas Hospital, Salisbury.

WORDSWORTH, late Rt. Rev. J., D.D., Hon. Fellow of Brasenose College, Oxford ; Hon. LL.D. Cambridge and Trinity College, Dublin ; Hon. D.D. Berne ; Bishop of Salisbury.

WORLLEDGE, A. J., M.A., formerly Scholar of Gonville and Caius College, Cambridge ; Canon and Chancellor of Truro Cathedral.

WRIGHT, W. M., M.A., St. John's College, Oxford ; J.P.

ALPHABETICAL LIST OF CONTRIBUTORS' SIGNATURES

A. C. D.	Davis, A. C.
A. F. L.	Leach, A. F.
A. J. W.	Wortledge, A. J.
A. L. P.	Poole, A. L.
A. L. W.	Woodard, A. L.
B. B.	Blaxland, B.
C. C. J. W.	Webb, C. C. J.
C. J.	Jenkins, C.
C. L. M.	Marson, C. L.
C. P. S. C.	Clarke, C. P. S.
C. O.	Ord, C.
C. W. C. O.	Oman, C. W. C.
C. W.	Wordsworth, C.
D. M. B. E.	Ellis, Miss D. M. B.
D. M.	Macleane, D.
D. S.	Stone, D.
E. C. G.	Gregory, Miss E. C.
E. C. M.	Mortimer, E. C.
E. M. B.	Blackie, E. M.
E. R.	Romanes, Mrs. G. J.
E. T. G.	Green, E. T.
E. W. W.	Watson, E. W.
F. E. B.	Brightman, F. E.
F. E. W.	Warren, F. E.
F. H. D.	Dudden, F. H.
F. H.	Hervey, Lord F.
F. M.	Morgan, F.
F. S.	Sanders, F.
G. B.	Baskerville, G.
G. C.	Crosse, G.
G. F. A.	Assinder, G. F.
G. V. P.	Portus, G. V.
G. W. E. R.	Russell, G. W. E.
H. C. B.	Beeching, H. C.
H. G.	Gee, H.
H. H. M.	Montgomery, Rt. Rev. H. H.
H. M. L.	Larner, H. M.
H. W. C. D.	Davis, H. W. C.
H. W.	Worcester, Bishop of.
J. E. P.	Prescott, J. E.
J. F.	Fisher, J.
J. G.	Gairdner, J.
J. H. F. P.	Peile, J. H. F.
J. N. F.	Figgis, J. N.
J. P. W.	Whitney, J. P.
J. T. F.	Fowler, J. T.
J. W.	Wordsworth, Rt. Rev. J., late Bishop of Salisbury.
L. P.	Pullan, L.
M. J. H. S.	Skrine, Mrs. M. J. H.
M. R. J.	James, M. R.
M. S.	Shaw, M.
R. B. R.	Rackham, R. B., the late.
R. G. D. L.	Laffan, R. G. D.
R. G. U.	Usher, R. G.
R. H. C.	Codrington, R. H.
R. L. P.	Poole, R. L.
S. L. O.	Ollard, S. L.
T. A. L.	Lacey, T. A.
T. B.	Barns, T.
W. H.	Hunt, W.
W. H. F.	Frere, W. H.
W. H. H.	Hutton, W. H.
W. H. V. R.	Reade, W. H. V.
W. M. W.	Wright, W. M.
W. W. C.	Capes, W. W.

.

LIST OF ABBREVIATIONS

A.C. . . . . . . Appeal Cases.
abp. . . . . . . archbishop.
Adm. and Eccl. . Admiralty and Ecclesiastical
           Cases.
al. . . . . . . aliter (otherwise).
Ambl. . . . . . Ambler's Reports.
Anglo-Cath. . . Anglo-Catholic.
Ann. Reg. . . . Annual Register.
app. . . . . . . appendix.
arch. . . . . . archaeological.
art. . . . . . . article.
A.-S. . . . . . Anglo-Saxon.
Ath. Cantab. . . Athenae Cantabrigienses.
Ath. Oxon. . . . Athenae Oxonienses.

B. Mus. . . . . British Museum.
B.N.C. . . . . . Brasenose College.
bdle. . . . . . bundle.
Bing. . . . . . Bingham's Reports.

c. . . . . circa.
C.C.C. . . . . . Corpus Christi College.
C.H. . . Constitutional History.
C.H.S. . . . . Church Historical Society.
C.J. . . Chief Justice.
C.M.H. . . . Cambridge Modern History.
C. Med. H. . . Cambridge Medieval His-
           tory.
C.Q.R. . . . . Church Quarterly Review.
C.S. . . . . . . Camden Society.
ch. . . . . church.
Ch. Ch. . . . Christ Church.
Ch. D. . . . Chancery Division.
Chron. . . . Chronicon.
Coll. . . . Collections.
cons. . . consecrated.
Cro. Car. . Croke's Reports of Cases in
           the Reign of Charles I.

d. . . . . died.
D.N.B. . . . . Dictionary of National Bio-
           graphy.
dep. . . . . . . deposed.

depr. . . . . . . deprived.
Dict. Hymn. . . Dictionary of Hymnology.
dio. . . . . . . diocese or diocesan.

E. and B. . . . Ellis and Blackburn's Re-
           ports.
E.H.R. . . . . English Historical Review.
eccl. . . . . . . ecclesiastical.
Eccl. and Mar. Ecclesiastical and Maritime
   Cas.   Cases.
ed. . . . . . . edited or edition.
Encyc. Brit. . . Encyclopaedia Britannica.
Eng. . . . . England or English.
Eng. Dict. . . English Dictionary.
Epp. . . . Epistolae, epistles.
Eq. . . . Equity.
Ex. . . . Exchequer.

Fasc. Ziz. . . . Fasciculi Zizaniorum.
Fr. . . . . . Frater (brother).

H.B.S. . . . . Henry Bradshaw Society.
H.E. . . . Historia Ecclesiastica.
H.L. Cas. . . House of Lords Cases.
Hagg. Con. . Haggard's Consistory Re-
           ports.
Hist. . . . . History, historical, historica.

Insts. . . . . Institutes.
Intro. . . . Introduction.

J.T.S. . . . Journal of Theological
           Studies.

K.B. . . . . King's Bench.

L. and P. . . . Letters and Papers.
L.R. . . . Law Reports.
L.T. . . Law Times.
Lib. . . Library.
Ld. Raym. . . Lord Raymond's Reports.

M.G.H. . . . Monumenta Germaniae His-
           torica.

Mem.	Memorial, Memorials.	Q.B.D.	Queen's Bench Division.
misc.	miscellaneous.	q.v.	quem vide (whom see).
mod.	modern.		
mod. rep.	modern reports.	R.S.	Rolls Series.
MSS.	manuscripts.	Raym.	Sir T. Raymond's Repor
		Regist. Sacr.	Registrum Sacrum A
N.E.D.	New English Dictionary.		canum.
N.S.	New Series.	Rep.	Reports.
nat.	national.	res.	resigned.
		Rob. Eccl.	Robertson's Ecclesiastic
(P.)	By Papal Provision.		ports.
P.	Probate.		
p.	page.	S.C.	Select Charters.
P.B.	Prayer Book.	Salk.	Salkeld's Reports.
P.C.	Privy Council.	Soc.	Society.
P.D.	Probate Division.	st.	statute.
P.S.	Parker Society.		
Parl.	Parliamentary.		
Patr.	Patrologia.	theol.	theology.
Pol. Hist. Eng.	Political History of England.	tr.	translated.
Phill. Eccl.	Phillimore's Ecclesiastical		
	Reports.	V.C.H.	Victoria County Histor
Q.B.	Queen's Bench.	W.R.	Weekly Reporter.

DICTIONARY OF
ENGLISH CHURCH HISTORY

A

ABBEYS (English). The abbeys for some nine hundred years played an important part in the religious, political, social, and economic history of England. But for the cataclysm of the sixteenth century there appears to be no reason why they should not have continued a useful existence up to the present time. Reforms were needed, and the system required readjustment, but that the abbeys were centres of idleness and vice has been refuted beyond question by recent research. An abbey was the home of a body of men or women living a communal life under rules, the main object of which was continual service of God, self-discipline, and work. All Religious Orders lived under the threefold vow of poverty, obedience, and chastity. Religious houses can be divided into four classes :—

1. The abbeys proper, *i.e.* monasteries practically independent of external control, which were ruled by an abbot. Abbots styled 'mitred' sat in the House of Lords. [PARLIAMENT, CLERGY IN.] But whether 'mitred' or not, they were great territorial magnates. (See B. Willis, *Mitred Abbies.*)

2. Priories and cells which were dependent on an abbey, to which they were attached as daughter houses. They were ruled by priors.

3. The great Augustinian priories, which were as powerful and influential as the abbeys, but subject to episcopal supervision.

4. The friaries, houses of the preaching or mendicant Orders of Friars (*q.v.*).

As all the Religious Orders were founded on the rule of St. Benedict either in a strict or modified form, so all the religious houses were built much after the same plan, with certain important variations.

As the type of an ideal abbey we take the magnificent remains of the Cistercian abbey of Fountains, near Ripon.

The abbey stood in its close or precincts surrounded by a wall with various postern doors. The great Gateway as main entrance was usually situated towards the south-west of the abbey church, and at right angles to the west front ; sometimes, however, as at Fountains, the great Gateway faced the west front. The Gateway was usually of considerable magnificence. The centre compartment of the lower stage was occupied by the main archway, large enough to allow access of a waggon, and had the porter's lodge at one side. The rooms above, and those adjoining the Gate-house, were often used as the Hospitium or Guest-house. At Fountains the Guest-house is a separate building of considerable size, lying between the main entrance and the abbey. Entering the Precincts, we see the façade of the great church at the northern end of the long western range of buildings. The church at Fountains, as was usual, stands on the north, so that the cloister court to the south of the nave might enjoy the full benefit of the sun. There are, however, numerous exceptions to this rule, as at Canterbury, Gloucester, Malmesbury, and Tintern. Monastic churches, with the solitary exception of Rievaulx, were always orientated.

The nave of Fountains is true to the severe early Cistercian style. The west front, pierced at a later date by a large perpendicular window, was preceded by a porch or narthex (an unusual adjunct in England which occurs also at Byland and Holm Cultram). Above the great west window stands the now headless statue of the Virgin, to whom all Cistercian houses were dedicated. The long nave has eleven pointed Norman arches (1135-47), supported by massive cylindrical piers. There is no Triforium below the simple line of Clerestory windows. The original low central tower, in strict accordance with the rules of the order, gave place at a later date to the superb transeptal tower of Abbot Marmaduke Huby, when Cistercian idealism had given way to the pious opulence of successful sheep farming.

The original east end was like that still standing at Kirkstall, a short square-ended aisleless choir. In the thirteenth century Abbot John of York and his two successors built a Presbytery of five bays, and terminated their work by the eastern transept or

'Chapel of the Nine Altars,' found elsewhere only at Durham. Those who now admire the fine perspective of arch and column hardly realise how divided up was the interior of the great church. The Conversi or Lay Brothers used the nave as their church. The Rood screen, which stood against the seventh pillar from the west end, served as reredos to their altar.

The two entrances at the south-west corner of the south aisle gave access to the quarters of the Conversi—the one to their dormitory, the other to the Cellarium or vaulted rooms beneath their dormitory used as their day rooms. The aisles were divided from the nave by stone screens. The stalls of the Conversi were placed east and west, with their backs to these screens, as were those of the monks in the Choir. The Rood screen had two doors on each side of the altar (such as still stand in St. Alban's Abbey). These doors were required for the Procession on Sundays and Feast days. The round stones marking the various positions of the monks in this Procession are still *in situ* down the nave. The space between the Rood screen and the Choir screen or 'Pulpitum' acted as a kind of ante-chapel, used by sick and infirm monks. There were two altars here, one on each side of the Choir door.

The Choir or church of the monks extended beneath the central tower to one bay westwards. The monks had two entrances into their part of the church: the Cloister door, which opened from the eastern alley of the Cloister into the south aisle, and the night entrance at the southern end of the south transept, which by means of 'the night stairs' connected the Monks' Dormitory with the church. All vestiges of the wooden screens have long vanished, but magnificent specimens of monastic stall work can be seen at Chester, Lancaster, and Christ Church, Hants.

After the church, the most important part of the abbey was the Chapter-house or 'Capitulum,' so called perhaps because a chapter of St. Benedict's rule was read in it daily after Terce. It was invariably built at the east side of the eastern alley of the Cloister. At Fountains it was separated from the south transept by a narrow chamber used as a sacristy or small library. The Chapter-house is a noble rectangular room built about 1150; eighty-four feet by forty-one, of six bays, divided by two rows of pillars into three vaulted aisles. It was entered from the Cloister. Against the east wall (except in the centre), and extending most of the length of the two side walls, are three stone benches,

rising one above another, for the monks. There are several tomb slabs of the abbots here. The rectangular form of Chapter-house divided by pillars appears to have been the usual Cistercian plan, the octagonal one at Margam being quite exceptional. Adjoining the Chapter-house on the south is the Parlour, where necessary conversation might be carried on, for silence was strictly enjoined in the Cloister. The Parlour was entered from the Cloister. Immediately to the south of the Parlour is a passage leading from the east alley of the Cloister to the Infirmary and Abbot's Lodging.

In the south-east corner of the Cloister is the entrance by a staircase to the Monks' Dormitory or 'Dorter.' This was a room one hundred and sixty-five feet long extending from the south transept over the Chapterhouse and Parlour, and on over a long vaulted basement to the south. At right angles to this southern end of the Dorter, and extending ninety-two feet east, was the 'Rere dorter.'

In the southern alley of the Cloister were three important rooms: the Calefactorium or Warming-house, the Refectorium or Frater, the Coquina or Kitchen. The Warming-house is a fine room with a stone vault supported by a central pillar, and with two enormous fireplaces. Over it is a stone-vaulted chamber, probably the Muniment-room. To the west of the Warming-house, and in the centre of the southern walk of the Cloister, stands the entrance to the Frater or Dining-room. On each side of the door are the remains of the Lavatory, often a feature of great beauty. In Cistercian abbeys the Frater instead of standing east and west against the Cloister, as in Benedictine, Cluniac, and Augustinian Canons' houses, stands north and south, with its ends only against the Cloister. Sibton and Cleeve are the only exceptions to this rule. At Fountains the Frater is a grand room built about 1200, one hundred and ten feet long by forty-six broad, lighted by tall lancets. It had a central arcade of five arches carried by four round pillars. The roof was of wood and of two wide spans with high gables. Besides the entrance from the Cloister there were openings into the Warming-house on the east and two in the west wall, the one to the Kitchen, the other to the wall pulpit, now a complete ruin. In the Frater at Beaulieu, now used as the parish church, is a fine example of such a pulpit. Against the south wall of the Frater, and extending down three-fifths of the side walls, are broad platforms, on which stood the tables of the brethren. At the end was the high table.

The tables stood on curious stone posts, good examples of which have recently been unearthed at Bardney. The service door or hatch from the Kitchen shows signs of an ingenious circular table, five feet in diameter, which would have several shelves. The Kitchen adjoined the Frater on the west, as was the Cistercian rule, possibly to bring it into direct communication with the Cloister, since Cistercian monks themselves acted as cooks. It was entered from the Cloister by a plain round-headed door. The fireplaces instead of being against the walls were placed back to back in the centre. As the remains of these fireplaces had almost disappeared, this room was mistakenly called the Buttery, and the Warming-house the Kitchen.

The western side of the Cloister at Fountains, as in all Cistercian houses, was occupied by the Cellarium or Cellarer's Building. It consists of two vaulted alleys three hundred feet long, supported by a long line of central pillars. This superb vista much impressed Montalembert. This block was for the accommodation of the Conversi. Their Frater and other offices formed the ground floors, whilst the upper floor acted as their 'Dorter.' These Conversi or Fratres Laici were practically monks who could not read. They had charge under the Cellarer of the secular and external affairs of the monastery. They kept certain of the Hours in their own church (the nave), but as they could not read they substituted for the regular offices certain prayers and psalms, which they learned by heart. They were peculiar to the Cistercian order, but after the fourteenth century they seem as a class to have died out, and to have been replaced by hired servants. The northern alley of the Cloister, that abutting on the church, was usually divided up into studies or 'Carrels,' where the monks could study and transcribe.

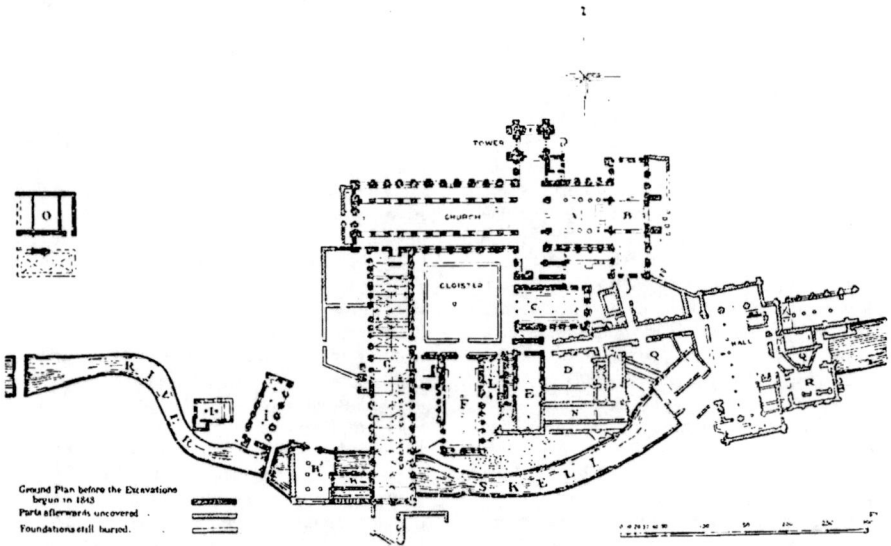

GROUND PLAN OF FOUNTAINS ABBEY

REFERENCES TO PLAN

A. Presbytery.
B. Nine Altars.
C. Chapter-house.
D. Yard.
E. Store-house, with Monks' Dorter over.
F. Frater.
G. Cellarium (formerly known as the Great Cloister), over which was the Dorter of the Lay Brethren.
H. Infirmary of Lay Brethren.
I. I. Guest-houses.
K. Garderobe or Necessarium.

L. Warming-house, over which is now the Museum.
M. Prisons.
N. Great Garderobe or Necessarium.
O. West Gate-house.
Q. Q. Ash-yards.
R. Kitchen of Infirmary.

N.B.—The Great Hall, to which this last building belongs, is the Infirmary, formerly supposed to be the Abbot's Hall. The Infirmary Chapel is just east of the middle of the hall.

The Infirmary or ' Farmery ' was not only the hospital for the sick, but also the abode of infirm monks or those who had been professed fifty years. It was a very important feature of every abbey. At Fountains there were two : one for the Conversi, situated to the south-west of the Cellarium ; and another for the monks at some little distance south-east of the church. The remains show that it was a splendid thirteenth-century hall, with chapel, kitchen, and offices.

The Abbot's House was placed between the Infirmary and the Monks' Dorter. A long covered passage connected the Abbot's Lodging with the east end of the church, and another connected the Infirmary with the south-eastern corner of the Cloister. There were besides a malt-house, a brew-house, and a mill (the latter still in use). The system of drainage was thorough and complete. The size of monastic drains has often given rise to the silly tales of underground passages to the nearest castle or nunnery, miles away.

Such, then, was an ideal abbey. It was almost a little town or village in itself, and contained and provided for all its own requirements.

The evidence for pre-Saxon monasticism is slight. There were certainly monasteries in Sussex and Devon, and historical criticism has still to prove that the stories which cluster round Glastonbury (q.v.) are mere legends. Soon after the conversion of the English abbeys arose, especially in the east and north, whose names are familiar in Church history : Hexham, Lindisfarne, Lastingham, Ripon, Whitby, Bardney, and Ely. These early Saxon monasteries appear to have contained the Missionary College, Clergy-house, and Sisterhood all in one, and were often ruled by a great lady, as St. Hilda (q.v.) at Whitby, or St. Etheldreda (q.v.) at Ely. This arrangement, when the first religious fervour somewhat cooled, had disadvantages, so we find St. Wilfrid (q.v.) at Ripon, and his friend Benedict Biscop (q.v.) at Wearmouth and Jarrow, trying to introduce the rule of St. Benedict, not, however, with success, and the Saxon style of comfortable country-house monasticism continued to flourish. In 734 Bede (q.v.) deplores the circumstances which led men to seek the tonsure instead of the exercise of arms. His warnings were fulfilled by the success of the Danes. In some cases the founder of a double monastery for men and women took over the charge of the men, often quite young relatives without any vocation, whilst his wife presided over the women. St. Aldhelm (q.v.) mentions gay young nuns dressed in purple or scarlet, trimmed with fur, who habitually used curling tongs. Even St. Edith of Wilton, whose piety is beyond question, startled good Bishop Aethelwold by the gaiety of her attire. Under these circumstances the wonder is not that there were scandals, but that they were comparatively few. King Alfred (q.v.) found it difficult to gather men with a vocation, and therefore imported foreign monks to fill his new foundation of Athelney.

In 959 Glastonbury and Abingdon alone maintained a semblance of true conventual life. In 960 St. Dunstan (q.v.) made a determined effort to restore the rule of St. Benedict, seconded by his pupil Aethelwold, Bishop of Winchester, and Oswald, Bishop of Worcester. During this period certain of the old secular cathedral foundations became monastic, and many abbeys destroyed by the Danes were restored, as Ely, Peterborough, and Crowland. Of the buildings of these Saxon houses practically nothing remains except small portions of their churches. At Ripon and Hexham interesting crypts survive. Parts of the Saxon abbey churches exist at Jarrow, Wearmouth, and Deerhurst.

The Norman Conquest inaugurated a great revival of monastic life. The introduction of foreign Churchmen by William led to the adoption of higher Continental ideals. The old Benedictine houses were rebuilt on a scale of unprecedented splendour : Durham, Gloucester, Winchester, Peterborough, Ely, Norwich, Bury, and St. Albans were among the finest Romanesque churches in the world, with their vast naves, apsidal chancels, and solemn central towers. Besides the rebuilding of these ancient shrines, new abbeys arose : Battle and Selby, founded by the Conqueror, and Shrewsbury by Roger de Montgomery, his lieutenant at Senlac. Other houses, like Lindisfarne and Bardney, arose once more from their ruins. The eleventh century was for the Benedictine order what the twelfth century was for monasticism as a whole, the Golden Age. Other great Benedictine monasteries were Canterbury, Rochester, Westminster, Chester, Tewkesbury, Malvern, Worcester, Pershore, Malmesbury, and Bath, the churches of which survive in whole or part. Glastonbury and St. Mary's, York, are only beautiful fragments, whilst Reading, Colchester, Ramsey, Evesham, and Abingdon have practically disappeared.

The Cluniacs, introduced eleven years after the Conquest, established a famous priory at Lewes. Of the great church, one of the finest in the country, hardly a vestige remains. They were never popular, and their houses did not exceed thirty-five in number. Castle Acre and Wenlock are their best preserved priories. Wenlock has remains of a thirteenth-century church four hundred feet long, ruins of a Norman chapter-house, portions of a unique octagonal twelfth-century lavatory, and an almost perfect example of a prior's house.

In 1128 the Cistercians were introduced into England by William Giffard, Bishop of Winchester, who built their first abbey at Waverley. The Abbot of Rievaulx (founded 1131) became the head of the Order in this country. They were the Puritans of their age. Their rule enjoined strict simplicity in buildings and ornaments. Their houses had to be situate *in locis a conversatione hominum semotis*, so we find the ruins of their exquisite churches hidden away in secluded valleys. Their very isolation, indeed, has saved them from the spoilers' hand. From 1130 to the middle of the thirteenth century the Cistercians spread far and wide. Their enthusiasm for building was in great degree responsible for the marvellous development of architecture during this period. One hundred abbeys arose to witness to the popularity of this order of pious sheep breeders. The Cistercian ruins mark particularly the period of transition from Norman to the early Pointed style. Fountains, Kirkstall, and Buildwas show the first signs of the coming change by the use of the pointed pier arch. Roche, Byland, and Jervaulx are examples of the transitional work of the later half of the twelfth century. The choirs of Rievaulx and Fountains are pure Early English. Netley and Tintern reach the Geometrical stage of the middle of the thirteenth century. The destruction of the thirteenth-century church of Beaulieu is an irreparable loss to architecture, as the plan shows a striking resemblance to Clairvaux, and, besides Croxden, it was the only Cistercian church with an apsidal ending. At the Dissolution all the churches of this Order were either destroyed or left to fall into ruins, the only exception being Holm Cultram, which was made parochial. Abbey Dore was restored to sacred uses in the seventeenth century after one hundred years of desolation.

The twelfth century saw also the rise of the Gilbertine order, founded by St. Gilbert of Sempringham (*q.v.*) in 1139. It was unique in its revival of the Saxon system of monks and nuns, sharing a common monastery, though rigorously separated. They had each a cloister, with its separ-

ate set of domestic buildings. The church, which was shared by both, was divided by a solid partition wall. The monks' rule was based on that of the Augustinians, and the nuns on that of the Cistercians. There were only twenty-five Gilbertine houses in the country, of which eleven were in Lincolnshire. The remains at Watton, near Driffield, give a good example of the curious plan of their abbeys. The church of Old Malton is a fragment of a Gilbertine church. There are also interesting remains of domestic buildings at Chicksands. The Carthusian Order came to England under Henry II., and was established at Witham, Somerset, under St. Hugh (*q.v.*). The extreme austerity enjoined by the rule of their founder, St. Bruno, seems to have deterred our forefathers from joining them. There were only nine houses in England. The Carthusians lived in solitude and silence. Each occupied a small detached cottage, standing in a garden surrounded by high walls, and connected by a common cloister. All met on Sundays and Feast days in the refectory. Their churches were small and without aisles. Mount Grace Priory in Yorkshire is the most complete example of their houses. Shene, with its cloister five hundred feet square, was one of their largest monasteries. The most celebrated Charterhouse was that in London, founded in 1371, and refounded as the famous school in 1611 by Sir Thomas Sutton.

The Canons Regular of St. Augustine, the 'Black Canons' or 'Austin Canons,' were regular clergy holding a middle position between the monks and secular canons, almost resembling a community of parish priests living under rule (that of St. Augustine of Hippo). The naves of their churches were often parochial, and so have often survived to this day. The prior's lodging was almost invariably attached to the south-west angle of the nave. This order came to England under Henry I., and quickly became the most popular of all. The head of an Augustinian house was almost always a prior. The naves of their churches were sometimes without aisles, as Kirkham, and sometimes had only one aisle, as Lanercost, Bolton, and Haughmond. The cathedral churches of Carlisle and of the two Tudor bishoprics of Bristol and Oxford were Augustinian priories. Other famous houses of this order were Waltham and Bridlington, whose huge naves still survive; of Thornton, Oseney, Walsingham, and Guisborough the scantiest fragments remain. St. Mary Overy (Southwark), St. Bartholomew's,

Smithfield, and Christ Church, Hants, still stand more or less complete.

The Premonstratensian order, a reformed branch of the Austin Canons (founded 1119 by St. Norbert), built their first house in England at Newhouse in Lincolnshire, 1143. They had thirty-four abbeys, of which Welbeck was the head. There are fine remains of their houses at Eggleston and St. Agatha's in Yorkshire, and at Bayham in Sussex. Their churches were often long and without aisles. 'Stern Premonstratensian Canons wanted no congregations, and cared for no processions, therefore they built their church like a long room' (Beresford Hope). The plan of the abbey of St. Agatha's is confusing by its irregularity.

With the coming of the friars in the thirteenth century the popularity of the abbeys waned. A *friary* was arranged on much the same plan as a small priory. The church was a long parallelogram unbroken by transepts. The vast hall-like nave provided the preaching space so necessary to their system. The cloister and domestic buildings were situated on the side of the church. Remains of their houses exist at Norwich, Gloucester, and Reading.

Cells such as St. Mary Magdalene, Lincoln, were the smallest of religious houses, and consisted of one long narrow range of buildings, terminating towards the east in a chapel.

The annual revenue of the various houses, including land and the proceeds from the spiritual benefices held by them, is reckoned by Speed at £171,312, 4s. 3½d. Nasmith reckons the total slightly higher. The annual value, therefore, of the eleven hundred and thirty monasteries and hospitals suppressed by the King must have been about £200,000, equal to £2,400,000 in present value (Blunt). [RELIGIOUS ORDERS.]

The houses raised since the revival of the religious life have been chiefly connected with sisterhoods. Religious brotherhoods are represented by the Cowley Fathers, the Benedictines of Caldey and Llanthony, and the Community of the Resurrection at Mirfield. [RELIGIOUS ORDERS, MODERN.] Their houses are mainly still in course of erection. The Church of the Society of St. John the Evangelist, Cowley, though of moderate dimensions, is a fine example of a simple conventual chapel. The sisterhoods rival the great Pre-Reformation Orders in the size and splendour of their houses. The chapel, refectory, kitchen, and cloisters of St. Margaret's Convent, East Grinstead (perhaps Street's finest design), form a superb group. The old traditional monastic plan forms the centre block, surrounded by vast ranges of buildings necessitated by the schools and orphanages which now form so important and useful an addition to the work of a modern sisterhood.

[W. M. W.]

ABBEYS Welsh. The history of monastic houses in Wales falls into two periods, roughly divided by the coming of the Normans. The earliest and most important house seems to have been that of Illtyd, 'of all the Britons best skilled in Holy Scripture, both the Old Testament and the New, as well as in every kind of learning, such as geometry, rhetoric, grammar, and the knowledge of all arts,' where Samson, afterwards Bishop of Dol, Gildas, Dewi, and even Maelgwn Gwynedd, were pupils. A little later Dewi founded his house—the modern St. David's—and, to mention only the most important, Dyfrig founded houses at Mochros and Henllan on the Wye, Cadog at Nantcarfan, Teilo at Llandaff, and Padarn at Llanbadarn. Similarly there were in North Wales Bangor Fawr, founded by Deiniol, its great offshoot, Bangor Iscoed on the Dee, Cyndeyrn's foundation, now St. Asaph, Cybi's at Holyhead, and that of Cadfan at Towyn. These early communities were characterised by an austere asceticism, and when this did not sufficiently mortify the flesh it was frequently the practice for saints to retire to eremitical seclusion in a cave or lonely island, such as Bardsey, Caldey, or Priestholm. Another feature of Celtic monasticism was manual labour, on which Dewi Sant and Gildas, as well as others, are said to have insisted. The Scriptures, too, were carefully studied, and much time was occupied in the regular services in the church, as in the later monasteries. The members of the community were admitted by a monastic vow, and the special virtues were humility, obedience, charity, and chastity. They dwelt within the sacred enclosure or 'llan,' apparently not in a single building, but in separate cells grouped around the church, the guest-house, and the other necessary out-houses. They were not, however, strictly confined to the precincts of the llan, but were despatched by the abbot on various missions, at first probably to spread the Gospel. In the time of the primitive Welsh laws there were two classes of church—mother churches and what may be called secondary churches. The former normally had an abbot (*abad*) and a community (*clas*), while in the latter there were only priests. The former were clearly monastic, and the clas was a closely bound community, receiving half of all payments to the church, succeeding to the movable property of the abad, and deciding all disputes among its members. By the tenth century Welsh monasticism was in decay: the early missionary fervour had died down: territorial and other endowments had crept in and brought with them wealth and luxury: celibacy had ceased to be observed: and in many cases monastic vocation had given way to hereditary claims, so much so that some abbots were laymen, as was the Abbot of Llanbadarn cited by Gerald de Barri (*q.v.*). There was in Wales, as in England, clear need of reform, but for some time after the Norman invasion the old Welsh monasticism subsisted. Bishop Bernard early in the twelfth century reformed the 'claswyr' of St. David's, and converted them into a body of canons; we hear of an Abbot of Towyn in 1147 and of Llandinam in the same century, and the memory of abad and claswyr at Llanynys survived even till the fifteenth century.

The coming of the Normans was of the nature of a crusade: they, with their religious minds and their love of order, did not appreciate the loose and—to them—vicious system of the Welsh monasteries, and at once began to found Benedictine houses, none of which can be traced prior to their arrival in Wales. The movement spread naturally from east to west, from Chepstow and Monmouth to Abergavenny, Ewias Harold, Brecon, Ewenny, Goldcliff, Llangennith, Kidwelly, and Cardigan. It is remarkable that all these Benedictine houses are in South Wales, this being due to the greater power of the North Welsh princes and their hostility to the new movement. Cluniacs were found only at St. Clears, but three Tironian houses were established in what afterwards became Pembrokeshire, at St. Dogmells, Pill, and Caldey. Augustinian canons were introduced by Bishop Bernard, who converted a cell at Carmarthen belonging to Battle Abbey into an Augustinian priory; another was set up at Haverfordwest, and a third in the wild and rugged solitudes of Llanthony, while later the old Welsh foundation of Beddgelert was appropriated by this Order. The Premonstratensians had one house in Wales at Talley, and that was founded and endowed by Welsh princes; in this way it forms a connecting link between the new monasteries founded by the Norman Marcher lords and the Cistercian abbeys which sprang up under the patronage of the Welsh princes. In 1144 the first Cistercian

community in Wales found a home at Little Trefgarn, near Haverfordwest, but soon moved to its future home at Whitland. In 1147 the amalgamation of the orders of Savigny and Citeaux brought Neath Abbey, founded in 1130, and Basingwerk to the Cistercians, who were in the same year given another house, at Margam, by Earl Robert of Gloucester. So far the foundations had been under Norman patronage, but the austere asceticism, the stern self-denial and the abstemiousness of the members appealed strongly to the Welsh, who saw in the plain, poor, and lonely houses something resembling the llans of the old Celtic saints. The Lord Rhys richly endowed Whitland. In 1170 a colony from Whitland was planted by Owain Cyfeiliog at Strata Marcella. In 1176 the abbey of Cwmhir was refounded by Cadwallon ap Madog; and a little later Ystrad Flur sent out its first colony, which settled at Caerleon or Llantarnam; while its second colony moved northwards and settled at Aberconway. Towards the end of the century the abbey of Cwmhir sent off a colony which, under the protection of Maredudd ap Cynan, found a home at Cymer; and in 1201 Madog ap Gruffydd established a community at Llyn Egwestl in Ial, which came to be known as Valle Crucis. It is curious that the two nunneries in Wales at Llanllyr on the Aeron, and at Llanllugan in Cydewain, were both Cistercian and both established by Welsh princes. The Knights Hospitallers founded a preceptory at Slebech in Pembrokeshire and a small house at Yspyty Ifan on the Conway. The thirteenth century saw a great development of the friars in Wales, as in England: Franciscans flourished at Carmarthen, Cardiff, and Llanfaes, the latter endowed by Llywelyn the Great; Dominicans were found at Haverfordwest, Brecon, Rhayader, Cardiff, Bangor, and Rhuddlan; and the Carmelites at Tenby, Denbigh, and Ruthin. Towards the close of the century Archbishop Peckham (*q.v.*), himself a friar, spoke in the highest terms of their work in Wales, but there, as elsewhere, they incurred the jealousy of seculars and monks; while the latter were themselves not united, for the Cistercians alone definitely threw in their lot with the Welsh princes. In Wales, as in England, monasticism played a great part, perhaps a greater part in Wales, which was in greater need of the civilising influence of the monastic institutions; thus in Wales the dissolution of the monasteries was especially disastrous. Not that the monastic houses in Wales were rich, for according to the *Valor Ecclesiasticus* (*q.v.*) only seven exceeded £150 in annual value, and not one exceeded £200 ; but their endowments, and those of other religious houses in England, had taken very largely the form of tithe, which otherwise would have been available for parochial incumbents. It is impossible to measure the value of the monasteries to Wales in religion, in literature, in history, in education, and in countless material services, but there is no doubt that the alienation of their endowments to laymen did irreparable harm to the Church in Wales. [ORDERS, RELIGIOUS.] [F. M.]

J. E. Lloyd. *A Hist. of Wales*: Bevan and Thomas, *Dio. Hist. of St. David's* and *St. Asaph*: Gould and Fisher, *Lives of the British Saints*: E. J. Newell, *Hist. of the Welsh Ch.*

ABBOT, George (1562-1633), Archbishop of Canterbury, was son of a Guildford cloth-worker, and entered Balliol College, Oxford, in 1578 ; became Master of University College, 1597. As Vice-Chancellor of Oxford, 1600, 1603, and 1605, he opposed the rising influence of Laud (*q.v.*). He was made Bishop of Lichfield and Coventry in 1609, and within a month translated to London, and in 1610 to Canterbury, though, according to Clarendon, he was 'totally ignorant of the true constitution of the Church of England, and considered the Christian religion no otherwise than as it abhorred or reviled popery.' Collier charges him with 'pro-phane indifference and remissness,' and Anthony Wood, who grants him an 'erudi-tion of the old stamp,' observes that Abbot's inexperience of the difficulties of parish priests 'was the reason (as some think) why he was harsh to them, and showed more respect to a cloak than a cassock.' He was of a morose and puritanical spirit, but his inflexible honesty was shown in the Essex nullity suit and his refusal to allow the *Book of Sports* to be read in Croydon church. He remon-strated with James upon the Spanish match, and constantly thwarted the King's wishes at the council board. But James respected him, and when the archbishop in 1621 accidentally killed a keeper with the cross-bow, did his best to extricate him from the canonical 'irregularity' which he had in-curred by this mischance. But he told Abbot that he owed his escape from seques-tration to Bishop Andrewes (*q.v.*), who would doubtless have succeeded him as archbishop. Coke and the lawyers, whose encroachments on the Church's rights he had firmly resisted, would have been pleased by his downfall. For a time he retired, for self-mortification, to the bede-house built by himself at Guild-

ford, but he resumed his functions before the death of James. He crowned Charles I., but was not in favour with that King, and the archiepiscopal authority was executed for a time by commission. Abbot's dis-affection to the ceremonial rules of the Church and his narrow divinity made his position a false one, and, though he was restored, his influence was at an end. He died, 5th August 1633, at Croydon, and was buried in the chapel of Our Lady, at Guildford, where his stately monument and his bede-house still remain.[1] He was a benefactor to Balliol College, and took part in the founding of Pembroke College, Oxford. His abiding title to remembrance, however, is as one of the translators of the four Gospels for the Authorised Version. [BIBLE, ENGLISH.] [D. M.]

S. R. Gardiner, *Hist. Eng.*; *D.N.B.*; Wood, *Ath. Oxon.*

ADRIAN IV., Nicholas Breakspear, Pope (d. 1159), the only Englishman to attain that eminence, was born at Langley, near St. Albans, where his father, a man of small means, became a monk while Nicholas was still a boy. According to one tradition, the future Pope was reduced to beg for alms at the abbey gate ; another relates that he applied for admission as a novice, but was rejected on the ground of illiteracy. His authentic history begins with his departure from England. He roamed through France begging his bread, entered Provence, and settled at Arles as a student. His education completed, he became a canon regular in the house of St. Rufus, near Valence. Here he established a reputation for learning and eloquence ; in 1147 he was elected abbot. A quarrel with his canons, who appealed against him to Rome, brought him into personal contact with Eugenius III., who, recognising his merits, created him Cardinal Bishop of Albano (c. 1150), a dignity which involved residence at Rome. In 1152 Nicholas was sent as legate to Scandinavia to reorganise the Swedish and Norwegian Churches, hitherto subjected to the Danish archbishopric of Lund. He fulfilled his com-mission with conspicuous ability, though the dissensions of the Swedish clergy made it impossible to give their Church an inde-pendent status. He erected an archiepisco-pal see at Drontheim, with jurisdiction over Norway and Iceland ; he reformed the Nor-wegian clergy, compelled them to accept the canon law, and induced both Norway and

[1] The monument is now in Holy Trinity Church Guildford.

Sweden to promise payment of Peter's pence. On his return to Rome (1153) he was hailed as the Apostle of the North, and on the death of Eugenius's successor, the feeble Anastasius IV., was unanimously elected by the cardinals, under the title of Adrian IV. (4th December 1154). His pontificate was brief and stormy; and, although on a few occasions he displayed some vigour, his policy in general was marked by timidity and hesitation. His chief success was won over the heretic, Arnold of Brescia, who since 1147 had been at Rome preaching against the hierarchy, and encouraging the Romans in their defiance of the temporal authority of the Pope. Adrian laid Rome under an interdict until the municipality agreed to banish Arnold. Frederic Barbarossa, the Emperor-elect, was then induced, as the price of his coronation, to assist the Pope in bringing Arnold to trial and execution (June 1155). But the alliance of Adrian with the Empire was hollow and barren of results. Frederic left him to subdue the Romans as best he could, and revived the question of Investitures (*q.v.*) by the bad faith with which he interpreted the Concordat of Worms (1122). Adrian was led by his adviser, Cardinal Roland, into a line of action which he had not the courage to sustain. He formed alliances with the Italian enemies of Frederic, while pretending to be the loyal supporter of the Empire. In 1157 he enraged the Emperor by an ambiguous letter which implied that the Empire was a papal fief; but he immediately explained away the obnoxious phrase on discovering that the German Church resented such pretensions. On the outbreak of war between Frederic and Milan the Pope assumed a bolder attitude, and presented to Frederic an ultimatum (1159), demanding that the Italian bishops should be freed from feudal obligations, that the Emperor should renounce the right of interfering in Rome, and that the Mathildine inheritance should be restored to the Holy See. This was taken as a declaration of war; but Adrian died on 1st September 1159, before his resolution had been put to the test.

Adrian IV. is remembered in English history as the Pope who granted Ireland in fee to Henry II. The bull *Laudabiliter*, which professes to be the authentic grant, is almost certainly forged. But the fact of the grant is attested by John of Salisbury (*q.v.*), a writer of unimpeached veracity, who was himself entrusted by the Pope with an emerald ring to be delivered to Henry II. in token of the grant. It is most probable that the grant was made in the winter of 1155-6.

Henry II. found no use for it, either through preoccupation with other schemes, or possibly because unpalatable conditions had been attached by the Pope. When the King resumed his Irish plans (1172), he obtained the approval of Alexander III., whose letters on the subject are still extant.

[H. W. C. D.]

J. D. Mackie, *Pope Adrian IV.*, 1907; J. H. Round, *Commune of London* (for *Laudabiliter*).

ADVERTISEMENTS, The, is the title of a set of Constitutions or Articles which were issued for the province of Canterbury in March 1566, with the signatures of Archbishop Parker (*q.v.*), three bishops who were on the Ecclesiastical Commission, and the Bishops of Winchester and Lincoln, 'with others.' They dealt with four subjects: (1) Doctrine and Preaching; (2) Prayer and Sacraments; (3) Ecclesiastical Policy; (4) Apparel of Ecclesiastics. And there were added to them eight Protestations to be made by those admitted to any ecclesiastical office. This document forms one of a series which begins with the Royal Articles of 1559. From these there flowed two streams: (*a*) a series of royal letters and orders in 1560 and 1561; (*b*) the Bishops' Interpretations of 1561, and the document in question, the Advertisements, which is based upon the Interpretations. The Advertisements were originally intended to have a royal sanction. They arose out of a letter of the Queen in 1565 directing Parker to ascertain the amount of varieties prevailing in the performance of Church services, and to secure a better enforcement of uniformity. The return of varieties was duly made, and a draft set of Articles, with a preface, was sent to the Queen, 8th March 1565, in the hope of obtaining her sanction, which was not given. Meanwhile, the bishops' conflict with rebellious Puritanism became more acute. On 12th March 1566 Parker made a fresh attempt to obtain a royal sanction for his draft, and, failing again, he recast it. He altered the preface so as to make the Advertisements rest upon the royal letter of 1565, though without claiming royal authority for them; and he altered the Articles so that they might claim no more than he was already authorised to claim; and in this form the document was issued.

It has attained great notoriety because of its bearing upon the controversy about the ornaments of the minister. Article 11 orders that in cathedral and collegiate churches the minister shall use a cope, with the gospeller and epistoller agreeably ; but that at all prayers to be said at the communion table no copes are to be used, but surplices. Article 12 orders the use of a surplice and hood in the choir, in similar churches. Article 13 orders that every minister in his ministration is to wear a surplice. It has been maintained that these three Articles, occurring thus in the middle of a whole group, have overridden the Ornaments Rubric (*q.v.*) by virtue of royal authority attached to them, and a provision of the Act of Uniformity (1559, 1 Eliz. c. 2). The Privy Council has in the past accepted this view ; but it is not now generally adopted, since historical investigation seems to prove that there was, as above stated, no royal sanction given to the Articles as a whole, and none therefore to these three. The Advertisements fell into their place in the series above mentioned, and were appealed to from time to time along with the Royal Articles. A later generation, misinterpreting Parker's preface, was inclined at times to assign to them royal authority, and the policy about vestments which they laid down was adopted in one of the canons of 1604. This canon, however, is not the last word upon the matter, since the rule for the ornaments of the minister is the present Ornaments Rubric, which dates from 1662, and was then enacted, in spite of all that had gone before.

[W. H. F.]

Gee and Hardy, *Documents*, p. 467 ; Dixon, *Hist. of Ch. of Eng.*, vi. 49-61, 89 *seqq.* ; Frere, *Hist. of Eng. Ch., 1558-1625*, p. 118 ; *Principles of Rel. Ceremonial*, c. xiv. ; Convocation Report, *Ornaments*, No. 416, 1908.

AELFEAH (St. Alphege (954-1012). Archbishop of Canterbury, was a monk of Deerhurst, Glos. (where an early window in the ancient church still commemorates him). He afterwards lived at Bath, first as an anchorite, then as abbot. He became Bishop of Winchester, 984, probably through the influence of St. Dunstan (*q.v.*). In 994 he met Olaf Trygwweson of Norway at Southampton, brought him to meet King Aethelred at Andover, and there confirmed him. The hatred which the heathen Norsemen had against the bishop for this is said to have been one of the causes of his death. In 1006 he became Archbishop of Canterbury. The canons of the Council of Enham (date not known) show him to have been a follower of Dunstan in encouraging but not enforcing the celibate life for clergy. The massacre of the Danes in 1002 embittered the hostility of the peoples, and was followed by many

reprisals. In 1011 Canterbury was taken, and Aelfeah made prisoner. He was kept captive on Danish ships at Greenwich for seven months, and at last, when he refused to be ransomed by taxing the poor, was murdered in a drunken bout. His teaching had brought many towards conversion, and even the murderers treated his body as sacred, and allowed it to be taken to London and buried at St. Paul's. In 1023 Cnut (*q.v.*) translated his remains to Canterbury. In 1078 Lanfranc (*q.v.*) argued against his claim to be regarded as a martyr, but Anselm (*q.v.*) urged that he was a witness to Christ, as he died for righteousness' sake rather than Christ's poor should suffer. His day in the Calendar is 19th April.	[W. H. H.]

A.-S. Chron. ; Thietmar ; Adam of Bremen ; Osbern, *Vita Elph.* ; Hunt, *Eng. Ch. to 1066* ; Hutton, 'Eng. Saints,' *Bampton Lectures*.

AELFRIC, Abbot (c. 955-c.1025), an eminent ecclesiastic (whose writings have been taken as typical of the opinions of the English Church in the half-century preceding the Norman Conquest, is not to be confused with Aelfric, Archbishop of Canterbury, who died in 1005, or Aelfric, who was elected archbishop of the same see in 1050 and never secured possession (Mr. Freeman, *Norman Conquest*, made the former error). Aelfric was sent from Winchester to instruct the monks of the house at Cerne in the Benedictine rule. He was a friend of important bishops and caldormen, and wrote much that has been preserved, including a heptateuch, a life of St. Aethelwold, Bishop of Winchester, treatises on the teaching of Latin, and homilies. Of the last two are of special importance : (1) 'On the birthday of St. Gregory, anciently used in the English-Saxon Church ' [translated and edited by Elizabeth Elstob, 1709], in which a full account of St. Augustine's work in converting the English is given, chiefly taken from Bede, but also derived from other sources ; (2) 'On the Sacrifice for Easter Day.' In this, while using the legend of the materialisation of the host, seen by two monks at Mass (the tale told also of St. Gregory; many mediaeval pictures of this exist ; cf. the 'Miracle of Bolsena '). he asserts a spiritual doctrine of the Real Presence in the Blessed Sacrament. He declares that 'great is the difference between the Body in which Christ suffered and the body which is hallowed for housel '—the latter 'His ghostly body, which we call housel, is gathered of many corns, without blood and bones, limbless and soulless, and therefore nothing is to be understood bodily, but all is to be understood spiritually. . . . Soothly it is, as we said before, Christ's body and blood, not bodily but spiritually. Ye are not to ask how it is done, but to hold to your belief that it is so done.' It is possible that he is indebted to Ratramnus of Corbie, who wrote against Paschasius Radbert. But transubstantiation was not a dogma of the Roman Church at this date, and Aelfric's doctrine is not incompatible with that of Bede. Aelfric became Abbot of Eynsham in 1005, and probably died there. [w. h. h.]

Aelfric, *Catholic Homilies*, ed. B. Thorpe (Aelfric Society), and *Lives of the Saints*, ed. W. W. Skeat ; S. H. Gem, *Abbot Aelfric*.

AETHELWULF (d. 850), King of the West Saxons, and father of Alfred. The 'donation of Aethelwulf' has been much discussed. It has been supposed to be the institution of tithes (*q.v.*) in England (Selden), but this has been shown to be unlikely, if not impossible. Various charters, confirmatory or illustrative of the grant, exist ; the most important is that in the *Textus Roffensis*, wherein the King grants certain lands *pro decimatione agrorum, quam, Deo donante, cæteris ministris meis facere decrevi.* This seems to have been a usual provision for the reward of a thegn and the endowment of a church. The 'Donation' may be regarded rather as a special than a general action, but Asser (*Vita Ælf.*) regards it as a perpetual grant over the whole land for the service of the Church. [w. h. h.]

Asser, xi. c. 2 ; see Stevenson's edition, pp. 186-91 ; Selden, *Hist. of Tithes*.

AIDAN, St. (d. 651), Bishop of Lindisfarne, an Irish Scot, was a monk of Hii, or Iona, when a bishop who had been sent at the request of Oswald (*q.v.*), King of Northumbria, to evangelise the Northumbrians returned, and declared to the assembled monks that he could do nothing with the people. Aidan asked whether he had not required too much of them, forgetting the Apostle's words, 'milk for babes.' All agreed that Aidan should take his place, and he was consecrated bishop. He went to Northumbria, probably in 635, and Oswald, having given him the island of Lindisfarne he built his church there, gathered helpers from Ireland, and had twelve English youths taught in his monastery that they might preach to their own people. Northumbria, where the Roman Paulinus (*q.v.*) had laid the foundations of a Christian Church, had largely relapsed into heathenism after the death of King Edwin ; only near Catterick had the deacon James carried on the Roman mission. Full of love and zeal, Aidan made missionary tours, generally on foot, preaching and talking with people on his way, urging them if they were heathens to accept the Gospel, and if already baptized to live as became Christians. Many devout Irish joined in his work ; churches were built and were crowded with hearers, and monasteries were founded in which the Scotic monks trained English youths in monasticism. Aidan had a church and bedchamber near the royal town, Bamborough, but his asceticism kept him from often appearing at the King's table. He was dining with Oswald one Easter Day when, beholding the King's boundless charity, he prayed that his hand might never decay, and it is said that centuries later it remained uncorrupted. Often he would retire to the little island of Farne and abide a while in solitude, as the Scotic saints loved to do. He was free from all pride, avarice, and anger, and was at once gentle and fearless, consoling the afflicted, and sternly reproving sinners, however powerful they might be. The gifts he received from the rich he spent on the poor or in redeeming captives, many of whom became his disciples and were ordained by him. Bede, who dwells on the beauty of his character, saw no fault in him save that he followed the rule of his own people, keeping Easter on the Celtic instead of the Roman date.

In 642 Oswald was slain fighting against Penda, the heathen King of Mercia. Northumbria was ravaged, and Aidan in his retreat on Farne Island cried to God as he saw the smoke rise from an attempt to burn Bamborough : then the wind shifted, and the fortress was saved. His work did not perish, for Oswald's brother Oswy (*q.v.*), who became King in Bernicia, the northern part of Northumbria, was a Christian, and Oswin, who reigned in Deira, the southern part, was a man of saintly life, to whom Aidan was deeply attached. Aidan remained bishop over both kingdoms. Once he reproved Oswin for blaming him because he had given to a beggar a horse with which the King had presented him, and, struck with Oswin's humility, prophesied that he would not live long. The incident illustrates the strain of extravagance in the Scotic saints and the submission they received, and indeed required, from their disciples. Soon afterwards Oswin was murdered by the order of Oswy. Twelve days later Aidan suddenly fell ill at Bamborough : men laid him on the ground and spread over him an awning, which they fastened to a wooden buttress of the church, and there he died on 31st August 651. He was buried in the cemetery of the monks in Lindisfarne. When after the Conference of Whitby in 664 most of the Scotic monks left to go to Ireland, Colman, their bishop, took with him some of Aidan's bones, and placed the rest in the sacristy of the church. [ENGLAND, CONVERSION OF.]   [W. H.]

Bede, *H.E.*; Bright, *Early Eng. Ch. Hist.*; Hunt, *Hist. of Eng. Ch. to 1066*.

ALCUIN was born of a noble Northumbrian family, *c.* 735 (730 according to Dümmler, *Neues Archiv*, xviii. 54). He was connected with St. Willibrord (*q.v.*), the first Bishop of Utrecht, and through this connection acquired by inheritance a small monastery founded by Willigis, the father of St. Willibrord (*q.v.*), on the Humber. At an early age he entered the cathedral school of York, where he received his education from its founder, Archbishop Egbert, a pupil of Bede (*q.v.*), and from the *scholasticus* Ethelbert. From Alcuin's poem *De pontificibus et sanctis Ecclesiae Eboracensis* much can be learnt of the education to be acquired at the school and of the books contained in the library at York, the most copious and valuable collection then existing. On Ethelbert becoming archbishop in 767 Alcuin was ordained deacon, and may have been appointed *scholasticus* of the school. When Ethelbert resigned the archbishopric in favour of Eanbald in 780 Alcuin became librarian. The new archbishop despatched him to Rome to fetch the *pallium* [PALL], and it was on this journey that he met Charles the Great at Parma in 781. He had twice previously visited the Continent, and on the first occasion, in company with Ethelbert, had appeared at the court of Charles. At his second meeting at Parma, Charles induced him to leave York for Aachen. On obtaining Eanbald's consent he returned to the Frankish court in 782, was given control of the monasteries of Ferrières and St. Lupus at Troyes, and took up his position as instructor at the Palace School. His class was composed of Charles himself, his family, and the most cultured men of the age, among them the royal biographer, Einhard. Alcuin taught by means of dialogue between master and pupil, and his treatise on Rhetoric, written in the form of a dialogue between Charles and himself, and his *Disputatio Pippini*, supply some idea of the style of discussion adopted. Alcuin was further employed to help the King in his ambitious design of educational reform. The famous Capitulary of 787, the first attempt to

promote education by legislation, bears the stamp of the English scholar. In 790 he returned to England, and was the means of restoring friendly relations between Charles and Offa. But his native country no longer offered a peaceful home for the student, and he returned to the Frankish court, there to begin his attack on the heresies then rife. He obtained the condemnation of the Spanish Bishop Felix of Urgel, the originator of the Adoptionist heresy, at the Council of Frankfurt, 794. Among Alcuin's writings an attack on this bishop is extant, *Liber Albini quem edidit contra Haeresin Felicis*. At the Council of Frankfurt the veneration of pictures, approved at the second Council of Nicæa and sanctioned by Pope Adrian, was also condemned. The famous *Libri Carolini* attacking this veneration were probably Alcuin's work. In 796 Charles acceded to Alcuin's desire to withdraw to the peace of the cloister by granting him the abbacy of St. Martin at Tours, the most important monastery in his gift. In his retirement he gave himself up to teaching and the transmitting of knowledge by means of copying MSS., many of which were borrowed from the library at York for that purpose. During this period he involved himself in a controversy with the Irish scholars, who after his retirement from court began to influence the mind of his patron. Indeed, a certain Clement of Ireland was placed over the Palace School in spite of Alcuin's bitter attack against that 'malignant pest,' the Irish scholar, 'who, though versed in many things, knows nothing for certain or true.' In 800 Charles visited him at Tours, and brought him back to Aachen to deal a final and victorious blow at the arch-heretic, Felix of Urgel, in a personal disputation. The last four years of his life he spent quietly at Tours, working with a large following of pupils in the monastic scriptorium. He died on 19th May 804, and was buried in the church of St. Martin.

Alcuin displayed no elements of originality either as a writer or teacher. His writings are rather compilations from the recognised sources—Boethius, Cassiodorus, Isidorus, St. Jerome, and Bede—than additions to mediæval learning. Besides the works already mentioned, his *Letters* supply a valuable source of information for the history and social conditions of his time. But to transmit to future generations what was already known was his avowed aim, and in accomplishing this he was eminently successful. It is impossible here to enter into the discussion as to whether Alcuin has a share in the formation of the Caroline minuscule. Delisle has shown that

a characteristic school of writing grew up
at Tours during the ninth century, but it is
difficult to prove that any of the numerous
Tours MSS. were written before Alcuin's
death in 804. Alcuin certainly paid great
attention to forms and accuracy in writing,
and the insular character of the ornamentation
lends support to the theory. But whether
the Caroline minuscule has its origin in
Roman antiquity or in Merovingian Gaul, as
Delisle and Traube respectively think, it
is dangerous to lay stress on the influence
of the English scholar.   [A. L. P.]

> The best edition of Alcuin's works is that
> of Froben, published at Ratisbon, 1777, and
> reprinted in Migne's *Patrologiae latinae cursus
> completus*, vols. c.-ci. The letters are ed. by
> Dümmler in the *Mon. Germ. Hist. Epist.*,
> vol. iv., and also with the anonymous biography
> of Alcuin and certain other works, in Jaffé's
> *Bibliotheca Rerum Germanicarum*, vol. vi.;
> *Monumenta Alcuiniana*, ed. Wattenbach and
> Dümmler; Lorentz, *Alcuins Leben*, 1829;
> Monnier, *Alcuin et Charlemagne*, 1863;
> Dümmler in *Neues Archiv*, vol. xviii., and
> article 'Alcuin' in *Allgemeine Deutsche Bio-
> graphie*; Mullinger, *The Schools of Charles the
> Great*; G. F. Browne, *Alcuin*.

ALDHELM, or **EALDHELM**, St. (640 ?-
709), first Bishop of Sherborne (705), son of
Kenten (Centwine), near relation of Ine, King
of Wessex, was probably first taught by an
Irishman, Maildubh, Maildulf, or Meldun,
founder of the school at Malmesbury (which
became an abbey under Aldhelm). He
names Abbot Hadrian, who came to Canterbury with Archbishop Theodore in 669, as
'preceptor of my rude infancy'—a strange
description of a young man of thirty. He
became Abbot of Malmesbury in 675, and
showed himself a scholar (with some knowledge of Greek and Hebrew), teacher, mission
preacher, founder, and builder. He built
two churches at Malmesbury, one or two at
Bruton, and one at Wareham (where he had
estates), perhaps on the site of St. Martin's,
by the north gate. It was roofless in the
twelfth century, but (by a miracle) no rain
fell within its walls. He also founded two
small monasteries at Frome and Bradford-
on-Avon, which he governed as well as
Malmesbury. The Saxon church of St.
Laurence, Bradford, discovered by Canon
Rich Jones, is commonly regarded as his
work. But some authorities believe it to be
much later—Professor Baldwin Brown dating it 950-1000, and Commendatore G. T.
Rivoira about the time of Edward the Confessor. Yet it may well be the *ecclesiola*
which William of Malmesbury (rightly or
wrongly) connects with his name. As
abbot he went to Rome as the guest of Pope

Sergius I., probably *c.* 700. It was in the
Lateran Church that his tossed-off chasuble
was (miraculously) supported by a sunbeam.
This red or purple vestment, on which black
rotulae were embroidered, bearing figures
of peacocks, was long preserved. While
still abbot he was asked at a council of
bishops, attended by 'priests from nearly all
Britain,' to compose a remonstrance addressed
to Gerontius, King of Damnonia. It touches
(1) the quarrelsomeness of the Britons
among themselves; (2) their wrong tonsure;
(3) their wrong Easter cycle; (4) the unfriend-
liness of the clergy across the Severn. Its
chief argument is the duty of accepting the
decrees of Blessed Peter and the tradition of
the Roman Church; for, without this, profession of right faith is no use. This letter
is said to have had a good influence.

When King Ine divided the see of Wessex
in the spring of 705 Aldhelm was called,
against his will, to rule the part west of
Selwood, which included a wedge of Wilts
(containing Malmesbury), the counties of
Somerset and Dorset, and that part of Devon
(Crediton and Exeter) which belonged to
Wessex. He visited his diocese diligently,
and built a very fine church at Sherborne,
which was unfortunately destroyed by Bishop
Roger. His descriptions of churches and
organs and church furniture show that there
were really good and well-filled buildings
erected in this period. Bishopstrow (Wilts)
marks a place where he planted his staff and
perhaps founded a church. He died in 709
at Doulting, near Shepton Mallet in Somerset,
and was buried at Malmesbury, stone crosses
(Bishop-stones) being erected where his body
rested on the way.

Aldhelm was a man of fine presence and
a good musician (on the lyre or harp) and
singer — like Caedmon attracting crowds
by his music, and then singing of religious
truths. He was a poet in his own tongue,
but unfortunately only Latin works are preserved. There is occasionally good stuff in
them, but much of the turgid crudity and
absurdity of the *Hysterica passio*. He was
the first to write Latin poetry in England,
and had much technical knowledge, which he
shows in his *Letter to Acircius, i.e.* King Aldfrith of Northumbria (lit. 'from the W.N.W.
wind').   [J. W.]

> His works may be found in Migne, *P.L.*, tom.
> 89, and (somewhat better) in Giles's edition.
> The other authorities for his life are Bede, and
> a life by Faricius of Malmesbury, Abbot of
> Abingdon, and a rather better one by William
> of Malmesbury. Modern accounts by Bishop
> G. F. Browne of Bristol (S.P.C.K.), and W. B.
> Wildman of Sherborne, *Life of St. Ealdhelm*,
> 1905, and W. Hunt in *D.N.B.*

ALFRED (Aelfred) 849-99, the greatest of our early kings, was a typical expression of the influence exercised by religion on the English people. He was the youngest son of Aethelwulf, King of the West Saxons, and his wife Osburh. He was born at Wantage, and was taken early to Rome, where he attracted the attention of Leo IV., and was given consular rank. In his fifth or sixth year he showed his future interest in learning by the zest with which he applied himself to a book of poems shown him by his mother, and (probably) learnt it by heart. He came into prominence in the reign of his brother Aethelred, to whom he was *secundarius*, or under-king, and he distinguished himself at the battle of Ashdown against the Danes. He succeeded his brother in 871, engaged in many battles with the Danes, and finally had to take refuge in the marshes of Somerset, and entrenched himself at Athelney. Gradually he recovered strength, defeated the Danes at Ethandun (878), compelled them to surrender and their King to be baptized ; defeated them at sea, repulsed their attack on Rochester, but was defeated in East Anglia. Again he recovered, and became overlord even of South Wales ; conquered London (885 ?); defeated the Danes at Farnham and at Exeter (893 ?). He lived to see the war ended, and England free and victorious at least for a while. He died on 25th October 899, and was buried in the new minster, afterwards called the abbey of Hyde, at Winchester, where in 1787 his ashes were scattered in the dust and his coffin sold for two pounds. Apart from his greatness as warrior, statesman, and reformer, Aelfred as a Christian king is notable for the care which he took to promote learning, especially religious education, and for his devotion to the interests of the Church. He induced Werfrith, Bishop of Worcester, to translate the *Dialogues* of St. Gregory; and in his own studies he was assisted by Werfrith, by Plegmund, Archbishop of Canterbury, and by two Mercian priests. He sent for foreign scholars, among them the priest John, who assisted the King in the translation which he afterwards made of St. Gregory's *Pastoral Rule.* He brought Asser, afterwards his biographer, from Wales, and became his close friend, granting him the monasteries of Congresbury and Banwell in Somerset. From Asser we learn the patience of the King in acquiring knowledge. As he learned he turned his knowledge to the practical profit of the clergy, translating for them Boethius's *Consolation of Philosophy,* as well as St. Gregory, Orosius, and possibly Bede. A warrior and a teacher, a craftsman and a hunter, a ruler who would not allow his judges to be illiterate, and who provided for the education of his clergy and nobles, Aelfred was, above all, a most devout Christian, setting aside half his time and half his revenue to the immediate service of God.'

It is curious that Aelfred, 'the Truth-teller,' as the chronicle of St. Neot calls him, should never have been canonised. Henry VI. applied to Eugenius IV. in vain. In earlier days reverence was paid to his memory in particular churches, and his name is found in at least one calendar.

The story of his life is the complete justification of his own words: 'I have always striven to live worthily, and at my death to leave to those who follow me a worthy memorial in my works.' The love and veneration of his contemporaries for ' England's darling,' as he was called, are vindicated by the judgment of modern historians, such as that of von Ranke : 'Alfred is one of the greatest figures in the history of the world ' ; and of Freeman: 'There is no other name in history to compare with his.' [W. H. H.]

Asser, *Life,* ed. W. H. Stevenson ; Plummer, *Life and Times of Alfred the Great.*

ANCHORITES. The term anchorite in its English form ' ancre,' ' ancress,' was almost restricted before the Reformation to such strict recluses as were forbidden by the terms of their vow ever to leave their cells. The practice of reclusion, which had grown slowly out of the monasticism of the desert, became common on the Continent during the sixth and seventh centuries, and was presumably practised in England before the Norman Conquest, but owing to the comparative rarity of records before that time we know little of English anchorites before the eleventh century. The will of one who calls himself ' Mantat the Anker ' has come down to us.

Many anchorites were professed monks and nuns, in which case they wore the habit and followed the rule of their order. Others took the vows of reclusion as seculars, and for these rules of more or less individual application were written. Two of these produced in England were the treatise written by Aelred of Rievaulx for his sister, and the well-known *Ancren Riwle.*

The Office *Ad Includendum Anachoritae* does not appear in English Service Books until the twelfth century, nor does it become common until the fourteenth. After that time, however, it is to be found in most Pontificals, as well as in the Sarum Manuals of 1506, 1515, and 1556. The Service included a Mass, sometimes *tanquam pro mortuis*, and was normally performed by the bishop, whose sanction, except in peculiars or cases of papal dispensation, was necessary. The door of the cell was sometimes built up, sometimes sealed by the bishop, and sometimes merely locked to admit of the entrance of a confessor, or in cases where the recluse was not a priest, but had a chapel forming an integral part of his cell, of a priest to say Mass. Usually the cell was attached to a church, either conventual or parochial, or to a private chapel, to which the anchorite had no access, and in these cases the occupant made his confession and communion through a hagioscope looking up to the high altar.

There were recognised rights of advowson in 'Ankerholds,' and a convent would sometimes present one of its members to a distant cell. Such anchorites were sometimes supported by their community or by a neighbouring convent, otherwise they were dependent upon alms. When secular persons sought enclosure the bishop's licence would often insist that provision should be made for the maintenance of the *includendus* before the ceremony of reclusion was performed. Anchorites, having no community goods to rely upon for food and clothing, were not strictly bound by the vow of poverty, and very frequently lived upon the revenues of lands, rent charges, or other property which they had received in charity or had possessed before their enclosure. Those who were priests often received the emoluments of a chantry. The early Pipe Rolls, the Close Rolls, and similar records contain many gifts of money, provisions, and firewood to anchorites. In the case of recluses on royal demesne a fixed alms of a penny a day or of a fraction or multiple of that sum was common. Anchorites were also frequent legatees in the wills of people in all ranks of life. They appear not only as recipients but as donors of money and other gifts to church purposes.

The anchorite did not, like the monk, become *civiliter mortuus*, but retained his individual rights unless he were already a member of a community. Thus we find an anchorite making a will four years after his enclosure, and an anchoress bringing a suit for the recovery of a rent charge which had been granted her upon certain lands, and not paid since the death of her benefactor. Anchorites, however, took the vow of obedience on enclosure, and were, from an ecclesiastical point of view, under the obedience of a superior then appointed.

It was generally admitted that the vow of 'constancy of abode' might be broken under fear of death or for the common good (*e.g.* to undertake the work of a bishop), but there are cases on record when neither consideration prevailed with the recluse to make him leave his cell. As a rule only the Pope could dispense from this vow or give permission for a change of cell, but we occasionally find recluses leaving their cells as an act of canonical obedience, *e.g.* to answer an accusation of Lollardy before the bishop. Cases of apostasy seem to have been rare.

Manual labour is enjoined by the rules, but the occupations of an anchorite were necessarily restricted. In early times a garden was often included in the cell, but this privilege became exceedingly rare. Recluses of both sexes copied service-books and wrote devotional works; anchoresses engaged in embroidery and charitable needlework, and took care of the altar vessels, though this was discouraged. One of the last references to the order before it vanished in the upheaval of the Reformation is the notice of payment to the anchoress of St. Margaret's, Westminster, for washing the Corporals in 1538.

[D. E.]

Volumes in *V.C.H.* under Religious Houses; Bloxam, *Gothic Architecture,* v. 163-85; Bridgett, *Hist. of the Holy Eucharist in Great Britain,* ii. ; Archæological Collections of Kent, Sussex, etc. ; *Archæol. Journal,* vol. lviii.

ANDREWES, Lancelot (1555-1626), prelate, preacher and apologist, styled by Laud 'a light of the Christian world,' was born in Thames Street, London, the son of a master-mariner, educated at Merchant Taylors'. Showing early aptness and industry, he was chosen at sixteen for a Greek scholarship at Pembroke Hall, Cambridge, whither his schoolfellow, Edmund Spenser, had preceded him. At Cambridge he led a lonely and studious life, addicting himself especially to the interrogation of nature, to such purpose that Bacon later submitted his writings to Andrewes's judgment. He had a gift for languages, and acquired a critical knowledge of fifteen. In 1576 he became Fellow of Pembroke, and in 1580 entered holy orders. The delivery of his Catechistical Lectures, with their plea for 'apostolic handsomeness and order' and conservative method, had an immense effect in the university, long the centre of the nonconformist movement. The Puritan party, according to Aubrey, 'had a great mind to drawe in this learned young man,' but they afterwards refused him his doctorate. Andrewes, however, would seem to have been attracted to the devotional side of Calvinism. He was himself 'deeply seene in all cases of conscience, and in that respect was much sought after by many.' The Puritan Earl of Huntingdon in 1586 took him northwards to confer with popish recusants, and his abilities were noted by Secretary Walsingham, who desired to make him Reader of Controversies in Cambridge, and procured his preferment to St. Giles's Cripplegate in London, as well as to a prebend in St. Paul's. Andrewes moved to London early in 1589. He was already chaplain to Whitgift and to the Queen, and in August 1589 became Master of Pembroke Hall. Most of his time, however, was spent in London. His stall also carried with it the office of penitentiary. In St. Paul's, St. Giles's and at court he preached a succession of striking sermons, so as to be styled ' *stella praedicantium* and an angell in the pulpit.' He declined in succession the sees of Salisbury and Ely as a protest against Elizabeth's policy of irreligious rapine, but in 1598 accepted the deanery of Westminster, which brought him into active connection with Westminster School. After the accession of James, over whom he exercised a lifelong influence, he ' by some persuasion ' accepted the bishopric of Chichester in 1605. He had not taken a prominent part in the Hampton Court Conference of 1604, but was one of the principal translators of the Authorised Version. In 1608 James sent him into the lists against Cardinal Bellarmine, wherein he asserted the divine right of regal authority independently of the Holy See, and the Catholic character of the reformed Church of England. In 1609 he was translated to Ely, and when the primacy became vacant the next year it was expected that he would succeed Bancroft. It may perhaps be doubted whether he was a strong enough helmsman for the troubled waters ahead. He was made High Almoner to the King and Privy Councillor; but, though his saintly intellectuality was a power in the circle of the court, he confined his activity as a councillor to ecclesiastical affairs. A stain rests on his career in connection with the Essex nullity suit (1618), yet he was not usually compliant to great persons. Being asked by James whether he agreed with Bishop Neile of Durham that the King might take his subjects' money without recourse to Parliament, he replied : ' Sir, I think it lawful for you to take my brother Neile's money because he offers it.' To the modern mind the worst action of Andrewes was his consent to the burning of the Anabaptist Leggat in 1612, which, however, even Casaubon approved. Casau-

bon, du Moulin and Grotius were among his friends. In 1617 Andrewes, with other prelates, attended the King to Edinburgh, where James persuaded the Scots clergy to accept five points of Catholic practice. Seven years earlier Andrewes had assisted in the consecration in London of bishops for three Scottish sees. In 1618 he was translated to Winchester. It is significant that he was not sent that year to represent the English Church at the Synod of Dort. During the next few years he is found enforcing reverence and order in his diocese, consecrating churches, and encouraging learning ; but he does not appear prominently in the controversy with Puritanism. Charles I. leaned on his judgment even more than his father had done. He died, 25th September 1626, being buried in St. Mary Overy, now Southwark Cathedral. The inscription on his tomb—which has been moved—records that ' unwedded he departed hence to a celestial aureole.' His saintly and apostolic character, his munificence, learning and reputation as a preacher, made him the foremost and most respected churchman of the day. The importance of Lancelot Andrewes in history, apart from his defensive writings, is his influence upon the conservative reaction of the end of the Tudor period, by which the Catholic character of the reformed Church was vindicated. The ritual of his chapel restored much dignified ceremonial to English worship. His writings are a storehouse of patristic theology, and his practice is referred to for many points of ceremonial. But his best-prized legacy to posterity is the book of devotions called *Preces Privatae*. A contemporary spoke of him as ' Doctor Andrewes in the school, Bishop Andrewes in the pulpit, Saint Andrewes in the closet.' [D. M.]

Works ('Library of Anglo-Catholic Theology'): *Lives* by Isaacson (1650), R. L. Ottley, D. Macleane ; R. W. Church in *Masters of Eng. Theology* ; J. H. Overton in *D.N.B.*

ANSELM, St. (*c.* 1033-1109), Archbishop of Canterbury, was a native of Aosta now in Piedmont, the son of a Lombard landowner, whose wife, Anselm's mother, was of Burgundian origin and noble, if not royal, descent. Anselm in his youth was delicate, studious, and visionary ; but, losing his mother at an early age, fell into wild courses, and quarrelled with his father. In 1056 he crossed the Alps to roam through Burgundy and France, as a penniless student, seeking education and a career. In 1059 he arrived at the Norman abbey of Bec, attracted by the fame of his fellow-countryman, Lanfranc (*q.v.*) of Pavia, then prior and *scholasticus* under Abbot Herluin. Under Lanfranc the school of Bec had become the resort of external students; Anselm joined their ranks, and by indefatigable studies soon qualified himself to act as Lanfranc's assistant. His original intention was to become a professional teacher; but Lanfranc and Archbishop Maurilius of Rouen induced him to take the monastic vows at Bec (1060). Three years later he succeeded Lanfranc as prior. He found the office an impediment to study, but was dissuaded by Maurilius from resigning; and he achieved a high reputation by his tact as a ruler of monks and his skill in teaching refractory pupils. He overcame opposition, and subdued the jealousy of his inferiors by the charm of a nature which was firm but gentle, lofty and yet sympathetic. As a spiritual director he was unrivalled, for he united moral enthusiasm with a profound knowledge of human nature; but for many years he found in metaphysical studies his most absorbing occupation. Like Lanfranc, he came to be regarded in his own lifetime as a Father of the Latin Church. But, while Lanfranc's genius was displayed in the exposition of authorities, Anselm attempted to find in natural reason a logical basis for theology, since he held that faith, to be perfect, must be established on reasonable grounds; *quod credimus intelligere* was the guiding principle of his meditations. His method was to discuss, in lectures and in conversation, some cardinal dogma, using the simplest language, discarding Scriptural proofs, and assuming only the received axioms of logic. His proofs, when satisfactorily developed, were committed to writing for the benefit of his pupils, but soon obtained a wider currency. Among the works so produced at Bec were (1) the *Monologium*, a discourse on the being and nature of God, in which he proclaimed himself a follower of St. Augustine, and identified God with the Platonic Idea of Good; (2) the *De Veritate*, a dialogue in which he explains and defends the conception of truth, or good, upon which the argument of the *Monologium* is founded; (3) the *De Libero Arbitrio*; and (4) the *De Casu Diaboli*, dialogues in which he considers the question whether predestination is compatible with freedom of the will; (5) the *Proslogium*, a work complementary to the *Monologium*, in which he claims to establish the existence of God by a single self-evident proof; (6) the *Liber Apologeticus*, addressed to a critic, the monk Gaunilo, who had impugned the argument of the *Proslogium*. The

two last treatises are remarkable essays in ontology, and justify Anselm's position as the first, and in some respects the most profound, of the Realist schoolmen. They anticipate, if they did not actually inspire, a famous proof of Descartes. Anselm urges that the very idea of a God implies His real existence, since we conceive of God as perfect —and He would not be perfect without the attribute of existence. Gaunilo raised the objection that the mind can create, by synthesis, the idea of a perfect being to which nothing corresponds in the realm of reality; and Anselm scarcely meets the difficulty by contending that the reality of God is implied in, and inseparable from, our idea of Him. But the *Proslogium* was received with universal praise; Anselm, who had published it anonymously, was commanded by a papal legate to affix his name to it. But he was soon distracted from these studies by official cares. In Herluin's old age he undertook the entire management of Bec, and on Herluin's death (1078) he reluctantly accepted the abbacy, to which he was unanimously elected. In the same year he paid his first visit to England, on business connected with the lands which his house held at Tooting Bec and elsewhere. Incidentally he renewed his acquaintance with Lanfranc, and showed his statesmanship by advising the archbishop not to expunge the name of Aelfeah (*q.v.*) from the Calendar, since that prelate, though only canonised by English sentiment, had incurred martyrdom in the cause of justice. Anselm also earned the esteem of many Anglo-Norman barons, and was received by William I. with singular respect. Thenceforth he was a frequent and honoured guest in England. He was specially summoned to the deathbed of the Conqueror (1087), though illness prevented him from appearing; and Rufus, after his accession, revered Anselm if not as a saint, at least as his father's friend. On Lanfranc's death (1089) the English laity and clergy concurred in desiring Anselm for their primate. The see was kept in the King's hand until 1093; when, the King lying sick at Gloucester, Anselm was invited by the bishops to give him ghostly counsel, and produced such an impression that Rufus promised to amend his life and government, and as an earnest of repentance invested Anselm with the see of Canterbury. Anselm, inspired by a well-grounded mistrust of the King's sincerity, made his acceptance conditional upon three promises: that the lands of Canterbury should be restored in full; that he should be accepted as William's chief counsellor in spiritual affairs; and that

B (17)

he might continue in the obedience of Urban II., whom the Norman Church had long since accepted by preference to Wibert, the Imperial antipope. The King granted the first condition, but evaded answering the second and third. He soon repented of his repentance ; he refused to let Anselm summon a Church council, though this was the traditional method of initiating ecclesiastical reforms ; he turned a deaf ear to remonstrances on his private life and his oppressions of the Church ; and finally told Anselm that he must repudiate Urban, and leave the Crown to settle which Pope should be recognised in England. On this last question Anselm appealed to the Great Council, pleading that no obedience was due to Cæsar in the things of God. His case was heard at Rockingham (1095). Both the bishops and the barons urged him to submit ; the King hoped that he would resign. But Anselm appealed from the Great Council to the Pope ; the bishops, though they renounced his friendship, declared themselves incompetent to depose him ; and the barons were won over by admiration for his courage. Rufus therefore, making a virtue of necessity, acknowledged Urban, but asked Urban's legate that Anselm might be deposed, or at least obliged to take the *pallium* [PALL] from the royal hand. Neither request was granted, and the King revenged himself by attacking Anselm in the forms of law for negligent discharge of feudal duties. The archbishop, finding himself powerless for good, demanded leave to go abroad ; this was grudgingly permitted, and he repaired to Urban at Rome (1097). In the days of tribulation before his departure, and during his stay in Italy, he composed the treatise *Cur Deus Homo*, to prove that the Incarnation was the only rational means by which the outrage on the honour of God, involved in sin, could be repaired. By Urban's desire Anselm attended the Council of Bari (1098) to defend the doctrine of the Double Procession against the Greeks ; his arguments are recapitulated in his treatise *De Processione Sancti Spiritus.* At Bari the Pope called public attention to his wrongs, and threatened Rufus with excommunication ; but Anselm interceded for delay, and no effect was given to the threat. Subsequently he took part in the Council of Rome (1099), which renewed the canons against those who received spiritual preferment from lay hands. It is incredible that he should have been ignorant of the earlier canons on this subject. But he had himself accepted Canterbury from the King's hands, and before 1099 had never questioned the propriety

of lay Investiture (*q.v.*). When recalled by Henry I. (1100) he at once refused either to renew the homage which he had rendered to Rufus, or to consecrate bishops whom Henry had invested. Anselm based his case on authority alone, and showed himself strangely passive in the dispute which he had raised. He granted Henry a truce until the invasion of Robert of Normandy had been repelled (1101), and in the interval did the King good service by sanctioning his marriage with Matilda of Scotland (a reputed nun), and by enlisting English sentiment against Robert and the baronial rebels. When the King stood firm on his prerogative Anselm went again into exile (1103-6), and ultimately threatened Henry with excommunication. But he willingly accepted the first overtures of peace, and welcomed the compromise which Paschal II. dictated to the English Church. His thoughts centred chiefly round practical reforms, such as the suppression of the slave trade and the enforcement of clerical celibacy. He asserted the liberties of the clergy and revived the practice of holding synods. But, apart from the Investitures question, he lived on good terms with the King, and readily forgave the bishops who had taken the King's part. He has been attacked by modern writers as a hypocrite who concealed his legal astuteness behind a veil of simplicity ; and as a papalist who attacked the royal prerogative and surrendered Anglican independence. These charges are gratuitous and unhistorical. Though Anselm may be idealised in the writings of his friend Eadmer, his own familiar letters prove the loftiness of his moral nature as indubitably as his philosophical writings attest the subtlety of his intellect.   [H. W. C. D.]

Eadmer. *Vita Anselmi* and *Historia Novorum* ; R. W. Church, M. Rule, and J. M. Rigg, modern *Lives* ; Freeman, *William Rufus* ; H. W. C. Davis, *Eng. under the Normans and Angevins.*

ARCHDEACON.

The office dates in germ from primitive times. No instance is known of a church in which the bishop had not at his service at least one deacon, and where there were more it became the custom for one to be chosen by the bishop as his confidential assistant in all save his purely spiritual duties. The 'bishop's deacon,' as he was styled in the third century, was the ancestor of the archdeacon. It is impossible to define his functions ; except so far as he was limited by his deacon's orders he administered the revenues and the discipline of the Church, superintending not only the laity, but also the clergy who were in deacon's orders or lower. The position of the 'bishop's deacon,' at any rate at Rome, carried with it the prospect of succession to the episcopate. In the third and fourth centuries this was rather the rule than the exception. St. Athanasius at Alexandria, it may be regarded as certain, held the same office. It was as 'bishop's deacon,' in the same sense in which St. Laurence, for instance, had been the deacon of St. Sixtus at Rome, that St. Athanasius attended the Council of Nicæa; and it was natural enough, apart from his peculiar gifts, that he should become the successor of Alexander. But we must bear in mind that the office was a personal one. It was held, and could be withdrawn, at the will of the bishop, and a new bishop was in no wise bound to continue in office the deacon of his predecessor.

When the need was felt of a definite title, Protodiaconus was tentatively used; but Archidiaconus, which first appears in Optatus (A.D. 370) found general acceptance. Yet for a good while 'the deacon,' with specification of the diocese, was a sufficient description. When Gregory the Great addressed a letter (*Ep.* i. 10), *ad Honoratum diaconum Salonitanum*, no one doubted who the 'deacon of Salona' was. As to the name finally adopted, it is open to the criticism that it fails to indicate the essence of the office. While an archbishop is essentially the head of a body of bishops, the characteristic of an archdeacon is that he is chosen by the bishop for a manifold office, of which his superiority over the other deacons is only an incidental part.

The office had its first development in the assignment of a local area within the diocese to the archdeacon. The first diocese to be thus divided is said to have been Strasburg in 774. Soon after this the office appears in England, where the Frankish Empire, at the height of its power and civilisation, was admired and imitated. The first known English archdeacon is Wulfred of Canterbury, who appears in 803 and was afterwards archbishop. But the line of Canterbury archdeacons does not seem to have been continuous before the Conquest, and the office gained no great importance, nor was it generally instituted in the English dioceses. In Canterbury diocese there appears to have been for a while a plurality of archdeacons; but this was exceptional there, and is not found elsewhere.

After the Norman Conquest archdeacons become general in England. Each prelate has at first not more than one; and the canons of English synods require him, as of old, to be in deacon's orders. The iteration of this command, which is given as late as 1127, proves that priests were beginning to assume the office. On the Continent such cases had been not uncommon from the eighth century onwards. By a more usual laxity the office was often conferred upon persons in minor orders, the diaconate being regarded as a maximum of clerical obligation, which need not be assumed at once by the archdeacon. It was not till the Act of Uniformity, 1662, that an archdeacon was compelled to be in priest's orders; since 1840 (3-4 Vic. c. 113) he, like a dean or a canon, must have been in such orders for at least six years.

The non-existence of episcopal registers till the thirteenth century makes it impossible to give dates for the foundation of the several archdeaconries; but it is certain that in some cases separate counties within a large diocese had their own archdeacons as early as 1200; on the other hand, many dioceses, including Canterbury, had but one at the close of the Middle Ages. And meanwhile the nature of the office changed. Soon after the Conquest, if not in some instances earlier, it came to be regarded as a benefice, with rights and duties, and often endowments, of its own. The endowments usually consisted in a share divided off, as a prebend, from what had been the joint cathedral estate. The archdeacon, thus having a life-tenure of his office, could no longer be regarded by the bishop as his personal agent in matters of litigation or administration. Hence came the appointment of officials and vicars-general, and the division of duties between the bishop, or his officers, and the archdeacon, by which the latter in most cases secured the control of church fabrics, with the power of ordering a rate for building or repair which lasted till 1868. He also had authority over all deacons and persons in orders lower than the diaconate, with the duty of watching not only over their conduct but also over their instruction. A survival of this in our Ordinal is the presentation by the archdeacon or his deputy to the bishop of persons to be ordained as deacons or priests. Another survival is the archdeacon's jurisdiction over parish clerks, who were originally in minor orders. No parish clerk, formally appointed in vestry meeting, can be deprived of his office save after judicial inquiry by the archdeacon. From time to time he has to sit in court to hear complaints against such officers, the parties being represented by solicitors, and has power to acquit, to reprimand, or to depose. His more general power over the clergy is exercised in the way of visitation. By a recent revival of activity, the archdeacons now actually visit the parishes under their charge. But in the later Middle Ages and down to the nineteenth century archidiaconal visitations were merely synodal, the archdeacon summoning the clergy to meet him at certain centres, and receiving from them a certain sum as 'procurations' (*q.v.*) in lieu of the cost of hospitality to himself and his attendants which would have fallen upon them had he paid them a personal visit. These procurations, in regard to which archdeacons were not modest or scrupulous, were a fruitful source of income, and of grievance, during the Middle Ages. At these visitations, then as now, churchwardens were admitted to office, and fees were charged for this service. The archdeacon also, as now, inducted new clergy into their benefices, in person or by deputy. He had also considerable and profitable powers in testamentary matters. But his most conspicuous function was that of judge of the moral delinquencies of the laity. Those offences were sought out by official informers and punished in most cases by fines. Thus the mediæval archdeacon and his court had a very unsavoury reputation. It must be borne in mind that the avowed purpose was the good of souls, and therefore it was regarded as lawful and desirable that offences should be sought out. The procedure was that of the canon law, which was borrowed from that of Rome, and rested on the assumption of the guilt of the person accused. Affiliation cases, among others, were heard before this tribunal; and its procedure, favourable always to those who could pay a smart fine, was further discredited by the opening it allowed to the officers of the court for the extortion of hush-money. This moral supervision of the laity caused the office of archdeacon to be regarded as a cure of souls; but its profitable nature, and the fact that it could be exercised by deputy, caused it to be among those types of benefice that were most often bestowed upon aliens. A bishop was the patron, and a bishop was always peculiarly amenable to papal pressure. Of all this jurisdiction very little survives. Since 1840 only the bishop has jurisdiction in penal proceedings against the clergy. The archdeacon has power, after hearing evidence, to correct parish registers —a power which is declining in importance since the institution of the state system of registration.

By the legislation of the nineteenth century,

as has been said, the archdeacon has been deprived of most of his powers, and what remains has been made uniform in all cases. In earlier times there was great diversity, some, *e.g.* the Archdeacon of Richmond in Yorkshire, having exercised very wide authority. The only conspicuous survival is the prerogative of the Archdeacon of Canterbury, who still enthrones every bishop of the southern province; his fees for this service were once no small part of an income which made him one of the wealthiest of English dignitaries. The incomes of the archdeacons have also been in most cases made uniform, at the sum of £200 per annum, including an estimated amount, which is never received, for their fees. Their former estates, when they had such, have been swept into the common fund of the Ecclesiastical Commissioners. We may regard the isolated case of the Bishop of Ely, who is his own archdeacon for the Isle of Ely, *i.e.* North Cambridgeshire, as an evidence of the former value of the office. The bishop occupies the place of the Abbot of Ely in this respect, as in others, and the abbey was exempt. Some other great monasteries: Glastonbury (*q.v.*), St. Albans (*q.v.*), and Westminster (*q.v.*), also nominated their own archdeacons. They also were free from any jurisdiction of the bishop or his officers over churches on their estates, but appointed an archdeacon instead of entrusting their abbot with the duty. The immunity of Westminster passed from the monks to the chapter, and remained till peculiar jurisdictions were abolished by 6-7 Will. IV. c. 77 and subsequent Acts. The archdeaconry survives as an honorary post.

The original purpose of Convocation (*q.v.*), as of the mixed clerical and lay assemblages which preceded it and Parliament, was taxation. At such assemblies the archdeacons, as prominent and wealthy ecclesiastics, appeared. This is especially noted in regard to that at London in 1177. When Convocation was constituted, and also in other Church councils of the thirteenth century, the archdeacons at first appeared as representatives of their subordinate clergy. They might be accompanied by elected delegates, yet still they appeared not in their own right but as part of the representation; or they might come without elected representatives, but with procuratorial letters from the clergy. The unreality of an official acting as a representative soon became apparent, and from 1277 onwards the clergy have appointed their own proctors, while the archdeacons have been summoned to Convocation in virtue of their office.

The present position of the archdeacon is one of influence with the clergy and people, and also with the bishop, rather than of administrative authority. He can advise the bishop because he has local knowledge, and in the course of acquiring that knowledge he has won the confidence of people and clergy. Much of his most important work is done not in the ordinary course of his duty, but as a commissioner *ad hoc*, appointed by the bishop. But there is a tendency to entrust suffragan or assistant bishops from time to time with tasks that would naturally and constitutionally fall to the share of the archdeacon.   [E. W. W.]

ARCHITECTURE. The history of English architecture differs very considerably from that of Continental Europe for two important reasons. (1) The complete overthrow of the Roman civilisation caused a break in its development from earlier models. (2) The spirit of insular independence has repeatedly exemplified itself in architecture.

Pre-Norman Period

The remains of Roman buildings, though numerous, are works rather of engineering than of architecture, chiefly consisting of walls or the foundations of buildings erected for military purposes. The great wall built by Severus early in the third century, from the Solway to the Tyne, to replace the turf wall of Hadrian, is the greatest of all Roman works in Britain. Here the ashlar work is of small stones almost cubical, laid in regular courses with rather wide joints. At Cilurnum, Borcovicus, and Amboglanna, stations on the wall, as also at Corstopitum, the foundations of buildings faced with large stones in the best traditional Roman manner can be seen. The Newport gate at Lincoln is also a fine example of this mode of construction. Another mode of building, unknown in Rome itself, but general throughout the provinces of the later Empire, consisted of rows of small stones alternating with courses of narrow bricks, as seen at Leicester, Lincoln, and York. Remains of Roman masonry exist at Burgh Castle, Richborough, Colchester, Porchester, Silchester, Pevensey, Caister, Worcester, Reculvers, Dorchester, Wroxeter, Aldborough, and London. The nearest approach to a perfect Roman building is the Pharos in Dover Castle.

Roman building material was often used again in later buildings, as at Brixworth and St. Albans. Of churches possibly Bosham and certainly St. Martin's, Canterbury, alone retain portions of this original Roman construction. At Silchester the foundations have been unearthed of a church erected probably about A.D. 350. It is forty-two feet long, consisting of nave, aisles, a western apse, and an eastern narthex.

The remains of Celtic architecture are very scanty. Cornwall furnishes a few examples. The best known is the oratory of Perranzabuloe, built before 450, and discovered in the sands in 1835. It is twenty-nine feet by sixteen, with gables twenty feet high, and side walls about thirteen feet high. There was an east window, a priest's door, and an entrance on the south. The masonry consisted of stones embedded in clay without mortar. The Saxon invaders destroyed many existing buildings, and exterminated most traces of older civilisation. When they were converted to Christianity they usually built their houses and churches of wood. About 680 Bede records the building of stone churches at Wearmouth and Jarrow ' in the Roman manner.' This is usually considered the starting point of the history of English architecture, which from this time to the Norman Conquest is known as the 'Saxon' or 'Anglo-Saxon' style. This term is misleading, for though English buildings may have had their own peculiarities, still there is little to entitle them to be classed as belonging to a style distinct from contemporary buildings on the Continent. The small and plain Saxon churches were simply ruder examples of the same Romanesque style which was general throughout Europe and was the common heritage of the West from Rome. In spite of the numerous Saxon remains few buildings have come down in anything like a complete state, and these are usually fragments of small churches, the larger Saxon minsters having been destroyed and rebuilt in later ages. The small church at Bradford-on-Avon is typical of the Saxon style: a simple rectangle for a nave, with a smaller rectangle to the east for a chancel, with a porch on the north and originally also on the south; narrow and lofty, with small windows set high up so as to keep off the draughts and to make the church a place of security in case of invasion. This church has been generally considered to be the work of St. Aldhelm (*q.v.*), 705. The similarity of the masonry to that of St. Wilfrid's crypt at Hexham seems to give strength to this view. Recent critics, however, hold that the excellence of its construction and the fine joints of the stone work point to a much later period. Some of the earliest Saxon work, however, as at Hexham and Ripon, under the influence of the Roman missionaries, shows work much superior to that which followed. Brixworth is an example of early Saxon construction, where Roman bricks are used up in the regular Roman manner. Brixworth, Wing, and Lydd are the only aisled Anglo-Saxon churches which survive.

One of the most general marks of Pre-Norman work is ' Long and Short work.' This consists of an alternation of tall upright and flat horizontal stones to form the angles of the building. Another mark is pilaster strips upon the surface of the walls. Of seventh and eighth century buildings Wing is especially interesting. It is a basilica with a polygonal apse ornamented externally with small pilasters, from which spring semicircular arches. Internally the apse has a raised floor, reached by a flight of steps. Underneath is the crypt or confessio ; the nave arches are semicircular on massive plain piers, and above them the lines of the ancient clerestory can be traced. The English fashion of square east ends seems soon to have replaced the earlier apse, transepts were added, and usually a western tower, though the central tower in the larger cross churches was not unusual. Worth, Barton-on-Humber, Earls Barton, Barnack, Sompting, Dover Castle Church, Repton, Holy Trinity, Colchester, are examples of Saxon work up to the beginning of the eleventh century.

The period immediately preceding and succeeding the Norman Conquest shows numerous examples of Saxon towers. St. Bennet, Cambridge; St. Mary and St. Peter, Lincoln; St. Michael, Oxford; Deerhurst, and a whole group of churches in the north-east of Lincolnshire. ' In all these Saxon buildings there is a closer tradition of Roman work than we see in the later Norman forms of Romanesque. There is a tendency to large stones, to flat jambs, to windows with a double splay, to the covering of walls with horizontal and vertical strips.' The towers are simply smaller and ruder examples of a type common in Italy and Germany up to a much later date. They are tall, slender, and unbuttressed, with small round-headed windows (sometimes triangular-headed), with curious baluster pillars set in the middle of the wall. The windows are set in groups of two or more, but are never grouped under a containing arch as in the Norman style. Saxon masonry is often very rough and rude. Herring-bone work peculiar to this style consists of flat stones or tiles placed like herring bones in rough walling. At Sompting is the original coping of the tower, a low four-sided spire.

Of the hundreds of churches standing at the time of the Conquest only about seventy preserve parts of their original Saxon work. The nave of Greensted Church, Essex, built about 1013, is the only example which survives of a timber church, a mode of construction at one time peculiarly Saxon.

The little church at Kirkdale, Yorks, has an inscription recording its destruction by the Danes and its restoration in the reign of Edward the Confessor.

NORMAN, 1060-1190

Under the Confessor's rule the Norman variety of Romanesque was first brought to England. In 1065 the church of Westminster was consecrated in a ' new style' (William of Malmesbury), and henceforth the earlier mode of building was displaced, though small churches continued for some years to be built in the old style, as at Lincoln and Oxford.

The Norman Conquest inaugurated a period of extraordinary architectural activity. The churchmen introduced by William began at once to rebuild their churches on a scale of unprecedented magnificence. St. Wulfstan (*q.v.*) of Worcester raised the only voice of protest against the destruction of the old Saxon minsters, yet he rebuilt his cathedral church later in the Norman manner. From the Conquest till the end of the twelfth century the Norman form of Romanesque prevailed. The style, however, continued to develop gradually from the clumsy, massive, and severe type of the early period (at first almost transitional from the Saxon) to the lighter and more ornamental features of the later period. This in turn becomes transitional to the Gothic or early pointed of the thirteenth century. The earliest Norman minsters are vast, massive, and plain. Their plan is that of the cross with boldly projecting arms or transepts. The western limb or nave is usually of immense length, as at Winchester, and St. Albans (*q.v.*), which has the longest nave in the world. The eastern limb is short, and terminated in the early examples with an apse. There were two forms of this apse :—

1. That in which the choir and lateral aisles had each a separate apse, the two lateral or smaller ones usually having square external walls, as at Romsey and originally at Durham and Selby.

2. That in which the central apse was encircled by the aisle called the ambulatory, with chapels radiating to the north-east, the east, and the south-east. This was the more common form, as originally at Westminster,

Bury St. Edmunds, and Norwich. The rectangular east end, however, soon began once
more to reassert itself at Old Sarum, Southwell, Sherborne, and Ely.

The chapels opening eastwards from the
transepts were usually apsidal. There was
usually a low central tower at the crossing
and often two more at the west end, as at
Durham and Southwell. Exeter and Canterbury, in a modified form, have transeptal
towers; Hereford, Ely, and Bury had single
western towers in conjunction with a central
lantern. The destruction of the abbey of
Bury St. Edmunds is an irreparable loss to
the study of Norman work. The church was
of gigantic proportions, with a western
transept of nearly two hundred and fifty
feet (the façade of Rouen is only one hundred
and ninety feet). The early Norman churches
have low massive piers with a triforium nearly
as large as the pier arches, as at Winchester,
where Walkelin's solemn transepts, 1079-93,
show what the great minster must have
been before the perpendicular casing was
thrown over its vast nave. Norwich, begun
1096, is rather more advanced; Gloucester,
1089-1100, has lofty piers with small triforium and clerestory; Tewkesbury, 1102-21,
is of the same style, but still more exaggerated. In Durham the high-water mark of
Norman work is reached in 1093 by William
St. Carileph and finished by Bishop Ranulph
Flambard, 1128. Here the pillars are not
so lofty as Gloucester, but the pier arches
are higher, and the triforium lower than at
Winchester and Norwich. Durham has hit
the happy mean, and is undoubtedly the
most magnificent Norman Romanesque
church in existence. Norman piers are
mainly of two kinds—the compound and the
cylindrical. The latter are too heavy to be
called columns. Columns proper rarely occur
except in crypts. The cylindrical piers are
found at Gloucester and Tewkesbury and
Southwell. At Durham and Selby they are
found alternating with compound piers. The
compound pier, however, is by far the most
common, as in the naves of Peterborough,
Ely, and Old St. Paul's. In Peterborough
choir cylinder piers alternate with octagons.
Durham presents the best example of the
compound pier, in which there is a separate
shaft for each order of the arch and for each
rib of the vault. In twelfth-century parish
churches the pier is almost always a cylinder.
These cylinders are sometimes ornamented
with a kind of fluting or zigzag pattern, as
at Waltham, Selby, Durham, Lindisfarne,
and the crypt at York. The capitals were
either the 'cushion,' peculiarly character-

istic of Norman work throughout the whole
period, or the 'scalloped capital,' a form
which was very general throughout the
twelfth century. Another early form of
capital was a kind of rude imitation of the
Ionic, as seen in the chapel of the White
Tower, London. The arches are generally
round-headed in early work, plain and
square-edged. Later they developed plain
round mouldings, and still later, especially
in the case of chancel arches and doorways,
they became loaded with ornament, the most
general form being that of the chevron or
zigzag moulding. The contrast between
the earlier Norman of Bishop Remigius,
1085-92, and the later elaborate work of
Bishop Alexander, 1146, can be studied
on the west front of Lincoln Cathedral.
Windows are often ornamented in the same
way as arches and doorways, they are generally long and rather narrow round-headed
openings, sometimes of two lights divided
by a shaft included under one arch, especially
in belfries. The earliest Norman vaults
are plain and of the barrel form; in the next
stage they have flat transverse arches only.
They then become groined, without ribs.
These occur over aisles or narrow spaces, and
belong to the latter half of the eleventh
century and the beginning of the twelfth.
At a later period the ribs are introduced, as at
Peterborough, 1117-43. The Norman architects preferred to cover their large spaces
with wooden ceilings, as in the naves of Ely,
Peterborough, and Selby. Early Norman
masonry is extremely rude and bad, with wide
joints between the stones, filled in with
mortar of a poor quality. The foundations
of their buildings were rarely securely laid.
The result has been a long list of disasters,
from the fall of the central lantern of Winchester, 1107, to that of Chichester, 1861.
At Winchester the rebuilding of the tower is
marked by much finer work, which is called
'fine-jointed masonry' to distinguish it
from the earlier and inferior form known
as 'wide-jointed masonry.'

EARLY ENGLISH, 1190-1245

The last quarter of the twelfth century
marks the period of transition from the
Norman to the Early English or 'Lancet' or
'First pointed.' All these terms are used
for the first type of Gothic. The process of
transition began, however, much earlier in
the use of the pointed pier arch at Malmesbury, Fountains, Kirkstall, and Buildwas.
The Cistercians, whose architectural energy
was at its height during the latter half of the
twelfth century, aided in no small degree

to develop the styles as at Byland and Roche.

The convenience of the pointed arch would soon suggest its use for windows and doors. Meanwhile under Henry II. the Norman style grows ever richer and lighter. The surface ornament is now wrought into elaborate shapes; columns are used wherever the weight will permit. Capitals become more elaborate, foliage is introduced, almost reproducing the richness of the ancient Corinthian capital. Famous types of this period are St. Peter's, Northampton, the nave of Wimborne Minster, the Galilee of Durham, the magnificent choir of Canterbury, the west end of Ely and Peterborough. St. David's Cathedral, and the shattered fragment of the great church of Glastonbury (*q.v.*), probably the most perfect example in the country. Here, although the pointed arch was used throughout (except in the earlier Lady Chapel), the mouldings are still Norman, though the caps nearly approach the beauty and grace of the succeeding style. At Ely and Peterborough, where the naves were built late in the twelfth century, the general effect of the earlier style is preserved, in harmony with the older model of choir and transepts. When, however, the west end was reached, there is found, especially at Peterborough, fully developed transitional work, very similar to that at Glastonbury. The great façade of Peterborough belongs, however, to the next century. By the end of the twelfth century the early pointed form of Gothic had been evolved. St. Hugh's (*q.v.*) work at Lincoln, 1188-1200, is usually considered the first example of pure Gothic in England. It is, however, now proved that the western end of the choir, the eastern end of the nave with the transepts, and exquisite north porch of Wells are the work of Bishop Reginald de Bohun, 1174-91. This work is undoubtedly Early English, with traces only of the earlier style in the mouldings and the square abacus. Also at Ripon and Bishop Auckland very early examples of Early English occur. The Early English or Lancet form of Gothic, 1190-1245, is distinguished from contemporaneous work abroad by the use of the round abacus (the square abacus is found only in early examples chiefly in the north); by the depth and richness of the mouldings of arch and pillars; by the freer and less conventional foliage of the capitals; and by the use of the detached shaft, usually of Purbeck marble, long and slender, connected with the central shaft at base and capital, also sometimes by one or two intermediate bands.

Another peculiar feature of Early English is its tenacious use of the tall lancet window either alone or in groups of two, three, or five. The space above is often pierced by a circle or quatrefoil. The west front of Ripon; the transepts of York, Beverley, and Hexham; the choirs of Ely and Southwell, Worcester and Rochester; the east end of Durham, Fountains, Rievaulx, and Whitby; the nave and choir of Lincoln: and, above all, the whole cathedral of Salisbury, are among the grandest types of this period. The choirs now become much longer, the square east end becomes almost universal. The few exceptions (as Westminster, St. Hugh's choir, Lincoln, Beaulieu and Croxden, Pershore and Tewkesbury) are often the results of foreign influence. A Lady Chapel at a lower level is now built out beyond the choir, as at Hereford, Chester, Salisbury, and Winchester. The central tower is heightened, and becomes the most important feature of great minsters, as does the western tower of parochial churches. The spire, originally an elongated roof, now develops into the true spire. The early examples, known as 'Broach spires,' rise from the tower much like a roof with eaves, as at Christ Church, Oxford. Just as, in the few cases where the apse occurs, the round has given place to the polygonal, so in the case of the chapter-house the circular becomes octagonal or decagonal, the earliest and largest example being that of Lincoln. Stone vaults with ribs on the angles of the groins, at first simple then more complicated, become general in great churches. The thrust of these vaults required heavier buttresses, which accordingly develop from the flat strips of the early Norman to the boldly projecting mass of the Early English. The Flying buttress used internally in Norman work now becomes a fine external feature. It is the Early English buttress which adds so much to the beauty of the buildings of this date. In France, where its use became exaggerated owing to the great height of the vaults, the effect produced is almost that of scaffolding. The Early English style can be very simple, as in the little chapel of Kirkstead, Lincolnshire, or very lavish in ornament, as on the west front of Wells. The moulding characteristic of the period is the so-called 'Dog-tooth' ornament—a pyramid cut into four leaves, meeting in the points. Sculpture now makes a great advance. The figures on the façade of Wells are especially admirable, though possibly carved under Italian influence.

By the middle of the thirteenth century, during the building of Westminster Abbey, the lancet began to give way to the Geometrical style. Its development was natural and almost inevitable. If two or more lancets are brought together under an arch, and the heads or spandrels pierced by circles, the simplest form of tracery is at once developed. Windows of this kind may be formed of any size, with circles, quatrefoils, and trifoils repeated on different plains. Such is the great east window of Lincoln and the whole eastern extension of the church known as the Angel Choir, one of the loveliest creations of the Middle Ages. The nave of Lichfield, the chapter-house and cloisters of Salisbury, the east end of Ripon, the ruined abbeys of Netley, Guisborough; above all, the magnificent church of St. Mary's Abbey, York, exhibit the style at its noblest. The destruction of this last masterpiece, built at the time when English architecture had reached its zenith of perfection, is the most deplorable loss in the whole history of English art.

DECORATED, 1245-1360

Towards the end of the thirteenth century the Geometrical style began to change into the ' Curvilinear ' or ' Flowing,' a style in vogue from about 1315-60. The Geometrical and Curvilinear styles are often included under what is known as the ' Decorated,' 1245-1360. In the Curvilinear style circles, quatrefoils, etc., no longer merely rest on the arches, but the mullions themselves are actually continued in the lines of the tracery, which now becomes more elaborate and varied. This style closely resembles the later French Flamboyant (so called from the flamelike forms of the tracery), but the mouldings, though shallower than in the preceding period, show no signs of that decadence so strongly marked in the French work. There was the usual transition between the Geometrical and Curvilinear styles. The choir of Merton Chapel, Oxford, 1280-90, the nave and chapter-house of York, the Lady Chapel of Lichfield, the chapter-house of Wells, show development from the simple to the more elaborate and varied form of Geometrical architecture, which soon culminated in the great west window of York, 1338, where the Curvilinear style is fully exemplified. The east windows of Carlisle and Selby are the finest examples of the style.

Exeter Cathedral, 1280-1370, provides the best study of the development of tracery; it also shows how the crushing lowness of the English vault can be partly retrieved by the rich effect produced by the additional ribs and bosses which came into fashion at the time.

The use of natural instead of conventional foliage is a feature of this period, as also the use in the mouldings of the ' Ball flower ' a globular flower half opened, showing within a small round ball. This ' Ball flower ' is used in the greatest profusion at Leominster, Hereford, Gloucester, and on the towers of St. Mary's, Oxford. Pillars are clustered, detached shafts disappear; doorways, sedilia, piscinas, niches, arcading, buttresses, and pinnacles show great variety of form and degrees of richness. The triforium often becomes absorbed with the clerestory or disappears entirely. Fine examples of the Curvilinear style are the choirs of Lichfield, Wells, and Tewkesbury; parts of Gloucester, Bristol, and Malmesbury; the great parish churches of Boston, Grantham, and Hull; and the smaller church of Heckington, Lincs. To this period also belong the magnificent group of towers at Lincoln; the towers and spires of Salisbury, Lichfield, Hereford, Wells, St. Mary's, Oxford; St. Mary Redcliffe, Bristol, Grantham, and the glorious octagon lantern of Ely.

PERPENDICULAR, 1360-1547

The last great period of Gothic architecture is usually known as the Perpendicular, 1360-1547. This has been subdivided into Rectilinear, 1360-1485, and Tudor, 1485-1547. Gloucester Abbey evolved Rectilinear architecture as early as 1330-7; it did not, however, come into general fashion till about 1360. It is a style peculiar to England alone, and its evolution from the Curvilinear is somewhat unaccountable. Probably the growing tendency to treat churches as mere frameworks for the gorgeous glass of this time is largely answerable for its popularity. [GLASS, STAINED.] It is the style, above all, of the great parish churches. The cathedrals and abbeys were as a whole completed when the ' Black Death ' devastated the country. When the architectural thread was once more taken up in the latter part of the fourteenth century, it was mainly parochial, not monastic. The great merchants now vie with churchmen in their zeal for church building. The distinguishing feature of the style is that the mullions are continued into the tracery in straight or perpendicular lines. This straight line appears first not in windows but in panelling in Abbot Wigmore's work at Gloucester, 1329-37. This panelling was used to case over the Norman work, and was carried up to the clerestory, which here appears to form simply part of the system of panelling with windows pierced in it. The two great builders who did most to popularise the style were Bishop Edington, who began to re-model the nave of Winchester, 1360, and his better known successor, Bishop William of Wykeham (*q.v.*), who finished the nave of that church and built his two colleges at Winchester and Oxford. At his death, 1404, Perpendicular had become the general style throughout the country. There was the usual period of transition between this and the preceding style, of which the best examples are the church of Edington, built by the bishop of the same name, and the choir of York (the work of Archbishop John de Thoresby). The leading principle of the Perpendicular style is the prominence given to the vertical line in everything, a promin-ence made more thorough by the presence of the strongly marked horizontal line. Mouldings on arch, pillar, or capital now become shallow and, as the style progresses, coarse. Panelling often seems to swallow up all ornamentation. It occurs on arcades, piers, windows, buttresses, and walls.

Ornaments are used at times lavishly, but they are added ornament, not constructive features brought into ornamental shapes. Windows attain a vast size, as at Winchester, Bath, Beverley, York, and Gloucester. The clerestory windows by their size often give great dignity, as at Sherborne; Christ Church, Hants; St. Mary Redcliffe, Bristol; Malvern. Square-headed windows used for convenience in the Decorated period now become very general, though their use for large eastern windows only occurs at Bath, where the style shows its very latest phase. In door-ways the square head with a depressed arch within becomes almost universal. This four-centred arch even occurs occasion-ally in pier arcades. Porches are often highly enriched with panel work, buttresses, pier arches, arcades, tabernacles, and figures. The roof and gables become low-pitched. The parapet, pierced or embattled, becomes an important feature. The three great characteristics which do much to raise this style into importance are the superb vaults, the fine wooden roofs, and the magnificent towers.

The Lierne vaults are those in which short transverse ribs or 'liernes' (French *lier*, to bind) are mixed with the ribs that branch from vaulting capitals. In the earlier and best examples the main constructional ribs are retained, as in the choir of Ely, the naves of Norwich, Winchester, Canterbury, and Tewkesbury. In later examples the ribs seem to run over the vault without much meaning, producing, however, a peculiarly

gorgeous effect, as in the choir of Wells or Gloucester, also in St. George's Chapel, Windsor, where it is often erroneously called a 'fan vault.' The 'fan vault,' another form peculiar to this period, is a natural development from the 'lierne.' It is so called from each sheaf of ribs branching out in the form of an inverted conoid, giving the appearance of a fan. This vault first made its appearance in Gloucester Abbey in the vaulting of the cloister, 1351-77. King's College, Cambridge, the Eastern Chapels of Peterborough, Sherborne Abbey, and above all Henry VII.'s Chapel, Westminster, are the best known instances of the fan vault. The wooden roofs of this period are no mere substitutes for the vault, but are often of equal dignity and splendour, and were deliberately chosen by preference. There are various shapes. The grand Hammer-beam roofs of East Anglia, as at St. Stephen's, Norwich; Wymondham; St. Wendreda's, March; and Westminster Hall are examples. The coved or cradle roofs of the west of England, the low-pitched tie-beam roofs common everywhere, show the same style.

'Perpendicular' towers were usually finished off with a rich parapet and pin-nacles. Some of the finest specimens are the great central lanterns of Canterbury, York, Gloucester, Durham, and Howden; the western towers of York and Beverley; the monastic towers of Fountains and Evesham, and those of the parish churches of Boston, Taunton, Wrexham, St. Neots, and St. John's, Glastonbury, with the collegiate towers of Merton and Magdalen Colleges, Oxford. Spires were, however, by no means rare; that at Louth is perhaps the most graceful in all Christendom. St. Michael's, Coventry; St. Mary's, Whittlesea; and Pat-rington and Norwich Cathedral also furnish fine examples. The unique mural crown of Newcastle also belongs to this period.

With the destruction of the monasteries and the spoliation of the Church ecclesiasti-cal building came practically to a standstill. By the middle of the sixteenth century Gothic architecture lay a-dying. The de-struction of hundreds of abbey churches and one fine cathedral (Coventry) can only be accounted for by the indifference of the great mass of the people to the architectural splendour of the past.

RENAISSANCE, 1510-1750

The Renaissance first makes its appear-ance early in the sixteenth century in Henry VII.'s Chapel, Westminster, where the Italian, Torrigiano, was called in to design the late

King's tomb. His work is wholly Renaissance in design, and the effigies of Henry VII. and his Queen are amongst the very noblest in Europe. The same artist was at work on the chantry of the Countess of Salisbury at Christ Church, Hants. In Layer Marney Church, Essex; in Bishop West's chantry, Ely; and in Bishop Gardiner's chantry at Winchester, Renaissance detail, with its scrolls, diaper work, and foliage, overlies the perpendicular design.

From the accession of Elizabeth to the reign of Charles I. there was a period of transition from expiring Gothic to ever-growing Renaissance. This has given us the styles known as Elizabethan (where the Gothic spirit, in spite of classical detail, still holds the ground), and Jacobean, where classicism has advanced but not yet eliminated Gothic.

This is the period of the great houses built with the confiscated wealth and often with the very stones of the despoiled church. No outline can be more picturesque than that of an Elizabethan house, with its great oriel windows, tall chimneys, and endless gables. Italian details are used after a Gothic fashion, classical or quasi-classical columns are inserted just as mediæval builders used their windows and blank arcades. Many ranges are placed one over the other. Longleat, possibly the earliest house of this kind, built in the reign of Edward VI.; Kirby Hall, Northamptonshire; Bishop Hall's house, Heigham; Ingestre Hall, Staffordshire; Burghley House, Hatfield House, Fountains Hall, are a few of the numberless examples of this style.

Meanwhile Perpendicular Gothic was dying hard, especially in Oxford, that ' home of lost causes.' The college chapels of Wadham, 1613; Jesus, 1621; Lincoln, 1631; St. Mary Hall, 1633; Oriel, 1637, show a determined effort to keep to the old style. The design and details of Wadham are so excellent that it might well have been erected a century earlier. The most remarkable example, however, of the Gothic Survival is the staircase of Christ Church Hall, with its central pillar and fan tracery, built as late as 1640. The Canterbury buildings of St. John's College, finished 1636, are among the most beautiful examples of the friendly meeting of the old and the new styles. The quadrangle, with its two arcaded cloisters, is mainly classical, but the exquisite ' Garden front ' is almost Tudor. This is probably the work of Le Sueur and not Inigo Jones, to whom it is popularly ascribed. Brasenose

Chapel, 1666, shows an effort to blend Gothic and Renaissance with the most charming effect. It is probably the latest example of Gothic as a living though an expiring tradition. Other churches showing good seventeenth-century Gothic are Bath Abbey, where Bishop Montagu added the fine fan vault to the roofless nave, 1608-16; St. John's, Leeds, 1632; Leighton Bromswold, restored 1632; Abbey Dore, restored 1634; the chapel of Peterhouse, Cambridge, 1639; St. Catherine Cree, London, 1630.

Inigo Jones was the first English architect of importance to free himself entirely from the Gothic tradition. The Banqueting-House at Whitehall (part of a vast design for a royal palace) and the portico of Old St. Paul's show design equal to Palladio and the great Italian masters. His work was unfortunately interrupted by the Great Rebellion.

The Restoration and the Great Fire of London inaugurated a period of building activity under the influence of Sir Christopher Wren. St. Paul's Cathedral, his masterpiece, ranks among the finest Renaissance buildings in the world, but like its great rival, St. Peter's at Rome, was dearly bought by the destruction of its magnificent predecessor. Of the fifty churches Wren built in London, St. Stephen's, Walbrook; St. Bride's, Fleet Street; St. Mary-le-Bow, St. Martin-upon-Ludgate are noteworthy either for their fine interiors or graceful spires. The chapels of Emmanuel College, Cambridge, and Trinity College, Oxford, and the northern walk of the cloisters at Lincoln are also well-known works of this great master. His interiors, though often dignified, are certainly more conducive to sitting in comfort than to kneeling in devotion.

Of Wren's contemporaries and immediate successors the following deserve remembrance :—Sir John Vanbrugh, the builder of great mansions, such as Blenheim, Castle Howard, and Duncombe Hall; Hawksmoor, who designed the new quadrangle of All Souls and the front of Queen's College, Oxford, and St. Mary Woolnoth, London; Dean Aldrich of Christ Church, Oxford, builder of All Saints in the High Street; Thomas Archer, whose church of St. Philip's, Birmingham, is now the pro-cathedral; Gibbs, the architect of the Senate House, Cambridge, and the Radcliffe Library, Oxford, St. Mary-le-Strand and St. Martin's-in-the-Fields, with a portico, second only to St. Paul's in all London; Henry Bell of King's Lynn. With the passing of these masters architecture fell on evil days—a period which lasted from the reign of George II. till the Gothic Revival. In every county may be seen the work of this unfortunate time: hideous towers and porches, barnlike churches fitted on to ancient towers.

The first quarter of the nineteenth century was marked by the revival of Greek models. St. Pancras Church, built by Messrs. Inwood in imitation of the Erechtheum at Athens; the British Museum; St. George's Hall. Liverpool, and numerous halls and institutes up and down the country, are types of this fashion.

GOTHIC REVIVAL FROM 1830

The revival of Gothic began early in the nineteenth century. Even in the eighteenth century, a time when mediæval architecture was, as the name Gothic shows, an object of general contempt, such men as Horace Walpole and the architect, James Essex, could appreciate its merits. To Sir Walter Scott more than any one is probably due the popularisation of mediævalism. At first there was a general opinion that Gothic was the right style only for churches. Those built in the early part of the nineteenth century, though bad in detail, are often excellent in outline, especially the towers and spires. 'The Martyrs' Memorial,' Oxford, erected 1839, was the most successful in point of detail of all the early attempts. With the building of the Houses of Parliament, 1840, from a plan of Sir Charles Barry in the late Perpendicular style, the Gothic Revival may be considered to have become general.

The names most associated with the revival from this time to the present day are, first and foremost, A. W. Pugin; Butterfield, best known for his work at Keble College; Sir Gilbert Scott, whose handiwork is visible in nearly every great church in the land; Street, whose greatest but not most satisfactory design is that of the Law Courts in the Strand. These great architects, with their correct reproductions of early forms, seem to have failed to catch the spirit of the past. Not so, however, Pearson, whose masterpiece, Truro Cathedral, is worthy to be compared with any work of the thirteenth century.

The churches designed by Bodley and his partner, Garner, breathe the very spirit of the fourteenth and fifteenth centuries. The church of Hoar Cross, Staffordshire, and the chapel of Clumber are magnificent. Amongst living church architects mention must be made of the younger Scott, whose stupendous design is gradually rising to completion above the busy dockyards of Liverpool.

[W. M. W.]

ARMINIANISM is a general term used to cover the whole High Church and Latitudinarian reaction against the intellectual tyranny of Calvinism (*q.v.*). Jacobus Arminius (or Hermann) (1560-1609) studied theology in Leiden. There he was greatly influenced by Koornhert, who argued for toleration in religion against the rigid uniformity imposed by the ministers. After some time spent at Geneva he became an important preacher in Amsterdam, and 1603 succeeded Franz Junius as Theological Professor at Leiden. On being appointed to refute Koornhert, who had attacked the doctrine of divine decrees, Arminius examined the whole matter, and developed his position in the direction of free will. His system was developed by his successor, Simon Episcopius. Its chief points are the denial of irresistible grace and the necessary final perseverance of the elect. While not denying the sovereignty of God, from which the whole Calvinistic scheme was deduced by rigid *a priori* reasoning, Arminius postulated that strong belief in the self-limitation of God's power, involved in the creation of free beings. He was violently opposed by his colleague, Gomarus, and 1610 a number of Dutch ministers, known as 'Remonstrants,' presented a list of articles formulating their dissent from Calvinistic orthodoxy. They secured an edict of the States-General in favour of the toleration of both opposing views in 1614. This, however, only served to bring the matter into the party quarrels between the partisans of the house of Orange and those of the *bourgeois* and republican ideals of Amsterdam. In 1617 Prince Maurice of Orange imprisoned the Arminian leaders, Oldenbarnevelt and Grotius, and summoned the famous synod of Dort to decide the controversy. This synod was attended by representatives of foreign churches, including some English clergy sent by James I. [REUNION, III.] It passed decrees condemning the Remonstrants, and asserting the main points of Calvinistic doctrine, but leaving open the infralapsarian position. The supralapsarian view asserts that the divine decree predestined the fall of Adam, thus denying all freedom to humanity; the infralapsarian denies this, and though repudiating freedom to all Adam's descendants is not fatal to free will in the abstract.

Whether or no it was due to the presence of English representatives at the synod, there is no doubt that from this time onwards there developed a strong intellectual movement in England against the rigid Calvinism in fashion. Laud (*q.v.*) and his friends were, in Mr. Gardiner's phrase, the 'broad Church-men' of the day. On a point so complex and profound as the relation of human freedom to divine grace they declined to dogmatise, and adopted the line afterwards suggested by Mozley (*q.v.*) in regard to this very controversy, that it were to be wished that on some subjects the human mind would admit its limitations. Like Arminius and his followers they revolted against the tenet of Calvinism that Christ did not die for all men, but only for the elect. With this negative position in regard to the prevailing Protestant orthodoxy there went for the most part other strong positive views about the nature of the Church and the value of external ordinances. With these we are not here directly concerned. These points, together with Laud's methods of enforcing conformity, enhanced the dislike of the Arminian or court clergy. But from the time of their first favour at the beginning of the reign of Charles I. there is no doubt that the Puritan party felt in them their true adversaries. This was seen in the passionate attack on Richard Mountague [CAROLINE DIVINES], author of the *New Gag for an old Goose*, and the contest that ensued between the Commons and the King, which was provoked by Mountague's *Appello Cæsarem*. This struggle, which lasted from 1625 to 1629, was closely connected with the general course of politics. Indeed, this case of Mountague alone affords strong evidence of the predominantly religious character of the conflict between Charles and the Puritans. A study of the Parliament which passed the Petition of Right reveals this most clearly. Mountague had been condemned for his *Appello Cæsarem* in 1625, and was made a bishop in 1628. Charles in December 1628 published the Declaration still prefixed to the Articles of Religion (*q.v.*), which endeavoured to prevent the imposing a purely Calvinistic sense on the Thirty-nine Articles. In this Charles was eminently justified, and was but continuing the policy which directed the whole Elizabethan Settlement (*q.v.*). The Commons, however, strong in Puritan prejudice, would have none of this. They drew up a Remonstrance, in which the spread of popery and the encouragement of Arminianism were totally condemned, along with the King's claim to levy tonnage and poundage.

Finally, in the next year, 1629, after Buckingham's assassination and Mountague's consecration (they took place on the same day), the great breach with the King took place when the Speaker was held down in his chair, and the three famous resolutions of

Sir John Eliot were passed, the first of which is in the following words: — ' Whosoever shall bring in innovation of religion, or by favour or countenance seem to extend or introduce Popery or Arminianism or other opinions disagreeing from the true and orthodox Church, shall be reputed a capital enemy to this Kingdom and Commonwealth.'

From that day began the eleven years' personal government of Charles, and the short-lived triumph of the 'Arminian' clergy. Associated in the popular mind with court favour, unpopular doctrine, and laxity of life, their position was never pleasant. Nor can it be denied that, until the cleansing fire of the Puritan persecution, the party contained in its ranks too many time-servers. Baxter's testimony in regard to the clergy of his youth is perfectly sincere, and may well be trusted. On the other hand, even apart from these other views, their position as opponents of the rigid predestinarianism in fashion was a courageous and necessary protest in favour of a truly Catholic faith against a view of God which made Him the worst kind of Oriental despot. [CALVINISM.]

[J. N. F.]

ARNOLD, Thomas (1795-1842). Headmaster of Rugby, youngest son of William Arnold, Collector of Customs at Cowes. The Arnolds came originally from Holland, and established themselves at Lowestoft, whence they removed to the Isle of Wight. It has been surmised, but never proved, that they were originally of Jewish origin. Arnold was educated at Winchester College. As a boy he seems to have been stiff and shy, fond of acting the Homeric battles, and reciting speeches from Pope's Iliad. His son, the celebrated Matthew Arnold, said in later years : ' My father's Latin verses were bad, not because he was a bad scholar, but because he was thoroughly unpoetical. He wrote excellent Latin prose, and his Greek you could not tell from Thucydides.'

In 1811 he was elected Scholar of C.C.C., Oxford, and 1814 graduated B.A. with a First Class in *Lit. Hum.*, and 1815 was elected Fellow at Oriel. He won the Chancellor's Prize for Latin and English Essays in 1815 and 1817. In 1818 he was ordained deacon, and in 1819 he established himself as a private tutor at Laleham, near Staines. In 1820 he married Mary Penrose, whose mother was the authoress of *Mrs. Markham's History of England*. Among his pupils at Laleham was W. K. Hamilton, afterwards Bishop of Salisbury, who always maintained his tutor's essential orthodoxy. Others, however, believed that his opinions tended towards Unitarianism. His scruples about subscription held him back from priest's orders till 1828. At the end of 1827 he had been elected Headmaster of Rugby. Dr. Hawkins, Provost of Oriel, predicted that he would change the face of education through all the public schools of England, but his brother-fellow, G. A. Denison (*q.v.*), said: 'Then they've got a fool for their headmaster.'

Public sentiment has confirmed Dr. Hawkins's view, and there can be little doubt that Arnold's influence, spreading through schoolmasters trained at Rugby, has tended to raise the tone of public schools, while his personal virtues have been extolled by his favourite pupils: by Dean Stanley (*q.v.*) in his *Life*, by Thomas Hughes in *Tom Brown's Schooldays*, and by A. H. Clough in *Dipsychus*. Before Arnold's headmastership the religious oversight of the boys had been entrusted to a chaplain. Arnold induced the trustees to make him chaplain, and the religion of the school was thus entirely in his hands. He preached every Sunday, with a singular eloquence, fervour, and directness, and his sermons were marked by an adoring devotion to the Lord Jesus Christ, which showed that his Unitarian tendencies had been left behind. But on such topics as the Church, orders, and sacraments he distinctly contravened the Prayer Book. He wished to expand the Church of England so as to include all denominations except the Jews. He believed that the head of a family could, as such, consecrate the Eucharist. His hatred of the Oxford Movement (*q.v.*) carried him beyond the bounds of courtesy, and sometimes even of decency. He peculiarly abhorred the idea of priesthood, and on his last night on earth he earnestly remonstrated with a former pupil (W. C. Lake, afterwards Dean of Durham) on holding the Catholic doctrine of the Holy Eucharist. He was strongly wedded to his own opinions, and his nature was dictatorial. His discipline was stern. His less attached pupils called him 'Tiger Tom,' and remembered to the end of their lives 'that black vein which came out across his forehead' when he was angered. Arnold laboured passionately to make the school a Christian society. Under his vigorous administration Rugby increased, rapidly and continuously, in numbers, improved immensely in tone and reputation, and acquired the place which it has always retained in the first rank of public schools.

In 1841 he was appointed Regius Professor of Modern History at Oxford, and accepted the post partly because it would afford him a sphere and a provision when he should resign Rugby. He delivered his Inaugural Lecture before a great audience on the 2nd December. The New Year found him and the school in great prosperity. He was now at the height of his fame, forty-six years old, and to all appearances perfectly well. On the 12th of June 1842 he died, after a few hours' illness, from *angina pectoris*. He is buried under the altar of Rugby Chapel.　　　　[G. W. E. R.]

Dean Stanley, *Life and Letters of Dr. Arnold*, and conversations with Dr. Bright, Dean Bradley, and Matthew Arnold.

ARTICLES OF RELIGION. The sixteenth century was marked by a general unsettlement in Western Christendom. The upheaval was caused partly by the revival of learning, which sent men back to the New Testament and the writings of the Fathers, so that they were led to contrast the Church as they knew it under papal dominion with the Church of the earliest days. The practical abuses of the later Middle Ages, especially such as were connected with scholastic theories as to human merit and with the discipline of souls in this world or the next, contributed to bring about a revolt from the central Church authority which administered so corrupt a system. A widespread change, however, in the attitude of Christians towards the Roman see was obviously attended with grave danger. Once the strong hand of central authority was shaken off, conflicting opinions on matters of faith were put forth, men assumed the right of private judgment and, refusing the guidance of Catholic tradition, worked out a theology *de novo* for themselves. The great heresies of early times were thus revived by sectaries, who went under the general name of Anabaptists. Under these circumstances responsible leaders in the new movement, both in England and on the Continent, naturally felt that definition of doctrine was necessary; it had to be made clear how far they were at one with the Church of the past, how much of the mediæval system they repudiated, and to what extent they agreed amongst themselves. Accordingly in various parts of Christendom at the Reformation more or less complete Confessions of Faith were issued. Zwingli's *Fidei Ratio* (1530) marked the extreme reaction of Swiss reformers, and the famous *Augsburg Confession*, issued in the same year, for which Melanchthon was mainly responsible, formed the charter of those who followed Luther. A few years later (1536) the youthful Calvin turned his mighty intellect to the working out of a complete system of theology in his *Institutes of the Christian Religion.*

The Reformation in England was at first a political rather than a religious movement. In 1535 negotiations were carried on with the Germans who had accepted the Augsburg Confession. [REUNION, III.] As a result of these attempts there appeared in 1536 the first English Articles of Religion, known as *The Ten Articles.* They did not mark any advance in the direction of doctrinal reformation, but contained a significant repudiation of the Papal Supremacy, for which the Royal Supremacy (*q.v.*) was substituted. That they were distasteful to the Lutherans is indicated by Melanchthon's remark that they had been 'put together with the greatest confusion.' In 1538, as an outcome of further negotiations with Lutherans, *The Thirteen Articles* were drawn up. These were never sanctioned by authority or even published, but have been found amongst papers belonging to Archbishop Cranmer (*q.v.*). They are important, however, because much of their language was adopted from the Augsburg Confession, and since they were used later in the compilation of the Articles of 1552, they formed the channel through which some of the language of the Lutheran formulary passed to our present Articles of Religion.

Under Edward VI. the current of the English Reformation was turned into a different channel. The influence of Lutheranism waned. Cranmer as early as 1548 appeared in the House of Lords as the spokesman of the view of the Eucharist held by the Geneva school of reformers. The leaders of the reforming party in England were in close touch with the same school through the residence of John à Lasco at Lambeth, and of Peter Martyr (*q.v.*) and Bucer (*q.v.*) at Oxford and Cambridge respectively. Cranmer seems at this time to have cherished the idea of drawing together the reformers on the Continent and uniting them with the English Church in the acceptance of a common Confession of Faith. The publication of Articles was for some time deferred in the vain hope of inducing the various reformed bodies to come to an agreement, but at length in 1553 there appeared *The XLII. Articles,* which formed the groundwork of our present XXXIX.

The title of *The XLII. Articles* runs thus : 'Articles agreed on by the Bishoppes and other learned menne, in the Synode at London, in the yere of our Lorde Godde MDLII. for the auoiding of controuersie in opinions and the establishement of a godlie concorde in certeine matiers of Religion.'

Though this title is misleading, as Cranmer admitted under examination at Oxford, in ascribing to these Articles synodical authority it well indicates their purpose and scope. For the Articles do not set out a system of divinity, and in this respect differ very much in character from the formularies of Continental reformers, which exhibit a more uniform body of doctrine. This important difference is accounted for by several causes. In the first place, the Continental reformers, though at first with more or less unwillingness, severed their connection with the Church of the past, and having thus rejected ecclesiastical authority it became necessary for them to re-erect the whole structure of Christian theology from its foundations in Holy Scripture. The aim of the English reformers, on the other hand, was simply the reformation of abuses. The Catholic Creed was assumed, the Primitive Church was taken as a pattern, and the Patristic writings were appealed to. Mediæval errors were attacked, but the organic identity of the Church was taken for granted, and it was, therefore, not considered necessary to construct a theology, but only to put forth Articles dealing, as their title states, with certain matters which were in controversy. Another reason why the Continental Confessions are more systematic than our Articles may be traced to the remarkable fact that they owe so much more to individuals. Since our formulary is the outcome of various influences at work in the nation and in Western Christendom generally, it does not evolve a logically complete theory of God's dealings with men, and some important subjects in theology are not treated at all. On the Continent it was far otherwise. The Reformation there owed almost everything to individuals of commanding personality with special central theories of their own. Thus Lutheranism is a system gathered round the doctrine of justifying faith, while Calvinism (*q.v.*) is a system turning on the absolute power of God as seen in election and reprobation, and other doctrines are subordinated to or influenced by these. In the English Articles it is remarkable that distinctively Lutheran language is avoided on Justification, and the Calvinistic catch-words are absent from the treatment of Predestination, the essential point of reprobation not even being mentioned. At the same time, the influence of the Geneva school, which was dominant in this country in the reign of Edward VI., may be traced in *The XLII. Articles,* particularly in those dealing with the Sacraments. Thus no mention was made of Confirmation, Penance, Orders, or Matrimony as Sacramental Ordinances of the Church, the doctrine that Sacraments take effect *ex opere operato* was repudiated, the practice of Infant Baptism was barely commended, and in the Article on the Lord's Supper it was expressly affirmed that a faithful man ought not either to believe or openly to confess the Real Presence. For four years after Queen Elizabeth's accession there was no authoritative doctrinal standard for the Church of England other than that contained in the Prayer Book, but to the Convocation which met in January 1562 XLII. Articles were presented. These were the Edwardian *XLII. Articles* revised by Archbishop Parker (*q.v.*), aided principally by Cox (Bishop of Ely) and Guest (*q.v.*) (Bishop of Rochester). Four Articles had been omitted, viz. on Grace, on Blasphemy against the Holy Ghost, on the Moral Law, and on the heretics called Millenarii. Four Articles had been added by the same committee : on the Holy Ghost, on Good Works, on the wicked at the Lord's Supper, and on Communion in both kinds. No less than seventeen Articles had been more or less modified. The Upper House of Convocation struck out three Articles dealing with Anabaptist errors no longer of much importance in the controversies of the time, and thus the number of the Articles was reduced to XXXIX. Two changes of importance were further made in the Latin Articles as sanctioned by the Queen (1563), viz. the first part of Article XX., on the authority of the Church, was added, and the Article on the non-participation of the wicked in the Eucharist was left out. This last was, however, reinserted in 1571, when a revision, in which Bishop Jewel (*q.v.*) was the most prominent figure, gave us *The XXXIX. Articles* in their present form.

In reviewing the changes made at the Elizabethan revision two noteworthy features call for remark. (1) As Cranmer had made the Confession of Augsburg his model, so in 1562, when our leading divines would consider their relation to Continental reformers, it was to the Lutheran school rather than to the Swiss that they turned. Many of the changes introduced by the Elizabethan revisers are traceable to the Würtemburg Confession, which was at the time the latest authoritative symbol of the Saxon school of reformers. Thus clauses added to Articles II., VI., and X., and the new Article V. are verbatim from the Würtemburg Confession, while additions to Articles XI. and XX. and the new Article XII. are in close agreement

with the same formulary. (2) In the modifications introduced at this time the Church of England parts company with those bodies which were influenced by the teaching of Zwingli and Calvin, and with which in the reign of Edward she had been closely associated. Among the indications in the Articles of a desire to return to a more Catholic position are the reference to the general consent of the Church as determining the Canon of Scripture (Article VI.), the emphasis on Good Works (Article XII.), the vindication of the authority of the Church in matters of faith (Article XX.), the refusal to condemn the doctrine that sacraments take effect *ex opere operato* (Article XXV.), the assertion that Infant Baptism is 'most agreeable with the institution of Christ' (Article XXVII.), the substitution of the statement that 'the Body of Christ is given' in the Lord's Supper for a repudiation of the Real Presence (Article XXVIII.), and the defence of the Ordinal (Article XXXVI.). The contents of the Articles may be summarised as follows:—

1. The Foundation Truths of Religion, accepted by all orthodox Christians (Articles I.-V.).

2. The Rule of Faith (Articles VI.-VIII.).

3. Individual Religion (Articles IX.-XVIII.). A philosophical group setting forth the theory of man's unregenerate and regenerate state, and dealing more particularly with points on which variety of opinion existed amongst those who had separated from Rome.

4. Corporate Religion (XIX.-XXXVI.). Dealing with the constitution, order, and authority of the Church, and setting out the doctrine of the Sacraments.

5. National Religion (XXXVII. - XXXIX.). Treating of the Church and the individual Christian in their relation to the State.

The Articles were intended to mark the agreement of the Church of England with the Church Catholic, to define its attitude towards Rome and the reformed bodies, to assert the power and independence of the English State in its relation to the Church as one of the forms of national life, and to preclude errors such as had arisen amongst those who had departed from Rome.

[E. T. G.]

Hardwick, *Hist.* : E. Tyrrell Green, *The Thirty-Nine Articles and the Age of the Reformation* ; B. J. Kidd, *The Thirty-Nine Articles* ; and commentaries by Bishop E. C. S. Gibson, Bishop Forbes, Maclear and Williams, and Bishop Harold Browne.

ASKEW, Anne (1521-1546), Protestant martyr, second daughter of Sir William Askew, or Ayscough, Knight, of an old

Lincolnshire family, was born, according to tradition, at Stallingborough, near Grimsby. She was highly educated, devoted to the study of the Bible, and much given to theological disputations, which she used to conduct with the clergy of Lincoln Cathedral. She married against her will one Thomas Kyme of Kelsey; but the marriage was unhappy, and she left her husband after two children had been born.

She was first charged with heresy concerning the Blessed Sacrament, and after Bonner (*q.v.*) had in vain tried to persuade her to sign an orthodox profession of faith was acquitted for want of witnesses. Soon afterwards she was again accused before the council at Greenwich, and met her accusers in an argumentative and most unconciliatory spirit. She refused to make any recantation, and being suspected of receiving support and encouragement secretly from persons of high position was racked in order that she might divulge their names. According to her own account, Lord Chancellor Wriothesley and Rich, the Solicitor-General, plied the rack with their own hands.

In June 1546 she was charged with heresy along with Dr. Shaxton, formerly Bishop of Salisbury, and two others at the Guildhall. All four were sentenced to be burnt, but Shaxton and one other recanted the next day. On 16th July she and three others were brought to Smithfield to be burnt. She was so crippled from the rack that she had to be carried in a chair. Shaxton preached a sermon at the execution. At the last moment Wriothesley offered her a pardon from the King if she would recant. But she maintained a marvellous resolution and composure, and remained firm to the end. Gunpowder was placed round the bodies of the victims to shorten their suffering.

[C. P. S. C.]

Bale, *Scriptores* ; Foxe, *Acts and Monuments* ; Wriothesley, *Chronicle.*

ATTERBURY, Francis (1663-1732), educated at Westminster and Christ Church, first attracted notice by *A Discourse concerning the Spirit of Martin Luther* (1687), written in opposition to the Romanising policy of Obadiah Walker, Master of University College, and became famous ten years later as the principal author of the attack upon Bentley's *Dissertations on the Epistles of Phalaris*, which went by the name of his pupil, Charles Boyle. Already he had become known in London as the most powerful preacher on the High Church side by his appointment as lecturer at St. Bride's, Fleet Street (1691), and preacher at Bridewell

(1693), the former of which posts he exchanged later for the preachership at the Rolls (1698). In 1697 he took up the cause of the silenced Convocations (*q.v.*) in the anonymous *Letter to a Convocation-man*, the first and most effective of a large number of tracts and treatises on the rights of Convocation in the controversy that ensued with the Whig divines. When the Convocation met in February 1700 he took his seat as Archdeacon of Totnes, and at once assumed the leadership of the High Church party in its constitutional conflict with the Upper House. In 1711 he was elected prolocutor, and distinguished his term of office by active support of the Parliamentary proposal for fifty new London churches. In 1713 he became Bishop of Rochester and Dean of Westminster, having already held in turn the deaneries of Carlisle (1704) and Christ Church (1711), in both of which his imperious temper had embroiled him with his colleagues. His refusal to recognise the statutes at Carlisle led to the passing of the Act (6 An. c. 21) to make valid the statutes of Henrician foundations. As Dean of Westminster he is remembered for the courage with which he carried through his scheme for building a new dormitory for the school in the college garden. He did much as bishop to raise the standard among his clergy by insisting upon the examination of candidates for holy orders. In the House of Lords he led the Tory and Jacobite interest. In 1717 he began a correspondence with the Pretender, which was discovered in 1722, and under a bill of pains and penalties he was sentenced to exile. For four years he undertook the ungrateful task of trying to bring some order into the Pretender's affairs, but, finding it impossible, he retired from the service. He died in Paris, 1732, and was buried in Westminster Abbey. He married early in life a Miss Osborne, and had a son and daughter, the latter of whom died under pathetic circumstances while visiting him at Montpellier. As a man of letters Atterbury has never received the credit he deserves. He edited Waller's poems in 1690, and promoted Tonson's folio edition of Milton, whose fame he was the first critic to revive. Many letters remain to Swift and Pope.

[H. C. B.]

Corresp. and Misc. Works, ed. J. Nichols, 5 vols., 1789-1798 ; H. C. Beeching, *Francis Atterbury,* 1909.

AUGUSTINE, St. (d. 604 ?), first Archbishop of Canterbury, was prior of St. Andrew's at Rome when he was sent by Pope Gregory (*q.v.*) in 596 as head of a mission of about

C

forty monks to convert the English. The missionaries were entertained at Lerins, and proceeded to Aix, where they heard of the fierce character of the English, and their courage failed. Augustine returned to Rome to obtain their recall. Gregory sent him back with an encouraging letter, appointed him abbot of the party, and gave him commendatory letters to the kings and bishops of Gaul. The missionaries again set out, and in the spring of 597 landed in Thanet, probably at Ebbsfleet, having with them Frankish interpreters. They advanced in procession, singing a litany, and bearing a silver cross and a picture of Christ, to meet Ethelbert, King of Kent, whose wife Bertha was a Christian. Augustine preached of the Redeemer's work, and Ethelbert, impressed by his words, gave them a lodging in his capital, Canterbury, where they used St. Martin's, the church of Bertha's chaplain, Bishop Liudhard. There on 1st June, the eve of Whit Sunday, Augustine baptized Ethelbert, and many others soon became Christians. Following Gregory's instructions Augustine sought the episcopate, crossed to Gaul, and probably in November was consecrated as archbishop of the English by Virgilius at Arles. On Christmas Day he baptized over ten thousand persons, probably in the Swale, near the mouth of the Medway.

Ethelbert gave him a dwelling at Canterbury and a ruined church, which he rebuilt as Christ Church, for the place of his see; another outside the walls he dedicated to St. Pancras, and near it he began the church of St. Peter and St. Paul (St. Augustine's) for a burying-place for the archbishops of Canterbury. He sent messages to Gregory with questions for the Pope's decision and a request for more workers. They returned in 601 with a fresh band of missionaries, with letters, answers to Augustine's questions, and a pallium [PALL] for him. Being told by Gregory that all the bishops of Britain were to be subject to him, he held a conference with British bishops at Augustine's Oak, perhaps Aust on the Severn, and invited them in brotherly terms to adopt Catholic usages and join in preaching to the heathen. They refused, and finally he proposed, it is said, an appeal to God through a trial of healing. Unwillingly they agreed: a blind Englishman was brought forth; they failed to heal him, but Augustine's prayer was heard, and he received sight. They asked for another conference, and to this, on the British side, came seven bishops and many learned men. Before coming they asked a holy anchorite how they might know whether Augustine was a

man of God. He said that if he rose to meet them he would show by his humility that he was a follower of Christ, but if he remained seated they might know that he despised them. Augustine did not rise at their coming, and they angrily refused his exhortations and denied his authority. Augustine threatened them, prophesying that as they would not preach the way of life to the English, they should suffer death at their hands, which years later came to pass.

Gregory's plan for dividing Britain into two provinces, each with twelve sees, the metropolitan sees being at London and York, was now impossible, and Augustine set aside the part of it which related to London and remained at Canterbury. In 604 he consecrated Justus as bishop of the West Kentings, with his see at Rochester, and Mellitus (*q.v.*) to be bishop of the East Saxons, over whom Saebert, a nephew of Ethelbert, ruled as under-king, with his see at London. Feeling that his end was near, he also consecrated Laurentius to be his successor at Canterbury. He died on 26th May 604, or perhaps 605; and his body was laid outside the church of St. Peter and St. Paul until the building was ready to receive it. He is said to have been tall and of stately bearing. That he was a man of somewhat narrow mind, with the closely restricted view natural to a monk, seems clear from some of the questions he asked Gregory. He seems also to have thought too much of his own dignity, adopting an unconciliatory attitude towards the British clergy. But his work proves him to have been courageous, self-sacrificing, and able, and his name should ever be gratefully revered by the nation for whose sake he dared and accomplished so much.

[W. H.]

Bede, *H.E.*; Dudden, *Gregory the Great*, ii.

AUTHORITY IN THE CHURCH

AUTHORITY IN THE CHURCH is based on the fact that Christianity is not a mere collection of abstract doctrines, but involves the existence of a definitely organised society, the Church. That Jesus Christ when on earth deliberately intended to found such a visible society, or kingdom, as He Himself most often called it, sufficiently appears from His recorded words in the Gospels and from the history of the early Church. From the earliest times we find it in existence, with definite members, the baptized, organised and ruled in a definite way by definite officers. And Christ not only founded such a society, but also bestowed upon it His own authority (Jn. 20$^{21\cdot3}$). All authority was resident in

Him (Mt. 28^{18})[1] in His threefold capacity of Prophet, Priest, and King; and He delegated it to the Church, which thus receives from Him as Prophet authority to teach, as Priest to administer the sacraments, and as King to govern. Further, Christ bestowed on the Church not only authority, but also a promise of the guidance of the Holy Spirit in exercising it (Jn. $14^{16\,17}$, 15^{26}, $16^{13\,14}$). This is an additional proof that the Church was intended to be an organised kingdom, not a fortuitous collection of individual believers, who would inevitably differ among themselves even in essentials. A divinely guided society must recognise some authority competent to declare the truth in important matters. Some truths indeed have been immutably laid down, such as the fundamental laws of morality and the truths embodied in the creeds. These the Church has no power to alter. But, apart from them, there are many matters with which it must deal for itself. Christ did not give it an unchangeable code of laws fitted to deal with any emergency that might arise, but authority to act for itself under the guidance of the Holy Spirit, to make its own laws, and to repeal, alter, or add to them as the changing circumstances of its history might require.

Such authority clearly could not, except in the very first days, be exercised by the whole body of believers. Ultimately the authority derived from Christ is diffused throughout the Church, but in practice it must be committed to definitely appointed officers. These, in the first instance, were the apostles to whom the words already cited were primarily addressed. But their authority did not expire with them. For, as has just been shown, it was necessary that it should continue throughout the Church's history. Both from Christ's words to them (Mt. $28^{19\,20}$) and from their subsequent actions it appears that they were commissioned to inaugurate a continuing ministry. In the New Testament this consists (1) of the apostles and apostolic men, and of presiding ministers appointed by them (1 Tim. 1^3; Tit. 1^5); (2) of local colleges of elders or presbyters, who are also called bishops, and are ordained by the apostles or their representatives (e.g. Tit. $1^{5\,7}$); and (3) of subordinate ministers called deacons (1 Tim. 3^{10}). The absence of records prevents us from following the steps by which this arrangement developed into the threefold ministry of diocesan bishops, priests, and deacons,

each with its distinct powers and functions, which we find established throughout the Church before the close of the second century. This system was introduced into the English Church at its foundation, and at the Reformation the English Church definitely adhered to it. This appears from the formularies then adopted (e.g. the Ordinal and Article XXXVI.) and from representative writers of the time. Individual divines, indeed, were inclined to undervalue episcopacy, but the mind of the English Church is seen in those who laid down the position which it has ever since held, that episcopacy was a form of government adopted by the primitive Church under the guidance of the Holy Spirit, and one from which the English Church had neither the will nor the power to depart. For a modern judicial statement of its position in this respect see *Bishop of St. Albans* v. *Fillingham* (1906, P. 163).

According to this view, the power of exercising authority in the Church resides in the episcopate, which is 'historically the continuation in its permanent elements of the apostolate.' This power is not delegated to the bishops by the clergy or the laity, but was given by Christ to the apostles, and has descended to the bishops. It is inherent primarily in the universal episcopate, but is also exercised by the bishops of any particular part of the Church acting together, who represent the whole Church [COUNCILS], and by each bishop, who in his diocese also represents the whole body. He has 'mission' to that part of the Church which has been entrusted to him, and thence possesses 'ordinary' or original jurisdiction therein. Yet his power is not absolute but constitutional, for it must be exercised in accordance with the law and mind of the Church, whose representative he is. [BISHOPS.] With these limitations the lower orders of the ministry are subject to the authority of their bishop, who represents the Church to them, and in its name gives them mission to their cures. Each order of the ministry possesses in its degree the threefold authority conferred by Christ upon the Church, to teach, to minister, to govern.

During the Middle Ages this system was impaired by the growth of the papal claims, which tended to depress the constitutional authority of the bishops and to introduce an absolutism foreign to the very idea of the Church. In the sixteenth century this process resulted in the English Church renouncing the Roman jurisdiction, but without explicitly rejecting any part of the faith or constitution of the undivided

---

[1] Without going into questions of New Testament criticism, it is here assumed that these passages rightly represent what Christ said and did.

Church. [CONTINUITY OF THE CHURCH OF ENGLAND.] Under these circumstances its bishops collectively and individually continue to represent the authority of the whole Church as they did before, with power to vary and add to its law in matters within the competence of a local Church : those of greater moment it refers to a free and impartial General Council; and in the words of Archbishop Laud (*q.v.*), ' when that cannot be had, the Church must pray that it may, and expect till it may, or else reform itself *per partes*, by *National* or *Provincial Synods*.'

All Church authority is spiritual in its nature, and is binding on the conscience of every member of the Church, *i.e.* baptized person. It may be enforced by spiritual penalties, culminating in expulsion from the Church. [DISCIPLINE.] The State, if it chooses, may add civil sanctions. Thus in 1571 an Act of Parliament enforced acceptance of the Thirty-nine Articles on all ministers (13 Eliz. c. 12). But this added nothing to the spiritual authority which they derived from Convocation. The State may in this and other ways support the Church's authority, or it may endeavour to hamper it ; but it cannot itself exercise that authority or in any way affect its validity, for that is altogether outside its sphere. [CHURCH AND STATE.]   [G. C.]

Gore, *The Ch. and the Ministry* ; Crosse, *Authority in the Ch. of England.*

B

BAMPTON, John (1690-1751), founder of the Bampton Lectureship at Oxford, was son of Jasper Bampton of Salisbury, gentleman. He entered Trinity College, Oxford, and graduated B.A., 1709; M.A., 1712. He was ordained, and became in 1718 Prebendary of the *Minor pars altaris* in the cathedral church of Salisbury and Rector of Stratford Toney, Wilts. By his will he left, subject to his wife's life interest, an estate (Nunton farm), situated in the parishes of Nunton, Downton, and Britford, to the University of Oxford to provide an endowment for a course of eight Divinity Lectures, to be delivered by a M.A. of Oxford or Cambridge on certain Sundays in term. The subjects of the lectures were specified, and their object was 'to confirm and establish the Christian faith and confute all heretics and schismatics.' No lecturer could be chosen a second time. The bequest in part owes its origin to a disagreement with Sir Jacob Bouverie, afterwards the first Viscount Folkestone, at Langford Castle. Mr. Bampton's Nunton lands lay ' contiguous to and greatly intermixed with ' the Bouverie property. Mr. Bampton refused to sell his land, and to prevent its being sold after his death he devised it to the University of Oxford, which became possessed of it after Mrs. Bampton's death, about 1778. The lectures began in 1779. Meanwhile the third Lord Folkestone (second Earl of Radnor) endeavoured in vain to buy or exchange the property, but in 1780 obtained a lease of it, and in 1805 he induced the University to accept in exchange an estate called Tinkersole at Wing, Bucks, and

obtained a private Act of Parliament (45 Geo. III.) authorising the exchange. Thus ' the intentions of Mr. Bampton, other than his concern for the Christian faith, were altogether defeated ' (Shadwell). The lectures were delivered annually until 1901, since which date they have become biennial, and Mr. Bampton's intentions further varied.

[S. L. O.]

Alumni Oxon. ; C. L. Shadwell, *The Universities and College Estate Acts*, 5, 6 (1898) ; MSS. in the University Archives.

BANCROFT, Richard (1544-1610), Archbishop of Canterbury, son of John Bancroft and Mary Curwyn, was born at Farnworth, Lancashire, 11th or 12th September 1544. He studied at the local grammar school, and entered Christ's College, Cambridge, about 1564 ; proceeded B.A., 1567, and removed to Jesus College, where he was Tutor till 1574 ; proceeded M.A., 1570, and D.D., 1585. In the meantime he had been appointed by his maternal uncle, the Archbishop of Dublin, Prebendary of St. Patrick's Cathedral, Dublin, with a leave of absence for six months in the year, but it is unlikely that he was much in Ireland. Apparently he hesitated about entering holy orders, for he was not ordained priest till 1574. He became at once chaplain to Bishop Cox of Ely, was soon made Prebendary of Ely Cathedral, Rector of Teversham, near Cambridge, and one of the twelve University preachers. In 1576 or 1577 he was archiepiscopal visitor of the diocese of Peterborough, and in 1581 of the diocese of Ely. In 1579 he became chaplain to Sir

Christopher Hatton, and now attracted the attention of Burghley, the Lord Treasurer, and of Elizabeth, partly by his preaching against the beginnings of Congregationalism at Bury (1581); partly by a negotiation regarding the revenues of St. Patrick's Cathedral (1584): but more particularly by revealing the truth about the flood of Puritan petitions which began to appear in 1584. The facts he had learned by long and patient investigation, and finally he was allowed to make them public in his famous sermon preached at Paul's Cross in February 1588-9, and in his more famous tracts, issued in 1593, *Dangerous Positions* and *A Survey of the Holy Discipline.* The movement, he showed, was the work of some hundred or two ministers, supported by a few thousand laymen, and led by Cartwright (*q.v.*), Travers (*q.v.*), Chaderton, John Knewstubbs, and others. Its aim, he proved, was not the reformation of the Church in a few minor matters, and the securing of a little toleration for tender consciences, but a thoroughgoing attempt to erect and practise Presbyterianism. The classis meant to transform, not to reform, episcopacy. The Marprelate Tracts (*q.v.*) were the work of the same coterie. He was instrumental in suppressing the tracts, in arresting and trying the classis leaders, and in breaking up their organisation for the time.

In 1587 he became a member of the High Commission (*q.v.*), and soon had given full expression to the tendencies already transforming it, made its inquisitorial functions less prominent, and developed it as a court for the trial of suits between party and party. He had shown, too, that its broad powers, unlimited discretion as to the legal means used, and its flexible constitution, made it the very instrument needed to strengthen the hands of the bishops and put life into the moribund ecclesiastical administration. These long years of varied activity had thus admirably equipped this brilliant man with rare and varied experience, made him cognisant of Church needs and difficulties, taught him administrative routine, shown him the attitude of gentry and common people towards the English Church, and, through his work against the classis and on the High Commission, given him a personal acquaintance with every important Puritan and Roman Catholic in England.

But now, when, eager to attack the abuses in the Church, he became Bishop of London (consecrated, 6th June 1597), he found his chief duties political rather than ecclesiastical; arresting recusants, examining priests suspected of treason, exercising the censor-ship of the press, supervising the universities, going on an embassy to Denmark (1600) to settle fishing rights and incidentally to prevent James VI. from securing Denmark's aid in his candidature for the English throne, supervising the preachers at Paul's Cross, and helping to quell the revolt of Essex (1601). These minor matters, he found, occupied far more of his time than the visitation (1598) and administration of his own see.

It was, however, as a statesman rather than as a bishop that he began a most delicate negotiation. He found the English Roman Catholics (*q.v.*) split up into two parties. The death of Mary Stuart and the defeat of the Armada had turned the thoughts of secular priests and laity to the establishment of some sort of organisation which would ensure the English Roman Catholics observance of their rites without endangering their lives or property, and without waiting for the overthrow of the Government, which seemed postponed indefinitely. What that organisation should be they could not agree, and a party of seculars, headed by Mush and Colleton, petitioned the Pope (1597) to establish an English bishopric, while the Jesuits, followed by the majority of the priests, wished for a missionary station. To appoint a bishop, argued Parsons, was to abandon the great plan of converting England and to come to terms with heretics. The Pope agreed, and established an Archpriest, George Blackwell, who was given practically absolute discretion in the government of the priests in England, and who proceeded to use it as the Jesuits directed. The discontented seculars now appealed to the Pope against this submissiveness to the Jesuits, and were again defeated.

Bancroft realised fully that if he could nurse this split in the Roman Catholic ranks the efficiency of the militant organisation intended to restore the papal power in England would be destroyed. He therefore freed the priests from prison, aided in a new appeal to Rome (1601), and allowed them to publish books openly attacking the Jesuits and expressing their scorn of the Spanish succession. Moreover, Bancroft, with Robert Cecil, Secretary of State, was planning the peaceful accession of James VI. of Scotland to the English throne, and was assuring that monarch that this secret negotiation with the priests would purchase the adhesion of the Roman Catholics to his cause. The appeal to Rome was partly successful, the scandal of a schism in the Roman Catholic ranks in England immensely successful, but neither gave any guarantee for the future.

James I. found himself at once confronted with the problem of the Church. In May 1603 the old classis party had delivered to the King the Millenary Petition, asking for a reform of the Church, and, thus assailed, the Churchmen threw the defence of their case upon Bancroft, who actually succeeded during the next few months in convincing James of its merits. Bancroft claimed that the reorganisation of the Church was not only imperative but was dangerous neither to Church nor State. James, however, insisted that in all fairness Bancroft and the bishops must refute the charges of the Puritans, and hence at the Hampton Court Conference (*q.v.*) in January 1603-4 Bancroft and Andrewes (*q.v.*), and some other divines, conferred at length with James, and then debated with Reynolds, the spokesman of the Puritans, in the presence of the King and a dignified assembly. Then, having answered the Puritans to the King's satisfaction, they received officially charge of the reconstruction of the Church, with some suggestions as to the direction the reforms should take.

With the evils Bancroft was only too familiar. The ' constitution ' of the Church consisted of such legislation as Henry, Edward, and Elizabeth had found time for, and was fragmentary, confused, contradictory, and even of dubious legality. The chief difficulty lay, however, in the condition of the clergy. The majority were without university degrees, and in consequence were ignorant, incompetent, and unable to preach ; about a seventh or eighth of them were pluralists, and about a tenth constantly non-resident.

A sweeping reconstruction of the whole fabric was inaugurated by Bancroft in the spring and summer of 1604, which in its breadth and completeness and in its subsequent influence may fairly be compared in importance to the breach with Rome or the changes of the nineteenth century. Most of this he executed as Bishop of London, for he was not elevated to the throne of Canterbury till 10th December 1604. In Convocation a new set of canons was prepared. [CANON LAW FROM 1534.] The Book of Common Prayer (*q.v.*) and the Thirty-nine Articles (*q.v.*) were confirmed, and a new translation of the Bible (*q.v.*) (the Authorised Version) was begun. A new seal was prepared for the bishops to answer legal objections of the Puritans, the ecclesiastical courts were reformed, and a project prepared for the remodelling of the High Commission. But in the two most essential points Bancroft's plans were defeated : Parliament refused to increase ecclesiastical incomes, and declined to increase the coercive power of the ordinary ecclesiastical courts. Instead, the House of Commons, led by the Puritan gentry, proposed to establish pure Calvinism (*q.v.*) (under the guise of the Lambeth Articles), and to transform the Church into a Presbyterian hierarchy of classes and synods. Without the assistance of Parliament (as the Puritans well knew) incomes could not be increased, and upon them hung the improvement of the character of the clergy and the abolition of pluralities and non-residence. Without its help the power of bishops and commissaries could not be made sufficient to coerce the refractory, ignorant, and disobedient clergy into obedience, and so do away with the nonconformity and irregularity of observance, then so common. Bancroft was compelled to accomplish as best he might these fundamental ends with the means already at hand.

With immense energy and resourcefulness he reorganised in 1605 the old visitatorial system, and actually produced from the system of presentments at visitations more tangible results than any agency had produced in the Church for generations. By selecting only experienced and active men he soon gathered round him a corps of workers who formed the backbone of the administrative life of the Church till the Civil War. With keen insight he declared that the visitation was less useful for punishing delinquents than for informing the clergy what the law was, and he insisted and proved that the vast majority were nonconformists from ignorance and carelessness rather than from conscientious scruples. In the method of visitation changes of the first importance were made, and the records of courts and parishes were corrected, mended, or kept (as need was) for the first time in many years.

Meanwhile during these busy years, 1604-5, the archbishop secured the submission of Puritans and Roman Catholics to the new settlement. He was in favour of mercy and leniency, on the ground that persecution alone could prevent internal quarrels from breaking the Puritans into sects. He therefore deprived about sixty (of whom ten or eleven were at once reinstated), and suspended about a hundred for a time. In the end all but a few submitted. The Roman Catholics, however, had cherished such expectations of royal clemency that Bancroft's earlier plans seemed for a time doomed to failure. But the Gunpowder Plot changed all. So frightened were the priests that the Archpriest himself (instigated by Bancroft) issued a circular letter execrating the plot and defying the Jesuits. As a result, the secular party received large accessions of strength from the priests and still larger from the laity. After long consultations and the discussion of several forms the oath of allegiance was evolved by Bancroft, consented to by the priests, and enacted in 1606 by Parliament. Bancroft meant the penal laws of 1606 to be an earnest to the Roman Catholics of what would happen if they did not accept his compromise, and swear temporal allegiance to the King in exchange for essential though not legal toleration. The compromise was after much hesitation accepted, and still forms the basis of the relations of the English Roman Catholics to the State and to the Church.

With the constitution codified, the administration, the visitations, and the ecclesiastical courts reformed, with the Puritans crushed and the Roman Catholics conciliated, Bancroft was at last free to devote his time to the two most important problems before the Church: inadequate incomes, inadequate coercive power in the hands of bishops and archdeacons to perform the real work entrusted to them. Social and economic causes had aided the Reformation in reducing most ecclesiastical incomes to a mere pittance. Nearly one-third of the benefices were worth £5 or less, and ninety per cent. were worth less than £26. The commutation of tithes (*q.v.*) into money, the decrease in the value of money in the sixteenth century, and the loss of many customary payments at the Reformation, reduced most clerical incomes to the wages of servants. Yet the Church had steadily increased the qualifications of incumbents, and demanded a better man for less money, while the Puritans complained bitterly that the standard was scandalously low. Finally, the Church had allowed the clergy to marry, but expected them to support a family on the income originally intended to support a single man. Here was the fundamental problem of the Church.

Bancroft's solution, first proposed at a secret conference of the bishops in February 1603-4, was the restoration of tithing in kind, so that the clergyman might once more receive an actual tenth of the produce of the community. This, he pointed out, would ensure a learned, able, resident clergy. But to such wholesale restoration the laity in and out of Parliament were unalterably opposed, and there remained only indirect means. Bancroft therefore turned to the courts. Many of the agreements between the priest and the parish in lieu of tithes in kind were known to be fraudulent, and much litigation

on the subject had gone on for a generation or more; others were not susceptible of legal proof. Bancroft now proposed to test in the ecclesiastical courts as many of these agreements as possible, and where they were not undoubtedly legal to declare them void, and restore tithing in kind. This plan was put into operation. Where it failed two poor benefices were united, and the scandal of plurality and non-residence lessened by an exchange of benefices among the existing clergy, so as to bring the pluralists' benefices as near each other as possible. All the old customary payments not actually abolished by law were also collected, and when necessary recourse was had to the courts.

Naturally this attempt to augment the income of the clergy was resented widely by the laity, who found ready to help them the old foes of the ecclesiastical courts, the common lawyers, armed with their old weapon, the prohibition, so long used to prevent the clergy from judging temporal questions. The battle was at once joined by the issue of a flood of prohibitions, on which the judges decided when possible against the jurisdiction of the Church, and actually threatened Bancroft's whole scheme of reform with annihilation. The archbishop, however, was not daunted. He complained to the King in Council that the judges issued writs which, according to their own standards, were bad, and also disregarded justice and equity (*Articuli Cleri*, 1605). The judges denied these charges, continued to issue the writs, assaulted the powers of the High Commission and its very right to exist at all, and began to demand practically a right to superintend the whole field of ecclesiastical law and administration under the guise of examining the limits of the ecclesiastical jurisdiction. So sharp became the controversy that finally in November 1608 James ordered judges and ecclesiastics to debate the case before him, and continued to hear arguments from time to time till the following July. Bancroft and his lawyers debated, argued, and pleaded in vain; the learning of Coke was too much for them; and in 1610 they had to consent to a tacit compromise, by which they admitted the claims of the common law, while the judges accepted most of the practical reforms in procedure demanded by the ecclesiastics, and allowed the testing of *modi decimandi* to go on under reasonable restrictions. [COURTS.]

The King had in the meantime given Bancroft no less difficult a task than the reconstruction of episcopacy in Scotland. Bancroft himself was during this year occupied with a deputation of eight ministers, headed by the two Melvills, whom James had summoned to London to answer for their conduct. Some of the most characteristic pictures of him we have are from their pens. But despite their opposition bishops were in 1608 given jurisdiction, and in 1610 made 'constant moderators' of the synods, and were to be assisted by two courts of High Commission. One of Bancroft's last acts was the consecration of these new Scottish bishops.

On 2nd November 1610 he died of the stone, from which he had suffered for thirty years. The harsh judgments usually given on his character have been traced to partisan statements, and are not borne out by other evidence. He was a great patron of men of letters, a lover of fine books, of manuscripts, and of the fine arts. In many ways he was a product of the Renaissance, and joined to genuine piety a thirst for power and p.eferment which often led him into unscrupulous acts. Like Bacon, Coke, and Parsons, he was a strange mixture of good and evil. Doctrinal disputes meant little to him, and while in early life he had leanings towards Calvinism, as a mature man neither Calvin nor Arminius attracted him ; he held firmly to the middle way which he and Hooker (*q.v.*) have made so famous. That he first propounded the doctrine of the divine right of bishops cannot be proved by any evidence now accessible. His great administrative gifts and his reconstruction of the administration of the Church, his strong love for it as an institution, and his great vision of its worth and position, will mark him for all time as one of its great builders.   [R. G. U.]

Usher, *Reconstruction of the Eng. Ch.*, 1910. 2 vols. Most of the materials are still in MS. Wilkins, *Concilia*: Cardwell, *Annals* and *Synodalia*; Strype, *Whitgift, Aylmer,* and *Annals,* contain many biographical details; and the Calendar of Cecil MSS. in *Hist. MSS. Com. Rep.* prints much of his correspondence.

BANGOR, See of, may be said to have had its origin in the monastic settlement made by St. Deiniol (early Welsh for Daniel) in the second half of the sixth century, probably on the spot where the cathedral church now stands. The little that is known of the abbot-bishop is of a fragmentary, legendary character. His Latin life is extant in one copy only, written in 1602, but is simply the 'Legenda' that was read on his festival (11th September). The date of his death is given as 584, and he was buried in Bardsey. The primary meaning of 'Bangor' was most probably 'a wattle-fenced enclosure'—thence 'a monastery.' This Bangor was, and is,

sometimes called by the Welsh 'Bangor the Great in Gwynedd.'

Of the diocese so called and its bishops we know next to nothing until we come to the Norman Bishop Hervey, 1092. It was originally conterminous, for the most part, with the old principality of Gwynedd ; and Bangor, being the great monastery within that principality, naturally became the cathedral city and centre of organisation. The diocese to-day comprises the Isle of Anglesey and portions of the counties of Carnarvon, Merioneth, and Montgomery, with an area of 985,946 acres and a population of 221,520. The old detached deaneries of Dyffryn Clwyd (and Cinmerch) and Arwystli were in no archdeaconry, but under the immediate jurisdiction of the bishop. The former, situated within a short distance of the cathedral city of St. Asaph, was in 1859 exchanged for that of Cyfeiliog and Mawddwy. An Order in Council of 1838 prospectively united the two northern Welsh sees to endow the proposed bishopric of Manchester (*q.v.*) with the episcopal income of one, but this arrangement was annulled in 1847.

The *Taxatio* of 1291 assessed the bishop's *Temporalia, i.e.* revenues from land, at £56, 1s. 10d. (the *Spiritualia* at this time appear to have been £100) ; the *Valor* of 1535 assessed the income at £131, 16s. 3d. It was fixed by Order in Council in 1846 at £4200. There were formerly three archdeaconries : Bangor (dating from 1120), Anglesey (1267), and Merioneth (1328). In 1685 the two former were annexed to the bishopric in perpetuity, and so continued to 1844, when they were restored and united to form one archdeaconry, Bangor and Anglesey, and a residentiary stall in the cathedral was assigned as an endowment. There are four residentiary canons, two being also archdeacons, each receiving £350 per annum. The cathedral, though its customs are those of the 'Old Foundation,' was, like the three other Welsh cathedrals, wrested into 'New Foundation' in 1843 (Welsh Cathedrals Act, 6-7 Vic. c. 77). The chapter consists of the dean (dating from about 1163), four canons residentiary, two prebendaries, treasurer, chancellor, precentor, and three canons—all in the bishop's patronage, as also are the two minor canons. There are fourteen rural deaneries.

LIST OF BISHOPS

The supposed early bishops were :—

1. Deiniol, *c.* 550. 2. Elbod, or Elfod, who induced the Church in North Wales to adopt the Roman cycle of Easter, 768

or 770; d. 809. 3. Mordaf, c. 930. 4. Morleis, or Morcleis; d. 945. 5. Duvan. 6. Revedun. 7. Madog Min, c. 1060; drowned at sea on his way to Dublin.

1. Hervey, 1092; first Norman bishop; driven from his diocese by the Welsh in 1109, when he was appointed by the King to be the first Bishop of Ely (*q.v.*). See vacant for eleven years, during which time its affairs were administered by Urban, Bishop of Llandaff.
2. David, 1120; elected by the Welsh, and cons. at Westminster; d. 1139.
3. Meurig, 1140; Archdeacon of Bangor; d. 1161.
4. William, 1162; Prior of St. Austin's, Bristol; there is great uncertainty respecting his association with the see.
5. Guy Rufus, 1177; Dean of Waltham Abbey; d. 1190. See vacant for over four years.
6. Alban, 1195; Prior of the Hospitallers of St. John of Jerusalem; d. 1196.
7. Robert of Shrewsbury, 1197; d. 1213. See vacant for nearly two years.
8. Martin, or Cadwgan, 1215; believed to be one and the same person; Abbot of Whitland, Carmarthenshire; retired in 1236 to Dore Abbey, where he died, 1241.
9. Richard, 1237; Archdeacon of Bangor; d. 1267.
10. Anian, or Einion, 1267; Archdeacon of Anglesey; a good, active bishop; baptized the first English Prince of Wales (Edward II.), 1284; to him belonged the Pontifical of Bangor; d. 1305, at a great age, and buried in the cathedral. There is no evidence that he was succeeded by a bishop named Cadwgan.
11. Gruffydd ab Iorwerth, 1307; d. 1309.
12. Anian or Einion Sais (the Englishman), 1309; Dean of Bangor and Archdeacon of Anglesey; d. 1328, and buried in the cathedral.
13. Matthew Englefield, 1328; Archdeacon of Anglesey; d. 1357.
14. Thomas Ringsted, 1357 (P.); a Dominican Friar of Oxford; d. 1366.
15. Gervase de Castro, 1366 (P.); another Dominican; d. 1370 at the Friary, Bangor, where he was buried.
16. Howel ab Gronwy, 1371 (P.); was elected by the chapter, but the Pope annulled the election and appointed him by papal Bull; Dean of Bangor and Archdeacon of Anglesey; d. 1372 on his way to Rome.

17. John Gilbert, 1372 (P.); a Dominican; tr. to Hereford, 1375.
18. John Swaffham, 1376 (P.); a Carmelite; tr. from Cloyne, Ireland.
19. Richard Yonge, 1400 (P.); tr. to Rochester, 1404; in fact, never took possession of the see.
20. Lewis or Llewelyn Biford, 1404; elected, but, owing to his attachment to Owen Glyndwr, never confirmed; ejected, 1408.
21. Benedict Nicholls, 1408 (P.); tr. to St. David's, 1418.
22. William Barrow, 1418 (P.); Canon of Lincoln; tr. to Carlisle, 1424.
23. John Cliderow, 1425 (P.); Canon of Chichester; d. 1434.
24. Thomas Cheriton, 1436 (P.); a Dominican Friar; d. 1447.
25. John Stanbery, 1448 (P.); a learned Carmelite; confessor to Henry VI. and first Provost of Eton; tr. to Hereford, 1452.
26. James Blakedon, 1453 (P.); tr. from Achonry, Ireland; d. 1464.
27. Richard Edenham, 1465; a Franciscan Friar; d. 1496.
28. Henry Dean, 1496; Prior of Llanthony; tr. to Salisbury, 1500.
29. Thomas Pigott, 1500; Abbot of Chertsey; d. 1504.
30. John Penny, 1505; Abbot of Leicester and Prior of Bradley; tr. to Carlisle, 1508.
31. Thomas Skevington, 1509 (P.); Abbot of Waverley and of Beaulieu; rebuilt the nave and added the western tower to the cathedral; d. 1533.
32. John Salcot, or Capon, 1534; Abbot of Hyde; tr. to Salisbury, 1539.
33. John Bird, 1539; suffragan Bishop of Penreth; tr. to Chester, 1541.
34. Arthur Bulkeley, 1542; Canon of St. Asaph; first of a series of native bishops; d. 1553, and buried in chancel of cathedral. See vacant for two years.
35. William Glynne, 1555; d. 1558, and buried in the choir.
36. Rowland Meyrick, 1559; Chancellor of St. David's; d. 1566, and buried in cathedral.
37. Nicholas Robinson, 1566; Archdeacon of Merioneth; d. 1585, and buried in cathedral.
38. Hugh Bellott, 1586; Dean of Bangor; tr. to Chester, 1595.
39. Richard Vaughan, 1596; Archdeacon of Middlesex; tr. to Chester, 1597.
40. Henry Rowlands, 1598; Dean of Bangor; d. 1616, and was buried in the cathedral.

41. Lewis Bayly, 1616 ; author of *Practice of Piety* ; d. 1631, and was buried in cathedral.
42. David Dolben, 1632 ; Prebendary of St. Asaph ; d. 1633, aged fifty-two, and was buried in Hackney Church.
43. Edmund Griffith, 1634 ; Dean of Bangor ; d. 1637.
44. William Roberts, 1637 ; sub-Dean of Wells ; suffered greatly during Civil War ; benefactor of the cathedral and educator of poor scholars ; d. 1665.
   Robert Price, Bishop of Ferns, was appointed to succeed him, but died before taking possession of the see.
45. Robert Morgan, 1666 ; Archdeacon of Merioneth ; d. 1673.
46. Humphrey Lloyd, 1673 ; Dean of St. Asaph ; ejected during the Commonwealth ; d. 1689, aged seventy-eight.
47. Humphrey Humphreys, 1689 ; Dean of Bangor ; tr. to Hereford, 1701.
48. John Evans, 1702 ; tr. to Meath, 1715.
49. Benjamin Hoadly (*q.v.*), 1715 ; the first Englishman appointed to the see since Bishop Bird ; tr. to Hereford, 1721.
50. Richard Reynolds, 1721 ; Dean of Peterborough ; tr. to Lincoln, 1723.
51. William Baker, 1723 ; tr. to Norwich, 1727.
52. Thomas Sherlock (*q.v.*), 1728 ; Dean of Chichester ; tr. to Salisbury, 1734.
53. Charles Cecil, 1734 ; tr. from Bath ; d. 1737.
54. Thomas Herring, 1738 ; Dean of Rochester ; tr. to York, 1743.
55. Matthew Hutton, 1743 ; tr. to York, 1747.
56. Zachary Pearce, 1748 ; Dean of Windsor ; tr. to Rochester, 1756.
57. John Egerton, 1756 ; Dean of Hereford ; tr. to Lichfield, 1769.
58. John Ewer, 1769 ; tr. from Llandaff ; d. 1774.
59. John Moore, 1775 ; Dean of Canterbury ; tr. to Canterbury, 1783.
60. John Warren, 1783 ; tr. from St. David's ; d. 1800 ; buried in Westminster Abbey.
61. William Cleaver, 1800 ; tr. from Chester ; tr. to St. Asaph, 1806.
62. John Randolph, 1807 ; tr. from Oxford ; tr. to London, 1809.
63. Henry William Majendie, 1809 ; tr. from Chester ; d. 1830.
64. Christopher Bethell, 1830 ; tr. from Exeter ; d. 1859.
65. James Colquhoun Campbell, 1859 ; Archdeacon of Llandaff ; res. 1890 ; d. 1895, aged eighty-two.
66. Daniel Lewis Lloyd, 1890 ; Headmaster of Dolgelly, Bangor Friars, and Brecon Schools ; res. 1898 owing to failing health ; d. 1899. He was the last bishop to occupy the old episcopal palace near the cathedral.
67. Watkin Herbert Williams, 1899 ; Dean of St. Asaph, 1892-8.   [J. F.]

Browne Willis, *Survey of Bangor* ; Hughes, *Dio. Hist.* ; Stubbs, *Registr. Sacr.* ; Le Neve, *Fasti.*

BARLOW, William, d. 1568, Bishop of Chichester, was an Augustinian canon of St. Osyth's, Essex ; educated there and at Oxford ; Prior of Tiptree, 1509 ; of Lees (or Lighes, Essex), 1515 ; of Bromehill, Norfolk, 1524 (a house suppressed by Wolsey), and Rector of Great Cressingham, 1525 ; later Prior of Haverfordwest, and of Bisham, 1534. Possibly owing to the suppression of Bromehill, he disliked Wolsey, but was employed by Henry VIII. on diplomatic business in France and Rome, 1529-30, and in Scotland, 1535-6. He was named and confirmed for the bishopric of St. Asaph, 1535, but before consecration was named for St. David's ; was confirmed, 20th April 1536, and took his seat in Parliament. No record remains of his consecration, but in the light of other considerations little significance belongs to that not uncommon case. The Lambeth Register, in which it might have been entered, was carelessly kept, and the St. David's Register is missing. There are other cases in which there is no evidence from Lambeth, *e.g.* that of Gardiner (*q.v.*), but in some of these cases the Diocesan Registers —where surviving—supply the lack. Had it not been that Barlow, along with Hodgkyns, Scory, and Coverdale (*q.v.*), consecrated Parker (*q.v.*), nothing would have been said as to his supposed lack of consecration. It is quite inconceivable that a bishop should have been admitted to Parliament, and to the discharge of various legal duties, without the consecration demanded both by the law of the Church and the State. Nor could such an objection have remained unnoticed by Gardiner, who spoke of him as a brother-bishop, or by Mary, who in 1554 accepted his resignation of Bath and Wells, which he then held. Furthermore, objections were urged against his views by the rebels in the Lincolnshire rising and by some who dwelt in his diocese. He had quarrels with the chapter at St. David's, and at Wells with his dean, Goodman, whom he deprived illegally, although the Council supported him. In none of these cases was anything said as to his lacking due consecration, and the story is first mentioned some eighty years later. It is true he was very lax in his earlier opinions as to the nature of the Church and the power of the sovereign in regard to ecclesiastical matters. This is shown by his answers before the commission of 1540, though he assented to other views in signing the *Institution of a Christian Man*; but the fact, even if true, that he did not regard consecration as necessary, does not prove his non-consecration. It should also be noted that his *Dialoge*—between Nicholas (a Lutheran in views) and William (representing Barlow himself), first printed 1531, and reprinted 1553—shows that he had then a strong dislike of Lutheran opinions and the abuses springing from them ; also, that he was certainly not Lutheran in his views on the Eucharist, and was cautious as to the introduction of a vernacular Bible and strongly against Tyndale's version. This makes it less surprising that at first under Mary he satisfied Gardiner of his orthodoxy. In Henry's reign he was active ; during the debates before the Act of Six Articles he advocated marriage of priests and Communion in both kinds ; he preached at St. Paul's against images, for which he was attacked by Gardiner ; he was on the Commissions of 1537 and 1540, which produced respectively the *Institution of a Christian Man* and the *Necessary Doctrine*, and on that (1542) which considered a new version of the Bible, taking as his share Galatians, Ephesians, Philippians, and Colossians ; for the Bishops' Bible he translated Esdras, Tobit, Judith, and Wisdom. He was also on the Commission (1551) for codifying the canon law. While at St. David's he stripped the lead from the palace, so causing its decay, and resided at Abergwili. In 1548 he was translated to Bath and Wells, about which date he married. Under Mary he was first imprisoned (probably for debt), resigned his see, was examined and submitted, January 1555 ; a little later he fled to Germany. As he had resigned his old see under Mary, on Elizabeth's accession he was named for a fresh see, Chichester, 1559. His career and his views illustrate the changing currents of the time : his energy was somewhat turbulent, but his interest in education genuine. [J. P. W.]

T. F. Tout in *D.N.B.*; Cooper, *Athenæ Cantabrigienses*; Denny, *Anglican Orders and Jurisdiction*; Pollard, *Cranmer*; Haddon, *Apostolical Succession in the Ch. of Eng.*

BARROW, Isaac (1630-77), divine, was son of Thomas Barrow, a London citizen, linendraper to Charles I., and nephew of Isaac

Barrow, Bishop of St. Asaph. He was educated at the Charterhouse, where ' his greatest recreation was in such sports as brought on fighting among the boys . . . for his book he minded it not.' Removed to Felsted school he made better progress, and in 1645 went to Trinity College, Cambridge. His father being impoverished through his devotion to the royal cause, Barrow was enabled to complete his University course by the liberality of Dr. Hammond, a royalist divine. He became B.A., 1648 ; Fellow, 1649 ; M.A., 1652. He proposed to follow the profession of physic, but decided it was not ' consistent with the oath he had taken as Fellow, to make divinity the end of his studies.' In 1654 he failed to obtain the Professorship of Greek, owing, it was said, to his religious and political views ; but when some of the Fellows urged his expulsion as a royalist the Master, Dr. Hall, replied : ' Barrow is a better man than any of us.' From 1655 to 1659 he travelled abroad. On his return he was ordained by Bishop Brownrigg of Exeter, was appointed Professor of Greek at Cambridge in 1660 ; Professor of Geometry at Gresham College, London, 1662 ; and first Lucasian Professor of Mathematics at Cambridge, 1663. This last chair he resigned to his pupil, Isaac Newton, in 1669, finding its duties hampered his study of divinity. In 1673 Charles II. made him Master of Trinity, in which position he was ' zealous and active.' ' He had always been a constant and early man at the chapel, and now continued to do the same.' ' The patent for his Mastership being so drawn for him, as it had been for some others, with permission to marry, he caused to be altered, thinking it not agreeable with the statutes, from which he desired no dispensation.' As Vice-Chancellor (1675-6) he proposed the building of a University theatre, schools, and library, ' by which we may come nearer in beauty to our dear and beautiful sister, Oxford.' The story goes that, piqued at the failure of this design, he declared he would build a stately library at his own college, and staked out its foundations ' with his gardener and servants ' that very afternoon. He died after a short illness in 1677.

Barrow's learning was encyclopædic. ' He seems always to have present to his mind the whole of ancient literature.' Though only forty-seven he had attained a unique reputation for scholarship, theology, mathematics, and natural science ; and his intellectual greatness was enhanced by an exemplary life. His vigorous style was enlivened by fertile and ingenious fancy. Charles II. declared that ' Barrow was the most unfair preacher he knew, for he never left anything for any one else to say on the subjects which he handled.' ' He was careless of his clothes even to a fault,' and ' very free ' in the use of tobacco, ' believing it did help to regulate his thinking.'

Barrow's chief literary work is his *Treatise on the Pope's Supremacy*, published posthumously in 1680. He allows to St. Peter a primacy of order, but denies that he possessed such a primacy as would confer superior power or jurisdiction. This primacy of order was personal to the apostle and not inherited by any one. It is doubtful whether St. Peter was Bishop of Rome. If he was, no result would follow in regard to the position of subsequent bishops of Rome. Moreover, history shows that the early bishops of Rome did not possess supreme jurisdiction. One bishop may exceed another in dignity, but in power all bishops are equal. In his writings on the Creed and the Sacraments Barrow is representative of many English Churchmen. On the central truths contained in the Creeds he held the orthodox beliefs which have been traditional in the English Church. Baptism is the means by which forgiveness, the gift of the Holy Ghost, regeneration, and the assurance of eternal life, if there is perseverance, are conveyed. The Eucharist is a commemorative representation of Christ's Passion whereby Christians are kept in mind of it; a means of receiving the benefits derived from the Passion and of union with Christ. The power of the keys committed to the ministry enables ministers to remit sins by inducing dispositions fit for forgiveness, by declaring God's mercy, by obtaining pardon through prayer, and by consigning pardon in Baptism and Absolution.

His theological works were edited by Tillotson (*q.v.*), 1678-87, with a *Life* by Abraham Hill. An able appreciation of ' Barrow and his Academical Times,' by Dr. Whewell, was included in A. Napier's edition, 1859. [G. C. and D. S.]

Works : T. A. Lacey, *Isaac Barrow* in *Revue Anglo-Romaine*, iii. 385-95.

BATH AND WELLS, Diocese of. The victories of Alfred resulted in a settlement. of which this diocese is one of the fruits. The see of Wells was founded in 909 by his son Edward, being taken out of the Sherborne diocese. [SALISBURY, SEE OF.] Its history naturally centres round Glastonbury (*q.v.*). First, it was the abbey's nursling, then its opponent, and at last its successor. King Ine, the warm friend to Glastonbury, had placed a small body of secular canons at Wells for parochial and missionary work,

under the shelter of the abbey. These had so prospered that their church of St. Andrew, with its central position, was marked out as the natural chair of the new see, which Edward and Archbishop Plegmund placed there, following the tribal boundaries of the Somerset folk. Except for the loss of Abbots Leigh and Bedminster to Bristol (*q.v.*), and Maiden Bradley and Stourton to Salisbury, the boundaries have been unchanged for a thousand years. There are three archdeaconries—Wells, Bath, and Taunton (all first mentioned in 1106). The cathedral church is governed by a dean and chapter of the Old Foundation. There are forty-nine prebends, including those held by the governing body. The extent of the diocese in 1912 is 1,043,050 acres ; the population is 437,635. The *Temporalia* were assessed by the *Taxatio* (*q.v.*) of 1291 at £541, 13s. 11d. (the only *Spiritualia* were £10 from the church of Burnham); the *Valor Ecclesiasticus* (*q.v.*) of 1535 assessed the revenues of the see at £1843, 14s. 5d.; and Ecton (1711) at £533, 1s. 3d. The present income is £5000. Of the earliest bishops all, with one exception, were Glastonbury men.

BISHOPS

1. Athelm, 909 ; a monk of Glastonbury ; tr. to Canterbury, 914.
2. Wulfhelm, 914 ; a monk of Glastonbury ; tr. to Canterbury, 923.
3. Aelfheah, 923 ; a monk of Glastonbury.
4. Wulfhelm, 938 ; a monk of Glastonbury ; appointed to thwart St. Dunstan.
5. Brihthelm, 956 ; tr. to Canterbury, 959 ; depr. and returned to Wells, 960.
6. Cyneward, 973 ; Abbot of Middleton.
7. Sigar, 975 ; Abbot of Glastonbury.
8. Aelfwin, 997.
9. Lyfing, 999 ; tr. to Canterbury, 1013.
10. Aethelwin and Brihtwin, 1013.
11. Merewit, 1027 ; Abbot of Glastonbury.
12. Duduc, 1033 ; a German ; appointed by Cnut : appointed to leaven the strongly English tone of the diocese ; began the quarrel with Glastonbury ; he left Congresbury and Banwell to the see ; d. 1060.
13. Gisa, 1061 ; a Frenchman ; nominee of Edward the Confessor ; found desolation and disorder, and left better order and revenue, but a sullen people; d. 1088.
14. John of Tours, 1088 ; a physician appointed by William Rufus ; unpopular ; this bishop moved the see to Bath, where he was a great builder and the patron of learning ; d. 1122.
15. Godfrey, 1123 ; a Dutchman ; d. 1135.

16. Robert, 1136; a Fleming from Lewes, and a disciple of Henry of Blois (*q.v.*); began the building of the cathedral church at Wells; d. 1166.

17. Reginald, 1174; built the nave, transepts, choir, and north porch at Wells; fostered the chapter and the town, and tried to heal the breach with Glastonbury by bringing the abbot into the chapter; elected to Canterbury, 27th November. d. 26th December, 1191.

18. Savaric, 1192; a violent man; tried to heal the breach by becoming Bishop of Bath and Glastonbury, of which house he was also abbot; first Bishop of Bath and Glastonbury; d. 1205.

19. Jocelin Trotman, 1206; a Somerset man; opponent of King John; second Bishop of Bath and Glastonbury until 1219, when, with the support of the diocese and country, the abbey was 'released,' and the see became of Bath; a great builder; d. 1242.

20. Roger, 1244; first Bishop of Bath and Wells; effected a compromise with Bath, and replaced the see in Wells.

21. William Button I., 1248; a Wells man; opponent of Glastonbury; d. 1264.

22. Walter Giffard, 1265; an opponent of the barons; tr. to York, 1266.

23. William Button II., 1267; canonised by the people, and patron of sound teeth; d. 1274.

24. Robert Burnell, 1275; chancellor of Edward I.; builder of the hall; d. 1292.

25. William of March, 1293; Edward I.'s treasurer; builder of the chapter-house; d. 1302.

26. Walter Haselshaw, 1302; reformer of abuses; d. 1308.

27. John Drokensford, 1309; Keeper of Edward II.'s Wardrobe; d. 1329.

28. Ralph of Shrewsbury, 1329; a great bishop; fortified the palace at Wells; supported the Statute of Labourers, 1351, and was besieged by the parishioners in Ilchester Church; the only bishop for the next two hundred years who was not a royal servant; a suffragan bishop appointed to assist him in 1362; d. 1363.

29. John Barnet, 1363; tr. (P.) from Worcester; tr. to Ely, 1366.

30. John Harewell, 1366 (P.); Chancellor of Gascony under Black Prince; helped to build south-west tower; d. 1386.

31. Walter Skirlaw, 1386; tr. (P.) from Lichfield; tr. to Durham, 1388.

32. Ralph Erghum, 1388; tr. (P.) from Salisbury; founder of a Wells college; d. 1400.

33. Henry Bowett, 1401 (P.); Treasurer of England; tr. to York, 1407.

34. Nicholas Bubwith, 1407; tr. (P.) from Salisbury; treasurer; builder of north-west tower, almshouses, and chantry; d. 1424.

35. John Stafford, 1425 (P.); tr. to Canterbury, 1443.

36. Thomas Beckington, 1443 (P.); Keeper of Privy Seal to Henry VI.; builder and benefactor of Lincoln College; d. 1465.

37. Robert Stillington, 1466 (P.); Yorkist chancellor; imprisoned for helping Lambert Simnel; d. 1491.

38. Richard Fox (*q.v.*), 1491; tr. (P.) from Exeter.

39. Oliver King, 1495; tr. (P.) from Exeter; chief secretary to Henry VII.; builder of Bath Abbey Church; d. 1503.

40. Adrian de Castello, 1504 (P.); tr. from Hereford; Borgian cardinal; absentee; depr. 1518.

41. Thomas Wolsey (*q.v.*), 1518 (P.).

42. John Clerk, 1523 (P.); favourer of royal divorce; creature of Henry VIII.; friend to Cranmer; d. 1541.

43. William Knight, 1541; ambassador; builder of Market Cross; d. 1547.

44. William Barlow (*q.v.*), 1549.

45. Gilbert Bourne, 1554 (P.); under him eighty-two clergy deprived, including the scurrilous Dean Turner, first of English herbalists; nine were burnt; depr. 1559, and lived ten years in captivity.

46. Gilbert Berkeley, 1560; opponent of townsmen of Wells and of Dean Turner; d. 1581.

47. Thomas Godwin, 1584; Dean of Christ Church; a physician; d. 1590.

48. John Still, 1593; Parker's chaplain; said to be author of *Gammer Gurton's Needle*; d. 1608.

49. James Montagu, 1608; editor of James I.'s works; tr. to Winchester, 1616.

50. Arthur Lake, 1616; a saintly and diligent bishop; d. 1626.

51. William Laud (*q.v.*), 1626; tr. from St. David's; tr. to London, 1628.

52. Leonard Mawe, 1628; Prince Charles's chaplain; d. 1629.

53. Walter Curll, 1629; tr. to Winchester, 1632.

54. William Piers, 1632; tr. from Peterborough; a faithful Laudian; much persecuted, but restored in 1660; one hundred and seven clergy sequestered under the Commonwealth; eighty ministers affected by the Act of Uniformity (*q.v.*); d. 1670.

55. Robert Creighton, 1670; restored cathedral after the profanation; his effigy represents him in cope and mitre; d. 1672.
56. Peter Mews, 1673; tr. to Winchester, 1684.
57. Thomas Ken (*q.v.*), 1685; depr. 1691.
58. Richard Kidder, 1691; 'a Latitudinarian traditor'; killed in the great storm, 1703.
59. George Hooper, 1703; tr. from St. Asaph; Ken dedicated the Hymnarium to this scholar; d. 1727.
60. John Wynne, 1727; tr. from St. Asaph; disciple of Locke; largely non-resident; d. 1743.
61. Edward Willes, 1743; tr. from St. David's; a courtier; little resident; d. 1773.
62. Charles Moss, 1774; tr. from St. David's; a disciple of Bishop Sherlock; little resident; d. 1802.
63. Richard Beadon, 1802; tr. from Gloucester; approved of Hannah More (*q.v.*); d. 1824.
64. George Henry Law, 1824; F.R.S. and F.S.A.; tr. from Chester; son of a Whig bishop, and disciple of Locke; founded diocesan societies and theological colleges at St. Bees, 1816, and Wells, 1840; d. 1845.
65. Richard Bagot, 1845; tr. from Oxford, where he had been a sympathetic critic of the earlier stages of the Tractarian Movement; d. 1854.
66. Robert John, Lord Auckland, 1854; chaplain to William IV.; res. 1869.
67. Lord Arthur Charles Hervey, 1869; on Committee of Revisers of A.V.; d. 1894.
68. George Wyndham Kennion, 1894; bought back for church the site of Glastonbury Abbey.   [C. L. M.]

BAXTER, Richard (1615-91), divine, son of a Shropshire freeholder who had gambled away his patrimony, but afterwards changed his life into one of pious seriousness. This serious influence, with but little teaching from negligent or immoral parish priests, prepared the boy for the work of his life. He was confirmed at the age of thirteen by Bishop Morton in the hasty, careless fashion inherited from the Middle Ages, when he was under the instruction of Wickstead, chaplain at Ludlow Castle, who grossly neglected him. In 1633 he was for a time at court; but he soon returned to Shropshire, and gave himself to the close study of theology, while he was much influenced by several Nonconformists of holy life. In 1638 he was ordained at Worcester. He first

ministered and taught school at Dudley, afterwards at Bridgnorth, where he avoided baptizing with the sign of the cross or celebrating the Holy Communion (because all were admitted who had not been formally excommunicated), but was, he says, 'in the fervour of my affections, and never preached with more vehement desires of man's conversion.' When by 'the *et caetera* oath' in 1640 obedience was required to the episcopal constitution of the English Church as then existing, Baxter made a study of the origin of church government, and decided that the primitive constitution was very different from that of his own day. In 1640 he was called to preach at Kidderminster, where he continued to labour for sixteen years with extraordinary success, living a life of great piety and devotion to the good of his parishioners. During the early part of the Civil War he was temporarily absent from his parish. He preached at Alcester on the day of Edgehill, 23rd October 1642. He was for a time chaplain to the Parliamentary troops at Coventry. He did not share the religious views of Cromwell, of whom he says that 'he would in good discourse pour out himself in the extolling of free grace, which was savoury to those that had right principles, though he had some misunderstandings of free grace himself.' He distrusted the extreme sectaries, and even believed that they were led astray by 'friars and Jesuits.' He did not approve of the Covenant or support the Engagement, and disliked the entire abolition of episcopacy and the King's execution. But he served as a chaplain in Whalley's regiment, and did not retire from active work till 1647, when for a time he was absent from Kidderminster at Rouse Lench, where he wrote part of *The Saints' Everlasting Rest*, his greatest book, published in 1650. In 1660 he went to London, where he obtained great influence, and no doubt gave powerful aid to the Restoration. He declined a bishopric, but Charles II. made him one of his chaplains, and though he was not allowed to return to Kidderminster he preached in London with the bishop's licence. On 16th May 1662, just before the passing of the Act of Uniformity, he 'bade farewell to the Church of England' in a sermon at Blackfriars. He continued to hope and work for the return to active ministry of those who could not fully accept the Prayer Book and had not been episcopally ordained. Living now again in seclusion he condemned the extremists of his party, but wrote a large number of important controversial works supporting the Puritan position against that of the English Church as represented by the divines of the Restoration period. He was committed to prison for preaching contrary to Act of Parliament, and procured his release, on the advice of the King himself, by applying to the Common Pleas for a *habeas corpus.* He now lived still more in retirement, but continued to preach from time to time in different meeting-houses. Under James II. he was more harshly treated. He was put in prison, 28th February 1685, on the charge of libelling the Church by some statements in his *Paraphrase of the New Testament,* and on 30th May was sentenced by Chief Justice Jeffreys to a fine of five hundred marks and imprisonment till it was paid. His imprisonment was not harsh, and he was released in 1686 when James attempted to propitiate the Nonconformists. He at once returned to the work of preaching, joined in the final opposition to James II., welcomed the Revolution, and took advantage of the Toleration Act. He died on 8th December 1691. Baxter's writings are numerous, and only part of them have been collected, in thirty volumes, edited by Orme, 1830. His chief works show great freedom and simplicity of style, with the charm of genuine piety, marred occasionally by a rigid Calvinism. His *Saints' Rest* is still among the most popular of religious writings.

[W. H. H.]

Reliquiae Baxterianae, 1696 : abridged by Calamy, 1702.

BEAUFORT, Henry (1374 or 1375-1447), Cardinal and Bishop of Winchester, was the son (legitimated in 1397) of John of Gaunt and Catherine Swynford. He appears to have studied both at Peterhouse, Cambridge, and Queen's College, Oxford, as well as at Aachen (in civil and canon law). He was made (before 1397) Dean of Wells, and in 1398 consecrated Bishop of Lincoln. He was also about this time Chancellor of the University of Oxford, possibly chosen as representing the Crown in support of the freedom of the University. His promotion to high public office was consequent on the accession of his half-brother, Henry IV., to the throne, and in February 1403 he was made chancellor. From the first, judging by his sermon at the opening of Parliament in 1404, he seems to have been an advocate of that constitutional rule with which the Lancastrian house was identified. In the next year he succeeded William of Wykeham (*q.v.*) as Bishop of Winchester, and resigned the chancellorship. His successor, Archbishop Arundel, was his formidable rival, and their quarrel came to a

head in 1411, when, after a close alliance with the Prince of Wales, who is said, by his advice, to have urged his sick father to resign the crown, he was dismissed from the council. When in 1413 Henry V. came to the throne he was at once made chancellor again ; and during his nephew's reign he remained one of his most important and trusted counsellors. In 1413 he was one of the assessors in the trial of Oldcastle, and in a sermon at the opening of Parliament he spoke strongly of public danger from the Lollards (*q.v.*). In 1417 he resigned the chancellorship, apparently in order to go on pilgrimage. He attended the Council of Constance garbed as a pilgrim, and mediating between the Emperor Sigismund and the cardinals, but holding no brief for general reform of the Church or of the constitutional position of England as regards the papacy. He appears to have ' come within measurable distance of being the new Bishop of Rome,' when Oddo Colonna was elected as Martin V. (1418), in whom the Council of Constance ' chose a head and found a master.' Beaufort was consoled with the cardinalate and a special appointment as legate (*q.v.*) for England, Wales, and Ireland. Archbishop Arundel lodged a formal protest against the appointment of a permanent legate *a latere,* and Henry prohibited the exercise of his functions or the acceptance of the cardinalate, but no breach of the friendship between uncle and nephew occurred. In 1420 he was fighting in Germany against the Hussites, but returned at the end of the year and was present at the coronation of Queen Catherine. He lent the King much money at a time of financial stress, and was named in Henry's will one of the guardians of the baby Henry VI. In 1422 he was appointed one of the Council of Regency, and ' withstood all the intent ' of Gloucester, who tried to be sole Regent. In 1424 he became chancellor for the third time. He was unpopular in London, and bitterly opposed to Gloucester, against whom he sought the help of Bedford. Gloucester made grave accusations against him at the ' Parliament of Bats,' February 1426, and a forcible pacification between the two was brought about by the Lords. In May he left England, again received the cardinalate, and served as legate in Germany, joining in the crusade against the Hussites. In 1428 he returned to England as legate, and enlisted soldiers for the Hussite Crusade. He took part in the coronation of Henry VI. : but Gloucester and indeed Parliament were suspicious of his power, writs of *praemunire* (*q.v.*) were issued against him, and he had to defend himself and obtain an act of indemnity. During the next few years he was much engaged in foreign policy, and was continually attacked by Gloucester, notably in 1439 ; but his accuser was discredited in 1441 through a plot of his wife's, and Beaufort came into power as one of the leaders of a peace party which eventually negotiated the marriage of the King. From 1443 Beaufort seems to have retired from political life, and resided at Winchester, where he died in the Wolvesey Palace on Palm Sunday, 1447.

He had one daughter, born probably before his ordination, for no scandal was breathed against his later life. He gave generous benefactions to his cathedral church, where he was buried, and to the hospital of St. Cross at Winchester. He was a typical mediæval statesman-clerk, not a scholar, but a wise and loyal politician.   [W. H. H.]

Radford, *Cardinal Beaufort.*

BECKET, Thomas (1118-70), Archbishop of Canterbury, the most famous English archbishop and saint of the Middle Ages, was the son of Gilbert Becket, a Norman trader of gentle birth, and Mahatz, or Matilda, his wife, a native of Caen (the legend of his birth from a Saracen mother has no historical foundation). He was born in Cheapside on St. Thomas's Day, probably in 1118. He was sent to school at Merton Priory in Surrey, and afterwards in London, where the sports of the time are vividly described by his biographer, William Fitz-Stephen. He was afterwards in an accountant's office, and then, about 1143, in the household of Theobald, Archbishop of Canterbury, with whom he came into great favour. He studied law at Bologna and Auxerre, held several livings while in minor orders, and in 1154 was ordained deacon and made Archdeacon of Canterbury. Soon after his accession Henry II., to whom he had already rendered political service, made him Chancellor of England. He now became a very important person, second after the King : took part in embassies (notably to Louis VII., King of the Franks, in 1158 to negotiate a marriage) and battles, and acted as itinerant justice in England. He was regarded (probably unjustly) as specially responsible for the heavy taxation placed on the Church for the Toulouse war of 1159. He was given charge of Henry II.'s eldest son : and, after an interval, he was raised to the primacy on the death of Theobald. He long hesitated, and even refused the office, for he saw the inevitable contest between his spiritual and the King's secular aims ; but at length he yielded, and he was

consecrated on Trinity Sunday, 3rd June 1162, in Canterbury Cathedral, having been ordained priest the day before. (The feast of the Holy Trinity was henceforth observed in England on the Sunday after Whit Sunday.)

He now ' cast off the deacon,' assumed the garb of the canons regular, resigned the chancellorship, set to work to recover the alienated property of the see of Canterbury, and stood forth as the champion of Church and people against unjust claims of the King to take certain dues to the sheriff for defence of the shires into the royal treasury (Woodstock, July 1163). He attended the Council of Tours held by Alexander III. in May 1163, and returned to England more than ever determined to preserve the rights of the Church. At Westminster, October 1163, Henry II. declared that he would enforce the ' customs ' of his grandfather, Henry I., and insist upon the adequate punishment of criminous clerks. The customs were drawn up by the King's lawyers and presented to a council at Clarendon, January 1164 [CLARENDON, CONSTITUTIONS OF]. Becket believed that he was ordered by the Pope to agree to the King's demands, and signed the Constitutions, but refused to seal them, being sure that they must prove the ground for contest. Henry determined to punish him, and brought charges against him relating to his tenure of the chancellorship, in a council at Northampton, October 1164. He was sentenced to pay very heavy fines, refused to recognise the authority of the council, pleading that he had at his consecration been freed from all the claims of his chancellorship, attended the council with his primatial cross in his hand, and was insulted by the barons of the King's court. Believing himself in danger of his life he fled to Flanders, 2nd November 1164, came to the Pope at Sens, and laid the whole matter before him. Alexander pronounced against all the Constitutions except six, and Becket retired to the Cistercian abbey of Pontigny in Burgundy, supported by the King of the Franks and most of the Frankish notables. Henry retaliated by confiscating his personal and ecclesiastical property and banishing all his relations and friends, and tried to alarm the Pope by entering into negotiations with the Emperor Frederic I., who was supporting an antipope. After several letters of warning Becket on Whit Sunday, 12th June 1166, at Vézelay excommunicated seven of the King's councillors, and solemnly warned Henry that a similar sentence might shortly fall on himself. Henry then declared that if the Cistercians continued to shelter him he would banish them from all his dominions, and Becket was obliged to leave Pontigny and seek refuge in the dominions of Louis VII. at the abbey of St. Colombe, Sens. He further demanded that legates should be sent to decide the questions at issue. Becket had on 24th April 1166 been appointed papal legate for all England, except the diocese of York. This made the position of the English bishops exceedingly difficult and a new legation anomalous. The bishops, especially Foliot (*q.v.*), wrote indignantly to Becket, and a vigorous letter fight continued for many months, both parties explaining their positions with lucidity and force. At last on 20th December Alexander appointed Cardinals William and Otto as legates, with power to judge and absolve. Becket declared that by this the Pope had suffocated and strangled the whole Church. Every difficulty was put in the way of the legates; it was not till November 1167 that they met Becket; and the whole mission was a failure. As the archbishop declared that the restoration of his see, from which he had been unlawfully driven, was a necessary preliminary, while Henry demanded a large sum of money still due, he said, from the ex-chancellor, Alexander tried to pacify Henry by ordering that Becket should not excommunicate King or nobles, and a new legation (two priors, and a monk that would never use pen or ink) was appointed in May 1168. In January 1169 all the parties met at Montmirail in Maine. Becket agreed to all things suggested, 'saving his order.' This, as a rejection of the Constitutions, drove Henry to fury, and the negotiations broke down. On 13th April 1169 Becket, now at Clairvaux, excommunicated Gilbert Foliot, Bishop of London, and the Bishop of Salisbury, and warned others, threatening an interdict for England on the Purification, 1170. Alexander issued a third commission to legates, Gratian and Vivian. They met both Henry and Becket at Montmartre, 18th November 1169, and again the negotiations broke down on 'saving my order.' A fourth legation was appointed in January—the Archbishop of Rouen and the Bishop of Nevers—and Alexander ordered that if the King did not admit Becket to the kiss of peace and restore the property he had confiscated within forty days an interdict should fall. But the whole point of this was removed by a saving clause, under which the legates absolved those who had already been excommunicated. They were suspected of having gone 'the Roman way' and taken Henry's money. A new cause of offence was given on 14th June 1170 in the coronation

of young Henry, the King's son, by Roger, Archbishop of York, in defiance of Canterbury's right and the Pope's order. At this everybody cried aloud, and Henry, beset by protesting kinsmen and clerks, saw that he must yield. On 22nd July 1170 at Fréteval he gave way entirely, promised to restore Becket and all his possessions, and said not one word of the Constitutions.

Becket crossed to England on 30th November. Henry had never given him the kiss of peace, and sent John of Oxford, one of his bitterest opponents, to escort him. Becket had suspended Roger of York for the coronation and excommunicated the two bishops. They hurried to the King, while Becket was received with extraordinary love and homage as he went to and when he arrived at Canterbury, 1st December 1170. There he was at once placed, by the court of the young King, in isolation and disgrace. His old pupil refused to receive him; his goods were stolen, his men insulted. On Christmas Day he excommunicated the thieves (notably the family of Broc, who had seized his castle of Saltwood). Meanwhile Henry had heard of his action towards the bishops, and burst into passionate rage. Relying on his words, four knights went to Canterbury (their names, for centuries remembered as infamous by all England, were Hugh de Morville, William de Tracy, Reginald Fitz-Urse, and Richard le Breton). They demanded that Becket should absolve the bishops. He refused to take off a Church sentence at their demand, protesting that there had been no word of submission. When he went to his cathedral church for vespers they followed him, and murdered him by the altar of St. Benedict in the north transept. The murder was heard with horror throughout the world. Pilgrims flocked to Canterbury, and sick were healed. When the choir of the cathedral was burnt down (1174) it was rebuilt largely by the offerings at his shrine, and his body was translated (1220) to a tomb behind the high altar, in a crypt under what came to be called 'Becket's Crown.' He was canonised on 24th February 1173. On 12th July 1174 Henry did public penance at his tomb. The Constitutions were entirely given up. All through the Middle Ages the stream of pilgrims to Canterbury continued. The pilgrimage became probably the most popular, and the shrine the richest, in Christendom. Becket was thought to have died for the liberty of the Church and the liberty of the people, threatened by a tyrannous King who was swiftly breaking down all freedom and all rights of separate estates before the omnipotence of the law, which meant the King's courts, and (in the case of a strong, unscrupulous monarch) ultimately the King's will. No one but the Church was able to stand up against the powers of Henry II. If the Church had not stood up and conquered, through the death of its leader, liberty in the future might never have been won. It is impossible to say that Henry might not have established a despotism like that of the French kings if so much of his reign had not been taken up with the contest against Becket. And it must be remembered that, apart from its temporary setting. the claim of Becket was one for the spiritual Body to be the judge of spiritual things, for the Church, not the State, to define the merits and the doctrine and the discipline of the Church. St. Thomas is commemorated on 29th December, his translation on 7th July; the latter feast still appears in the Oxford University Calendar.

[W. H. H.]

Materials for the Hist. of Becket, 7 vols., R.S.: Hutton, *Thomas Becket*.

BEDE, or BAEDA (673-735), 'the father of English history,' was the most shining example of the learning of the Northumbrian monasteries in the days of the kingdom's greatness. For his life he himself supplies practically the only material. What he says may be thus translated :—

'These things concerning the Church history of Britain, and more especially of the people of the English, I, Baeda, a servant of Christ and priest of the monastery of the blessed apostles, St. Peter and St. Paul, which is at Wearmouth and at Jarrow, have, the Lord helping me, undertaken, so far as I could learn it, either from the writings of the ancients, or from the tradition of the elders, or from my own knowledge. I was born in the territory of the said monastery, and at the age of seven I was, by the care of my kinsfolk, given for education to the most reverend Abbot Benedict, and afterwards to Ceolfrid. From that time, dwelling all my life in that monastery, I have given all my labour to the study of the Scriptures ; and amid the observance of monastic discipline and the daily charge of chanting in the church, I have ever held it sweet to learn. or teach, or write. In the nineteenth year of my life I was admitted to the diaconate, in my thirtieth to the priesthood, both by the hands of the most reverend Bishop John. and at the bidding of Abbot Ceolfrid. From which time of my receiving the priesthood to the fifty-ninth year of my age I have en-

deavoured, for my own use and that of my brethren, briefly to annotate the holy Scripture, out of the works of the venerable fathers, or to add something of my own in conformity with their meaning and interpretation.'

He then adds a list of his works—his commentary on Genesis, Samuel to the death of Saul, and so on throughout the Bible; his historical writings up to that date (731), and the like; and he ends : 'And I pray Thee, good Jesus, that to him to whom Thou hast graciously given to drink in with delight the words of Thy knowledge, Thou wouldst mercifully grant to come one day even unto Thee, the fountain of all wisdom, and to appear for ever before Thy face.'

Bede was indeed, for the time, a most voluminous writer. Alcuin (*q.v.*), little more than half a century after his death, spoke of him as receiving great praise from men, but more from God, for his works. Some forty can be specified, the most important being his *Church History of the English Nation*, his lives of the Abbots and of St. Cuthbert, and his letter to Egbert, Archbishop of York ; but much value attaches also to his commentaries on the Bible as illustrating the learning of his own age and race. His life was throughout that of a simple scholar and teacher ; but he came, as such persons often do, to exercise a very wide and important influence. The monastery of Wearmouth was founded in 674, that of Jarrow probably in 681, both by Benedict Biscop (*q.v.*), a learned scholar who had travelled abroad and brought back from Italy Lombardic craftsmen, and who had intended to preside over both. While he was away on his many visits to Rome Eosterwine took his place at Wearmouth, Ceolfrid at Jarrow, and at one time the plague slew all in the latter house who could take part in the religious offices, except the abbot and Bede, then a child, who there learnt a lesson of the duty of clerks which he never forgot. Years later he said to the monks of Wearmouth: 'I know that angels are present at the canonical hours and the congregations of the brethren. How if they find me not among them ; will they not say, Where is Bede ? Why cometh he not to the ordered devotions of the brothers ?' Benedict died in 689 or 690, and Ceolfrid succeeded him as abbot of both houses. Ceolfrid resigned in 716, and died on his way to Rome. Hwaetberht succeeded him, and was still abbot when Bede died. It seems unlikely that Bede ever went outside Northumbria : we know that he visited Holy Island and York. He was, in fact, a perfect example of the concentration of interests, religious and educational, afforded by the monastic life, and the abundant evidence of his contemporaries and successors shows how very important and widespread was his influence. And his life was very strict and exact in obedience to the rule of his order, but transfigured by friendship and Christian love. Many early stories tell of his lovable, simple nature, and he fitly died as he had finished his commentary on the gospel of the beloved disciple, on Ascension Day, 26th May 735, and was buried at Jarrow. Within a century the title of Venerable was affixed to his name. His bones were translated to Durham in the eleventh century. They were scattered in 1541, but a stone in the Galilee Chapel of the cathedral church still bears the words:—

'Hac sunt in fossa Baedae venerabilis ossa,'

and a legend says that the epithet was originally added by an angel. Bede is commemorated on 27th May. [W. H. H.]

Hunt. *Hist. of Eng. Ch. to* 1066; Bright, *Early Eng. Ch. Hist.*; Plummer, *Baedae Opera Historica*.

BENEFIT OF CLERGY, or the exemption of persons in holy orders from the usual penalties of the criminal law, is not found in England before the Conquest. The separation of the civil and ecclesiastical courts by William I. paved the way for the introduction into England of the claim to immunity from the civil law which the clergy had already established abroad, and which, under the growing influence of the Canon Law (*q.v.*), developed early in the twelfth century into a demand that no clerk should be tried for any offence save in the spiritual court. Under Stephen this claim was allowed in practice, but it was one which could not be admitted by a strong king, and naturally came into dispute between Henry II. and Becket (*q.v.*). Henry seems to have desired that when a clerk accused of an offence against the civil law pleaded exemption he should be tried in the church court, and if convicted should be degraded from his orders and returned to the temporal court, which, now that he was a clerk no longer, could inflict the usual lay penalty. [CLARENDON, CONSTITUTIONS OF.] This proposal was apparently founded on the practice of Henry I.'s reign, but in the reaction which followed the death of Becket it had to be abandoned save for breaches of the forest law, and a procedure more favourable to the Church's claims came into use. When a clerk was charged with felony his bishop demanded that he should be delivered to the Church, and became responsible for his safe custody until his trial before the justices. He then either pleaded his clergy or the bishop again demanded him, and he was again handed over to be tried in the bishop's court. Here he was allowed to purge himself by finding compurgators, usually twelve in number, to swear to his innocence. If he failed in this, an event apparently of rare occurrence, the bishop could inflict imprisonment as well as spiritual penalties. This procedure did not apply to misdemeanours, nor to the more serious forms of treason. But it was allowed by the State as covering all charges of felony with some few exceptions, and attempts were made to ensure that the purgation and the punishment inflicted by the bishop should be serious matters instead of mere formalities. [COURTS.]

This exemption from ordinary criminal process, extending to all ordained persons and members of religious orders, covered a very large proportion of the population, including many who, though in minor orders, were for all practical purposes laymen. Before the end of the Middle Ages all who could read were assumed to be clerks, and the judges did not require strict proof even of this qualification. The general immunity thus gradually introduced was first restrained by a statute of 1488 (4 Hen. VII. c. 13), which provided that, whereas 'divers persons lettered have been the more bold to commit murder' and other crimes 'because they have been continually admitted to the benefit of the clergy,' criminals who could not prove that they were really in holy orders should, on being allowed this privilege, be branded in the hand, and not admitted to it again.

In 1513 murderers and robbers who were not really in holy orders (defined in 1532 as 'of the Orders of Subdeacon or above') were deprived of benefit of clergy altogether (4 Hen. VIII. c. 2). This led to warm controversy, the Abbot of Winchcombe declaring at Paul's Cross that by the law of God all clerks were exempt from temporal punishment. The Act was allowed to lapse, but was renewed in 1532 (23 Hen. VIII. c. 1). In 1536 all criminals, whether in orders or not, were limited to a single plea of clergy (28 Hen. VIII. c. 1). In 1575 the last distinction between clergy and laity was removed by the abolition of the solemn farce of compurgation (18 Eliz. c. 7). Henceforth benefit of clergy was merely an incident of criminal procedure, the repetition of the 'neck-verse' (Ps. 51[1]), which saved the prisoner from the gallows, being accepted as proof of his ability to read. In Blackstone's words, the 'noble alchemy' of the legislature had converted 'an unreasonable exemption of particular popish ecclesiastics into a merciful mitigation of the general law,' and this was itself abolished in 1827. Benefit of clergy now only survives in the privilege of resident members of the Universities of Oxford and Cambridge to be tried for misdemeanours in the vice-chancellor's court.   [G. C.]

Pollock and Maitland, *Hist. of Eng. Law*, II. ii.; Blackstone, *Commentaries*, IV. xxviii.

BENSON, Edward White (1829-96), Archbishop of Canterbury. His ancestors were not (as was often stated) Jews, but substantial Yorkshire yeomen. He was educated at King Edward's School, Birmingham, by James Prince Lee, afterwards first Bishop of Manchester. From Birmingham he went to Trinity College, Cambridge, where his diligence and high character won the favourable regard of Mr. Francis Martin, Fellow of Trinity, whose liberality enabled him to complete his academical course in spite of poverty. In 1852 Benson came out eighth in the First Class of the Classical Tripos, and was Senior Chancellor's Medallist. He became Fellow of Trinity and an assistant master at Rugby under Dr. Goulburn. In 1854 he was ordained deacon, and in 1856 priest. In 1858 he was appointed Master of Wellington College, which had been founded, at the instance of Prince Albert, as a memorial to the Duke of Wellington. His administration was vigorous, his success in teaching considerable, and his æsthetic interests and acquaintance with Fine Art left their permanent impress on the college and its buildings, especially the chapel. At Wellington, as at Rugby, he was noted for severity, which he justified on the ground that his boys were a rude and riotous community. In 1873 he was appointed by Bishop Christopher Wordsworth (*q.v.*) Chancellor of Lincoln Cathedral, with a canon's stall. He threw himself with great energy into religious and educational efforts for the benefit of the working classes of Lincoln, and acquired much popularity. In 1877 he was chosen by Lord Beaconsfield to be the first Bishop of Truro (*q.v.*), and it was known that this nomination was peculiarly acceptable to Queen Victoria, who knew the high estimation in which Prince Albert had held Benson. He was a thoroughly vigorous and effective bishop. His skill in organisation enabled him to weld all the parts of a remote, neglected, and in

some respects almost foreign, county into a united and harmonious diocese, and by gathering round himself a company of mission - preachers he contrived to spread the message of the Church through districts where down to that time all spiritual religion had been identified with Nonconformity. The enduring memorial of his episcopate is Truro Cathedral, which, thanks to his boundless zeal and activity, was evolved out of the old parish church of Truro.

Archbishop Tait (*q.v.*) died in 1882, and Mr. Gladstone (*q.v.*), after most careful deliberation, chose Bishop Benson for the primacy. He told the present writer that his reasons were two: first, that it was desirable, in view of possible changes impending over the Church, that the new archbishop should be a man young enough to hold the primacy for a good many years; and second, that Benson had given him proofs of capacity and sound Churchmanship in organising a new diocese and building a cathedral. 'All,' he said, ' has been done on ecclesiastical lines.' The appointment was much censured by the Liberal party. The bishop was known to be a fanatical Tory, and he had just given his name to the Tory committee at a by-election for the University of Cambridge. Some mischief-maker eagerly reported this fact to Mr. Gladstone, who replied : 'Is it so ? Then it is very much to the bishop's credit. A worldly man, or an ambitious man, or a self-seeking man would not have joined a Tory committee when Canterbury was vacant and I was Prime Minister.'

As primate Benson was exactly what he had been as schoolmaster and bishop: intensely hard-working, copious in great designs, eager to extol the Church as the divine safeguard of our national life, intolerant of contradiction or criticism, and, as far as circumstances permitted, imperious. The main events of his primacy were three: (1) his revival of 'the court of the Archbishop of Canterbury' for the trial of Bishop King (*q.v.*) of Lincoln, who had been charged with illegal practices in divine worship. The constitution and procedure of this 'court' were held by great authorities to be defective. Bishop Stubbs (*q.v.*) said : 'This is not a court—it is an archbishop sitting in his library'; and Dean Church (*q.v.*) called the precedent on which the archbishop relied 'fishy,' but described the court itself as 'a distinctly spiritual court of the highest dignity.' The archbishop's judgment in the Lincoln case was important, apart from the particular points at issue because it assumed the continuity of the Church before, through, and after the Reformation, and based its decisions not on the dicta of the Judicial Committee, but on the rubrics of the Prayer Book and the traditional practice of the Church. [COURTS, RITUAL CASES.] (2) In 1894 an attempt was made by some well-meaning but unauthorised persons to obtain from the Pope a formal recognition of Anglican orders. Archbishop Benson resolutely declined to enter, directly or indirectly, into secret negotiations with Rome. And the result, which was the formal condemnation by Rome of Anglican Orders, showed him to have been right. [REUNION.] (3) In organising the forces of the Church against the Bill for disestablishing the Welsh Church, which was brought in by the Liberal Government in 1895, Benson allied the Church more closely than it had ever been allied before with the aims and methods of the Tory party, and thereby intensified that hostility of Liberalism to the Church which it had long been the anxious endeavour of more statesmanlike Churchmen to avoid.

It is difficult to define precisely Benson's theological position. With the whole Oxford Movement and the men who led it he was completely out of sympathy, and he thought Newman 'a weak man.' His closest associates were his old school-fellows, Westcott (q.v.) and Lightfoot (q.v.); but he was free from the mistiness of Westcott, and was much more of a sacramentalist than Lightfoot. In his early days at Wellington, although he used the mixed chalice and took the ablutions, he celebrated in the afternoon and stood at the north end of the Holy Table. He affirmed the identity of the Holy Eucharist with the Mass, and framed some admirable devotions for the use of the celebrant, but he assailed the practice of fasting communion as 'materialistic.' He commended the departed to God at the altar, and offered the Eucharist with special intentions, but his doctrine of the Eucharistic Sacrifice seems to have been something peculiar to himself. He believed intensely in the Apostolic Succession, but favoured the recognition of Presbyterian Orders. He believed that the Church is a spiritual society, but his devotion to the principle of Establishment was a monomania. He was an æsthete, an artist, an antiquary, a ritualist as long as ritual conveyed no doctrine, and withal a man of fervent piety.

Benson married in 1859 his cousin, Mary Sidgwick, by whom he had three sons and two daughters. He died suddenly in Hawarden Church, when on a visit to Mr.

Gladstone, on the 11th of October 1896, and was buried in Canterbury Cathedral.

[G. W. E. R.]

A. C. Benson, *Life.*

BIBLE, History of English. Until the end of the fourteenth century no one vernacular translation of the Bible would have been widely intelligible. There was no uniform standard English language until at least the days of Wyclif (q.v.). The history of English translations falls into six periods.

(1) *Pre-Conquest Translations.*—No complete translation was made in Anglo-Saxon days in any English dialect. In the seventh century Cædmon had turned parts of the Latin Bible into Northumbrian metre. Bede (q.v.) translated St. John into the same dialect. Interlinear Saxon translations of the Latin Gospels survive, and paraphrases of other parts. These earliest versions exerted no influence upon later.

(2) *Early English Translations.*—The dominance of the Latin Bible was supreme after the Norman Conquest, whilst knowledge of Greek and Hebrew had died out. Traces of occasional translations of some portions of Scripture appear in the twelfth and thirteenth centuries; chiefly of those parts most used and known, e.g. the Psalms. Thus the metrical *Ormulum*, paraphrasing Gospels and Acts, probably belongs to the twelfth century. Prose translation in this period is found in Richard Rolle's (q.v.) *Psalter.* These works and others are relics of a probably wide fashion of translation, nor must we forget versions and paraphrases undertaken for miracle plays.

(3) *Wyclif Translations.*—We now come to a great epoch in the evolution of the English Bible. Standard English was crystallising at the end of the fourteenth century. Wyclif, the greatest English scholar and teacher of the time, was perhaps the first man in England to plan a translation of the whole Bible. The great task was completed in or about 1382. The first edition was due mainly to him, but in part to his friend, Nicholas Hereford, who uses a somewhat different dialect of English. The work was revised by another friend, called Purvey or Purday, and the revision came out in 1388. Both versions existed, of course, in manuscript only, and despite rigorous suppression many copies survived, and were used in secret right down to the time of the Reformation. The whole trend of events was to check the circulation of the book. When translation on any large scale was

again attempted, the English of Wyclif was largely unintelligible.

(4) *Reformation Translations.*—With the great changes of the sixteenth century the translation of the Bible was undertaken by a series of scholars whose attempts mark successive steps in the formation of the ultimate standard version. Printing, which was then a rapidly improving invention, spread widely the fruits of their labours. (*a*) William Tyndale (*q.v.*) led the way. The attitude of the ecclesiastical authorities towards amateur translation of the Scriptures made it necessary for him to carry on his work abroad, whence the printed books were brought into England. His New Testament was complete and published in 1525, and at once made its way to London and elsewhere. The story of the careful watch kept by spies, and of their attempts to stop the work of printing and transmission, is well known. Notwithstanding their zeal he managed to get several editions of the New Testament through the press before 1529. He then began the Old Testament, but was unable to complete it. Portions were printed and published. In 1534 a revised edition of the Pentateuch and of the New Testament appeared. The bishops were hostile to these books, and many were destroyed. One great cause of uneasiness lay in the marginal notes, in which Tyndale expressed his own doctrinal views. Mistranslations, supposed in many cases to be wilful, were also marked. Sir Thomas More (*q.v.*) attacked Tyndale for what were considered dangerous errors. And yet Tyndale's is the basis of all future important English versions. His very words and phrases still survive. No Englishman's actual words are better known to the English-speaking race than his. (*b*) Miles Coverdale (*q.v.*) introduces the next stage. So far, translation had been unauthorised, but the way was being paved towards an authorised version. In 1530 the King promised that such a work should be undertaken. In 1534 the Convocation of Canterbury petitioned for it. Meanwhile Coverdale was encouraged by Cranmer to take in hand the task of translating the Scriptures. This he did in retirement on the Continent, and in 1535 published a complete translation from the German and Latin Bibles. He made some use of Tyndale's work. He did not translate from the original but from translations. Notwithstanding this defect, his version is not without merit. Our version of the Psalms in the Prayer Book is still mainly Coverdale. Many of his translations of words and phrases still survive in the

Authorised Version of 1611. The book was without note or comment, but contained a 'prologue unto the Christian reader.' A second slightly altered edition was licensed by the King in 1537. (*c*) In 1537 appeared a second complete English Bible, the work of one Thomas Matthew, now known to have been really John Rogers (*q.v.*). He became Tyndale's literary executor, and in this capacity was able to make use of the latter's works. Accordingly he re-edited Tyndale's translation, filling up the untranslated gaps in the Old Testament. In this he made large use of Coverdale, occasionally altering words or phrases. It will thus be seen that Rogers was rather an editor than translator, but as an editor he is excellent. He added prologues and other helps. Cranmer (*q.v.*) warmly welcomed the book, and urged Cromwell (*q.v.*) to get it licensed by royal authority. It was then the first actually authorised English version, and formed an important link in the history, as it constituted the direct basis of later versions. [It should be added that in 1539 a private revision of Matthew's Bible was issued by Richard Taverner. This book was certainly consulted by the later translators.] (*d*) Cranmer's, or the Great Bible : Coverdale's Bible was inaccurate, and Matthew's being largely based on Tyndale might incur the hostility of critics. Consequently Cromwell, who had so largely helped Coverdale, got him to undertake a new translation. It was based upon Matthew, with such other help as the famous Complutensian Polyglot could supply. The first edition was ready in 1539. It was the text only, in folio form, as all the English versions of the whole Bible so far had been. It comprised the whole Bible and Apocrypha. The recent Injunction of 1538 to set up in churches ' one book of the whole Bible in English in the largest volume ' soon gave this handsome book the name of the Great Bible. In 1540 a second edition was ready, and Cranmer added a preface to it. Thus the archbishop's name is introduced in this connection. A still later edition in 1541 gained some episcopal sanction. (*e*) The Geneva Bible : during Mary's reign many English scholars had taken refuge abroad [MARIAN EXILES]. Among them was Whittingham at Geneva. Here he translated the New Testament, making much use of Tyndale, and of Beza's Latin New Testament, publishing his work in 1557. For the first time in an English Bible verse numberings were introduced. It was revised at Geneva, and a translation of the Old Testament was added in 1560. Notes were added of considerable historical significance. All the previous Bibles had been folios, but this was compendious in form, and with good clear type. These merits, over and above the notes, made the book specially attractive, and it had a great influence upon religion in England, where it was current for a long period. The version of 1611 was, to some extent, indebted to it. (*f*) The Bishops' Bible : Archbishop Parker (*q.v.*), in hopes of superseding the Geneva Bible, conceived the idea of forming by co-operation an Anglican revision of the English Bibles. The task was distributed among various scholars, and was complete in 1568. The first edition was a folio, but there were smaller shapes afterwards. Verse numberings and notes were introduced, as in the Geneva version. It was not so good in character as the Genevan. It contained the whole Bible, including the Apocrypha. [We may also note here that the English Romanists abroad published an English Bible. The New Testament appeared at Rheims in 1582. The Old Testament was published at Douai in 1609-10. The revisers of 1611 made some use, at all events, of the New Testament.]

(5) *The Authorised Version* of 1611.— When the Hampton Court Conference (*q.v.*) was held in 1604, an incidental promise was made by the King to the Puritan Dr. Reynolds that a new revision should be undertaken. A representative list of scholars was drawn up, and instructions were issued to the members of the boards of revision. We know the names of some forty-seven. Six companies met, two at each centre, viz. Oxford, Cambridge, Westminster. The revisers had the English efforts of nearly a century before them. They consulted the work of all their predecessors, as well those above named as Continental translators. Much co-operation and mutual consultation went on, and at last the printed book appeared in 1611, with an interesting preface, and a fulsome dedication to James I. The first edition was a folio, but smaller shapes soon appeared. The revisers took the Bishops' Bible in the 1572 edition as their basis. No marginal notes were allowed. How successful their work was three centuries have testified. At the same time, it must be remembered that they were essentially conservative : ' Truly we never thought to make a new translation, nor yet to make of a bad one a good one, but to make a good one better, or out of many good ones one principal good one.' This version is called 'authorised,' but it never received formal licence ; it superseded the others by sheer excellence.

(6) *Revised Version.*—More than two cen-

turies passed, during which constantly increasing light fell upon the text and meaning of the Bible. The magnificent English of the version of 1611 was discovered by degrees to be deficient in accuracy. A science of textual criticism had been gradually built up. Critical texts of the Greek Testament had been issued by Tischendorf (1815-74) and others. It was felt that a new translation worthy of the growth of Greek scholarship ought to be undertaken. From time to time the question of revision was mooted. At last in 1870 Convocation took it up. Committees of Anglicans and Nonconformists were appointed to revise the Old Testament and the New. American co-operation was invited. The changes were to be as few as possible, and in Bible language, with some reference to the necessary correction of the underlying original text. The revisers met at the Jerusalem Chamber. The New Testament was issued in 1881. Its foes were more numerous than its friends ; but a considerable change of sentiment has been perceptible of late. The Old Testament was ready in 1884. The Old and New Testaments were published together in 1885. The Apocrypha was added in 1895. All through, American suggestions were considered, often used, and those not used were placed in an appendix. In 1898 a revised reference edition of the whole Bible appeared.   [H. G.]

H. W. Hoare, *Our Eng. Bible* ; A. W. Pollard, *Records of the Eng. Bible* ; Mombert, *Eng. Versions of the Bible.*

BINGHAM, Joseph (1668-1723), born at Wakefield, September 1668, and educated at Wakefield Grammar School and University College, Oxford (matriculated, 26th May 1684 ; B.A., 1688 ; Fellow, 1689 ; M.A., 1691). He was ordained deacon in 1691, priest in 1692. The ' Trinitarian Controversy' was then in process ; Sherlock (*q.v.*) had published his *Vindication* in 1691, and South (*q.v.*) in the *Animadversions*, 1693, had, with some justice, charged him with tritheism. On SS. Simon and Jude, 1695, Bingham preached before the University at St. Peter-in-the-East a sermon on the Holy Trinity in Sherlock's sense, and was immediately delated to the vice-chancellor by J. Beauchamp, B.D., Fellow of Trinity, commonly known as ' the heretic-hunter.' On 25th November the Hebdomadal Board condemned two propositions contained in the sermon as ' false, impious, and heretical ' ; and South in his *Short History of Valentinus Gentilis* denounced Bingham as a follower of Sherlock. Meanwhile Bingham had been nominated by Dr. J. Radcliffe to the rectory of Headbourne Worthy, Hants, and had resigned his fellowship. On 12th May 1696, in a visitation sermon at Winchester, he defended his University sermon. Both these sermons, with a second visitation sermon of 1697, and a preface explaining the circumstances, were prepared for publication, but did not see the light till 1829. In 1702 he married Dorothea, daughter of Richard Pococke, Rector of Colmer; and by her he had two sons and eight daughters, one of whom married Thomas Mant, and became the grandmother of Richard Mant, Bishop of Down and Connor. In 1706 Bingham published *The French Church's Apology for the Church of England*, in which he showed that dissenters 'act and go upon such principles as would oblige them to separate from the French [Huguenot] Church and perhaps all other Protestant Churches,' and exhorted the Huguenot immigrants to discountenance, in accordance with their own principles, the English dissidents, and to conform to the Church. In 1708-11 he published the first three volumes of the *Origines Ecclesiasticae*, begun in 1702. In 1712 he issued *A scholastical history of the practice of the Church in reference to the administration of Baptism by Laymen*. Part I., a criticism of Roger Laurence's *Lay-baptism invalid*, 1708 (2nd ed., 1710). He was answered by T. Brett in *An enquiry into the judgement and practice of the Primitive Church*, and by Laurence in a second part of *Lay-baptism invalid* (1712-13). Bingham replied to this in *A scholastical history*, Part II. (1714), and to Laurence's further *Supplement* (1714) in *A dissertation on the Eighth Canon of the Council of Nice* (1714). In reply to Burnet's (*q.v.*) strictures (1710) on *Lay-baptism invalid*, Laurence had written *Sacerdotal Powers, or the Necessity of Confession, Absolution*, etc. (1711, 1713); and in 1711 Brett had published his *Sermon on the Remission of Sins*, which was attacked and almost censured in the Lower House of Convocation. It was apparently in relation to the question here discussed that in 1713 Bingham published *Two sermons and two letters to the Lord Bishop of Winchester* (Trelawney, who had consulted him about 'the indispensable necessity of absolution in all cases whatever') *concerning the nature and necessity of the several sorts of absolution*. In 1712 he had been collated by Trelawney to the rectory of Havant, which he held in plurality with Headbourne till his death. In 1715 the publication of the *Origines* was resumed, and the remaining seven volumes appeared at

intervals up to 1722. Meanwhile Bingham had lost all his money in the bursting of the South Sea Bubble, 1720. He began to prepare a second edition of the *Origines*, and had in view a popular abridgment and a supplement on minor rites; but he died, 17th August 1723, at the age of fifty-five, and was buried at Headbourne Worthy.

Bingham was essentially a student and a scholar, but he was also an excellent parish priest. In character he was modest, gentle, and unworldly, but firm and independent; and in discussion he contrasts strongly with such controversialists as South and Sherlock. As a divine he was of the Caroline type, strongly anti-Roman, and with a marked sympathy with the foreign reformed bodies, and especially the French. 'The peace of the Church' was what he had 'always had at heart, and could be content to sacrifice any interest of his own in order to effect it'; and his preface to the projected second edition of the *Origines* is still a valuable argument for possibilities of reunion on the basis of a real and primitive episcopacy. His fame rests chiefly on the *Origines*, a great work, and the first of its kind, on the hierarchy, the ecclesiology, the territorial organisation, the rites, the discipline, and the calendar of the primitive Church, drawn from the original sources, but betraying an immense erudition in the later literature of the subject. It was translated into Latin and published (1724-8) by the Lutheran, J. H. Grischow of Halle, with a preface by the distinguished J. F. Budde; and an abridgment in German by a Roman Catholic editor was issued at Augsburg, 1788-96. There is no portrait of Bingham.

[F. E. B.]

R. Bingham, *Life*, prefixed to *Works*, 1821-9 (of which the article in *D.N.B.* is only an abridgment); Hearne, *Collections*. Bingham's *Works* were published in 2 vols. fol., London, 1726; in 9 vols. 8vo., 1821-9, ed. by his great-grandson, Rich. Bingham; and in 10 vols. 8vo., Oxford, 1855.

BIRINUS (d. 649 ?), apostle of the West Saxons, was probably an Italian by nation, of Teutonic descent. After taking counsel with Pope Honorius he resolved to preach the Gospel in the inland country of the English, which had not been visited by any teacher, and was consecrated a regionary bishop (one without an assigned diocese) by Asterius, Bishop of Milan, at Genoa. He landed in the country of the Gewissas, afterwards called West Saxons, in 634, and finding them sunk in the darkest heathenism worked among them. Their King, Cynegils, hearkened to him, and was baptized at Dorchester (Oxon) in 635. Oswald (*q.v.*) of Northumbria, then overlord of Britain, who had come to Wessex to marry the daughter of Cynegils, acted as the King's sponsor, and received him at the baptismal font. Cynegils and Oswald then joined in giving Dorchester to Birinus that he might make it his episcopal see. In 636 Cwichelm, the under-king, the son of Cynegils, was baptized, and died the same year; and in 639 Birinus baptized Cwichelm's son Cuthred, the under-king, standing sponsor for him himself. He built churches among the West Saxons, and converted many. His work may have received a temporary check about 642, for Cynegil's son and successor, Coenwalch, refused to accept Christianity. Coenwalch, however, was driven from his kingdom by the Mercians, and while in exile in East Anglia was converted. He regained his kingdom in 647 or 648, and built a church in his royal city, Winchester, the predecessor of the present cathedral, which Birinus is said to have dedicated. After having firmly established Christianity in Wessex, Birinus died at Dorchester on 3rd December 649 or perhaps 650, and was there buried. Dorchester having become a Mercian see, Haeddi, Bishop of Winchester, translated his body to Winchester in or after 676. Bishop Ethelwold is said to have placed the relics of the saint in a shrine when he rebuilt the church about 980, and a portable shrine, or feretory, was provided for them by Canute in 1035. They were again translated in 1150.

[w. h.]

J. E. Field, *St. Berin of Wessex.*

BIRMINGHAM, See of.

The first step towards the foundation of the see was taken in 1888, chiefly at the instance of Bishop Philpott of Worcester, who presided over a large meeting, at which Archbishop Benson (*q.v.*) and Bishop Westcott (*q.v.*), both Birmingham men, were present. A committee was formed to promote the project, and the bishop promised £800 a year from the income of the see towards the endowment, a promise which was not renewed by his successor. The scheme was abandoned in 1892 after Dr. Philpott's resignation, but revived after the accession of Dr. Gore in 1902. An Endowment Fund was inaugurated, and though only £105,000 was asked for, in two years £118,000 had been raised, including £10,000 offered anonymously by Canon Freer in a letter to the *Times* (14th April 1902). The see was established by Order in Council, 12th January 1905, under the Southwark and Birmingham

Bishoprics Act, 1904 (4 Edw. vii. c. 30). The income of the see was fixed at £3000, with £500 for a house. The diocese consists of Birmingham and the surrounding districts, and includes parts of the counties of Worcester, Warwick and Stafford. It was taken mainly from the diocese of Worcester, but partly also from that of Lichfield. It is divided into the archdeaconries of Birmingham and Aston, the latter having been constituted in 1906. The population is estimated at 1,050,000. St. Philip's Church built 1711, became the pro-cathedral of the see. As the diocese has no recognised chapter, the bishop is appointed by Letters Patent from the Crown.   [A. C. D.]

BISHOPS

1. Charles Gore, 1905; tr. from Worcester; tr. to Oxford, 1911.
2. Henry Russell Wakefield, 1911; Dean of Norwich.

BISCOP, Benedict

(c. 628-90) came of a noble family of Angles. If he is the Biscop mentioned by Florence of Worcester (*Genialogia*), he was related to the royal house of the Lindisfari. He began life as a thegn of Oswy (*q.v.*), King of Northumbria, but at the age of twenty-five he resolved to devote himself to the work of the Church. He therefore went to Rome in 653, travelling as far as Lyons with Wilfrid (*q.v.*), whom he met at Canterbury. After some years he returned to Northumbria to promote religion and learning, but in 665 he again set out for Rome. Shortly after he withdrew to the monastery of Lerins, an island off the coast of Provence, where he took the monastic vow and received the tonsure. When he returned to Rome two years later he was bidden by Pope Vitalian to conduct Theodore (*q.v.*), who had just been elected archbishop, and his followers to England. They arrived at Canterbury in May 669, and Benedict was then appointed abbot of the monastery of SS. Peter and Paul, over which he ruled for two years. He left Canterbury to buy books on the Continent, and having purchased a large number at Rome and Vienne returned in 672 to Northumbria. King Egfrith was so much struck by his work that he gave him seventy hides of land near the mouth of the Wear on which to build a monastery. To carry out this work he secured the services of masons and glaziers from Gaul. The monastery at Wearmouth was completed in 674 and dedicated to St. Peter. About 678 he again journeyed to Rome to obtain relics, pictures, and books with which to furnish it. He secured also from Pope Agatho its exemption from external control, and gained the services of John, the Arch-chanter of St. Peter's and Abbot of St. Martin's at Rome, who came with him to teach the monks of Wearmouth the Roman choir office. Shortly after he began to build the sister abbey at Jarrow, for which Egfrith granted him forty hides of land. This was completed in 682 and dedicated to St. Paul. Over the second foundation he placed Ceolfrith, who had long helped him in his work, while at the same time he took a colleague, his cousin Easterwine, to help him in ruling Wearmouth. When these arrangements had been completed he made his fifth journey to Rome to procure relics, books, pictures, and vestments for the church of Jarrow. In his absence Easterwine died, and a certain Sigfrith was chosen abbot. Soon after his return to England, Benedict became paralysed, and remained so for the last three years of his life. His colleague, Sigfrith, died a few months before him, and Ceolfrith was set over the two sister monasteries. On 12th January 690 Benedict died, and was buried in the church of St. Peter at Wearmouth. In 964 his bones were removed by Aethelwold, Bishop of Winchester, to his abbey at Thorney. His life was written by Bede (*Vita Abbatum*, ed. Plummer), who at the age of seven was placed under the abbot's care. See also *Acta Sanctorum* under 12th January.

[A. L. P.]

BISHOPS as the chief ministers of the Christian Church are as old as any record of its life as an organised body. The New Testament and other early writings show that the apostles appointed presbyters to preside over local churches, with power to provide for the continuance of the ministry. And during the first two centuries this system developed into the monarchical and diocesan episcopacy which has ever since been the rule of the Catholic Church, has existed in the English Church from its foundation, and was expressly accepted by it in the sixteenth century at the most important crisis in its history. [AUTHORITY IN THE CHURCH.]

Appointment of Bishops.—At first the right to elect a bishop rested with the people of the vacant see. At a later stage the bishops of the province appointed, subject to the veto of the metropolitan, which in the fourth century developed into a separate process, the confirmation of the election. From the sixth century a profession of obedience to the metropolitan was required before confirma-

tion. Before Christianity reached England the share of the clergy in the appointment had dwindled to an almost nominal right of election by the cathedral clergy. In 796 Alcuin (*q.v.*) urged that chapters should have freedom of election, and throughout the Middle Ages attempts were made by them to assert this right, with only occasional success. In 1214, for instance, King John granted freedom of election, and confirmed it in Magna Carta (*q.v.*), 1215. In practice such freedom usually led to disputed elections and appeals to Rome. After the acceptance of Christianity by civil rulers the bishops became personages in the state, and Christian emperors and kings were allowed first a veto on the choice of bishops, and ultimately a right of appointment, which to a great extent superseded the older methods of election and entirely swallowed up the primitive rights of the laity.

In England before the Norman Conquest bishops were usually appointed by the King in and with the consent of the Witenagemot, a mixed assembly of lay and clerical notables. Sometimes the clergy and even the laity of the vacant diocese were consulted. After the Conquest the feudal theory of the episcopal office appears. The bishop added to his former character that of the 'King's man,' holding his temporalities directly of the Crown as overlord and doing homage for them. [INVESTITURES.] The see of Sodor and Man [MAN] alone was held of a subject (a 'mediate' bishopric). This relationship of the bishops to the Crown strengthened the royal claims to their appointment, the only serious rival being the Pope, who claimed first the right to decide disputes over episcopal appointments as part of his general appellate jurisdiction, then that of confirming the election, and lastly a power of direct appointment. [PROVISORS.] As a rule, King and Pope respected each other's nominations, at the expense of the chapters. The normal mode of appointment was for the King to send the chapter a *congé d'élire* (permission to elect), which usually contained the name of the person to be elected, whom, as a rule, they accepted. The election must then be confirmed by the Pope, the bishop-elect taking an oath to him and paying fees. He also made a profession of obedience to his metropolitan. The election needed also the formal consent of the King, who restored to the bishop on his doing homage the temporalities of the see (which reverted to the Crown at a vacancy). If any dispute arose between King and chapter or between parties in the chapter the only appeal was to the Pope, who either confirmed the election of one of the candidates or, more frequently, annulled the whole proceedings and provided either one of the candidates or a nominee of his own. So it came about that even a candidate duly elected without opposition was willing that his position should be made quite secure by the Pope's quashing the election and providing him. Apparently the fourteenth-century Popes deliberately aimed at making their consent indispensable to the validity of every episcopal appointment. And the kings, somewhat short-sightedly, acquiesced in this policy by applying for papal provision for their own nominees. They were content that the popes should have the desired power so long as a reasonable proportion of royal nominees were appointed, and they could safeguard the temporal jurisdiction by compelling the bishop to renounce all words prejudicial to it in the Bull of Provision. Thus the real power of appointment was shared between Pope and King, and after the breach with Rome the Crown was left in sole possession.

The procedure was laid down by statute in 1534 (25 Hen. VIII. c. 20), which empowers the Crown on the vacancy of a bishopric to send the chapter a licence to elect ' with a letter missive containing the name of the person whom they shall elect.' If they delay above twelve days the Crown shall appoint by Letters Patent. Thus the mediæval abuse by which the chapters had lost their rights was made permanent. After the election the bishop-elect shall take an oath of fealty to the King, who shall signify the election to the archbishop, requiring him to confirm it and consecrate the elect, giving him ' pall [if an archbishop], benedictions, ceremonies, and all other things requisite ' without obtaining any Bulls or other instruments from Rome. If he fail to do so, or the chapter fail to elect the person nominated, they are liable to *Praemunire* (*q.v.*). The Act 1 Edw. VI. c. 2 (1547) abolished this procedure on the ground that ' such elections be in very deed no elections,' and substituted appointment by Letters Patent. This Act was repealed in 1554 (1-2 Ph. and M. c. 8). Under Mary there are several instances of papal provision, but the Act of Supremacy, 1559 (1 Eliz. c. 1), restored the procedure of 1534, under which bishops are still appointed.

After election the King sends his mandate to the archbishop, who holds a court (in which the Vicar-General presides) and cites objectors to appear. At the confirmations of Drs. Hampden (*q.v.*), Temple (*q.v.*), and Gore (1902, 2 K.B. 503), the Vicar-General refused to hear objectors, holding that confirmation was a ministerial duty, and the only relevant objections would be against the formality of the election or the identity of the elect. Objections to fitness for the office must be made at an earlier stage. At confirmation the bishop-elect takes the oaths of allegiance and of canonical obedience to the archbishop, and the declaration against simony, and the vicar-general commits the spiritualities of the see to him, and orders him to be enthroned. Enthronement in the southern province is the right of the Archdeacon of Canterbury: in the northern province the Archbishop of York appoints *ad hoc*. After confirmation the bishop-elect has *potestas iurisdictionis*, and can perform all episcopal acts except those which depend on consecration. This is given usually by the archbishop and at least two other bishops, its essential form being the simultaneous laying on of the hands of the consecrators. It confers *potestas ordinis*, and is preceded by an ' oath of due obedience ' to the archbishop. By ancient custom no consecration of a bishop of the southern province may take place out of Canterbury Cathedral save by licence of the dean and chapter of Canterbury. Finally, the new bishop sues for his temporalities, which are restored on his taking an oath of homage, acknowledging that he holds the bishopric ' as well the spiritualities as the temporalities thereof ' from the Crown. ' Spiritualities ' in this sense means the emoluments from ecclesiastical sources such as tithes, as opposed to the income from purely temporal sources, manors and the like. These are the only spiritualities which are in the King's hands and can be given by him. The spiritualities of jurisdiction are vested during vacancy in the guardian of the spiritualities, by canon law the dean and chapter, but by custom usually the archbishop.

There are three processes in the appointment of a bishop. (1) He must be *chosen*. In almost every country at every age since the conversion of Constantine the State, with the acquiescence of the Church, has had a large share in the choice. In England until the end of the Stuart period the sovereign's personal will was the chief factor. William III., not being a churchman, was advised by a commission of divines. Sir Robert Walpole was the first lay minister to acquire the regular power of choosing bishops. In election and confirmation the Church accepts the State's choice. A Bill to abolish election as merely an unedifying formality failed to pass the House of Commons in 1880. Mr. Gladstone (*q.v.*) urged that the existence of the ceremony constituted a check on improper appointments, and alluded to the case of Thomas Rundle, whose nomination to the see of Gloucester in 1733 was so vigorously opposed by Gibson (*q.v.*) and others on the ground of his alleged Deism, that though it had been published it was withdrawn. It was also pointed out that election gave the chapter an opportunity to protest against an unfit nominee by refusing to elect him and braving a *Praemunire*. (2) He must be *placed*. The State has a large share in deciding to what diocese a particular person shall be appointed ; but the Church, through the archbishop, gives him mission to it by committing the spiritual jurisdiction to him at confirmation. (3) He must be *made* a bishop. This is done by the Church alone at consecration. And if an improper appointment were made, it would be the Church's duty to withhold consecration at the risk of temporal penalties.

Where there is no chapter the Crown appoints by Letters Patent, and the Church gives the nominee mission, as well as making him a bishop, at consecration. The canonical qualifications of a bishop are that he must be thirty years of age at least, born in wedlock, a learned presbyter, and of good life and behaviour.

Removal of a bishop from his see may take place in the following ways :—

1. Translation to another see. This was forbidden in early times as likely to proceed from improper motives. A bishop was held to be bound to the see, to which he was consecrated by a tie comparable to that of wedlock. In England translation was hardly known before the tenth century, and was rare until the fourteenth. From 1066 to 1300 only fourteen instances of English sees being vacated by translation are recorded ; during the fourteenth century thirty-four, and during the fifteenth fifty-five. The increase was chiefly due to the practice of papal provision. It was held that the Pope alone could remove a bishop from his original see, and had a special duty to appoint a bishop for the church so bereaved. Consequently the papal claim to provide to all sees vacated by translation was admitted, and the number of translations increased. In later times translations to wealthier and more important sees became the rule. From 1609 to 1836 every bishop of the rich see of Ely held it by translation. Of seventeen bishops of Bangor between 1689 and 1830 thirteen were translated to other sees. A relic of the earlier feeling may be found in the refusal of Bishop T. Wilson (*q.v.*) to desert his wife (*i.e.* his see) in his old age because she was poor. In modern times translations are common.

2. Resignation on grounds of incapacity was permitted though not encouraged in early times. As the notion of a matrimonial tie between bishop and see grew stronger resignation was looked on with disfavour. In 1256 Pope Alexander IV. reluctantly permitted Bishop Wescham of Lichfield to resign on account of paralysis. But it was more usual for incapacitated bishops to be assisted by coadjutors.

By canon law any cure can only be resigned into the hands of the authority from whom it was received. Therefore since the Reformation an English bishop could apparently only tender his resignation to his metropolitan who had given him mission, and the metropolitan could accept it with the consent of the Crown. As the procedure was uncertain a special Act was passed in 1856 (19-20 Vic. c. 115) to allow the sees of London and Durham to be declared vacant on the resignation of Bishops Blomfield (*q.v.*) and Maltby. The Bishops Resignation Act, 1869 (32-3 Vic. c. 111), allowed the Crown to declare any see vacant and proceed to fill it, if satisfied that the bishop ' has canonically resigned ' on account of incapacity arising from old age, mental or permanent physical infirmity. The retiring bishop is to retain a portion of the income. If a bishop is incapacitated by permanent mental infirmity a coadjutor bishop may be appointed to perform his episcopal functions, and to succeed to the bishopric (except London, Winchester, or Durham) at his death. No such appointment has yet been made. This scheme was approved in outline by Convocation early in the same year.

3. Deprivation or deposition from a see could originally only be decreed by the provincial synod. From the sixth century the popes claimed this jurisdiction. In fact, however, it fell into the hands of the kings. Archbishop Theodore (*q.v.*) apparently exercised it on his own responsibility, but as a rule unworthy bishops before the Norman Conquest were deprived by King and Witan. In 1070 Stigand was deposed as schismatic by a national council, at which papal legates were present. Later deprivations were made by papal authority, but were few in number. A more usual method of removing an obnoxious or unfit bishop was by compulsory translation to a remote or unimportant see. Several instances occur in the fourteenth century. The civil power can deprive a bishop of the temporal incidents of his see, and can also prevent him from exercising spiritual jurisdiction. Instances of this are the deprivation of the Italian bishops of

Salisbury and Worcester by Act of Parliament in 1534 (25 Hen. VIII. c. v.), and of the Nonjurors (*q.v.*) under 1 - 2 W. and M. c. 8. Bishop Watson of St. David's, on the other hand, was deprived by the spiritual authority of his metropolitan (see below).

4. *Degradation.* A bishop, like a priest, can apparently be degraded from his orders for serious offences. [DISCIPLINE.] Naturally there are few instances of so grave a proceeding. Cranmer (*q.v.*) was degraded from bishop to layman by virtue of a papal commission. In 1590 Bishop Middleton of St. David's, having been found guilty by the Star Chamber of simony and other offences, was handed over to the High Commission, by whom, according to Heylyn (*Hist. Examen*, 221), he was 'degraded from all holy orders' at Lambeth 'by a formal devesting of him of his episcopal robes and priestly vestments.'

The Functions of the Episcopate are, firstly, to provide for the continuance of the ministry by consecration of bishops and ordination of ministers of lower degree (Tit. 1[5]). From the earliest times this power has been confined to the highest order of the Christian ministry. Secondly, provision being thus made for the continuance of the Church, it is their duty to see that it fulfils the purpose for which it was founded : to maintain the faith against error and schism, and generally to keep the Church not merely in order but in life. The authority by means of which these duties are performed is exercised by the English bishops under present circumstances either (*a*) collectively by the bishops of each province in synod [CONVOCATION, COUNCILS], or (*b*) individually by each bishop in his diocese. In early times each local church was a self-contained community over which a single bishop presided, the clergy working under his direction. But as the Church grew it became necessary for him to give them mission to particular districts. This system was followed in England, the circumstances of the conversion leading to the formation of large dioceses. After the Council of London, 1075, bishops' seats which had sometimes been fixed in villages were removed to principal towns, and from the twelfth century their duties were more definite and their control over their clergy more complete than in Anglo-Saxon times.

A bishop's first duty is to provide for the spiritual needs of his diocese by ordaining clergy to work in it, instituting presentees to benefices (which involves the power to reject those who are unfit) and licensing the unbeneficed clergy. Other purely spiritual functions are confirmation, the consecration of churches and churchyards, and certain powers of dispensation.

The bishop's executive power is largely exercised through officers whom he appoints, both clerical, as the archdeacon (*q.v.*) and lay, as the chancellor. Formerly he also exercised it in person by means of visitations. During a visitation all inferior authority was suspended. Peculiars (*q.v.*) were exempt from episcopal visitation. The practice of visitation was reorganised and made more effective by Bancroft (*q.v.*). By Canon 60 of 1604 confirmations were to be held at visitations, which were to take place every third year. In modern times the practical work of visitation is performed by the archdeacon, the bishop's visitation consisting mainly of the delivery of a charge. By virtue of his inherent authority a bishop administers, interprets, and where necessary supplements the Church's law, both by constitutions formally promulgated in diocesan synod [COUNCILS] and by giving directions to meet particular needs. An instance of this is the *ius liturgicum*, to which the preface to the Prayer Book refers, the power to interpret and supplement the written law of public worship.

From primitive times a voluntary jurisdiction appears to have existed in the Church to avoid the scandal of law-suits before unbelievers (1 Cor. 6[1-6]). In later times much of the bishop's judicial power has been exercised in formal Courts (*q.v.*). But he is not a mere judge, bound to decide every case brought before him. The nature of his authority requires him always to keep in mind the spiritual interests of the parties and of the Church. Therefore he rightly possesses the power of stopping by his veto a suit which might injure those interests. And he can, if need be, exercise jurisdiction and discipline more privately and informally *in foro domestico*, bringing his paternal and pastoral authority to bear.

Bishops and the Temporal Power.—As the conversion of England was mainly achieved through the acceptance of Christianity by the kings, the bishops of the English Church from its very foundation have held an important position in the state. The pagan priests by virtue of their office had been prominent among the royal counsellors. And to this position the Christian bishops succeeded, with the additional prestige of representatives of a higher morality and of the superior civilisation of Rome. As a rule, each bishopric was originally conterminous with a kingdom, and so the bishop quickly became the most important man after the King. Owing to the peculiarly close connection of the Anglo-Saxon Church and State the position of the bishops constituted them leaders in government, in the Witan, and even in the battlefield; while their ecclesiastical jurisdiction was supported by the secular power. After the union of the kingdoms they retained their position as leaders in the national life without becoming independent potentates like the prince-bishops of Germany. Odo was the first Archbishop of Canterbury (942-59) to become chief counsellor to the Crown of England, 'a position,' says Bishop Stubbs, 'which he leaves to Dunstan (*q.v.*) and a long series of successors.' From the eleventh century it became common for the kings to use their power in episcopal appointments to promote their favourites, or men who had earned preferment by administrative work, and, being ecclesiastics, could conveniently and cheaply be rewarded with bishoprics. Thus there grew up a class of bishops who were primarily state officials, administrators, financiers, or diplomatists; men of high character as a rule, and good churchmen, but not specially fitted for spiritual or ecclesiastical distinction. This type practically ended with Wolsey (*q.v.*). Nicholas Wotton (1497 ?-1567), a typical diplomatist of his time, who held the deaneries of Canterbury and York simultaneously, more than once refused a bishopric as a reward for his services, holding himself unfit for the office. Many mediæval bishops, also, were great feudal nobles, levying aids from their clergy, administering secular justice, and ruling their large estates as temporal lords. After the Reformation they appear shorn of much of this greatness, mere ecclesiastics, far more dependent on the Crown and its ministers than before. The events of the first half of the nineteenth century produced another change. Dignified and comfortable prelates gave way to hard-working leaders of a revived spiritual life in the Church and the nation—a process that was much affected by the increase in the number of dioceses. Until 1847 every diocesan bishop sat in the House of Lords. [PARLIAMENT, CLERGY IN.] The changes that have since taken place in this as in other respects have tended to emphasise the spiritual and ecclesiastical aspects of the episcopal office.

Archbishops.—The organisation of the Church into provinces under metropolitans was established before Christianity came to England. Pope Gregory I. (*q.v.*) intended that the country should be divided into two provinces, but the course of events has modified his scheme in some particulars. During the Middle Ages the metropolitan tended to develop, from *primus inter pares* into a ruler, though this tendency was checked by the growth of the papal power. The history of the appointment of English archbishops has followed the same course as that of bishops. The custom of sending them the pall (*q.v.*) died away with the necessity of confirmation of their election. Under 25 Hen. VIII. c. 20 the election is signified to four or more bishops of the province, or to the other archbishop and two bishops, who confirm it and consecrate the archbishop-elect if he be not already a bishop. The special functions of an archbishop are :—

1. To summon and preside in provincial synod, over the acts of which he has a veto. [CONVOCATION.]

2. To confirm election of bishops.

3. To hear appeals from the diocesan courts. [COURTS.]

Two further duties have been the subject of dispute, namely :—

4. To try charges brought against a bishop. In early times the bishops were tried in provincial synod. In the Middle Ages the popes claimed this jurisdiction, and it has never been effectively recovered by Convocation; the proceedings of which against Bishops Cheyney and Goodman (*q.v.*) of Gloucester in 1571 and 1640 were not trials. At the end of the seventeenth century the metropolitans assumed jurisdiction. In 1684 Bishop Wood of Lichfield was suspended by Sancroft (*q.v.*) for neglect of duty after a trial by two bishops as arbitrators. Archbishop Tenison, with other bishops as assessors, tried Bishop Thomas Watson of St. David's for simony, and in 1698 sentenced him to deprivation. This was upheld by the Court of Delegates and by the King's Bench on an application for prohibition (14 State Trials, 447 ; 1 Ld. Raym., 447 and 539). In 1700 Tenison tried Edward Jones, Bishop of St. Asaph, for the same offence, and in 1701 suspended him. In *Read* v. *Bishop of Lincoln* (1889, 14 P.D. 88) Archbishop Benson (*q.v.*) held that the jurisdiction over his suffragans lay in the metropolitan, who can exercise it alone, with assessors, or in synod. But high authorities have thought that it may not be exercised apart from the synod.

5. To visit all the dioceses in his province. This right was exercised by some mediæval archbishops, but met with resistance. In 1322 Bishop Grandison of Exeter caused the doors of his cathedral to be shut against his metropolitan, and prepared to resist his visitation by force. Such visitations were

held in the sixteenth and seventeenth centuries. Laud (*q.v.*) visited his province by means of commissioners, 1634-7, since when the practice has fallen into abeyance. Laud also successfully asserted his right to visit the Universities (Wilkins, *Conc.*, iv. 525).

Suffragans.—The word means an assistant, and is used of a diocesan bishop in his relation to his metropolitan, but more commonly of an assistant to a diocesan bishop. Such assistant bishops, called *chorepiscopi*, were appointed in the third century to supervise the outlying parts of large dioceses. Their position gave rise to controversy, and their appointment was forbidden in the ninth century. In the later Middle Ages the numerous diocesan bishops who were occupied in affairs of State required assistants to perform their episcopal duties, and suffragans were appointed with titles taken from Irish and Eastern sees. Dr. Stubbs enumerates over a hundred such bishops who acted in English dioceses between 1306 and 1535. They were appointed by the Pope. An Act of 1534 (26 Hen. VIII. c. 14; repealed 1554, 1-2 Ph. and M. c. 8; revived 1559, 1 Eliz. c. 1) gave a list of twenty-six places for which suffragans might be appointed. The diocesan was to present two candidates to the King, who was to choose one for consecration. Under this Act seventeen suffragans were appointed down to 1592, after which it was disused until 1870, though the canons of 1604 assume the existence of suffragans. The Suffragans Nomination Act, 1888 (51-2 Vic. c. 56) allowed other places to be added to those named in the Act of 1534. The appointment of suffragans is now common, but is a less satisfactory method of relieving overburdened bishops than the division of dioceses. By custom bishops suffragan do not sit in Convocation unless they hold some position entitling them to a seat in the Lower House. The appointment of coadjutor bishops with right of succession was not regarded with favour in the Middle Ages, as interfering with the right of election, and occurred rarely in England; but the principle was admitted by the Bishops Resignation Act, 1869 (above).

[G. C.]

For the early centuries see C. H. Turner, in *C. Med. Hist.*, i. vi.; *Dict. Christian Antiquities*, articles 'Bishops,' A. W. Haddan; 'Metropolitans,' B. Shaw. For Middle Ages Stubbs, *Const. Hist.*, chaps. viii. and xix.; *Hist. Eng. Ch.*, ed. Stephens and Hunt, vols. i.-iii. For modern times Phillimore, *Eccl. Law*; *Laws of Eng.*, article 'Eccl. Law.' See also Gibson, *Codex*; Stubbs, *Reg. Sacr. Ang.*; J. W. Lea, *Bishop's Oath of Homage*.

BLOMFIELD, Charles James (1786-1857), Bishop of London, son of a schoolmaster at Bury St. Edmunds, was educated at the Grammar School there and at Trinity College, Cambridge, where he was Scholar, and later Fellow. He won many University distinctions, working twelve and sometimes fifteen hours every day, and soon became famous as one of the most finished scholars in England. He graduated B.A., 1808, and was ordained deacon in March, priest in June, 1810 by Dr. Mansel, Bishop of Bristol, and Master of Trinity, and became Curate of Chesterford, where he took pupils. Later in the year he became Vicar of Quarrington, Lincs. but was non-resident. In 1811 he became Rector of Dunton, Bucks, still holding Quarrington, and was an active magistrate. 1817 he was made Rector of Great and Little Chesterford (Cambs), Rector of Tuddenham, Suffolk, and chaplain to Howley (*q.v.*), Bishop of London. In 1819 he married a second time, and became Rector of St. Botolph's, Aldgate, retaining Chesterford, however, where he resided for three months in each year; at other times an account of the parish was sent him weekly by his curate 'in the vegetable basket.' At Aldgate he ceased to take pupils, and became an active parish priest. 1822 he became Archdeacon of Colchester, and 1824 Bishop of Chester, retaining his London living *in commendam*. He began to infuse vigorous life into his diocese, seeking to abolish non-residence and to raise the standard of clerical life, being specially careful about ordination. His attempt to abolish the episcopal wig was frustrated by George IV., but permitted by his brother. In 1828 he became Bishop of London. His politics had undergone great changes. Early a Whig, and owing his first preferments to Whig lords, he had become opposed to Roman Catholic emancipation (1828), and in 1829 apologised in the House of Lords for voting against the Duke of Wellington, to whom he 'owed a debt of gratitude for his favourable opinion, and for a recommendation to his sovereign for an advancement in the Church.' He absented himself from the critical division when the Reform Bill was lost in the House of Lords in 1831. He supported it, however, in 1832. He was the leading spirit of the Ecclesiastical Commission, and actively promoted Church reform. Sydney Smith (*q.v.*) accused him of 'an ungovernable passion for business.' In 1836 he issued an appeal for funds to build fifty new churches in London, which met with wonderful success. During his episcopate nearly two hundred new churches were consecrated one of which (St. Stephen's, Hammersmith) was built and endowed at his own expense. In dealing with theological problems he was less successful. ' He was not at his best as a divine, and . . . singularly unsure of his own mind. He knew . . . that when the questions raised by the Tracts [for the Times] came before him he was unqualified to deal with them' (R. W. Church). Though describing himself as in church principles ' in entire agreement' with Joshua Watson (*q.v.*), he gave no support to the Oxford Movement, and in the early stages of the ritual controversy drove W. J. E. Bennett from St. Paul's, Knightsbridge (1851). He forbade flowers on the altar (especially when their colour harmonised with that of a saint's festival) as being ' worse than frivolous, and to approach very nearly to the honours paid by the Church of Rome to deified sinners.' In a famous charge (1842) he had urged obedience to the rubric and enjoined the use of the surplice in preaching, a weekly ' offertory,' and the reading of the Church Militant prayer. Protests from Evangelical clergy induced him to recede from this position. He was deeply involved in the Jerusalem Bishopric (*q.v.*) scheme of 1841. He supported the revival of Convocation (1851), signed a protest against Dr. Hampden's (*q.v.*) appointment to Hereford (1847), and as an assessor dissented from the judgment of the Privy Council in the Gorham (*q.v.*) case (1850). He was a friend and ally of Bishop S. Wilberforce (*q.v.*), and dissuaded him from resigning his see when his brother, R. I. Wilberforce (*q.v.*), became a Roman Catholic (1854). He was an admirable preacher, ' very effective in manner,' only ' he flings his head at you too much,' but on occasion in preaching ' he was affected to tears.' His incessant activities and his early overwork at Cambridge undermined his health. An accident at a Council at Osborne (1846) produced an illness from which he never quite recovered. He became paralysed, October 1855, and he resigned his see (by special Act of Parliament), 1856. He made gallant but unsuccessful attempts to establish a satisfactory Final Court of Appeal for ecclesiastical cases. He is bitterly attacked by Disraeli in *Tancred*.

[S. L. O.]

Memoir by his son: Memoir of Joshua Watson; Life of Bishop S. Wilberforce.

BONIFACE, St., or **WYNFRITH** (680-754), the apostle of Germany, was born at Crediton in Devon. He received his early education at Exeter, but soon left it for the monastery of Nursling, near Winchester, where

he gained a reputation as a preacher. He was ordained priest at the age of thirty, and in 716 made his first missionary journey to Frisia. But he failed to win any success. Radbod, the heathen king, was at war with Charles Martel, and checked in every way the progress of Christianity in his territory. Under these circumstances Boniface was compelled to return to Nursling in 717. He did not, however, give up the idea; indeed, he refused to accept the abbacy of Nursling, on the ground that his work lay in a different sphere. In the following year, accompanied by a few friends, he went to Rome, bearing a letter of introduction from Daniel, Bishop of Winchester (*Ep.* 11). Gregory II. received him with favour, and gave him authority to evangelise Germany. Boniface then returned through Bavaria and Thuringia, when he heard of the death of Radbod, and immediately hastened to Frisia. Here he worked with increasing success for three years with Willibrord (*q.v.*), the English Bishop of Utrecht, who urged him to become coadjutor to his bishopric; but Boniface declined, on the ground that he was not yet fifty years of age. In 722 he went to Hesse, where he founded a church at Amöneburg. His success became known to the Pope, who summoned him to Rome, and on 30th November 723 consecrated him bishop after he had taken a solemn oath of allegiance to the apostolic see. Armed with commendatory letters to Charles Martel and the clergy and princes with whom he was likely to come in contact (*Ep.* 17-21), Boniface left Rome to continue his missionary work. Charles gave him permission to preach the Gospel in Hesse and Thuringia, but it is doubtful how much real assistance Boniface received from him. The saint's well-known letter to Bishop Daniel (*Ep.* 63) is ambiguous: ' Without the protection of the prince of the Franks I can neither rule the people of the Church nor defend the priests or clergy, monks or nuns.' These words, commonly considered as an acknowledgment of his dependence on the Frankish king, may equally mean that he is handicapped by lack of support from the temporal ruler. This interpretation would explain the fact that during Charles's lifetime Boniface made no attempt to organise the Church in the East Frankish or Austrasian districts, but confined his energies to Bavaria, where no doubt he was assisted by Prince Odilo.

Hesse and Thuringia, whither Boniface now turned his attention, were partially Christian, but still maintained much of their pagan rites. Boniface struck at the heart of the mischief : he felled the oak dedicated to Thor which stood at Geismar, not far from Fritzlar. Out of its timber he erected a missionary chapel, and shortly after founded a monastery at Fritzlar. The effect of this action on the minds of the pagans seems to have been considerable, and large numbers were converted. In 732 Gregory III. raised Boniface to the dignity of archbishop, thus giving him a wider authority over the clergy of Germany. In 738 he paid his third visit to Rome, probably to make arrangements for the reorganisation of the Church in Bavaria, which was soon carried out. The duchy was divided into four bishoprics, Salzburg, Passau, Freising, and Regensburg. On the death of Charles Martel in 741 Boniface set to work to reform the Frankish Church. In this he received great assistance from Carloman and Pippin, the successors of Charles, and his powers were at the same time increased by Pope Zacharias, who created him legate. Four bishoprics were set up in Hesse and Thuringia, at Würzburg, Buraburg, Erfurt, and Eichstadt. A marked advance was made in carrying out Church reform when on 21st April 742 the first Austrasian Council was held. This was followed by a series of similar councils. At the Council of 744 heresy was attacked. Adalbert, a fanatic who dedicated churches to his own honour, and Clement, an unorthodox Irish priest, were condemned. They, however, continued to preach and to influence a considerable following. Another Irish priest, Virgil, afterwards Bishop of Salzburg, was attacked by Boniface, but, supported by the Pope, he escaped condemnation. In 745 a council was held for the entire Frankish dominions. Boniface presided, and it was probably on this occasion that he was given the diocese of Cologne. But before he had been installed the see of Mainz fell vacant, and was granted to Boniface with the primacy over all Germany. But a desire to return to missionary work in Frisia, the scene of his first activities, was always strong with him. In 753, therefore, he resigned his archbishopric to his fellow-countryman, Lul, and departed northward. On the 5th of June, Whitsun Eve, 754, at a place near Dokkum, where he had arranged to meet some Christian converts, Boniface and his companions, fifty-two in number, were massacred by a band of heathens. Boniface's remains were afterwards laid in the church at Fulda, which he had founded ten years before.

To evangelise the heathen parts of Germany, to reform and organise the Frankish Church

already existing, to bring the whole under the authority of the Roman see, were the objects Boniface set out to perform. Few missionaries have been rewarded with a larger measure of success or achieved more for Christianity in Europe. Though he left England early in life he never lost touch with it, and more than once he sent thither for recruits to assist him in his work. Moreover, throughout his career he kept up a frequent correspondence with his fellow-countrymen ; and his letters, which have been preserved, are of profound interest as illustrative both of the times and of the character of the saint himself. The few other writings that have been preserved are of comparatively little interest. St. Boniface is commemorated on 5th June. [A. L. P.]

Letters, ed. by Dümmler, in *Mon. Germ. Hist. Epistolae,* iii. and also by Jaffé, *Bibl. Rer. Germ.,* iii. The references given above are to the former edition. The Life by Willibald, together with five shorter lives ed. by Levison, in *Scriptores Rer. Germ. Vitae S. Bonifatii* ; Werner, *Bonifacius der Apostel der Deutschen* ; and Bishop G. F. Browne, *Boniface of Crediton and his Companions.*

BONNER, Edmund (*c.* 1500-69). Bishop of London, is said to have been a priest's son. Bachelor of both Laws at Oxford (Pembroke College), and Doctor (1524). Chaplain to Wolsey (*q.v.*) ; much employed by Henry VIII. on business abroad (1521-43) in Italy, France, and Spain ; presented (1532) to Clement VII. Henry's appeal to a General Council. Rector of Cherry Burton, of East Dereham, and Archdeacon of Leicester. Bishop of Hereford (1538) and of London (1539), a promotion due to Cromwell (*q.v.*) and distasteful to Gardiner (*q.v.*), with whom Bonner had quarrelled, and from whom he differed in his policy about the English Bible. His knowledge of law and ability as a subordinate led to his frequent employment in legal business, such as enforcing the Six Articles, and under Mary for degradation of ecclesiastics. On the accession of Edward VI. he at first resisted the Visitation and Injunctions of 1547, and was sent to the Fleet for two months. Later on he was lax in enforcing the use of the First Prayer Book. He was ordered to preach at St. Paul's Cross on certain heads given him, including the Mass and the full power of the King, even as a minor. A long process followed, in which Bonner showed himself very firm on Transubstantiation, while not resisting the Royal Supremacy, and, indeed, he appealed to the King. His defence was ingenious and bold. He had tried to get on with the administration, but being out of sympathy with them the attempt failed. In the end he was deprived by a commission, partly of laymen, but including Cranmer (*q.v.*). He was hardly dealt with, and the council rejected the appeal he had made. Under Mary he was restored, a commission, partly of laymen, declaring his deprivation illegal. He, along with Thirlby, was sent to Oxford to degrade Cranmer, and his behaviour there compared badly with Thirlby's. As Bishop of London he bore a chief part in the persecutions, and was once urged by the Queen to greater stringency (1555). Rough and violent-tempered, he yet gave prisoners chances of recantation, but although by no means the instigator of severity or cruel by nature, he showed no dislike of his subordinate but public part in the persecutions. Elizabeth at once showed disfavour to him. He acted as President of the Southern Convocation, there being no archbishop, and under her was firmer in resistance than he had been under Edward vi. He ordered the old use to be kept up at St. Paul's even after the Act of Uniformity, and he was deprived and placed in the Marshalsea. Horne, Bishop of Winchester (1564), urged him to take the oath under the Act of Supremacy. His refusal and subsequent objections raised interesting points. Apart from purely technical matters he contended that Horne was no bishop either by ecclesiastical or civil law. As a matter of fact, the Edwardine Ordinal had not been sanctioned by Parliament when Horne was consecrated. To get rid of this legal objection an Act was passed (8 Eliz. c. 1) legalising the consecration retrospectively, but a proviso added in the debates excluded from this retrospective sanction acts such as tendering the oath. Bonner was thus saved by his ingenuity from further trouble. Too much evil has been said of him, but his training and character made him more at home in Henry's diplomacy than in spiritual matters. Pliant to begin with as regards royal authority, he felt strongly upon Eucharistic doctrine, and when he made a stand he was firm and bold in his utterances. He died in the Marshalsea prison, September 1569, and is buried in the churchyard of St. George's, Southwark.   [J. P. W.]

Collier, *Eccl. Hist.*; Gairdner in *D.N.B.*; S. R. Maitland, *Essays on the Reformation*, xvii.-xx.

BOYLE, Hon. Robert (1627-91), was the ideal lay churchman of the later seventeenth century, devout, learned, popular, eminent. He was the fourteenth child of the first Earl of Cork (1566-1643), and was brought up by a pious elder sister during his earlier years, afterwards travelling abroad till the death of his father, when he returned to England. Here he became one of the members of the Philosophical (which eventually became the Royal) Society, at first in London and afterwards at Oxford, where meetings were held alternately at Wadham College and at Boyle's lodgings in the High Street. He was deeply engaged in the study of chemistry, mechanics, and physics, and, no less, in theology, and especially in the Old and New Testaments. He was a voluminous writer and a brilliant talker. 'Mr. Cowley and Sir William Davenant both thought him equal in that respect to the most celebrated geniuses of that age.' He lived in London with his sister, Lady Ranelagh, for nearly thirty years, and was a constant attendant at St. Martin-in-the-Fields, where Tenison (afterwards archbishop) was rector. Burnet (*q.v.*), to the expense of publication of whose *History of the Reformation* he generously contributed, was another of his clerical friends, and when he died (30th December 1691) preached his funeral sermon in warm eulogy. He gave 'a large account of Mr. Boyle's sincere and unaffected piety; and more especially of his zeal for the Christian religion, without having any narrow notions concerning it, or mistaking, as so many do, a bigoted heat in favour of a particular sect for that zeal which is an ornament of a true Christian.'

In natural science Boyle was a Baconian, and the famous Boerhave of Leiden said of him: 'Mr. Boyle, the ornament of his age and country, succeeded to the genius and inquiries of the great chancellor Verulam. Which of all Mr. Boyle's writings shall I recommend? All of them. To him we owe the secrets of fire, air, water, animals, vegetables, fossils; so that from his works may be deduced the whole system of natural knowledge.'

By his will he founded annual Boyle Lectures 'for the defence of the Gospel against infidels of all sorts.' Bentley preached the first course in 1692. Addison spoke of him as 'an honour to his country,' and the dissenter Calamy described him as 'one of the two great ornaments of Charles II.'s reign.'   [W. H. H.]

Birch, *Life of Boyle*; Overton, *Life in the Eng. Ch.*, 1660-1714.

BRAY, Dr. Thomas (1656-1730), deserves an honoured place in the history of the Church of England for his efforts on behalf of education and of missions. He took his degrees at

Oxford (All Souls, Hart Hall, and Magdalen College), and was from 1690 Rector of Sheldon, where he published *Catechetical Lectures*, which won him considerable fame. From 1695 he was interested in America, and in the provision of libraries both there and at home, towards which he induced the archbishops and others ' cheerfully to contribute.' In England he succeeded in founding eighty libraries, in North America thirty-nine. In England the scheme was advocated by a vigorous *Essay towards promoting all necessary and useful Knowledge, both divine and human, in all parts of his Majesty's Dominions* (1697). In this he advocated his plan for the benefit of the laity thus : ' For our younger gentry, I cannot but think it would tend extremely to furnish their minds with that useful knowledge as will render 'em serviceable to their families and countries, and will make 'em considerable both at home and abroad, and will keep 'em from idle conversation and the debaucheries attending it, to have choice collections of such books dispersed thro' all the kingdom, and waiting upon 'em in their own parlours, as will ennoble their minds with principles of virtue and true honour, and will file off that roughness, ferity, and barbarity which are the never-failing fruits of ignorance and illiterature.' His advice to the clergy was of a similar character. ' The truth is,' he wrote, ' there are a sort of writers which are traditionally handed down from one old study to another, who are not such a good-humoured and inviting society as to make one delight much in their conversation. But what man of spirit or education, had he a Justin Martyr, a Tertullian or Cyprian ; a Sanderson, a Hammond or Tillotson come to visit him, would leave such men of sense for the society of the sons of Belial ! '

From these libraries seemingly grew the Society for Promoting Christian Knowledge, of which he was one of the original five members. At the end of 1699 he sailed for North America as commissary of the Bishop (Compton) of London, working for the establishment of the Church and for the education of clergy. Returning to England he obtained the passing of an Act for the establishment of the Church in America, but he laboured in vain to secure the appointment of a bishop. The S.P.C.K. had grown during his absence, and in 1701 he procured a charter for the creation of a new society to extend and supplement its work, the Society for the Propagation of the Gospel. In 1723 he founded the society of ' Dr. Bray's Associates for founding clerical libraries and supporting

negro schools,' which still continues and publishes a yearly account of its work. From 1706 he was Rector of St. Botolph's, Aldgate, where he was famous for his catechising of children. He was also one of the first to pay special attention to inmates in prison, for whom he organised special ministrations. One of his last works was to design a colony in America for English unemployed. He was a vigorous and humorous writer and a parish priest of exemplary devotion, and to no one in the seventeenth and eighteenth centuries does the practical work of the English Church owe a greater debt.

[w. h. h.]

Reports of Dr. Bray's Associates; Overton, *Life in the Eng. Ch.*, 1660 1714.

BRISTOL, See of, was founded by Letters Patent, 5th June 1542, under the power to erect new sees conferred upon the Crown by 31 Hen. VIII. c. 9 (1539). It consisted of the county and archdeaconry of Dorset, taken from the diocese of Salisbury (*q.v.*); the city and county of Bristol, taken from the dioceses of Gloucester (*q.v.*), Bath and Wells (*q.v.*), and Worcester (*q.v.*); and the manor of Leigh in Somerset (which last was surrendered to the Crown by Bishop Bush in 1549). The monastery of St. Augustine, Bristol, a house of Augustinian canons, founded, 1142, by Robert Fitzhardinge, had been liberally endowed, its income in 1539 being £692, 2s. 7d. It became a mitred abbey, 1398. In 1534 the abbot and eighteen canons subscribed the Royal Supremacy ; in 1535 it was visited by Layton (*q.v.*), and surrendered in 1539, the abbot and eleven canons being pensioned. In 1542 its church was made the cathedral church of the new see, with a dedication to the Holy Trinity. According to Browne Willis, it ' is truly no elegant structure, being reputed one of the meanest cathedrals in the kingdom.' Restorations, including a complete rebuilding of the nave, undertaken in the nineteenth century at a cost of over £100,000, have only partly removed this reproach. The other monastic buildings were transformed into residences for the bishop and chapter, which was to consist of a dean, six major and six minor canons, deacon, sub-deacon, master of the choristers, two masters of the grammar school, sub-sacrist or sexton, butler, two cooks, and others—in all thirty-nine. There are now a dean, four residentiary, twenty-five honorary, and three minor canons.

The see was originally endowed with lands estimated to produce an income of £383, 8d. 4d., and was one of the poorest in

England, which accounts for the frequency of translations. Ecton (1711) gives the value as £327, 5s. 7½d. The present income is £3000. In 1835 the Ecclesiastical Commissioners recommended that the see should be united with Llandaff (*q.v.*). Objection was taken to this, and also to their second suggestion, that the city of Bristol should be transferred to Bath and Wells. Eventually by an Order in Council of 5th October 1836 Dorset was restored to Salisbury, and the sees of Gloucester and Bristol were united, the diocese to consist of the county of Gloucester, and the deaneries of Malmesbury and Cricklade in the county of Wilts. which with four deaneries in the county of Gloucester constituted the new archdeaconry of Bristol. Bedminster was added to it by transference from Bath and Wells in 1845. The chapters of Gloucester and Bristol were to elect the bishop alternately. The Bishopric of Bristol Act, 1884 (47-8 Vic. c. 66). provided that a separate diocese should be formed as soon as the necessary endowment was secured. This was effected in 1897, largely through the energy of Archdeacon Norris. the income of the see being £3000. of which £700 was taken from Gloucester. The diocese was constituted by Order in Council of 7th July 1897.´ It consists of the deaneries of Bristol, Stapleton. and Bitton, the portion of Wilts already in the united diocese, and three parishes in Somerset transferred from Bath and Wells. It is divided into the archdeaconries of Bristol and North Wilts (constituted 1904). and has a population of 583,000.

BISHOPS OF BRISTOL

1. Paul Bush, 1542 : Provincial of the ' Bonhommes,' a reformed order of Austin friars, and last Provost of their house at Edington, Wilts ; he was a strong Conservative, defending the Mass in Latin. Having married, he was deprived after Mary's accession, but resigned before the sentence was executed, and died Rector of Winterbourne, near Bristol, 1558. The inscription on his monument in the cathedral ends with the words *cuius animae propitietur Christus.*

2 John Holyman. 1554 ; formerly a monk of Reading ; learned and a famous preacher ; opposed Henry's divorce ; was on the commission to try Ridley (*q.v.*) and Latimer (*q.v.*), but ' lived peacefully, not embrewing his hands in Protestants' blood ' (Fuller) ; d. 1558.

3. Richard Cheyney, 1562 ; disputed against Transubstantiation in Convocation, 1553 ; the citizens of Bristol complained to Cecil of his belief in the Real Presence and the freedom of the will ; was excommunicated for refusing to sign the Thirty-nine Articles, 1571, but apparently submitted ; approved of pictures and crucifixes in churches ; Campion the Jesuit tried to convert him to Rome ; he held the see *in commendam* with Gloucester ; d. 1579.

4. John Bullingham, 1581 ; appointed to both sees after two years' vacancy ; res. Bristol, 1589.

5. Richard Fletcher, 1589 ; tr. to Worcester, 1593. See vacant ten years.

6. John Thornborough. 1603 ; tr. from Limerick ; tr. to Worcester, 1617.

7. Nicholas Felton, 1617 ; tr. to Ely, 1618.

8. Rowland Searchfield, 1619 ; d. 1622.

9. Robert Wright, 1623 ; tr. to Lichfield, 1632.

10. George Coke, 1633 ; tr. to Hereford, 1636.

11. Robert Skinner, 1637 ; tr. to Oxford, 1641.

12. Thomas Westfield. 1642 : refused the bishopric, 1617, but now accepted because he was rich enough to ' adorn it with hospitality out of his own estate ' ; fainted with agitation when preaching before Charles I. ; though a Royalist, was allowed by Parliament to retain his emoluments ; attended the Westminster Assembly, 1643 ; d. 1644.

13. Thomas Howell, 1644 ; the last bishop consecrated in England for sixteen years ; d. 1646 in consequence of rough treatment at the capture of Bristol, 1645 ; his wife had died earlier from the same cause. The citizens of Bristol undertook the education of his children, ' in grateful memory of their most worthy father.' See vacant fifteen years.

14. Gilbert Ironside I.. 1661 ; treated nonconforming ministers with forbearance ; d. 1671.

15. Guy Carleton, 1672 ; Dean of Carlisle ; tr. to Chichester, 1679.

16. William Gulston, 1679 ; d. 1684.

17. John Lake, 1684 ; tr. from Sodor and Man ; instituted weekly Eucharist in the cathedral ; one of the Seven Bishops (*q.v.*) ; tr. to Chichester, 1685.

18. Sir Jonathan Trelawney, Bart., 1685 ; one of the Seven Bishops; tr. to Exeter, 1689.

19. Gilbert Ironside II., 1689 ; son of the fourteenth bishop ; tr. to Hereford, 1691.

20. John Hall, 1691 ; Master of Pembroke College, Oxford ; a Puritan who ' could bring all the theology of the Westminster Assembly out of the Church Catechism ' ; d. 1710.
21. John Robinson, 1710 ; Dean of Windsor ; tr. to London, 1713.
22. George Smalridge, 1714 ; friend of Atterbury (*q.v.*), whom he succeeded in the deanery of Christ Church, holding it *in commendam* with the bishopric ; d. 1719.
23. Hugh Boulter, 1719 ; tr. to Armagh, 1723.
24. William Bradshaw, 1724 ; held the deanery of Christ Church *in commendam* ; d. 1732.
25. Charles Cecil, 1733 ; tr. to Bangor, 1734.
26. Thomas Secker, 1735 ; tr. to Oxford, 1737.
27. Thomas Gooch, 1737 ; Master of Caius and Gonville College, Cambridge ; tr. to Norwich, 1738.
28. Joseph Butler (*q.v.*), 1738 ; tr. to Durham, 1750.
29. John Conybeare, 1750 ; Dean of Christchurch ; d. 1755.
30. John Hume, 1756 ; tr. to Oxford, 1758.
31. Philip Young, 1758 ; tr. to Oxford, 1761.
32. Thomas Newton, 1761 ; Dean of St. Paul's ; endeavoured to reform the diocese, and complained of the nonresidence of the cathedral clergy, and that he was ' there for months together without seeing the face of dean or prebendary, or anything better than a minor canon ' ; d. 1782.
33. Lewis Bagot, 1782 ; Dean of Christ Church ; tr. to Norwich, 1783.
34. Christopher Wilson, 1783 ; d. 1792.
35. Spencer Madan, 1792 ; tr. to Peterborough, 1794.
36. Henry Reginald Courtenay, 1794 ; tr. to Exeter, 1797.
37. Ffolliot Herbert Walker Cornewall, 1797 ; tr. to Hereford, 1803.
38. George Pelham, 1803 ; tr. to Exeter, 1807.
39. John Luxmoore, 1807 ; Dean of Gloucester ; tr. to Hereford, 1808.
40. William Lort Mansel, 1808 ; Master of Trinity, Cambridge ; famous for jests and epigrams ; d. 1820.
41. John Kaye, 1820 ; Master of Christ's College, Cambridge ; tr. to Lincoln, 1827.
42. Robert Gray, 1827 ; father of Bishop Robert Gray (*q.v.*) of Capetown ; refused to postpone service in the cathedral during the Reform Riots, 1831 ; his palace was burnt to the ground by the rioters ; d. 1834.
43. Joseph Allen, 1834 ; tr. to Ely.

44. James Henry Monk, 1836.
45. Charles Baring, 1856.
46. William Thomson, 1861.
47. Charles John Ellicott, 1863.

} Bishops of the united see of Gloucester (*q.v.*) and Bristol.

48. George Forrest Browne, 1897 ; tr. from Stepney. [a. c.]

Le Neve, *Fasti* ; Browne Willis, *Cathedrals* ; *V.C.H. Gloucester* ; *D.N.B.*

BRITISH CHURCH. By the British Church is meant the Christian Church which existed in England and Wales before the foundation of the English Church by St. Augustine (*q.v.*), and after that event to a limited extent in Wales, Cornwall, Cumbria, and Strathclyde. There are not sufficient facts known about this Church to enable a continuous history of it to be constructed. The only contemporary British historian, Gildas, who died *c.* A.D. 550, composed an extremely verbose and diffusive diatribe against British kings and clergy, from which only a limited amount of historical facts can be gleaned. It is here proposed to treat the subject chronologically, mentioning what is known about the British Church century by century.

The first century is a blank, broken only by legends connecting various apostles, and other Scriptural personages, especially St. Joseph of Arimathaea, with Britain. These legends may be dismissed at once. They first appear in very late writings, and have no historical foundation. Full information is given about them in the first two chapters of Archbishop Ussher's *Britannicarum Ecclesiarum Antiquitates.*

The second century is also a blank so far as ascertained facts are concerned. But to it belongs a story which has obtained some credence because it is told by Bede (*q.v.*) (*H.E.*, i. 4). It is to the effect that a British king, named Lucius, applied to Pope Eleutherus in A.D. 156 to be made a Christian, that the application was granted, and that the King and nation were then converted to Christianity. This story first appears in a sixth-century recension of the *Liber Pontificalis* at Rome, whence Bede must have borrowed it. It was unknown to the British historian Gildas, and is entirely without support. Bede's version of it involves chronological errors, and Professor Harnack has recently disposed of it by the brilliant suggestion or discovery that Lucius was not a British king at all, but King of Birtha (confused with Britannia) in Edessa, a Mesopotamian realm, the sovereign of which was Lucius Aelius Septimus Megas Abgarus IX. (*E.H.R.*, xxii. pp. 767-70).

But while all attempts to connect the introduction of Christianity into Britain with definite dates and names in the second century have proved fruitless, there is indirect and outside evidence that Christianity had penetrated Britain before or about the close of this century. The evidence is patristic in its source and general in its character. Tertullian, writing c. 208, speaks of there being places in Britain inaccessible to the Romans yet subject to Christ. Origen, about thirty years later, refers in two passages to the British people having come under the influence of Christianity. But how did they so come ? In the absence of precise information the most probable supposition is that Christianity came through Gaul, between which country and Britain commercial intercourse was going on. There may, too, have been individual Christians among the numerous Roman soldiers who were then stationed in Britain. The almost universally Latin, or at least non-Celtic, names of such British martyrs, bishops, and others as have been preserved point to a preponderating Roman rather than Celtic element in the personnel of the British Church ; though against this inference it must also be remembered that, as in the cases of Patricius and Pelagius, the names known to us may be assumed Christian names superseding some earlier Celtic names of which, in most cases, no record has survived. Possibly the British Church consisted at first of converts to Christianity among the Roman invaders, and of such natives as came into immediate contact with them ; and the native element only preponderated gradually when the Roman troops were withdrawn, and when civilian Roman settlers would for their own safety leave the island as well.

Third century.—British martyrs, whose names are known to us, may be assigned to this century. By far the most famous of them is St. Alban, martyred, as Gildas asserts, or according to another reading conjectures, in the Diocletian persecution (*Hist.*, cap. viii.). But as the Diocletian persecution is not known to have reached Britain, it is more likely that the persecution in question was that of Decius in 250-1, or that of Valerian in 257-60. Bede tells the story at considerable length (*H.E.*, i. 7), and says that the martyrdom took place at Verolamium, now St. Albans. Both Gildas and Bede evidently quote from some early but now lost *Passio Sancti Albani*. The details may be unhistorical, as is frequently the case in such *Passiones*, but it is not necessary to doubt the existence and the

martyrdom of St. Alban. We have the fifth-century evidence of the Gallican presbyter Constantius, who, writing a life of St. Germanus c. A.D. 480, describes a visit of SS. Germanus and Lupus to his sepulchre at St. Albans, and sixth-century evidence in a line of the poetry of the Gallican Venantius Fortunatus.

In the martyrology of Bede, and in many later martyrologies and calendars, 17th September is marked with *In Britanniis* [*natale*] *Socratis et Stephani*, and in Baronius's edition of the Roman martyrology this has grown to *Sanctorum martyrum Socratis et Stephani*. But there is no early authority for the existence of these saints, and nothing is known of their history. It may be supposed that, if they existed, they were martyrs in one of the above-named early persecutions. Augulus, Bishop of Augusta (London), is another martyr of this period whose name is preserved in early martyrologies (Oman, *Hist. of Eng. to 1066*, p. 178).

Fourth century.—A church has recently been discovered at Silchester (*Calleva Atrebatum*), which there is every reason to believe to be a fourth-century Romano-British church. Little more than the structural foundations now remain, but they are sufficient to enable us to reconstruct the whole of the ground plan, and to take the measurement of its component parts. The church bears a close resemblance to fourth-century churches discovered in Italy, Syria, and Africa. Traces of the foundations of Roman basilicas have been found underneath the churches of Reculver and Lyminge in Kent, and of Brixworth in Northamptonshire ; but whether those basilicas were used for secular or ecclesiastical purposes is not known. The only claim of the above-named churches in their present state, and of a few other churches, such as St. Martin at Canterbury, to be regarded as Romano-British, lies in the fact that they have a few stones or bricks of Romano-British date used up a second time in their construction.

Distinctively Christian emblems have been found in other places than churches. The X P monogram has been found in mosaic pavements or on building stones of villas at Frampton in Dorset, Chedworth in Gloucestershire, and Harpole in Northamptonshire ; on a silver cup at Corbridge in Northumberland ; on two silver rings from a villa at Fifehead Neville in Dorset ; on some bronze fragments at York ; on some masses of pewter found in the Thames, on one of which it is associated with A and Ω, and with the words *spes in deo* ; on the bezel

of a bronze ring found at Silchester, though
the nature of the ornament in this last case
has been doubted. There was also found
at Silchester a fragment of white glass with
a fish and a palm roughly scratched upon it.

In this century three British bishops are
recorded to have been present at the Council
of Arles in 314—namely, Eborius, Bishop of
York; Restitutus, Bishop of London; and
Adelfius, Bishop of Lincoln, if Londinensium
is rightly interpreted as an error for Lindu-
mensium; and they were accompanied by a
priest named Sacerdos and a deacon named
Arminius. There is no evidence for the
suggestion sometimes made that British
bishops may have been present at the Council
of Nice in 325. There is the direct testimony
of St. Athanasius that British bishops were
present at the Council of Sardica in 345 and
voted in his favour, but he mentions neither
the names of these bishops nor the names of
their sees. British bishops were present
again at the Council of Ariminum in 359.
This rests on the authority of Sulpicius
Severus, who, while he mentions neither their
names nor their sees, adds a statement which
throws some light upon the financial position
of the British Church at that time—namely,
that 'there were three bishops from Britain,
who, because they lacked private means,
made use of the public bounty, refusing
contributions offered to them by the rest.'
The public bounty refers to the provision for
their entertainment which the Emperor had
ordered to be offered at the public expense
(*Hist. Sac.*, ii. 41).

Fifth century.—A British bishop whose
name, and but little else, has come down to
us, but who must be assigned to this century,
is Riocatus. He made two journeys from
Britain to Gaul to see Faustus, a Breton if
not a Briton, and Bishop of Riez, *ob. c.* 492,
and carried certain works of Faustus back to
Britain. Another British bishop of whom
we know little more than the name is Fasti-
dius. He wrote a book, or possibly two
books, to a widow named Fatalis in the first
half of the fifth century. His writings have
been accused of semi-Pelagianism, but his
semi-Pelagian tendency is of the slightest
possible character. There is no authority for
the conjecture associating him with the see
of London.

Though Pelagius was born *c.* 370, yet the
active life of this heretic belongs to the fifth
century. Italy, Africa, and Palestine were
the scenes of his labours; but Pelagianism
would naturally expect to establish a footing
in Britain because Pelagius, who from
Jerome's description has been thought to be

an Irishman, was most probably a Briton by
birth, a member of one of those Gaelic
families who had crossed from Ireland and
settled themselves on the south-western
coast of Great Britain (Bury, *Life of St.
Patrick*, p. 15). His companion Coelestius,
no doubt, was an Irishman; and an Irish
or British origin may be surmised for a
certain Agricola, the son of a Pelagian
bishop named Severianus, who taught and
spread Pelagianism in Britain, as Prosper
tells us, *sub an.* 429. Both names here have
a Roman rather than a Celtic sound, but that
fact, as has been already pointed out, cannot
be pressed to prove a Roman nationality.
That the inroad of this heresy was serious
may be gathered from the fact that in the
year 429 two Gallican ecclesiastics, Germanus,
Bishop of Auxerre, and Lupus, Bishop of
Troyes, were sent by a Gallican synod
according to Constantius, but by Pope
Coelestine according to Prosper, to Britain
to stem it; and that in 447 the same Germanus and Severus, Bishop of Troyes, came
to Britain for the same purpose. Their efforts
were completely successful.

The last recorded communication between
the British Church and Western Christianity
took place in 455, in which year, according
to an entry in the *Annales Cambriae*, the
British Church changed its ancient mode of
calculating Easter, and adopted the mode
of calculation then in use at Rome. This
was shortly afterwards exchanged at Rome
for the Victorian cycle of five hundred and
thirty-two years, and that cycle was changed
again there, in the next century, for the
Dionysian cycle of nineteen years; but neither
the Victorian nor the Dionysian cycle was
ever adopted in the British Church, which
still adhered, when St. Augustine arrived, to
an older Roman cycle of eighty-four years
(Bury, *Life of St. Patrick*, p. 376).

Sixth century.—Apart from Wales, and
so far as that part of Great Britain now
called England is concerned, there are few
facts to record. This is the more remarkable, because the only early British historian
belongs mainly to this century. The chronology of Gildas's life is very uncertain, but it
must be placed between A.D. 450-550, and his
literary activity belongs to the sixth rather
than the fifth century. His prolix work,
including both *Historia* and *Epistola*, while
it contains a fierce denunciation of the
morality of British princes and clergy,
unfortunately yields a minimum of facts
about them. Two incidents gleaned from
an Irish authority may be here recorded.
Two bishops of the Britons came from Alba

to sanctify St. Bridget, *ob.* 523 (*Leabhac Breac.* fol. 62). Fifty bishops of the Britons of Cell Muine visited St. Maedoc of Ferns, *ob.* 626 (*ibid..* fol. 81).

There are in existence lists of early British, Welsh, Manx, and Cornish bishops, for the majority of whose lives no certain evidence can be produced. The very existence of many of them is doubtful. These lists may be seen in Stubbs, *Registr. Sacr. Ang.,* 2nd ed., app. vii. Some of them, such as St. David (*q.v.*), first Bishop of Menevia ; Dubritius, first Bishop of Llandaff, together with his immediate successors, Teilo and Oudoceus ; Kentigern and Asaph, the first two Bishops of St. Asaph ; Deiniol, the first Bishop of Bangor, together with a few less known names on the lists, are historical personages. But no early lives of them are extant. Existing lives date from the twelfth century or later, and are mixed with much fable, and they belong to the history of the Welsh rather than the British Church, if the two may be distinguished.

[F. E. W.]

BUCER, Martin (1491-1551), reformer, was born at Schlettstadt (Alsace), and at the age of fifteen entered the Dominican Order. At the University of Heidelberg he came under the influence of Luther, and from 1523 he laboured as a reforming pastor with Capito at Strasburg. The special characteristic of his career as a reformer was his consistent policy of mediation in a vain endeavour to reconcile the Lutheran and Calvinistic schools of thought. With Capito he was responsible for the Tetrapolitan Confession (1530), presented at the Diet of Augsburg by representatives of the four cities : Strasburg, Constance, Meiningen, and Linden. This formulary holds an intermediate position between the views of Saxon and Swiss reformers, with a leaning towards Zwinglianism. Throughout his life Bucer was distrusted by both the parties he sought to unite. Luther at Marburg is said to have cried to him : ' Thou art a rogue '; and amongst the Swiss he was known as ' the limping Strasburger.'

In 1542 Bucer was invited with Melanchthon by Hermann, Archbishop of Cologne, to inaugurate the Reformation in that city. One important outcome of their joint labours was the ' Church Order,' known as *Hermann's Consultation* (1543), from which were derived some features of the English Order of Communion (1548), and of the Book of Common Prayer (*q.v.*) of 1549. Exiling himself from the Continent on account of the *Interim*,

Bucer came to England at Cranmer's invitation, where he was honourably received, and appointed Regius Professor of Divinity at Cambridge, a post which he held until his death in 1551.

After the publication of the Prayer Book of 1549 Bucer's opinion was sought by the leaders of the reforming party apparently with a view to further revision. His reply was given in a *Censura* of twenty-eight chapters. The most notable things objected to were kneeling at the Communion, prayers for the dead, the sign of the cross in consecrating the Eucharist, the chrisom, the anointing and the sign of the cross in Baptism, the anointing of the sick, any commendation of the soul of the departed at burial. In this criticism Bucer started objections afterwards taken up and repeatedly urged by the Puritan party against the Book of Common Prayer. In one other respect has Bucer influenced our service-book. In the Ordinal of 1550, while the structure of the service was preserved, the old Pontifical was largely departed from. The new matter was based on a work of Bucer's, *De Legitima Ordinatione* in his *Scripta Anglicana.* The questions put to candidates for the ministry in particular are borrowed from this source, and the address to candidates for the priesthood is based on a like feature in Bucer's form. [E. T. G.]

References in Calvin's *Letters* and Jacobs's *Lutheran Movement in England.*

BULLS, Papal. The word bull (*bulla*) denotes strictly the leaden seal, bearing as a rule representations of the heads of the apostles Peter and Paul on the one side, and the name and number of the Pope on the other, by which papal letters were authenticated. In the later Middle Ages it was commonly applied also to the document itself, and in particular to letters of the type described below, Section 3. Papal rescripts are described by various names, some of which indicate the form of the document (*litterae* or *epistola*), others the nature of the contents (*auctoritas, privilegium, decretum, litterae decretales,* etc.). But in their general plan they all agree : the popes carried on the forms employed by the Roman emperors and their officers, and uniformly drew up their documents in the shape of letters. They were written on papyrus down to the early part of the eleventh century, and afterwards on parchment : but not one is preserved in the original earlier than Paschal I. (819), with the exception of a fragment of one of Hadrian I. (788). The 2400 documents of the time preceding Hadrian are only preserved in transcripts. At an early date a selection was made of letters which were deemed of special importance as defining points of law. These are the *decreta*, beginning with the pontificate of Siricius in the last quarter of the fourth century, which were put together in the collection of Dionysius Exiguus and are printed in Justel's *Bibliotheca Juris Canonici Veteris*,[1] i. 181-274 (Paris, 1661).

Papal rescripts fall into the following classes :—

1. *Privilegia*, Solemn Bulls, or Great Bulls, beginning in the form, *Gregorius episcopus servus servorum Dei venerabili fratri A. X episcopo, In Perpetuum*, with the first line (except in the earliest examples) written in tall, laterally compressed, letters. Under Hadrian I. begins the custom of a double dating: first, the *Scriptum*, in the hand of the notary who wrote the document in the ' curial ' character : secondly, the *Data*, written by one of the higher officers of the chancery, who delivered it to be sealed, and before long written in a beautiful minuscule hand. The Pope himself authenticated the document with an autograph greeting, usually *Bene valete*. Under Leo IX. (1049) this autograph was replaced by a monogram on the right of the foot of the document, matched on the left by a rota or circle containing as a rule the names of the apostles Peter and Paul and that of the Pope, surrounded by a motto taken from the Bible. From the time of Victor II. the Pope begins to resume the practice of writing his own subscription, but not in the old form of a greeting, but *e.g. Ego Paschalis catholice ecclesie episcopus ss.*, between the rota and the monogram. The cardinals also write their subscriptions under the Pope's. As the Pope's personal official staff grew in importance, the notarial date (*Scriptum*) was gradually given up ; it is never found after the death of Callixtus II. (1124). Great Bulls are mostly the instruments of grants of privileges to churches and religious houses, drawn up in a grand style to serve as title-deeds, and made imposing by means of elaborate formulæ and attestations. They are especially abundant in the eleventh and twelfth centuries ; in the latter half of the thirteenth they were more rarely issued, and they almost cease with the establishment of the papacy at Avignon in 1309. When

revived for special purposes in the sixteenth century this form of document is called a *Bulla Consistorialis*.

2. *Letters*, or Little Bulls, open with the same form of title and address as Privileges, but the address is followed not by *In Perpetuum*, but by a greeting, which in time assumes the form *Salutem et apostolicam benedictionem*. They are devoid of the imposing features of Great Bulls ; they have no rota or monogram, no subscriptions of Pope or cardinals ; and they bear a simple date of place, day, month, and usually indiction, but in 1188 the indiction was abandoned and the year of the pontificate took its place. In the second half of the twelfth century they were distinguished into two classes, according as the seal was attached by red and yellow silk ties or by hempen strings. The former came to be known as *Litterae de Gratia* or *Tituli* : they granted favours, rights, privileges, benefices ; they were usually intended to have an enduring or permanent force : and the writing was characterised by an ornamentation which was strictly regulated. The other class consisted of *Litterae de Justitia* or *Mandamenta*, issuing a command or ordering a commission for hearing a cause, and were commonly of a temporary nature ; and the writing was free from embellishment. Little Bulls from the eleventh to the middle of the fifteenth century formed the regular vehicle of the Pope's correspondence. The great series of decretals and all the letters which are of importance for political history are drawn up in this form.

3. As the Great Bull fell into disuse an intermediate form, known specifically as *Bulla*, was invented towards the middle of the thirteenth century which combined some of the features of the two earlier models. The first line of the document was written in elongated letters, but *In Perpetuum* was replaced by a formula which crystallised into the words *Ad perpetuam* (or *futuram*) *rei memorium* : but all the rest follows the pattern of the Little Bull sealed with silk. This form was used specially for decrees and excommunications.

All Bulls are dated in the ancient manner by kalends, nones, and ides.

From the last years of the eleventh century papal documents are characterised by a peculiar style of rhythmical diction, which is traced to the chancellorship of John of Gaeta, afterwards Pope Gelasius II. ; this is called the *Cursus*. It was a restoration in a modified form of the *clausula rhetorica* of ancient times. Its most obvious feature is that every sentence or principal clause, with certain admitted exceptions, must close with

---

[1] This small collection must be carefully distinguished from the pseudo-Isidorian book of decretals, which was compiled and largely forged about 847, and contains (1) fifty-nine letters, from St. Clement to the beginning of the fourth century, all spurious ; (2) canons of councils, etc., mainly genuine ; (3) a continuation of letters from Silvester I. to Gregory II., of which thirty-five are forgeries.

two words or groups of words of one of the three following types, the metre being reckoned by accent not by quantity, with a cæsura at the prescribed interval:—

(*a*) *Cursus velox*, —◡◡ —◡—◡, as '*néverit incursurum*';

(*b*) *Cursus planus*, —◡ ◡—◡, as '*scripta mandamus*';

(*c*) *Cursus tardus, ecclesiasticus,* or *durus*, —◡ ◡—◡, as '*vestro discedere*.'

The first element in the clausula may be the termination of a longer word, as ' providerint éligéndum,' ' dilatióne compléndum,' ' ultióni | subiáccat.' This system prevailed in the chancery, though from the latter part of the thirteenth century it was less rigidly observed, until it broke down altogether under the influence of the revival of classical learning in the fifteenth.

4. Broadly distinguished from the Bull is the *Brief*, which was sealed not with lead, but with the Pope's secretum or privy seal on red wax. Though found earlier, it does not come into common use until the pontificate of Martin V. It begins with the name of the Pope, styled *papa*, with his number (as *Eugenius papa* IIII.), and continues with the name of the person addressed in the vocative (*dilecte fili*), followed by *Salutem et apostolicam benedictionem*. The date, which is given in the modern style, contains a clause which soon becomes fixed in the form *sub annulo piscatoris*. This became the normal vehicle of the Pope's official correspondence.

5. The *Motu Proprio*, introduced under Innocent VIII., bore no seal, and was often written in Italian. It opened like a brief, but the address was generally followed by the words *Ad futuram rei memoriam*. The date was given in the ancient manner. This form of document was principally employed in the administration of the Papal States.

[R. L. P.]

BURGON, John William (1815-88), Dean of Chichester, was son of a London merchant, and was born at Smyrna. His mother was a daughter of the Austrian Consul there, and had Smyrniote blood in her veins. He destined himself for holy orders; but, his father's business becoming involved in difficulties, he felt it a duty to enter the paternal counting-house. In 1841 the house suspended payment, and Burgon was free to follow his own bent. Friends enabled him in 1842 to enter Worcester College, Oxford, where he ' toiled terribly,' and obtained a Second Class in *Lit. Hum.* He won the Newdigate Prize with a spirited poem on Petra, which

contained one famous couplet; and in 1846 he was elected to the Fellowship at Oriel vacated by J. H. Newman (*q.v.*). He was ordained deacon, 1848; priest, 1849; and, while still residing at Oriel, served various curacies in Berkshire. These pastoral experiences ended in 1853, and Burgon became absorbed in theological research. In 1854 he published anonymously *A Plain Commentary on the Four Holy Gospels*, in which a minute and reverent study of the Sacred Text was reinforced by constant reference to patristic and Anglican tradition. In 1863 he was made Vicar of St. Mary-the-Virgin, Oxford, and in 1867 was appointed Professor of Divinity at Gresham College, London. On assuming this office he graduated B.D., choosing for the required Theological Exercises ' A Vindication of the Genuineness of the Last Twelve Verses of St. Mark's Gospel.' The subject was highly controversial, but controversy was to Burgon as vital air. He conducted it by sermons, by pamphlets, and in the press. Among the subjects which he handled polemically were *Essays and Reviews* (*q.v.*); the Doctrine of Inspiration ; the relation between the University and the Colleges, and between the Colleges and the Parish, at Oxford ; the Consecration of Bishop Temple (*q.v.*) : the enforcement of a New Lectionary ; the admission of a Unitarian to a share in the Revision of the New Testament and to Communion ; the development of Ritualism in Oxford, and the election of Dean Stanley (*q.v.*) to a Select Preachership. The first election of a woman to serve on a school-board elicited from Burgon a protest which, on account of the admirable lady to whom it referred, was long remembered in Oxford as ' Miss Smith's Sermon.' His polemical vigour, combined with his varied erudition, procured him from Dean Church (*q.v.*) the nickname of ' The dear old learned Professor of Billingsgate.'

In 1875 Burgon was appointed Dean of Chichester. The Revised Version of the New Testament appeared in 1881. [BIBLE, ENGLISH.] Burgon attacked it in four articles, which he republished in 1883 as *The Revision Revised*. His principal aim was to establish the *Textus Receptus* as against the Westcott-Hort recension ; he enlivened his task and attracted a wide circle of readers by his attack on the grotesque English of the revisers. His trenchant comparison of the Revised Version of 2 St. Peter $1^{5,6,7}$, with the beautiful language of the Authorised Version drew an emphatic compliment from Matthew Arnold. ' By merely placing these versions side by side, the Dean of Chichester thinks that he has done enough to condemn the Revised Version. And so, in truth, he has.'

Burgon's last days were occupied in compiling some terse and admirable biographies of *Twelve Good Men*, and by constant labour at his treatise on *The True Principles of Textual Criticism*. The foundation of Burgon's theology was the Bible as accepted and interpreted by the Universal Church. No one was a keener champion of the supreme claim of the written Word, but no one more vigorously opposed the notion that every man is at liberty to make his own theology. For working purposes he referred all questions to the Book of Common Prayer. He was an English Churchman to the backbone. His horror of Romanism, as the *corruptio optimi*, was fanatical, and his feeling towards Dissent, as a rebellion against authority, was angry and contemptuous. Even within the English Church his sympathies were eclectic and exclusive. Evangelicals offended him by their indifference to Sacramental doctrine, and by their external slovenliness. He dreaded the Romanising tendencies which he thought he perceived in Ritualism, and he regarded the Broad Church party as steeped in heresy.

[G. W. E. R.]

Personal recollections: E. M. Goulburn, *Life*; G. W. E. Russell, *Household of Faith*.

BURNET, Gilbert (1643-1715), Bishop of Salisbury; M.A. Aberdeen, June 1657; D.D. Oxford, 1680; was born at Edinburgh, son of Robert Burnet, a moderate episcopalian, who had refused to take the covenant. His mother was a violent Presbyterian. He studied at Marischal College, Aberdeen. In 1665 he began his ministry at Saltoun, fifteen miles east of Edinburgh, as a probationer, and, receiving a call, was ordained by George Wishart, Bishop of Edinburgh. He ministered acceptably for five years, giving the sacrament four times a year, and using ' the forms of Common Prayer, not reading but repeating them.' Visiting London in 1673 he became chaplain to Charles II., but was soon dismissed as ' too busy.' He found a place as preacher at the Rolls (1675-84) and lecturer at St. Clement Danes, where his sermons were greatly admired, *e.g.* by John Evelyn (*q.v.*). In 1679 he published vol. i. of his *History of the Reformation*, for which he received the thanks of Parliament and a request to continue it. On 29th January 1680 he wrote a remarkable letter to the King, warning him that what he needed was not a change of ministry or alliance, etc., but a change in his own heart and course of life. Charles read the letter, but made no

reply. After a two hours' 5th November sermon in 1684 on Psalm 22 21 he was dismissed from the Rolls, because of the supposed disloyal allusion to the Lion and the Unicorn in his text. In 1685, on the accession of James II., he got leave to go abroad, and resided at The Hague in close intercourse with the Prince and Princess of Orange, to the latter of whom he became deeply attached; married a Dutch wife of Scottish extraction, and became a naturalised Dutch subject. He helped William to write his ' Declaration,' and got him to alter the passage which implied Presbyterianism. On 5th November 1688 he landed with the prince at Torbay, a place which he suggested in preference to Exmouth. He went with him to Salisbury, where he disturbed the congregation in the cathedral during the prayers for the King. On the whole he gave very useful and conciliating advice to the prince at this period. He was consecrated Bishop of Salisbury ' after a week of complete retirement and a night of solemn vigil.' Easter Day, 31st March 1689. He preached the coronation sermon, 11th April. His first pastoral letter to his diocese gave great offence, since he implied that William and Mary were sovereigns by right of conquest. He was also active on the Commission for comprehension and the revision of the Prayer Book, which High Churchmen dreaded. Notwithstanding blunders and faults of taste he was a very efficient bishop, far before his age in his conception and standard of duty. His plan was to live eight months every year in Salisbury and four at Windsor in the archdeaconry of Berks (Dorset was then in Bristol diocese). Every year he made a perambulation of three weeks or a month. In twenty years he had confirmed in two hundred and seventy-five churches in the diocese. He did what he could to promote clerical residence and to check pluralities, and his method of visitation by short residences at small centres was excellent. He was the first English bishop to establish a theological college, under Precentor Daniel Whitby, at Salisbury, at his own expense: but the opposition from the universities forced him to drop it after five years. In 1692 he had published *A Discourse of the Pastoral Care*, in 1694 his *Four Discourses to the Clergy of the Diocese* (on Christian evidences, Socinianism, Romanism, and Nonconformity), in 1699 his *Exposition of the Thirty-nine Articles*, and in 1710 *An Exposition of the Church Catechism*—all intended at first for the edification of his own diocese. The first was generally approved, but the second led to an unfair charge of

Socinianism, and the third was censured as Latitudinarian by the Lower House of Convocation in 1701. He attended King William's death-bed. His influence with the new Queen led to the transfer of the first-fruits and tenths paid by the clergy (originally to the Pope and then to the Crown) to the governors of Queen Anne's Bounty (*q.v.*) for the increase of small livings. He had advocated the plan under William as likely to attach the clergy to the Crown. Burnet now became more political in his fear of Rome and anxiety for the Hanoverian succession. In February 1709 he lost his third wife, and retired very much to her house in Clerkenwell. He lived long enough to see the accession of George I., and died in Clerkenwell, where he lies buried. His *History of his own Time*, his most important work, was published after his death (vol. i., 1723-4; vol. ii., 1733-4, with a most important *Supplement*, including his *Autobiography*, ed. H. C. Foxcroft, Oxford, 1902).

He was a very early riser, a hard student, a great smoker and tea-drinker; a man of splendid physique, tall and burly, with superabundant health. His strongest characteristics were quick observation and good memory, great self-confidence and outspokenness, insatiable activity, religious tolerance (though he approved political suppression of Roman Catholics), and a strong and simple love of religion and religious men. He had many obvious faults. He was deficient in refinement, reserve, and imagination; inquisitive, impertinent, and petulant, vain and over-busy; a thoroughgoing and formidable partisan, but quickly impressionable, and therefore somewhat changeable in opinion. He was, however, generous and forgiving, and sincerely anxious for comprehension in matters of religion. His public and private charities were great. His chief services to the Church were his example of episcopal diligence and his success in attaching the great Whig party to the Church.   [J. W.]

The best edition of the *Own Time* is by Dr. Osmund Airy (author of the memoir in *D.N.B.*). The best *Life* is that by Rev. T. E. S. Clarke, minister of Saltoun (the Scottish portion), and Miss Foxcroft. The *Life*, appended by his son Thomas to the *Own Time*, is practically superseded.

BURY ST. EDMUNDS, Abbey of. About 903 the remains of St. Edmund (*q.v.*) were translated from their original resting-place at Hoxne to Beodricsworth, afterwards known as Bury St. Edmunds, and placed in a large wooden church. The shrine was in the charge of a college of four priests and two deacons, to whom Edmund the Magnificent made a grant of lands in 945. Many miracles were now attributed to St. Edmund. In 1010 his relics were removed for fear of the Danes to London, where their power of working cures caused Bishop Aelfhun to try to keep them. He was baffled by a miracle, and the body was restored to Bury about 1013. In 1014 Sweyn, the Danish king, died in torment, as was believed, after beholding a vision of St. Edmund advancing to slay him. His son Cnut (*q.v.*) became a benefactor to Bury, and the foundation of the monastery dates from his reign. At his command a new stone church was begun in 1020, when Aelfwine, Bishop of Elmham, replaced the secular clerks by a body of twenty Benedictine monks. In 1028 a charter of Cnut granted the monastery exemption from episcopal control and other privileges, including a gift of four thousand eels a year. In 1044 Edward the Confessor enlarged the lands and jurisdiction of the abbey and gave it the privilege of free election of its abbot; and in 1065 that of coining its own money, which it retained until the reign of Edward III. In 1065 the name St. Edmund's Bury first appears. Under William I. the abbey continued to enjoy royal favour. Herfast, Bishop of Thetford, wished to remove his see to Bury, but Abbot Baldwin defeated this project, visiting Rome in 1071 and inducing Alexander II. to take his house under the special protection of the Holy See. Its freedom from episcopal control was confirmed by a charter of William I., 1081. Its wealth had now doubled since the death of King Edward; it is noted in Domesday as possessing about three hundred manors, a larger number than any other religious house in the country. Baldwin marked the increasing prosperity of the abbey by building a splendid stone basilica, of which some fragments still remain. The relics of St. Edmund were translated thither in 1095.

During the twelfth century the abbey had a chequered history. New buildings were raised, and in 1146 were almost entirely burnt. Henry I. granted the privilege of a fair to be held yearly for six days about the feast of St. James. Abbot Hugh vowed canonical obedience to Archbishop Theobald, but in 1172 a Bull of Alexander III. made the abbey immediately subject to Rome. During the remainder of its history the abbey was constantly at feud with the bishops of Norwich, but succeeded in maintaining its independent position.

Hugh's death in 1180 was followed by the

best-known episode in the history of the abbey—the election and rule of Samson the sub-sacrist, famous as the hero of the *Chronicle of Jocelin de Brakelond*, and of Carlyle's *Past and Present*. Jocelin, who was probably a native of Bury, entered the monastery in 1173, and his *Chronicle* gives a vivid picture of its life. He tells how the royal mandate to elect a new abbot was received, the excitement it caused among the monks, and how, after much negotiation, Samson was elected, and, though unknown to the king, was accepted by him. Samson was a Norfolk man, born 1135; he became a monk, 1166. Elected abbot, he received a mitre from the Bishop of Winchester, who said he knew the abbots of St. Edmund's were entitled to this dignity. Samson proved an able and masterful ruler. The monks sometimes resented his high-handed rule, and especially disliked his granting privileges to the town of Bury, which was now beginning to assert itself and demand its liberties, a demand with which Samson sympathised. He brought the affairs of the abbey into a state of efficiency and improved the buildings. He wished to go on crusade, but was refused permission by Henry II. In 1193 he opposed the rebellion of Prince John, both by excommunicating him and by taking the field at the head of his knights, and he visited Richard I. in his prison in Germany. After filling a large space in the history of his time, he died in 1208, and was buried in unconsecrated ground owing to the Interdict. His remains were transferred to the chapter-house in 1214.

The abbey plays a prominent part in thirteenth-century history, being by now one of the richest and most powerful Benedictine houses in England, or indeed in Christendom. The shrine of St. Edmund was a favourite resort of pilgrims, partly no doubt because it lay on the route from London to the Low Countries; just as Canterbury owed part of its popularity among pilgrims to its position on the high road to France: in either case the merchant could combine business with devotion. In 1214 the abbey church of Bury was the scene of a meeting between Archbishop Langton (*q.v.*) and the barons who were resisting King John. The story, that in the war that ensued St. Edmund's relics were removed by Louis the Dauphin to Toulouse, is without foundation. It first appears in 1644, and was revived in 1901 when the alleged relics were brought from Toulouse for the new Roman Catholic Cathedral at Westminster, but were afterwards admitted to be spurious. After

Evesham, 1265, the abbey sheltered some of the adherents of Simon de Montfort. It continued to receive favours from the kings. Henry III. granted two fairs at Bury, of which one was abolished in 1871: the other still continues. By this time a flourishing town had grown up around the abbey, and jealousies and conflicts arose between the monks and the townsmen supported by the Franciscan friars, who had established themselves at Bury in 1257. The monks were more than once constrained to appeal to the King against the violence of the townsmen, which culminated in the great riot of 1327, when the abbey was plundered, and Abbot Richard of Draughton, who had apparently broken some agreement with the townsmen, was kidnapped and carried to Diest in Brabant. Laxity of discipline had apparently caused the abbey to forfeit the respect of its neighbours; eventually peace was made by commissioners appointed by the King, but the reputation of the abbey did not improve. 'Many of the monks, it is said, lived in the surrounding villages away from the monastery; they wore the dress of laymen; they were engaged in abductions, fightings, riots, and other unlawful practices; they had many illegitimate children as "walking witnesses" (*testes gradientes*) against them.' The riots broke out again at the time of the Peasants' Revolt (1381), when the prior, Richard de Cambridge, was among those murdered by the mob at Bury. Contrary to what might be expected, the moral tone of the house seems to have been higher in the fifteenth century than in the fourteenth, and no more is heard of scandals. Many noble laymen and women sought the honour of being enrolled among its associates. Henry VI. visited the abbey at Christmas 1433 and stayed till St. George's Day (23rd April) 1434. In 1447 a Parliament met at Bury, and during its sitting Duke Humphrey of Gloucester met his mysterious end. During this period a number of external misfortunes fell upon the abbey. The western tower fell in 1430. In 1439 a great storm did much harm, and in 1465 a fire completely gutted the church, but left, it was said, the shrine of St. Edmund uninjured.

In 1535 the abbey was visited by Sir Thomas Legh (*q.v.*) and John ap Rice, who, failing to find any cause of complaint against the monks, assumed 'that they had so confederated and compacted together before our coming that they should disclose nothing.' An attempt to bribe Cromwell (*q.v.*) having failed, the abbey was again visited in 1538, and plundered of many of its treasures; and on 4th November 1539 it was surrendered, the abbot receiving a pension of £333. 6s. 8d., and forty other members pensions varying from £30 to £6, 13s. 4d. The spoils of the abbey included 1553 oz. of gold plate and 10,433 oz. of silver plate, besides precious stones. Lead was stripped from the roofs to the value of £3302.

In the *Taxatio* of 1291 the abbey is shown as possessed of a greater income in *Temporalia* than any other house in England, namely £774, 16s.; it also had £152, 13s. 4d. in *Spiritualia*; and the offerings at St. Edmund's Shrine were valued at £40 a year. The *Valor Ecclesiasticus*, 1535, gives the net income, after all deductions, as £1656, 7s. 3½d. But there were heavy outgoings. The income yearly distributed to the poor amounted to £398, 15s. 11½d., besides generous doles of food and clothing. The tithes belonging to the abbey in Bury St. Edmunds and the lordship of Bury St. Edmunds were annexed by the Crown in 1539, and enjoyed by the Crown till the sixth year of King James I., when they were given to the aldermen and burgesses of Bury St. Edmunds.

The site and precincts of the monastery were sold by the Crown to John Eyer, Esq., for £412, 19s. 4d. on 14th February 1560. Since then they have passed through many hands, and are now the property of the Marquis of Bristol.

In the second half of the thirteenth century the household consisted of eighty monks, twenty-one chaplains, and a hundred and eleven servants; by 1535 the number of monks stood at sixty-two, and at the time of the surrender at about forty-five. The abbey had a famous library, consisting of over two thousand volumes. Among its special privileges was the abbot's power of conferring minor orders on his monks, and the right to call in any bishop to admit them to the higher orders. Before the Dissolution the wills of burgesses of Bury St. Edmunds were proved before the sacrist, the monastery being exempt from episcopal and archidiaconal authority. After 1539 the town remained still exempt from the jurisdiction of the Archdeacon of Sudbury, and wills were proved before a commissary of the Bishop of Norwich until 1844, when by an Order in Council the town was made to form part of the archdeaconry of Sudbury.

The abbey lay on the slope of a hill, and its precinct, a rough oblong, included the whole of the mediæval town. The great church, of which only a few fragments remain, lay south of the monastery, not north as was usual; probably on account of the slope. The churches of St. James and St. Mary are still standing, and there are remains of the abbey gateway and of the abbot's house [ARCHITECTURE, RELIGIOUS ORDERS].

LIST OF ABBOTS

1. Uvius, 1020; Prior of Holme; d. 1044.
2. Leofstan, 1044; d. 1065.
3. Baldwin, 1065; a French monk of St. Denis, physician of Edward the Confessor. Under him the power and wealth of the abbey greatly increased, and a new church was built; d. 1097. Three years' vacancy, William II. keeping the abbacy in his own hands.
4. Robert I., 1100; son of Hugh, Earl of Chester, appointed by Henry I.; deposed, 1102, by Archbishop Anselm as not having been canonically elected.
5. Robert II., 1102; not consecrated till 1107, probably for lack of the king's consent; d. 1107. Seven years' vacancy.
6. Albold, 1114; Prior of St. Nicasius, Meaux; d. 1119. Two years' vacancy.
7. Anselm, 1121; nephew of St. Anselm; elected Bishop of London, 1128, but, failing to obtain the royal consent, was not consecrated; desired to go on pilgrimage to Santiago in Spain, but was persuaded by the monks to build the church of St. James, still standing at Bury, instead; d. 1148.
8. Ording, 1148; formerly prior; called by Jocelin *homo illiteratus*, but an able ruler; obtained privileges from King Stephen, whose tutor he had been; d. 1156.
9. Hugh, 1157; Prior of Westminster; under his inefficient rule the abbey decayed both morally and financially; d. 1180.
10. Samson, 1182; most famous of all the abbots; d. 1211. Two years' vacancy.
11. Hugh of Northwold, elected 1213; refused confirmation by King John till 1215; became Bishop of Ely, 1229.
12. Richard de l'Isle, 1229; Abbot of Burton, formerly a monk of St. Edmunds; d. 1234 at Pontigny, while returning from Rome, whither he had gone to appeal against visitors sent by Gregory IX. to reform the abbey.
13. Henry of Rushbrook, 1235; excused from attendance at the Council of Lyons on account of the gout; d. 1248.
14. Edmund of Walpole, 1248; a weak man; was ridiculed for taking the cross in spite of his monastic vow; d. 1256.

15. Symon of Luton, 1257 ; d. 1279.
16. John of Northwold, 1279 ; d. 1301.
17. Thomas of Tottington, 1302 ; d. 1312.
18. Richard of Draughton, 1312 ; a learned theologian and canonist : kidnapped in the riot of 1327 ; d. 1335.
19. William of Bernham, 1335 ; a man of bad character, under whom scandalous immorality prevailed ; d. 1362.
20. Henry of Hunstanton, 1362 ; d. 1362 on his way to Avignon to obtain papal confirmation.
21. John of Brinkley, 1362 ; appointed by Pope Innocent vi. ; president of provincial chapter of English Benedictines ; d. 1379. Five years' vacancy owing to a disputed election ; Pope Urban v. providing Edmund de Bromefield, who was imprisoned under the Statute of Provisors, and the monks electing
22. John of Tymworth, who at last succeeded in obtaining papal confirmation in 1384 ; d. 1389.
23. William of Cratfield, 1390 ; d. 1415.
24. William of Exeter, 1415 ; attended the Council of Constance ; d. 1429.
25. William Curteys, 1429 ; trusted counsellor of Henry vi. ; appointed by the general chapter of the Benedictines visitor of all their houses in East Anglia, 1431 ; d. 1446.
26. William Babington, 1446 ; d. 1453 : no registers appear to have been kept by the later abbots, and little is known of the abbey's history at this time.
27. John Bohun, 1453 ; d. 1469.
28. Robert of Ixworth, 1469 ; d. 1474.
29. Richard of Hengham, 1474 ; d. 1479.
30. Thomas Rattlesden, 1479 ; described as *pius* ; d. 1497.
31. William Cadenham, 1497 ; d. 1513.
32. John Reeve of Melford, 1513 ; became a member of the Privy Council, 1520 ; said by the visitors to live too much at his country houses, and to be fond of cards and dice : but being found ' very conformable,' he was recommended for a pension which he did not live to enjoy, for the misfortunes of his house and order ' affected him so nearly, that he gave way to Fate within less than half a year,' and died 31st March 1540. [G. C.]

V.C.H., Suffolk: *Memorials of St. Edmund's Abbey*, R.S. ; B. Willis, *Mitred Abbies* ; *The Chronicle of Jocelin of Brakelond*, ed. Sir Ernest Clarke.

BUTLER, Joseph (1692-1752), was born at Wantage of Presbyterian parents, and after passing through the local Grammar School entered an academy for the education of ministers at Tewkesbury. Here he was a fellow-student with Thomas Secker, afterwards Archbishop of Canterbury ; Edward Chandler, his predecessor as Bishop of Durham, having also been educated there. While here, in his twenty-second year, he entered into a correspondence with Dr. Samuel Clarke, not yet suspect of Arianism, in criticism of the *a priori* argument contained in his Boyle Lectures on *The Being and Attributes of God*. The acuteness of the young man's reasoning was extraordinary, and Dr. Clarke printed the correspondence in later editions of his work. Not less remarkable is the complete anticipation of the qualities most characteristic of his mature writings. ' I design the search after truth,' he wrote, ' as the business of my life ' ; and to a compliment on his manner he replied : ' I have aimed at nothing in my style, but only to be intelligible.' His unaffected simplicity redeems the remark from all priggishness.

His search after truth led him to abandon Presbyterianism, and shortly after the closing of this correspondence, in 1714, he entered Oriel College, Oxford, as a candidate for holy orders. There he became acquainted with Edward Talbot, son of the Bishop of Durham, through which connection came most of his subsequent promotion. In 1718 he was appointed to the preachership at the Rolls Chapel, which he retained till 1726, delivering there the great series of Sermons which made his reputation. The chief of them upheld the contention, not so familiar then as now, that vice is ' a violation or breaking in upon our own nature.' He justified, in a Christian sense, the Stoic doctrine that virtue is a life conformable to nature, setting himself especially to correct a misapprehension of Wollaston's remark that ' to place virtue in following nature is at best a loose way of talk.' Against the hedonism of Shaftesbury, then much in vogue, he maintained the supremacy of conscience, regarded as an endowment of man no less natural than the passions and appetites.

A volume of fifteen of these Sermons was published in 1726, with a preface containing an apology, not unneeded, for issuing under that title such abstruse treatises. Six others were added in later editions. In 1722 the Bishop of Durham had collated him to the rectory of Houghton, which he exchanged three years later for the valuable benefice of Stanhope, where he kept close residence for some years. Queen Caroline asked on one occasion whether he were not dead, to which the Archbishop of York replied: 'No, madam, but he is buried.' In 1733 Charles Talbot, son of the Bishop of Durham, becoming Lord Chancellor, made him his chaplain, and presented him to a prebend at Rochester. In 1736, mainly through Secker's influence, he became Clerk of the Closet to Queen Caroline, and attended her constantly until her death in 1737. About the same time was published the work by which he is best known, *The Analogy of Religion, Natural and Revealed, to the Constitution and Course of Nature*, with its momentous introduction on the argument of Probability. The preface contained the famous sentence : 'It is come, I know not how, to be taken for granted by many persons that Christianity is not so much as a subject of inquiry; but that it is, now at length, discovered to be fictitious.' The direct sequence of this great treatise upon the Sermons depends on the observation that probability alone sufficiently establishes a moral obligation which the conscience can recognise—a position denied by Toland and other Deists. [DEISTS.] In 1738 Butler was appointed Bishop of Bristol, being consecrated on 3rd December. There he came into unpleasant relations with John Wesley (*q.v.*), whose exaggerated supernaturalism he disliked, and with Whitefield (*q.v.*), whose teaching of total depravity seemed to him intolerable. In 1740 the slender income of his see was supplemented with the deanery of St. Paul's.

and he resigned the rectory of Stanhope. In 1746 he was made Clerk of the Closet to the King; in 1750 he was translated to the bishopric of Durham. In 1747 he is said to have refused the archbishopric of Canterbury on the ground that it was 'too late for him to try to support a falling church.' In his primary charge he discoursed of religion in a strain very different from the dry intellectualism of his Sermons and of the *Analogy*; he noted 'the general decay of religion in this nation'; he insisted once more on the moral force of probability; but he attributed the general lack of religion not so much to 'a speculative disbelief or denial of it,' as to 'thoughtlessness and the common temptations of life.' The remedy was to be found in greater attention to public and private forms of devotion. He referred to Mohammedan and Romanist practice, by virtue of which 'people cannot pass a day without having religion recalled to their minds.' These remarks brought upon him a ridiculous charge of being a crypto-papist, supported by reference to a marble cross which he had placed behind the altar in his chapel at Bristol, and it was even asserted afterwards that he had died in the communion of Rome. His friend Secker, the Archbishop of Canterbury, was at pains to make a solemn refutation of this calumny. Butler died unmarried at Bath on the 16th of June 1752, and was buried in Bristol Cathedral.   [T. A. L.]

Works: R. W. Church, *Pascal and other Sermons*, pp. 25-51 : T. Bartlett, *Life*.

C

CALVINISM. The name given to the complex of doctrines, which were supposed to be especially characteristic of the Genevan reformers. As a matter of fact, John Calvin, who was not an original thinker, but a systematiser, did not originate the doctrines connected with his name; while in England at least Calvinism is by no means necessarily connected with Calvin's system of Church government. It is tenable with or without a belief in episcopacy, and indicates no more than a belief in the rigid doctrines of predestination and reprobation, and a dislike of all ceremonial in religion, coupled with the denial of any final authority outside the Bible. In regard to predestination, Calvin's *Institutio* did but state in a more systematic and scholastic form what had been the belief of Luther. In the latter's reply to Erasmus, *De Servo Arbitrio*, and in numerous other

writings, Luther makes it clear that he, equally with Calvin, denied all freedom or responsibility to man, and asserted the entirely predetermined nature of human life, including the sin of Adam. In this, again, the reformers were merely following a tendency that had been very prevalent at the close of the Middle Ages. Wyclif (*q.v.*) used to say: *Omnia quae eveniunt, de necessitate eveniunt,* although it is not quite certain how far Wyclif included in this the action of the human will. Bradwardine, his master, had been a very strong predestinarian. So, as in other sides of Puritanism (*e.g.* the dislike of the drama), the position taken up by extreme Protestantism was not so much an innovation on the mediæval *Anschauung* as the exaggeration and emphasising of one or more elements within it.

Calvin's system as developed in his

Institutio Christianae religionis is a logical and compact doctrine, lucid, harmonious, and horrible. It starts from one tenet, and from that argues deductively without any qualification. That tenet is the sovereignty of God. The system is an intellectualist construction, entirely regardless of the facts of life. Since God can only be conceived as sovereign, and since no limits can be set to His omnipotence, for to do so is to deny His freedom, there can be no place for any real choice on the part of a created being; and the place of man in the universe is necessarily decided by *divine decree*. God's predestination is something more than His foreknowledge, and no consideration is given to the possibility of His limiting Himself by the creation of free beings. There never was nor will be any freedom save that of God's eternal will. It is not merely the case that Adam's descendants all share his nature and therefore his guilt. This view the infralapsarian, while denying freedom to the individual, asserts it for the race, and is in reality, as proved in the case of Arminius, destructive of the sheer monism to which Calvinism leads. But this is not the doctrine of Calvin or Luther. Not merely is sin the corruption of Adam, but Adam's own sin was predetermined, and he had no real choice. At the same time, since human nature is thus evil, it has no rights; every man is *ipso jure* damned; nor can he complain of the fortunate Jews or Christians, who are elect. Salvation being a matter not of right but of grace, God's freedom is not to be judged, but His abundant mercy praised. In this view Christ died only for a few, and those few, being predestined to glory, cannot by any outward sin sever themselves from their destiny.

Although Calvinism naturally and historically leads on to determinism, it must not be confused with it. The determinist starts with an analysis of human life, and with the conception of cause and effect, mathematically understood. He arrives, in consequence, at a universe which from start to finish is a network of inevitable relations, and has no place for spirit. Calvin, on the other hand, starts from the idea of freedom found in its perfection in God, and so anxious is he to preserve this intact that he allows no real place for that or any other element in the universe of being. This is more *naïf* in Luther, but there is no doubt of it being present in both. It is the conception of sovereignty unlimited by law, which had governed the minds of the great civilians, and was applied to the Papacy (also to the modern State) transferred to the sphere of religion. In Calvin's work the notion of God as essentially Love simply does not occur.

It is customary to attribute the strength of this system to its logical coherence. But that is surely to allow too much to mere formal consistency, when it is remembered that for so long a time it dominated Protestant Europe. Rather we should be justified in seeing it in the tremendous experience of Luther, repeated *in petto* in thousands of lesser men. The sense of the 'elect,' that he was in God's hands, that he was being swept in the force of a current stronger than himself, the intimate experience of being one cared for, chosen by a heavenly Father, coupled with the knowledge that many had no such security, and many more no hope of it, and set against a background of a religion that could be construed purely externally, was probably the leverage which gave the new system such strength. It is 'the godly and comfortable doctrine of election.' Strength of one kind or another it undoubtedly had. Few were the minds in the English Church in the mid-sixteenth century whom it did not dominate, and its power in the other reformed communions was little short of tyrannical. Fortunately for England, it failed of complete expression. The Thirty-nine Articles are almost certainly patient of a purely Calvinist interpretation; but they are so adroitly framed that it can be eluded, and despite the ruling influences in the Church of Elizabeth, sheer Calvinism never became authoritative. Often, indeed, have attempts been made to deny this. But the facts are against such denial. If the articles had excluded a non-Calvinist interpretation, why were they never held sufficient by the extreme party? The strongest evidence of all is that afforded by the Lambeth Articles of Whitgift (*q.v.*). Though a stern upholder of uniformity and no friend to the Presbyterian movement led by Thomas Cartwright (*q.v.*), he was willing, if not to give the extreme Calvinists all they wanted, at least to go a great deal further than the existing formulæ. The Thirty-nine Articles were then to be supplemented by the following. These propositions, generally known as the Lambeth Articles, are as follows:—

1. God from eternity hath predestinated some to life, some He hath reprobated to death.

2. The moving or efficient cause of predestination to life is not the prevision of faith, or of perseverance, or of good works, or of anything which may be in the persons predestinated, but only the will of the good pleasure of God.

3. Of the predestinated there is a fore-limited and certain number which can neither be diminished nor increased.

4. They who are not predestinated to salvation will be necessarily condemned on account of their sins.

5. A true living and justifying faith, and the Spirit of God sanctifying is not extinguished, does not fall away, does not vanish in the elect either totally or finally.

6. A truly faithful man, that is one endowed with justifying faith, is certain by the full assurance of faith, of the remission of his sins and his eternal salvation through Christ.

7. Saving grace is not given, is not communicated, is not granted to all men, by which they might be saved if they would.

8. No man can come to Christ except it be given to him, and unless the Father draw him. And all men are not drawn by the Father that they may come unto the Son.

9. It is not placed in the will or power of every man to be saved.

But for the prescience of Elizabeth, and the strong common-sense of the lay mind as shown in Burleigh, these would have become the law of the Church. Later on, in the light of the Arminian controversy, the House of Commons endeavoured to maintain that they were the official interpretation of the existing formularies. To this the reply was the Declaration of Charles I. Thus, first the clerical party and afterwards the laymen failed in imposing them on the Church of England. With the summoning of the Westminster Assembly, however, and the imposition of 'The Solemn League and Covenant,' it seemed as though the day of final triumph had come. That the Westminster Confession and Catechism enshrined the pure Calvinistic faith has never been questioned. Fortunately, however, these were imposed only by the Erastian House of Commons, and the Assembly of Divines had no real ecclesiastical authority. Along with the Directory they may have been held to be the secular law for the Establishment during the period of triumphant Puritanism. Even then it may be doubted whether they any more than the ' Holy Discipline' had any wide practical predominance outside London and Lancashire. The provisions of the *Instrument of Government* and the *Humble Petition and Advice* made distinctly for toleration in this matter, if not in others. The whole fabric, however, was swept away at the Restoration, and with the Act of Uniformity of 1662 vanished the last danger of a church officially Calvinistic.

In the Methodist and Evangelical revival of the eighteenth century the old controversy arose again. It was largely the ground of the quarrel between Lady Huntingdon (*q.v.*) and her chaplain, Whitefield (*q.v.*), and John Wesley (*q.v.*). Wesley was a strong Arminian, and frequent expressions of disgust at the narrowness of the Calvinist offer of salvation only to a few are to be found in his *Journal*. The Calvinistic Methodists of Wales testify by their title to the nature of the quarrel and to their difference from other Methodists.

It is impossible to follow the fortunes of Calvinism in other countries. In Scotland the trial of J. M'Leod Campbell (1800-72) for heresy in 1830 because he asserted that Christ died for all is a proof of how greatly the old doctrine still dominated men's minds even in the nineteenth century. In the recent changes, however, even its official authority has been done away. The basis of Union of the Free Kirk and the United Presbyterian, and the fifth clause of the Scottish Church Act, 1905 (5 Edw. VII. c. 12), remove from both established and non-established bodies any obligation to hold to Calvinism in the old literal sense.

The springs of modern philosophic determinism, as expounded by Spinoza and Hegel, have sometimes and with some justice been traced to the denial of human freedom set out by Luther and Calvin. This influence, however, must only be a matter of conjecture, and is at most indirect. Neither is there space here to discuss the exact relation between the predestinarianism of Calvin and that of St. Augustine. It may, however, be said that St. Augustine, even at the cost of some inconsistency, refused to draw the extreme conclusion of either total depravity or divine reprobation in the Calvinistic sense.

[J. N. F.]

CAMBRIDGE PLATONISTS. The greatest corporate mystical reaction that England has ever known owes itself to the group of men in the seventeenth century, called the Cambridge Platonists. Educated, all but one, at Emmanuel College, Cambridge, the seat of Puritanism, they summarise and express rather what Puritanism fell short in than what it represented. Concrete, sharp-cut dogma had held the field in the Westminster Assembly; men's minds had been fixed on formulas and formularies; and the mystics came to the rescue of vital, inward truth, and the adjustment of the outer to the inner life. They claimed supremely to be illuminated by Reason; and this, far from degrading it, as in the following century, to the sum of man's opinions as a perceptive animal, they understood to be the entire faculty of apprehension; and most especially its extension by continuity and analogy to those matters the proofs of which are drawn from experience rather than from demonstration. The kinship, established by this attitude, with the Platonic and Neo-Platonic schools of thought, they further strengthened by a study, amounting almost to a revival of, the philosophy of those (especially of the latter) writers. Principal Tulloch thus describes the task to which they set themselves. 'They sought to marry · philosophy to religion, and to confirm the union in the indestructible basis of reason and the essential elements of our higher humanity. . . . It was the first elaborate attempt to wed Christianity and philosophy made by any Protestant school ; and it may even be said to have been the first true attempt of the kind since the days of the great Alexandrine teachers.' The writings of those men are sown with quotations from Pythagoras, Plato, Plotinus, Philo, and Clement of Alexandria. In more modern times the greatest sympathetic influence they confessed was that of Descartes ; while they ranged themselves with more or less neutrality to that of Bacon, and in active hostility to the philosophy of Hobbes. The axioms of the author of the *Leviathan* (1651), that morality consists only in seeking each man his own advantage : and that, as Bishop Burnet puts it, 'religion has no other foundation than the law of the land,' were naturally intolerable to the Cambridge Platonists. Cudworth, in especial, took the field against the *Leviathan*, and was among its most damaging critics. The calm, reasonable, practical side of their teaching is sometimes dwelt on to the exclusion of the enthusiasm and the passion for an undivided devotion to the Person and Example of Jesus Christ, that is a no less marked feature. If, in some of their writings, the lack of controversial style, and the occasional prolixity and adherence to obsolete beliefs, should lead people to misjudge the value of their contribution to English religious life, it may be safely asserted that there exists nothing more finely characteristic of English piety at its best than the flower of the writings of Whichcote, John Smith, and Culverwel ; while the powerful intellect and critical acuteness of Cudworth have placed him for ever among the English philosophers.

Benjamin Whichcote, 1609-83. Fellow of Emmanuel, 1633 ; Rector of North Cadbury, Somerset, 1643 : returned to Cambridge in 1644 as Provost of King's, succeeding Dr.

Collins, who was deprived by Parliament. Whichcote accepted the office with great reluctance, and under pressure, on condition of being allowed to share the stipend with its banished holder. At Cambridge, and especially as lecturer in Trinity Church, he exercised a far-reaching influence on the religious thought of his time. He preached, we are told, from very short notes, so that the matter rather than the manner of his sermons is what survives to us. He appears to have been one of the born teachers and inspirers of men who are most instrumental in forming the mind of their times, although in such fashion that after ages are apt to underestimate their power, shaping as it did more living, but less directly traceable material than paper folios. At the Restoration, he, in his turn, was deprived of the Provostship, but was appointed in 1662 to St. Anne's, Blackfriars. Thence he removed, on the burning of his church in the Great Fire, to a living in Cambridgeshire ; but returned to London in 1668 to the living of St. Lawrence, Jewry, which he held till he died in 1683. Tillotson (*q.v.*) preached his funeral sermon. As is natural for a mind of Whichcote's stamp, recoiling from the coining of formularies and declarations of faith, in the sphere of religion viewed as a life principle, he dwells in his teaching on the peculiarly mystical doctrine of the necessity for Christ's Redemption to be worked *in* us as well as *for* us. The antecedent goodness of God as shown in the Atonement is also a favourite topic. All the mystics unite in repelling with passion the hateful Calvinist doctrine of an angry God, satisfied only with utmost vengeance on a vicarious Victim. Whichcote, no less than his fellows, proclaims the unalterable love of God to be the true and only moving cause of Christ's coming. His aphorisms, collected from his MSS., were published with his sermons after his death. Many of them and of his sayings are of great value. 'If a man has wrong suppositions in his mind concerning God, he will be wrong through all the parts of his religion.' 'Heaven is *first* a temper, and *then* a place.' 'To go against reason is to go against God ; . . . reason is the divine governor of man's life ; it is the very voice of God.' '*We are, none of us, at all better than we mean*; . . . and the truth is here, there is no dispensation for failure in intention. For misapprehension God doth grant allowance, and dispense with human frailties ; but for a failing of intention there is no dispensation.'

Ralph Cudworth, 1617-88. Matriculated at Emmanuel, 1632 ; held the living of North

Cadbury, Somerset, for the two years immediately preceding Whichcote; became B.D. and Master of Clare Hall, 1644; Regius Professor of Hebrew, and Master of Christ's, 1654. He had friendly dealings with the Commonwealth officials, but maintained his position at the Restoration, and was given a living in Herts. In spite of this, and of subsequently being made a prebendary of Gloucester, he remained in Cambridge, and died there. As a young man he attracted attention by two remarkable sermons; and in 1647 he preached before the House of Commons, by no means mincing his words, but giving them some very plain, hard truths to digest. But Cudworth's life-work, and that which renders him the most famous of all the Cambridge Platonists, is his refutation of Hobbes's *Leviathan*, which he undertook in a work entitled *The True Intellectual System of the Universe*. The lack of system and discipline in the presentation of his thought has prevented full justice always being done to his vigorous and destructive criticism of the rival philosophy, and of the writer's immense and varied learning. 'These three things,' he says in a characteristic passage, ' are the fundamentals and essentials of true religion—namely, that all things do not float without a head and governor, but there is an omnipotent understanding Being presiding over all ; that God hath an essential goodness and justice ; and that the differences of good and evil moral, honest and dishonest, are not by mere will and law only, but by nature ; and consequently, that the Deity cannot act, influence, and necessitate men to such things as are in their own nature evil ; and lastly, that necessity is not intrinsical to the nature of everything, but that men have such a liberty or power over their own actions as may render them accountable for the same, and blameworthy when they do amiss; and, consequently, that there is a justice distributive of rewards and punishments running through the world.'

John Smith, 1618-52. Smith was Whichcote's pupil at Emmanuel; graduated B.A. in 1640, and became Fellow of Queens' in 1644. Gifted with a remarkably beautiful disposition, he was held in high esteem as a tutor, alike for his character and for his learning, and the ready command in which he held it always at his disposal. He was the most naturally eloquent, and possessed the most felicitous style of all the Cambridge Platonists, as is witnessed by his volume of *Select Discourses*, the only work that has survived, probably the only one he ever wrote. In the first of these occurs the

pregnant aphorism : ' Such as men themselves are, such will God Himself seem to be ' ; and throughout this, and the sermon on the Nature of God, it is taught that the most direct road to a knowledge of the Supreme Being is by reflection upon 'our own originals,' upon the divine spark that inhabits, or that *is* the consciousness of every man. John Smith's definition of the eternity and omnipresence of God is an admirable antidote to the vagueness and the pantheism whereinto some mystics have fallen : ' We may also know God to be eternal and omnipresent, not because He fills either place or time, but rather because He wanteth neither.' He paraphrases Whichcote when he says : ' Hell is rather a nature than a place ; and heaven cannot be so truly defined by anything without us, as by something that is within us.'

Henry More, 1614-87. After a brilliant career at Eton entered Christ's College, 1631; became M.A. and Fellow, 1639. Nothing would induce him to leave Cambridge permanently, and there he lived and died, a student, with many friends of every sort. Greatly troubled in his youth by the problems of life, he found their solution in the mystical writers, especially Plotinus, Hermes Trismegistus, and the *Theologia Germanica*, ' that golden little book, that first so pierced and affected me.' He was also a great student of the Cabbala. His writings are numerous, but of much less present interest than those of the rest of his school. At one time an enthusiastic Cartesian, he discovered in later years a more material than spiritual tendency in the French philosopher, and cast him aside. More was beyond doubt the most picturesque figure in the group : charming, fantastic, intellectual, and deeply religious, he held a unique position. He has more affinities than the other Cambridge Platonists with the Nature mystics—those who hold the correspondence of the visible with the invisible throughout all things in the universe. The *Life of More* was a favourite book with William Law (*q.v.*).

Nathaniel Culverwel, d. 1651, entered Emmanuel College in 1633, and in time became Fellow, preaching in its chapel his famous sermons. The favourite text of the Cambridge Platonists, 'The spirit of man is the candle of the Lord ' (Prov. 20[27]), is very dear to him, and a noble sermon on Reason is based upon it. 'The Creator,' he says, ' furnished and beautified this lower part of the world with Intellectual lamps, that should shine forth to the praise and honour of His Name, which totally have their dependence upon Him both for their being, and for their perpetual continuation of them in their being. 'Twas He that lighted up these lamps at first; 'tis He that drops the golden oil into them. Look then a while but upon the Parentage and Original of the soul, and of Reason, and you'll presently perceive that 'twas the *Candle of the Lord.*'

John Worthington, 1618-71. probably contemporary at Emmanuel with John Smith, whose *Discourses* he edited, became Master of Jesus College; lecturer at Hackney, 1670.

The following are two Oxford disciples:—

Joseph Glanvill, 1636-80, the ally and satellite of More; a scholar of great promise and brilliancy; died at the age of forty-four.

John Norris, 1657-1711. Rector of Bemerton; corresponded with More, and was, like William Law, a fervent disciple of Malebranche. Principal Tulloch calls him 'The solitary Platonist of the Revolution era'; and he is also singular among English mystics for the manner in which he espouses the Dionysian teaching of the 'Divine Dark' —Walter Hilton indeed alluding to it, but in a slightly different sense. [E. C. G.]

Tulloch, *Rational Theology in Eng. in Seventeenth Century,* vol. ii.; J. H. Overton, *Life and Opinions of the Rev. William Law*; Whichcote, *Sermons, Aphorisms*; John Smith, *Select Discourses*; Culverwel, *Light of Reason*, etc.; More, *Mystery of Godliness, Divine Dialogues*; Norris, *Sermons, Miscellanies*; *Cam. Hist. Eng. Lit.,* VIII. chap. xl.

CAMPEGGIO, Lorenzo (1472-1539), Cardinal and Bishop of Salisbury, belonged to a noble Bolognese family; studied law, and married, but after the death of his wife was ordained, and was created cardinal by Leo X., 1517. He twice visited England as Legate, and on both occasions Henry VIII. (*q.v.*) insisted that Wolsey (*q.v.*) should share his Legatine functions and authority. In 1518 he was sent to persuade Henry to join in a crusade against the Turks; in 1528 to try the question of the validity of Henry's marriage with Katherine of Aragon. He suffered much from gout, which Bishop Gardiner (*q.v.*) said was the only objection to his position as Legate. He was under instructions from Clement VII. not to deliver judgment without referring the matter to Rome. Wolsey meantime was pressing for an immediate decision. The difficulty was settled by the case being recalled to Rome, and his mission terminated. As an affront, Henry had his baggage searched by the customs officers at Dover. He had been appointed Bishop of Salisbury, 1514, but was deprived by Act of Parliament, 1534

(25 Hen. VIII. c. XXVII.) on the ground of non-residence. [C. P. S. C.]

Brewer, *Reign of Henry VIII.*; Dr. J. Gairdner in *D.N.B.*; Cassan, *Lives of the Bishops of Salisbury.*

CANON LAW IN THE ENGLISH CHURCH TO 1534.

A *canon* is a rule of conduct, and specifically a rule laid down by the Christian Church for its members. There is a theory of the origins of Christianity, recently stated with great force by Rudolf Sohm, according to which the formulation of such rules is foreign to the principles of the Gospel, and should be regarded as an aberration. Sohm has been effectively criticised by Harnack, who shows that 'probably never in the history of religion has a new society appeared with a more abundant and elaborate equipment.' Indeed, much was taken over from the Synagogue, the *Ecclesia* of Christ being regarded as the true succession of the *Ecclesia* of the Old Testament. The assembly of apostles and presbyters, recorded in Acts 15, made an express canon; we find St. Paul doing the same in his epistles; the word κανών first appears in this sense in Gal. 6¹⁶. In addition to such formulated rules, the Church, like any other human society, recognised a mass of unwritten custom which should not be transgressed, and St. Paul could cut short a debate by saying: 'We have no such custom (συνήθεια), neither the Churches of God' (1 Cor. 11¹⁶). There were therefore from the first the elements of a systematic order in the Church, and these pointed almost inevitably, along the ordinary lines of human development, to a codified *Ius canonicum.*

But this was remarkably slow in arriving. The law of the Church was supposed to reside in the breast of each bishop, as pastor and judge, who was guided by custom and by sparse records, chiefly those of the canonical Scriptures. Councils of bishops for exercising discipline are obscurely indicated by the writer quoted by Eusebius (v. 16) as concerned with the Montanist heresy in the second century. In the third century they became frequent, and authentic records begin; from the fourth century onward they were in full working order. The exercise of an authority that can properly be called *jurisdiction,* whether by individual bishops or by councils, is evident from the second century. It involves the two functions of *discipline* and *dispensation.* Both are obscurely indicated in Hermas, *Mand.* iv. 3, where a single penance after baptism is treated as a dispensation from the severity of strict law. Early in the third century the growing practice of dispensation led to the revolt of St. Hippolytus against the looser discipline of Callistus of Rome: the later and more extended schism of Novatian was due to a like impulse.

Collections of canons for general use began to appear in the fourth century. The sources were not identified, and there was a general tendency to refer them back to the apostles. The *Statutes of the Apostles*, now preserved only in Coptic and Ethiopic, and in part also in Latin, are partly derived from a source which is probably of the third century, and is also represented in a somewhat different form by the *Canons of Hippolytus*, extant only in Arabic. The eighty-five Greek *Canons of the Apostles* are a late fourth-century collection, in part derived from earlier sources, in part no doubt the invention of the collector. The canons of councils were carefully preserved, the earliest of which completely extant are those of a synod held at Illiberris (*circ.* 305). Most of them had only a local currency, but the canons of Ancyra (*circ.* 314), of Nicæa (325), of Sardica (*circ.* 344), and of Laodicea (*ante* 381), secured universal acceptance. After the year 381 the distinction of general and particular councils was more clearly marked, but the rejection of the twenty-eighth canon of Chalcedon (451) by Rome and the whole West shows that the constitutions even of an œcumenical council were not invariably accepted.

In the sixth century the work of collectors became more systematic. John the Scholastic, Patriarch of Constantinople in 565, not only gathered canons from all sources, but also digested their substance into fifty titles, thus doing for the Eastern Church what was not done for the West until six centuries later. Dionysius Exiguus in 550 brought out a Latin translation of the whole collection of Greek canons, adding those enacted by a long series of African councils. Neither of these collectors, however, confined himself to conciliar constitutions: they included the sixty-eight canons of St. Basil the Great, or decisions of vexed questions made by that eminent Father; Dionysius added the decretal letters of the Bishops of Rome, preserved in the Roman archives from the time of Siricius (384-98). This collection of Dionysius became the foundation of the subsequent Canon Law of the Western Church. In the seventh century a collection of the same kind, doubtfully attributed to St. Isidore of Seville, was made and published in Spain.

The ninth century saw the production of the Forged Decretals, supposed Epistles of the Popes anterior to Siricius, which immensely strengthened the growing authority of the Roman See. Early in the twelfth century Ivo of Chartres compiled his *Panormia*, or *Pannonica*, in imitation of the Pandects of Justinian.

Christianity was planted in England at a time when Canon Law was already well organised in Rome. The correspondence of St. Gregory the Great (*q.v.*) with St. Augustine (*q.v.*) of Canterbury, and the *Penitential* of Theodore, show how hard it was to apply this to the rough circumstances of the North, and what grave compromises were sometimes necessary, but the whole of it was applied in principle. Canons were made by local councils in England, as elsewhere, but it is a mistake to think of them as forming the whole or even the main part of the Canon Law here in use: they were supplementary. We must think of a great body of custom, reinforced by a great but indeterminate mass of written law, the whole of which was more or less current throughout the Western Church, and kept in approximate uniformity by frequent appeals and references to Rome. We have also to face the fact that the distinction of Church and State had by the tenth century entirely disappeared in the West. St. Gregory the Great could still contrast the laws of the Commonwealth with the laws of the Church, but there supervened the conception of a unitary *Respublica Christiana*, in which both are merged. There follows a new differentiation of function within the one society, which leads to the great conflict of *imperium* and *sacerdotium*, and supplies the familiar English division of *Spiritualty* and *Temporalty* in one body politic; the term *Ecclesia* being constantly used of the Spiritualty alone, as in Magna Carta and in Henry VIII.'s Statute for Restraint of Appeals. Henceforth Canon Law is no longer the law of the Church as distinct from the State: it is part of the law of the whole community—that part precisely which is specially administered by the Spiritualty. *Canones* and *Leges* are carefully distinguished, the former being made by spiritual authority, the latter by temporal authority, or more frequently by Temporalty and Spiritualty acting together; both alike were in force over the whole community, though there were frequent attempts, sometimes successful, to withdraw spiritual persons from the operation of laws made or administered by the Temporalty.

The work of Ivo of Chartres (d. 1116)

heralded an important movement. Bishops and councils, in administering canonical justice, had always borrowed freely from the methods and the *regulae iuris* of Roman law, as also latterly from the barbaric methods of German law. In the twelfth century the revival of the study of the *Corpus Iuris Cirilis*, especially at Bologna, threatened a serious growth of the Imperial authority, an undigested mass of canons and decretals being unable to hold its own against such rivalry. This fear seems to have suggested the production of Gratian's work, *Concordantia Discordantium Canonum*, commonly known as the *Decretum*, in which the whole collection of known canonical legislation, genuine and spurious, was reduced under orderly titles, with comments reconciling or explaining discrepancies (*circ.* 1150). The *Decretum* had an immediate success; adopted at once as a text-book at Bologna, it rapidly spread thence, and within a short time was being read in the new schools at Oxford. With glosses and additions (*Palea*), it acquired almost as much authority in the courts as in the Universities, and made Canon Law a practicable system. In 1253 Gregory IX. commissioned Raymond of Peñafort to make a similar digest of the papal decretals accumulated since the time of Gratian, which he promulgated to the Universities under the title of the *Five Books of Decretals*. In 1298 Boniface VIII. added the *Sext* (*i.e.* sixth book), and in 1313 Clement V. put out the *Clementines*, constructed on the same plan. Later decretals down to 1483 were similarly edited under the title of *Extravagants* (*i.e.* decretals as yet ' wandering outside ' the official collections). These compilations together make up the *Corpus Iuris Canonici* as it existed in the sixteenth century.

These books have been improperly described as a Code, or as the Statute-book of the Church. They were, in fact, no more than a text for study, put out by the highest authority. Canons and decretals gained nothing but a wider publicity by being included, and others which were not included had exactly the same authority, if they could be produced on occasion. Many of those contained in the *Decretum* were obviously obsolete, or superseded by later legislation; decretals of the thirteenth or fourteenth century could equally be abrogated. Those canons and decretals alone which were from time to time currently enforced formed the actual body of Canon Law. They were current with exactly the same force throughout the whole of Western Christendom, and new decretals ran with exactly the same force everywhere. These were the *Ius Commune*. But this must be understood subject to an important qualification. Written law was superimposed from the first, as we have seen, upon a mass of customs, and the practice of the Church down to the end of the Middle Ages recognised the force of local *consuetudo* as being such that with forty years' prescription it could set aside the obligation of the *Ius Commune*, unless the custom were in express terms reprobated. Thus the *Ius Commune* was everywhere limited by a fluid mass of custom, recognised by canonists as good, doubtful, or bad law, according to circumstances.

England, as a part of united Christendom, shared this common law. Here, as elsewhere, there were customs of the realm limiting its operations. Here, as elsewhere, there was some local legislation supplementing it. Many English canons of a date anterior to the thirteenth century passed into complete oblivion, except in so far as their effect survived in local custom. The canons and constitutions made in the councils held under the legates Otho (1236-7) and Ottobuoni (1268) were annotated by John of Ayton; a long series of constitutions made in synods of the province of Canterbury from 1222 to 1433 was digested in the *Provinciale* by William Lyndwood (*q.v.*) in the manner of the *Corpus Iuris*, with an immense gloss relating it all to the *Ius Commune*. There was thus a valuable body of national and provincial Canon Law; but the importance of this must not be exaggerated; it was merely supplemental. An erroneous opinion once attributed to the mediæval Church of England a separateness and independence which the theory and practice of the time would have made impossible; the Roman Canon Law, the *Ius pontificium*, was supposed to have been current in England only in so far as it was with more or less of formality accepted and incorporated into the native Canon Law. This error seems to have been due partly to a misapplication of the principle underlying the Reception of the Roman Civil Law by the states of Germany in the sixteenth century, which is perhaps responsible for some of the language used in the legislation of Henry VIII., partly to a misunderstanding of the canonical effects of *consuetudo*. It is not true that the *Ius Commune* was current only when *received*, but it is true conversely that its effect might be barred by a contrary custom of the realm. In his brilliant refutation of this error, Professor F. W. Maitland went some distance astray in the opposite direction, speaking of decretals as ' absolutely binding statute law,' which they were not in face of contrary custom, and treating the restraint imposed by such custom as an external constraint put upon the Church by the State. This is anachronistic, for Church and State were not then distinguished; a custom of the realm of England, which might be recorded in the judicial year-books, in an Act of Parliament, in a royal charter, or in any other way, was a local custom of a part of Christendom, and therefore integrated in Canon Law. Maitland has shown, however, from the crucial instance of the law regarding the legitimation of natural-born children by subsequent matrimony, that the courts spiritual would go far in ignoring a custom of the realm which the temporal authorities maintained against the protest of the Spiritualty. On the other hand, Mr. Ogle has shown, from the crucial instance of Peckham's (*q.v.*) constitution *Audistis* against pluralities, that in the thirteenth century the English Spirituality could venture to legislate contrary to the tenor of a recent decretal, where this was found to be ill adapted to local circumstances. Peckham excused himself humbly to the Pope for this audacity; two centuries later Lyndwood judged it an impossible liberty.

For the sake of illustration, it may be well to note four striking variations from the *Ius Commune* established in English practice. (1) Questions of the right of advowson were partly remitted to the temporal courts. (2) Lapse of patronage was subject to special rules. (3) Legitimation of children *per subsequens matrimonium* was not entirely allowed. (4) The church courts had cognisance of testamentary matters. This last peculiarity was inexplicable to Lyndwood, who could only refer it (*Prov.*, pp. 176, 263) to some unknown origin, founding it 'super consensu Regis et suorum Procerum in talibus ab antiquo concesso.'

We find then in England, as in other countries, a normal qualification of the general Canon Law by the effect of local custom, together with a limited and diminishing liberty of canonical legislation supplementing or even modifying the *Ius Commune.* Otherwise that *Ius Commune* was law in England.   [T. A. L.]

Carlyle, *Mediæval Political Theory in the West*; Gierke (Maitland's translation), *Political Theories of the Middle Age*; Maitland, *Roman Canon Law in England*; Ogle, *Canon Law in Mediæval England*; Pollock and Maitland, *History of English Law*; Stubbs, *Seventeen Lectures on Mediæval and Modern History*; Wood, *The Regal Power of the Church.*

CANON LAW IN THE ENGLISH CHURCH FROM 1534.

In 1532 Convocation (*q.v.*), by assenting under pressure from Henry VIII. to the document called the Submission of the Clergy, undertook (1) not to enact canons in future without the royal licence and assent, and (2) that the existing canons should be examined by a commission, and such as were found 'to stand with God's laws and the laws of your realm' should continue in force, and the rest should be abrogated 'by your grace and the clergy.' This undertaking never having been repudiated by the Church, and having been confirmed by Parliament in 1534 (25 Hen. VIII. c. 19), is the law both of Church and State, and forms the starting point for any consideration of the present canon law of the English Church.

Canons passed since 1534.—The commission foreshadowed in 1532 eventually produced the *Reformatio Legum* (*q.v.*) in 1553. This compilation never became law. In 1556 Cardinal Pole (*q.v.*) as legate promulgated twelve canons on matters of discipline. But when Elizabeth came to the throne it was obvious that the project of a revised canon law had come to nothing, and Parker (*q.v.*) and his immediate successors contented themselves with issuing small bodies of canons dealing with matters of discipline which required immediate attention. In 1563 an unsuccessful attempt at such legislation was made by Parker in Convocation. In 1571 ten canons were passed by the Upper House, and though not sanctioned by the Queen were enforced by virtue of their spiritual authority. In 1576 the Convocation of Canterbury enacted fifteen canons or 'articles,' of which thirteen received Elizabeth's assent. She also allowed further sets passed in 1584 and 1597 to be issued, with a statement that they had received her confirmation. This was held to sanction them only for her life. Therefore at her death Church legislation since 1534 was in a state of confusion, existing only in scattered and fragmentary codes of canons and other documents of uncertain authority. Bancroft's (*q.v.*) policy required a full code of undoubted validity, and under his influence one hundred and forty-one canons were passed by the Convocation of Canterbury in 1604, by that of York in 1606, received the royal assent, and have remained the principal legislative achievement of the English Church since the breach with Rome. They are based on mediæval canons, on those passed in the sixteenth century (including Pole's), and on the Tudor Injunctions (*q.v.*), Advertisements (*q.v.*), and Articles (*q.v.*). The canons drawn up in 1606 when Overall (*q.v.*) was prolocutor did not receive the royal assent, and were never promulgated. The seventeen canons passed in 1640 received the royal assent. Their alleged invalidity rests on the fact that Convocation continued to sit after Parliament was dissolved. A project to re-enact them in 1661 came to nothing. In Anne's reign it was intended to reform the Church by means of canons, and a draft set was under consideration in 1714, but the suppression of Convocation in 1717 deprived the Church of the power of reforming itself.

Henry VIII.'s legislation put an end to the scientific study of the old canon law. Henceforth practitioners in the Church courts were no longer 'steeped and soaked . . . in the papal law-books.' Nor could this be said of the great English canonists of the seventeenth and eighteenth centuries, as Spelman (*q.v.*), Wilkins (*q.v.*), Gibson (*q.v.*), and John Ayliffe (1676-1732), author of the *Corpus Juris Canonici Anglicani*. The reprinting of Lyndwood's *Provinciale* at Oxford in 1679 marks a revival of the study of the canon law, but it was mainly academic, and languished after the middle of the eighteenth century — the Church courts (*q.v.*) being mainly engaged in marriage, slander, and will cases, which were increasingly recognised as falling within the sphere of secular law.

With the revival of Convocation came a demand for the revision of the canons. In 1865 two new canons were enacted under royal licence, and several of those of 1604 amended. Canons 62 and 102 were amended in 1888, and a new canon on clergy discipline enacted in 1892. Committees for revision of the whole code were appointed by both Convocations in 1866, and in 1874 presented a draft revised code of eighty-nine canons. An amended version of it in ninety-four canons followed in 1879, but no synodical action was taken, and the canons of 1604, though in some respects obsolete and inapplicable to modern conditions, remain for the most part unrevised.

Modern English Church Law.—The provincial canons enacted since 1534 form but a small part of the law now in force in the English Church. The constituent parts of that law may be thus enumerated :—

1. Pre-Reformation canon law. Under 25 Hen. VIII. c. 19 all existing canons have the same force as they had before, provided they are not contrary to the laws of the realm or the King's prerogative. With this proviso the general body of the canon law and the provincial canons of the English Church have the same force as they had before 1534, except

in so far as they have been varied or abrogated by lawful authority. Accordingly the courts of Church and State alike have admitted the validity of these canons and been guided by them (1825, *Rennells v. Bishop of Lincoln*, 3 Bing. 323 ; 1848, *Burder v. Mavor*, 1 Rob. Eccl. 614).

2. Canons enacted since 1534, if they comply with the terms of the Submission of the Clergy, form part of the King's Ecclesiastical Law, and will be enforced by the courts ; otherwise they have only the spiritual authority which they derive from enactment by the synod.

3. Enactments which, though not in the form of canons, have been sanctioned by the Church through Convocation, such as the XXXIX. Articles (*q.v.*) and the rubrics of the Prayer Book.

4. The decisions of the Church courts (*q.v.*), which are valid until overruled by competent authority.

5. Custom possesses greater authority in ecclesiastical than in civil law. No canon is valid until it is accepted by the Church, and many positive enactments are based upon prevailing usage. There is thus an unwritten law of the Church, *ius commune ecclesiasticum*, which is of full validity although it has never been formally enacted, but rests on the unexpressed will of the Church. This law has been fully recognised by the courts in modern times, and they have laid down that in administering it works of history and theology may be taken into account. The law may be illustrated by the history that lies behind it.

6. Secular law, whether contained in statute or otherwise, may form part of Church law if it is accepted by the Church and deals with matters over which the State has authority. The Church's acceptance may be express : *e.g.* the Clergy Discipline Act, 1892 (55-6 Vic. c. 32), which deals with the deprivation of criminous clergymen, was expressly accepted by Convocation, which passed a canon in accordance with its provisions ; or it may be implied : *e.g.* the Acts dealing with the manner of paying Church rates (*q.v.*) before their final abolition were accepted and acted on by the Church courts without any formal ecclesiastical enactment. Both these instances deal with matters of temporal property on which Parliament is competent to legislate, and its enactments, being accepted by the Church, form part of the ecclesiastical law. But such a measure as the Public Worship Regulation Act (*q.v.*), dealing with matters outside the civil sphere, and having been definitely repudiated by

Convocation, forms no part of the Church's law. [CHURCH AND STATE.]

Abrogation.—Canon law may be abrogated by express repeal, or it may be implicitly repealed by the enactment of other law superseding it. When the Church accepted the transfer of the jurisdiction over matrimonial suits to the State in 1857, the canons dealing with the procedure of the Church courts in such cases were by implication repealed. Or it may be abrogated by force of custom; that is to say, by falling into desuetude. 'The canon law of a Church is that which is in fact in use and force therein.' But to express the mind of the Church such desuetude must be the result of deliberate intention. Mere non-user without such intention may weaken the force of a law, but cannot express the mind of the Church so as to abrogate it altogether.

Force of the Canon Law.—The civil courts have decided that the canon law in force in the English Church is fully binding on the clergy; that is to say, the mediæval canons which are in force under 25 Hen. VIII. c. 19, and the canons which have since that time been enacted by Convocation with the royal assent. It is fully established that all these canons bind the clergy without any confirmation by Parliament. Lord Hardwicke's judgment in *Middleton* v. *Crofts* (1736, 2 Atkyns, 650) is the accepted authority on this point. It also lays down that the canons do not *proprio vigore* bind the laity, but that many of them 'are declaratory of the ancient usage and law of the Church of England, received and allowed here,' which do bind the laity. In 1604 Parliament seems to have been apprehensive on this point, and Bills were introduced then, in 1606, and in 1610 to declare the canons not binding unless confirmed by Parliament. They failed to pass, however, and it was clearly Bancroft's intention that in matters of discipline (*q.v.*) the laity should be subject to the canons. This is expressly laid down in Canon 140. Gibson, commenting on Coke's contention that the temporalty are not bound because they are not represented in Convocation, remarks: 'As if the laity had nothing to be saved but their estates; nor the clergy anything to do but to save themselves.' It must be remembered (i) that the secular courts allow that canons which are declaratory of accepted Church law, or have been in any way confirmed by statute, are binding on the laity; (ii) that in 1604 all the laity were supposed to be faithful members of the Church, and Canon 140 assumes this; (iii) that all validly enacted canons are binding on the conscience of

Church people. But much canon law on the subject of discipline has been allowed to fall into desuetude. And now that so many members of the State are not members of the Church, the State naturally refrains from enforcing Church law on the laity by the secular arm, preferring to leave it to the Church's spiritual authority. The bulk of the ecclesiastical law now recognised by the State deals with matters immediately affecting the clergy only.   [G. C.]

Cardwell, *Synodalia*; Gibson, *Codex*; Usher, *Reconstruction of the Eng. Ch.*; Collins, *Nature and Force of the Canon Law*; Wood, *Regal Power of the Ch.*; Crosse, *Authority in the Ch. of Eng.*

CANTERBURY, See of. Before the coming of St. Augustine (*q.v.*) Canterbury was the seat of a bishop named Liudhard. He had been sent by the King of the West Franks with his daughter Bereta when she became wife of Aethelberht, the Kentish King. He had probably been in Kent many years before Augustine came, but as the country was heathen can hardly be described as a diocesan bishop. The church of St. Martin, Canterbury, built, says Bede, when the Romans still dwelt in Britain, was used by Bereta for her worship, but it seems probable that Liudhard had become aged and unable to minister. In any case, the mission of Augustine forms the starting point of the historic see of Canterbury. The diocese may be regarded as beginning with the baptism of Aethelberht on the eve of Whit Sunday, 597, probably in St. Martin's Church. It was originally conterminous with the kingdom of Kent, but the north-west portion became the diocese of Rochester (*q.v.*) in 604. The diocese was organised as soon as Augustine had received consecration in Gaul. The advice sent to him by Gregory the Great (*q.v.*) involved the creation of a metropolitical see with diocesan bishops. There were to be archbishoprics of York and London. But this arrangement was never made, and Canterbury continued metropolitan of the south, with the title (from 1353) of primate of all England. On Aethelberht's death in 616 the kingdom was in grave danger of lapse into paganism. Mellitus (*q.v.*) and Justus fled from their sees, and Laurentius, Augustine's successor, was preparing to follow them when a vision enabled him to bring the young King Eadbald to accept the faith. With Justus (624) the archbishopric may be said to have passed from its period of insecurity into that of settled authority. But the first five bishops were all in some way associated with Gregory the Great, and it was not till Theodore of Tarsus (*q.v.*), 668, that the primatial authority was clearly recognised. Gradually the customs connected with the papal idea of legation grew up and became fixed. In later centuries the archbishops of Canterbury were recognised as papal legates (*q.v.*), but it was not till the time of Stephen Langton (*q.v.*) that this dignity was habitually conferred on them as of right. Nor was the custom in itself regarded as abating the power of the archbishop. Anselm was welcomed by the pope of his day as *alterius orbis papa* ; and England was continually, now more, now less, regarded as being outside the 'world' of which the German King was Roman Cæsar and the Bishop of Rome universal ordinary. The position of Canterbury was, in fact, to a considerable extent that of a patriarchate, and if the comparison with the Eastern patriarchates is not a close one, that with Aquileia is more exact. Great though the power of the see in the Middle Ages was in itself, it was immensely increased by the succession of great men who possessed it. Some were saints, some men of learning, many were great leaders of men, skilled in the practice of civil government. And with few exceptions they were men who rose to the high ideal of their great office, and whose hearts were set on the things of God. Their secular work was undertaken that through it they might the better serve the Church ; and, like Langton (*q.v.*), Edmund Rich (*q.v.*), Winchelsey, they were leaders in the assertion of English political liberty. The register of Archbishop Peckham (*q.v.*)(R.S., and now being printed completely by the Canterbury and York Society) illustrates at once the wealth and the activity of a mediæval primate. The manors of the archbishop which he visited extended from Croydon and Otford in the west to Canterbury, Witham, and Ford in the east; from Northfleet and Reculver in the north to Romney, Aldington, Lyminge, and Saltwood in the south. An itinerary of the manors enabled the archbishop to make an almost complete visitation of his diocese, and the registers show that this was generally done with minuteness and severity. At Canterbury and at Lambeth the archbishops lived in great state. Till the nineteenth century they kept practically open house, and crowds of beggars were in the Middle Ages fed daily from their tables. Their households were very large, containing besides chaplains and secretaries, knights and men-at-arms, and children of great personages sent there to be nurtured in piety and learning. The Canterbury school from the days of Archbishop Theodore was famous. Becket (*q.v.*) was the tutor of Henry II.'s eldest son. Sir Thomas More (*q.v.*) was brought up in the household of Morton (*q.v.*). After the Reformation the households of prelates such as Whitgift (*q.v.*), Laud (*q.v.*), Sheldon (*q.v.*), and Sancroft (*q.v.*) were famous nurseries of scholars and young nobles. The archbishop's court was recognised by the Constitutions of Clarendon (*q.v.*) as being the supreme court of ecclesiastical judicature within the realm, and not subject to any right of appeal. But throughout the Middle Ages, from the time when Dunstan (*q.v.*) disobeyed a papal injunction to the Reformation, the position of the archbishop became increasingly difficult, as set between the Roman Church and the English State, and it was only through his double capacity as *legatus domini papae* and yet *papa alterius orbis* that he managed to retain not a little independence. With the Reformation the powers of the archbishop became more clearly defined by law. But though the archiepiscopal court exercised jurisdiction in 1699 (*Lucy* v. *Bishop Watson* of St. David's, who was sentenced to deprivation for simony), the jurisdiction cannot be said to have been settled till the time of Archbishop Benson (*q.v.*) and the Lincoln case, if then. [COURTS.]

The Archbishop of Canterbury is primate of all England, and has metropolitan jurisdiction over twenty-seven dioceses. In the Middle Ages he had much strife for precedence with the see of York (*q.v.*). The mediæval archbishops administered their dioceses through bishops suffragan, with titles of sees *in partibus*. Under the Suffragans Act, 1535 (26 Hen. VIII. c. 14), bishops suffragan of Dover were consecrated in 1537, 1539, and 1569 ; this title has been revived since 1870, and there has been a bishop suffragan of Croydon since 1904. From 1375 to 1558 Calais and the surrounding district formed part of the diocese of Canterbury. An Order in Council of 8th June 1841 abolished about a hundred Peculiars of Canterbury in other dioceses ; and by an Order of 8th August 1845 the diocese was made to include the whole of Kent, except the city and deanery of Rochester and certain parishes in the diocese of London. But at the formation of the diocese of Southwark (*q.v.*) the western portion of Kent was transferred to Rochester. Canterbury now consists of the eastern part of Kent and the rural deanery of Croydon. It has a population of 589,656 and an acreage of 634,242. There was only one archdeaconry, that of Canterbury (first mentioned, 798), until 4th June 1841, when that of Maidstone was constituted by Order in Council. The *Temporalia* of the see were assessed by the *Taxatio* of 1291 at £1355, 8s. 1d., and the *Spiritualia* at £250; by the *Valor* of 1534 the income was £2682, 12s. 2d.; it is now £15.000.

The cathedral church of Canterbury owes its splendour to the work of many archbishops. Augustine consecrated a church, Bede tells us, which had formerly been built by the Romans but had fallen into decay. This was a basilica. Beside it grew up the monastery of Christ Church. The church had a precarious existence for centuries from fire and Danes, and at the time of the Norman Conquest was in ruins. Lanfranc began to rebuild it, and was followed by Anselm. The building was finished in 1130, when the prior, Conrad, completed 'the glorious choir.' This choir was burned down in 1174, and the new choir was begun by William of Sens and completed by William the Englishman (1174-80). The ancient Norman nave with the transept remained till the fourteenth century, when the Perpendicular work was undertaken (1378-1410), and completed by Prior Chillenden (1390-1421). The central 'Bell Harry' tower was added in 1495, and the north-west tower is of the nineteenth century. The Norman crypt remains. The extensive eastern chapel is called Becket's Crown, where at one time the relics of St. Thomas of Canterbury were shown.

Till the Reformation the monks of Christ Church formed the chapter of the cathedral, though in the election of an archbishop a claim was made by the suffragans of the province. Henry VIII., when he confiscated the other monasteries within the diocese (Cranmer transferred to him four of his manors, 1540), created a dean and chapter, and planned a grammar school and a school of divinity to be connected with the cathedral. This latter was to have readerships in the five chief subjects, with forty free scholars to be sent to Oxford and Cambridge. But the foundation was not completed, and the new foundation, incorporated by Letters Patent, 8th April 1542, consisted of a dean and twelve canons. Six canonries were suspended by the Cathedrals Act, 1840 (3-4 Vic. c. 113), and two more annexed to the two archdeaconries.

ARCHBISHOPS OF CANTERBURY

1. Augustine (*q.v.*), 597; d. *c.* 604.
2. Laurentius, 604; d. 619.

3. Mellitus (*q.v.*), 619; tr. from London.
4. Justus, 624; tr. from Rochester; cons. Paulinus as bishop for the north; d. 627.
5. Honorius, 627; cons. by Paulinus, and established the see firmly; received pall from Rome, 634; d. 653. A year and half's interregnum followed.
6. Deusdedit, 655; the first English archbishop; cons. by Ithamar of Rochester; d. 664.
7. Theodore (*q.v.*), 668; d. 690.
8. Berchtwald, 693; d. 731.
9. Tatwine, 731; a Mercian from the Worcestershire monastery of Bredon, and a man of learning, who wrote Latin hexameters; d. 734.
10. Nothelm, 735; visited Rome, and gave information to Bede for his *History of the English*; d. 740.
11. Cuthberht, 741; tr. from Hereford; had been Abbot of Lyminge; held the famous Clovesho Council in 747; friend of Winfrid (Boniface) (*q.v.*); d. 758.
12. Bregowine, 759; was an 'old Saxon' (*i.e.* one born in the land whence the invaders had come); d. 765.
13. Jaenberht, 766; had been Abbot of St. Augustine's (the house founded by St. Augustine as St. Peter and St. Paul's), a house which gradually came into conflict with the mother church of Canterbury; in his time the jurisdiction of the see was much reduced by Offa's creation of the Lichfield (*q.v.*) archbishopric; d. 790.
14. Aethelheard, 793; elected in 791 on Jaenberht's death, but kept two years without consecration because the men of Kent regarded him as a creature of the Mercians: with them again he took refuge, 797-8, but Ecgberht recognised him as metropolitan in 803; d. 805.
15. Wulfred, 805; he threw off the Mercian influence, and was friendly to Wessex; d. 832.
16. Feologild, 832; a Kentish man who held the primacy less than a year, dying in 832.
17. Ceolnoth, 833; he in 864 adopted the disastrous policy of buying off the Danes; d. 870.
18. Aethelred, 870; formerly a monk of Christ Church, Canterbury; d. 889.
19. Plegmund, 890; the friend and adviser of King Alfred (*q.v.*); a Mercian who exemplified the religious union of England and twice visited Rome; d. 914.
20. Athelm, 914; tr. from Wells; d. 923.
21. Wulfhelm, 923; tr. from Wells; d. 942.

22. Oda, 942; tr. from Ramsbury; adopted by an English noble, who took him to Rome, where he was ordained; the friend of Aethelstan, he became an important political factor in the reigns of Eadmund and Edred; he revived the monastic rule at Canterbury, in which he was followed by Dunstan; d. 959.

[23. Aelfsige,[1] 958; tr. from Winchester; died on his way to Rome, 959.

24. Brithelm,[1] 959; depr. by Eadgar.]

25. Dunstan (*q.v.*), 960; tr. from London.

26. Aethelgar, 988; tr. from Selsey; d. 990.

27. Sigeric, 990; tr. from Ramsbury; d. 994.

28. Aelfric, 995; tr. from Ramsbury.

29. Aelfheah (*q.v.*), 1005; tr. from Winchester.

30. Lyfing, 1013; tr. from Wells; d. 1020.

31. Aethelnoth, 1020; of the kin of the West Saxon kings, but chaplain of Cnut (*q.v.*), and supporter of Danish rule; d. 1038.

32. Eadsige, 1038; also a philo-Dane, and supporter of Harthacnut; d. 1050.

33. Robert of Jumièges, 1051; came with Eadward Confessor to England; Bishop of London, 1044, and became head of the opposition to Earl Godwine; for a time successful, but when Godwine returned he was forced to fly, and was outlawed and deposed by the witan.1052.

34. Stigand, 1052; had been chaplain to Cnut; was Bishop of Elmham, 1043, and of Worcester, 1047; was appointed to Canterbury uncanonically, Robert being still alive, and received the pallium from the antipope, Benedict x.; it was probably a Norman fable that he crowned Harold; he accepted William, but was deprived, 1070; d. 1072.

35. Lanfranc (*q.v.*), 1070; d. 1089.

36. Anselm (*q.v.*), 1093; d. 1109.

37. Ralph d'Escures, 1114; tr. from Rochester; administered the see of Canterbury on Anselm's death in 1109, but could not obtain election for more than four years; with him the contest with York for profession of obedience became acute; d. 1122.

38. William de Corbeil, 1123; a Norman, and pupil of Anselm; after holding several English offices was chosen by Henry I. to be primate; he continued the dispute with York, and crowned Stephen. Henry of Huntingdon says his glories could not be described, because they did not exist; d. 1136.

39. Theobald, 1139; revived the Canterbury school of clerks; played a judicious

part in the troubled politics of Stephen's reign, but was a supporter of Matilda, and eventually secured the succession for her son, Henry II.; d. 1161.

40. Thomas Becket (*q.v.*), 1162; d. 1170.

41. Richard, 1174; Prior of St. Martin's, Dover; was elected by the bishops in defiance of the monks of Christ Church; was a careful primate, strict in preserving the rights of his see; d. 1184.

42. Baldwin, 1185; tr. from Worcester; a Cistercian; was the first to secure the supremacy of Canterbury over Wales, where he preached the crusade; he crowned Richard I., and died in Palestine, 1190. Alexander Llewellyn, who had been cross-bearer to these three primates, said that on arriving in the city Thomas went first to the court, Richard to the grange, and Baldwin to the church.

43. Hubert Walter (*q.v.*), 1193; tr. from Salisbury; d. 1205.

44. Stephen Langton (*q.v.*), 1207 (P.).

45. Richard le Grant (or of Wethershed), 1229; who opposed Henry III. in politics, though it was he who had chosen him archbishop, and excommunicated his minister, Hubert de Burgh; he died, 1231, at Rome, where he had gone to appeal.

46. Edmund Rich (*q.v.*), 1234; d. 1240.

47. Boniface of Savoy, 1245; the uncle of Henry III.'s Queen, who, though much hated at first, did good work for his see, visited his province, and played no bad part in the settlement of the constitutional dispute; d. 1270.

48. Robert Kilwardby, 1273 (P.); a Dominican, who was provincial of his order in England, 1261; crowned Edward I.; a philosopher and theologian, but driven from England by the power of Edward I., and became cardinal and Bishop of Porto, 1278, dying the next year; he took away all the registers, etc., of Canterbury, and thus Peckham's is the first register extant in England.

49. John Peckham (*q.v.*), 1279 (P.); d. 1292.

50. Robert Winchelsey, 1294; Rector of the University of Paris and a D.D. and Chancellor of Oxford, also a Prebendary of Lincoln and of St. Paul's; he published the famous Bull *Clericis laicos*, and was outlawed by Edward I.; he was in continual dispute with Edward I., and was in banishment when the King died; Edward II. restored him; he was one of the Lords Ordainers, and excommunicated Gaveston; d. 1313.

---

[1] These archbishops were held to be intruded, and are not reckoned by Bishop Stubbs among the regular holders of the see.

51. Walter Reynolds, 1313 ; tr. (P.) from Worcester ; was a politician under Edward I. ; liked by Edward II., who made him Chancellor : on Winchelsey's death Thomas of Cobham was elected primate by the monks, but Pope and King set him aside and appointed Reynolds, who, after supporting the King in his worst acts, turned against him and crowned Edward III. ; d. 1327.

52. Simon Meopham, 1328 ; cons. at Avignon ; held many Church councils, and was an active and religious prelate, who was finally excommunicated for refusing to appear before the Pope's special legate in regard to his dispute with the abbey of St. Augustine ; d. 1333.

53. John Stratford, 1333 ; tr. (P.) from Winchester ; a doctor of both laws at Oxford ; as Bishop of Winchester took a prominent part in the deposition of Edward II., and became chief minister, and in 1330, 1335, and 1340 Chancellor to Edward III., with whom he afterwards quarrelled, but was reconciled before his death in 1348.

54. Thomas Bradwardine, 1349 (P.) ; like his predecessor of Merton College, Oxford, and as a philosopher was called *doctor profundus* ; after serving in important political and ecclesiastical posts was consecrated at Avignon, but died before the end of the year.

55. Simon Islip (*q.v.*), 1349 (P.) ; d. 1366.

56. Simon Langham, 1366 ; tr. (P.) from Ely ; Chancellor of England, 1363 ; had been a monk, and then Abbot of Westminster and Bishop of Ely, 1360 ; took an active part against Wyclif when he was archbishop ; made a cardinal in 1368, he was forced to resign Canterbury ; was made Bishop of Præneste ; died, 1376, at Avignon.

57. William Wittlesey, 1368 ; tr. (P.) from Worcester ; nephew of Islip, and his vicar-general ; held various offices ; left no mark as primate ; d. 1374.

58. Simon Sudbury (*q.v.*), 1375 ; tr. (P.) from London.

59. William Courtenay, 1381 ; tr. (P.) from London ; son of Hugh, Earl of Devon ; had risen rapidly in the Church, and was prominent, when Bishop of London, against Wyclif ; visited the province, and was an active suppressor of the Lollards ; though he opposed the second statute of Provisors, 1391, he accepted that of *Præmunire*, 1393 ; d. 1396.

60. Thomas Arundel, 1397 ; tr. (P.) from York ; Bishop of Ely, formerly Chancellor ; was a prominent politician, and as an opponent of Richard II. was impeached in Parliament and banished in 1397, but was given the see of St. Andrews.

61. Roger Walden (P.), 1398 ; a favourite of Richard II. ; held the see only a year, then deposed on the fall of that King, but was given the see of London in 1400, after

62. Thomas Arundel was restored, 1399 ; he crowned Henry IV. ; was three times his Chancellor, and stoutly resisted Lollardy, trying Sir John Oldcastle for heresy, convicting him, and handing him over to the State ; d. 1414.

63. Henry Chichele (*q.v.*), 1414 ; tr. (P.) from St. David's ; d. 1443.

64. John Stafford, 1443 ; tr. (P.) from Wells ; partisan of the Beaufort house ; d. 1452.

65. John Kemp, 1452 ; tr. (P.) from York ; a Fellow of Merton College, Oxford, who rose from elevation to elevation through his political services to Henry V. and his support of the Beauforts ; he was Bishop of Rochester, 1419 ; of London, 1421 ; Archbishop of York, 1426 ; made cardinal, 1439, and took a prominent part in the politics of the reign of Henry VI. ; d. 1454.

66. Thomas Bourchier, 1454 ; tr. (P.) from Ely ; brother of the Earl of Essex ; Chancellor of the University of Oxford ; Bishop of Worcester and then of Ely ; a supporter of the Yorkists, and crowned Edward IV., 1461 ; persuaded Queen Elizabeth to give up her children to Richard, whom he afterwards crowned ; he lived to marry Henry VII. ; d. 1486.

67. John Morton (*q.v.*), 1486 ; tr. (P.) from Ely.

68. Henry Dean, 1501 ; tr. from Salisbury ; a politician and councillor of Henry VII. ; d. 1503.

69. William Warham (*q.v.*), 1503 ; tr. (P.) from London ; d. 1532.

70. Thomas Cranmer (*q.v.*), 1533 (P.).

71. Reginald Pole (*q.v.*), 1556 (P.) ; d. 1558.

72. Matthew Parker (*q.v.*), 1559 ; d. 1575.

73. Edmund Grindal (*q.v.*), 1576 ; tr. from York ; d. 1583.

74. John Whitgift (*q.v.*), 1583 ; tr. from Worcester ; d. 1604.

75. Richard Bancroft (*q.v.*), 1604 ; tr. from London ; d. 1610.

76. George Abbot (*q.v.*), 1611 ; tr. from London ; d. 1633.

77. William Laud (*q.v.*), 1633 ; tr. from London ; d. 1645.

78. William Juxon (*q.v.*), 1660; tr. from London: d. 1663.
79. Gilbert Sheldon (*q.v.*), 1663; tr. from London: d. 1677.
80. William Sancroft (*q.v.*), 1678; d. 1693.
81. John Tillotson (*q.v.*), 1691; d. 1694.
82. Thomas Tenison, 1695; tr. from Lincoln; Fellow of C.C.C., Cambridge, and a good parish priest there and in London; a critic of Hobbes and an anti-Roman controversialist; founded the first public library in London when he was Rector of St.-Martin-in-the-Fields; ministered to Monmouth and Nell Gwynne; he was a moderate Whig, and had a good influence over William III., but was out of favour with Anne; he strongly supported the Hanoverian succession, and was one of the founders of the S.P.G.; d. 1715.
83. William Wake (*q.v.*), 1716; tr. from Lincoln; d. 1737.
84. John Potter, 1737; tr. from Oxford; Fellow of Lincoln and Regius Professor of Divinity, Oxford; he was one of those who began the journey towards the archbishopric by being the archbishop's chaplain, and was an editor, classic, and patristic scholar; d. 1747.
85. Thomas Herring, 1747; tr. from York; D.D. of Cambridge and Fellow of C.C.C.; Archbishop of York during the '45, and a strong supporter of the Government, but a man of no great knowledge or abilities; d. 1757.
86. Matthew Hutton, 1757; tr. from York; of a Yorkshire family; Fellow of Christ's, Cambridge, and D.D.; succeeded Herring at Bangor, York, and Canterbury; d. 1758.
87. Thomas Secker, 1758; tr. from Oxford; originally a dissenter, and trained for the dissenting ministry, but after studying medicine went to Oxford and graduated at Exeter; he was chaplain to George II.; Bishop of Bristol and of Oxford, and Dean of St. Paul's; a careful, studious, moderate man; d. 1768.
88. The Honble. Frederick Cornwallis, 1768; tr. from Lichfield; a son of the fourth Lord Cornwallis; Fellow of Christ's, Cambridge, and D.D.; Dean of St. Paul's; a handsome and agreeable personage, but rebuked by George III. for intending to give a ball at Lambeth; d. 1783.
89. John Moore, 1783; tr. from Bangor; son of a Gloucestershire farmer; tutor to the young Churchills, and owing much to their patronage. He became Dean of Canterbury and Bishop of Bangor, and thence when Hurd and Lowth refused was made Archbishop of Canterbury; he was a supporter of all philanthropic effort and a friend of Wilberforce, and though he refused to consecrate Seabury, afterwards consecrated two bishops for America; d. 1805.
90. Charles Manners Sutton, 1805; tr. from Norwich; D.D. Emmanuel College, Cambridge; after serving several cures he was Dean of Peterborough, Bishop of Norwich, and Dean of Windsor, and intimate with the family of George III.; d. 1828.
91. William Howley (*q.v.*), 1828; tr. from London.
92. John Bird Sumner, 1848; tr. from Chester; Fellow of King's College, Cambridge; Canon of Durham; introduced to favour through his brother Charles, who was liked by George IV.; he was an Evangelical of piety and distinction and a Whig, though made Bishop of Chester by Peel; he supported Mr. Gorham (*q.v.*) against the Bishop of Exeter, and was at first 'wildly denunciatory' of the Oxford Movement; d. 1862.
93. Charles Thomas Longley, 1862; tr. from York; Student of Christ Church; Headmaster of Harrow; Bishop of Ripon, 1836; Durham, 1856; Archbishop of York, 1860; d. 1868.
94. Archibald Campbell Tait (*q.v.*), 1868; tr. from London; d. 1882.
95. Edward White Benson (*q.v.*), 1883; tr. from Truro; d. 1896.
96. Frederick Temple (*q.v.*), 1896; tr. from London; d. 1902.
97. Randall Thomas Davidson, 1903; tr. from Winchester; Dean of Windsor, 1883.

[W. H. H.]

Jenkins, *Dio. Hist.*; Stanley, *Memorials of Canterbury*; Le Neve, *Fasti*.

CARLISLE, See of, was founded by Henry I. in 1133 at the instigation of Thurstin, Archbishop of York, from whose diocese its territory was taken. It was conterminous with the land of Carlisle, which was added to England by William II. in 1092. It consisted of the portion of Cumberland north of the Derwent (except the parish of Alston) and the northern portion of Westmorland. It was enlarged in 1856, under an Order in Council of 10th August 1847, by the addition of the southern portions of Cumberland and Westmorland and that part of Lancashire called ' Lonsdale North of the Sands,' taken from the diocese of Chester (*q.v.*).

A priory of Regular Canons of St. Augustine, founded by Henry I. about 1123, and dedicated to the Blessed Virgin Mary, became the cathedral church (the only English cathedral held by this order), and so remained until the reign of Henry VIII. The surrender to the Crown took place on 9th January 1540. Out of the dissolved priory, by charter bearing date 8th May 1541, the King founded the cathedral church of the Holy and Undivided Trinity. and created a dean and four prebendaries or canons, under the name of the dean and chapter of the said church. The church was endowed with the property of the priory, with the addition of the revenues of the priory of Wetheral. At first the bishop and the priory held their property conjointly. The first division was made under the direction of the papal legate Gualo about 1216 : the final distribution was completed in 1249 in the time of Bishop Silvester. The temporalities of the see are given in the *Taxatio* of 1291 as £126, 7s. 7d. and the spiritualities as £22, 19s.; the *Valor Ecclesiasticus* gives the income as £541, 4s. 11½d. Ecton (1711) gives the value as £531, 4s. 9½d. The present income of the bishop is £4500. The see is divided into the archdeaconries of Carlisle (1133), Westmorland (1856), and Furness (1882). It has an acreage of 1,642,897 and a population of 401,280. A bishop suffragan of Barrow-in-Furness was appointed, 1899.

BISHOPS

1. Athelwold, 1133 ; the first prior of the Augustinian convent of Carlisle ; had been Prior of St. Oswald's, Nostell ; was witness in 1136 to the Charter of Liberties granted by Stephen ; d. 1156. A vacancy for nearly fifty years.
2. Bernard, 1204 ; Archbishop of Ragusa ; appointed by King John at the request of Innocent III.
3. Hugh, 1218 ; Abbot of Beaulieu in Hampshire ; appointed by the influence of the legate Gualo to coerce the rebellious canons ; deputed by Henry III. to arrange the marriage of Alexander II. of Scotland with Johanna, the King's sister ; d. at La Ferte in Burgundy, 1223.
4. Walter Malclerc, 1223 ; a diplomatist who held high offices in the State ; the great patron of the friars when they first came to England ; Henry III. gave him the manor of Dalston, 1230, the manor-house becoming Rose Castle, the

present episcopal residence ; res. 1246, and joined the Dominican order in Oxford, where he d. 1248.
5. Silvester de Everdon, 1247 ; Archdeacon of Chester ; much engaged in political matters ; one of the four prelates chosen in 1253 to confront Henry III. in defence of the liberties of the Church ; killed by a fall from his horse, 1254.
6. Thomas de Vipont, or Veteri-ponte, 1255 ; d. 1256.
7. Robert Chause, 1258 ; Archdeacon of Bath ; was engaged in continual lawsuits concerning questions arising in his diocese : d. 1278.
8. Robert Ireton, 1280 (P.) ; Prior of Gisburne ; was much employed by Edward I. in the affairs of Scotland ; a commissioner in 1290 to arrange for the marriage of Prince Edward with Margaret. the Maid of Norway ; commissioner in 1291 to adjust the claims to the crown of Scotland ; d. 1292.
9. John de Halton, 1292 ; Governor of Carlisle Castle in 1302 ; by commission of Pope Clement V. he excommunicated Robert Brus in Carlisle Cathedral in 1305 ; took a great part as diplomatist and soldier in the wars of that period ; was present in the Parliament held in Carlisle when the first antipapal statute was passed in January 1307 ; present at the great Council of Vienne in 1311 when the Order of the Templars was dissolved : d. 1324.
10. John Ross, 1325 (P.) ; Archdeacon of Salop : cited by the prior and convent of Carlisle in 1330 for seizing the profits of their churches : he excommunicated the prior ; d. 1332.
11. John Kirkby, 1332 (P.) ; Prior of Carlisle ; was a militant and quarrelsome bishop; much engaged in the Scottish wars ; he conveyed Joan, daughter of Edward III., betrothed to Peter of Castile, on her ill-fated journey in 1348 ; d. 1352.
12. Gilbert Welton, 1353 (P.) ; one of the commissioners to arrange the ransom of David II., King of Scots, in 1357 ; also later for acknowledging his sovereignty ; a warden of the Western Marches ; d. 1362.
13. Thomas Appleby, 1363 (P.) ; a warden of the Western Marches ; appointed in 1384, and from time to time, to treat of peace between Richard II. and Scotland and France ; d. 1395.
14. Robert Reed, or Reade, 1396 (P.) ; tr. from Waterford, and the same year tr. to Chichester.

15. Thomas Merks, Merke. or Sumestre, D.D., 1397 (P.); famous for the speech which he is said to have made in Parliament in defence of the deposed King, and which Shakespeare preserves in his play of *Richard II*. (iv. 1); tr. 1400, *ad ecclesiam de Samastonam in qua clerus seu populus Christianus non habetur* (P.R., 2 Hen. iv.); suffragan of Winchester, 1403-4; Rector of Sturminster Marshall, 1403; of Todenham, 1404; d. 1409.

16. William Strickland, 1400 (P.); did much for ecclesiastical architecture both in the cathedral and in rebuilding Rose Castle and its chapel; d. 1419.

17. Roger Whelpdale, D.D., 1420 (P.): a native of Cumberland; Provost of Queen's College, Oxford, to which, and to the University, he bequeathed some of his property; d. 1422 at Carlisle Place, London, and directed that he should be buried in the church of St. Paul.

18. William Barrowe, D.C.L., 1423; tr. (P.) from Bangor; Chancellor of the University of Oxford in 1413; a commissioner to arrange the truce with Scotland in 1429; d. 1429.

19. Marmaduke Lumley, LL.B., 1430 (P.); Archdeacon of Northumberland; tr. to Lincoln, 1450.

20. Nicholas Close, D.D., 1450 (P.); Chancellor of the University of Cambridge in 1450; tr. to Coventry and Lichfield, 1452.

21. William Percy, 1452 (P.); Chancellor of the University of Cambridge, 1451-5; d. 1462.

22. John Kingscote, 1462 (P.); had been a creditor of Edward iv. before his appointment; d. 1463.

23. Richard Scroope, 1464 (P.); Chancellor of the University of Cambridge in 1461; d. 1468.

24. Edward Story, D.D., 1468 (P.); Master of Michaelhouse, Cambridge; a commissioner to treat with Scotland in 1471; tr. to Chichester, 1478.

25. Richard Bell, 1478 (P.); Prior of Durham; res. 1495; d. 1496. A remarkable brass of the bishop in full pontificals is in the choir of the cathedral.

26. William Sever, 1496 (P.); Abbot of St. Mary's, York; a commissioner to arrange the truce with Scotland, 1497, and the marriage in 1502 of James iv. with Margaret, daughter of Henry vii.; tr. to Durham, 1502.

27. Roger Leyburn, or Leybourne, 1504 (P.); Master of Pembroke Hall, Cambridge, and Archdeacon of Durham; d. 1507.

28. John Penny, LL.D., 1509; tr. (P.) from Bangor; d. 1520; buried in St. Margaret's, Leicester.

29. John Kyte, or Kite, 1521; tr. (P.) from Armagh; sent by Henry vii. as ambassador to Spain; the friend and agent of Cardinal Wolsey; attended Henry viii. at the Field of the Cloth of Gold; made titular Archbishop of Thebes in Thessaly; took a strong position on the side of the King in the matter of the royal divorce; d. in London 1537; buried in Stepney Church, where there is a long inscription.

30. Robert Aldrich, D.D., 1537; Archdeacon of Colchester; chaplain to Queen Jane Seymour; one of the authors of the Bishops' Book, 1537; one of the two bishops who protested against the second Act of Uniformity; d. 1556; buried at Horncastle.

31. Owen Oglethorpe, D.D., 1557; Dean of Windsor; President of Magdalen College, Oxford; a disputant in 1554 with Cranmer, Latimer, and Ridley; crowned Queen Elizabeth, Canterbury being vacant and Heath of York having refused; dep. 1559 for refusing the oath of supremacy; d. the same year; buried in St. Dunstan's in the West, London.

32. John Best, B.D., 1561; had difficulties with the clergy of the diocese about the oath of allegiance; he termed them 'wicked imps of Antichrist,' 'ignorant, stubborn, past measure, false, and subtile'; d. 1570.

33. Richard Barnes, 1570; tr. from suffragan bishopric; held an important visitation of the diocese and of the cathedral, backed by the High Commission, in 1571; tr. to Durham, 1577.

34. John Meye, D.D., 1577; Master of Catherine Hall, Cambridge; Archdeacon of the East Riding; d. of the plague, 1598; buried in Carlisle.

35. Henry Robinson, D.D., 1598; a native of Carlisle; Provost of Queen's College, Oxford; d. of the plague in 1616, and was buried in Carlisle Cathedral, where there is a curious brass, similar to one at Queen's, to which college he was a benefactor.

36. Robert Snowden, D.D., 1616; preached before James i. on his visit to Carlisle in 1617; d. 1621.

37. Richard Milbourne, 1621; tr. from St. David's; a native of Cumberland; had been Dean of Rochester; d. 1624.

38. Richard Senhouse, D.D., 1624; chap-

lain to James I. and Dean of Gloucester ; preached the coronation sermon of Charles I. ; killed by a fall from his horse, 1626.

39. Francis White. D.D., 1626 ; Dean of Carlisle ; tr. to Norwich, 1629.

40. Barnabas Potter, D.D., 1629 ; Provost of Queen's College, Oxford ; d. 1642, and buried in London.

41. James Ussher (*q.v.*), 1642. See vacant until the Restoration.

42. Richard Sterne, D.D., 1660 ; Master of Jesus College, Cambridge ; ministered to Archbishop Laud (*q.v.*) on the scaffold ; tr. to York, 1664.

43. Edward Rainbow, D.D., 1664 ; Master of Magdalene College, Cambridge, and Dean of Peterborough ; d. 1684 ; buried at Dalston.

44. Thomas Smith, D.D., 1684 ; native of Asby, Westmorland ; Dean of Carlisle ; most generous in his gifts ; d. 1702 ; buried in the cathedral church.

45. William Nicolson, D.D., 1702-18 ; a native of Orton, Cumberland ; Archdeacon of Carlisle ; a distinguished man of letters and antiquary ; his controversy with Dean Atterbury (*q.v.*) resulted in the passing of the Act (6 Anne, c. 21) which established the validity of the statutes of the cathedrals of the New Foundation ; tr. to Derry in 1718 ; thence to Cashel ; d. 1727.

46. Samuel Bradford, D.D., 1718 ; Master of Corpus Christi College, Cambridge ; tr. to Rochester, 1723.

47. John Waugh, D.D., 1723 ; a native of Appleby; Dean of Gloucester ; d. 1734, and buried in London.

48. George Fleming, D.C.L., Bart., 1735 ; a native of Rydal, Westmorland ; Dean of Carlisle ; d. 1747 ; buried in the cathedral church.

49. Robert Osbaldeston, 1747 ; Dean of York ; tr. to London, 1762.

50. Charles Lyttelton, 1762 ; Dean of Exeter ; d. 1768 in London.

51. Edmund Law, D.D., 1769 ; a native of Cartmel, Lancashire ; Master of Peterhouse, Cambridge ; eminent in letters ; of his sons, one was Lord Ellenborough and two were bishops ; d. 1787, and buried in the cathedral church.

52. John Douglas, 1787 ; Dean of Windsor ; tr. to Salisbury, 1791.

53. Edward Venables Vernon, D.C.L., 1791 ; assumed the name of Harcourt ; tr. to York, 1807.

54. Samuel Goodenough, D.C.L., 1808 ; Dean of Rochester ; famous as a botanist ;

d. 1827 ; buried in Westminster Abbey.

55. Hugh Percy, D.D., 1827 ; tr. from Rochester ; Dean of Canterbury ; d. 1836.

56. Henry Montagu Villiers, D.D., 1856 ; tr. to Durham, 1860; a strong Evangelical.

57. Samuel Waldegrave, D.D., 1860 ; Fellow of All Souls, Oxford ; also a strong Evangelical ; d. 1869.

58. Harvey Goodwin, D.D., 1869 ; Dean of Ely ; d. 1891.

59. John Wareing Bardsley, D.D., 1892 ; tr. from Sodor and Man ; d. 1904.

60. John William Diggle, D.D., 1905.

[J. E. P.]

Bishops' registers, 1293-1386, 1561-1643, 1660 *seq.* ; Nicolson and Burn, *Hist. of Cumberland and Westmorland* ; Bishop Nicolson's MSS. in Dean and Chapter Library ; *Papal Letters*, R.S.

CAROLINE DIVINES, The. This name has been given to the theological writers of the seventeenth century who had been trained in the generation succeeding that of the Elizabethan Settlement of religion in England and looked at the theology and discipline of the Church from something like a common standing point. It is impossible to draw a strict line ; but roughly it may be said that the reign of Charles I. marks one period of their activity, while the second is that which is covered by the lifetime of his sons. Convenient dates are from 1625 to 1700. But the school which flourished in those three-quarters of a century, to which in its earlier stage was applied the famous eulogy, *clerus Angliae stupor mundi*, had its definite forerunners in the days of Elizabeth and James I. Some of the writers lived to a great age ; and some who were not actually Carolines in date were certainly of the same spirit.

The common bond which unites them is a consciousness that the Catholicity rather than the Protestantism was the decisive feature of the English Church. The separation from Rome had come because Roman pressure on English allegiance had become practically intolerable. It was a practical Reformation which had taken place. But, no less, the vigour of theological study, which in England took its inspiration and its tone from Erasmus rather than from Luther, had directed the attention of scholars to the divergence of mediæval teaching from the teaching of the Bible and the fathers of the primitive Church. There was a very strong spirit of Protestantism, which came to a climax under Elizabeth in the power possessed by Calvinism at the Universities and at Lambeth. But Universities have always been apt to be attracted by a system or a 'movement.' Theological freedom is rarely encouraged there. And archbishops, in a Church so undermanned in bishops as the English Church was, can rarely find time to be close students. Thus a reaction came rather from solitary scholars, who rose to high fame, than from men who were seated in positions of authority. They read the Bible and the Fathers for themselves, and then found that their theology was of a piece with what was ancient rather than with the modern. They could not submit to Rome until Rome ' was other than she is ' (as Laud (*q.v.*) said), but they found themselves widely separated from the 'new theology' of their day. The school which became prominent under James I. and for a time dominant under Charles I. started then from the Bible and from the definite statements of the existing English formularies, that the Church did not desire to dictate to churches abroad or to depart from them in matters where they followed ancient rule, and that the interpretation of Holy Scripture was to be in accordance with that of the ancient doctors. As regards organisation, the school as a whole believed in episcopacy being of the *bene esse* of the Church ; and much the larger part of it believed that it was even of the *esse*. The Caroline Divines may be said to trace their origin to (1) Hooker (*q.v.*), in his definite opposition to the Puritans' view that all rules of Government were laid down exactly in Holy Scripture ; (2) Bilson, 1546-1616, who declared that the English disagreement with Rome on the critical subject of the Holy Communion was ' only *de modo praesentiae*' ; (3) Andrewes (*q.v.*), who said that the English Church granted Christ to be truly present in the Eucharist and truly to be adored ; and (4) Overall (*q.v.*), who pointed out that the English Church no longer ' called them creatures of bread and wine' after consecration. Here was a position most clearly belonging rather to the old than to the new theology. And it was this which linked together the school of which Andrewes was perhaps most clearly the father and Laud the most prominent member. It is not proposed in this article to analyse the opinions of the theologians who will be named. On many points of detail and of expression they differed among themselves, but in the main principles of Church government and Church doctrine they were decidedly of one mind.

The following is a rough list of those who most influenced the reign of Charles I. : - Christopher Sutton, 1565-1629. Prebendary of Westminster ; famous for his *Disce Mori* (1600) and *Disce Vivere* (1608), and for his *Godly Meditations upon the most Holy Sacrament* (1613)—all three constantly reprinted during the seventeenth century, and revived in the nineteenth. William Laud, 1573-1645. Archbishop of Canterbury, the disciple of Andrewes and editor of his sermons, who carried out his principles, theological, practical, and ceremonial, in his work as dean, bishop, and primate. Richard Mountague, 1577-1641, who added to the sacramental doctrine a Catholic view of the Communion of Saints and a powerful anti-Calvinist attack. Thomas Jackson, 1579-1640, President of Corpus Christi College, Oxford, and Dean of Peterborough, who was bitterly attacked by Prynne. Originally a Puritan, his theological studies led him to a definitely Catholic position. William Forbes, 1585 - 1634, Bishop of Edinburgh, whose *Considerationes Modestae* shows a thorough understanding of ancient theology and of the harmony of Anglican formularies with it. George Herbert (*q.v.*), 1593-1640, who was the poet of the school as well as its typical country parson. Both in poetry and prose he taught high sacramental doctrine. He was ordained by Archbishop Laud, and no doubt was greatly influenced by him. In connection with Herbert it is natural to mention Nicholas Ferrar (*q.v.*), 1592-1637, who, though he was not strictly a divine, was the founder of the ' Arminian nunnery' at Little Gidding, which ruled its life by the formularies of the English Church and the theology of the Laudian school. John Bramhall, 1594-1663, who was Strafford's chaplain in Ireland, became Bishop of Derry, 1633, and Archbishop of Armagh at the Restoration ; he was especially emphatic on the identity of the English Church before and after the Restoration. John Cosin (*q.v.*), 1594-1672, who belonged to the school in its later as well as its earlier period. In 1627, at the request of Charles I., he drew up for the ladies of the court a book of Private Devotions (1627), which followed the ancient models. This beautiful volume, preceded as it was by Bailey's *Practice of Piety*, originally dedicated to Charles I. when he was Prince of Wales, set the tone for Anglican devotion, and encouraged it to proceed on ancient models, for centuries. Its devotions for the seven hours of prayer were followed by Dr. Richard Sherlock in the *Practical Christian* and observed by the holy Bishop Thomas Wilson (*q.v.*). Editions appeared throughout the seventeenth century, a tenth in 1719, and in 1838 an eleventh—another link between the Carolines and the Tractarians. As Prebendary of Durham and Rector of Brancepeth he introduced ceremonial suggesting pre-Reformation usage, and again as Master of Peterhouse, Cambridge. Cosin's works, especially his *History of Papal Transubstantiation*, mark the Anglican position very clearly. He saw that in many respects the English Church agreed much more with the doctrines of the Romanists than with the foreign Protestants; and yet he was not prepared to 'unchurch' the latter, as Laud was and most of those who thought with him. Herbert Thorndike, 1598-1672, was a thorough English Catholic, but he was a convinced supporter of the Reformation in England as a Catholic movement, as in his *Reformation of the Church of England better than that of the Council of Trent* (1670). He was a learned scholar and a student of liturgies, and he advocated many doctrinal and liturgical principles which were by no means generally accepted in his day, or later. Henry Hammond, 1605-60, whom Keble so nobly commemorated, was another of the Laudian school, but tolerant rather than polemical. The divines of the later Caroline age were such as Anthony Sparrow, 1612-85, who became Bishop first of Exeter and then of Norwich after the Restoration, and was another liturgiologist. His very important *Rationale* of the Book of Common Prayer (1657) explains and illustrates the Prayer Book from Catholic sources, and was reprinted by Newman (*q.v.*) in 1837. But a greater name than any of these is that of Jeremy Taylor (*q.v.*), 1613-67, who may be said to have gloried in the English Church, and was the most notable of all the influences which turned men's minds the Anglo-Catholic way. He was a thorough priest, as well as a great man of letters. His *Worthy Communicant* (1660), side by side with his *Holy Living* (1650) and *Holy Dying* (1651), show him to have thoroughly assimilated the wide Catholicism of Laud. 'Tradition, authority, faith, liberality, were harmonious, not contending, in his mind.' He is perhaps the last of the Carolines who decisively belongs to the period before the wars. Others who survived them were not so conspicuously of Laud's school; for example, John Gauden (*q.v.*); and Isaac Barrow (*q.v.*), who, without being clearly a Latitudinarian, was notably a Laudian. Daniel Brevint, 1616-95, was another scholar whose sympathies lay more with Protestants, and whose *Missale Romanum, or the Depth and Mystery of*

the Roman Mass, and the *Christian Sacrament and Sacrifice* (1673), do not place him clearly with this school. But Sheldon (*q.v.*) and Sancroft (*q.v.*), the one a practical man, the other a trained theologian, were both conspicuously anti-Calvinist, and were followers of the doctrine and discipline of the Laudian school. The Church of the Restoration took tone from them, but remained conspicuously anti-Roman, and vindicated its position under James II. Among the later Caroline Divines conspicuous figures are John Pearson (*q.v.*), 1613-86, Bishop of Chester, whose *Exposition of the Creed* is a work of massive learning, and who splendidly defended the Church against Puritans and Romanists. He has been considered the greatest English theologian of the seventeenth century, though Ussher (*q.v.*) has by some been placed beside him. Both stand rather apart from the main course of the Caroline Divines. Thus, similarly, we do not include among them the Latitudinarians, such as Wilkins and Burnet (*q.v.*), or the Cambridge Platonists (*q.v.*). We may conclude rather with Thomas Ken (*q.v.*), 1637-1711, most conspicuously a Catholic Churchman, and John Johnson, 1662-1725, the author of the *Unbloody Sacrifice*, who definitely teaches the Real Presence and Sacrifice in the Eucharist.

Great as were the services which the Caroline Divines (of whom but a few conspicuous names have here been recorded) rendered to English theology, their services to English literature were almost as great. Taylor made the riches of Elizabethan style the property of religion, and the post-Restoration theologians led the way to the simplicity of later times.

It should be added that so soon as Romanism under Charles II. began to be aggressive in England, and when the negotiations for reunion, which were at least broached during the Cabal Ministry (when Rome seems to have been willing to accept the Prayer Book and a married clergy), broke down, and were replaced by the bitterness of the Popish Plot and the determined efforts of James II. to re-establish Romanists in power, English theology became again deeply tinged with anti-Roman opinions. It is impossible, however, to say that the change is more than one of emphasis.   [W. H. H.]

The works of the chief divines were republished in the Library of Anglo-Catholic Theology; see also *Cam. Hist. Eng. Lit.*, Vol. VII. chap. vi.

CARTWRIGHT, Thomas (1535 ?-1603), Puritan divine, was born in Hertfordshire about 1535, and matriculated as a sizar of Clare Hall, Cambridge, in 1547. During Mary's reign he served as a lawyer's clerk, and on the accession of Elizabeth returned to Cambridge as Minor Fellow of Trinity. He held in rapid succession a Fellowship at St. John's, the Junior Deanship of that college, a Major Fellowship at Trinity, and in 1564 a Senior Fellowship, thus becoming one of the governing body. He was a hard student and a very popular preacher, but aroused so much opposition by his radical ideas that he went to Ireland in 1565 as chaplain to his friend Loftus, just made Archbishop of Dublin, who tried to get for him the see of Armagh. In 1567 he was back at Cambridge, proceeded B.D., and was elected by his triumphant friends Lady Margaret Professor in 1569. His lectures on Church government, however, heightened the old opposition to him, and after a long struggle between his party and that of Whitgift (*q.v.*) Elizabeth made Whitgift vicechancellor, and gave him the support of the State. Cartwright was at once deprived of his professorship, and went to Geneva, returning to England in 1572, only to get into further trouble. He visited Field and Wilcox, two Puritans, then in gaol for writing the *Admonition to the Parliament*, and published a *Second Admonition* supporting them. Whitgift published an elaborate answer to this, and a long controversy ensued, ended by a proclamation ordering the suppression of Cartwright's tomes, and by a warrant of the ecclesiastical commissioners for his arrest. He left England, sojourned for a time at Heidelberg, and finally became minister of the English congregation at Antwerp and Middleburgh. He translated Travers's (*q.v.*) books on Church discipline and wrote on the subject himself, and married (1577) the sister of John Stubbe, who was later convicted of seditious writing. In 1585 Leicester and Burghley aided his return to England.

He came back to join his Puritanical brethren, many of whom were his former pupils and associates, in setting up in England Presbyterianism as outlined in his own and Travers's books. A beginning had already been made. Small conferences of ministers existed in Essex, Suffolk, and Northamptonshire, and thus actually formed the first rank of the hierarchy which Cartwright believed was the form of Church government divinely ordained by Christ. To knit these small assemblies of ministers together; to form provincial and national synods; to prepare and secure the acceptance of a book of discipline which should be more than a theoretical

phantasy—this was his great scheme. Exactly how this was accomplished we do not know, but it was certainly well under weigh by 1587. To induce the State to impose this scheme upon the Church they had petitioned freely, and even offered a draft of the scheme to the House of Commons. To make the bishops ridiculous, and thus show their inefficiency to govern, the Marprelate Tracts (*q.v.*) were issued. That State or Church should countenance such doings was not to be expected, but so cleverly did Cartwright handle the movement that, when he and some of the leaders were arrested in 1590, neither the High Commission (*q.v.*) nor the Star Chamber could prove their guilt. That they were guilty in all but formal law is clear; and the posturing of Cartwright before the High Commission, his letters, petitions, and protestations, filled with a casuistry worthy of a Jesuit, cannot longer be credited against the actual record of the Dedham classis. The inability of the lawyers to produce conclusive evidence and the influence of Burghley set Cartwright free in 1592. Shortly after he was allowed to preach, and went with Lord Zouch to the Channel Islands, keeping in touch with the members of the party, who were planning to renew the attempt to establish the discipline on Elizabeth's death. In March 1603 Cartwright was once more in London in the Puritan conference, drawing up the Millenary Petition with the other brethren. The success of this document started a campaign of petitions and meetings, in which Cartwright had a prominent part, but one which cannot now be separated from the work of the other leaders. In particular he wrote letters asking for support from his old friends among the statesmen and gentry. He was to have argued at the Hampton Court Conference (*q.v.*), and doubtless he would have been spokesman. He died, however, 27th December 1603, in the midst of the final preparations. His loss to his party was irreparable. He was unquestionably the most notable Puritan of his generation, and perhaps the most learned and cultured man the sect has ever produced.   [R. G. U.]

Cooper, *Athenae Cantabrigienses*, ii. ; 'The Minute-Book of the Dedham Classis' printed in Usher's *Presbyterian Movement*, etc., C.S., 1905 ; Usher, *Reconstruction of the Eng. Ch.*, i. 290-312 ; Strype, *Life of Whitgift*.

CARTWRIGHT, Thomas (1634-89). Bishop of Chester, son of a schoolmaster, and grandson of the famous Puritan, Thomas Cartwright (*q.v.*), entered at Oxford under the Commonwealth, became tabardar and then chaplain of Queen's College, his tutor being Thomas Tully, afterwards Principal of St. Edmund Hall and Dean of Ripon, in which latter post Cartwright succeeded him in 1675. Notwithstanding his Puritan training, Cartwright sought ordination from the Bishop of Oxford under the Commonwealth, and became ' a very forward and confident preacher.' At the Restoration he came out as an ardent Royalist, and preferments were showered upon him, ending with the see of Chester, in 1686. He had for long been much attached to James II., who esteemed him highly. His appointment to Chester was much disliked, both Archbishop Sancroft (*q.v.*) and Jeffreys opposing it. An accident at his consecration (Archbishop Sancroft fell while communicating the people) was ill-omened. From his *Diary* Cartwright appears to have been a hard-working bishop, entertaining freely, preaching and celebrating frequently, keeping careful record of his confirmations and ordinations. He was in frequent communication with Roman Catholics in England, and attended as a spectator the consecration of a bishop at St. James's Chapel, 1st May 1687. His devotion to James II. and his unbounded belief in Divine Right led Cartwright to assist the King in his unconstitutional acts. He became a member of the Ecclesiastical Commission, 1687, and conducted the famous Visitation of Magdalen College, Oxford. In 1688 he strongly favoured the Declaration for Liberty of Conscience, and opposed the Seven Bishops (*q.v.*). He became so unpopular that he followed James II. to St. Germains, December 1688, and accompanied him to Ireland; and there he died of dysentery, 15th April 1689, and was buried with great ceremony in Christ Church, Dublin. Friendly to Roman Catholics as Cartwright was (at Chester he endeavoured to secure for them a chapel in the city), he never wavered in his churchmanship. He died, having ' taken the Blessed Sacrament and the Church's absolution,' and on his death-bed in Dublin, when two Roman Catholic clergy urged upon him that ' there was but one God, one Church,' the bishop replied, 'somewhat short': ' I know all this as well as you, but I am not able to answer you for the failing of my spirits, and therefore I desire you to forbear talking with me any more about this, for I have done already what, I hope, is necessary for my salvation.' Though neither as learned, ascetic, nor devout as the foremost Caroline divines, Cartwright seems to have in no way merited the attacks of Whig historians—Burnet, Mackintosh, and Macaulay. Portraits of Cartwright exist in the Provost's Lodgings, Queen's College, Oxford, and the National Portrait Gallery.   [S. L. O.]

Diary, C.S.; Wood, *Ath. Oxon.*; Perry in *D.N.B.*

CEDD, or **CEDDA, St.** (d. 664), Bishop of the East Saxons, an Angle of Northumbria, was, like his younger brother Chad (*q.v.*), brought up at Lindisfarne under Aidan, and acquired a great reputation for sanctity and learning. In 653 Peada, overlord of the Middle Angles, asked Oswy (*q.v.*) King of Northumbria, to send four priests to assist in the conversion of his subjects. Cedd came with them then, and the mission seems to have been most successful. Their preaching was listened to eagerly, multitudes were baptized, and even the heathen Penda let them preach in his kingdom. Cedd was, however, recalled in the same year by Oswy, and sent to preach in the country of Sigebehrt, King of the East Saxons. His preaching was again successful, and in the following year he was consecrated Bishop of the East Saxons by Finan. Many churches were built and clergy ordained, and before long the East Saxons became Christians. He built two monasteries, one at Ithanchester, near Malden, and one at West Tilbury, where the severe discipline of Lindisfarne was practised. When Sigebehrt went to a feast at the house of a thegn who was living in sin Cedd refused to pardon him. ' Because thou hast not refrained from visiting that lost and accursed man, thou wilt have death in thine own house.' Sigebehrt was soon afterwards murdered—a fulfilment, as every one thought, of the prophecy. His successor was baptized by Cedd before he was allowed to ascend the throne. Cedd also founded a monastery at Lastingham, near Pontefract. He was present at the synod of Whitby, and gave his assent to the Catholic custom of keeping Easter. He seems to have gone thence to Lastingham, and to have sickened of the plague, and died there on 26th October. He was buried at Lastingham, and thirty of his monks who came from Ithanchester that they might live or die near his body caught the infection and, with the exception of one lad, died of the plague.

He has been placed second to Mellitus (*q.v.*) in the list of the bishops of London, but Bede (*q.v.*) never speaks of him under that title, but only as Bishop of the East Saxons. The city may have been independent of the East Saxons at the time, or Cedd may have preferred, like most Scotic bishops, to fix his seat in a remote part of the country away from London.

After the death of his brother Chad an Anglican inmate of an Irish monastery professed to have seen in a vision the soul of Cedd descending from heaven in the midst of angels to conduct Chad's soul back to the celestial country. [C. P. S. C.]

Bede, *H. E.*; *D. N. B.*

CHAD, or CEADDA, St. (d. 672), was a Northumbrian. He and his three brothers, Cedd (*q.v.*), Cymbill, and Caelin, were all ordained priests, and he and Cedd became bishops. In 664 he succeeded Cedd, Bishop of the East Saxons, as Abbot of Lastingham. In the same year Wilfrid (*q.v.*) was elected Bishop of Northumbria, and went to Gaul to be consecrated, but stayed there so long that Oswy (*q.v.*), King of Northumbria, became impatient, and determined to make Chad bishop instead. He went to Canterbury for consecration, but found the see vacant by the death of Deusdedit, and went on to Wessex, where he was consecrated by Wini, Bishop of Winchester, and two British bishops. He ruled the see of Northumbria nobly, according to Bede (*q.v.*), for those years, and was distinguished for his piety and devotion, travelling always on foot. In 669 Archbishop Theodore (*q.v.*) declared his consecration invalid. Chad meekly submitted, and retired to Lastingham, but in the same year was sent to be Bishop of the Mercians, and fixed his see at Lichfield (*q.v.*), where he built a church to eastward of the present cathedral, and dedicated it to St. Mary. He built a house near the cathedral for himself and seven or eight brethren. Their life was apostolic and devoted to prayer, study, and the ministry of the Word. He also founded a monastery at Barrow in Lincolnshire. He still made his journeys on foot, though on one occasion Archbishop Theodore is said to have made him ride, and helped him on to his horse with his own hand. After two years and a half a pestilence visited his neighbourhood, and several of his clergy died. Seven days before his own death he sent for a disciple, and told him that he had been warned by the song of angels of his approaching end, and with great joy bade him ' go back to the church and tell the brethren to commend by their prayers my departure to God.' He died seven days afterwards, on 2nd March 672, a day which is still marked in the calendar of the English Church. His reputation for saintliness was so great that numbers visited his tomb, and many miracles were said to have been wrought at it. 'The things,' says Bede, ' which he had learned from Scripture, these he diligently sought to do.' He soon became one of the most popular English saints. A copy of the gospels which is said to have belonged to him is preserved at Lichfield. Over forty churches are dedicated under his name, including Lichfield Cathedral, dedicated to St. Mary and St. Chad. [C. P. S. C.]

Bede, *H. E.*; *D. N. B.*

CHAPTERS, Cathedral. The cathedrals of the English Church are distinguished as those of the Old and of the New Foundation, the two classes having been during the Middle Ages under the direction of members of the secular and regular clergy respectively, till the government of the latter was reconstituted at the opening of the Reformation. The former were ruled in early times by the bishops, with the services of a body of clergy who were entirely under their control. These, however, gradually gained a more independent status, and before the Conquest some division of the estates belonging to the see had commonly been effected in their interest. This change was carried further soon afterwards, when the organisation of the cathedral chapters was completed on the model, as it seems, of Bayeux by Norman prelates. Those of York, Lincoln, and Salisbury were first formed on the same lines, and then Chichester, Exeter, Hereford, Lichfield, St. Paul's, and Wells followed at no long interval for the most part on the same lines, together with the churches of the Welsh bishoprics, Bangor, St. Asaph, St. David's, and Llandaff, though without deans in the last two cases and with exceptional features here and there. The dean, whose title was borrowed from convents of the Benedictine rule, became the head of the governing body in the cathedral ; the precentor regulated the musical services ; the chancellor regulated the schools of the city or even of the diocese, and dealt with official acts and correspondence ; while the treasurer, with sacristans under him, had the care of the precious vessels, relics, and vestments, and the supplies of wine and tapers. A varying number of canons completed the official staff.

The bishop by his own gift, or leading laymen of the diocese, sometimes perhaps through his influence, provided further endowments for the general uses of the governing body, as also for the formation of separate prebends. Each canon, so called at first from his official status, or obligations under the rule of Chrodegang of Metz, received his share of the general fund, usually in the early form of daily commons of bread and beer while in actual residence ; as prebendary he had the exclusive right to the income of a manor or a landed estate. When serving the church of his prebend, or engaged, as might be, in one of the offices of the State, his place was taken in the services of the cathedral by his vicar-choral, appointed at first by the prebendary himself and subject only to him, but included afterwards in a regular body recognised by the chapter, which acquired in course of time separate estates, and in the fourteenth century a definite status regulated by royal charter. The numerous chantries which were founded were for the most part divided among the vicars, and the monopoly of interment within the Close provided further work and emoluments for their support. A grammar school required by canon law for each cathedral to be under the chancellor's care, together with a song school for a few choristers under the succentor or deputy of the precentor, together with an organist, vergers, and sextons, completed the foundation. [EDUCATION.]

The dean and chapter acted together as the ordinary for the church; the dean being the chairman and executive officer was elected by the canons and presented to the bishop for his sanction.

The bishop had relinquished all direct control over the chapter, but claimed visitatorial powers, which were frequently contested by appeals to Rome, but finally were secured in all cases, though with some formal limitations, except at Hereford, which maintained its independence in this respect up to the Reformation.

As time went on fewer of the canons continued to reside; many canonical houses were vacant and gradually disappeared; and by a series of changes in the fourteenth and fifteenth centuries a limited number of residentiary canons ousted from power and share of the general fund all the other prebendaries, fixing their own number and term of residence, and practically co-opting to the places that fell vacant. The acceptance of this change by the dispossessed canons has never been adequately explained, for the chapter act books of that early period have either disappeared or not given up their secrets. No royal sanction was procured, and several popes, it is known, expressed disapproval of the changes. Remonstrances were urged at Hereford, but without result.

In 1840, after long inquiry by the Cathedral Commissioners [COMMISSIONS, ROYAL], the number of residentiary canons was limited by 3-4 Vic. c. 113 in each case, and a definite income of varying amount was provided for the dean. All the separate estates of the dignitaries and prebendaries, together with the incomes of the suspended canonries, were taken as they became vacant to swell the general fund of the Ecclesiastical Commissioners.

In what are called the cathedrals of the New Foundation a monastic community had till the Reformation the practical control, subject to the authority of the bishop, who was nominally the abbot, while the prior actually ruled. This was an arrangement almost peculiar to England. It was not commonly so harmonious as were the relations between the bishop and the chapter of the other class. The monks, relying on their influence at Rome, resented all the attempts of their ecclesiastical superior to interfere with the dignity or the interests which they prized. The monks of Canterbury were engaged for long years in bitter feud with Archbishops Baldwin and Hubert, and ultimately wrecked by their narrow jealousies the schemes of educational progress. The strife at Durham between Bishop Bek and his convent was also extremely bitter.

After the Dissolution of the Monasteries (*q.v.*) it was necessary to make provision for the maintenance and ministries of the cathedrals to which religious bodies had been attached, and it was proposed also to establish more bishoprics and cathedral churches. In pursuance of the power granted by 31 Hen. VIII. c. 9 the King placed secular canons in place of the monks who had been ejected, and the bodies thus regulated are called the deans and chapters of the New Foundation; such are Canterbury, Winchester, Worcester, Ely, Carlisle, Durham, Rochester, and Norwich. Besides these he constituted five more cathedrals, and endowed them out of the estates of dissolved monasteries, viz. Chester, Peterborough, Oxford, Gloucester, and Bristol. Westminster (*q.v.*) was also made an episcopal see, but this was again altered, and it became a collegiate church under Queen Elizabeth.

In the new chapters a dean took the place of the prior of the religious house which had been dissolved, and a limited number of canons was provided to act with him on the model of the older chapters, but with larger powers commonly for the dean as ordinary. In 1707, doubts having arisen as to the validity of the statutes of cathedrals of the New Foundation, they were confirmed by Act of Parliament (6 An. c. 75, commonly cited as c. 21).

The Act of 1840 founded a new institution of honorary canonries as distinctions to be bestowed upon deserving clergymen, to be entitled to stalls and take rank next after the canons, without emolument or other place in the chapter. These were to be twenty-four in number in the cathedrals of the New Foundation, where they are called canons; while in the others the term prebendary is used, and the number is determined by the ancient custom.

For the Welsh chapters a special Act was passed (1844, 7-8 Vic. c. 77) by which the provisions of the earlier Act were to extend to Bangor and St. Asaph. [See also separate articles for each SEE.]   [W. W. C.]

Phillimore, *Eccl. Law*; *Essays on Cathedrals*, ed. Dean Howson (art. by E. A. Freeman); *Epistolae Cantuarienses*, introd. by W. Stubbs.

CHARLES I. (1600-49), King of Great Britain and Ireland, and martyr, the only person formally canonised by the English Church since the Reformation, was born at Dunfermline, and did not come to England till 1604. He was a delicate child, and only gradually grew strong and athletic, becoming a good rider, as well as interested in books, particularly theology and plays, in music and in painting. On the death of his brother Henry in 1612 he came more prominently into public life. After a boyish quarrel in 1618 he became a great friend of his father's friend, George Villiers, Duke of Buckingham, to whom he remained attached till his murder in 1628. In 1623 they went to Madrid (taking full provision for the performance of the English Church services in a private chapel) with a view to negotiate a marriage with the sister of Philip IV. The obdurate demands of the Spaniards for the recognition of Romanism in England caused the negotiations to break down, and Charles married Henrietta Maria, daughter of Henry IV. of France, on 1st May 1625 (by proxy). On 27th March he had become King by the death of his father. From the first he was in difficulties with his Parliament, largely through the policy of Buckingham, and partly through the attack of the Commons on Richard Montague, an anti-Calvinist writer, whom Charles made his chaplain. Parliament met again in 1628, and in the Petition of Right condemned a number of illegal or unconstitutional practices, and accused Bishops Laud (*q.v.*) and Neile of favouring popery. Charles gave his special favour to Montague and Mainwaring (who had published sermons in which he declared that those who did not pay sums demanded by the Crown should receive damnation, i.e. in modern language, condemnation), and translated Laud to the see of London. In 1629 Parliament was dissolved, and a period

of personal government began. Money was obtained in many unusual ways. 'Obsolete laws were revived,' says Clarendon, 'and rigorously executed,' and 'unjust projects of all kinds, many ridiculous, many scandalous, all very grievous, were set on foot.' Year by year the Government in consequence became more and more unpopular. Charles was now advised by Thomas Wentworth (afterwards Earl of Strafford) and Laud, the former an advocate of benevolent despotism, the other tolerant towards liberty of opinion within the Church, but anxious to enforce the formularies to which she was committed. Church preferment was given according to a list of names supplied by Laud, in which the O (Orthodox) were distinguished from the P (Puritan) among the clergy. In 1633 Wentworth was made Lord Deputy of Ireland and Laud Archbishop of Canterbury.

In 1634 the King endeavoured to raise a sum of money, primarily for a fleet to keep off pirates, by 'ship money,' from maritime shires and London, which in the next year he ordered to be exacted also from inland counties. In 1637 in Hampden's case the judges (except Coke and Hutton) gave judgment in favour of the Crown in regard to the legality of this. Meantime the Star Chamber was active in suppressing libels against the King, Queen, and bishops (cases of Prynne, Burton, and Bastwick): the severe punishments were attributed by the Puritans to Laud. In 1637-8 the attempt to introduce a liturgy into Scotland caused riots in Edinburgh, the signing of a Solemn League and Covenant to resist innovations, and a revolution took place. In 1639 Charles went to York, but failed to gather an army strong enough to coerce the Scots. In 1640 the Scots entered England, and he was obliged to yield. On 13th April the Short Parliament met, and it was dissolved on 5th May because it would not grant supplies before the redress of grievances. Charles summoned, by the advice of Wentworth and Laud, a Parliament, which met on 3rd November 1640. At the beginning of 1641 the Commons ordered that 'commissions be sent into all counties for the defacing, demolishing, and quite taking away of all images, altars, or tables turned altar-wise, crucifixes, superstitious pictures, monuments, and reliques of idolatry, out of all churches or chapels.' On 11th November 1640 Strafford was impeached: on 18th December Laud. The trial of the former failing, a Bill of Attainder was brought in, which was passed on 7th May by the Lords, and Charles on 10th May gave his assent. Bishop Williams (*q.v.*) had advised him that his ' public conscience ' might do what his personal conscience forbade, but he was probably most influenced by the riot in London which threatened the Queen's life. From that moment the whole fabric of presonal government was broken down. Charles made an ineffectual visit to Scotland. A rebellion (largely due to dread of Puritanism) broke out in Ireland. The Grand Remonstrance, against all the King's policy in recent years, was passed (22nd November 1641). On 4th January 1642 Charles made matters much worse by endeavouring to arrest five members who were opposed to him. During the next three months the chief dispute was on the control of the militia, which the Parliament wished to secure for itself.

On 8th April Charles issued from York a declaration against the demands and conduct of Parliament. and on 23rd August he set up his standard at Nottingham. On 23rd October he fought an indecisive battle at Edgehill. Throughout the war which followed he showed considerable military capacity, and though not successful in his object at Newbury (20th September 1643), he won the fight at Cropredy Bridge (29th June) and secured the capitulation of Essex at Lostwithiel (12th September). In 1643 at Oxford and in 1645 at Uxbridge negotiations were entered into, which broke down because Charles was determined to preserve episcopacy, while the Scots, who now controlled the policy of Parliament. were determined on its destruction. Charles was willing, on the advice of his chaplains. to grant toleration. but he said: ' Let my condition be never so low, I resolve by the grace of God never to yield up this Church to the government of Papists, Presbyterians, or Independents.' On 22nd February 1645 the negotiations were broken off. On 9th May Charles left Oxford. on 15th May relieved Chester. on 1st June took Lancaster. but on 14th June he was totally defeated at Naseby, and all hope of success in the war was at an end, and the King found himself face to face with the Independents as the dominant party among his opponents. He returned to Oxford. 6th November, and remained there with failing fortunes till 5th May 1646. when he gave himself up to the Scots. ' Then came months of difficult negotiation. The King was willing to allow the establishment of Presbyterianism, for a time, and the suppression of the Independents, in whom men like Baxter as well as the Scots already saw their most dangerous foes ; but he insisted on the maintenance of some at least of the sees,

as a security for freedom of Church worship and for the continuance of apostolic succession.' Charles. in the course of negotiations at Newcastle with Alexander Henderson. applied to Juxon (*q.v.*). Bishop of London. to advise him as to how far he might allow the temporary cession of episcopacy. ' which absolutely to do is so directly against my conscience that by the grace of God no misery shall ever make me.' Juxon and Brian Duppa, Bishop of Salisbury. agreed that a temporary compliance might be justified, and the King offered to accept the establishment of Presbyterianism for three years, after which a ' regulated episcopacy ' was to return. ' How can we expect God's blessing if we relinquish His Church ? ' said the King when he was pressed to further concession. On 30th January 1647 he was delivered up by the Scots, and remained at Holmby House, where he again agreed to the establishment of Presbyterianism for three years. On 3rd June. seized by Joyce on behalf of the army, he was removed from Holmby, and after moving about was taken to Hampton Court. There the ' Heads of Proposals ' put to him by the army included the abolition of ' all coercive powers, authority. and jurisdiction of bishops, and all other ecclesiastical officials whatsoever, extending to any civil penalties upon any.' Charles preferred this to the proposal of Parliament that Presbyterianism should be established. with no toleration for the use of the Common Prayer ; but he arrived at no definite settlement with the army. On 11th November he escaped to Carisbrooke Castle, where he soon became a strict prisoner. On 26th December he signed a secret treaty with the Scots, agreeing to the establishment of Presbyterianism in England for three years and the suppression of the other sects ; but the second Civil War failed, and after a new attempt at settlement (the treaty of Newport, 18th September) had come to nothing because the King refused entirely to abandon episcopacy, he was again seized by the army, imprisoned in Hurst Castle. 4th December ; moved to Windsor, 19th December : and brought to trial at Whitehall, 19th January 1649.

He refused to plead before an illegal tribunal, but was sentenced to death on 27th January, and executed on 30th January in front of Whitehall. He was attended during his last hours by Juxon. who confessed and absolved him at Whitehall. ' There they permitted him and the Bishop to be alone for some time, and the Bishop had prepared all things in order to his receiving the Sacrament ; and, whilst he was at his private devotions, Nye and some other bold-faced ministers knockt at his door . . . to offer their services to pray with the King. [But he said]: "They that have so often prayed against me shall never pray with me in this agony." When he had received the Eucharist he rose up from his knees with a cheerful and steddy countenance. . . . They at Whitehall had prepared two or three dishes of meat for him to dine upon, but he refused to eat anything . . . resolved to touch nothing after the Sacrament. But the Bishop let him know how long he had fasted . . . and how some fit of fainting might take him upon the scaffold . . . which prevailed with him to eat halfe a manchet of bread and drinke a glass of wine ' (Sir Philip Warwick's *Memoires of the Raigne of King Charles I.*). He went boldly to the scaffold, and in his last speech said : ' For the people ; and truly I desire their liberty and freedom as much as anybody whosoever ; but I must tell you that their liberty and freedom consists in having of government those laws by which their life and their goods may be most their own. It is not having share in government, sirs ; that is nothing pertaining to them.' He was buried in St. George's Chapel at Windsor by Juxon, but permission to use the Prayer Book service was refused.

Charles undoubtedly died because he would not abandon the Church, and this was formally recognised at the Restoration. On 25th January 1661 it was ordered that 30th January should be kept as a public fast, and a form of prayer was drawn up by Bishop Duppa. This contained a prayer that by ' a careful, studious imitation of this Thy blessed saint and martyr, and all other Thy saints and martyrs that have gone before us, we may be made worthy to receive benefit by their prayers, which they, in communion with the Church Catholic, offer up unto Thee for that part of it here militant.'

The form of prayer, after revision, was issued by the authority of both Convocations, annexed by the authority of the Crown to the Prayer Book, and sanctioned by Parliament in 12 Car. II. c. 14. Royal proclamation at the beginning of each reign ordered its use, but in 1859 it was withdrawn from the Prayer Book by Royal Warrant. In the Calendar ' King Charles, Martyr ' was inserted on 30th January, and no action has ever been taken by Crown, Convocation, or Parliament to remove the words, though the printers have omitted them.

Charles was thus formally canonised by the Church of England. Sermons were preached annually in his memory, often reaching a high pitch of devout eulogy. Churches were dedicated to his memory (Arnold Forster, *Studies in Church Dedications*, ii. 346-8). Keble's (*q.v.*) poem in the *Christian Year* is well known, and in a sermon he declared that ' it is as natural that the Church of England should keep this day as it is that Christ's Universal Church should keep St. Stephen's martyrdom.' And Bishop Creighton (*q.v.*) in 1895 said that by his death Charles saved the Church of England for the future. [EIKON BASILIKE.] [W. H. H.]

King Charles's Works, 1661 : S. R. Gardiner in *D.N.B.* : Hutton, *Hist. of Eng. Ch.*, 1625-1714.

CHEKE, Sir John (1514-57), one of the most learned men of the sixteenth century, famous as the chief patron of Greek learning in England, commemorated as such by Milton in a sonnet, a considerable writer and translator, and tutor of Edward VI. A Cambridge man by birth, he entered St. John's, where he gained renown as a classic. He was one of the many Cambridge men who espoused Reformation doctrines, and probably had great influence upon the development of William Cecil, afterwards Lord Burghley. He was the recognised leader of Greek studies, and was the first Regius Professor of Greek in 1540. His championship of classical learning went hand in hand with his vindication of reformed opinions. The *State Papers Domestic* contain several of his papers on the pronunciation of Greek. Bishop Gardiner (*q.v.*) was his adversary in this, and the trend of church opinion at the time probably had great influence in promoting the English pronunciation of Greek which he espoused. In 1544 Cheke became tutor to Prince Edward, then six years old, and left Cambridge. His chief place of abode was for some time at Hertford, where he and Sir Anthony Cooke encouraged the precocity of their pupil. The course of study was ample enough, including reading aloud from Cicero, Aristotle, and other classical authors. Henry made Cheke a lay canon of Christ Church, Oxford, and when the new foundation of the college was established Cheke obtained a pension by way of compensation. When Edward came to the throne he loaded his tutor with gifts, and continued his studies under Cheke's guidance. In 1548 Cheke became Provost of King's by royal dispensation, and held the office until Mary's reign. It was natural that he should be a member of the University Commission in 1549. A little later he was on the commission which drew up the *Reformatio Legum* (*q.v.*). It is supposed that he was ordained about this time. All through Edward's reign he was a great supporter of the Reformation movement, and the close friend of Ridley (*q.v.*) and others. His influence with the King continued unabated, though his enemies conspired to undermine his authority. He took some part in the distinctive changes of the period, *e.g.* in the sacramental disputations of 1552; in the shaping of the XLII. Articles, 1553. Resigning his provostship in 1554, he went into exile in Italy and Germany, where he lectured. He was brought back to England by order of Philip, and under fear recanted his Protestantism in the most public way. Ashamed of his cowardice, he fell ill, and after a period of gradual decline died in 1557.   [H. G.]

Strype, *Life*, 1705.

CHESTER, See of, was one of the dioceses founded by Henry VIII. Bishops of Chester are found in earlier times, but the old Mercian bishopric was variously styled Lichfield (*q.v.*), Coventry, or Chester, and the bishop had cathedrals in all three cities, the church of St. John containing his chair in Chester. The diocese as constituted by Letters Patent of 4th August 1541 consisted of the archdeaconries of Chester (founded before 1135, and now taken from Lichfield), and Richmond (first mentioned, 1088; taken from York, *q.v.*), and comprised the counties of Chester and Lancaster, with large portions of Yorkshire, Cumberland, and Westmorland, and a few parishes in Wales. At first it formed part of the province of Canterbury, but in 1542 was transferred to York. The Benedictine abbey church of St. Werburgh became its cathedral.

The enormous extent of the diocese remained unaltered till 1836, when the Yorkshire territory was taken to form part of the new see of Ripon (*q.v.*). By Order in Council of 10th August 1847 the territory of Chester in Westmorland and Cumberland was assigned to the see of Carlisle (*q.v.*), together with the part of Lancashire which lies to the north of Morecambe Bay. This rectification did not take effect till 1856. By the Order of 10th August 1847 all the remainder of Lancashire north of the Ribble was assigned to the new see of Manchester (*q.v.*), and the archdeaconry of Liverpool was constituted. In 1849 the Welsh portion of the diocese was transferred to St. Asaph (*q.v.*). In 1880 the diocese of Liverpool (*q.v.*) was formed out of the part of Lancashire remaining in the diocese of Chester, which retained only the county of Chester, with some outlying portions of parishes extending into Flintshire and Lancashire.

The original inadequate endowment of the bishopric necessitated its occupant holding some benefice *in commendam*. Six bishops held the rich rectory of Wigan. At the creation of the see its value was estimated at £420, 1s. 8d., but it was subsequently considerably reduced under George I. Bishop Gastrell (1714-26) computed the net revenue at £955, 4s. 2¾d. This small income led to constant translations. From the death of Peploe in 1752 to the accession of Graham in 1848 every bishop was translated, giving origin to the saying: ' The bishop of Chester never dies.' The episcopal income is now £4200.

The diocese is divided into the two archdeaconries of Chester and Macclesfield (constituted, 1880) and into thirteen rural deaneries. The population is 816,020. The cathedral church of Christ and the Blessed Virgin Mary is ruled by a chapter dating from 1541, now consisting of a dean and four canons, two prebends having been suspended in 1840 (3-4 Vic. c. 113). The full number of honorary canons is twenty-four, each of whom has since 1903 received on his appointment a honorarium of £100.

BISHOPS OF CHESTER

1. John Bird, 1541; tr. from Bangor; previously the last Provincial of English Carmelites and Bishop suffragan of Penreth; an episcopal ' Vicar of Bray '; warmly promoted changes under Edward VI.; depr. under Mary as married, but separated from his wife, and became assistant Bishop to Bonner (*q.v.*); d. Vicar of Dunmow, 1558.
2. George Cotes, 1554; Master of Balliol; an active Marian; d. 1555.
3. Cuthbert Scot, 1556 (P.); Master of Christ's College, Cambridge, and Vice-Chancellor; a strong Marian; incurred obloquy by burning the bones of Bucer and Fagius; imprisoned on Elizabeth's accession, but escaped, and d. at Louvain, 1564.
4. William Downham, 1561; an inactive prelate; d. 1577.
5. William Chaderton, 1579; tr. to Lincoln, 1595.
6. Hugh Bellot; tr. from Bangor, 1595; a strict celibate; d. 1596.
7. Richard Vaughan; tr. from Bangor, 1597; tr. to London, 1604.
8. George Lloyd; tr. from Sodor and Man, 1605; favoured Puritans; d. 1615.
9. Thomas Morton, 1616; tr. to Lichfield, 1619.
10. John Bridgeman, 1619; a Laudian pre-

late; a vigorous administrator; at beginning of siege of Chester withdrew to Wales: d. at Morton Hall, near Oswestry, 1652.

11. Brian Walton, 1660; a learned legist and divine; suffered much from Puritans; edited the *Polyglot Bible*, the great work of the 'silenced clergy'; d. 1662.

12. Henry Ferne, 1662; an able pamphleteer on Royalist side; chaplain to King Charles, and with him throughout his campaigns; Master of Trinity College, Cambridge, 1660; Dean of Ely, 1661; d. five weeks after consecration.

13. George Hall, 1662; son of Bishop Joseph Hall of Norwich; very unpopular with Nonconformists; d. from accidental knife wound, 1668.

14. John Wilkins, 1668; a great experimenter in natural philosophy and real founder of Royal Society; Warden of Wadham, Oxford, and Master of Trinity, Cambridge; married Cromwell's sister; Dean of Ripon, 1660; friend of Evelyn (*q.v.*); very lenient to Nonconformists and desirous of comprehension; d. 1672.

15. John Pearson (*q.v.*), 1673.

16. Thomas Cartwright (*q.v.*), 1686.

17. Nicholas Stratford, 1689; previously Warden of Manchester and Dean of St. Asaph; an excellent bishop; d. 1707.

18. Sir William Dawes, 1708; tr. to York, 1714.

19. Francis Gastrell, 1714; wrote several valuable works in defence of revealed religion; an excellent bishop, who compiled a record of every parish, church, school, and ecclesiastical institution in his diocese; d. 1725.

20. Samuel Peploe, 1726; a strong Hanoverian; Warden of Manchester and Vicar of Preston; a contentious prelate; d. 1752.

21. Edmund Keene, 1752; tr. to Ely, 1771.

22. William Markham, 1771; tr. to York, 1777.

23. Beilby Porteous, 1777; tr. to London, 1787.

24. William Cleaver, 1788; tr. to Bangor, 1800.

25. Henry William Majendie, 1800; tr. to Bangor, 1809.

26. Bowyer Edward Sparke, 1810; tr. to Ely, 1812.

27. George Henry Law, 1812; tr. to Bath and Wells, 1824.

28. Charles James Blomfield (*q.v.*), 1824; tr. to London, 1828.

29. John Bird Sumner, 1828; tr. to Canterbury, 1848.

30. John Graham, 1848; Master of Christ's College, Cambridge, 1830; a great friend of the Prince Consort; d. 1865.

31. William Jacobson, 1865; Regius Professor of Divinity at Oxford; a learned theologian and 'single-minded' bishop; res. 1884; d. 1884.

32. William Stubbs (*q.v.*), 1884; tr. to Oxford, 1889.

33. Francis John Jayne, 1889; Principal of Lampeter, and Vicar of Leeds.

[F. S.]

Stubbs, *Registr. Sacr.*; *D.N.B.*; *Chester Dio. Gazette*, vols. v.-x.

CHICHELE, Henry (1362-1443), Archbishop of Canterbury, son of a Northamptonshire yeoman, was educated on the foundations of William of Wykeham at Winchester and Oxford. He graduated as a doctor of the civil law, and practised for some time in the Court of Arches. In 1396 he entered priest's orders; in the following year he became an archdeacon in the diocese of Salisbury; and in 1404 obtained the chancellorship of Salisbury Cathedral. Under Henry IV. he was employed as a diplomat at the courts of Paris and Rome, and attracted the favourable notice of Pope Gregory XII., who appointed him to the see of St. David's (1408). In 1414 he was selected by Henry V. to succeed Archbishop Arundel. His promotion was due to his capacity for practical affairs, and he is chiefly remembered as an ecclesiastical statesman. He continued the persecution of the Lollards (*q.v.*) which his predecessor had commenced, though it would seem that he showed more leniency to the heretics than Arundel or Henry V. He induced Convocation to support the policy of war with France; but the common statement that he did so to divert attention from the abuses of the Church, is a mere conjecture; and the famous oration in favour of the war which Shakespeare, following Hall the chronicler, puts into his mouth is a literary exercise of the sixteenth century. In 1437-8 he founded the college of All Souls, Oxford, in which prayers were to be offered for the souls of Henry V. and all Englishmen who perished in the French wars. This has been construed as evidence of his remorse, but the inference is questionable. Though a trusted counsellor of Henry V., the archbishop was not connected with the management of the war. Both in this reign and the next he was chiefly occupied in defending the privileges of the English Church against papal interference. His relations with Rome were difficult, since

Martin v. and Eugenius IV. complained bitterly that he did not procure the repeal of the statutes of Provisors (q.v.) and *Praemunire* (q.v.). He did his best to satisfy Rome in 1428, when, with tears in his eyes, he begged the House of Commons to surrender the obnoxious laws. But his sincerity was doubted, and several attempts were made to limit his power over the English Church. In 1417 Martin v. made Henry Beaufort (q.v.) a cardinal, with legatine powers over Great Britain. Chichele persuaded Henry v. to prohibit Beaufort from accepting the office ; but his own legatine commission was suspended in 1424, and two years later Beaufort accepted the cardinal's hat, with the office of legate *a latere*. To this no objection was taken so long as Beaufort was engaged in the Hussite Crusade. But when he returned from Bohemia the Privy Council came to Chichele's rescue, and issued a *praemunire* against the cardinal. Beaufort was glad to purchase an Act of Indemnity by paying a large sum and renouncing all claims to legatine power in England (1432). But his friend Kemp, Archbishop of York, was in 1440 created a cardinal, with precedence over Chichele. The latter meditated resigning, but died before the necessary formalities were completed, at the age of eighty-one. He was buried at Canterbury, where his tomb (recently restored) may still be seen. Besides All Souls he founded two other colleges : one for secular priests in his native village of Higham Ferrers ; the other at Oxford for Cistercians, on the site now occupied by St. John's College. Both were suppressed at the dissolution ; but the buildings of the Cistercian house (dedicated to the Virgin and St. Bernard) were granted in 1555 to the founder of St. John's. At All Souls the kin of Chichele had special rights, in respect of fellowships, until the year 1858, when his statutes were revised by a Royal Commission.   [H. W. C. D.]

Hook, *Lives of the Archbishops*, v. : Duck, *Life of Chichele*, 1617 ; Radford, *Cardinal Beaufort*.

CHICHESTER, See of, owes its origin to St. Wilfrid (q.v.), who after his expulsion from Northumbria in 680, failing to find refuge in Mercia and Wessex, came to Sussex. The King (Aethelwalch) and Queen were Christians, and there was a little settlement of Celtic monks under Dicul at Bosham, but the people were stubbornly heathen. Owing to Wilfrid's preaching many thousands were baptized, *quidam voluntarie, alii vero coacti regis imperio*. Aethelwalch granted Wilfrid his own vill of Selsey, where he built a

church, dedicated to St. Peter, and a monastery. In 686 Cadwalla of Wessex conquered Sussex, but was converted by Wilfrid, and confirmed his possession of Selsey. St. Lewinna was a Sussex martyr of the conversion. In 688 Wilfrid was recalled to York, his clergy remaining at Selsey, and the see was merged in Winchester (q.v.) ; 709 Winchester was divided, and Sussex was replaced under Selsey ; 1075 the bishopric was moved to Chichester by Bishop Stigand.

The see included originally all Sussex, but the grant of the manor of Old Malling to Canterbury in 823 gave the archbishop jurisdiction over a belt of land stretching north-east across the county, including the rural deaneries of Pagham and South Malling. The Bishops of London and Exeter also had peculiars (Lodsworth and Bosham). These and others were in 1841 reunited to the see, which now includes all Sussex as at first. The population is 605,202. A bishop suffragan of Lewes was appointed in 1909.

The *Taxatio* of 1291 assessed the bishop's *Temporalia* (i.e. revenues from land) at £462, 4s. 7¾d.: as in most old sees the bishop had no *Spiritualia* save Boxley (Bexhill), which was assessed with the *Temporalia*. Under Henry VI. the *Spiritualia* (from the church of Houghton) were £6, 13s. 4d. ; the *Valor Ecclesiasticus* of 1536 assessed the income at £677, 1s. 3d., and the value was unchanged in 1711. It is now £4200. The diocese is divided into three archdeaconries—Chichester (first mentioned, 1156) and Lewes (first mentioned, 1180) ; the third, Hastings, was constituted 1912. Rural deaneries lasted apparently well into Queen Elizabeth's reign, and seem to have been revived in 1812. The cathedral church is ruled by a chapter of the old foundation, the deanery, precentorship, and other dignities dating from Bishop Ralph, 1115. There are twenty-seven prebendaries and four Wiccamical prebendaries (founded, 1520-3). The practice of having four residentiaries began in 1574. From that time until 1840 they were co-opted, though throughout the eighteenth century the dukes of Richmond exercised great influence over the appointments. By the Act of 1840 (3-4 Vic. c. 113) the canons are appointed by the bishop.

BISHOPS OF SELSEY

1. St. Wilfrid (q.v.), 681 ; returned to York, 688.
2. Eadhberht, 709 ; President of St. Wilfrid's monastery at Selsey, and one of his priests.

3. Eolla, c. 714.
4. Sigga, 733.
5. Aluberht.
9. Wiohthun, 789 ; d. c. 805.
10. Aethelwulf, 811 ; d. c. 816.
11. Coenred, 824 ; d. c. 838 ; in 825 successfully reclaimed land from Beornuulf, King of Mercia.
12. Gutheard, 860 ; d. c. 862.
13. Beornege, 909 ; d. c. 929.
14. Wulfhun, 931 ; d. c. 940.
15. Aelfred, 914 ; d. c. 953.
16. Ealdhelm, c. 936 ; d. c. 979.
17. Aethelgar, 980 ; tr. to Canterbury, 988.
18. Ordbriht, 989 ; d. 1009.
19. Aelfmaer, 1009 ; d. c. 1031.
20. Aethelric I., 1032 ; d. 1038.
21. Grimketel, 1039 ; d. 1047 ; said to have bought the see.
22. Heeca, 1047 ; d. 1057 ; a royal chaplain.
23. Aethelric II., 1058 ; dep. 1070 uncanonically (see *Florence of Worcester*) and confined at Marlborough, but 1072 appears *antiquissimus* as an expert in English laws at the trial on Penenden Heath, being driven there in a carriage with four horses.
24. Stigand, 1070 ; a royal chaplain ; 1075 removed the see to Chichester ; d. 1087.

6. Osa, c. 765.
7. Gislehere, 780.
8. Tota, 785.

Bishops of Chichester

25. Gosfrid, or Godfrey, 1087 ; d. 1088.
26. Ralph I., Luffa, 1091 ; founder of present cathedral church, 1108, which, damaged by fire, 1115, he again repaired ; created the four great dignities in his chapter, and was an active, courageous, and good bishop ; d. 1123.
27. Seffrid I., d'Escures, 1125 ; formerly Abbot of Glastonbury ; brother of Archbishop Ralph of Canterbury ; quarrelled with abbey of Battle ; dep. 1145, probably for opposition to Stephen ; retired to Glastonbury.
28. Hilary, 1147 ; a partisan of Stephen ; able and eloquent : tried unsuccessfully to gain jurisdiction over Battle Abbey ; opponent of Becket (*q.v.*) ; d. 1169.
29. John, 1174 ; surnamed Greenford (on doubtful authority) ; d. 1180.
30. Seffrid II., 1180 ; formerly archdeacon and dean ; almost rebuilt the cathedral after the great fire, 1187 ; most of the present church is his work ; d. 1204.
31. Simon of Wells, or Simon Fitz-Robert, 1204 ; Archdeacon of Wells and a royal official ; was on good terms with John ; continued rebuilding of the cathedral ; d. 1207.
32. Richard Poore, 1215; tr. to Salisbury, 1217.

33. Ralph of Wareham, 1218 ; Prior of Norwich ; d. 1222.
34. Ralph Neville (*q.v.*), 1224 ; d. 1244.
35. St. Richard Wych (*q.v.*), 1245 ; d. 1253.
36. John of Clymping, or John Bishop, 1254 ; d. 1262.
37. Stephen of Berksted, or Burghsted, 1262 ; sided with Simon de Montfort ; blind in later life ; d. 1288.
38. Gilbert of St. Leofard, 1288 ; formerly treasurer of the church ; builder of the Lady Chapel ; a strong bishop and saintly man ; d. 1305.
39. John Langton, 1305 ; twice Chancellor (1292-1302, 1307-10) ; a strong ruler, built the great south transept window, and was a benefactor ; d. 1337.
40. Robert Stratford, 1337 ; brother of the Archbishop of Canterbury ; a statesman ; twice Chancellor ; d. 1362.
41. William of Lynn, 1362 (P.) ; formerly dean ; tr. to Worcester, 1368.
42. William Rede, or Reade, 1368 (P.) ; Fellow of Merton ; fortified Amberley Manor-House ; d. 1385.
43. Thomas Rushook, 1385 ; tr. (P.) from Llandaff ; partisan of Richard II. ; 1388 banished to Ireland ; tr. to Kilmore ; d. 1388-9.
44. Richard Metford, 1390 (P.) ; tr. to Salisbury, 1395.
45. Robert Waldby, 1396 ; tr. (P.) from Dublin ; tr. to York, 1397.
46. Robert Reade, or Rede ; tr. (P.) from Carlisle ; his register is the earliest surviving ; d. 1415.
47. Stephen Partington ; tr. (P.) from St. David's, 1417 ; Provincial of the Carmelites and rigorous anti-Lollard ; present at the Council of Constance, 1417, and died in the same year.
48. Henry de la Ware, 1418 (P.) ; Canon of Chichester ; d. 1420.
49. John Kemp, 1421 ; tr. (P.) from Rochester ; tr. to London, 1421.
50. Thomas Polton, 1421 ; tr. (P.) from Hereford ; tr. to Worcester, 1426.
51. John Rickingale, 1426 (P.) ; formerly Chancellor of Cambridge ; d. 1429.
52. Simon Sydenham, 1431 (P.) ; Dean of Salisbury ; d. 1438.
53. Richard Praty, 1438 (P.) ; Fellow of Oriel, Dean of the Chapel Royal, and active in visiting the Sussex monasteries ; d. 1445.
54. Adam Moleyns, or Molyneux, 1446 (P.) ; Dean of Salisbury ; a favourite of Henry VI., and unpopular ; murdered at Portsmouth, 9th January 1450.

55. Reginald Pecock (*q.v.*), 1450 (P.); tr. from St. Asaph; dep. 1457.
56. John Arundel, 1459 (P.); Fellow of Exeter, Oxford; chaplain and physician to Henry VI.; built the Arundel screen in the cathedral; d. 1477.
57. Edward Story, 1478 (P.); tr. from Carlisle; formerly Chancellor of Cambridge; built the Market Cross and founded the Prebendal School; d. 1503.
58. Richard Fitz-James, 1503; tr. (P.) from Rochester; tr. to London, 1506.
59. Robert Sherborn, 1508; tr. (P.) from St. David's; Wykehamist and Fellow of New College; held large preferments, including two prebends in Chichester, and was a royal official; a noble benefactor to the cathedral and city; res. June 1536; d. six weeks later.
60. Richard Sampson, 1536; tr. to Lichfield, 1543.
61. George Day, 1543; an Etonian and Provost of King's; a Conservative; disliked the changes of Edward VI.; declined to remove stone altars, 1550; dep. 1551; restored (P.), 1553; d. 1556; a learned and good bishop.
62. John Scory, 1552; tr. from Rochester; a Dominican who had married; on Mary's accession separated from his wife, and did penance, but fled later to Friesland; appointed to Hereford, 1559.
63. John Christopherson, 1556 (P.); Master of Trinity, Cambridge; an active Marian; d. 1558.
64. William Barlow (*q.v.*), 1559; d. 1568.
65. Richard Curteis, 1570; formerly dean; d. (poor and in debt) 1583.
66. Thomas Bickley, 1585; Warden of Merton, Oxford; had fled under Mary; beloved in the diocese; d. (unmarried) 1596.
67. Antony Watson, 1596; Dean of Bristol; quiet and unambitious; d. (unmarried) 1605.
68. Lancelot Andrewes (*q.v.*), 1605; tr. to Ely, 1609.
69. Samuel Harsnett, 1609; tr. to Norwich, 1619.
70. George Carleton, 1619; tr. from Llandaff; M.A. St. Edmund Hall, Oxford, and Fellow of Merton; at the Synod of Dort, 1618, maintained Apostolical Succession; d. 1628.
71. Richard Montague, 1628; tr. to Norwich, 1638. [CAROLINE DIVINES.]
72. Brian Duppa, 1638; tr. to Salisbury, 1641.
73. Henry King, 1642; Dean of Rochester; friend of Isaac Walton; captured at siege of Chichester, 1643; released, and

lived at Langley, Bucks, till Restoration, when he returned and restored the cathedral and palace; d. 1669.
74. Peter Gunning, 1670; tr. to Ely, 1675.
75. Ralph Brideoake, 1675; d. suddenly on Visitation, 1678.
76. Guy Carleton, 1678; tr. from Bristol; a Cavalier; called by a Chichester mob 'an old popish rogue'; d. (aged eighty-nine) 1685.
77. John Lake, 1685; tr. from Bristol; a devout Royalist officer, who became Vicar of Leeds; one of the Seven Bishops (*q.v.*); refused the oaths, 1689, and dep.; d. in same year.
78. Simon Patrick (*q.v.*), 1689; tr. to Ely, 1691.
79. Robert Grove, 1691; d. 1696 from his carriage overturning.
80. John Williams, 1696; a royal chaplain; d. 1709.
81. Thomas Manningham, 1709; a Wiccamical prebendary and treasurer; d. 1722.
82. Thomas Bowers, 1722; son of a Shrewsbury baker; Archdeacon of Canterbury; d. 1724.
83. Edward Waddington, 1724; an Etonian; repaired the palace; d. 1731.
84. Francis Hare, 1731; tr. from St. Asaph; a scholar and a friend of Walpole and Marlborough; married two heiresses in succession; lived chiefly in Buckinghamshire; d. 1740.
85. Matthias Mawson, 1740; tr. from Llandaff; tr. to Ely, 1754.
86. Sir William Ashburnham, Bart., 1754; formerly dean; eldest son of an ancient Sussex family; held the see forty-four years; reduced the number of choristers; d. 1798.
87. John Buckner, 1798; revived rural deaneries, 1812; d. 1824.
88. Robert James Carr, 1824; tr. to Worcester, 1831.
89. Edward Maltby, 1831; tr. to Durham, 1836.
90. William Otter, 1836; first Principal of King's College, London; founded the Diocesan Association, 1836, and (with Dean Chandler), the Theological College, 1837; d. 1840.
91. Philip Nicholas Shuttleworth, 1840; Warden of New College; a Low Churchman, but made Manning (*q.v.*) archdeacon; d. 1842.
92. Ashurst Turner Gilbert, 1842; Principal of Brasenose College; strongly opposed to the Oxford Movement [NEALE, J. M.]; d. 1870.

93. Richard Durnford, 1870; a scholar and High Churchman; founded Diocesan Conference and many other organisations; greatly beloved; d. 1895, aged ninety-four.

94. Ernest Roland Wilberforce, 1895; tr. from Newcastle, where he organised the diocese; previously Canon of Winchester and missioner; son of Bishop S. Wilberforce (*q.v.*); a strong and good ruler; d. 1907.

95. Charles James Ridgeway, 1908; Dean of Carlisle.   [S. L. O.]

Stephens, *Memorials of See of Chichester* and *Dio. Hist.*; Stubbs, *Registr. Sacr.*

CHURCH AND STATE are two distinct organisations independent of each other, though to some extent composed of the same individuals. Each is autonomous, and has authority over its members: the Church a spiritual authority [AUTHORITY IN THE CHURCH], the State a physical authority, which, however, rests on divine sanction as well as on force (Rom. 13[1-7]). The civil power may assume three attitudes towards any religious association of its subjects. (1) It may refuse to recognise it as lawful. This policy may vary from active persecution—the profession of such religion being a punishable offence—to mere disabilities, certain positions in the State being closed to its adherents. Such an attitude may be justified on the ground that the religion in question ought not to be tolerated for reasons of public policy, *e.g.* that its adherents are necessarily disloyal subjects, as was alleged of the Roman Catholics under Elizabeth. It was formerly thought to be the State's duty, when it was convinced of the truth of a religion, to enforce it on all its subjects for their souls' good. A statute of 1414 (2 Hen. v. st. 1, c. 7) imposes civil penalties on heretics. The formal title of the Act of the Six Articles (1539, 31 Hen. VIII. c. 14) is 'An Act for Abolishing of Diversity of Opinions in . . . Religion.' But with the gradual growth of the idea of liberty of conscience such action has come to be held to be outside the sphere of civil government. [TOLERATION.] (2) The State may adopt an attitude of impartial recognition, holding that a religious body has the right to the same treatment from the State as any other lawful association. It is protected by law in the possession of property, and the contracts of its members with each other will be enforced. (3) A religious body may receive not merely recognition but a privileged position as the official religion of the State, which will accordingly recognise

and enforce its laws and admit its officers to a position in the civil constitution. At the conversion of Constantine (313) the Christian Church entered into this relationship with the State. And though the State claimed no spiritual authority in consequence, yet the fact that it enforced the Church's law, and allowed high official rank to its bishops, inevitably led to its seeking some control over the Church. This was increased by the tendency of the Church to invoke the aid of the secular power for the settlement of disputes and the coercion of heretics. Hence the Christian emperors came to be credited with an ecclesiastical and, by analogy with the godly kings of the Old Testament, theocratic character. The Emperor was held to be not only ordained of God as civil ruler but also Vicar of God in the ecclesiastical sphere, with a duty to maintain religion and piety, to protect the Church, to assist it in doing its proper work, and to see that it does it. This naturally involved the assumption by the civil power of considerable control and voice in the Church's affairs.

Matters were at this stage when the conversion of England began. And the fact that, as a rule, Christianity was first accepted by the kings, and by them imposed upon their subjects, led to a close connection of Church and State, which was maintained throughout the Anglo-Saxon period. The kings issued mixed codes of civil and ecclesiastical laws with the sanction of both Church and State, and nominated the bishops, who were among their leading advisers in secular as well as religious matters. This era of a national Church practically identical with the State came to an end with the Norman Conquest (*q.v.*), by which the English Church was drawn more closely into the organisation of Western Christendom, which involved a less intimate connection with the secular power at home.

For the next five hundred years Church and State in England, though in theory the distinction between them was less clearly marked than it has since become, are often found in conflict, the Church by virtue of its sacred character claiming various privileges and exemptions from the civil law; the State endeavouring, with varying success, to maintain its temporal supremacy over the persons and property of all its citizens. And while the State was autonomous, the Church formed part of a great international system with its centre at Rome, so that members of the State were also, in their capacity as churchmen, the subjects of a foreign power, which claimed to be supreme even over temporal rulers. William I. first asserted the right of the civil powers to control the Church in its relations with Rome, in its Councils (*q.v.*), and in its Courts (*q.v.*). All through the Middle Ages the conflict was kept up. Its varying fortunes may be traced in the struggles over Investitures (*q.v.*) and criminous clerks [BENEFIT OF CLERGY], and in the Mortmain (*q.v.*), Provisors (*q.v.*), and *Praemunire* (*q.v.*) legislation. Yet the Church did not altogether lose the national character it had won in the days when its organisation pointed the way to the union of the Anglo-Saxon kingdoms. Men like Langton (*q.v.*) and Grosseteste (*q.v.*) resisted the usurpations of kings and popes alike. And many statesmen-bishops played a prominent part in the national life without violating their allegiance to the Pope.

The breach with Rome and Henry VIII.'s (*q.v.*) formal assertion of the Royal Supremacy (*q.v.*), 1531-4, considerably affected the relations of Church and State. The Tudor theory of Church and State is formally set out in the preamble to the Statute of Appeals (1533, 24 Hen. VIII. c. 12). England is an independent, self-contained community under two aspects—civil, the State, and spiritual, the Church—neither subject to any foreign interference, but each managing its own affairs under the supremacy of the Crown, which must be exercised constitutionally by means of the civil and ecclesiastical machinery respectively. With all his despotism Henry was careful to observe constitutional forms, and in this he was followed by Elizabeth (*q.v.*), who after the first year of her reign consistently forbade Parliament to interfere in Church matters, which, she insisted, should be dealt with by the ecclesiastical authorities subject to the visitatorial power of the Crown. This power did not greatly differ from that claimed for the Crown by William I. and the stronger among his successors, save that it had no longer to reckon with the claims of the papacy. Now that this disturbing factor in the relations of Church and State was removed those relations had to be restated, and the civil control formally defined. In this process the Crown succeeded to some of the papal prerogatives and methods of action. But the Tudors claimed no spiritual powers for the Crown. This was stated in various public documents, *e.g.* Article XXXVII.: 'We give not to our princes the ministering either of God's Word or of the sacraments,' but only the power 'to rule all states and degrees committed to their charge by God, whether they be ecclesiastical or temporal.' The action of Elizabeth and James I. showed

that this included controlling the State when it sought to encroach upon the Church's sphere; and it is inevitable that the civil power should exercise a similar control over the Church, to restrain its courts and councils if they exceed their spiritual functions to the prejudice of the civil rights of the subject. These are matters which fall within the duty of the State. It is bound to deal with them, and is not open to the charge of Erastianism (*q.v.*) for doing so. It must also, if appealed to, deal with questions arising out of the possession of temporal property by a religious body.

All religious functions are exercised only by *leave* of the State, though the *power* to exercise them is derived solely from the Church. The State gives the metropolitan leave to consecrate a bishop, gives Convocation leave to enact canons, gives every clergyman leave to minister in his parish. But the power to consecrate, to make canons, to administer the sacraments is given by the Church. All religious bodies, whether 'established' or not, thus carry on their functions by leave of the State, and as long as Church and State confine themselves to their proper spheres no conflict of duties can arise. If, however, the State were to seek to prevent the Church from performing the work committed to it by God, the spiritual and temporal laws would come into conflict, and it would be the duty of those who are subject to both to obey the higher. For the civil law within its proper sphere is binding on the conscience, and can only conflict with the spiritual law by exceeding its sphere. In such a case the Church must obey the spiritual law even if this involves disobeying the temporal, and must submit to whatever penal consequences may ensue. [ESTABLISHMENT; SUPREMACY, ROYAL.]   [a. c.]

Pusey, *Royal Supremacy*; R. W. Church. *Relations of Ch. and State*; J. W. Lea, *Letters*; Crosse, *Authority in the Ch. of Eng.*

CHURCH, High, Low, Broad. The terms 'High Church' and 'High Churchman' are first found in the late seventeenth century, and were originally 'hostile nicknames.' The *New English Dictionary*, *s.v.* 'High Churchman,' states that the term originally applied to 'those who, holding a *de jure* Episcopacy, opposed a comprehension or toleration of differences in Church polity, and demanded the strict enforcement of the laws against Dissenters. . . . With these were then associated the doctrine of the divine right of kings (of the House of Stuart), and the duty of non-resistance. . . . The appellation was, in fact, practically synonymous with Tory.' It appears to have been derived from the term 'High-flier,' which occurs in a pamphlet of 1680, the *Honest Cavalier*. 'The honest Divines of the Church of England who for their Conscience and Obedience are termed High-fliers.' The term 'High Churchman' is found first in a pamphlet (*Good Advice*) of 1687. It came slowly into general use, but may be said to have attained the place of an almost official term when it was specially noticed by South (*q.v.*) in the Dedication to Narcissus Boyle, Archbishop of Dublin, prefixed to the third volume of his famous *Sermons*, 1698. South reprobates the terms 'High Church' and 'Low Church' as 'odd' and 'new,' 'maliciously invented' to cause division. 'The ancienter members of' the English Church 'who have all along owned and contended for a strict conformity to her rules and sanctions . . . have been of late . . . *reprobated* under the inodiating character of *high Churchmen*.' The terms appear clearly in a pamphlet of 1699, *Catholicism without Popery, an Essay to Render the Church of England a Means and a Pattern of Union to the Christian World*. In this 'the true Difference between the High Church and Low Church (as they are called to this Day)' is said to turn chiefly on their attitude towards Reunion. The clergy fell into two parties after 1559: 'one Party were for finding out Means of Reconciliation with Rome, and bringing the Pope to Terms; the other Party were for accomodating matters and forming an Union between the English Church and Foreign Protestant Churchmen.' High Churchmen are further distinguished : 'They were for allowing Sports on the Lord's Day, and for Holidays, and a Religion that men might wear Genteely; for singing Prayers which makes little difference between Latin and English in point of Edification. . . . They were fond of God fathers and God mothers, Bowing at the Name of Jesus, and to the Altar, and getting the Communion-Table Altar-wise. On the other side the Pious Puritan Bishops were for Union with the Protestants abroad, who scrupled most of these things.' Under Queen Anne the term is in general use. Burnet (*q.v.*) speaks of 'those men who began now [1704] to be called the high church party.' A tract of 1704, *A Letter to a Friend concerning the New Distinction of High and Low Church*, asserts (p. 19) that 'it is the character of a High Churchman never to admit of the least alteration of the Establish't Worship upon any pretence whatever; and those are thought very Low Church

Men who think it Reasonable to consent to any Alterations, though they were for the better. . . .' 'Some very discerning men suspected' that 'all this Noise about High and Low Church . . . signifies no more than Whig and Tory.' The term was not always regarded with pleasure, for Sacheverell (*q.v.*) in a sermon (5th November 1709) regarded the division into High and Low Churchmen as 'villainous.' During the eighteenth century the term retained a political rather than an ecclesiastical meaning, and was often synonymous with 'Tory.' But an ecclesiastical meaning also remained, for Michael Johnson, father of Dr. Johnson (*q.v.*), is described by Boswell as 'a zealous High Churchman and Royalist.' Early in the nineteenth century the term seems again to change its meaning. Bishop E. Copleston writing, 29th January 1814, from Oxford, says: 'This place is the headquarters of what is falsely called *high church principles* . . . the leading partisans who assume that title appear to me only occupied with the thought of converting the property of the Church to their private advantage, leaving the duties of it to be performed how they can' (*Memoir*, 47). He considers himself 'more a high churchman than most of them,' as he 'would have much greater exertions made to preserve the unity of our Church and to make it in *effect* as well as in *name* a national Church.' The content of the term seems here to be equivalent to that of the 'high and dry' Churchmen who were Tory in politics and opposed to 'enthusiasm' in religion. The Evangelical Bishop D. Wilson (*q.v.*), writing from Calcutta, 21st May 1833, seems to use the term in the same sense of opprobrium when he writes: 'My mild and, I hope, firm Churchmanship, which I have maintained all my life at home, in the face of *High* Church principles and *No* Church principles, is of infinite importance.' From the Oxford Movement (*q.v.*) in 1833 the term became used in an exclusively ecclesiastical sense, and was shorn of political meaning. Dean Hook (*q.v.*) in his *Church Dictionary* (1837) regards the term as 'the nickname given to those . . . who regard the Church, not as the creature and engine of State policy, but as the institution of Our Lord.' To this belief in the divine origin of the Church must be added a belief in the apostolical succession and in the importance of sacraments in the Christian life.

Low Church has denoted in turn two schools in the English Church. It was used originally as an antithesis to 'High Church' at the end of the seventeenth century. Thus South in his Dedication (*supra*), 1698, speaks of 'the fashionable, endearing name of *low church-men*,' who are so called, he says, ' not from their affecting we may be sure a *lower condition* in the *church* than others . . . but from the low condition ' they ' would fain bring the church itself into.' H. Bedford, 1710, writes : ' He is known to be so wretched a

Low Churchman as to dispute all the Articles of the Christian Faith.' The term was thus synonymous with Latitudinarian (*q.v.*), and ' Low Churchmen ' were also termed ' No Churchmen.' *Ne'er a barrel the better herring between Low Church and No Church* is a tract of 1713. In *The Distinction of High Church and Low Church* (1705) the author defines a Low Churchman (p. 26) as ' one but coldly and indifferently affected towards the Church, and not much concerned what becomes of her '; and again (p. 27), those ' also are call'd Low-Church-Men who make a shift to keep in the Communion and Bosom of the Church . . . but at the same time have no inward liking to her Constitution.' Sacheverell, *Character of a Low Churchman*, 1702, defines the term in much the same way: ' He looks upon the censuring of False Doctrine as a Dogmatical Usurpation, an Intrusion upon that Human Liberty, which he sets up as the Measure and Extent of his Belief.' The term fell into disuse during the eighteenth century, and when revived in the nineteenth century was applied as a rule to the ' Evangelicals ' (*q.v.*).

The term Latitudinarian (*q.v.*) appears to have been continuously used throughout the eighteenth and in the nineteenth century to denote the original ' Low Church,' until *c.* 1850 the term 'Broad Church' came into use, owing its origin according to B. Jowett to A. H. Clough, at Oxford. It is found in the *Edinburgh Review* in 1850 (in an article by A. P. Stanley), and in the same magazine is used as a regular party term in 1853. Dryden (*Hind and Panther*, 1687) had called Latitudinarians ' your sons of breadth.'

The term Evangelical to describe a school of thought in the English Church began after the Methodist Revival of the eighteenth century. It is used indeed in 1532 by Sir Thomas More (*q.v.*) to describe the followers of the German Reformation—Tyndale (*q.v.*) and his friends—in irony, but from 1747 it is used regularly as denoting the doctrinal school which followed the Methodists, the chief points being that ' the essence of " the Gospel " consists of faith in the atoning death of Christ, and denies to " good works " or to sacraments a place in the scheme of salvation.' When the term ' Low Church ' was revived

in the nineteenth century it was applied to the ' Evangelicals,' and has since been used as practically synonymous with it. The *New English Dictionary* (1903) defines ' Low Church-man ' as ' a member of the Church of England holding opinions which give a low place to the claims of the episcopate and priesthood, to the inherent grace of sacraments, and to matters of ecclesiastical organisation, and thus differ relatively little from the opinions held by Protestant Nonconformists.' The difference between ' Low Church ' and ' Evangelical ' in current usage is that the latter connotes as a rule more zeal and spirituality, the former coldness and lack of enthusiasm. But doctrinally the content of both terms is the same.   [S. L. O.]

New Eng. Dict.; J. H. Blunt, *Dict. of Sects*, etc. ; Balleine, *Hist. of Evangelical Party.*

CHURCH RATES. By the common law and custom of England, differing in this respect from general canon law, every parish was liable for the upkeep of its church (except the chancel, for which by an ancient English custom the rector was responsible) and churchyard, and for providing the necessary fittings and ornaments. By the fourteenth century it was established that owners of land in the parish were parishioners for this purpose whether they lived in it or not. In the sixteenth century regular rates began to be levied for these purposes. In the seventeenth it was sometimes thought that while the repair of the fabric was a charge on all the land of the parish (except its own glebe), the provision of furniture, bells, sexton's wages, and the like were a personal charge on those who actually lived in the parish (2 *Rolle's Rep.*, 262, 270). But other decisions showed that this distinction was not good, and that all parishioners were liable for such expenses whether they lived in the parish or not (*Jeffrey's Case*, 1589; Coke, *Rep.*, v. 67 ; see also 1 Bulstrode 19, 1 Salk. 164). In 1677 the temporal courts held that the church court could by monition compel a parish to repair its church, but could not itself make the rate (*Mod. Rep.*, i. 236; ii. 222). That could only be done by the churchwardens and parishioners at a vestry meeting summoned by the churchwardens. The majority of those present could bind the parish, and if no one came the churchwardens alone could make a rate for expenses the neglect of which would expose them to penalties. Under *Circumspecte agatis* (1285) church rates were within the jurisdiction of the church courts (*q.v.*)

They could enforce payment by excommunication. [DISCIPLINE.] The first dissenters to oppose compulsory church rates were the Quakers, who objected to them under Charles II., but did not actively resist. In 1696 an Act was passed empowering justices of the peace to compel Quakers to pay church rates (7-8 Will. III. c. 34). This Act was renewed in 1714 (1 Geo. I. st. 2. c. 6), and in 1813 all church rates were made recoverable before the justices (with an appeal to quarter sessions) where the amount did not exceed £10 and the validity of the rate was not disputed; in other cases the church courts retained their jurisdiction (53 Geo. III. c. 127). Meanwhile Dissenters had increased in numbers and influence, their civil rights had been recognised, and it was difficult to resist their contention that it was unjust that they should be compelled to contribute to the church from which they dissented as well as to their own places of worship. It was answered that the rites of the Church were provided for all who chose to claim them, and that owners of land had acquired it subject to the liability for church rates. The movement against them, however, spread, especially in large towns, and vestries often became the scenes of violence. A Bill for the abolition of the rates was introduced in 1837, but in the same year the centre of interest was shifted to the law courts by the opening of the celebrated Braintree cases. The majority of the vestry of Braintree (Essex), while admitting that the church needed repair, carried an amendment declaring against the compulsory principle. The churchwardens afterwards made the rate themselves, and sued a defaulting parishioner in the consistory court, which held the rate valid; but the civil courts granted a prohibition, holding that the churchwardens could not act against the majority of the vestry (*Veley* v. *Burder*, 1837-41, 9 L.J.Q.B. 267, 10 L.J. Ex. 532). The churchwardens, being monished by the consistory court to repair the church, made the rate on behalf of the minority of the vestry instead of on their own responsibility, and the case again went leisurely from court to court, till in 1853 the House of Lords declared the rate invalid (*Veley* v. *Gosling*, 1841-53, 4 H.L. Cas. 679). By this time the victory over compulsory rates was practically won. It had been aided by the feeling roused by the imprisonment of Thorogood, a Chelmsford shoemaker, for contempt of the ecclesiastical court in refusing his rate in 1839. Henceforth church rates were only collected in country districts where dissent was comparatively weak. In large

towns they were systematically refused, and could not be enforced. From 1853 Bills for their abolition were continually brought in, and met with varying measures of success. That of 1861 was only lost on third reading by the Speaker's vote. In 1864 a Bill to commute them for a rent-charge on land was defeated. The Bill of 1867 passed the Commons, and was rejected in the Lords, all the bishops present voting against it. In 1868 the Compulsory Church Rate Abolition Act (31-2 Vic. c. 109) was passed through Mr. Gladstone's (*q.v.*) influence. Payment of church rates could no longer be enforced by law except in so far as, though called church rates, they were applied to secular purposes. But the vestry might still levy a voluntary rate, and parishioners refusing to pay it had no voice in its expenditure. Voluntary church rates have since been generally superseded by pew rents and voluntary contributions. But compulsory church rates are still levied in a few parishes under private Acts of Parliament. [PARISH.]   [G. C.]

Burn, *Eccl. Law*; Law Reports (the Braintree cases are also published in volume form); Hansard, *Parl. Debates*, 1834, '37, '39, '53-'68; Cornish, *Eng. Ch. in the Nineteenth Century*, I. viii.; Cannan, *Local Rates in Eng.*

CHURCH, Richard William (1815-90). Dean of St. Paul's, born in Lisbon, eldest son of an English merchant, who until his marriage had been a member of the Society of Friends. His early years were spent in Italy, where his uncle, afterwards General Sir Richard Church, held a command in the kingdom of Naples. He was educated at Exeter, and at Redlands, near Bristol, a school of strictly Evangelical principles. He went to Wadham College, Oxford, then a centre of Evangelicalism, in 1833, but was influenced by his brother-in-law, G. Moberly, later Bishop of Salisbury, then Fellow of Balliol, a High Churchman. He won a First Class in Classics, 1836, and a Fellowship at Oriel, 1838. In the interval he had come to know Newman (*q.v.*) and C. Marriott (*q.v.*), and translated (for the 'Library of the Fathers') St. Cyril of Jerusalem (published, 1838). On his election to Oriel, R. Michell, an Oxford tutor, said: 'There is such a moral beauty about Church they could not help taking him.' Church was now a convinced adherent of the Oxford Movement and an intimate friend of Newman. In this year he formed the other great friendships of his life, with Sir F. Rogers (later Lord Blachford) and with J. B. Mozley (*q.v.*).

He was ordained deacon Advent, 1839. In 1842, on account of his agreement with

Tract No. 90, which the Provost of Oriel (Dr. Hawkins) bitterly opposed, he offered to resign his tutorship, an offer which was finally accepted. In 1843 he was warned by the Provost that in the event of his applying for priest's orders a college testimonial might be refused him. March 1844 he became Junior Proctor. The most important event of his proctorship was his veto (in conjunction with his colleague, Mr. Guillemard of Trinity) of a censure on Newman's Tract No. 90 in Convocation on 13th February 1845. Newman's secession, October 1845, was a heavy blow to him, but he never wavered in his belief in the Catholicity of the English Church. In January 1846 he joined with J. B. Mozley, Lord Blachford, Thomas Haddan, and M. Bernard in founding *The Guardian* newspaper as the weekly organ of Church principles. An article by Church on Le Verrier's discovery of the planet Neptune first called popular attention to the distinction of the paper, and made its position secure. In Advent 1852 he was ordained priest, and in January 1853 he became Vicar of Whatley, Somerset, where he married, July 1853, and remained for eighteen years. From 1864 his intimacy with Newman (broken since 1846) was renewed in its former freedom and affection. In 1869 Mr. Gladstone (*q.v.*) offered him a canonry at Worcester, which he declined because he had been defending the Liberal policy as to the Irish Church in *The Guardian*, and he wished to show that his support was disinterested. In July 1871 he declined the deanery of St. Paul's, but pressure from Dr. Liddon (*q.v.*) and Mr. Gladstone caused him to accept. He came to London 'with fears and with repugnance.' He celebrated and preached for the first time in the cathedral in December 1871. Henceforward until his death he was one of the chief influences in ecclesiastical affairs. He detested controversy and shunned public meetings, for he was a shy and sensitive scholar, but his passion for righteousness and truth burnt like a flame and was felt on all sides. He became, as it were, 'a standard conscience by which men tested their motives and their aims.' This moral authority was felt in 1874-8, the period of struggle over the Public Worship Regulation Act (*q.v.*) and the Ritual Cases (*q.v.*). The dean felt so keenly the injustice of the policy pursued that he was prepared to resign his deanery as a protest (May 1877). His attitude caused Archbishop Tait to pause, by showing him the strength of feeling behind High Churchmen. At the end of his life, in the agitation over Biblical criticism, by his wisdom and courage 'he did much to prevent a serious split between old and young.'

Aided by Liddon, R. Gregory (who succeeded him), and later by H. S. Holland, he transformed St. Paul's Cathedral from a piece of ecclesiastical lumber into the great central church of London. As a preacher and man of letters he was famous, and his words and judgments had great weight. He remained 'a man apart, unique, against whom no one could say a word. Pure, reserved, austere, he yet won the praise of the world,' and he was described by an unbeliever as 'the finest flower of the Christian character.' His last act in St. Paul's was to bury his colleague, Dr. Liddon. He died at Dover 9th December 1890, and was buried at Whatley. [S. L. O.]

M. C. Church, *Life and Letters*; D. C. Lathbury, *Life*; H. S. Holland, *Personal Studies*.

CLARENDON, Constitutions of (1164). This name was given to the document containing the customs of the realm in regard to the relations between Church and State which was presented to a council held at Clarendon, Wilts, 13th-28th January 1164. The party of Becket (*q.v.*) said that the document did not represent the law or custom of the realm, but had been drawn up in accordance with Henry II.'s wishes by Richard de Luci and Jocelin de Balliol, two of his lawyers. Becket only signed the customs after much demur, and afterwards withdrew his assent, and suspended himself from the exercise of his ecclesiastical functions till he should have been absolved by the Pope. But the document claims to bear the acceptance of the Archbishop of York and twelve bishops in the presence of a large number of barons. The first clause orders that suits concerning church patronage shall be tried in the King's not the church court. This was objected to as bringing before secular men the decision of matters relating to the cure of souls, contrary to the edict of William I. The third ordered that accused clerks should be summoned before the King's court, there plead their clergy, be tried in the church court (a King's officer being present), and if found guilty, sentenced, after degradation, to a layman's punishment in a lay court. This was objected to as bringing clerks before lay judges and as punishing twice for one offence. The fourth ordered that clergy should not leave the realm without the King's assent and giving sureties: objection, it prevented access and appeal to Rome. The fifth ordered that excommunicates should not give pledge to obey the Church's order: objection, the State interfered in a purely spiritual matter. The seventh said that no tenant in chief of the Crown should be excommunicated without the consent of the King, or in his absence the justiciar: objection the same. The eighth ordered that appeals should be from the archdeacon's to the bishop's, bishop's to archbishop's court, and then, 'if the archbishop should fail in doing justice,' the case should be sent to the King, so that *by his order* the archbishop should conclude the case without its going further: objection, similar to the above, and also to the implied check on appeals to Rome. The ninth ordered that trials concerning property in which clergy were concerned should be decided by jury as regards the question whether the property were of lay or ecclesiastical tenure, and according to that decision be tried, as regards the question of right, in the lay or church court. The tenth was similar in point, and the objection to it was the same as to the fifth and seventh. The twelfth ordered that the King should have all the revenues of vacant prelacies, and that elections to the vacancies should be in his chapel: objection, the order was simoniacal and prevented free election to bishoprics and abbeys. The fifteenth ordered that suits concerning debts should be heard in the King's court: objection, debt was a moral offence, and should fall under the moral jurisdiction of the Church. The other clauses (2, 6, 11, 13, 14, 16) were 'tolerated' eventually by the Pope. They embodied points in the relations between Church and State which were not in serious dispute. But one of them forbade the ordination of sons of villeins without the lord's consent, and this (though it recognised a principle which is at least as old as the fifth century and the 'Constitutions of the Apostles') was felt by some to limit unduly the freedom of man, and to prevent those serving as ministers of Christ for whom Christ died. The Constitutions remained the chief matter of dispute between King and archbishop till the reconciliation at Fréteval. [BECKET.] When Henry finally submitted after the archbishop's murder he gave way on every point, save that he insisted on the trial in his courts of archbishops, bishops, or any other clergy caught poaching in his forests. Many of the points were never settled till the Reformation; some are not settled yet. But the claim of Henry that the State might order the archbishop's court to rehear a case, but might not itself give the final decision, appears to be the true con-stitutional principle, though in the nineteenth century exceptions to it were recognised by the secular courts. [COURTS.] [W. H. H.]

Stubbs, *S.C.* ; Pollock and Maitland, *H. L. of Eng. Law* ; W. H. Hutton, *Thomas B. L.*

CNUT, or **CANUTE** (c. 995-1035), King of England, Denmark, and Norway, was a younger son of Sweyn Forkbeard, King of Denmark, by a Polish princess, Gunhilde. He accompanied his father on the great expedition of 1013 against Aethelred the Redeless of England. Sweyn died in the hour of victory (3rd February 1014), and Cnut was proclaimed King of England by the army, while his elder brother Harold was recognised as their father's successor in Denmark. Expelled for the moment by Aethelred, Cnut brought a new army to England in 1015, and overran most of the country. On the death of Aethelred (23rd April 1016) the Dane was acknowledged as King by most of the English magnates. Eadmund Ironside, the heroic son of Aethelred, maintained the national cause for some months with such vigour and military skill that Cnut agreed to divide the kingdom with him. But Eadmund died or was murdered in November 1016 ; and from that date the position of Cnut was secure, though two other sons of Aethelred were living in Normandy under the protection of their uncle, Duke Richard. Cnut married their mother Emma, the sister of Richard, thus averting the danger of Norman intervention. The first acts of the new reign were designed to conciliate English feeling. Cnut dismissed his Scandinavian host, except the crews of forty ships, whom he retained as his huscarls or bodyguard. He caused the witan to re-enact the laws of Eadgar. He promoted some Englishmen to high offices ; notably Aethelnoth, to whom he gave the see of Canterbury; Lifing, whom he made Abbot of Tavistock and Bishop of Crediton, and employed as a confidential minister ; and Godwin, to whom he eventually entrusted the earldom of Wessex. In time Cnut became the ruler of a great northern empire. He succeeded Harold in Denmark (1019) ; he evicted St. Olaf from the throne of Norway (1028) ; and extended his power along the south shore of the Baltic. But England remained the centre of his power, and in England he showed his best qualities as a ruler.

At the beginning of his reign he crushed his real or supposed enemies with brutal violence, temporised with the heathenism of his Danish followers, and was regarded, perhaps unjustly, as himself a heathen. A new policy was, however, outlined in a proclamation to the English which he published about 1020. The King states in this document that he had taken to heart the admonitions which Archbishop Lifing of Canterbury had brought to him from the Pope. He announces his intention of governing righteously ; he commands his ealdormen to co-operate with the bishops in punishing offenders against the law of the Church, and his sheriffs to pay attention to the advice of the bishops in doing justice. Such enactments signified the revival of the old alliance between Church and State. Cnut needed the help of the English Church both in ruling England and for missionary work among the inhabitants of Denmark ; he seems to have treated Canterbury as the ecclesiastical metropolis of his wide dominions. This policy bore remarkable fruits in Denmark and in Norway. In England it was responsible for the benefactions which Cnut lavished upon such foundations as Bury St. Edmunds and the minster church at Winchester. He also conferred less material benefits on the English Church. In 1027, when visiting Rome in the guise of a pilgrim, he protested against the heavy fees which English archbishops were required to pay for the pallium (*q.v.*) ; and he obtained safe-conducts for English pilgrims travelling to Rome through the lands of Burgundy and the Empire. He commanded his officials to enforce the payment of tithes (*q.v.*) and other ecclesiastical dues. He enforced the observance of Sunday as a day of rest from secular business and amusements. He ordained that the clergy, especially those in priests' orders, should remain celibate ; and that no man should marry within the forbidden degrees. He required that all his subjects in England should learn at least the Creed and the Lord's Prayer. He interdicted every form of heathen worship, with a minuteness of detail which implies that heathenism was still rampant among the Danish immigrants. He commanded that sorcerers and soothsayers should be banished or put to death. He is naturally praised by the chroniclers, who were ecclesiastics. But his rule appears to have been also popular with the laity. [H. W. C. D.]

Freeman, *Norman Conquest*, vol. i. ; J. R. Green, *Conquest of England* ; L. Larson, *Canute the Great*.

COLENSO, John William (1814-83), born in Cornwall of parents in humble circumstances, obtained a Sizarship at St. John's College. Cambridge, where he was Second Wrangler in 1836, and was elected Fellow of his col-

lege in 1837 ; was mathematical master at Harrow, 1839-42 ; returned to Cambridge as Tutor of his college, 1842-6; and was Vicar of Forncett St. Mary, 1846-53. In 1853 he was consecrated first Bishop of Natal, taking the oath of canonical obedience to the Bishop of Capetown as metropolitan, though that dignity was not yet created. Of a combative disposition, he incurred grave censure for tolerating polygamy in Kaffir converts, and maintaining his position by argument with little regard for tradition or authority. In 1861 he published a *Commentary on the Epistle to the Romans*, to which exception was at once taken, especially on account of his treatment of the Atonement and the Sacraments. This was followed in 1862-3 by the two volumes of *The Pentateuch and Book of Joshua critically examined*, a work which he frankly traced back to questions of detail, especially about numbers, addressed to him by an intelligent Zulu. Colenso attempted, with entirely inadequate equipment, to solve the problems which have since his day engaged more competent scholars in what is called the Higher Criticism. Disciplinary proceedings were taken against him by the metropolitan, Robert Gray (*q.v.*). The English bishops, urged by Bishop Gray to condemn the *Commentary*, were unable to agree on any course of action, but when the book on the Pentateuch appeared they almost unanimously inhibited Colenso, then in England, from preaching in their dioceses. In February 1863 forty-one bishops, English, Irish, and Colonial, addressed him a letter, drafted by Tait (*q.v.*). advising him to resign his see on the ground that he professed himself unable in conscience to use the baptismal and ordination services as in the Prayer Book. ' We will not abandon the hope,' they wrote, ' that through earnest prayer and deeper study of God's Word you may, under the guidance of the Holy Spirit, be restored to a state of belief in which you may be able with a clear conscience again to discharge the duties of your sacred office.' In May the bishops of the province of Canterbury in Convocation, Thirlwall (*q.v.*) alone dissenting, adopted resolutions declaring the book to ' involve errors of the most dangerous character,' but declining to take further action on the ground that the book would shortly be submitted to the judgment of an ecclesiastical court. Colenso's case became doctrinally involved with that of *Essays and Reviews* (*q.v.*), and his book received an attention exceeding both its merits and its faults. He refused to resign, though in his preface he had intimated his intention of doing so. Deposed and excommunicated by the South African bishops, he obtained more than one judgment from law courts evacuating that sentence of all legal effect, and he retained possession of the endowments of the see and of other property held in trust for the Church in Natal. At the first Lambeth Conference [COUNCILS] in 1867 fifty-five out of eighty bishops declared their acceptance of the judgment pronounced upon him 'as being spiritually a valid sentence.' Visiting England again in 1874, Colenso was once more inhibited by some of the bishops, but was invited to preach in Balliol College Chapel and at Westminster Abbey. He died still excommunicate, but left an honoured name for his efforts, sometimes more earnest than wise, on behalf of the social and moral welfare of the Zulus, by whom he was affectionately known as *Sobantu*, 'Father of the People.' [T. A. L.]

G. W. Cox, *Life*.

COLET, John (1466-1519), Dean of St. Paul's, born in London in 1466 or early in 1467, was the son of Sir Henry Colet of the Mercers' Company, who, after being twice Lord Mayor, purchased a pleasant country house at Stepney, and died there in 1505, leaving a widow who had borne him no less than eleven sons and as many daughters. Of these, however, John was ultimately the sole survivor. He had been sent to Oxford, where he graduated M.A. after seven years' study, and devoted himself to the Church. He enlarged his mind by travel in Italy, where he first met Erasmus. After his return he was ordained (deacon in 1497, priest in 1498), and resided in Oxford, where he gave Latin lectures on the Epistle to the Romans, which at once attracted much attention. His mind was certainly under the influence of the new Platonism of Ficino and Pico della Mirandola, the former of whom he may possibly have met in Italy; yet there was something very English in his direct study of St. Paul which drew doctors and abbots to attend his lectures with note-books. He himself, in a letter to the Abbot of Winchcombe (Richard Kidderminster), gives an interesting account of a visit paid him by one of his hearers, a priest, who sought him out in his own chamber, inspired by a like love of the Apostle's writings. A curious monument of his efforts to interpret Scripture is bound up with his MS. exposition of Romans at Corpus Christi College, Cambridge. This is a set of letters on the six days of Creation in Genesis, written in answer to a student's question—not about them, but

about dark places in Scripture generally the *first* dark place in Scripture being, in his friend's opinion, the words of Lamech in Gen. 4[23, 24]. Colet considered the opening chapter far more difficult, and confessed that he only made, in his ignorance of Hebrew, a doubtful attempt at a solution. But it is clear that he discarded literalism altogether: for God, he considered, created all things at once in His eternity, and the language about material things was merely adapted to the instruction of an unlearned people, to raise them to higher views of God and His worship. The six days were merely a poetical arrangement of edifying matter.

Colet was much influenced at first, like others of his time, by the writings attributed to Dionysius the Areopagite. He found matter in them to rebuke corruptions of his own day in a book which he wrote on the sacraments, first published in 1867. But, apparently in the very last years of the fifteenth century, his friend Grocyn became convinced that the so-called Dionysian writings, though old, were not of such very high antiquity, and Colet speedily agreed with him in a conclusion which is now universally admitted. In this matter, as about the book of Genesis, his simple honesty in the pursuit of truth is conspicuous. And it is gratifying to find that it was no impediment to his receiving the degree of D.D., which was bestowed upon him at Oxford, unsought, in 1504. At some uncertain date, but scarcely before 1500, his father's influence had procured for him, among other benefices, the vicarage of St. Dunstan and All Saints, Stepney. There was a rector as well as a vicar here; and it was not the profits of the living that attracted Colet, for he gave it up in 1505, the year of his father's death. His mother, Dame Christian, continued to live at Stepney not only after her husband's death, but after her son's, fourteen years later; and Colet himself was much attached to the place, as shown by a letter addressed to him by Sir Thomas More, urging him to come back to London, notwithstanding the attractions of smiling fields and the society of simple rustics who scarcely needed a physician for body or mind.

In May 1505, some months before resigning his Stepney vicarage, he was made Dean of St. Paul's. This drew him back to London, where he from that time seems to have given his chief energies to preaching at the cathedral, expounding Holy Writ in a way that drew up Lollards from long distances to hear him, and afforded plausible ground for a suspicion of Lollardy against himself. But, in fact, he was a staunch maintainer of old church principles, and while hating abuses and contemptuous of superstitions, believed that the Church herself had the power to deal with these things, if all her excellent laws and canons were but honestly enforced. There was some appropriateness in his connection with a cathedral dedicated to St. Paul. He delivered lectures there himself, and invited other divines to lecture also (among them the Scotsman, John Major or Mair), on St. Paul's Epistles. He put new life into the study of the Scriptures, and certainly undervalued that of the Schoolmen. He reformed the statutes of the Guild of Jesus in 1507, and was evidently planning from the first the foundation of his celebrated school in St. Paul's Churchyard for the free teaching of one hundred and fifty-three poor men's children, under the supervision of his father's company, the Mercers, which he endowed for the purpose out of his father's lands ' to the value of £120 or better,' as Stowe puts it. The building seems to have been completed in 1510. He framed statutes for the school on the 18th June 1518.

It did not escape notice that this new foundation was inspired by unconventional ideas, being placed under the control of a lay society ; and Bishop Fitzjames, having doubts about the teaching and some things said by Colet himself against images and against written sermons, cited his dean before Archbishop Warham (*q.v.*) for heresy. Warham dismissed the charge ; but the aged bishop was never quite satisfied with his energetic dean, who, nevertheless, was so far from being a real heretic that in the year 1511 his name is included by John Foxe (*q.v.*) in a list of ' persecutors and judges ' of heretics, *i.e.* of persons who conducted their trials. On the 6th February 1512, when the Convocation met at St. Paul's, Colet was appointed by the archbishop to preach the opening sermon, and delivered a most eloquent discourse, from Romans 12², against the evil conditions which the world imposed upon the Church. It was in this sermon that he insisted that the Church's ailments were the same as of old, and no new laws were necessary to counteract them if old ones were put in force ; but the Church must not be ' conformed to this world.' It is to be feared, however, that the four dismes granted by the clergy in this Convocation, ostensibly for the defence of the Church and Realm of England, and for the extirpation of heresies and schisms everywhere (see Seebohm, p. 224 n.), were mainly used for the war with France, to which Colet was greatly opposed. And,

moreover, being called on to preach before the King on Good Friday, 1513, he denounced the evils of war in a way that Henry himself thought likely to discourage his soldiers. But, having called the preacher to a private audience, after an hour and a half's familiar conversation he dismissed him honourably, desiring him merely to explain himself in public, lest it should seem that he considered no war justifiable to a Christian.

Although thus supported by the King against insinuations that he was thwarting the King's policy, he was still harassed by the Bishop of London, and was thinking in 1514 of retiring among the Carthusians of Sheen ; which it would seem that he actually did, apparently building a house for himself within their precincts. About this time he went with his friend Erasmus to Canterbury, a pilgrimage of which the Dutch scholar gives a lively account, describing his companion, who was certainly very disrespectful to old musty relics, by the name of Gratianus Pullus. In 1518 Colet was three times attacked by the sweating sickness, and was left a mere wreck. He died on the 16th September 1519. [J. G.]

Seebohm, *Oxford Reformers* (2nd edit., 1869).

COLLIER, Jeremy (1650-1726), Nonjuror, became scholar of St. John's, Cambridge, 1669 ; graduated B.A., 1673 ; M.A., 1676 ; was ordained deacon in the latter year, and priest, 1677. 1679 he became Rector of Ampton, Suffolk, resigned, 1685, and went to live in London, where he was made chaplain at Gray's Inn. He refused the oaths to William and Mary, 1689, and thus became a Nonjuror. He was the first to attack the settlement of 1689, in a pamphlet in answer to Burnet (*q.v.*), in which he argued that James II. had not abdicated. For this he was imprisoned six months in Newgate, and then released without trial. He continued to write brilliant pamphlets, but in 1692, having gone to Romney Marsh, he was suspected of designing communications with King James, and was again imprisoned. No evidence being found against him, he was admitted to bail and released. Fearing lest by giving bail he recognised the existing government, he returned to prison, but was released at the intercession of his friends. On the 3rd April 1696 he with two other Non-juring priests publicly at the scaffold absolved Sir John Friend and Sir William Parkyns, condemned for plotting to assassinate William III. Parkyns was a penitent of Collier, and having made his confession to him had desired absolution on his last day. The primates and eleven bishops published a strong condemnation, as if Collier had condoned the crime for which the accused were executed, and they laid unnecessary stress on the imposition of hands which accompanied the absolution. Collier avoided arrest, and was outlawed, but later returned to ordinary life without molestation.

He is specially famous for his protest against the immorality and profaneness of the English stage, 1698. Dryden admitted his contention, and Vanbrugh and Congreve, after a contest, acknowledged their defeat. Under Anne he was pressed to leave the Nonjuring body, but refused, and officiated regularly at the Nonjurors' Oratory in Broad Street, London. He published in 1708 the first volume of his *Ecclesiastical History of England*, still a valuable work, being 'honest and impartial,' and based on original authorities. 3rd June 1713, Ascension Day, he was consecrated bishop (with N. Spinckes and S. Hawes) in Bishop Hickes's (*q.v.*) Oratory in Scroop's Court, Holborn, by Hickes and two Scots bishops, Campbell and Gadderar, and on Hickes's death, 1715, became the leader of the body. His primacy was marked by the unhappy division between Usagers and Nonusagers [NONJURORS], Collier being the leader of the Usager party, 1717, and by an attempt at reunion with the Eastern Church [REUNION], which lasted 1716-25. In the formal documents, 1722, Collier signs himself *Primus Anglo-Brittaniae Episcopus*. Collier, who wrote some forty-two works, has by his splendid gifts and blameless life won the praise of so strong an opponent as Lord Macaulay, who says : ' He was in the full force of the words a good man . . . a man of eminent abilities, a great master of sarcasm, a great master of rhetoric.' He is buried in St. Pancras Churchyard, London.

[S. L. O.]

Life by Lathbury prefixed to *Eccl. Hist*. vol. ix. ; Overton, *The Nonjurors*: Lathbury. *Hist. of the Nonjurors* ; Dr. Hunt in *D.N.B.*

COMMISSIONS, ROYAL, are bodies appointed by the Crown either (1) to exercise the Royal Supremacy (*q.v.*) in matters of administration : this was a common device in the sixteenth century, and has been revived in modern times (see below); or (2) to inquire into certain specified matters in order that their Reports, which possess no authority of themselves, may serve as a basis for legislation. The earliest commission of this kind was that appointed in 1551 to revise the canon law. [REFORMATIO LEGUM.]

Commissions to revise the Prayer Book so as to make it acceptable to dissenters, and thus bring about reunion, were appointed in 1661 [SAVOY CONFERENCE] and 1689, when ten bishops and twenty other divines were bidden (17th September) to prepare alterations of the liturgy and canons, and proposals for the reform of the church courts, to be submitted to Convocation, 'and when approved by them' presented to the Crown and Parliament, ' that if it shall be judged fitt they may be establisht in due forme of law.' The Commission met on 3rd October, sat eighteen times, and with the aid of six sub-committees produced a scheme of alterations in the Prayer Book by 18th November. Nine of its members attended few or no meetings, and these were the ' most rigid ' against comprehension, some of them also questioning the validity of the Commission. Of those who remained William Beveridge was the most active in resisting changes in favour of dissenters, Burnet (*q.v.*), Tenison, Tillotson (*q.v.*), Stillingfleet (*q.v.*), and Simon Patrick (*q.v.*) being among the leaders in favour of comprehension. Among the chief features of the scheme presented were the omission of many black-letter saints from the Calendar, of the apocryphal Lessons, and of the mention of absolution in the Exhortation in the Communion Service, the substitution in many places of ' Minister ' for ' Priest,' and of ' Lord's Day ' for ' Sunday ' ; the surplice, kneeling at communion, and the cross in baptism were to be optional : many of the collects were altered and lengthened. These proposals proved distasteful to the Lower House of Convocation, and nothing came of the Commission. [COMMON PRAYER, BOOK OF.]

Church Building Commissioners.—In 1711 Parliament, apparently at the instance of Convocation, passed the Church Building Act (9 An. c. 17, commonly cited as c. 22), allotting the proceeds of certain coal duties for building fifty new churches in or near London, and empowering the Queen to appoint commissioners to carry it out, which was done in September 1711. After Anne's death the scheme was allowed to drop, only some fourteen of the proposed churches having been built. In 1818 Parliament (by 58 Geo. III. c. 45) set apart a sum, not to exceed £1,000,000, for new churches, and again empowered the Crown to appoint commissioners, who existed as a separate body till 1856, when their powers and duties were vested in the Ecclesiastical Commissioners (19-20 Vic. c. 55).

The Ecclesiastical Courts Commission, 1830, seems to have been due as much to Brougham's restless love of reform, and ambition to increase the dignity and authority of his office, as to the inconveniences caused by the cumbrous system of Church Courts (*q.v.*) into which it was to inquire. It was appointed, 28th January 1830, and reappointed with some additional members, 5th July. As finally constituted it comprised sixteen members, including Archbishop Howley (*q.v.*) and five bishops. On 12th January 1831 Brougham, apparently in a hurry to substitute the Privy Council for the Court of Delegates, bade the Commission report at once on the expediency of that change; and on the 25th it presented a Special Report, assenting to rather than recommending the proposal, for the witnesses who had been examined were generally doubtful whether the change would be an improvement. The General Report (February 1832) gave an exhaustive account of the jurisdiction and procedure of the ecclesiastical courts, and proposed drastic reforms, including the transference of the contentious jurisdiction of the diocesan to the provincial courts, and the introduction into the ecclesiastical courts of oral evidence and trial by jury. It also suggested the abolition of the provincial courts of York, so that those of Canterbury should exercise jurisdiction over the whole kingdom. But the main object for which the Commission was appointed, the abolition of the Delegates, had now been achieved, and less attention was paid to its other recommendations, though some of them were incorporated into later Acts dealing with the church courts.

The Ecclesiastical Revenues Commission.— The revenues of the Church could hardly escape the notice of the reformers of that age. Violent attacks were made on the abuses of pluralities, sinecures, and gross inequalities of income. On 23rd June 1832 a Commission of twenty-four, including the two archbishops and several bishops, was appointed to inquire into Church revenues and patronage. Its Report (16th June 1835) consisted mainly of tabular statements, covering more than a thousand pages, and supplied much of the materials for the Reports of

The Ecclesiastical Commission, which was appointed, 4th February 1835, to inquire into the distribution of episcopal revenues and duties, to consider how the cathedral and collegiate churches might be made more efficient, 'and to devise the best means of providing for the cure of souls, with special reference to the residence of the clergy in their respective benefices.' The Commission consisted of the two archbishops, three

bishops, and seven laymen, including Sir Robert Peel, to whom its appointment was chiefly due. Its first Report, 17th March 1835, made proposals for the rearrangement of dioceses under the three headings of Territory, Revenue, and Patronage. The second, 4th March 1836, dealt with cathedral and collegiate bodies, and proposed the restriction of non-residence and pluralities. The third, 20th May 1836, proposed further reconstitution of dioceses, and recommended that Parliament should appoint commissioners to carry out the rearrangements, and that the Crown should be empowered to give their schemes the force of law by Order in Council. This was done by the Established Church Act, 1836 (6-7 Will. IV. c. 77), which appointed a permanent body of thirteen 'Ecclesiastical Commissioners for England' to lay schemes before the Crown, which was empowered to confirm them by Order in Council. The original Commissioners were the two archbishops, three bishops, five holders of great offices of State, and three other laymen. All the Commissioners must subscribe a declaration of membership of the Established Church. Later Acts have extended the membership of the Commission, which now consists of the Archbishops of Canterbury (chairman) and York, the bishops, nine great officers of state, the Deans of Canterbury, St. Paul's, and Westminster, seven lay commissioners appointed by the Crown and two by the Archbishop of Canterbury, and three 'Church Estates Commissioners' appointed under an Act of 1850 (13-14 Vic. c. 94). The original Commission submitted its fourth Report, 24th June 1836. It recommended the reorganisation of cathedral chapters, the application of a part of their revenues to other ecclesiastical purposes, and the suppression of a number of canonries. The Cathedrals Act, 1840 (3-4 Vic. c. 113), was based on this Report. A fifth Report was drafted but not presented. Numerous Acts have carried out various recommendations of the Commissioners, and extended their powers and duties, which may now be summarised thus: to prepare schemes (which are carried out by Order in Council) for the rearrangement of the boundaries of existing dioceses, archdeaconries, rural deaneries, and parishes, and for the creation of new ones; to hold and administer the property of ecclesiastical persons and corporations, or to superintend its administration by its holders, and to receive and administer private gifts for ecclesiastical purposes. These are all functions which concern the material side of the Church's work, with which the State is necessarily concerned, its territorial boundaries and temporal property, and can be carried out by suitable persons appointed by the State without any taint of Erastianism attaching to the Church, or interference with its spiritual character.

The Cathedrals Commission, 1852.—After the Act of 1840 (above) it was felt that while some abuses and inequalities in cathedral chapters had been reformed, the general result had been to reduce their dignity without increasing their efficiency, and on 10th November 1852 a Commission of thirteen members, including Archbishops Sumner and Musgrave, Bishops Blomfield (*q.v.*) and Wilberforce (*q.v.*), and Dr. Hook (*q.v.*) was appointed, to report how the cathedral and collegiate churches might be made 'more available for promoting the high and holy purposes for which they were founded.' Its first Report (6th April 1854) is a statement, based on the evidence supplied by the various chapters, of the history and constitution of the cathedral and collegiate bodies. Its second (16th March 1855) recommends the erection of a see of Cornwall, to be fixed at St. Columb Major, the rector of which had made a liberal offer towards its endowment. In its third Report (10th May 1855) the Commission returned to its main subject, and submitted a plan for the reorganisation of the constitution, functions, and revenues of chapters. It further recommended that an enabling Act should be passed to provide for the creation of new dioceses as required and as funds became available. No legislation followed immediately from this Commission.

The Clerical Subscription Commission, 1864.—In 1863 Mr. C. Buxton moved in the House of Commons that it was desirable to relax the subscription to the formularies required of the clergy by the Acts of Supremacy and Uniformity (*q.v.*) and other statutes, and by the Thirty-sixth Canon, alleging that they were too stringent, and debarred many from holy orders. A Commission of twenty-seven members, including eight archbishops and bishops, was appointed (8th February 1864) to report how these forms might be altered and simplified while still securing conformity with the doctrine and ritual of the Church. On 9th February 1865 it presented a unanimous Report, the most important recommendation being that Declarations of Assent to the Prayer Book and the Articles of Religion and against Simony should be substituted for the forms hitherto in use. On this Report Parliament founded the Clerical Subscription Act, 1865 (28-9 Vic. c. 122), and

Convocation amended the canons to bring them into harmony with it. The result was to substitute a general assent to the doctrine of the formularies for a particular acceptance of everything contained in them.

The Ritual Commission, 1867, was due to the rapid growth of ceremonial in the 'sixties and of the heated controversy to which it gave rise. Lord Shaftesbury desired to restrain the use of vestments (*q.v.*) by statute, but Lord Derby's government considered it advisable to inquire into the subject before legislating. The project of a Royal Commission was supported by Gladstone (*q.v.*), then in opposition, and by S. Wilberforce (*q.v.*), who wished to check Shaftesbury's 'short and easy method of persecution.' The Government declined to limit the scope of the Commission to vestments or ornaments as Wilberforce and Archbishop Longley wished. It was appointed (3rd June) to inquire into differences of practice which had arisen from varying interpretations of the rubrics, with a view of amending them so as to secure uniformity of practice in matters deemed essential, and to report upon the advisability of revising the Table of Lessons. Its twenty-nine members included Longley, Archbishop Beresford of Armagh (for its scope extended to the Irish Church, not yet disestablished), Bishops Tait (*q.v.*), Thirlwall (*q.v.*), and Wilberforce, Dean Stanley (*q.v.*), and Sir R. Phillimore (*q.v.*). Shaftesbury declined to serve because he owned that he could not consider the subject impartially, and he objected to the inclusion of Wilberforce as a partisan on the other side. Eight of the Commissioners, including Wilberforce, Phillimore, and J. G. Hubbard, founder of St. Alban's, Holborn, formed themselves into a private committee to guide the proceedings. They seem to have been successful in making the first two Reports less adverse to the 'ritualists' than they would otherwise have been. The first Report (19th August) was drafted by Hubbard and inspired principally by Wilberforce. It deals solely with vestments, and states that though some witnesses regard these as important none consider them essential, while they give offence to many. It therefore recommends that an easy and effective method of restraining variations from established usage should be provided. What this was to be was revealed by the second Report (30th April 1868). The bishop, or on appeal the archbishop, was to hear complaints from responsible parishioners aggrieved by departures from established usage, and to enforce their discontinuance by summary process. There was to be an appeal to the Privy Council on points of law only. Wilberforce, the leading spirit of the Commission, and nine other members dissented wholly or in part from this Report, after 'hot fights' against its 'tyranny and unfairness.' Shaftesbury, demanding in the House of Lords that legislation should follow these Reports, declared that 'the very fate of the Church of England was trembling in the balance.' Lord Salisbury deprecated haste and excitement upon so serious a matter, and said that to listen to Shaftesbury's 'tone of menace' they might imagine 'he had an enormous physical force in the country at his back—a Barebones Parliament sitting in the other House, and a Puritan Minister storming at their Lordships' Bar.'

The remainder of the Commission's history was less controversial. In January 1869 it was reappointed with some changes. Its third Report (12th January 1870) presented a revised Table of Lessons, based on the desirability of varying and shortening many of those previously in use. The Lessons taken from the Apocrypha were reduced from one hundred and thirty-two to forty-four. The Ordinary was to have power to sanction the substitution of other Lessons for those appointed. These proposals were considered and approved by Convocation, and became statute law by the Prayer Book (Table of Lessons) Act, 1871 (34-5 Vic. c. 37). Meanwhile, the Commission had presented its fourth and last Report (31st August 1870), which dealt with the whole of the rubrics and recommended a number of alterations. It left the Ornaments Rubric untouched, but suggested that an explanatory note be appended to the Athanasian Creed, a proposal which raised a storm of controversy. Phillimore and Lord Carnarvon withheld their signatures from the Report, and every one of the other Commissioners dissented from it on one or more points. No fewer than seventeen qualified their assent to the recommendation as to the Athanasian Creed, most of these, including Tait, wishing to discontinue its public use. From such inconclusive and divided counsels little practical result could be expected. Letters of Business were issued to the Convocations to consider the revision of the rubrics, which they did at great length but without practical result. A few of the less important proposals of the fourth Report formed the basis of the Act of Uniformity Amendment Act, 1872 (35-6 Vic. c. 35). The failure of the Commission to solve the ritual problem made legislation inevitable, and so prepared the way for the Public Worship Regulation Act (*q.v.*).

The Benefices Commission, 1878, was the outcome of flagrant abuses of church patronage. The laws against simony were systematically broken or evaded. Livings were 'publicly advertised and privately sold' by agents, who issued periodical catalogues under such names as *The Church Preferment Gazette,* a system, said Bishop Magee (*q.v.*), 'which combines the worst scandals of publicity with the worst evils of privacy.' Chiefly at his instance a Commission of twelve was appointed, 1st June 1878, which in its Report (14th August 1879) acknowledged the existence of flagrant abuses. Its chief recommendations, based on the principle that patronage is a trust to be exercised for the spiritual benefit of the parishioners rather than a mere right of property, were that the sale of advowsons by public auction and the sale of next presentations should be forbidden, and restrictions placed on secret trafficking in livings; that the Declaration against Simony should be amended; that the bishop's power to refuse institution to an unfit presentee should be extended, and some opportunity of objecting given to parishioners; and that Donatives [PECULIARS] should be abolished. The subject was much discussed in Parliament, but without practical result till 1898, when an Act was passed incorporating most of these recommendations (Benefices Act, 61-2 Vic. c. 48).

The Ecclesiastical Courts Commission, 1881, had a very different task from that of its predecessor of 1830. The quasi-ecclesiastical jurisdiction to which the earlier Commission gave almost exclusive attention had been abolished. The church courts were now confined to purely ecclesiastical matters. And the methods by which they dealt with cases of doctrine and ritual, which in 1830 were almost unknown as subjects of litigation, had produced more than one serious crisis. [COURTS, RITUAL CASES.] The policy of prosecutions had broken down, and the Public Worship Regulation Act, so far from strengthening this policy, had conspicuously failed 'to put down ritualism.' The 'ritualists' had repudiated the authority of the courts, and the imprisonment of four of them had produced a reaction in their favour. At this point Archbishop Tait, wearied with ritual disputes, on behalf of the bishops and of Convocation, formally asked the Government to appoint a Commission. Mr. Gladstone, then Prime Minister, and Lord Chancellor Selborne willingly agreed, and on 16th May 1881 the Commission was appointed 'to inquire into the constitution and working of the Ecclesiastical Courts as created or modified under the Reformation Statutes of the 24th and 25th years of King Henry VIII. and any subsequent Acts.' It was felt that this would give those who objected to the existing courts an opportunity of stating their case. The Commission was a strong one of twenty-five members, including Archbishops Tait and Thomson, Bishop Benson (*q.v.*) of Truro, who succeeded Tait as president of it in February 1883, two other bishops, Lord Chief Justice Coleridge, Lord Penzance, Sir R. Phillimore, several other lawyers, and two eminent historians, Drs. Stubbs (*q.v.*) and Freeman. It examined fifty-six witnesses, and the minutes of evidence contain much that is still of interest and value. Besides taking oral evidence, it published a body of information concerning the judicial procedure of other Churches. But its most notable and permanent work is to be found in the Historical Appendices to the Report. Five of these are by Dr. Stubbs, whom Freeman called 'the hero' of the Commission. They contain some of his most valuable historical work, and as a summary of the history of ecclesiastical jurisdiction in England, its true nature and relation to the State, are not likely to be superseded. The Report (July 1883) proposed a complete scheme of ecclesiastical judicature, consisting of diocesan, provincial, and final courts. It draws a distinction between cases involving doctrine or ritual, and others, such as prosecutions for misconduct, which may be tried by the Official Principal. Doctrinal or ritual suits may be tried by the bishop or archbishop in person with legal and theological assessors. The final court is to consist of five lay judges to be appointed by the Crown, each of whom is to make a declaration that he is a member of the Church of England as by law established. Only nine commissioners signed this Report without qualification. Fourteen expressed dissent on various points. Lord Penzance submitted a separate Report. Convocation objected to the proposed final court and no legislation followed. The most important result of the Commission, apart from the historical work of Dr. Stubbs, was that both evidence and Report showed the strength of the case against the Privy Council and Lord Penzance's court. It thus helped to justify those who had resisted them, and played its part in bringing to an end the period of ritual prosecutions.

The Ecclesiastical Discipline Commission, 1904, was the result of an agitation carried on with vigour, both inside and outside Parliament, against the alleged increase of ceremonial excesses. To satisfy the supporters of this movement who were anxious for legislation, the Prime Minister, Mr. A. J. Balfour, appointed a Commission, 23rd April 1904. It comprised Sir M. Hicks-Beach (afterwards Lord St. Aldwyn) as chairman, Archbishop Davidson of Canterbury, Bishop Paget of Oxford, Sir Lewis Dibdin, Dean of the Arches, and ten other members. It was 'to inquire into the alleged prevalence of breaches or neglect of the law relating to the conduct of Divine Service in the Church of England and to the ornaments and fittings of churches; and to consider the existing powers and procedure applicable to such irregularities.' It held 118 meetings, examined 164 witnesses, and the minutes of evidence extend to 23,638 questions and answers, many of considerable length. A feature of the evidence was the reports supplied by the Church Association [SOCIETIES, ECCLESIASTICAL] and others on over 550 churches where illegal ceremonial was alleged to be in use; and more would have followed had not the Commission intimated that sufficient evidence of this class had been given. The witnesses included some twenty bishops and a number of authorities on liturgiology and ecclesiastical law and history. The Report, which was unanimous, was presented, 21st June 1906. It summarised the evidence on illegal ceremonial, distinguishing those breaches of the law which appeared to the Commission to possess doctrinal significance. A historical survey from 1840 followed, designed to show how the present disregard of the letter of the law arose. The Commissioners arrived at two main conclusions: (1) 'the law of public worship in the Church of England is too narrow for the religious life of the present generation,' and the Church possesses no sufficient powers to adjust its law to meet the changing requirements of various ages in matters of ceremonial and the like; (2) 'the machinery for discipline has broken down.' The law of public worship is so rigid and the methods of applying it so unsuitable that it cannot be enforced. The Commissioners, however, believed that 'in the large majority of parishes the work of the Church is being quietly and diligently performed' in loyalty to the principles of the Prayer Book. The recommendations may thus be summarised. Convocation should prepare a new Ornaments Rubric and a general revision of the rubrics with a view to their enactment by Parliament. The system of courts proposed by the Commission of 1883 is again recommended, with the exception that questions of doctrine or ritual not clearly governed by 'documents having the force of Acts of Parliament' are to be referred to the whole bench of bishops, whose decision is to bind the final court. More power to regulate ornaments and the conduct of divine service should be given to the bishops, their veto should be abolished, illegal practices significant of doctrine 'should be promptly made to cease,' and the decisions of the courts enforced by deprivation. Machinery should be provided for the creation of new dioceses. In consequence of this Report Letters of Business were issued to the Convocations on 10th November 1906, bidding them report upon the desirability and form of a new Ornaments Rubric, and other modifications of the law relating to the conduct of divine service and the ornaments of churches.   [G. C.]

> The principal authorities are the official proceedings of each Commission : those of 1689 were reprinted by order of the House of Commons in 1854. See also for it Burnet's *Hist. of His Own Time*; for the nineteenth-century Commissions, Hansard, *Parl. Debates, passim*, and (since its revival) *Chronicle of Convocation*; for the Ritual Commission see also *Life of Bishop Wilberforce*, and for the Courts Commission, 1881, Hutton, *Memoir of Bishop Stubbs*.

COMMON PRAYER, Book of. At the beginning of the sixteenth century, with two local exceptions, the Roman rite prevailed throughout the Western Church. This did not mean simple uniformity ; dioceses and religious orders, and even particular churches, had their own 'uses,' diverse from one another in respect of both rite and ceremony, though all conforming to the ' Roman ' type. The local exceptions were the diocese of Milan, where the 'Ambrosian,' a half-Romanised Gallican rite, was in use ; and Spain, where in a few churches the old Spanish rite, commonly called the 'Mozarabic,' survived, and was reinvigorated by Cardinal Ximenes by the publication of the Missal in 1500 and of the Breviary in 1502. But there were several forces making for liturgical reform. (1) The Renaissance : the fastidious Ciceroni-anism of the Italian humanists and the Roman court was shocked by the latinity of the service-books, and Ferreri, Bishop of Guardia Alferi, was commissioned by Leo X. to rewrite the hymns and to reform the Breviary. The hymns were rewritten and published : but the Breviary never saw the light ; and the whole scheme was wrecked by the sack of Rome in 1527 and the downfall of the humanism of the Curia. (2) The longstanding dissatisfaction with the condition of the Breviary, on the ground of the inadequate recitation of the Psalter through

the multiplication of festivals and octaves, which interrupted the course by the constant repetition of the festal Psalms ; the excessive shortening of the lessons from Holy Scripture, and the unedifying character of the lessons from the lives of saints ; the burdensomeness of added devotions : and so on. This dissatisfaction resulted in two reforms—by commission of Clement VII.—one that of Carafa, afterwards Paul IV., of which little is known ; the other that of Quignon, Cardinal of St. Cross. Quignon's *Breviarium Romanum* was approved by Paul III. and published in 1535 ; but it was so drastic in its simplification of things that it was immediately condemned by the Sorbonne, and in consequence a second recension was issued in 1536, in which some old features were restored. This Breviary was in wide-spread use until it was displaced by the reformed Breviary of Pius V. (1568). (3) The Reformation, which everywhere, along with changes in other respects, implied liturgical reform. In Germany the foundation was laid by Luther, for the Mass in his *Formula Missae* (1523) and *Deutsche Messe* (1526), for baptism in *Taufbüchlein* (1523, 1526), for marriage in *Traubüchlein* (1534), for ordination in *Ordinationis Formula* (1537), and in his Litany (1529). The principles here involved were embodied, with varying divergence in detail from the traditional rites, in the multitude of *Kirchenordnungen*, in which the Lutheran reformation was applied to the several areas in which it was accepted. More drastic and revolutionary changes resulted from Zwingli's reforms in Zurich and Calvin's in Geneva. But all these reforms agreed in one respect, viz. in the more or less complete substitution of the vernacular for Latin as the liturgical language, thus relating themselves to the growing *sense of nationality*, which was otherwise operative in the Reformation, and may perhaps be reckoned as a fourth, if subordinate, force making for liturgical reform. But there was reform apart from the Reformation, if springing out of the same causes. Such moderate and Catholic reform is represented by the Council of Cologne, 1536, and that of Mainz in 1549, both of which enjoined some measure of liturgical emendation, and urged or hinted that the people should be instructed in the meaning of ceremonies, providing material for such instruction in the *Encheiridion* of Cologne and the *Institutio* of Mainz, and perhaps suggesting the vernacular instructions inserted into the later sixteenth-century German *Ritualia*. In Cologne a few years later the archbishop, Hermann von Wied, went over to Lutheranism, and endeavoured to enforce a Lutheran reformation, regulated by the *Einfaltigs Bedenken*, 1543 (*Pia deliberatio*, 1545; Eng. trans., *Consultation*, 1547), the work mainly of Bucer (*q.v.*) and Melanchthon. This was resisted by the chapter of Cologne, who replied to it in the *Antididagme Coloniense*, 1544, a moderate Catholic counter-statement and defence. Hermann's attempt failed, and he was ultimately excommunicated. Meanwhile, as part of the revival of Greek letters, the principal Greek liturgies had been printed, and had come to the knowledge of Western scholars and divines. Such was the general situation when liturgical reform began to be undertaken in England; and most of these movements and measures influenced or found their parallel in the English movement.

Some beginnings of change were made in Henry VIII.'s reign. (*a*) It was proposed in 1542, and again in 1543, to amend the service-books by purging them of unauthentic and superstitious texts; and meanwhile the Sarum Breviary was enjoined on the whole province of Canterbury. (*b*) The *Ten Articles* of 1536 included an exposition of the nature of ceremonies and of the meaning of several of them; and this exposition was, with the rest of the *Ten Articles*, incorporated in the *Bishops' Book* of 1537 and the *King's Book* of 1543, catechisms parallel to those of Cologne and Mainz, which contributed something to the Book of Common Prayer. A parallel exposition was contained in the *Thirteen Articles* of 1538. In 1540 certain bishops were commissioned by the King 'to separate pious from impious ceremonies and to teach the true use of them'—a commission which resulted in the so-called *Rationale* or *Book of Ceremonies*, an exposition of existing usages influenced by the *Ten Articles*, and still more by the *Encheiridion* of Cologne. (*c*) The Bible [BIBLE, ENGLISH] was translated into English, and the several translations and revisions issued in the *Great Bible* of 1539 and 1541, which became the liturgical text; and in 1543 it was required that this Bible should be read through publicly by means of a lesson to be added to Matins and Evensong on all holy days. (*d*) In view of the Scottish and French wars of 1544, the usual processions of general intercession were enjoined to be used on Wednesdays and Fridays, and the English Litany, the work of Cranmer (*q.v.*), was issued for the purpose (27th May). This was not a mere litany, but a ' rogation ' or ' procession.' It consisted of the Litany proper, followed by a procession-anthem, the traditional prayers ' in time of war ' (' From

our enemies,' etc.), and concluded by the priest's versicle and its response, and a series of Collects. Its basis is the Sarum Litany and Rogation for Rogation Monday, with the omission of the invocations of individual saints; modifications in detail and a considerable number of suffrages are derived from Luther's *Litany* of 1529, and some details, including the ' Prayer of St. Chrysostom,' from the Greek Liturgy of Constantinople (ed. 1528); while some elements are new or derived from unknown sources. Later in the year Cranmer was engaged in an attempt to translate and adapt the whole Sarum *Processional*; but the attempt failed, and in 1545 a royal injunction directed the use of the English ' Procession ' and ' none other ' on all Sundays and holy days, and thus abolished the *Processional*.

Edward VI. succeeded on 28th January 1547, and further changes soon followed. In 1547 and 1548 English was increasingly used—first at Compline in the King's chapel (11th April 1547), then for Epistle and Gospel in High Mass (August), and for the *Gloria*, *Credo*, and *Agnus Dei* in the Mass at the opening of Parliament (4th November); in May 1548 it was adopted for Mass and Divine Service in St. Paul's and many parish churches in London, and before September in the royal chapel. The Royal Injunctions (August 1547) besides directing the use of English in the Epistle and Gospel at High Mass, and a lesson in English from the New Testament at Matins, and from the Old Testament at Evensong, again abrogated all processions except the English Litany, requiring this to be sung before High Mass kneeling and without perambulation; and prescribed the form of Bidding Prayer. Early in 1548 the Council forbade the distinctive ceremonies of Candlemas, Ash Wednesday, and Palm Sunday, and the veneration of the cross on Good Friday. In December 1548 the Convocation of Canterbury approved of Communion in both kinds, and an Act was passed in Parliament in the same sense. To carry this measure into effect, a company of bishops and divines compiled *The Order of Communion*, which was issued by royal proclamation on 8th March 1548. This Order was in English, and contained (after a notice of Communion and a warning to prepare for it, to be used on some day preceding that of the Communion) an exhortation at the time of Communion and the invitation; a general confession, absolution, and comfortable words; the prayer *We do not presume*; the form of administration, and *The peace of God*. This was to be inserted into the Latin Mass immediately after the Communion of the priest. Part of the confession, three of the ' comfortable words,' the opening of the absolution, and the added ' which was given for thee,' ' which was shed for thee' in the administration, are derived from Hermann's *Consultation*; the body of the absolution and of the words of administration are translated from the Latin ; the *We do not presume* is a compilation from the New Testament, the Greek liturgy of St. Basil, and mediæval commonplaces.

FIRST BOOK OF EDWARD VI., 1549.—In the autumn of 1548 it was made known that the preparation of an English service-book was already in hand. ' Certain bishops and notable learned men,' ' some favouring the old, some the new learning,' were assembled at Windsor and then at Chertsey for the settlement of ' a uniform order of prayer.' It is unknown precisely who they were. It is probable that much of the book was already in existence, and it is possible that it had been used in the English services already mentioned. Cranmer had long been busy. As we have seen above, in 1544 he had experimented on an English *Processional*, and in the following years he composed two experimental schemes for a reformed *Breviary*. In any case some part of the new book, and in particular the Canon of the Mass, was ready apparently in October, and was discussed and signed, with reservations, by all the bishops but one ; and the whole book was ready by the middle of December. It was read to the Commons on 19th December ; and the Act of Uniformity (*q.v.*) enforcing it was passed in the Lords on 15th January, in the Commons on 21st January, and received the royal assent on 14th March. The records of Convocation for these years have perished, and there is some conflict of evidence as to whether the book received the consent of Convocation, but it is more probable that it did not. The ' First Book of Edward VI.' was quite new in two respects : first, that it was wholly in English ; and secondly, that it combined in a single volume the ' Common Prayer' which had hitherto been contained in separate volumes, the *Breviary*, the *Processional*, and the *Missal*, and the ' other rites and ceremonies' of the Church,' contained in the *Manual* and part of the *Pontifical*, ' according to the use of the Church of England,' which thus becomes one and the same everywhere. The basis of the whole is the Roman rite according to the Sarum use ; but it includes contributions from the Greek rite of Constantinople, from the Mozarabic rite, and from the Lutheran, while

avoiding distinctively Lutheran doctrine. The Preface on the Divine Service is largely derived from Quignon's Breviary ; the rules as to the recitation of the Psalter and the reading of Holy Scripture are from Cranmer's second experimental Breviary scheme ; the Calendar is considerably simplified, chiefly by omission of all names except those derived from the New Testament ; Divine Service is reduced to Matins (combining features of the old Matins, Lauds, and Prime) and Evensong (similarly derived from Vespers and Compline), and in general structure follows Lutheran models ; the Litany is that of 1544, with the omission of all invocation of saints and the reduction of the collects ; the Mass reproduces the structure and much of the content of the Roman, the admirable paraphrase of the canon (affected considerably by the *Antididagma* of Cologne), making explicit the commemorative character of the act, and including an invocation of ' the Word and Holy Spirit' (from the liturgy of St. Basil) before the Institution, and incorporates the *Order of Communion* of 1548 ; the orders of Baptism are largely affected by the *Consultation* of Hermann, and in the consecration of the font by the Mozarabic rite ; the order of Confirmation includes a short catechism on the Creed, the Decalogue, and the Lord's Prayer, abolishes the use of chrism, and borrows a prayer from Hermann ; the order of Matrimony almost wholly reproduces the traditional use, but introduces a new feature, the declaration of the marriage, from Hermann ; the Visitation of the Sick closely follows the old order, with some simplification, but Extreme Unction is reduced to its simplest essentials, and the Commendation of the dying is wholly omitted ; the Burial of the Dead is a masterly condensation of the old rite, bringing out its essential structure as an Office of the Dead (three psalms, lesson, Lord's Prayer, preces, and collect), a procession, the committal of the body (affected by Hermann), and a Mass ; the Purification of Women is practically unchanged ; the rite for Ash Wednesday follows the old rite but substitutes the comminations and the penitential homily for the imposition of ashes ; and the book ends with a long note, ' Of Ceremonies,' in the sense of the *Thirteen Articles* of 1538, and ' Certayne Notes' on vestments, gestures, and other points. The book was variously received : some accepted it eagerly and anticipated the date prescribed for its adoption ; others accepted it grudgingly and adapted it as far as possible to the traditional usage ; while the rebels in the West put the abolition of all that it involved in the forefront of their demands.

No provision was made in the book for any pontifical office except Confirmation. On 31st January 1550 an Act was passed empowering the King to appoint six prelates and six other learned men to draw up forms of Ordination, and on 2nd February an Order of Council appointed the commissioners, whose names are unknown. The forms had obviously been already compiled, for the work of the commission was completed before 8th February, and *The forme and maner of makyng and consecratyng of Archebisshoppes, Bisshoppes, Priestes and Deacons* was published at the beginning of March. Though the Act had mentioned 'bishops, priests, and deacons and other ministers,' the new book provided only for the three orders, thus abolishing the sub-diaconate and the minor orders. In structure the new forms followed the traditional scheme, with slight changes in order; but in two ways the scheme was simplified, viz. first, by the omission of the vestings and of the unctions of priests and bishops; and secondly, the act of ordination was unified in contrast with the duplication in the Latin rite resulting from the combination of Gallican with Roman forms. On the other hand, certain additions were made, viz. the Oath of the King's Supremacy is required; the element of instruction is greatly enlarged, particularly in the long exhortation of priests; and deacons and priests are publicly examined, which hitherto had only been done in the case of bishops. As to the content of the scheme, a large part of the matter, especially in the ordination of priests, is derived from Bucer's *De ordinatione legitima*, and particularly the introits, most of the selection of lessons, the long exhortation, most of the examination of deacons and priests and part of that of bishops, and the central prayer for priests and the address of that for bishops; the Litany is that of the book of 1549; the rest is either new, or translation, paraphrase or modification of Latin matter. A characteristic of the whole work is its strong emphasis on the ministry of the word.

SECOND PRAYER BOOK OF EDWARD VI., 1552.—The First Book was not a final measure, and was perhaps never intended to be so by its chief promoters. In the three years following its publication a new and extreme type of reformer, inspired from Switzerland, was gaining influence; the moderating influence of Somerset was withdrawn and was succeeded by the violence of Warwick; the bishops of the old learning were mostly elimi-

nated; Ridley (*q.v.*) was carrying things with a high hand in ordering, spite of the rubrics of the Prayer Book, the destruction of altars in the diocese of London, and his cue was followed by the Council, which ordered the destruction of them everywhere; and two of the foreign divines who had come to England, P. Martyr and Bucer, wrote criticisms of the book, Bucer's *Censura* being a long review of it in detail. In the end the book was drastically revised. Now again nothing is known of the details of the process, except that it was effected by Cranmer, Ridley, and 'a great many bishops and other the best learned within the realm and appointed for that purpose.' The second Act of Uniformity, enforcing the new book, was finally passed in Parliament on 14th April 1552, to come into operation on 1st November. Convocation had nothing to do with it. In consequence of a violent sermon of Knox's against kneeling at Communion, the Council suspended the printing of the book (27th September) and required Cranmer to reconsider the question of kneeling. Cranmer protested, but on 27th October the Council ordered the declaration on kneeling (the 'Black Rubric') 'to be joined unto the book.'

In this revision the principal changes were that the sermon 'Dearly beloved brethren,' with its text, and a general confession and absolution, were prefixed to Matins and Evensong, and psalms alternative to *Benedictus*, *Magnificat*, and *Nunc dimittis* were added; the second Masses of Christmas and Easter, and that of St. Mary Magdalen, were deleted, the introits and 'post-communions' were abolished, the *Gloria in excelsis* was put after the communion, the *Kyrie* was farsed with the decalogue, the canon and communion were broken up, the intercession being attached to the offertory, and the Lord's Prayer and the oblation put after the communion, the confession, absolution, and comfortable words before the preface, and *We do not presume* after the preface and sanctus, and a new and unscriptural form of administration was substituted for the traditional form; in Baptism the exorcism, the white vesture, and the unction were removed, the cross shifted to follow the baptism, and a thanksgiving was added; the cross was omitted at Confirmation; Extreme Unction and reservation were ignored; the psalms were omitted in the Visitation of the Sick and in Burial, and prayers and the Mass for the departed omitted; in the Ordinations, which were now made part of the Book of Common Prayer, though still with a separate title-page, the introits and the delivery of chalice and paten to priests and of the crozier to bishops were abolished. As to the origins of these changes, other than the drifting of the minds of those who were concerned in them, two can be indicated : the *Censura* of Bucer, many of the suggestions of which were adopted, and the perverse desire to cut the ground from under some passages of Stephen Gardiner's (*q.v.*) treatise on the Sacrament of the Altar (1551) in reply to Cranmer's book on the same subject (1549), in which Gardiner had argued that the Mass of 1549 was consistent with the traditional doctrine. In England this book was in use for less than a year.

THIRD PRAYER BOOK OF 1559.—On the accession of Mary (10th July 1553) the English book continued in use for some months alongside of a partial restoration of the Latin ; but late in the year the first Act of Repeal abolished the Act of Uniformity, and restored, on and after 20th December, the liturgical situation of the last year of Henry VIII. (*i.e.* the Latin rite with the English Litany), and forbade all other use. For the rest of the reign such history as there is of the Book of Common Prayer shifts to Frankfort, where one party of the English exiles fought successfully for the use of the Second Prayer Book as against a Swiss type of service. [MARIAN EXILES.] On the accession of Elizabeth (17th November 1558) no change was made for some time, except that the English Litany, which had obviously fallen into disuse in Mary's reign, was restored in the royal chapel, and a proclamation (27th December) allowed the use of English in the Lord's Prayer, the Creed, the Decalogue, and for the Epistle and Gospel, besides the Litany. Meanwhile, in view of the meeting of Parliament in January, negotiations and deliberations were in progress, of which the history is obscure. There appears to be no certain evidence that, as has been often asserted, it was seriously contemplated to restore the book of 1549 ; in any case, it was the book of 1552 with three specified changes that was, in fact, enjoined by the third Act of Uniformity, which was passed early in 1559. These changes were, the provision of proper first lessons for all Sundays, the omission of the petition against the Pope in the Litany, and the addition of the words of administration of the communion of 1549 before those of 1552. But, in fact, other changes were made, notably the insertion of the 'Ornaments Rubric' (*q.v.*). The Injunctions of 1559 ordered and regulated the use of Rogation-tide processions, enjoined the use of wafer-bread, prescribed the use of Plain-

song, while allowing a hymn in figured music before or after service, and provided a new and enlarged form of Bidding Prayer. In 1561 the Ecclesiastical Commissioners were directed by the Crown to revise the Calendar and the Table of Lessons ; very little change was made in the Lessons, but a number of names were added to the Calendar. Nothing more need be related for this reign except that a number of small verbal changes were made in the text, apparently without authority, and that the Puritan party formulated their objections to the book.

FOURTH PRAYER BOOK OF 1604.—On the accession of James I. (24th March 1603) the Puritan party presented (April) the 'Millenary Petition,' in which they set forth their grievances generally and in particular as against the Book of Common Prayer. In consequence the Hampton Court Conference (*q.v.*) was summoned, and met 14th, 16th, 18th January 1604. The result was that a number of changes were made, ostensibly by way of 'explanation,' most of them of no importance, a few of them more notable, especially the requirement of a ' lawful minister ' for the administration of private baptism, and the addition to the Catechism of a section on the Sacraments, mostly derived from A. Nowell's short catechism, *Christianae pietatis prima institutio* (1570). These changes were ratified by Convocation in the eightieth canon of 1604. During the rest of the reign of James I. and during that of Charles I. the introduction of unauthorised verbal changes continued.

In 1637 was issued the—for the moment ill-fated—Scottish Prayer Book, which only concerns us in so far as it influenced in some details the last revision of the English book. On 1st March 1641 the Lords appointed a committee ' to take into consideration all innovations in the Church respecting religion ' ; and a sub-committee drew up a paper recommending the consideration of the current Puritan objections and of other points ; but nothing came of this. On 13th January 1645 Parliament abolished the Prayer Book and substituted the *Directory*, and on 23rd August they made the use of the Prayer Book in public or in private punishable with fine and imprisonment. For the next fifteen years the book was in abeyance. But equivalent forms were tolerated so long as they were not formally identical with those of the Book of Common Prayer. Accordingly Jeremy Taylor and Sanderson drew up forms, which had some influence on the subsequent revision ; and Sanderson, as a casuist, had occasion to justify his procedure as against the scruples of those ecclesiastics who felt themselves bound by the Act of Uniformity (*Nine cases of Conscience*, 1685, p. 157).

FIFTH PRAYER BOOK OF 1662.—At the Restoration the Puritan divines again presented their grievances, and Charles II. summoned the Savoy Conference, which sat from time to time from 15th August to 24th July 1661, with the result that a few unimportant concessions were made to the Puritans. [SAVOY CONFERENCE.] Meanwhile a serious revision had been undertaken by the bishops in Convocation, and it made such progress that when on 21st November a King's letter directed a revision, and a committee was appointed for the purpose, the committee at once reported that the proposals were ready for the consideration of the House ; and after discussion and amendment the revised book was signed by the members of both Houses of both Convocations, and the fourth Act of Uniformity, with the revised and signed book (the 'Book Annexed') attached to it, received the royal assent on 19th May 1662. The work of the revision was carefully done, and most of its about six hundred changes were improvements. In some respects the text marks a return to 1549 ; and the revision was affected by Cosin's *Private Devotions* (1627), by the Scottish book of 1637, and notably by Cosin's *Particulars to be Considered* (*Works*, v. 502), and still more by a paper drawn up by M. Wren (*q.v.*) in 1660 (Jacobson, *Fragmentary Illustrations*). In some minor points suggestions of the Lords' Committee of 1641 and of the Puritan divines at the Savoy Conference were adopted, but no serious concessions were made in this direction. The changes made are mostly small ones, by way of improving the sense or the language, or by way of explanation, or to make directions more explicit ; a new office for the Baptism of those of Riper Years, and the Forms of Prayer to be Used at Sea, are provided, and offices for 30th January, 29th May, and 5th November are directed to be added, but did not, in fact, appear in the printed book ; by way of minor additions, the five prayers after Matins and Evensong are added, after the Scottish book of 1637 ; further occasional prayers and a general thanksgiving are provided ; in the Order of Holy Communion, collect, etc., are provided for a sixth Sunday after Epiphany, the placing of the elements on the altar at the offertory, a commemoration of the departed in the prayer for the Church, and the manual acts at consecration, are restored, and the 'Black Rubric' with modifications is again inserted ; in Baptism the consecration

of the water is restored ; the renewal of baptismal vows is prefixed to Confirmation : special prayers are added to the Visitation of the Sick ; psalms are restored to the Order of Burial, but unhappily the structure of the office is disarranged so as to be unintelligible ; the psalms in the Purification of Women are changed ; the arrangement of parts in the Ordinations is in some respects modified, and to the 'forms' of ordination of priests and bishops words are added to make it clear, as against Presbyterian contentions, that the two orders are distinct. Further, the Psalter is for the first time officially included in the volume, and the version of 1611 is substituted for the Great Bible in all lessons from Holy Scripture. The superintendence of the printing of the book was entrusted to Sancroft (*q.v.*) ; and, as directed by the Act of Uniformity, certain copies of the printed book, corrected by the Book Annexed, and certified, along with copies of the Act of Uniformity, under the Great Seal (the 'Sealed Books') were distributed to be laid up in cathedrals and elsewhere.

The book has not been seriously altered since 1662, though efforts have been made to get it changed. A Royal Commission in 1689 drew up lengthy and elaborate proposals for changes with a view to the reconciliation of dissenters, but nothing came of them. [COMMISSIONS, ROYAL.] Agitation for revision was prolonged throughout the eighteenth century, mainly in the Latitudinarian (*q.v.*) interest. The Ritual Commission of 1867 had three results. (1) A new Lectionary was prepared, approved by Convocation and consented to by Parliament in 1871 (34-5 Vic. c. 37). In some respects it was an improvement on the existing Lectionary, but, judged on its merits, it leaves much to be desired. (2) The Act of Uniformity Amendment Act of 1872 (35-6 Vic. c. 35) gave statutory force to a measure of Convocation for the allowance of shortened services and of other liberties in the use of the Prayer Book. If in some respects useful, this measure at the same time went clean contrary to the principles of divine service explicitly laid down in the book itself. (3) In response to royal Letters of Business, Convocation proposed (1879) a number of emendations of the rubrics, but nothing came of this. In 1906, in consequence of the report of the Royal Commission on Ecclesiastical Discipline, Letters of Business were issued to the Convocations, enjoining them to report on the desirability of change of the Ornaments Rubric and of other changes in the law relating to the conduct of divine service and the ornaments of churches. No reply has as yet been returned to the Letters.   [F. E. B.]

Cardwell, *Conferences, Documentary Annals, Synodalia*; Gasquet and Bishop, *Edward VI. and the Book of Common Prayer*; Procter and Frere, *A New History of the Book of Common Prayer*; Gee, *The Elizabethan Prayer Book and Ornaments*.

COMMONWEALTH, Church under the. The story of the Church's fortunes under the Commonwealth literally begins after the death of the King (Charles I.), but the church reforms of the Long Parliament began soon after its meeting, 1641. Numerous petitions were sent in asking for church reform. In answer to one of these —the Kentish petition—a declaration was issued promising 'necessary Reformation of the Government and Liturgy of the Church.' At the outset a majority of those who were ready to reform the Church had no very clear idea what they wished to do except that (1) Parliament was to be supreme in religious as well as civil matters, and (2) 'innovations' should be taken away, and the condition of things under Queen Elizabeth should be restored. 'This Reformation would only take away what was justly offensive and at least unnecessary and burdensome.' This gives us the key to the Parliament's action with regard to the Church up to the King's death, and explains much in the lengthy debates which went on in both Houses from 1642 to 1649.

Some members resented the discipline of the Church as exercised in the Church Courts (*q.v.*), and wished to bring under Parliamentary control all such power as had previously been exercised by the bishops. A large number of the country gentry were jealous of clerical influence, and also disliked the reforms of Archbishop Laud (*q.v.*), but only a small minority really wished to destroy the Church. But this minority knew exactly what it wanted, and desired to get rid of the bishops and the liturgy, and 'to bring the Church into agreement with other Reformed Churches.' This party was able in the end to get its way owing to the necessity of an alliance with the Scots, who were called in to help the Parliament to stem the tide of the Royalist successes in the war.

The English Parliament at first desired to make a civil alliance, but the Scots insisted on their price—a religious agreement between the two countries. Two things stood in the way: episcopacy and the liturgy. At first the reformers in the Commons declared that they desired to return to the primitive form of episcopacy; but in the end they gave way, and in 1643 an Act was passed abolishing episcopacy.

The liturgy still remained. This, they thought, might be amended, as many, probably the majority, still regarded the Prayer Book with affection. The Scots, however, and their friends in Parliament were determined to end the use of what they called the idol of the English people. On the day of Laud's execution, 10th January 1645, the Book of Common Prayer was abolished, and the Directory, a Parliamentary service book drawn up by the Westminster Assembly, was substituted as the 'legal' Prayer Book of the country. The Book of Common Prayer was at first forbidden by an ordinance with no penalties attached; but as this proved ineffective the following penalties were prescribed:—for first offence, £5; for second offence, £10; for third offence, one year's imprisonment without bail, and the minister who failed to use the Directory was to pay forty shillings each offence. Parliament was careful in this, as in other things, to follow the precedent of the Tudor sovereigns.

The Archbishop of Canterbury was imprisoned as soon as the troubles began, and executed in 1645. Williams (*q.v.*), the other primate, with eleven bishops protested against their exclusion from the House of Lords, and were in consequence imprisoned. They were, however, liberated on bail after six months, and returned to their bishoprics to find their palaces used as prisons, and the property of their sees confiscated in those parts where the Parliament held sway. The bishops were unable to carry on the Church's system of worship and discipline owing to the Penal Laws. Some, as Juxon (*q.v.*) of London, were men of property. They lived on their estates, and helped their poorer brethren who were in poverty and distress. Others, as the Puritan Winiffe of Lincoln and Prideaux of Worcester, were reduced to great straits. All suffered alike—men of the Laudian school, moderate men, and men of Puritan inclinations. Bishop Hall of Norwich, for instance, a prelate of moderate opinions and gentle character was expelled from his house, and although a pension of £400 was allowed, it was paid irregularly, and never in full. During the latter years of the period the surviving bishops began to discuss plans for preserving the succession. Proposals were made to consecrate bishops, but legal difficulties were suggested by Royalist laymen, and nothing was done. Priests and deacons, however, were ordained in private, *e.g.* by Skinner of

Oxford, who promised that the letters of orders should be given when the Church was restored.

Many priests were obliged to leave their benefices very early in the war. (1) A grand committee and a sub-committee of the Long Parliament received petitions against the parochial clergy, the charges being generally (*a*) ceremonial or (*b*) evil living. (2) Another committee, *i.e.* for 'plundered ministers,' ejected clergy of Royalist sympathies who had taken the place of men favourable to the Parliamentary cause. (3) When, however, that cause had triumphed, and the Solemn League and Covenant had been agreed to by both Houses, it was made impossible for any loyal clergy to remain at their posts. All above the age of eighteen were to subscribe to the Covenant ' that we shall without respect of persons endeavour the extirpation of Popery, Prelacy' (*i.e.* Government of the Church by Archbishops, Bishops, etc., etc.). Hence many were already expelled under (1); some more under (2); a far larger number under (3) were ejected by local country committees nominated by Parliament.

The Universities.—The two Universities were strongholds of the Church and the training-ground of her ministry. In 1644 a commission under the Earl of Manchester dealt with Cambridge. Masters, fellows, students, members of the university said to be ' scandalous and ill-affected to Parliament,' were summoned before them. They were to lose their places and revenues and to be replaced by ministers approved by the Westminster Assembly: the Covenant was to be offered, and all who refused it were to be deprived. The colleges which had been affected by the Laudian movement, *e.g.* Peterhouse, St. John's, Queens', Jesus, naturally received particularly severe treatment; while others are said to have been more leniently dealt with, sometimes on account of personal influence, *e.g.* Benjamin Whichcote saved many of the Fellows of King's, or because of their well-known Puritan tradition, *e.g.* Emmanuel.

Oxford, as the centre of the Royalist interest, could expect small mercy, and Heads of Colleges and Fellows were treated as at Cambridge. In 1647 a special ordinance was passed for the visitation and reformation of the University by a commission of fourteen laymen and ten divines under the Chancellor, the Earl of Pembroke. The Covenant was to be enforced, the Directory used, and an inquiry made about those who had carried arms against Parliament. There was a Court

of Appeal, in the form of a standing committee, under Sir N. Brent, Warden of Merton, formerly Laud's vicar-general. Nearly five hundred Heads, Canons, and Fellows were expelled, and their places filled by Presbyterians and Independents. Oxford, however, remained in spite of all this a rallying-point for the Church, as the deprived Dean of Christ Church performed the Church services near his college, and they were largely attended by graduates and undergraduates, apparently without much hindrance from the new authorities.

This Oxford congregation is an example of what was going on in Church centres in the country. The mass of the people were under Parliamentary discipline, and obliged to worship according to the Directory, in the parish church. In many places they obviously did so with reluctance. The old Church Feasts were supplanted by the Sabbath and Days of Thanksgiving or Humiliation ordained by the authority of Parliament. Penalties were inflicted upon those who did not observe them, so that, again following precedent, religious worship was made compulsory. In general the people seem to have reluctantly acquiesced, though they occasionally expressed their feelings against the suppression of Christmas, *e.g.* at Canterbury, and Ipswich in 1647, when the churches were again decorated with green, and some attempt was made to restore the old festivities. There is not, however, a sign of the same devotion to the Church among the poorer classes which in later days inspired large numbers of people in France at the Revolution to gather on moorland or in barns to take part in the Church's worship. The scattered congregations of Church people seem to have consisted mainly of the upper and educated class. Sometimes attempts were made to interrupt them — a well-known example being given in Evelyn's (*q.v.*) *Diary* under Christmas Day, 1657, when Peter Gunning's service at Exeter Chapel in London was disturbed by the soldiers. Evelyn's experience is a good example of what was liable to happen to less known Churchmen. He was taken to Whitehall to be examined, and was asked how, ' contrarie to an Ordinance made that none should any longer observe the superstitious time of the Nativity, I durst offend, and particularly be at Common Prayers, which they told me was but the Masse in English. . . . As we went up to receive the Sacrament the miscreants held their muskets against us as if they would have shot us at the Altar, but yet suffering us to finish the Office of Communion, as perhaps not having instructions what to do in case they found us in that action.' So at other times he goes to hear Jeremy Taylor, who preached at a private house in London.

Some Churchmen were allowed to hold benefices, and seem to have used the Prayer Book or parts of it, as George Bull in Bristol ; Hacket (*q.v.*), afterwards Bishop of Lichfield, who omitted such parts of the service as were offensive to those in authority ; others, as Pearson (*q.v.*), preached church doctrine, but did not use the Prayer Book. His lectures at St. Clement's, Eastcheap, have come down to us as *Pearson on the Creed*, and were a means of preserving the foundations of the faith at a time when many were in danger of losing all hold upon the Catholic faith and falling into error.

The temptation to accept the claims of Rome was another danger to the Church. In France, where many Church people were in exile, bishops and clergy held very moderate opinions about the claims of the Holy See, and had a true conception of the rights of a national Church. In Paris the English ambassador's chapel was the spiritual home of many exiled churchmen. Here the Prayer Book was continuously used ; and Cosin (*q.v.*) preached there often, helping ' certain ladys of great qualitie who were then to be discharged from our Queen Mother's service unless they would go over to the Roman masse.' There, too, Morley, afterwards Bishop of Winchester ; Dr. Stewart, Dean of St. Paul's ; Dr. Earle, and many other eminent divines ministered to the faithful; while the Bishop of Galloway conferred holy orders. So when men might have become faint-hearted and almost in despair of the life of the English Church, Cosin, Morley, Sanderson, Bramhall, and Hammond, with others less well known, by their preaching and teaching and solid controversial writings saved many who might have been tempted to find refuge in the Roman Communion. As a matter of fact, very few deserted the Church of England during this crisis: Goodman (*q.v.*), Bishop of Gloucester ; only four clergy belonging to cathedral or collegiate bodies ; and as far as we know no member of the parochial clergy ; while only a very small and insignificant number of laity submitted to the Roman See—a proof, if it were needed, of the falsity of the accusations of popery so freely brought against bishops and clergy during the days of Laud.

The deprived clergy naturally suffered much from poverty. They were supposed, under certain conditions, and if they had not offended, according to the judgment of the

committees, against certain regulations, to receive one-fifth of their benefice as a pension. The restrictions were so severe that very few received any compensation.

Many went abroad, many were confined as prisoners in hulks on the Thames, or in bishops' palaces then used as prisons. Fortunately for themselves, many clergy were able in those times to practise medicine ; while a large number found refuge in the houses of noblemen or gentry, and taught their children or acted as chaplains. We find here and there a rare instance of a churchman being presented to a benefice by a Puritan patron. The best known instance is Dr. Laurence, Master of Balliol and Margaret Professor at Oxford, receiving Somersham from Colonel Walton, whom he had protected after the battle of Edgehill. In some districts—according to Dr. Stoughton the whole of Craven in Yorkshire—the clergy accommodated themselves to the changes and retained their livings.

Five years before the Restoration the clergy suffered the last and in the view of many contemporaries their death-blow from the Government. In 1655, by an edict of the Protector, the deprived clergy who had acted as schoolmasters, chaplains, or tutors were no longer allowed to keep school, preach, or administer sacraments, under pain of imprisonment for the first two offences and banishment for the third offence. ' This was the mournfullest day that in my life I had scene or the Church of England herself since the Reformation ; to the great rejoicing of both Papist and Presbyter.' Such is Evelyn's lament on Christmas Day, 1655, when he went to London for service and heard Dr. Wild ' preach the funeral sermon of Preaching.'

Buildings and Property.—Cathedrals and churches naturally suffered during the war. In 1643 Parliament began to deal with ornaments : altars, candlesticks, basins, etc., were to be removed, and there was much destruction of crosses, statues, and pictures, but monuments of those not reputed saints were to be spared. This was repeated in 1644, when surplices, superstitious vestments, roods, rood-lofts, and holy-water fonts were not to be used any more. Under these ordinances much of the damage popularly ascribed to Cromwell and his army was done. Windows were broken and brasses and bells taken away from the churches. The cathedrals suffered even more than the parish churches—Winchester being a notable exception owing to the Parliamentary leader being an old Wykehamist. At the close of the war, when the country was settling down under the Protector, and the churches were being used by the preachers of the new establishment, an ordinance provided that rates should be levied by churchwardens and overseers for the repair of the buildings.

Parliament also took over the control of the endowments and the patronage when it was in the hands of Royalists. It acted on the principle that all their rights were forfeited, and also confiscated the property of the sees. The episcopal estates were used to pay for war expenses, and the property of deans and chapters who had assisted the King were also used by the government. Parochial tithes, however, were still used for the maintenance of the Parliamentary ministers and of the Protector's establishment. They were, however, no longer recovered in ecclesiastical courts, but before two J.P.'s, who might examine defendants on oath and adjudge the case with costs. The ordinance which touched episcopal property and rights did not affect advowsons, and lay patrons who were on the side of Parliament did not lose their rights.

Church reforms of some value were also suggested and partly tried, such as equalisation of incomes, division of large parishes, increase of income of poor preachers, which were to be benefited from 'impropriate tithes,' 'first fruits,' and tenths: while very large sums were expended upon the Parliamentary committees and individuals who administered Church property.   [B. B.]

John Walker, *Sufferings of the Clergy* (1714); Shaw, *Hist. Eng. Ch.*, 1640-1666; Blaxland, *The Struggle with Puritanism*; W. H. Hutton, *Hist. Eng. Ch.*, 1625-1714.

CONTINUITY OF THE CHURCH OF ENGLAND.

This phrase implies that since St. Augustine (*q.v.*) extended the organisation of the Holy Catholic Church to England in 597 its existence here has been continuous: that the body known to-day as the Church of England is still the Holy Catholic Church in England, looking back on an unbroken life since the day when Augustine planted it. This continuity has been attacked from very different points of view. It is undeniable that the Church of 597 continued unbroken down to 1534, and it is equally undeniable that the Church of 1559 is still in existence to-day. But between those points 1534 and 1559 a break is alleged in the continuity. The ultimate underlying question is, In what does the identity of the Church consist? The English Church is clear that there must be continuity of faith and doctrine as contained in the Apostles'

and Nicene Creeds, and in Holy Scripture as 'the rule and ultimate standard of faith'; of the two Sacraments of the Gospel; and of jurisdiction, the 'historic Episcopate.' This was laid down by the Lambeth Conference of 1888. [REUNION.] This premised, the subject may conveniently be considered under four heads:—

1. *Continuity of Law.*—The question at issue is not whether in the sixteenth century the Church repealed or amended some part of its law. A far greater matter of principle is at stake, and it may conveniently be expressed in the words of the late Professor F. W. Maitland (1850-1906), whose *Roman Canon Law in the Church of England* (1898) contains the most lucid and brilliant statement of the case for a breach of continuity in this respect. The Ecclesiastical Courts Commission [COMMISSIONS, ROYAL] had reported in 1883 that 'the Canon Law of Rome, although always regarded as of great authority in England, was not held to be binding on the courts,' meaning apparently not that it might be overridden in the secular courts, but that it was not binding in English Church courts unless it had been 'received'; that the Papal Law Books were regarded 'as manuals but not as codes of statutes.' This contention Maitland set himself to controvert, relying mainly on the mediæval English canonists, and especially on Lyndwood (*q.v.*), whose writings, he contends, assume that the Roman Canon Law, the *ius commune* of the Church, was regarded by the English Church courts as 'absolutely binding statute law' without any reference to its 'reception' here; and that it was merely eked out at a few points by the purely English ordinances of the archbishops. Lyndwood's attitude is that of a lawyer commenting on and reconciling, where necessary, with a supreme body of law the edicts of an 'inferior legislator,' the archbishop, who may make for his province statutes which are merely declaratory of the *ius commune* of the Church, and may supplement the papal legislation, but has no power to derogate from, far less to abrogate, the laws made by his superior. Such, Maitland argues, were the respective positions of the Roman and the purely English canon law in the English Church before the breach with Rome. At that point we come upon 'a sudden catastrophe in the history of the spiritual courts. Henceforth they are expected to enforce, and without complaint they do enforce, statutes of the temporal legislature. . . . Not only is their sphere of action limited by the secular power—that is a very old phenomenon—but their decisions

are dictated to them by Acts of Parliament—and that is a very new phenomenon.' And these very statutes impose on the Church courts 'not merely new law but a theory about the old law. . . . Henceforth a statutory orthodoxy will compel all judges to say that it was only "by their own consent" that the people of this realm ever paid any regard to decretals or other laws proceeding from any "foreign prince, potentate, or prelate."' Bishop Stubbs in reply pointed out (*Lectures on Med. and Mod. Hist.*, ed. 1900, pp. 335-6) that the difference between his position and Maitland's was not so great as it might appear. But he could not agree that the canon law had a 'vitality and force analogous to that of the national law in temporal matters—that is, that the Corpus Juris stood, in the strict ecclesiastical courts, on the same footing as the Statute Book in the temporal courts. . . . What authority it had it owed rather to tacit assumption than to formal and constitutional acceptance by Church or State.' It is well known that in earlier times canons were regarded as having no force of themselves apart from the mind of the Church, shown by their acceptance. It is true that as the mediæval Church tended to become a State its law came to be regarded as more and more analogous to civil law, and as deriving its force not from the assent of the law-keeper, but from the centralised authority of the lawgiver, the Pope. But, on the other hand, as Mr. Ogle has shown (*Canon Law in Mediæval England*, 1912), such phrases as 'absolutely binding statute law' suggest a misleading analogy when applied to mediæval conditions. They presuppose a central authority with power to enforce its decrees, and ignore the important position occupied, more especially in ecclesiastical affairs, by local law and custom. Moreover, Maitland has throughout both misapprehended and exaggerated the effect of Lyndwood's testimony. In reality Lyndwood treats the archbishops' constitutions as valid. And further, the papal decrees could only operate in England so far as they were admitted by the temporal power—a limitation in which the English Church was content to acquiesce. In 1532-4 this control over legislation was more definitely asserted by the State and accepted by the Church than before. Much of the existing canon law, both papal and national, was to (and still does) remain in force; and the power of making English canon law was to remain as before in the archbishops with their provincial synods. [CONVOCATION, CANON LAW FROM 1534.] But even if the more extreme papalist view

be adopted, it does not follow that there was any break in continuity, any more than there was when the Popes to some extent succeeded in imposing their authority on a church which from the time of Archbishop Theodore (*q.v.*) to the twelfth century had been practically independent as far as legislation was concerned. A synod of 747 laid down that matters which could not be settled by a bishop should be referred to the archbishop in provincial synod, and no mention is made by the synod of any further appeal. In 1115 Pope Paschal II. complained bitterly of the independence of the English Church, and there was no breach of continuity when it succeeded in reasserting that ancient independence in the sixteenth century.

2. *Continuity of Jurisdiction.*—By the constitution of the Catholic Church authority is inherent in and exercised by the episcopate. [AUTHORITY IN THE CHURCH.] During the Middle Ages much of this authority was gradually, and to a large extent insensibly, acquired by the Popes. The civil power as a rule resented this usurpation, and tried, when it could, to check it. Henry VIII., unlike his predecessors, was strong enough to prevent the Popes from exercising not merely excessive but any authority over the Church in his kingdom. The papal jurisdiction had been exercised very largely in ecclesiastical suits, as a court both of first instance and of final appeal. The exercise of this power was forbidden by statutes of 1533 and 1534, with the acquiescence of the Church, which thus reverted to its earlier system, which had been to a great extent overthrown by papal usurpation. [COURTS.] Here again there was clearly no breach of continuity. As to the question of the continuity of orders in the English Church see ORDINATIONS, ANGLICAN.

3. *Continuity of Faith and Doctrine.*—Neither under Henry VIII. nor under Elizabeth was there any intention either in Church or State to vary from the Catholic faith. As Sir Thomas Browne (1605-82) wrote in *Religio Medici*, 'It is an unjust scandal of our adversaries and a gross error in ourselves to compute the nativity of our religion from Henry VIII. ; who, though he rejected the Pope, refused not the faith of Rome, and effected no more than what his predecessors desired and essayed in ages past.' This is borne out by legislation. The first Annates Act, 1531 (23 Hen. VIII. c. 20), declares that the King and his people are 'as obedient, devout, catholick, and humble children of God and holy church, as any people be within any realm christened.' Section 19 of the

Peter Pence Act, 1534 (25 Hen. VIII, c. 21), runs: 'Provided always, that this act, nor any thing or things therein contained, shall be hereafter interpreted or expounded, that your grace, your nobles, and subjects intend by the same to decline or vary from the congregation of Christ's Church in any things concerning the very articles of the Catholick Faith of Christendom, or in any other things declared by Holy Scripture and the Word of God, necessary for your and their salvations, but only to make an ordinance by policies necessary and convenient to repress vice, and for good conservation of this realm,' etc. In the sixth of the canons of 1571 the Church enjoins that preachers shall teach nothing 'but that which is agreeable to the doctrine of the Old Testament and the New, and that which the Catholic Fathers and ancient bishops have gathered out of that doctrine.' In 1609 Archbishop Bancroft (*q.v.*) quoted this canon to show that 'this is and hath been the open profession of the Church of England, to defend and mainteine no other Church, Faith, and Religion, than that which is truly Catholike and Apostolike, and for such warranted, not only by the written word of God, but also by the testimonie and consent of the ancient and godly Fathers.' In matters of faith the English Church took its stand on primitive antiquity. In the words of Sir Roger Twysden (1597-1672), 'The Church of England having with great deliberation reformed itself in a lawful synod, with a care as much as possible of reducing all things to the pattern of the first and best times, was enterpreted by such as would have it so, to desert from the Church Catholic; though for the *manner*, they did nothing but warranted by the continued practice of their predecessors; and in *the things amended* had antiquity to justify their actions: so that nothing is further off truth than to say that such as reformed this church made a new religion; they having retained only that which is truly old and catholic, as Articles of their faith' (Wordsworth, *Eccl. Biog.*, iv.).

4. *Continuity of Possession.*—It must be remembered that in the eyes of the law there is no such body as 'the Church of England,' capable of holding property. All Church property is vested in a number of corporations sole or aggregate, *i.e.* consisting of one person, as the rector of a parish, or of a number, as a dean and chapter. The only ecclesiastical corporations dissolved in the sixteenth century were the religious houses. [MONAS-TERIES, SUPPRESSION OF.] The process was completed by the Acts of 1539 (31 Hen. VIII. c. 13) and 1559 (1 Eliz. c. 24). which

transferred their property to the Crown. And with some comparatively small exceptions it ceased to be Church property at all. All other ecclesiastical corporations continued to hold their endowments and other property by precisely the same tenures and titles as before. There was never any act of transfer, and as far as the possession of property is concerned the continuity is unbroken. [G. C.]

CONVERSION OF THE ENGLISH.

The evangelisation of the English was effected first by Roman and then by Scotic (Irish) missions; the Britons took no part in the work. From Rome, directly or indirectly, the Kentish and East Anglian peoples received the Gospel, and so, too, the East Saxons, but they turned from it; the people of Lindsey heard it; the Bernicians had some knowledge of it, and it gained a hold in Deira; Wessex was won by Birinus (*q.v.*), an Italian bishop; and later the South Saxons were converted by Wilfrid (*q.v.*), the leader of the Roman party. Wars, apostasy, and a lack of new preachers checked the work begun by Augustine (*q.v.*), and it was taken up by the Scots from Iona: they carried it on with success, and in the Midlands broke new ground. Their missions lasted from 635 to 664. The adoption of Christianity generally depended on State action: the king and his nobles were baptized, and the people largely followed their example. The predominance of a Christian king over other kings, and royal marriages, were important factors in the spread of the Gospel, and the influence of royal and noble ladies on the infant Church is specially noteworthy. The people were quick to receive baptism; their heathenism, which was largely impregnated with nature-worship, had lost its hold upon them. Though the Britons would not preach to them they knew that the conquered people, many of whom dwelt among them in slavery or wretchedness, had another faith; and some of them had come into contact with the Christians of Gaul and desired to know their religion, but the Gallican bishops had neglected to teach them.

Christianity was rendered easier to the English by Gregory's (*q.v.*) direction that heathen customs, not in themselves evil, should as far as possible be adapted to the new religion—a course which may have contributed to the long prevalence of heathen superstitions in the Christianised country. The converts were not persecuted by the heathen, though wars such as those of Penda of Mercia, and acts of violence, as the murder of Earpwald of

East Anglia, no doubt had a religious side. The wholesale conversions, which were more or less dependent on royal action and in many cases could not have implied individual conviction, were sometimes followed by widespread apostasy, as in Essex and East Anglia, when the civil power, which had favoured Christianity, was overthrown. While the success of both the Roman and the Scotic missionaries was largely due to the favour of kings, there seems reason to believe that the Scots and their English disciples sought in a greater degree than the Romans to obtain individual conversions by constantly travelling and appealing to people by the way. Zealous and warm-hearted, they accomplished a noble work, but they magnified asceticism unduly, and they could not have established a church government of the best type; that, like the first tidings of salvation, came to the English from Rome, and came through the instrumentality of Archbishop Theodore (*q.v.*).

Approximate dates of conversion :—

Kent, 597; Roman mission.

East Saxons, 604; Roman. Relapse; re-conversion, 665; Scots.

Northumbria, partial, 627; Roman. Completed, 635; Scots.

Lindsey, 628; Roman, 653; Scots.

East Anglians, 628; Edwin of Northumbria (Roman). Relapse; reconversion, 631; Felix from Rome.

West Saxons, 635; Birinus; Italian.

Middle Anglians, 653; Scots.

Mercians, 655-8; Scots.

South Saxons, 681; Wilfrid.

Wight, 686; through Wilfrid. [W. H.]

Bede, *H.E.*; Bright, *Early Eng. Ch. Hist.*; Hunt, *Hist. of Eng. Ch. to 1066.*

CONVOCATION. ORIGIN AND DEVELOPMENT.—The two Convocations of the English Church are the provincial synods of Canterbury and York. [COUNCILS.] But from Edward I.'s reign they have also formed part of the constitution of the realm. In that reign they became the recognised representatives of the Church in its relations with the State. Direct representation of the clergy first appears in 1225, when Archbishop Langton (*q.v.*) ordered the chapters of all cathedral and collegiate churches and religious houses to send proctors to the provincial synod. After various experiments Archbishop Peckham (*q.v.*) in 1283 summoned a council consisting of the bishops of his province, the abbots, priors, and other heads of religious houses, the deans of cathedral and collegiate churches, the archdeacons, one proctor for

the chapter of each cathedral and collegiate church, and two proctors to be elected by the clergy of each diocese. This scheme was drawn up at a council held by the King at Northampton earlier in the same year, and was never embodied in a canon, though it was afterwards considered to possess canonical authority. Within a few years the Convocation of York was organised in the same manner, except that it included two proctors for the clergy of each archdeaconry instead of each diocese. Both Convocations have ever since remained as they were then constituted, except for some temporary minor variations, and for the disappearance of the heads of religious houses in the sixteenth century. In the following table typical Convocations of the Middle Ages and of the seventeenth century are compared with those of the present time.

CANTERBURY, UPPER HOUSE

	1452	1640	1911
Archbishop,	1	1	1
Bishops,	16[1]	21	26

LOWER HOUSE

Heads of religious houses,	295	...	...
Minor dignitaries,	62	77	99
Capitular proctors,	18	24	25
Clergy proctors,	35	44	54
Total of both Houses,	427	167	205

YORK, UPPER HOUSE

	1424	1628	1911
Archbishop,	1	1	1
Bishops,	2	3	9

LOWER HOUSE

Heads of religious houses,	49	...	...
Minor dignitaries,	20	13	31
Capitular proctors,	6	7	8
Clergy proctors,	18	31	49
Total of both Houses,	96	55	98

The Convocation of Canterbury is summoned by the archbishop's mandate addressed to the Dean of the Province, the Bishop of London, who issues a summons to each bishop for himself and the clergy of his diocese. In the northern province there is no dean; the summons goes direct from the metropolitan to each bishop. The writ of 1283 directed that the proctors should be chosen by the whole clergy of the diocese. In later times this has been understood to mean that only the beneficed clergy have the right to vote in an election of proctors. Stipendiary curates were unknown in the thirteenth century, and there is no historical precedent for their having been admitted to vote at any later time, although the royal writ to the archbishop bids him summon his 'whole

[1] The see of Llandaff, although in existence at the time, is for some reason omitted from the enumeration in both Houses. Wilkins, *Conc.*, I. xi.

clergy' to Convocation. As the unbeneficed clergy were not taxed by Convocation, they had not the same claim as the beneficed to be represented directly. Archbishop Arundel appears to have attempted to tax unbeneficed clergy in 1404, but to have failed because they were unrepresented in Convocation. But since it ceased to be a taxing body (see below) there is no ground but that of long-standing custom for refusing unbeneficed clergy the vote. The mode of election of proctors by the beneficed clergy varies in different dioceses. In 1888 the Queen's Bench Division decided that the archbishop was the final judge of questions arising out of the election of proctors, and that the civil courts had no jurisdiction to review his decision, nor to interfere in the internal affairs of Convocation, 'an ancient body as old as Parliament and as independent' (*R. v. Archbishop of York*, 20 Q.B.D. 740). At first all the members sat together. The division into two Houses came about gradually, being sometimes caused by the desire of the bishops to deliberate in private, more often by the reference of particular matters to the lower clergy for their separate consideration. By the early part of the fifteenth century the separation had become a custom. The abbots and priors sat sometimes in one House, sometimes in the other. Since the dissolution of the monasteries the archbishop and diocesan bishops alone have constituted the Upper House. But Convocation is constitutionally a single body though, as a matter of custom and convenience, it sits in two Houses. On solemn occasions, such as its formal opening or the promulgation of new canons, the two Houses sit together in full synod. The archbishop is president of the whole Convocation, and of the Upper House when sitting separately; and by ancient custom no act of Convocation is valid without his assent. The Lower House elects a prolocutor to preside over it, and to be its representative in dealing with the Upper. An ancient and important privilege and duty of the Lower House is that of initiating synodical action by presenting schedules of grievances or other matters which they think need consideration. These are known as *gravamina* and *reformanda*. Any member or members of the Lower House may present a *gravamen* to the Upper through the prolocutor. But if adopted by the Lower House as a body the *gravamen* becomes an *articulus cleri*, and is presented as such.

The primitive rule of the Council of Nicæa that provincial synods should meet twice a year was adopted by the Council of Hertford (673), with the proviso that once should suffice. The Convocations now meet three or four times a year. Each day's meeting is termed a session. And when, as is usual, the business lasts for three or four days, they are called a group of sessions. In modern times, however, much of the work of Convocation is done by committees, which are not tied to particular times or modes of meeting. Their reports are designed to be the basis of synodical action. Convocation is prorogued from one group of sessions to another by the archbishop, but it is doubtful whether he has the power to do this without the assent of his brother bishops. Since the breach with Rome it has usually been assumed that Convocation must be dissolved at the dissolution of Parliament. The grounds for this opinion are not clear, and it was not followed on a famous occasion in 1640 (see below). It is doubtful whether Convocation is automatically dissolved by the demise of the Crown. The question was raised after the death of William III. in 1702, when the attorney-general advised that the Convocation then in existence expired with the sovereign. It continued to sit, however, after the death of Queen Victoria in 1901, and again after that of Edward VII. in 1910.

The place of meeting formerly varied, but since the middle of the fourteenth century the Northern Convocation has usually met at York, and the Southern at St. Paul's, whence, in modern times, it adjourns to Westminster for deliberation. The privilege of members of Convocation to the same freedom from arrest as is enjoyed by members of Parliament dates from 1429. Historical and geographical reasons have caused the Southern Convocation to play a more prominent part in the life of the English Church than the Northern, which has usually been, in Fuller's phrase, ' but the hand of the dial moving and pointing as directed by the clock of the province of Canterbury' (*Ch. Hist.*, bk. xi., sec. 23).

FUNCTIONS.—1. *Legislative and deliberative.* Originally the primary function of a provincial synod was to promulgate in the province the general law of the Church. The extent to which the canon law was in force in England until it had been formally accepted by the English Church is disputed. [CANON LAW.] But there is no doubt that parts of it were so accepted by the English synods. They also enacted provincial canons, or assented to those which were placed before them by the archbishop, who was said to ' decree and ordain' them, ' with the assent ' of the synod.

Since the breach with Rome, and pending the assembling of a General Council whose authority the English Church can recognise, the Convocations have been the only bodies whose legislation can be accepted by English Churchmen as canonically valid. Thus it has been their duty, though they have been hampered in its fulfilment, to adapt or add to the provincial law as changing circumstances require, without bringing it into conflict with the general law of the Church. The legislative power of a synod is inherent in the bishops alone [BISHOPS, COUNCILS], though in the English Convocations the lower clergy have acquired by custom the negative right of veto. Nevertheless, the actual legislative power for a province resides in its bishops assembled in synod. But, apart from legislation, Convocation should act as the living voice of the Church, and express by its resolutions the Church's mind.

2. *Judicial.*—In the early centuries the bishops of a province exercised judicial powers while assembled in synod. But later regularly constituted Church Courts (*q.v.*) came into being, to apply the law to individual cases. Before 1066 English provincial synods exercised jurisdiction in important cases, such as disputes between dioceses. In the later Middle Ages the judicial activities of Convocation were usually confined to the trial of heretics, a matter which, at any rate at first, might well be considered to raise points too novel and too grave to be left to the usual ecclesiastical judges. Dr. Stubbs (*q.v.*) was of opinion that Convocation as a court was merely 'attendant on and assessing to the archbishop,' in whom and not in the synod the jurisdiction resided. In any case the tendency was for the synod to confine itself to deliberation and legislation, leaving judicial functions to the courts. The Statute of Appeals, 1533 (24 Hen. VIII. c. 12), provided that in cases touching the King a final appeal should lie to the Upper House of Convocation. But this jurisdiction was never exercised, and was superseded in the following year by the statute 25 Hen. VIII. c. 19. [COURTS.] The *Reformatio Legum* (*q.v.*) proposed the Upper House as the final court of appeal, but this scheme never became law. On various occasions in the sixteenth and seventeenth centuries writers or preachers of heretical doctrine were summoned before Convocation and compelled to retract. But the practical result of Whiston's (*q.v.*) case was to show that the present extent of its jurisdiction is to condemn heretical books and opinions, but not to try or punish their authors. This course was followed in the synodical condemnation of the writings of Bishop Colenso (*q.v.*) in 1863, and of *Essays and Reviews* (*q.v.*) in 1864. In 1891 an unsuccessful attempt was made to deal with *Lux Mundi* in the same way.

3. *Financial.*—During the twelfth century the clergy occasionally protested against the taxation of church land and property for secular purposes. But this was a position which could not be maintained, and in the thirteenth century the Convocations granted subsidies to the King on behalf of the clergy. Edward I. sought to form a Parliamentary estate of the clergy for this purpose. [PARLIAMENT, CLERGY IN.] But they resisted, and preserved the right of taxing themselves in Convocation. This refusal had important results. Had the clergy become an estate of Parliament, the provincial synods might have been unhampered by connection with the State. By insisting on their financial claims the Convocations became part of the national constitution as well as spiritual assemblies, and the results of this dual character are to be observed throughout their history.

In 1296 Boniface VIII., by the Bull *Clericis laicos*, forbade the clergy to pay taxes to the secular power. The King, in reply, threatened them with outlawry, and they were obliged to evade the Pope's command. As a rule the self-taxation of the clergy worked well, and they paid their share towards the national revenue, occasionally (as in 1374 and 1377) insisting on the redress of grievances as the condition of their contribution. From 1540 onwards their grants were always ratified by Parliament. In 1664 the arrangement, being found to press hardly on the clergy, was brought to an end by a verbal agreement between Archbishop Sheldon (*q.v.*) and Lord Chancellor Clarendon, to which the clergy tacitly assented, 'as it was a great relief to them in taxations' to be taxed by Parliament like other citizens. The first Act which taxes them contains a proviso that nothing in it is intended 'to the prejudice of the ancient rights' of the clergy (16-17 Car. II. c. 1). This surrender by Convocation of its financial powers (called by Bishop Gibson (*q.v.*) 'the greatest alteration in the constitution ever made without an express law') greatly facilitated the suppression of Convocation in the next century, now that its existence was no longer necessary to the financial well-being of the State.

CONVOCATION AND THE CROWN.—The power of summoning Convocation resides in the archbishop of the province. But its privilege of voting the taxes of the clergy caused the mediæval kings to bid the archbishops summon their Convocations whenever Parliament was called for financial purposes. Thus it became customary for Convocation to be summoned concurrently with Parliament. During the Middle Ages it was frequently summoned by the archbishops, independently of the Crown, to transact ecclesiastical business only. But as the demand for money was more regular and frequent than the demand for canons, the Convocations summoned primarily for financial purposes were more numerous than those held solely to meet spiritual needs. Both assemblies alike were summoned by the archbishop, in the former case at the instance of the Crown, and in the latter of his own mere motion. The kings from William I. onward also claimed a power of veto over the acts of church synods. William I. decreed that nothing should be enacted in a synod save what was agreeable to his will and had first been ordained by him. Anselm (q.v.) acquiesced in William II.'s refusal to allow him to hold a council. In 1279 Edward I. compelled Archbishop Peckham to revoke certain decrees which he had promulgated in a provincial council at Reading. As a rule, however, the kings left the archbishops free to summon their synods, and the synods free to carry on their spiritual work. The royal veto over the meeting and proceedings of Convocation was a weapon in reserve, only to be used if the Church seemed to encroach on the secular sphere. Under Henry VIII. the relations between the Crown and Convocation were restated, and placed on the footing on which they still remain. In 1532 Convocation, under pressure from Henry VIII., agreed to 'The Submission of the Clergy,' in which the clergy promise that they will not in future enact or put in force any canon in Convocation, 'which Convocation is, always has been, and must be assembled only by your highness' commandment of writ, unless your highness by your royal assent shall licence us to assemble our Convocation,' and to make canons. An Act of 1534 (25 Hen. VIII. c. 19) gave this arrangement Parliamentary authority.

These two Acts of Convocation and Parliament respectively lay down the terms which still govern the relation of Convocation to the State. It must be observed that the body which the clergy admit 'always has been' assembled by the royal writ is Convocation as a part of the constitution, meeting at the same time as Parliament for financial purposes, not the purely ecclesiastical provincial synods which also met from time to time

during the Middle Ages. But this distinction is now obsolete. The two bodies are fused into one, which is a constitutional Convocation as well as a provincial synod; and the King's writ is essential to its assembling (the writ is addressed to the archbishop, who on receiving it issues his mandate as described above). Moreover, it cannot now enact any canon without the King's licence, though this is not necessary for the transaction of other business. It appears from the 'Submission' that after a canon has been enacted it must receive the royal assent, though this is not perfectly clear from the words of the statute. And, further, no canon can be enacted which is contrary or repugnant to the laws of the realm.

In modern times, beginning from the reign of Anne, it has been customary for the Crown to issue 'Letters of Business' to the Convocations, requesting them to take into consideration certain specified matters. These Letters must be distinguished from the royal licence just mentioned. They are not a necessary preliminary to the action of Convocation, and are in no way binding upon it. [CHURCH AND STATE, ROYAL SUPREMACY.]

LATER HISTORY.—After the Submission of 1532 Convocation continued to be summoned concurrently with Parliament, and took its part in the work of the Reformation (q.v.). Henry VIII. always preferred to attain his ends where possible by means of legal and constitutional forms, and it is probable, though not certain, that most of the ecclesiastical statutes of his reign were laid before Convocation. He also consulted it in 1533 on the validity of his marriage with Katherine of Aragon, and in 1534 on the papal supremacy. In 1547, after the accession of Edward VI., Convocation declared the marriage of the clergy and communion in both kinds to be lawful. It co-operated in the reaction under Mary (q.v.), and after Elizabeth's (q.v.) accession presented articles in favour of papal supremacy and the Romish doctrine of the Mass. Consequently it had to be ignored in the Elizabethan Settlement (q.v.) till 1563, when a new Convocation assembled and resumed its proper place in the constitution of the Church, the Queen being careful to protect it from the encroachments of Parliament. In 1571, for instance, she forbade the House of Commons to consider any 'Bills concerning religion' 'unless the same should be first considered and liked by the clergy.' And this was her consistent policy. In 1563 Convocation revised the Articles of Religion (q.v.) of 1553, finally sanctioning them in their present form in 1571. It passed bodies of canons which were mostly enforced in practice, though some of them failed to receive the royal assent. This legislative activity culminated in the code of canons of 1604 [CANON LAW FROM 1534]. In 1606 the royal licence to make further canons resulted in those known as Bishop Overall's (*q.v.*) Convocation Book, to which the royal assent was refused. In 1640 the right of Convocation to continue sitting after the dissolution of Parliament was questioned. The judges were referred to and admitted the right. Accordingly it sat for more than three weeks after Parliament was dissolved, and enacted seventeen canons, which were confirmed by the Crown. Their authority has been questioned at various times, but there can be no doubt that before the Submission the sittings of Convocation by no means necessarily synchronised with those of Parliament, and there seems to be no good legal or constitutional ground for supposing that any change has been made. The point has never been definitely settled. After 1640 Convocation did not meet till 1661, when royal letters were issued directing it to revise the Prayer Book. For this purpose the Convocation of York appointed delegates to act on its behalf in that of Canterbury, and this combined synod sanctioned the revised book. The period 1688-1717 was a busy and acrimonious one in the history of Convocation. The bulk of the clergy were High Churchmen [CHURCH, HIGH, LOW], and some were Jacobites. The Lower House reflected these opinions, and found itself frequently at variance with the Upper, composed largely of Low Church and latitudinarian divines who had been appointed to bishoprics because they favoured the Revolution and the Hanoverian succession. In 1689 a Comprehension Bill, designed to promote the union of Protestant dissenters with the Church, was introduced into Parliament. [REUNION IV.] At this the Church party in the House of Commons was 'much offended' because a Bill affecting the Church had been introduced ' in which the representative body of the clergy had not been so much as advised with ' (Burnet). Accordingly they petitioned the King to call a Convocation, thus showing that they realised the rightful position of that body in the constitution. When Convocation met the Lower House showed itself ' stiff for the Church of England,' and declared through its prolocutor: '*Nolumus leges Angliae mutari*.' The attempt at comprehension was accordingly abandoned. After this Convocation was not allowed to meet except formally till 1700. From this foretaste of the longer

suppression which was soon to follow, the southern Convocation was rescued by Atterbury's (*q.v.*) vigorous championship of the synodical rights of the clergy. That of York only met formally between 1698 and 1861. A succession of controversies between the two Houses of the Convocation of Canterbury followed. Some of these were concerned with their respective rights, and especially the claim of the Lower House to adjourn as it pleased independently of the Upper House and of the archbishop, a claim which could not be constitutionally maintained. Others were caused by attempts of the Lower House to censure latitudinarian books and opinions. The last and most famous of these was an attack on Bishop Hoadly (*q.v.*), which induced the Government to prorogue Convocation in order to avoid a formal censure upon him. This prorogation of Convocation against its will by the exercise of the Royal Supremacy was followed by its suppression for all practical purposes for one hundred and thirty-five years. It was summoned as before at the beginning of every Parliament, but after formal proceedings, varied only by such mild activities as the passing of an address to the Crown, it was again adjourned. At the time of the suppression it had many useful reforms in contemplation, and had it been permitted to effect them the stagnation which characterises the life of the Church for the next hundred years might, to some extent, have been avoided. Although the State was primarily responsible for the suppression, the Church is by no means free from blame. Save in one or two isolated instances no attempt was made to enable Convocation to resume its functions. In 1703 Wake (*q.v.*) had written that if the sovereign should ever neglect his duty so far as not to summon Convocation, the bishops should urge him to do so ; and if he still refused, Convocation should meet and act as seemed best for the Church, 'and be content to suffer any loss, or to run any danger for their so doing.' But as archbishop he scarcely acted up to his own counsel, and his successors were not the men for heroic measures. A few zealous churchmen like Dr. Johnson (*q.v.*) might lament the enforced silence of the constitutional voice of the Church, but the great majority acquiesced in it as the normal state of things until the general revival of church life which followed the Oxford Movement (*q.v.*). It was then felt that the Church's synod ' ought to be a real living and active one, instead of a piece of lumber dragged out one day and dragged back into its closet the next.' In 1837 a motion that it should be made 'efficient for the purposes for which it was recognised by the constitution' was defeated in the House of Commons by 24 to 19, Lord John Russell remarking that he 'could not see the advantage of reviving the religious disputes of the reign of Queen Anne.' Later efforts to revive Convocation met with much Erastian opposition in the press and elsewhere, while a considerable section of the clergy was suspicious, not to say hostile. After the Gorham (*q.v.*) judgment it was seen to be necessary that the voice of the Church should express itself freely. Owing largely to the exertions of Bishop S. Wilberforce (*q.v.*) and of Henry Hoare (1807-65), a well-known banker and the leading spirit of the 'Society for the Revival of Convocation,' the Canterbury Convocation was allowed to resume the active exercise of its functions in 1852. The opposition of Archbishop Musgrave prevented the northern synod from following this example during his life, but it met under his successor in 1861. Since then both Convocations have continued to meet, and have to some extent resumed their normal place in the life of the Church. In 1865, 1888, and 1892 Convocation passed canons, under royal licence, and it has been shown to be possible for Convocation and Parliament to work together by legislating concurrently for Church and State. In 1872 Letters of Business were issued requesting the Convocations to take into consideration the recommendations of the Ritual Commission [COMMISSIONS, ROYAL]. And the fact that they had been thus consulted, and had reported to the Crown, was recited in the preamble to the Act of Uniformity Amendment Act (35-6 Vic. c. 35). In 1879 Convocation presented to the Crown a complete revision of the rubrics, but requested that it should not receive Parliamentary sanction until the method of legislating for the Church should have been reformed. During part of the debates on this subject the two Houses of the Southern Convocation sat together in full synod. In other ways apart from legislation Convocation has made good its claim to be the living voice of the Church, not only in such matters as the drawing up of special forms of service, but also and more notably at the time of the Vatican Council (1870), when it passed decrees setting forth the position of the English Church against the papal claims, and formally communicated them to the orthodox churches of the East.

REFORMS.—It has been felt that Convocation could take its place more effectively in the life of the Church if its constitution were reformed. This subject has constantly occupied it since its revival. Most of the proposals made have tended towards increasing the number of clerical proctors and their election by the whole body of the clergy. It has been suggested that such reforms could be made by the archbishop on the authority of the writ which directs him to assemble 'the whole clergy' of his province. But as the present arrangement is fixed by long-standing custom, the suggested power of altering it without the authority either of Convocation or of Parliament must be held doubtful. In 1855, and again in 1865, the royal licence to make a canon reforming the representation of the clergy was refused on the ground that there was no precedent, and that Convocation could not be reformed without the authority of Parliament. The refusal was repeated in 1897. Dr. Stubbs, whose opinion upon such a matter carried great weight, considered that, as the synod was not organised in its present form by canon, the constitutional method of reform would be to proceed by obtaining an Act of Parliament to give recognition on behalf of the State to changes introduced by the archbishop. For, as Convocation is not merely an ecclesiastical synod, but also a part of the constitution, any reforms made in it would require civil sanction. Bills to enable it to reform itself have been introduced into Parliament, but have failed to pass. Yet, however Convocation may be organised, its authority resides in the bishops alone. This fact tends to be somewhat obscured because the course of history, and especially the importance of the Lower House in voting money and the prominence it has attained in doctrinal disputes, have tended to place it in an anomalous position. But by the constitution of the Church the lower clergy in a provincial synod are only a consultative body, whose function is to advise and, if necessary, to check the bishops, who alone can exercise the spiritual authority of the synod. In 1888 the Upper House of Canterbury refused to consider a proposed supplement to the Catechism presented by the Lower, on the ground that synodical action upon matters of doctrine should proceed from the Upper House, the function of the Lower being to suggest the consideration of such matters by way of petition or address. The Lower Houses, however, have acquired by custom an absolute veto on the acts of the Upper, which are not valid without their consent.

In 1857 Convocation discussed the advisability of taking steps whereby 'the counsel and co-operation of the faithful laity' might be secured to its proceedings. But no action was taken till 1885, when both Houses of the Convocation of Canterbury agreed on a scheme for the constitution of a House of Laymen, to be appointed by the lay members of the diocesan conferences, and by the archbishop, to act as a consultative adjunct to Convocation on all subjects except the definition and interpretation of faith and doctrine. The Canterbury House of Laymen first met in 1886, and that of York in 1892. Both now sit concurrently with the Convocations, but are not constituent parts of them, and their decisions do not affect the validity of the acts of the synods. [G. C.]

Wilkins, *Concilia* ; Cardwell, *Synodalia* ; *Journal of Convocation, Chronicle of Convocation* ; for an outline of its development see Stubbs, *C.H.*, III. chap. XV. For its revival Warren, *Synodalia* ; Hansard, *Parl. Debates*, 1837, 1851. 1852 ; *Life of S. Wilberforce*, II. iv.-vii. ; Sweet, *Memoir of H. Hoare*. On the subject generally see (among many other works) Wake, *Authority of Christian Princes* and *State of the Church* ; Atterbury, *Rights of Convocation* ; Gibson, *Synodus Anglicana* ; Lathbury, *Hist. of Convocation* ; Joyce, *England's Sacred Synods* ; Stubbs. *Hist. Appendices to Report of Eccl. Courts Commission*, 1883 ; Beeching, *Francis Atterbury* ; *Records of the Northern Convocation*, Surtees Soc., 113.

CORONATION. The earliest recorded coronations in England are those of Egferth, son of Offa of Mercia, and Eardwulf of Northumbria (*A.-S. Chron.*, ann. 785, 795). In the line of Wessex the record is continuous from Edward the Elder (902) down to the present, except for Edmund (940) and Cnut (*q.v.*) (1016), and for Matilda (1135) and Edward V. (1483), who were never crowned. Before the Confessor the coronations were generally at Kingston : his own was at Winchester. From Harold onward all have been crowned at Westminster.

A 'Coronation' is the creation and inauguration of a monarch ; and such an act naturally includes (1) the choice, or at least the identification, of the person to be inaugurated : (2) his pledge to fulfil his trust ; (3) the act of creation by consecration : (4) the investiture of the monarch with his insignia ; (5) the setting of him in his official place ; (6) the acknowledgment of him by his subjects. Accordingly the English order of coronation in its developed form, apart from details, consists of the following elements :—(1) The nobles and prelates assemble in Westminster Hall ' to consult about the election and consecration ' of the monarch, and the confirmation by him of the laws and customs of the realm — a survival of the old debates of the Witan—and the prince is ' elevated ' on to his seat. Then they all conduct him in solemn procession, with the *regalia*, to the abbey, and there, standing on the ' theatre,' he is presented to the assembly, and their final assent is demanded and given by acclamation. (2) After a sermon the elect is interrogated by the Archbishop of Canterbury, and swears to confirm the laws and customs granted by his predecessors ; to preserve peace for the Church, the clergy, and the people ; to do justice with mercy ; and to enforce the laws that shall be made ; and in answer to the petition of the bishops he promises to conserve their rights and those of the churches committed to them. (3) He is consecrated (*a*) by prayer—*Veni Creator*, the Litany, and a series of ' benedictions ' ; (*b*) by unction : he is anointed with oil on hands, between the shoulders, on the shoulders and the elbows, and with both oil and chrism on the head ; while the choir sing Psalm 21, with the antiphon, *Zadok the priest*. (4) The King is invested with his insignia—the two tunics, the buskins, shoes, and spurs ; the sword, the *armillae*, and the *pallium* ; the crown, the ring, the sceptre, and the rod ; and then he is solemnly blessed. (5) He is taken to the throne by the bishops and the nobles, and there seated, while *Te Deum* is sung ; and then the archbishop admonishes him in the *Sta et retine*. (6) The bishops do their fealty and the nobles their homage. Then, if so be, the Queen is consecrated by prayer, anointed on head and breast, and invested with ring, crown, sceptre, and rod. The Mass and Communion follow. Lastly, after depositing part of the *regalia* on the altar of St. Edward's Chapel, they proceed to Westminster Hall, where the banquet is held, in the course of which the mounted champion enters and challenges any who question the King's right to the crown.

There are four successive recensions of the Order of Coronation, which mark the development of the rite. *A*. That of the *Pontifical* of Egbert of York and the Leofric Missal, which may be as old as the eighth century. Here the coronation follows the creed in the Mass, and consists of three ' benedictions ' ; the unction of the King's head, during the singing of Psalm 21, with its antiphon, *Zadok the priest*, and followed by a prayer ; the delivery of sceptre, rod, and crown, each with a prayer ; the acclamation and the kiss ; after which the Mass is continued. *B*. In the second recension *Te Deum* is sung as soon as the King has prostrated himself before the altar; the prayers of *A* are partly rearranged and new ones added: the ring and the sword are added to the insignia, and there is a formula of delivery for each of the insignia; a solemn blessing follows the delivery of the rod; and the enthronement follows, with the admonition, *Sta et retine*; and the unction of the Queen, and her investiture with ring and crown, each with a formula of delivery and a prayer. Then the Mass begins. Some of the new matter of this recension occurs in the coronation of the Emperor Lewis II. (877), some in the Roman Imperial Coronation of the tenth century; and the whole order is closely akin to that of the coronation of the Emperor at Milan as King of Italy (Martène, *de ant. eccl. rit.*, II. ix. ord. 5). The detailed description of the coronation of Eadgar (Whitsunday, 972) in the *Vita S. Oswaldi* (R.S., lxxi. p. 426) makes it clear that this order was then used, at least as far as the delivery of the rod, and it may well have been compiled for that occasion and reflect the imperialism of the moment. *C.* The third is contained in several Pontificals of the twelfth century. While in structure almost identical with *A* and *B*, in content it departs widely from them. It retains only one prayer of *A* and thirteen formulæ of *B*, and it has ten new formulæ. It adds the Litany before the oath, and the presentation and recognition of the elect after it; the breast, shoulders, and elbows are anointed besides the head; the delivery of the *armillae* after the sword is new; the ring is not delivered till after the crown; and *Te Deum* is delayed till after the blessing. This order is nearly akin to that of the tenth-century *Ordo Romanus* of Hittorp (*de Off. eccl.*, p. 96), and the coronation of the Emperor as German King at Aachen (Martène, II. ix. ord. 4). *D.* The fourth recension, the fully developed form, is in part a fusion of *B* and *C*; but it adds further prayers and ceremonies (as indicated above), and in its fullest shape, in the *Liber regalis* and the Westminster Missal, it gives detailed rubrics. This form, which has been affected by the later Western Imperial coronation, and indirectly by the Eastern, was in use from perhaps the early fourteenth century till Elizabeth. For James I. it was translated into English, and was so used for Charles I., and with little change for Charles II. For James II. Sancroft (*q.v.*) made some changes of order, omitted several prayers, altered and mutilated other formulæ, and by a blunder which has been perpetuated provided for the de-

livery of the orb as well as the sceptre, with which it is identical. For William and Mary, Compton, Bishop of London, made further changes and omissions; reduced the unctions to those on hands, breast, and head; and added a new ceremony, the delivery of the Bible. Little change has been made since, except that the processions from and to Westminster Hall, and the banquet, have been omitted from William IV. onward; the unction on the breast was omitted in the cases of William IV. and Victoria; and some slight changes and abridgments were made for Edward VII., which were mostly continued for George V.

Two further points may be noticed. (1) In *A* there is no recognition of hereditary claim; but in some of the new matter which appears first in *B*, while election is asserted, there is also a recognition of hereditary right. In *D* the prince is presented to the people as 'the rightful and undoubted inheritor' of the crown, but also as 'elect, chosen, and required' by the three estates, and the consent of the people to his coronation is asked. This continues down to James I. From Charles I. to James II. he is described as the 'rightful inheritor,' without allusion to election, and those present are only asked whether they are willing to do their homage. William and Mary are the first to be presented as already 'undoubted King and Queen of this realm.' (2) It is commonly said that the prayers and ceremonies of the coronation imply that the consecrated King is, what by some he has been held to be, a *mixta persona*, both cleric and lay; and this mainly on two grounds. (a) The similarity in structure and the identity of certain formulæ as between the order of coronation and that of the consecration of a bishop. But, besides that the similarity is not perhaps so close as is suggested, of the common formulæ *Veni Creator* is quite indeterminate, and the intention of the Litany is only determined by proper suffrages, which are different in the two cases; while such assimilation of rites is natural and common, and it implies no more than that both rites are consecrations of persons to office and status. (b) The regal vestments are said to be 'sacerdotal'; and in particular the 'armil' is identified with the stole, the 'pallium' with the cope. But there can be no doubt that the 'armil' is the *loros* or *diadema* of the Byzantine emperors, and is ultimately a folded *toga*; while the 'pallium' is no more like a cope than one cloak is necessarily like another; it is quadrangular, and is properly buckled on the right shoulder, not on the breast; it is the 'imperial purple,' and ultimately the *paludamentum* of the Roman general in the field. And. in fact, the whole series of regal vestments. from buskins to pallium. is identical term by term with the Byzantine series. and was no doubt derived through the Western Empire from Constantinople. On the other hand, such a petition as that the King 'may nurture, teach, defend. and instruct the Church,' etc., seems to imply something like what Article XXXVII. repudiates. [F. E. B.]

Selden, *Titles of Honour*; A. Taylor. *The Glory of Regality*: Maskell. *Monumenta ritualia* (1882). ii. ; C. Wordsworth, *The manner of the Coronation of Charles I.*; J. W. Legg, *Missale Westmonasteriense* and *Three Coronation Orders*; L. W. Legg, *English Coronation Records*; H. Thurston, *The Coronation Ceremonial*.

COSIN, John (1594-1672), an influential leader of the Laudian reaction in the north of England under Charles I.. a refugee during the Protectorate, and later an eminent liturgiologist and Bishop of Durham. In his earlier days as Prebendary of Durham, and the moving spirit in the ecclesiastical changes under Charles I. (*q.v.*), his tone was far more uncompromising than at a later date. Born at Norwich and educated in the Grammar School of that city, Cosin passed to Caius College, Cambridge, and became Fellow. He was already a man of conviction, and both Andrewes (*q.v.*) and Overall (*q.v.*) offered him work. After a brief time with the latter at Lichfield he became domestic chaplain to Neile, appointed Bishop of Durham, 1617. This appointment was epoch-making in Cosin's fortunes. Neile, already in the confidence of James I., was one of the foremost of the little circle of eminent men who became the centre of Church influence. As Talbot brought Butler to Durham a century later, so Neile brought Cosin at the age of thirty to Durham, and with the diocese Cosin's name now became imperishably linked. First as Master of Greatham Hospital and then as Prebendary of the cathedral, Cosin came into the front rank of the clergy in the diocese. He became Archdeacon of the East Riding in 1625. Thus his influence began to extend outside the diocese. though it is uncertain how long he held the office. Next year he married his predecessor's daughter. Frances Blakeston. In 1627 the first-fruits of his liturgical studies appeared in the shape of his *Collection of Private Devotions.* [CAROLINE DIVINES.] The rising temper of the opposing school of thought soon marked these 'Cozening devotions.' In Durham changes had been rife

under a little knot of like-minded prebendaries. A strong opposition was led by the senior prebendary, Peter Smart (*q.v.*), who delayed public protest until his old schoolfellow Neile was translated to York. Preaching the Assize Sermon in 1628, Smart attacked the Arminian changes in general and Cosin in particular. When in 1633 Charles I. stayed in Durham Castle, Cosin adroitly managed that the King should visit the cathedral with much ceremony, and throw over all that had been done in the way of 'innovations' the mantle of his authority and sanction. Cosin has left a minute account of the proceedings on that occasion. Next year he was appointed Master of Peterhouse. He introduced into the college chapel the alterations which had given so much offence at Durham. He was, apparently, away from Durham in 1639-40, when the Scottish troubles began and the prebendaries' houses were rifled after Newburn Fight. He was thus spared witnessing the fate of his ornaments within the cathedral. He was immersed in University business at Cambridge. Vice-Chancellor in 1639, in 1640 Charles made him Dean of Peterborough. The Long Parliament deprived him of all his ecclesiastical benefices. Remaining at Cambridge he was ejected in 1644 from the Mastership for sending the college plate to the King. A time of exile followed. In Paris he acted as chaplain to Henrietta Maria's household at the Embassy. Here he carried out the services in his own way without hindrance for nineteen years, defending the Anglo-Catholic position against Romanist adversaries. Despite the help of friends Cosin was in some straits in Paris, yet he managed to collect books and to pursue his studies. To this quiet period we doubtless owe much of his liturgical knowledge. At the Restoration he returned to his deanery. His other benefices were restored by degrees (*Corresp.*, vol. ii. pp. 3-4). In December 1660 he was consecrated Bishop of Durham, and began the eleven years of diocesan administration which gave him so great a name as prelate. His energy and strong personal influence wrought a great change. as Basire's funeral sermon attests. His visitations were very carefully conducted. His minute interest in all the details of building and planning at Durham, whether in castle, library, or elsewhere, is shown in his correspondence. At length, after a long illness, he died in London in 1672, and was buried in the renovated chapel at Auckland.

His most important work is the *History of*

Papal Transubstantiation, written in Paris; published, 1675. His 'corrected copy' of the Prayer Book, the so-called 'Durham Book,' was printed in 1619, but annotated and corrected by Cosin, probably as secretary of the revision committee, in 1660 and 1661, and represents a stage in the process of revision then in hand. (J. T. Tomlinson, *Prayer Book, Articles, and Homilies.*)

[H. G.]

Works (Lib. of Anglo-Cath. Theol., 5 vols.); *V.C.H.,* Durham, ii. 13-58; *Correspondence,* Surtees Soc., vols. 52 and 55.

COUNCILS as a feature of Church government date from apostolic times. The Council of Jerusalem, c. A.D. 49 (Acts 15), is called by Jeremy Taylor 'this first copy of Christian councils.' Assemblies for deliberation and decision are essential to the life of any society. The Church, though divinely founded, forms no exception to this rule. Its spiritual authority has been normally exercised through councils. It was a natural consequence of the episcopal constitution, by which the authority of the whole body was especially committed to the bishops (*q.v.*), that they should meet and take counsel both for decision of difficulties and for preservation of unity, the rule of each in his own diocese being guided by the results of deliberation in common. [AUTHORITY IN THE CHURCH.]

Constitution.—It follows, therefore, that the authority of a council resides in the bishops who compose it. This authority is exercised, as a rule, in the presence of certain inferior clergy and laity, whose function it is to be 'at once a means of counsel and information, and a check on inconsiderate action.' The clergy have normally taken part in the debates, and the counsel of the learned is naturally sought. In later times the growth of the idea of government by representation has had its effect on the Church. But, according to the original constitution of councils, the sole duty of the inferior clergy and of the laity was to advise the bishops, and to aid them in ascertaining the general feeling of the Church, and thus to influence their decision. The traditional right of the laity to be present at councils, and to take part in debate if called upon, survived in the canonists until the twelfth century, although it had become obsolete in practice. And at no time had their presence implied any co-ordinate authority in the council, the acts of which derived their validity from the bishops, who alone were its constituent members. It must be remembered that the

government of the Church is neither democratic nor despotic. Its rulers do not depend on the multitude for their authority; neither are they 'lords over subjects; but divinely commissioned leaders of a divine society' (Report of Committee of Convocation on *The Position of the Laity,* 1902, p. 7). From this it followed at first that the practice of voting and carrying resolutions by bare majorities was not recognised. The intention always was to secure something like unanimity. Nothing else could fulfil the idea that a council was an assembly in which . . . the Holy Spirit prevailed to guide the Church into all truth. . . . Hence it is a sort of anachronism to discuss . . . whether the laymen [and clergy] had or had not "votes." . . . It was quite enough for them if they in a greater or less degree influenced the general decision' (*ibid.,* p. 25). The acts of a council when passed must be published to the Church at large, and are not finally binding until they have won its acceptance. The whole body of the faithful, 'the Church diffusive,' is thus the ultimate authority, and has the power of informally ratifying or rejecting the acts of a council. This ratification usually follows as a matter of course, but it has occasionally been withheld when the acts of a council have proved to be clearly contrary to the mind of the Church.

Relation to Civil Rulers.—The conversion of Constantine (A.D. 312), and the recognition of Christianity as the official religion of the Empire, affected the status of councils. The assembling of General Councils, including bishops from all parts of the Empire, became possible. The Christian emperors summoned General Councils from time to time, both at the request of the Church and also at their own discretion. The English Church in the sixteenth century recognised this right of the civil power. 'General Councils may not be gathered together without the commandment and will of princes' (Article XXI.). The emperors also assumed the right to preside in General Councils, either in person or by a representative. But they only acted as moderators, and directed the course of the proceedings. They made no claim to be constituent members of the councils, nor to take part in the debates or decisions. Several General Councils, however, requested the emperors to ratify their decisions, and so give them the force of civil law, though this ratification added nothing to the spiritual validity by virtue of which they were binding on the conscience of Christians. This supremacy of the emperors over the councils of the early centuries is in harmony with the position allowed to Christian rulers throughout the history of the Church, and still exercised by the English Crown over Convocation. It includes the right to command or to forbid the assembling of a council, to prescribe, within limits, the subjects for discussion, and the right to give civil sanction to its decrees. [CONVOCATION; CHURCH AND STATE; SUPREMACY, ROYAL.]

General Councils.—The most illustrious councils in ecclesiastical history are the General Councils of the undivided Church, and especially the first four, of Nicæa (325), Constantinople (381), Ephesus (431). and Chalcedon (451), whose canons have always been considered to possess œcumenical authority in an especial degree. The Act of Supremacy, 1559, recognises ' the first four General Councils ' as standards of doctrine in the English Church equal in authority to ' the canonical Scriptures.' The Lambeth Conference of 1867 (see below) bore formal testimony to its belief in the faith ' as affirmed by the undisputed General Councils.' And Archbishop Benson (*q.v.*) expressly stated that the canons of the first four were binding on the English Church in matters of faith and doctrine (*Read v. Bishop of Lincoln*, 1889. 14 P.D., p. 109).

A General Council must include a sufficient number of bishops to ensure that its acts shall represent the mind of the whole Church. The decrees of any valid council bind all who are subject to its jurisdiction whether present at it or not (Canon 140 of 1604). The Roman Church holds that the Pope alone can summon a General Council, and that he is not subject to its authority. Neither contention is borne out by early church history. The English Church has always recognised the supreme authority of ' a lawful, free and well-composed General Council ' (Laud, *Conference with Fisher*). In 1246 a council of bishops held at London appealed against the Pope's extortions to the authority *concilii universalis aliqui tempore per Dei gratiam convocandi* (Wilkins. *Conc.*, i. 688). And in 1427 Archbishop Chichele (*q.v.*) appealed *ad sacrosanctum concilium generale* against a papal suspension from his legateship (*ibid.*, iii. 485). Since the Reformation the English Church has consistently appealed against the pretensions of Rome to the authority of a free General Council. Its position is summed up by Laud in the *Conference* referred to above. There are ' some Businesses,' he says, ' (Is not the setling of the Divisions of Christendom one of them ?) which can never be well setled but in a General Council. . . . And when that cannot be had the Church must

pray that it may, and expect till it may, or else reform itself *per partes* by National or Provincial Synods ' (p. 139). A General Council is the supreme legislature of the Church on earth. Nevertheless, the English Church recognises that General Councils ' may err and sometimes have erred even in things pertaining unto God ' (Article XXI.). Their decrees vary in authority according to the nature of the subjects with which they deal (some being concerned with faith and doctrine, others with less important matters), and according to the reputation of the council enacting them, and their ability to win acceptance from the Church at large.

The nature of General Councils made it impossible that they should meet at regular or at frequent intervals. Their function was to deal with grave crises, reconcile schism, or define doctrine. Legislation on minor matters, which required meetings at stated periods, could be left to the less majestic and less unwieldy assemblies now to be described.

National Councils.—As Christianity spread dioceses were grouped into provinces, and these again into patriarchates and exarchates. These arrangements usually followed the civil divisions of the Empire. And it became usual for the bishops of each division to meet together in synod. Apart from Provincial Councils, which are considered below, the only assemblies of this kind which directly concern the history of the English Church are the National Councils, which for centuries disputed the position of its chief assembly with the separate councils of the two provinces, and at times seemed likely permanently to supersede them. In the words of Dr. Stubbs (*q.v.*), ' From the first ages of English Christianity to the latest date at which a body of canons was promulgated, the idea of a National Synod has been present to the mind of the Church.' In the Anglo-Saxon period we find two kinds of National Councils. There are the purely ecclesiastical synods, such as those of Hertford (673) and Hatfield (680). These do not materially differ in constitution and functions from Provincial Councils, but such of them as were held after the recognition of the independence of the York province in 735 include the bishops of two provinces instead of one, under the presidency of the Archbishop of Canterbury. After the eighth century their history becomes obscure. It does not appear that they were held often, if at all, after the Danish wars. In earlier times they were assembled without any permission from the secular power. The bishops of England were already meeting in synod when the civil government was still divided among a number of independent kings, none of whom could authorise the holding of a National Council. Their decrees were not thought to require any secular ratification. Kings and nobles were sometimes present, and attested their acts to add secular to their spiritual authority. Secondly, the witenagemots, although they were mixed assemblies of clergy and laity, meeting primarily to transact secular affairs, yet played a part in the history of the English Church, and must be included among its councils. The bishops were recognised members of them, and abbots were sometimes present also. Dr. Stubbs (*C.H.*, vi.) gives lists typical of the proportions of the clerical and lay elements in a national witenagemot. In 931, 2 archbishops, 2 Welsh princes, 17 bishops, 15 caldormen, 5 abbots, and 59 King's thegns. In 966 the King's mother, 2 archbishops, 7 bishops, 5 caldormen, and 15 King's thegns. The bulk of the ecclesiastical legislation from 827 to 1066 is the work of these mixed assemblies. Church and State were in complete harmony, and it was part of the work of these assemblies to enforce by their decrees the law laid down by spiritual authority. Consequently their enactments on such subjects as 'the enforcement of Sundays and festival holydays, the payment of tithe, the establishment of the sanctity of oaths, of marriage and of holy orders' (*ibid.*, p. 144) possessed the authority of Church and State alike.

Here as elsewhere the Norman Conquest (*q.v.*) separated more completely the spheres of civil and ecclesiastical authority. National synods continued to be held, but were quite distinct from the great council of the nation. Thus in 1085 the King held a council at Gloucester which sat for five days, and included the prelates as well as the lay councillors, and immediately afterwards the archbishop and bishops held a synod by themselves which lasted for three days more. In 1102 a council of bishops and lay nobles held by Henry I. at Westminster was followed by a synod of archbishops and bishops alone. A synod held at Windsor, 1072, provided that such assemblies should be held in future at the will of the Archbishop of Canterbury. But they failed to become a permanent feature in the constitution of the English Church owing to the jealousy of the Archbishops of York, who disliked the priority allowed in them to the southern metropolitan. This rivalry between the two archbishops, together with the growing claims of the papacy, resulted in the introduction of national synods over which a papal legate

presided [LEGATES]. In the twelfth and thirteenth centuries these legatine councils became to some extent the recognised assemblies of the Church. They were regarded with some resentment, and were not successful in composing the differences between the two metropolitans. At a council held at Westminster, 1176, Roger of York, finding the Archbishop of Canterbury already seated on the right of the presiding legate, rather than take his place on the left sat down on his rival's knee, and an undignifying scene ensued. About the middle of the thirteenth century the period of foreign legates came to an end, save for a few unimportant exceptions. National Councils being thus rendered impossible by the mutual jealousies of the two archbishops, the separate synods of the two provinces became the normal councils of the English Church from the latter part of the thirteenth century, and few attempts have been made to revive the use of National Councils. The most important was that of Wolsey (*q.v.*), who, using his commission as legate to supersede the authority of Canterbury, held a synod of the bishops of the two provinces in 1518, and in 1523 united the two Convocations in a national synod. Cardinal Pole (*q.v.*), as legate, held a national synod in 1555. By Canon 139 of 1604 'the Sacred Synod of this Nation' is 'the true Church of England by representation.' And though this canon was passed by the two Convocations separately, yet its wording, and its title, 'A Nationall Synode the Church representative,' show that, in Dr. Stubbs's phrase, 'the idea of a National Synod' was still 'present to the mind of the Church.' Since then there has been no National Council in England. There have been joint action of the two Convocations and more or less informal meetings of their members, but the most usual form of co-operation between them in modern times has been that of simultaneous or concerted action, as when canons were enacted by the Convocation of Canterbury in June 1865, and in exactly the same form by that of York a week later. The most recent attempt to give effect to the desire for a National Council is the Representative Church Council (*q.v.*).

Provincial Councils.—Towards the end of the second century the Church in each province was organised under the primacy of a metropolitan, who summoned the bishops of the province to its synod, in which he presided. His presence was soon considered essential to its complete validity. The bishops brought certain presbyters with them, and deacons and lay people were also present.

The functions of a provincial council were to receive and publish the decrees of General Councils, and also to enact canons to meet local needs not covered by the general law of the Church, which it could supplement but not contravene. Within these limitations its decrees were binding in the province, and sometimes won acceptance beyond its borders and passed into the general church law. Provincial synods exercised judicial functions in early times. They heard appeals from the diocesan courts, and acted as courts of first instance in cases which were beyond the competence of an inferior body, such as the trial of a bishop, or the settling of disputes between dioceses. Provincial synods formed on the primitive model and wielding authority in spiritual matters existed in the English Church from the time of Theodore (*q.v.*). At times their importance was overshadowed by National Councils. But they rose into prominence again in the thirteenth century. [CONVOCATION.]

Diocesan Synods are probably as old as the organisation of the Church in dioceses, though they are not mentioned until the third century. They apparently existed in England shortly after the Conversion, and remained a normal part of the Church's constitution throughout the Middle Ages. A National Council held at Windsor in 1076 ordered that each bishop should assemble his synod every year. And there is evidence that in theory the diocesan synod was expected to meet twice a year. It normally consisted of the bishop and the whole priesthood of the diocese, but sometimes, both in the Middle Ages and more recently, only representative priests have been summoned. Deacons were also present, but did not form part of the synod. Laymen were specially summoned in order to give information of any disorders among clergy or people with which the synod could deal. They were known as *Testes Synodales*, or in English questmen, or sidemen (there is no authority for the belief that this word is a corruption of synodsmen). Their duties are defined by the canons of 1604, but they lost their synodical position from about the middle of the seventeenth century. The synod was summoned by the bishop's mandate, and he could at his option either preside over it in person, or appoint deputies to do so. Its functions were to elect proctors for Convocation, to receive and publish the decrees of councils of higher authority, and to supplement the general and provincial law by diocesan constitutions. These emanated primarily from the bishop. They were then discussed in the synod, the function of the clergy being to assist the bishop with their advice. The bishop himself, however, was the legislative authority for the diocese, just as its assembled bishops were for the province. But although he was not bound by the opinion of the clergy, it was customary for him to enact nothing without their consent. And this being obtained, the constitutions were promulgated as the law of the diocese. Canons thus enacted were sometimes accepted by the Church at large, on account of the reputation of the bishop who made them or of their inherent merit, and so passed into the general law. It was also the duty of the clergy, as well as of the lay questmen, to bring forward complaints which might form the subject of diocesan legislation. The synod also furnished an opportunity for the bishop to deliver a charge, and for systematic inquiries to be made into the state of the fabrics of the churches and the morals and discipline of the clergy. In these respects it has been to some extent replaced in modern times by episcopal visitations. It was occasionally used as a place of trial, the bishop being the judge, and the clergy acting as assessors.

Diocesan synods in England have had little connection with the State, though in the Middle Ages they were occasionally summoned under royal writ. Before Convocation was finally recognised as possessing the power of taxing the clergy, the diocesan synods were sometimes separately consulted on this subject. The last recorded instance of this took place in 1280. These synods were not affected by the restrictions placed upon Convocation by the Submission of the Clergy. And that it was intended that they should continue to hold their place in the Church's life is amply proved by the *Reformatio Legum* (*q.v.*), which provides for their annual session in every diocese. From the second half of the sixteenth century, however, they fell into disuse. Occasional examples can be found during the seventeenth, after which they ceased (save in the diocese of Man) until 1851, when Bishop Phillpotts (*q.v.*) summoned a synod at Exeter. They were discussed in the Canterbury Convocation in 1864, 1865, and 1867, but the proposal to revive them did not find favour with the Upper House, the bishops preferring the mixed conferences of clergy and laity which were then coming into use. Formal synods, however, have been and still are occasionally held in various dioceses, *e.g.* Lincoln, 1871; Southwark, 1905; Birmingham, 1910.

Ruri-Decanal Chapters.—For the sake of

completeness these assemblies, which date from Anglo-Saxon times, may be noticed. They consisted of the rural dean (*q.v.*) and the beneficed clergy. Their duties were to receive and publish the decrees of higher authorities, to inquire into and report upon wrongs and abuses, and to transact other minor business. They were also courts having jurisdiction in certain small matters. At the close of the Middle Ages they fell into disuse. There were attempts to restore them in the seventeenth century, and in the second half of the nineteenth they were very generally revived as deliberative assemblies of the clergy.

Modern Quasi-Conciliar Bodies. — The second half of the nineteenth century was an age of conferences. The revival of church life led to a general desire for common deliberation. Convocation, when revived, proved to be archaic, unrepresentative, and hampered by legal restrictions ; and its proceedings had, for many, an air of unreality. Diocesan synods were even more unfamiliar, and their effectiveness for the purpose required was doubted. Accordingly Ruri-Decanal and Diocesan Conferences of clergy and representative laymen were brought into being soon after the middle of the century, and have continued to fulfil the functions for which they were intended, namely, to exchange, to reveal, and to form the opinions of church people upon questions affecting the Church.

A more prominent assembly is the Church Congress, which dates from 1861, when the Cambridge Church Defence Association invited about three hundred delegates from similar associations to meet at Cambridge to discuss Church defence. The meetings were held, 27th to 29th November, under the chairmanship of the Ven. F. France, Archdeacon of Ely. The second congress met at Oxford in 1862, Bishop S. Wilberforce (*q.v.*) presiding. Since then it has met annually in some important town. In 1869 the Ven. W. Emery, Archdeacon of Ely, 'Father of the Congress,' became its permanent secretary, and in 1873 a standing committee was appointed. The membership of the London Congress of 1899 reached eight thousand. The 'Jubilee Congress' was held at Cambridge in 1910, with a membership of over three thousand five hundred. It is a loosely organised national Church Conference. Any member of the Church, clerical or lay, may take part in it. Since its early days it passes no resolutions, but merely discusses. Its chief work has been to stir up and maintain in various parts of England a sense of corporate church life. It is worth noting that

it has always been organised on national, not on provincial lines.

Finally, the 'Pan-Anglican' Conferences, which have been held at Lambeth once in every decade during the past half-century, must be mentioned. The first Lambeth Conference was indirectly an outcome of the cases of Bishop Colenso (*q.v.*) and *Essays and Reviews* (*q.v.*). In 1865 the Provincial Synod of Canada prayed Archbishop Longley of Canterbury to summon ' a General Council ' of the Anglican communion to counteract the disturbing effect of those episodes. The Convocation of Canterbury approved the design. It was found, however, that the original intention to convene a council which should define doctrine would provoke opposition, and could not be carried out. And a conference to serve as ' a demonstration of union ' between the different Churches in communion with Canterbury was substituted. In summoning the conference Archbishop Longley expressly stated that it would not be competent to define doctrine, but that united worship and common counsels would tend to maintain the unity of the faith. Invitations were sent to the whole Anglican episcopate, 144 bishops, of whom 76 attended. The Conference met at Lambeth, 24th September 1867. It was admittedly an experiment, and its programme had been drawn up with a view to the avoidance of controversy. A stormy debate on the Colenso question was probably inevitable, but with this exception the proceedings were confined to such subjects as the powers of metropolitans, and the constitution and functions of synods and ecclesiastical courts. Committees were appointed to consider these matters, and the Conference met again in December to consider reports and to draw up and issue an ' Address to the Faithful.' An important result of the Conference was that in uniting the American and colonial bishops on equal terms with the English as members of a world-wide communion, it supplied a practical refutation of the theory that the Established Church is merely a creature of the State and dependent upon it. Archbishop Tait (*q.v.*), on succeeding to the primacy, found that bishops in all parts of the world were in favour of holding a second Conference, which he therefore convened in 1878. It was attended by 100 bishops. As before, an Encyclical Letter was issued. The Conference of 1888 was attended by 145 out of 211 bishops invited, and followed the lines of that of 1878, as did that of 1897, which coincided with the thirteen hundredth anniversary of the landing of St. Augustine.

To this Conference about 240 bishops were invited, and 197 came. The Conference had now assumed 'a certain measure of continuity,' and had justified itself as a means of maintaining unity and corporate life. A Central Consultative Body was formed, to which any Church may resort for information or advice. The Conference of 1908 was attended by 242 bishops, and preceded by a 'Pan-Anglican Congress' of 7000 clerical and lay delegates from all parts of the world.

[G. C.]

For councils in the early Church see the article Councils by A. W. Haddan in *Dict. Christian Antiq.*, and Bright, *Age of the Fathers*; for the place of the laity, J. W. Lea, *Evidence of Primitive Ch.*, and the Report of Convocation referred to in the text. For English Church Councils the authorities cited for the article on Convocation; for the quasi-conciliar bodies *Lambeth Conferences* (S.P.C.K.), and annual Reports of the Church Congress.

COURTS for the interpretation of the law and its application to particular cases are an essential part of the organisation of any society. In the primitive Church the bishop, either alone or sitting with his presbyters in diocesan synod, acted as judge in his diocese, with an appeal if necessary to the synod of provincial bishops [COUNCILS], which in some cases of greater importance was itself the court of first instance. After the organisation of Patriarchates in the fifth century an appeal lay from the provincial synod to the Patriarch. And the primacy allowed to the Pope gradually and almost insensibly developed into a claim to constitute a court of final appeal from the whole of Christendom. The recognition of the Church by the civil power, and the growth of a system of Canon Law (*q.v.*), produced regularly constituted courts imitated from those of the State and exercising the power it allowed them as well as their inherent spiritual jurisdiction.

Courts in the Anglo-Saxon Period were similar to those of primitive times, coloured by the peculiarly close relations of Church and State then prevailing in England. The bishop exercised jurisdiction in the shire-moot, the general assembly of the shire, where he sat with the aldorman and expounded the law and pronounced the sentence in ecclesiastical cases. The bishop, and apparently the archdeacon as well, took the same part in the hundred court. And the bishop exercised a more private and informal, as well as a more spiritual, jurisdiction in his personal tribunal, *forum domesticum*. Suits which were either begun in the provincial synod, or taken thither or to Rome on appeal, were few and exceptional.

Courts in the Middle Ages.—The Norman Conquest introduced a system more in accordance with the ideas of reforming churchmen and canonists. William I. decreed that no bishop or archdeacon should henceforth hold pleas of the episcopal laws in the hundred court, nor bring to the judgment of secular men any cause concerning the government of souls, but such causes should be decided by the bishop according to the canons and episcopal laws. The effect of this policy was to separate the ecclesiastical jurisdiction from the civil and to organise it in a regular system, which may thus be outlined :—

1. The Court of the Rural Dean (*q.v.*) transacted some petty business in subordination to that of the archdeacon.

2. The Court of the Archdeacon (*q.v.*) now first appears as a regular part of the system.

3. Diocesan Court. The bishop continued to exercise jurisdiction privately, in visitation, and sometimes in diocesan synod. But a more formal court was required to administer the canon law, and the consistory court of the diocese appeared and became the normal court of the first instance. The most important development in it during the Middle Ages was the appointment of the bishop's Official as judge (see below).

4. Provincial Courts. The chief of these were the Court of Arches and the Chancery Court, the Consistory Courts of Canterbury and York respectively under the Official Principal of each archbishop. The southern court received its name, Court of the Arches, from the Church of St. Mary-le-Bow (*de Arcubus*), in which it was usually held. The Dean of the Arches was originally the judge of the archbishop's Court of Peculiars which sat in that church. But after a time this position was always held in conjunction with that of Official Principal, and the holder of both offices came to be known by the title of the less important. The Archbishop of Canterbury had also a Court of Audience, in which, apparently, he originally exercised his legatine jurisdiction in person, both as a tribunal of first instance and on appeal from the Arches. He had certain assessors, called auditors, eventually reduced to one, who became judge of the court, which sat at St. Paul's, and for a time exercised co-ordinate jurisdiction with the Arches. An unsuccessful attempt was made to abolish it in 1536. It disappeared in the seventeenth century. A similar court at York seems to have been soon merged in the Chancery Court.

There was also in each province a Prerogative Court exercising the archbishop's testamentary jurisdiction. The judge was called the Master, Keeper, or Commissary. His jurisdiction was distinct from that of the Official Principal, but the two offices were sometimes held in conjunction. The Archbishop of Canterbury had also his Court of Peculiars, mentioned above. For the provincial synods as courts see CONVOCATION. The subject of the judicial powers of the Archbishops of Canterbury is complicated by the fact that almost continuously from 1127 to 1534 they were also papal legates, and it is doubtful how much of their jurisdiction was exercised in that capacity [LEGATES].

5. Peculiars (*q.v.*). There were numerous peculiar jurisdictions which broke in upon the hierarchy of church courts. Before the Norman Conquest some religious houses had acquired exemption from episcopal control, and their abbots exercised ordinary jurisdiction. During the Middle Ages many other exempt jurisdictions arose, such as Royal Peculiars, Peculiars belonging to various bishops, deans, and chapters, and others. Districts of varying extent, covered by these exemptions, lay outside the jurisdiction of the usual courts, and were subject to their own judges, from whom an appeal lay to the Pope.

Appeals in the Middle Ages.—The notion of appealing from one court to another naturally followed the introduction of an ordered system of courts administering a recognised body of law. In the twelfth century appeals lay from archdeacon to bishop, bishop to archbishop, and thence to the Pope. This last step was an inevitable result of the recognition of the canon law as a world-wide system, not limited by national boundaries; but it was regarded with jealousy by the kings as introducing an outside jurisdiction over which they had no control, and they sought to restrict it as much as possible. William I. suffered no one to receive letters from the Pope unless they were first shown to himself. And in the Constitutions of Clarendon (*q.v.*) Henry II. laid down that if the archbishop failed to do justice recourse should be had to the King, that by his order the case might be settled in the archbishop's court, and not carried further without the King's leave. This attempt to establish a veto over appeals to Rome had to be abandoned after the death of Becket (*q.v.*), and the Crown could only hinder them by exercising its undoubted right of forbidding the intercourse of its subjects with a foreign power [PRAEMUNIRE]. They were generally permitted by the kings, and became very numerous. Towards the end of the Middle Ages they decreased in number, and were almost entirely confined to questions of wills and marriages. Apart from their appellate jurisdiction the Popes claimed a universal jurisdiction of first instance, exercised through legates with general powers, and delegates specially appointed to decide particular cases.

The Jurisdiction of the Church Courts in the Middle Ages was based on William I.'s principle that cases touching the government of souls should not be tried in the secular courts. But the difficulty of applying it in practice led to constant rivalry between the ecclesiastical and secular courts, the results of which may be summarised as follows:—

1. The right of the church courts to deal with purely spiritual matters, such as the celebration of divine service, was never questioned by the State.

2. They claimed to deal with all questions of church property, but the temporal courts succeeded in asserting jurisdiction over advowsons and questions of patronage, the church courts retaining disputes about church revenues, tithes (*q.v.*), and land given in 'free alms' to the Church. Their right to deal with portable ecclesiastical property, as church ornaments, was not contested.

3. The Church had jurisdiction over all questions connected with marriage (*q.v.*).

4. The close connection of the Church with a man on his deathbed led to a claim to dispose of his goods according to the wishes he had then expressed, or for the good of his soul if he had died intestate. The church courts thus acquired testamentary jurisdiction over personal property but not over land, which could not be devised by will, but passed to the heir in accordance with the secular law.

5. The Church failed to enforce its further claim that all promises and obligations resting on good faith came within its jurisdiction. It was allowed to deal with such matters as perjury, and to punish breaches of faith as sins, but not (except by the wish of the parties) to settle disputes rising out of them.

6. The church courts also exercised a disciplinary jurisdiction over the laity for sins which were not punishable in the temporal courts as crimes. [DISCIPLINE.]

7. All breaches of the ecclesiastical law by the clergy were cognisable by the ecclesiastical courts.

8. Their claim to jurisdiction over clerks accused of crimes punishable in the temporal courts was only partially successful [BENEFIT OF CLERGY; CLARENDON, CONSTITUTIONS OF.]

9. Both clerks and laymen were subject to the disciplinary jurisdiction of the church courts over heresy (*q.v.*).

The Reformation.—The close of the Middle Ages saw the church courts fallen into weakness and corruption. Their spiritual censures lacked moral weight, and their excessive fees, their delays, and vexatious procedure also weakened their authority. Moreover, practically all important jurisdiction was now in the hands of judges whose authority was directly delegated to them by the Pope. The constitutional courts of the Church thus fell into disuse, and had to be restored almost *de novo* when the papal encroachments were thrown off.

In 1532 the Statute of Citations (23 Hen. VIII. c. 9) forbade the summoning of parties outside their own diocese except in certain cases. Its object was to define the jurisdiction of the provincial courts, and to restrict the authority exercised by the archbishop over the whole of his province, which, it was alleged, had been used oppressively ' by calling of poore men from the farthest part of the realme to London for an half-penny candell, or for a litell obprobious word.' This statute was confirmed by Canon 94 of 1604.

More important legislation followed. The Statute of Appeals, 1533 (24 Hen. VIII. c. 12), lays down the principle that all spiritual and temporal causes should be decided within the realm by the spiritual and temporal courts respectively, and recites the attempts of the mediæval kings to resist the papal intrusions. Its provisions are confined to matrimonial, testamentary, and tithe cases, which had recently been almost the only subjects of appeals to Rome. In these there shall be no appeal from the archbishop's court save to the Upper House of Convocation in cases touching the King. The Act for the Submission of the Clergy and Restraint of Appeals, 1534 (25 Hen. VIII. c. 19), which applied to all ecclesiastical cases, added an appeal ' for lack of justice ' in the archbishop's court to the King in Chancery. This was the origin of the Court of Delegates (below). The appeal in cases touching the King is not mentioned, but has been held to have been superseded by the creation of the new final court. Appeals from exempt jurisdictions were transferred from the Pope to the King in Chancery. Any appeal to the Pope was made an offence liable to the penalties of *praemunire*. The obtaining of dispensations from Rome was forbidden by the Peter Pence Act, 1534 (25 Hen. VIII. c. 21). Dispensations, licences, and faculties which had previously been granted by the Pope were to be henceforth (and still are) granted by the Archbishop of Canterbury in both provinces. This jurisdiction, which does not derogate from the ordinary dispensing and licensing power of the Archbishop of York and the bishops, is exercised in the Court of Faculties by the Master of the Faculties, who is usually but not necessarily the same person as the Dean of the Arches. These Acts were repealed in 1554 (1-2 Ph. and M. c. 8), but revived by the Act of Supremacy, 1559 (1 Eliz. c. 1), which again formally renounces the papal jurisdiction, reaffirms the visitatorial supremacy of the Crown, and provides for its exercise by means of commissioners. Neither in Henry's reign nor Elizabeth's did Parliament profess to bestow any ecclesiastical jurisdiction. The effect of this legislation on the church courts was to restore them to their constitutional position, to give them Parliamentary authority, and to provide for the carrying out of their decisions by the secular arm; to abolish the papal jurisdiction in England, and to set up two new courts, through which the Royal Supremacy was to be exercised, the Courts of Delegates and High Commission (*q.v.*).

The Court of Delegates was created by the Act 25 Hen. VIII. c. 19, which provides ' for lack of justice at or in any of the courts of the archbishops of this realm . . . it shall be lawful to the parties grieved to appeal to the King's majesty in the King's Court of Chancery, and that upon every such appeal a commission shall be directed under the great seal to such persons as shall be named by the King's highness . . . like as in cases of appeal from the Admiral's Court to hear and definitely determine such appeals, and the causes concerning the same.' This provision has some affinity with the eighth Constitution of Clarendon. Henry VIII., like Henry II., desired that appeals from the archbishop should come to his own court ' for lack of justice,' a phrase which implies that it was not intended to give the right of appeal as a matter of course, but only that the Crown should intervene when the archbishop's court had clearly failed in its duty. Therefore no permanent court was set up, but special persons were to be appointed by the Crown to hear each case as it arose. They were to be experts in ecclesiastical law, just as those who heard appeals from the Admiral's Court were experts in admiralty law. These Delegates, as they were called, were to give the final decision, not, as in Henry II.'s scheme, to remit the case to the provincial court. This device of appointing delegates to hear appeals had been normally adopted by the Popes, and was probably intended only to apply to the matrimonial and testamentary cases which had been the usual subjects of appeals to Rome. There is no evidence that the Delegates were meant as a court of appeal in cases of doctrine or discipline, which, in fact, were monopolised by the Court of High Commission until its abolition in 1641. And for two centuries after that there was little need for such a court. Only seven cases involving doctrine or discipline are known to have come before the Delegates during their whole history (1534-1832), and in none of these did they reverse the decision of the provincial court. No permanent Court of Delegates was formed, but individuals were appointed to hear each appeal as it arose. At first they were frequently civilians only, though sometimes bishops, judges, and occasionally peers were added. From the middle of the eighteenth century the court was normally made up of three common law judges and three or more civilians chosen from a rota without regard to their fitness for the position. If the court were equally divided, or the majority included no common law judge, more Delegates were added by a Commission of Adjuncts. Although there was no appeal, the case might be reheard by a stronger body of Delegates under a Commission of Review. It is uncertain whether the statute which set up this court received any formal assent from Convocation. But in practice the Church accepted it as a convenient means by which the Royal Supremacy could be exercised in the quasi-ecclesiastical matters to which its jurisdiction was, in fact, confined.

Church Courts in Modern Times.—During the seventeenth and eighteenth centuries the church courts remained practically unchanged. Coercive ecclesiastical jurisdiction was abolished, 1641 (17 Car. I. c. 11), but, except that of the High Commission, restored, 1661 (13 Car. II. st. 1, c. 12). In the nineteenth century they underwent considerable modification; their present position may thus be summarised:—

1. The Archdeacon's Court gradually fell into abeyance after the middle of the seventeenth century, partly because an appeal lay from it to the diocesan court, to which suitors therefore preferred to resort in the first instance; partly because of the decrease in the number of disciplinary charges against the laity, in which its activity chiefly lay. The Parish Clerks Act, 1844 (7-8 Vic. c. 59), gave it jurisdiction over charges of misbehaviour against Parish Clerks. Under the Church Discipline Act and later statutes

charges against the clergy can only be heard in the diocesan and superior courts.

2. The Diocesan Court was unaffected by legislation until the Church Discipline Act, 1840 (3-4 Vic. c. 86). This was only concerned with the machinery for dealing with charges against the clergy, and provided for a preliminary commission of inquiry, after which the bishop might either hear a case in person with three assessors, of whom one must be a lawyer, or send it by letters of request to the provincial court. In practice bishops have generally done this, and so the diocesan court has tended to drop out of its place in the constitution of the Church. By forcing assessors on the bishop the Act further interferes with the free exercise of his personal jurisdiction. The Clergy Discipline Act, 1892 (55-6 Vic. c. 32), restored the jurisdiction of the diocesan court over charges of immorality against the clergy. But in other cases it is still unduly overshadowed by frequent recourse in the first instance to the provincial courts.

3. Provincial Courts. The Court of Arches and the Chancery Court of York retain their former position, except in so far as they may have been affected by the Public Worship Regulation Act (*q.v.*). In consequence of that Act the same judge presides in both, but as he is properly qualified according to the canons, his ecclesiastical jurisdiction does not appear to be affected by the fact that he is also judge of the secular court set up by the Act. The Prerogative Courts were abolished in 1857, but the Court of Faculties remains unaltered.

4. Peculiars, about three hundred of which had survived to the nineteenth century, were abolished in part by the Church Discipline Act, 1840, and finally, for all practical purposes, by the Ecclesiastical Jurisdiction Act, 1847 (10-11 Vic. c. 98).

5. Court of Final Appeal. Down to 1832 the Court of Delegates continued to do its work unobtrusively and without arousing dissatisfaction. But at that time a restless spirit of reform prevailed, and naturally fastened on the church courts as cumbrous and antiquated. The first recommendation of the Ecclesiastical Courts Commission, 1830 [COMMISSIONS, ROYAL], was that an appeal to the King in Council should be substituted for that to the King in Chancery, on which the jurisdiction of the Delegates was based. The reasons given for the change, which was effected in 1832 by 2-3 Will. IV. c. 92, were the manner in which the Delegates were appointed, their costly and dilatory procedure, and the fact that they gave no reasons for their decisions, which were therefore not

uniform. The change was not in itself objectionable. The Crown might exercise its Supremacy as constitutionally in Council as in Chancery, by appointing suitable judges from among the Privy Councillors. But in 1833 a new court, the Judicial Committee of the Privy Council, was created to hear appeals to the King in Council (3-4 Will. IV. c. 41). It was to consist of the Lord Chancellor and a number of judges and ex-judges, of whom only the judge of the Prerogative Court of Canterbury (besides the Lord Chancellor) need be a churchman or even a Christian. Thus the right and duty of the Crown to appoint suitable persons through whom to exercise its Supremacy was taken away, and a new secular court set up. This 'very bungling piece of work,' which Charles Greville attributed to Brougham's 'ambitious and insatiable desire of personal aggrandisement,' was 'smuggled through' unobserved. Convocation was suspended, and no bishop or other representative of the Church seems to have taken any notice of the Act. The Church Discipline Act, 1840, made all archbishops and bishops who were Privy Councillors members of the Judicial Committee for the hearing of appeals under that Act. The Appellate Jurisdiction Act, 1876 (39-40 Vic. c. 59), repealed this provision, and by rules made under it three bishops chosen from a rota must be present at the hearing of ecclesiastical appeals as assessors, not as members of the court. This change was beneficial in helping to deprive the court of its false semblance of spiritual authority.

The first case of note which came before it was that of Gorham (q.v.), when it adopted the principle that in doctrinal cases 'its duty extends only to the consideration of that which is by law established to be the doctrine of the Church of England, upon the true and legal construction of her Articles and Formularies, and we consider that it is not the duty of any court to be minute and rigid in cases of this sort.' It interpreted this principle in such a manner as to condone laxity of doctrine, and thus first attracted the attention and hostile criticism of churchmen. In 1850 Bishop Blomfield (q.v.) introduced into the House of Lords a Bill providing that on doctrinal questions the Judicial Committee should take the opinion of the bishops, which should be binding upon it. Brougham then admitted that the court 'had been framed without the expectation of questions like that, which produced the present measure being brought before it. It was created for the consideration of a totally different class of cases.' The Bill was defeated, but church-

men gradually destroyed the moral authority of the court by a process of ignoring, and, when necessary, defying it. The most important objection was that which went to the root of its jurisdiction. It was created solely by Parliament, which could bestow no spiritual authority. And Parliament's claim to set up an ecclesiastical court was a breach of the terms of alliance between Church and State. The court was therefore unconstitutional, as well as devoid of spiritual authority, which can only be given by the Church. Objection was also taken to the manner in which it exercised the jurisdiction it claimed. Under the plea of interpreting documents, its judgments had the effect of defining doctrine. And as they were held to bind the ecclesiastical courts, it assumed in effect the power of legislating for the Church. In 1882 it expressly stated that its judgments formed part of the constitution of the Church of England as by law established (*Merriman* v. *Williams*, 7 A.C. 510). And it claimed spiritual powers by purporting to inflict spiritual censures such as monition, although its members were not, as a rule, versed in ecclesiastical law. It applied legal technicalities to matters to which they were inappropriate; it made no distinction between serious and trivial breaches of the rubrics; it treated any divergence from the common usage with pedantic harshness, and deliberately confessed to having two standards, a strict one for ceremonial and a lax one for doctrinal offences (*Sheppard* v. *Bennett*, 1872, L.R. 4 P.C., at p. 404). To the plain man this seemed, as Dean Church (q.v.) said, 'unjust, unconstitutional, and oppressive.' The effect it produced is shown by the words of Bishop S. Wilberforce (q.v.): 'It is a very serious thing to have the Supreme Court decide to satisfy the public, and not as the law really is'; and by the even weightier condemnation of Bishop Stubbs (q.v.): 'I do not care about the vestments themselves, nor for a *mistake* in the interpretation of the law, but there is no mistake here; it is a falsification of documents.' The general verdict was officially recorded in the Report of the Discipline Commission, 1906 [COMMISSIONS, ROYAL]. 'A Court dealing with matters of conscience and religion must, above all others, rest on moral authority if its judgments are to be effective. As thousands of clergy with strong lay support refuse to recognise the jurisdiction of the Judicial Committee, its judgments cannot practically be enforced.'

Another result of its claims has been to weaken the foundations of law and authority in the Church. A widespread refusal of obedience to a tribunal claiming to be the final court of appeal, however justifiable, must tend to weaken the sense of authority. And as the provincial and diocesan courts considered themselves bound by the Privy Council's decisions, churchmen lost their respect for these also. Even the spiritual authority of the bishops was weakened, for there was a widespread, and often well-founded, belief that their directions represented not their own mind or that of the Church, but that of the Judicial Committee.

In 1892 its domination was to some extent broken by the judgment in *Read v. Bishop of Lincoln* [BENSON; KING; RITUAL CASES]. The archbishop's court did not consider itself bound by existing judgments of the Privy Council, but allowed the points at issue to be argued afresh, and came to its conclusions without regard to previous decisions. And in forming these conclusions it did not confine itself to narrow rules of interpretation, holding that important points of church law could not properly be decided unless considerations of history and liturgiology were admitted. On appeal both these principles were admitted by the Judicial Committee, which thus tacitly withdrew from its previous position. It has, however, survived all schemes to set up an appeal court of spiritual validity. It is generally assumed that such a court is essential to the Church's judicial system. But if that system could be so reformed that the diocesan and provincial courts exercised a jurisdiction of undoubted spiritual validity, it is questionable whether further appeal would normally be required. Both in the twelfth and in the sixteenth century it was thought that an appeal beyond the provincial court was only needed in exceptional cases. And any appeal to a final spiritual court might well be confined to specially difficult or important matters.

The Benefices Act, 1898 (61-2 Vic. c. 48), set up a new court, consisting of an archbishop and one lay judge, to hear appeals against a bishop's refusal to institute a clerk for any reason except doctrine or ritual. Its decision is final.

Ecclesiastical Judges.—Since the twelfth century it has been the exception for bishops to preside in their consistory courts. The work of these courts, having then become too great for the bishops, tended to fall to the archdeacons, whose courts thus enlarged their jurisdiction. The bishops, regarding such encroachment with jealousy, sought to preserve the jurisdiction of their own courts by delegating their judicial functions to Officials, namely, the Official Principal, who

had jurisdiction in contested suits, and the Vicar-General, who exercised non-contentious jurisdiction, institutions, the granting of licences, and the like. It became usual to unite these two offices in one judge, commonly called the bishop's Chancellor. The custom of appointing these judges became so general in the Middle Ages that the temporal courts have held that a bishop must appoint a Chancellor (*ex parte, Medwin*, 1853, 1 E. and B. 609; *R. v. Tristram*, 1902, 1 K.B. 816). And the canonists maintained that he could be compelled to do so by the metropolitan.

The Official's is not an inferior jurisdiction, but that of the bishop himself, exercised by delegation. No appeal lies from the Official to the bishop, but the bishop in appointing him can limit his jurisdiction or reserve to himself either certain kinds of cases or 'a general right to exercise in person the offices otherwise deputed' (*R. v. Tristram, supra*). Canon 11 of 1640 recognises this power in the bishop, and it is in accordance with the common law and practice of the Church. And even if no reservation is expressed, it is doubtful whether by canon law a bishop may part with the whole of his jurisdiction. Similar considerations apply to provincial judges, except that their jurisdiction apparently cannot be limited in the manner described. The Official Principal and Vicar-General of an archbishop are usually different persons.

Where there is a dean and chapter the judge's appointment is confirmed by them as representing the clergy. It is a freehold, and is binding on the bishop's successors. In the Middle Ages no ecclesiastical judge might be either a layman or married. A Bill to override this rule of the canon law was withdrawn from Parliament at the request of Convocation in 1542, but passed in 1545 (37 Hen. VIII. c. 17), and in 1633 was said by the King's Bench to be merely declaratory of the common law (*Walker v. Lamb*, Cro. Car. 258). The present rule of the English Church on the subject is to be found in Canon 127 of 1604, which lays down that an ecclesiastical judge must be not less than twenty-six years of age, learned in the civil and ecclesiastical laws, at least a Master of Arts or Bachelor of Law, reasonably well practised in the course thereof, well affected and zealously bent to religion, touching whose life and manners no evil example is to be had, and must take the Oath of Supremacy, and subscribe the Articles of Religion. The validity of his jurisdiction depends on his appointment by the bishop. Any further qualifications may be varied from time to time.

A bishop may also appoint a commissary to exercise jurisdiction in distant parts of the diocese. And under Canon 128 any judge may appoint a duly qualified deputy, called a Surrogate.

The Bishop's Veto.—A bishop is not merely a judge to try any case brought before him, but a father in God, bound to consider the whole interests of the Church and the spiritual benefit of the accused person. Therefore he is himself the prosecutor in criminal cases. But from early times it has been customary for him to permit others to prosecute, or, in the technical phrase, ' to promote his office ' of prosecutor ; and he has always had power to refuse this permission if he sees fit. For the ecclesiastical jurisdiction ' is not to be exercised without discretion, or to be left entirely to the judgment and passions of private persons ' (*Maidman* v. *Malpas*, 1794, 1 Hagg. Cons. 205). In this, as in other respects, the bishop's functions were exercised by his Official, and the practice was to allow an action to proceed if the prosecutor could show that it was one of which the church court could properly take cognisance, and that he was able to pay the costs. The Church Discipline Act, 1840, placed this discretion on a statutory basis. The bishop has an absolute right to allow proceedings to be taken under that Act or not, as he thinks fit (*Julius* v. *Bishop of Oxford*, 1880, 5 A.C. 215). The Public Worship Regulation Act gives him power to veto proceedings taken under it (*Allcroft* v. *Bishop of London*, 1891, A.C. 666). When the bishop has vetoed a prosecution no *mandamus* will lie from the temporal courts to compel him to allow it to proceed ; nor can those courts enter into the merits of the case, or consider whether he has exercised his discretion wisely.

Ecclesiastical Jurisdiction in Modern Times has been greatly diminished ; partly because coercive spiritual jurisdiction, at any rate over the laity, is not in accordance with modern ideas ; partly because much of their former jurisdiction is now more suitably exercised by secular courts. As litigation increased the system of a multiplicity of minor courts all over the country became very inconvenient. Their procedure was costly, antiquated, and cumbrous. It was not till 1854 that they were enabled to receive oral instead of written evidence (17-18 Vic. c. 47). The portions of their former jurisdiction which have been abolished, may be arranged in three groups :—

1. Their criminal jurisdiction over offences now cognisable in the temporal courts has been withdrawn, and their disciplinary

powers over the laity have fallen into abeyance [DISCIPLINE].

2. Over Church property. That over tithes (*q.v.*) was abolished by a series of statutes, the most important being the Tithes Act, 1836 (6-7 Will. IV. c. 71), that over Church rates (*q.v.*) by 31-2 Vic. c. 109 (1868), and practically the whole of that over questions of dilapidation by the Ecclesiastical Dilapidations Act, 1871 (34-5 Vic. c. 43).

3. The testamentary and matrimonial jurisdiction, which formed the bulk of their work, was abolished (except the granting of marriage licences) in 1857 by the Probate Act (20-1 Vic. c. 77) and the Divorce Act (20-1 Vic. c. 85).

Their existing jurisdiction is as follows :—
A. Criminal (or Disciplinary) : (i) over the clergy for offences against the ecclesiastical law, including heresy ; (ii) over the clergy for offences against morality ; (iii) over lay church officers for certain breaches of the ecclesiastical law ;
B. Civil : (iv) over church property, the fabrics, their contents, and churchyards : this consists mainly of faculty cases ; (v) over certain cases of patronage ; (vi) marriage licences.

Church Courts and the State.—Under the relationship of Church and State in England the church courts form part of the constitution as ' the King's Ecclesiastical Courts.' They not only enjoy spiritual jurisdiction, derived solely from the Church but exercised with the sanction of the State, but also temporal or coercive powers conferred on them by the State, which therefore has the duty of (1) controlling, and (2) supporting them.

1. Its control is enforced by the writ of prohibition, by which the temporal forbids the ecclesiastical court to proceed further in a particular case, on the ground that it is violating natural justice, contravening the civil law, or exceeding its jurisdiction. The temporal court may, without Erastianism (*q.v.*), protect its own jurisdiction, or interfere if flagrant injustice is done. The process was also known as *appellatio tanquam ab abusu*, or *appel comme d'abus*. It is first found in England under Henry I. The clergy protested against it without success, but its limits were defined at various times, notably by *Circumspecte agatis* (1285), an ordinance in which Edward I. enumerates the cases which as *mere spiritualia* are properly subject to ecclesiastical jurisdiction. The clergy strenuously opposed it under James I. [BANCROFT ;

HIGH COMMISSION, COURT OF], but the State courts succeeded in maintaining the principle laid down by Coke in Fuller's case (1606, 12 Rep. 41): 'When there is any question concerning what power or jurisdiction belongs to ecclesiastical judges in any particular case, the determination of this belongs to the judges of the common law.' Prohibition does not enable the temporal court to act as a court of appeal if the church court has wrongly interpreted the church law. In that case recourse must be had to the ecclesiastical court of appeal. ' It is without precedent to grant a prohibition to the ecclesiastical court because they proceed there contrary to the canons ' (Holt, C. J., in *Watson* v. *Lucy*, 1699, 1 Ld. Raym. 539 ; see also *Mackonochie* v. *Lord Penzance*, 1880, 6 A.C. 424). *Mandamus* is the kindred proceeding by which the temporal courts compel those of the Church to exercise jurisdiction if they have wrongly refused to do so.

2. The State may fulfil its duty of enforcing the authority of the courts of an Established Church either (i) by granting them coercive powers to be used at their discretion : thus in the Middle Ages the church courts had their own prisons; or (ii) by holding its coercive power in readiness to enforce their decision when they apply for it in particular cases : this procedure is now regulated by the Act of 1813 (53 Geo. III. c. 127). [DISCIPLINE.]   [G. C.]

The best single history of church courts in England is contained in Stubbs's *Hist. Appendix I.* to the *Report of the Eccl. Courts Commission*, 1883. For primitive church courts see articles *Appeals* and *Bishops* by A. W. Haddan in *Dict. of Christian Antiq.*; for the Anglo-Saxon period, Stubbs, *C.H.*, viii.; for the Middle Ages, *ibid.*, xix.; Pollock and Maitland, *Hist. Eng. Law*; Maitland, *Canon Law in Eng.*; Hale, *Precedents*; for the Court of Delegates, Rothery, *Return of Appeals to the Delegates*, and the *Report and Proceedings of the Eccl. Courts Commission*, 1832 ; on the other periods and the subject generally, Gibson, *Codex*; Phillimore, *Eccl. Law*; article *Eccl. Law* in *The Laws of Eng.*; Crosse, *Authority in the Ch. of Eng.*; proceedings of the Royal Commissions already mentioned, and of the *Discipline Commission*, 1906 ; the statutes and cases quoted, and Gee and Hardy, *Documents*.

COVERDALE, Miles (1488-1569), Bishop of Exeter, translator of the Bible [BIBLE, ENGLISH], was born in Yorkshire, perhaps in that dale of Richmondshire whose name he bore, in 1488. He studied at Cambridge, and was ordained priest in 1514. He joined the Austin Friars at Cambridge, and was secretary to Robert Barnes, their prior, at the time he was prosecuted for

heresy before Wolsey (*q.v.*) in 1526. Next year he is in correspondence with Thomas Cromwell (*q.v.*). In 1528 he preached against images, and became what was called an apostate—that is, he abandoned his order and fled. For over five years little or nothing is known of him, though one of his surname took a degree at Cambridge in 1530 or 1531. It is stated, indeed, with some appearance of truth, that he was at Hamburg with Tyndale (*q.v.*) in 1529, helping (somehow) in the translation of the Pentateuch. It is probable, however, that he had first fled to the Low Countries, where, by a later tradition, he received some help from Jacob van Meteren at Antwerp. Hoker's statements about Coverdale are mostly true, with some confusion of dates and circumstances, though at times they are very perplexing. It is possible that Coverdale was at this time an agent for Tyndale at Antwerp—a hypothesis that would agree pretty well with the alleged meeting of the two at Hamburg in 1529.

If so, we may presume that he was narrowly watched, and at length compelled to leave the Low Countries. Perhaps he received aid from Cromwell in England to translate the Bible into English; but if so, it was secret aid, and it is curious that there should be no documentary evidence of the fact. But somewhere he completed the work in MS., translating simply from the Latin text compared with Luther's German Bible, and internal evidence shows that he got it printed by Froschover at Zurich. It was finished in October 1535, and sent to England, where Cromwell prepared to force its sale. For in August 1536 a set of Injunctions (*q.v.*) was issued in which every parish clergyman was required to procure a whole Bible in Latin, and also one in English, to be placed in the choir of his church. This order does not seem to have been pressed. But in 1537 Coverdale's Bible gave place to that called Rogers's, which was a combination of Tyndale's and Coverdale's. Coverdale, meanwhile, had come home; but a new project was started in 1538, and he was sent to Paris to superintend, along with Richard Grafton, the printing of a large Bible there in the best typography. The work was interrupted by the Inquisition ; but by the aid of Bishop Bonner (*q.v.*), the English ambassador, the printers escaped, and were able to carry away their plant and a company of French compositors, by whose aid the printing was completed in London in April 1539. In 1540 Cromwell was beheaded, and Coverdale once more fled abroad. He received the degree of D.D. at Tübingen, and in 1543 he settled at Bergzabern in the Rhine Palatinate, where he became pastor and schoolmaster, translating into English the works of Bullinger and others. Before settling there he had married Elizabeth Macheson, whose sister, the wife of Dr. Johannes Macchabæus (Macalpine), helped to translate the first Danish Bible.

In England a proclamation was issued on the 8th July 1546 against receiving or keeping Tyndale's or Coverdale's translation of the New Testament. But the death of Henry VIII. in 1547 soon brought about a change, and Coverdale, returning in 1548, was made King's chaplain and almoner to the Queen Dowager, Katherine Parr. In 1549, when Lord Russell was sent against the western rebels, he was sent also to aid him by his preaching. In 1551 he was appointed Bishop of Exeter by Letters Patent, the more aged Bishop Voysey having been induced to resign. He was also named in the commissions of 1551-2 for revising the canon law. To assist him in his ecclesiastical jurisdiction he procured the services of Dr. Robert Weston as his Chancellor, a lawyer, who was afterwards Chancellor of Ireland—a very necessary aid, as the people of his diocese, accustomed to the old religion, could not easily endure a married bishop of the new school.

In 1553 the death of Edward VI. brought about another change. Coverdale was deprived; but in February 1554 he obtained a passport to leave the country for Denmark, as the King there made special intercession for him. In Denmark, however, he found that he could not be useful. He went to Wesel, and from thence once more to Bergzabern; later on to Geneva. There it is thought that he assisted in the preparation of the Genevan Bible; but this only came out in 1560, whereas in 1559 he had returned to England. On the 17th December 1559 he assisted at Archbishop Parker's (*q.v.*) consecration. In 1563 he was made a D.D. of Cambridge, and was given by Bishop Grindal the rectory of St. Magnus by London Bridge; but he prayed for, and obtained, release of the first-fruits, which were over £60. Nevertheless, in 1566 he was driven to resign this living by the Queen's determination to maintain a stricter observance of the liturgy. His death appears to have occurred on the 20th January 1569. He was buried in St. Bartholomew's Church, which was pulled down in 1840 for the building of the Royal Exchange.

[J. G.]

Hoker, *Bishops of Exeter* (1584); *Mem. of Coverdale*, Anon. (1838); Gairdner, *Lollardy and the Reformation*.

CRANMER, Thomas (1489-1556). Archbishop of Canterbury, of an old Lincolnshire family settled in Nottinghamshire, was born at Aslacton, 2nd July 1489. His father was no less anxious for his son's physical than for his mental training, and all his life Thomas was an excellent horseman. But his father died during his boyhood, and his mother sent him to Cambridge at fourteen. There he graduated B.A. in 1512, and M.A., 1515. He obtained a fellowship at Jesus, which he lost by marriage, though he sent his wife to the Dolphin Inn, as she was related to the landlady, to prevent interference with his studies. A year after his marriage his wife died in childbirth, and his fellowship was restored to him. He proceeded D.D., and declined an offer of one of the foundation fellowships of Wolsey's new college at Oxford. He had been common reader at Buckingham (now Magdalene) College, had the readership given him of a newly founded divinity lecture at Jesus, and was chosen by the University public examiner in theology.

In the summer of 1529, a year of great pestilence, he withdrew from Cambridge with two scholars to the house of their father, a Mr. Cressy of Waltham Abbey. Cardinal Campeggio (*q.v.*) had just prorogued the legatine court, and every one knew that the King could not get his divorce from Katherine in that way. The King himself too, as it happened, was coming to Waltham on a progress, and his two chief agents in the divorce, his secretary, Gardiner (*q.v.*), and his almoner, Dr. Foxe, had lodgings assigned for them in Cressy's house. They were college friends of Cranmer's, and the three discussed together how the King could attain his object. Cranmer suggested the plan of taking opinions from Universities on which Henry might act without further delay; and the King, delighted with the suggestion, got him made chaplain to the Earl of Wiltshire, Anne Boleyn's father. This gave him a start in life such as he little expected. He accompanied Wiltshire to the Emperor when he met the Pope at Bologna in 1530; and after his return home he himself was sent as ambassador to the Emperor in 1532, having a secret mission also to some of the German princes, which proved a failure owing to the pacification of Nuremberg. While with the Emperor at Mantua, he received his recall, as on Warham's (*q.v.*) death the King had determined to make him Archbishop of Canterbury. This was awkward, as he had just married in Germany a niece of Osiander of Nuremberg—a union, of course, unrecognised by the Church. He delayed his return, as he afterwards said, by at least seven weeks, in the hope that the King would change his purpose. But the King had his own views in the matter, and obtained for him the necessary Bulls at Rome. He was consecrated on the 30th March 1533, having made a very disingenuous protest beforehand that the oath of obedience to the Pope which he was about to take would not bind him to anything against the King. His temporalities were restored on the 19th April, and he took an oath to the King renouncing all grants to the Pope that might be prejudicial to royalty. Already he had taken a first step towards the King's object by a letter which he wrote on the 11th April for leave to try his cause of matrimony; and with Henry's consent he summoned both the King and Katherine before him at Dunstable. He pronounced Katherine contumacious for not appearing, though he had been seriously afraid of her doing so, and gave judgment on the 23rd May that the marriage was invalid. Five days later, as the result of a secret inquiry, he pronounced the King to be lawfully married to Anne Boleyn. There is nothing to be said in defence of such conduct except that it was the result of pressure which no ordinary flesh and blood could resist; and Cranmer felt from this time that Royal Supremacy (*q.v.*) was a principle to which the Church must perforce submit, trusting that justice must rule in the end. His examination of Elizabeth Barton shows also a painful subservience; and he presently restricted licences to preach to those who would inveigh against the Pope's authority and keep a discreet silence for a while about Purgatory and some doctrines then under consideration. But, committed as he was to Anne Boleyn's cause, he did his best to mitigate the King's severity against More (*q.v.*) and Fisher (*q.v.*) and others whom Henry put to death for her sake in 1535. Next year, 1536, she herself was executed, to Cranmer's undoubted pain and perplexity; but before she suffered he obtained from her in the Tower a confession of certain facts, on the strength of which, though they were not revealed to the public, he pronounced that her marriage to the King had been invalid from the first.

Now began the framing of formularies—the Ten Articles of 1536, which in 1537 were extended into *The Institution of a Christian Man* (otherwise called *The Bishops' Book*), as that again was in 1543 revised into *The Necessary Doctrine and Erudition of a Christian Man* (also called *The King's Book*). Cranmer's part in these publications is not definite—in

some it seems to have been mainly that of a critic, and he professed that he was never satisfied with the last, though he had prepared the way for it in 1540 by presiding in a commission on doctrines and ceremonies. But earlier than all these, owing to a resolution of Convocation, he had set on foot a project for an English Bible (*q.v.*), which had not advanced very far when that of Coverdale (*q.v.*) made its appearance in 1535; but this was set aside in favour of that of Matthew (or Rogers, *q.v.*) in 1537, of which Cranmer desired the authorisation, declaring that he believed the bishops would never produce a better. Yet it was, after all, but a patchwork of Tyndale's (*q.v.*) and Coverdale's translations, neither of which had been approved.

In 1538 Cranmer and some other English divines were deputed to confer with certain German theologians sent over to discuss terms of union between England and the Protestants. In the same year his cathedral of Canterbury was rifled of its most costly treasures—the shrine of St. Thomas, the gold and jewels of which, packed in two great chests for the King's use, were as much as six or eight men could carry. In November John Lambert, or Nicholson, having been brought before Cranmer for heresy touching the Sacrament, made his appeal to the King, who heard the case in person. The King called in Cranmer to reply to the arguments of the accused, which he did. But Gardiner was not satisfied with the primate's arguments, and supplemented them by some of his own. Lambert was condemned and burnt. In 1539 was passed 'the Act of the Six Articles,' which Cranmer did his best to oppose in Parliament. He felt it necessary to dismiss his wife, whom he had hitherto kept in seclusion; and if the story be not an invention of contemporaries, he had her carried about in a chest, which once nearly led to a mishap. Next year he married the King to Anne of Cleves, took part afterwards in her divorce, and interceded for Cromwell (*q.v.*) as far as he dared. In 1541 the duty was imposed on him of giving the King the bitter information of Katherine Howard's infidelity.

In March 1541 the cathedral priory of Christ Church, Canterbury, was altered into a deanery and chapter. By that time 'the Great Bible' had been already set up in parish churches by an order of the previous year. This edition is known as 'Cranmer's Bible,' from his having written a preface to it. But in 1542 it was strongly objected to in Convocation, especially by Bishop Gardiner.

His secretary, Morice, writes of three · conspiracies' against Cranmer towards the close of Henry VIII.'s reign. These were, in truth, complaints against him for heresy which it was thought the King would listen to, for the King's zeal for orthodoxy was always acute when there seemed to be danger from abroad; but in each case he supported his archbishop, and disappointed his adversaries. One of these cases was a complaint by the prebendaries of his own cathedral in 1543; but the King made the primate judge in his own cause to investigate the matter. Another has been dramatised by Shakespeare, in which the archbishop was nearly committed to the Tower, but saved himself by exhibiting the King's ring. In 1544 the general use of prayers in English was ordered by royal mandate, and an English litany was published just before the King's expedition to Boulogne. [COMMON PRAYER, BOOK OF.]

After the death of Henry VIII. in 1547 Cranmer showed himself eager to keep up the doctrine of Royal Supremacy by making all the bishops take out new licences to exercise their functions, himself leading the way. Being primate of all England, he was the real supreme head in church matters now, as the Protector Somerset left these entirely to him. He was, indeed, rather conservative at first, and felt that it was dangerous in the King's nonage to make such changes as the late King might have enforced by supreme authority. He even opposed the Act for the suppression of colleges and chantries which was passed in the end of Edward's first year. But he had previously set on foot a general visitation of the realm in the King's name, promoting the sale of a new book of Homilies and a translation of Erasmus's *Paraphrase of the New Testament* for use in churches. He also obtained in Convocation a vote to permit marriage of the clergy, which, however, was only authorised in Parliament next year. More ready effect was given to a unanimous resolution of Convocation in favour of Communion in both kinds, which, being ratified in Parliament, led necessarily to some revision of the liturgy of the Church. A royal commission was issued in January 1548 to Cranmer and twelve other divines, six of whom were bishops, to prepare an Order of Communion, which appeared on 8th March 1548. Earlier in the year a number of old Church ceremonies were forbidden by proclamation; and in that year also, but probably later, he published his so-called *Catechism*, which was not really his, but a translation from the German of a Lutheran treatise with higher eucharistic doctrine than he himself somewhat later professed. In 1549 was passed the first Act of Uniformity, enforcing the use of a Prayer Book in English for public worship. This produced a serious insurrection in Devonshire and Cornwall. The rebels set forth their complaints in fifteen articles, requiring the revival of the Latin Mass, the use of images, the Act of the Six Articles, and the old Church order. Cranmer drew up an elaborate answer, reproaching them for insolence of tone, and pointing out that while some of their demands involved serious inconsistencies, one was at variance with old church principles, which had been far too long neglected.

After the fall of Somerset a religious reaction was expected; but that did not suit Warwick's policy, and change went on more than ever. Cranmer, at the head of a commission, had already deprived Bonner (*q.v.*) of his bishopric of London (the proceedings were by no means equitable), and he did the like to Bishop Gardiner in 1551; while in the latter year also, without his direct agency, Bishops Heath (*q.v.*) and Day were likewise deprived; and in 1552 Bishop Tunstall (*q.v.*) of Durham, though Cranmer had stoutly opposed a Bill for his deprivation in Parliament, was deprived by a commission consisting largely of laymen. It is really impossible to vindicate the fairness of these proceedings, and one must suppose Cranmer to have been carried on for his part by an irresistible sense of expediency. His idea, at this time, was to form a new Catholicism in England by a general agreement of divines there and abroad who disowned papal jurisdiction. To this he was stimulated all the more by the fact that eminent refugees came over from Germany to avoid the Interim of 1548; and besides Germans like Bucer (*q.v.*) he offered hospitality at Lambeth to Italians like Peter Martyr (*q.v.*), to the Pole, Laski, and to various others. He also invited Melanchthon to England, but he could not come. He was at this time receding further from Lutheranism in one important matter, and he wrote a book on the Sacrament, repudiating alike Transubstantiation and the Real Presence. This gratified most of the foreign divines, but shocked Gardiner, who, though in prison, managed to publish an answer to it, which drew a further reply from Cranmer.

At this time (1551) the zeal of reformers in England stood in awe of a serious political danger. Somerset had allowed the Princess Mary to continue to have the Latin Mass in her household; but this being opposed to the Act of Uniformity was a privilege Warwick would no longer permit. 'The Mass,' he is reported to have said, 'is either of God or of the Devil.' But when the Imperial ambassador, in his master's name, demanded toleration for Mary as the Emperor's cousin, Cranmer and some other bishops were called, and their counsel required whether such a concession was lawful. Painfully impressed with the danger of the Emperor declaring war against England, they resolved that although licensing sin was sin, conniving at it for a time might be permissible. [MARY.]

In 1552 Parliament passed a new Act of Uniformity to authorise a Second Prayer Book, which was mainly the result of criticisms on the first by Cranmer's friends, the foreign reformers. In the autumn he made some final corrections on 'the XLII. Articles' (afterwards reduced to the well-known XXXIX.), which he had previously submitted to the Council, and they were published in May 1553 for subscription by the clergy.

On Edward VI.'s death Cranmer, though unwillingly, was committed to the cause of Lady Jane Grey, for which he had to undergo a trial for treason in November following. The usual sentence was passed, but his life was spared; and in April 1554 he, Ridley, (q.v.), and Latimer (q.v.) were taken to Oxford to justify their heresies in a theological disputation. Of course, they were all declared vanquished in argument, but great respect was shown to Cranmer by his opponents. The three remained in prison till they could be put on their trial as heretics, after Pole (q.v.) had come to England as legate and the old spiritual jurisdiction restored. Ridley and Latimer were first tried under a special commission of the legate. Cranmer, as one who had been primate, was cited to appear at Rome in eighty days, but was informed that Cardinal du Puy, who had charge to try him, had delegated his functions to Brookes, Bishop of Gloucester. He was brought before Brookes in St. Mary's Church, Oxford, 12th September, but refused to recognise his authority, as he had once sworn never again to acknowledge papal jurisdiction. This was futile, and the charges were examined, but no judgment was passed. The proceedings were reported to Rome, and Cranmer remained months in prison, one day seeing Latimer and Ridley carried to the stake. His case was heard at Rome after the eighty days had expired, and judgment was given against him.

On 14th February 1556 he was brought before Bonner and Thirlby in Christ Church to be degraded. He made some fruitless protests. In prison he was pressed hard to recant, and at first signed a declaration accepting the Pope's authority, as the King and Queen had done so. This not being held satisfactory, he made others successively more and more explicit. He in vain tried to save his adhesion to Royal Supremacy, or to reserve a point for the decision of some future General Council. His two first submissions were made before his degradation. The fourth was distinctly dated 16th February, and declared his full submission to the teaching of the Catholic Church on the Eucharist as in other things. A writ for his execution was issued on the 24th, and he was told that he should die on the 7th March; but further time was given him at his own request for preparation, and he made what seemed to be a final submission (the sixth) on the 18th, full of penitence for his past life. He was evidently sore perplexed. His own doctrine of Royal Supremacy had driven him to accept the Pope again as the King and Queen did, and even the sacramental doctrine of the Church, which his own mind could not see, and which he might have hoped that the Church itself would ultimately define otherwise, but that the matter had been already settled a few years before at Trent. On this subject he had conferences with orthodox divines in prison, and he seemed, even on the 20th, to be quite sincere in his conversion. Next day he was to die. It was a wet morning, and Dr. Cole, who was to have preached at the stake, delivered his sermon in St. Mary's Church. Cranmer was moved even to tears, and drew tears from the spectators. After the sermon he addressed the people, as he was expected to do, declaring first his full belief in the Catholic faith and then the thing that troubled his conscience most. But here came a surprise to the audience; for the thing that troubled his conscience most, he said, was having made writings contrary to his convictions; and those writings were not his books on the Sacrament but the bills which he had written or signed since his degradation—that is to say, all but his first two submissions. And as in this his hand had written contrary to his heart, he was resolved that at the stake the offending hand should first be burned. He ran to the stake and fulfilled this promise, putting his right hand into the flame when it began to rise; and very soon all was over.

[J. G.]

Gairdner, *L. and P. of Henry VIII.*; *Cranmer's Remains* (Parker Soc.).

CREIGHTON, Mandell (1843-1901), Bishop of Peterborough and London, historian of the papacy, was born in Carlisle, educated at Durham under Dr. Holden, and at Merton College, Oxford, of which he was elected Fellow in 1866. gaining first classes in Mods. and *Lit. Hum.* and a second in Law and History. After living for some few years in Oxford as a Tutor and a very brilliant historical lecturer, he retired to the college living of Embleton in Northumberland in 1875. Besides taking a great part in local activities he was a Guardian of the Poor, and at one time secretary of the Church Congress, and having much to do with the organisation of the new diocese of Newcastle (*q.v.*). Creighton continued his historical work. In 1882 he published the first two volumes of his *History of the Papacy during the Reformation*. This work, of which the fifth and final volume went down to the sack of Rome in 1527. forms his main title to fame as a historian. But he published during his lifetime many smaller books, of which those on Wolsey and Queen Elizabeth are the best known. At Embleton, no less than at Cambridge afterwards. Creighton did almost as much historical teaching as learning, frequently having undergraduates as pupils. To Cambridge he removed in 1884, being the first Dixie Professor of Ecclesiastical History. In this capacity Creighton probably did more than any one else (not excluding Lord Acton) to stimulate the study of history in a University in which it was not the fashion. His lectures, and more especially his conversational classes, were an inspiration to many, while with the actual conduct of the school and the remodelling of the Historical Tripos he had much concern. His part in the social and academic life of the University was large, but it was lessened by his appointment in 1885 to a canonry at Worcester. There he rapidly won influence, partly as a preacher and partly through his interest in all local affairs. His influence in the cathedral chapter was predominant, and he was the main instrument of the improvement at the west end and the river front. In 1886 Creighton became the first editor of the *English Historical Review*.

In 1890 he had been promoted to a canonry at Windsor, but before he was installed he was nominated to the bishopric of Peterborough. His life was now mainly, though not entirely, occupied with diocesan and ecclesiastical duties. The geniality and sympathy which were so strongly marked in his character combined with his amazing grasp and quickness to win him the respect of his diocese. Before he left it respect had ripened into affection. With the working men of Leicester he was especially popular, and through this fact he was able to exercise a decisive influence in the settlement of the boot strike in 1895. Outside functions were not neglected. He represented the English Church at the coronation of the Czar, Nicholas II., in 1896, just as ten years earlier he had represented Emmanuel College at the tercentenary of Harvard. He delivered in 1893-4 the Hulsean Lectures at Cambridge, producing a very characteristic volume on *Persecution and Tolerance*. He was Rede Lecturer at Cambridge, 1895, and Romanes Lecturer at Oxford, 1896.

In 1897 he was translated to London. It does not appear that he ever enjoyed his work in London as he did that at Peterborough; and indeed it was fraught with difficulties. He complained of the enormous amount of administrative work and of the lack of human relations with his clergy, owing to the fact that he had only to drive to a church for a function and then drive on to another, whereas in the country diocese of Peterborough it was commonly necessary to stay the night. He was also subject to attacks on all sides owing to the violent agitation against 'ritualism.' This began almost immediately after his appointment by the interference of the late John Kensit, and was stimulated by the Erastian Whig, Sir W. Harcourt. This agitation, in part the natural result of Temple's (*q.v.*) *laissez-faire* policy, tested all Creighton's powers of statesmanship and sympathy. In a situation in which entire success was out of the question, he achieved results far more satisfactory than would have fallen to the lot of most of his colleagues on the bench. The whole controversy had one good result: it enabled Creighton to bring his vast store of historical learning and imagination to bear on the problem. He set himself definitely to find out what was the relation of National Churches, of the English Church in particular, to Christendom as a whole. He developed with much acumen the view which scholars like Casaubon had commended in the seventeenth century, that the Church of England is 'based on sound learning,' and in this lies her distinctive quality alike against Rome and Geneva. Creighton, who had, as he put it, 'almost a craze for liberty,' was ever in favour of using persuasion rather than coercive power. While he held that it was wrong for a priest in his diocese to disobey his orders and presumptuous to disregard his expressed wish, he was not prepared to punish this wrong by direct action; and at the close of his life and after much misgiving he interposed his veto against the attempt of a Baron Porcelli to get up a prosecution against the incumbent of St. Peter's, London Docks. Partly for this reason he was never understood by either side, while his epigrammatic humour irritated those persons who think a sense of humour out of place in a clergyman. It was on a reference from Creighton to the archbishop, as interpreter of the rubric, that the famous Lambeth Opinions on incense and reservation were promulgated by Dr. Temple. Worn out with his manifold tasks, Creighton died on 14th January 1901 after an illness of a few months. Shortly before his death he had summoned the representatives of both parties to a conference on the Holy Eucharist.

Both by temper and conviction Creighton was tolerant—a quality which came out in his teaching no less than his rule. This tolerant quality meant a readiness to understand all views, but in no way implied haziness or indefiniteness in his own. A strong High Churchman, with a belief in the sacramental system and the authority of the Church, he hailed the publication of *Lux Mundi*. Sensitive to all the currents of intellectual life, his hold on the Incarnation and its attendant miracles was never shaken. His breadth of mind and sense of humour made him one of the most brilliant talkers of the day, and he was hailed by Lord Rosebery as the ' most alert and universal intelligence in this land.' He had a wide circle of those who felt for him not merely respect but love. His premature death was mourned in London as that of few of his predecessors had been. Posthumous works have served but to enhance his fame, and the *Life*, published by his widow, has taken rank among the six best biographies in the language.

[J. N. F.]

CROMWELL, Thomas (1485?-1540), called by Dixon ' the greatest enemy of the Church of England,' was son of a Putney blacksmith. According to John Foxe's (*q.v.*) romantic but untrustworthy account, he used to declare ' what a ruffian he was in his younger days' when he travelled much abroad. He afterwards became a successful tradesman, lawyer, and money-lender, and by 1514 attracted the notice of Wolsey (*q.v.*), who employed him in the suppression of the smaller monasteries, in which, says Foxe, ' he showed himself very forward and industrious,' and acquired odium by his ' rude manner and homely dealing,' and, it may be added, his rapacity. He thus stood in some danger at Wolsey's

fall. Cavendish (*Life of Wolsey*) tells how at ' Asher ' (*i.e.* Esher) on ' All-Hallows Day,' 1529, he found Cromwell in tears, ' saying of Our Lady matins ; which had been since a very strange sight'; and learned his intention to ride to London, ' where he would either make or mar or he came again, which was always his common saying.' While deserting Wolsey's service for the King's he contrived to pose as the champion of his fallen master, who called him ' mine only aider.' Cromwell had probably ascertained that his pleading Wolsey's cause in Parliament (which he had first entered in 1523) would not be displeasing to the King.

He had learned his political ideals from Machiavelli's *Prince*, which he recommended to Pole (*q.v.*), telling him that a councillor's first duty was to study not the honour but the inclination of his prince. By appealing to Henry's greed for money and despotic power he became his most powerful minister and adviser for ten years, during which time his principal achievements were the Suppression of the Monasteries (*q.v.*), the abolition of the papal jurisdiction, and the establishment of the Royal Supremacy (*q.v.*). Throughout he showed himself able, cunning, unscrupulous, and tyrannical. He became Privy Councillor, 1531 ; Chancellor of the Exchequer, 1534 ; Secretary to the King, 1535. In 1535 he was also appointed Vicegerent or Vicar-General in causes ecclesiastical, to carry out the Act of Supremacy (1534, 26 Hen. VIII. c. 1), with power to supersede the ordinary jurisdiction of bishops and archbishops. This was a following of papal precedent. He presided in Convocation both in person and by deputy. He was chiefly responsible for the Injunctions (*q.v.*) issued in 1536 and 1538. At his house in Austin Friars he abused his power to set back his neighbours' fences by twenty-two feet and to remove the house of one of them on rollers. Gifts and honours were heaped on him, including a prebend at Sarum and the deanery of Wells. He became Lord Privy Seal, 1536 ; Knight of the Garter and a Baron, 1537. Yet he only retained his power by abject servility. Henry ' beknaveth him twice a week and sometimes knocks him well about the pate.' By 1539 Henry's supremacy was firmly established, and he desired to emphasise his orthodoxy ; whereas Cromwell was identified with Protestantism by policy, and probably by such sympathies as he had, and was seeking to counterbalance France and the Emperor by an alliance with the Lutheran states of Germany, and by a marriage between

Henry and Anne, sister of the Duke of Cleves, which was solemnised, 6th January 1540. The King's resentment at this policy was increased by his bride's lack of personal attractions. Yet Cromwell's skill as a financier, and packer and manager of parliaments, enabled him to reassert his influence as against the Catholic party headed by Gardiner (*q.v.*). In April he was made Earl of Essex and Lord Chamberlain. But his usefulness was at an end, and Henry followed Cromwell's policy in destroying a tool which had done its work. On 10th June he was arrested at the council on a charge of treason, the Duke of Norfolk tearing the ribbon of St. George from his neck. An Act of Attainder was passed, and he was beheaded, 28th July.

[G. C.]

Merriman, *Life and Letters*; Dr. Gairdner in *D.N.B.*; H. A. L. Fisher, *Pol. Hist. Eng., 1485-1547*.

CRUSADES, or wars waged in the name of the Cross against infidels, heretics, and schismatics, were frequently raised in Western Europe from the closing years of the eleventh to the middle of the fifteenth century. Indeed, some even later enterprises against Mohammedan powers were dignified with this name; as, for example, the expedition of Charles V. against Tunis (1535), and the raids of the Knights of Malta upon the strongholds of the corsairs. Crusades began, as they ended, with projects for expelling Islam from the borders of the Mediterranean; and at first the name was reserved for expeditions having this aim in view. They were raised at the invitation, or at the least with the approval, of the Pope, were usually directed by his legates, and in theory were recruited from all Christian peoples, though, in fact, they sometimes assumed a national complexion. The volunteers enrolled themselves under princes of repute, and the military command was put in commission among those leaders who brought the largest contingents or could boast of the greatest reputation. The members of a crusading army styled themselves the soldiers of Christ, were distinguished from other men by the badge of the cross which they wore on the left shoulder, and, as being dedicated to the service of God, enjoyed various privileges, of which the most considerable were immunity from attacks by personal enemies, inviolability for their property of every description, and exemption for the term of the Crusade from the ordinary laws of debt. These privileges were not infrequently abused, and men took the Cross to escape from their

creditors or the consequences of a feud, without the slightest intention of fulfilling their vow. Still, the crusading impulse was strong and genuine in the twelfth century; and for another hundred years, at least, it appealed to a considerable minority of conscientious men. So long as any Christian strongholds still held out in the Holy Land, there was a regular stream of pilgrims from Europe, who came to take part in one or more campaigns, and enrolled themselves under the princes of the Latin colonies. Fleets of transport vessels sailed at more or less regular intervals from the seaports of Italy and Southern France; and the business of carrying pilgrims to and from Palestine was highly profitable. But though many crusaders discharged their obligation in this manner, the Church continually pressed upon European rulers the duty of raising the larger and more highly organised expeditions to which alone the name of Crusade is properly applied. Historians commonly notice eight Crusades, although the catalogue might be enlarged by the inclusion of other expeditions little, if at all, inferior in size to some of those which have been thus distinguished. The eight are as follows:—(1) The Crusade, proclaimed by Urban II. at the Council of Clermont (1095), which captured Jerusalem and founded the Latin Kingdom. (2) The Crusade preached by St. Bernard to avenge the fall of Edessa; this set out in 1147 under the leadership of the Emperor Conrad III. and Louis VII. of France. (3) The Crusade which was raised after the capture of Jerusalem by Sultan Saladin (1187). This was joined by the Emperor Frederic Barbarossa (who died on the outward march), by Philip Augustus of France, and by Richard Lionheart of England; it resulted in the recovery of Acre, but left Jerusalem in the hands of Saladin. (4) The Fourth Crusade, proclaimed by Innocent III., was diverted by Philip of Suabia and the Venetians against the Greek Empire of Constantinople (1202-4), which it destroyed and replaced by the short-lived Latin Empire. (5) The Fifth Crusade, chiefly recruited from the German and Hungarian nations, attacked Egypt and captured Damietta (1219), but was subsequently defeated and compelled to surrender this conquest. (6) The Crusade of the Emperor Frederic II. (1228), who succeeded, without recourse to arms, in obtaining a treaty under which Jerusalem, Bethlehem, and Nazareth were ceded to the Christians. But, after his departure, the Kharismian Turks attacked and took Jerusalem. (7) The Seventh Crusade was led by Louis IX.

of France, who incurred a crushing defeat in Egypt, and was taken captive (1250), but proceeded to Syria after he had been ransomed, and spent three years there in attempts to organise the defence of the Christian coast towns. (8) The Eighth Crusade, led by the same prince, was diverted against Tunis by the influence of his brother, Charles of Anjou. The army was decimated by the plague, to which Louis himself fell a victim (1270); the greater part of the survivors then returned to France. But Prince Edward of England, who reached Tunis after the death of the French King, went on to Acre with a few followers, and remained there for two years. His return marks the close of the crusading period in the strict sense. Acre fell in 1291, and the Latin occupation of Palestine came to an end. For years the Franks and the military orders [RELIGIOUS ORDERS] had been confined to one or two strong places. Little sympathy was now felt for them in Europe, and no attempt was made to reinstate them. Cyprus remained a Christian state, under the Lusignans; Rhodes was held by the Knights of St. John until 1522. But the Teutonic Knights had returned from Palestine to Europe in the first half of the thirteenth century. They founded a state on the Vistula, at the expense of the heathen Prussians, and for more than two centuries lived the life of crusaders on the shores of the Baltic. The Templars returned to their European estates, devoted themselves to banking operations, and were finally suppressed by Pope Clement V. at the instigation of Philip IV. of France (1312). Apart from the Prussian Crusades, those against the Hussites of Bohemia and the Turkish invaders of Hungary are the last considerable manifestations of the crusading spirit. The Hussite Crusades were raised, chiefly from the German nation, in the years 1420-34. The most famous of the Hungarian Crusades were that of 1396, annihilated at Nicopolis by Sultan Bajazet, and that of 1456 which raised the siege of Belgrade.

England's share in the Crusades was relatively slight. Though Richard I. and Edward I. earned personal distinction in the Holy Land, they were unable to raise large forces among their own countrymen; and those Englishmen who followed them were drawn chiefly from the upper classes. English volunteers played some part in most of the eight great Crusades. They were particularly prominent in that branch of the Second Crusade which was diverted to Portugal and effected the capture of Lisbon; and the Fifth Crusade was joined by a number of barons who had fought against King John on the side of his French rival. Many of those who followed Edward were moved by a desire to do penance for their part in the Barons' War of 1264-5. But in England, as elsewhere, the Church allowed the humbler sort of crusaders to commute their vow on easy terms. The crusading ideal was, like that of chivalry, a foreign importation, though it long remained part of the creed of the English aristocracy. In the fourteenth and fifteenth centuries this island still produced eminent crusaders. One such was Henry Despenser (*q.v.*), the fighting Bishop of Norwich, who led a Crusade from England to Flanders to maintain the cause of Urban VI. against his rival, Clement VII. (1383). Henry IV., before his accession, served with the Teutonic Knights in Lithuania: we gather from Chaucer's *Prologue* that such an adventure was not uncommon for an English knight. Henry V. cherished hopes of recovering Jerusalem, and his uncle, Henry Beaufort (*q.v.*), earned a cardinalate by placing himself at the head of a Hussite Crusade. It is easier to enumerate the English crusaders than to trace the effects of the Crusades on English society and the English Church. Whoever reads the best of our mediæval chroniclers—say Hoveden or Matthew Paris—will at once perceive how interest in the Holy War widened the outlook of the ordinary Englishman. Whether the Crusades more immediately affected the development of scientific knowledge is problematical, to say the least. Arab mathematics, Arab medicine, Arab philosophy came into Western Europe by way of Toledo and Palermo through the peaceful intercourse of curious *savants*; this exchange of ideas was hindered not helped by the Crusades. Adelard of Bath, Michael Scott, and Roger Bacon owed little, if anything, to the Moslems of the Levant, who were inferior in culture to their brethren of Spain.

The Fourth Crusade produced in England, as in Paris, a premature renaissance of Greek studies; but in England this appears to have begun and ended with the famous Grosseteste (*q.v.*). In the economic sphere the Crusades co-operated with many other causes to cause the transition from *Natureconomie* to *Geldeconomie*, from serfdom to the cash nexus, from rural life to town life; but they produced no dramatic change in the relative importance of social classes. They neither destroyed the English baronage nor made the fortunes of the English serf and burgess. In the ecclesiastical sphere they were the occasion for some outbursts of emotional revivalism and of anti-Jewish feeling; but the Jews were detested more for their usury than for their religion. The papacy found in the crusading movement a new pretext for the taxation of the English clergy, and for squeezing money out of the feeble Henry III. But the money was used for other purposes, and could almost as well have been obtained on other pleas. In fact, the importance of the Crusades for English history is much slighter than the picturesque school of historians will allow.

[H. W. C. D.]

Von Sybel, *Hist. of the Crusades* (Eng. trans.); Archer and Kingsford, *The Crusades*.

CUTHBERT, St. (d. 687), Bishop of Lindisfarne, a native of Bernicia, was as a boy warned by a little child that boyish sports did not become him, and a disease in his knee being cured soon afterwards by an angel, as he believed, his thoughts turned heavenwards. While keeping sheep upon the Lammermuir Hills in 651 he saw in a vision the soul of Aidan (*q.v.*) borne to heaven. Forthwith he rode to (Old) Melrose, and received the tonsure of the Scotic shape from the Abbot Eata. As a monk he was humble, became learned in the Scriptures, and being physically strong was constant in fastings. He migrated with Eata to Ripon, where he became Hostillar, but returned to Melrose in 661 when the Scotic monks were deprived of Ripon. He was attacked by the plague, recovered, and was made prior. In 664 he moved with Eata to Lindisfarne, adopted the Roman usages, and persuaded the other monks to do the same. He frequently retired into solitude on the mainland, and in 676 built himself a hut on the desolate Farne Island, and as far as possible cut himself off from his fellow-men, giving himself up to prayer and ascetic practices. In 684 he was chosen Bishop of Hexham, but was unwilling to accept the office. Finally Eata resigned the bishopric of Lindisfarne in his favour, himself taking that of Hexham, and in 685 Cuthbert was consecrated at York by Archbishop Theodore (*q.v.*) and seven other bishops. For nearly two years he actively performed his duties as bishop, travelling about his diocese and preaching with apostolic zeal and love, until at the end of 686, finding his end near, he again retired to Farne Island, where he died on 20th March 687. He was buried in the church of Lindisfarne, and in 698 his body was translated and was found uncorrupted. During the Danish invasions in 875 it was removed, and those in charge of it after many wanderings brought it to Chester-le-Street in 883, whence in 990 it was again removed for fear of the Danes, and a few months later was brought to Durham. A church, the predecessor of the present cathedral, was built, and the saint's body was placed there in 999. The grave was opened, and his bones discovered, in 1827. He was the most famous saint of Northern England, and was commemorated on 20th March. His festival disappeared from the English Calendar in 1549, but was replaced in that of the Scottish Book of 1637.   [W. H.]

The anonymous life used by Bede, together with Bede's two lives of Cuthbert, in prose and verse, are in Bede's *Opera Hist. Minora* (Eng. Hist. Soc.); J. Raine, *St. Cuthbert, etc.*, 1828.

D

DAVENANT, John (1572-1641), Bishop of Salisbury, was son of a city merchant-prince. One of his sisters (Judith) was mother of Fuller (*q.v.*) (who styles his uncle 'the second *Jewell* of Salisbury'), and another (Margaret) was wife of Bishop Townson, who held the see of Sarum only ten months, and, dying of a fever contracted by 'unseasonable sitting up to study' (as Fuller says), left his widow and fifteen children impoverished, to be provided for by his brother-in-law and successor. Davenant was educated probably at Merchant Taylors' School, and certainly as a 'pensioner' at Queens' College, Cambridge. He became Fellow there in 1597; President, 1614; and he was Margaret Professor of Divinity, 1609.

In 1618 he was chosen by James as a delegate to the synod of Dort or Dordrecht along with Joseph Hall (then Dean of Worcester), Samuel Ward, Master of Sidney, and G. Carleton, Bishop of Llandaff (and Chichester), where he took a leading part, and with the other English delegates attempted to moderate the high Calvinism of the Continental Protestants. Soon after his return, 1621, though after some delay occasioned by Archbishop Abbot's untoward accident with the cross-bow, he was consecrated to Sarum.

At Salisbury the bishop had a contention with the corporation, 1631-6: in 1629 H. Sherfield, their Puritan recorder, had broken with his staff the coloured glass in St.

Edmund's Church in defiance of the bishop's express monition, for which he was sentenced in the Star Chamber in 1633. Davenant, who was a keen logician and controversialist, had himself incurred the displeasure of Charles I. by his sermon preached before the court in Lent, 1631, in which he disregarded the terms of 'his Majesty's declaration,' prefixed in 1628 to the XXXIX. Articles of Religion (*q.v.*), wherein 'all further curious search' into those points which had been hotly discussed among Arminians and Calvinists is prohibited.

In his contribution to J. Durie's *eirenicon, de pace ecclesiastica inter evangelicos* (1634), he left, as Bishop Hall says (in his *Peacemaker*), 'a Golden Tractate' as his legacy to Christendom. In a second treatise, included in the English translation of the *Exhortation to Brotherly Communion* (London, 1641), he treats as the three main difficulties the questions of (1) the Presence of Christ in the Eucharist; (2) the Ubiquity of Christ's Humanity and 'the communication of properties'; (3) Predestination and Free Will. As perfect agreement is impossible with imperfect knowledge, he considers acceptance of the Apostles' Creed should be a sufficient basis for communion, and appears not to consider the differences between Episcopalians and Presbyterians a difficulty. [REUNION.]

In the administration of his diocese Davenant loyally supported Laud's directions as to the placing of the Holy Table; and his injunction on that subject and on holding twelve communions a year (viz. on four consecutive Sundays thrice a year), directed to the vicar and churchwardens of Aldbourne, Wilts, 17th May 1637, is entered in the extant parish register, and is printed in the *Memoir* by M. Fuller, pp. 424-7. [c. w.]

J. Wordsworth, *National Church of Sweden* (1911), pp. 293-6.

DAVID, St. (d. 589?), abbot-bishop, Patron of Wales. In Welsh he is known as Dewi Sant. The earliest authority for his life is a *Vita S. Davidis*, by Ricemarchus (Rhygyfarch), Bishop of St. David's, 1088-96. All the other lives are amplifications or abridgments of this. His father was Sant (a *regulus* of Ceredigion, in south-west Wales), descended from Cunedda Wledig, who, with his sons, migrated from North Britain in the early fifth century and settled in Wales. His mother was Non, the daughter of Cynyr, a man of some importance in the neighbourhood of (afterwards) St. David's. On his father's side he was Brythonic or Welsh, and on his mother's Goidelic or Irish. His birth-date is nowhere given, but in the *Annales Cambriae* he is made to have died in 601. This, however, is too late; it was probably in 589, possibly earlier.

Many legends have clustered round St. David's name; in fact, his whole life, as we have it, is legendary, and it is with the greatest difficulty that one is able to sift the few facts it contains. The legends are all calculated to enhance his glory, and manifest his pre-eminence over the other Welsh saints, and, no doubt, justify his canonisation.

At a suitable age he was sent to be instructed at 'The Old Bush' or Ty Gwyn (not Whitland), near St. David's, a monastic school presided over by St. Paulinus (the Welsh saint of the name), with whom he remained for ten years. Afterwards he became a monastic founder himself, and, among other monasteries, founded that of Ty Ddewi or St. David's, his principal foundation, where he gathered round him a number of disciples or monks, bound by the severe rule of the Celtic Church.

He was a man of retiring disposition. When the Synod of Brefi was held, about 545, to enact canons of discipline for the clergy and laity—not to suppress the Pelagian heresy, as generally supposed—it was only after great pressure that he was induced to attend; but in the legend of the rising of the ground under him into a hill, his biographer could not resist the temptation to establish the apocryphal supremacy of the saint and his see over the entire British Church. The story of his pilgrimage with SS. Teilo and Padarn to Jerusalem to be consecrated bishop by the Patriarch is a fiction invented to establish the independence of the Welsh Church in relation to the see of Canterbury. David together with SS. Gildas and Cadoc was invited by Ainmire, the High King of Ireland, to restore the flagging Christianity of the island, which was in danger of succumbing to the revived paganism. To the trio the Church of Ireland is indebted for a form of the Mass. It is a mistake to say that he was bishop of a diocese in the ordinary sense. He did not form the diocese of St. David's (*q.v.*); what he did was to plant centres of religious and monastic influence, thereby laying the foundations of the great diocese of a later period.

Dedications in Wales under his name, up to 1836, numbered fifty-three, of which forty-two were in the diocese of St. David's alone, and not one in the whole of North Wales. He was emphatically a South Wales saint, and the dedications make him the third most popular saint in Wales, being preceded by the Blessed Virgin and St. Michael the Archangel. There are a number of early dedications under his name in Devon and Cornwall, and in Brittany, especially in Léon.

There is no evidence whatever that St. David is entitled to the designation of archbishop, either of Wales or of Menevia (as in the Anglican Calendar), or of Caerleon.

He died on the 1st of March ; at what age is unknown ; but his biographer's one hundred and forty-seven years is impossible. Archbishop Arundel in 1398 ordered his festival to be observed in every church throughout the province of Canterbury, and to be duly marked in the Calendar. It is not known for certain how the leek became his emblem. There is nothing about leeks in his life. St. David is still the one purely Welsh saint who has been formally enrolled in the Calendar of the Western Church. It is believed that his canonisation took place in the time of Pope Calixtus II., 1119-24. It was then that his cult, from being that of a merely local saint, became that of the Patron of Wales. But during his lifetime, and for centuries after, he can only be regarded as the supreme or chief saint of the principality of Dyfed, with which the diocese roughly coincides. Of the four patrons of Great Britain and Ireland, St. David is the only native saint.

He was buried at St. David's, and his plain but empty shrine now occupies a very modest position in the choir of the cathedral. Two pilgrimages to his shrine were esteemed equivalent to one to Rome.   [J. F.]

DAVIES, Richard (1501-81), Bishop of St. David's, was the son of Dafydd ab Gronw, Vicar of Gyffin, near Conway, and was educated at New Inn Hall, Oxford, graduating in 1530. In 1549 he was presented by Edward VI. to the rectory of Maidsmorton, and in 1550 to the vicarage of Burnham, both in the diocese of Lincoln. Of these he was deprived by Queen Mary, and he retired with his wife into exile in Geneva, where he suffered much privation. On the death of Mary he returned, and was restored by Elizabeth to his preferments, and made Bishop of St. Asaph in 1560. In 1561 he was translated to St. David's. He was the leader of the reforming party in Wales, and the trusted adviser of Parker (q.v.) and Cecil on matters affecting the Church in Wales.

Davies was a good scholar and linguist. During his exile he had lived in an atmosphere of Biblical translation, and he was instru-mental in providing the Welsh people with the Prayer Book and New Testament in the Welsh tongue, both of which appeared in 1567. In 1562 an Act had been passed (5 Eliz. c. 28), in which, no doubt, Davies had had a principal hand, requiring the four Welsh bishops and the Bishop of Hereford to have the Old and New Testaments and the Prayer Book translated into Welsh and placed in every church before the 1st of March 1566, but making no provision for the costs of either translation or publication. The time was much too short in which to execute such an arduous task. In 1567, however, such portion of the task as could reasonably be expected was accomplished. Davies seems to have been entirely responsible for the Prayer Book, whilst the New Testament was mostly the work of William Salesbury (q.v.). The portions translated by Davies were 1 Timothy, Hebrews, St. James, and 1 and 2 St. Peter. He also wrote the 'Epistle to the Welsh' prefixed to it. The expense of printing both was equally borne by Davies and Salesbury. They had intended also to bring out the Old Testament, and had translated a considerable portion of it, but owing to an unfortunate rupture between them over 'the general sense and etymology of some one word,' as Sir John Wynn tells us, it was abandoned. There is a MS. translation of the Pauline Pastoral Epistles in Davies's autograph at Gwysaney, near Mold, which was published in 1902 by Archdeacon Thomas. This is not identical with the portion he translated in the New Testament, but was probably a revision, as it is smoother and more finished. Davies also translated for the Bishops' Bible, 1568, the books of Joshua, Judges, Ruth, and 1 and 2 Samuel. He died, 7th November 1581, aged eighty, at Abergwili Palace, and was buried in the parish church there.

[J. F.]

DEISTS (Latin *Deus*, God), literally believers in God, a group of writers of the latter part of the seventeenth and earlier half of the eighteenth century, who granted the existence of God, but endeavoured to limit all belief in God's liberty to reveal Himself. Like the semi-Christian Arians of the fourth century, the Deists did not form a compact and coherent party, and were chiefly united by their negations. But though differing widely among themselves, they may be justly grouped together on account of the appeal which they all made to 'reason,' their attack on mysteries and miracles, their rejection of the doctrine of the Trinity and of any divine intervention such as the Christian finds in the Incarnation, and their criticism of the infallibility of the Bible.

The pedigree of Deism can be traced back to LORD HERBERT OF CHERBURY (1583-1648), who endeavoured to find in a supposed 'religion of nature' an authority to which all rational minds would submit. But the typical characteristics of Deism first appear full-blown in the writings of CHARLES BLOUNT, published in 1678 and 1680. He openly attacked priestcraft and the Pentateuch, and indirectly assailed the mediatorship and miracles of our Lord by a criticism of alleged similar phenomena in pagan belief. He was a vindictive adversary, a literary plagiarist who appropriated the labours of Herbert and Milton, and having fallen in love with his deceased wife's sister, ended his life by suicide.

JUNIUS JANUS TOLAND (1670-1722) was a more capable writer, and the author of the celebrated *Christianity not Mysterious.* Brought up as a Roman Catholic near Londonderry, he became a Protestant before he was sixteen. He was somewhat vain, but versatile and well read. He affirmed that he knew ten languages, including Irish, which a hundred years after his death was still widely spoken in the north of Ireland. He studied in Leyden and Oxford, and in 1701 visited the courts of Hanover and Berlin, and in England he was employed by the free-thinking Whig nobles to write in the interest of themselves and the House of Hanover. His small but notorious book, published in 1696, provoked the serious controversy between the Deists and the orthodox which lasted for a generation. To strip Christianity of mystery, to bring it 'within the conditions of nature,' is its task. He admits those parts of the New Testament revelation which seem to him to be comprehensible by reason. While he affirms that the value of religion does not consist in what is unintelligible, he hints, not obscurely, that what he does not understand ought not to be believed. His own religion appears to have combined Pantheism and a form of Unitarianism. In harmony with the latter is his view of early Church history, expressed in his book, *Nazarenus,* where the Catholic Church appears as the result of an amalgamation between Jewish Unitarian Ebionites and a Pauline party of Gentile origin.

ANTHONY ASHLEY COOPER, third Earl of Shaftesbury (1670-1713), was a patron of Toland, but stands outside the ordinary groove of Deism. He was liberal and generous. He was somewhat sceptical, and held that 'Religion is capable of doing great good or harm; and Atheism nothing positive in either way.' But he was a profound admirer of Plato, and held that it was right to submit, 'with full confidence and trust, to the opinions *by law establish'd.*' His famous book, *Characteristicks,* is a gentlemanly exhortation to follow a virtue which cannot fail to be its own reward.

MATTHEW TINDAL (1653 ?-1733) calls for special notice. Like Toland, he was for part of his life a Roman Catholic. He was the son of a minister, and at Oxford was elected to a law Fellowship at All Souls College. In the time of James II. he 'turn'd Papist,' and 'went publickly to Mass in Oxford.' But early in 1688, when the accession of William III. to the English throne seemed more than possible, Tindal became alive to 'the absurdities of popery,' and received Holy Communion in his college chapel. Hearne describes him as 'a most notorious ill Liver' and 'a noted Debauchee,' but 'sedate in company, and very abstemious in his Drink.' He became an ardent 'Williamite,' and gained a pension by maintaining that certain prisoners could be tried as pirates, though they pleaded that they were acting under a commission from James II. He wrote various pamphlets in the Whig and Low Church (*i.e.* Latitudinarian, *q.v.*) interest, including one on *The Rights of the Christian Church,* which was specially intended 'to make the clergy mad.' As an irritant it attained an unqualified success, but it was eclipsed by his *Christianity as old as the Creation, or the Gospel a republication of the Religion of Nature,* published in 1730. This work, which came to be known as 'the Deist's Bible,' marks the highest intellectual achievement of English Hanoverian Rationalism. Like Toland, Tindal assumes a decent Christian mask in the title and even in the chapter headings of his book. But the mask is almost transparent, for the book is undeniably directed against Christianity. He regards certain things as 'mutable,' as being merely 'means to ends,' other things as 'so indifferent as not to be consider'd either as means or ends.' The observance of these indifferent things is superstitious. Other and more important things, 'by their internal excellency, show themselves to be the will of an infinitely wise and good God.' 'The Religion of Nature' consists in observing these last things, and 'the Light of Nature' is our sufficient guide. The book is well written, and garnished with quotations from English divines, the classics, and the Bible. The Fathers of the Church are ridiculed for allegorising the Old Testament. And though Tindal refers to this practice as a proof that by allegorising they 'sufficiently acknowledg'd the sovereignty of reason,' he allows in 'the Religion of Nature' 'no Mysteries, or unintelligible Propositions, no Allegories.' The essence of his doctrine, as of the other Deists, is that God has given a moral law to man, and this law is simply the conditions of our actual existence, plain to every one alike, whether his capacity is high or mean. To this law God has added nothing, and it is absurd to suppose either that He has added anything or declared it in a manner which admits of any obscurity. The statement of Tindal's contemporary, Proast, that Tindal privately admitted that he had abandoned Christianity, is therefore not unjustified. Nor can we wonder that, long before his death, an Oxford wag composed an epitaph for Tindal, ending with the lines :—

'And now that his Body 's as rotten as pelf,
Pray for his soul who ne'er prayed for 't
  himself.'

THOMAS WOOLSTON (1670-1733) specially directed his efforts towards discrediting the miracles of the New Testament. He bitterly attacks the clergy, speaking of them as the physicians under whose care the woman with an issue grew worse. The taste of the age required attacks upon Christianity to be veiled, but relished outspoken satire of the clergy. At the beginning of the reign of George III. they were most disliked when they were austere ; before that time they were reproached for their ignorance and their love of drink and games. Woolston's tracts were popular enough, as the lines of Swift testify : - -

'Here's Woolston's tracts, the twelfth
  edition,
'Tis read by every politician ;
The country members, when in town,
To all their boroughs send them down ;
You never met a thing so smart,
The courtiers have them all by heart.
Those maids of honour who can read
Are taught to use them for a creed.'

He thus expounds the heart of his doctrine : 'Be no longer mistaken, *Good Sirs*, the History of Jesus's Life, as recorded in the Evangelists, is an emblematical representation of His Spiritual Life in the Soul of Man ; and His Miracles are Figures of His mysterious Operations. The four Gospels are in no Part a litteral Story, but a System of mystical Philosophy or Theology.' He hopes that 'the letter' of the stories of Christ raising

the dead will receive 'a Toss out of the Creed of a considerate and wise Man.'

ANTHONY COLLINS (1676-1729) especially attacked the theory that the Christian revelation was a fulfilment of Jewish prophecies. He maintained the now widely accepted view that the Book of Daniel is not the work of a prophet of the time of the exile but of a much later writer, contemporary with the violation of the Temple by Antiochus Epiphanes. He was educated at Eton and King's College, Cambridge, and his defective scholarship exposed him to the merciless ridicule of Bentley.

THOMAS CHUBB (1679-1747) was a disciple of Samuel Clarke, the Arian, but forsook Arianism (*q.v.*) for Deism. It was not, however, an extreme Deism, but a religion resembling the form of Unitarianism current in England about one hundred years after his death. He makes religion consist in the belief that morality alone makes a man acceptable to God. He insists on 'the supremacy of the Father' and the inferiority of Jesus Christ to the Father, and opposes the full Christian doctrine of the Atonement. He was a person of mild and inoffensive character, and regularly attended his parish church.

HENRY SAINT-JOHN, Viscount Bolingbroke (1678-1751), took some part in the religious controversies of the time, but did not greatly influence the course of Deism. Celebrated for his statecraft, eloquence, and extreme licentiousness, he won fame in other fields than theology. He attacks both the history and morality of the Old Testament. He says: 'As theists we cannot believe the all-perfect Being liable to one of the greatest of human imperfections, liable to contradict Himself.' He claimed, therefore, to be a 'theist,' the word not yet being distinguished sharply from 'deist.' The nastiness of Bolingbroke's line writing agrees better with his own character than with his assertion of a belief in One who cannot contradict Himself.

The coincidences between the English Deism of the eighteenth century and the German rationalism of the nineteenth are too significant to be ignored. Toland and Morgan anticipated F. C. Baur in their views about the relations between St. Paul and the original apostles, and in asserting the right of the Unitarian Ebionites to a place in the Church. Woolston anticipated Strauss by trying to find inconsistencies in the Gospel account of the miracles, and by treating all miracles as no more than allegory. Chubb, by assailing the divinity of our Lord, and throwing doubt on prayer and a future life in works of a popular character, anticipated the present phase of rationalistic propaganda in England and Germany. It is also remarkable that the Deists, like the self-styled 'Modern Protestants' or 'Liberal Protestants,' adopted the disingenuous method of using Christian phraseology while attacking all the distinctive doctrines of Christianity, and were sometimes under the delusion that the moral fruits of Christianity would continue to grow when the tree had been plucked up by the roots.   [L. P.]

Works of Deists: *Encyc. Brit.*, 10th ed.; M. Pattison in *Essays and Reviews*.

DENISON, George Anthony (1805-96), 'the militant Archdeacon of Taunton,' was the fourth of nine brothers, of whom one became Bishop of Salisbury and another Speaker of the House of Commons. Educated at Eton and Christ Church, after a distinguished University career he became Fellow of Oriel (1828), where he found the famous Common Room 'as dull a place socially as I can remember anywhere; men were stiff, and starched, and afraid of one another; there was no freedom of intercourse.' In 1845 he was appointed Vicar of East Brent, where he ruled with kindly despotism for fifty years, and originated the custom of 'harvest thanksgivings.' In 1851 he was made Archdeacon of Taunton. Always a convinced High Churchman, in his later years he approved and defended a more elaborate ceremonial than he himself adopted. In sermons preached in Wells Cathedral, 1853-4, he maintained that the Body and Blood of Christ are really present in the consecrated elements, independently of worthy reception, and are to be worshipped. On this Mr. Ditcher, Vicar of South Brent, prosecuted him for heresy. The case was heard by Archbishop Sumner (acting for the diocesan, who was patron of Denison's preferments) and four assessors, and sentence of deprivation was pronounced. Denison appealed on the technical point that the suit had not been begun within the legally prescribed time, and the Privy Council upheld the objection, without dealing with the doctrinal issue. The result of the proceedings, which lasted from September 1854 to February 1858, was to bring high eucharistic doctrine into public prominence.

Holding strong convictions against liberalism in doctrine and politics alike, and maintaining them with singular pugnacity, Denison took part, usually a leading part, in every church controversy, from the opposition to Hampden (*q.v.*) in 1847 to the dispute over *Lux Mundi*, which caused him to leave the

English Church Union [SOCIETIES, ECCLESIASTICAL] in 1892. A strong Tory in politics, he opposed Mr. Gladstone (*q.v.*), and contributed materially to his defeat at Oxford in 1865. He stoutly resisted State interference in church schools, and abhorred the conscience clause. In the Act of 1870 he recognised the defeat of his ideals in education, but no Government inspector was ever allowed to show his face in the school at East Brent. He was a prominent figure in Convocation, where in 1870 he came into violent collision with Dean Stanley (*q.v.*) on the question of the Athanasian Creed. Impetuous and combative as he was, his genial and kindly nature kept him on friendly terms with his opponents.   [G. C.]

G. A. Denison, *Notes of My Life*; L. E. Denison, *Fifty Years at East Brent*; *Proceedings against the Archdeacon of Taunton* (Bath, 1857); *Chronicle of Convocation*, 1855-92.

DESPENSER, Henry (1341?-1406), Bishop of Norwich, was grandson of Edward II.'s favourite, Hugh Despenser the younger, and from his early years showed a taste for warfare, and he developed into one of the condottiere ecclesiastics typical of the fourteenth and fifteenth centuries. During the revolt of 1381 he won distinction by his effectual suppression of the disturbances in East Anglia, but his name has acquired greater prominence from his connection with the 'Flemish Crusade' of 1383. In 1382 Count Louis of Flanders, who was at strife with his principal towns, having been defeated by the men of Ghent, under their regent, Philip Van Artevelde, sought the help of his suzerain, the King of France. This was granted, and Van Artevelde turned to the English Parliament for support. The quarrel furnished England with an opportunity of manifesting her traditional enmity to France. About this time Urban VI. proclaimed a crusade against the antipope, Clement VII., appointing Despenser as its leader. Since the King of France was a prominent supporter of the antipope, it was easy for English Churchmen to regard a favourable response to Van Artevelde in the light of a holy war. Parliament sanctioned the campaign, and in 1383 Despenser went to Calais at the head of an army of, for the most part, adventurers and fanatics. It was a disgraceful affair, prompted either by lust of fighting or superstitious devotion to the Roman pontiff. Since the Flemings themselves were Urbanists, the expedition was the more immoral. Some in Despenser's army urged that the attack should be made upon France rather than Flanders. But the bishop was a man of no scruples. He had determined to fight in Flanders, and his will carried the day.

The campaign was at first successful. But fortunes changed, and Despenser was compelled to raise the siege of Ypres, and to take refuge in Gravelines, whence he fled to England. Parliament condemned him, and he was deprived for about two years of the temporalities of his see. Yet the guilt was as much that of his judges as of the condemned. The campaign not only furnished an indictment against its leader, but was a revelation of the moral degradation to which England had sunk. Despenser, however, retained the favour of Richard II., and on the accession of Henry IV. was imprisoned for his loyalty to the late king. He died in 1406, and is buried in Norwich Cathedral.

[E. M. B.]

Walsingham, *Historia Anglicana*, vol. ii., R.S., 1864; Capgrave, *De Illustribus Henricis*, R.S., 1858; Froissart, *Chronicles*, Book 11.

DICETO, Ralph de (d. 1220), Dean of St. Paul's, derived his surname possibly from Dissay in Maine, and was born probably before 1130. He was perhaps a chorister of St. Paul's, or at any rate attached in early life to the Church. He succeeded Richard de Belmeis as Archdeacon of Middlesex in 1162, being, it seems likely, of his kindred, and possibly the son of his brother Ralph, who had been dean till 1160, a competitor for the post being John the Kentishman, afterwards Bishop of Poitiers, who corresponded with him till his death. He studied at St. Geneviève, Paris. He took kindly to the new Bishop of London, Gilbert Foliot (*q.v.*), but never definitely opposed Becket (*q.v.*). In 1180 he became Dean of St. Paul's, and immediately made a survey of all the property of the cathedral, built largely, and was generous in benefactions. His chief works are the *Abbreviationes Chronicorum* and the *Imagines Historicorum*, which carry the history through his own time up to 1202. Many MSS. of his works exist at St. Paul's. He was a cultivated scholar, acquainted with the Latin classics and the writers of the Silver Age; a careful chronicler, well informed as to public events; and in the words of his canons' record, *bonus decanus*.

[W. H. H.]

R. de Diceto, ed. Stubbs (R.S.).

DISCIPLINE. Some method of enforcing its laws and punishing offenders is necessary to an organised body. The Church being a spiritual society can only inflict spiritual censures, namely, the withdrawal of spiritual privileges, culminating in expulsion. The primary object of this discipline is the spiritual benefit of the offender, his repentance and restoration. It is *pro salute animae*. It is based on Scripture and apostolic practice (Mt. $18^{15.18}$; 1 Cor. $5^{3.5}$; 1 Tim. 1^{20}; Tit. 3^{10}), and soon developed into a system of public penitence and restoration by absolution, which from about the seventh century was largely superseded by private confession and absolution. After the recognition of the Church by the State spiritual penalties were enforced by the coercive power.

A. PUBLIC DISCIPLINE. 1. *Jurisdiction.*— In the Anglo-Saxon period there was little distinction between the ecclesiastical and civil jurisdictions. The Church had to enforce on her converts the observance of the moral law. And not only breaches of that law, but also such offences as neglecting to have a child baptized, or to observe Sunday or Lent, were punishable under the civil law. After the Norman Conquest the church courts (*q.v.*) acquired a wide disciplinary jurisdiction over the clergy for crimes which in laymen would be punishable in the secular courts [BENEFIT OF CLERGY], and over clergy and laity alike for sins which were not crimes, such as sexual immorality, usury, or perjury; for heresy (*q.v.*) and sorcery, and for such breaches of ecclesiastical decorum as lying in bed during church time, or habitually rejoicing at seeing priests in trouble. The State also gave to the church courts the duty of enforcing by spiritual penalties the collection of taxes and debts from clerks. The application of ecclesiastical penalties to such matters, the ease with which they could be commuted for money, and the vexatious use of the disciplinary jurisdiction brought it by the end of the Middle Ages into weakness and contempt. The efforts of Grindal (*q.v.*) and others to restore it were ineffective until it fell into the hands of the High Commission (*q.v.*). After the abolition of that court it again decayed. *The Rector's Book, Clayworth, Notts* (ed. Gill and Guildford, 1910), shows the rector in 1676 publishing an excommunication sent out of the archdeacon's court against two persons for marrying within the time prohibited and refusing to appear to give account of the same. Their absolution was published a week later. Early in the eighteenth century Johnson of Cranbrook maintained that dissenters were still subject to church discipline for 'uncleanness,' but admitted that 'there is not now a spirit in the English people to put the

Penal Laws against Vice in execution. . . . If a wealthy man be presented he gets the information withdrawn by feeing some officer : if a poor man . . . the churchwardens will not be at twenty shillings charge to bring an offender to penance.'

Nevertheless, fines and penances continued to be inflicted. In 1787 the church courts were violently attacked in the House of Commons as rapacious, oppressive, and even ' infernal ' ; and their activity was checked by an Act ' to prevent frivolous and vexatious suits ' by limiting the time for beginning a suit for defamation to six, and for fornication, incontinence or brawling to eight months after the offence (27 Geo. III. c. 44). Spiritual penalties for non-payment of tithes (*q.v.*) and church rates (*q.v.*) disappeared when those matters were removed from the church courts. In 1855 their jurisdiction over defamation was abolished on the ground that it had ceased to be a means of enforcing spiritual discipline, and become oppressive (18-19 Vic. c. 41). In 1860 the jurisdiction over the laity for brawling was transferred to the temporal courts (23-4 Vic. c. 32). In 1876 their long-disused power of punishing perjury was held to have been withdrawn by the statutes which made it punishable at common law, and the jurisdiction over the laity for moral offences was declared not to be ' in harmony with modern ideas, or the position which ecclesiastical authority now occupies ' (*Phillimore* v. *Machon*, 1 P.D. 481). The church courts now exercise disciplinary jurisdiction over the clergy for immorality, and over clergy and lay church officials for breaches of church law.

2. *Procedure.*—In the Middle Ages the bishop's visitation was a special time for seeking out and presenting offenders. The duty of presentment, which formerly lay with the officials of the court and the laity generally, was by the canons of 1604 confined to the churchwardens and sidesmen, with whom in theory it still rests. In modern times the bishop is either himself the accuser, or allows any one who is willing to undertake the duty, to promote his office. Apart from definite accusation, ' common fame ' was a sufficient reason for summoning a man before the church court and putting him to purgation. He had to take an oath that he was innocent, and to produce some half-dozen compurgators who would swear that they believed him. If he failed he was held guilty without further trial, ' inasmuch as that person must be owned to be ripe for the censures of the Church who, in a whole parish, cannot find so small a number to declare their belief of his

innocence ' (Gibson, *Codex*). This ' oath *ex officio* ' was ' a discipline too wholsom to be digested ' in the seventeenth century, and was abolished, 1661 (13 Car. II. st. 1, c. 12).

3. *Censures.* In the Middle Ages the church courts could inflict whipping, fine, and imprisonment. Clerks guilty of notorious crimes were not allowed to purge themselves, but were kept in the bishop's prison. The obstinate heretic was in the last resort burned. The canon law claimed that the Church had power to inflict this penalty ; and in 1401 the Lollard, William Sawtre, was burned under this power before the passing of the Act (2 Hen. IV. c. 15) which gave it civil sanction. In actual fact no temporal punishment can be inflicted on an unwilling culprit without the consent, active or passive, of the State, in which all temporal and coercive power ultimately resides. The Act of 1401 was repealed in 1534 (25 Hen. VIII. c. 14), but revived in 1554 (1-2 Ph. and M. c. 6), and again repealed, 1559 (1 Eliz. c. 1). The writ *de heretico comburendo* was finally abolished in 1677 (29 Car. II. c. 9), with an express proviso that the Church might still impose ecclesiastical censures.

Spiritual censures, to some of which temporal consequences have been and still are attached, are as follows :—

(i) Penance. Public penance (appearing barefoot in church, or in the streets, carrying a taper or a faggot) was sometimes enforced in the Middle Ages even on persons of high rank. But it and excommunication could, as a rule, be escaped by a money payment, so that, as Chaucer said (*Cant. Tales, Prol.*), a man need have no fear of them unless his soul were in his purse, ' for in hys purs he sholde y-punysshed be, 'Purs is the Ercedekenes [archdeacon's] helle.' This jurisdiction over the laity was chiefly exercised by the archdeacon (*q.v.*). We find warnings against the practice of commutation as early as the eighth century ; the canon law sought to restrict it by providing that money should not be taken for grave sins, or from relapsed offenders, and when taken should be applied to pious uses. In 1413 the House of Commons protested in vain against the practice ; and Convocation tried to regulate it in 1597, in 1640, and in 1710. Penance continued to be inflicted in the nineteenth century. In 1812 Sir William Scott told the House of Commons that in cases of defamation ' persons were not asked to go into church in a white sheet, or anything of that sort ; but merely to retire into the vestry-room, and in the presence of two or three friends of the injured party, to ask pardon and promise to be more guarded in future.' In 1816 a man found guilty of incest was sentenced by the Court of Arches to do penance in church ' whilst the greater part of the congregation might be assembled to see and hear the same ' (*Blackmore* v. *Brider*, 1 Phill. Eccl. 359). Persons refusing to perform penance might be imprisoned for contumacy; instances of this are found as late as 1830 (*Proceedings of Eccl. Courts Commission*, 1832, pp. 568-9). In 1856 Sir R. Phillimore (*q.v.*), as Chancellor of Chichester, claimed but did not exercise the power to inflict penance. It may now be considered obsolete.

(ii) Excommunication, the ultimate spiritual penalty, in its lesser form involved exclusion from Mass and Communion ; the greater was complete deprivation of Christian privileges and fellowship. Both were accompanied by temporal disabilities. Before the Norman Conquest an excommunicate was out of the protection of the civil law. Afterwards he could not sue or perform any legal act, but he could be sued. If he did not submit within forty days the ecclesiastical might signify the fact to the temporal court, which would imprison him under the writ *de excommunicato capiendo*. This procedure was not always followed. William I. forbade that any ecclesiastical penalty should be laid on any of his barons or servants without his leave ; and there were various exemptions. The punishment being used for offences for which it was inappropriate was not regarded. John Keyser, when excommunicated for debt in 1465. ' openly affirmed that the said sentence was not to be feared, neither did he fear it.' For at harvest ' he had as great plenty of wheat and other grain as any of his neighbours, saying to them in scorn . . . that a man excommunicate should not have such plenty of wheat ' (3 Insts. 42). The Millenary Petition, 1603, asked ' that excommunication come not forth under the name of lay-persons, chancellors, officials, etc. That men be not excommunicated for trifles and twelvepenny matters.' And Bacon wrote: ' For this to be used irreverently, and to be made an ordinary process, to lackey up and down for fees, how can it be without derogation to God's honour, and making the power of the keys contemptible ? ' The scandal continued, however, until 1813, when excommunications were abolished except as 'spiritual censures for offences of ecclesiastical cognisance,' when they were not to involve any civil incapacity or penalty save imprisonment for not more than six months (53 Geo. III. c. 127). Its existence as a spiritual censure is shown, *e.g.*, by the rubric which

forbids the Burial Service to be used for excommunicates. The rubric before the Communion Service gives the clergy a limited power of imposing the lesser excommunication, subject to appeal to the ordinary.

The procedure under the writ *de excommunicato capiendo* was reformed in 1563 (5 Eliz. c. 23). In 1605 Bancroft (*q.v.*) complained of the interference of the temporal courts in releasing excommunicates without their making submission. The Act of 1813 (amended in 1832 by 2-3 Will. c. 92) abolished the writ and empowered the church courts to signify any contumacy or contempt to the Court of Chancery, which should issue the writ *de contumace capiendo* for the offender's imprisonment. By 3-4 Vic. c. 93 (1840) the church court, with the consent of the other parties to the suit, may release him without his submission. Several clergy were imprisoned under this procedure, 1877-87. [RITUAL CASES.] It enables the church court to call in the secular arm to punish contumacy without pronouncing sentence of excommunication.

(iii) Monition. A warning not to repeat the offence ; disobedience to it entails the penalties of contempt. But the court is not obliged even to issue a monition if it is satisfied the offence will not be repeated.

(iv) Suspension, for a limited period, either *ab officio*, from performing clerical duties, or *ab officio et beneficio* from the temporal benefits of the offender's preferments as well. Under this head may be included the inhibition from performing divine service or exercising the cure of souls, provided by the Public Worship Regulation Act (*q.v.*).

(v) Sequestration of the profits or income of a benefice. In the Middle Ages the church courts enforced payment of civil debts by this process. In modern times it may be classed with the pecuniary forfeitures imposed under 1-2 Vic. c. 106 for such offences as plurality and non-residence.

(vi) Deprivation of preferment. To this in certain cases incapacity to hold further preferment is added (Clergy Disc. Act, 1892, 55-6 Vic. c. 32). Under Canon 122 sentence of deprivation can only be pronounced by the bishop in person. It has, however, been customary for the Dean of the Arches to pronounce it. Under the Felony Act, 1870, it is incurred *ipso facto* by conviction in the temporal court for felony.

(vii) Degradation, or deposition, from holy orders may be inflicted summarily by pronouncing the sentence, or solemnly by divesting the culprit of the robes and instruments (a book or vessel) pertaining to his order. It was thought to be a condition precedent to the punishment of a clerk by the temporal court. In 1630 the Star Chamber ordered Leighton to be degraded before sentencing him to the pillory, because ' this court for the reverence of that calling doth not use to inflict any corporal or ignominious punishment upon any person so long as they continue in Orders.' In 1686 the King's Bench ordered one Samuel Johnson to be degraded before being pilloried and whipped for a seditious libel. Three bishops took from him a Bible, his cap, gown, and girdle, but not his cassock, which omission was afterwards held to invalidate the degradation (see *State Trials*, xi. 1339). For the degradation of Bishop Middleton in 1590 see BISHOPS.

B. PRIVATE DISCIPLINE through private confession and absolution became common from about the seventh century. At first the power of reconciling penitents was thought to reside only in the bishop, who could delegate it to priests or deacons. Afterwards priests also were recognised as possessing this power except in cases of grave sin. In the Anglo-Saxon Church the penances enjoined in private confession were largely regulated by the ' Penitentials ' ascribed to Theodore (*q.v.*) and others, which laid down the appropriate penalties for various sins. Later, the practice was regulated by the canon law. The Lateran Council, 1215, ordered that every one should go to confession at least once a year, and breaches of this rule were punishable in the church courts. Contributions of money or labour towards works of piety were frequently imposed as penances, which gave rise to the system of indulgences, or remissions of penance in return for such works or for money payments. They were popularly believed also to carry remission from the guilt of sin, and a traffic in them arose. Thomas Gascoigne, in the middle of the fifteenth century, wrote that men would declare they could easily get plenary remission from any sin for fourpence or sixpence or a game at tennis. Private confession was retained in the English Church at the Reformation. Neglect of it was made punishable by fine and imprisonment by the statute 31 Hen. VIII. c. 14 (1539). Canon 113 of 1604 forbids the priest to reveal anything he has heard in confession. During the seventeenth century it was fairly commonly practised, and it was retained by the Nonjurors (*q.v.*). The tradition of the advisability of deathbed confession survived well into the Hanoverian period, and appears as a subject of mockery in the eighteenth-century novelists. In 1793

Henry Best, Fellow of Magdalen, Oxford, in a University sermon advocated the revival of the practice, which actually came about through the Oxford Movement (*q.v.*).

[G. C.]

N. Marshall, *Discipline of the Primitive Ch.*, 1711; Gibson, *Codex*; Hale, *Precedents*; Phillimore, *Eccl. Law*; S. Johnson, *Works* (*Some Memorials*), 1710; H. C. Lea, *Hist. of Auricular Confession*.

DOLLING, Robert William Radclyffe (1851-1902), priest, was educated at Harrow and Trinity College, Cambridge, which he left without a degree owing to ill-health, and became assistant to his father, an Ulster land agent. Living much in London, he became attached to St. Alban's, Holborn, and as ' Brother Bob ' was warden of a branch of St. Martin's League of Postmen. Ordained deacon in 1883, he was almost at once given charge of St. Martin's Mission, Stepney, which he resigned in 1885, soon after his ordination as priest, owing to difficulties with Bishop Temple (*q.v.*) as to his relations with his parish church. In August 1885 he was appointed to the charge of the Winchester College Mission, St. Agatha's, Landport, and flung himself into the work of a garrison and dockyard town, its exuberant evil and possibilities for good, with an energy as exuberant as its own. With the help of his sisters and a band of workers, whom he infected with his own enthusiasm, he organised and extended the work of the Mission. His burly presence, his jovial personality, and gift of good fellowship made him the central and inspiring figure whether in gymnasium, dancing class, or mothers' meeting, and all alike were sanctified by his great-hearted sympathy, his zeal for Christ, and love of souls. He carried the same qualities into his work on the School Board and Board of Guardians, his crusades against brothels and intemperance, his Christian Socialism, and championship of the cause of labour. To him ' every social question was a question of the Lord Jesus Christ.' It was his nature to keep open house, and soldiers and sailors, thieves out of gaol and tramps out of work, members of Parliament, inebriate clergymen whom only he could reclaim, training-ship boys, and Winchester prefects gathered round the common table. He always maintained the close connection of the Mission with Winchester, and the school in return supported him with whole-hearted confidence. His sermons in chapel, his speeches in ' School,' the week-end visits of the senior boys to Landport, and his practice of spending a day a week at Winchester, all contributed to make Dolling and his work a part of the school life.

His religion was a fervent evangelicalism, expressed partly in his methods of extempore prayer and mission services, partly in the gorgeous ceremonial of the Catholic faith. It culminated in the magnificent basilica which was the outward crown of his ten years' work. 'A sturdy beggar,' as he called himself, he had during that time raised nearly £50,000 for the Mission. His 'ritual' involved him in difficulties with successive bishops of Winchester, which reached their height at the time of the dedication of the new St. Agatha's in 1895. Bishop Randall Davidson refused to allow a third altar specially for Eucharists for the departed, and rather than give up the principles which he thought involved, viz. prayers for the dead and non-communicating attendance at Holy Communion, Dolling resigned, leaving Portsmouth in January 1896. Always a striking and powerful preacher, he now devoted himself to raising money by preaching to pay off a debt on St. Agatha's, and visited America, where he preached four hundred sermons in ten months. In 1898 he became Vicar of St. Saviour's, Poplar, where his chief work was done among the children, whom he loved. But his health was now broken by continual overwork, and from his coming to Poplar he was 'a man spent.' The bishops under whom he worked in London—Creighton (*q.v.*) and Winnington-Ingram—gave him generous support, and the bishops of London and of Stepney took part in his funeral service.

[G. C.]

Personal recollections : Dolling, *Ten Years in a Portsmouth Slum*: C. E. Osborne, *Life.*

DRAMA IN THE ENGLISH CHURCH.

The Church has always sought to teach by the use of symbolism and dramatic representation in public worship. Early instances of this are the Palm Sunday procession, the reading of the Gospels in Holy Week by several ministers representing the various actors in the Passion ; above all, in the Eucharist, by the solemn reproduction of the words and actions of our Lord at the Last Supper. From about the ninth century short scenes, called 'tropes,' were introduced into the services on certain days, representing in dialogue and action the events commemorated. In an Easter trope used at Winchester in the tenth century one priest, vested in an alb to represent an angel, sat in the Easter Sepulchre, and was approached by three others in copes, bearing thuribles, and personating the holy women bringing spices. A dialogue, closely following the words of Scripture, led up to a hymn of praise. This originally formed the introit at Mass, but was afterwards transferred to the choir offices. Similar tropes recalled the Adoration of the Shepherds at Christmas, the dialogue between the Apostles and the Angels on Ascension Day, and other events of the Christian Year. They were sacred dramas in an elementary form, and were elaborated as time went on by the introduction of other characters : St. Peter, St. John, and the Risen Lord at Easter ; and at Christmas the Magi and Herod, whose ranting became so popular as to pass into a byword.

Strictly speaking, plays on Scriptural subjects (including the apocryphal gospels, which supplied a very popular episode, the Harrowing of Hell, or deliverance of spirits in prison) were called 'Mysteries,' perhaps from their original place among the ceremonies of the Mass, and those on the lives of post-Scriptural saints 'Miracles.' But in England this word was used for both. Plays on the lives of the saints were only introduced here after the Norman Conquest. A *Ludus de S. Katarina* was performed at Dunstable about 1100. Hilarius, a twelfth-century writer, probably an Englishman, wrote as well as a *Raising of Lazarus* and a *Daniel* a miracle of St. Nicholas which is frankly comic. A heathen finding his goods stolen beats the image of St. Nicholas, in whose charge he had left them. The indignant saint appears in person, compels the robbers to restore their booty, and the owner is converted.

Meanwhile the Scriptural plays were undergoing further development. It was natural to play the Passion and the Resurrection consecutively, and to precede them by the Old Testament stories which foreshadow the events of the Gospel. A twelfth-century Norman play of the Fall and the death of Abel is extant. Cycles were thus formed which, even in the twelfth century, were too long and elaborate to be played in church, and were transferred to the open air. The ecclesiastical drama had · now reached a stage at which it could be further developed only by elaboration of the dramatic and comic elements, which made it unsuitable for liturgical purposes. Consequently, while the tropes retained their place in the services, the interest of the subject is transferred to the great cycles representing the sacred story from the fall of Lucifer to the Last Judgment, which the trade guilds of York, Chester, and other places represented at Corpus Christi with much elaboration of humour, horseplay, and sometimes of pathos. The Church still encouraged these developments of its drama, as means of edification and a counter-attraction to the ribaldry of purely secular entertainments. The Lollards (*q.v.*) opposed them on what would now be called ' puritanical ' grounds. They were at their zenith in the fourteenth and fifteenth centuries, and survived till the close of the sixteenth.

The remaining kind of ecclesiastical drama, the Morality or moral play, dealt allegorically with the struggle between good and evil for the soul of man, the characters being personified qualities. Dialogues such as that between Mercy, Peace, Truth, and Righteousness, founded on Ps. 85 and attributed to Archbishop Langton (*q.v.*), are purely didactic. The dramatic Morality only appears in the fourteenth century ; the earliest extant example, *The Castell of Perseverance*, dating from the first half of the fifteenth, shows *Humanum Genus* attacked by the World, the Flesh, the Devil, and the Seven Deadly Sins, who are resisted by the Virtues. The well-known *Everyman* is another example. In the sixteenth century Moralities were turned to controversial purposes, as when Dissimulation appears as a monk calling himself Devotion. The later history of the Morality is chiefly important for its part in the development of English drama. The various kinds of religious drama were sometimes united with each other or with secular elements in the same play. The fifteenth-century *Mary Magdalene* combines the events of the saint's life, both Scriptural and legendary, with the Morality element of the attack of the powers of evil upon her soul. And *The Historie of Jacob and Esau* (*c.* 1557) adds many of the features of both classical and native comedy to its Scriptural plot.

[G. C.]

A. W. Pollard, *Eng. Miracle Plays*; Chambers, *Mediæval Stage*; *Camb. Hist. Eng. Lit.*, v.

DRESS OF THE CLERGY. The everyday dress of the clergy has been the subject of a long series of enactments, from the sixth century downwards; and notably of Canon 16 of the Fourth Lateran Council in 1215 (which is incorporated in the *Decretals*, III. i. 15), and in England of the *Constitutions* of Otho (1237) and of Ottobon (1268), and the Canons of 1460, 1463, and 1604 ; besides the statutes of Universities and Colleges which regulate academical dress, and whatever rules govern English legal dress, both of which are only varieties of the traditional clerical dress of the West. These enactments tend to be

rather negative than positive, prohibiting gaiety, luxury, expensiveness, and conformity with current secular fashions, and rather assuming than explicitly describing what was to be worn. But certain positive principles emerge ; in particular, the garments are to be long (*talaris*), loose, closed, *i.e.* not open in front, of one colour, and that neither green nor red. The clerical dress derives from the Roman suit of the fourth century, the *tunica* and *pænula,* which through the change of secular fashions and the adoption of a new type of costume by laymen became ecclesiastical, and then split up and developed on two lines, the one that of liturgical dress [VESTMENTS], the other that of the everyday clerical dress. Accordingly in the ninth century we find the clergy ordinarily wearing the *alb* or tunic and the *cappa*, the full chasuble, with (later if not already) side-slits, through which the arms were passed ; and from the ninth to the eleventh century priests were required always to wear stoles. In the fourteenth century, and no doubt a century or two earlier, the complete clerical suit consisted of an under-tunic (*subtunica*, the cassock), an over-tunic (*supertunica*, the gown), and a hood (*caputium*), *i.e.* a cape and a headpiece with a lengthened ' poke ' (*liripipium*, *tippet*). Beneficiaries, dignitaries, and graduates had gown and hood lined with fur, or later, in summer, with silk ; and between the gown and the hood they wore a ' habit,' either a *cappa*, with two side-slits (*chimaera*, chimere) or a single central slit through which to pass the arms ; or a *tabard*, a tunic with short, pointed sleeves : or, especially if they were lawyers, a *mantle* (*armilausa*) fastened on the right shoulder ; and dignitaries and doctors added a *cap*, which, originally, it seems, a loose skull-cap turned up round the edge, took on a different form in some countries, in France and Italy developing into a fez, while in England remaining a skull-cap ; and the higher lawyers wore a coif, a linen cap tied under the chin. Bishops wore a linen *rochet* over the gown and under the *cappa*. In the latter half of the fifteenth century changes began to be made. The over-tunic or gown was divided up the front, and the sleeves were often widened : the hood, instead of being put on, was either thrown loosely over one shoulder, or ' squared,' as it is still called at Cambridge, *i.e.* laid over the shoulders, the liripipe falling over one, the cape over the other ; or, like the secular hood, it was converted into the *chaperon*, with a streaming liripipe, and then the liripipe was detached and became the tippet or scarf ; and the skull-cap developed four corners, no doubt at the outset accidentally and merely because it was made of four pieces ; and this square cap was by the middle of the sixteenth century worn by all ecclesiastics. Besides this, in the first half of the sixteenth century the tabard, and, except for lawyers, the mantle disappeared ; and the cappa fell into disuse except in the universities and by bishops ; and the bishops split both forms of cappa up the front ; whence the open chimere and the 'parliament robe.' English bishops also turned up their fur-lined gown sleeves to form a cuff over their rochet sleeves. Further, the old variety of colour generally disappeared, except for graduates in the universities and on formal occasions, and black took its place. This was taken for granted in England, but was enacted on the Continent in the second half of the sixteenth century. In the middle of the sixteenth century, then, the ordinary clerical dress is that depicted on the title-page of the Great Bible of 1539 and in the great portrait of Cranmer in the National Portrait Gallery. This traditional costume is enforced by the Thirtieth *Injunction* of 1559. But meanwhile it had been abandoned in Geneva, and the lay gown, with its 'false' sleeves, and the round bonnet had been adopted ; and this costume was affected by the returned exiles and the Puritan party, as it was also adopted by the lay faculties, law and medicine, in the universities. One side of the 'vestiarian' difficulty of the reign of Elizabeth was the enforcement of the traditional dress as against the Genevan fashion. One chapter of the *Advertisements* (*q.v.*) of 1566 was devoted to this ; and the final enactment which governs the dress of the clergy is the 74th Canon of 1604, which requires bishops to wear their accustomed apparel, that is, rochet, chimere, tippet, and cap ; dignitaries and graduates, cassock, gown, hood or tippet, and cap ; and all other clerics the same, except the tippet. But there have been further changes of form. Canon 74 requires gowns with sleeves either 'strait' at the wrists or wide. The wide sleeve is that of the ordinary bell shape, gathered at the shoulder ; the 'strait' sleeves were either ordinary close sleeves, in this period a little puffed at the shoulders, or full 'balloon' sleeves gathered in at the shoulders and again at the wrist ; and subsequently both forms were made too long, and then a slit was made at the elbow and the arm put through the slit, leaving the sleeve to fall from the elbow, and from this resulted the modern M.A. sleeve of the universities : or in the latter form the wristband was pushed up the arm and pro-

duced the 'pudding sleeve.' In the second half of the sixteenth century the hood, when it was not displaced by the tippet, was again 'put on' and not thrown over the shoulders ; but it was greatly enlarged, and so fell low down at the back ; and though shortened in front, it so continued throughout the seventeenth century ; but with the advent of wigs in the eighteenth century it was slit down the front and a ribbon inserted, so that it hung wholly on the back. And after the Restoration, the identity of hood and tippet being forgotten, both came to be used together, except by doctors in full dress, and by bishops until S. Wilberforce (*q.v.*), who initiated the fashion of wearing the hood over the black chimere. But the use of the hood for everyday wear seems to have been displaced in practice by that of the tippet since the end of the sixteenth century ; and by the end of the seventeenth century the tippet itself seems to have fallen into disuse, except in church, by all but doctors and chaplains. Meanwhile the square cap developed its squareness : by about 1640 it had become on the continent the modern biretta ; in England it assumed a more flexible and graceful form. But both here and elsewhere it was worn over a skull-cap ; and the 'mortarboard' of the end of the seventeenth century apparently combined the square cap and the skull-cap in one piece. In the reign of Elizabeth the clergy wore the current ruff at the neck and wrists. Consequently a frill appeared below the turned-up linings of the sleeves of bishops ; hence the modern frill beneath the black wristband of the rochet : the red wristband now worn with the red chimere is, unless the prelate be an Oxford D.C.L., a mere folly, perhaps invented by Wilberforce. The neck-ruff gave place to the square collar or band in about 1640, and this was gradually reduced till it became the 'bands' in about 1730. The bishops apparently abandoned the use of rochet and chimere as their ordinary dress after the Great Rebellion, and adopted the ordinary clerical dress which continued in use till late in the eighteenth century, when bishops and the higher dignitaries adopted the short cassock ('apron') under a coat, while the clergy generally adopted the professional dress, common to them with doctors and lawyers, viz. black with a white neckcloth, to which later, in some cases, was added the 'stand-up' collar. About the middle of the nineteenth century the plain ('M.B.') waistcoat came into use, and somewhat later the Roman collar. As to the hair both on head and face (apart from the tonsure, which in England was disused from the sixteenth century), the clergy have followed the lay fashions, while lagging somewhat behind the rest of the world. They grew their hair long after about 1650, and adopted the wig early in the eighteenth century, and in England at least retained it in some cases till after the middle of the nineteenth century. In respect of the hair of the face, in the Middle Ages they were generally clean-shaved, but sometimes wore beard and moustache; and this became general in about 1530 and lasted till about 1620, when the moustache and imperial succeeded and lasted till about 1700, when again they shaved clean, and continued to do so down to the middle of the nineteenth century, after which in England they continued to follow the lay fashion, which now no longer required uniformity, and did as they pleased. [F. E. B.]

DUNS SCOTUS (d. 1308). The materials for a biography of Joannes Duns Scotus are slender. Even the land of his origin is disputed, but, although both Scotland and Northumberland have claimed him, the claim of Ireland, vigorously asserted in the seventeenth century by the Franciscan annalist, Father Luke Wadding, is probably the strongest. The date of his birth is variously given as 1266 and 1274, but it is certain at least that he died at Cologne in October 1308. At some unknown date and place he became a Franciscan, and at an early age went to Oxford, where his reputation as a teacher was to be made, and where also he would naturally fall in with the tradition most hostile to the Dominican influence. From Oxford he passed to Paris, where he carried on his many battles from 1304 until the year of his death. In its main outlines the intellectual career of Duns Scotus resembles that of the other great scholastics. In studying mathematics he was by no means peculiar. His largest work, the *Opus Oxoniense*, took the accustomed form of a commentary on the *Sentences* of Peter Lombard; and most of his labours, collected in the *Opus Parisiense*, deal with the topics already handled at Oxford. There are also commentaries on some of Aristotle's works, a treatise, *De Rerum Principio*, and a *Grammatica Speculativa*, which is thought to be genuine. The antithesis of Scotist and Thomist, and the survival for some centuries of Scotist chairs of philosophy, are the most notorious tributes to his influence. But the title of *doctor subtilis*, once imposed as a mark of honour, has mainly survived as a reproach. The fact is that he was not happy in the moment of his birth. The new

world revealed by the translations of Aristotle had been so thoroughly surveyed by the great Dominicans that, unless he was prepared either to relapse into antiquated paths or to plunge into heresy, little was left for a man of wide learning and restless ingenuity but the business of differing from others. Duns Scotus was in his very essence a controversialist. We need not question his sincerity, nor suppose that his advocacy of the doctrine of the Immaculate Conception was prompted by his opposition to the rival doctors, but we can hardly escape the impression that to agree with his enemies, or even with his friends, was pain and grief to him. Possibly, too, this is the deepest and truest antagonism between Scotus and Aquinas, for if it was an instinct with St. Thomas to arrive by way of criticism at harmony, it was not less an instinct with Scotus to prove that such harmony was unreal. The tendency of some modern students (especially P. P. Minges) is to diminish the differences between the two champions. Often, indeed, it seems as though, after long and laborious argument, Scotus had succeeded only in slightly readjusting the balance among the elements already recognised by Aquinas. For instance, it has been said by many writers that Aquinas is 'intellectualist,' but Scotus 'voluntarist'; yet nothing could be much more erroneous than to suppose that Scotus was in sympathy with 'voluntarism' of the modern kind. He does reject the Aristotelian or Dominican doctrine of the will in its relation to the *ultimus finis*, and on this basis rests his opinions that theology is *practica* rather than *intellectiva*, that *voluntas* is nobler than *intellectus*, and that beatitude consists in *fruitio* rather than in *visio*. Nevertheless, a modern reader is not unlikely to feel that, whereas Aquinas has made ample allowance for the satisfaction of the will, Scotus has denied the supremacy of intellect on grounds pre-eminently intellectualistic. His position is determined not by temperament but by logic, and there is little in him of Bonaventura's inclination towards the 'affective' or mystical life. Another wide field of controversy is opened up by theories relating to matter, to form, and to the manner of their inter-connection. It must suffice to note that by carrying the union of form and matter into regions beyond human observation, Scotus deprives the angelic individual of its Thomist privilege of constituting a distinct species, while in the sphere of more earthly speculations he assaults the argument that would find in matter alone the *principium individuationis.* He might, however, have been wiser to content himself with destructive criticism, for the Scotist doctrine, sometimes known as *haecceitas*, amounts to little more than the assertion that an individual is individual because of the individuality belonging to it. On the whole, the glory of Duns Scotus would seem to be a departed glory. A revival of Thomism is even now, for good or evil, in process, but a revival of Scotism in this or any future age is almost beyond imagination. [W. H. V. R.]

DUNSTAN, St. (924-88), was born at or near Glastonbury in the West Saxon kingdom. His parents were of noble blood, and his mother was connected with the court. He received a good education, and took the clerical tonsure at Glastonbury while still a boy, but was afterwards placed in the household of King Athelstan. His attainments earned him the reputation of a wizard; and being traduced to the King by jealous kinsmen, he was expelled from the court with brutal violence. After a severe illness he turned his thoughts to religion and became a fully professed monk at Glastonbury, though much of his time was spent at Winchester in the household of Bishop Aelfheah, his kinsman. He devoted himself to the arts of calligraphy, illumination, and metal work; he also became a proficient harper, and composed antiphons — among others the well-known *Kyrie rex splendens.* In Eadmund's reign (940-6) he returned to court, and, in spite of new calumnies, was made Abbot of Glastonbury. As abbot he made the monastic school a famous seminary of religion and learning; many of his pupils rose to high positions in the Church. It would seem that Dunstan introduced the Benedictine rule at Glastonbury; in any case, he was influenced by the Benedictine ideal. He showed a tendency to the strictest asceticism; his chamber was 'not so much a room as a tomb,' low and narrow, and lighted only by a lattice in the door. Under King Eadred (946-55) Dunstan became a trusted minister and the custodian of the royal treasures; but he refused the see of Crediton on the plea of unworthiness (perhaps as being under the canonical age), and still lived much at Glastonbury. At the coronation feast of Eadwig (955) he was one of the messengers whom the Witan sent to recall the King from his paramour's company; and Eadwig afterwards revenged himself by confiscating Dunstan's property. Dunstan, fearing still more extreme measures, escaped to Flanders,

where Count Arnulf placed him in charge of the newly restored monastery of St. Peter at Ghent. But in 957 Eadgar, brother of Eadwig, having been elected King by the Mercians and Northumbrians, recalled Dunstan to be his adviser, and gave him the sees of Worcester and London, which he held together. Two years later Eadgar succeeded Eadwig in Wessex, and made Dunstan Archbishop of Canterbury, expelling the archbishop-elect, Brihtric, Bishop of Wells, who was of exemplary character but a partisan of Eadwig. The irregularity of Dunstan's appointment was condoned by the notorious Pope John XIII., to whom Dunstan applied in person for the *pallium.* Apparently this visit to Rome opened an epoch of more regular correspondence with the papacy. John XIII. gave his approbation to the reforming movement in the English Church, with which the names of Dunstan and Eadgar are closely connected. The first object of the reformers was to purify the older religious houses by introducing monks in place of secular canons. They carried out this policy, not without violence, in Wessex, Mercia, and East Anglia, and were cordially supported by the King. Dunstan, though a friend of monasticism, was more cautious. The leaders of the reforming clergy were his friends: St. Aethelwold had been his pupil; St. Oswald received the sees of Worcester and York through his influence. But it is significant that Dunstan left secular canons in possession of his own metropolitan church. Nor did he feel that unqualified respect for Rome which characterised the new monasticism; on one occasion he refused point-blank to pardon an offender against the marriage laws for whom the Pope had interceded. Dunstan acted as Eadgar's chief minister in secular affairs, and was preoccupied with that policy of consolidation and construction which gave his master, by 973, a quasi-Imperial position in Great Britain. Legend makes Dunstan responsible for delaying Eadgar's coronation till 973; and we can hardly doubt that it was his influence which induced the King to obtain in that year the Pope's benediction. We may also attribute to Dunstan's advice the ecclesiastical laws of Eadgar. But these contain few novelties, are moderate in tone, and lend no support to the story that Dunstan persecuted the married clergy. He took, however, a strong line against the ecclesiastical reaction which followed Eadgar's death. During the interregnum, when the throne was in dispute between Eadward the elder, and Aethelred the younger, son of Eadgar, the lay magnates of Mercia and East Anglia took up arms, some to attack and some to defend the monks of the reformed houses. Dunstan and St. Oswald threw the weight of their names into the scale against Aethelred, the candidate of the reactionaries; and they finally procured the election of Eadward. The Church reforms of Eadgar were then triumphantly vindicated in three successive synods. The last of these, held at Calne in Wiltshire (977), was disturbed by an accident which rumour exalted into a miracle. The floor of the council chamber, which was an upper room (*solarium*), gave way; and the assembled prelates except Dunstan, who was standing on a beam, fell violently to the ground. At Calne the controversy ended in favour of the reformers. But shortly afterwards Eadward was assassinated at Corfe (978), and Aethelred succeeded him. Dunstan performed the coronation; but in 980 he assisted in translating the remains of Eadward from Corfe to Shaftesbury Abbey (*q.v.*), where they were buried with the honours due to a martyr. After this date Dunstan seems to have been viewed with disfavour by Aethelred, and disappears from political history. In 986 Aethelred laid waste the bishopric of Rochester, which was under the special patronage of Canterbury, and Dunstan was obliged to buy peace by payment of a heavy sum. Two years later the archbishop died at Canterbury. He was at once revered as a saint, though he only owes his place in the Calendar to a law of King Cnut (*q.v.*), who ordained that 19th May should be kept as Dunstan's Mass Day. His shrine at Canterbury enjoyed high repute as a resort of pilgrims and a sanctuary for malefactors, until it was overshadowed by that of St. Thomas: his intercessions were also highly valued by the Canterbury schoolboys when in danger of a whipping. Dunstan left no writings; the *Concordia Regularis*, a contemporary exposition of the Benedictine rule, has been attributed to him; but it refers to him in the third person, and is probably the work of Abbot Aelfric (*q.v.*). The Bodleian Library boasts of several manuscripts which were formerly in his possession; one of these is a commonplace book, illustrated by his own hand.　[H. W. C. D.]

Stubbs, *Memorials of St. Dunstan*, R.S.; E. W. Robertson, *Hist. Essays*, 1872; Hook, *Lives of the Archbishops of Canterbury*, i.

DURHAM, See of, must be distinguished from the palatinate or bishopric of Durham. Diocese and bishopric were not conterminous. The bishopric was a large franchise containing Durham and parts of Northumberland, with members in Yorkshire. It was founded before the Conquest, organised in the twelfth century, and became a kind of buffer state between England and Scotland, over which the bishop ruled as a king. His secular power was somewhat diminished in 1536, and was finally annexed to the Crown in 1836 (6-7 Will. IV. c. 19). The see of Durham was formed in 995. Before that year the local metropolis of the Church had been at Lindisfarne and Chester-le-Street successively. Simeon, the Durham historian (*c.* 1130), is careful to trace this succession. St. Aidan (*q.v.*) is the founder of the see, which was afterwards moved to Durham. With the help of King Oswald (*q.v.*) he established his see at Lindisfarne, where his successors ruled until the invasions of the Danes. The boundaries of the diocese were not strictly fixed, but probably contracted and expanded according to the fluctuations of the royal power in Northumbria. Roughly it included Northumberland and Durham, but Hexham was taken out of it, and was a separate see from 678 to 821. In 854 the bishopric of Hexham was divided between Lindisfarne and York, Lindisfarne taking the district between Tyne and Aln, and York that between Tyne and Tees. This connection of Hexham with York continued until 1836, when it was added to Durham by Order in Council of 22nd December. The Danish invasions were a grave source of trouble in the ninth century, and in 875 the Lindisfarne monks abandoned the island, carrying with them the body of St. Cuthbert (*q.v.*), the most famous of their bishops and saints. After seven years of wandering they settled at the old Roman town of Chester-le-Street, and this became the headquarters of the Congregation of St. Cuthbert, as the followers of the body of the saint were called. Here for one hundred and twelve years the see was established under a succession of eight bishops, in whose time the patrimony of St. Cuthbert, or the bishopric, was gradually formed. Its confines were probably still ill-defined. With the final outburst of Danish ferocity at the end of the tenth century, the congregation took the saint's body to Ripon for a short time. Returning towards Chester-le-Street in 995, they determined to make Dunholm their residence. Its impregnable position suggested the choice, and from that day to this Dunholm, or Durham, has been the ecclesiastical capital of the see. Here a church was raised to enshrine the saint, and became a widely sought centre of pilgrimage. The Norman Conquest brought great changes.

A castle was built for the Lotharingian Bishop Walcher from which to rule his diocese and to exercise the secular jurisdiction which had begun in Saxon days and was now being consolidated under Norman influence. The successors of Walcher developed this palatine power. William of St. Calais built the new cathedral in 1093, and placed Benedictine monks in possession. The organisation of parishes and rural deaneries was carried out by degrees in the twelfth century. The pastoral supervision of the diocese was inefficiently performed owing to the bishops' absorption in secular duties, and to their frequent absence from the north. Scottish raids greatly interfered with church work, particularly in the fourteenth century, though they recurred at intervals until the end of Elizabeth's reign. The bishops built castles or fortified houses at various points in their little kingdom. Their power was much abridged by the centralising action of Henry VIII. In his reign great changes came to the diocese. In 1540 the monastery surrendered to the Crown, and prior and monks were replaced by a dean and twelve canons. Hugh Whitehead, the last prior, a man of virtuous and religious life, became first dean. The attractions of St. Cuthbert's shrine were destroyed. Under Edward VI. a plan was made to divide the see, establishing a new centre at Newcastle. The accession of Mary (*q.v.*) brought back the old order, and this change was delayed for over three hundred years. The Elizabethan bishops had a heavy task in carrying out the religious alterations of the period. In 1569 the Northern Rebellion well-nigh succeeded in restoring the former system. The diocese was a great centre of recusancy, and never settled down to a whole-hearted acceptance of the Reformation until the days of Bishop Cosin (*q.v.*). The Wesleyan movement had much influence, and in the early nineteenth century, at a time when Bishop Barrington was striving to extend the work of the Church, Primitive Methodism gained a great hold upon the miners. The enormous increase of population introduced a problem of Church extension with which bishop after bishop grappled. Barrington, Van Mildert, and later bishops strove to build new churches, to cut up parishes, to keep pace with the rapid growth of Sunderland, Gateshead, and Stockton. The perplexing industrial questions of the last thirty years have exercised the thoughts and studies of clergy and laity alike. Nowhere have there been such impressive and influential Church leaders as Bishops Lightfoot (*q.v.*) and Westcott (*q.v.*). The division of the diocese in 1881 was

carried through by Bishop Lightfoot. [NEWCASTLE, SEE OF.] The population of the reduced diocese, which was 867,258 in 1881, is now much increased. It was 1,114,590 in 1901.

The see of Durham, shorn of its Yorkshire members in 1841, was restricted to the county of Durham in 1881 (save part of Sockburn, in Yorkshire). The archdeaconries and rural deaneries had been fixed before the *Taxatio* of 1291, in which we first trace the completed mediæval organisation of the diocese. The archdeaconries of Northumberland and Durham corresponded to the two counties. In the latter county there were the deaneries of (1) Durham with 35 parishes; (2) Auckland, including the Aucklands and the prebends of Auckland; (3) Lanchester, including Lanchester and the prebends of Lanchester; (4) Chester-le-Street, with corresponding inclusion; (5) Darlington, including 20 parishes. Some modification was introduced before the *Valor* (*q.v.*) of 1535, but the process cannot be traced. By Order in Council, 27th August 1842, Northumberland was divided into the archdeaconries of Northumberland and Lindisfarne. In 1881 the reduced diocese was divided into two archdeaconries—Durham and Auckland. The rural deaneries were rearranged thus: Durham had the rural deaneries of Jarrow, 23 parishes; Chester-le-Street 20 parishes; Gateshead 15 parishes; Durham 17 parishes; Houghton-le-Spring 15 parishes; Wearmouth 26 parishes; Easington 20 parishes; Lanchester 13 parishes. Auckland had the rural deaneries of Auckland, 23 parishes; Stanhope 16 parishes; Darlington 28 parishes; Stockton 16 parishes; Hartlepool 15 parishes. (For some account of the arrangement see Bishop Lightfoot, *Charge*, 1882.) These 247 parishes have now been increased to 254. Many of them were the result of the redistribution carried out by the nineteenth-century bishops. The income of the see was assessed by the *Taxatio* of 1291 at £2666, 13s. 4d. *Temporalia*, and there were £40 *Spiritualia*: and by the *Valor Ecclesiasticus*, 1534, at £2821, 1s. 5¼d. Ecton (1711) gives the value as £1821, 1s. 3d. It had increased to nearly £50,000 by 1836, when the Ecclesiastical Commissioners reduced it to £8000; and it was further reduced to £7000 on the founding of the see of Newcastle.

The cathedral church, reconstituted in 1541, and dedicated to Christ and the Blessed Virgin Mary, consisted of a dean and twelve prebendaries, with other officers. (See Hutchinson, *Hist. Durh.*, ii. 102.) Mary bestowed the patronage of the prebends upon the bishop. The cathedral is governed by the statutes of Philip and Mary, 1554, as limited by the Act of 1707, dealing with chapters of the new foundation (6 Ann. c. 21). The original and ample list of officers, ninety-six in number, has been modified by subsequent Acts, notably the Cathedrals Act, 1840 (3-4 Vic. c. 113), which suspended six canonries, and the Bishoprics Act, 1878 (41-2 Vic. c. 68), and is now reduced to about fifty persons. One canonry is annexed to the Professorship of Greek and another to that of Divinity and Ecclesiastical History in the University of Durham. The dean and chapter have twenty-nine benefices in their gift, of which five are within the city of Durham. There has been a bishop suffragan of Jarrow since 1906.

BISHOPS OF LINDISFARNE

1. St. Aidan (*q.v.*), 635; cons. by Scoto-Irish bishops; d. 31st August 651.
2. Finan, 651.
3. Colman, 661; retired after the Whitby Council in 664; d. 676.
4. Tuda, 664.
5. Eata, 678; exact date of death unknown.
6. St. Cuthbert (*q.v.*), 685.
7. Eadberct, 687.
8. Eadfrith, 698; d. 721.
9. Aethelwold, 724.
10. Cynewulf, 740; d. 782.
11. Hygbald, 781; d. 802.
12. Ecgbert, 803.   14. Ecgred, 830.
13. Heathored, 821.   15. Eanbert, 845.
16. Eardulf, 854; d. 899. Under him the wanderings of the Congregation of St. Cuthbert took place from 875 until the establishment of the see at Chester-le-Street, 883.

BISHOPS OF CHESTER-LE-STREET

17. Cutheard, 900; added to the patrimony of St. Cuthbert (*V.C.H.*, ii. 6).
18. Tilred, 915.   21. Sexhelm, 947.
19. Wigred, 928.   22. Ealdred, 957.
20. Uhtred, 944.   23. Elfsige, 968.
24. Aldhun, 990; the flight to Ripon took place under his direction, and under him, with the help of the Earl Uhtred of Northumbria, the see was established at Durham in 995. The Congregation of St. Cuthbert settled at Durham (*Sim. Durh.*, i. 78).

BISHOPS OF DURHAM

24. Aldhun, 995; built the White Church, and the first cathedral which superseded it; his daughter m. Earl Uhtred; d. 1018.

25. Eadmund, 1020.
26. Eadred, 1041; bought the bishopric from Harthacnut; perhaps never cons.
27. Aethelric, 1042; res. 1056; d. 1072; unpopular; nominee of Earl Siward.
28. Aethelwin, 1056; brother of previous bishop; submitted to the Conqueror feignedly; cons. at Winchester.
29. Walcher, 1071; a Lotharingian appointed by the Conqueror; occupied Durham Castle, built for him by Earl Waltheof; developed palatinate; murdered, 1080.
30. William of St. Carileph (or St. Calais, in Maine), 1081; built the existing cathedral; substituted Benedictine monks for the Congregation of St. Cuthbert; d. 1096. See vacant, 1096-9 (*Sim. Durh.*, i. 119).
31. Ralph Flambard, 1099; minister of William II.; developed the palatinate and city (*Sim. Durh.*, i. 138); completed the nave of cathedral; d. 1128.
32. Geoffrey Rufus, 1133; attempts made by the Scots to wrest the palatinate; d. 1140. Cumine, a usurper, held Durham, 1141-4, defying the canonically appointed bishop.
33. William de St. Barbara, 1143; d. 1152.
34. Hugh de Puiset (*q.v.*), 1153; d. 1195.
35. Philip of Poitou, 1197; confidential friend of Richard I.; introduced a period of great disputing between bishop and prior; cons. at Rome by Pope Celestine III.; d. 1208. A long vacancy, 1208-17.
36. Richard Marsh, 1217 (P.); appointed after long disputes; Chancellor of King John; convent dispute prolonged; appeal to Rome; d. 1226. A vacancy of more than two years.
37. Richard le Poor, 1229; first elected in 1215, and set aside; tr. from Salisbury; ended the conventual strife by the *Convenit*, 1229; completed the cathedral by adding the Nine Altars; d. 1237; buried at Tarrant, Wilts.
38. Nicolas Farnham, 1241; Prior Melsamby elected, but set aside; Farnham, the King's physician, elected; res. 1248.
39. Walter Kirkham, 1249; controversy with the King as to forfeitures; bishop engaged in disputes with bishopric feudatories; d. 1260.
40. Robert Stichill, 1260; Prior of Finchale; d. in France, 1274; his heart buried at Durham.
41. Robert of Holy Island, 1274; Prior of Finchale; d. 1283.

42. Antony Bek, 1284; the palatine power begins to reach its height; employed by Edward I. in the Scottish negotiations; the period of Scottish invasion begins; Bek made King of Man and Patriarch of Jerusalem, 1306; d. 1310.

43. Richard Kellaw, 1311; a man of learning and high character; the diocese suffers severely from the Scots; d. 1316.

44. Lewis de Beaumont, 1318 (P.); kinsman and nominee of Queen Isabella; the Pope overrode a different election, and promoted Beaumont; a man of extraordinary character and ignorance; d. 1333.

45. Richard of Bury (d'Aungerville), 1333 (P.); superseded the chapter's election of Graystanes; Bury, tutor of Edward III., is famous for his *Philobiblon*; d. 1345.

46. Thomas Hatfield, 1345 (P.); was elected by the chapter, but the Pope annulled the election and provided him; Keeper of the Privy Seal; the most famous of the palatine bishops of the period; his throne is in the cathedral; the battle of Durham, 1346, and the Black Death, 1349, mark his episcopate; d. 1381.

47. John Fordham, 1382 (P.); Canon of York; tr. to Ely, 1388.

48. Walter Skirlaw, 1388; tr. (P.) from Bath and Wells; Canon of York, 1370; Archdeacon of Northampton, 1380; a great builder; d. 1406; cons. (to Lichfield) 14th January 1386 by seven prelates in the presence of the Kings of England and Armenia and many nobles.

49. Thomas Langley, 1406 (P.); Dean of York and Chancellor of England; cardinal, 1411 (the only Durham cardinal save Wolsey); restored the Galilee and built the Northern Gateway and Gaol; founded schools at Durham; d. 1437.

50. Robert Neville, 1437 (P.); son of first Earl of Westmorland; uncle of Edward IV. and Richard III.; built the Exchequer near the castle; d. 1457.

51. Laurence Booth, 1457 (P.); nominee of Queen Margaret; tr. to York, 1476.

52. William Dudley, 1476 (P.); Dean of Windsor; d. 1483.

53. John Sherwood, 1484 (P.); patron of the Renaissance; d. in Rome, 1494.

54. Richard Fox (*q.v.*), 1494 (P.); tr. from Wells.

55. William Senhouse, 1502 (*al.* Sever or Sinews); tr. (P.) from Carlisle; previously Warden of Merton; d. 1505.

56. Christopher Bainbridge, 1507 (P.); Dean of York; tr. to York, 1508.

57. Thomas Ruthall, 1509 (P.); tr. to Winchester, 1528 (*Script.*, iii.).

58. Thomas Wolsey (*q.v.*); tr. (P.) from Bath and Wells, 1523; tr. to Winchester, 1529.

59. Cuthbert Tunstall (*q.v.*), 1530; tr. (P.) from London; built chapel in castle; dep. and d., 1559.

60. James Pilkington, 1561; Master of St. John's, Cambridge; a refugee at Geneva; returned under Elizabeth; d. 1576.

61. Richard Barnes, 1577; tr. from Carlisle; tried to promote conformity; d. 1587. After a vacancy

62. Matthew Hutton, 1589; tr. to York, 1595.

63. Tobias Matthew, 1595; Dean of Durham; tr. to York, 1606.

64. William James, 1606; Dean of Durham; friend of James I.; tried to repress increasing recusancy; d. 1617.

65. Richard Neile, 1617; tr. from Lincoln; led the Arminian changes at Durham; tr. to Winchester, 1627.

66. George Monteigne, 1628; tr. to York, 1628.

67. John Howson, 1628; tr. from Oxford; took a more moderate position than his two predecessors; d. 1632.

68. Thomas Morton, 1632; tr. from Coventry and Lichfield; of great learning and, on the whole, anti-Arminian; received Charles I. at Durham, 1633 and 1639; pensioned off, 1646, and then ejected; acted as tutor; d. 1659.

69. John Cosin (*q.v.*), 1660; d. 1672. After a vacancy

70. Nathaniel Crewe, 1674; Bishop of Oxford; Jacobite in sympathy at first; Baron Crewe on death of his brother in 1691; left various benefactions, and estates under trust; d. 1722.

71. William Talbot, 1722; tr. from Salisbury; patron of Butler (*q.v.*); father of Charles, first Baron Talbot; d. 1730.

72. Edward Chandler, 1730; tr. from Coventry and Lichfield; d. 1750.

73. Joseph Butler (*q.v.*), 1750; d. 1752.

74. Richard Trevor, 1752; tr. from St. David's; d. 1771.

75. John Egerton, 1771; tr. from Coventry and Lichfield; father of seventh Earl of Bridgewater; d. 1787.

76. Thomas Thurlow, 1787; tr. from Lincoln; brother of Lord Chancellor Thurlow; d. 1791.

77. The Hon. Shute Barrington, 1791; tr. from Salisbury; a vigorous diocesan organiser; interested in agriculture; d. 1826.
78. William Van Mildert, 1826; tr. from Llandaff; the last of the palatine bishops; very liberal; in favour of moderate reforms; great patron of the new University; one of the old High Churchmen; d. 1836.
79. Edward Maltby, 1836; tr. from Chichester; formerly Headmaster of Harrow; 'a Greek play bishop'; res. 1856.
80. Charles Thomas Longley, 1856; tr. from Ripon; tr. to York, 1860.
81. The Hon. Henry Montague Villiers,

1860; tr. from Carlisle; d. 1861, after much suffering; a leader of the Evangelical party.
82. Charles Baring, 1861; tr. from Gloucester and Bristol; an Evangelical of much practical piety; res. 1878; d. 1879.
83. Joseph Barber Lightfoot (*q.v.*), 1879; d. 1889.
84. Brooke Foss Westcott (*q.v.*), 1889; d. 1901.
85. Handley Carr Glyn Moule, 1901; formerly Hulsean Professor and Fellow of Trinity College, Cambridge.

[H. G.]

Bede, *H.E.*; Simeon of Durham, *Scriptores Tres.* (Surtees Soc.); *V.C.H.*, vol. ii.; Canon Low Low, *Dio. Hist.*

E

EALDRED, or ALDRED, Archbishop of York (d. 1069), is first mentioned as a monk at Winchester. About 1027 he became Abbot of Tavistock, and in 1046 was nominated to the see of Worcester. A capable administrator and on good terms with the family of Godwin, he was a conspicuous figure in the English episcopate under Eadward the Confessor. In 1050 he represented the King at the Council of Rome, convened by Pope Leo IX.; and in 1054 he was sent on a mission to the Emperor Henry III., whose help he invoked for the purpose of bringing home Eadward Aetheling, son of Eadmund Ironside, from exile in Hungary. Ealdred spent a year at Cologne with Archbishop Hermann; and it may have been on this visit that he became familiar with the rule of Chrodegang of Metz, which he afterwards imposed upon the canons of York, Beverley, and Southwell. In 1058 he made a pilgrimage to Jerusalem through Hungary, following a fashion which was then popular on the Continent, but to which no English bishop had hitherto conformed. In 1060 he was appointed to the see of York, with the King's permission to hold Worcester as before. Next year he went to Rome for his pallium [PALL]; but Nicholas II. refused to grant it until he had resigned Worcester, and persisted in this decision even though Earl Tostig, who had accompanied Ealdred, threatened that the payment of Peter's Pence (*q.v.*) should cease. Papal legates returned with Ealdred to enforce the surrender of Worcester: and Wulfstan (*q.v.*) was appointed to that see on their recommendation. But Ealdred contrived to

retain for some time a large part of the Worcester estates. On the death of the Confessor he adhered to Harold, and it is said that Harold was crowned by him, though Norman writers allege that the ceremony was performed by the schismatic Stigand. After Harold's death Ealdred desired to crown Eadgar Aetheling at London. But finding himself deserted by Earls Eadwine and Morcar, he made peace with the Conqueror, whom he crowned in Westminster Abbey on 25th December 1066. He afterwards crowned Queen Matilda when she came to England. Tradition represents Ealdred as defending with spirit both his own property and the rights of his fellow-countrymen against Norman greed. He is even said to have rebuked William I. face to face. But he died on 11th September 1069, before he had been able to give any signal proofs of the patriotism with which he was credited.   [H. W. C. D.]

Freeman, *Norman Conquest*, vols. ii., iii., iv.

EASTER OFFERINGS were due by canon law to the priest from every parishioner when he received Communion at Easter. Similar offerings were payable at Christmas, Whitsuntide, and the feast of the dedication of the parish church. They might not be less than 2d. a head, but by custom might be more. At Croydon they were 4d. for a man, 3d. for a woman, 5d. for a married couple; at Batley 'every communicant, 2d.; every cow, 2d.; every plough, 2d.; every foal, 1s.; every hive of bees, 1d.; every house, 3½d.' In 1749 the Court of Chancery held they were due 'of common right' (*Carthew v. Edwards*, 1 Ambl. 71). The Tithe Act, 1839 (2-3 Vic. c. 62), provided for their commutation. In recent years the name has been applied to a voluntary offering customarily made to the parish priest at Easter.

[G. C.]

Phillimore, *Eccl. Law*.

EDMUND, St., king and martyr (841-70), was born in 841, and while still a boy was designated for the East Anglian throne. The story runs that the King of East Anglia (to whom a twelfth-century writer, with no support, however, from known records, gives the name of Offa), being about to make a pilgrimage to the Holy Land, paid a visit to his relative, the King of ' Saxony ' (probably Kent), the father of Edmund, and adopted the boy as his own son. The East Anglian King then went his way, but died on his journey homewards (about A.D. 853-4), after nominating Edmund, who is said to have been his nephew, as his successor. The 'Saxon' King reluctantly permitted Edmund to sail for Norfolk, there to be trained for the duties of kingship.

The education of the young prince lasted for a year or more, during which period we seem to trace him at Hunstanton and Attleborough in Norfolk, and perhaps on 5th November 855 at Winchester on the occasion of Aethelwulf's (*q.v.*) much-canvassed grant to the Church. On Christmas Day, 855, he was chosen King, at first probably by the North-folk only ; but exactly a year later he was solemnly crowned in Suffolk at Bures, on the River Stour. Probably the ceremony was hastened through fear of the rival ambitions of Mercia and Wessex, and anxiety caused by Danish irruptions. It does not appear that his sovereignty was disputed, or that the Danes did at that time trouble East Anglia. By the benignity and justice of his rule Edmund won the hearts of his subjects as well as by the purity and gentleness of his disposition, his care of the poor, and his steady repression of wrongdoing.

But in 866 a great host of Danish freebooters, under chiefs called Inguar and Hubba, landed and wintered in Edmund's territories. War did not, however, at once break out ; the strangers made a pact with the natives, procured horses from them, and in the following spring went northwards to York. Returning south in 868, they were besieged at Nottingham, which they had taken, by an English force under Alfred (*q.v.*) of Wessex and Burrhed, King of Mercia. If a

charter ascribed to Burrhed can be trusted, Edmund was present at the siege, but this is not certain. Later the Danes withdrew to York, but in 870 once more appeared in southern districts as a conquering army, the fleet under Inguar, the land forces under Hubba. The former entered the mouth of the ' Alde,' and the Danes sacked Oxford. Edmund marched from ' Haegelisdun ' against the invaders, but was defeated. His whole kingdom did not extend, probably, over more than Norfolk and Suffolk, with the addition of Cambridgeshire, or at least the Isle of Ely, and it was only with a part of his ' fyrd ' that he could encounter the marauders. Edmund was pursued and taken in or near a village called Sutton. His captors had at first offered to spare his life if, as a dependant, he would share his kingdom with Inguar. The terms were refused, though Humbert, Bishop of Elmham, the northern diocese of East Anglia, advised compliance. The King was bound to a tree and beaten ; he was made a target for the arrows or javelins of the Danes; and finally, while still asserting his faith in Christ, was beheaded by Inguar's order (20th November 870). Returning to their boats, the pagans disdainfully flung the head of Edmund into the intervening thicket.

When peace had been in some degree restored the East Anglians recovered the martyr's head, which they found guarded by a wolf, and laid it with the body in a humble grave in Sutton, and built over it a little bede-house, close to the spot where their King had been killed.

The legend usually related places the final catastrophe not at Sutton, which is near Woodbridge, but at Hoxne, on the borders of Suffolk and Norfolk, and some chroniclers speak of a battle near Thetford. Whichever was the scene of Edmund's death and first burial, it was not many years before the fallen hero acquired the repute of sanctity. This certainly occurred during the reign of Ælfred, as is proved by four coins found at Cuerdale, and either in Alfred's lifetime or early in the reign of Edward the Elder the sacred body was removed to a new mausoleum at Bedericesworth, now Bury St. Edmunds (*q.v.*), in which town the martyr was venerated for many ages.

Much of the accretion of legend and marvel which attach to the memory of St. Edmund must be discarded from serious history. The story of the wolf, and of the lifeless head of the saint calling the searchers with the repeated exclamations, ' Here ! Here ! Here !' must be treated as fables. The tale that the tree to which he was bound by the Danes stood in Hoxne Wood till 1848 is both mythical and modern, and a local legend that, under pursuit by his enemies, the King took refuge beneath a bridge, and was detected by his gilt spurs, is too silly almost to notice.

[F. H.]

Corolla Sancti Edmundi, ed. Lord F. Hervey.

EDMUND (St.) RICH (*c.* 1170-1240), Archbishop of Canterbury, was elected archbishop in 1233, in succession to Richard Weathershed, after three elections to the vacancy had been quashed, on various grounds, by the Pope. He was elected at Rome by certain monks of Canterbury who had been ordered by their convent to present the name of John Blund. Gregory IX., having rejected Blund, instructed the envoys to make another choice, that the primatial see might be filled without further delay. The election was approved by Henry III. on 10th October 1233 ; Edmund was consecrated at Canterbury on 2nd April 1234. On the day of consecration he received his pallium [PALL], which had been sent to him from Rome.

The new archbishop was deservedly renowned for piety, asceticism, and theological scholarship. But his previous career had been uneventful, and is only outlined in the vaguest manner by his biographers. He was born at Abingdon. His father died while he was a youth. His mother, a woman of saintly character, gave him a careful training in religion, and sent him to study at Paris. Returning to England not later than the year 1200, he lectured in arts for six years at Oxford. He then studied theology at Paris, and became a famous teacher there. About 1222 he accepted the office of Treasurer to Salisbury Cathedral, and devoted himself earnestly to meditation and good works. Already a preacher of some note, he enhanced his reputation by preaching a crusade (? in 1227) at Oxford, Worcester, Gloucester, and Leominster.

As archbishop he offered a steady, though ineffectual, resistance to royal misrule and papal exactions. A week after his consecration he threatened to excommunicate Henry III. unless the King would amend his government; and in the same year he accused Henry of connivance at the treachery by which Richard Marshal, leader of the baronial opposition, had been done to death. In 1237 he supported an agitation in the Great Council for the dismissal of the foreign councillors who had misled the King. Such behaviour, strange in our eyes, was then not only warranted but demanded by public opinion. By long usage the Archbishop of

Canterbury ranked as the first adviser of the Crown and the special champion of popular liberties. But henceforth Edmund was chiefly occupied in resisting the schemes of King and Pope for the taxation of the clergy and the exploitation of ecclesiastical patronage. In furtherance of these schemes Henry III. invited the Pope to send a papal legate into England, and Cardinal Otho accordingly arrived in 1237. Edmund protested that the invitation was prejudicial to the liberties of his see. He met the legate with due respect, and attended the legatine council of St. Paul's (November 1237), in which Otho promulgated some important constitutions to be permanently observed by the English Church (Wilkins, *Concilia*, i. 649-56). But soon afterwards the archbishop paid a visit to Rome, ostensibly on judicial business, in defiance of a mandate from Otho to remain at home. He failed to secure the recall of Otho. The legate continued to reside in England until 1241, and extorted large sums from the clergy. In 1240 he demanded a fifth of their movables from the prelates ; the demand was at first resisted by Edmund and others ; but the courage of the archbishop failed him, and in the end he paid the sum of eight hundred marks which was required of him. Shortly afterwards the Pope demanded that three hundred benefices should be assigned to Romans of his nomination. Edmund, despairing for the liberties of the English Church, resolved to imitate the flight of his predecessor, Becket (*q.v.*). He went overseas to the monastery of Pontigny, and there devoted himself to religious exercises and self-mortification. His health failed rapidly. He removed to Soisy for a change of air, but sank rapidly, and died, 10th November 1240. His body, which was buried at Pontigny, was credited with miraculous virtues from the very day of his death. It is still preserved in an elaborate shrine behind the high altar, having survived the storms of the Huguenot risings and the French Revolution. In spite of objections raised by Henry III., he was canonised by Pope Innocent IV. in 1247. The honour was not ill-bestowed. Though little of a statesman, Edmund Rich was remarkable for the virtues of his private life. No man of his generation was so widely beloved or so deservedly revered. His name is perpetuated by St. Edmund Hall at Oxford, the chapel of which was dedicated in his honour by Bishop Fell (*q.v.*) in 1682.

[H. W. C. D.]

Matthew Paris ; the lives printed by Surius, by Martène, and Durand in *Thesaurus Anecdotorum*, vol. iii., and by Dom Wallace in *St. Edmund of Canterbury*, 1893.

**EDUCATION, THE CHURCH IN RE-
LATION TO.** In England Education was
from the first the child and creature of the
Church, in whose exclusive care it remained
until the Reformation, and in its almost
exclusive care until the Restoration. From
Bede (*q.v.*) we can infer that education was
introduced into England by St. Augustine
(*q.v.*), and that he founded the first English school as a part of the first English
Church at Canterbury. He tells how Sigebert, King of the East Angles, who had
become a Christian, when he came to the
throne in 631, 'wishing to imitate what
he had seen well ordered in the Gauls,
set up a school in which boys could be
taught grammar, with the help of Bishop
Felix, whom he had got from Kent, and
provided them with masters and ushers after
the Canterbury custom.' This custom could
not have originated with any one but
Augustine.

When in 598 the school at Canterbury was
established, the episcopal control of schools
was a comparatively recent development.
Until the sixth century the schools, both the
grammar and rhetoric schools, were endowed
by and under the control of the emperors
(or their successors, the barbarian kings)
and the municipalities, and were since the
days of Quintilian, in the strict sense,
'public schools.' How new a departure it
was for a bishop to teach school may be
gauged by Gregory the Great's (*q.v.*) letter
to Desiderius, Bishop of Vienne, introducing
Augustine's emissaries Lawrence and Mellitus
(*q.v.*) returning from a mission to Rome.
The Pope actually rated the bishop for
'teaching grammar, . . . since the praise of
Christ cannot be in one mouth with the praise
of Jupiter. Consider yourself what a crime
it is for a bishop to recite what would be
improper in a religious layman.' This
letter shows that though the schools had
come under ecclesiastical, that is episcopal, control, the classics, with their heathen
mythology, still remained the medium of
education, and in spite of Gregory's remonstrance fortunately always continued to be
so. The Psalms indeed, with the Creed,
the Lord's Prayer, and the Ten Commandments, became the staple for teaching
children to read, and prevailed in the song
school, which until the Reformation performed the function of an elementary school.
But when the boys were moved on from
reading to the grammar school, the classical
authors and the Latin grammar formed the
staple of education. The Greek Archbishop
Theodore (*q.v.*), in his twenty years of
strenuous rule and teaching, added Greek,
a fact which undoubtedly contributed largely
to make the English the leaders in the
educational world throughout Europe in the
seventh and eighth centuries. Greek continued to be taught in England, at all events
at Canterbury and Winchester, until the
eleventh century.

In connection with Canterbury Cathedral
under the governance and, certainly with
Archbishops Theodore and Dunstan (*q.v.*),
under the actual teaching of the archbishop, the school established by Augustine
remained until the secular clergy were
replaced by monks in the eleventh century.
Then it was removed outside the cathedral
precincts, which had become monastic, and
established in or by the church of St. Alphege,
where until 1540 it was taught by a secular
schoolmaster appointed by the archbishop,
who invested him with powers resembling
those of the chancellor of a university,
including exclusive jurisdiction over his
scholars in all civil cases in which scholars
were concerned, whether as plaintiff or defendant, and in all criminal cases, except those
of life and limb, with power of enforcing his
judgments by excommunication. A series of
cases in the fourteenth century, fortunately
collected and preserved among the cathedral
muniments, show this power being actively
exercised. In 1540 this school ceased on
the establishment of the present Cathedral
Grammar School, called (since the eighteenth
century only) the King's School, where the
last master of the City Grammar School,
John Twyne, was made the first master of
the Cathedral School. The master and usher
were made integral parts of the cathedral
foundation, with rank and pay immediately
after the canons, while for the first time fifty
King's scholars were provided, on the model
of the scholars of Winchester and Eton,
to receive their education free, also lodging and board in the common hall of the
new college of canons, and clothing and
handsome stipends at the expense of the
common fund.

Such in brief is the history not only of
Canterbury School but of all the other schools
which formed the earliest and chief provision
for education in England and are still among
the chief secondary schools of the country,
the cathedral schools, established by the
bishops in their episcopal sees, the chief
cities of the time. But the schools varied
in development according as the cathedrals,
like Canterbury, were transferred from the
clergy to the monks, or, following the normal
course everywhere but in England, remained

with the secular canons. In this respect Winchester (till 1540, when in view of Winchester College no cathedral grammar school was set up), Rochester, Worcester, and the later Durham, Norwich, Ely, with the Augustinian Canons' church of Carlisle, were alike. In the secular cathedrals, on the other hand, the primeval St. Paul's, York, Chichester, Lichfield, Hereford, and the later Exeter, Lincoln, Salisbury, Wells, the bishops devolved the care of the school on the chapter, and particularly on the resident officer, called the schoolmaster, who in early days was the second, and in later days the third or fourth, person in the church. Only in default of the schoolmaster and the chapter did the bishop himself resume control. Thus at Hereford in 1384 the schoolmaster, then called chancellor, being a papal nominee, a non-resident Italian, having made default in appointing a grammar schoolmaster and paying him, and the chapter having failed to make him do so, the bishop intervened and appointed one himself: an incident unfortunately misinterpreted by careless local historians as the foundation of the school. At the Reformation these schools of the cathedrals of the old foundation went on as before, but those which had not, like Chichester and St. Paul's and Lichfield, already acquired new and special endowments, and did not, like York and Lincoln, subsequently acquire such endowments, disappeared for lack of sustenance, as at Exeter, Salisbury, and Wells—the governing body, the canons, failing to increase the ancient stipends or provide new buildings in accordance with the fall in the value of money and modern educational demands.

THE SONG SCHOOLS.—From the first it would appear that chanting or singing and music were taught by different masters and in separate schools. Bede records that James the deacon, whom Paulinus (*q.v.*) had taken with him to York, 'became master of ecclesiastical singing to many, after the fashion of Rome and Canterbury,' while under Wilfrid (*q.v.*), Aeddi, surnamed Stephen, also went from Canterbury as 'singing master to the Northumbrian churches.' Canterbury, again, provided a master to teach 'church songs,' in the person of Maban, at Hexham, when Acca became bishop there in 709. Yet in the famous account by Alcuin (*q.v.*) of the episcopal school at York under Archbishop Albert (*c.* 735) and Alcuin himself, they as 'masters of the city' taught not only 'the art of the science of grammar' and 'the tongues of orators,' *i.e.* rhetoric, but also 'singing together in Aeonian

chant and playing on the flute of Castaly,' *i.e.* song and music. Alcuin, however, writing after he had become master of Charles the Great's Palace School to his old pupil, Eanbald II., when he had become archbishop, recommends a division of the schools, the teachers of writing and song being differentiated from the grammar schoolmaster. In later times, from the eleventh century onwards, the two schools of grammar and song were distinct and separate in all the great towns—the song schoolmaster (*Magister Scolae cantus* or *musicae*) being under the precentor and appointed by him, while the grammar schoolmaster was appointed by the chancellor and responsible to him. So at Winchester College the school of the master of the choristers, who taught singing and music not only to the choristers but to the scholars, was distinct from that of the grammar schoolmaster, who also taught grammar to the choristers as well as to the scholars. At Eton the song school was perhaps more important, as besides the seventy scholars there were twelve scholars of a lower grade, a kind of servitors or sizars, who were a sort of choral scholars. In both cases the choristers were almost probationary scholars, and were usually promoted to scholarships in due course. In the collegiate churches and in chantry schools it was the rule to find two canons or officers, as in the collegiate church of Hastings about 1080, one to teach the grammar school, the other the song school; or as at Durham in 1414 and Alnwick in 1448, one chantry priest to teach the grammar school and the other the song school in separate buildings. Occasionally in smaller places the teaching of grammar and song was entrusted to one person as at Northallerton in Yorkshire, where in 1377 the Prior of Durham, to whom Northallerton belonged, appointed John Pudsey, clerk, to teach boys grammar and song in the school there; while about the same time at Howden the prior appointed different persons to the song and reading school and the grammar school.

BISHOPS' AND PRIESTS' SCHOOLS BEFORE THE CONQUEST.—The common custom for bishops to keep schools and superintend education was in 826 crystallised into the common law of the Church by a canon of Eugenius II. in Council. 'Complaints have been made to us of some places that in them neither masters nor care for the study of letters are found. Therefore in all seetowns care and diligence are by all means to be had that masters and teachers be established to teach assiduously the study of letters and of the liberal arts.' The so-called 'Canons of King Edgar' of 960 and the 'Ecclesiastical Laws' of 994 purported to extend this law to all priests. 'We enjoin that priests diligently teach youth and educate them in crafts '—technical education—' that churches may have help from them.' 'Priests ought always to have schools of schoolmasters in their houses, and if any of the faithful wish to entrust his children to them for instruction they ought willingly to receive them and teach them kindly.' This last is copied from Theodulf, Bishop of Orleans, so that it probably represents a pious wish rather than actual English practice at the time. Still, there is no doubt that besides the great schools established in the great cities and other large centres of population in connection with the cathedrals and the great collegiate churches, whether those which had been bishops' sees like Hexham and Ripon, Thetford or Crediton, or were almost secondary cathedrals like Beverley and Southwell Minsters, a certain number of parish priests, and in later days parish clerks, also kept schools of a humble kind. Moreover, the wandering scholars, the knights-errant of education, sometimes set up schools for a time in likely places, such as the one who 'by some chance, or rather by the grace of God,' settled at Rotherham in Archbishop Rotherham's youth (c. 1435), and gave him the education which enabled him to be appointed one of the first scholars of Eton in 1443 and admitted to King's College, Cambridge, the same year. The bishops' duties to education were certainly carried out in later Anglo-Saxon days as they had been in earlier. Aelfric's (*q.v.*) Saxon-Latin grammar (c. 1005) tells us how he taught grammar as he had learnt it in the school of Bishop Aethelwold at Winchester, while Dunstan's name is used by him as that of the typical schoolmaster. The account of Cnut (*q.v.*), after his conversion, going round and providing exhibitions at the cost of the privy purse to send clever boys, including even those who were not sons of freemen, to school in any notable city or borough he visited, testifies to the adequacy of school supply. The foundation of the college of Holy Cross, Waltham, by Earl Harold (c. 1060), with, as its second person next to the dean, Master Athelard, imported from Holland, educated at Utrecht, and teaching school at Liége, shows that the English authorities were as well aware as the Normans of the importance of education.

REACTIONARY INFLUENCE OF LANFRANC. —Curiously enough, the advent of the ex-schoolmaster Lanfranc (*q.v.*) as archbishop was adverse rather than favourable to education. His later monastic zeal had made him an enemy to the wider views of the secular philosophers. He resisted the restoration of the monasticised cathedrals of Canterbury and Winchester to the secular clergy. While some Normans founded collegiate churches with grammar schools attached, like Henry, Count of Eu, at Hastings, or gave them a firmer basis by placing them under new collegiate churches, like Ilbert de Lacy at Pontefract, Lanfranc encouraged the prevailing tendency to monasticism. The transfer of the government of schools from the secular clergy to the Cluniac monks, as at Eye and at Reading, or to the new order of Augustinian canons, as at Gloucester, to Llanthony Abbey, and to Darley Abbey, which went on from 1070 to 1180, was a reactionary movement. The schools were not taught by the monks or the regular canons themselves, and when the first burst of enthusiasm in each successive new order was over, they were less qualified than the most idle and worldly of the secular clergy to preside over educational institutions.

THE UNIVERSITY MOVEMENT.—The growth of the Universities, due to the existence of churches of secular canons at Paris and Oxford respectively, and the partial preservation of competition thereby, manifested in the lives of Abelard and others, stayed the dry-rot that threatened education. The University Movement was, in England as in France, almost wholly clerical, and mainly theological. It was a spontaneous movement, not emanating from the governors of the Church, and owed its development to the protection of the Church Universal, as embodied in the distant power of the Pope, which emancipated it from the nearer power of the bishops. It immensely increased the numbers of the clergy and the power of the Church. But in an age in which school teaching was a matter of strict monopoly, enforced by excommunication, the Universities set an example of free trade in education and competition between rival teachers. While the cathedral chancellor's licence to teach was usually restricted to one school, or at least to the privileged churches, in each place, the University Chancellor's licence was given to all who could pass the examination prescribed.

THE CATHEDRAL CHANCELLORS' THEO-LOGICAL SCHOOLS.—The bishops seem to have been alarmed for their cathedral schools, and partly because of this, partly following the fashion for elevating dialectic and philosophy above literary instruction.

these schools were differentiated into the Chancellor's school, which, like the University schools, devoted itself to theology, and the grammar school, which confined itself to literary instruction. The new movement was recognised by the Lateran Councils of 1179 and 1215, which gave an impetus to the separate endowment of schools apart from a share in the general endowment of the churches to which they were attached. The former provided that every cathedral church should provide a benefice for a master to teach the clerks of the Church and other poor scholars gratis; the latter said that not only in every cathedral church, but in every other where means suffice, a fit master should be endowed to teach grammar and other things, and in every metropolitical church also a theology master. At the same time the exaction of fees for granting a licence to teach, which was what a University degree meant, was forbidden. The earliest separate endowments of schools, as apart from the churches to which they belonged, were at St. Paul's in 1127 and at Salisbury in 1137. A large augmentation was given to that of St. Paul's in 1198, and in 1205 we find the schoolmaster no longer called by that name, but by that of chancellor. A similar grant of a separate endowment to the schoolmaster of York about 1180 was followed by a similar change of title, he appearing as Chancellor in 1191. Thenceforward the Chancellor restricted his own teaching to that of the theological school, which became known as the chancellor's school, for attendance at which the parochial clergy received dispensation from residence in their parishes.

THE COLLEGE MOVEMENT.—The ordinary cathedral school, the grammar school, was thenceforward devolved on a deputy appointed and paid by the chancellor, called the grammar schoolmaster (*Magister scholarum grammaticalium*). One bishop, the Bishop of Salisbury, seems to have tried to set up a rival to Oxford and Cambridge at his own cathedral city. A movement for establishing houses and endowments for poor scholars had begun at Paris at the end of the twelfth century with the establishment of beds in hospitals for poor scholars. This was improved on by separate establishments in the Oriental College founded by Pope Innocent in 1248, and the House of the Scholars of the Sorbonne by Robert of that name in 1257. These were promptly imitated in England in the House of the Scholars of St. Nicholas, founded at St. Nicholas Hospital in Salisbury by Bishop Giles Bridport, under the wardenship of one

of the canons of the cathedral, in 1262. Two years later the ex-Chancellor of England, Walter of Merton, Bishop of Rochester, founded at Maldon the House of Scholars for scholars studying at Oxford. In 1269 a second college at Salisbury, called the House of the Valley Scholars, was founded for theologians only by Bishop Walter de la Wyle. Next year Merton moved his house to Oxford, appropriated to it the parish church of St. John, making the Warden and Fellows the chapter of the church. Ten years afterwards the first college at Cambridge was founded by the Bishop of Ely, at first in connection with a hospital, that of St. John (itself two centuries later bodily transformed into St. John's College), but in 1285 moved out to Trumpington Gate, by the church of St. Peter, which was appropriated to it, and collegiated, the college thence deriving its name of Peterhouse. All over the country during the last half of the thirteenth and the first half of the fourteenth century, pious founders, mostly bishops, or kings and queens acting on their advice, founded collegiate churches of the secular clergy, those at Oxford and Cambridge *ad studendum et orandum*, and those elsewhere *ad orandum et studendum*; in the former with University students as Fellows in the place of canons, in the latter with a public grammar school, taught by a canon or a deputy, attached. Stopped for a generation by the Black Death, the movement was resumed on a larger scale by William of Wykeham (*q.v.*) in the foundation of New College, Oxford, in 1379, and the first grammar school founded as an independent ecclesiastical foundation in Winchester College in 1382.

THE EDUCATIONAL MOVEMENT OF THE FIFTEENTH CENTURY.—Meanwhile the spirit of free inquiry and discussion which the unlimited competition of Oxford and Cambridge had produced, reached a development which threatened the very system of ecclesiastical authority in education. How far Wycliffe (*q.v.*), one of the greatest of the schoolmen, would have succeeded in dominating Oxford permanently, as he did for a time, if politics had not intervened, and so effected the Reformation peacefully through educational institutions, it is idle to speculate. As it was, the Lollard schools, if they were anything more than chapels, were denounced by Act of Parliament, and the bishops were converted into heresy-hunters, and newly founded colleges and schools were specifically directed, like Eton, to the extirpation of heresy and the increase of the Catholic faith.

In the fifteenth century efforts were made to break the monopoly of the authorised grammar schools and establish free trade in schools everywhere as at the Universities. It has been suggested in some quarters that this was a Lollard movement and anti-clerical. But the persons concerned and the facts alleged show conclusively that there was no religious motive at work. In 1393 the Mayor's Court in London had tried to stay proceedings taken in the ecclesiastical courts by the masters of the three ancient authorised schools : St. Paul's, St. Martin's-le-Grand, a collegiate church, and St. Mary-le-Bow. The masters had sued not on religious grounds, but against ' certain strangers feigning themselves masters in grammar, not being sufficiently learned in that faculty.' The Archbishop, Bishop, and Chancellor of St. Paul's asked (and no doubt obtained) a writ of Privy Seal to the Lord Mayor to stop his interference with a ' Court Christian.' In 1410 the masters of Gloucester Grammar School sued a rival master in the Common Pleas for damages for setting up an unlicensed school, which had reduced their fees from three shillings or two shillings a quarter to one shilling or less. As the Prior of Llanthony, the licensing authority, joined in the action, it is clear there was no anti-church movement involved. The court held the action would not lie because schools were a spiritual matter, and therefore for the ecclesiastical and not the common law courts. The London monopoly was again attacked in 1447, on the ground that ' where there is great number of learners and few teachers, and all the learners be compelled to go to the same few teachers, the masters wax rich in money and the learners poor in learning.' But as the petition was presented by four London parsons, who asked to be allowed to set up schools in their own parishes, it is clear there was nothing anti-clerical in the movement. The petition was granted ' so it be by the orders of the ordinary or otherwise by the archbishop,' the one being interested in the monopoly of St. Paul's School and the other in that of St. Mary-le-Bow, his Peculiar. A year before, 6th May 1446, two new schools had been allowed in London, one in St. Dunstan's in the East, the other in St. Anthony's Hospital in Threadneedle Street, which for the next century was a successful rival of St. Paul's School. This school was established under royal and episcopal patronage, with statutes made by William Waynflete (*q.v.*), then Provost of Eton, on the lines of Eton. Eton was, in fact, only the greatest of a

large number of free grammar schools and university colleges established during the reign of Henry VI., who much more than Edward VI. deserves to be considered the royal patron-saint of education. Ewelme, Oxfordshire ; Newport, Salop ; Towcester, Northants ; Alnwick, Northumberland ; Sevenoaks, Kent, are some amongst the many grammar schools established under him, all free schools, in the sense of being free from tuition fees, while that of Newland, Gloucestershire, was to be ' half-free, that is to saie, to take of scolars lernynge grammer 8d. the quarter, and of other lernynge lettres and to rede. 4d. the quarter.' A unique college was founded at Cambridge in 1439 called God's House, now merged in Christ's College, the first Secondary Training College, for the training of grammar schoolmasters. A remarkable protest was made by ex-schoolmaster Bishop Waynflete in founding Magdalen College and Magdalen College School at Oxford, against taking boys from grammar and plunging them into dialectic and philosophy before they were of sufficient learning and age. These schools and colleges were the first products of the Renaissance in England. They marked the reaction against excessive scholasticism and the revival of literary study as opposed to that of logic. After a pause during the Wars of the Roses, the foundation of free grammar schools went on with increasing volume till the first year of Edward VI. The successful churchman, especially if a bishop, was expected to found, and did found, a grammar school in his native place if it had not such a school before, or to endow it on a more substantial scale like Archbishop Chichele at Higham Ferrers, or Cardinal Wolsey at Ipswich, and Dean Colet in London, if a school had existed there before.

REVOLT AGAINST CLERICS AS EDUCATORS BEFORE THE REFORMATION.— Incipient revolt against clerical educators may perhaps be seen in the provision at Sevenoaks (1437) that the master was by no means to be in holy orders ; and in John Abbott's giving his school at Farthinghoe in Northants to the government of the Mercers' Company in 1443. It appears more prominently in the municipal by-law passed at Bridgnorth in 1502 that ' no priest shall teach no school after the common (*i.e.* public) schoolmaster cometh to the town ' ; and in Dean Colet's taking St. Paul's School in 1510 out of the hands of the Chancellor of St. Paul's and of himself as dean and his chapter to give it, like Abbott, to the Mercers' Company because he ' found less corruption in a body of married laymen than in any other order or degree of mankind,' while appointing a layman headmaster.

RESTORATION OF CLERICAL INFLUENCE AFTER THE REFORMATION. The Act for the dissolution of colleges and chantries, which vested the endowments of all colleges and chantries in the Crown from Easter 1548, expressly exempted the University colleges, with Winchester and Eton, and made provision for the reconstitution of those grammar schools which had been attached to the dissolved collegiate churches and chantries by a commission. But the commission was never constituted, an interim order only being made for the continuance of the grammar schoolmasters at a salary equal to the net income they had received from the dissolved houses. The song schools, the chief provision for elementary education, were abolished altogether. Some half a dozen grammar schools were reconstituted by Act of Parliament, about a dozen by letters patent, placing them in the hands of newly constituted municipal corporations, which took the place of confiscated gilds, and about two dozen by patents creating new corporate governing bodies *ad hoc*, styled 'Governors of the goods, possessions, and requirements of the Free Grammar School of King Edward the Sixth in the town of Sherborne,' or wherever it might be. It has been represented that these bodies were solely lay bodies, and that, in the charters of Edward VI. and the much more numerous charters of Queen Elizabeth alike, the freedom of the schools was freedom from the Church and from ecclesiastical control. This is an entire mistake. The freedom given was freedom from tuition fees simply. It was almost invariably the case that the rector or vicar of the parish church was made an ex-officio governor, and invariably the case that the statutes to be made should be made with the advice and consent of the bishop of the diocese. Moreover, in Henry VIII.'s Injunctions in 1528, repeated in Queen Elizabeth's Injunctions in 1559, it was provided that 'no man shall take upon him to teach but such as shall be allowed by the ordinary.' This was only a re-enactment of the old system of licensing, but it was accompanied by a proviso that the appointee should not only be found meet for learning and dexterity in teaching and in conduct, but also 'for right understanding of God's religion.' It was to the bishops too that in 1580 was committed the power of examining schoolmasters and displacing recusants. After the clergy had been reformed by the abolition of the obligation of celibacy, the jealousy manifested

of priests' teaching disappeared. While it was a common thing in the fifteenth and the first half of the sixteenth century to find schoolmasters even in cathedral schools like York, or in collegiate schools such as Winchester laymen or clerks who had at all events not advanced as far as holy, *i.e.* subdeacon's, orders, it is almost unknown from 1559 onwards to 1640, and again from 1660 to 1850, to find any but men in holy orders appointed masters of any endowed grammar school. In secondary education, therefore, the Church acquired or retained even more control after than before the Reformation. So, too, in the universities. Though the courts held in 1619 that colleges were lay foundations, they, nevertheless, consisted (with a few exceptions of legal and medical fellows) almost wholly of men in holy orders until the University Commission of 1854. It is only within the present century that the precedent, set by the legal college of All Souls' in 1881, of electing a lay head, has been followed by a substantial number of other colleges at both the old universities.

THE CHURCH AND ELEMENTARY SCHOOLS AFTER THE REFORMATION.—In elementary education the loss of the song schools was largely repaired by making the lower classes in grammar schools elementary, or by adding a quasi-independent writing school, or lower school. In such cases the school was often promoted and in effect ruled by the Church. But after Bates's case in 1670 and Low's case in 1700 had practically decided that only grammar schoolmasters required a licence from the ordinary, the exclusive control of elementary education by the Church ceased. From that time a large number of private adventure schools sprang up.

The Church, however, made a determined and persistent effort to establish a system of elementary education for the lowest classes, the gutter poor who had grown up in the large towns, then almost untouched, by the charity schools initiated by the Society for Promoting Christian Knowledge in 1699. By 1705 35 such schools had been founded in or near London, which by 1718 had grown to 1378 schools, with 28,610 scholars, while there were 241 other schools, the numbers in which had not been ascertained. In these schools reading, writing, and arithmetic for boys, reading, writing, knitting, and sewing for girls, were subordinate to the chief design, education in the rules and principles of the English Church. Clothing as well as instruction was provided, and the schools were a sort of lower-grade Christ's Hospital of 'blue-coat' boys. The boys were apprenticed on leaving, the girls sent into domestic service. Many of them were boarding schools, and became rich in endowments. In 1782 another step in educating the lower orders was made under Church auspices by Robert Raikes in the establishment of Sunday schools, in which instruction in secular as well as religious subjects were given. Attempts had been made before by J. Wesley (*q.v.*) in 1737, Lindsay and Hannah More (*q.v.*) in 1769; but Raikes first organised the movement (which founded them everywhere under the Society for the Support and Encouragement of Sunday Schools in the different counties of England), which became the Sunday School Union in 1803. In 1834 there were a million and a half children in these schools. They prepared the way, as child labour began to be relaxed, for the day schools.

It is questionable whether the organised movement for day schools, rendered economically possible by the monitorial system, in which pupils acted as teachers, was first initiated by Joseph Lancaster, son of a private soldier, a Calvinist become Quaker; or by Dr. Bell, who son of a barber, who became an army chaplain, and head of an orphan asylum at Madras. Lancaster opened his first school in 1796, and the famous Borough Road school in 1798. Dr. Bell published his book, *An Experiment in Education*, in 1797, and his method, known as the Madras system, was adopted in St. Botolph's, Aldgate, in 1798. The monitorial system was not really new. It had prevailed largely in the grammar schools of the Middle Ages and the sixteenth century, and even at Winchester and Eton. But applied upon the new scale, and to the lower orders, it came and spread with all the force and rapidity of a new discovery. The National Society, founded in 1811 in rivalry with the undenominational Royal Lancastrian Institution established in 1808, and merged in the British and Foreign School Society in 1814, soon outdistanced its rival. By 1831 the latter had 490 schools, the National Society over 3000, with an average attendance of 409,000. Parliament began to make grants for building schools in 1832. In 1837 it was stated in Parliament that the National Society had received £70,000 from Parliament, had raised £220,000 by subscriptions, and built over 700 more schools, with accommodation for 130,000 more children. When the Education Act of 1870 was passed, it was ascertained that there were 4165 National Schools, or schools in connection with the Church, which had cost rather

more than a million and a quarter of money in Parliamentary grants, and slightly more than three millions in subscriptions. Of a total of 8919 schools receiving grants in 1870, 6954 were Church schools. They were supported by £418,839 in subscriptions, £502,023 in school pence, or fees paid by the parents, and one and a half millions in Parliamentary grants. The average subscription per child came to 7s. 3½d., as against 9s. 7d. in grants. By 1890 the subscriptions had fallen to 6s. 7½d. a child, as against 17s. 6½d. in grants, with an average attendance of almost two million children. In 1904 the Church schools reached their highest recorded total of 11,874, from which, partly through change of classification, partly by transfer to local education authorities, there was a decline of nearly 1000 to 10,952 in 1911, with an average attendance of one and three-quarter million children. Only in 1900 did the average attendance in Board schools reach the figure of those in Church schools. In 1911 the Council schools numbered 8006 only, but with an average attendance of well over three million children. In training colleges for teachers the Church is still supreme.

[A. F. L.]

A. F. Leach, *Educational Charters and Documents*, *Eng. Schools at the Reformation*, *Early Yorkshire Schools*; *Yorks. Archæol. Soc.* (Record Series); article 'Schools' in *V.C.H. of Beds, Bucks*, etc.; H. Holman, *Eng. National Education*; *Board of Education Reports*.

EIKON BASILIKE. This book, with for second title *The Pourtraiture of his Sacred Majesty in his Solitudes and Sufferings*, was published immediately after the murder of Charles I. (*q.v.*) (January 1649). It is said to have been on sale the next day. It achieved enormous popularity, and very soon went through forty-seven editions. Milton answered it in *Iconoclastes* (1649), and a controversy as to authorship began which was resumed at the Revolution of 1688. The book professes to be the work of Charles, and to contain verses and meditations inspired by the events of his last years. There are added 'Prayers used by His Majesty in the time of His Sufferings. Delivered to Dr. Juxon, Bishop of London, immediately before His Death,' which are no doubt genuine. But it is doubtful how much of the rest of the book was actually written by the King. It is not like his ordinary style, and it is very like the style of Gauden (*q.v.*), who definitely claimed the authorship in a letter to Clarendon, 21st January 1661. Clarendon answered: 'The particular which you often renewed I do confesse was imparted to me under secrecy, and of which I did not take myself to be at liberty to take notice, and truly when it ceases to be a secret I know nobody will be glad of it except Mr. Milton. I have very often wished I had never been trusted with it.' If Gauden wrote it, it was at least a masterpiece of dramatic presentment. He gave a wonderful picture of a character (which may be compared to that of Calderon's *Principe Constante*) of idealised royalty, devoted to his people and to the Church, and holding his power as a trust from God. And ' it is quite possible that he had before him when he wrote actual meditations, prayers, and memoranda of the King, which perished when they had been copied and found their place in the masterly mosaic.' A few extracts will best illustrate the ideal which is represented. Thus in the view taken of church endowment we have : ' No necessity shall ever, I hope, drive me or mine to invade or sell the Priests' lands. . . . I esteem it my greatest Title to be called, and my chiefest glory to be, the Defender of the Church, both in its true Faith and its just Fruitions, equally abhorring Sacriledge and Apostasie. . . . O Lord, ever keep Thy Servant from consenting to perjurious and sacrilegious Rapines, that I may not have the brand and curse to all Posterity of robbing Thee and Thy Church of what Thy Bounty hath given us and Thy Clemency hath accepted from us, wherewith to encourage Learning and Religion. Continue to those that serve Thee and Thy Church all those incouragements which by the will of the pius Donors and the justice of the Laws are due unto them ; and give them grace to deserve and use them aright to Thy glory and the relief of the Poor ; that Thy Priests may be cloathed with righteousness and the Poor may be satisfied with bread ' (*Eikon Basilike*, xiv.). This exactly represents Charles's known views. Again, as to the manner in which he bore his defeats and misfortunes, the writer makes him say: ' God may at length shew my Subjects that I chose rather to suffer for them than with them. Haply I might redeem myself to some shew of liberty, if I would consent to enslave them. I had rather hazard the ruine of one King than to confirm many Tyrants over them ; from whom I pray God deliver them, whatever becomes of me, whose Solitude hath not left me alone ' (*Eikon*, xxiii.). And the position of ' Defender of the Faith ' as held by the English King is very happily expressed, as Charles may well have expressed it, in the words: 'Thou, O Lord, seest how much I have

suffered with and for Thy Church. Make no long tarrying, O my God, to deliver both me and It. As Thou hast set me to be a Defender of the Faith and a Protector of Thy Church, so suffer me not by any violence to be overborn against my conscience. Arise, O God, maintain Thine own cause. Make me, as the good Samaritan, compassionate and helpful to Thy afflicted Church. As my Power is from Thee, so give me grace to use it for Thee ' (*Eikon*, xvii.). It seems probable that Charles I. at least saw the collection in manuscript ; it was sent to him at Carisbrooke—at least that is the assertion of Gauden, his wife, and his assistant curate at Bocking. On the whole the external evidence as to authorship is inconclusive, but the internal is strongly in favour of Gauden. [GAUDEN, JOHN.]   [W. H. H.]

E. Almack, *Bibliography of the King's Book*, 1896 ; Chr. Wordsworth, *Who wrote Eikon Basilike*, 1824 ; C. E. Doble, *Academy*, 1883, pp. 330, 367, 402, 457 ; *Camb. Hist. of Eng. Lit.*, vol. vii. pp. 161-2.

ELIZABETH, Queen (1533-1603). Two questions are treated here : (*A*) the religious views of the Queen ; (*B*) her influence upon the English Church.

(*A*) Her parentage brought her into connection with the ' Divorce ' of Henry VIII. and his repudiation of the Pope. She was thus naturally biassed against the papacy ; both her respect for her father and her experience of the too rapid changes under Edward VI. would incline her against extreme changes in doctrine or ritual ; Mary's reign, and her difficulties during it, seem to have strengthened both these tendencies. On her accession she was at once popular, as she saved the nation from the rule of Spain. But there is not evidence that even the religious change made was popular ; the system set up had to win its way, which in the end it did. But it is clear that from the first a repudiation of the papacy was intended ; here both the Queen and the ministers she had chosen were agreed. Nevertheless, the Queen—whose duplicity in negotiations was notorious—was not above representing her views as either strongly mediæval or strictly Reforming, as suited the moment. And she probably understood the advantage to her of the hopes that each party held of her taking its side more decisively. At the outset of her reign the ceremonies and ritual of her chapel, with its crucifix and lighted candles, set up a standard and were eagerly discussed. Later on (1564) she was disturbed by the laxity of clerical dress. It seems probable that at her coronation the elevation of the host was omitted, but that she communicated. This would fit in with her later acts. She had strong opinions in favour of the celibacy of the clergy, and she certainly disliked the tendency of the Puritans to encourage Parliamentary interference with the Church. It was her fixed view that Church matters should be settled under the Royal Supremacy by the bishops and Convocation; hence Church matters she excluded, along with the delicate matter of her marriage and the succession, from the discussion of Parliament. More than once—as in 1566—difficulty thus arose. It may be said with truth that the Church history of her reign depended upon the personalities and views of the archbishops, but both Parker (*q.v.*) and Grindal (*q.v.*) had differences with the Queen. Parker wished to reduce the ceremonial of her chapel for the sake of example. He remonstrated with her for her action against the marriage of cathedral clergy (1561); she refused her assent to the Canons of 1571, so that the bishops had to enforce them upon their own responsibility, and she suppressed two of the Canons of 1576. With Grindal she had a difference as to the suppression of 'prophesyings'; she disliked their encouragement of Nonconformity, while Grindal liked their evangelical character. The archbishop was sequestered for six months, and afterwards only partly restored to active ministrations, and this state of things lasted up to his death (1583). Under Whitgift (*q.v.*)—partly because of his policy and partly because the aims of the Puritans were more clearly seen—matters went more smoothly. One curious result of the relations between Queen and archbishop is to be found in the Advertisements (*q.v.*) of 1566, which Parker issued on his own authority as an attempt to enforce discipline at the wish of the Queen, although she refused her authority to his suggestions. It was supposed at the time, and since, that she had given them her authorisation.

(*B*) What has been said may make clear the difficulty of deciding exactly how far Elizabeth influenced the Church; her own wishes largely agreed with the policy of Parker and Whitgift as they tried to shape the Church and direct its future. She had a genuine dislike of Puritanism because it worked against Church organisation and opposed traditional order and ritual; on the other hand, she had a firm determination not to admit the papacy into England. Thus the same limiting lines on two different sides were drawn both by her inclination and by

the episcopal policies; the future of the English Church was thus kept within these definite lines. But it is hard to say exactly how much was due to the Queen herself; political expediency impelled her in the same direction as her wishes; she urged the bishops to action, but she disliked to take responsibility. Of her personal convictions it is harder still to speak. Like other sovereigns of the day, she viewed religion as a force in politics; her considerable learning, her experiences in delicate positions before her accession, and as a skilful negotiator after it, made her disinclined to lay stress upon minor matters. In the greater issues her wishes and her proper policy agreed. Her private character has often been judged too harshly. From her father she inherited self-will, and from her mother caprice; her vanity was great, and her conduct towards her many admirers, from Seymour down to old age, was lacking in refinement. But there is no reason to charge her with anything worse. She often injured the revenues of the Church for her own advantage, and her treatment of the episcopal lands was disgraceful. But she, herself very learned in an age of learned women, appreciated learning in the clergy, and her national enthusiasm made her understand the needs of a national Church. This national enthusiasm and pride joined with her wisdom in helping to mould a Church which was thoroughly national, and in the course of her reign became efficient. Her church policy was thus in agreement with her secular policy, and had the same result. In Church as in State she often chose her ministers well, and if she did not always support them as they expected, it was often difficult to discriminate between what was due to them and due to her. But something of the greatness of a great age belongs to her.

[J. P. W.]

A. F. Pollard, *Hist. of Eng.*, 1547-1603; W. H. Frere, *Hist. Eng. Ch.*, 1558-1625; Dixon, *Hist. Ch. of Eng.*, vols. v. and vi.; A. O. Meyer, *England und die Katholische Kirche unter Elizabeth und den Stuarts*, vol. i., Rome, 1911; Gee, *The Elizabethan Clergy*, 1558-64; Birt, *The Elizabethan Religious Settlement*; F. W. Maitland, *C.M.H.*, vol. ii. chap. xvi.

ELIZABETHAN SETTLEMENT, The.

The term is used to express the state of comparative finality in ecclesiastical affairs which was reached in the reign of Elizabeth (*q.v.*). The Settlement in many respects was a real one, though not seen to be so at first. Under Henry (*q.v.*), Edward, and Mary (*q.v.*) the pendulum had swung backwards and forwards, but in Elizabeth's reign it came to rest. The Reformation Settlement is not the work of Henry VIII., for that work was entirely undone by Mary ; nor is it that of Edward VI., and still less of Mary : it is Elizabethan. Again, the Elizabethan Settlement represents the triumph of the idea of a reformed Catholicism which is neither papal nor, in the strict sense of the terms, 'Protestant' or 'Reformed.' The Lutheran Protestant and the Swiss Reformed Calvinist derided, as did the Recusant, the attempt which England made to establish a reformed Catholicism ; but the ecclesiastical history of the reign showed that such an achievement was possible ; and the history of three centuries since has confirmed it.

The Elizabethan Settlement rests upon both a civil and an ecclesiastical basis. The Acts of Elizabeth's first Parliament gave it its civil basis, especially the Act of Supremacy and the Act of Uniformity (*q.v.*). The administrative orders of the Crown contributed also to this. Its ecclesiastical basis was given by the hierarchy in Elizabeth's reign through constitutions, canons, and the like. It may therefore be said to represent, in a more or less documentary form, one part of that complex partnership between Church and State which is called by the vague term of 'Establishment,' though the greater part of the partnership has its roots far behind the sixteenth-century Reformation, and was unaltered by it. In all these respects the Elizabethan Settlement was a real one.

It was, however, a settlement in which no absolute finality was reached ; sometimes with more and sometimes with less of justification, considerable modification has been made as time has gone on. The Elizabethan period was but a stage in a long history. There was no point in the reign at which things were stationary, and change has gone on ever since. Further, there are important points in which the Settlement has been altered, or at any rate has not been observed. Neither Church nor State has shown an entire loyalty to the situation as then defined. For example :—

1. In regard to the Book of Common Prayer : it is only in recent years that the worship, as there prescribed, has begun to be seriously carried out. The Settlement made by the Elizabethan Act of Uniformity introduced a type of service which was to consist of the Rite according to the Second Prayer Book of Edward in the main, but with ornaments and the external appearance of the First Prayer Book of 1549. It was soon found in Elizabeth's reign that it was im-

possible to carry out this arrangement in any complete degree so far as the external appearance of the service was concerned, and it is only since the revival of the eucharistic vestments in the nineteenth century that the law of the Elizabethan Settlement has begun to be observed. [VESTMENTS.]

2. With regard to ecclesiastical discipline and the relation of the church courts to the civil courts : the church courts (*q.v.*) have been continually the victims of the jealousy of the civil courts. In Elizabeth's reign and later they were hampered by vexatious prohibitions, and finally in the nineteenth century they were thrown into complete confusion when the present unconstitutional court of final ecclesiastical appeal was established by Parliament without the concurrence of the Church. The fault of this, however, must largely be laid to the door of the Ecclesiastical Commission, which was part of the Elizabethan Settlement, established in accordance with the Act of Supremacy of Elizabeth. [HIGH COMMISSION, COURT OF.] The present state of ecclesiastical disorder, so far as courts are concerned, is an entire departure from the Elizabethan Settlement.

3. The relation of the Church to Crown and Parliament : here also, through aggression of the State, the bargain of the Elizabethan Settlement has not been faithfully observed. The Elizabethan Settlement postulated the Crown as supreme over two machineries of government, ecclesiastical and civil—that is, over the legislative and judicial functions belonging to each, *i.e.* Convocation (*q.v.*) and Parliament in the legislative sphere, the ecclesiastical courts and the civil courts in the judicial sphere. Elizabeth maintained against the growing Puritan opposition the integrity of Convocation, and insisted that ecclesiastical legislation should be initiated there and not in Parliament. But the Stuart dynasty in its unwise conflicts with Parliament for an untenable royal prerogative involved the Church in its own defeat, with the result that in the eighteenth century Convocation was silenced, and the Settlement was entirely upset. This also has only been partially recovered in the nineteenth century. The present Parliamentary jealousy of Convocation, and all its consequences, are a departure from the Elizabethan Settlement.

The Elizabethan Settlement was thus both an enduring settlement and an unenduring one. It could not be expected that it would always survive, but it is not creditable to the English Constitution that many vital changes that have been made have come about for the most part not through joint action of the Church and Parliament with the Crown, but through civil aggression and a disregard of the essence of the compact between Church and State.   [W. H. F.]

Frere, *Hist. of Eng. Ch., 1558-1625*: R. W. Church, *Pascal and other Sermons*, pp. 52-96.

ELY, See of. The Isle of Ely, then in the diocese of Lincoln (*q.v.*), being extremely easy to defend, and containing the rich abbey of St. Etheldreda (*q.v.*), was not. Henry I. decided, to be left under monastic government, and the diocese of Lincoln being too large for a single bishop, and the interests of religion therefore requiring a division, he and Archbishop Anselm (*q.v.*) desired to found a new see in the abbey. This desire was approved by the Council of London, 1108, was agreed to by Robert, Bishop of Lincoln, sanctioned by Pope Paschal II., and carried out in 1109. The monks became the chapter of the bishop, and were thenceforth governed immediately by a prior. In 1541, on the surrender and dissolution of the monastery, a dean and chapter of eight major canons, etc., was founded, the last prior becoming first dean. By the Cathedrals Act, 1840 (3-4 Vic. c. 113), the canonries were reduced to six, two being annexed to the Ely Professorship of Divinity and to the Regius Professorship of Hebrew at Cambridge respectively, the patronage of the remaining four stalls being left to the bishop.

The diocese originally consisted of the Isle of Ely and the county of Cambridge. By an Order in Council of 12th April 1337 it was enlarged by the transference to it of the counties of Huntingdon and Bedford from the diocese of Lincoln, and of part of the archdeaconry of Sudbury (the western part of Suffolk) from that of Norwich; and by another Order, dated 10th April 1839, certain other parishes from Lincoln were added. It is now divided into four archdeaconries: Ely (first mentioned, 1110), Bedford (first mentioned, c. 1078), Huntingdon (first mentioned, c. 1078), and Sudbury (first mentioned, c. 1126). It consists of 1,357,765 acres, and has a population of 531,000. The revenues of the see were assessed in the *Taxatio* of 1291 at £2000, and in the *Valor Ecclesiasticus* of 1534 at £2134, 18s. 5d. Ecton (1711) gives the value as £2134. 8s. 6½d. The present income is £5500.

BISHOPS

1. Hervey, 1109; a Breton: tr. from Bangor; had been unable to persuade the Welsh either by spiritual or carnal weapons to receive him, and in 1107, on the death of Richard, abbot of Ely, was made administrator of the abbey; he divided the estates of the abbey between the monks and the see, securing, the monks complained, the larger share for the see; d. 30th August 1131.

2. Nigel, 1133; nephew of Roger (*q.v.*), Bishop of Salisbury; was Treasurer; when Stephen arrested his uncle and brother in 1139 he escaped, and held Ely against the King; in 1143 he went to Rome, being accused of wasting the property of the see on knights, but was acquitted; after his return the civil war brought him further trouble; he was much employed by Henry II., and bought the Treasurership for his son, Richard Fitz-Neal, Bishop of London; an excellent official, he was bishop only in name; d. 30th May 1169.

3. Geoffrey Ridel, 1174; as Archdeacon of Canterbury a prominent opponent of Becket (*q.v.*); he was constantly employed in secular matters, and was proud and violent; he was liberal to his cathedral, almost completing the new building to the west and building the lower part of the western tower; d. 21st August 1189.

4. William Longchamp (*q.v.*), 1189; d. 21st January 1197.

5. Eustace, 1198; on his nomination to the bishopric he was made Chancellor, but held that office less than two years; after pronouncing the interdict in 1208 fled from England, but was restored in 1213; he was much employed both in civil and ecclesiastical business; he built the western part, probably the Galilee, of the cathedral; d. 3rd February 1215. There was a disputed election between Geoffrey de Burgh, Archdeacon of Norwich, and one Robert of York, who held the spiritualities for nearly five years without consecration, but Honorius III. quashed both the elections in 1219, and appointed

6. John of Fountains, 1220 (P.); Abbot of Fountains and Treasurer; a pious man; d. 6th May 1225.

7. Geoffrey de Burgh, 1225; again elected; was brother of Hubert de Burgh, the Chief Justiciar; d. 17th December 1228.

8. Hugh of Northwold, 1229; Abbot of St. Edmund's; devout and magnificent, is described as 'the flower of Black monks'; he built the presbytery of

his church, the episcopal palace, and a fine tower, and dedicated the cathedral in September 1252 ; he opposed the King's encroachments on the liberties of the Church ; d. 6th August 1254.

9. William of Kilkenny, 1255 ; Keeper of the Great Seal ; of high character ; d. in Spain on an embassy, 22nd September 1256.

10. Hugh Belsham, 1257 ; had been sub-prior ; the King refused his election, but Hugh obtained his confirmation from Alexander IV., who consecrated him at Viterbo : he founded Peter-house, the earliest of Cambridge colleges, after the model of Merton College, Oxford ; d. 15th June 1286.

11. John Kirkby, 1286 ; had held office in the King's Chancery, and in 1283 was elected Bishop of Rochester, but Arch-bishop Peckham (*q.v.*) refused the election on the ground of plurality ; he was appointed Treasurer in 1284 : on his election to Ely, Peckham did not re-new his opposition : he gave himself wholly to secular business ; d. 26th March 1290.

12. William de Luda, or Louth, 1290 ; learned and magnificent ; d. 25th March 1298.

13. Ralph Walpole, 1299 ; tr. (P.) from Nor-wich ; had made himself unpopular as Archdeacon of Ely, for all the diocese of Norwich ' abused the convent ' for electing him ; on Bishop Kirkby's death there was a double election ; Boniface VIII. quashed both and trans-lated Walpole to Ely in 1299 ; he revised the statutes of the convent, and was probably set on monastic reform, which may perhaps account for the notice of his unpopularity in Norwich by the monk Cotton ; d. 20th March 1302.

14. Robert of Orford, 1302 (P.) ; was Prior of Ely ; Archbishop Winchelsey re-fused to confirm his election on the ground of his illiteracy, but he obtained confirmation from Boniface VIII., and returned home after spending, it is said, £15,000 ; d. 21st January 1310.

15. John Keeton, 1310 ; also a monk of Ely ; in 1314 Edward II. visited Ely and decided against the claim of the con-vent to have the body of St. Alban ; d. 14th May 1316.

16. John Hotham, 1316 ; was Chancellor of the Exchequer ; Treasurer, 1317 ; and Chancellor, 1318-20 ; he was present at the battle of Myton, 1319, and in 1320 was arrested and fined, probably for

some civil cause ; he joined Queen Isabella in 1326, and in 1327-8 was again Chancellor ; after being paralysed for two years, d. 15th January 1337. In his time the convent built the octagon of the cathedral with its dome and lantern, and he rebuilt three bays of the presbytery.

17. Simon Montacute, 1337 ; Archdeacon of Canterbury ; tr. (P.) from Worcester by Benedict XII., who quashed the monks' election of their prior ; was a younger brother of William, Earl of Salisbury, and in 1318 had been recommended to the Pope by Edward II. on the plea of his poverty ; at Ely he was a liberal benefactor to his cathedral ; d. 20th June 1345.

18. Thomas de Lisle, 1345 (P.) ; Clement VI. having quashed the monks' election of their prior, Alan Walsingham, a famous architect and goldsmith ; Thomas had been a Dominican prior ; he was en-gaged in a quarrel with Lady Wake, daughter of Henry, Earl of Lancaster, some of whose estates adjoined his manors ; was fined for abetting in-cendiarism, and was found guilty by a jury of harbouring a murderer ; his temporalities were seized and he fled to Avignon ; there he d. 23rd June 1361.

19. Simon Langham, 1362 (P.) ; tr. to Canter-bury, 1366.

20. John Barnet, 1366 ; tr. (P.) from Bath ; d. 7th June 1373.

21. Thomas Arundel, 1374 (P.) ; tr. to York, 1388.

22. John Fordham, 1388 ; tr. (P.) from Durham ; a favourite of Richard II., who made him Treasurer in 1386, but Parliament insisted on his dismissal ; the lords ordered his banishment from court, 1388, and his translation from Durham to Ely by Urban VI. was pro-cured by them as a punishment ; d. 19th November 1425.

23. Philip Morgan, 1426 ; tr. (P.) from Worcester by Martin V. ; a Welshman and an eminent lawyer ; had been fre-quently employed in diplomacy by Henry V. ; was Privy Councillor in 1419 and one of the Council of Government during the minority of Henry VI. ; he was elected to York, 1423, but the Pope set aside the election and granted him Ely ; he insisted on his visitatorial authority over the University of Cam-bridge, and the University obtained a Bull declaring it free from episcopal jurisdiction ; he was a vigorous re-

former of clerical abuses in his diocese ; d. 25th October 1435.

24. Louis of Luxemburg, 1438 (P.) ; Bishop of Térouanne, 1415 ; Archbishop of Rouen. 1436 ; held Ely *in commendam* : was the brother of the Count of St. Pol ; as Archbishop of Rouen had upheld the English interest in France. and was uncle of Jacquetta. second wife of the Duke of Bedford ; on the death of Bishop Philip the monks elected Thomas Bourchier, Bishop of Worcester, but the King refused the election. and at his request Eugenius IV. granted Louis the administration of the see ; he was appointed cardinal priest in 1439 and cardinal bishop in 1442 ; he was seldom in his English diocese, but d. there 18th September 1443.

25. Thomas Bourchier, 1443 ; tr. (P.) from Worcester ; tr. to Canterbury. 1454.

26. William Grey. 1454 (P.) ; of the family of Grey of Codnor ; had held rich preferments ; had studied at Oxford and Ferrara, where he was a patron of learned men and became a prominent humanist ; Nicholas V. appointed him Apostolic Notary and Referendary and nominated him to the see of Ely ; he was Treasurer, 1469-70 ; he was hospitable and magnificent ; to his college, Balliol, he was a liberal benefactor, among his gifts to it being his valuable collection of manuscripts ; and he also gave largely towards the restoration and adornment of this cathedral ; d. 14th August 1478.

27. John Morton (*q.v.*), 1479 ; tr. (P.) to Canterbury, 1486.

28. John Alcock, 1486 ; tr. (P.) from Worcester ; was Master of the Rolls. 1462, and was employed in diplomacy ; in 1474 he was joint Chancellor, and as President of the Council of the Prince of Wales from 1473 had much to do with the principality ; he was again Chancellor, 1485 ; learned and pious, he desired the reformation of ecclesiastical abuses ; he founded Jesus College, Cambridge. endowed Peterhouse, restored Great St. Mary's Church, and carried out fine works at Ely and elsewhere ; d. 1st October 1500.

29. Richard Redman, 1501 (P.) ; tr. from Exeter ; Abbot of Shap, Westmorland ; rebuilt the cathedral of St. Asaph ; in 1487 was suspected of complicity in Lambert Simnel's rebellion, but evidently cleared himself ; he was profusely charitable ; d. 24th August 1505.

30. James Stanley. 1506 (P.) ; a younger son of Thomas, Earl of Derby ; had studied at Oxford and at Paris ; he held rich preferments ; he took part with his stepmother, Margaret Beaufort, in her foundation of St. John's and Christ's Colleges, Cambridge ; he had a family by a mistress who dwelt in one of his episcopal residences ; d. 22nd March 1515.

31. Nicholas West. 1515 (P.) ; said to have been the son of a baker at Putney ; was educated at Eton and King's College, Cambridge ; he was much employed in diplomacy both before and after his consecration ; he reformed the convent of Ely. which had fallen into grievous disorder ; he was chaplain to Queen Katherine of Aragon, and was a Churchman of the old school, but was interested in literature ; magnificent in his daily life, he was also extremely liberal, built exquisite chapels at Ely and Putney. and was a benefactor to King's College ; d. 28th April 1533.

32. Thomas Goodrich (*q.v.*), 1534 ; d. 10th May 1554.

33. Thomas Thirlby, 1554 ; tr. from Norwich ; cons. 1540 to Westminster ; the only bishop of that see ; owed much to Cranmer's favour ; he was employed by Henry VIII., and 1542-8 and 1553-4 was ambassador to the Emperor ; at Norwich he complied with the law, but secretly disliked changes ; he was favoured by Queen Mary, and took part, weeping, in the degradation of Cranmer ; only three persons seem to have suffered death for heresy in his diocese, and in two of these cases he was not concerned ; in 1559 he was deprived for refusing the oath of supremacy. was imprisoned, 1560, and d. 26th April 1570. He was generally absent from his diocese.

34. Richard Cox, 1559 ; a prominent reformer ; first Dean of Christ Church, Oxford. 1547 ; Dean of Westminster, 1549 ; held both deaneries and other preferments together ; was Chancellor of Oxford, 1547-52, and from his destruction of books at Oxford was nicknamed 'cancellor' ; after a short imprisonment on Mary's accession he fled to Frankfort. where he defended the English liturgy from the attacks of other refugees ; as bishop he desired to see the clergy more powerful in secular jurisdiction ; his resistance to the cupidity of Elizabeth and her

courtiers earned him the reputation of parsimony, and he was warned that it would not be well for the Queen to learn ' how great a grazier, how marvellous a dairyman, how rich a farmer ' he was; his see was so terribly despoiled that he resigned in vexation, 1580; d. 1581. A vacancy of eighteen years, during which the revenues were taken by the Crown, and the diocese administered by commissioners appointed by the archbishop.

35. Martin Heton, 1599; accepted the see with the condition of assenting to further serious spoliation; learned, and a good preacher; d. 14th July 1609.

36. Launcelot Andrewes (*q.v.*), 1609; tr. from Chichester; tr. to Winchester, 1619.

37. Nicholas Felton, 1619; tr. from Bristol; a close friend of Andrewes; held the Mastership of Pembroke College, Cambridge, along with the see of Bristol; was one of the translators of the Bible, and a man of piety, learning, and sound judgment: d. 6th October 1626.

38. John Buckeridge, 1628: tr. from Rochester; President of St. John's College, Oxford, 1605-11, and Laud's (*q.v.*) tutor and friend; was a sound and learned churchman, an eminent defender of episcopacy and Royal Supremacy against the Presbyterians, and a man of exemplary piety; d. 23rd May 1631.

39. Francis White, 1631: tr. from Norwich; was an able disputant, who as Dean of Carlisle distinguished himself in a controversy with ' Fisher the Jesuit '; d. February 1638.

40. Matthew Wren (*q.v.*), 1638; tr. from Norwich: d. 1667.

41. Benjamin Laney, 1667; tr. from Lincoln; was Master of Pembroke Hall, 1630-44, and was chaplain to Charles I.; was deprived, 1644, and followed Charles II. in exile; on the Restoration he regained his mastership, and received a canonry at Westminster and the see of Peterborough; he was munificent, a High Churchman, but lenient with Nonconformists; d. 24th January 1675.

42. Peter Gunning, 1675; tr. from Chichester; suffered deprivation and a short imprisonment at the outbreak of the Civil War; later conducted Church services at Exeter House, Strand, which were winked at; on the Restoration was made Master of Clare Hall and a Divinity Professor at Cambridge, and in 1661 Master of St.

John's College and Regius Professor: he disputed with Baxter at the Savoy Conference; was learned and pious, a good preacher, an active bishop, a ' hammer of schismatics,' and a liberal giver; d. 6th July 1684.

43. Francis Turner, 1684; tr. from Rochester; was Master of St. John's College, Cambridge, 1670; Dean of Windsor, 1683; was one of ' the Seven Bishops ' (*q.v.*); as a Nonjuror (*q.v.*) he was deprived, 1690, and he was arrested as a Jacobite, 1696; d. 2nd November 1700.

44. Simon Patrick (*q.v.*), 1691; tr. from Chichester: d. 1707.

45. John Moore, 1707; tr. from Norwich: the son of an ironmonger; a popular London preacher; was a Low Churchman and a Whig; he collected a famous library, which after his death was bought by George I. and presented to the University of Cambridge; d. 31st July 1714.

46. William Fleetwood, 1714; tr. from St. Asaph; a good Churchman, though a Whig; published a preface to four sermons in 1712, in which he attacked the doctrine of non-resistance; the House of Commons ordered it to be burned by the hangman; it was republished as No. 384 of the *Spectator*: he was tolerant, and was much liked by his clergy, though the majority of them were Tories; d. 4th August 1723.

47. Thomas Green, 1723; tr. from Norwich; was Master of Corpus Christi College, Cambridge, 1698-1716; he pronounced sentence of deprivation on Dr. Bentley, Master of Trinity, in 1734; he was a ' finical ' man, with no special claim to be remembered as bishop: d. 18th May 1738.

48. Robert Butts, 1738; tr. from Norwich; a rough, hasty man; said to have been addicted to swearing; resided little in either diocese, and was much disliked: he was a good preacher; d. 26th January 1748.

49. Sir Robert Gooch, Bart., 1748; tr. from Norwich; was Master of Caius College, Cambridge, from 1716 to his death; was dignified, liberal, and thrice married; his translation to Ely was the result of pressing solicitation by himself and his brother-in-law, the Bishop of Salisbury (Sherlock), to the Duke of Newcastle; d. 14th February 1754.

50. Matthias Mawson, 1754; tr. from Chichester: the son of a wealthy brewer: was Master of Corpus Christi College,

Cambridge, 1724-44, and refused the see of Gloucester, 1734; he was an awkward, retiring man, very rich and very liberal ; d. 23rd November 1770.

51. Edmund Keene, 1771 ; tr. from Chester ; was Master of Peterhouse, 1748-54 ; he declined the Irish primacy, 1764. ' disliking so public a situation '; Horace Walpole accuses him of base conduct on more than one occasion; as bishop he was inactive, good-humoured, and liberal ; he rebuilt the palace at Chester, and to a large extent that of Ely, and built Ely House, Dover Street ; d. 6th July 1781.

52. James Yorke, 1781 ; tr. from Gloucester ; fifth son of the first Earl Hardwick ; was Dean of Lincoln ; offered Paley the headship of Jesus College, and Paley dedicated his *Evidences* to him ; he advocated a revision of the Articles ; d. 26th August 1808.

53. Thomas Dampier, 1808 ; tr. from Rochester ; famous as a book collector ; d. 13th May 1812.

54. Bowyer Edward Sparke, 1812 ; tr. from Chester ; owed his elevation to his having been tutor to the Duke of Rutland ; was Dean of Bristol, 1803 ; he is said to have received as bishop revenues which in the aggregate amounted to nearly £200,000 (*Times*, 7th April 1836) ; and he provided for his two sons and a son-in-law out of the most valuable preferments in his gift, the three being said to have derived incomes from ecclesiastical sources amounting to £12,200 a year between them (*Black Book*, pp. 24-6); d. April 1836, aged seventy-six.

55. Joseph Allen, 1836 ; tr. from Bristol when that see was united to Gloucester ; was tutor to Earl Spencer; Vicar of Battersea, 1808 ; Rector of St. Bride's, Fleet Street, 1829 ; as bishop he was diligent, was interested in attempts to promote religion and morality, and specially in the religious education of the poor, and was a man of independent character ; d. 20th March 1845.

56. Thomas Turton, 1845 ; was Senior Wrangler, 1805 ; a Professor of Mathematics at Cambridge, 1822 ; Regius Professor of Divinity, 1827 ; Dean of Peterborough, 1830 ; and Dean of Westminster, 1842 ; he published several controversial pamphlets and composed some good church music. For some years before his death he was incapacitated by sickness ; d. 7th January 1864.

57. Edward Harold Browne, 1864 ; tr. to Winchester, 1873.

58. James Russell Woodford, 1873 ; an impressive though not eloquent preacher ; was appointed Vicar of Leeds, 1868 ; as bishop he was diligent and respected ; he established a diocesan fund for increasing church accommodation and the augmentation of poor livings ; was zealous as a restorer of churches, and founded the Ely Theological College ; he was a High Churchman, but in sympathy with other forms of thought, and was a man of great personal holiness ; d. 24th October 1885.

59. Lord Alwyne Frederick Compton, 1886 ; a younger son of the second Marquis of Northampton ; was Dean of Worcester, 1879, and Prolocutor of the Lower House of Convocation, Canterbury ; he was conscientious, courtly, and kind ; a High Churchman who, though he endeavoured to propagate his opinions, showed no unfair bias ; he resigned the see at the age of eighty, 1905 ; d. 1906.

60. Frederick Henry Chase, 1905 ; formerly President of Queens' College, Cambridge.
[w. h.]

ERASTIANISM. The principles expounded by Erastus, on the predominance of the civil power in ecclesiastical concerns, have won this name in England owing to the controversies in the Westminster Assembly. They are not known by this name on the Continent. Byzantinism or Cæsaro-Papism would be a more accurate term.

Thomas Lüber (or Erastus) was born at Baden in 1524 ; matriculated at University of Basel in 1542. He became a scientific physician of distinction, and in 1557 was made Professor of Therapeutics at Heidelberg by the Elector Palatine, Otto Henry. In 1559 Otto Henry died, and the new elector proscribed both Catholicism and Lutheranism. The latter had been previously the dominant faith. There now ensued a violent controversy on the subject of the ' Holy Discipline.' An attempt was made by the extremer Calvinists to introduce this brightest jewel of the Puritan crown, and establish ruling elders and the whole paraphernalia made so famous in Geneva and afterwards in France and Scotland. Erastus was the leader of the party who were opposed to this. In 1568 an English refugee, George Wither, offered some theses on the discipline of excommunication, insisting that it existed *jure divino* entirely apart from the civil magistrate. Erastus developed his opposition in his *Explicatio Gravissimae Quaestionis*, which includes his seventy-five theses, and also in the Confirmatio or reply to Beza, who had, not unnaturally, entered the lists on the other side. In spite of this protest the discipline was introduced, and Erastus was himself excommunicated in 1574. Under a new elector a Lutheran revolution followed, and Erastus left Heidelberg for Basel, where he lectured on ethics, and died in 1583.

In Erastus's lifetime neither his work nor that of Beza was published. What made it famous was the similar controversy in England. In 1589 the *Explicatio* was published nominally at Pesclavium, really at London, and the real editor was the husband of Erastus's widow. There is evidence that Wolf, the publisher, was rewarded by the Council. There seems little doubt that the publication was an attempt by Whitgift (*q.v.*) to produce an effective reply to the claim of the Presbyterian leaders in England, Cartwright (*q.v.*) and Travers (*q.v.*), to introduce the holy discipline. From this time forth Erastianism became the name for that view, which asserted the entire possession of coercive authority by the civil power in the Church, and denies any to the clergy or to the Church as organised separately from the State. The name of Erastus was involved in the Arminian controversy, and Grotius was the most famous name on that side in his treatise *De Imperio Summarum Potestatum Apud Sacra* (1614).

What finally naturalised the term in England was the controversy in the Westminster Assembly. The attempts of the Presbyterian divines to introduce excommunication and to make it entirely independent of the civil power were opposed by Selden and others, and were never entirely successful. The theses of Erastus were translated into English, and appeared in 1659 under the title, *The Nullity of Church Censures*. The controversies which led to the disruption in Scotland in 1844 led Dr. Lee to republish the old translation with an elaborate preface of his own, vindicating Erastus from the charge of Erastianism as commonly understood.

Erastianism in the sense of the teaching of Erastus must be distinguished from its later forms. In Erastus's view, and the same should be said of nearly all the Erastian divines of the sixteenth and seventeenth centuries, there was no claim to set a purely secular power above the Church. What they claimed was an entire recognition of the coercive jurisdiction of the civil authority in a state which tolerated *but one religion and that the true one*. What they refuse to allow is any competing jurisdiction. Its later developments are due partly to Selden and Hobbes, partly to the growth of toleration. Selden asks: 'Whether is the Church or the Scripture the judge of religion?' and replies: 'In truth neither, but the State.' This is precisely the view of Hobbes, and would make all religious truth the sport of political expediency. But it is not the view of Erastus; what he claims is that in a Christian state the magistrate is the proper person to punish all offences, and since excommunication is of the nature of punishment, it ought not to be imposed without his sanction. With the development of toleration Parliament has come to consist of men of all religions and of none. Modern Erastianism claims the right of a body so composed to adjudicate on matters of belief either in person or by deputy, and would allow ecclesiastical causes to be decided by civil judges, who might every one of them be agnostics.

At the same time Erastus, like Luther or Hooker (*q.v.*), in his endeavour to maintain the rights of the laity very much exaggerates the function of the civil power. The error of all the parties at this time arose from two causes: (*a*) the disbelief in religious toleration; (*b*) the conception of the State as a single uniform society which allowed no inherent rights in any other society. The supporters of the discipline were right in claiming inherent rights for the religious society and denying that they were all derived from the civil power. They were wrong in attempting with such a claim to make the religious society coextensive with the nation, and to use the civil power for that end. The controversy has thus more than one aspect. Inside the body, which may be regarded either as Church or State according to the aspect uppermost at the moment, it is a controversy between the rights of the laity and those of the hierarchy (for ruling elders, though laymen, are part of the hierarchy). Outside these limits it is the controversy between those who push the principle of the unity of the State to an extreme, and those who assert the inherent, underived authority of other societies. It is only finally to be settled by the recognition (*a*) of the liberty of the individual to choose his religion; (*b*) the rights of the corporate personality, the Church or family, as guaranteed and controlled but not created by the State.

[J. N. F.]

ESSAYS AND REVIEWS. Early in the year 1860 was published under this title a volume containing essays by seven writers: Frederick Temple (*q.v.*), the Headmaster of Rugby, wrote on *The Education of the World*; Rowland Williams, Vice-Principal of Lampeter and Vicar of Broad Chalk, on *Bunsen's Biblical Researches*; Baden Powell, Savilian Professor of Geometry at Oxford, on *The Study of the Evidences of Christianity*; H. B. Wilson, Vicar of Great Staughton and formerly Bampton Lecturer, on *The National Church*; C. W. Goodwin, a lay graduate of Cambridge, on *The Mosaic Cosmogony*; Mark Pattison, Rector of Lincoln College, Oxford, on *Tendencies of Religious Thought in England, 1688-1750*; Benjamin Jowett, Fellow and Tutor of Balliol and Regius Professor of Greek, on *The Interpretation of Scripture*. A notice to the reader explained that each author was responsible for his own essay alone, and continued: 'The volume, it is hoped, will be received as an attempt to illustrate the advantage derivable to the cause of religious and moral truth, from a free handling, in a becoming spirit, of subjects peculiarly liable to suffer by the repetition of conventional language and from traditional methods of treatment.' The writers expected severe criticism; A. P. Stanley (*q.v.*), then Regius Professor of Ecclesiastical History at Oxford, though entirely sympathetic, thought the project inopportune, and refused to take part in it. Jowett wrote to him: 'We do not wish to do anything rash or irritating to the public or the University, but we are determined not to submit to this abominable system of terrorism, which prevents the statement of the plainest facts and makes true theology or theological education impossible.' The terrorism referred to was the work of the dominant faction at Oxford, which, having trampled on the Tractarians, was now turning upon its former Liberal allies; Wilson had been one of the Four Tutors who in 1841 procured the condemnation of Tract 90. This demand for freedom of discussion was the only ground common to the seven authors. Temple's essay provoked little opposition; it was a temperate account of the progressive understanding of revelation in the light of the conscience, its only fault being that the writer underestimated the permanent value of ecclesiastical dogma. Williams discussed, in what even Stanley called a 'flippant and contemptuous tone,' those human elements in the Old Testament which are now all but universally recognised. Baden Powell's paper resolved itself into an attack on the

idea of miracle, which he took to mean 'something at variance with nature and law,' pronouncing it flatly impossible, since 'even an exceptional case of a known law is included in some larger law'; thus alleging against miracles the very consideration by which they are now commonly defended. Wilson maintained against Evangelical individualism the 'multitudinism' or nationalism which he found asserting itself at Geneva; to secure this, he demanded the greatest possible freedom of teaching for the clergy, as of belief for the laity, and consequently the relaxation of subscription to formularies; in the meantime he proposed a mode of dealing with the Thirty-nine Articles which drew upon him many reminders of the part which he had himself taken in denouncing the 'non-natural interpretation' of Tract 90. Goodwin's essay was a mere negative criticism of various attempts to reconcile the Mosaic story of Creation with ascertained facts of astronomy and geology; he insisted on the literal interpretation of the story, saying that 'it has nothing in it which can be properly called poetical,' and that 'it bears on its face no trace of mystical or symbolical meaning'; this narrative was 'the speculation of some Hebrew Descartes or Newton, promulgated in all good faith as the best and most probable account that could then be given of God's universe.' Pattison, a lost disciple of the Tractarians, wrote as a brilliant humanist, with unbounded scorn for all past apologetic except Butler's (*q.v.*), and much implied derision of all attempts to find a basis of belief in his own day. Jowett's essay was the longest and weightiest of all; he criticised various methods of interpretation with thin acumen and complete lack of sympathy, and distinguished with real insight the demands of popular and of critical exegesis. The true interpreter, he said, will 'read Scripture like any other book, with a real interest and not a merely conventional one.' The words 'like any other book' were taken, apart from their context, as the one definite suggestion of the essay, destroying all special reverence for the Bible. How slight was Jowett's real departure from orthodoxy may be judged by his remark: 'A true inspiration guarded the writers of the New Testament from Gnostic or Manichean tenets; at a later stage, a sound instinct prevented the Church from dividing the humanity and Divinity of Christ.' To the description, put out by 'an eminent English prelate,' of the Nicene definition as 'the greatest misfortune that ever befell the Christian world,' he replied that 'a different decision would have been a greater misfortune.'

Small notice was taken of the volume until an enthusiastic welcome in the *Westminster Review* called attention to it. Several editions then rapidly appeared. Bishop S. Wilberforce (*q.v.*) fiercely attacked it in the *Quarterly*; Stanley made a tepid defence in the *Edinburgh*, to the editor of which he wrote privately some extremely severe strictures on four of the writers. Opponents unfairly insisted on treating the seven authors as jointly responsible for the whole volume, and stirred up a general indignation which refused discrimination; the few who kept their heads did not spare condemnation; Tait (*q.v.*), who was afterwards reckoned the chief defender of the book against formal censure, wrote: 'I deeply deplore, indeed execrate, the spirit of much of the *Essays and Reviews*.' A meeting of bishops was held at Fulham in February 1861, at which was adopted a remonstrance, drawn up by Wilberforce, and afterwards issued by the Archbishop of Canterbury as an encyclical with the signatures of twenty-four bishops, including Tait, Hampden (*q.v.*), and Thirlwall (*q.v.*), whose reputation for Liberalism gave it the greater weight. This letter did not name the book, but reflected on some of the negations of its authors, and hinted at the need of personal censure. A little later, the Lower House of the Convocation of Canterbury addressed the bishops on the subject, and a synodical condemnation of the book was proposed. A committee, presided over by Archdeacon Denison (*q.v.*), reported that there were good grounds for condemnation, complaining of the principle found running through the book that the truth of Holy Scripture should be determined by the measure of modern thought. In the meantime legal proceedings had been instituted. For this purpose the writers had to be dealt with individually; Bishop Hamilton of Salisbury took action against Dr. Williams, and the Rev. James Fendall against Mr. Wilson. In December 1862 the Dean of the Arches, Dr. Lushington, condemned each of the accused on three special counts, one of these in Mr. Wilson's case being the expression of a hope that all souls alike may 'find a refuge in the bosom of the Universal Parent,' and that 'a judgment of eternal misery may not be the purpose of God.' They were sentenced to suspension *ab officio et beneficio* for one year, but appealed to the Judicial Committee of the Privy Council, and after a hearing before Lords Westbury, Cranworth, Chelmsford,

and Kingstown, with the two archbishops and the Bishop of London (Tait), the sentence was reversed on 8th February 1864, the archbishops alone dissenting from part of the judgment. As in the Gorham (*q.v.*) case, the judges disclaimed all power of deciding what is the true doctrine of the Church, nor did they pronounce on the general tendency of the book; they found only that the appellants had not, in the passages alleged, directly contradicted the formularies. This left it open to the ecclesiastical authorities to declare that doctrine, and protests against the judgment were at once organised. Pusey joined hands with Lord Shaftesbury and the Evangelicals. A declaration on the Inspiration of Scripture and on Eternal Punishment was signed by 11,000 of the clergy; on 16th March an address of thanks for their dissent from the judgment was presented to the archbishops with the signatures of 137,000 laymen. On 20th April Bishop S. Wilberforce moved in Convocation that the bishops should consider the opinion expressed by the clergy on 21st June 1861, that there were sufficient grounds for a synodical condemnation of the book. Thirlwall objected to treating it as a whole; Tait warned the House against promulgating new Articles of Religion. A committee was appointed by the casting vote of the archbishop, which reported on 21st June. Wilberforce then moved: 'That this Synod . . . doth hereby synodically condemn the said volume, as containing teaching contrary to the doctrine received by the United Church of England and Ireland, in common with the whole Catholic Church of Christ.' This was adopted with only two dissentients, Tait and Jackson of Lincoln. On 15th July Lord Houghton in the House of Lords questioned the lawfulness of this action, when the Lord Chancellor (Westbury) attacked the bishops in a tone of offensive banter, describing ' the thing which they call a synodical judgment' as 'a well-lubricated set of words, a sentence so oily and saponaceous that no one can grasp it,' and received a weighty rebuke for his ribaldry from Wilberforce. From that date the excitement gradually died down, though there was some renewal of it five years later, when Temple was appointed Bishop of Exeter. But in spite of the ineffectiveness of the courts in dealing with doctrine, it was felt that the false teaching was sufficiently condemned, and the doctrine of the Church sufficiently asserted.   [T. A. L.]

ESTABLISHMENT is a particular relationship of the Church to the State, under which its machinery is a recognised part of the civil constitution. Until the sixteenth century Church and State in England were composed of the same persons, and there could be no question of one religious body being in a privileged position. Since that time other religious bodies have been in existence, and the Church is said to be ' established ' in contradistinction to them. The phrase is first used in Canon 3 of 1604 : ' The Church of England by Law established under the King's Majesty.' But this does not mean that the Church was chosen by the State out of a number of religious bodies and placed in a privileged position. Its relations to the State remained as they had always been, subject to such modifications as were rendered necessary by the renunciation of papal jurisdiction. The Church was never ' established ' by any specific Act or Acts of Parliament. In this, as in other respects, the English constitution was the result of slow and natural growth. During the long period in which Church and State were co-extensive the Church's officers were recognised by the State, and its councils and courts were as much part of the national constitution as were the secular assemblies and tribunals. The law which the synods enacted was the King's Ecclesiastical Law, and it was administered by the King's Ecclesiastical Courts. And this is still the case (see Lord Blackburn's judgment in *Mackonochie* v. *Lord Penzance*, 1881, 6 A.C. 446). Besides their spiritual authority derived from the Church, this law and these courts possess temporal authority, as part of the law and judicature of the realm, and are therefore subject to the conditions which the State imposes in return for the support of the secular arm. The most important of these conditions are that the Church accepts as valid Acts of Parliament dealing with ecclesiastical subjects, provided they do not conflict with the spiritual law [CANON LAW]; that the State chooses the persons to be appointed to bishoprics [BISHOPS] and certain other offices in the Church ; that Convocation (*q.v.*) cannot meet or enact canons without the permission of the Crown; and that the Church Courts (*q.v.*) are in some respects subject to the control of those of the State. Should these conditions hamper the Church in its spiritual work, or be intolerably abused by the State, it would be the Church's duty to free itself by severing its connection with the State and giving up whatever privileges it derives therefrom.

It has been maintained that the Church which accepts such privileges from the State becomes a mere ' department of public worship,' bound in its doctrine and ceremonial by whatever laws Parliament may enact. This view finds no support in history, which shows that the Church is a spiritual society with jurisdiction of its own anterior to the State and independent of it. [AUTHORITY IN THE CHURCH.] The fact that the State recognises the Church's spiritual law as of divine origin and sanction, and agrees to enforce it, does not give it power to abrogate or amend that law. The State may withdraw its support if it chooses. It may by force of the civil law impose upon its subjects whatever religion it pleases ; but if such legal religion conflicts with that of the Church, the Church can only refuse to adopt it and face the temporal consequences.

Nor does establishment create a ' national Church ' in the sense of a comprehensive body which would include all members of the State whatever their religious views. Dr. Arnold (*q.v.*) desired to see the Church hold this position, but differences of opinion are now too wide and too strong for such a body to be formed except on lines of the vaguest undenominationalism. The Church could only occupy such a position by renouncing its distinctive doctrines. The Church, however, is national in that it is the official representative of the State in matters of religion. By 12-13 Will. III. c. 2 the sovereign must be in communion with it.

Though the Church was not established by statute, Disestablishment, or the severance of the present connection of Church and State, could only be effected by statute abrogating the State's control over the Church. This would give the Church greater liberty, *e.g.* Convocation could legislate more freely, and bishops would be chosen without any reference to the civil power. The Church's law and the decisions of its courts would possess the same spiritual validity as before, but would not be enforced by the secular arm, unless the parties had entered into a civilly valid contract to abide by them, when they would be carried out by the civil courts like the decisions of any other arbitrators (*Long* v. *Bishop of Capetown*, 1863, 1 Moo. P.C. N.S. 461-2).

Yet the fact that a Church is not established does not necessarily give it complete freedom from secular control. It must almost necessarily own temporal property, such as funds and buildings, in respect of which it is subject to the temporal law. And if such property is held on terms which include matters of doctrine, and disputes arise, the civil courts must inquire into and decide them. The history of non-established religious bodies affords numerous instances of doctrines being the subject of litigation in the secular courts (*e.g. Jones* v. *Stannard, Times,* 2nd February 1881 ; *Free Church of Scotland (General Assembly of)* v. *Lord Overtoun.* 1904, A.C. 515). All questions concerning property must ultimately be decided by the civil power ; but the necessity of thus referring matters of doctrine to it may be avoided by inserting a clause in the trust deeds of property referring disputes to a voluntary tribunal of spiritual validity, and reserving power to the Church, acting through its proper authority, to vary them in points of doctrine.

The question of property raises the subject of Disendowment, which is popularly associated with Disestablishment. All property is held under the sanction of the State. Morally the property of the English Church is on the same basis as that of any other religious or secular body. Any part of the Church's income which can be shown to be given by the State in return for services rendered would naturally cease with those services. But apart from the question of the origin of tithes (*q.v.*), nearly the whole of that income arises from voluntary gifts made to the Church either now or in the past, and not from public funds. [CHURCH AND STATE, SUPREMACY, ROYAL.] [G. C.]

Brewer, *The Establishment and Endowment of the Ch. of Eng.* (ed. Diblin); authorities cited for CHURCH AND STATE.

ETHELDREDA, St., or **AETHELTHRYTH** (d. 679), a daughter of Anna, a Christian king of the East Anglians, is said to have been born at Exning, Suffolk, and was married to Tondbert, alderman of the South Gyrwas, receiving from him the Isle of Ely. He died, leaving her a virgin, and five years later, in 660, she was married to Egfrid, the son and successor of Oswy (*q.v.*), King of Northumbria. Encouraged by Bishop Wilfrid (*q.v.*), she preserved her virginity against her husband's will, and after twelve years, 672, obtained his consent to her retirement. She received the veil from Wilfrid at Coldingham, a double monastery of men and women, where Egfrid's aunt, Ebbe, was abbess. After residing there a year she journeyed to the Isle of Ely. According to legend, she left Coldingham because her husband sought to regain her, and her flight from him was blessed by miracles. In Ely she built and ruled over a double monastery, like Coldingham, practising severe asceticism in dress, fasting, prayer, watching, and

abstinence from the bath. She was attacked by the plague, which was accompanied by a large tumour below the jaw ; it was lanced by a physician, but she died the third day after, on 23rd June 679. By her direction her body was buried in a wooden coffin among the graves of the monastery. Her sister Sexburga succeeded her, and on 17th October 695 translated her body, which was found incorrupt, placing it in a richly wrought marble sarcophagus brought to her by some of her monks from the ruined city of Grantchester, close to the modern Cambridge. While suffering in her neck Etheldreda spoke of the time when she loaded it with costly necklaces. Her name became popularised as Audrey, and her pious words bringing it into connection with necklaces which were sold at the fair held on 17th October, and by pedlars to women of the lower class (*Winter's Tale,* iv. 3), gave us the word tawdry (St. Audrey). Her monastery perished during the Danish invasions, and was rebuilt by Bishop Ethelwold. A new church, now Ely Cathedral, was begun by Abbot Symeon (1082-93), and continued by his successor, who again translated the saint's body. She is commemorated on 17th October. [W. H.]

Besides Bede's account, a twelfth-century life in *Liber Eliensis* (Anglia Chr. Soc.).

EVANGELICALS. The two religious revivals in England during the eighteenth century were almost simultaneous, and had much in common both in cause and characteristics. The debased condition of social life under George II. called for such movements not only within the Church but also outside it. The general tone of the higher classes was vicious and profane, that of the lower classes brutal and irreligious. It was chiefly in the middle classes that the quiet piety of former generations continued. Except in some country parishes the spiritual heritage from the past slumbered. Church fabrics were neglected, the services were perfunctorily performed, the days of observance were disregarded. The clergy, who were often absentees, were wanting in sanctity and devotion; special zeal was resented and discouraged. The awakening came through the ardent preaching and tireless energy of the leaders of the two movements, and the terms Evangelical and Methodist, at first frequently interchangeable, came into use. In past times the former expression had been confined to the distinctive doctrines of the Gospel and to the counsels to attain a saintly life; but in the middle of the eighteenth century it began to be attached to Churchmen who laid special stress on personal conversion and the vicarious Atonement of Christ. With other names it has undergone a change of meaning, and has come to be used of those who are spiritually-minded without reference to any particular body of Christians. The use of it in combination with other terms is now frequent, and Liberal Evangelical, Evangelical Catholic, and Neo-Evangelical, first coined in 1868, are adopted variations. [CHURCH, HIGH, LOW.]

The two movements soon began to diverge, not so much at first in doctrine as in method. The Evangelical revival, which remained within the Church, held in a modified form the Calvinism of Whitefield (*q.v.*), but did not adopt the organised intrusion of Wesley (*q.v.*) into other parishes. The independence of it can be traced in the work of the pioneers, as Thomas Walker (1719-60) at Truro, Thomas Adam (1701-81) at Winteringham, and Daniel Rowlands (1713-90) in Wales. The work of the Wesleys and of Whitefield undoubtedly exercised a strong influence on Evangelicals not only from personal contact but from religious sympathy. The saintly John Fletcher (1729-85) of Madeley, who confined himself to his Shropshire colliers, was at one time designated as the successor of John Wesley. James Hervey (1714-58) of Weston Favell, a college pupil of John Wesley, was a staunch Evangelical. William Grimshaw (1708-63) of Haworth on the Yorkshire moors, and John Berridge (1716-93) of Everton in the Midlands, both itinerated; but Henry Venn (*q.v.*) during his eleven years at Huddersfield acknowledged the irregularity of preaching in unconsecrated places. John Newton (1725-1807), at one time a blasphemous slave-dealer, spent nine years among the Methodist leaders before his ordination, and came to be the spiritual director of Evangelicals at Olney, and then at St. Mary Woolnoth in London.

The Evangelical leaders took their parishes for their world, and formed their own little societies round them. Centres of activity were established, and whole districts became quickened into new life. The work advanced against constant persecution and opposition, though in the next century this experience did not cause toleration to be extended to the Oxford Movement (*q.v.*). With the well-disposed there was the attachment to 'genteel' conventions, and the dread of religious enthusiasm to be overcome. The scholarly William Romaine (1714-95) endured hardness before he triumphed over the prejudices of the middle-class congregations at St. Dunstan's, Fleet Street, and St. Andrew's, Blackfriars. Charles Simeon (*q.v.*) at Holy Trinity, Cambridge, passed through an ordeal of contention until he secured first toleration and then recognition as the greatest spiritual force in the University. At an earlier date, 1768, six students of St. Edmund Hall suffered expulsion from Oxford for 'too much religion.' But an increasing number of devoted clergy gradually won their way by sheer force of piety and character. Not that positions of importance were given to them; the only one who attained high preferment was Isaac Milner (1751-1820), a brilliant Senior Wrangler, who became Dean of Carlisle. Another Senior Wrangler, Henry Martyn (1781-1812), a spiritual son of Charles Simeon, was not allowed to preach in any church in his native county except that of his brother-in-law. At the close of the eighteenth century the Evangelicals were the most definite and the most active influence in the Church; but they were not the dominant party, and even at the end of the nineteenth century a favourable estimate of their numbers is not more than one-fourth of the clergy. In 1822 there were not a dozen Evangelical clergy in London; and ten years later Daniel Wilson (1805-86), on succeeding his father at Islington, said that the Evangelical party were 'few in number, and holding for the most part subordinate positions.' The refined Richard Cecil (1748-1810) at St. John's, Bedford Row; the practical David Woodd (1785-1831) at Bentinck Chapel; and the able Thomas Scott (1746-1821) at the chapel of the Lock Hospital, had to be content with proprietary chapels, which later deteriorated into commercial speculations. Some of the most efficient Evangelical clergy remained unbeneficed almost to the end of their lives, while men of indifferent attainments obtained by influence important livings. To remedy this, 'spheres of work' were purchased, and gradually the Simeon Trustees have acquired the right of presentation to more than a hundred parishes. With the second generation the influence of the Evangelical clergy increased, their position was accepted, and their manifold activities produced devout lives and good works that are eminent in religious history.

The conspicuous work of the Evangelicals in the nineteenth century is found in the voluntary societies they founded. Some contain the term 'Church' in their title and are more distinctive in their principles, while others without this qualification are more general in their range. In 1783 the Eclectic Society was formed in London ' for religious intercourse and improvement.' The numbers were small, but their influence was far-reaching. A discussion in 1796 on the best method of promoting the knowledge of the Gospel among the heathen, with a view to the disposal of a legacy of £4000, led to the foundation of the subsequently world-wide Church Missionary Society (1799). Its title until 1812 was ' The Society for Missions to Africa and the East.' In 1802 Josiah Pratt (1768-1844) became secretary at an annual salary of £60, which later on was increased to £300, and during the twenty-one years he held this position its expansion became assured. The first bishop to join the society was Henry Ryder (1777-1836) of Gloucester, who was also the first decided Evangelical raised to the bench (1815). The Newfoundland Society (1823) owed its inception to a votive offering of a west-country merchant who survived shipwreck. In 1861 it was joined with the Colonial Church Society (1838) to form the Colonial and Continental Church Society. The South American Missionary Society was instituted in 1844 to forward the heroic labours of Allen Gardiner. Originating at Bristol, the Missions to Seamen (1856) had as its founder W. H. G. Kingston, the author of sea stories for boys. The Church Pastoral Aid Society (1836), for the purpose of ' increasing the number of working clergymen and encouraging the appointment of pious and discreet laymen as helpers to the clergy in duties not ministerial,' had to pass through considerable criticism. The matters objected to were the proposed inquiries into the qualifications of the clergy and the employment of lay assistants. The last experiment of this kind had been Wesley's lay preachers. In 1875 the Church Parochial Mission Society, with William Hay Aitken as its first leader, resulted from the Moody and Sankey Mission, and promoted the movement for holding services in unconsecrated buildings. Until 1855 it was illegal by the Toleration Act of 1812 (52 Geo. III. c. 155) for more than twenty persons to meet for religious worship in any building but a consecrated church or licensed dissenting chapel. The spiritual equipment of the Evangelical party was strengthened in 1861 by the establishment of the London College of Divinity, in 1877 by the foundation of Wycliffe Hall at Oxford, and in 1881 by that of Ridley Hall at Cambridge. [THEOLOGICAL COLLEGES.]

Other societies established by the Evangelicals were based on the principle of devotion to a common Master without reference to the Church's system. To these Nonconformists were admitted. The clergy in general in the early part of the nineteenth century were not regarded as among the converted, and on their part, after the spread of dissent through the Methodist revival, an agreement would not have been practicable. In the second and third quarters of the century the general bond between Evangelicals became more that of a vigorous antipathy to Rome and the Oxford Movement, the apparent resemblance of which had readily alarmed them. Their persecuting tendency was also shown in their hostility towards Dr. Thomas Arnold (*q.v.*), who seemed to them to tolerate Agnosticism, and to his successors, F. W. Robertson of Brighton and Charles Kingsley (*q.v.*). The earlier Evangelicals did not deny, far less persecute; they were content to affirm. In the last thirty years co-operation with Nonconformists has been found mostly in social and literary work. The Religious Tract Society (1799) publishes writings of an elementary character, while the British and Foreign Bible Society (1804) circulates the Scriptures in all languages and to all parts of the world. In 1845 the Evangelical Alliance was supported by the partisan section. The Church Association (1865), prominent at one time, declined through its prosecutions under the Public Worship Regulation Act (*q.v.*), and new organisations were started, which have been since united with others to form the National Church League. [SOCIETIES, ECCLESIASTICAL.] William Pennefather (1816-73) opened the Mildmay Deaconess Home in 1860 for ' women desirous of labouring in the Lord's vineyard as Phœbe did of old.' Five years later, after a close study of the Lutheran deaconesses in Prussia, the Mildmay deaconesses appeared in their quiet uniform, and though at first disturbing to some of the elder clergy, met with a speedy success. Other interdenominational societies in which the Evangelicals have the greater influence are the Cambridge Inter-Collegiate Christian Union (1877), to band together men in ' dead earnest ' for the spiritual good of their brother students; the Children's Scripture Union (1879), with its seaside services; and the Keswick Convention (1875), for the promotion of practical holiness. The Young Men's Christian Association (1844), the Young Women's Christian Association (1855), the Railway Mission (1881), the Navvy Mission (1883) are also spheres in which Evangelicals and Nonconformists work together. But co-operation was not found possible in the

London Mission Society (1795), the London Society for Missions to the Jews (1809), and the Indian Female School Society (1861), from which the Church of England Zenana Missionary Society was divided off in 1880.

A notable annual gathering of Evangelicals is the Islington Conference (begun 1827), which at first consisted of thirty to fifty of the clergy, but which is now attended by as many as a thousand. The list of Evangelical leaders who have here addressed their brethren contains most of those who have been prominent in this school. First, Edward Bickersteth, Hugh Stowell, Hugh M'Neile, John W. Cunningham. H. M. Villiers; then John Miller, John Charles Ryle (*q.v.*), E. Garbett, William Cadman, the Bardsleys; then W. H. Barlow, T. P. Boultbee, E. Hoare, J. Richardson, W. Lefroy; then H. W. Webb-Peploe, H. C. G. Moule, and H. Wace, their leaders of to-day. In 1899 the centenary of the Church Missionary Society was a great event. The 'Policy of Faith,' the unbounded development, the missionary enthusiasm, though sometimes said to ' over-monopolise efforts and gifts,' yet has made this society, more than all others, the institution to which Evangelicals are attached, and with which they are especially identified in the twentieth century.

On the nation the effect produced by the Evangelical movement was seen at first in the fresh spirit of moral zeal carried to the hearts of the poor. It checked the revolutionary and sceptical ideas at the close of the eighteenth century. In 1780 Robert Raikes by his Sunday schools gave the first impulse to popular education. The slave - trade was overthrown by Thomas Clarkson and William Wilberforce (*q.v.*) after many years of unwearied exertions. The Factory Acts were due to the philanthropic labours of Lord Shaftesbury. In both centuries many of the ' serious ' laity gathered round the Evangelicals. Of John Thornton (1720-90) it was said: ' Few have ever done more to feed the hungry, clothe the naked, and help all that suffer adversity.' One of the wealthiest merchants in Europe, his purse was always open to schemes of charity, besides the distribution of Bibles, Prayer-Books, and other religious publications. Another of their most influential supporters was Lord Dartmouth (1731-1801), President of the Board of Trade and later Colonial Secretary, who with the elder Thornton secured benefices for Evangelical clergy. In the nineteenth century Lord Shaftesbury (1801-85) stands out beyond all others in his life of godliness and devotion to the poor and

friendless. Ragged schools and every sort of Home Mission agency had his special support. As bishop-maker for nine years from 1855, when his relation, Lord Palmerston, became Prime Minister, his influence was supreme; but of his fourteen nominations not all were strictly Evangelical, though none were Tractarian. At the close of the century his place as lay leader was taken by Sir John Kennaway. The ' Clapham Sect ' was for many years the most remarkable group of Evangelical laymen. John Venn (1759-1813) was vicar of Clapham, then with three miles of meadows separating it from London, and a population of two thousand. In the ' holy village ' were the residences of Henry Thornton (1760-1815), banker; William Wilberforce, M.P. for Yorkshire; Charles Grant (1746-1823), Chairman of the East India Company; James Stephen (1759-1832), the famous advocate; Zachary Macaulay (1768-1838), formerly Governor of Sierra Leone; Lord Teignmouth (1751-1834), a just and generous but not inspiring Governor-General of India; and Granville Sharp (1735-1832), a pioneer in the suppression of the slave-trade. Combined in this coterie were piety, wealth, eloquence, knowledge of men, legal acumen, business experience, and Parliamentary influence such as made their united action irresistible. They lived in the world, but realised the presence of God in all their ways; their time and wealth were regarded in the light of a trust from God; their inspiration was drawn from diligent study of the Bible and fervent prayer, public, family, and private. Evangelicals looked to the ' Clapham Sect ' not only because of their position and influence, but because of the beauty of holiness that dwelt in them. Though many despised them, to ' sit under ' a popular preacher became a recognised custom of the day even with the fashionable world. Their example quickened the spirit of philanthropy among the middle classes, the section of the community to which the Evangelicals had widely appealed. A standard was represented by them which impressed itself on all who came in contact with it. The effect produced is measured in its influence on the family rather than in the Church. The particular type of life both before and after this time continued through two or three generations, and the tradition was carried on from father to son. The Venns, the Scotts, the Thorntons, the Bickersteths, the Bardsleys are notable instances. To the intimacy of such circles admission was only obtained by the ' converted,' and for these it was an essential to ' witness.' Dancing, card parties, and the theatre were rigorously banned. Fiction, unfit as much of it was in those days, was also not allowed because of the time it occupied which otherwise might have been given to the Scriptures, sermons, and books such as Bunyan's *Pilgrim's Progress.* Interest in Foreign Missions and the May Meetings held in Exeter Hall, Strand (1831-1907), provided a diversion in their ordered lives. If in earlier generations aloofness from the world produced austerity, later the mark of consecration was more manifest. Their phraseology at first had been peculiar, and the familiarity with which they spoke of holy things may have appeared to lack reverence, but their anxious inquiries after the welfare of the souls of others and their terms of endearment came from a sincere zeal and love in the cause of their Master. Their very earnestness constrained them to improve every occasion in season and out of season. The frequent use of ' D.V.' did but express their belief in divine interposition. At times they were censorious. A touch of quiet worldliness in their comfortable homes showed itself amid their not always consistent protest against pomps and pastimes. Their strict observance of Sunday, when social hospitality was neither given nor accepted, and their clothes and meals and books and conversation and relaxations were of a precise order, was a power in the national life. The waning of this and the decline of home training are more noticeable in the present day because of the standard they reached two generations ago. Works of benevolence and mercy, visiting and Sunday-school teaching, were fruitful products of their religion. Changes have come in their methods as in other directions. But a level of saintliness was obtained that expressed their personal devotion to the Saviour, and made them in their day the salt of the earth.

The distinctive feature of the Evangelical clergy has been their preaching, directed to arouse their congregations to a state of personal conversion. The depravity of human nature, the conviction of sin, the Atonement. Justification by faith and not by works. Sanctification by the Holy Spirit, have been the doctrines on which they have most insisted.

In earlier days the subject of Predestination and Election was pushed to extremes by some, though few held the tenets of the New Birth and Christian Perfection. The Evangelicals were then mostly moderate Calvinists. and did not to any great extent take part in the controversy that led to the

first cleavage in the Methodist movement. Later there were many who repudiated Calvinism and advocated the doctrine of Universal Redemption. The power of their preaching came from a passionate love of souls and longing to promote the love of God. Not so much the desire to escape from the wrath to come as the worthlessness of everything which did not begin and end in God moved men to self-surrender. The sense of helplessness and the need of grace have found a permanent expression in the words of Toplady (*q.v.*) :—

'Nothing in my hand I bring,
Simply to Thy Cross I cling.'

But a tendency of their preaching was to produce an inclination rather to rest in the certitude of salvation than to feel the need of spiritual progress. The constant exposition of texts only with regard to favourite doctrines, without reference to a system of order and doctrine, did not uplift the Church as a whole. They had little interest in the search for theological truth or in the experience of historical tradition. Philosophy, except that which centred in the Crucifixion, was not found amongst them. Undue exaltation of preaching caused them to undervalue liturgical worship, the creeds, and the sacraments. the last in teaching rather than in practice. They made little study of the Prayer Book, though they asserted their affection for it. They were content with the Thirty-nine Articles and the Liturgy, and at no period did they agitate for revision. The introduction of hymn-singing and the innovation of evening services are their two contributions in the way of worship. The mutilation at one period of the Baptismal Service in view of the question of Regeneration, and the adoption in 1852 of Evening Communions, are phases that represent ideas held by them on these subjects. Some parishes, however. as Islington under the elder Daniel Wilson (*q.v.*), had already revived early Eucharists. the use of the Litany on Wednesday and Friday, and a service on each saint's day. In their churches the pulpit was the central object, and the font and altar had scant dignity given to them. Not that lack of ceremonial implied irreverence or slovenliness. Evangelistic preaching, pastoral visiting, prayer meetings, were not supplemented by corporate action and Church authority. The revival of Convocation (*q.v.*) was opposed by them because of the exclusion of laymen. whose services were a growing feature in their work. They did not favour the establishment of Church

Congresses. The Oxford Movement was alien to them through the emphasis it laid on Church order and discipline. Like the Latitudinarians (*q.v.*), they were unable to produce ecclesiastical leadership or power, though in their own organisations they showed cohesion and vitality. Nevertheless, they transformed innumerable lives. They delivered men from the bondage of sin. They inspired them with a hope of heaven. They won souls to a knowledge of Christ ; and with them to know Christ was ' to believe in Him, and to love Him, to walk with Him, to work for Him, to watch for His second coming.'

Few books of merit have been produced by the Evangelicals, and these have not outlived their generation. They relied on the living message rather than on the printed page. No great divine arose among them. Hervey's *Theron and Aspasio* and *Meditations among the Tombs*, both of a Calvinistic cast, were popular in their day. J. H. Newman (*q.v.*) in his *Apologia* says that, ' humanly speaking, he almost owed his soul to the writings of Scott,' whose *Force of Truth* and *Commentaries* were sold in their thousands. Cecil's *Remains* is still remembered. Joseph Milner (1744-97) of Hull wrote a *History of the Church of Christ*. Venn's *Complete Duty of Man* and Wilberforce's *Practical View* were read in all Evangelical houses for many years. Henry Thornton's *Family Prayers* was an accepted household office. Hannah More's (*q.v.*) writings to the highly placed served their purpose in quickening many to a sense of their responsibility. *The Christian Observer*, started in 1802 as a monthly magazine, under the auspices of the Clapham circle, continued until 1880. *The Record*, begun with the violent editorship of Alexander Haldane in 1828, is now the weekly organ of moderate Evangelicals. But the literary force has been chiefly with hymn-writers. Thomas Robinson (1749-1813) of Leicester, in one of the many congregational collections of Psalms and Hymns, excluded all Psalms from the old version of Sternhold and Hopkins. The *Olney Hymns* (1779), composed by William Cowper (1731-1800) and John Newton, though without the gladness of the Psalms, appealed to the heart through their intense love of the Saviour, and ' enriched the hymnody of all time.' The *Hymnal Companion*, edited by E. H. Bickersteth (1870), rapidly became the recognised hymn-book of Evangelical congregations, and in 1893 was in use in 1478 English churches. The Parker Society (1840) was formed to meet an attack on the Reformation divines by a reprint of their works.

Books that influenced the early Evangelicals frequently belonged to a different school. Thomas à Kempis marked the turning-point in the life of John Newton. Bishop Thomas Wilson's (*q.v.*) *Lord's Supper* taught Charles Simeon the meaning of the Atonement. William Law's (*q.v.*) *Serious Call* changed the lives of John Wesley, Thomas Adam, Henry Venn, and Thomas Scott ; and this book beyond all others may be counted as a source of the revival.

[H. M. L.]

Balleine, *Hist. of the Evangelical Party* ; W. E. Gladstone, *Gleanings*, vii. ; J. H. Overton, *Evangelical Revival in the Eighteenth Century* ; Eugene Stock, *Hist. of the Church Missionary Society* ; and others.

EVELYN, John (1620-1706), one of the most notable lay churchmen of the seventeenth century, was born of a Surrey family, became a student of the Middle Temple, and a fellow-commoner of Balliol, where he seems to have chiefly studied dancing and music. He travelled in Holland, and served in the army there ; returning to England, he spent three days in November 1642 with Charles's army, and then settled at Wotton, his family seat in Surrey. After spending most of the next ten years abroad he settled at Sayes Court, Deptford, in 1652, compounding with the Parliament. He now devoted himself to gardening and natural science, and was one of the founders of what became the Royal Society, being a great friend of John Wilkins and Robert Boyle (*q.v.*). He kept up correspondence with Charles II. in exile, and remained firm in his allegiance to the Church, being one of those who were arrested for receiving the Holy Communion on Christmas Day, 1657. He worked hard for the Restoration, and was in favour at court after the King's return. He had been generous to the dispossessed clergy, and supported many of them by money and kindness, especially Jeremy Taylor, who became his confessor. He now became prominent in Church matters, a commissioner for the rebuilding of St. Paul's, and aiding the establishment of the Church in the plantations. He was frequently at the court, but regarded its vice and dissipation with growing disgust. ' What contentment can there be in the riches and splendour of the world purchased with vice and dishonour ? ' he wrote in his *Diary*; and his description of the last Sunday of Charles II.'s life is one of the most famous records of the luxury and frivolity of the court. He was a friend, however, of artists and musicians, and interested in all the culture of his age.

Besides the chief clergy of the time he was intimate with Bentley and Pepys, Gibbons and Hollar. He was famous as a gardener, his own garden at Sayes Court being one of the most perfect examples of the formal style of the age. His *Life of Mrs. Godolphin* contains a delightful picture of the life of a religious lady of the court, and his own *Diary* throws abundant light on social, political, and religious history. A devout man, respected by all, a most strict follower of the rules of the Church, he represented the Caroline divines in their breadth, piety, and catholicity in a way which made him universally respected even among those who disliked his opinions and did not imitate his conduct. There was not a good work of his age with which he was not associated.

[W. H. H.]

Memoirs, ed. by H. B. Wheatley.

EXETER, See of, can be traced from the subdivision of that of Sherborne [SALISBURY, SEE OF] by Archbishop Plegmund in 909. Plegmund established the three dioceses of Cornwall, Devon, and Somerset. In 1040, on the death of Burwold, Bishop of Cornwall, that diocese was united with Crediton. The bishops of Devon for the first hundred and forty years held their see at Crediton, whence it was removed to Exeter by Bishop Leofric in 1046 on account of the defenceless position of Crediton against the Danish pirates. Leofric recovered alienated property at Culmstock, Branescomb, and Saltcomb, and the Conqueror granted him the estate of Holcombe. By Order in Council of 30th July 1838 the Scilly Isles were declared to be within the diocese of Exeter and archdeaconry of Cornwall. In 1876 the ancient diocese of Cornwall was revived by the establishment of the see of Truro (*q.v.*), with jurisdiction over the territory of the former archdeaconry of Cornwall.

The see includes all the county of Devon (with the exception of five parishes and a hamlet in the diocese of Truro, and two parishes in the diocese of Sarum) and one parish in the county of Somerset. The population is 658,273.

The *Taxatio* of 1291 assessed the *Temporalia* (*i.e.* revenues from land) at £461, 18s. 4¾d.; the *Valor Ecclesiasticus* of 1536 assessed the income at £1566, 14s. 6d., but the survey of Bishop Veysey of November of the same year returned it as £1391, 1s. Ecton (1711) gives the value as £500. It is now £4200. The diocese was formerly divided into four archdeaconries: Exeter (first mentioned, 1083), Totnes (first mentioned, 1140), Barn-

staple (first mentioned, 1143), and Cornwall (first mentioned, 1089), but that of Cornwall ceased to exist on the formation of the see of Truro. There are twenty-three rural deaneries. The cathedral church is ruled by a chapter of the Old Foundation; the deanery and chancellorship were founded by Bishop Briwere in 1225: the offices of treasurer and precentor date from 1133 and 1154 respectively. There are twenty non-residentiary prebendaries. By the Cathedrals Act, 1840 (3-4 Vic. c. 113), the number of canons residentiary was reduced from eight to five. An Order in Council of 11th August 1837 annexed one canonry to the archdeaconry of Exeter. An Order of 30th November 1882 suspended one of the five canonries and transferred its endowment to Truro. A bishop suffragan of Crediton was appointed in 1897.

BISHOPS OF CREDITON

1. Eadulf, 909; d. 931.
2. Aethelgar, 934; d. 953.
3. Aelfwold, 953; cons. by advice of Dunstan (*q.v.*); d. 972.
4. Sideman, 973.　6. Aelfwold II., 988.
5. Aelfric, 977.　7. Eadnoth, 1008.
8. Lyfing, 1027; on death of Burwold, Bishop of Cornwall, c. 1040, that see was united with Crediton; Lyfing also held the see of Worcester; accompanied Cnut to Rome; d. 1046.

BISHOPS OF EXETER

9. Leofric, 1046; chaplain and Chancellor to Edward the Confessor; a zealous defender of his flock against piratical ravages; moved the see to Exeter in 1050, and there maintained the cathedral staff from his private resources; a learned and generous bishop; d. 1072.
10. Osbern, 1072; had property in Sussex, Hampshire, Surrey, Berkshire, Gloucestershire, Norfolk, and Oxfordshire; d. 1103.
11. William Warelwast, or Warawast, 1107: an obsequious courtier, whose consecration was delayed by Anselm (*q.v.*) owing to the contest about Investitures (*q.v.*): made generous use of his property; resigned on becoming blind, and retired to Plympton Priory; d. 1137.
12. Robert Chichester, 1138; Dean of Salisbury; d. 1155.
13. Robert of Warelwast, 1155: nephew to William Warelwast: Dean of Salisbury; d. 1160.

14. Bartholomew of Exeter, 1161; Dean of Chichester and Archdeacon of Exeter; cons. by the Bishop of Rochester, the see of Canterbury being vacant; named by Alexander III. ' the luminary of the English Church '; formerly an opponent of Becket (*q.v.*), he afterwards desired to remain with him in voluntary banishment, and was chosen to preach in Canterbury Cathedral after the murder; a saintly and learned bishop; d. 1184.

15. John Fitz-Duke, 1186; Precentor of Exeter; d. 1191.

16. Henry Marshall, 1194; son of Gilbert, Earl Marshall; a noble prelate, who completed the cathedral as designed by William Warelwast; d. 1206.

17. Simon de Apulia, 1214; avowed partisan of John; not cons. till 1214 in consequence of the interdict; fixed boundaries of the city parishes; d. 1223.

18. William Briwere, or Bruere, 1224; founded in 1225 the deanery and precentorship, appropriating churches for the new offices; pious and charitable; d. 1244.

19. Richard Blondy, or le Blund, 1245; Chancellor of Exeter; d. 1257.

20. Walter Bronescombe, 1258; cons. while a deacon; commenced the episcopal registers; heads the list of twelve bishops and barons appointed after the battle of Evesham, 1265 (*Dictum de Kenilworth*); collected and revised the cathedral statutes, and obtained confirmation of charters for the past two hundred and seventy-six years; a bishop of unwearied industry and unsullied integrity; d. 1280.

21. Peter Quivil, or Wyvill, or Peter of Exeter, 1280; built the cathedral transepts by breaking through the Norman towers and joining arches; annexed lands for precentorship and chancellorship; presided over an important synod in Exeter, 1287; d. 1291.

22. Thomas de Button, or Bitton, 1292; Dean of Wells; d. 1307.

23. Walter Stapeldon, 1308; Precentor of Exeter and Doctor of Canon Law; chaplain to Pope Clement V.; benefactor to cathedral fabric to the extent of £1800; vaulted a large part of the choir and erected the sedilia in south of sanctuary; treasurer to Edward II., with whom he was a high favourite; founded Hart's Hall and Stapeldon's Inn at Oxford, afterwards consolidated in Exeter College; established St.

John's Hospital Grammar School in Exeter; murdered in London, 1326.

24. James de Berkeley, 1327 (P.); elected first by the chapter, but provided by the Pope; d. 1327.

25. John de Grandison, 1327 (P.); chaplain to Pope John XXII.; found the cathedral in a state of poverty and confusion, but by careful administration restored it; resisted the visitation of the diocese by the metropolitan, Simon Meopham, ' *nequiter vi armata* '; in 1337 compiled the *Ordinale*, regulating the cathedral offices; wrote a life of St. Thomas of Canterbury; d. 1369.

26. Thomas Brentingham, or de Brantyngham, 1370 (P.); Treasurer of the Exchequer; added west façade; d. 1394.

27. Edmund Stafford, 1395 (P.); Chancellor of England, 1396 and 1401; benefactor to Exeter College; d. 1419.

28. John Catterike, 1419 (P.); cons. at Bologna, 1414; tr. from Lichfield and Coventry; d. 1419.

29. Edmund Lacey, 1420; tr. (P.) from Hereford; accompanied Henry V. to Agincourt; composed an office in honour of the Archangel Raphael; built the hall in Exeter House, London; d. 1455.

30. George Neville, 1458 (P.); tr. to York.

31. John Bothe, 1465 (P.); traditional donor of the bishop's throne; d. 1478.

32. Peter Courtenay, 1478 (P.); tr. to Winchester.

33. Richard Fox (*q.v.*), 1487 (P.); tr. to Bath and Wells.

34. Oliver King, 1493 (P.); King's secretary; formerly Dean of Hereford; tr. to Bath and Wells, 1495.

35. Richard Redmayn, 1496 (P.); tr. from St. Asaph; tr. to Ely, 1501.

36. John Arundel, 1502; tr. (P.) from Lichfield and Coventry; d. 1504.

37. Hugh Oldham, 1505 (P.); former chaplain to Margaret Beaufort; successfully opposed encroachment upon his ordinary jurisdiction; a munificent patron of education; completed St. Saviour's Chapel; d. 1519.

38. John Voysey, or Veysey, 1519 (P.); formerly dean; President of the Council of the Marches of Wales; tutor to Princess Mary, and in agreement with Henry on the Divorce and Supremacy questions; in 1551 the Privy Council peremptorily required him to surrender the see, and he submitted *propter corporis metu*, retiring on a pension.

39. Miles Coverdale (*q.v.*), 1551.
    John Voysey (*sup.*). 1553; reinstated by Mary; d. (aged ninety-two) 1554.
40. James Turberville, 1555; restored to the see the borough and manor of Crediton; deprived and imprisoned by Elizabeth for not subscribing to the Act of Supremacy, 1559.
41. William Alley, or Allein, 1560; owing to impoverishment he reduced the number of canons from twenty-four to nine; 'Ho bought a commyssion to be a Justice of the Peace within the citie, contrary to the lybertes of the same' (Hoker, *History*); instituted a 'Poor Man's Library'; d. 1570.
42. William Bradbridge, 1571; former Dean of Salisbury; allowed to hold two benefices *in commendam* owing to impoverishment; ruined at the age of seventy by agricultural speculation; 'he died £1400 in debt to Queen Elizabeth, and had not wherewith to bury him'; d. 1578.
43. John Wolton, 1579; a scholar, who remodelled the statutes; in 1585 the Crown restored to the chapter lands and rents which had been appropriated, reserving an annual pension of £145; d. 1594.
44. Gervase Babington, 1595; tr. from Llandaff; surrendered manor of Crediton to Elizabeth; tr. to Worcester, 1597.
45. William Cotton, 1598; hostile to Puritanism and a rigorous exactor of conformity; d. 1621.
46. Valentine Carey, 1621; former Dean of St. Paul's; d. 1626.
47. Joseph Hall, 1627; tr. to Norwich, 1641.
48. Ralph Brownrigg, 1642; Master of the Temple; was never installed at Exeter; d. 1659.
49. John Gauden (*q.v.*). 1660.
50. Seth Ward (*q.v.*), 1662; former dean; tr. to Salisbury, 1667.
51. Anthony Sparrow, 1667; former Master of King's College, Cambridge; tr. to Norwich, 1676.
52. Thomas Lamplugh, 1676; tr. to York, 1688, as reward for loyalty to James II.; when established there he became an enthusiastic supporter of William of Orange.

53. Sir Jonathan Trelawny, Bart., 1689; tr. from Bristol; one of the Seven Bishops (*q.v.*); a supporter of the Revolution; tr. to Winchester, 1707.
54. Offspring Blackall, 1708; former chaplain to Queen Mary; an opponent of Hoadly (*q.v.*); d. (aged sixty-six) of a fall from his horse, 1716.
55. Launcelot Blackburn, 1717; former dean; tr. to York, 1724.
56. Stephen Weston, 1724; an excellent scholar and wise bishop; he introduced the custom of keeping the registers in English; d. 1742.
57. Nicholas Claggett, 1742; tr. from St. David's; d. 1746.
58. George Lavington, 1747; d. 1762.
59. Honble. Frederick Keppel, 1762; formerly Canon of Windsor; son of the second Earl of Albemarle; d. 1777.
60. John Ross, 1778; a Fellow of the Royal Society; d. 1792.
61. William Buller, 1792; formerly Dean of Canterbury; d. 1796.
62. Henry Reginald Courtenay, 1797; tr. from Bristol; d. 1803.
63. John Fisher, 1803; formerly Canon of Windsor and tutor to Princess Charlotte of Wales; tr. to Salisbury, 1807.
64. Honble. George Pelham, 1807; younger son of the first Earl of Chichester; tr. from Bristol; tr. to Lincoln, 1820.
65. William Carey, 1820; formerly Headmaster of Westminster; a strong and good bishop; tr. to St. Asaph, 1820.
66. Christopher Bethell, 1830; tr. from Gloucester; tr. to Bangor, 1830.
67. Henry Phillpotts (*q.v.*), 1831; d. 1869.
68. Frederick Temple (*q.v.*), 1869; tr. to London, 1885.
69. Edward Henry Bickersteth, 1885; a well-known composer of hymns; res. 1900; d. 1906.
70. Herbert Edward Ryle, 1901; tr. to Winchester, 1903; Dean of Westminster, 1911.
71. Archibald Robertson, 1903; formerly Fellow of Trinity College, Oxford, and Principal of King's College, London.

[E. C. M.]

Oliver, *Lives of the Bishops of Exeter* and *Ecclesiastical Antiquities of Devon*; Reynolds, *Ancient Diocese of Exeter*; Le Neve, *Fasti*; Hingeston-Randolph, *Episcopal Registers of the Bishops of Exeter*; Stubbs, *Registr. Sacr.*

F

FECKENHAM, John de, *alias* **Howman** (*c.* 1515-84), Abbot of Westminster, was one of the chief of the Marian ecclesiastics who survived into Elizabeth's reign, and, refusing to conform, were deprived of their positions and imprisoned. He was a monk at Evesham, and on the suppression of the monastery in 1540 returned to Oxford, where he had been educated; held the benefice of Solihull as a secular priest, and was chaplain to Bishop Bonner (*q.v.*). Under Edward he was involved in the bishop's disgrace, and spent some time in the Tower. At Mary's (*q.v.*) accession he was released and made Dean of St. Paul's. His power in preaching and disputation made him a prominent character in the ecclesiastical world. He sighed, however, for his monastery, and in 1556 he was entrusted with the task of restoring the convent at Westminster. This Benedictine refoundation was on the lines of the Italian congregation rather than on old English lines; but its career was short. Abbot Feckenham was one of the leading opponents of the Elizabethan changes both in Parliament and elsewhere; he and his monks were among the first to refuse the Oath of Supremacy, and they were thereupon ejected, 12th July 1559. The abbot himself after ten months was sent to prison, and passed nearly the whole of the remaining twenty-four years of his life in some sort of imprisonment or custody. He maintained to the last his reputation as a man not merely of ability, but of singular generosity both in matters of money and matters of belief. His controversy with Horne, Bishop of Winchester, when he was quartered upon him (1563), became historic; and it was probably in consequence of it that he was sent back to the worse durance of the Tower. After a short period of comparative liberty and three years spent with the Bishop of Ely, to their mutual discomfort, he was sent to Wisbeach Castle, newly become a special prison for recusants, where in 1584 he died. His life is a fine and faithful representation of the vicissitudes and hardships of those who could not fall in with the English Reformation.   [W. H. F.]

Taunton, *English Black Monks,* t. c. ix.

FELL, John (1625-86), was one of the most notable of the militant clergy of the seventeenth century. He was son of Dr. Samuel Fell, Dean of Christ Church, and became a Student of that house when he was only eleven, taking the degree of M.A. when he was fifteen. He was in arms for the King, lost his Studentship, was ordained, and remained in Oxford during the Commonwealth. He lived in Beam Hall, opposite Merton College, and there kept up the services of the Church, with Dolben and Allestree (there is at Christ Church a famous picture of the three). At the Restoration he became canon, 27th July, and dean, 30th November 1660, of Christ Church, and quickly restored both cathedral and college to conformity. He was, says Anthony Wood, 'the most zealous man of his time for the Church of England, and none that I yet know of did go beyond him in the performance of the rules belonging thereto'; and Burnet, who first came to know him in 1663, said that he and Allestree 'were two of the devoutest men I saw in England: they were much mortified to the world and fasted and prayed much' (original form of his *History,* published by Miss Foxcroft in 1902). He did much building at Christ Church, including 'Tom Tower,' much for University discipline, much for the University Press, and was a generous patron of scholars. In 1675 he was made Bishop of Oxford, retaining the deanery and the mastership of St. Oswald's, Gloucester. He rebuilt the bishop's house at Cuddesdon, expelled Locke (by James II.'s order) from his Studentship, and died in 1686. He was a learned scholar, editing St. Cyprian and many other ancients; he was also a writer and editor of books of devotion; his friend Allestree probably wrote *The Whole Duty of Man.* But Anthony Wood shows that the opinion expressed in the well-known epigram was not peculiar to its writer.   [W. H. H.]

Wood, *Athenae Oxonienses*; Evelyn, *Diary.*

FERRAR, Nicholas, born in London on 22nd February 1593, was the third son of Nicholas Ferrar, a rich East India merchant, and of Mary (born Woodnoth), his wife. Never was mother more truly the maker of a son, her life deserving its record almost as well as his. The family were all 'zealous lovers of the Church,' and Nicholas showed almost from his infancy a strong religious bent. He had early a great devotion to the Scriptures, and 'could repeat perfectly the history of his near kinsman, Bishop Ferrar' (*q.v.*) from Foxe; we must hope that this fact of kindred may harmonise with the rest of his character and thought, the lifelong affection of his delicate soul for that grisly classic. At Clare Hall, Cambridge, where he graduated in 1610, subsequently becoming Fellow, he was known as a serious and very charming person and as a scholar of rare gifts. But his health was always frail, and travel being prescribed for it he left England in the train of Elizabeth, the newly married Princess Palatine, apparently as secretary, and on retiring from her service wandered in Europe for several years, spending lengthened periods at Hamburg and afterwards at Padua, Venice, and Rome. On his return followed the remarkable episode of his employment in important public business connected with the Virginia Company; which exhibits this student and mystic in the light of a sagacious man of business, who came out of a dangerous undertaking the poorer, but with clean hands and a high reputation for capacity. In 1625 the main interest of his life begins. The outbreak of plague causing Mary Ferrar and her sons to leave their 'great house in the parish of St. Bennett Sherehogge in St. Sythe's Lane in London,' they sought refuge at the manor lately bought by her in Huntingdonshire, 'a very good air but a depopulated place.' They first saw Little Gidding in June of that year, and she, it seems, scarcely left it again save for the farewell visit to London, during which Nicholas, early on Trinity Sunday, 1626, was privately ordained deacon by Laud (*q.v.*) in Henry VII.'s Chapel. He never sought priest's orders. Friends in high life thought that by this step he threw away a career; others offered livings he did not want. The Ferrars returned quietly to their green Midland meadows; where the tiny church, now to become the centre of their lives, stood under the shadow of 'a fair house fairly seated'; there to create and develop a new thing in religious history. Here three generations, represented by the families of her son John and her daughter Susanna Collet, knelt nightly for Mary Ferrar's blessing, after a day spent in good deeds and in the devout practice of a ruled and ordered life of prayer and work. A picture, redolent of the seventeenth century, of their life, of themselves, and their servants, 'forty persons in all,' remains for us in John Ferrar's life of Nicholas, 'the soul that inspirited the whole family.' Nicholas Ferrar's attractive and elusive personality belongs emphatically to his own age. The 'exceeding dear Brother' of George Herbert; the ascetic contemplative, with his passion for feast and fast and

vigil, for lovely ritual and 'good and grave Cathedral music'; the eager restorer of impropriated tithe and glebe, is, doubtless, ancestor after the spirit of the Tractarians. His deed and word for the world meant the creation of a thing, which never has been seen save at Gidding. 'Mr. Ferrar's religious house' was not, according to the popular idea, a kind of convent, with Mary Collet as its first sister. It was no less than a new company of the life devout, which, drawing together 'the kindred points of heaven and home,' adapted to a definitely religious rule the uses of a large and varied family both of men and women. Its days, alive with busy charity, were ruled by two capable mothers, and fragrant with the wholesome joys, the innermost devotions, of a deeply united family. The 'Levite in his own house,' as Nicholas the deacon named himself, their spiritual head and director, a 'most dear and honoured father,' called his system of 'canonical hours' and 'particular praiers' 'the rule by which he ordered his family.' Beside him 'his good mother, the veritable foundress and governess of their religious life,' obeyed, with the sympathy of a perfect self-effacement, the child who had once obeyed her. Gidding of its nature needed two makers. The cloister asks the saint; the home is 'not a hearth, but a woman.' Every figure in the picture repays study: the two heads; the two vowed 'maiden sisters,' Mary and Anna—Nicholas's joy and 'ever his great care'; the younger Nicholas yielding up 'most cheerful' his life of splendid promise; the busy girls at their exquisite bookbinding that we still may handle, and their 'dressing of poor people's wounds'; the harassed King and the soldierly 'Palsgrave' visiting and envying.

That Gidding was in no merely picturesque sense but truly a 'religious house,' where a real and strenuous 'rule' of devotion and practice was strictly followed, is clear from the minute directions for it recorded in Nicholas's life; from the exquisite picture of the family procession to church in Lenton's letter; far more, from the evident fact that these busy men and women, who came and went, married and bore children, yet never returned to Gidding without instantly submitting themselves to the order of its hours and the guidance of its head. This ordered life did not cease with Nicholas's death in 1637. In 1646 the scurrilous tract called *The Arminian Nunnery*, having drawn Puritan attention to it, a raid was made on Gidding, before which the family fled, and much damage was done; but that they ventured back is evident from contemporary letters and also from specimens of their bookbinding. The house has now disappeared; but the calm little church, very much as it was, and still enshrining Ferrar's altar, lectern, and brass font, still stands, remote in 'a solitary wooded place' amid the rural landscape, 'a green thought in a green shade.' The grave of Nicholas is before its west door. It is a spot to attract the pilgrim. A final word must be given to Mr. Shorthouse's exquisite picture of Little Gidding in *John Inglesant.* It is unhappily somewhat inaccurate, and unwarranted liberties are taken with the real and fragrant life of that gentle saint, Mary Collet.   [M. J. H. S.]

Nicholas Ferrar (two lives), ed. Mayor, Camb., 1855; *Chron. of Peter Langtoft,* ed. T. Hearne, app. cxix. and cxxv.

FERRAR, Robert, Bishop of St. David's, a Yorkshireman, educated chiefly at Oxford, became an Augustinian Canon, but in 1528 was involved in a charge of heresy, and had to recant. After accompanying Barlow (*q.v.*) on an embassy to Scotland he became Prior of St. Oswald's, Nostell, near Pomfret, apparently to carry out the surrender, and then chaplain to Cranmer, whose example he followed by marrying. At the accession of Edward VI. he became chaplain to the Protector Somerset, who appointed him Bishop of St. David's by letters patent in 1548. At his consecration he took a new oath, 'very full and large,' renouncing the Pope and acknowledging the Royal Supremacy. On St. Martin's Day he preached at Paul's Cross, clothed 'not as a bishop but like a priest,' and 'spoke all manner of things against the Church and the Sacrament of the Altar, and against vestments, copes, altars, and all other things.' He was one of the few bishops who in Hooper's (*q.v.*) opinion 'entertained right opinions on the matter of the Eucharist.' But as Bishop of St. David's he refused to communicate after breaking his fast. In his diocese he met with great difficulties. The chapter, led by Thomas Yonge and Rowland Meyric, quickly made his position impossible; he was accused of not preaching and studying sufficiently, of sanctioning superstitious practices, of stirring up envy between Welsh and English, and more frivolously that 'he useth bridle with white studs and snaffle, with Scottish stirrups, with spurs, a Scottish pad with a little staff of three-quarters long'; that he whistled to 'a seal-fish tumbling' in Milford Haven; and that 'he daily useth whistling to his child and says he understood his whistle when he was but three days old.' On the fall of

Somerset—which, says Fuller (*q.v.*) shrewdly, was his chaplain's greatest fault—fifty-six formal complaints were laid before the Privy Council; in 1551 a commission was issued, and one hundred and twenty-seven witnesses were examined. Ferrar was kept in prison till Mary's accession, when he fared worse. In May 1554 he was deprived of his bishopric, and early in 1555 was roughly examined by Gardiner (*q.v.*), who charged him especially with the breach of his monastic vow, though Ferrar pleaded that his vow was to live chaste, not to live single. He was sent down to Carmarthen and tried before Morgan, his successor in the diocese; he declined to subscribe to articles 'invented and excogitated by men'; and was condemned and burnt on 30th March, 'on the South side of the market Cross.' 'His firmness and sufferings raised his character more than his conduct in his diocese'; he told a bystander that 'if he saw him once to stir in the pains of his burning he should then give no credit to his doctrine'; he bore his sufferings unflinchingly until he was struck down. A poor, feckless, contentious, but sincere man, he was, according to Fuller, 'not unlearned, but somewhat indiscreet or rather uncomplying, which procured him much trouble; so that he may be said, with St. Laurence, to be broiled on both sides, being persecuted both by Protestants and Papists.'   [F. M.]

Burnet, *Hist. of the Reformation*: Fuller, *Worthies of Eng.*; Foxe, *Acts and Monuments.*

FIELD, Richard (1561-1616), born at Hemel Hempstead, member of Magdalen Hall, and later of Queen's College, Oxford, and afterwards Lecturer of Lincoln's Inn, Rector of Burghclere, Prebendary of Windsor, and Dean of Gloucester. Recognised as a man of great learning during his lifetime, he is now chiefly remembered by his famous treatise, *Of the Church.* Of this work the first four books were published in 1606, the fifth in 1610; a considerably enlarged second edition was issued in 1628. It contains his permanent contribution to Anglican theology. He defines the Church as 'the multitude and number of those whom Almighty God severeth from the rest of the world by the work of His grace, and calleth to the participation of eternal happiness, by the knowledge of such supernatural verities as concerning their everlasting good He hath revealed in Christ His Son, and such other precious and happy means as He hath appointed to further and set forward the work of their salvation' (I. vi.). He regards the Church as being 'at the same time both visible and invisible in divers respects,' since it is visible 'in respect of the profession of supernatural verities revealed in Christ, use of holy sacraments, order of ministry, and due obedience yielded thereunto, and they discernible that do communicate therein,' and invisible 'in respect of those most precious effects and happy benefits of saving grace wherein only the elect do communicate' (I. x.). He describes the ' notes ' of the Church as three : (1) the complete profession of the revealed supernatural verities ; (2) the use of the appointed Christian ceremonies and sacraments ; and (3) the union of men in this profession and use under 'lawful pastors and guides, appointed, authorised, and sanctified ' (II. ii.). The ' power of ordination ' he ascribes to ' bishops alone,' so that ' no man may regularly do it without them '; but he adds that ' bishops and presbyters are in the power of order the same,' and that in an extreme case, such as the apostasy of ' the bishops of a whole Church or country,' the presbyters ' remaining Catholic ' might choose one of themselves as their chief, and with him continue to ordain (v. lvi.). He admits six, and with some reservations seven, Œcumenical Councils (v. li.). He allows a ' primacy of honour and order found in blessed Peter,' but sharply distinguishes this from the ' amplitude of power ' alleged by the Church of Rome (v. xxiii., xxiv.). He maintains that ' the whole Church (comprehending all the believers that are and have been since the apostles' time) ' is ' freed from error in matters of faith,' and that in matters of faith it is ' impossible also that any error whatsoever should be found in all the pastors and guides of the Church thus generally taken '; but that all might be deceived ' in things that cannot be clearly deduced from the rule of faith and word of divine and heavenly truth ' (IV. ii.). His antagonism to the Church of Rome, which he describes as ' the synagogue of Satan, the faction of antichrist, and that Babylon out of which we must fly unless we will be partakers of her plagues ' (Appendix, III. viii.), is extreme. He teaches that baptism is ' the ordinary and set means of salvation,' 'so that no man carelessly neglecting or wilfully contemning it can be saved,' and that Christians are ' justified, sanctified, and made the temple of the Holy Ghost,' and ' have the beginning, root, and seed of faith, hope, and love' ' when they are baptized ' (III. xxi., xliv.). Concerning the Eucharist, he held that the elements are changed in use at the consecration so as to signify and exhibit and contain and communicate the Body and Blood of Christ, and

that there is a sacrificial commemoration of Christ's passion and death like to the heavenly presentation of Himself to the Father by our Lord in heaven ; and though he denied that the Eucharist is a ' propitiatory sacrifice for the quick and the dead,' he thought that the mediæval canon of the Mass did not involve any doctrine contrary to that held in the Church of England since the Reformation (III. xxxviii., and Appendix). He denounces as ' an invention of their own ' the ' kind of absolution imagined by the papists ' ' giving grace ' and ' remitting sin,' and restricts the absolution, which is ' an apostolical and godly ordinance,' to freeing from censures and Church punishments, and ' the comfortable assuring of men upon the understanding of their estate that they shall escape God's fearful punishments ' (Appendix to III. xxiv.; Appendix, III. vii.). While rejecting Purgatory and ' the Romish manner of praying for the dead,' he affirms that prayer for the departed is in itself ancient and right (III. xvii.). Invocation of saints he repudiates as ' not known in the first ages of the Church ' (III. xx.). In the general theological position which has been illustrated above Field is very fairly representative of many post-Reformation Anglican divines.

[D. S.]

FISHER, John (d.1535), Bishop of Rochester, eldest son of a rich and devout mercer of Beverley, was educated probably at the Minster School and at Michael-House, Cambridge, where he graduated B.A., 1487; M.A., 1491; and became Fellow, and, 1497, Master. In 1494 he was Senior Proctor, and having business at court, won the esteem of the King's mother, Margaret, Countess of Richmond, who made him her confessor, 1497.

Fisher became Vice-Chancellor of his University, 1501, and began a thorough reformation, Cambridge being then poor and lifeless. The Lady Margaret generously furthered his plans, and by his advice founded Christ's and later St. John's Colleges, as well as the Divinity Lectureships and Preachership which still bear her name. Fisher (who became President of Queens', 1505-8) founded four Fellowships at St. John's, besides scholarships and Greek and Hebrew lectureships. It was due to his influence that Greek at Cambridge met with none of the opposition displayed towards it at Oxford; and he brought Erasmus to Cambridge. 1504 he was elected Chancellor of the University, and held the post for life. In the same year he was consecrated Bishop of Rochester. Henry VIII., in earlier life, was proud of him, and would say: ' No King in Christendom hath a bishop worthy to be compared with Rochester.'

He took no part in politics, save that, 1514, he went on an embassy to the Pope, and until the ' King's Business ' began, 1527, he was known chiefly as a very learned and holy student, secluded in his palace at Rochester. In July 1527 Wolsey (*q.v.*) sounded him as to the King's project to get rid of Katherine of Aragon, and found him firmly opposed. Fisher appeared at the legatine court (1529), handed in a book he had written against the King's plea ' to avoid the damnation of his soul and to prove himself not unfaithful to the King.' Henry attacked him with great scurrility, and marked him for ruin. Later in the year, Fisher in the House of Lords protested against the tendency of the Church legislation which emanated from the Commons, describing it as the result of a cry of ' Down with the Church,' which was due to ' lack of faith only.' He accepted the Supreme Headship, 1530, and the Submission of the Clergy, 1532. In 1530 he was nearly poisoned by his cook, it was thought at the instigation of the court. The unsuccessful poisoner was disavowed, and by a cruel and retrospective act was boiled alive (22 Hen. VIII. c. 9). In 1534 Henry accused Fisher, with five others, of misprision of treason (*i.e.* of not revealing matters politically dangerous) in connection with the half-crazy Elizabeth Barton, the Nun of Kent. His perfectly just plea, that he had not thought it necessary to reveal matters which the nun herself had told the King, availed nothing. Absent from the trial through illness, he was sentenced to imprisonment and forfeiture, but was subsequently fined £300. Three months later he refused to swear to the first Succession Act (25 Hen. VIII. c. 22), which entailed the crown on the issue of Anne Boleyn. He was willing to swear to the succession, but not to the preamble of the Act, which stated that the marriage with Katherine was contrary to the laws of God, and contained expressions contrary to his belief about the papal power. According to Chapuys, for two years Fisher had been urging the Emperor to invade England ; of this, however, the Government knew nothing (Pollard, *Henry VIII.*, 322, note 2, for references). He was condemned to death, 17th June 1535, under the Verbal Treasons Act (26 Hen. VIII. c. 13). His fate was sealed by the action of Paul III., who had created him cardinal a few weeks before. Fisher, who retained to the last the sturdy resolution of a Yorkshireman, made a very noble end, 22nd June 1535, calling his

execution ' his wedding day.' His body was buried in All Hallows, Barking ; his head, by Henry's order, was exposed on London Bridge. [S. L. O.]

Brewer, *Henry VIII.* : J. B. Mullinger in *D.N.B.* : Dixon, *Hist. of Ch. of Eng.* : Gairdner, *Hist. of Eng. Ch.*, 1485-1558, and *Lollardy and the Reformation.*

FOLIOT, Gilbert (d. 1188), Bishop of London, was born in England of a Norman family, and became a monk at Cluny, where he rose to be prior. He was thence transferred to Abbeville, and became Abbot of Gloucester in 1139. In 1148 he was made Bishop of Hereford, possibly through the influence of kindred in the district. He was probably by this time nearly forty years of age, and was renowned for his learning, activity, and austerity. He never took meat or wine. Already men began to say that he aspired to be archbishop. In 1161, however, he refused to administer the see of London during the infirmity of the bishop, Richard de Belmeis, and in 1162 he took a decided attitude of opposition to the election of Becket to Canterbury, declaring that he had been a persecutor of the Church and a destroyer of her goods. The Bishop of London died in the next year, and Foliot now accepted the see, though apparently with reluctance (28th April 1163). He was greatly in the favour of Henry II., and Becket warmly eulogised him. But a dispute at once broke out between them, for Foliot claimed that, as he had already vowed canonical obedience when he was consecrated to Hereford, he need not repeat the vow. Before long he extended this claim into one for actual independence, and a declaration that London was a metropolitan see. He took his claim back to Roman times, and based it on the political eminence of the city. John of Salisbury (*q.v.*) pointed out that this resort to pre-Christian times could not convince, and satirically accused him of being willing to be an arch-flamen as he could not be an archbishop. At Clarendon and again at Northampton he was strongly opposed to the archbishop [BECKET], endeavoured to take his cross from his hand, and told him that he always had been and always would be a fool. He was one of Henry's envoys to Alexander III., and was rebuked by the Pope at Sens for his intemperate language. During Becket's exile Henry gave him the diocese of Canterbury to administer, and he was charged with great severity against the archbishop's kindred and supporters and with allowing bribery by clergy wishing to marry. He continued to denounce Becket before the Pope and attack him in most vigorous letters. Becket was anxious to excommunicate him, but was restrained by the Pope till Whit Sunday, 1169. when the sentence was formally pronounced at Clairvaux. It was delivered by a French clerk named Beranger to the celebrant at High Mass in St. Paul's on Ascension Day. Foliot at once appealed to Rome, with his dean, archdeacon, canons, and parish priests. and at Michaelmas crossed the sea, with the King's licence, to prosecute the appeal in person. The Pope empowered the Bishop of Exeter and the Archbishop of Rouen to absolve him (Easter, 1170). On 14th June he joined in crowning Henry's son, in defiance of the rights of Canterbury. For this Becket on his reconciliation with Henry again excommunicated him, or rather replaced him under the sentence from which he regarded him as having been irregularly released. Foliot crossed to Normandy to entreat Henry's protection the same day that Becket returned to England (1st December 1170). Though he was not in any way responsible for the archbishop's murder he was not absolved till May 1172. He remained a close adviser of the King, and at his pilgrimage to Canterbury in 1174 preached a sermon declaring that Henry was in no way responsible for the crime. He remained prominent till his death in 1188, taking part in the elections of Archbishops Richard of Dover and Baldwin. He was undoubtedly an ambitious and stern man, and was much embittered by disappointment at the preferment of one whom he must have regarded as thoroughly secular, when he, who represented the most rigid monastic ideal, deserved (as he thought) the primatial throne. His bitter animosity to Becket coloured his whole later life. As a prelate he was exact in the discharge of his duties, but narrow and occasionally timeserving, as well as obscurantist.

[W. H. H.]

Materials for the Hist. of Becket, R.S.: Gilbert Foliot, *Epistolae* (Migne, *Patr. Lat.*, cxc.).

FOX, Richard (1447 or 1448-1528), Bishop of Winchester, was born at Ropesley, Lincolnshire. One tradition says his early education was at Boston Grammar School, another that he was a scholar of Winchester. He probably studied for a time at Magdalen College, Oxford. In any case, he passed on to the then greater opportunities of the University of Paris, and there took the degree of Doctor of Canon Law, and was ordained priest. At this time he became secretary to Henry, Earl of Richmond. His abilities at once made him notable among the adherents of the exiled prince, and Richard III. wrote to prevent his institution to the vicarage of Stepney on the ground that he was with that 'great rebel Henry ap Tuddor.' In 1485 Fox accompanied Henry to England, and was present at Bosworth Field. Henry at once appointed him principal Secretary of State and Keeper of the Privy Seal. For nearly thirty years Fox retained his great place in the counsels of the nation, an admirable example of the type of ecclesiastical statesmen which culminated and ended in Wolsey (*q.v.*). Passing rapidly from one bishopric to another, he was for a time content to administer the spiritual affairs of his diocese by deputy, while he devoted himself to the service of the State, and was constantly employed in the negotiation of treaties and other secular business. He retained his influence under Henry VIII. (*q.v.*), and was one of the commissioners who concluded the treaty with Louis XII. in 1510. The outbreak of the French war in 1513 marks the beginning of the rise of Wolsey, and from this time Fox gradually withdrew from public affairs to the spiritual care of his diocese and to the encouragement of learning. He resigned the Privy Seal in 1516, and died on 5th October 1528, having been blind for some years.

His most abiding work was the foundation of Corpus Christi College in Oxford, of which the first statutes are dated 1517. He was a man of liberal mind and a friend of all sound learning whether Old or New; and even in the busiest times of his life was zealous in his care for education, and maintained a connection with both the English Universities. At Cambridge he was Master of Pembroke in 1507 and afterwards Chancellor; at Oxford he was a benefactor of Magdalen, and assisted to draw up new statutes for Balliol, of which college he was elected Visitor in 1511.

As a builder Fox cannot compare with some of his great predecessors, and if the completion of King's Chapel at Cambridge was indeed his work, it is a striking contrast to the unpretending architecture of his own foundation at Oxford. His first care at Winchester was the roofing of the choir, in which his screen and chantry still bear his device, the Pelican, impaling the arms of his four sees: Exeter (1487-92), Bath and Wells (1492-4), Durham (1494-1501), and Winchester (1501-28).   [J. H. F. P.]

FOXE, John (1516-87), martyrologist. There is singularly little in the record of the early career of this famous writer that we can safely trust. A biography of him, erroneously believed to have been composed by one of his sons in the seventeenth century, seems, for the most part, little better than a romance. It is certain that he was born at Boston in Lincolnshire in 1516, and also that he went to Oxford, where he perhaps entered at Brasenose ; he became Fellow of Magdalen in 1539, graduated B.A. in 1537, M.A. 1543 ; declining to comply with college rules, he and five others resigned their fellowships. He then seems to have found employment as tutor with the Lucy family at Charlecote, where he married, 7th February 1547, Agnes Randall of Coventry. Shortly afterwards he went to London, where, it is said, he found it hard to make a living, and had to walk in St. Paul's, lean and starved, till some one came to him with a gift from the Duchess of Richmond. It is certain that he became tutor to the orphan sons of that lady's unhappy brother, the poet Surrey, and that he stayed with the family, mostly at Reigate, during the reign of Edward vi. In 1550 he was ordained deacon by Bishop Ridley (*q.v.*) in St. Paul's. He was not ordained priest till 1560 by Bishop Grindal (*q.v.*).

In 1554 the old Duke of Norfolk died, and his grandson Thomas, who had been Foxe's pupil, became duke. The times were inconvenient for a married clergyman, even if that were all, and Foxe fled to the Continent. He had already written and published some books in London, but he took abroad with him the MS. of a work which in 1554 he published at Strasburg—a Latin history of the Church from the times of Wyclif to A.D. 1500. This became afterwards the nucleus of a larger undertaking.

On the 3rd December 1554 he was at Frankfort, where he was one of seventeen (Knox and Bale being two of the others) who signed a reply to a letter from the English congregation at Strasburg deprecating unnecessary alterations in the last book of Common Prayer. This was virtually the beginning of those 'Troubles at Frankfort' which affected so deeply the English reformers in exile before the reign of Elizabeth, and laid the foundation of similar troubles in England all through that reign. [MARIAN EXILES.] When Knox and his adherents were driven out of Frankfort, Foxe withdrew with some of them to Basle, the rest going to Geneva. He reached Basle in November 1555, where he earned his bread as a reader for the press in the printing-office of Oporinus, who also befriended him in publishing his *Christus Triumphans* and in the great

project he had further in hand. For news had already come from England of the burnings of martyrs, which had begun in February 1555, continuing on to the end of Mary's reign, and Foxe obtained much intelligence, especially from his friend Grindal, as to the lives and fates of the sufferers. He remained at Basle for some months after Elizabeth's accession, seeing his great work (in its original Latin form) through the press, and he only left for England in October 1559.

This work had doubtless been a severe strain upon him, and lack of adequate funds must have increased the strain ; for his old pupil, the Duke of Norfolk, to whom it was dedicated, had for some time withheld pecuniary support, and Foxe wrote to him after his arrival in England that he was dying of hunger. The duke, on this appeal, at once ordered provision to be made for him, and when he came himself to London received him into his house at Aldgate. Here he turned the great work into an English form, and saw the first edition of the *Acts and Monuments* through the press of John Day in 1563. Criticism came slowly. The very magnitude of the huge folio made it difficult to handle with care, while the letter-press, with the appalling woodcuts of martyrs enveloped in the flames, served sufficiently the grand purpose of filling superficial readers with a deep detestation of Rome. Answers, moreover, could only be printed abroad, and the first was the *Sex Dialogi* of Harpsfield, which appeared under the name of Alan Cope at Antwerp in 1566. But in England Foxe's work won the esteem naturally due to a great undertaking fully carried out, and in 1571 Convocation ordered that every bishop should have a copy in his house. It was also chained to desks in many parish churches for general perusal. It was doubtless all the more popular after the papal excommunication of Queen Elizabeth in 1570. That year, though, being in feeble health, he felt scarcely equal to the task, he was called on to preach a Good Friday sermon at Paul's Cross on the 24th March, which was not only printed at the time but reprinted several times in later years.

On the 2nd June 1572 he had the painful duty of attending his old pupil, the Duke of Norfolk, at his execution on Tower Hill. The duke left him a pension of £20, which was continued by his son. Of Foxe's later years the most conspicuous incidents are his ineffectual intercession for two Dutch Anabaptists condemned to the flames in 1575, and his sermon on the conversion of a

Spanish Jew in 1577. We would also gladly believe his anonymous biographer, who says that he wrote many letters to influential persons to prevent Campion being put to death in 1581. Foxe died in London on the 18th April 1587, and his tomb is still to be seen in Cripplegate Church. His *Acts and Monuments* was republished three times before his death, in 1570, 1576, and 1583. A fifth edition appeared in 1596-7, and there have been many since. Of his other works not yet mentioned, the most notable was his completion of Haddon's answer to the Portuguese Jesuit Osorius.

To form any estimate of Foxe as a historian it is necessary to consider his general conception of church history. He dated the chief corruptions of Christianity from 'the loosing out of Satan, which was about the thousandth year after the Nativity of Christ.' From that time in about four hundred years sound doctrine and purity of life were almost extinguished until they were revived by Wyclif and Huss. Following these were abundant martyrs for the truth, and, generally speaking, all whom 'the Pope's Church' condemned as heretics were such martyrs. The fact that though opposed to the Church they differed vitally on doctrines of high importance did not prevent Foxe placing their names in a new martyrology; and the industry with which he collected information was amazing. Some of his mistakes were ludicrous, especially about Grimwood of Hitcham, whom he not only accused of swearing away a man's life on a false charge of treason, but represented to have been visited for so doing by an awful judgment in a sudden and quite impossible kind of death, his bowels falling out of his body. Grimwood, however, was actually alive when Foxe wrote, and many years afterwards, hearing this strange story about himself related from the pulpit as a warning against perjury, brought an action against the parson for slander. Yet really, considering the size of the work and the credulity of the author (who, by the statement of a contemporary, was given to strange delusions about himself), positive errors are few in the *Acts and Monuments*. It is rather that the facts are generally discoloured. But when we have made allowance for the bias with which it was written, the information in the book is full and valuable.

It is strange that even about Foxe's life we are left so much in the dark. For no trustworthy memoir was ever written, and almost all the facts which can be safely stated are derived from documents, for which see Sir S. Lee's notice of him in *D.N.B.*

[J. G.]

FRASER, James (1818-85), Bishop of Manchester, was educated at Shrewsbury and Lincoln College, Oxford, and became Fellow of Oriel in 1840. His work as Assistant Commissioner to the Education Commission (1858) and in similar capacities induced Mr. Gladstone (*q.v.*) in 1870 to offer him the bishopric of Manchester, a centre of the religious education controversy, upon which Fraser's views were in accordance with the Act of that year. He quickly proved himself a hard-working bishop. 'Striding about his diocese on foot, carrying his own blue bag containing his robes, stopping runaway carts, and talking familiarly with every one he met,' he took the diocese by storm. He addressed meetings of railwaymen, actors, cab-drivers, medical students, slaughtermen, and others, interested himself in social questions, and was arbitrator in more than one trade dispute. He married in 1880.

Fraser professed himself a churchman of the school of Hooker, but his broad sympathies did not include a toleration of so-called 'extreme' High Churchmen, though they won him the title of 'bishop of all denominations.' He refused preferment to a clergyman of whose belief in the deity of Christ he was not satisfied. In 1879 he allowed proceedings to be taken under the Public Worship Regulation Act (*q.v.*) against S. F. Green, Rector of St. John's, Miles Platting. Mr. Green conscientiously disregarded the judgment of Lord Penzance, and his imprisonment in Lancaster Castle caused much scandal and distress. He refused to purchase his release by any recognition of the jurisdiction under which he had been condemned. Eventually his living became vacant by lapse, and in 1882 he was discharged on Fraser's application, after an imprisonment of nineteen months. As the priest presented to the vacant living declined to modify the ceremonial, Fraser refused to institute him, and successfully defended legal proceedings brought to compel him to do so. [RITUAL CASES.]

[G. C.]

Hughes, *Memoir*; Diggle, *Bishop Fraser's Lancashire Life*. For the Miles Platting case see *Dean v. Green* (8 P.D. 79); *Heywood v. Bishop of Manchester* (12 Q.B.D. 404; *Eccl. Courts Commission*, evidence 5710 6020, 6205-51, 7704-92.

FRIARS, The, represent one side of the great revival of religion in the thirteenth century, with its earnestness and democracy. The monks had for object the cultivation of religion as a corporate life ; the friars aimed at renouncing worldliness and at helping others.

1. The Franciscans followed the rule of St. Francis: absolute poverty, living upon alms (mendicancy), and the relief, spiritual and bodily, of distress. Although living as mendicants they soon needed central habitations, which at first were of a rough kind in poor parts of towns (thus the rafters for their Cambridge chapel were set up by one man in a day). Later on their buildings became larger, and even magnificent, and caused criticism. The Franciscans (or Friars Minor, Minorites, Greyfriars) were authorised in 1210, their new rule in 1223. The Second Order of St. Francis, intended for women (Poor Clares), and the Friars of Penitence, or Third Order (Tertiaries), increased the popularity and use of the Order. They came to England (1224) (London, Stinking Lane ; York, Bristol, Lynn, Cambridge, etc.) as missionaries living simple lives, not open to the reproach of wealth like the secular (parish) clergy and the monks, they quickly became popular and influential. As the social condition of the towns—where the Franciscans first settled—improved, the Order became wealthier. The pathetic interest of the founder's life belongs to his Order also. But in carrying the Gospel to men they had to seek and to give training—hence we find them at the Universities ; their care for the sick and lepers turned them to natural science. Before the thirteenth century was over they had great power at the Universities (at Oxford, Grosseteste (q.v.) as chancellor favoured them), and were foremost in science (e.g. Roger Bacon). This, although inevitable, was a departure from the founder's rule, which had forbidden them books. At Oxford a long struggle began against them, in which Fitz-Ralph, Archbishop of Armagh, bore part, and on this much academic history hinges. They tried to get freedom for their own teaching, and then to gain control of the University, and met with resistance. At Cambridge they gained the privilege of lecturing in their own halls to their own students. Like the Dominicans, in reviving religion they revived learning also.

2. The Dominicans (Friars Preachers; from their black cloak over white habit called Black Friars), founded by St. Dominic for the conversion of the Albigenses, and authorised by Honorius III. in 1216 for preaching, became a mendicant order (1220), but kept much of their former organisation as canons, and were less democratic than the Francis-

cans. Gregory IX. (1233) used them largely for the newly introduced Inquisition. England was made (1221) one of the eight provinces, and after a visit to Canterbury the first Dominicans in England settled at Oxford, where they gained great influence, and whence they spread rapidly. Their intellectual energy was great, especially in formal theology. These two leading Orders were part of the rich life of the thirteenth century, but the same energy and the same attempt to meet the conditions of the day which produced them was also seen in other ways.

3. The Carmelites, founded on Mount Carmel (1156), came to Europe (1240) at the time of these new mendicant orders, and gave up their hermit life for a community life as mendicants (from their white cloak over a brown habit called White Friars).

4. There were many congregations of hermits under the Augustinian rule [RELIGIOUS ORDERS], especially since the twelfth century. These were joined by Alexander IV. (1256): marked by a black habit.

5. There were other lesser Orders, such as the Servites, the Crutched Friars (from a red cross on their dress), the Brethren of the Sack (from their coarse dress), who came to London (1257), and others. The formation of new Orders was forbidden (1215), and (1274) only the four great Orders were allowed to receive new members, although the latter decree was not enforced. Papal policy towards the friars varied in the Middle Ages much as it did centuries later towards the Jesuits.

The friars had great effect upon social and intellectual life. As popular mission preachers they went everywhere, and from this and their hearing confessions generally—under papal encouragement given first to Dominicans and Franciscans, then to other mendicants—friction arose with parish priests. They were accused of a share in the Peasants' Revolt, and complaints were made of their over-much begging. (The ' limitours ' were so called from their begging within a limited district.) There were jealousies among the orders, as described in Piers Plowman's Creed. But for their usefulness Peckham (q.v.), himself a friar, and Grosseteste encouraged them. Boniface VIII. restricted their preaching without leave from parish priests, but the old quarrel remained. It was easy to satirise them, but their popularity—as shown by bequests—continued down to the Reformation. Their defenders, e.g. Aquinas, interpreted poverty to apply to the individual not to the Order.

On the intellectual side the Franciscans

and Dominicans furnished the leading school-men, many of whom were English. Alex-ander Hales (1245) from Gloucestershire, Bonaventura (1274), Duns Scotus (*q.v.*), William Ockham (*q.v.*) from Surrey, were Franciscans. Albertus Magnus, a German, St. Thomas Aquinas, were Dominicans. The Franciscans for the most part were Realist in their philosophy, but the Dominicans followed Aquinas; hence the difference between Scotists and Thomists (followers of Scotus and Aquinas) was partly a difference between the two great Orders.

A division among the Franciscans between the advocates for the strict rule and for relaxation went on—like the quarrel between Franciscans and Dominicans—through the Middle Ages. The second Franciscan general, Elias of Cortona, relaxed the rule, and dissensions began. These parties were called respectively Observants and Community brethren. The English Franciscans were (1230) for strictness when those on the Continent were for laxity. Many Franciscans who were eager for poverty followed the Apocalyptic views of Abbot Joachim, looking for a speedy earthly kingdom of God. These were the 'Spiritual Franciscans,' often at conflict with authorities and popular with the masses. Some of the more extreme of these separated themselves and, as Fraticelli, formed a heretical sect. John XXII., by condemning the popular Franciscan view that our Lord and the apostles had no property, but lived on alms, came into conflict with the Order (1322). The Franciscans then supported the Emperor Lewis the Bavarian in his struggle with the Pope, and William Ockham and Marsiglio of Padua, by their controversial writings in support of the Emperor, laid the foundations of a new mediæval political school. Their writings, both on the political and the philosophical side, greatly affected English thinkers—notably Wyclif (*q.v.*), who, it is worth noting, remained friendly with the Franciscans after his quarrel with the monks, and expected some of them to join him. In 1515 the Franciscan Warden in London (Standish) defended the citizens for their attacks on foreigners, and also strongly advocated the royal power against the ecclesiastical—a striking proof of the democratic and political tendencies of the Order. At the time of the Dissolution of the Monasteries the Franciscan Observants (a strict and reformed branch founded by St. Bernardino of Siena, introduced into England by Henry VII.), especially those at Greenwich, were treated with great cruelty. They had become the fashionable court order. At the suppression there were

60 Franciscan houses, 53 Dominican, 42 Austin, 36 Carmelite; with the other lesser Orders, about 200 friaries in all, and probably about 1800 friars. (Gasquet's estimate in *Henry VIII. and the English Monasteries,* vol. II. chap. vii.).   [J. P. W.]

Best general account in Heimbucher, *Die Orden und Kongregationen der katholische Kirche,* vol. ii. (1907). On English Franciscans best account is *Tractatus Fr. Thomæ de Ecclestun,* ed. A. G. Little (Paris, 1909). For St. Francis, see *Eng. Hist. Rev., passim ;* Brewer, *Monumenta Franciscana,* R.S.; Helyot. *Hist. des Ordres Monastiques;* Jessopp, *Coming of the Friars ;* Capes, *Hist of Eng. Ch. in Fourteenth and Fifteenth Centuries,* chap. xv.

FRIDESWIDE, St. (d. *c.* 735), virgin and abbess, is said to have been daughter of a Mercian king or under-king ruling at Oxford. She took a vow of virginity, and when wooed by a neighbouring king took refuge in a pigsty. Her suitor on approaching Oxford was smitten with blindness, but, according to one writer, his sight was restored at her prayer. Returning to Oxford, she was met by a leper, who was healed by her kiss. She founded a convent at Oxford, became its abbess, and died there.

Many of the legends of St. Frideswide are the common property of hagiology, and the earliest extant lives of her date from the twelfth century. But there is no reason to doubt her existence, and her foundation of a religious house in or near Oxford, probably at Binsey. The monastery bearing her name is known to have existed during the Danish wars. At the Domesday survey it was occupied by secular canons, who were replaced by regulars (Austin Canons) early in the twelfth century. Her relics were translated in 1180, from which time she was regarded as the patron saint of the City and University of Oxford. In 1434 Archbishop Chichele (*q.v.*) ordered her festival, 19th October, the traditional date of her death, to be observed as that of the special patroness of the University (Wilkins, *Conc.,* iii. 524). Her shrine (which was again removed in 1289) became a centre of devotion, and received many rich gifts. It was plundered in 1538, and in 1552 Peter Martyr's (*q.v.*) wife was buried in or near it. In 1557 these bones were removed by Dean Marshall at the orders of Cardinal Pole (*q.v.*) and buried in a dunghill. After Elizabeth's accession they were restored and mingled with those of Frideswide under the epitaph *Hic requiescit religio cum superstitione.* In 1525 her monastery had been suppressed by Wolsey (*q.v.*), who replaced it by a college built on the same site, and known as 'Cardinal College.' After his fall this was refounded by Henry VIII., and in 1546 its church became the cathedral of the new diocese of Oxford, with the title of Christ Church. Churches are dedicated to St. Frideswide in Oxford, at Frilsham (Berks), at the Christ Church (Oxford) Mission in Poplar, and, under the name of St. Fréwisse, at Borny, near Boulogne. Her festival still retains its place in the Oxford University Calendar, though it disappeared from that of the English Church in 1549.   [G. C.]

Parker, *Early Hist. of Oxford*; Wood, *City of Oxford*; Foxe, *Acts and Monuments*, ed. 1868, viii. 296.

FRITH, John (1503-33), martyr, was a victim of the evil cross-currents, political and theological, that arose out of Henry VIII.'s secret encouragement of heresy in his desire to marry Anne Boleyn. He seems to have been born in 1503. He studied at King's College, Cambridge, where Stephen Gardiner (*q.v.*) was his tutor. He graduated B.A. in 1525, and being a precocious young divine was immediately called by Wolsey (*q.v.*) to Oxford, and made a Fellow of his new college there. He was one of a number of that college who were committed to custody in 1528 on a charge of heresy. Four of the prisoners died, apparently from the unwholesome conditions of an underground prison, and Frith and the others were released on condition that they would not go farther than ten miles from Oxford. Frith, however, escaped beyond sea. Returning two years later, he was put in the stocks at Reading; but giving evidence of scholarship to the schoolmaster, he was released. He had been seeking out the Prior of Reading, a large purchaser of heretical books, with whom, apparently, he went abroad again, as Sir Thomas More (*q.v.*) was now Lord Chancellor and bent on prosecuting heretics. He was in Holland, a newly married man, in the spring of 1531; but he returned to England once more in July 1532, lured by the King, who at this time felt that heretics might be useful to him, however much his Chancellor was against them. He ventured even to write and circulate in MS. a book against the Real Presence in the Eucharist, of which Sir Thomas More obtained two copies. He was seized and lodged in the Tower, not for punishment but rather for his security, and was not loaded with irons. Tyndale (*q.v.*) wrote him a sympathetic letter from abroad, urging him to be wary in disclosing his mind, lest it should create division among those opposed to the papacy; for Dr. Barnes in England,

like his master, Luther, would be hot against him if he denied the Real Presence. He should treat that subject as an open one. And this was the line he actually took when examined upon the subject. He was examined on the 20th June 1533 both upon Purgatory and on the Eucharist by Stokesley, Bishop of London, and others at St. Paul's. His old tutor, Gardiner, now a bishop, did his utmost to show him that his views were erroneous, even after sentence was passed on him as a heretic, but to no effect. He and a disciple of his named Andrew Hewet, a tailor's apprentice, were burned at Smithfield, 4th July 1533. His writings, some of them anonymous or pseudonymous, are rather numerous for so young a man, and mostly controversial.

[J. G.]

FROUDE, Richard Hurrell (1803-36), priest and author, eldest son of R. H. Froude, Archdeacon of Totnes, was educated at Ottery and Eton. He entered Oriel College, Oxford, 1821, and gained a double Second Class (Classics and Mathematics), 1824. He became Fellow, 1826 (with R. I. Wilberforce, *q.v.*), and Tutor, 1827. As an undergraduate he was pupil of John Keble (*q.v.*), and was his devoted friend, learning his High Churchmanship from him. He came to know J. H. Newman (*q.v.*) well, 1828-9, when they were Tutors together, but was shy of him at first. He wrote (7th September 1828): 'Newman is a fellow that I like more. the more I think of him; only I would give a few odd pence if he were not a heretic.' He brought Newman to know Keble; from that friendship the Oxford Movement (*q.v.*) sprang. Froude realised the importance of the act, and said, with death in prospect: 'Do you know the story of the murderer who had done one good thing in his life? Well, if I was ever asked what good deed I have ever done, I should say I had brought Newman and Keble to understand one another.' Froude, together with his colleagues, resigned his Tutorship in 1830 owing to their differences with the Provost (Dr. Hawkins). Froude was ordained deacon, 1828; priest, 1829. He spent the winter of 1832-3 in Southern Europe, accompanied most of the time by Newman. At Rome with Newman he began the *Lyra Apostolica*; his poems are initialled β, and are of great beauty. He took part in the formal beginning of the Movement at the conference at Hadleigh [ROSE, H. J.], July 1833. He was in the West Indies for his health, November 1833 to May 1835, lecturing for some months at Codrington College,

Barbados. He died of consumption at Dartington, 28th February 1836.

Froude was an enthusiastic English Catholic ; he reverenced the Caroline divines (*q.v.*) and the Nonjurors (*q.v.*). He was drawn strongly to the mediæval Church, and disliked the sixteenth-century reformers; his strictures upon them first began the historical criticism of the English Reformation, but horrified the British public at the time. He believed in the celibacy of the clergy, and had a deep devotion to the Real Presence and reverence for the Blessed Virgin. Yet he felt deep disgust at Roman Catholicism as he saw it abroad, and thought its followers 'wretched Tridentines.' He was a brilliant talker, a bold rider, a daring sailor, and a very handsome and gallant figure. There was about him 'an awful reality of devotion,' and probably his merciless self-discipline hastened his death. ' No one,' Dean Church thinks, ' ever occupied Froude's place in Newman's heart.' The publication of his *Remains*, Part I. (2 vols., 1838), edited by Keble and Newman, in which his strong expressions about the Reformers and injudicious extracts from his journal were printed, caused a storm. Part II. (2 vols., 1839) contains various essays and his history of Archbishop Becket. It was arranged and prepared for publication by J. B. Mozley (*q.v.*).   [s. l. o.]

Remains, Part I., 1838 ; Church, *Oxford Movement* : Newman, *Apologia* : L. I. Guiney, *R. H. Froude*.

FULLER, Thomas (1608-61), Church historian, entered Queens' College, Cambridge, when just thirteen, graduated B.A., 1624 ; M.A., 1628, and was appointed by his uncle, Bishop Davenant (*q.v.*), to a prebend at Salisbury, 1631 ; Rector of Broadwindsor, 1634. As proctor in Convocation (*q.v.*), 1640, he opposed its continuance after the dissolution of Parliament. In 1641, though not formally sequestered, he relinquished his preferments, became curate at the Savoy Chapel, London, and used his influence as a popular preacher in the cause of peace. In 1643 he retired to Oxford, where his advocacy of conciliation brought him into disfavour, though not, it would seem, with Charles I. (*q.v.*), before whom he preached a remarkable sermon on Jacob's vow, in reference to the King's promise to restore his abbey lands to the Church. He was in Exeter as chaplain to the infant Princess Henrietta at its surrender, 1646. Under the Commonwealth he lived unmolested, owing to influential friends, of whom the Earl of Carlisle presented him to the living of Waltham Abbey (*c.* 1649), and Earl Berkeley to that of Cranford, 1658. Though a ' stout Church-and-King man ' Fuller had not the martyr's temperament, and his ingrained moderation and easy good-nature lend some colour to Heylyn's (*q.v.*) accusation of complying with the times, and South's (*q.v.*) picture of him with his big book under one arm and his little wife under the other, running after his patrons for invitations to dinner in exchange for the dull jests of his conversation. To such attacks he replied with dignity and good humour, maintaining that his was a ' sinless compliance ' without compromise of principle. At the Restoration he returned to his prebend, but refused to disturb the minister in possession at Broadwindsor.

As a historian Fuller is prejudiced and uncritical, but his quaint felicity of style, continual flow of wit, and easy, vivacious narrative have won him a reputation among English prose writers only below the highest. His marvellous memory caused his earliest biographer to style him 'a perfect walking library.' His chief works are *The Church History of Britain*, 1655 ; *The Worthies of England*, 1662, and numerous volumes of sermons and quasi-devotional moralisings.

[g. c.]

Works: anonymous *Life*, 1661 : modern *Lives* by J. E. Bailey and J. M. Fuller.

G

GARDINER, Stephen (1493 ? - 1555), Bishop of Winchester, was born at Bury St. Edmunds perhaps in 1493. The date commonly given, 1483, is impossible, but may be a misreading of some inscription. Many stories of his parentage and early years are fabulous. He was the eldest son of John Gardiner, a substantial cloth merchant of Bury, and was educated mostly at Cambridge. But in the year 1511, perhaps before he went to that University, he visited Paris as one of a certain Mr. Eden's household, and there, as appears in a letter which he wrote to Erasmus in 1527, he met the great Dutch scholar, and dressed him some salads in a way that particularly pleased his palate.

Returning home, and pursuing his studies at Cambridge, he became a doctor of civil law in 1520, and of canon law next year. Leland says that he gave new vigour to the study of law at Cambridge, clearing it from a mass of obsolete pedantries; and also that he set on the stage the comedies of Plautus, or one of them at least. He himself refers to this in a letter of much later date to Sir William Paget (who was his early pupil), reminding him of a time when they both took parts in a performance of the *Miles Gloriosus*. In 1526 we find him acting, along with two bishops, the Abbot of Westminster and others, under a commission from Wolsey (*q.v.*) as legate, for the examination of certain German heretics. In 1527 he is designated as Archdeacon of Taunton in a treaty made with Francis I., in which he and Sir Thomas More (*q.v.*) were commissioners, to act in conjunction with two Frenchmen. Just before this, in May, he had been present at the secret proceedings by which it was first proposed to inquire into the validity of Henry VIII.'s marriage with Katherine of Aragon. In July he went into France with his master, Wolsey (*q.v.*), who on his return found that the King had been seeking to attain his object at Rome without his instrumentality. Henry found out his mistake, and was obliged once more to trust everything to the cardinal, who in 1528 despatched Gardiner, then his secretary, and Edward Foxe to the Pope. They were to procure the sending of Cardinal Campeggio (*q.v.*) to England with a decretal commission to enable him and Wolsey to determine the question of the validity of the King's marriage. This was a peculiar demand, and taxed Gardiner's ingenuity to the utmost to procure it, backed up by strong letters from Wolsey as to the extreme importance of the concession. The envoys took the Pope at a disadvantage, for he was not then at Rome, having escaped in December from durance in the castle of St. Angelo, and they found him in the dilapidated city of Orvieto (*Urbs Vetus*, as Gardiner said it was truly called), where hunger, bad lodgings, and ill air kept him as much a prisoner as ever. But Clement, in a bishop's palace, with ante-rooms 'all un-hanged' and the roofs fallen down, was not to be overcome by circumstances. Gardiner did his best, and the mission of Campeggio was conceded; but he was obliged, even after much insistence, to accept only a general commission instead of a decretal one. Wolsey saw that this was insufficient, and urged Gardiner to press the Pope still further, in a way that was indeed quite improper, till the Pope at length yielded to what was orally demanded, and no more, with some special precautions against abuse.

In this bad business Gardiner had done his best as a lawyer for a client; and the King, taking him from Wolsey's service, made him his own secretary. In 1530 the King sent him to Cambridge to obtain opinions against the lawfulness of marriage with a brother's widow, which he did, not without some amount of artifice. In May he was among the learned convoked to de-nounce Tyndale's (*q.v.*) books, and in July, as a doctor, he signed the letter of the lords to Clement VII. urging him to give a speedy de-cision in the King's favour. His old master, Wolsey, was by this time in disgrace, and relied much on Gardiner's intercession with the King, which in some small ways was effectual, but not as regards the cardinal's colleges, on the erection of which he had bestowed so much thought and expense. In 1531 the King gave Gardiner the bishopric of Winchester, telling him that he had often ' squared ' with him, but loved him none the worse—a fine evidence both of Gardiner's freedom of judgment and Henry's appre-ciation of good service. Gardiner was now sent on a mission to France to cultivate closer relations with Francis I. and counteract the Emperor's influence at Rome. On his return in 1532, being a bishop, he took undoubtedly the main part in drawing up ' the Answer of the Ordinaries,' which he knew could not be acceptable to the King. But the ' Submission of the Clergy ' ended their opposition to the Crown.

Henry continued all his days to use Gardiner's services, which he valued highly, in embassies and otherwise. But in April 1534 the more subservient Thomas Cromwell (*q.v.*) supplanted him as the King's secretary. Under Royal Supremacy Churchmen no longer ruled, and Gardiner, against the grain, took the oath of supremacy, like other bishops, in 1535. He also, like the other bishops, wrote a treatise to vindicate the doctrine, which at the time he no doubt considered defensible, though he regretted his action afterwards. But he soon found himself driven to a more un-gracious task. For he was set to compose an answer to a papal brief in which Paul III. declared to Francis I. his intention to deprive Henry of his kingdom; and such an answer involved a vindication of the executions of Fisher and More as traitors. It seems, how-ever, to have been meant only for diplomatic use, not to be shown unless needed. Gardiner himself was sent to France to use personal arguments with Francis, and engage him in a common opposition with Henry alike to the Pope, the Emperor, and a proposed General Council. While on this embassy his opinion was asked in 1536 about a political alliance between Henry VIII. and the Lutheran princes of Germany, which he strongly dissuaded, though he did not object to their being subsidised by the King. He remained abroad three years, and in 1539, a year after his return, though Cromwell had got him excluded from the Council, his influence was increasing. Next year Dr. Barnes, being allowed to preach at Paul's Cross, brought himself into trouble by insulting Gardiner. For Cromwell, on whose support the Protestant preachers relied, was now tottering to his fall.

In November 1540 Gardiner was sent to Charles V. in the Low Countries, and followed him into Germany. The fall of Cromwell and the divorce of Anne of Cleves had smoothed the way for a better understanding with the Emperor. But Charles was then more intent on arriving at an understanding with the Protestants at the diet at Ratisbon; and it was really to prevent his doing so that Henry had sent Gardiner thither as a strong opponent of Lutheran theology. So Gardiner's mission was not acceptable, and met with some hindrances. But it was impossible to shake him off, except on the plea that he was the emissary of a heretical King who had divorced the Emperor's aunt, Katherine of Aragon, despised the Pope's authority, and even now showed no desire to be reconciled to the Holy See. When Granvelle met him with these reproaches Gardiner had some difficulty in answering them. He laid the blame of the past on Cromwell, but said it was a capital offence for an Englishman to talk of reconciliation with Rome. This was quite true; but it was no less true that if the Protestants, who were disgusted at the divorce of Anne of Cleves, became loyal to the Emperor, Henry had not a friend upon the Continent. Charles, however, could not rely on the Protestants, and Granvelle assured Gardiner that he was willing to intercede for his master with the Pope. And such was Henry's feeling of insecurity at the time that he actually instructed Gardiner to thank Granvelle for an offer of mediation conveyed through the Imperial ambassador in England.

This very private matter led to an incident, which was the source of much gossip, and was remembered long to Gardiner's disadvantage by men who did not understand the circumstances. It became known that Gardiner had actually received a letter from the Pope

at Ratisbon, and people thought that he would be put to death as soon as he came home. But Henry knew the value of his services, and received him very well. In England while he was away a great change had been made in his cathedral, which was converted from a monastic into a secular foundation with a dean and twelve prebendaries. At Canterbury, where he first heard Mass after landing, a similar change had taken place, and on inquiring about the new establishment he found that the prebendaries did not agree. One of them, a namesake of his own, told him men got into more trouble by opposing heresy than by promoting it.

In the Convocation of 1542, which condemned the use of the Great Bible, Gardiner took a prominent part, and gave in a list of a hundred words and phrases which he considered ought to be retained in translation in a form as near the Latin as might be. But the King put an end to the revision project indirectly, and gave Anthony Marlar sole authority to print the Bible in English for four years. In the same year Gardiner, as Chancellor of the University of Cambridge, condemned the new system of pronouncing Greek that had been introduced by John Cheke (q.v.) and Thomas Smith.

Near the end of Henry's reign he was with the Emperor again, negotiating the treaty of Utrecht, which was concluded on the 16th January 1546, to define more closely the mutual relations of the two sovereigns in the event of joint hostilities against France. While on this embassy he made his influence felt at home, warning Henry that it would be fatal to the treaty to adopt certain reforms on which Cranmer was bent, pulling down roods in the churches, and suppressing the ringing of bells on All-Hallows' night. As a diplomatist it is clear that his services were highly valued by Henry to the last; yet he was not named in the King's will. It is said that when some expected that he would have been included among the executors, the King distinctly refused, for a reason that was certainly characteristic. 'Marry,' he said, 'I myself could use him and rule him to all manner of purposes as seemed good unto me; but so shall you never do.' The ecclesiastical revolution which Gardiner would have opposed had gone too far to be repressed; and as it was clear that in the coming reign Church matters must go on under Cranmer as archbishop, the presence of Gardiner in any high councils could only lead to unpleasant contentions.

Innovations, indeed, against which

Gardiner protested in vain, began immediately after Henry's death. All the bishops had to take out fresh licences to exercise their functions in the new reign. Images began to be broken and maltreated, when as yet the orders were only to remove them if 'abused' by pilgrimages and worship. Afterwards came a royal visitation, to which both Gardiner and Bonner (*q.v.*) raised very natural objections, and though neither bishop insisted on his own view they were both sent to the Fleet. Bonner was soon released, but after two years more he was deprived of his bishopric. Gardiner remained over three months in the Fleet when he was released by a general pardon, with an admonition; but the Council required him to preach before the King to make his position clear. This he did (29th June 1548) in a way that he thought could give no offence. But next day he was arrested and sent to the Tower. And he not only remained a prisoner during the rest of the reign, but was deprived of his bishopric after a long-drawn-out trial on a flimsy pretence of disobedience to royal authority.

On the accession of Mary he was liberated and appointed Lord Chancellor. He was also restored to the Chancellorship of Cambridge University, which he had held from 1540 to the death of Henry VIII.; and in 1556 he was made Chancellor of Oxford as well. He was Mary's most trusted councillor, and though opposed to her wishes in her marriage with Philip, he yielded, and himself solemnised the marriage. From the first he did his best for the old religion, but it could not be fully reinstated till the coming of Cardinal Pole (*q.v.*) in November 1554 and the reconciliation of England to Rome. When, unhappily, the old heresy laws were revived, he did what was possible to induce the heretics brought before him to accept the pardon offered. But though he sat on the legatine commission before which the first heretics were tried, he soon gave up the thankless task. On the meeting of Parliament in October 1555 he addressed the two Houses with an eloquence that was all the more astonishing because he was already far gone in mortal illness. He died on the 13th November, and his body was carried with great solemnity to Winchester and buried in his cathedral.

Accounts of Gardiner's life have been defective and prejudiced, being founded mainly upon Burnet, who followed Foxe's extremely unfair reports of what he did. Even before the publication of the Calendars of State Papers in the last century, Dr.

Maitland's *Essays on the Reformation* had gone far to counteract these misrepresentations, and modern research has opened ample stores of information, which put a very different aspect on his career. For some results of this see Gairdner's *Lollardy and the Reformation*.   [J. G.]

GAUDEN, John (1605-62), divine, took his Arts degree from St. John's College, Cambridge, and those in Divinity from Wadham College, Oxford. He was private tutor to the sons of Sir W. Russell, and married their sister; was chaplain to Rich, Earl of Warwick, and in 1642 became Rector of Bocking, where he continued the use of the Prayer Book for some time. He asserts that he was a member of the Assembly of Divines, but was turned out because he was against the extirpation of bishops. From the time of the execution of the King he began to publish pamphlets against the proceedings of the army, in favour of religious marriage, and in defence of the ministry of the Church. But he conformed to Presbyterianism, and continued to hold his living. In 1660 he succeeded Brownrigg as preacher at the Temple, and at the end of the year, after the Restoration, followed him also as Bishop of Exeter. During the years 1660-1 he published several important pamphlets, notably *Anti Baalberith*, a vindication of his own conduct and an attack on the covenant and covenanters. In 1662 he was translated to Worcester, but died on 20th September of the same year. He is buried in his cathedral church. His chief claim to fame is his reputed authorship of *Eikon Basilike* (*q.v.*). It seems that both Charles II. and James II. admitted his claim, though there is much evidence that Charles I. did write prayers and memoranda, which, however, were not produced till many years after the death of Charles II. and of Gauden. According to Burnet it was mainly by Gauden's influence that the 'Black Rubric' was reinserted in the Prayer Book of 1662. [COMMON PRAYER, BOOK OF.]   [W. H. H.]

Wood, *Athenæ Oxonienses*; Oliver, *Lives of Bishops of Exeter*.

GERALD DE BARRI (Giraldus Cambrensis) (1146-1223), chronicler, born at Manorbier, near Tenby, was the youngest son of a Norman lord and grandson of Nest, famous as the Helen of Wales and the ancestress of the Fitzhenries, Fitzgeralds, and Fitzstephens. Trained first by his uncle, David, Bishop of St. David's, then at Gloucester, and finally at Paris, Gerald in later life played many parts. As commissioner of Archbishop Richard he in 1172 enforced on the refractory Flemings of Roose the payment of tithe on wool and cheese; as a royal chaplain he acted as intermediary between Henry II. and the Welsh princes in 1184, accompanied Prince John to Ireland in 1185, and Archbishop Baldwin on his tour through Wales to preach the Third Crusade in 1188. As Archdeacon of Brecon, or as he preferred to say *Archidiaconus Menevensis*, he proved a vigorous administrator not only of his archdeaconry from 1175 to 1203, but also of the diocese on several occasions, and a bold champion of its rights against Bishop Adam of St. Asaph when in 1176 he tried to assert his claim to Kerry as part of the kingdom of Powys. He was a candidate for the bishopric of St. David's on three occasions —1176, 1198, and 1214. On the second of these occasions he fought a bitter and determined fight, which lasted five years and involved three journeys to Rome, not only for his own claim to the see, but also for its independence of Canterbury and for its rights as a metropolitan church, with not only the Welsh bishops as suffragans, but also, as Gerald claimed, those of Chester (*i.e.* Lichfield). Hereford, Bath, and Exeter. He had to contend against the bitter hostility of Archbishop Hubert Walter (*q.v.*); against the influence of the King, who saw in Gerald not only a scion of powerful Norman-Irish families, but also a Welsh patriot; and against the cynical indifference of Innocent III. (*q.v.*). It is strange that Gerald, who was probably responsible for the assertion of the claim in 1175, did not support the chapter in their opposition to Archbishop Baldwin's celebration of the Mass at the high altar of St. David's in 1188. It is now agreed that Gerald's assertion of the metropolitan claims of St. David's had no historical basis; but it is also true that, though actuated to some extent by personal ambition, he strove manfully for what he and others regarded as 'the honour of Wales.' As an author he discussed geography, history, ethics, divinity, canon law, biography, and, above all, Gerald de Barri, and has left memorials of his prolific ability in eight bulky volumes in the Rolls Series. Trenchant, and even spiteful in his criticisms, credulous of miracles and fables, vain to the last degree, he appeals to us by his intense humanity, his fearless courage, his stubborn determination, his witty and humorous anecdotes, and his shrewd judgment of men and things.   [F. M.]

H. Owen, *Gerald the Welshman*; J. E. Lloyd, *A Hist. of Wales*; *Works* in R.S.

GIBSON, Edmund (1669-1748), Bishop of London, entered Queen's College, Oxford, as 'a poor serving child' in 1686, became Fellow, and was ordained, 1694. He showed an early aptitude for antiquarian studies, publishing an edition of the *Chronicon Saxonicum*, 1692, of Camden's *Britannia*, 1695, and of the works of Spelman (*q.v.*), 1698. As librarian at Lambeth under Archbishop Tenison he joined in the Convocation (*q.v.*) controversy, and in 1702 published his *Synodus Anglicana*, a work of permanent value, though overshadowed by his more famous *Codex Juris Ecclesiastici Anglicani*, 1713, a digest of English Church law which is still a standard authority. Industry, learning, and good sense rather than originality or genius were the distinguishing characteristics of 'Dr. Codex,' as he was nicknamed, and they enabled him to fill with credit one of the chief places in the church history of his time. Appointed Bishop of Lincoln in 1716 through the influence of Wake (*q.v.*), he was translated in 1720 to London, where he combated immorality, opposed 'infidelity and enthusiasm,' published devotional and controversial works, interested himself in missionary work in the colonies, and refused translation to Winchester. Although he classed Methodists with papists and deists as 'disturbers of the Kingdom of God,' John Wesley called him 'a great man,' 'eminent for piety and learning.' During the last years of Wake's primacy 'there was committed to him a sort of ecclesiastical ministry.' Sir Robert Walpole, charged with treating Gibson as pope of the English Church, replied, 'and a very good pope he is too.' But his successful opposition to the Quakers' Relief Bill, 1736, designed to reform the mode of recovering tithe and church rates, lost him the minister's confidence and the primacy on Wake's death in 1737. In 1747 he refused it on the score of age and infirmity.   [G. C.]

Works; Smallbrooke, *Some Account*, 1749; Wood, *Athenae Oxonienses*; Abbey and Overton, *Eng. Ch. in the Eighteenth Century*.

GILBERT, St., OF SEMPRINGHAM (1083-1189), was the son of a Lincolnshire knight of Norman blood and an English woman of lower condition. He studied abroad, and then returned to England, and set himself to teach what he had learned. He had a passion for education, and set to work to teach both boys and girls and to make them while learning live by rule. 'Though they were still seculars and Gilbert himself was in secular dress,' says his early biographer,

' he not only taught his scholars the rudiments of learning, but also morals and monastic discipline. He restrained the boys from their liberty of playing and wandering at will, and, according to the monastic rule, he compelled them to be silent in church and to sleep together as in a dorter, to speak and to read only in the places which he chose out for them.' By his father's patronage he was admitted to the livings of Sempringham and West Torrington. Soon his fame reached Robert Bloet, Bishop of Lincoln, and he called Gilbert to live with him as one of his clerks, an association which was continued with the next bishop, Alexander, nephew of the great Roger of Salisbury, ' for he judged it good to live under episcopal rule.' It was not till 1134 that he was allowed by the bishop to return to Sempringham. Meanwhile he had been ordained priest, much against his will. He had given the income of his benefice of Torrington to the poor. He was now able to minister there himself, and to set up a house for virgins to engage in study and prayer, as seculars, near the church of Sempringham. The community soon attracted attention, and through gifts of various knights it spread, and before 1154 Gilbert had built eleven houses for his order. He endeavoured to subject them to the Cistercians, but the general chapter of that order, 1147, declined to rule over women. But he made friends, in his visit to Gaul, with St. Bernard, with whom he stayed at Clairvaux, and who helped him to draw up the institutes of his order, so that Innocent III. (*q.v.*) described Gilbert and Bernard as the two founders of Sempringham. Eugenius III., St. Malachy of Armagh, and other eminent ecclesiastics gave him every encouragement, and Eugenius confirmed the order, ' having found no fault in it.' On his return to England he surrendered his control to Roger, Provost of Malton, and received a canon's dress from him. During the Becket (*q.v.*) contest he supported the archbishop, but without losing the favour of Henry and Eleanor. As he grew old some weakness and even corruption arose in his order, and some of the lay brothers treated him very badly, but he lived among them till the last. It was only in his later years that he himself actually entered the order, and indeed it is possible that Roger of Malton was not appointed till this time. The founder died at Sempringham at the age of one hundred and six, having lived from the reign of the Conqueror to the last year of Henry II., a length of life unparalleled in feudal times. The order regarded him with the greatest reverence, and told how ' kings and

princes honoured him, pontiffs and prelates received him with devotion, kinsmen and strangers loved him, and all the people revered him as a saint of God. We have seen bishops on their knees asking for his blessing and coming from a great distance to beg fragments of his clothing.' He was canonised by Innocent III., 1202. He had founded thirteen conventual churches, nine of which were for men and women together, four for canons only, and at his death the order had 700 men and 1500 women in it. He had also built a number of hospitals for sick and poor, lepers, widows and orphans. The order was unique in being founded on English soil and having no houses outside England, unique also, in this period, in its arrangement for ' double monasteries.' Up till the fourteenth century the order grew in members and riches. Its revenues in 1278 were £3000. At the dissolution they were but £2421, 13s. 9d., while the numbers of the professed showed that decay had set in. There were then only 143 canons and 139 nuns, with 15 lay sisters. [RELIGIOUS ORDERS.]

[W. H. H.]

Dugdale, *Monasticon*; Rose Graham, *St. Gilbert of Sempringham*.

GILPIN, Bernard (1517-83), called ' The Apostle of the North,' was a type of the class of clergy who, though more satisfied with religion as it had been in Mary's reign, were content to abide in the Church of England and accept the Elizabethan changes. After sixteen years at Oxford he became one of the public preachers of King Edward's day ; but under Mary, after further study abroad, he took up work under his great-uncle, Tunstall (*q.v.*), the venerable Bishop of Durham ; was Archdeacon of Durham and Rector of the great parish of Houghton-le-Spring. Before long he was in trouble, but as a reformer of morals rather than of doctrine. The Marian persecution threatened him, but he survived the attacks then made upon him. At the opening of the new reign he refused the bishopric of Carlisle, and devoted his life to apostolic labours in the north. Not content with caring for his own immense cure, he made great missionary journeys through the neglected areas in the northern province, winning the people by preaching and acts of personal and munificent charity. It was only with great difficulty that he had brought himself at the royal Visitation of 1559 to take the Oath of Supremacy ; but his example won the adhesion of countless clergy who looked to him as their leader. He remained independent, outspoken, and soundly attached to the doctrines of primitive antiquity, which he had learnt to distinguish from the Roman-ensian views of the day. But his position was a difficult one; and he was wise in absenting himself from home during the time of the Northern rising. All along his attitude brought him into suspicion and conflict from time to time with the episco-pate, but no one dared touch him; and Father Gilpin died a popular hero at the age of sixty-six.   [W. H. F.]

Vita by Bishop Carleton, 1628, etc.; printed in English in Wordsworth, *Eccl. Biog.*, iii. 370-432.

GLADSTONE, William Ewart (1809-98), statesman, was the fourth son of Sir John Gladstone, first Baronet, a God-fearing man of an old-fashioned type, by his marriage with Anne Robertson, a fervent Evangelical. He was born on the 29th December 1809. Ten years later Mrs. Gladstone said in a letter to a friend that she believed her son William had been 'truly converted to God.' At eleven William Gladstone went to Eton. Seventy years later T. T. Carter (of Clewer) wrote: 'I remember him at Eton, a pure and noble boy.' In 1828 he went up to Christ Church, where the blameless schoolboy developed into the blameless undergraduate —diligent, sober, regular alike in study and devotion: giving his whole energies to the duties of the place, and quietly abiding in the religious faith in which he had been reared.' Bishop Charles Wordsworth said that no man in the University read his Bible more regularly, or knew it better. Cardinal Manning (*q.v.*) remembered him as walking to Church 'with his Bible and Prayer Book tucked under his arm.' He was conspicuously moderate in the use of wine, and Archbishop Temple (*q.v.*), who followed him to Oxford ten years later, de-clared that undergraduates drank less in the 'forties because Gladstone had been courage-ously abstemious in the 'thirties. At Christ-mas 1831 he got his Double First. He earnestly desired to take holy orders. Cardinal Manning said in old age: 'He was nearer to being a clergyman than I was. He was as fit for it as I was unfit.' But his father overruled his desire, and forced him into Parliament, to which he was elected in December 1832.

Gladstone left Oxford before the Oxford Movement (*q.v.*) began; and his first acquaintance with that movement came to him through his friendship with James Robert Hope (Scott). Hope stated his opinion that ' the Oxford writers were right '; and Gladstone determined to study the question for himself. He began with a close examination of the Occasional Offices of the Prayer Book. 'Those offices,' he said, 'opened my eyes.' From Bishop Phillpotts (*q.v.*) he learned that the opinions of the Reformers were nothing to us, and that for the authoritative interpretation of the Prayer Book we must go to the divines of 1662. His previous study of Hooker had prepared him for the change of view. He had already acquired (during a visit to Rome) the conception of a Universal Church, and Sir William Palmer's *Treatise on the Church of Christ* confirmed and defined that concep-tion. From this process of independent examination he emerged—what he remained to the end of his life—an English Catholic Churchman. There was no break with his religious past. He was from first to last an Evangelical. But Catholic doctrine and practice were superimposed on the Evan-gelical foundation. In 1838 he published his first book, *The State in its Relations with the Church*. It was mainly a political book, in that higher sense of politics which is con-cerned with the nature, functions, and well-being of the State. But it contains some theological passages of great interest, in which the writer criticises the actual work-ing, as distinct from the formal teaching, of the Church of Rome.

In 1846 he published *Church Principles considered in their Results*. This book maintains the visibility and office of the Church, the mathematical certainty of the Apostolic Succession, and the nature and efficacy of the sacraments. It defines the relations between authority and private judgment, and vindicates the Church of England as the divinely-appointed exponent of Christian truth for the people of this country.

His private life was ruled in strict con-formity with his public profession. By his marriage in 1839 with Catherine Glynne, he gained a zealous and devoted supporter in all good works of charity and benevolence. With his friend, James Hope, he joined himself in a lifelong effort to reclaim the fallen sisters of humanity. He joined in guaranteeing the maintenance of the first Sisterhood established in the English Church in modern times. He rigidly limited his hours of sleep and amount of food. His almsgiving was profuse and systematic. He observed Fridays. He 'reserved the Sunday for sacred uses.' He was a weekly communicant.

In 1850 he was moved, by the judgment of

the Privy Council in the Gorham case (*q.v.*), to address to the Bishop of London an Open Letter in which he sought to prove that, as settled at the Reformation, the Royal Supremacy was not inconsistent with the spiritual life and inherent jurisdiction of the Church, and urged that the recent establishment of the Judicial Committee as the ultimate Court of Appeal in religious causes was ' an injurious, and even dangerous, departure from the Reformation Settlement.'

Hardly had the commotions connected with the Gorham case died down, when an attack on the doctrine of the Holy Eucharist was begun by the prosecution of Archdeacon Denison (*q.v.*) for teaching the Real Objective Presence. In 1856 Gladstone wrote: ' My mind is quite made up, that if belief in the Eucharist as a Reality is proscribed by law in the Church of England, all I hold dear in life shall be given and devoted to over-setting and tearing in pieces such law, whatever consequences, of whatever kind, may follow.'

These words touch one of Gladstone's central convictions. No one ever had a more profound or more childlike faith in the Reality of the Most Blessed Presence under the forms of Bread and Wine. The Real Objective Presence, depending on the Lord's act in Consecration, independent of the receiver, and prior to the act of Communion—' the Presence of the Lord upon the Christian altar '—this characteristic truth of Catholic theology was held and taught by Gladstone with all his heart, and soul, and mind, and strength. To see him at Communion was an object-lesson in adoring worship. This devotion to the Blessed Sacrament, together with his belief in the Eucharistic Sacrifice and in the doctrine of the Keys, led some to imagine that he was tending towards Rome. This was a signal delusion. He used to say : ' I am the strongest antipapalist in the world. The papacy is a tyranny all through—a tyranny of the Pope over the bishops, of the bishops over the priesthood, of the priesthood over the laity.' The Temporal Power he always regarded as a kind of anti-Christ.

Gladstone had begun life, as his treatises show, with a strong belief in the virtues of the union between Church and State; but the lapse of years profoundly modified his view. As far back as 1845, he wrote to his friend, Samuel Wilberforce (*q.v.*), his apprehension that ' The Irish Church is not in large sense efficient '; and to the appeal—' Have faith in the ordinance of God '—he

replied that he must see in that Church ' the seal and signature of ecclesiastical descent ' ; and whether she could show them. as against the Roman claim, he evidently thought doubtful. The Act of Irish Disestablishment, which he carried in 1869, was the gradual outcome of these and similar misgivings.

Some traces of sympathy with the Broad, Liberal, or Latitudinarian, School may perhaps be seen in his high regard for Charles Kingsley (*q.v.*), whom he twice promoted ; in his vigorous efforts to defend F. D. Maurice (*q.v.*) against official persecution ; in his admiration of *Ecce Homo* ; in his early and persistent confidence in Frederick Temple (*q.v.*) ; in his disparagement of the Athanasian as compared with the Nicene Creed ; in his increasingly lenient judgment on the nature of culpable schism. But his most conspicuous departure from the rigid traditionalism of his early theology was his adoption, in *Studies Subsidiary to the Works of Bishop Butler*, of the doctrine which is commonly called ' Conditional Immortality.' He came to the conclusion that the human soul is not necessarily indestructible, but that immortality is the gift of God in Christ to the believer.

Gladstone's last illness, which began in 1897, was declared incurable in March 1898. As soon as he knew his fate, he began to make systematic preparation for death. He summoned Bishop Wilkinson (*q.v.*) of St. Andrews to Hawarden, and the Bishop said, with reference to what then ensued: ' I wish that every young man could have seen him as he weighed his life, not in the balances of earth, but of heaven, as he reviewed the past and anticipated the future.'

By Easter Gladstone was far gone in weakness, and it was doubtful whether he could endure the strain of a private Celebration. ' It will be the first Easter since I was confirmed,' he said, ' that I have not made an Easter Communion.' When his son, the Rector of Hawarden, proposed to bring the Holy Sacrament from Church, he inquired, with characteristic dutifulness, whether the practice was strictly consistent with the Church's order ; and, being assured on that point, he received it with the utmost fervour of thankful devotion. He died on Ascension Day, 19th May 1898, just as the earliest Eucharists were going up to God.

[G. W. E. R.]

Personal recollections : Morley, *Life* ; *Correspondence on Church and Religion*, ed. Lathbury ; G. W. E. Russell, *Household of Faith*.

GLASS, Stained. The coloured glass in our church windows is sometimes called 'stained' and sometimes 'painted,' but these terms are not synonymous. The same glass is, as a rule, both stained and painted. The glass as first made is what is called 'white,' that is, either colourless, or slightly green owing to the accidental presence of oxide of iron. The various colours are produced by adding to the melted glass in a crucible or 'pot' certain metallic oxides, each of which stains the glass some particular colour. The ruby stain, however, was so dark that glass of the same thickness as the rest would have been practically opaque, while if it had been made thin enough to give the required shade it would have been too fragile and inconvenient in every way. So the craftsman dipped the lump of white glass at the end of his blowing tube into a pot of melted ruby, and then blew his bubble and spread it out in the form of a plate. The glass so made was white, coated with a thin and inseparable layer of ruby, or sometimes the glass was so managed that the white and ruby formed alternate layers in the finished material. Coated glass is often called 'flashed ruby,' and this, as well as flashed blue or yellow coated in the same way, was in common use. It was not found practicable to mix coloured glass with white, as wine is mixed with water, the melted glass being too stiff and viscid to combine, and the product would be too streaky. The diamond as a cutting instrument being unknown to the early glaziers, they drew a line on the glass with a red-hot iron, causing it to crack in the required direction, and then the edges were chipped to the precise shape that was wanted with a notched iron instrument called a grozing iron. Ancient fragments always show these chipped edges. So far the glass was only stained, but before the thirteenth century it was found that the effect could be greatly heightened by painting lines or shading upon the 'pot metal' or stained glass. The paint used consisted of peroxides of copper, iron, or manganese, ground up with powdered flint glass, which is the most fusible kind of glass, mixed with oil or gum or some such medium, and applied with a brush. Then the glass was placed in a suitable furnace, and so the paint was fused on to it, and, if done properly, indelibly fixed. If insufficiently burnt the paint soon peeled off, as in some modern glass, especially in the work of amateurs. Thus were indicated the features, folds in garments, or veins in leaves. The next step was to fasten the pieces together by the process called leading. The glazier's lead is a rod of about a quarter of an inch in diameter, deeply grooved on two sides so as to be like the letter II in section; the grozed edges of the glass were fitted into these grooves, the lead was soldered together where necessary, some sort of putty or paint was rubbed in, and thus the glass mosaic was completed. These methods have continued substantially the same up to the present time, only that the cutting diamond superseded the ruder method in the seventeenth century. Windows with geometrical and interlacing patterns were sometimes executed wholly in white glass, depending for their ornamental effect solely on the lead lines. The early craftsman, whether in pattern work or in figures, not only painted in glass, he drew in lead. His designs were often emphasised by touches of colour, while consisting mainly of 'white' glass of various tints, resulting from methods of manufacture which were chemically imperfect, but which greatly improved the general effect, for anything like the evenness of tint that we see in the modern 'cathedral glass,' so called, is most unsatisfactory. Pattern glass chiefly 'white,' relieved here and there by lines or jewels of colour and by opaque painting, is called *grisaille* (grey). The 'Five Sisters' at York, and some windows at Salisbury, afford the finest English examples of this; but no one can form any idea of their beauty who has not seen them through a field-glass, without which help, indeed, no ancient glass can be properly examined in detail.

The austere Cistercian regulation issued in 1134 against coloured glass shows that it had then become common in France. There is comparatively little English glass of the twelfth century now left; there may be some fragments in the nave at York, and perhaps elsewhere. The earliest glass of any great importance is of the thirteenth century, and there are considerable amounts of it at Canterbury, York, Salisbury, and Lincoln, while smaller portions remain elsewhere, as at Beverley Minster and at Brabourne Church in Kent. The characteristics of style follow one upon the other much as in architecture. The broad distinctions are between Gothic, Renaissance, and Modern. Gothic may be divided into (1) thirteenth century and before; (2) fourteenth century; and (3) fifteenth century and after, though naturally the three 'styles' run one into the other in a sort of evolution.

The *thirteenth-century glass*, often called '*Early English*,' may be taken as including any little remains that there may be of Romanesque or twelfth-century work. Its main characteristics are groups of figures in medallions of circular or other geometrical forms, set in backgrounds and borders of conventional foliage. When large and broad Norman windows have been glazed in this style, the medallions are of corresponding size, and subdivided so as to hold four or more separate subjects. In the narrower Lancet windows the medallions are proportionately small, and each one is devoted to a single subject. The figures in the medallions are, as a rule, few in number, and so stand out clearly against a plain background, with sometimes a conventional tree or building to suggest a scene. The lead lines form the outlines of the figures, etc., but often have to cross them, always, of course, when two pieces of glass either of the same or of different colours require to be joined. Figure and canopy windows of this period are sometimes found, the figures rude and stiff and the canopies small and simple. The border is a prominent feature in most early windows; it sometimes occupies half the area of a medallion window, and may include, together with its foliated ornament, little medallions with figures. Ornamental detail is always strictly conventional. Sometimes heraldry is modestly introduced, and shields are of the ' heater ' form. Colour is uneven and of an infinite variety of tone. The glazing is a mosaic of small pieces. Painting is limited to the one opaque pigment for lines, cross-hatching, and shading. Grisaille usually contains more or less coloured glass, but the general effect is grey and silvery. In *Jesse windows* the tree branches out so as to enclose spaces in which are set the figures of ancestors of Christ, with attendant prophets and apostles at the sides. As in medallions, the figures stand out distinctly against the ruby ground if the background of the window is blue, and vice versa. In the latter part of this period the foliage became less conventional—a sign of transition. In inscriptions Lombardic letters alone are used.

In the *fourteenth-century*, or ' *Decorated*,' period, together with windows divided by mullions into two or more lights, came a different arrangement of the glass. Figures and figure subjects commonly occur together with grisaille in the same window. Or the subjects or figures are piled one above the other in panels with very rudimentary canopies. Canopies, however, soon became conspicuous features, where there was room enough for them, taking the form of flat, tall gables with crockets and finials, over cusped arches, with pinnacles beside them. They are made chiefly of yellow pot-metal glass, and

are set in one or more rows across the window. In the larger windows the canopy had an elaborate architectural design above and behind it, sometimes growing to quite absurd proportions. In grisaille windows with figures or subjects these are placed in panels or under canopies, forming coloured bands across a light window. Any attempt at perspective in the canopies is a sign of transition to the next period. Borders are narrower than in the earlier windows, and are often still narrower in the tracery-lights. The borders frequently contain heraldic, allusive, or fancy devices, alternating one with another, as crowns, fleurs-de-lis, castles, covered cups, and squirrels nibbling at nuts. It was in the fourteenth century that the process of staining white glass yellow on the surface was discovered. In this process the yellow stain was laid on in the same way as paint where required ; white and yellow on the same piece of glass is always Middle Gothic or later. The hair and head-circlets of angels are stained yellow upon white glass, as also are monograms or other devices, as in figured ' quarries ' or lozenge panes. Figures are still rudely drawn, and appear in strained attitudes. In Decorated grisaille the foliated pattern runs all over the window, and is overlaid, as it were, by the white or coloured strap work; whereas in the work of the thirteenth century it is confined within the spaces of the main pattern, or at any rate within the panels. In the centres of the panels are coloured bosses or heraldic shields. Foliation now imitates nature so closely that the different plants represented can be at once recognised. Colour becomes more even and uniform in the same piece of glass, and often lighter in hue, ' streaked ' ruby ceasing to be used about the middle of the century. Flesh tint passes on from the decided pink of early glass to the white of late Decorated. and heads are better drawn than hands and feet. More green and yellow come in, and pale blue is sometimes converted into a greenish colour by the application of yellow stain. Outline painting is still practised, becoming more delicate as time goes on. Shading continues to be smeared on. But in the latter part of the century the smear begins to be stippled with the point of a brush held at right angles to the glass; the effect of which was that the opaqueness was mitigated. and it became possible to deepen the shadows without affecting the transparency, and so to relieve the flatness which marked the earlier work. Inscriptions are at first in Lombardics, then in black letter with Lombardic capitals. Mitres are gabled and crosiers foliated. Fourteenth-century glass marks a transition from rude and archaic drawing to the later and more artistic pictorial manner, from conventional to natural foliage, and from strong, rich colour to the delicate silvery effect of the later coloured glass.

The *late or fifteenth-century* Gothic glass corresponds in date with the 'Perpendicular' Gothic architecture, including as it does transitional characteristics appearing about twenty years before the century, and for about thirty years after it. The typical fifteenth-century windows contain much more white and less coloured glass than those of the fourteenth century, during which, as we have seen, the white was coming in. The figure and canopy is the favourite arrangement, and it can be carried into the tracery of perpendicular windows. Canopies are commonly like elaborate tabernacles such as those of the stalls in a great choir, of white glass with some yellow stain and brown shading, and often drawn in good perspective. There is white in the draperies, and the flesh is represented by white. There are commonly blue and ruby backgrounds in the alternate lights, but so much space is occupied by the subjects and tabernacles that comparatively little blue or ruby appears, there being just enough to enrich the prevailing white. With so much white glass the general effect is all the more bright and silvery. There was a marked improvement in drawing all through the fifteenth century. The faces are pencilled in fine lines, and as beautifully executed as any paintings of the time. The figures are in natural and dignified attitudes, and groups are more artistically disposed than before. The St. Cuthbert and St. William windows at York are among the finest examples of subject windows. In these, except at the tops of the lights, the canopies are very much reduced, so as to give more room for the groups. The lights with red backgrounds have blue backgrounds to the canopies, and vice versa. In the St. Cuthbert window are three red backgrounds alternating with two blue; in the St. William, three blue and two red. Such alternate backgrounds were a usual arrangement. In the great east window at York, apart from the tracery, are one hundred and seventeen subjects in its twenty-seven lights, but the canopies are so insignificant that they hardly separate the subjects. In subject panels trees, flowers, grass, rivers, sea with fishes, rocks with starfishes, buildings, etc., are introduced with more or less skill so as to suggest scenes. Grisaille such as that of the thirteenth and fourteenth centuries no

longer occurs, but there are windows all in white, or all in white with yellow stain, with delicate painting, and backgrounds of painted and stained quarry work. Towards the end of the period Renaissance details begin to come in. Shading is carried further than in the previous century, and is sometimes done on both sides of the glass. Heraldry becomes very gorgeous and elaborate. Shields are at first lengthened at the sides, while later they become almost square at the bottom. Inscriptions are in black letter, sometimes with Lombardic capitals. Mitres are tall and crosiers elaborate.

Early in the *sixteenth century* the Renaissance in art reached this country, and, as in architecture, so also in glass, we find much work that is wholly Gothic in feeling, though containing many Renaissance details. There was a great improvement both in colour and in drawing up to about 1535. The windows have much less the character of mosaics than any that came before them, and in their distinctness, relief, and perspective are more like other pictures. The architectural representations are Italian in character. Many new tints are employed, and these are due not only to new kinds of glass, but to the free use of the yellow stain not only on white but on coloured glass, producing most rich and varied hues, and sometimes the stain was applied twice over so as to produce two shades. Canopies are drawn in correct perspective, with both Italian and Gothic details, and they sometimes extend over several lights, and enclose well-executed landscape backgrounds. Heraldry is very elaborate. Roman letters and Arabic figures begin to appear.

The Reformation put an end to the making of coloured windows for churches for many years, and when coloured windows were again required the art had been lost. There was a sort of revival in the *seventeenth century*, as may be seen in windows at Wadham, Lincoln, and Balliol Colleges in Oxford and elsewhere, but these, owing to heavier shading and inferior glass, are dull and heavy in effect as compared with pre-Reformation glass. The art, both in colour and in design, fell still lower in the *eighteenth century* and in the early *nineteenth*, and then came that great revival in all the ecclesiastical arts which affected glass as much as anything else. It began with imitation of thirteenth-century glass, and has gone through all phases, until now we sometimes have imitation Renaissance, though some designers have aimed, with more or less success, at something 'original.' It seems best, in ancient or indeed in any churches, to have any new glass in the style of the window in which it is placed, though any servile imitation of the old or affectation of archaic grotesqueness should be avoided. We ought not to put mosaic medallions into a fifteenth-century window, nor figures with elaborate canopies into a lancet. Nevertheless, subject glass in the Decorated style, with restrained canopy work and broad borders, has been put into the wide Norman and Lancet windows of Durham Cathedral with excellent effect. The best *modern glass* is quite worthy to stand beside the old, but should never be put in its place. Much invaluable ancient glass has been thrown away in order to insert modern 'memorial' or other windows. Every remaining portion of ancient glass should be carefully preserved, releaded if necessary, as is often the case, but dealt with by a skilled person. If it cannot be preserved in the church it should be sent to a museum. The outer surface of old glass is always more or less corroded by the action of air, rain, frost, noxious vapours, etc.; hence its whitish opaque appearance outside. This does not affect the translucency of the glass so much as might be expected; indeed, it has a good effect in toning down strong colours. The less done at such decayed surfaces the better. 'Cleaning' means destruction.   [J. T. F.]

Lewis F. Day, *Windows, etc.*. 1909 ; Winston, *An Inquiry, etc.*, 1847. 2nd ed. 1867 ; *Memoirs, etc.*, 1865 ; Westlake, *Hist. of Design in Painted Glass*, 1881-6 ; J. Fowler, *Archæologia*, xlvi. ; *Yorks. Archæol. Journal*, iii. ; J. T. Fowler, *Yorks. Archæol. Journal*, iv., xi. ; Wm. Fowler's magnificent hand-coloured engravings, 1802-22.

GLASTONBURY is a much disputed name (perhaps from *clas*, a monastery.) Ynyswitrin, the British name, means *insula vitrea*, the glass - green island. Avalon, perhaps Semitic (אבל, *abel*, grassy place).

The mass of late Celtic discoveries at the lake village seems to bear out the suggestion that Glastonbury was for long a great emporium and treasure island, whose labourers lived on the smaller islands, the treasure being the Mendip minerals. The approach to this fortified island was by waterways, past the fortresses along the coast, which guarded the Axe, Brue, and Parrett. The Phœnician trade with 'the Isles' probably ended here, and it is not impossible that Hiram of Tyre fetched lead from this very spot. The trade by Poseidonius' time (135 B.C.) was carried on through Vannes. When Cæsar broke the Veneti this route was naturally also broken, and the Claudian conquest driving roads to the north, to carry the minerals through Southampton, took away the commercial importance of the shining island, which is now known to have been surprisingly civilised long before the Roman conquest. The first name in history is the King Arviragus, who seems to have given the Romans some trouble. In his day, and thirty-one years after our Lord's passion, St. Joseph of Arimathæa is said to have been sent here by St. Philip and to have been given a grant of land. Many small tokens give colour to this tale. The early ritual agrees with the Philippine tradition. The remains of a wattle hut have been found in the abbey grounds; a Levantine dropstone sepulchre, some 'Egyptian or Syrian' tiles, all attest the connection of Britain with the Eastern Mediterranean. The simplicity of the story makes falsehood unlikely, and the ancient Church is five times mentioned before the coming of St. Augustine. In spite of troubles and temporary abandonment the place seems to have been a focus of Christian love and worship. St. Patrick of Ireland, his successor Benignus, and many other Celtic missionaries were here laid to rest. The Saxon invasion for a century and a half threatened to reconquer for heathenism the holiest earth in England, during which time begins the history and subsequent poetry of King Arthur, who with Guinevere is said to be buried near the old church. A few years before Cenwalch stormed the last British strongholds in Wessex he had been converted to the faith, so the old, but often restored, church and the additions of St. David were saved. But the British Church became Latinised. Ine renewed and enlarged the privileges of the Tomb of Saints, and perhaps laid the foundations of the church of SS. Peter and Paul which afterwards grew to such magnificence. Kentwine in 673 first introduced the rule of St. Benedict. The house shared not a little in the work of the eighth-century missions, and began to educate bishops for all England. Nine of its sons were promoted to Canterbury before the Norman Conquest. The fierce struggles of three Danish wars left the holy spot still unburnt, and Alfred (*q.v.*) endowed it with lands and relics after his memorable victories. Athelstan brought here the bones of Pope Urban I., and Edmund the Elder collected relics of the northern saints. Both these last Kings were buried in the abbey. The greatest son of the house was perhaps St. Dunstan (*q.v.*). Edgar also upheld and advanced this privileged 'second Rome.' Cnut (*q.v.*) confirmed the charters, fixing his seal in the wooden church, which was still standing in 1022; but the later Anglo-Saxon abbots seem to have wasted the goods and the fame of the place.

The transfer of so unique and cherished a treasure to the Normans was made with much friction. The displacement of the old church music, inherited from Dunstan, by the newer Latin plain-song, caused riot and bloodshed even at the altar, and William I. made peace by a grant of land and banished Turstan, the high-handed abbot, who returned and redeemed his fame by buildings, of which small trace, if any, remains. Herlwin, his successor, is the first abbot whose work has survived in burnt red stones and chevron mouldings in the south transept. Henry of Blois (*q.v.*) built, endowed, enlarged, and enriched the place, and established the anti-episcopal policy which had such evil effects in later years. Henry II. kept the abbey without an abbot from 1178-84, when a dreadful fire burnt not only the venerable wooden church with all its shrines, but the new Norman buildings as well. Ralf Fitz-Stephen, the King's chamberlain, Reginald, Bishop of Bath, and others helped to set up the chapel of Our Lady (still called St. Joseph's from its history) in the Transition style. Among the relics saved were the bones of St. Patrick, and Gildas, and St. Oswald's arm, and some of the more doubtful relics of St. Dunstan. From this time until the days of the last abbot the abbey church rose little by little. To the west is St. Mary's Chapel, its door carving still unfinished because Henry II. died too soon. Then comes the Early English Galileo and west door to the great church, which is of astonishing dimensions; the nave, ending in the huge arch; the choir; the chapel of St. Edgar, in the style of Henry VII.'s Chapel at Westminster; and at the last an apse, make up a grand total of five hundred and ninety-four feet. Of this splendid house of God only a few shards and wrecks remain, but what is left is reverently and jealously preserved. The history of the house after Henry II. is that of a learned, art-loving Benedictine monastery composed of from fifty to sixty monks and a great number of retainers. With land in five counties and in sixty-four parishes, with many livings in its gift, with a school which helped to feed the University of Oxford, it had a great interest in weaving, jewellery, field sports, bell casting, clock making, music and organs, weaving, painting, and all ecclesiastical art-work. With much almsgiving, with hospitals, fisheries, deer parks, and manors, it maintained a power and organisation that must

have made the diocese almost impossible to work. One bishop, Savaric, tried to solve the problem of this great division by getting himself nominated as Bishop of Bath and Glastonbury and forcing the monks to elect and obey him. But even in the reign of John this high-handed, though statesman-like, solution was found impracticable, and after two abbot-bishops the interests were again divided, and Glastonbury became both the wonder of the land and the great difficulty of the Church. It was so beloved by the poor that, unlike the bishop, it had no need of fortification until after Cade's rebellion. It was so privileged that even law-loving monarchs like Edward I. (who came to see King Arthur's bones put in a shrine) could not act officially in its precincts. Henry VII. had to deal leniently with it. Erasmus and Sir Thomas More found much pleasure in the learning of the last abbot but one, Beere; and Leland, the antiquary, was astonished at its splendid library. At last the crash came. Abbot Whiting, an old, weak man, refused to surrender his princely house, though he surrendered almost everything else. A charge of treason was made against him—probably he had supported the Northern rebellion—and he was ignominiously butchered on the Tor, 14th November 1539. Then began a shameful and barbarous pillage. The work of centuries of artists, poets, and saintly men was destroyed to make roads, pigsties, and secular buildings. The holiest place in England was defiled and destroyed. Except for the labours of Hearne, the antiquary, the abbey was almost forgotten in England until 1826, when Warner wrote its history, and 1908, when Dr. Kennion, Bishop of Bath and Wells, acquired its sacred acres once more for the Church.

There is but little left now to see beyond the ruins of St. Mary's, the Galilee, the remains of the great church, and the foundations of the abbey. A fragment of the almonry a piece of the great wall, the abbot's kitchen and his barn, rise solitary from the green turf. In the town may be seen the old gateway; the Pilgrims' Inn, built to accommodate the wealthier travellers; and the tribunal, erected by Abbot Beere; and the museum contains a few relics of the departed glories. The Tor is still crowned by a solitary decorated tower of St. Michael, and Chalice Hill speaks of the legends of the Holy Grail.

The holy thorn, a Levantine variety, which sprang from St. Joseph's staff, was cut down by the Puritans for flowering upon Christmas Day. It has left many descendants, one in the abbey grounds and others throughout the county.

ABBOTS OF GLASTONBURY

Joseph of Arimathaea, his son, Faganus, and Diruvianus, presidents.

1. Worgret, sixth century.	35. Robert of Winchester, 1171.
2. Lademond.	36. Henry de Soliaco, 1189.
3. Bregoret.	
4. Beorthwald, seventh century.	37. Savarie, 1192.
5. Hemgesel.	38. Jocelin of Bath, 1206.
6. Berwald, eighth century.	39. William Vigor, 1219.
7. Albert.	40. Robert of Bath, 1223.
8. Aethfrid.	
9. Cengil.	41. Michael of Amesbury, 1235.
10. Tumbert or Cumbert.	42. Roger Ford, 1253.
11. Tican.	43. Robert Petherton, 1261.
12. Cuban.	
13. Waldun.	44. John of Taunton, 1274.
14. Bedwulf.	45. John of Kent, 1291.
15. Cuman, ninth century.	46. Geoffrey of Fromont, 1303.
16. Muean.	
17. Guthlac, 824.	47. Walter of Taunton, 1322.
18. Elmond, 851.	48. Adam of Sodbury, 1322.
19. Herefrith, 867.	
20. Elfric, 916.	49. Walter of Monington, 1342.
21. Stiward, 922.	
22. Aldhun.	50. John of Chinnock, 1374.
23. Dunstan, 943-55.	
24. Elsi, 956.	51. Nicholas of Frome, 1420.
25. Egelward I.	
26. Sigebar, 965.	52. Walter More, 1445.
27. Berred, 1000.	
28. Brithwin, 1017.	53. John of Selwood, 1457.
29. Egelward II., 1027.	
30. Egelnoth, 1053; deposed by William I.	54. Richard of Beere, 1493.
31. Turstan, 1078.	55. Richard Whiting, 1525-39.
32. Herlwin, 1101.	
33. Sigfrid, 1120.	[C. L. M.]
34. Henry of Blois (q.v.) 1126.	

Adam de Domerham; John of Glaston; Eyton, *Monument*; Hearne, *Hist.*; Warner, *Hist.*; and many modern handbooks, of which Mr. Bligh Bond's is best for the architecture.

GLOUCESTER, See of. From the seventh till the sixteenth century the lands which had been originally settled by the tribe of the Hwiccas, all along the lower course of the Severn, remained united as the bishopric of Worcester (q.v.). When the South Midland shires were created in the tenth century, the bishopric of Worcester practically corresponded to Worcestershire and Gloucestershire, with half Warwickshire. But there was one exception: the part of Gloucestershire west of Severn, in and about the Forest of Dean, had never been settled by the Hwiccas, and did not form part of their tribal bishopric. It belonged to the see of Hereford (q.v.). Gloucestershire in the later Middle Ages, therefore, included a considerable fragment of the bishopric of Hereford, viz. the whole of the 'Deanery of the Forest' (*Decanatus de Foresta*), and some small parts of the deaneries of Ross and Irchenfield.

When Henry VIII. in partial fulfilment of his pledge to create and endow new sees from the revenues of the suppressed monasteries, decided in 1541-2 to make new dioceses, with Gloucester and Bristol (q.v.) as their centres, a considerable rearrangement of boundaries became necessary. The King here, as in most of his other creations, took the secular frontiers of the counties as his general working base, and not the old ecclesiastical limits. Roughly speaking, his new diocese of Gloucester, constituted by Letters Patent of 3rd September 1541, was to coincide with the county. But Bristol, chosen as a see-town because of its size and wealth, was taken out of Gloucestershire in 1542, and with it went its large rural deanery along the estuary of the Severn. But while losing this city and its dependent district, the new bishopric of Gloucester acquired a large addition, which had never been before under the same ecclesiastical jurisdiction as the rest of the shire, viz. the lands beyond Severn. These though remaining in the archdeaconry of Hereford, were henceforth in the diocese of Gloucester, and made two rural deaneries those of the Forest and of 'Ross and Irchenfield'; the fragments of these two old Hereford rural deaneries which lay within the Gloucester border being joined as a single unit, though separate rural deaneries of Ross and of Irchenfield continued to exist within the diminished diocese of Hereford.

The vagaries of the shire boundary between Gloucestershire and Worcestershire are well known[1]: each county pushes irregularly shaped peninsulas and headlands into the other, and outlying fragments of each are also found lying as islands wholly surrounded by alien territory. Henry VIII. made but a partial effort to simplify this confusion

[1] For an illuminating paper on the origin of these eccentric limits, see C. Taylor's 'Northern Boundary of Gloucestershire' in *Proceedings of the Bristol and Gloucestershire Archeological Society* for 1910.

which had been of little practical importance so long as Gloucestershire and Worcestershire were parts of the same see. Hence the new bishopric, following the old county boundary, had a most fantastically jagged northern boundary; but one simplification was made: in the midst of the new diocese lay a large patch of Worcester see-land, ' Blockley Jurisdiction,' and a smaller patch, Cutsdean, which had in the later Middle Ages been under the Archdeacon of Gloucester, though they appertained to the shire of Worcester. Now, though remaining part of the shire of Worcester, they were placed within the see of Gloucester. Gloucestershire owned some outlying fractions scattered eastward, and these, *e.g.* Widford in the heart of West Oxfordshire, and Shenington under Edgehill in Warwickshire, became part of the new Gloucester bishopric. On the other hand, some small islands of Wiltshire land enclosed in South Gloucestershire, such as Pulton, remained in the bishopric of Salisbury. The new diocese contained thirteen rural deaneries—Hawkesbury, Dursley, Stonehouse, Gloucester, the Forest, Ross and Irchenfield, Winchcombe, Chipping-Camden, Blockley, Stow-on-the-Wold, Cirencester, Bibury, and Fairford. But these by the eighteenth century had been reduced to ten only. The record of 1779 gives us as existing only Hawkesbury, Dursley, Stonehouse, Gloucester, the Forest, Winchcombe, Chipping-Camden, Stow, Fairford, and Cirencester. Ross and Irchenfield has merged in the Forest (which was transferred from the archdeaconry of Hereford to that of Gloucester in 1836). Bibury in Fairford, Blockley in Stow. There was only one archdeaconry, that of Gloucester (first mentioned as part of Worcester diocese, 1122).

The bishopric of Gloucester, as thus composed, was one of the smaller English dioceses, and also one of the least well endowed. Ecton (1711) values it as £315, 7s. 3d., and later in the eighteenth century it was estimated to be worth no more than £900 a year. During its early history it was more than once allowed to be held *in commendam* along with a neighbouring bishopric. In 1552 the see was dissolved, and became for two years an archdeaconry in the diocese of Worcester, Hooper (*q.v.*) being given the title of Bishop of Worcester and Gloucester. The separate see of Gloucester was restored in 1554. Bishops Cheyney and Bullingham under Elizabeth both held Bristol as well as Gloucester. But these pluralities ceased in the reign of James I., and the only mark of the poverty

of the diocese that remained was that its bishop was nearly always willing to be translated to a greater see. Of the twenty-three bishops of Gloucester between 1604 and 1862 no less than thirteen were moved on, after a short tenure of the diocese, to larger charges. Only three of the twenty-three are buried in Gloucester Cathedral (Bishops Miles Smith, Nicholson, and Benson).

In 1616 James I., hearing that there was ' scarce ever a church in England so ill governed and so much out of order' as Gloucester, appointed Laud (*q.v.*) dean to reform it. Laud had the Holy Table placed altar wise, at the east end of the church, which so offended Bishop Miles Smith that he never entered his cathedral afterwards, though he lived eight years longer.

The boundaries remained unchanged from 1541 to 1836, when at the recommendation of the Ecclesiastical Commissioners the sees of Bristol and Gloucester were amalgamated by Order in Council of 5th October 1836. But only Bristol city and rural deanery of the territories of the Bishop of Bristol came back to Gloucester. Dorsetshire was given to Salisbury (*q.v.*), while Salisbury in return ceded to Gloucester its northern Wiltshire rural deaneries, Cricklade and Malmesbury, by Order in Council of 19th July 1837. A second archdeaconry was created at the same time, that of Bristol, including the rural deaneries of Bristol, Hawkesbury, Dursley, Fairford, and Cirencester.

This arrangement lasted till 1897, when on the recreation of a separate bishopric of Bristol (by Order in Council of 7th July), the see of Gloucester gave up Bristol city, and its extensive rural deanery, with those of Stapleton and Bitton—both nineteenth-century creations taken out of Hawkesbury—and the two recently acquired Wiltshire rural deaneries, to make up the new diocese of Bristol. Thus in 1912 the see of Gloucester is again a shire diocese, save that it lacks the three rural deaneries next to Bristol, and owns the island of Worcestershire, which formed ' Blockley Jurisdiction.' It has two archdeaconries: Gloucester, and Cirencester (created 1832, and including the old rural deaneries of Cirencester, Fairford, Stow, and Stonehouse). It has 320 benefices, served by 410 clergy. Its population is 320,924, and its extent 687,456 acres. The income of the bishop was at its union with Bristol in 1836 raised to £5000. But when Bristol was taken out of it in 1897 the bishop resigned £700 of his income, and the see is now worth £4300 annually.

There had been a religious house at

Gloucester] *Dictionary of English Church History* **[Gloucester**

Gloucester from 681. In 1022 it was re-founded by St. Wulfstan, Bishop of Worcester, as a Benedictine abbey. Henry III. was crowned in its church, 1216. In 1283 Gloucester Hall was founded at Oxford as a college for its monks. But the exclusive connection of the Hall with Gloucester Abbey only lasted a few years. The building of the abbey church continued through the Middle Ages, and culminated in the erection of the beautiful central tower in the fifteenth century. The church was extensively restored in the nineteenth century. The last abbot, William Parker, died in 1539, and on 2nd January 1540 the abbey surrendered to the Crown, the prior receiving a pension of £20, and twelve monks from £5 to £10 each. The total revenues amounted to £1846, 5s. 9d. It was refounded by Henry VIII. with a dedication to the Holy Trinity, and the chapter was made to consist of a dean and six canons, besides minor canons and others. It did not absorb that of Bristol in 1836, but the latter cathedral retained its own establishment. By an Act of 1713 (13 An. c. 6) one canonry is annexed to the mastership of Pembroke College, Oxford. The Cathedrals Act, 1840, suppressed two canonries, leaving four. In 1890 the number was increased to five by an endowment being left for a canon-missioner.

BISHOPS OF GLOUCESTER

1. John Wakeman, 1541; last Abbot of Tewkesbury, which he had surrendered, 1540, and where he has a monument; 'an intriguing and servile ecclesiastic'; d. 1549.
2. John Hooper (*q.v.*), 1550.
3. James Brooks, or Broks, 1554 (P.); d. shortly after Elizabeth's accession, 1558. The see vacant four years.
4. Richard Cheyney, 1562; held the bishopric of Bristol *in commendam*; d. 1579. The see vacant two years.
5. John Bullingham, 1581; held the bishopric of Bristol *in commendam*; d. 1598.
6. Godfrey Goldsborough, 1598; d. 1604; has an altar-tomb in the cathedral.
7. Thomas Ravis, 1605; tr. to London, 1607.
8. Robert Parry, 1607; tr. to Worcester, 1610.
9. Giles Thompson, 1611; d. 1612, before entering his diocese.
10. Miles Smith, 1612; a favourer of Puritans; d. 1624.
11. Godfrey Goodman (*q.v.*), 1625; depr. 1640; d. 1656. The see vacant four years.

12. William Nicholson, 1661; restored Church order and reformed abuses, but treated Nonconformists with consideration; d. 1672.
13. John Pritchet, 1672; d. 1681.
14. Robert Frampton, 1681; a zealous Churchman; arrived half an hour too late to join in the action of the Seven Bishops (*q.v.*); depr. 1691 [NONJURORS], but allowed to retain the living of Standish, worth £40 a year; d. 1708.
15. Edward Fowler, 1691; a Whig; 'Puritanically brought up,' but 'wheel'd about with the times'; d. 1714.
16. Richard Willis; tr. to Salisbury, 1721.
17. Joseph Wilcocks, 1721; tr. to Rochester, 1731.
18. Elias Sydall, 1731; tr. from St. David's; d. 1733.
19. Martin Benson, 1735; refused higher preferment; the friend of Bishop Butler; Porteous, Bishop of London, wrote: 'His purity, though awfully strict, was inexpressibly amiable'; d. 1752.
20. James Johnson, 1752; tr. to Worcester, 1759.
21. William Warburton (*q.v.*), 1760; d. 1779.
22. Honble. James Yorke, 1779; tr. from St. David's; tr. to Ely, 1781.
23. Samuel Halifax, 1781; tr. to St. Asaph, 1789.
24. Richard Beadon, 1789; tr. to Bath and Wells, 1802.
25. George Isaac Huntingford, 1802; tr. to Hereford, 1815.
26. Honble. Henry Ryder, 1815; tr. to Lichfield, 1824.
27. Christopher Bethell, 1824; tr. to Exeter, 1830.
28. James Henry Monk, 1830; became Bishop of Gloucester and Bristol, 1836.

BISHOPS OF GLOUCESTER AND BRISTOL

28. James Henry Monk, 1836; revived Church life; restored rural deans; augmented small livings; cons. fifty-four new churches; d. 1856.
29. Honble. Charles Baring, 1856; tr. to Durham, 1861.
30. William Thomson, 1861; tr. to York, 1862.
31. Charles James Ellicott, 1863; Hulsean Professor of Divinity, Cambridge, 1860; Dean of Exeter, 1861; appointed bishop by Palmerston on Lord Shaftesbury's advice, because of his share in answering *Essays and Reviews* (*q.v.*), Disraeli wished to appoint him to Canterbury, 1868; Chairman of New

Testament Revision Company ; a hard-working bishop ; res. and d. 1905.

BISHOPS OF GLOUCESTER

31. Charles James Ellicott, 1897-1905.
32. Edgar Charles Sumner Gibson, 1905 ; Principal of Wells Theological College, 1880-95 ; Vicar of Leeds, 1895.
[C. W. C. O.]

V.C.H. Gloucester ; Browne Willis, *Cathedrals.*

GOODMAN, Godfrey (1583-1656), Bishop of Gloucester, took his degrees at Trinity College, Cambridge, held the living of Stapleford Abbots in Essex, 1606-20; became Prebendary of Westminster, 1607 ; B.D. at Oxford, 1615 ; and had a number of livings in Berks, Gloucester, and Wales. He became a disciple of Andrewes, and a good preacher in his style, and rose to be Canon of Windsor, 1617; Dean of Rochester, 1621; Bishop of Gloucester, 1625. A sermon at court, 1626, was supposed, says Heylin (*q.v.*), 'to trench too near the borders of popery,' and many complaints were made against him for 'excessive ritual,' such as pictures and hangings decorated with the crucifix and the restoring of the cross in Windsor. He seems to have been a negligent bishop, for Laud (*q.v.*) opposed his translation to Hereford, and ordered him to retire to his own diocese. He neglected to report on his see in 1633, 1636, 1637, and resided at Windsor preferably to Gloucester. He became more and more Romanist in his views. Panzani, the Pope's agent, 1636, thought him a convert, because he used the breviary and declared that he wished to keep a Roman priest in his house. But it was not till his refusal to sign or accept the canons of 1640 that matters came to a crisis, and the Convocation of May 1640 declared him deprived of his see. He then submitted, and was restored, but expressed a desire to resign as soon as his debts were paid. He was now obnoxious alike to Laudians and Puritans, and was beset by both. He joined in the protest of the bishops against their intimidation, December 1641, and was committed to the Tower on a charge of high treason. He was released and ordered to return to Gloucester, where his house was sacked in 1643, when he took refuge in Wales. He finally retired to Westminster, and died there on 19th January 1656, and was buried at St. Margaret's. He declared himself a Romanist in his will. His theological works are of no value, but his account of the court of James I. (not published till 1839) is useful. The defects of Goodman's personal character and his dis-ingenuous concealment of his opinions—there is no certainty when he 'went over to Rome,' if he ever formally did—prevented his undoubted abilities being useful to religion or learning.   [W. H. H.]

Wood, *Athenae Oxonienses* ; Walker, *Sufferings of the Clergy.*

GOODRICH, or GOODRICKE, Thomas, D.D. (d. 1554), Bishop of Ely and Lord Chancellor, younger son of Edward Goodrich of East Kirkby, Lincs ; entered C.C.C., Cambridge, and became Fellow of Jesus, and was Proctor in 1515. He was presented by Wolsey to the rectory of St. Peter, Cheapside, London, in 1529. He was one of the divines consulted by Convocation as to the legality of Henry VIII.'s marriage with Katherine, and on the commission appointed by the University of Cambridge to consider the same question. He was soon after appointed a royal chaplain ; made Canon of St. Stephen's, Westminster ; sent on an embassy to France ; and in 1534 made Bishop of Ely. As bishop he laboured to maintain the Royal Supremacy, but at the end of the reign fell under suspicion of favouring the reformed religion further than the King allowed. On the accession of Edward VI. he was sworn of the Privy Council, put on a commission for the visitation of Cambridge University, and possibly on that which drew up the First Prayer Book [COMMON PRAYER, BOOK OF]. He was sent on an embassy to France, and made Lord Chancellor in 1552. He signed the letter of the Council refusing to acknowledge Mary's right to the throne, but soon afterwards submitted ; signed the declaration ordering Northumberland to disarm, was pardoned by Mary, and allowed to retain his bishopric.

Burnet (*q.v.*) says that 'he was a busy, secular-spirited man and gave himself up wholly to faction and intrigues of State ; and though his opinions always leaned to the Reformation it was no wonder if a man so tempered would prefer the keeping of his bishopric to the discharge of his conscience.'

Hooper (*q.v.*) mentions him as one of six bishops who were 'favourable to the cause of Christ and held right opinions on the Eucharist' ; Hooper had conversed with him, and 'discovered nothing but what was pure and holy.'   [C. P. S. C.]

Strype, *Eccl. Memorials, Cranmer* ; *D.N.B.*

GORHAM, George Cornelius (1787-1857), divine, was educated at Queens' College, Cambridge, of which he became Fellow in 1810. In 1811 Bishop Dampier of Ely threatened, ineffectively, to refuse to ordain him on account of unsoundness on baptismal regeneration. He attained distinction as a botanist and an antiquary, and in 1846 became Vicar of St. Just in Penwith, Cornwall, being instituted by Bishop Phillpotts (*q.v.*), who shortly afterwards rebuked him for advertising for a curate ' free from Tractarian error.' In 1847 he was presented to Brampford Speke in the same diocese, when the bishop insisted on his right to examine him before institution (Canon 39). The examination comprised one hundred and forty-nine questions, and occupied eight days, lasting in all fifty-two hours. Gorham frequently protested against the intricate and vexatious nature of the questions as virtually a ' penal inquisition,' and against allowing ' the valuable hours of life (already so advanced in each of us) ' to ' roll away in unprofitable discussion.' The point at issue was baptismal regeneration. Gorham held that it was conditional upon worthy reception of the sacrament, and that infants never benefited in baptism except by virtue of some other gift of grace. His views, coloured by his peculiar Calvinism, were distinct from those held by most Evangelicals. As the bishop eventually refused to institute him, he brought the almost obsolete action of *Duplex Querela* in the Court of Arches, where the Dean, Sir H. Jenner Fust, decided that his view was opposed to that of the Church, and that therefore the bishop was justified in his refusal. The Privy Council reversed this decision on appeal, and the bishop having failed to obtain a prohibition, and still refusing to perform the institution, Gorham was instituted by Archbishop Sumner. He complained that the bishop stirred up ill-feeling in his parish, bidding his parishioners ' be on the watch for occasions of complaint,' but he retained the living till his death.

' The Great Gorham Case ' raised a storm of controversy. Over sixty books and pamphlets dealing with it are catalogued in the British Museum, and a foreign visitor congratulated a country which knew no more serious revolution than that of ' *le père Gorham.*' The Privy Council did not profess to define doctrine, but only to lay down the ' true and legal construction ' of the Church's formularies, without being ' minute and rigid ' in their interpretation. The doctrine which it attributed to Gorham and declared to be lawful was that the grace of regeneration does not so necessarily accompany the act of baptism that regeneration invariably takes place in baptism. But this was not what he really held. Dr. Pusey (*q.v.*) and the Tractarian leaders, though they supported

the bishop, thought his action ill-advised. Eventually Archdeacon Manning (*q.v.*) and others seceded to Rome in consequence of the ' vile judgment.' But such men as Keble (*q.v.*), S. Wilberforce (*q.v.*), and Gladstone (*q.v.*) realised that it was a mere State decision, which did not compromise the Church. Nor was it without good results. It was an important factor in the revival of Convocation (*q.v.*), and it drew attention to the character of the Privy Council as an ecclesiastical court of appeal [COURTS].

[G. C.]

Works: Moore. *The Gorham Case*; Liddon, *Life of Pusey*, vol. iii.

GRANVILLE, or **GRENVILLE, Denis** (1637-1703), Dean of Durham and later chaplain to James II. at the Court of St. Germans, an active organiser in the diocese of Durham as Archdeacon of Durham, also an interesting writer of letters. He was of distinguished family and connection. He was great-grandson of Sir Richard, whose name is undyingly associated with the *Revenge*, and youngest son of Sir Bevil, the famous Cornish royalist. He was descended from the Corbeil family, and in his exile delighted in tracing his French ancestry and connection with many noble families of ancient lineage. From a Cornish school Denis passed to Eton, and then became a gentleman-commoner at Exeter College, Oxford. Here he fell into debt, and was afterwards rarely free from money troubles, despite his preferments. He was a convinced Churchman, and naturally attracted attention at the Restoration. Bishop Cosin (*q.v.*) was the source of his promotion. Granville married the bishop's daughter, Anne, who was little help to her husband, and soon became the victim of intemperance. After holding a country living, and then a prebend in York Cathedral, Granville was given a prebend at Durham in 1662. Almost coincidently he was made Archdeacon of Durham, and held in turn the rectories of Elwick and Sedgefield. Such multiplied preferment deserved the criticism of Archbishop Sancroft (*q.v.*). Granville managed to keep much of it during the whole of his connection with Durham. Bishop Crewe contrived his further appointment to the deanery in 1684, and with this he still held the archdeaconry and the rectory of Sedgefield. His efforts for the improvement of the cathedral services and personnel were effective. He constantly set Cosin before him as his model. His principal effort was to promote the more frequent celebration of the Holy Communion, and by his efforts weekly Eucharists were restored in several cathedrals, and he desired to restore the daily Eucharist. At the Revolution he had the courage of his convictions and strove to promote Jacobite sympathy in the diocese. He fled from Durham and his goods were distrained upon for debt. Save for one short visit to England he spent the rest of his life in France, partly at the Court of St. Germans. Like Cosin he resisted all efforts to make him submit to the Church of Rome. He presently withdrew to other places of retirement, where friends in England aided him with gifts of money, as also did Mary of Modena. He occupied himself in his exile with writing and preaching and tracing his French pedigree. He died and was buried in Paris in 1701. His wife had not shared his troubles, but remained with friends at Durham, and was buried in the cathedral in 1691.   [H. G.]

V.C.H., Durham, ii. 58-62; D.N.B. and authorities there cited; *The Remains of Denis Granville*, Surtees Soc., vols. xxxvii. and xlvii.; *Life* by Roger Granville, 1902.

GRAY, Robert (1809-72), Bishop of Capetown, was the son of Robert Gray, Canon of Durham, and afterwards Bishop of Bristol, where the palace was burnt during the Reform Bill riots. He graduated from University College, Oxford, in 1831, was ordained in 1832, and after serving various cures was appointed by Letters Patent of the Crown first Bishop of Capetown in 1847. His strenuous labours as founder and pastor belong to the history of the South African Church, but a series of untoward events brought him into important relations with the authorities of the Church of England. In 1853, other bishoprics being founded in South Africa, he resigned his see to facilitate the division of the diocese, and by new Letters Patent was both reappointed bishop and declared metropolitan, the extent of his jurisdiction being defined in accordance with the general law of the Church. A clergyman named Long having contested his episcopal authority, recourse was had to the courts of the colony, and on appeal to the Judicial Committee of the Privy Council, which ruled (29th June 1863) that the Letters Patent of 1853 were null and void, so far as concerned the creation of any ecclesiastical jurisdiction, because granted after the establishment of constitutional government in the colony. The Church in South Africa was a merely voluntary association, the members of which were bound as by contract, and might set up purely spiritual tribunals with-

out any coercive jurisdiction (*Long v. Bishop of Capetown*, 1 Moore P.C. N.S. 411). This judgment put an end to the legal contention that the Church of England, as a body established by law, extends to all the dominions of the Crown.

In the meantime a further difficulty had arisen. Colenso (q.v.), Bishop of Natal, had been delated for heresy to Gray as metropolitan, and was cited to appear on 17th November 1863; in October, on the strength of the judgment in Long's case, he publicly denied the metropolitan's jurisdiction, and refused to appear, afterwards petitioning the Crown to set aside the judgment of deposition pronounced against him. The petition was referred to the Judicial Committee, which gave the same ruling as before, adding that the oath of canonical obedience to the metropolitan taken by Colenso at his consecration could not set up any right to exercise jurisdiction which the law would recognise (*In re Bishop of Natal*, 1864, 3 Moore P.C. N.S. 115). These judgments of the Privy Council are not to be confounded with those given in cases carried on appeal from the English courts spiritual. The Judicial Committee was not on this occasion acting as an Ecclesiastical Court of Appeal, and the questions before it concerned only the legal constitution of the South African colonies. But some of the *obiter dicta* delivered by Lord Westbury on the second occasion aroused great indignation, and contributed much to the ruin of the moral authority of the tribunal. He spoke of the sovereign as ' head of the Established Church and depositary of the ultimate appellate jurisdiction.' He laid it down that ' pastoral or spiritual authority may be incidental to the office of bishop, but all jurisdiction in the Church, where it can be lawfully conferred, must proceed from the Crown.' He said accordingly that ' in the case of a settled colony the Ecclesiastical Law of England cannot . . . be treated as part of the law which the settlers carried with them from the mother country,' and this because ' the erection of a new court with a new jurisdiction cannot be without an Act of Parliament.' All this was in close agreement with the legal theories of a past age, and especially with those of Sir Edward Coke, from whom the last quotation was borrowed, but its revival in this exaggerated form and its application to the oversea dominions of the Crown was an express denial of the Church's inherent powers of discipline, and the implied revival of the long-abandoned title of ' Head of the Church ' stirred a lively antagonism. These judgments therefore, though dealing directly only with the merest legal niceties of colonial constitutions, gave rise to vigorous controversy in England. In South Africa their legal effect was accepted without demur, and the Church was there organised in complete independence of the State, and in proper provincial independence of the Church of England. Some malcontents having followed Colenso in declaring themselves members of the 'Church of England in South Africa,' and having made good their legal title as such to certain buildings and endowments (*Bishop of Natal* v. *Gladstone*, 1866, L.R. 3 Eq. 1), the Bishop of Capetown, in accordance with ancient precedents, put to the provincial synod of Canterbury the formal question whether they held communion with Colenso or with the orthodox bishops who had deposed and excommunicated him. S. Wilberforce (*q.v.*) moved the synod (in June 1866) to declare that the Church of England was in communion with Gray, and not in communion with Colenso; but other bishops deprecated an open collision with the State, and the synod affirmed its communion with the Bishop of Capetown only, saying nothing about Colenso. After Colenso's death the Archbishop of Canterbury and his comprovincials refused to recognise and consecrate the priest elected by his followers to succeed him, and in 1891, on the resignation of the bishop (Macrorie) consecrated at Capetown to replace him, Archbishop Benson (*q.v.*) persuaded both parties in Natal to entrust him with the choice and consecration of a new bishop. The consent of the South African episcopate being obtained, the schism was thus healed.

Of Robert Gray's personal character an unfriendly witness, in whose judgment 'it is not to be desired that the Church of England should have many prelates of his type,' bears the following testimony :—'Bishop Gray was entirely one with that section of the Church of England which denied the dependence of the Church upon the State, or deplored it so far as it could not be denied ; the party of Pusey and Keble, of Anselm and Becket ; in doctrine, but not in politics, the party of Sancroft and Cosin. His courage and perseverance are worthy of all praise, and in most trying circumstances his temper does him honour' (Cornish, *The English Church in the Nineteenth Century*, ii. 262).

[T. A. L.]

H. L. Farrer, *Life*.

GREGORY, St. (*c.* 540 to 12th March 604), entitled the Great—'Gregory our father

who sent us baptism'— the first pope of his name, and the last of the Four Doctors of the Latin Church, was born in Rome. Of the earlier part of his life few details are preserved, and almost all the dates are conjectural. His father was Gordianus, the *regionarius*, a man of good family and considerable wealth, owning large estates in Sicily and a palace on the Cœlian Hill in Rome ; his mother was St. Silvia (*Acta Sanctorum*, 3rd November). Gregory received the best education to be had at the time, and was distinguished for his proficiency in the arts of grammar, rhetoric, and dialectic. He entered upon an official career, and *c.* 573 became Prefect of the City. Soon afterwards, however, *c.* 574, feeling irresistibly drawn to the 'religious' life, he resigned his office, devoted the greater part of his wealth to founding six monasteries in Sicily and one in Rome, and in the last—the famous monastery of St. Andrew—became himself a monk.

But he was not permitted to remain long in retirement. Probably in 578 he was ordained 'seventh deacon' (? archdeacon) of the Roman Church, and in the following spring Pope Pelagius II. appointed him *apocrisiarius*, or resident papal ambassador at the court of Constantinople. On his return to Rome, *c.* 586, he was made Abbot of St. Andrew's. It is to this period of his life that the incident of the English slave-boys (if it be accepted as historical) must be assigned. The famous story of the punning abbot and the Angles with angel faces is derived from English sources (the S. Gallen *Life of Gregory*, 9 ; Bede, *H.E.*, ii. 1, from whom it is copied by the biographers Paul. Diac., *Vita Greg.*, 17 ; Johann. Diac., *Vita Greg.*, i. 21). According to the earliest version the young Angles are not described as slaves and Gregory is represented as conversing with them directly. Gregory himself, however, nowhere alludes to the incident, and it is strange that if he was really fond of punning on names he does not indulge his fancy in his familiar letters. The tradition has probably been elaborated, but there is nothing improbable in the supposition that Gregory first became interested in Britain through a meeting with some Angles in Rome. This at any rate would account for what followed. Gregory resolved personally to undertake the conversion of Britain, and having obtained the reluctant consent of the Pope he set out with a small band of monks upon the mission. On the third day of his journey, however, he was overtaken by messengers from the Lateran, who ordered him to return.

In 590 Pelagius II. died, and the clergy and people unanimously chose Gregory as his successor. He did everything in his power to avoid the dignity, but while he was preparing for flight he was seized and carried off to the basilica of St. Peter, and there consecrated bishop, 3rd September 590.

His pontificate was marked by extraordinary energy and activity. 'He never rested; he was always engaged in providing for the interests of his people, or in writing some composition worthy of the Church, or in searching out the secrets of heaven by the grace of contemplation' (Paul. Diac., *Vita*, 15). He persevered in the ascetic discipline. Having banished all lay attendants from his palace he surrounded himself with clerics and monks, with whom he lived as though still in a monastery. To the spiritual needs of his people he ministered with pastoral zeal, arranging for the regular performance of the services in the Roman basilicas, frequently appointing 'stations,' and delivering eloquent and practical sermons, in which we get for the first time a distinct approach towards a systematic use of anecdote and illustration. Nor was he less solicitous in providing for the temporal welfare of his flock. Deaconries, guest-houses, hospitals, and other charitable institutions were liberally endowed, and free distributions of food were made to the poor at the convents and basilicas. The funds for these and similar purposes were provided from the patrimony of St. Peter—the estates of the Roman Church in Italy and the adjacent islands, Africa, Gaul, and Dalmatia. In superintending these domains Gregory exhibited remarkable capacity, and his letters dealing with the management of the property of the Church are of extraordinary interest (see especially *Ep.*, i. 39a, 42). Gregory was one of the best of the papal landlords. His only fault as a man of business was that he was inclined to be too lavish in his expenditure, and after his death it was said that by his excessive liberality he had actually impoverished the treasury of the Roman Church.

Within the strict bounds of his patriarchate, *i.e.* the Churches of Central and Southern Italy and the islands, it was Gregory's policy to watch with particular care over the election and discipline of the bishops. Apart from this he abstained as far as possible from interfering in the concerns of the several dioceses. He encouraged the bishops to assemble in synods, and enforced throughout the patriarchate the regulations that clerics in holy orders should not cohabit with their wives or permit any women, except such as

were allowed by the canons, to reside in their houses, and that the revenues of each church should be divided into four equal parts, to be assigned respectively to the bishop, the clergy, the poor, and the repair of the fabric of the church.

In his relations with the Churches which lay outside the limits of his patriarchate—in Northern Italy, Spain, Gaul, Africa, Illyricum, and the East—Gregory used his influence with much skill to promote the power and pretensions of the Roman see. He claimed for it a primacy, not of honour merely, but of authority, in the Church Universal. In his view Rome, as the see of the Prince of the Apostles, was by divine appointment (*Ep.*, iii. 30) 'the head of all the churches' (*Ep.*, xiii. 50). The decrees of councils would have no binding force 'without the authority and consent of the Apostolic See' (*Ep.*, ix. 156). The Bishop of Rome was called to undertake 'the government of the Church' (*Ep.*, v. 44); appeals might be made to him against the decisions even of the Patriarch of Constantinople; and all bishops, including the patriarchs, if guilty of heresy or uncanonical proceedings, were subject to his correction (*Ep.*, ix. 26, 27). Such claims, even when accompanied by the Pope's assurances that he had no desire to interfere with the canonical rights of bishops (*Ep.*, ii. 52; xi. 24), could not be put forward without encountering opposition. Three notable disputes—with the bishops of Ravenna concerning the use of the pallium [PALL]; with Maximus, the 'usurping' bishop of Salona; and with the Patriarchs of Constantinople over the title 'Ecumenical Bishop'—prove that even the greatest of the early popes found it impossible always to enforce his authority. Yet Gregory's frank assertion of this lofty claim, and the firmness and consistency with which he upheld it, undoubtedly contributed greatly to build up the system of papal absolutism. The line which he took prepared the way for such successors as Gregory VII. and Innocent III. (*q.v.*).

Further, this consolidation of spiritual authority coincided with a remarkable development of the temporal power of the papacy. Italy was distracted between the Lombards and the Imperialists, and Gregory, availing himself of a unique opportunity, soon won a position that was almost regal. For the first time in history the Pope appeared as a political power. He appointed governors to cities, issued orders to generals, provided munition of war, sent ambassadors to negotiate with the Lombard King, and even ventured to conclude a private peace. He determined with sovereign authority what was to be done in Rome, and outside the city he had no hesitation in encroaching on the prerogatives of the Imperial government, which was too weak to prevent such invasion of its rights. Probably he did not consciously aim at usurpation; circumstances compelled him to assume the functions of a secular potentate. But his action created a precedent, of which his successors were not unwilling to avail themselves.

The first monk to become Pope, Gregory was naturally a zealous supporter of monasticism. He laboured to diffuse the monastic system by the foundation and endowment of new monasteries, and undertook to reform the older institutions, many of which were in a very unsatisfactory condition, by enforcing a strict observance of the Rule of St. Benedict. He protected the monasteries from the encroachment of the bishops by issuing *privilegia* or charters in restraint of abuses, whereby the episcopal jurisdiction in the monasteries was confined strictly to spiritual matters. He further sought to emphasise the distinction between monks and secular clergy, prohibiting the former from ministering in parish churches, and ordaining that a monk who was promoted to an ecclesiastical cure should lose all rights in his monastery. Two slight innovations introduced by him may be noticed: the minimum age of an abbess was fixed at sixty, and the period of novitiate was prolonged from one year to two.

Gregory takes high rank among the great organisers of missionary enterprises for the conversion of heathens and heretics. The spread of Catholic Christianity among the Lombards is to be attributed largely to his influence: he took measures also for the suppression of paganism in Gaul, Italy, Sicily, Sardinia, and Corsica; of Arianism in Spain, of Donatism in Africa, of Manichaeism in Sicily, of the Schism of the Three Chapters in Istria and Northern Italy. Most important, however, was the twofold mission to Britain. First in 596 he sent out a band of monks, headed by Augustine (*q.v.*), Prior of St. Andrew's monastery. These missionaries do not appear to have been selected on account of any particular personal qualifications for the work. They were utterly ignorant of the character and customs of the people to whom they were sent, and could not speak a word of their language. Further, by an extraordinary oversight, they seem to have been furnished with no written instructions or even letters of introduction. After journeying as far as Aix their courage failed, and they

sent Augustine back to Rome to beg that they might be recalled. Gregory, however, would not allow the scheme to drop. He directed them to take some Franks to act as interpreters, provided them with letters of recommendation to the chief persons in Gaul, and to ensure discipline among the missionaries themselves appointed Augustine abbot, and gave him full authority over his companions. In 598 Augustine sent Laurentius and Peter to Rome to report what had been done, to ask advice on certain difficult points, and to request that more workers might be sent. Strangely enough, Gregory delayed no less than three years before replying. In June 601, however, a fresh band of missionaries set forth from Rome, bearing, together with presents, some remarkable letters from the Pope to Bereta, Aethelberht, and Augustine. Bereta was thanked for the help she had given to the mission, and flattered with the assurance that her good works had attracted the notice of the Emperor (*Ep.*, xi. 35); Aethelberht was urged to put down the worship of idols among his people and destroy the temples (*Ep.*, xi. 37). After the departure of the missionaries, however, Gregory changed his mind on the last point, and despatched a courier after them with fresh instructions. The idols were to be destroyed, but the shrines were to be purified with holy water and dedicated to Christian worship, while the heathen sacrifices were to be transformed into religious feasts (*Ep.*, xi. 56). Of the three letters to Augustine the first contains an exhortation to the archbishop not to be uplifted on account of his gift of miracles (*Ep.*, xi. 36); the second confers on him the pallium [PALL], to be worn only during Mass, and develops a scheme for the constitution of the English Church. Augustine, whose metropolitan see is assumed to be not Canterbury but London, was to ordain twelve bishops, who should be subject to his jurisdiction, in the southern part of the island. Another bishop was to be sent to York. If the people in that part of the country received the Gospel, the Bishop of York was also to consecrate twelve suffragans, and act as their metropolitan. During Augustine's lifetime all the bishops in the island were to be subject to his authority, but after his death the archbishops of London and York were to be independent of each other, the senior taking precedence, but each ruling in his own province as metropolitan, each receiving the pallium from Rome, and each being ordained by his own suffragans (*Ep.*, xi. 39). This scheme was at the time impracticable, yet the wisdom with which it was conceived has since been justified. With the substitution of Canterbury for London, and some other inevitable changes of detail, it represents in outline the constitution of the English Church as it is in the present day. The third document addressed to Augustine was the famous *Responsa*, consisting of replies to a number of questions on points of ecclesiastical organisation and discipline (*Ep.*, xi. 56*a*). With the writing of these letters and the sending of the second band of missionaries Gregory's labours for the conversion of the English came to an end. The English have not been unmindful of the debt of gratitude which they owe to this great Pope. Already in the beginning of the eighth century he was invoked in England as a saint, and the Council of Clovesho decreed that the festival of ' our father Gregory ' should be kept as a holiday of obligation (Haddan and Stubbs, iii. 368). Among the numerous titles bestowed on him, Bede's designation of ' apostle ' is the best known and most appropriate. ' For we rightly may and ought to call him our apostle, because, whereas he bore the pontifical primacy in the whole world, and was placed over the churches already converted to the true faith, he made our nation, till then given up to idols, a Church of Christ. Though to others he may not be an apostle, yet he is to us. For the seal of his apostleship are we in the Lord ' (Bede, *H.E.*, ii. 1).

Gregory was a prolific writer. Among his extant works are more than eight hundred etters, a commentary on Job in thirty-five books, a manual for the use of bishops, a collection of miraculous stories of saints together with a life of St. Benedict, and a large number of sermons. Tradition further ascribes to him a reform of the Liturgy, a revision of the Antiphonary, and the revision and rearrangement of the system of Church music. But as regards the Liturgy the extent of his work has undoubtedly been exaggerated. The undisputed Gregorian innovations amount only to this, that he ordered the Alleluia after the Gradual to be chanted more frequently than formerly, and that he introduced two slight modifications into the Canon, inserting some words into the prayer *Hanc igitur*, and altering the place of the *Pater Noster*. Further, in the ceremonial of the Mass he forbade sub-deacons to wear chasubles when they proceeded to the altar for the celebration, and forbade deacons to perform any musical part of the service, with the single exception of the chanting of the Gospel. It is practically certain he revised the Antiphonary. The tradition that he was the founder of the Roman Schola Cantorum

has been proved to be an error, while the attribution to him of certain hymns—among them the familiar ' Blest Creator of the light ' —is equally mistaken.

Finally, as Fourth Doctor of the Latin Church, Gregory claims the consideration of theologians. The last of the great Latin fathers and the first representative of mediaeval Catholicism, he is the link which connects the theology of Tertullian, Ambrose, and Augustine with the scholastic speculation of a later period. His teaching, indeed, is not philosophical, systematic, or truly original. Its importance lies mainly in its simple, popular summarisation of the doctrine of Augustine, and in its detailed exposition of various religious conceptions which were current in the Western Church, but which had not hitherto been defined with precision. In his exposition, *e.g.*, of the ideas of Purgatory, of the Eucharistic Sacrifice, of Angels, of the efficacy of relics, Gregory made a distinct advance upon the older theology, and influenced profoundly the dogmatic development of the future. From his time to that of St. Anselm (*q.v.*) no teacher of equal eminence arose in the Church.

While his greatness as a man is universally admitted, there are some who call in question his greatness as a saint. Certainly he had faults. He was harsh at times almost to cruelty. He was inclined to be too subservient to persons of rank. His flattery of the murderous usurper Phocas is repulsive. Yet the careful student of Gregory's life and writings can scarcely fail to be impressed with the nobility of his character. Never certainly was there a more unselfish man, never one more genuinely religious. His faults were in many instances those of his age ; his virtues were his own.   [F. H. D.]

Works ; the complete works of Gregory in Migne's *Pat. Lat.* ; the *Epistolae* in the *M.G.H.*, Berlin, 1887-99. The *Pastoral Care* and a selection of the *Letters* have been translated into English in the series of *Nicene and Post-Nicene Fathers* ; the *Morals* in the *Library of Fathers*. See also *Dialogues of St. Gregory*, ed. E. C. Gardner ; the Whitby *Life of Pope St. Gregory the Great*, ed. F. A. Gasquet, London, 1904 ; F. Homes Dudden, *Gregory the Great* ; T. Hodgkin, *Italy and her Invaders*, vol. v. cc. 7-10 ; H. K. Mann, *The Lives of the Popes*, vol. i. pp. 1-250 ; F. Gregorovius, *Rome in the Middle Ages* (E.T.), vol. ii. pp. 16-103 ; E. G. P. Wyatt, *St. Gregory and the Gregorian Music*. For other literature see O. Bardenhewer, *Patrology* (E.T.), pp. 655-7.

GRINDAL, Edmund (c. 1519-83). Archbishop of Canterbury, succeeded Parker (*q.v.*) in 1575, having been previously Bishop of London, 1559-70, and Archbishop of York,

1570-5. A Cumbrian by origin, he was educated at Cambridge; and through the patronage of Bishop Ridley (*q.v.*) he attained a prominent position, and was likely to be nominated bishop by Edward. At Mary's accession he went abroad, and he remained there till January 1559. On his return he came back to his former influential position and reached the episcopate. His rule, however, in London was lax, not through any moral defects, but owing to his sympathy with the recalcitrants, who, under foreign influence, were opposing the Church settlement. His attempts at discipline were therefore half-hearted. His diocese was one of the most difficult and most crucial. Owing to his weakness and incapacity Parker had frequently to intervene; and it was thought a good way out of an embarrassing situation to transfer him to York in 1570. Here the diocesan's task was to repress Recusancy rather than coerce Nonconformity, and Grindal was more in his element. But ill-fortune led him to Canterbury five years later. There were many persons about the court who were anxious for a policy more favourable to Nonconformity, and even to the nascent Presbyterian views, than Parker had been. The new archbishop was in a sense their man; but some found him too honourable, some too obstinate, for their taste, and he soon was in trouble with the Queen because of his tactless handling of the problem caused by the clerical meetings called 'prophesyings.' On his refusal to suppress these gatherings at the Queen's orders he was suspended from the exercise of his functions; and though he was allowed later to undertake certain of his spiritual duties he never recovered from the disgrace, and he was about to resign on account of his blindness and failing health when he died, 6th July 1583. His career showed plainly the futility of the policy of concession to the Nonconformist Churchmen and others who were going further still than they to overturn the episcopal Church polity. The only possible result, if it had been successful, would have been a revolution, which would have been as disastrous politically as ecclesiastically. In private life Grindal made many friends, and he was graced by personal charm as well as piety and learning; but his conscientiousness was often misplaced, and his weakness of character flew to obstinacy, and thus the hopes of his earlier years ended in failure.

[W. H. F.]

Strype, *Life*; W. H. Frere, *Hist. Eng. Ch.*, *1558-1625*; White, *Lives of the Elizabethan Bishops*; Bishop Creighton in *D.N.B.*

GROSSETESTE, Robert (1175-1253), Bishop of Lincoln. The character and history of Grosseteste do not belie the promise of his name. Among the great English churchmen of his age he has left the highest reputation for dominant character and varied attainments. Born at Stradbroke, Suffolk, of humble parentage, he was a distinguished 'master' at Oxford in 1199. He graduated also at Paris, studying there Hebrew and Greek, and returned to Oxford, where he afterwards became *rector scholarum*, a position corresponding to that of the later Chancellor. Whilst holding this high office he received successively the archdeaconries of Wiltshire, Northampton, and Leicester, and a prebend at Lincoln—all of which, except the last, he resigned in 1232·owing to chronic ill-health. The main interest of his Oxford career lies in his relations with the newly arrived Franciscans. Always inclined to be critical of the monks, Grosseteste joyfully threw in his lot with the new order of Friars (*q.v.*), and became the first *lector* of their Oxford community. In so doing he helped to frustrate the purpose of St. Francis, who had hoped to found a brotherhood of simple, unlettered saints. The dangers of laziness were illustrated by the older Religious Orders, and Grosseteste accordingly encouraged learning, though he did not cease to exhort the friars to the life of poverty. Their well-worn and patched habits delighted him, and we still have one of his sermons in praise of mendicancy. The connection with Grosseteste was maintained after he had left the University, and the friars eventually received the gift of his library. To the influence of their great patron may be attributed in part the constitutionalist sympathies of the Franciscans in the disputes of the thirteenth century.

In 1235 the chapter of Lincoln elected Grosseteste bishop, and he entered upon the administration of the most populous diocese in England. In spite of the claims of the chapter of Canterbury, the consecration took place at Reading. Henceforward so much of his time was spent in strenuous conflict with monastic bodies, the Pope, and sometimes the King, that Matthew Paris compares him to Ishmael, with his hand against every man. These controversies were largely concerned with monastic exemptions from episcopal visitation and the monastic tenure of benefices. In 1239 the chapter of Lincoln disputed his right to visit them, and later produced a pretended history of their church in support of their contention. The question was referred to arbitrators, but no decision was made, until

Grosseteste, followed in haste by the dean and some of the canons, visited the Pope at Lyons in 1244 and obtained papal approval of his claim. In 1243 occurred a quarrel with the chapter of Canterbury. Grosseteste in his zeal for discipline had deposed and excommunicated the Abbot of Bardney for not answering a citation. As the see of Canterbury was vacant, the abbot appealed to the chapter, who took the opportunity to exercise metropolitan rights, and excommunicated the bishop. Grosseteste was furious. 'So may these ever pray for my soul to eternity,' was his only comment upon the sentence. His open defiance of the chapter received the sanction of a papal letter ordering the excommunication to be withdrawn. Seven years later Grosseteste made a second visit to the papal court to protest against the appropriation by religious houses of the tithes belonging to benefices in their gift. But the old bishop was unable to combat the venality of which he accuses the Roman court, and he returned to England unsuccessful. Probably Matthew Paris is just when he says that Grosseteste was unduly severe in dealing with the monasteries, though he admits that such severity arose entirely from a sense of responsibility for the souls entrusted to his care.

In his relations with the apostolic see Grosseteste is thoroughly representative of English churchmanship. His loyalty to the Pope is shown in his adherence to the unpopular constitutions of the legate Otho, although his local sympathies led him to protect the students of Oxford who attacked the papal emissary. At the Council of Merton he supported the papal proposals against the English barons. In 1241 he joined in sending a message from several bishops to the Emperor Frederick II., urging him to terminate his disputes with the papacy. But along with his submission to the supremacy of Rome, Grosseteste was vigorous in resisting practical abuses. The popes had lately begun to claim presentations in England on a large scale, and nominated Italians, often of unsuitable character or not even in priests' orders. Such nominees Grosseteste 'hated as though they were the poison of the serpent.' In the year of his death he refused to institute the Pope's young nephew, Federigo di Lavagna, to a canonry at Lincoln, arguing that the papal plenitude of power was for edification, not destruction. Again, in matters of finance zeal for liberty caused him to refuse the demands of the Pope in 1244, unless the consent of the whole body of bishops was obtained.

In the politics of his age Grosseteste played a consistent, if inconspicuous, part. He inherited the traditions of Stephen Langton (*q.v.*) and the Great Charter, and was the friend and adviser of Simon de Montfort. The King was to him suspect as a lover of foreigners and of arbitrary power. Thus he persuaded Nicholas of Farnham to accept the bishopric of Durham, lest the King should appoint some *alienigenum et degenerem*. He engaged in several disputes with Henry over Church appointments with varying success, according as the King received papal support. The most remarkable case concerns the sheriff of Rutland, whom Grosseteste ordered to arrest Ranulf, a clerk of the Lincoln diocese, deprived for incontinence. The sheriff refused to intervene, and the bishop excommunicated him. Whereupon the King appealed to Rome, and received the support of papal letters declaring against the citation of royal bailiffs before courts christian in secular matters.

In 1244 Grosseteste was appointed a clerical representative to discuss the financial needs of the Crown. In 1252 the royal demand of a tenth, nominally for crusading purposes, met with his vehement opposition. It mattered nothing, he argued, what the French gave their King; two cases would create a custom, and the precedent once established, the power of refusing supply would be gone. In the same year Grosseteste joined in securing the confirmation of the charters, and threatened excommunication against all who should violate them.

In the summer of 1253 his last illness overtook him at Buckden. Characteristically he called to his bedside a friar, who was at once his confessor and his medical adviser. The dying speeches attributed to him are chiefly censures on his beloved friars for not sufficiently combating heresy, on the corruption and nepotism of the Roman court, on the growing financial power exercised by the Caursins, on the attempted arbitrary government of Henry III. He bewailed the growing luxury, and prophetically declared the signs of coming strife, which should, however, free the Church from her bondage to the world.

At Grosseteste's tomb in Lincoln Cathedral miracles were soon recorded, but repeated attempts to secure his canonisation failed. His public career had not recommended him for papal approval; but in England he was canonised informally by the people. Matthew Paris describes him as pleasant and jovial 'at the table of bodily refreshment; at the spiritual table devout, tearful, penitent'; as a bishop diligent and honourable. Food, sleep, and merriment were his prescription for bodily welfare. The *Monumenta* of the friars record the case of a scrupulous brother who asked for a penance and was told to drink a cup of the best wine. 'Dear brother,' said Grosseteste, 'if you often performed a penance like that you would have a better-ordered conscience.' His close relations with Oxford gave Grosseteste frequent opportunities of befriending necessitous students, as, for instance, when he induced the University to lend small sums to its poorer members. It is remarkable that Grosseteste was among the few who appreciated the importance of Foreign Missions (*q.v.*). He told the friars not to mourn the departure of Adam of Oxford for the East, for 'the light of his knowledge is so bright that it ought to be concentrated most where it may dissipate the thick darkness of infidelity.' He offered himself to preach the Gospel to the Saracens, if commanded by the Pope and cardinals.

As a man of learning, he seemed to his own age a universal genius and magician. Roger Bacon, who attended his lectures, says: 'One man only, the Bishop of Lincoln, really knew the sciences.' Matthew Paris calls him *vir nimis literatus, a primis annis scholis educatus.* An enormous number of treatises, sermons, translations, and commentaries bear his name. He appears in the rôles of lawyer, philosopher, French poet, physicist, agriculturalist, as well as theologian. For the next two centuries his name is frequently quoted as the greatest English authority on every subject of learning. Though more interested in natural science, to which he applied himself with diligence and honest research, he supervised translations or commentaries on many famous works, including Aristotle's *Ethics*, his *Physics*, the *Testament of the Twelve Patriarchs*, the *Ignatian Epistles*, Walter de Henley's treatise on husbandry. But this constituted only one side of a career conspicuous in the active revival of religion and the national life; as the guide and counsellor of the Franciscans and the moral reformer of his diocese; in the forefront of the learning of the day as the teacher of the young University of Oxford; as the nationalist statesman who used his influence to avert the threatened disruption of the kingdom and to secure truth and justice in the State, Grosseteste is an embodiment of the best influences in the public life of the thirteenth century.

[R. G. D. L.]

Matthew Paris, *Chronica Majora*; Grosseteste, *Letters*; *Monumenta Franciscana*, i.—all in R.S.; Felten, *Robert Grosseteste, Bischof*

con Lincoln, 1887; Stevenson, *Robert Grosseteste*; Creighton in *Historical Lectures and Addresses*; Bigg in *Wayside Sketches in Ecclesiastical History*, 1906; H. R. Luard in *D.N.B.*

GUEST, Edmund (*c.* 1518-77), Bishop of Salisbury, son of Thomas Guest, Gheast, or Gest, of Northallerton, Yorks, but of a Worcestershire stock, was educated at York and Eton; Scholar, 1536; Fellow, B.A. (with Aylmer), 1541; M.A., 1544; and Vice-Provost of King's College, Cambridge; B.D., 1551. In the University grace-book his name is spelt 'Gest' and 'Jest.' Fuller (*q.v.*) apparently pronounced it as 'guest.' In King Edward's time the Vice-Provost came forward on the Reformers' side, and dedicated to his Provost, Cheke (*q.v.*), the King's 'schoolmaster,' in 1548 *A Treatise againste the preuee Masse in behalfe and furtheraunce of the mooste holye communyon* (printed by T. Reynold, 8vo). On 24th June 1549 he took part in the second day's disputation before the Visitors of the University. Dr. Glyn, afterwards Marian Bishop of Bangor, maintained Transubstantiation and the Eucharistic Sacrifice, and Guest followed Perne and Grindal (*q.v.*) on the Protestant side, with Pilkington as third opponent, Ridley (*q.v.*) acting as moderator. Guest's argument has been printed by Foxe, *Actes and Mon.*, ed. 1610, cols. 1258*b sqq.* Though ten years later Jewel (*q.v.*) on his return to England in March 1559 could write of him (*Works*, Parker Soc., ii. p. 1199) to P. Martyr (*q.v.*) as 'a Cambridge man, called Ghest,' he was like others who took part in those disputations marked out for the episcopate. Licensed to preach in 1551, he had in 1552 a controversy with Christopher Carlile of Clare Hall, who at Cambridge commencement in July maintained a position against the Descent into Hell. Under Mary (*q.v.*) Guest, like Parker (*q.v.*), remained in England in concealment, and on Elizabeth's accession he was made domestic chaplain to the new archbishop. It has been generally supposed that he filled his place at some meetings of Prayer Book revisers about February 1559, when illness prevented Parker from attending. An undated paper by Guest, which Cecil afterwards forwarded to Parker, is among Parker MSS. (cvi. art. 137) at C.C.C., Cambridge. Strype (*q.v.*) and others supposed it to belong to 1559, when the Elizabethan Prayer Book was being drafted. Dr. Gee, *Elizabethan Prayer Book*, has reprinted it (pp. 215-24), arguing that it belongs to a stage in the history of the Second Book of Edward VI., about March 1552 (*ibid.*, p. 50). The *C.Q.*

Reviewer (liv. p. 346, July 1902) maintains Strype's opinion. Guest was prepared to take part on the Protestant side in the public disputation in Westminster Abbey, March 1559, and he has left writings on the three questions proposed ; but the proceedings were brought to a close before his turn came to speak. Dorman, a papist, in his *Disproufe* (Antwerp, 1565) gives testimony to Guest's personal character and (setting aside his so-called heretical opinions) his fitness ' to beare the office of a true bisshop.' Harpsfield (*q.v.*) being deprived after the disputation, Guest was appointed Archdeacon of Canterbury, 13th October, and Rector of Cliffe in Kent, and when consecrated to the see of Rochester, 24th March 1560, was allowed to hold these preferments *in commendam*. The Queen made him also her almoner ; ' and he,' says Fuller, ' must be both a wise and a good man whom she would trust with her purse.' He remained unmarried. He had assisted Parker with the Articles of Religion (*q.v.*) in 1563, and signed the xxviii. on 29th January. He also as a commissioner in causes ecclesiastical signed the Advertisements (*q.v.*). About 1565 he prepared a conservative translation of the Psalms for the Bishops' Bible, which appeared in 1568. In May 1571

he wrote to Cecil (ineffectually), urging in the interest of peace and charity some modifications of Articles xvii., xxv., and xxviii., the last of these having been penned by him in its original form. He desired also the excision of Article xxix. (*S.P. Dom.*, lxxviii. 37). He preached in his cathedral at Rochester in favour of the Presence in the Eucharist. Dr. Frere has printed Guest's Articles and Injunctions for Rochester Cathedral (1565) and diocese (1565 and 1571), and likewise those for Salisbury Cathedral (1571)—*Alcuin Club Collection*, xvi. (1910). After Jewel's death Guest was translated in December 1571 to Sarum. He had no trouble with Roman Catholic recusants in either of his dioceses, owing presumably to his adherence to the true principles of the English Reformation. He died at Salisbury, 28th February 1577, leaving to the Cathedral library, according to his epitaph (which dates his death incorrectly), a vast quantity of excellent books, some of which Mr. Malden has identified. His brass effigy, showing a mild and benevolent countenance, was removed from the choir in 1684 to the south-east transept.

[c. w.]

H. Geast Dugdale, *Life*, 1840 ; *D.N.B.*

H

HACKET, John (1592-1670), Bishop of Coventry and Lichfield, son of a London tailor, was born in the parish of St. Martin's, Strand, and educated at Westminster and Trinity College, Cambridge, where he became Fellow. He was ordained in 1615, and soon afterwards became chaplain to Bishop Williams (*q.v.*), and received among other benefices St. Andrew's, Holborn, and Cheam in Surrey—the one, he was told, being given for wealth and the other for health. He resided in London in the winter, and was an active parish priest and a popular preacher; a large sum collected by him to rebuild the church was afterwards confiscated. He was appointed Archdeacon of Lincoln in 1631, and Canon of St. Paul's in 1641. He took an active part in the proceedings of the earlier sessions of the Long Parliament as a representative of the moderate and conciliatory part of the Church, and pleaded for the retention of deans and chapters, at first with success. He was appointed a member of the Westminster Assembly of divines, but soon retired. His Holborn

living was sequestrated, but he was allowed to retain Cheam, and seems to have continued to use the Prayer Book publicly, and remained loyal to the King.

At the Restoration he once more became prominent as a preacher, and was offered the bishopric of Gloucester, which he refused, but accepted that of Coventry and Lichfield in 1661. The cathedral was in ruins, but he set himself to restore it with the utmost energy, and raised a sum of £20,000, of which he contributed £3500 himself. He was opposed by Wood, the dean, whom he excommunicated in consequence. But success crowned his efforts, and a solemn service of consecration was held on Christmas Eve, 1669. He died on 25th October 1670.

[c. p. s. c.]

Plume, *Life of Hacket*, ed. Walcot, 1865.

HAMPDEN, Renn Dickson (1793-1868), Bishop of Hereford, was educated at Oriel College, Oxford, and became Fellow, 1814. In 1833 he was appointed Principal of St. Mary Hall, Oxford, where he introduced reforms and spent £4000 of his own money on the buildings. A pamphlet advocating the admission of dissenters to the University (1834), but especially his Bampton Lectures of 1832 on 'The Scholastic Philosophy considered in its relation to Christian Theology,' brought his orthodoxy into suspicion. Their theme was the injurious effect of the survival of scholasticism on Protestant truth, as involving excessive veneration for the sacramental system, tradition, and church authority. The lectures were thought to have been inspired by Blanco White, and to be heretical on the subjects of the Blessed Trinity and the Atonement. His appointment as Regius Professor of Divinity in 1836 met with vigorous opposition, led by J. H. Newman (*q.v.*) and Dr. Pusey (*q.v.*), and supported by Mr. Gladstone (*q.v.*), who in 1856 expressed his regret for his action. 'A shower of pamphlets . . . descended from Oxford over the land.' Evangelicals joined in the protests, but Lord Melbourne refused to let Hampden withdraw, saying: 'Be easy, Doctor; I like an easy man.' A statute to exclude the Professor from the boards which inquired into heresy and nominated select preachers, though delayed by the proctors, was carried in Convocation. An attempt to repeal it in 1842 was defeated. Hampden was learned, but his style was obscure and his manner unattractive; 'he stood before you like a milestone and brayed at you like a jackass.' His dislike of Tractarianism led him in 1842 to require a Tractarian candidate for the degree of B.D. (R. Macmullen) to maintain a low and questionable doctrine of the Eucharist. In this act of tyranny he was supported by the courts (*Hampden v. Macmullen, Notes of Eccl. and Mar. Cas.*, iii., supp. 1).

In 1847 Lord John Russell raised a storm of protest by offering him the see of Hereford. Thirteen bishops signed a remonstrance. It was proposed to prosecute Hampden for false doctrine, but Bishop S. Wilberforce (*q.v.*) withdrew his consent to the suit. Evangelicals and Liberals alike protested against throwing 'a fresh firebrand into our unhappy Church.' But the minister, a strong Erastian and Low Churchman, intended the appointment as a blow to the High Church party, and when the Dean of Hereford, Dr. Mereweather, protested that he would not vote in the chapter for Hampden's election to the see, merely replied: 'I have had the honour to receive your letter of the 22nd inst. in which you intimate to me your intention of breaking the law.' Hampden was duly elected, the dean and one canon voting

against him; and the election was confirmed, the Queen's Bench deciding (though the judges were divided) that the vicar-general was right in refusing to hear objectors to the confirmation (*R. v. Archbishop of Canterbury*, 1848, 11 Q.B. 483). Thus ended the many Hampden controversies. Henceforth he was 'buried alive' in his diocese, which he administered peaceably but without distinction. [BISHOPS.]   [G. C.]

Works; H. Hampden, *Memorials of Dr. Hampden*; T. Mozley, *Reminiscences*; R. Jebb, *The Case of Dr. Hampden.*

HAMPTON COURT CONFERENCE, The,

was called by James I. in the summer of 1603 to give the Puritans an opportunity of discussing with the bishops the reform of the Church. In December the Puritan ministers held a conference in or near London to decide on their demands. The moderates defeated the radicals, who wished to 'modify' episcopacy sufficiently to make it Presbyterianism, and pledged the speakers to ask simply for the reform of abuses and minor matters. The bishops spent the autumn preparing their case. On 14th January 1603-4, the first day of the conference, the bishops were alone with the King, and were really forced to defend themselves. This, however, they did to James's satisfaction, and agreed to reform many abuses. On the second day, 16th January, the majority of the bishops in committee drew up in form the points concluded at the first day's debate with the King, while Bancroft (*q.v.*), Bishop of London, and Bilson, Bishop of Winchester, aided by several deans, debated the question of reform with five Puritans—Reynolds, Spark, Chaderton, Knewstubbs, and Feilde. As spokesman, Reynolds demanded purity of doctrine, an able clergy, the government of the Church 'sincerely ministered according to God's word,' and the correction of the errors in the Book of Common Prayer and the amendment of the Thirty-nine Articles. All these points he elaborated at great length, insisting paradoxically that they were things of no importance which it was highly essential to change.

Bancroft, with great keenness of insight, tore the thin mask from these demands. What they asked really included, he said, the adoption of the full Calvinistic doctrine of predestination, thus abandoning the position the English Church had always held. The change desired in confirmation was meant to place in the hands of the ordinary clergy the right to confirm, and hence the right to admit, new members to the Church. To declare that the minister's intentions were not of the essence of the Eucharist, as Reynolds asked, was to permit the Puritan clergy to administer to their flocks a sacrament which they did not believe was a sacrament at all, which, however, they must perform in order legally to hold their cures. To say that they might perform the highest rite in the ritual without believing it was to sanction the violation of the law of the Church in its most essential point. An addition to the Catechism and a new translation of the Bible were readily granted. But the sign of the cross in baptism James declined to omit, and he flatly told the Puritans that he and the bishops desired a learned clergy as much as any Puritan, but that without better incomes, better clergy were not to be hoped for. He added that he thought all these requests slight and unimportant.

Nettled at last by this reception, Reynolds finally brought forth the radical proposals, and asked for the modification of episcopacy. He asked that the bishops and archdeacons should share their functions with a council of learned ministers. The archdeacon's visitation would thus become a classis, the bishop's a provincial, and the archbishop's a national synod. Hence, without changing the law of the English Church, the substance of the true Church government instituted by Christ could be introduced. James had had too much experience of Scottish presbyters not to see the meaning of this proposal, and told Reynolds he would never grant it till he was 'pursy and fat.' Rising, he said that if this was all the Puritans had to say he saw no crying need for reform; they should conform, or he would 'harry them out of the land.' So ended the second day.

On 18th January, the third day, a large and imposing assembly of dignitaries met, and James, presiding, first listened to reports from the various committees of the points to be reformed. (A list of them is in Prothero, *Statutes and Const. Documents*, 416.) Then the Puritan advocates were called, who came accompanied by a representative group (thirty-two in all) of the most prominent of the party from all over England. The royal decisions were announced, they promised to obey them, the King agreed to tolerate tender consciences for a while, and the Conference ended. The positive result of the Conference itself was a list of points which several committees of the bishops and privy councillors were to put into execution, and later, in 1611, the so-called Authorised Version. [BIBLE, ENGLISH.] [R. G. U.]

Barlow, *Summe and Substance of the Conference*; Usher, *Reconstruction of the Eng. Ch.*; Cardwell, *Conferences.*

HARPSFIELD, Nicholas (c. 1519-75), was the younger and more distinguished of two brothers who held high ecclesiastical office in Mary's reign. Both were Wykehamists, Oxonians, and learned writers; but while John (1516-78), the elder, went into retirement soon after Elizabeth's accession, published nothing further, and took no part in controversy, Nicholas, who, being Archdeacon of Canterbury had earned an unenviable reputation as an ecclesiastical judge, became one of the chief disputants on the Conservative side. His life was spent in prison from his arrest, while attempting to escape abroad, in August 1559 to his death; but he wrote considerably nevertheless. Some of his books were published by friends, *e.g.* his *Dialogi* by Cope and his *Defence of Feckenham* (*q.v.*) by Stapleton; others only appeared after his death, or remain still in MS. His earlier work, a treatise on Henry's first divorce, is of considerable historic value.

[W. H. F.]

Pocock, introd. to Harpsfield's *Treatise on the pretended Divorce* (C.S.). Catholic Rec. Society, *Misc.*, i. 41, 48, 53.

HEATH, Nicholas (c. 1501-78), Archbishop of York; after being appointed Archdeacon of Stafford in 1534 was in 1535 sent with Edward Fox, Bishop of Hereford, to the princes of the Smalcaldic League to negotiate for a doctrinal alliance between them and Henry VIII. The mission failed, but Heath's 'humanity and learning' made a favourable impression. [REUNION WITH THE FOREIGN REFORMED.] In 1539 he was appointed Bishop of Rochester, and in 1543 translated to Worcester. In Edward VI.'s reign the devastation of altars and churches induced him, like many others, to turn back to the Conservative side. In 1548 he attacked in the House of Lords the manner in which the First Prayer Book treated the doctrine of the Mass. Yet in 1551 he was one of the commission appointed to draw up the new Ordinal, which, when finished, he refused to endorse, though he professed himself ready to use it. He was consequently imprisoned, and eventually deprived, but was allowed to live in the house of Ridley (*q.v.*).

On Mary's accession he was restored, and in 1555 translated to York, where he procured the return of much of the former property of the see. In 1556 he became Lord Chancellor, in which capacity, on Mary's death, he proclaimed Elizabeth 'undisputed heir' to the Crown. Soon afterwards he resigned the seal, and Sir Nicholas Bacon, a layman, became Lord Keeper, an appointment significant of the difference in policy of the two Queens. Heath did his best to go with the new order, but the Royal Supremacy (*q.v.*), even in the modified form in which Elizabeth exercised it, was more than he could approve. Speaking on the Supremacy Bill in the House of Lords, he admitted that to withdraw obedience from Paul IV., 'a very austere stern father unto us,' was a comparatively unimportant matter. But the title 'Supreme Head,' then proposed, was one which Parliament could not confer nor the Queen receive (Strype, *Annals*, I. ii. 399). He had already refused to officiate at Elizabeth's coronation, and now became the leader of the main body of Marian prelates who declined the Supremacy Oath. He was deprived in July 1559, but after three years' imprisonment (June 1560 to September 1563) was allowed to retire to his house at Chobham, Surrey, where he lived 'many years in great quietness of mind to my singular comfort.' He was included in the official returns as a recusant, and Mass was known to be said at his house. But he was apparently not molested, and Elizabeth occasionally visited him.   [W. H. F.]

Bridgett, *Catholic Hierarchy*, vii. ; Burt, *Elizabethan Religious Settlement* ; *D.N.B.*

HENRY VIII. (1491-1547), King of England, born at Greenwich, 28th June, was third child and second son of Henry VII. and his wife Elizabeth, eldest daughter of Edward IV., and thus in his person united the rival houses of York and Lancaster. He was baptized at Greenwich in the Church of the Friars' Observants (reformed Franciscans, then and earlier an order specially beloved by the Tudors) by Bishop R. Fox (*q.v.*). In pursuance of his policy of keeping the great offices out of the hands of the old nobility and conferring them on his sons (the work being done by capable dignitaries, civil servants of less exalted rank), Henry VII. made the baby prince, 1492, Warden of the Cinque Ports ; 1494, Lord Lieutenant of Ireland (where Sir E. Poynings was his Deputy) ; and December 1494, Warden of the Scottish Marches. Brought up strictly by clever parents, Henry was from his very early years carefully educated. Erasmus, writing 1st April 1529, bears clear witness to Henry's intellectual ability and training (*Epistolae*, London, 1642, p. 1269), *puellus admodum studiis admotus est*. He was trained in Mathematics and spoke Latin, French, Spanish, and a little Italian. In 1499, when only eight, his writing astonished Erasmus, and the precocious boy sent the great scholar a note challenging something from his pen.

All his life he was devoted to music ; when four years old (1495) he had a band of minstrels of his own, distinct from those of his father and elder brother. He practised the art he so much loved, and played on the lute, the organ, and the harpsichord. He brought to England the organist of St. Mark's, Venice, one Dionysius Memo, and on one occasion listened to an organ recital by him for four hours without a break. Henry was also a composer (vocal and instrumental pieces of his composition are among the MSS. in the British Museum), and one of his anthems, 'O Lorde, the Maker of all thyng,' is still sung in English cathedrals.

Henry was also remarkable for his prowess as an athlete. Erasmus, in the letter above quoted, witnesses to it. In riding, tilting, wrestling, and archery, Henry was among the foremost in his realm. Hunting was a passion with him, and he would tire eight or ten horses in the day, stationed beforehand along the line of country he meant to take ; and Giustiniani, the Venetian ambassador, in a secret despatch of 1519, describes also Henry's 'extravagant fondness for tennis—at which game it is the prettiest thing in the world to see him play, his fair skin glowing through a shirt of the finest texture.'

The story that Henry was intended by his father for high ecclesiastical office and was therefore specially trained in theology, appears to rest only on the authority of Lord Herbert of Cherbury, whose life of Henry was published, 1649, and is probably only an inference from the King's theological interests. These were throughout his life considerable. According to the contemporary, Polydore Vergil, Wolsey induced Henry to study St. Thomas Aquinas. In 1518 the King appears to have defended 'Mental and *ex tempore* Prayer' as against those who confined their devotions to fixed forms, and in 1521 he composed his treatise, *Assertio Septem Sacramentorum*, in reply to Luther, and the work is no contemptible performance. On 11th October 1521 Leo X. gave him the title *Fidei Defensor* for his book against Luther. Henry had pressed for some such title as early as 1515, and in January 1516 he had suggested that particular title (Pollard, 107). Henry displayed his theological side in his examination of Lambert (or Nicholson) at his trial for heresy, November 1537, and, according to Cromwell (*q.v.*), 'benignly essayed to convert the miserable man' to belief in the corporeal presence in the Eucharist. The later formularies of his reign (the Articles of 1536, the *Bishops' Book*, 1537, and the so-called *King's*

Book, 1543) doubtless owe something to his interest in the subject. The last contains a preface by the King, in which, after a brief and excellent summary of the Christian faith as expounded in the book, he warns his people that the reading of the Old and New Testament is ' not so necessary for all those folks ' who belong to the class that needs teaching. They are to hear and not to read; and the King concludes his warning by insisting on his own interpretation of the text: ' Blessed are they that *hear* the Word of God and keep it,' *i.e.* hearing the doctrine, not reading the Scriptures, is best for most men. Henry was reckoned religious by some observers. ' Very religious,' Giustiniani calls him in 1519, and describes how he used to hear three Masses on the days on which he hunted, and sometimes five on other days, and he used to attend the Office, *i.e.* Vespers and Compline, in the Queen's chamber. To the end of his life ' Henry seldom neglected to creep to the Cross on Good Friday, to serve the priest at Mass, and to receive holy bread and holy water every Sunday ' (Pollard, 388, quoting *L. and P.*, xiv. i. 967). Nicolas Sander in his *De Schismate Anglicano* (ed. 1628, p. 166) admits that Henry ' always held the sacrament of the Eucharist in the highest honour,' and relates how when a little before his death he was about to communicate, and finding it extremely difficult to rise from his chair and kneel, ' the Zwinglians around him were assuring him that in his state of health he might communicate sitting, the King replied that if he did not cast himself to the earth before the most holy sacrament, he should be derogating from its due honour.' But in the sixteenth century orthodoxy of belief and practice did not necessarily involve a Christian purity of life.

Henry had been brought up in a good home, and the married life of his parents was a model of happiness and fidelity. He himself married on 11th June 1509 (he had succeeded to the Crown on 22nd April) Katherine, daughter of Ferdinand and Isabella of Castile and Aragon, the nominal widow of his brother Arthur, who had died in April 1502. At the time of her union with Henry, Katherine was twenty-four and Henry not quite eighteen, and she was sufficiently beautiful for the King to be very much in love with her. The first years of their married life were years of real happiness. Doubtless if Katherine had possessed tact she would have kept her husband's love. Unfortunately for her, her lack of tact made her unable to manage him (as Katherine Parr did in later years), and more than once she seriously

wounded his vanity, and to do so was to invite his jealousy and dislike. The marriage was singularly unfortunate in another respect. By June 1514 she had borne the King three sons and a daughter, but they were either born dead or survived their birth only a few days. A fourth son was born prematurely at the end of the year, dead—a fact Peter Martyr attributed to the King's brutality to the Queen at the time, as he vented on her his rage with her father. In February 1516 a daughter, Mary, was born. In the next year the Queen seems to have had a miscarriage; and in November 1518, when Henry was again hoping for a male heir, a daughter was born dead. This was the last of Katherine's children. There can be no doubt that Henry's desire for a male heir to continue the direct succession was a serious passion with him.

Henry, despite his high interests, was not a faithful husband, and the best that his apologists urge for him is that he was not as licentious as his contemporaries. Yet he fell immeasurably below the standard set him by his father, or by his friend, Sir Thomas More (*q.v.*). As early as 1510 scandal connected his name with a married sister of the Duke of Buckingham. In October 1513 he brought back with him from Calais Bessie Blount (daughter of Sir John Blount), a maid of honour to Katherine, and gave her a splendid establishment at New Hall in Essex. She bore him a son, Henry Fitzroy, 1519, who was created Duke of Richmond. About 1521 Mary Boleyn, sister of Anne Boleyn, became his mistress, and in 1533 the Duke of Norfolk told the Imperial ambassador, Chapuys, that Henry had always been inclined to *amours* (*L. and P.*, vi. 241), and even in 1515 it was said that ' he cared only for girls and hunting ' (*L. and P.*, ii. 1105). In this connection an odious story, still current (cf. Lewis, Introduction to Sander's *Rise and Progress of the Anglican Schism*, 1877), alleges that Henry was himself the father of Anne Boleyn. It was stated by Sander in his book, on the authority of Mr. Justice Rastall, a brother-in-law of Sir T. More; but it had an earlier currency, as some such story was being repeated in England in 1533 (Pocock, *Records of the Reformation*, ii. 468; Brewer, *Henry VIII.*, ii. 240 n.). Henry himself denied it to Sir George Throgmorton, though he admitted his affinity to Anne through his connection with her sister. Mary Boleyn was married later to one of Henry's courtiers, Sir W. Cary, who died 1528. Notwithstanding his grosser pleasures, ' Henry was a keen man of business, and even under Wolsey (*q.v.*) took a large share in foreign politics: but after 1525, when Francis I. was captured at Pavia by Charles V., foreign politics ceased to be interesting. Wolsey's own policy of the balance of power had become impossible, and the King turned to other subjects. Uppermost was the question of his wife. It was now certain that he could no longer hope for a male heir, and Katherine herself was becoming repugnant to him. Since 1524 (so he told Grynaeus in 1531: Brewer, ii. 162, n. 2) he had ceased to treat her as his wife, and he began to develop scruples as to the legality of his marriage. Brewer supposed that the matter began to be discussed secretly by the King in 1525 and 1526, but it is now clear that he misunderstood a reference to *istud benedictum divortium* (Pollard, 197, n. 1). How the doubts arose is not known. Shakespeare records the tradition that they were suggested to Henry by his confessor, Longland, Bishop of Lincoln (1521-47). Henry told the Lord Mayor and aldermen of London later that they arose from the death of his children, together with his own Bible reading. In 1527 Henry and Wolsey both stated that doubts as to the validity of the King's marriage had been suggested by a French envoy, the Bishop of Tarbes, when concluding a treaty which involved the marriage of the Princess Mary and Francis I. Whatever the origin, on 17th May 1527, with great secrecy, a trial was held before Wolsey as legate and Archbishop Warham (*q.v.*) as assessor, at which Henry appeared to answer a charge of living with his brother's wife. The court came to no decision, and Katherine never knew of it. Henry opened negotiations with Rome on his own account apart from Wolsey, and in 1528 sought a dispensation 'to have two wives'; 'whereof some great reasons and precedents appear, especially in the Old Testament' (*L. and P.*, iv. 2157 and 2161). This clumsy device was bound to fail, but Wolsey succeeded in gaining a Legatine Court in England to try the case under a decretal commission, *i.e.* a commission laying down the law by which the case was to be determined, without further appeal. To hold this court Cardinal Campeggio (*q.v.*) was associated with Wolsey, and reached London on 28th October 1528. The court began its sessions in the great hall of the Black Friars in London, 31st May 1529, and sat intermittently until 23rd July, when it was supposed that sentence would be given; but following the use of the Roman courts, Campeggio adjourned it for the summer until

1st October. Meanwhile Pope Clement VII. had made up his mind to become an Imperialist, and on 15th July revoked the cause to Rome. The immediate result was the fall of Wolsey, who was charged with *Praemunire* in October, and stripped of most of his possessions. The question was complicated by Henry's passion for Anne Boleyn (a lady of the court and sister of his former mistress). Some sixteen of his love-letters to her survive, written in the period 1527 to December 1528 (printed in the *Harleian Misc.*, iii. 45, and in *The Pamphleteer*, 1823, vols. xxi. and xxii.). These documents—now in the Vatican—are disgraced by some gross allusions, and are discreditable alike to the writer and to the lady who received them. After the break up of the Legatine Court Henry was at first at a loss, but finally entered upon a policy of coercing the Pope and the English Church. His greatest *tour de force* was when he accused the whole English Church clergy and then the laity of *Praemunire* for acquiescing in Wolsey's legatine authority in December 1530. Henry himself had caused the *Praemunire*, had clamoured for Wolsey to be made legate, and in 1528 had prayed for a Legatine Court to try his own case, and had pleaded before it. Yet in 1530 he was the only man in the realm not guilty of *Praemunire*. His use of the statute was characteristic: 'It was conservative, it was legal, and it was unjust' (Pollard, 284).

The result of this action was the recognition of the Royal Supremacy (*q.v.*) by the Convocations. In November 1532 Henry was married to Anne Boleyn, probably by George Brown, a Franciscan friar (*Edinburgh Review*, January 1886), and she was crowned at Westminster, 31st May 1533. On 7th September 1533 her daughter Elizabeth was born at Greenwich (her birthday seems to have been the cause of the addition of the Festival of St. Enurchus to the English Calendar in 1604, as during her reign the day was probably a holiday). On 23rd May 1533 Cranmer (*q.v.*) had declared the marriage between Henry and Katherine void *ab initio*, and on 28th May he pronounced that with Anne Boleyn good and lawful. Henry had treated Katherine with singular callousness. Until 14th July 1531 he had been to see her every three days, but on that date he left Windsor without bidding her farewell, and never saw her again. He bade her withdraw to various, somewhat malarious, manor-houses in turn, took her daughter Mary from her, and never allowed them to meet again. At Rome, 11th July 1533, the marriage with Anne was declared void, and on 23rd March 1534 Clement VII.

declared that with Katherine to be legal. After the birth of Elizabeth, Queen Katherine was declared Princess Dowager of Wales, and the Princess Mary lost her title and pre-eminence. On 7th January 1536 Katherine died at Kimbolton, conscious, dignified, and devout to the end. The story that she wrote at the last a touching letter to Henry is a pure invention. When the news of her death reached Henry he and Anne dressed themselves in yellow, and the King danced with the ladies of the court 'like one mad with delight.' Katherine's request to be buried among the Franciscan Observants was neglected, and her body was laid in the Benedictine abbey church of Peterborough.

From 1534 the breach with Rome widened, and in 1535 a reign of terror began. Sir T. More and Bishop Fisher were executed, and Henry reached a height of absolutism unknown in previous history. On 2nd May 1536 Anne Boleyn was arrested on charges of incest and adultery, and after a trial before her uncle, the Duke of Norfolk, and twenty-six peers, was found guilty, and executed on 19th May. Two days before Cranmer declared in a formal court at Lambeth the marriage between her and Henry to be utterly null and void *ab initio*, and by an Act of 1536 the Princess Elizabeth was declared, like Mary, illegitimate. Henry was now 'a Christian bachelor, mishandled by fate' (H. A. L. Fisher). He had in appearance been married some twenty-seven years, and had begotten two daughters, but so far was appearance from reality that Cranmer decided that he had never yet been legally married, and was still without lawful offspring. On the day of Anne's execution Henry received a dispensation to marry Jane Seymour, one of the maids of honour; next day they were secretly betrothed, and were married on 30th May. Jane Seymour is the one Queen of Henry whom all unite in praising, save Alexander Aless, a Scots reformer, who denounced her as 'an enemy to the Gospel.' Cardinal Pole described her as 'full of goodness,' and she did much to alleviate the hard lot of the Princess Mary. She exercised no political power, and died twelve days after giving birth to a son, Edward VI., at Hampton Court, 24th October 1537.

Henry's health was now (1538) bad. He had a fistula in one leg, his face at times grew black, and he himself speechless from pain. He proceeded, however, with the Dissolution of the Monasteries (*q.v.*) and with overtures to the reforming princes of the Empire. In 1539 he resolved to marry Anne of Cleves

with a view to strengthening his position in Europe. She was thirty-four years old, a plain, heavy woman, destitute of every accomplishment save needlework, and knowing no language but her own. Henry married her most unwillingly on 6th January 1540, calling her (so Burnet alleges) ' no better than a Flanders mare.' The result of the wedding was the fall and death of Cromwell (*q.v.*) in July 1540, and on 7th July 1540 the united Convocations declared the marriage between Henry and Anne of Cleves null and void, on the ground of her precontract and Henry's defective intention. Anne was pensioned, and was, wrote Marillac, the French ambassador, in August 1540, 'as joyous as ever, and wears new dresses every day.' She lived happily in England until her death in 1557. On 28th July 1540 Henry married a young girl, Katherine Howard, niece of the Duke of Norfolk. His old spirits returned, and he began a new rule of life, rising between five and six A.M. even in winter, hearing Mass at seven, and then riding until ten. In November 1541 Cranmer disclosed to him the unchastity of the Queen. She was condemned by Act of Attainder and executed, 11th February 1542. On 12th July 1543 he married his last wife, Katherine Parr, already the widow of two husbands (Edmund Brough and Lord Latimer), and destined to be the wife of a fourth (Sir Thomas Seymour). Her character was beyond reproach; she nursed Henry tenderly during his closing years, and 'succeeded to some extent in mitigating the violence of his temper' (Pollard, 411). His increasing infirmities did not, however, deter Henry once more from going to war with France, and from July to the end of September 1544 he conducted the campaign in person, and captured Boulogne. Financial exigencies drove him to debase the currency, though he coined his own plate to meet the cost of the war; and in June 1546 he made peace, England retaining Boulogne for eight years longer.

His diseases, however, grew upon him. The fistula which was at last to slay him grew worse, and his bulk was so unwieldy that he could with difficulty walk and stand. In January 1547 he became mortally ill, but was 'loath to hear any mention of death.' He died at two A.M. on 28th January, being fifty-five years and seven months old. According to Sander, he had in his last hours constantly moaned out the word 'monks' (*De Schismate*, ed. 1628, 173), and his last act was to ask for a cup of white wine. Having drunk it he said: 'We have lost everything'; and so died. It is clear that he sent for Cranmer, who arrived two hours before the end, when Henry was speechless and could only grasp the archbishop's hand in response to his appeal that he trusted in Christ. By his will he was buried at Windsor, and money was left for a great number of Masses to be said for the repose of his soul; and it is stated that until the Revolution in 1792 Mass was said annually for him, under the will of Francis I., at the cathedral of Notre Dame in Paris.

Henry's character, like that of his father, shows a break in middle life. In 1530 Wolsey, as he lay dying, said to Sir William Kingston: 'He is a prince of royal courage and hath a princely heart, and rather than he will miss or want part of his appetite he will hazard the loss of one half of his kingdom. I assure you, I have often kneeled before him in his privy chamber, the space of an hour or two, to persuade him from his will and appetite, but I never could dissuade him' (Cavendish, *Life of Wolsey*). In 1534 Sir T. More said to Cromwell: 'You are entered into the service of a most noble, wise, and liberal prince: if you will follow my poor advice, you shall in your counsel given to his Majesty ever tell him what he ought to do, but never what he is able to do . . . for if a lion knew his own strength, hard were it for any man to rule him' (More, *Life of More*, 260). These were judgments of able men who knew him well. After More the King's ministers were of a lower type, and Henry became more and more the capricious tyrant. But he carefully clothed his despotism with the forms of law, and doubtless his strange matrimonial experiences were in part due, as he averred, to his own 'scrupulosity of conscience.' Yet 'when Henry made a voyage of exploration across that strange ocean his conscience, he generally returned with an argosy' (Fisher). To the end of his days he seems never to have lost his self-respect, and his intense belief in himself and in his kingship seems in his later years his strongest support. At the beginning of his reign radiantly popular, by the bloodshed of the years following his marriage with Anne he lost his popularity, but never, it would seem, the confidence of the nation. He judged with unerring accuracy the need of a strong monarchy and the price which his people were willing to pay for it; he erected the despotism and exacted the price.

Memorable in English Church history as the 'majestic lord who broke the bonds of Rome,' his chief acts were the assertion of the Royal Supremacy and the Dissolution of the Religious Houses. He was in a real sense the creator of a Royal Navy, and his love

for England was indubitable. His personal character is described by Dixon as one of 'degraded magnificence,' his court was fierce and foul, and the justest estimate of his private life is that of Pollard: 'Every inch a King, Henry VIII. never attained to the stature of a gentleman' (*Life*, 335).

[S. L. O.]

A. F. Pollard, *Henry VIII.*; J. Gairdner, article in *D.N.B.* and *Lollardy and the Reformation*; H. A. L. Fisher, *Pol. Hist. of Eng.*, 1485-1547; Brewer, *Reign of Henry VIII.*; Stubbs, *Lectures on Mediæval and Modern Hist.*; the documents of the reign have been completely calendared in the *Letters and Papers of Henry VIII.*; J. A. Froude, *Hist. of Eng.*, wrote as an apologist for the King.

HENRY OF BLOIS (d. 1171), Bishop of Winchester, was a grandson of the Conqueror and brother of King Stephen. He was educated at Cluny, where, if he failed to develop in himself the monastic type of character, he at least formed a lasting admiration for the monastic ideal. His uncle, Henry I., gave him the abbacy of Glastonbury (1126) and the see of Winchester (1129); and he obtained a papal dispensation to hold these preferments together. But he first became prominent in politics when his brother came forward as the rival of the Empress for the throne. He declared for Stephen, and persuaded Archbishop William to do the same, pledging himself that Stephen would maintain the liberties of the clergy. Stephen accordingly made in his second charter of liberties (1136) an express grant to the bishops of exclusive jurisdiction over ecclesiastical persons and property. But when the see of Canterbury fell vacant it was refused to Bishop Henry, although he made strenuous efforts to obtain it. Stephen's choice fell upon Theobald, Abbot of Bec; but Henry was consoled by the Pope with a legatine commission which made him, for some purposes, the superior of the primate (1139). [LEGATES.] In the same year Henry asserted his new authority by citing the King before a synod to answer for his rough treatment of Roger of Salisbury (*q.v.*). Stephen refused to give satisfaction, and stayed the proceedings of the council by an appeal to Rome. There was no open breach between the brothers, but the ill success of Stephen in the civil war soon convinced the bishop that it was God's will to depose the persecutor of the clergy. When Stephen was captured at Lincoln (1141) the Empress made overtures to Henry. He admitted her to Winchester, proclaimed her the Lady of England, and held a council of the clergy, from which he obtained a declaration that Stephen had forfeited the kingly title. The bishop accompanied the Empress to London for her coronation, which never took place, and shared her flight when she was expelled from the city. But on discovering that she paid no heed to his advice, and would grant no terms to his family, he opened negotiations with Stephen's friends. The Empress, discovering his intrigues, besieged him at Winchester. But he was relieved by the King's party, and shared their triumph when Stephen was set at liberty. The bishop justified his last change of front in a third council, held at London (December 1141), to which he stated that the Empress had broken faith with him and that the Pope had censured him for deserting Stephen. The sincerity of the explanation may be doubted. Henry was not so black as he is painted by the biographer of Stephen. He was too impetuous to be an accomplished hypocrite; his taste for war and politics was tempered by a genuine devotion to the interests of his order, and even by a desire to ensure the peace of the kingdom. But he was consequential, hot-headed, and autocratic; he could not tolerate a rival or swallow an affront. After 1141 he remained loyal to Stephen, but still indulged his factious temper in ecclesiastical quarrels. Until he lost his legatine commission he waged an unseemly warfare against his rival, Theobald; and he is traditionally credited with the ambition of making Winchester an archiepiscopal see. He pushed his nephew, William Fitzherbert, into the see of York, and supported the election against the Pope and St. Bernard. He encouraged Stephen in an anti-papal policy, and was consequently suspended for a time. But age appears to have softened his imperious temper. He promoted the reconciliation between Stephen and Henry of Anjou (1153), which deprived his own family of the succession. He was loyal to Henry II., although their relations were far from cordial. In the Becket controversy he showed to better advantage than at any other time of his life; for he endeavoured to play the part of a mediator, and gave public evidence of his sympathy with the archbishop. Though he remained in England and deprecated Becket's more violent acts, he steadily supported the privileges which the King had attacked. He died a few months after Becket's murder. It is related that on his death-bed he reproached Henry II., who had come to see him, with the responsibility for that crime. In his latter years he was a munificent benefactor to Cluny; and at Winchester, besides

adding to the cathedral and in part rebuilding St. Swithin's monastery, he founded the hospital of St. Cross.   [H. W. C. D.]

Norgate, *Eng. under the Angevin Kings*; Ramsay, *Foundations of Eng. and Angevin Empire*.

HERBERT, George (1593-1633), divine and poet, was fourth of the seven sons whom, with their three sisters, Magdalen (daughter to Sir Richard Newport) bore to Richard Herbert of Montgomery Castle, the eldest of her children being the statesman and philosopher, Edward, Lord Herbert of Cherbury. Of the younger brothers, Sir Henry was Master of the Revels; Thomas (a posthumous son) was a brave seaman, and author of pasquinades, etc.; Richard, who had some reputation as a duellist, was, like William, a soldier; while Charles was educated at Winchester, and became ultimately Fellow of New College. Of himself, George Herbert, in the first among five of those poems which are entitled *Affliction*, thus addresses God :—

‘ Whereas my birth and spirit rather took
    The way that takes the town ;
Thou didst betray me to a lingering book,
    And wrap me in a gown.’

He was a Queen's Scholar of Westminster School, while Andrewes (*q.v.*) was dean. There he began his boyish ‘ apologetic epigrams ’ against the Scottish Presbyterian, Andrew Melville. Thence in 1609 he passed to Trinity College, Cambridge, under Dr. Nevile, where in 1614 he became Fellow. In 1618 he was appointed Deputy Orator for the University. In 1620 he became Public Orator, in which capacity he composed for the University Latin congratulatory or complimentary letters, *e.g.* to King James, to thank him for a presentation copy of *Basilicon Dôron*, or to Bacon (1620), for whom he translated part of the *Instauratio*, and who in return complimented the youthful orator by dedicating to him his collection of Psalms in verse. Through his mother and his elder brother Herbert came to know Dr. Donne, who became a lifelong friend, and influenced his tastes and style as well as his religious character. About the time of James I.'s death and other changes at court he turned resolutely to the study of divinity. Bishop J. Williams (*q.v.*), who was Donne's patron, in July 1626 gave Herbert his earliest Church preferment, viz. the prebend of Leighton Bromswold, Hunts (with a stall, ‘ Layton Ecclesia,’ in Lincoln Cathedral). He took serious thought for the parish on the estate, and with the help of John and Nicholas Ferrar (*q.v.*) in the neighbouring parish of

Gidding, and contributions from Lord Pembroke, made the dilapidated church which he found at St. Mary's Leighton to become, though he did not live to see it finished, 'for decency and beauty . . . the most remarkable parish church in this whole nation' at that day. With characteristic earnestness of purpose and love of detail he gave his directions for the construction of its plain but solid furniture. On collation to the prebend he was only in deacon's orders, but his health and his occupations led him in 1627 to part with the post of Orator, which he had thought so desirable. In 1629, being on a visit to his stepfather's brother, the Earl of Danby, he fell in love with Jane Danvers, who, from her father's report of her future husband, became (says Walton) 'so much of a Platonick, as to fall in love with Mr. Herbert unseen'; and, becoming an orphan very shortly after the marriage was arranged, 'Jane . . . changed her name into Herbert the third day after their first interview.'

With commendable humility Herbert doubted at first whether he ought to accept the rectory of Fugglestone with Bemerton, near Wilton and Salisbury, which Charles I. offered him, while the recently married poet was contemplating a lifelong diaconate; he was, however, persuaded by Laud (*q.v.*) to accept the benefice and to put off his courtly silk attire and lay aside his sword. 'A tailor was sent for to come speedily from Salisbury to Wilton to take measure, and make him canonical clothes against next day; which the tailor did'; and Bishop Davenant (*q.v.*) as expeditiously instituted Herbert into 'the good and more pleasant than healthful parsonage of Bemerton.' Lying before the altar in the locked church at his induction he made those solemn vows for his own conduct which he exemplified no less in his brief but saintly life there (1630-3) than in his charming prose manual, *A Priest to the Temple, or Countrey Parson, his Character and Rule of Holy Life,* finished apparently in 1632, but not published till twenty years later. This little treatise was accompanied by a reissue of Herbert's collection of 'outlandish proverbs,' named *Jacula prudentum,* some of which no doubt had enlivened the music parties which he frequently attended on his way back from the cathedral evensong on week days. His religious poems, some of them probably known to his friends in his lifetime, and married to the sweet tones of his own voice and lute or viol, were given by Herbert on his death-bed to Nicholas Ferrar, who at first met with some difficulty on submitting the MS. (now in the Bodleian),

in obtaining the licence of the vice-chancellor of Cambridge by reason of the lines :—

'Religion stands on tip-toe in our land,
Readie to passe to th' American strand.'
The Church Militant.

Three editions of the poems were issued in 1663, and more than seventy thousand copies had been sold by 1670. They have comforted many, from King Charles in his captivity and Richard Baxter (*q.v.*) in the seventeenth century, to our own times. A few lyrics, such as 'Throw away thy rod' and 'Sweet day, so cool' (in Walton's *Compleat Angler*), 'I got me flowers,' etc., are still occasionally sung. J. and C. Wesley (*q.v.*) recast forty of them for congregational use, but they dropped in time out of the Wesleyan hymn-book. One finished jewel alone was admitted into *Hymns Ancient and Modern,* 'Let all the world' (No. 548).

On 3rd March 1632-3, while the singing men of Sarum chanted 'the singing service of the dead,' as he desired (Aubrey), George Herbert's delicate frame was laid beneath the altar of the little church or chapel of St. Andrew, Bemerton, in restoring which, along with his prebendal church in Lincolnshire and his parsonage houses, he spent his moderate income. [CAROLINE DIVINES, MYSTICS, POETRY IN ENGLISH CHURCH.] [c. w.]

Works; I. Walton, *Life*; Julian, *Dict. Hymn.*

HEREFORD, See of, was carved out of the vast Mercian diocese of Lichfield (*q.v.*) in the seventh century, but its boundaries were for a long time ill-defined, and have been subject to many changes. It now includes the whole county of Herefordshire, and nearly all Shropshire south of the Severn, together with twenty-one parishes which are wholly or in part in Worcestershire, eight parishes in Radnorshire, and eight in Montgomeryshire, with parts of four others of which the remaining portions are in Shropshire. In early times the diocese stretched much farther southwards, including Cheltenham and Monmouth, and until the see of Gloucester (*q.v.*) was formed, the Forest of Dean.

Before the Norman Conquest the see of Llandaff (*q.v.*) seems to have embraced all Herefordshire west of the Wye, where the population was chiefly Welsh, and for a century and a half it claimed, by repeated appeals to the Pope, the district of Irchinfield, which it had lost during the old age of Bishop Herwald. The disputed parishes were not regained, but Dixton, Stanton, and Monmouth were restored in 1844. In 1852 the

Ewyas deanery, of which Llandaff had been stripped by St. David's, was assigned to Hereford. In 1905 the rural deanery of Condover, with its fifteen parishes, was transferred from the diocese of Lichfield to that of Hereford, and also Quatt, Worfield, and Mathon from the diocese of Worcester (*q.v.*), while Badger, Beckbury, Bobbington, Meole Brace, and Sutton were transferred to Lichfield, and Shelsley Walsh to Worcester. The population is now 218,874.

The *Taxatio* of 1291 assessed the *Temporalia* of the see at £149, 1s. 5d. and the *Spiritualia* at £20. In the *Valor Ecclesiasticus* the income appears as £768, 10s. 10½d. The present income is £4200, with a house. It was said by Swinfield to be the worst endowed bishopric in England, and if men of influence and ambition were appointed to it, they were commonly soon translated to other spheres. Of the early bishops for three centuries scarcely anything but their names have been recorded, and those with variations of detail.

The diocese is divided into two archdeaconries: Hereford (first mentioned, 1109) and Ludlow (first mentioned as Salop, 1162, renamed Ludlow, 1876). The deanery dates from about 1140. The chapter when fully developed in the thirteenth century consisted of a dean and twenty-seven canons, who were also called prebendaries from the separate estates enjoyed by each in addition to a share of the general revenue. The dignities of the precentor, treasurer, and chancellor were also held commonly by canons. The division of the estates of the church between the bishop and the chapter took place very early, the manors being retained by the former, while the latter was mainly supported by the great tithes of dependent churches, the dean and dignitaries having also a large number of pensions charged on other parishes. A distinct provision, however, for the chapter was made even before the Conquest by the gift of four manors by two Saxon ladies, and smaller benefactions followed in later days.

From the first the distribution of the corporate funds was arranged so as to encourage constant residence. It was made for the most part in the shape of daily commons given in kind to every canon near at hand, and stated quantities of corn were charged on the neighbouring manors, to be delivered at the canons' bakehouse. Funds were assigned early in the thirteenth century for division, under the name of mass-pence, among the canons who were present at Mass in the cathedral, and many lists of attendances still exist in the archives. There were like distributions at many obits or anniversary services to all who officiated or were present on such occasions. Gradually titular residentiaries ousted, as in other cathedrals, all the rest from powers of management and benefits of office, except the possession of the prebends. The term 'residentiary' first appears in 1356, but there was no fixed usage as to the number before 1569, when a rule was made that there should be six only, bound to six months of residence, which the Caroline statutes reduced to three. Finally the number of canons was limited to four.

A peculiar privilege of the chapter of Hereford was the monopoly of all rights of interment, not merely of the inhabitants of the city, but of the villages for some miles around. This caused friction with the neighbouring parishes, which did not, in the city at least, have any separate churchyards until comparatively recent times. The duties which this privilege involved furnished work and emolument for the vicars, originally twenty-seven, to correspond to the number of the canons, whose deputies they were. The numerous chantries that were founded provided a definite status and more income.

A characteristic of the chapter was the pertinacity with which they resisted all attempts of their bishops to hold visitations of the cathedral. Other chapters showed at times the same repugnance, but at Hereford the resistance was successfully maintained for many centuries. Popes might sanction or disallow the episcopal claim, but the chapter's attitude remained the same, and till the sixteenth century it held its own. Its plea, which it did not always take the trouble to urge, was that the cathedral stood within the Peculiar of the dean, which was a group of more than twenty parishes and chapelries in and round the city, in which he had large powers, instituting the incumbents, and having testamentary and matrimonial jurisdiction. [PECULIARS.] Under Elizabeth the papal sympathies of the chapter were fatal to its independence. Bishop Scory implored the Crown to intervene; a commission was appointed which introduced some drastic changes; and at a later date the Caroline statutes superseded the ancient *Consuetudines*, which had been in force from the middle of the thirteenth century. They reduced the number of the vicars-choral to twelve—all to be in holy orders—and made them responsible for the vocal part of the musical services of the cathedral, other than that of the boy choristers, giving them also a life tenure of office, and independent management of their estates, subject to the control of the dean and chapter as visitors.

The cathedral school existed at a very early date, not as a mere song school for choristers, but as a grammar school attached to the cathedral in accordance with the canon law. It was certainly not founded by Bishop Gilbert, as has been supposed, for he merely appointed a master when the chancellor, who was then a Roman cardinal, neglected to discharge his duty in the matter. It was formally reconstituted under Elizabeth.

Bishops

* *Buried in the Cathedral or Lady Arbour.*

1. Putta, 676.
2. Tyrhtel, 688.
3. Torhthere, 710.
4. Walchltsod, 727.
5. Cuthbert, 736; tr. to Canterbury in 740.
6. Podda, 741.
7. Hecca, 747.
8. Ceadda, 758.
9. Aldberht, 777.
10. Esne, 781.
11. Ceolmund, 787.
12. Utel, 793.
13. Wulfhard, 800.
14. Beonna, 824.
15. Eadulf, 825.
16. Cuthwulf, 837.
17. Mucel, 857.
18. Diorlaf, 866.
19. Cynemund, 888.
20. Eadgar, 901.
21. Tidhelm, 930.
22. Wulfhelm, 934.
23. Alfric, 941.
24. Athulf, 951.

25. *Ethelstan, 1012; said by a twelfth-century writer to have rebuilt the cathedral, which was set on fire by the Welsh in 1055; d. 1056.
26. Leofgar, 1056; 'Earl Harold's mass-priest'; d. 1056. Four years' vacancy.
27. *Walter of Lorraine, 1061; d. 1079.
28. Robert Losinga, 1079; a skilful mathematician; began to build a cathedral after the pattern of that of Aix-la-Chapelle; abridged the chronicle of Marianus Scotus; d. 1095.
29. Gerard, 1096; tr. to York, 1100.
30. *Reinelm, 1107; d. 1115.
31. *Geoffrey de Clive, 1115; 'agriculturae studens'; d. 1120.
32. *Richard de Capella, 1121; clerk of the signet to Henry I.; d. 1127.
33. *Robert de Bethune, 1131; Prior of Llanthony, to whose support when plundered by the Welsh he devoted four prebends of his cathedral, for which reason perhaps he lived on bad terms with the dean and chapter, though famous for his saintly virtues; completed the fabric of the cathedral, the nave and south transept of which still remain; d. 1148.
34. Gilbert Foliot (*q.v.*), 1148; tr. to London.
35. Robert de Melun, 1163; Prior of Llanthony; a theologian of high repute,

whose works were found long afterwards in mediæval libraries; d. 1167.
36. *Robert Foliot, 1174; Archdeacon of Oxford; d. 1186.
37. *William de Vere, 1186; credited by tradition with the erection of the Lady Chapel, for which perhaps he prepared by the actual removal of the eastern apse; gave liberal help to the endowments of the chapter; d. 1198.
38. *Giles de Braose, 1200; prominent in the strife of the barons with John; d. 1215.
39. *Hugh de Mapenor, 1216; Dean of Hereford; d. 1219.
40. Hugh Foliot, 1219; founder of the hospital of St. Katherine at Ledbury; d. 1234.
41. Ralph of Maidstone, 1234; Dean of Hereford; gave to the see his inn, Mounthalt in London; res., 1239, to become a Franciscan friar at Oxford.
42. *Peter d'Aigueblanche, 1240; detested by the clergy for his schemes of exaction in the interest of Pope and King; disputed the rights of the dean and chapter, and with papal aid forced reluctant canons to contribute to rebuild the north-west transept; seized at Hereford by the insurgent barons, and imprisoned at Eardisley Castle; left liberal benefactions for the poor, but also elements of strife in the Savoyard kinsmen whom he had lodged in offices of dignity around him; d. 1268.
43. *John Breton, 1269; d. 1275.
44. *Thomas Cantilupe, 1275; the only canonised Bishop of Hereford, and the last Englishman canonised at Rome; eminent as scholar and Chancellor of Oxford, and Chancellor of England during the ascendancy of Simon de Montfort; lived in ascetic rigour, and maintained the rights of his see against all aggression; disputes with Archbishop Peckham (*q.v.*) moved him to appeal to Rome, but he died on his way thither near Orvieto, 1282, whence his bones were carried to Hereford. Numbers of sick folk believed that they were cured at his tomb, and the beautiful tower of the cathedral was largely paid for by the offerings of pilgrims to his shrine.
45. *Richard Swinfield, 1283; a notable preacher and careful administrator, whose Register is full of historical and antiquarian notices; d. 1317.
46. Adam Orleton, 1317 (P.); tr. to Worcester, 1327.

47. *Thomas Charleton, 1327 (P.); Treasurer of England in 1329; Chancellor and Keeper of Ireland; d. 1344.
48. *John Trilleck, 1344 (P.); ruled his diocese with unfailing care, deserving the eulogy of 'gratus, prudens, pius' placed on his grave; d. 1360.
49. *Lewis Charleton, 1361 (P.); d. 1369.
50. William Courtenay, 1370 (P.); tr. to London, 1375.
51. John Gilbert, 1375 (P.); tr. (P.) from Bangor; tr. to St. David's, 1389.
52. *John Trevenant, 1389 (P.); Auditor of the court of Rota at Rome; long busily engaged with proceedings against notable Lollards, especially William Swynderby and Walter Brut, which fill a large part of his Register; d. 1404.
53. Robert Mascall, 1404 (P.); a Carmelite friar; confessor to Henry IV.; contributed to the building of the Bishop's Cloister: d. 1416.
54. Edmund Lacy, 1417; Master of University College, Oxford; tr. to Exeter, 1420.
55. Thomas Polton, 1420 (P.); tr. to Chichester, 1421.
56. Thomas Spofford, 1422 (P.); Abbot of St. Mary's, York, to which he finally retired; res. 1448.
57. Richard Beauchamp, 1449 (P.); tr. to Salisbury, 1450.
58. Reginald Boulers, 1451 (P.); tr. to Lichfield, 1453.
59. *John Stanbury, 1453; tr. (P.) from Bangor; a Carmelite friar chosen by Henry VI. to be his confessor and first Provost of Eton; gave the site and large help for the Vicars' College; built the Stanbury Chantry: d. 1474.
60. Thomas Milling, 1474 (P.); Abbot of Westminster; friend and patron of Caxton; d. 1492.
61. Edmund Audley, 1492; tr. (P.) from Rochester; built the Audley Chantry; tr. to Salisbury, 1502.
62. Hadrian de Castello, 1502 (P.); tr. to Bath and Wells, 1504.
63. *Richard Mayew, 1504 (P.); second President of Magdalen College, Oxford, and Chancellor of the University; d. 1516.
64. *Charles Booth, 1516 (P.); Chancellor of the Welsh Marches; built or completed the north porch of the cathedral; d. 1535.
65. Edward Foxe, 1535; 'the principal pillar of the Reformation' (Fuller); Provost of King's College, Cambridge; sent with Gardiner to negotiate with the Pope for the King's divorce; tried to persuade the Queen to renounce her

title; sent to Smalcald to induce the German princes to unite with the Church of England; one of the compilers of 'the Bishops' Book'; d. 1538.
66. Edmund Bonner (q.v.), 1538; removed to London before consecration.
67. *John Skip, 1539; almoner to Anne Boleyn; last Abbot of Wigmore; Master of Gonville Hall, Cambridge; took part in the composition of 'the Bishops' Book' and 'the King's Book'; possibly one of the committee appointed to draw up the First Prayer Book of Edward VI., but protested against it; d. 1552.
68. John Harley, 1553; dep. under Mary as a married and 'pretensed Bishop of inordinate life and conversation'; d. 1554.
69. *Robert Parfew, or Wharton, 1554; Abbot of St. Saviour's, Bermondsey; tr. (P.) from St. Asaph; d. 1557.
   [Thomas Reynolds; Dean of Exeter; nominated, 1558, but not consecrated; d. in the Marshalsea.]
70. John Scory, 1559; a Dominican friar; Bishop, under Edward VI., of Rochester and then of Chichester; recanted 'with tears and groans' before Bonner, but retracted his submission, and fled to Friesland; elected to Hereford, he found the cathedral clergy 'dissemblers and rank Papists,' and little sympathy in the city with reforms, being himself 'abhorred for the most part for religion'; he desired to rebuild his palace, but, much to his indignation, the dean and chapter refused to consent; grave charges were brought against him of abuses in the management of the property of the see; assisted in consecration of Parker (q.v.); d. 1585.
71. *Herbert Westfaling, 1586; Dean of Windsor; d. 1602.
72. *Robert Bennet, 1603; Dean of Windsor; d. 1617.
73. Francis Godwin, 1617; tr. from Llandaff, 1601; author of the work *de praesulibus Angliae*; 'a pure Latinist and incomparable historian' (Fuller); said by Wharton (q.v.) to have devoted more pains to the Latin than to the matter; d. 1633.
   [William Juxon (q.v.); elected, but tr. to London before consecration.
   Godfrey Goodman (q.v.); Bishop of Gloucester; elected, but the royal assent being refused he was obliged to resign his claim to the see.]
74. *Augustine Lindsell, 1634; tr. from Peterborough; d. 1634.

75. Matthew Wren (*q.v.*), 1635; tr. to Norwich.
76. *Theophilus Field, 1635; tr. from St. David's; d. 1636.
77. George Coke, 1636; tr. from Bristol; committed to the Tower in 1641 for protest against proceedings in the House of Lords during the enforced absence of the bishops; d. in retirement, 1646, soon after the sequestration of his estates.
78. Nicolas Monk, 1661; Provost of Eton; d. 1661.
79. *Herbert Croft, 1662; Dean of Hereford before the Commonwealth; a Jesuit in early life; d. 1691.
80. *Gilbert Ironside, 1691; Warden of Wadham College, Oxford; tr. from Bristol; d. 1701.
81. *Humphrey Humphreys, 1701; tr. from Bangor; d. 1712.
82. *Philip Bisse, 1713; tr. from St. David's; expended much in questionable taste on the cathedral and palace; d. 1721.
83. Benjamin Hoadly (*q.v.*), 1721; tr. from Bangor; tr. to Salisbury, 1723.
84. Henry Egerton, 1724; pulled down the ancient chapel of St. Mary Magdalene adjoining the cloisters; d. 1746.
85. *Lord James Beauclerk, 1746, in whose time the west tower fell; d. 1787.
86. John Harley, 1787; d. 1788.
87. *John Butler, 1788; tr. from Oxford; d. 1802.
88. *Ffolliot Herbert Cornewall, 1803; tr. from Bristol; Dean of Canterbury; tr. to Worcester, 1808.
89. John Luxmore, 1808; tr. from Bristol; tr. to St. Asaph, 1815.
90. George Isaac Huntingford, 1815; Warden of Winchester College; tr. from Gloucester; d. 1832.
91. Edward Grey, 1832; Dean of Hereford; d. 1837.
92. Thomas Musgrave, 1837; tr. to York, 1847.
93. Renn Dickson Hampden (*q.v.*), 1848.
94. *James Atlay, 1868; Vicar of Leeds; Canon of Ripon; d. 1894.
95. John Percival, 1895; Headmaster of Clifton and Rugby Schools; President of Trinity College, Oxford.

[w. w. c.]

Browne Willis, *Survey*; Havergall, *Fasti Herefordenses*; *Episcopal Registers* (Cantilupe Society); Phillott, *Dio. Hist.*

HERESY is a word derived from the Greek αἵρεσις, meaning 'a sect,' which is actually so translated in Acts 5[17], 15[5], and 24[5].

It ought also to have been translated 'a sect,' as it actually is in the R.V. (24[14]), to make St. Paul's answers relevant to the charge against him in 24[5]. But a sect among Christians was a wrong thing from the first, because all are members of one body; and sects or 'heresies' are placed by St. Paul in Gal. 5[20] among the 'works of the flesh,' which are as 'manifest' as they are evil. St. Paul accordingly instructs Titus (3[10]) to reject, or refuse, a heretical man 'after a first and second admonition,' simply because he is perverse and factious. Heresies, moreover, are shown to be utterly destructive of the faith in 2 Peter 2[1], where it is said that they will be introduced by false teachers, 'denying the Lord that bought them.' On this subject the apostolic instruction was still followed in the Middle Ages. But Christianity having by that time become the general religion of European nations, it was not found easy to deal with heretics merely by church censures and by instructing Christians to avoid their company. So in the thirteenth century Aquinas (*Secunda Secundae*, qu. xi.) maintains that a heretic who remains obstinate after a first and second admonition is rightly punished, first by anathema (or excommunication), and afterwards by death.

Here we trace the beginning of evils abhorrent to more humane times. The truth, it was felt, was in the keeping of the Church, that is to say, of a well-instructed clergy, and in doubtful questions there was an appeal from bishops to the Pope. The scholastic method of reasoning in very subtle questions might not be so infallible as men thought; but to raise opposition to what seemed well-founded decisions was real factiousness on the part of any one but a well-qualified divine. Certainly to persist obstinately in maintaining one's own opinion in the face of the Church was a course calculated to engender strife; and if the Church had no other remedy but to excommunicate the offender, what could the civil authority do with such a mischief-maker? There was but one opinion in the Middle Ages—that he should be burnt. And this view the Church virtually approved, for perverse heretics seemed to deserve no mercy, though there are cases in the twelfth century of bishops actually protecting heretics from popular fury ('Tanon, *Histoire des Tribunaux de l'Inquisition en France*, p. 15).

It would seem, indeed, that Church censures were for a long time held to be sufficient. The late M. Julien Havet considered that burning for heresy was first provoked by the extravagances of the Cathari after the year 1000; but possibly it may be traced farther back. In England, in the earliest notice of the coercion of heretics, they were dealt with not by burning but by severe enough measures ordered simply by despotic power. At a council at Oxford in 1166 some thirty heretics who came from Germany were condemned; and Henry II. ordered them to be branded in the face (their leader in the chin also), and whipped out of the town in winter, no man being allowed to offer them food or shelter. This severity was said to have purged the realm completely of an unwonted pest brought in by aliens (R. Howlett's ed. of *William Newburgh*, R.S., i. 131-4). The first recorded instance of burning in England was in 1210, when we are told (without particulars) that an Albigensian was burnt in London (*Liber Niger*, p. 3, C.S.). In 1222 occurred the more celebrated case of a deacon who was burnt as an apostate, having turned Jew for the love of a Jewess. By that time a methodical way of dealing with heretics had been indicated by the Lateran Council of 1215, which directed that they should be condemned by the ecclesiastical authorities in presence of the secular powers, or their bailiffs, and delivered up to them for punishment, clerks being first degraded from their orders. Some English bishops who had attended this council took part in one at Osney by Oxford in the spring of 1222, at which judgment was pronounced on the apostate deacon; and the condemned man was accordingly degraded by the court christian and forthwith burnt by the lay power. No sentence of death seems to have been passed; at least there is no evidence of any condemnation by a lay court, and the earliest accounts read otherwise. But apparently the lay power must get rid of such an offender, if the nation would not incur interdict.

At his coronation in 1220 the Emperor Frederick II. was pledged to punish heretics by banishment and confiscation of goods; and he not only published a 'constitution' to that effect, but followed it up in later years with others more severe. One of these, issued in 1231, expressly sanctioned punishment by fire, and governed from that time the practice in the Empire and of European princes generally (*Lyndwood*, p. 293, note *d*). In 1298, the recent papal law being codified in 'the Sext' by Boniface VIII., the kind of obedience which the Church expected of Christian princes in this matter was made still more obvious. About that time in England we find it was a principle recognised by law that

various felonies ought to be punished by burning, and that among others sorcerers, sodomites, and unbelievers 'openly attainted,' when reported to the King should be put to death by him 'as a good marshal of Christendom.' Yet for nearly two hundred years after the date of the Judaised deacon not one actual case of burning for heresy in England seems to be on record: and it was generally believed till recent times that there were none before the first year of the fifteenth century, when the statute *de heretico comburendo* (2 Hen. IV. c. 15) was passed. This, however, is rather doubtful; for in sermons attributed to Wyclif (*q.v.*), and certainly of Richard II.'s time, there are very distinct allusions to heretics being persecuted and burnt. There is also in the *Chronicle of Meaux* (ii. 323) a retrospective notice of the persecution of some Franciscans in various countries in 1318 for their opposition to Pope John XXII.; and among those in England were fifty-five men and eight women burnt 'in a certain wood.' Possibly this may have been the wooded district of the Chiltern Hills, which in a later period became a noted refuge for heretics.

It seems probable, however, that there was very little heresy in England before the days of Wyclif, and therefore very little burning. Wyclif himself, moreover, was no real heretic, for it was always a question while he lived whether his teaching would not ultimately prevail. But existing order was threatened by his strong denunciation of abuses; and a few years after his death we have the rare spectacle of an enthusiast named William Swynderby appealing both to the King and to Parliament against an episcopal sentence. For this departure from customary practice he gave reasons not a little interesting. The bishop, he said, after excommunicating a man, could do no more without help of the King's law: yet a cause of heresy involved judgment of death. For the bishop would say, as the Jews did to Pilate: 'It is not lawful for us to put any man to death': and Swynderby hoped that no justice would pass an untrue judgment, as the bishop had done.

Lollardy was at this time very strong, and was largely favoured by influential men: but it was soon found dangerous, especially after Henry IV.'s accession, when the statute *de heretico comburendo* was passed. And even before that Act had become law William Sawtré was burned in Smithfield under the authority of a King's writ dated 26th February 1401 but not issued till the 2nd March, when it bore the words: 'By the King and

Council in Parliament.' In this writ it was set forth that the Archbishop of Canterbury, with the consent of his suffragans and the whole clergy of his province, had in due order of law condemned Sawtré as a heretic who had relapsed after being abjured, and had therefore degraded him and left him to a secular tribunal, as the Church had nothing more to do with him. The King accordingly, seeing that such heretics, by divine and human law and canonical usage, ought to be burnt, directed the mayor and sheriffs of London to have it done in some public place within their liberty ' in detestation of such a crime, and as a warning to other Christians.' Such was the tenor of the writ, which was duly entered on the Parliament Roll as issued to the mayor and sheriffs on Wednesday, 2nd March. Later, apparently on Thursday, the 10th of the same month, the last day of Parliament, was passed the Act above mentioned, which, however, was not mainly intended to authorise the burning of heretics, though it did authorise such punishment in extreme cases, but rather to give the bishops (for it was passed at their request, and that of the clergy generally) more complete control over such men, seeing that heretics easily escaped from one diocese to another and evaded episcopal jurisdiction. In fact, the most important provision of this Act was one for putting down all unlicensed preaching; for this was the check chiefly relied on to meet the evil. And measures of Convocation afterwards strengthened the discipline of the Church in this matter by laying under interdict not only unlicensed preachers in churches or churchyards, but the very churches and parishes that allowed them.

Open heresy thus lost favour. Sir John Oldcastle, the last renowned knight to give it any support, added treason to heresy, and was burnt by a special sentence of Parliament at St. Giles's, being suspended by a chain over a blazing fire (1417). The Church was really getting into order as the Great Schism was ended, and heretics who were disturbers of order were of small account till the day when Henry VIII. encouraged them for his own purposes and brought on the Reformation.

The very essence of heresy was an attempt to disturb order. Opinions were not heresy so long as they were held with due respect for the decisions of the Church, and it was only reasonable that private opinion should show deference to the faith which had been expounded and discussed for centuries. Private opinion may even have been right in some things; for a view of orthodoxy resting on a seeming Biblical foundation, and developed by mere logical syllogisms from a hypothesis which might itself be questioned, is no such entirely safe guide as men too readily imagine. Philosophers may build upon figures of speech and raise an edifice which common men cannot inhabit or make real use of. The danger, moreover, was serious, when the Church, founding itself, to all appearance, both on reason and on Scripture, insisted on Aristotelian views about physical things before the truths of physical science had really been investigated. Thus the common faith of all Christendom was made to include theories about ' substance ' and 'accidents' and the stability of the earth, which do not harmonise well, or, it may be, at all, with advancing scientific knowledge. Religion must not shut out the light of experience on any subject whatever; and the attempt to do so in religion's name only paralyses faith without being able to shackle investigation.

Nevertheless, it must be owned that the emancipation of the human mind in the sixteenth century was not largely due to divines or philosophers of the highest rank. Luther almost stands by himself. Calvin can scarcely be called a friend of freedom. And when we turn to England the best theologian we have to show is Cranmer (*q.v.*), whose internal history was evidently a painful struggle reflected in a life of marked inconsistencies. The Reformation here began with a royal despotism which wilfully stirred up heresy to help in destroying that supreme power at Rome on which existing church order depended. And when once that work was done heresy could no longer be coerced so easily as it had been. Very flagrant repudiations of what was vital to the faith of all Christendom were still for a time put down by the fiery remedy. But the faith of a nation, measured by dogmatic standards, could no longer be upheld by penal laws. After a long struggle, in which for a time old heresies got the upper hand, men were allowed to form themselves into dissenting communions. From that time forward the faith has only vindicated itself by its own inherent consistency, and men who stand apart from the Church from no love of schism scarcely deserve to be reputed heretics. Their opinions, indeed, may be heretical, but conscientious acts are not. And the injurious effects of wrong opinions so entertained lose themselves in the general body of Christianity. Indeed, it may well be believed that though popular theology must go astray to some extent, it is better that the laity should cultivate thinking than merely accept dogmas on authority. [LOLLARDS.]

[J. G.]

HERMITS. The hermit differed from the anchorite (*q.v.*) in that the former was *solivagus*, the latter *conclusus*. The vow of the anchorite forbade him to leave his cell, that of the hermit held him only to a solitary life of celibacy and a rather easily interpreted poverty.

The first hermits in this country were probably those Celtic solitaries of both sexes of whom traces abound in Cornwall and in other districts, but whose legends are generally puzzling and doubtful. Like these their successors, the earlier English hermits, of whom St. Guthlac is the most famous, took up their abode in lonely places, in fens, caves, and forests, where they imitated as closely as possible the life of their forerunners in the Thebaid in the fourth century. Before the twelfth century, however, we find that this feature of eremitic life had quite ceased to be characteristic. The majority of hermits now lived by high roads, or even in towns. This change was probably due in great measure to the Berengarian controversy, and to the increased stress laid upon Easter 'duties.' The devout hermit could no longer live in places where, unless he were a priest himself, he was unable to receive the sacraments.

Moreover, as life became more complex the hermit's temptation to rely less upon his own exertions than upon the alms of the charitable would increase, and this consideration helped to bring his hut to the bridge or the roadside. When the idea of flight from the haunts of men had dwindled thus, hermits became useful to the community as menders of roads and bridges and succourers of travellers. Indeed, this semi-religious duty became characteristic of their order, and the 'bridge-hermit' of the Middle Ages was a thoroughly familiar figure. The manner of life thus developed was open to considerable abuse. Thus we find hermits bracketed with beggars and vagabonds in a statute of Richard II. From this condemnation, however, are excepted such 'approved' hermits as have letters testimonial from the ordinary. The same distinction is made in one of the numerous wills which leave money to hermits to pray specially for the testator's soul. These 'approved' hermits obtained formal permission from the bishop to 'serve God in that order,' and received the episcopal benediction in an Office which was, however, much simpler than that of enclosure, and did not include Mass. Letters were sometimes issued to the clergy of the diocese announcing that the profession had been made, and requesting them to recognise the new hermit and see to his support. In some cases there was a right of advowson to recognised hermitages, and hermits were formally appointed by the bishop or patron. Hermits were seldom priests, but they often had chapels attached to their cells, and we find episcopal licences for Mass to be celebrated in such chapels. In the very rare case of a monk becoming a hermit after his profession, he seems to have lived under the obedience of the nearest abbot of a monastery. The same cell was not infrequently inhabited at different times by hermits and by strict recluses, and there are cases of two cells existing attached to the same church, of which one was occupied by a hermit and one by an anchorite. Proximity to a church was not, however, necessary for hermitages. Sometimes a regularly constituted hermitage would be submitted to the rule of a neighbouring convent, and would develop in process of time into a cell of the house. Several small communities, such as Writtle and St. James, Cripplegate, had this origin.

The profession of poverty did not forbid a hermit to collect money as well for charity as for his own support. Fixed 'wages' of five shillings a quarter were paid to a hermit at Hunstanton by the L'Estrange family, probably in consideration of his praying for them. He might also possess cattle and lands, as is proved by the will of more than one hermit—for hermits were able to make legal wills. A certain amount of land seems generally to have accompanied a hermitage, and there the occupant would keep at least one cow, as well as grow vegetables for his table.

Hermits probably said the Hours in the shorter form used by lay brethren in religious houses. They had often a servant, or disciple, who was trained to succeed his master. And when they died they were buried in their cells. A knell would be rung for an 'approved' hermit at the nearest church. How numerous these 'poor hermits' became we can guess as well from the strictures of *Piers Plowman* as from such romances as the *High History of the Holy Graal*. To this day a few of their more permanent cells exist—the famous Royston Cave, the rock-dwelling of St. Robert at Knaresborough, and another, partly of masonry, at Warkworth. In the seventeenth century a larger number survived, for Weever writes that there were then 'solitarie little cells or cabbins in divers places of this

S

Kingdome which carrie still the name of Hermitages.' [D. E.]

Besant. *Medieval London*, ii. 170 ; Jusserand. *Eng. Wayfaring Life*, p. 137 ; Cutts. *Scenes and Characters* ; Fosbrooke, *British Monachism* ; *Episcopal Registers, passim* ; *Office for Blessing a Hermit* in Bp. Lacy's *Pontifical* ; *Works of Richard Rolle*, ed. Horstmann.

HEYLIN, Peter (1600-62), born at Burford, went from the grammar school there to Hart Hall, and then to Magdalen College, at Oxford. B.A., 1617 ; Fellow of Magdalen, 1618 ; ordained, 1624 : D.D., 1633. In 1627 he disputed in the Divinity School, maintaining that the Church of England came from the ancient Catholic Church and not from Wycliffites, Waldenses, and the like. Patronised by Laud, he received various preferments (Meysey Hampton, near his birthplace, was offered him, but Bishop Goodman (*q.v.*) did not allow him to accept it), and in 1631 was made a prebendary of Westminster, where later as treasurer he did much for preservation of the fabric. In 1633 he became Rector of Alresford, Hants ; in 1635 he was one of the prebendaries of Westminster who complained against the dean (Williams, Bishop of Lincoln) ; in 1636 he wrote and published an anti-Puritan *History of the Sabbath*. In the latter year he began a famous controversy with Williams by his *Coal from the Altar*, directed against the order to keep the altars in churches table-wise, *i.e.* extending east and west, not north and south. Williams replied in *The Holy Table, Name and Thing*, and Heylin answered again in *Antidotum Lincolnense*. He held various livings till the outbreak of the war, and meanwhile was very active in controversy, taking a prominent part in the Convocation of 1640, and advising that it might constitutionally continue to sit and act after Parliament was dissolved. [CONVOCATION.] He was for some time with the King in Oxford, engaged on the news-sheet of the King's party, *Mercurius Aulicus*, but lost his livings, was declared a delinquent, and for a long time had great difficulty in procuring support for his family. Up till 1660 he wrote continuously on every subject of public interest from geography to church history and the life of Charles I. His most notable books are the *Cosmographie*, a brilliant geographical survey ; the *History of Presbyterianism*, a vigorous attack on the politics and religion of the Calvinists ; the *History of the Reformation*, a justification of the Anglican point of view ; and the *Cyprianus Anglicus*, a bright and sympathetic life of Laud. At the Restoration it was he who

advised the summoning of the Convocation, and he was much consulted by the Church party during the ecclesiastical settlement. He returned to his house at Westminster, but he was infirm and blind, and he died on 8th May 1662, and was buried in the Abbey.

To Heylin's learning, good memory, and sharp wit the Laudian party owed a great deal. He was a consistent defender of the position of the Church as inherited from the earliest days, and he conclusively vindicated the loyalty of his patron, the archbishop.

[W. H. H.]

Wood, *Athenae Oxonienses* ; Walker, *Sufferings of the Clergy*.

HICKES, George (1642-1715), bishop and Nonjuror, educated first at Thirsk, later at the Grammar School, Northallerton, entered St. John's College, Oxford, 1659, but his ardent Royalist and Church views involved him in trouble with Thankful Owen, the Puritan President, and he was sent down. 1660 he returned as a ' servitor ' to Magdalen, whence he graduated B.A., 1663. He migrated to Magdalen Hall, but, 1664, was elected to a Yorkshire Fellowship at Lincoln College. 1665 he became M.A., and for seven years was what is now called a college tutor. 1675 he became Rector of St. Ebbe's, Oxford. 1678 he was made D.D. at St. Andrews, and, 1679, at Oxford. He became Prebendary of Worcester and Vicar of All Hallows, Barking, 1680 ; a royal chaplain, 1681 ; and Dean of Worcester, 1683. In 1686 he resigned All Hallows, Barking, but accepted the living of Alvechurch to hold with his deanery. In 1684 he refused the see of Bristol. He opposed James II.'s measures, and did not read the Declaration, but he was staunch in his loyalty, and refused the oaths to William and Mary. He was consequently suspended and then deprived, but allowed to remain at his deanery till May 1691, when, a new dean being appointed, he affixed with his own hand a strong protest to the choir gates of his cathedral church, an act which compelled him to remain hidden for some time to avoid arrest. He took refuge with a strong political opponent, White Kennett, later Bishop of Peterborough, at Ambrosden, Bucks, where he pursued his studies in Saxon and Icelandic. For some time he was compelled to adopt the disguise of a major in the army. When it was decided to continue the episcopal succession Hickes went to James II. at St. Germans to select men. He was one of those chosen, and was consecrated bishop (of Thetford) with Wagstaffe (*q.v.*), 24th February 1693. In 1699 Lord Chancellor Somers procured a *nolle prosequi,* which stayed further proceedings against him, on account of his great services to learning on non-controversial subjects. Hickes lived for many years in Great Ormond Street, London, and officiated regularly at the oratory in Scroope's Court, near St. Andrew's, Holborn. Here, in celebrating the Holy Eucharist, he used the Office in the Prayer Book of 1549. Hickes was in learning and ability the equal of the greatest of the Caroline divines. His *Thesaurus of the Ancient Northern Tongues* (1703-5) is ' a stupendous monument of learning and industry.' His contributions to theology were no less learned. His *Christian Priesthood* and his *Constitution of the Catholic Church* show his patristic scholarship. He was of necessity driven into controversy. His works on the Roman question are among the best defences of the Anglican position. A well-known book of *Devotions in the Way of Antient Offices,* compiled by Susanna Hopton, printed 1701, was revised and has a preface by him, and is often called by his name. Hickes was after Bishop Lloyd's death, 1709, the unquestioned leader of the Nonjuring body, and was affectionately called by them ' the good Father Hickes.' Though he had many friends among conforming Churchmen, Hickes was a determined advocate of the continuance of the succession and the separation, in contrast with Ken (*q.v.*) and Dodwell. He regarded the ' Revolution Church' as a schismatic body. He died, 15th December 1715, and is buried in St. Margaret's, Westminster. His elder brother, John Hickes, held opinions diametrically opposed to those of the bishop, was ejected from his living, 1662, and executed for his share in Monmouth's rising, 1685. [NONJURORS.]

[S. L. O.]

HIGH COMMISSION, Court of. ORIGIN. —The Commissioners for Causes Ecclesiastical originated in the small and temporary commissions created for the trial of heretics by T. Cromwell (*q.v.*) as Vicegerent. Some traces of commissions somewhat similar in composition and procedure are to be found in the preceding half-century, and it is probable that Henry and Cromwell only completed the transformation of the mediæval heresy trial. The summary procedure of the mediæval trial, sanctioned partly by lay and partly by ecclesiastical authority, was continued ; the decision was as before final, and appeal was impossible ; the penalty of fine and imprisonment reflected the old maxim that the State alone might inflict the penalty of death. The inquisitorial powers of the Commis-

sioners Ecclesiastical (as their official title ran till 1611, though the popular name, ' High Commission,' superseded it before 1580) were old, and the procedure in all essentials older. Edward VI., following a still older administrative habit, put into commission the powers Cromwell had exercised as Vicegerent, and his first body of Commissioners exercised their authority by creating smaller bodies to conduct the actual trial. Mary, however, by Letters Patent of 1556 gave the Commission the form it preserved till 1583 - a body of bishops, statesmen, and lawyers, endowed with almost plenary authority and practically unlimited discretion in causes ecclesiastical. Elizabeth expressly sanctioned the Commission by a clause of the Act of Supremacy (1 Eliz. c. 1, s. viii.), which has long been erroneously regarded as the beginning of the Commission. Indeed, the Commission was not a creation at all, but a growth, and its origin was the necessity of exercising in some way the amplitude of authority invested in the Crown by Henry's assumption of the Supreme Headship. Henry had used it against Roman Catholic and Protestant ; Edward VI. had persecuted the Catholics, Mary the Protestants, and Elizabeth actually expelled some of Mary's bishops and priests by an instrument which Mary herself had developed. The High Commission received its final form at Elizabeth's hands because her settlement was the first to be permanent.

HISTORY OF THE HIGH COMMISSION. 1. 1535-83. *An Inquisitorial Instrument for the repression of Heresy.* —During these years the Commission was wholly under the control of the Privy Council, and its members were more often statesmen and civil lawyers, who could be trusted, than ecclesiastics, whose allegiance was usually dubious. Indeed, it was a temporal body for quasi-political work, and was a tool of the Privy Council, devoid of any institutional life or traditions of its own. Its chief duty was the enforcing of the religious tests of temporal loyalty as laid down in the Acts of Supremacy and Uniformity and in the Thirty-nine Articles. It was busily supporting the State, not the Church. Its powers were as broad as the royal prerogative, and its procedure as indeterminate as that of the Privy Council, but the Commissioners were not allowed to exercise such discretion themselves. The orders from the Privy Council were of the most minute description, telling them what to do and how to do it. (See *Privy Council Register,* New Series, xi. 137, 149, 174, 182, 212, 456 ; xii. 336 ; xiii. 72, etc.) Coupled to these were duties connected with the censorship of the press, later handed over to the Bishop of London and the Star Chamber.

2. 1583-1611. *Development into a Law Court.* — Gradually as the Commission became more and more permanent, its duties more regular, its term of office longer, its membership more numerous, it developed more and more the aspect of a court, and began to have more and more an institutional life and spirit of its own. The questions before it became in the 'seventies less and less political; every year reduced the possibility of popular revolt; Norfolk was executed, Mary Stuart in prison; the Roman Catholics seemed cowed; and the work of the Commission became more and more ecclesiastical, requiring a knowledge of ecclesiastical law and administrative routine rather than of the precepts of state-craft. The force of circumstances was emancipating the Commission from the close control of the Privy Council, and tending to bring into prominence its legal rather than its inquisitorial aspect. Indeed, it had always been treated as a court, albeit a court untrammelled by precedent and the usual rules of procedure, and exercising rather the residual jurisdiction of the Crown than an ordinary competence to try suits between party and party. But in 1576 the new aspect as a court becomes evident, by 1583 the development is clearly under way, and by 1592 was certainly completed.

This change seems to have been chiefly due to Richard Bancroft (*q.v.*), aided by Richard Cosin, Edwin Stanhope, and John Aylmer, Bishop of London. From now on until its dissolution in 1640 its judicial functions in suits between party and party dwarf every other power it has. The old inquisitorial functions fell into practical abeyance, and were used only occasionally. The registrar and the few notaries, at first the whole staff, had now expanded into an army of clerks, while proctors and advocates were regularly licensed to practise before its bar, and clients so thronged its doors that the plea rolls could hardly be kept clear. Its procedure became regular and firm, but was popular with suitors because of its promptitude, and its freedom from the vexatious delays and useless forms so common in litigation in the courts of that time. Its jurisdiction was extended to cover the usual competence of ecclesiastical courts (*q.v.*). The most interesting aspect of its work appeared in its development of an equitable jurisdiction in ecclesiastical cases, and in the broad use of pleading *in forma pauperis*,

whereby it performed most of the functions of an ecclesiastical Court of Requests. The possibility of securing a decree of specific performance, sanctioned by temporal pains of fine and imprisonment, made the Commission exceedingly popular among litigants.

Another aspect of the Commission's work was especially developed by Bancroft. The ordinary ecclesiastical officials were lacking in coercive power; they might censure and admonish, and even excommunicate, but neither laity nor clergy paid much attention to such feeble pains and penalties. At the same time, the clergy were ignorant and disobedient, but could not be displaced, partly because the stipends were so poor that better qualified men refused the benefices, and partly because the Queen, for reasons of state, usually forbade the removal for simple ecclesiastical delinquencies of clergy who were loyal to the State. The work of the Church had to be done by means of unwilling hands, and the hierarchy did not possess in itself the requisite powers to coerce them into obedience. The Reformation had nominally added nothing to the legal powers of bishop or archbishop, and extraordinary authority had hitherto always come from Rome in the form of bulls, decrees, or legates. For want of such authority in the reformed Church matters had gone from bad to worse for half a century in the administration of dioceses and provinces. Now, about 1590, Bancroft seems to have made clear to Whitgift (*q.v.*) and Burghley that the needed coercive power existed in the High Commission, which could itself enforce specific performance of any order and compel obedience from the most refractory. Hence the Commission became also an administrative organ of the greatest importance, and, in fact, the key of the whole ecclesiastical fabric. By its means order and decency were finally evolved by Whitgift, Bancroft, and Cosin in a thousand details of ecclesiastical routine.

It was unlikely, however, that the common law courts would view with favour the powers, authority, and ever-growing popularity of this new court. Cawdry in 1587 had questioned the legality of the new administrative functions of the Commission, but the judges had upheld them. The right of the Commission to hear ordinary suits at ecclesiastical law, and indeed cases which trenched very nearly, if not completely, on the territory claimed by the common law judges, was another matter. On this ground Sir Edward Coke, Chief Justice of the Common Pleas, began in 1607 and 1608 a strong attack on the Commission, and insisted that its powers exceeded the authority granted by the statute of Elizabeth, and that it had no right to try every and any case ecclesiastical, but only those of extremely serious nature. The blow struck at the Commission's position as a law court also imperilled its administrative functions, which Bancroft (now archbishop) felt were of the first and greatest consequence. The archbishop and his lawyers fought hard in Fuller's case (1607) and on various prohibitions, as well as in debates before the King, but were neither defeated nor victorious. Some sort of compromise, whose exact terms we do not know, was patched up in 1611.

3. 1611-40. *A Law Court for the Trial of Suits between Party and Party.*—In 1611 Archbishop Abbot (*q.v.*) carried out Bancroft's scheme for a reorganisation of the Commission. The period of growth was ended, and the Commission stood forth as a law court with a fixed procedure, a broad though not unlimited jurisdiction, and a regular staff of officials to execute its orders. Further, it had attained institutional strength and an *esprit de corps* of its own. All this was openly recognised in the Letters Patent of 1611. Procedure and organisation were officially sanctioned, and the name High Commission was formally adopted. Dignity was lent by the presence among the Commission's members of a crowd of divines and statesmen, but it was understood that they would rarely, if ever, sit. Its decisions were, however, to be no longer final, and Commissions of Review were to be issued by the Crown in case of appeal. By the restoration of the earlier form in 1625 this provision was repealed, and the Commission took on again some of its aspects of unlimited power and arbitrary procedure. Moreover, between 1583 and 1633 the old inquisitorial functions were so seldom used, and the judicial sessions were so regular and so crowded with suitors, that the resumption under Laud (*q.v.*) of only a part of the Commission's earlier activities, and the exercise of a little of its early authority, were thought scandalous innovations and unwarranted abuses of law. In fact, a few decrees in individual cases, for which abundant precedent existed, have generally been treated by historians as conclusive evidence of the usual functions of the Commission (such as Leighton's case), in complete neglect of the Act Books crowded with ordinary law-suits and a Court Calendar so long that only the unceasing activity of Laud and his lawyers could keep pace with it. Whatever opinion

we may hold as to the justice of the Commission's decrees in some few cases, there can be no doubt that its legal and administrative activity was the backbone of the administration of the Church from 1583 to 1640, and that to it was mainly due such efficiency and vigour as were displayed.

PROCEDURE. 1. *Party and Party.*—(1) Articles formed by the plaintiff's proctor were submitted, scrutinised, and must be accepted and signed by the plaintiff's advocate and by a Commissioner. (2) Letters missive were then granted against the defendant, or if he were a fugitive an attachment issued to apprehend him. (3) Affidavit of messenger or pursuivant of the serving of the letters or attachment. (4) Defendant appearing took oath *ex officio* to answer truly the Articles Original (No. 1). (5) Three days allowed the plaintiff's proctor to bring in Articles Additional. (6) The defendant answers these articles before his proctor and a Commissioner. The case might now be followed in two ways: (*a*) the plaintiff might attempt to prove his contention by the defendant's answers; the hearing comes at once; all the articles and the answers are read in open court; advocates heard for both sides; the Commissioners, beginning with the youngest, give individual opinions; the registrar issues the decree in accordance with the majority opinion: or (*b*) when the plaintiff cannot prove his case from the answers of the defendant and must prove his contention by witnesses, etc. (7) Terms probationary: to the plaintiff to prove his articles, and then to the defendant to prove his defence; the evidence of each to be signed by an advocate duly licensed to practise in the High Commission; each to put in interrogatories, which the other must answer in writing. When each had asked and had answers to all his questions, the counsel for the plaintiff moved to go to report, and the Commissioners issued to the defendant a monition to appear on a date fixed. Both advocates then put in briefs of their arguments, and each received the other's. On the morning of the hearing came informations, an informal hearing before three Commissioners, the registrar, the advocates, and proctors concerned in the case. The briefs were read by the advocates, objections adduced by either side, proof furnished when demanded, witnesses produced, and finally the briefs were signed by the Commissioners present, and when thus approved could no longer be questioned for matters of fact. In the afternoon, before the full court, came the hearing, which consisted of the reading of the formal papers, of the briefs, of a speech by each advocate, and of the opinions of the Commissioners, delivered in order of seniority, beginning with the youngest. The majority decided, and the registrar issued the decree in accordance with their decision.

2. *Cases of Office.* — The procedure was the same as in cases between party and party, except that the part of the plaintiff was taken by the court or an advocate appointed to act for it. In Laud's time a King's Advocate was appointed to prosecute cases of office.

[R. G. U.]

Usher, *Reconstruction of the Eng. Ch.*, treats its history in outline to 1610. The commissions are abstracted in Prothero, *Statutes and Constitutional Documents*. The only remaining Act Books are fully calendared in the *State Papers Domestic*, 1634-6, 1639-40. The *Privy Council Register*, New Series, contains much on the early history of the commission. The bulk of the material is in manuscript.

HILDA, St., or HILD (614 ?-80), abbess, daughter of Hereric, nephew of King Edwin (*q.v.*), was born about 614, and was baptized by Paulinus (*q.v.*) in 627. When thirty-three she assumed the monastic habit, and spent a year in East Anglia, intending to imitate her sister Hereswid, a nun of Chelles, near Paris. Aidan (*q.v.*) called her back to Northumbria, and after a year spent as a nun she became Abbess of Hereteu, or Hartlepool, and ruled her house with wisdom gained from learned men, many of whom, and among them Aidan, visited her. In 657 she founded a monastery at Streaneshale, or Whitby, where, as at Hartlepool, she presided over a double community of men and women. Under her wise and holy governance her monastery exhibited the characteristics of the Church in the Apostolic Age. All called her 'Mother.' She taught the Scriptures diligently. Five Whitby monks became bishops, and she received the poet Caedmon into her house. Kings and nobles asked counsel of her. She attended the conference held at Whitby in 664 [WILFRID] on the Scotic side, but probably adopted the Catholic Easter. She took part against Wilfrid in his dispute with Archbishop Theodore. After an illness of six years she died on 17th November 680, having that year founded a monastery at Hackness as a dependency of Whitby.

[W. H.]

Bede, *H.E.*; Eckenstein, *Woman under Monasticism.*

HOADLY, Benjamin (1676-1761), bishop, was educated at Clare Hall, Cambridge.

He became Rector of St. Peter-le-Poor, London, holding later in plurality the rectory of Streatham. In 1705 he preached before the Lord Mayor against Passive Obedience and Non-Resistance. The Lower House of Convocation complained of this sermon as dishonouring the Church, but without result. Hoadly soon became the champion of the Whig clergy against Atterbury (*q.v.*) and the High Churchmen. In 1709 the House of Commons voted an address praying the Queen to ' bestow some dignity ' on him as a reward for ' his eminent services both to Church and State ' in supporting the principles of ' the late happy revolution.' In 1715 George I. made him Bishop of Bangor, and he was allowed to hold both his livings *in commendam*. In 1716 he attacked the Nonjurors (*q.v.*), and in 1717 he preached before the King on ' The Nature of the Kingdom or Church of Christ.' Its argument, from the text. ' My kingdom is not of this world ' (Jn. 18³⁶), is directed to prove that the Gospels afford no warrant for the existence of any visible church authority. In the Kingdom of Christ He is King, and this excludes all other authority. The laws of the Kingdom are plainly fixed, and no one has authority to alter, add to, or interpret them in such manner as to be binding on others. This sermon, said to have been suggested by the King, gave rise to the Bangorian controversy. Hoadly's own contributions to it fill between five and six hundred folio pages of his *Works*, which also contain a list, admittedly incomplete, of more than a hundred pamphlets and writings by other authors on this subject during 1717 and 1718 alone. Among his antagonists were Law (*q.v.*) and T. Sherlock (*q.v.*), who was one of several royal chaplains deprived of their posts for writing against Hoadly. The most important outcome of the controversy was the suppression of Convocation (*q.v.*). A committee of the Lower House had extracted from his works a number of propositions alleged to be subversive of Church government. A synodical condemnation of his opinions would have emphasised the opposition of the clergy to the government. Accordingly it was thought expedient, in Hallam's phrase, ' to scatter a little dust over the angry insects,' and Convocation was prorogued in 1717, and not allowed to meet again, except formally, till 1852.

Hoadly, ' cringing from one bishopric to another,' was rewarded with the see of Hereford in 1721, translated in 1723 to Salisbury, and in 1734 to Winchester. In 1735 he published anonymously *A Plain*

Account of the Nature and End of the Lord's Supper, maintaining that sacrament to be a mere commemorative rite. His theological position is shown by his low and latitudinarian views on matters alike of church government and doctrine ; his conception of his pastoral duties may be gathered from the fact that during his six years as Bishop of Bangor he never set foot in the diocese. He is memorable as a strong and skilful controversialist, but in spite of the adulation with which he sets forth views acceptable to those in power, there is no reason to doubt that he conscientiously held them.   [G. C.]

Works, with *Life* by his son ; Wilkins, *Concilia.*

HOLGATE, Robert (1491-1555), Archbishop of York, joined the order of St. Gilbert of Sempringham (*q.v.*), and was probably educated in their house at Cambridge. He became Master of Sempringham, Prior of Walton, Yorks, and Vicar of Cadney, Lincolnshire. Owing to a dispute with Sir Francis Ascough at Cadney he came to London, and was made chaplain to Henry VIII. In later life he stated that but for this he would have remained a poor priest all his life. He was consecrated Bishop of Llandaff in 1537, receiving the royal licence to hold the Mastership of Sempringham and the Priory of Walton *in commendam.* He became President of the Council of the North in 1535, and was henceforward much occupied in secular business. In 1540 he surrendered Walton to the King, and received in exchange a grant of all its lands. In 1545 he was translated to York, and at confirmation received a pall (*q.v.*) from Cranmer—the sole instance of an Archbishop of Canterbury conferring the pall under the authority given him to do so by 25 Hen. VIII. c. 20 (Stubbs, *C.H.,* iii. 305 n., and *Gent. Mag.,* 1860, 522 ; Dr. Wickham Legg, *Yorks. Archæol. Journal,* 1898, 121). He alienated to the King sixty-seven manors belonging to the see, in return for large grants from dissolved monasteries. By such means, while he impoverished the see, he became the wealthiest bishop in England.

In 1549 he was married publicly, though it is stated that the marriage had been previously performed privately. He had differences with Warwick, and had to resign the Presidency of the Council of the North. In 1551 one Anthony Norman complained that Holgate's wife had been previously married to himself, and demanded her restitution. The Council appointed commissioners to go into the matter. Their report is not known, but the lady was described as his wife in a grant of lands from the King after the inquiry.

He appears not to have had any strong religious convictions and to have been ready to conform to the opinions of the party in power. In Edward's reign he passed as a Reformer, ordered the vicars-choral of the cathedral to have each a New Testament in English, that the works of Calvin and Bullinger should be included in the library, forbade the playing of the organ during service, and directed that all carving and images behind the high altar should be removed and texts substituted.

On Mary's accession he was imprisoned and deprived for being married, but obtained his release by declaring that he repented of his marriage, that he had only married for fear of being thought a papist, and offering to put his wife away, obey the Queen's laws, and pay £1000. His petition was granted, but his death soon followed. His wealth was enormous, but no mention is made of his wife in his will.   [C. P. S. C.]

Strype, *Eccl. Memorials, Cranmer* : W. Hunt in *D.N.B.*

HOLY EUCHARIST, Doctrine of, in English Church. There is no reason for supposing that the Eucharistic beliefs ordinarily held in the Church of England before the Reformation differed from those customary in the rest of the Western Church. The teaching of the Venerable Bede (*q.v.*) in the eighth century that the Eucharist is a sacrifice in which the Body and Blood of Christ are offered to God on behalf of the living and the dead, and that the Body and Blood of Christ are received by Christians by means of Communion, is substantially the same as that of St. Gregory the Great (*q.v.*), which was probably brought to England by St. Augustine (*q.v.*) at the end of the sixth century. That the same beliefs were held by the Celtic Christians, to whom other strains of English Christianity are due, may be illustrated from the *Bangor Antiphonary* of the seventh century (i. 10 *v,* 11 *r* ; ii. 10, 11, H.B.S. ed.), and the *Stowe Missal* in the eighth (i. 45, 46, H.B.S. ed.). The teaching of Aelfric (*q.v.*) in England in the tenth century, with the doubt whether his meaning is that there is a gift of spiritual union with Christ, bestowed inwardly only on the communicant, or that the means of the gift is that the elements are made by consecration spiritually to be the Body and Blood of Christ (*Homilies,* ii. 268-73, Aelfric Society ed.), is a reproduction of that contained in the treatise of Ratramn of Corbey and Orbais in the ninth century in his treatise, *On the Body and Blood of the Lord*. The theological instruction and the devotional writings of Lanfranc (*q.v.*) and Anselm (*q.v.*) in the eleventh and twelfth centuries are representative of England and Normandy alike ; and the provision in the Canterbury statutes of the eleventh century for the carrying of the Sacrament in procession on Palm Sunday and for acts of adoration in connection with the procession, as well as for the placing of the Sacrament in the Sepulchre and the consequent adoration on Maundy Thursday and Good Friday, are probably expressive of customs which were also Norman (*Decreta pro Ord. S. Benedicti*, i. 4 ; *Ordinarium Can. Reg. S. Laudi Rotomagensis* ; John of Rouen, *De off. eccl.* ; Martene, *De ant. mon. rit.*, xii. 13-15 ; xiii. 46 ; xiv. 39). In the thirteenth century the teaching of Alexander of Hales, who, an Englishman by birth, filled various ecclesiastical offices in England before his removal to Paris, with its scanty treatment of the Eucharistic sacrifice and its minute discussion of the doctrine of Transubstantiation, its merits in the assertions of the objective value of consecration, of the reality of the Presence and gift of the Body and Blood of Christ, and of the need of worthy reception if there is to be spiritual profit, as well as its demerits in over-elaboration of the nature and method of the Presence so as to bring it into accordance with the Aristotelian philosophy (*S.T.*, IV. v. x. xi.), affords a characteristic instance of the general tendencies of the time. The thirteenth-century English directions for the adoration of our Lord at the elevation of the Host and when the Sacrament is carried do not differ from the contemporary instructions abroad. William of Ockham (*q.v.*), also a native of England and a teacher at Paris, who became Provincial of the English Franciscans in 1322, taught that all that Holy Scripture and the true tradition of the Church and considerations of reason really supported was that the Body of Christ is under the species of bread ; but he accepted the current doctrine that the substance of the bread and wine ceases to be on the authority of the Church of his day (*Quodl. sept.*, iv. 34, 35) ; John Wyclif (*q.v.*) questioned very much in the ordinary scholastic teaching concerning the nature and results of Transubstantiation (*Trial.*, iv. 1-10 ; *De Euch.*, passim ; *Fasc. Ziz.*, R.S., v. 105, 115-17, 131) ; the Lollard statement of 1395 followed Wyclif (*q.v.*) (*Fasc. Ziz.*, R.S., v. 361, 362) ; Sir John Oldcastle, representing the best of the Lollards (*q.v.*), in 1413 explicitly explained

that 'the most worshipful Sacrament of the altar is Christ's Body in the form of bread, the same Body that was born of the Blessed Virgin, our Lady Saint Mary, done on the cross, dead and buried, the third day rose from death to life, the which Body is now glorified in heaven,' but that 'as Christ when dwelling on earth had in Himself Godhead and manhood, yet the Godhead veiled and invisible under the manhood, which was open and visible, so in the Sacrament of the altar there is real Body and real bread, that is, the bread which we see, and the Body of Christ veiled under it which we do not see' (*Fasc. Ziz.*, v. 438, 444). These all were giving utterance to lines of thought which were being developed outside as well as within England. So also were the more extreme Lollards, who maintained that the Eucharist was 'nothing but a morsel of dead bread and a tower or pinnacle of antichrist' (see the statement of Sir Louis de Clifford quoted in Walsingham, *Historia Anglicana*, R.S., ii. 252, 253 ; xxviii. *b*). The reply of the official representatives of the Church in England was no less in accordance with the lines adopted abroad. Care was taken in the declaration of the University of Oxford in 1381, at the Council of London in 1382, and in other official actions to maintain not only that the consecrated Sacrament is the Body of Christ, but also that after consecration the substances of bread and wine do not remain ; and the theological attitude thus adopted was enforced by such steps as the burning of William Sawtré in 1401 and of Richard Wyche about 1439. On the other hand, while devotions of the people and the instructions of the clergy in the fourteenth and fifteenth centuries imply that the consecrated Sacrament is the Body and Blood of Christ, they are unaffected whether, the continuance of the bread and the wine is affirmed or denied. The intense devotion of Mother Julian of Norwich's *Revelations of Divine Love*, the teaching of John Myrc of Lilleshall in his *Festival Book* and his *Instructions for Parish Priests*, Langforde's *Meditations for Ghostly Exercise in the Time of the Mass*, the discourse addressed to the York Guild of Corpus Christi in the fifteenth century, would lose their meaning if the consecrated Sacrament were not the Body and Blood of Christ ; whereas they make no suggestion as to the nature of the physical change in the elements, and they would gain nothing or lose nothing according as the spiritual doctrine of Transubstantiation which the great Schoolmen had formulated were affirmed or denied. So in the century preceding the Reformation the official representatives of the Church in England were bent on enforcing that doctrine of Transubstantiation which, designed to protect the spiritual character of the Eucharistic Presence of Christ, carried with it a denial of the continuance of the substance of the bread and wine in the consecrated Sacrament; the care of pastors and the love of people were not much concerned with the technicalities of the doctrine from one point of view or another, provided that their mental conceptions allowed to their souls the truth that the living Lord who was born of Mary and died on the cross was present and adored and offered in sacrifice and received. The New Learning of the Renaissance had its votaries in England as abroad. John Colet (*q.v.*), Dean of St. Paul's, who died in 1519, was one of its pioneers. In caution, in restraint, in mysticism, in the evident dread of anything carnal or mechanical or unreal, in the devout belief that the consecrated Sacrament is the Body and the Blood of Christ, Colet may well represent the most refined and cultivated minds in the wonderful opening years of the sixteenth century. Throughout the reigns of Henry VIII., Edward VI., Mary, and Elizabeth different and contradictory beliefs were struggling for mastery. A doctrine of the Eucharistic Presence which, whether called by the name of Transubstantiation or not, was substantially that officially affirmed by the Church of Rome at the Council of Trent may be seen in the writings of King Henry VIII. (*q.v.*) and Bishop Fisher (*q.v.*), the *Six Articles* of 1539, and the *King's Book* of 1543; in the writings of Gardiner (*q.v.*) and others during the reign of Edward VI.; in the official acts of Mary's reign; and after the accession of Elizabeth in the proceedings of the Convocation of Canterbury in 1559. A doctrine which affirmed that the consecrated elements are the Body and Blood of Christ without deciding anything in regard to Transubstantiation is in the *Ten Articles* of 1536, the *Bishops' Book* of 1537, the *Thirteen Articles* of 1538, and the First Prayer Book of Edward VI., issued in 1549. A doctrine which does not connect the Presence of Christ with the consecrated Sacrament before Communion, but maintains that the faithful communicant receives either the Body of Christ itself or the power and virtue of the Body, is suggested by some features of the Second Prayer Book of Edward VI., issued in 1552, by the draft *Forty-five Articles* of 1551, by the *Forty-two Articles* of 1553, by *Poynet's Catechism* of 1553, and by the writings of Ridley (*q.v.*), Cranmer (*q.v.*), and Latimer (*q.v.*). In Elizabeth's reign, in accordance with her

well-known policy, the tendency is to make room for different doctrines. The Prayer Book of 1559 is not incompatible with a belief either that the elements become the Body and Blood of Christ at consecration, or that faithful communicants receive the Body and Blood of Christ at their Communion without these having been previously present, though perhaps slightly inclining to the former belief; the teaching of the *Thirty-eight Articles* of 1563, the *Thirty-nine Articles* of 1571 [ARTICLES OF RELIGION], and the *Homilies* of 1563, while denying Transubstantiation and Zwinglianism alike, is in the direction of asserting that faithful communicants really receive the Body and Blood of Christ, and leaving open the further question whether the Body and Blood are present at the consecration or only to the communicant at communion; and the tendency thus seen in the documents may be illustrated from the differences in the writings of individual theologians. In subsequent reigns the same tendency continues, though the emphasis mostly tends towards asserting the gift to the communicant and either denying or being careless about a presence in virtue of consecration. The additions made to the Catechism in 1604 and the Prayer Book of 1662 require belief that faithful communicants receive the Body and Blood of Christ, and incline towards the doctrine that the Body and Blood are present at consecration and before reception, without explicitly asserting this latter doctrine. Till 1688 a minority among theologians asserted a presence in the Sacrament before Communion; the large majority are content to say that the Body and Blood are received by the faithful communicant. In the teaching of John Hales in his tract, *On the Sacrament of the Lord's Supper*, published probably soon after 1635, there is an instance of the Zwinglian doctrine that the communicant receives only bread and wine as signs of Christ, which, in defiance of the formularies, was in later years to be widely prevalent and strongly influential in the English Church.

Through the long period from the accession of Henry VIII. to the departure of James II. the doctrine of the Sacrifice does not always follow the doctrine of the Presence; but for the most part those who affirmed that the consecrated Sacrament is the Body and Blood of Christ recognised also the specifically sacrificial character of the Eucharist, though as a rule without much definition of sacrifice, and those who rejected the Presence at consecration tended to deny any more distinct Sacrifice than a mere memory of the cross and such as is to be found in all acceptable prayer.

In the closing years of the seventeenth century and in the eighteenth the chief points of interest lay in the growth of Zwinglianism and in the teaching of the Nonjurors (*q.v.*). It was at this time that Zwinglianism obtained that hold in English thought which has hardly yet altogether ceased to influence doctrine and practice in the English Church. The Nonjurors, who shared with the best divines of the English Church a horror of Zwinglianism, were not entirely agreed among themselves as to a positive doctrine ; but there was developed among them a characteristic belief, which eventually became more influential in Scotland and America than in England, that the elements are made at the recital of the institution to be representative symbols of the Body and Blood of Christ, that as such symbols they are then offered in sacrifice, and that at the later invocation of the Holy Ghost the elements become the Body and Blood of Christ in virtue and power and effect. It was the natural outcome of this doctrine that the group of the Nonjurors known as the Usagers were eager to use the Liturgy which they published in 1717, in which the recital of the institution, the commemoration of Christ, and the invocation of the Holy Ghost were placed in an appropriate order. The nineteenth century inherited from the earlier times denials, vagueness, and beliefs. The best representatives of the Evangelical Movement [EVANGELICALS] emphasised the blessedness of the spiritual participation in Christ which the faithful communicant enjoys.

The Tractarians [OXFORD MOVEMENT] reaffirmed the value of the Eucharistic sacrifice and of the doctrine that by virtue of the consecration the living and spiritual Body and Blood of Christ are present in the Sacrament under the form of bread and wine. Later writers placed the doctrine in closer touch with other characteristics of Christian thought by their emphasis on the spiritual nature of the risen Body of Christ, and on the intimate connection between the earthly offering in the Church's Eucharist and the heavenly pleading of our Lord. During the long and at times bitter controversies of the last sixty or more years the Church of England itself has not given any authoritative interpretation of its formularies ; and the general tendency has been to acquiesce in a position that the formularies exclude Zwinglianism and at any rate a gross and carnal form of Transubstantiation, but are patient of very different doctrines between these two extremes. Meanwhile the progress of positive Eucharistic truth within the English Church has been

no less than marvellous. The Zwinglianism once so common has almost disappeared, though time, of course, is needed to remove all its effects. In each generation receptionist and virtualist opinions, if still held, take a stronger and more effective form. There has been a vast increase in the number and influence of those who believe that the consecrated Sacrament is the Body of Christ and that the Eucharist is the sacrificial pleading of Him who for our redemption took human life and died and rose again.   [D. S.]

Stone, *Hist. of the Doctrine of the Holy Eucharist* and *Holy Communion*.

HOOK, Walter Farquhar (1798-1875), Vicar of Leeds and Dean of Chichester, was educated at Winchester and Christ Church, Oxford, leading a solitary life at both owing to his studious habits and love of seclusion. After working at Whippingham, Birmingham, and Coventry he was elected Vicar of Leeds by the trustees in 1837 in spite of the strong opposition of the Evangelicals. Though he never identified himself with the Oxford Movement (*q.v.*), his learning caused him to welcome it, and he was on friendly terms with its leaders, whom he often defended against misrepresentation. His sermon, 'Hear the Church,' preached before the Queen in 1838, a defence of the authority of the Church apart from its connection with the State, caused some sensation and controversy. The early history of St. Saviour's, a church given anonymously to Leeds by Dr. Pusey (*q.v.*), intensified his mistrust of the Movement in some of its aspects. For between its consecration in 1845 and 1851 nine of its clergy seceded to Rome. This brought about a temporary breach of his friendship with Pusey, of whom, however, he spoke in later years as 'that saint whom England persecuted.' Hook maintained his position as a sober, 'historical Church of England man' so consistently against opposition from every quarter that Bishop S. Wilberforce (*q.v.*) compared him to a ship at anchor, which, though stationary, always swings round to breast the tide.

He was the first to apply the principles of the revival of church life to practical work in a large town, and his example affected the whole of the north of England. During his incumbency twenty-one churches were built in Leeds. About 1851 he adopted for a short time the then novel practice of evening Communion. He took part in public affairs, and advocated a secular system of State education. He was a hard worker, commonly rising before five in the morning. His sturdy independence of character and shrewd humour broke down all opposition, and won the devotion of Yorkshiremen. He published sermons, pamphlets, and works of popular church history, the best known being his *Lives of the Archbishops of Canterbury*, to which he devoted much time after becoming Dean of Chichester in 1859.   [G. C.]

W. R. W. Stephens, *Life*.

HOOKER, Richard (1553-1600), 'a poor obscure English priest,' author of the *Ecclesiastical Polity*, of which Pope Clement VIII. declared that 'it had in it such seeds of eternity that it would abide till the last fire shall consume all learning.' Hallam justly describes it as 'the first great original prose work in our language.' At Exeter Grammar School Hooker showed such a grave modesty and sweet serenity that at the request of his uncle, John Hooker, Bishop Jewel (*q.v.*) took him under his care, and in 1567 procured him a 'clerk's place' at C.C.C., Oxford, in which condition he continued till his eighteenth year, 'still increasing in learning and prudence, and so much in learning and piety that he seemed to be filled with the Holy Ghost.' Restored from a dangerous sickness by his mother's prayers, he started on foot to visit her, also visiting Jewel on the way, who sent him forward with his blessing, good counsel, twenty groats, and a horse which had carried him many a mile (his walking-staff). On Jewel's death Hooker discovered another patron in the President of Corpus, Dr. Cole, who found him pupils. Walton gives an exquisite picture of the young tutor's saintly life, he all the while 'enriching his quiet and capacious soul with the precious learning of the Philosophers, Casuists, and Schoolmen . . . restless in searching the scope and intent of God's Spirit revealed to mankind in the Sacred Scripture. . . . Nor was this excellent man a stranger to the more light and airy parts of learning, as musick and poetry.' In 1577 he was chosen Fellow of his college, and in 1579 Reader in Hebrew to the University. In that year, for some unknown reason, probably some point of Church observance, he and other Fellows were expelled the college, but were reinstated on appeal to the Visitor. In 1582 Hooker was ordained, and soon after was appointed to preach at Paul's Cross. The lodging for preachers, called the Shunamite's House, was then kept by John Churchman, whose wife made Hooker good cheer, and told him 'it was best for him to have a wife that might prove a nurse to him . . . and such a one she could and would provide.' This

turned out to be her own daughter Joan, 'who brought him neither beauty nor portion.' By this marriage he 'was drawn from the tranquillity of his colledge . . . into the corroding cares that attend a married Priest and a countrey parsonage; which was Drayton-Beauchamp in Buckinghamshire.' Here his old pupils found him tending sheep and reading Horace, whence he was called indoors to rock the cradle. But in 1586 he became, somewhat unwillingly, Master of the Temple, where the controversies gathered round him that gave birth to the *Ecclesiastical Polity*. The afternoon lecturer was Walter Travers (*q.v.*), a vehement Calvinist, so that it was said 'the forenoon sermon spake Canterbury, and the afternoon Geneva.' Inhibited by Archbishop Whitgift, Travers began a pamphlet war, among his charges being that Hooker had said 'he doubted not but that God was merciful to many of our forefathers living in popish superstition, inasmuch as they sinned ignorantly.' 'Weary of the noise and oppositions' of one whom he called 'a good man,' Hooker solicited the archbishop to remove him to some quiet spot where he could devote himself to a justification of the Church's system. In 1591 Whitgift presented him to Boscombe, near Salisbury, and the same year he became prebendary of Netheravon. Within eighteen months he had finished the first four books of the *Ecclesiastical Polity*, though publication was delayed till 1594. In 1595 Queen Elizabeth presented him to Bishopsbourne, near Canterbury, where he 'gave a holy valediction to the pleasures and allurements of earth,' devoting himself to prayer and mortification and the duties of his office. Many turned out of the road to see one so famous, but they found only 'an obscure, harmless man . . . in poor clothes . . . of a mean stature and stooping, and yet more lowly in the thoughts of the soul.' He had at this time a close friend in Dr. Adrian Saravia, who was his confessor. Hooker died on All Souls Day 1600, 'meditating,' he said, 'the number and nature of the Angels.' He had published the fifth book of the *Ecclesiastical Polity* in 1597, and seems to have left the last three in a state of forwardness. His widow was accused of allowing Puritan hands to garble the MS.

Hooker met an anarchic Puritanism, not with its own abusive violence, but with a broad theory of the order of the world and a large elucidation of the nature of law, whose 'seat is the bosom of God and her voice the harmony of the world.' Behind the decrees of Pope or council, and even behind the

Sacred Scriptures themselves, stands the Eternal Reason, expressing itself in regular and constant law, which reaches from the throne of God to the life of the meanest worm. Yet, because God reveals Himself in many ways, our reason arrives at the knowledge of His will, not by merely asking what is written, but by a number of concurrent means and faculties. Puritans thought they found in the Bible a methodical code of rules, so that it was sinful to do anything in religion without express Scriptural direction. Hooker, on the other hand, maintained that it is no derogation to the perfection of the Sacred Scriptures to hold that they leave many things to the discretion and tradition of the Church, a 'supernatural Society,' which is illuminated by the heavenly Wisdom and has by means of Councils General the authority of a mother over private judgments. As a 'politic Society' the Church has 'full dominion over itself,' and the use which it has made of this autonomy in decreeing rites and ceremonies Hooker shows, especially in the famous Fifth Book, to be in accordance with reason. He asserts the continuity of the Church of England with the historic Catholic Church— 'To reform ourselves is not to sever ourselves from the Church we were of before : in the Church we were and we are so still'—and describes the 'rites, customs, and orders of ecclesiastical government,' derided as 'popish dregs,' as 'those whereby for so many ages together we have been guided in the service of the true God.' But such customs, even when of apostolic origin, 'have the nature of things changeable,' though he admits that not only the law of nature but even some positive laws are immutable.

It is when Hooker applies this luminous doctrine of the law-making power of human society, and especially of the Spirit-guided Church, to the organic structure of the Church itself that he is a somewhat dangerous guide. The Gospel ministry stands on the same footing as the Gospel sacraments rather than on that of mere ceremonies. In Hooker's time, however, it was regarded as a question of the best form of Church administration and government, rather than as one of the transmissory devolution of stewardship and ambassadorship for Christ. Hooker loses sight of Apostolic Succession, as the covenanted channel of grace and truth, in the discussion of ecclesiastical polity, and places it on the level of wearing surplices or keeping Lent. 'I conclude,' he says, 'that neither God's being author of laws of government for His Church, nor His committing them into Scripture, is any reason sufficient wherefore all

churches should for ever be bound to keep them without change.' Hooker roundly denied the Calvinistic minor premiss that the original form of Church polity had been Presbyterian. A strange thing, he says, if it were so, that no part of the Church had ever found it out. But even were it true, the Calvinistic major assumption that the Church is bound always by its first constitution is challenged. Here Hooker's contemporaries of the close of the Tudor period, such as Saravia, Bilson, and Bancroft (*q.v.*), parted company with him. They perceived the application to the Divine Society of a *contrat social* theory, which regarded the institutions of the kingdom of God as evolved out of the general will of the Christian people, to be impossible, for the Church is prior to its members, and its fundamental principles are not derived from consent. But also it was seen that a confusion had arisen between the question of the 'form of episcopal regiment' and the issue how the ministerial commission is conveyed. To escape condemning the ordinations of the Continental Protestants, Hooker held that though 'the whole Church visible hath not ordinarily allowed any other than bishops alone to ordain,' yet cases of 'inevitable necessity' might arise for departing from that rule. But, apart from the question whether the whole visible Church ever made or ever relaxed any such rule, the real point was whether ordination can in any case proceed from below, that is to say, from popular or lay appointment. Elsewhere Hooker extols the unearthly derivation and authority of the priesthood in the most exalted language, *e.g. E.P.*, v. lxxvii., secs. 1, 2, 3. Episcopacy, again, is a 'sacred regiment, ordained of God' (VII. i., sec. 4). This is a far higher view than the Erastian one of Cranmer and Whitgift, and Hooker was a Church champion of a more spiritual order than his predecessors.

His exposition of the doctrine of the Incarnation in the Fifth Book is of profound value, and the consequent sacramentalism of the Gospel dispensation is uncompromisingly drawn out as regards the 'sacrament of new birth.' The 'Food of Immortality,' too, is stated to be 'a true and real participation of Christ and of life in His Body and Blood,' so that 'these holy mysteries do instrumentally impart into us, in true and real though mystical manner, the very Person of our Lord Himself, whole, perfect and entire.' But for these words the statement just before that we receive 'the grace of' Christ's Body and Blood might seem to lean to virtualism. Similarly, in spite of the much-debated expression (*E.P.*, v. lxvii., sec. 6) that 'the real presence of Christ's most blessed Body and Blood is not to be sought for in the Sacrament, but in the worthy receiver of the Sacrament.' Hooker's teaching, though unsatisfactorily expressed, was not a mere receptionism. He does not deny an objective verity of the Body and Blood 'externally seated in the very elements themselves,' but only that it should be speculatively 'sought for' there rather than, where we are certain it is, in the soul of the believing recipient. Hooker alludes to fasting reception as a thing not controverted (IV. ii., sec. 3). He also speaks firmly of the profitableness before communion of auricular confession to 'God's appointed officer and vicegerent,' to whom are committed the keys of remission and retention of sins. It will be seen that Hooker represents a conservative reaction from the excesses of the earlier Reformation, preparing the way for the fuller recovery attained by the school of Andrewes (*q.v.*), Herbert (*q.v.*), and Laud (*q.v.*). His master mind checked and turned the tide of revolution. And he rescued theological controversy from the gutter, investing it with a solemn dignity, richness, and grandeur.

[D. M.]

Works. ed. Keble. Church, and Paget : Izaak Walton, *Life* : Vernon Staley, *Life*.

HOOPER, John (d. 1555), Bishop of Gloucester and Worcester, born towards the end of the fifteenth century in Somersetshire. His father did not favour the Reformation. 'My father, of whom I am the only son and heir, is so opposed to me on account of Christ's religion, that should I refuse to act according to his wishes, I shall be sure to find him for the future not a father but a cruel tyrant.' Even in 1550 he writes: 'My father is yet living in ignorance of the true religion, but I hope that the grace of God will at length teach him better.'

He is said to have been a Cistercian monk at Gloucester. On the Dissolution he went to London, was converted to the new doctrines by the writings of Zwingli and Bullinger, returned to Oxford in order to propagate them, and 'eftsoons fell into displeasure and hatred of certain who began to stir coals against him,' and would have been prosecuted for heresy under the Act of the Six Articles, but escaped, and became steward in the household of Sir Thomas Arundell, who discovering his opinions sent him to Bishop Gardiner (*q.v.*) that he might be converted, but without effect, though he kept him some days, and

commended his learning and wit. He shortly afterwards fled to Paris, and returning was compelled to fly again to the Continent by way of Ireland.

In 1546 he married an Antwerp lady at Basle, and in 1547 removed to Zurich, where he remained for two years, and became intimate with Bullinger. Before this he had adopted extreme Zwinglian views. In a letter to Bullinger, probably in 1546, he lamented the state of religion in England. 'England has at this time ten thousand nuns, not one of whom is allowed to marry. The impious mass, the most shameful celibacy of the clergy; auricular confession, superstitious abstinence from meat, and purgatory, which was never before held by the people in greater esteem than now.' He objected to the Lutheran doctrine of the Eucharist as much as to the Roman. Though in a letter to Bucer (*q.v.*) he disclaimed a belief that the sacraments were only bare signs, it is difficult to see that he understood anything else by them. 'The minister gives what is in his power—namely, the bread and wine, and not the Body of Christ ; nor is it exhibited by the minister, and eaten by the communicant, otherwise than in the word preached, read, and meditated upon. And to eat the Body of Christ is nothing else than to believe, as He Himself teaches in the sixth of John.'

He returned to England in May 1549, became chaplain to the Protector Somerset, and was prominent among a section of the more extreme Reformers. He devoted himself to preaching, and, according to Foxe, 'the people in great companies and flocks came daily to hear his voice, and often were unable to get into the church on account of the crowd ; he used continually to preach, most times twice, at least once, every day.'

He took part in denouncing Bonner (*q.v.*) to the Council for a sermon, and in 1550 preached a course of Lent sermons before the King, in which he attacked the Ordinal just published on account of the vestments and the form of oath, and was in consequence brought before the Council by Cranmer (*q.v.*) and admonished. In the same year he was nominated by Northumberland to the see of Gloucester. He refused on account of the oath, which the King himself altered to remove the objectionable allusion to saints and the gospels. He also objected to the vestments. A long and bitter discussion took place, in which the foreign Reformers at Zurich and Basle were consulted and took different sides. The King and six of the Council sent a letter to Cranmer authorising him to consecrate Hooper without them, but this he refused to do. At one period Hooper was confined to the Fleet for contumacy, after which he submitted, and was consecrated, 8th March 1551. The bishopric was thus forced upon him because the mandate for his consecration had been issued. As bishop he showed great activity. He preached three or four times a day, issued many injunctions, and endeavoured to organise the diocese on the Zurich model, with superintendents instead of rural deans and archdeacons. At his visitation of 1551 he found that of 311 clergy 10 could not say the Lord's Prayer, 27 did not know who was its Author, 30 could not tell where it was to be found (*E.H.R.*, January 1904). In the same year Sir Anthony Kingston, being rebuked by Hooper for adultery, struck him on the cheek, for which he was fined and compelled to do penance, which resulted in his conversion.

In 1552 he resigned the see of Gloucester, which was dissolved and amalgamated with Worcester, to which Hooper was appointed with the title of Bishop of Worcester and Gloucester. He consented under pressure to alienate the revenues to the Crown. He administered his new diocese on the same lines, but met with more opposition, and two of the canons denounced his articles as illegal.

On the accession of Mary he was one of the first against whom proceedings were taken on account of religion, though as the laws against heresy were not yet re-enacted he was apprehended on a charge of owing money to the Queen, and committed to the Fleet on 11th September 1553. He seems to have remained there fifteen months, and by his own account was treated with great harshness, ' having nothing appointed to me for my bed but a little pad of straw and a rotten covering with a tick and a few feathers therein, the chamber being vile and stinking.' In March 1554 he appeared before the commission, and was deprived. The charges were principally that he was married and did not believe in the corporal presence in the Eucharist. In January 1555 he again appeared before the commissioners at St. Mary Overy, Southwark; two examinations were made, but he refused to recant, and was sentenced to be degraded and delivered to the sheriffs. He was sent to Gloucester for execution, and was burnt on 9th February 1555. His suffering was extreme, but his constancy was unshaken.

Hooper was a voluminous writer as well as an indefatigable preacher, and did much to popularise extreme Protestant views. His moral character was high; he was liberal to the poor, and his zeal was great if not always according to knowledge. His character was austere, stern, and unbending. Foxe relates that ' a worthy citizen came to his door for counsel, but being abashed at his austere behaviour durst not come in but departed, seeking remedy of his troubled mind at other men's hands.' He was stiff in his opinions, incapable of admitting himself to be in the wrong, unable to see any good in his adversaries, and to judge by his eulogies on Somerset, Warwick, and other members of the council almost incapable of seeing any evil in those who shared his opinions. He was a man to extort respect rather than to win love, but his cruel death must have gone far to promote the opinions for which he laboured so remorselessly in his life.   [c. p. s. c.]

Strype, *Memorials*; Foxe, *Acts and Monuments*; *Works, Original Letters* (Parker Soc.).

HORNE, George (1730-1792). Bishop of Norwich, second son of Samuel, Rector of Otham, Kent, born at Otham, 1st November 1730; educated at Maidstone School; Exhibitioner of University College, Oxford, 1746; B.A., 1749; M.A., 1752; B.D., 1759; D.D., 1764; ordained deacon by Bishop Secker of Oxford, 1753; and priest presumably in 1754. In 1750 he was elected Kent Fellow of Magdalen College; and it is Horne to whom Gibbon refers in the *Autobiography* as ' the only student, a future bishop ' among the Fellows in 1752-53. Gibbon adds that he was ' deeply immersed in the follies of the Hutchinsonian system '; along with his friend, W. Jones (*q.v.*), of University College, afterwards of Nayland, and his cousin, W. Stevens (' Nobody '), and with other eminent members of the University, he accepted much of ' Hutchinsonianism,' without being committed to its more fantastic developments, attracted by its reverent and spiritual treatment of Holy Scripture as contrasted with the general attitude of the moment, and regarding it as the antidote to the contemporary rationalism and Deism (*q.v.*). He wrote in defence of the so-called Hutchinsonians, especially in reply to the anonymous strictures of Kennicott. In 1768 he was elected President of Magdalen, and in the same year he married Felicia, daughter of Philip Burton of Eltham. From 1771-81 he was chaplain in ordinary to George III. In 1776 he published his best known work, *A Commentary on the Psalms*, a devotional exposition, simple and devout, with a learned introduction vindicating the Christian use of the Psalms as interpreted of our Lord and the Church. J. Wesley in his *Journal* (27th March 1783), says of the *Commentary*: 'I suppose [it is] the best that ever was wrote.' It has been reprinted whole or in extract between twenty and thirty times. From 1776-80 Horne was Vice-Chancellor of the University, and in this capacity was brought into close relation with the Chancellor, Lord North, by whose influence he was nominated to the deanery of Canterbury in 1781. On 21st May 1790 he was elected to the see of Norwich, and was consecrated at Lambeth on 6th June. Failing health had made him reluctant to accept the see, and led him to resign the Presidency of Magdalen in 1791. He found some relief by repeated visits to Bath, but he died there, 17th January 1792. He was buried at Eltham, Kent, and his epitaph (reproduced in his cathedral church) was written by his friend and biographer, Jones of Nayland. The charm and the integrity of Horne's character are sufficiently marked in the phrases by which he became known to a younger Oxford generation—'True as George Horne,' 'Sweet-tempered as George Horne.' He was a high churchman of a profoundly religious and devotional temper; and it may be noted that he re-edited Stanhope's version of Andrewes's *Preces Privatae* and prepared an edition of the *Manual for the Sick*; and other devotional tractates and versions are among his works. 'He conformed himself in many respects to the strictness of Mr. Law's rules of devotion'; but he was disquieted by Law's advocacy of J. Böhme's mysticism. Horne was an eminent preacher, and published a large number of sermons. His sympathy was keen and practical with the Scottish bishops—'Better bishops than I am'—and their flocks; he told W. Jones that if St. Paul were on earth, he thought he would communicate with the Scottish Church as most like the people he had been used to; and he used his influence in promoting the repeal (1790) of the penal laws which oppressed them. Of Methodism, Horne spoke severely and even contemptuously in a University sermon in 1761 (cf. Wesley, *Journal*, 8th March 1762); but he disapproved of the expulsion of the Six Students from St. Edmund Hall in 1768; and when at Norwich he refused to interfere with Wesley's ministrations. Among his friends were Hannah More (*q.v.*) and S. Johnson (*q.v.*); Boswell notes that in March 1776 he and Johnson 'drank tea with Dr. Horne': and in a letter of 1791 Horne writes: 'I sooth my mind and settle my temper every

night with a page or two of Bozzy, and always meet with something to the purpose.' Besides the works already mentioned, he wrote a good deal, mostly in pamphlet form: among other things the anonymous *Letter to Adam Smith, LL.D.*, *on the life, death, and philosophy of D. Hume*, *Letters on Infidelity*, and a *Letter to Dr. Priestly*; a collection of *Aphorisms and Opinions*; and contributions to *The Scholar armed* and *The Orthodox Churchman* (the precursor of the *British Critic*). There are two portraits of Horne at Magdalen College and one at University College, and several engravings.   [F. E. B.]

W. Jones of Nayland, *Memoirs of George Horne, D.D.*: Macray, *Register of Magdalen College*, N.S., v.

HORT, Fenton John Anthony (1828-92), scholar and divine, was born in Dublin and educated at Rugby and Trinity College, Cambridge, of which he became Fellow in 1852, after being Third Classic, 1850, and gaining First Classes in both Moral and Natural Sciences, 1851, as well as becoming President of the Union. Ordained deacon, 1854; priest, 1856, he was Vicar of St. Ippolyts (Herts). 1857-72; Fellow and Lecturer of Emmanuel College, 1872-8; was a member of the New Testament Revision Company, 1870-80, and Apocrypha, 1880-92; Hulsean Professor (*vice* Perowne), 1878-87, and Lady Margaret Reader (*vice* Swainson), 1887-92.

The least known of the great Cambridge triumvirate of the nineteenth century [LIGHTFOOT, WESTCOTT], Dr. Hort exercised an influence more easily underestimated than justly appraised. The pupil of Westcott, the friend of Maurice (*q.v.*), Kingsley (*q.v.*), Lightfoot, Bradshaw, and Clerk-Maxwell; a writer on botany and a textual critic of supreme ability; an original member of the Alpine Club; a devoted parish priest and a University professor, he touched life on many sides. In Cambridge his influence was that of a master; outside it a constitutional difficulty in expressing his thought and an extreme sensitiveness as to the responsibility of judgment confined his reputation to the circle of scholars. But his share in the New Testament Revision was probably greater than that of any other, and his joint edition of the Greek Testament (first projected with Dr. Westcott in 1853 and published in 1881) opened a new era in textual criticism. Its introduction, despite severe compression, is a masterpiece of analysis and reconstruction, and, if subsequent studies have tended to claim for the Western Text a greater importance than Westcott and Hort allow, the book still remains one to which all Biblical scholars unhesitatingly acknowledge their obligations. Besides articles on Gnostic heretics in *Dict. Christ. Biog.*, the only other work published in his lifetime was the *Two Dissertations* (1876) on Jn. 1^18 and the Constantinopolitan Creed—a book of permanent value. Of posthumous works the Hulsean Lectures (delivered 1871, published 1893), entitled *The Way, the Truth, and the Life*, though difficult in style and in the last part without final revision, are a real contribution to theology. The studies of *Judaistic Christianity* and *The Anti-Nicene Fathers* are of less importance, but the fragments of commentaries on 1 Peter and the Apocalypse and the *Prolegomena to Romans and Ephesians* well repay study. His last work was the 'Life' of Bishop Lightfoot for the *D.N.B.*

[C. J.]

Sir A. F. Hort, *Life and Letters.*

HOW, William Walsham (1823-97), first Bishop of Wakefield, was educated at Shrewsbury and at Wadham College, Oxford. In 1851 he became Vicar of Whittington in Shropshire, where for twenty-eight years he carried on the active pastoral work in which he excelled and delighted. His speech at the Wolverhampton Church Congress, 1867, setting forth the Anglican position as he conceived it, made a marked impression, and gave him the position which he ever after retained of a leader among moderate High Churchmen. In 1879 he was appointed suffragan to the Bishop of London, with special charge of the East End, under the title of Bishop of Bedford, with a canonry at St. Paul's and the living of St. Andrew, Undershaft. He did valuable work in leading and welding together the revival of church life and work which had already begun in the East End. In 1888 he became first Bishop of Wakefield (*q.v.*), and spent his remaining years in organising the new diocese. He declined in 1890 the rich see of Durham. To a devout and loving spirit he joined great gifts of organisation, simple straightforward preaching and writing, a talent for hymn-writing, and a genial humour. Among his works are *Plain Words, Pastor in Parochia*, and other manuals, and many hymns. [G. C.]

F. D. How, *Life.*

HOWLEY, William (1766-1848), Archbishop of Canterbury, son of the Vicar of Bishop's Sutton, Hants, was educated at Winchester College, where he 'knocked Sydney Smith

(*q.v.*) down with the chess-board for checkmating him,' and this is said to have been the only violent action of his life. In 1783 he was admitted a Scholar of New College, Oxford, of which society he became Fellow and Tutor, proceeding B.A., 1787, and M.A., 1791. His scholarship is said to have been admirable, but he never displayed it. In 1804 he was appointed Canon of Christ Church, and in 1809 Regius Professor of Divinity. He held also the vicarages of Bishop's Sutton and Andover and the rectory of Bradford Peverell. In 1813, through the good offices of Lord Abercorn (1756-1818), to whose son he had been tutor, he was appointed Bishop of London. Though no orator, he took an active part in the House of Lords whenever ecclesiastical matters were discussed. He supported the Bill of Pains and Penalties against Queen Caroline, laying stress on the dogma that 'The King can do no wrong either morally or politically' (which last word the *D.N.B.* absurdly renders ' physically '). His loyalty did not lack its reward, for in 1828 he was raised to the see of Canterbury. He was enthroned by proxy, thereby drawing down upon himself the amused reprobation of Sydney Smith : ' A proxy sent down in the Canterbury Fly, to take the Creator to witness that the archbishop, detained in town by business or pleasure, will never violate that foundation of piety over which he presides— all this seems to me an act of the most extraordinary indolence ever recorded in history.' In 1829 Howley led the opposition to the Roman Catholic Relief Bill, and in 1831 he opposed the Reform Bill; but in the critical session of 1832 he changed his tactics like a wise man, and offered no further opposition to the Bill. In 1833 he opposed the Irish Church Reform Bill, and moved the rejection of the Bill for removing Jewish disabilities. In 1839 he triumphantly carried Six Resolutions against Lord John Russell's very mild scheme for National Education.

As Bishop of London he had baptized Princess Victoria, and in the early morning of 20th June 1837 he posted from Windsor, where he had attended the death-bed of William IV., and, together with the Lord Chamberlain, announced to the princess at Kensington Palace her accession to the throne. On the 28th of June 1838 he crowned her in Westminster Abbey. Dean Stanley remembered his ' tremulous voice asking for the Recognition.'

Howley was the last Prince-Archbishop of Canterbury, for on his death the Ecclesiastical Commission reduced the income of the see to £15,000 a year. When he dined out no one left the room till he rose to go; and at Lambeth he presided in state over public banquets, to which the guests invited themselves, and where ' the domestics of the Prelacy stood, with swords and bag-wigs, round pig, and turkey, and venison.' He drove abroad in a coach and four, and when he crossed the courtyard of Lambeth Palace from the chapel to ' Mrs. Howley's Lodgings ' he was preceded by men bearing flambeaux.[1] His gold shoe buckles descended to Archbishop Benson (*q.v.*).

In character Howley was humble, modest, and benevolent—' gentle among the gentle,' said Mr. Gladstone, ' and mild among the mild.' Sydney Smith, even when opposing the Cathedral Reforms which the archbishop sanctioned, testified to his ' gentleness, kindness, and amiable and high-principled courtesy to his clergy.' When, having made himself obnoxious to the populace by his opposition to the Reform Bill, he was mobbed in the streets of Canterbury, and the chaplain in attendance complained that a dead cat had hit him in the face, the archbishop replied that he should be thankful it was not a live one. All testimony points to his deep and practical piety ; and Mr. Gladstone used to quote him as one of the persons of high authority who dated the revival of religion in England to the horror aroused by the excesses of the French Revolution in its later stages. Dean Church (*q.v.*) says, rather tepidly, that he ' might be considered a theologian.' He accepted the dedication of *The Library of the Fathers.* He charged earnestly against the Unitarians. He said he would rather resign than consecrate Dr. Arnold. In old age he allowed his younger and more vigorous suffragan, Bishop Blomfield (*q.v.*), to hurry him into responsibility for the ill-starred Jerusalem bishopric (*q.v.*) ; but in 1847 he told Lord Aberdeen that he ' would rather go to the Tower than consecrate Bishop Hampden.' This strong profession he was not required to make good, for he died on the 11th of February 1848, within one day of completing his eighty-third year. He had ' used, without abusing, a princely revenue,' and left £120,000.

He died at Lambeth, and was buried at Addington. His body was conveyed to its burial-place by road ; the hearse was drawn

by six black horses, and ' a plume of black feathers ' (instead of a mitre) was borne in front of it. [G. W. E. R.]

HUGH, St. (*c.* 1135-1200), Bishop of Lincoln, son of William, a knight of Avalon, near Pontcharra, in Burgundy, who died a monk. His mother Anna was also of great piety and active holiness ; so that from his earliest youth he learned the valour, simplicity, and single-hearted devoutness which made him a power with his contemporaries. He entered the priory of Villarbenoit at an early age ; and after ordination was put in charge of the mission chapel of St. Maximin ; but finding himself unfitted for parish work fled to the austere rule of the great Charter-House, where his fervour and learning soon made him distinguished among a distinguished company. He was elected procurator, and in that office dealt with all outsiders during the troubled times of the Becket (*q.v.*) controversy. After the murder of St. Thomas, Henry II. agreed, as part of his penance, to found three religious houses, of which one was a Carthusian house at Witham, a work which was done so indefinitely and half-heartedly that the new Carthusians were brought into conflict with the inhabitants of the district. Hugh was recommended to the King as an ornament to the Church, one to whom there were no foreigners, no outcasts, and no enemies, whose virtues would soothe the soreness of the wounded people. Reginald, Bishop of Bath, had the honour of fetching the reluctant Hugh into his diocese and country. Here, with infinite tact and patience, the two houses and churches were built, after the population, nearly as large as it is at present, had been settled elsewhere on generous terms. The secular church, still standing, was finished at the time when the great fire burnt down ancient Glastonbury. The likeness to Avalon Church, and the still closer likeness of the Galilee at Glastonbury to St. Hugh's Lincoln work, make his influence clear in this lovely art. As a teacher he rather set his face against miracles, as compared with 'the unique miracle of holiness.' He was elected to the bishopric of Lincoln at the order of the King in 1186 ; but refused it, until he was freely chosen by the chapter and commanded thereto by the head of his order. After a humble entry that was the jest and wonder of all men, he entered upon fourteen years of active life, always bounteous in alms, rigorous and clean-handed in rule, and careless about the consequences of offending the mighty. He surrounded himself with eminent scholars and promoted learning greatly.

He was entirely fearless in differences with Henry II., Richard, and John even about forest law, which he hated. He excommunicated and flogged wrongdoers, refused prebends to courtiers, and was a tender friend not only to all little children, but to animals, birds, and to the outcast lepers, to the very dead, and (not without danger at times) even to the persecuted Jews. Lincoln Cathedral, a comparatively new Romanesque building, had been shattered by the fall of a tower, and with an incredible audacity he built it up in the form of a cross. If not the sole inventor of the Early English style, he was one of its earliest and chief exponents. His work, some of it done with his own hands, is still to be seen. If a wall were not stable enough he buttressed it from outside after it was already reared. If that were not sufficient he arcaded it inside. The work has a bold, amateur waywardness that is perplexing in contrast to the finished and ordered excellence of the Angel Choir, built in his honour. St. Hugh opposed vigorously the demands of the kings to reward secular officials with sinecures at the expense of the Church. He also resisted the policy of employing church officers in civil functions, showing that he sharply distinguished the bodies civil and ecclesiastical; but as a landlord and master he used his civil powers with an unfeudal mercy and generosity which provoked great remonstrance. He refused to exact fines and heriots from the needy, laughing at customs which infringed mercy, and defying them. His passionate love of relics alone seems to divide him from the holiest men of our own time, but his life and advice were of the sanest and wholesomest of all time. In his last year he went into Normandy to help in the treaty of peace between John and the King of France. He then visited his old haunts, fell ill at Clermetz, and got home to die. In appearance he was blue-eyed, with red-brown hair, of middle height, strongly built, and because of his excessive fasts inclined to fatness. He was buried at Lincoln, the Kings of Scotland and England, with many notable men, bearing his pall. In art St. Hugh is usually represented with his favourite swan, as for instance in the sculpture of the tower of St. Mary's Church in Oxford.

[c. l. m.]

Magna Vita, R.S.; *Metrical Life*, ed. Dimock; Migne, *Patrologia*, vol. 153, contains an abridgment of the first; *Lives* by Perry, Thurston, and Marson.

HUNTINGDON, Selina, Countess of (1707-91), daughter of the second Earl Ferrers. Her mind, even in very early infancy, was of a serious cast, and when she was nine years old the funeral of a child of her own age made a deep impression on her. In 1728 she was married to Theophilus, ninth Earl of Huntingdon (1696-1746). The marriage was entirely happy. Both Lord and Lady Huntingdon were excellent people according to their lights, setting an example of virtuous living in a profligate age, and abounding in practical benevolence. The Methodist Revival [METHODISM] under Whitefield (*q.v.*) and the Wesleys (*q.v.*) was now beginning to spread; and among its adherents was Lady Margaret Hastings, who communicated the Methodist doctrines to her sister-in-law, Lady Huntingdon. Shortly afterwards Lady Huntingdon had a dangerous illness, and, when the sense of sin and the fear of death lay heavily on her, she remembered some words of Lady Margaret's about the joy and peace which spring from faith in a Personal Saviour. Her conversion dated from this illness, and as soon as she recovered she sent a message to the brothers Wesley, who happened to be preaching in the neighbourhood of Donington Park, in Leicestershire (Lord Huntingdon's home), and assured them of her adhesion to their doctrines. Lord Huntingdon did not share this change of view; but he accompanied his wife to the meetings of the Methodist Society in Fetter Lane, and together they frequented the vigorous preaching of George Whitefield in London, at Bristol, at Bath, and wherever they could follow him. By 1740 Lady Huntingdon had acquired so leading a position among her new associates that she procured permission from John Wesley for a young layman called Maxfield to 'expound' in public. Maxfield soon became the first itinerant lay-preacher of the Methodist Society, and thus Lady Huntingdon was 'the honoured instrument of sending this new and unwearied sickle into the harvest.' About 1744 she formed a personal acquaintance with Whitefield, which determined the subsequent tenor of her life. Whitefield's passionate piety, forcible eloquence, and unwearied zeal in the Master's service gave him a deserved influence over his followers; but the vulgarity which was ingrained in his nature is painfully apparent in his relations with Lady Huntingdon. However, that excellent lady did not dislike religious flattery; she became Whitefield's staunch ally, and made him her chaplain. Lord Huntingdon died in 1746, and Lady Huntingdon, being now mistress of her own movements and fortune, established herself at Ashby-de-la-Zouch, and devoted herself wholly to the work of evangelisation. For twenty years she and Whitefield continued to provoke each other to good works.[1] While he was preaching she was organising, and really, though unconsciously, laying the foundations of a new church. She is said to have spent on religious objects £100,000, and she sold her jewels to swell the sum. She built or acquired chapels in several parts of London, and in all quarters of England, Wales, and Ireland. When no chapel was available she had prayers and preaching, and even the Holy Communion, in her own house. Exercising her rights as a peeress, she appointed several clergymen as her chaplains, and employed them as itinerant ministers for the service of her scattered congregations. In 1768 she bought an ancient mansion, called Trevecca House, in the parish of Talgarth, South Wales, and converted it into a College for the religious and literary instruction of intending ministers, proposing to admit only such as were truly converted to God and resolved to dedicate themselves to His service. They were at liberty to stay there three years, during which time they were to have their education gratis, 'with every necessary of life and a suit of clothes once a year.' They might seek Orders in the Church of England, or become ministers in any of the orthodox Protestant communions.[2] The theology taught at Trevecca was rigidly Calvinistic; and in the controversy concerning Calvinism and Arminianism which raged between Wesley and Whitefield, Lady Huntingdon was strongly on Whitefield's side. The controversy came to a head in 1770, when the minutes of the Methodist Conference affirming the doctrine of universal redemption were denounced by the Calvinists as popery in disguise. For adhering to the doctrine contained in them the headmaster of Trevecca was promptly dismissed by his patroness, and henceforth the breach between the Methodist Society and 'Lady Huntingdon's Connexion' was complete. Just at this juncture Whitefield died. The removal of this powerful personality left Lady Huntingdon completely uncontrolled. There was no one in her connexion qualified by age, character, and intellectual powers to counsel or restrain her, and from this time till her death she ruled with undisputed sway. She gathered round her a company in which rank, wealth, and education were represented, but all were in strict

subordination to herself. Her chaplains were her servants, and her chief lieutenants were certain 'Honourable Women.'

The fact that Lady Huntingdon admitted candidates for the Nonconformist ministry to her college at Trevecca shows that she was already sitting very loose to the English Church, and in this respect again she differed widely from the Wesleys; but she did not actually separate herself from the Church till 1779, and then the decisive act was forced upon her by clerical opposition. In 1779 she bought a disused place of public amusement, called 'The Pantheon,' at Spa Fields, Clerkenwell,[1] and proposed to convert it into a chapel. However, the vicar of the parish objected, as he had the right to do, to the erection of an Anglican chapel of ease in his parish and not under his control. Lady Huntingdon had no mind to have her chapels and chaplains under any control except her own, so, in order to secure independence of the ecclesiastical authorities, she registered her chapels as dissenting places of worship under the Toleration Act. After this decisive act of separation (though she tried to make out that it was something less) those of her chaplains who held English livings of course resigned their chaplaincies. Meanwhile their places were supplied by the 'ordination' of students from Trevecca. These recruits could receive at the best only Presbyteral ordination; but this was conferred on them on the 9th of March 1783, and so Lady Huntingdon's Connexion 'lapsed into open schism.'

Apart from the affairs of her own church, for such it soon became, Lady Huntingdon often exercised a salutary influence over the personages and events of her day. Her position and connections gave her easy access to the highest ranks of society, and she sedulously preached the Gospel, or caused it to be preached, to her noble kinsfolk and acquaintance. She took an active part in defeating that movement for relaxation of subscription to the Prayer Book which was fomented by the Latitudinarian party. When the Archbishop of Canterbury and Mrs. Cornwallis turned Lambeth Palace into a place of revelry and dissipation, she invoked and obtained the powerful aid of King George III., who very soon brought the scandal to an end. When gross abuses had arisen in the charities of Repton School and Etwall Hospital (of which Lord Huntingdon was a hereditary trustee) it was Lady Huntingdon who urged the rights of the poor,

[1] In his will he described her as 'that Elect Lady, that Mother in Israel, that mirror of true and undefiled Religion, the Right Hon. Selina, Countess of Huntingdon.'
[2] The college was transferred in 1792 to Cheshunt, Herts, and in 1905 to Cambridge.

[1] The site is now occupied by the church of the Holy Redeemer.

and suggested the drastic set of questions by which the truth was elicited. In everything to which she put her hand she was energetic, thorough, and business-like. Her latter years were much occupied with schemes for carrying on after her death the work to which she had given her life, and for uniting what were quaintly called ' The Societies in the Secession patronised by Lady Huntingdon ' in an independent and permanent church. She spent her time between the College at Trevecca and her house, close to the chapel, at Spa Fields ; but she was still so keen on evangelistic work that as late as 1786 she promised to pay a visit to Brussels, attended by one of her favourite ministers, with a view to introducing the Gospel into a benighted land, and ' had a new equipage prepared for the occasion.' The invitation from Brussels seems to have been something of a hoax or a plot, and the visit did not take place, but the energy which even contemplated it demands our admiration. Lady Huntingdon died at Spa Fields in her eighty-fourth year on the 17th June 1791. She is buried at Ashby-de-la-Zouch.   [G. W. E. R.]

Life and Times, 2 vols., 1839.

HYMNS IN THE ENGLISH CHURCH.

The hymns used in the English Church before the Reformation were those of the usual cycle, which (with some minor differences) prevailed in most of the Latin Breviaries of the West. England had possibly had a distinguished share in the original formation of this cycle ; it added a few hymns for local festivals at a later date, but it was less productive of novelties than other countries in the fourteenth century. The same is true of the sequences in the Missal, if they may be classed as hymns. There was but little available in England of versions in the vernacular, though English carols were common and popular as well as Latin ones ; and a few of the hymns and sequences which most resembled carols were translated and sung in English by the people. Hymnody proper, however, was so far not a popular and voluntary addition to church services, but a fixed and unchanging item in the Latin clerical offices of the Breviary.

When the attempt was made to provide in the Prayer Book a popular form of these offices, reduced in number and complexity so as to suit the laity, attempts were made to include versions of the Latin hymns. But Cranmer (*q.v.*) had no gift of versification, and no one who was available for the task ; consequently the English offices of

Morning and Evening Prayer appeared devoid of any official hymnody ; and so they have continued ever since. The only ancient hymn preserved in the Prayer Book (apart from psalms, canticles, and the *Te Deum*) is the *Veni Creator* in the Ordinal, which is represented by two versions, one (1550) probably by Cranmer, and the other taken in 1661 from Cosin's *Collection of Private Devotions,* 1627. Thus, almost by an accident, the English Church was reduced to the same loss of hymnody which many of the foreign reformers took as a duty, through their prejudice against the use of anything but Holy Scripture in public worship. While Geneva, France, and that part of Germany which followed Switzerland took this line, and confined their attention to metrical psalms, the case was very different with Lutheranism ; for that movement owed much, both in its origin and thenceforward, to its continuance and development of the vernacular hymnody. Luther's hymns won a place where otherwise his influence would hardly have penetrated. They threatened for a moment to make a successful invasion of England, when Coverdale (*q.v.*) about 1539 published versions of the favourite German chorales in his *Goostly Psalmes.* But the tide turned, and the German influence became suspect, and vanished, condemned to wait for Hanoverian days before it had another opening.

The Genevan influence, on the contrary, came to stay ; when Sternhold and his followers had provided a metrical version of the Psalter, copying the example of Marot and Beza in the French psalms, the book soon received an official sanction ; and from 1560 onwards it became almost a companion volume to the Prayer Book. Psalms and paraphrases thenceforward occupied the field to the almost complete exclusion of hymns ; only Cranmer's version of the *Veni Creator* and some half-dozen hymns were admitted into the early Metrical Psalters. It was a nucleus that was enlarged very slowly ; a hymn before sermon, some penitential hymns (among them the familiar ' O Lord, turn not away Thy face '), and a thanksgiving after Communion were the most noticeable.

The attempt to provide a church hymn-book was first made by George Wither, with the help of the music of O. Gibbons in 1623. His *Hymnes and Songes of the Church* was not a compilation, but a set of hymns from his own hand ; and this fact, besides indiscreet royal patronage, raised obstacles in the way of its success. The ' Old Version ' of the psalms continued on its way without a rival.

or a companion in Church circles, and only began to lose ground when the New Version of 1696 appeared. Thus psalmody competed with psalmody; but the day of the return of hymns was still deferred. However, the *Supplement to the New Version* offered an opportunity which was not wasted; and the appearance there of 'While shepherds watched their flocks' foreshadowed a change that was coming, though still only slowly. Musical development, meanwhile, was going ahead rapidly, but it was still mainly concerned with metrical psalms rather than with the small group of hymns that was in use.

The real father of English hymnody is Isaac Watts, the Independent minister, who leapt into fame at the beginning of the eighteenth century. The Nonconformist bodies had been making some experimental moves in hymnody for some time, being not tied, as the Church seemed to be, to a semi-official psalm-book; and now at a burst there came from Watts's pen such masterpieces as 'When I survey the wondrous Cross' and 'O God, our help.' A new age had begun; but still prejudices were strong against any non-biblical hymns both among Nonconformists and Churchmen.

The next era was inaugurated by the Wesleys (*q.v.*); and they developed the English hymn, as formed by Watts, having the advantage of an intimate knowledge and appreciation of the treasures of German hymnody. While John Wesley figured chiefly as a translator, his brother Charles produced native compositions; and among the countless hymns which he wrote during his long career are some of the best established of our favourites, *e.g.* 'Jesu, Lover of my soul.' At first the use of these hymns was confined to the Methodist Societies, and they found little place in church worship; but the delight in hymn-singing was infectious. The London charitable institutions for Orphans and Magdalens took it up, and the singing in their chapels became so famous that bishops exhorted the parishes to practise congregational singing, and the Charity Children were trained to lead the rest of the worshippers. Some of the more stiff-necked were declaiming still against non-biblical compositions; but more liberal Churchmen were steadily introducing the hymns of Watts and the Wesleys.

Meanwhile the character of the books changes; for collections of 'Psalms and Hymns' begin to supersede the Metrical Psalter (in either version), or the books of mere selections from the psalms. Gradually

the proportion of the two ingredients alters, till the hymns oust the bulk of the psalms; the book becomes a hymn-book, and only a few versions of psalms find a place there, disguised as hymns.

So far there was nothing which had been produced for church worship comparable with the hymns of Watts and the Wesleys; but in 1779 the *Olney Hymns* appeared, the joint production of John Newton and William Cowper; and this book, in some degree, made good the deficiency. At the beginning of the nineteenth century materials had accumulated from many quarters; the 'Collections' that appeared were improving in quality; but they had not yet come into any liturgical shape, though schemes for special psalms distributed according to the calendar had been for some time in existence. The change, which was to give modern church hymn-books their form, was made by Bishop Heber, who, while still a parish priest, drew up for his parishioners his *Hymns written and adapted to the weekly Church service of the year.* It was published by his widow in 1826. Half the hymns included were Heber's own; the rest were gathered from many sources, and included some of the earliest of modern versions from Latin office hymns. Thenceforward such translations became increasingly prominent, especially under the influence of the Oxford Movement (*q.v.*), until Dr. Neale (*q.v.*) and his companions issued in 1852 the *Hymnal Noted*, both words and tunes being drawn from the Latin Offices. Meanwhile Neale was also writing English hymns, in company with Keble (*q.v.*) and Lyte and other representative Churchmen; with Faber and Caswall, who had passed over to the Roman communion; with Miss Havergal and Mrs. Alexander, representing the other sex. Further translations became available—from the Greek, a department in which Neale was again conspicuous, and from the German, especially through the versions of Miss Winkworth and Miss Cox. In the multiplicity of 'Selections' that were formed from these materials three lines of gradual development have led to three of the chief hymn-books of the day : (1) Edward Bickersteth's *Psalmody* of 1833 was the forerunner of his son's *Psalms and Hymns* (1858), and that has developed into the *Hymnal Companion* (1870); (2) the S.P.C.K. *Psalms and Hymns* of 1855 has grown into *Church Hymns*; (3) by the withdrawal of Mozley's *Hymnal, Hymns and Introits*, and a number of other current books, the way was opened for the launching of *Hymns Ancient and Modern* in

1861. These are the chief books in use throughout the Anglican communion, but the Churches of Ireland, Canada, and the United States have official hymn-books of their own. [MUSIC IN THE CHURCH, POETRY IN THE CHURCH.]   [W. H. F.]

Julian, *Dictionary of Hymnology; Hymns Ancient and Modern* (Historical Edition).

I

INJUNCTIONS are orders given by administrative authority for the observance of Church law and customs in places where there is need of such a reminder. When the bishop visits his diocese, or even the archdeacon his archdeaconry, he first investigates by Articles of Inquiry, and then calls attention to the irregularities that have been 'detected' and gives such Injunctions as seem necessary to correct them. The practice runs back to a distant past, and is a valuable piece of administrative machinery. It applies also to other spheres of jurisdiction such as a monastery or a college. From time to time Injunctions have had a special significance. When Henry VIII. undertook the task of ecclesiastical visitation he issued Injunctions (1536) through Cromwell (*q.v.*) as his vicar-general, and thus began a series of Royal Injunctions which played an important part in the changes during the sixteenth century. Edward VI., Mary, and Elizabeth all followed his example in this respect. Edward and Elizabeth were more precise than their father, for they issued Articles of Inquiry as well as Injunctions. Mary was less precise, for her Injunctions (1554) were not only based on no Articles of Inquiry, but they were arbitrarily issued apart from any visitation.

Injunctions must be distinguished from legislation; they are merely reminders of existing law and custom, and a notification that obedience and conformity are expected. Such action is specially necessary, because otherwise Canon Law might fall into desuetude, and might cease to be binding, through mere neglect, unless kept in vigour by such Injunctions. Properly speaking, there is no opportunity in them for innovation; but they were used in the middle of the sixteenth century as a means of altering and innovating both by the Crown and by the bishops. The Crown set the example, and it was not unnatural, since the Tudors were used in the civil sphere to act thus personally by proclamation. But it was a less tolerable abuse when bishops followed the royal example; for constitutional government, not arbitrary action, was the tradition in Church affairs. Their excuse, no doubt, was that, since Henry had paralysed the action of Convocation, the constitutional procedure of legislating by canon was not open to them, and that changes were therefore necessarily to be made arbitrarily. The Elizabethan Injunctions, the last of the series, had a permanence which was denied to those which preceded them. They were regarded as having a special authority; and the Elizabethan bishops, flouted by Puritans, countermined by courtiers, and liable to be left unsupported by the Queen if they outran her humour, were glad to take shelter behind them in administering discipline. But as Convocation recovered its power of making canons, and issued, in fact, the codes of 1571, 1585, and 1597 (the last two with special royal sanction), the Injunctions of 1559, which had been invaluable in the *interim* between the Marian and the Elizabethan episcopates, declined in value. Many of their provisions became obsolete, and others were incorporated in the canons. After the publication of the complete code in the next reign (1604) this decline was still more evident and rapid. In the early days the Injunctions were read in church every quarter, and to the end of the reign they were kept in print; but subsequently there was no call for fresh editions; the canons occupied the printer instead, and were appended, like the Articles of Religion, to the Prayer Book. They were read in church, and the bishops appealed to them where formerly they had cited the Royal Injunctions; and this document became of historical rather than of legal value.

Episcopal Visitation and Injunctions continued to do good service when the royal action had ceased and its provisions fallen into obscurity. But Articles and Injunctions became rarer in the eighteenth century and ceased, as Visitation became no longer a legal inquiry but only the occasion of a formal appearance, a synodal payment, a charge, and a luncheon. A revival, however, came in the second half of the nineteenth century; and the machinery now recovered is likely to prove useful again in maintaining discipline and efficiency, provided it is kept to its proper use and not made an opportunity for arbitrary action.   [W. H. F.]

Frere, *Visitation Articles and Injunctions* (Alcuin Club).

INNOCENT III., Pope. Lothar dei Conti (c. 1161-1216), belonged to a noble family of Latium ; his father was of German, his mother of Roman, descent. In his youth he studied at Paris and Bologna ; when scarcely of full age he earned distinction as a jurist in the Curia. In 1190 he was made a cardinal by his uncle, Clement III., and although viewed with less favour by Celestine III. (1191-8), he earned such a reputation that on Celestine's death he was unanimously elected to the papacy by his colleagues (1198). At this date he was known outside Rome chiefly as a writer upon religious subjects ; among his works the *De Contemptu Mundi* achieved some popularity, and is not without biographical value ; and the *De mysteriis Missae* is a liturgical treatise of some importance. But he was essentially a politician and a leader of men—quick of wit, ready of tongue, an impressive orator, an erudite publicist and lawyer. He became Pope at a critical juncture in the fortunes of the Holy See. Henry VI., who had succeeded in uniting the Sicilian to the Imperial Crown, died a few months before Celestine, leaving Sicily and Naples to an infant heir : and the Empire was now in dispute between two rival claimants. There was thus an opportunity of freeing the States of the Church from German tyranny, of reasserting the papal suzerainty over Sicily and Naples, of playing off the Saxon against the Hohenstauffen party in the Empire until both were fatally weakened. Innocent made a skilful, if unworthy, use of his favourable situation. He restored the tottering edifice of the temporal power ; he abused his position as guardian of Frederic of Sicily to strengthen his own influence in that kingdom ; in Germany he supported Otto IV. against Philip of Suabia and Frederic against Otto. No Pope since Gregory VII. had counted for so much in European politics. The pontificate of Innocent was, in a sense, the golden age of the mediæval papacy. But the results of his activity were not commensurate with his hopes. He was deceived several times by his chosen allies, by Otto, by Frederic, by Philip Augustus. The Fourth Crusade and that against the Albigensians were raised in his name, but escaped from his control and brought his office into disrepute. The decadence of the papacy in the next hundred

years must be attributed to the effects of the policy which his genius imposed upon his successors from Honorius III. to Boniface VIII. Though pious and disinterested, Innocent attached excessive weight to material resources and visible dominion. He treated the national Churches as provinces of an ecclesiastical monarchy ; he asserted in new and startling forms the time-honoured principle that kings should acknowledge themselves the servants of the Church.

His relations with the Plantagenets have been often misrepresented. He endeavoured to use England as a pawn in the politics of the Empire. He supported Richard Cœur de Lion, and he treated John with unusual forbearance, because they were, or might be, valuable allies. But on more than one occasion he threw prudence to the winds, in his dealings with these sovereigns, that he might assert the liberties or the dignity of the Church. He peremptorily commanded Richard to deprive Hubert Walter (*q.v.*) of the justiciarship, and consistently sided with the monks of Canterbury against that powerful minister. He supported the turbulent Geoffrey of York against both Richard and John. He took John to task for the repudiation of Hadwisa-Isabelle of Gloucester ; and, at a time when John was peculiarly desirable as an ally, he protested against his lawless maltreatment of the Bishop of Limoges and the Archbishop of Dublin. The nomination of Stephen Langton (*q.v.*) to the see of Canterbury (1206) was a high-handed act, but certainly not suggested by political motives ; Innocent endangered the cause of his own party to vindicate the principle of free election. His later measures against John were neither precipitately undertaken nor excessive, considering the brutal measures by which the King sought to intimidate the English clergy. The interdict was not enforced until 1208 ; the sentence of personal excommunication was only published late in 1209 ; and yet another three years elapsed before Philip of France was invited to execute the sentence of deposition. The terms imposed upon John, when he at length submitted (1213), were extremely light : for there is no reason to believe that Innocent demanded the oath of vassalage. John appears to have offered his homage of free will, to obtain support against the baronial opposition. It was the successors of Innocent who abused the papal suzerainty over England. Innocent can hardly be blamed for interfering in the constitutional crisis of the next two years. He was invited to do so by the barons, and he appears to have mediated in good faith. That he should quash Magna Carta (*q.v.*), which his commissioner had approved, seems only natural when we remember that he had consistently forbidden the barons to coerce the King and that Pandulf (*q.v.*) was no plenipotentiary. It is true that Stephen Langton was against the King, and appeared at Rome to explain the position of the barons. But by this time Stephen himself stood convicted of disobedience—the one offence for which Innocent admitted no excuses ; and it is improbable that he received a fair hearing. Innocent lived long enough to witness the overthrow of his *protégé* ; but the merits of Magna Carta as a constitutional settlement were not demonstrated in his lifetime. He died on 16th July 1216 at Perugia, while Louis of France and the English rebels were in the full tide of success.　　　　　　　　　　[H. W. C. D.]

Luchaire, *Innocent III.* ; Norgate, *John Lackland* ; Stubbs, *C.H.*, i. ; H. W. C. Davis, *Eng. under the Normans and Angevins.*

INVESTITURES CONTROVERSY, The (1059-1122), was the result of a vicious system of patronage which developed *pari passu* with feudalism in Western Europe. By the eleventh century it was the practice of sovereigns to treat the more important ecclesiastical benefices as a species of fief, which was held from the Crown and escheated on the death of the occupant. The ruler claimed the right of appropriating the revenues of such a benefice during a vacancy, and nominated a successor as and when he pleased. The newly appointed prelate received seisin of his office by the delivery into his hands of its spiritual insignia, the ring and staff ; and in return he rendered the same homage as any other vassal. He was not competent to exercise his office until he had been canonically elected and consecrated ; but the effect of the royal investiture could not be safely called in question. The natural consequence was that benefices were sometimes sold, and frequently conferred as rewards for political services. Churches were impoverished to satisfy the demands of the sovereign upon his nominee, and ecclesiastical discipline was ill enforced by prelates who had been selected for any cause rather than their fitness. Against this abuse the reformed papacy made a determined protest in the second half of the eleventh century, denouncing simony in the first place, and then lay investiture as a practice which led inevitably to simony. Lay investiture was also disliked, on more abstract grounds, because it seemed to imply the supremacy of the State over the Church. The ring and the staff denoted a spiritual office, and he who gave the symbols plainly claimed the right to give what they denoted. The controversy was raised by reformers such as Cardinal Humbert and Peter Damiani. The papacy declared for the cause of reform in 1059, when a Roman synod held by Nicholas II. condemned every form of lay patronage : *ut per laicos nullo modo quilibet clericus aut presbyter obtineat ecclesiam nec gratis nec pretio.* This proved too sweeping to be enforced. For some time the papacy was content to make war merely on the grosser forms of simony. But in 1078 a synod held by Gregory VII. condemned the practice of receiving ecclesiastical benefices as fiefs ; and laymen who gave investiture were declared excommunicate by another decree in 1080. The new legislation was aimed in the first instance at the Emperor ; it opened a bitter quarrel with Henry IV. and Henry V., which was protracted until 1122, when the exhaustion of both parties made a compromise possible. The Concordat of Worms (1122) provided that, in the Imperial dominions, there should be free and canonical elections to vacant bishoprics and abbacies ; that the elections should take place in the presence of the Emperor ; that, if the electors disagreed among themselves, he should have the power of choosing between the rival candidates ; that the prelate-elect should be invested by the Emperor with the temporalities of his office, and should perform the services due from them. These terms left to a disingenuous Emperor a loophole for evasion ; and the Imperial prerogative of arbitration was grossly abused by Conrad III. and Frederic Barbarossa ; so that the chief result of the Concordat was to change the form rather than the inward nature of the dispute between papacy and Empire. But the terms arranged at Worms were the best that conciliatory statesmen on either side could devise. For Englishmen the concordat has a peculiar interest since it followed the lines of an earlier agreement between the English crown and the papacy (1107). This was negotiated by Archbishop Anselm (*q.v.*), but his correspondence with Paschal II. shows that he only executed instructions which came to him from Rome. In England the question of investitures was raised comparatively late, and was settled with less friction than might have been expected. William I. and Lanfranc (*q.v.*) were able to disregard the papal legislation on the subject, since Gregory VII. stood in need of England's support, and was satisfied that the King exercised his objectionable prerogative in an unobjectionable manner. Rebuking a too zealous legate, the Pope writes (1081) that William, though not immaculate, neither sells nor plunders the churches of his kingdom. Under William Rufus the case was different. The new King kept vacant bishoprics and abbacies in his own hands, or sold them for ready money, or used them to reward such ministers as Robert Bloet and Ranulf Flambard. Against such abuses there was general indignation, and Archbishop Anselm rebuked the King to his face. But even Anselm did not yet dispute the King's rights of appointment and investiture, from which these evils followed as a logical corollary. Anselm was himself nominated and invested by Rufus; and, though he begged to be excused, he took no exception to the manner of his appointment. But towards the end of the reign, when Anselm was in exile, he took part in a council at Rome (1099) which issued sentences of excommunication against all who gave or who received lay investiture. Though Anselm did not feel strongly on the subject, he proceeded to enforce the decree on his return. He refused to do homage to Henry I. and to hold intercourse with those who violated the decree; and, since the King stood firm, Anselm went into exile for the second time (1103-5). The English bishops, for the most part, made light of his scruples, and begged him to give way. But he stood firm until Paschal II. gave him leave to make a compromise. Negotiations were opened in 1105, but the final settlement was delayed until 1st August 1107, when terms were formulated in the Council of London. They are only known to us at second-hand, and there is some variation between our different accounts. But Paschal conceded that the King might receive homage and grant investiture of the temporalties before the consecration of the prelate-elect. In writing to Anselm the Pope expressed a hope that the King might be ultimately induced to forego these rights. But they were tenaciously maintained by Henry and his successors. The King, on his side, recognised the principle of free election. We learn from the later Constitutions of Clarendon that elections, in the time of Henry I., took place in his chapel and in his presence. He did not claim in so many words the right of arbitrating if a dispute arose among the electors. But no one could be elected without his previous approval; and consequently the King had an opportunity of reducing the election to a mere form if he wished. To this extent the

English settlement of 1107 was, no less than the Concordat of Worms, a defeat for the papacy and the reforming party. In regard to the question of homage, they had only withdrawn from an untenable position. But another battle had to be fought before freedom of election was legally guaranteed in England. This concession was made at length by King John, and was afterwards incorporated in Magna Carta (*q.v.*).

[H. W. C. D.]

W. R. W. Stephens, *The Eng. Ch., 1066-127*; M. Rule, *Life and Times of St. Anselm*; H. W. C. Davis, *Eng. under the Normans and Angevins*.

ISLIP, Simon of (d. 1366), Archbishop of Canterbury, born probably at Islip, Oxon, was Fellow of Merton College, Oxford, in 1307, became a doctor both of canon and civil law, and was made Archdeacon of Canterbury in 1343. As chaplain to Edward III., he was closely attached to him for many years, and employed in various offices, political as well as ecclesiastical. After two persons who had been nominated to succeed Stratford as Archbishop of Canterbury had died of the Black Death before consecration, he was elected by the chapter, and provided by the Pope, to the primacy. He was an energetic archbishop, pursuing and punishing abuses in every direction, but incurring much blame (probably undeserved) for personal hardness and avarice. In 1350 he put forth a canon which formed an exact parallel to the Statute of Labourers, requiring priests to serve for the same wage as before the Black Death. He appears to have approved thoroughly of the independent attitude of the English State in regard to Rome; the statutes of Provisors (*q.v.*), 1351, against papal 'provision' to benefices, and of *Praemunire* (*q.v.*), 1353, against papal jurisdiction, being passed in his time. He concluded the ancient dispute between the two primates by the agreement ordered by Edward III., 1353, that the northern metropolitan might have his cross borne erect before him within the southern province, if he gave to the shrine of St. Thomas at Canterbury a gold effigy of an archbishop worth £40, or gems of equal value. The arrangement seems to be no longer maintained. He was a generous benefactor to Canterbury and Cambridge, and at Oxford he founded a college of clerks secular and regular, which he attached to Christ Church, Canterbury; it was later absorbed in Christ Church, Oxford. Islip was buried in his cathedral church.

[W. H. H.]

Wharton, *Anglia Sacra*.

J

JERUSALEM, Bishopric in. The import-ance of this is largely due to its effect on J. H. Newman (*q.v.*). It was one of 'the three blows which broke' him in the autumn of 1841, and 'which finally shattered his faith in the Anglican Church.'

The project began with Frederic William IV., King of Prussia, who felt great interest in the Holy Land. He was grieved that Protestants had no head or rallying point there. Further, he admired English institu-tions, including, apparently, the English Church, but it seems that one ultimate object of the scheme was to introduce the episco-pate into the national Church of Prussia. To promote these ends he sent Chevalier Bunsen as special envoy to London, June 1841, to negotiate for a bishopric in Jerusalem, to which the English bishops should conse-crate. The English Government favoured the design, and the Archbishop of Canterbury (Howley) (*q.v.*) and the Bishop of London (Blomfield)(*q.v.*) supported it. Bunsen gained the help of Lord Palmerston and Lord Ashley (afterwards Shaftesbury), the leader of the Evangelicals. A statement was later issued explaining the scheme as a step towards the unity of discipline and doctrine between the English Church and 'the less perfectly constituted of the Protestant Churches of Europe, and that, too, not by the way of Rome,' while it was to establish 'relations of amity with the ancient Churches of the East.' A treaty between the two Governments was signed, 15th July 1841.

Bunsen by August had arranged matters with the bishops, and 30th August 1841 Howley introduced the Bill creating the bishopric into the House of Lords. It became law on 5th October (5 Vic. c. 6). By this Act the bishop was to have jurisdiction not only over Anglican churches, but also 'over such other Protestant con-gregations as may be desirous of placing themselves under his authority.' By Royal Warrant he could exercise jurisdiction over congregations in Syria, Chaldea, Egypt, and Abyssinia. The Prussian King gave £15,000 towards an endowment; £20,000 was to be raised by subscription in England. Mr. Gladstone (*q.v.*) (whom Bunsen had been at special pains to conciliate) promised to act as one of the trustees, but later withdrew. Bunsen used every art to gain his support,

including a dinner at the Star and Garter at Richmond (15th October 1841), where he induced him to propose a toast: 'Prosperity to the Church of St. James at Jerusalem and to her first bishop.'

Other features of the scheme were that the Crowns of England and Prussia were to nominate in turn to the bishopric, the bishop was to ordain German ministers on their sub-scribing the Confession of Augsburg, Angli-cans on subscribing the XXXIX. Articles and the Prayer Book, but Anglicans and Prussians were to use their separate formu-laries in their services.

The Evangelicals welcomed the scheme, as did Dr. Arnold (*q.v.*) and his school. 'Thus,' Arnold wrote (23rd September 1841), 'the idea of my Church Reform Pamphlet, which was so ridiculed and so condemned, is now carried into practice by the Archbishop of Canterbury himself.' The project was reso-lutely opposed by High Churchmen, especially Bishop Phillpotts (*q.v.*), J. R. Hope (later Hope-Scott), a distinguished barrister, and even by the *Times* (19th October 1841).

Newman (11th November 1841) sent a solemn protest to his own bishop and the Archbishop of Canterbury, on the grounds that Lutheranism and Calvinism were heresies repugnant to Scripture, and that the English Church was admitting such heretics to communion without renunciation of their errors. 'On these grounds, I, in my place, being a priest of the English Church and Vicar of St. Mary the Virgin's, Oxford, by way of relieving my conscience, do hereby solemnly protest against the measure afore-said, and disown it, as removing our Church from her present ground and tending to her disorganisation.'

The later history of the scheme is summed up in Newman's words: 'As to the project of a Jerusalem bishopric, I never heard of any good or harm it has ever done except what it has done for me; which many think a great misfortune, and I one of the greatest of mercies.' Only two Germans were ever ordained under the scheme. On their return to Germany their ordination was not acknow-ledged by the Prussian Evangelical Church, and pastorates could not be found for them, and this effectually checked the scheme. The first German pastor in Jerusalem did not arrive till 1853, and then had a congregation of twenty-three persons.

BISHOPS

1. Michael Solomon Alexander; cons. at Lambeth by Archbishop Howley, 7th November 1841; an Israelite, born 1799 at Tronzka, in the Grand Duchy of Posen, who, having been a Rabbi, was converted and baptized at Plymouth, 1825, and was later ordained in Ireland; he worked for the conversion of the Jews, and (1832) became Professor of Hebrew at King's College, London; after his consecration he was conveyed to Jaffa with his suite in a ship of war (the *Devastation*), provided by the Government through Lord Ashley. He did little to realise the hopes of his patrons, and died in Egypt (on his way to England), 23rd November 1845, leaving a large young family slenderly provided for.

2. Samuel Gobat, who was nominated by the Prussian King on Bunsen's recommendation, was by birth a Swiss (born at Crémine, 1799); Bishop Phillpotts presented a solemn protest against his consecration with seven weighty objections, 23rd May 1846; it was disregarded, and Gobat, who had been ordained deacon, August 1845, was privately ordained priest by Bishop Blomfield, 30th June, and cons. bishop by Archbishop Howley, 5th July 1846, the preacher being Bishop Daniel Wilson (*q.v.*); in 1851 it appeared that he was proselytising from Eastern churches; J. M. Neale (*q.v.*) sent to the Eastern Patriarchs an address and protest against such efforts; this was signed by the leading High Churchmen, Pusey, Keble, Marriott, I. Williams, and more than a thousand others; to it the Archbishops of Canterbury (Sumner), York (Musgrave), Armagh, and Dublin replied with an address of sympathy with Gobat; in 1856 he intruded into Scottish dioceses and performed episcopal functions, evoking a strong protest from the Primus (Skinner) to the Archbishop of Canterbury; his career was unfortunate; he had differences with his own clergy and with the English residents in Jerusalem, and when he died in Jerusalem, 11th January 1879, the see seemed likely to end. He used as his official signature the strange form 'S. Angl-Hierosol.'

3. Joseph Barclay was nominated by Lord Beaconsfield and cons. by Archbishop Tait, 25th July 1879; he was an Irishman, and graduate of Trinity College, Dublin, and the first native of Great Britain to hold the see; he had been an active missionary among the Jews, and had worked in Jerusalem, 1861-70; he died, 22nd October 1881.

No attempt was made by the Prussian King to fill the see, and the treaty of 1841 was finally dissolved in 1886. Germany withdrew from the affair, receiving back the £15,000 given by Frederic William IV., and the passionate prayer of Newman in 1843 was answered (*Sermons on Subjects of the Day*, 335, note 1): 'May that measure utterly fail and come to naught, and be as though it had never been.'

In 1887 the bishopric was reconstructed on different lines by Archbishop Benson (*q.v.*) in spite of opposition from Liddon (*q.v.*) and others. Dr. George Popham Blyth, then Archdeacon of Rangoon, was chosen in spite of Low Church protests, and consecrated to represent the English Church in the Holy City. His work has issued not only in growing friendliness between the Eastern and English Churches, but in the building of the beautiful church and college of St. George (consecrated 1910).   [S. L. O.]

W. H. Hechler, *The Jerusalem Bishopric*; *Memoirs* of Bishop Blomfield, J. R. Hope-Scott, Bishop Barclay, Bunsen, and Bishop Gobat; MS. collections of Dr. Bloxam at Magdalen College, Oxford; *Reply to Two Pamphlets* (Vindication of Bishop Gobat), London, 1859.

JEWEL, or **JUELL**, John (1522-71), Bishop of Salisbury, one of a family of ten; born on an ancestral farm in Berrynarbor parish, North Devon; passed from Barnstaple school well prepared in logic, etc., to Merton College, Oxford, July 1535. Parkhurst becoming his tutor, made him 'postmaster' (*portionista*), and in 1539 recommended him to a better scholarship at Corpus, where he became B.A., and in 1542 Fellow; B.D., 1552; and 1565 D.D. *in absentia*. About 1548 he came under Peter Martyr's (*q.v.*) influence, attending his divinity lectures, and assisting in his supplementary Protestant teaching. Licensed Preacher, 1551; Archdeacon of Chichester and Rector of Sunningwell, Berks, where he preached and catechised. He held the office of Public Orator just long enough to compose (in general terms) the University's congratulation to Queen Mary (*q.v.*) on her accession, 1553, and to hear St. Mary's bell ring for the restored Latin Mass while showing his draft letter to the vice-chancellor. He declined to attend Mass at Corpus, lost his Fellowship, and after a touching valedictory address to his class removed for a while to Broadgate Hall (later Pembroke College). He had a very good memory and used a system of short-hand; acted as notary to Cranmer (*q.v.*) and Ridley (*q.v.*) at their disputation in April 1554. When pressed to subscribe a popish test he gave way, hastily took the pen, and smiling, said: 'Have you a mind to see how well I can write?' His life was yet en-dangered, and learning that Parkhurst had left the country he made his escape, with assistance from Augustine Bernher (Lati-mer's Swiss servant), Sir N. Throgmorton, and Laurence Humphrey, whom Jewel, when bishop, declined to institute because he refused to wear the legal vestments. At Frankfort, Edwin Sandys (who shared bed and board with him), seconded by Chambers and Sampson, persuaded Jewel to make public confession of his frailty in subscribing. He took part with Cox against Knox and other extreme Calvinists [MARIAN EXILES], and went to Strasburg, where Peter Martyr repaid to him the kindnesses which he had received when in England. He also in 1556 took him to Zurich (where Jewel lodged with Froschover the printer), and probably helped him to visit Padua, his former home, where Jewel met the Venetian Scipio, with whom he afterwards had a con-troversy about the English attitude towards the Council of Trent. At Zurich Jewel suc-ceeded Pellican as Hebrew professor.

Hearing of Elizabeth's (*q.v.*) accession, he reached England in March 1559 in time to assist his former tutor, Parkhurst, who had been robbed while travelling, and to be pre-pared to oppose the papists in the disputation at Westminster. He served on the Royal Commission of the West under the Earl of Pembroke, thus visiting his own county, Devon, and Salisbury, where he came into contact with Gardiner's chaplain, T. Harding, and more or less directly with H. Cole. He was consecrated to the impoverished bishop-ric of Sarum, and gave, besides the Royal Injunctions (*q.v.*) of 1559, Articles of Visi-tation to the cathedral (visited by deputy) in 1560, 1562, and 1568, with statutes on the two last dates (Alcuin Club Collection, xvi.). He called in the Latin service-books about the end of March 1560. He preached at Paul's Cross, 15th June and 26th November 1559, and 31st March 1560. On the second and third occasions, as also when preaching before the court, 17th March 1560, he re-peatedly challenged the champions of specific-

ally Roman doctrines and practices to bring forward one clear proof from the first six centuries A.D. An answer was essayed by Dr. Cole, and, after the appearance of Jewel's *Apologia pro Ecclesia Anglicana*, 1562, an-other by Harding (1564) from Louvain. Sermon, Letter, Reply, Confutation, and Defence followed one another in regular suc-cession in a seven years' war of controversy. The *Apologia* was translated into English and other languages—Anne Bacon's version being edited, 1564, by Archbishop Parker (*q.v.*), who desired to append it to the Articles of Religion which Jewel in 1571 revised. Bancroft (*q.v.*) directed his works to be in every parish, 1610. Jewel denounced the 'seditious Bull' of Pius V., which was handed to him when preparing to preach in his cathedral. Ill-health kept him latterly in his diocese, where he befriended promis-ing boys; among them Hooker (*q.v.*). He died at Monckton Farley, 23rd September 1571, after riding to preach at Lacock, and is buried in his cathedral church. Bishop John Wordsworth was convinced that the *bibliotheca* which, according to Fuller and others, was raised (*exstructa*) at Jewel's cost in Sarum Cathedral was merely a book-case.

[C. W.]

J. Ayre, *Works* and *Memoir* (Parker Soc.), 1845-50 : *D.N.B.*

JOHN OF BEVERLEY, St.

JOHN OF BEVERLEY, St. (d. 721), Bishop of York, was educated under Arch-bishop Theodore (*q.v.*), and became a monk of Whitby. He was consecrated Bishop of Hexham probably in 687, and conferred deacon's and priest's orders on Bede (*q.v.*), who writes warmly of his sanctity. He was diligent in teaching, and was beloved by the band of scholars he gathered round him. Often, like Cuthbert (*q.v.*), he sought retire-ment, especially during Lent, and dwelt with a few friends in a wood near Hexham, at a place believed to be St. John's Lee, where he had a church and cell. In 705 he was trans-lated to York, then claimed by Wilfrid (*q.v.*) as his see. He built a monastery at Indera-wood, afterwards Beverley, and when he became too old for his episcopal duties he consecrated Wilfrid II. as his successor at York, retired to Beverley, and there died on 7th May 721. He was canonised in 1037. Many miracles are recorded of him, and his fame was great in the north. [W. H.]

All that is certain about John's life comes from Bede. Folcard (eleventh century) wrote a life, *ap. Historians of York*, R.S.; see also Raine, *Hexham* (Surtees Soc.).

JOHN OF SALISBURY (c. 1120-80), Bishop of Chartres, was born at Old Sarum. He studied logic at Paris under Abelard, and grammar at Chartres in a school maintaining the traditions of the eminent humanist, Bernard. Returning to Paris about 1140, he studied theology and philosophy, and soon after became domesticated with his lifelong friend Peter, then Abbot of Moutiex la Celle. In 1148 he was present at the Council of Rheims. There St. Bernard presented him to Archbishop Theobald of Canterbury, whose secretary he eventually became. When his friend Thomas Becket (*q.v.*) became archbishop John espoused his cause against the King and shared his exile. He was prominent in negotiations between archbishop, Pope, and King. While unwavering in his loyalty to Thomas and to Alexander III., he severely criticised the former's want of tact and the latter's vacillation. He was present at the archbishop's murder. In 1172 he became Bishop of Chartres *divina dignatione et meritis S. Thomae martyris*.

John, in Bishop Stubbs's words 'the central figure of English learning' in his time, was first and foremost a humanist. Educated at Chartres, the nursery of the short-lived humanistic movement of the twelfth century, he became possessed of a conception of the ancient world which, however limited in comparison with that of the Renaissance scholars, was the same in kind as theirs, and free from the fantastic distortion and false perspective so common after the literary scholarship of his time had given way to the tyranny of the scholastic philosophy, for which his own encouragement of Aristotelian studies had prepared the way. Except for a few words he knew no Greek, but eagerly learned from those who did; with the Latin writers available he was thoroughly familiar. His intimate knowledge of the Bible is apparent on every page he wrote; he had an extensive acquaintance with such of the Fathers as could be read in Latin. With his humanism went a deep sense of the spiritual significance of the international unity of Christian civilisation; in such ecumenical institutions as the Roman law and the papal jurisdiction he recognised a divine ordinance against the separatist tendencies of national kingdoms, in which the ultimate sanction was neither reason nor revelation, but force. Hence his unwavering support of Becket against Henry II. and of Alexander III. against Frederick Barbarossa. This loyalty to Christendom did not exclude a lively English patriotism and a pride in his native city and country; indeed, in many qualities of his mind he was typically English. He united a universal curiosity with a steady common-sense; strong moral convictions and genuine piety with a capacity for many friendships, and a genial tolerance where principle was not at stake. He wrote an admirably simple and vigorous style; he knew his world well, and did not spare the faults of the powerful and the fashionable; and his philosophy, if not original or profound, is always learned, appreciative, and sensible.

Writings.—(1) Letters: some official, and giving a vivid impression of the various business of the court of Canterbury; others personal, mostly of the period of his exile, charmingly written, thoroughly alive, and full of information. (2) *Entheticus de dogmate Philosophorum* ('Introduction (?) on the doctrine of Philosophers'), an elegiac poem, including a satirical account, under symbolical names, of the most prominent figures in English politics during Stephen's reign. (3) *Policraticus* ('Statesman's Handbook') *de nugis curialium et vestigiis philosophorum* ('of the trifling pursuits of courtiers and the tradition of the philosophers'), in eight books, the fullest expression of the author's mind, and with its sequel (4) *Metalogicon* ('Plea for Logic'), which contains John's intellectual autobiography, and describes the methods and results of the philosophical teaching of his day, a storehouse of information as to the learning and thought of the age. These works were offerings to Becket, whose copy still exists in the library of C.C.C., Cambridge. (5) *Historia Pontificalis*, a fragment in continuation of Sigebert's chronicle. (6) *Vita S. Anselmi*, written for the process of St. Anselm's canonisation, which, however, did not take place at this time. (7) *Vita S. Thomae.* [C. C. J. W.]

Opera Omnia, ed. J. A. Giles, Oxford, 1848 (reprinted in Migne's *Patrologia Latina*, tom. cxcix.; *Historia Pontificalis* (not in Giles), ed. W. Arndt, in *Monumenta Historiae Germaniae*, tom. xx. pp. 615 seqq., without author's name; *Vita S. Thomae* and many letters in Robertson's *Materials*, R.S.; *Policraticus*, ed. C. C. J. Webb; R. L. Poole, *Illustrations of the Hist. of Mediaeval Thought*, pp. 201 tol.

JOHNSON, Samuel (1709-84), writer and critic, son of a Lichfield bookseller, entered Pembroke College, Oxford, where the bitterness of poverty made him 'rude and insolent,' but a perusal of Law's (*q.v.*) *Serious Call* rescued him from laxity of principle. He left Oxford without a degree owing to his father's insolvency, and became a schoolmaster, but in 1737 came to London. After a period of privation and struggle his poems, his *Rambler* (1750-2), and his *English Dictionary* (1755) placed him at the head of the literary profession. In his later years he wrote little except the *Lives of the Poets* (1779-80). Ill-health largely explains the sloth and irregular habits of which he bitterly accuses himself. 'This is not the life to which Heaven is promised,' he writes in his journal, which, with his *Prayers and Meditations*, reveals his deep piety, penitence, and humility, and his careful and solemn preparation for his annual Communion, at Easter, at St. Clement's Danes. He employed his great authority and vigorous powers of argument against infidelity and laxity of every kind. 'Obscenity and impiety have always been repressed in my presence,' he said. In an age of looseness of belief and practice the unswerving faith and earnest piety of the dictator of literature produced a great effect.

He was a convinced churchman, and astonished his biographer by declaring that he would ' stand before a battery of cannon to restore the Convocation to its full powers,' as well as by his preference for Roman Catholicism over Presbyterianism on the ground that 'the Presbyterians have no church, no Apostolical Succession.' In Scotland he refused to attend a Presbyterian place of worship. He had a respect for Roman Catholicism, and doubted the sincerity of converts from it, though ' an obstinate rationality ' prevented him from joining that Church. In spite of his dictum, ' No reasoning papist believes every article of their faith,' he defended its controverted doctrines with much force. ' Sir, there is no idolatry in the Mass; they believe God to be there, and they adore Him.' He practised fasting and prayer for the departed, and would not condemn invocation of saints, though he did not practise it.

Johnson ' had nothing of the bear but his skin.' His roughness of manner covered much tenderness and practical charity. His natural melancholy, which he fought against, but only partially overcame, accounts for his morbid horror of death and damnation. But he bore much suffering, and at last encountered death with Christian fortitude.

[G. C.]

Boswell's *Life* and *Tour to the Hebrides*; G. B. Hill, *Johnson Miscellanies*.

JONES, Griffith (1683-1761), founder of the Circulating Welsh Charity Schools, was born in the parish of Cilrhedyn, situated in the two counties of Pembroke and Car-

marthen. He evinced a strong desire to take holy orders, and was accordingly sent to the Elizabethan Grammar School at Carmarthen, from which he was ordained directly, it would appear, in 1708 by Bishop Bull of St. David's. In 1711 he was promoted to the vicarage of Llandilo Abercowyn, and in 1716 to the rectory of Llanddowror, both in the county of Carmarthen.

The S.P.C.K., originated in 1698, had among its founders three influential Welshmen, whose zeal for the society resulted in the establishment in Wales of charity schools for the education of the young and illiterate, and its agents were very active in the circulation of cheap Bibles, Prayer Books, and wholesome literature generally. It was a laudable effort to establish a system of elementary education. But it was not sufficient, and there was a thirst for education. Griffith Jones stepped in to supplement these schools with a system known as the Circulating Welsh Charity Schools, the first of which he started in 1730. It had been his custom to catechise his congregation in a homely manner before the Sunday on which Holy Communion was administered, and the ignorance he found led him to adopt some means of instructing them, as well as others generally. He first trained teachers, and then sent them on circuit from parish to parish, remaining for a few months only at a time in each, and then moving on to the next centre. The schools were not confined to children, but were attended by adults, who were regularly catechised. In the undertaking he received much financial support from Madam Bevan of Laugharne in Carmarthenshire. He published annual reports of the schools, under the name *Welsh Piety*, from 1738 to 1760, and these were continued by Madam Bevan till her death.

The number of schools opened in his lifetime amounted to nearly four thousand, and the number of scholars to over a hundred and fifty thousand. It was work done in the education of the masses in the principles of the Church of England ; and in his day he did more than any other man in Wales in promoting the study of religious literature in the mother tongue. He died in 1761, and was buried at Llanddowror, of which he had been rector for forty-five years. Madam Bevan carried on the schools till her death in 1777, and in her will made provision for continuing them, but owing to the validity of the will being questioned the fund was not released until 1804. The work however, which had been carried on for nearly half a century, had by then come to an end. [J. F.]

JONES, William, of Nayland (1726-1800), divine, was descended from Colonel John Jones, the brother-in-law of Oliver Cromwell and a regicide, a descent of which he was not proud, and which led him to keep 30th January as a day of special humiliation for the sins of his ancestor. He was educated at the Charterhouse and at University College, Oxford, where he formed a lifelong friendship with George Horne (*q.v.*), and he lived to be his chaplain and biographer. He was attracted by the writings of John Hutchinson (1674-1737), whose philosophy, as laid down in *Moses' Principia*, found a complete system of science and revealed truth in the mystical interpretation of the Hebrew language, and especially of the Old Testament. Jones held 'that the Hebrew is the primæval and original language; that its structure shows it to be divine; and that a comparison with other languages shows its priority'; but both he and Horne repudiated the name Hutchinsonian. Jones's defence of the Catholic Doctrine of the Trinity brought him to the notice of Archbishop Secker. After holding various curacies in Northamptonshire he was preferred by Secker to livings in Kent: Bethersden, 1764; Pluckley, 1765. In 1777 he became perpetual curate of Nayland in Suffolk, which has provided him with a distinguishing title, and exchanged Pluckley for Paston in Northamptonshire, which he visited annually; 'but he set up his staff at Nayland for the remainder of his days.' Nayland became a rallying point for the old High Church party. In 1792 he helped to found a 'Society for the Reformation of Principles,' which was to counteract the influence of the French Revolution. It resulted in the publication of the *British Critic*. He was never entirely free from poverty, which obliged him to take pupils until 1798, when Archbishop Moore gave him the sinecure rectory of Hollingbourne, Kent. His constant friend, William Stevens, paid the stipend of a curate for 'the old boy,' as his friends called him.

Jones was learned in many subjects, and was a skilful controversialist. As a musician he is remembered as the composer of the familiar tune 'Nayland,' which he called 'Stevens' after his friend. Hence it appears in collections sometimes as 'St. Stephen's.' Jones retained to the last 'the lively spirit of a boy, with more than a common share of manly wisdom'; his scientific knowledge caused him to be made F.R.S.; but his chief fame is his rigid adherence to the Catholic tradition in the English Church,

based on profound theological knowledge. His works were edited in six volumes by his biographer, W. Stevens. His *Letters from a Tutor to his Pupils*, republished in 1816, show his sterling good sense, his admirable taste, and his deep piety, and in these respects anticipate the spiritual letters of Bishop E. King. His orthodox high churchmanship was joined to 'a more spiritual tone than was common in his day,' and he is remembered as a leader of 'the school, more numerous than is commonly supposed, which formed the link between the Nonjurors' and the Oxford Movement.

[S. L. O.]

Works, with *Life*, by W. Stevens; J. H. Overton in *D.N.B.* and *Eng. Ch. in Eighteenth Century*; Churton, *Memoir of Joshua Watson*.

JUXON, William (1582-1663), Archbishop of Canterbury, was born at Chichester, went to school at Merchant Taylors', London, and became Scholar of St. John's College, Oxford, in 1602. He chiefly studied law, and took the B.C.L. degree. After his ordination he became in 1609 Vicar of St. Giles's, Oxford, where his 'edifying way of preaching' drew large congregations. On 10th December 1621 he was unanimously elected President of St. John's, to succeed Laud (*q.v.*); became Dean of Worcester, 1627; Vice-Chancellor of the University, 1626 and 1627. He actively aided in the Laudian reform of the University statutes, was made Clerk of the Closet, 1632, and Dean of the Chapel Royal, 1633. Laud had all along been his friend, admirer, and patron, and had the highest opinion of his wisdom and integrity. No doubt it was through Laud's influence that he was nominated to the bishopric of Hereford in 1632, but it was to London that he was consecrated at Lambeth on 27th October 1633. As bishop he was scrupulous in visitation and in enforcing the law, but was successful and popular until the growth of Puritanism spread difficulties in his way. He was active in the restoration of St. Paul's, concerned in the revision of the Scots Prayer Book (from which he anticipated trouble), and energetic in every kind of public work. So much was he trusted that Laud was able to procure his appointment as Lord High Treasurer, 6th March 1636, in which post he worked with regularity and unselfish devotion to duty. He was actively engaged in the collection of ship money and forced loans, yet no one attributed the measures to him, and Falkland, when most bitterly criticising the bishops, said of him 'that in an unexpected place and power he expressed an equal moderation and humility, being neither ambitious before, nor proud after, either the crosier or the white staff.' When Charles came to Oxford in 1636 to open the new buildings Laud had given to St. John's, Juxon was present, having superintended most of the building and found the marble at Bletchington. He (with Ussher. *q.v.*) advised Charles I. to refuse his assent to the attainder of Strafford, and was the constant adviser of the King after Laud was imprisoned, and Charles declared that he 'was ever the better for his opinion.' [CHARLES I.] During the last year of the King's life Juxon was continually with him, was present during his trial, ministered to him before his execution, received his prayers from his hand [EIKON BASILIKE], and attended him on the scaffold. ' You are exchanging a temporal for an eternal crown; a good exchange,' were his last words, and Charles replied : ' Remember.' He took the body to Windsor for burial, but the church service was not allowed. During the Commonwealth he remained in seclusion at Little Compton, reading the church service at Chastleton House, and hunting with his own pack of hounds. On the Restoration he was made Archbishop of Canterbury with universal thankfulness and rejoicing, being elected, 13th September 1660, and confirmed on 20th September in Henry VII.'s Chapel, a large concourse being present. The actual crowning of Charles II. was performed by him, but he was unable from infirmity to conduct the whole service ; and, after beginning many fine works of generosity and charity, he died on 4th June 1663. He had been bitterly disappointed with Charles II., being ' so much struck with what he observed in him that he lost both heart and hope.' He was buried with great pomp in St. John's College Chapel, where Laud's remains were soon laid beside him, that the college might still possess all that was mortal of the two who had been ' sometime and successively Archbishops of Canterbury and Presidents of that Society.' Juxon was in opinions a thorough Laudian, but he was a gentle and tactful as well as a tolerant man. Lloyd in his *Memoirs of those that Suffered* says he was ' the delight of the English nation, whose reverence was the only thing all factions agreed in, by allowing that honour to the sweetness of his manners that some denied to the sacredness of his function, being by love what another is in pretence, the universal bishop.'   [W. H. H.]

S. R. Gardiner, *Hist. of Eng.* ; Sir Philip Warwick, *Memoirs.*

K

KEBLE, John (1792-1866), divine and poet, eldest son of John Keble, Vicar of Coln St. Aldwyn, Glos., was born at Fairford, where his father resided. Educated at home, he was elected Scholar of C.C.C., Oxford, in December 1806, being only fourteen years old. In 1810 he graduated with a double First Class (*i.e.* in Classics and in Mathematics), and 1811 was elected Fellow of Oriel, then the intellectual centre of the University. In 1812 he won the English and the Latin Essays, being still under twenty-one. He became famous rapidly as one of the ablest men in a brilliant college. held various University appointments, and became Tutor at Oriel in 1817. He resigned his Tutorship and left Oxford, 1823, going to aid his father, then in failing health. He had been ordained deacon, Trinity Sunday, 1815 ; priest, Trinity Sunday, 1816, by Bishop W. Jackson of Oxford. He had worked since his ordination in various Cotswold parishes, and was curate of Southrop, 1823-5. where Isaac Williams (*q.v.*), R. H. Froude (*q.v.*), and R. I. Wilber- force (*q.v.*) were his pupils. T. Arnold (*q.v.*) had been his close friend at Corpus, and they were Fellows together at Oriel. Keble was godfather to Arnold's distinguished son Matthew. In 1831 Keble became Professor of Poetry at Oxford, and held the chair until 1841. His lectures, delivered in Latin, were published in 1844, and contain a sympathetic criticism of the chief Greek and Latin poets. An English translation of them is now (1912) in the press. From 1819 he had begun to write poems, and in 1827 he published them anonymously as *The Christian Year*. Their success was instantaneous, and before his death there had been ninety-five editions, which increased in the year after he died to one hundred and nine. Arnold, who had seen them in manuscript in 1823, declared that ' nothing equal to them exists in our language.' Keble had been brought up as a churchman of the school of the Caroline Divines (*q.v.*), and had learnt from his father the old Catholic doctrines of the Real Presence, the Power of the Keys, belief in the visible Church and in the Apostolical Succession, and to these he held fast through life. These teachings, mediated through R. H. Froude, touched Newman (*q.v.*), and the close friendship of the three begun in 1829 resulted in the Oxford Movement (*q.v.*). That Movement was begun by a sermon preached by Keble on 'National Apostasy' (on the text, 1 Sam. 12²³) before the Judges of Assize in St. Mary's, Oxford, 14th July 1833 ; and Newman in the *Apologia* describes Keble as 'the true and primary author of the Oxford Movement.' There is little doubt that the sermon was prompted by the preacher's study of the works of Charles Leslie [NON-JURORS], reprinted by the University Press 1832. In the *Tracts for the Times* which followed Keble took his share, writing Nos. 4, 13, 40, 52, 54, 57, 60, 78, and 89. He was, however, chiefly occupied with his great edition of the *Works of R. Hooker*, 3 vols., 1836. With Newman he edited Froude's *Remains*, Part I. (2 vols.), 1838 ; Part II. (2 vols.), 1839 ; and wrote the strong Preface to vol. i. of Part II. In 1838 he became with Newman and Pusey (*q.v.*) joint editor of the *Library of the Fathers*. For this he translated St. Irenæus and revised some of the volumes of St. Augustine and St. Chrysostom. He strongly urged on Newman the publication of Tract No. 90 (1841), and in 1844 pressed Pusey to publish an English translation of the Breviary. He was the close friend and adviser of Newman, and strove wisely, but in vain, to avert his secession in 1845. His own confidence in the English Church never wavered, and with the danger his spirit rose higher. He believed unhesitatingly in the essential unity of the Catholic Church and in the English Church as a living part of it. Hence, despite the prejudices of the time, he claimed in its fulness all that could be justly reckoned Catholic. His view of the position of the English Church was resolutely true to facts. ' "Under appeal and doing penance," that is the English Church's place in the kingdom of heaven ; we are not saying it of her in comparison with other Churches, but positively—whatever other Churches are, such, we firmly believe, is our place.' He took a leading part in the struggles after 1845 ; strengthening the confidence of waverers after the Gorham Judgment (1850); refusing to hear of Pusey withdrawing two adapted Roman Catholic books which had displeased Bishop S. Wilberforce (*q.v.*), 1851 ; printing in 1857 two strong pamphlets protesting against the Divorce Act, and in the same year publishing his treatise on *Eucharistical Adoration*, which defended in the

clearest terms the doctrine of the Real Objective Presence attacked in the case of Archdeacon Denison (*q.v.*) and in that of Bishop A. P. Forbes in Scotland at the same time. To this treatise he is said to have devoted more time and trouble than to any other of his works. In 1863 he produced his great *Life of Bishop T. Wilson* as an introduction to Wilson's *Works*.

Keble had married in 1835, and ceased to be Fellow at Oriel. In 1836 he became Vicar of Hursley, near Winchester, where he remained till his death, which occurred at Bournemouth, 29th March 1866. He is buried at Hursley.

From the beginning of the Oxford Movement in 1833 until his death no dignity in the English Church was ever conferred upon him (he had been offered a colonial archdeaconry in 1824, but refused it on account of his father's need of help, and he was created Hon. Canon of Cumbrae in Scotland in 1854), and this grave reproach is a vivid illustration of the party spirit and narrowness of the authorities of the time. His own bishop, C. Sumner, refused in 1841 to ordain his curate, Peter Young, priest, and Mr. Young remained a deacon at Hursley until ordained priest by Bishop S. Wilberforce (for the Bishop of Exeter) in 1857. After Mr. Keble's death his work was recognised, and the great college at Oxford which bears his name was founded in his memory and opened in 1870.

Mr. Keble, apart from his genius and learning, was remarkable for the rare distinction of his nature. 'Without a particle of the religious cant of any school, without any self-consciousness or pretension or unnatural strain, he literally passed his days under the quick and pervading influence . . . of the will and presence of God' (Dean Church). And the same authority declares that 'to the last' he kept 'a kind of youthful freshness, as if he had not yet realised that he was not a boy. . . . He was the most refined and courteous of gentlemen, and in the midst of the fierce party battles of his day' he was 'always a considerate and courteous opponent' (*Occas. Papers*, ii. 296-9). He was especially devoted to children, and was the friend and playmate of the large family of his neighbour, Dr. (later Bishop) Moberly, whose Memoir (*Dulce Domum*, 1911) specially illustrates this side of Keble's character. When he was a young tutor with his pupils at Southrop the old gardener used to say: 'Master is the greatest boy of the lot' (I. Williams, *Autobiog.*, p. 18).

Another feature of Mr. Keble was his

inspired common-sense. This made him a sound spiritual guide, and as Church principles revived hearing confessions and directing consciences became a real part of his work. He became in 1846 the spiritual guide of Dr. Pusey, and in 1854 of Dr. Liddon. He spoke out strongly on the need of the revival of sacramental confession in 1850. His *Letters of Spiritual Counsel*, first published 1870, illustrate this side of his character. It is generally understood that Dr. Moberly was Mr. Keble's own confessor.

Mr. Keble's especial influence in times of panic in the Church, when men were being driven over to Rome (1845 and 1850-1), was intellectually his distrust of what was cut and dried—the lesson he had learnt from Nature. *A priori* views, like those of W. G. Ward in his *Ideal of a Christian Church* (1844), never shook him. A body *totus teres atque rotundus* was unlike anything in Nature, and a human and artificial rather than a divine and natural creation, so that anomalies in the English Church were to his mind no proof that she had ceased to be divine. His view was in direct antithesis to that which prefers 'mathematics applied to things eternal,' and seeks a refuge from the anomalies of the English Church in the sharp and clear uniformity of Rome. This teaching is stamped upon *The Christian Year*. With it is combined a very deep personal love to our Lord as a living friend. 'Generally speaking, religious men, before Mr. Keble, spoke of Him in a more distant way, as One holding the central place in a dogmatic system' (Principal Shairp, *Studies*, etc., 1868, p. 329).

Keble's poems besides *The Christian Year* were those contributed to the *Lyra Apostolica*, 1836, written under the signature γ; *The Psalter in English Verse*, 1839; *Lyra Innocentium*, 1846; *Miscellaneous Poems*, 1869 (which included the verses from *Lyra Apostolica*). Archbishop Benson (*q.v.*) delighted in his poetry, and insisted that in it is to be found 'the common ground where poetry and religion meet' (*Life*, i. 592).   [S. L. O.]

Memoir by Sir J. T. Coleridge: Lives by Dr. Lock and Hon. E. Wood ; Dr. Liddon, sermon (No. xiii.) in Clerical Life and Work ; Church, Oxford Movement, chap. ii. ; Dr. W. Lock, Introductions to The Christian Year and Lyra Innocentium (Library of Devotion, Methuen, 1898-9) ; Isaac Williams, Autobiography.

KEN, Thomas (1637-1711), Bishop of Bath and Wells, son of an attorney in the Court of Common Pleas, of an ancient Somerset family. His eldest sister married,

1646, Isaac Walton, who on Ken's father's death, 1651, became his guardian. 30th January 1651 Ken was admitted scholar of Winchester, where he formed a lifelong friendship with Francis Turner, later Bishop of Ely, and one of the Seven Bishops (*q.v.*). 1656 he was elected to New College, Oxford, but there being no vacancy he entered at Hart Hall, succeeding to a vacancy at New College, 1657. At Oxford he was known for his 'excellent genius' in music. He was a skilful lutanist, and sang well. Becoming Fellow of New College he graduated B.A., 1661 ; M.A., 1664 ; was ordained, and became Rector of Little Easton, Essex, 1663-5. He became chaplain to his friend, Morley, Bishop of Winchester, and in 1666 Fellow of Winchester, resigning his Fellowship at New College. 1667-9 he was Rector of Brightstone. 1669 he became Prebendary of Winchester and Rector of East Woodhay, resigning Brightstone, since he resolutely declined to hold livings in plurality. 1672 he resigned his living, and went to reside in Winchester, where in 1674 he published his famous *Manual of Prayers* for Winchester scholars. 1679-80 he was chaplain to the Princess Mary at The Hague, where he rebuked William of Orange for his treatment of his wife, and earned his further dislike by causing one of his friends, Count Zulestein, to marry one of Mary's Maids of Honour whom he had wronged. Returning to England in 1680 he was made chaplain to Charles II., to whom he showed the same firmness, refusing when the court came to Winchester to allow Nell Gwyn the use of his prebendal house. 1683-4 he went as chaplain to the fleet sent to dismantle Tangier. November 1684 he was offered the see of Bath and Wells, and was consecrated, 26th January 1685. A week later he attended the King's death-bed 'without any intermission for three whole days and nights,' and gave him absolution, for which act he was censured by Burnet (*q.v.*).

He attended the Duke of Monmouth the night before his execution and on the scaffold, and was unremitting in his care for the prisoners taken in his rebellion, which took place in Ken's diocese.

He petitioned against the Declaration of Indulgence (1687), and was one of the Seven Bishops (*q.v.*). He was personally loyal to James II., and voted in the Convention for a regency. When the Prince of Orange became king Ken was unable, though after much hesitation, to take the oath to the new sovereigns. Petitions were sent praying that he might be allowed to remain, as he was dearly loved in his diocese, but though allowed much delay he was deprived, 1691, having made a solemn protest against the act in his cathedral church and in the market-place at Wells. His generosity, especially to the French Protestants, had been lavish, and the sale of his effects left him with only £700 and his books, which he never sold. He retired to Longleat, the seat of his friend, Lord Weymouth, who, to avoid the appearance of patronage, received his £700, and allowed him an annuity of £80. 1695 he openly officiated in his robes at the funeral of John Kettlewell, a saintly Nonjuror. He consented, with great reluctance, to the continuation of the succession of Nonjuring bishops. He took a prominent part in appealing for funds for distressed Nonjurors in July 1695, for which he was summoned before the Council, but defended the action with his customary simplicity and courage, and the affair dropped.

1703, when Kidder, his intruded successor, was killed at Wells in the great storm, Queen Anne wished to restore Ken. He declined, but his friend Hooper being appointed he resigned to him the rights of canonical jurisdiction which he had hitherto claimed. 1704 Anne granted him a pension of £200 a year for life. Ken was anxious to close the schism, and by his advice Robert Nelson (*q.v.*) and others ceased to be Nonjurors. He continued to live chiefly at Longleat, where 'in a large upper room' with his books he 'wrote hymns, sang them to his viol, prayed,' and finally died, after some years of ill-health, 19th March 1711. He was buried, as he directed, 'in the Church-yard of the nearest Parish within his Diocese (which happened to be Frome Selwood), under the east window of the Chancel, just at sunrising.' He was unmarried. His name is best known by his familiar morning and evening hymns. [S. L. O.]

Lives, by 'A Layman' (London, 1851), Dean Plumptre; Overton, *The Nonjurors*.

KING, Edward (1829-1910), Bishop of Lincoln, second son of Walker King, Rector of Stone and Archdeacon of Rochester. Born in London 29th December 1829, he was privately educated till he matriculated at Oriel College, Oxford, 1848 (B.A., 1851; M.A., 1855; B.D. and D.D., 1873). At Oriel he was a disciple of Charles Marriott (*q.v.*), of whom he said, 'If there is any good in me, I owe it to Charles Marriott. He was the most Gospel-like man I ever met.' After visiting the Holy Land, he was ordained at Cuddesdon by S. Wilberforce (*q.v.*), deacon on 11th June 1854, priest 3rd June 1855, as assistant curate of Wheatley, where his characteristic gifts at once found scope: his love for the poor and simple and his sympathy and influence with young men. In 1858 Wilberforce made him chaplain of Cuddesdon College, and in 1859 pressed him, but in vain, to succeed Liddon as Vice-Principal; but on the death of H. H. Swinny in 1863 he became Principal of the College and Vicar of Cuddesdon, and so continued till 1873. Here he exercised an enormous influence on many generations of ordinands, and inspired an enthusiastic loyalty which still lives. In 1873 Mr. Gladstone (*q.v.*) nominated him to succeed Dr. Ogilvie as Regius Professor of Pastoral Theology and Canon of Christ Church. Archbishop Tait (*q.v.*) had done his best to prevent the appointment, which was elsewhere criticised; but the result more than justified Mr. Gladstone's judgment. Dr. King's professoriate was a brilliant one. His lectures on *Parochialia* were perhaps as good as such lectures can be; while, apart from the technical duties of his chair, he became the most potent religious force in the University, a force which widely and characteristically exerted itself through the 'Bethel' (a wash-house in his garden which he cleaned out, and put into it 'cocoa-nut matting and chairs and a harmonium—very simple, but very lovely'), where on Friday nights in term he gave spiritual instructions on such subjects as the Lord's Prayer, the Deadly Sins, and the Ten Commandments. Missionary work 'stirred him up to the very bottom,' and he had much to do with the foundation in 1876 of St. Stephen's House in Oxford (in memory of Stephen Fremantle of Christ Church) as a hostel for graduates preparing for the mission field, which, standing opposite the King's Arms Hotel, became known as 'Canon King's Arms'; and in 1878 with that of the Missionary College at Dorchester, Oxon, of which for some years he was visitor; while he was keenly interested in the Oxford Mission to Calcutta, founded in 1880. Meanwhile he was the confessor and director of many souls, and the general adviser of as many more. In 1885, to the joy of Christopher Wordsworth (*q.v.*), who had resigned the see of Lincoln, Mr. Gladstone nominated Dr. King to succeed him. He was elected with enthusiasm on 20th March, confirmed on 23rd April, consecrated by Archbishop Benson and nine assistants on 25th April, Liddon preaching the sermon, *A Father in Christ*, and enthroned on 19th May. He at once made the same impression in his diocese as he had made elsewhere. But in 1888 he was attacked, mainly from outside. The Church Association, with the concurrence of a layman of the diocese, petitioned the metropolitan to cite him for alleged illegalities committed in the Minster and at St. Peter-at-Gowts in December 1887, viz. the use of the eastward position, altar lights, the mixed chalice, *Agnus Dei*, the sign of the cross at the absolution and the blessing, and the ablution of the sacred vessels at the altar. On 4th January 1889 the archbishop cited the bishop to appear before him on 12th February in his court, which had been in abeyance for two hundred years, and of the competence of which there was considerable doubt. [COURTS.] Immediately from all over the diocese, England, and the English-speaking world, messages of sympathy and promises of prayers and Eucharists poured in on him, and a defence fund was raised more than sufficient for his expenses. On 12th February he appeared before the archbishop and five episcopal assessors, and on the advice of friends, both ecclesiastical and legal, he read a protest against the procedure, claiming his right to be heard, not by the metropolitan alone, but by all the bishops of the province. The archbishop overruled the objection, and the trial began on 5th February 1890. The judgment, which was delivered on 21st November, was generally in favour of the bishop. It was described by R. W. Church (*q.v.*) as ' the most courageous thing that has come from Lambeth for the last two hundred years,' and was received with general satisfaction. The prosecutors appealed to the Judicial Committee of the Privy Council, which dismissed the appeal on 2nd August 1892, only attempting to save its face by the absurd contention that the vicar of the parish and not the bishop was responsible for the lights on the altar. The troubles of these four years, while they did not visibly disturb his serenity, aged the bishop; but for seventeen years more he administered his diocese, better loved than ever. He founded a Diocesan Fund for church building and spiritual aid; promoted Houses of Rescue; and formed the Grimsby Church Extension Society to meet the needs of the largest and most growing town population in the diocese. In the early years of the new century he enforced in his diocese the archiepiscopal 'Opinion' on Incense, and within limits that on Reservation; and on the legalising of marriage with a deceased wife's sister he directed his clergy to refuse to solemnise such marriages or to allow them in their churches; while he felt himself

bound, in view of the *data* of the New Testament, the practice of the Eastern Church, and the decision of the Lambeth Conference, not to treat as excommunicate an innocent party married after divorce, though not consenting to such marriage in church. On his eightieth birthday, 29th December 1908, he received from his diocese a birthday present of £2000 for Grimsby. On 30th November 1909 he alone of the bishops voted in the House of Lords against the Finance Bill of that year. In January 1910 his health began definitely to fail, and by the end of February he knew that his end was near, and with characteristic simplicity he made his final arrangements and preparations, and died on 8th March. On 11th March his funeral in the cloister garth of his cathedral church was attended by a vast throng, the Archbishop of Canterbury officiating.

Edward King was a great man; a rare distinction was the mark, as of his face, so of his person and his life. Spiritually he was a saint, simple, sane, sensible, strong, and a saint who made saintliness infinitely attractive: with all the Tractarian seriousness and solemnity, and with a French capacity for making it seem not impossible to be good. Intellectually he has sometimes been depreciated, perhaps because he won no academic distinctions. But those who knew him will perhaps think that he was among the most intellectual persons they have ever known: only, as was perhaps the case with St. Anselm, to whom he has been compared, his intelligence was so much a part of his character, so wholly himself, that it might easily escape notice in the simplicity and charm of his personality. He had a singularly alert mind, and was interested in everything: no one ever saw him bored, and ' he never touched a topic without displaying an original view '; and he was keenly alive to the intellectual difficulties of his day. He knew and could talk French, German, and Italian; and in a mixed company he could talk in at least three languages at once—no small accomplishment; while his English was admirable. And he read widely to the end. Socially he was amazing: he moved up and down the social strata without effort: or rather he seemed to have no sense of social distinctions, and could talk to every one ' in the language wherein he was born,' so that the ploughboy could say he must have been a ploughboy himself. He was so absolutely a gentleman that his rustics could say there was nothing of the gentleman about him. He published nothing except a *Letter to the Rev. Charles John Elliott* in reply to *Some strictures on a book entitled*

'*The Communicants' Manual*' *with two prefaces by the Rev. E. King, D.D.,* and his episcopal charges. A few sermons were published for him in his lifetime. Since his death a collection of spiritual letters and some volumes of sermons have appeared. Of portraits, there is a convincing crayon drawing of him at the age of twenty-six by J. Drummond (1855); a sketch (1873) and a portrait (1874, now at Cuddesdon College; engraved 1877) by G. Richmond, and a portrait (in the Palace at Lincoln) by Mr. Ouless (1900)—neither of them like him.   [F. E. B.]

G. W. E. Russell, *Edward King*; B. W. Randolph has edited *Spiritual Letters. The Love and Wisdom of God. Sermons and Addresses.* and *Duty and Conscience.*

KINGSLEY, Charles (1819-75), divine, was son of a landed proprietor in the New Forest, who lost his fortune, took to holy orders as a profession, and died Rector of Chelsea.

Charles was a high-spirited and active boy, fond of natural history and the open air, but not good at games. He had no aptitude for accurate scholarship, but read discursively, and wrote English verse and rather rhapsodical prose. In 1836 he entered King's College, London. He went up to Magdalene College, Cambridge, 1838, where he won a scholarship, but, in his own words, he was 'very idle and very wicked' during his first two years at Cambridge. In 1839 he met his future wife, Frances Grenfell. She exercised a deep influence on his character, and indeed altered the whole tone and purpose of his life. He abandoned all the rough sports and base pleasures in which he had delighted, read very hard, and, in spite of lost time, secured a first class in the Classical Tripos, and a second in Mathematics. He had resolved to seek holy orders, and in 1842 he was ordained to the curacy of Eversley in Hampshire, and soon afterwards made acquaintance with Maurice's (*q.v.*) *Kingdom of Christ,* a book which permanently coloured his theological thinking. In 1844 he was appointed Rector of Eversley by the squire, Sir John Cope of Bramshill, and Eversley for the rest of his life was his home. He was a zealous parish priest, but his activities extended far beyond parochial bounds. He felt an irresistible impulse towards authorship. Most of his books were in effect pamphlets. The poem which first made his name, *The Saint's Tragedy,* and his story, *Hypatia,* were attacks on asceticism. His hatred of Romanism effervesced in *Westward Ho.* His sympathy with the agricultural poor was expressed in *Yeast,* with the citizens of the town in *Alton Locke. Two Years Ago* was a plea for sanitary reform. His prose writings were interspersed with delightful verses, many of which became popular songs. Maurice's influence drew him into the 'Christian Socialist' movement, and he contributed a good deal to the journals connected with it, signing himself 'Parson Lot.' A sermon on 'The Message of the Church to Labouring Men,' which he preached at St. John's, Fitzroy Square, in 1851, seemed so revolutionary in tone that the incumbent of the church rose in his place and denounced it.

Kingsley's writings attained a wide popularity. His theory of practical religion, which laid excessive stress on the culture of the body, acquired the nickname of 'Muscular Christianity.' He soon cast aside the socialistic or radical opinions of his early life, became, or found that he had always been, a devotee of the Crown and the aristocracy. He became a favourite of Prince Albert, and in 1859 he was made Chaplain in Ordinary to the Queen. In 1860 he was appointed Regius Professor of Modern History at Cambridge, and it soon became apparent that he was very imperfectly acquainted with the subject which he had to teach; but his lectures were attended by the Prince of Wales, afterwards King Edward VII. He was now attaining a wide influence, but in 1864 he made a fatal slip. He had published in *Macmillan's Magazine* an article in which he roundly accused the Roman Catholic Church in general, and Dr. Newman (*q.v.*) in particular, of teaching systematic lying. When Newman challenged him for proof he failed abjectly to produce it, but had not the grace to apologise or withdraw. His lumbering attempts at self-justification elicited Newman's *Apologia pro Vita Sua.* Newman's sincerity was triumphantly vindicated, and Kingsley stood displayed as a rash and reckless accuser of his brethren, and a most unskilful controversialist.

From that time his influence palpably declined, but his worldly fortunes mended. Mr. Gladstone (*q.v.*) made him a Canon of Chester in 1869, and of Westminster in 1873. His last prominent intervention in public controversy was in 1873, when he came forward as a champion of the Athanasian Creed, laying special stress on the testimony which it bears to the doctrine of the Intermediate State.   [G. W. E. B.]

Charles Kingsley: His Letters and Memories of his Life, by his wife; J. H. Newman, *Apologia pro Vita Sua.*

KITCHIN, Anthony (1477-1563). Bishop of Llandaff, was originally a Westminster Benedictine, and later Abbot of Eynsham. He was made Bishop of Llandaff in 1545, and held the see uninterruptedly till his death in 1563. He sided with the Marian bishops in their Parliamentary opposition to the Elizabethan changes, but then he parted company from them. He took the Elizabethan oath of supremacy, and was one of the commission appointed for Parker's (*q.v.*) consecration in 1559, but did not act. He preferred to retire to the obscurity of his diocese, from which he scarcely emerged, till his death four years later at the advanced age of eighty-six. He and Stanley, the Bishop of Sodor and Man, were the only two Marian bishops who retained possession of their sees : but Barlow (*q.v.*) and Scory were other links with the Edwardine past, the latter consecrated with the new Ordinal in 1551, but the former in 1548 with the Latin Pontifical. Kitchin was made to figure in the more developed form of the Nag's Head fable, as being present in the tavern and refusing to consecrate Parker. His character has been much attacked by those who disapproved of him for the line which he took ; it is difficult to say with how much justification.

[W. H. F.]

White. *Lives of the Elizabethan Bishops.* 11-13 ; Collins, *Eng. Reformation*, 65.

L

LANFRANC (d. 1089). Archbishop of Canterbury, belonged to a leading family of Pavia. He was educated in the famous law-school of that city, and won considerable reputation as a jurist ; some of his opinions are cited as authoritative by the glossators of a later age. His legal studies left a profound impression on his essentially practical mind ; their influence may be traced in his political career, and even in his theological writings. But while still young he migrated to Normandy, and set up a school at Avranches, 'having heard that the study of letters had much decayed among that barbarous race, and understanding that he might there obtain great glory and profit.' After two or three years his thoughts turned to religion, and he entered the abbey of Bec, which under Herluin, its founder and first abbot, was then regarded as a pattern of monastic organisation and a school of saints (1042). Herluin discerned the abilities of Lanfranc, and about 1045 promoted him to be prior. But Lanfranc devoted himself chiefly to theological studies, and to the direction of the monastic school, which in his time, and owing to his fame, attracted students even from Gascony and Italy. Many of his pupils rose subsequently to high places in the Church ; among them were Ivo of Chartres, the celebrated canonist, and Anselm of Badagio, afterwards Pope Alexander II. As a theologian Lanfranc is chiefly remembered for his intervention in the controversy, raised by Berengar of Tours, concerning the Eucharist. Lanfranc was accused at Rome of sympathising with the heresiarch. He not only cleared himself before Leo IX., but also undertook to state the orthodox position against Berengar at the Council of Vercelli (1050). It is stated, on doubtful authority, that he repeated this performance at the Councils of Tours (1055) and Rome (1059). But his principal contribution to the long dispute was a treatise, *De Corpore et Sanguine Domini*, written at some time after the final recantation of Berengar (1079). Berengar, according to Lanfranc, had maintained that the elements in the Eucharist were not changed by consecration, and treated the sacrament as merely symbolic. Lanfranc argues, from Scripture and the Fathers, that the earthly substances are incomprehensibly converted through consecration into the Lord's Body and Blood, while the external form and appearance remain. This work, and some commentaries on the Epistles of St. Paul, are his only considerable writings on theology. While still the Prior of Bec he became a friend and counsellor of Duke William ; and his career is henceforth that of a statesman in whom the taste for affairs perpetually conflicts with a sincere reverence for the monastic ideal of seclusion. Between 1053 and 1059 he incurred William's displeasure by public condemnation of the marriage which the duke had contracted, in defiance of a papal prohibition, with Matilda of Flanders. He was ordered to quit Normandy, and actually started for Rome. But, happening to meet William by the way, he obtained forgiveness by his ready wit and imperturbable good humour. He was afterwards instrumental in persuading Pope Nicholas II. to remove the interdict which had been laid upon Normandy and to condone the objectionable marriage (1059). In token of penitence, the duke founded the monastery of St. Stephen at Caen ; and he nominated Lanfranc as the first abbot (1066). Soon afterwards Lanfranc was elected to the see of Rouen, left vacant by the death of Archbishop Maurilius (1067). But he declined the honour with the consent of the duke, who may have already singled him out as the fittest successor to Archbishop Stigand. Lanfranc was nominated to Canterbury in 1070. Though he only accepted the see under pressure from the Pope's legate, he at once threw himself into the work of reforming the English Church. [NORMAN CONQUEST.] In his zeal for the purification of English monasticism, and for the enforcement of clerical celibacy, he showed himself a true son of Bec and a partisan of the Hildebrandine movement. But his zeal was tempered by respect for custom and vested interests. He raised no protest against the custom of lay investiture, even after it had been condemned by a papal council (1078). He refused to persecute those parish priests who had contracted marriages before the decree of the Council of Winchester (1076). He passively supported his master in resisting the claim of Gregory VII. to feudal suzerainty over England, and remained neutral during the papal schism which began in 1080 ; and it would seem that he shared in the mistrust which other bishops in other countries had conceived of Gregory's too autocratic policy. If Lanfranc had hardly formulated the conception of a national Church, he was unwearied in defending the rights of Canterbury. In 1070 he raised a claim to the obedience of the see of York, which was strenuously resisted by Archbishop Thomas, disliked by William, and dubiously received by Alexander II., Lanfranc's former pupil. But the archbishop won over the King, induced the Pope to refer the matter to an English council, and obtained at Winchester (1072) from the assembled clergy a favourable verdict which, unhappily for his reputation, he owed to spurious charters. On a smaller stage, before the shire-moot of Kent, he defended the estates of his see with complete success against the formidable earl-bishop, Odo of Bayeux (*q.v.*). In works of piety and charity he showed a commendable zeal. He was a liberal benefactor to the poor and to the monks of Canterbury and St. Albans : he rebuilt his cathedral ; he founded the hospital of St. John outside Canterbury, and the leper-house of St. Nicholas, Harbledown.

Though hampered in his studies by want of leisure, he devoted himself to textual criticism ; under his supervision the Vulgate and the writings of the Fathers were purged of the errors which careless copyists had introduced. But it may not unfairly be said that, next to ecclesiastical reform, politics were the chief subject of his thoughts. He sometimes acted as justiciar when William I. was absent in Normandy, and showed energy and courage in crushing the revolt of the Earls of Hereford and Norfolk in 1074-5. His influence secured the recognition of William II. as King of England at a time when many of the baronage would have preferred the feeble Robert Courthose (1087) ; and he kept the Church and the native English loyal to their allegiance in the rebellion of 1088. It is remarkable that so staunch a Churchman twice identified himself with the State in resistance to claims of episcopal privilege. In 1082 he asserted the right of the Conqueror to deal with Odo of Bayeux as with a disloyal baron ; and in 1088 he took the same attitude in regard to William of St. Calais, Bishop of Durham. But the principle on which he acted in these cases was afterwards accepted by the Church ; and he may be awarded the credit for anticipating the one satisfactory solution of the Investitures Controversy (*q.v.*). Lanfranc died in May 1089, and was buried in Canterbury Cathedral.

[H. W. C. D.]

Freeman, *Norman Conquest* ; W. R. W. Stephens, *The Eng. Ch., 1066-1272* ; Antoine Charma, *Lanfranc* (Paris, 1849) ; H. W. C. Davis, *Eng. under the Normans and Angevins.*

LANGTON, Stephen (d. 1228), Cardinal and Archbishop of Canterbury, was of English extraction, but received his education in the University of Paris, where he graduated as a doctor in theology and afterwards lectured. He earned a reputation as a copious and original commentator on the Old Testament ; tradition affirms, but apparently without foundation, that he was the first to divide the Vulgate into chapters. Innocent III. (*q.v.*) made him a cardinal in 1206, and he had not been long at Rome before he was elected, on the same Pope's nomination, to the see of Canterbury. The election was made at Rome by a delegation of the Canterbury monks, after Innocent had refused to accept either Reginald, whom they had elected irregularly, or John de Grey, who had been forced upon them by John. As the King would not recognise Innocent's nominee, Langton remained on the Continent until 1213. He at first acted as a restraining force upon

Innocent; but, when John had shown his contempt of an interdict and a sentence of personal excommunication, the archbishop demanded a sentence of deposition (1212). Hereupon John yielded, and Langton was allowed to enter England in 1213. He soon evinced a sympathy for the baronial opposition. It is even stated that he suggested to them the policy of taking their stand upon the charter of Henry I., which afterwards served as the model of Magna Carta (*q.v.*). But in public he preserved the attitude of a mediator. In the conferences which preceded the signing of Magna Carta he negotiated with the barons on the King's behalf and in his name (1215). In the preamble to the charter Langton heads the list of the counsellors by whose advice John states that he is acting; and the insertion of the first clause, guaranteeing the liberties of the Church, was probably his work. Late in 1215 he was suspended by papal commissioners for refusing to enforce a sentence of excommunication against the baronial party. He went to Rome in person, and pleaded his cause before Innocent III., with the result that the sentence was relaxed. But he was not allowed to revisit England until the close of the civil war. Returning in 1218, he lent the support of the English Church to the Regency in its struggles against papal claims and baronial insubordination, procuring the recall of Pandulf (*q.v.*), and assisting Hubert de Burgh to crush Falkes de Bréauté. His last political act of importance was to obtain from Henry III. the fourth and final edition of Magna Carta (1225). In his ecclesiastical capacity he distinguished himself by asserting the privileges of Canterbury. In 1220 he obtained from the Pope a promise that no more legates (*q.v.*) should be sent to England in his lifetime. This did not prevent the Holy See from commissioning a nuncio, the sub-deacon Otho, to collect money from the English clergy and to demand rights of presentation for his master (1225). But upon a protest from Langton the nuncio was withdrawn; and from this time the archbishops of Canterbury were allowed to hold, as of right. the dignity of a *legatus natus*. Langton left his mark on the law of the English Church. In 1222 he held at Oseney a provincial synod in which, besides the decrees of the Fourth Lateran Council (1215), he promulgated special constitutions for the English Church (Wilkins, *Concilia*, i. 585.) One of these provided that all Jews should wear a distinctive badge; another excluded the concubines of the clergy from participation in the sacraments.

This same synod also set a memorable precedent by condemning an apostate deacon, who had Judaised, and handing him over to the secular arm to be burned at the stake. The procedure could be justified by the Lateran decrees, but was novel to English jurists. It is fortunate for Langton's fame that his successors found no occasion to act upon the precedent. He died at Slindon, in Sussex, in July 1228. His disinterestedness and moderation, his piety and learning, made a profound impression on contemporaries. But the chronicles of the period are singularly deficient in anecdotes of his private life. Scholarly, reserved, and self-restrained, he had a marked capacity but little liking for political affairs, and never courted the public eye. But he undoubtedly ranks among the foremost men of his age, and is perhaps the greatest of our mediæval archbishops.   [H. W. C. D.]

Stubbs, preface to *Walter of Coventry*, vol. ii.; C. E. Maurice, *Life* in 'English Popular Leaders,' vol. i.; H. W. C. Davis, *Eng. under the Normans and Angevins*.

LATIMER, Hugh (1485-1555), Bishop of Worcester. was born at Thurcaston, Leicestershire. 'My father was a yeoman and had no lands of his own, only he had a farm of three or four pound a year at the uttermost and hereupon he tilled so much as kept half a dozen men. He had walk for a hundred sheep and my mother milked thirty kine. He was able and did find the King a harness with himself and his horse. I can remember that I buckled his harness when he went into Blackheath field (1497). He kept me to school or else I had not been able to have preached before the King's majesty now.' According to Foxe, 'he so profited at the common school of his own country that at the age of 14 years he was sent to the University of Cambridge.' Nor were bodily exercises neglected. 'In my time my poor father was as diligent to teach me to shoot as to learn me any other thing; he taught me how to draw; how to lay my body in my bow, and not to draw with strength of arms as other nations do, but with strength of the body.'

At Cambridge he became a Fellow of Clare Hall, and, having been ordained, attracted the attention of Thomas Bilney by a sermon against Melanchthon. Bilney 'was the instrument by which God called me to knowledge; for I was as obstinate a Papist as any was in England. Bilney heard me at the time and perceived that I was zealous without knowledge; and he came to me afterwards in my study and desired me to hear his confession. I did so, and by his confession I learned more than before in many years. So from that time forward I began to smell the word of God and forsook the school-doctors and such fooleries.'

Being suspected of Lutheran tendencies he was inhibited in 1525 by Bishop West of Ely from preaching in that diocese. He was afterwards examined by order of Cardinal Wolsey (*q.v.*) acting as Legate, and on disowning Lutheran errors was given permission to preach throughout the kingdom.

In December 1529 his two sermons ' on the card ' provoked hostility, as he deprecated pilgrimages and other external observances as compared with works of mercy. He won the royal favour as a supporter of the divorce. In 1530 his name appears as favourable to the King's purposes on a committee of divines appointed at Cambridge to report on the validity of the marriage with Katherine. He was immediately afterwards appointed to preach before the King. In 1530 he was presented to West Kington, in Wiltshire, where he seems to have resided. Foxe says that ' his diligence was so great, his preaching so mighty, the manner of his teaching so zealous that he could not escape without enemies.' In 1532 he was accused of saying that Our Lady was a sinner, of forbidding invocation of saints, of denying purgatory and hell fire, and stating that almost all the bishops and clergy in England were thieves, and that there was not enough hemp in England to hang them with. His own bishop, Campeggio (*q.v.*), was an absentee, and in the end he was cited to appear before Bishop Stokesley of London, and after some delay made a complete submission, but was summoned to appear again almost immediately, and confessed that he had erred in doctrine. In 1533 he was in trouble again for a sermon preached at Bristol, and was inhibited by the Bishop of London. However, in the next spring, 1534, he was appointed to preach before the King on Wednesdays in Lent, and was active in supporting the marriage with Anne Boleyn. In 1535 he was made Bishop of Worcester, and issued injunctions ordering every priest and religious to have a whole Bible in English or at least a New Testament; he ordered the clergy not to lay aside preaching for any religious observance, to admit no one to Communion who could not say the Paternoster in English, and to instruct the children of their parishes to read English. He had the image of the Virgin in Worcester Cathedral, ' our great Sibyll,' as he called it,

stripped of its jewels and ornaments and eventually burned in London. ' She herself with her old sister of Walsingham, her young sister of Ipswich, with their other two sisters of Doncaster and Penrice would make a jolly muster in Smithfield.'

In 1536 he was at Lambeth examining heretics with Cranmer (*q.v.*) and Shaxton. He preached the opening sermon at Convocation, denouncing the bishops and clergy, and asking what good they had done during the past seven years. They had burnt a dead man, William Tracy, and tried to burn a living one (himself); ' this other ye would have raked in the coals because he would not subscribe to certain articles which took away the supremacy of the King.' In 1537 he took part in the committee which produced *The Institution of a Christian Man*, or *Bishops' Book*—work which he found difficult and uncongenial. ' It is a troublous thing to agree upon a doctrine in things of such controversy, with judgments of such diversity, every man meaning well and yet not all meaning one way.' In 1538 he was on a commission to examine Forest, and afterwards preached, or, as he callously put it. ' played the fool,' at his execution. He was also one of the commission to examine the famous ' Blood of Hailes.' When the Act of the Six Articles was passed he and Shaxton, Bishop of Salisbury, resigned their sees. He was kept a prisoner for more than a year in the house of Sampson, Bishop of Chichester. When liberated he was ordered not to preach or to visit London, either University, or his diocese. He was brought before the Council in 1546 on a charge of having encouraged Dr. Crome, and he remained a prisoner in the Tower until the accession of Edward VI. in 1548.

The few years of Edward's reign were perhaps the most fruitful of his life. In the words of his servant, ' then most of all he began to set forth his plough and to till the ground of the Lord and sow the good corn of God's word. In the which his painful travails he continued all King Edward's time, preaching for the most part every Sunday two sermons. . . . For he being a sore bruised man and above threescore and seven years of age took notwithstanding all these pains in preaching, and besides this every morning ordinarily winter and summer about two of the clock in the morning he was at his book most diligently.' He was one of the commission which condemned Joan Bocher the Anabaptist, who was burnt in consequence. He refused to resume his bishopric, but had a great vogue as a preacher. He preached a course at St. Paul's, beginning 1st January 1548, including his famous sermons on the Plough, in which he inveighed against un-preaching and non-resident prelates, and held up the devil as an example. ' He is the most diligent preacher of all others ; he is never out of his diocese ; he is never from his cure ; he is ever in his parish ; the diligentest preacher in all the realm ; he is ever at his plough.' In Lent. 1549, he preached a course before the King, mainly dealing with current abuses, especially the wrong-doing of the rich and their oppression of the poor. He did not scruple to take a strong partisan line in his sermons in support of Somerset, and attacked Lord Seymour, justifying his execution, and hinting not obscurely at his eternal damna-tion.

Soon after Mary's accession a summons was issued for his apprehension. He was given six hours' notice of the intended arrest in order that he might escape. But this he refused to do, and said to the pursuivant : ' My friend, you be a welcome messenger to me ; and be it known to you and to the whole world that I go as willingly to London at this present, being called by my prince to give an account of my doctrine as ever I was to any place in the world.' He appeared before the Council, and was committed to the Tower. In March 1554 he was sent down to Oxford with Ridley (*q.v.*) and Cranmer (*q.v.*) to dispute with divines from both Universities on the doctrine of the Mass.

After some delay, and several appearances before the Bishop of Lincoln and other commissioners, he was condemned for heresy and delivered to the secular arm. On 16th October he and Ridley were led to execu-tion ' upon the north side of the town in the ditch over against Balliol College.' Latimer was dressed ' in a poor Bristow freez frock much worn and a kerchief on his head.' When they came to the stake bags of gun-powder were tied round their necks by Ridley's brother-in-law. A lighted faggot was then laid at Ridley's feet, and Latimer said : ' Be of good comfort, Master Ridley, and play the man ; we shall this day light such a candle by God's grace in England as I trust shall never be put out.' Soon the flames reached Latimer, and he died without much suffering. He was perhaps the most widely influential of the English Reformers, owing to his vigorous, aggressive personality, combined with a very popular style of preaching ; homely, vigorous, and often vulgar, but never dull or obscure. He had the courage of his convictions, and did not hesitate to rebuke vice or to speak plainly

to kings and great nobles. His sermons preached before Edward VI. in 1549 were published in that year, and six more editions appeared in that century. He attached an exaggerated importance to preaching : ' Take away preaching, you take away everything.' He was unmarried, and, unlike some of the Reformers, his private life will bear inspection. He was honest and sincere, and was ever the champion of the poor. At his first sermon before Henry VIII. he begged the life of a poor woman unjustly condemned to death at Cambridge. He wished poor children taught to read, poor scholars sent to Universities, chaplains provided for prisons. He was bitterly hostile to the Inclosures.

His interest in the Reformation movement was the interest of the practical man who wished abuses removed rather than that of the theologian. But his self-confidence and hasty temper made him a violent partisan, lacking in judgment and foresight. He be-came a loyal supporter of Henry VIII., Anne Boleyn, Cromwell (*q.v.*), and Somerset, rather through want of balance and judgment than want of principle. He upheld the Royal Supremacy blindly, without seeing that it was used to maintain abuses as much as to remove them. He was never tired of denouncing ' monkery,' set pilgrimages and such ' fooleries,' yet states that there are now (1549) ' none but great men's sons in colleges,' and predicts that ' the realm will come to a very barbarousness and utter decay of learning ' ; that poor men are woefully oppressed ; that livings are sold and given to servants ; that there is more open immorality than ever before—though he appears to have been unconscious that the alterations in religion had, to say the least, not been as successful as he had hoped.

[c. P. S. C.]

Sermons (Parker Soc.) : Strype, *Memorials* ; Foxe, *Acts and Monuments*.

LATITUDINARIANS. The word was ' first hatch'd at Cambridge,' apparently near the middle of the seventeenth century, to de-scribe those who favoured latitude of opinion in religious matters and treated forms of Church government and worship, or even doc-trine, as indifferent. As a rule, this indifference was allied with hostility towards much of the doctrine and practice sanctioned by the universal Church. Old writers give caustic definitions of the name : Wycherley, 1676, ' Thou dost side with all men, but wilt suffer for none ' ; Butler, 1680, ' A Latitudinarian . . . believes the Way to Heaven is never the better for being strait ' ; *Dict. Cant. Crew,*

1700. '*Latitudinarian*, a Churchman at large, one that is no Slave to Rubrick . . . and in fine looks towards Lambeth, and rowes to Geneva.' The terms 'Latitudinarians' and ' Latitude-men ' were abusively applied to the group of Cambridge Platonists (*q.v.*) who opposed ' superstitious conceits and a fierceness about opinions.' They, in Burnet's words, ' loved the constitution of the Church, and the liturgy, and could well live under them. . . . They were all very zealous against Popery.' One of the earliest apologies for Latitudinarianism is the *Free Discourse*, 1670, by Edward Fowler (1632-1714), formerly a Presbyterian minister. In 1691 he was consecrated bishop to fill the see of Gloucester, ousting Frampton, who was deprived as a Nonjuror. In the Commission for revising the Prayer Book in 1689 Fowler had proposed that the use of the Athanasian Creed should be optional. Soon after he had grasped the crosier he taught a semi-Arian doctrine of the Trinity, and revived Origen's theory that the soul of Jesus Christ existed before the Incarnation. Nearly contemporary with Fowler was Daniel Whitby (1638-1726), Precentor of Salisbury. He urged dissenters to conform, and denied Apostolical Succession. He was author of a commentary which upheld Christ's deity, a doctrine which he later privately abandoned, though he retained his clerical office and preferments.

Arianism, which reduces the Son of God to the position of a pagan demi-god, was strongly favoured by the theological works of Dr. Samuel Clarke (1675-1729). He was criticised by Waterland (*q.v.*), who, in opposition to Clarke's insistence on the use of Scripture only, justly declared that ' the sense of Scripture is Scripture.' Clarke was once silenced in the presence of Queen Anne by Dr. Hawarden, who asked him : ' Can the Father destroy the Son ? ' — a question to which no Arian could reply except by a blasphemous affirmative.

The accession of the Hanoverian dynasty to the English throne gave the party their chance. George I. and Walpole wished to weaken the Church, and Walpole, with consummate skill, chose as his instrument Benjamin Hoadly (*q.v.*), who published in 1716 an attack on the doctrine of a visible Church, and followed it by a sermon before the King, in which he declared that Christ ' left behind no visible, human authority.' The King retained Samuel Clarke as a chaplain, and rid himself of four chaplains who opposed Hoadly.

By the middle of the century there was a serious, though by no means universal, decay of church life. Morals, faith, and worship had alike declined. Herring (1693-1757), Archbishop of York and afterwards of Canterbury, though an active worker, commended the writings of Hoadly and Clarke. In 1743 the Bishop of Chester succeeded in stopping weekly Eucharists at the collegiate church of Manchester. On clerical life a lurid light is thrown by the correspondence of Edmund Pyle, a Latitudinarian chaplain in ordinary to George II. The clergy of his party appear as vultures in their greed for preferment, negligent of their duty, seeking gain by political sermons, and supporting anti-Christian opinions. Pyle's father, who held many preferments, was almost suffocated ' with distemper and indignation' at the sight of an emblem of the Trinity in Unity on a new pulpit in his church of St. Margaret's, Lynn. Pyle also describes as ' an excellent member of our church ' an ecclesiastic named Sykes, who was loaded with preferment, though he supported Arianism and attacked the doctrine of the Resurrection.

In 1751 Clayton, Bishop of Clogher, attacked the Athanasian and Nicene Creeds. He was followed in 1754 by Archdeacon Blackburne, who started the ' Anti-subscription ' movement. Apparently Arian at heart, he opposed the need of episcopacy, confirmation, and confessions of faith. Cornwallis, Archbishop of Canterbury (1768-83), being essentially a courtier rather than a prelate, Blackburne circulated in 1771 a petition for application to Parliament for relief from subscription to the Liturgy and Articles. The petition was rejected by Parliament, and though Cornwallis was not adverse to a revision of the Prayer Book, the bishops feared that it would disturb the peace, and sagaciously dropped the scheme. The rise of Evangelicalism (*q.v.*) checked the progress of Latitudinarianism, but it prepared for its recrudescence because it was, as one of the greatest of Evangelical Nonconformists declared, ' satisfied with fellowship of an accidental and precarious kind. It cared nothing for the idea of the Church as the august Society of saints. It was the ally of individualism ' (Dale, *The Old Evangelicalism and the New*, pp. 16, 17).

Between 1820 and 1833 there was in many quarters a revival of Church life, and this revival seems to have provoked a violent anti-clerical attack not only on real abuses but on the Church itself. New democratic principles were leavening the minds of the people, a new popular literature which ignored religion was at work, and the government was unfriendly. Dr. Arnold (q.v.) of Rugby, who though reckoned as a Broad Churchman was as much opposed to secularism as he was devoted to the Divine Person of our Lord, was in favour of fighting the evils of the day by admitting dissenters into the Church. The Oxford Movement (q.v.) showed a more excellent way, and advanced against theological 'Liberalism,' as it now began to be called, with the weapons of learning and spiritual experience. The opponents of the Tractarians had little or no respect for the living collective tradition of the Church, the deposit of the faith handed down by obedient love. And when the Church in Oxford was weakened by the secession of some of the Tractarians, the Latitudinarian spirit throve aggressively. It found a cultured expression in *Essays and Reviews* (q.v.), 1860. We here only note the essay on *The National Church*. It cautiously assails the Athanasian Creed and the Church's doctrines of the sacraments and the ministry, and advocates a relaxation of subscription to the Thirty-nine Articles in the interests of those who are reluctant 'to enter an Order in which their intellects may not have free play.' It anticipates the most recent Modernism by urging that Jesus Christ has not revealed His religion 'as an historical faith,' and that 'a uniformity of historical belief . . . can never exist.' The book was condemned by Convocation as 'containing teaching contrary to the doctrine received by the united Church of England and Ireland, in common with the whole Catholic Church of Christ.'

We may connect with *Essays and Reviews* the controversy about Bishop Colenso (q.v.), who after long discussions was excommunicated in spite of the State, and was superseded in the see of Natal by Bishop Macrorie in 1869. The case of Colenso is not unlike that of the ancient heresiarch, Nestorius, with whom he had much in common. We can put a more favourable interpretation on some of his statements than they received from his contemporaries, but other statements prove that his condemnation was inevitable. Colenso's letters to English newspapers in 1866 show that he objected to prayers offered to Jesus Christ (*Life of Bishop Gray*, ii. pp. 264, 278), though he had protested to the Bishop of Cape Town that he believed in His divinity. In the immediately succeeding years the sermons of Dr. Liddon (q.v.) and the fruitful researches of Dr. Lightfoot (q.v.) in primitive Christian literature inflicted severe wounds on Lati-

tudinarianism. To some extent it was fostered in Oxford by Professor Jowett, and by Dr. Hatch, whose revolutionary theories with regard to the origin of the ministry were refuted by Dr. Gore. Hatch's work marks the transition from the older to the more recent theological 'Liberalism.' The old Latitudinarianism was, on the whole, English. It was also mainly content to appeal to the well educated. The modern 'Liberalism' or 'Liberal Christianity' or 'Liberal Protestantism' draws its inspiration from Germany. And it conducts an active propaganda, endeavouring to reach all classes. It is aided by a copious supply of translations from foreign rationalistic books. A bold attempt to utilise the writers of such works was made in the *Encyclopædia Biblica* (1899-1903). 'Liberalism' of this foreign type has especially assailed the miracles of our Lord, His Virgin birth, and His bodily resurrection. Within the Church of England it is mainly a small clerical movement, and the laymen who care for religion are as a rule solidly opposed to it. [L. P.]

Murray, *Eng. D.*; *D.N.B.*; Tulloch, *Rational Theology in the Seventeenth Century*; *Memoirs of a Royal Chaplain*, ed. by A. Hartshorne (John Lane, 1905); Perry, *Student's Eng. Ch. Hist.*, 1717-1884.

LAUD, William (1573-1645), Archbishop of Canterbury, the son of William Laud, a clothier, was born at Reading, 7th October 1573, and was educated at the free school there and at St. John's College, Oxford, matriculating when he was ten days over his sixteenth birthday. He became Reading Scholar of the college, 1590, and Fellow, 1593; B.A., 1594; M.A., 1598; B.D., 1604; D.D., 1608. For the degree of B.D. he discussed the doctrine of baptism, taking views opposed to the extreme Protestant teaching, and for that of D.D. the divine right of episcopacy. (It is worth noting that Dr. S. R. Gardiner in the *D.N.B.* made an error on this point, still uncorrected in the new edition; Laud's *Works*, iii. 262.) At St. John's Laud's tutor was John Buckeridge, who no doubt influenced his opinions in the direction they took, for both built their theology, as Heylin (q.v.) says, 'upon the noble foundations of the fathers, councils, and the ecclesiastical historians,' and both represented the consequent reaction against the Calvinism which had for some years been in power at Oxford. St. John's itself, however, was an example of the way in which the repudiation of Roman supremacy had been carried out in England. Several of the Fellows had left the country and accepted the papal obedience. The original President had retired from or been deprived of his college office, but had continued to hold his ecclesiastical benefices. But the founder of the college himself, Sir Thomas White, had all the while directed the fortunes of the young society, accepting the Reformation, and providing for the performance of divine service in the college chapel, with no sign of violent breach with the past. The college founded under Mary went on under Elizabeth, with its founder still in charge of it. This is significant, for it shows that Laud was brought up at Oxford under influences unfavourable to the development of Puritan opinions, and representative rather of that theory which is known as 'the continuity of the English Church.' Laud went through the ordinary duties of a college Fellow; he was Proctor in 1603-4. He became chaplain to Charles, Earl of Devon, and in this office consented to marry his master to Lady Rich, who had been divorced in consequence of her adultery with him. It was a grievous breach of his duty to the Church, and Laud repented bitterly of what he had done. Ever after he observed St. Stephen's Day, the day on which he had committed this sin, as a strict fast. A tract of his remains in the Record Office, which shows that he repudiated all defence of the action and endeavoured to bring the earl at last to repentance. As a preacher at Oxford Laud maintained the Catholicism of the English Church, and one of his sermons was accused to the vice-chancellor; but the Chancellor intervened, and proceedings ceased. In 1608 Laud became chaplain to Neile, Bishop of Rochester, 'a man who very well understood the constitution of the Church of England.' He was given several benefices, and in 1610 a prebend in Westminster Abbey in reversion. He then resigned his Fellowship. When Buckeridge, who had become President of St. John's, became Bishop of Rochester in succession to Neile, Laud was elected to the Presidency after a hot contest, which had to be referred to the Visitor, the Bishop of Winchester (Bilson), who referred it to the King. James decided in Laud's favour, and before long made him his chaplain. Returning to Oxford, Laud became the leader of those opposed to Calvinism, and as such was attacked by Abbot (Regius Professor of Divinity) from the University pulpit as 'a papist in point of free will, inherent righteousness and the like, . . . and in the doctrine of the Sacrament.' But Laud was able to fight down opposition, and gradually to influence the whole University.

In 1616 he was made Dean of Gloucester, where he offended the bishop, Miles Smith, a Calvinist, by getting the chapter to remove the altar to the east end of the cathedral. In 1617 he went to Scotland with James VI., and shocked the Presbyterians by wearing a surplice. In 1621 the Westminster reversion fell in, and he at once became a leading member of the chapter. He was consecrated Bishop of St. David's on 18th November 1621, giving up his Oxford headship but retaining his Westminster prebend. In 1622 he took part in a famous 'controversy with the Jesuit Fisher,' attempting to secure the mother of the favourite, Buckingham, in allegiance to the English Church. The book which resulted from this was published in 1624, and went through several editions. It is an admirable summary of the English seventeenth-century arguments against Rome. It points out that the Greek Church is a standing disproof of the papal claim to exclusive authority, and resists the Roman view that all points defined by the Church are fundamental. On one side his work is an anticipation of Chillingworth (*Religion of Protestants*), on another it is a development of Hooker; but, above all, it is an assertion of the position of the English Church as essentially loyal to the doctrine and discipline of the undivided Church. Laud visited the diocese of St. David's twice, was enthroned in his then almost inaccessible cathedral, and built and consecrated a chapel in his palace at Abergwili, near Carmarthen. On the accession of Charles I. Laud, who was already the confessor of the King's friend, Buckingham, became the sovereign's chief ecclesiastical adviser. He showed that he claimed for the Church a wide tolerance, and yet that he believed her ministers to be definitely bound by her definite enactments. Then he defended Richard Mountague [CAROLINE DIVINES] against the House of Commons in 1628, as in later years he supported Chillingworth; promoted the Latitudinarian 'ever memorable John Hales'; and was responsible for the Declaration prefixed (1628) to the Thirty-nine Articles, which ordered silence on points of controversy and the acceptance of the words of the document in their plain sense; but he enforced, in whatever position he was placed, the obedience of the clergy to the Prayer Book, Articles, and canons of the Church. He advised, or assisted, Charles and Buckingham in political matters, and thus soon began to share in their unpopularity. The King rewarded him with the bishopric of Bath and Wells, 1626, and London, 1628, and in 1633, on the death of Abbot, he became in fact, what he had long been in practice, primate of all England. At Charles's coronation he had been deputy for the Dean of Westminster (Williams (*q.v.*), Bishop of Lincoln, who was his lifelong enemy, now in disgrace) ; he had succeeded Andrewes (*q.v.*) as Dean of the Chapel Royal; and he had been for eight years most intimate with the King. In 1628 he was elected Chancellor of the University of Oxford, where (as later at Dublin) he gave new statutes, which were in force for over two hundred years, and greatly reformed the studies and discipline of the place. His interest in learning was very near his heart, and he was a munificent benefactor to the Bodleian Library, employing agents to hunt up books all over Europe and elsewhere ; and he built a new quadrangle for his own college. As Archbishop of Canterbury his political duties were considerable. He sat on many committees, and in all of them worked hard. He was a member of the Courts of Star Chamber and High Commission (*q.v.*), and his conduct in each exposed him to great unpopularity and to misrepresentation. In the former he was concerned with many cases of criminal libel, such as those of Prynne (against the King and Queen, in *Histriomastix*), Leighton (against the bishops and church system), and Prynne, Burton, and Bastwick for further libels against the Church, and is said (though the evidence is not complete) to have pressed for a severe sentence on these civil offences. In the Court of High Commission, which dealt only with offences against morals and against church law, he was extremely severe against moral offenders. The laxity which had come into English life with the Reformation needed sharp treatment, and the High Commission did not spare the most exalted persons. In regard to offences against the Prayer Book, its procedure seems to have been moderate. The most stringent measures were taken to secure conformity in those who held benefices, but few seem to have been deprived. Laud's determination to introduce order extended over every province of public life with which he was concerned. He tried to stop corruption in the civil service by procuring the appointment of Lord Treasurer for Juxon (*q.v.*) (his successor as President of St. John's and as Bishop of London). He held a metropolitical visitation, visited the cathedrals and the University of Oxford, reporting annually on the state of his province to the King, and making every effort to enforce obedience to the canons or statutes by which the clergy, parochial or

cathedral, were bound. He was, indeed, throughout a practical reformer, seeking to make the Church effective in its work and loyal to its standards. Thus he got the King in 1633 to urge the bishops to ordain only those who had definite cures or titles— an attempt to stop a pre-Reformation abuse; and urged everywhere the placing of altars at the east end of the churches, severely reprehending Bishop Williams's book, *The Holy Table, Name and Thing*, which had upheld a different practice. His activities were not limited to his political and religious duties in England. He corresponded with foreign Protestants, welcoming political alliance, but showing no desire to admit intercommunion with non-episcopal bodies. He endeavoured to provide a bishop for the British dominions in the New World, but the matter was not carried through before his fall. He supported the restored episcopacy of Scotland, went with Charles to Edinburgh, and took care for the restoration of churches and of parochial endowments, and assisted the bishops in the issue of a new Prayer Book containing the 'Scottish Communion Office.' 1637. In Ireland he cordially supported his friend the Lord Deputy, Thomas Wentworth, Earl of Strafford, agreed with him against persecution of the Romanists and in excluding their bishops, and got the Church to accept the English Articles, as a clear repudiation of extreme Calvinism. He took measures to bring foreign Protestant settlers to accept after the first generation the doctrine and usage of the national Church, and he provided carefully for the spiritual wants of English merchants abroad. In fact, he kept an eye on every side of British activity. He filled so large a space in public life that he could not fail to attract attention overseas. Papal emissaries endeavoured to attract him, but he replied that Rome must be other than she was before he could see any possibility of English reunion with her ; and he did much to bring many 'perverts' back to the Anglican Church. The Greek Church also entered into relations with him. Lascaris, afterwards Patriarch of Constantinople, visited him, and they discussed hopes of reunion. He was indeed by far the greatest ecclesiastical figure of his age. With less truth, he was taken to be a great political figure, and he was so closely associated with the King that when political troubles came to a crisis he was involved in the King's fall. He was indeed almost driven to take sides with the party of absolutism. His studies in political science were in the direction of obedience to authority. Thus after the Short Parliament his notes show that he distinctly advised unconstitutional means of raising money if no others could be taken. 'Tried all ways, and refused all ways. By the law of God and man you should have subsistence, and lawful to take it.' From 1633 to 1638 Laud's measures may be said to have been in active progress. From 1639 they broke down. The Bishops' War gave Scotland to Presbyterianism and utterly routed the Laudian party in the Church. Against his better judgment and the advice he had given to Charles, Convocation was prolonged after the dissolution of the Short Parliament, 1640, and gave the King supplies which Parliament refused. New canons were passed, distinctly anti-Roman, but equally anti-Puritan and anti-popular. The unfortunate requirement of an oath from office-holders never to ' consent to alter the government of this Church by archbishops, bishops, deans, archdeacons, etc.,' caused even more laughter than indignation. Then the High Commission Court was broken up on 22nd October 1640. Within ten days the Long Parliament met, and on 18th December Laud was impeached. He was sent to the Tower, 1st March 1641. He bade a pathetic farewell from the window of his prison to Strafford on 12th May, giving him his blessing as he was led to the scaffold. He was then kept in prison for three years without trial. On 12th March 1644 the few remaining Lords heard in Westminster Hall the charges of the Commons against the Archbishop of Canterbury as a traitor to the sovereign against whom they were engaged in civil war. The charges were of great width ; everything almost that he had done as an ecclesiastic, and a good deal that he had not done, was brought in evidence that he had endeavoured to alter the constitution of the Church, and was thus a traitor to the Crown. He defended himself with extraordinary patience and acuteness. His counsel, Hearn, argued that no act alleged fell within the statute of treason, and when the reply was made that though no single act was definite treason yet all together were treasonable, answered: 'This is the first time that e'er I heard that a thousand black rabbits did make one black horse.' The Lords, it was clear, could not accept that view ; no lawyer could support it. Then other measures were taken. A mob petitioned that the archbishop should be executed, and on 22nd November the Commons substituted for the impeachment a Bill of Attainder. After hesitation and conference the Lords passed this on 4th January 1645. Not more than fourteen peers at the utmost were

concerned. On the same day the Book of Common Prayer was disestablished, and the Directory substituted for it, also by the Lords and Commons. 'Thus,' wrote a member of the Lower House, ' the archbishop and the Prayer Book died together.' It was on 10th January 1645 that the archbishop met his death on Tower Hill. In a touching speech he asserted his loyalty to 'the Church of England established by law.' He was buried at All Hallows, Barking, by the Tower. After the Restoration his coffin was exhumed, and it was interred under the altar in St. John's College Chapel at Oxford on 24th July 1663.

Laud was unquestionably the greatest prelate the English Church had produced since the Reformation. He was a theologian of the type of Andrewes, a convinced Anglican, but a believer that Anglicanism was fundamentally Catholic. He has been styled a reformer ; and such he was in that he desired to bring back the Church from Calvinistic teaching, which seemed to him to limit the love and mercy of Almighty God. But he was also eminently conservative ; he strove for uniformity of usage, but only in obedience to the formularies to which he and the Church were pledged. Thus he gave a coherence to the Anglican position which men could understand, which gave Charles a party who would fight and die for him, and enabled the restoration of the kingship in 1660 to bring with it a restoration of the Church as Laud had endeavoured to organise and represent it. Personally, Laud was a warm and generous friend, a tolerant thinker, a strenuous worker, a bibliophile, a musician, a lover of animals. He saw his own aim with unusual clearness, and he set about realising it by the methods of an experienced teacher. But he was dictatorial and impatient. People forgot his real tenderness of heart in the abruptness of his outward manner. He saved the Church of England, and probably he could not have saved his own life had he been ever so conciliatory in the expression of the opinions which he and she held. But his personal defects went a long way to condemn him. Clarendon, who greatly admired him, writes : 'He did court persons too little, nor cared to make his designs and purposes appear as candid as they were, by showing them in any other dress than their own natural beauty and roughness, and did not consider enough what men said or were like to say of him. If the faults and vices were fit to be looked into and discovered, let the persons be who they would that were guilty of them, they were sure to find no connivance of favour from him. He intended the discipline of the Church should be felt as well as spoken of, and that it should be applied to the greatest and most splendid transgressors, as well as to the punishment of smaller offences and meaner offenders; and thereupon called for or cherished the discovery of those who were above the reach of other men or their power and will to chastise.' Thus his honesty was no small element in his condemnation. But he left a school of devoted admirers, and loyalists justly regarded him as a martyr for the Church.   [W. H. H.]

Heylin, *Cyprianus Anglicus*; Laud, *Works*; S. R. Gardiner, *Hist. of Eng.*, and in *D.N.B.*; W. H. Hutton, *William Laud*.

LAW, William (1686-1761), was born at King's Cliffe, Northamptonshire, of a commercial stock, with good traditions of refinement and learning; entered Emmanuel College, Cambridge, as a Sizar in 1705; was elected Fellow, and was ordained in 1711. He was suspended from his Fellowship for a public speech reflecting on the Government. On the death of Anne he refused the oath of allegiance to George I., and remained a Nonjuror (*q.v.*) to the end. In 1727 he entered the family of Mr. Gibbon of Putney as tutor to Edward Gibbon, father of the historian. Advanced to the position of family friend, monitor, and general authority, he remained there for twelve years, till the death of Mr. Gibbon broke up the household. In 1740 Law retired to his native village, and there lived till his death, having been previously associated for some years with two ladies, Mrs. Hutcheson and Miss Hester Gibbon, who under his direction founded schools and almshouses, and lived a life of practical piety and devotion. It is doubtful whether Law ever officiated in church after becoming a Nonjuror. His life was one of almost monastic simplicity, regularity, and—save for the times when he threw himself vigorously into controversy—of seclusion.

He is chiefly known as the author of the *Serious Call*; as perhaps the most brilliant English ecclesiastical controversialist; and a mystic, the disciple of Jacob Böhme. The *Serious Call* stirred the hearts of the two Wesleys (*q.v.*). Gibbon, the historian, speaks of it as 'a popular and powerful book of devotion'; and Dr. Johnson (*q.v.*) as that which first caused him to think in earnest. As controversialist he combated successively Dr. Hoadly (*q.v.*), who denied to the Church all superhuman origin or function; Dr. Mandeville, who practically did the same for man-

kind; Tindal the Deist, who exalted a low conception of Reason to be the rule and measure of all things; Hoadly, who, writing anonymously, degraded 'the Nature and End of the Sacrament of the Lord's Supper'; Dr. Trapp, who extolled the excellence of a half-hearted devotion; and Dr. Warburton (*q.v.*), who maintained that the Mosaic system and the Old Testament took no account of man's immortality. As mystic and constructive theologian Law has received far less attention than he deserves. His great thesis was the unalterable love of God; and, like all mystics, he rejects absolutely as a grotesque fable and invention the notion of a vengeance-loving God, and of a debtor-and-creditor theory of payment exacted and extorted in the Atonement. From the same motive, and in obedience to his keen logical instinct, he absorbed and reproduced in a more acceptable form the teachings of Jacob Böhme, finding as others have done, in the doctrine of a primarily perfect Creation, its necessary shattering into chaos and warring elements by the Fall of the Angels, and its progressive emergence from this state unto the consummation of all things, an anchor for the Christian mind, in view of the apparently blind and malevolent forces of Nature. The truly mystical idea that Self—self-will instead of God's Will—is the root of all sin, and of man's apostasy from God, is very forcibly expressed by Law; and by no one is the *reasonableness* of redemption, its restoring to man exactly that thing he had lost, more lucidly set forth. The *Spirit of Love* and the *Spirit of Prayer* are two of his works that deserve a far wider recognition than has been accorded them. The *Way to Divine Knowledge* and the *Grounds and Reason of Christian Regeneration* will carry the reader still further into the depths of his thought; while his polemical works contain much of enduring interest. His *Three Letters to the Bishop of Bangor* (Hoadly) are probably the most brilliant pamphlets in all English Church history.   [E. C. G.]

Works; J. H. Overton, *The Life and Opinions of the Rev. William Law*.

LAYTON, Richard (1500 ?-1544), Dean of York, and the chief agent in the visitation of the monasteries, was educated at Cambridge; seems to have been in the employment of Wolsey (*q.v.*); held several preferments, but lived in London. He was employed by Cromwell (*q.v.*) in the suppression of Syon, and afterwards wrote to him: 'You will never know what I can do till you try me.' On 1st August 1535 he began visiting the smaller monasteries from Evesham, passing thence to Bath and the west, and later into Sussex. [MONASTERIES, SUPPRESSION OF.] To judge by his letters to Cromwell, he was thoroughly unscrupulous, and anxious only to please his employer. Finding that he had given offence by praising the abbey of Glastonbury, he wrote an abject letter of apology, and promised not to offend again. The lack of time alone would have made even a pretence at an impartial visitation a farce. Confessions were extorted by every kind of pressure, and considerable money payments were taken. In the same year he visited the northern monasteries, taking those in Northamptonshire, Bedfordshire, and Leicestershire on the way. He made himself so unpopular that his execution was demanded by the leaders of the Pilgrimage of Grace (*q.v.*). He took part in the trial of Anne Boleyn and the divorce of Anne of Cleves.

In 1537 he became Rector of Harrow-on-the-Hill, where he pressed Cromwell to stay with him with the words: 'Surely Simeon was never so glad to see Christ his master as I shall be to see your Lordship.' He was made Dean of York in 1539, and died in 1544. After his death it was discovered that he had pawned the minster plate. From his many letters which survive he seems to have been a coarse, foul-minded man, rough and violent towards those weaker than himself; a supple time-server to Cromwell, whom he called his *Maecenas et unicus patronus*; greedy and unscrupulous at all times, and an almost worthless witness so far as the monasteries were concerned. [C. P. S. C.]

Narratives of the Reformation, C.S.: *Letters on Suppression of Monasteries*, C.S.: Gasquet, *Henry VIII. and the Eng. Monasteries.*

LEGATES, papal envoys to local churches and governments, were appointed from early times. *Presbyteri a latere* are mentioned in a canon of the Council of Sardica (343); the *apocrisiarius*, whom the popes kept at Constantinople in the sixth century, may be called a resident legate. The Anglo-Saxon Church was visited by legates as early as 786, when the Bishops George and Theophylact arrived with commendatory letters from Adrian I. to the Kings of Wessex, Mercia, and Northumbria. Their object was to obtain the promulgation of certain reformatory canons, and these were duly approved by the Mercian and Northumbrian Witans. In and after the time of Hildebrand the legatine office acquired a new importance. Legates became the instru-

ments through whom the Pope signified his commands to Churches and sovereigns, or on occasion interfered directly in the detail of ecclesiastical administration. Three kinds of legatine commission may be distinguished in the mediaeval period. The *legatus missus*, or nuncio, was despatched on a special mission with limited powers. To this class belonged some of the papal tax collectors who visited England under Henry III. and Edward I.: as, for instance, William Testa, appointed in 1306 to administer the vacant see of Canterbury. Testa was summoned before Parliament, compelled to refund the money which he had collected, and forbidden to continue his exactions. The *legatus natus*, or perpetual legate, held his commission by virtue of occupying some privileged episcopal see. He was empowered in general terms to visit and reform the Churches placed beneath his jurisdiction. A commission of this kind was obtained in 1126 by William of Corbeil, then Archbishop of Canterbury. It was a personal grant, which expired with his death. The next English legate of this type was Henry of Blois (*q.v.*), who held the office in 1139-43. But Archbishop Theobald subsequently received it (c. 1150), and it was granted, though sometimes after a long delay, to his successors. Becket (*q.v.*), Richard, Baldwin, and Hubert Walter (*q.v.*). Stephen Langton (*q.v.*) did not obtain it until he made a special journey to Rome for the purpose in 1220. But from his time until Cranmer in 1534 renounced the title (Wilkins, *Concilia*, iii. 769), the commission was regularly granted to the archbishops of Canterbury. It was also granted to the archbishops of York from 1352 onwards. But the *legati nati* were liable to be temporarily superseded by a legate sent from Rome. The *legatus a latere* was a papal plenipotentiary, and his mandates could only be resisted by an appeal to the Pope. He was usually sent to hold a council of the national Church, or to transact political business of exceptional importance. Of legatine councils held in England the most noteworthy are: (1) that of 1071, held by Ermenfrid of Sion to depose Bishop Aethelric of Selsey. This was held at the instance of William I., who had, however, reserved the more important case of Archbishop Stigand to be heard in the Great Council; (2) the Council of Westminster (1125), held by the notorious Cardinal John of Crema to enact reforming decrees (given by Florence of Worcester's continuator, *s.a.*); (3) the Council of St. Paul's, held by Cardinal Otho in 1237; and (4) the Council of St. Paul's, held by Cardinal Ottobuoni in 1268. The constitutions passed in the two last-named assemblies were of considerable importance, and are commonly cited as the Constitutions of Otho and Ottobon. They relate more particularly to pluralities, the enforcement of clerical celibacy, the farming of benefices, and the procedure of courts christian. The practice of sending legates *a latere* was resented by the English archbishops, who claimed for themselves ·the exclusive exercise of legatine authority in the English Church. The attitude of the Crown on the subject was fluctuating. Henry I. obtained from Calixtus II. a promise that no legate should be sent to England without the royal assent. But the promise was broken even by the Pope who gave it ; and although Henry I. claimed the right of excluding uninvited legates, it was rarely exercised either in his time or afterwards. Legates were occasionally invited for political purposes by John, by Henry III., and even by Edward I. Of those who interfered in political affairs the most important are : Gualo (1216-18), who was sent to check the invasion of England by the French Prince Louis, and remained as guardian of the infant Henry III. : Pandulf (*q.v.*) (1218-21), who claimed supreme power in the Regency, till recalled at the request of Stephen Langton; and Ottobuoni (1265-8), who mediated between Henry III. and the defeated Montfortians. Of English legates the most remarkable is Cardinal Wolsey (*q.v.*) who was created *legatus a latere* jointly with Campeggio (*q.v.*) in 1518 to preach a crusade, but was continued in the office, from 1519 onwards, with large powers for the visitation of the monasteries. In 1554 Cardinal Pole (*q.v.*) came to England as legate to effect the reconciliation of the English Church with Rome, and remained to direct Mary's policy. His special commission was cancelled in 1557 by Paul IV., though he was allowed, as Archbishop of Canterbury, to retain the rank of *legatus natus.* The Archbishop of Canterbury still retains a fragment of his legatine power in his right to grant degrees, such degrees being—before the breach with Rome—degrees in the University attached to the papal court.

[H. W. C. D.]

Stubbs, *C.H.*, xix. ; G. Phillips, *Kirchenrecht*, vol. vi.

LEGH, Sir Thomas (d. 1545), probably a member of the Cheshire family of Legh, was one of the two principal agents in the visitation of the monasteries [MONASTERIES, SUPPRESSION OF]. He became an advocate in 1531, and went as ambassador to Denmark, 1532, when he was described by Chapuys as

'a doctor of low quality.' In 1535 Layton (*q.v.*) wrote to Cromwell to ask that he and Legh might be appointed to visit the northern monasteries ; he was first sent with John ap Rice to Worcester, Malvern, and other places in the west and south. He wrote to Cromwell to complain of Layton's leniency, but was himself complained of by ap Rice, who declared ' that he was too insolent and pompatique ' ; ' handleth the fathers very roughly,' was ' satrapique,' of intolerable elation of mind, and extortionate in his pecuniary exactions. He wished this information to be kept secret from Legh, as otherwise he feared ' irrecoverable harm from Legh's rufflers and serving men.'

Legh then made a visitation in the eastern counties, joined Layton at Lichfield, and accompanied him on his northern tour. He was so unpopular in the north that his cook was hanged, as he was out of reach himself. The plan of action was to extort confessions when possible ; failing that to accept any report adverse to the monks without allowing time for investigation, and to make the conditions of life as odious as possible by enforcing obsolete statutes, by pecuniary exactions, and in other ways to persuade the religious that their wisest course was to surrender their house. For the province of York and the diocese of Coventry and Lichfield Legh and his colleagues made up a list of enormities of appalling foulness. No credence can be placed in these ' comperts.' Many of the houses, painted most blackly, were afterwards well reported on by the neighbouring gentry, and in the Act for suppressing the smaller monasteries (27 Hen. VIII. c. 28) the preamble expressly thanks God that in the larger houses religion was ' right well kept and observed.' When the preamble was drawn up the King and his advisers possibly had before them the ' comperts ' in which the larger monasteries are traduced as well as the small.

Legh became rich by the acquisition of monastic and other Church property, was knighted in 1544, and died, 1545. He seems to have been a greedy, unscrupulous man, subservient to his employers, and was ' one of the vilest instruments that Henry ever used ' (Dixon).

[C. P. S. C.]

For authorities see LAYTON.

LICHFIELD, See of, represents the seventh-century Mercian see, which has sometimes been thought to be a survival of a British see. Peada, sub-King of the Middle Angles, was baptized, 653, by Bishop Finan of Lindisfarne, who in 656 consecrated Diuma, an

Irishman, Bishop of the Middle Angles. He was followed by several bishops of Scotic consecration, but the diocese reveres the name and memory of St. Chad (*q.v.*), who made Lichfield his episcopal see. It was now conterminous with the kingdom of Mercia, covering practically the whole of the Midlands from the Humber to the Wye, and stretching south nearly to London. Under Bishop Seaxwulf this huge area was divided and sees were formed, at Lichfield for the Mercians, Leicester for the Middle Angles, Sidnacester for Lindsey, Worcester for the Hwiccians, Hereford for the Hecanas, and possibly also Dorchester for the South Angles. Bishops Headda and Ealdwine held Lichfield and Leicester together, but from about 737 they were again separated.

Offa (757-796) raised the Mercian kingdom to the height of its power. He took advantage of his overlordship to constitute Lichfield an archiepiscopal see. At the Synod of Cealchythe (Chelsea, near Leighton Buzzard) in 785 Jaenbyrht of Canterbury was forced to give up some portion of his province. Offa was supported by Pope Adrian I., and Hygebeorht was appointed by Offa. Adrian, fearing that Offa would set up a rival papacy, perhaps at Canterbury, acceded to Offa's request, thus flattering the pride of Lichfield, which could never be looked on as a rival to Rome, and at the same time humbling that of Canterbury. Hygebeorht signs as archbishop several times between 786 and 801.

Offa and Ecgferth, his son and successor, died in 796. Coenwulf, a distant cousin, succeeded (796-821). He decided on the advice of his bishops to restore the see of Canterbury to its former dignity. Alcuin in a letter to Aethelheard, Archbishop of Canterbury, in 797 begs that Hygebeorht of Lichfield be not deprived of his pall during his lifetime, but says that the consecration of bishops must come back to the holy and primatial see.

The diocese of Lichfield now embraced roughly Staffordshire, Cheshire, Lancashire, Shropshire, Warwickshire, and Derbyshire. The see was removed from Lichfield to Chester by Bishop Peter in 1075. His successor, Robert de Limesey, removed it to Coventry in 1095. The bishops held the title sometimes of Chester, sometimes of Coventry, and later of Coventry and Lichfield. But Lichfield seems to have been throughout the real centre of episcopal life and work. In 1541 the bishopric of Chester (*q.v.*) was formed, and the county and archdeaconry of that name taken from Lichfield. At the Restoration, Bishop Hacket took the title

Lichfield and Coventry. By Order in Council, 22nd December 1836, the archdeaconry of Coventry, covering the greater part of Warwickshire, was cut off and given to Worcester. Bishop Butler and his successors have been Bishops of Lichfield. By Order in Council, 19th December 1846, the deanery of Bridgnorth was added to Hereford. The archdeaconry of Derby was separated in 1884 to form part of the new diocese of Southwell (*q.v.*). The diocese contains 1,174,196 acres, and has a population of 1,222,312. It is divided into the archdeaconries of Stafford (first mentioned, *c.* 1135), Salop (first mentioned, 1083), and Stoke (created 1877). A bishop suffragan of Shrewsbury was consecrated in 1537 under 26 Hen. VIII. c. 14, but did not work in the diocese. There was a suffragan with the same title, 1888-1905, and since 1909 there has been a bishop suffragan of Stafford.

The revenue of the see in 1182 was £165 (W. Salt, *Coll.*, i. 109-10); the *Taxatio* of 1291 estimates it at £349, 2s. 10d. In 1468 it was £984. 13s. 1¾d. The *Valor Ecclesiasticus*, 1534, estimates it at £703, 5s. 2d. Ecton (1711) gives the value as £559. 17s. 3½d. In 1806 it was £559, 17s. 3d., and by the Ecclesiastical Commissioners it has been fixed at £4200.

Bishop Aethelwald is said to have instituted a body of twenty secular canons at Lichfield in 822. The number of prebends was increased in the twelfth and thirteenth centuries to thirty-one, of which two were suspended by the Cathedrals Act, 1840 (3-4 Vic. c. 113), since when there have been four canons residentiary, three of whom hold the offices of precentor (which dates from the twelfth century), treasurer (first mentioned, 1140), and chancellor (first mentioned, 1223).

The church traditionally ascribed to Jaruman, and dedicated by Headda, 700, was probably that of St. Peter, to which the body of St. Chad was translated before 731. No trace of it remains, but the foundations of the Norman cathedral of the eleventh and twelfth centuries still exist. The present cathedral, dedicated to St. Mary and St. Chad, is Early English and Early Decorated, and dates chiefly from the thirteenth century. Its warm, soft colour is due to the New Red Sandstone of the Hopwas and Lichfield quarries. The western spire was built, *c.* 1350. The cathedral was wrecked by the Puritans, 1643; restored by Bishop Hacket, who built the central spire; and was reconsecrated, 24th December 1669. It was restored, 1788-1822, and under Sir Gilbert Scott in the second half of the nineteenth century.

LIST OF BISHOPS

1. Diuma, 656; cons. by Finan of Lindisfarne; d. 658.
2. Ceollach, c. 658; Irish; cons. by Finan; returned to Iona.
3. Trumhere, c. 658; akin to royal house of Deira; cons. by Irish bishops; probably withdrew in 659.
4. Jaruman, 662; built church in the Close, 666; sent at head of a mission to Essex to restore Christianity; d. 667.
5. Ceadda (St. Chad) (*q.v.*), 669.
6. Wynfrith, 672; deacon to St. Chad; dep. by Theodore, 675.
7. Seaxwulf, 675; first Abbot of Peterborough, c. 664-675; encouraged growth of monasticism; d. 691.
8. Headda, c. 691; dedicated cathedral of Lichfield, 700.
9. Ealdwine (Wor), c. 721 (? 715); d. 737.
10. Hwitta, 737.   11. Hemele, 752.
12. Cuthfrith, 765.
13. Beorhthun, c. 768. Kent recovered by Offa in 775; this led to overshadowing of the see of Canterbury.
14. Hygeberht, 779; Bishop of Lichfield, 779-785; Archbishop, 785-c. 802.
15. Ealdwulf, c. 803; by consent of King and by authority of Leo III. renounced archiepiscopate, and at Synod of Clovesho, 803, signed as Bishop of Lichfield.
16. Herewine, c. 815.
17. Aethelwald, 818; in 822 instituted the canons of Lichfield under the provost, Hwitta; eleven priests and nine deacons; d. 828.
18. Hunbeorht, 828.   20. Tunbeorht, c. 843.
19. Cyneheorht, c. 833. 21. Eadbeald,[1] c. 860.
22. Eadbeorht,[1] c. 869. The silence of the register tells of the wreckage wrought by the Danes.
23. Wulfred,[1] c. 877. In 878 Aelfred made Aethelred caldorman of the Mercians. Wulfred probably made bishop at same time. Mercia alone preserved remains of old learning. In 895 the Danes crossed Mercia to Chester.
24. Wigmund,[1] c. 895.
25. Aelfwine (Ella), c. 910. The succession in the lists recovered.
26. Aelfgar (Wulfgar), c. 937.
27. Cynesige, 949. This may have been the occasion of the gift or recovery of the Codex of St. Chad's Gospel to the cathedral of Lichfield. The note on the title-page reads: 'Kynsy (or Wynsy) Praesul.' The title 'Praesul' is not usual. It may have been assumed

[1] Not in old episcopal lists.

by Cynesige in connection with the recovery of Mercian independence.
28. Wynsige, c. 963.   30. Godwine, c. 1003.
29. Aelfheah, 973.   31. Leofgar, 1020.
32. Beorhtmaer, 1026; d. 1039.
33. Wulfsige, 1039. In 1043 the nuns turned out of Coventry and monks established under Abbot Leofwine; d. 1053.
34. Leofwine, 1053; Abbot of Coventry, 1043-1053; cons. abroad; d. 1067. See vacant, 1067-1072. Staffordshire in rebellion in 1069. William wasted the country. In 1070 he built castles at Stafford and Chester. [The bishops from 973 to 1067 appear from their names to be related to the Mercian houses.]
35. Peter, 1072; cons. by Lanfranc; removed see to Chester, 1075, partly from wasted condition of Staffordshire, partly for safety.
36. Robert de Limesey, 1085; chaplain to William I.; removed see to Coventry, 1102; d. 1117. See vacant till 1121.
37. Robert Peche, 1121; chaplain to Henry I.; began work of restoration at Lichfield; d. 1127. See vacant, 1127-1129. Farmed during vacancy by Geoffrey de Clinton, the Chancellor.
38. Roger de Clinton, 1129; nephew of Geoffrey de Clinton; ordained priest, 21st December 1129; cons., 22nd December 1129, by Archbishop William; encouraged foundation of religious houses, and himself founded Benedictine nunnery at Farewell in 1140, and Cistercian house at Buildwas in 1135; restored the cathedral at Lichfield, increased the number of prebends, fortified the castle, and entrenched the city; he took the cross in 1147, and d. at Antioch in 1148. [The three bishops from 1085 to 1148 were all chosen from the families of Mercian landowners.]
39. Walter Durdent, 1149. The King granted right of election for first time to monks of Coventry and canons of Lichfield. They failed to agree, and King appointed Walter Durdent Prior of Canterbury; d. 1159. See vacant till 1161.
40. Richard Peche, 1161; son of thirty-seventh bishop; Archdeacon of Chester, 1125; Archdeacon of Coventry, 1126-1161; elected by chapters of Coventry and Lichfield; increased endowment of deanery and community of Lichfield; founded St. Thomas's, Stafford; retired there on pension, Michaelmas, 1182; d. 6th October 1182. Thomas Noel held rents during vacancy.

41. Gerard la Pucelle, 1183; chaplain and legal adviser to Richard, Archbishop of Canterbury: Canon of St. Thomas's, Stafford: elected by chapters of Coventry and Lichfield; d. at Lichfield, perhaps by poison, 13th January 1184.

42. Hugo de Nonant, 1188; nominated, January 1185: received temporalities, 1184; cons. 1188: expelled monks from Coventry, 1190; Sheriff of Staffordshire, 1190-1194; forfeited temporalities, c. 1196; monks of Coventry restored, 1197; d. 1198.

43. Geoffrey de Muschamp, 1198: Archdeacon of Cleveland, 1194-1198; elected by chapters of Coventry and Lichfield on nomination of Archbishop Hubert; d. 1208; buried during interdict. See vacant, 1208-1214.

44. William de Cornhill, 1215; disputed election: monks of Coventry elected Prior Josbert, 1208; canons of Lichfield elected Walter de Gray, 1210; Pandulf (*q.v.*) cancelled both, and by his advice both chapters elected William de Cornhill Archdeacon of Huntingdon; appointed receiver of forfeited church property in 1208; royal assent, 6th August 1214: cons. at Reading, 25th January 1215; gave canons of Lichfield right to elect dean; d. 1223.

45. Alexander de Stavenby, 1224 (P.); provided by Honorius III. on appeal after disputed election: ordained priest, Easter Eve, 1224; cons. at Rome, Easter Day, 14th April 1224; in 1228 Gregory IX. ordered that elections should be made by the united chapters at Coventry and Lichfield alternately; restored and endowed church at Lichfield; founded Franciscan house at Lichfield; d. 1238.

46. Hugh de Pateshull, 1240; Canon of St. Paul's; Clerk of the Exchequer; Treasurer of England, 1234; d. 1241.

47. Roger de Weseham, 1245 (P.); Dean of Lincoln; provided by Innocent IV. on nomination of Grosseteste (*q.v.*); monks of Coventry and canons of Lichfield agreed in 1255 that the greater chapter for election of bishop consist of equal number from each chapter; res. 1256; d. 1257.

48. Roger de Meyland (Longespee), 1258: son of William of Longespee, Earl of Salisbury; Canon of Lichfield: ignorant of English, and lived abroad; admonished by Archbishop Peckham (*q.v.*) to reside, 1282: in 1284 Archdeacon of Derby made coadjutor; d. 1295.

49. Walter de Langton, 1296; Dean of Bruges; Canon of Lichfield; Treasurer of England, 1295-1307; trusted counsellor of Edward I.: on an embassy when elected: imprisoned under Edward II.: built new palace in the Close, made shrine for St. Chad, rebuilt Eccleshall Castle; paved streets of Lichfield; d. 1321.

50. Roger de Norbury, 1322 (P.); Canon of Lincoln, 1316; Chancellor of Cambridge University, 1321; Treasurer of England, 1327; tr. body of Bishop Langton to tomb on south of altar; d. 1359.

51. Robert de Stretton, 1360; chaplain to Black Prince; became blind in 1384; restored shrine of St. Chad; d. 1385.

52. Walter Skirlaw, 1386 (P.); tr. to Bath, 1386.

53. Richard Scrope (*q.v.*), 1386 (P.); tr. to York, 1398; buried at Lichfield.

54. John Brughill, 1398; tr. (P.) from Llandaff; Dominican confessor to Richard II.; enthroned at Lichfield, 8th September 1398; Richard II. present, and held a feast in bishop's palace; by his will house built for the chantry priests; d. 1414.

55. John Catterick, 1415; tr. (P.) from St. David's; tr. to Exeter, 1419; one of thirty electors of Martin V. in Council of Constance, 11th November 1417.

56. William Heyworth, 1420 (P.); Abbot of St. Alban's; gave land in Bacon Street to sacrists and St. Mary's Guild in city for the rent of a rose on Midsummer Day; this the old foundation of Milley's Hospital; d. 1446.

57. William Booth, 1447 (P.); tr. to York, 1452.

58. Nicolas Close, 1452; tr. (P.) from Carlisle; Chancellor of Cambridge University, 1450; d. 1452.

59. Reginald Bolars, 1453; tr. (P.) from Hereford; d. 1459.

60. John Hales, 1459; Provost of Oriel, 1446; built canons' houses in west of Close; gathered round him a group of great men: Thomas Heywood, builder of the library, dean, 1457-1492; John Morton (*q.v.*), Archbishop of Canterbury, Archdeacon of Chester, 1474-1478; Nicolas West, Bishop of Ely, Archdeacon of Derby, 1486-1515; d. 1490. See vacant, 1491-1492.

61. William Smith, 1493 (P.); tr. to Lincoln, 1495; Dean of Chapel Royal, St. Stephen's, Westminster: founded Grammar School at Lichfield, 1495.

62. John Arundel, 1496 (P.); tr. to Exeter, 1502.

63. Geoffrey Blythe, 1503 (P.); Dean of York, 1498; President of Council of Wales, 1512; opened aqueduct in Close; d. 1533.
64. Rowland Lee, 1534; comm.-gen. to Wolsey in Visitation of 1529; President of Council of Wales, 1534-1543; in 1539 shrine of St. Chad granted to use of cathedral church; failed to save cathedral priory of Coventry from destruction; d. 1543.
65. Richard Sampson. 1543: tr. from Chichester; President of Council of Wales, 1543-1548; conservative in church matters; d. 1554.
66. Ralph Bayne, 1554; repaired cathedral; refused oath to Elizabeth; depr. 1559; d. at Islington. 1559.
67. Thomas Bentham. 1559; had been in exile in Zurich and Basel; d. 1579.
68. William Overton, 1580; d. 1609.
69. George Abbot (*q.v.*), 1609; tr. to London. 1610.
70. Richard Neile, 1610; tr. from Rochester; tr. to Lincoln, 1613.
71. John Overall (*q.v.*), 1614; tr. to Norwich. 1618.
72. Thomas Morton. 1619; tr. from Chester; tr. to Durham, 1632.
73. Robert Wright, 1632; tr. from Bristol; first Warden of Wadham College, Oxford; committed to the Tower, 1641; held Eccleshall Castle for the King, 1642; d. 1643.
74. Accepted Frewen, 1644; tr. to York, 1660.
75. John Hacket (*q.v.*), 1661; d. 1670.
76. Thomas Wood, 1671; Dean of Lichfield, 1664-1671; excommunicated by Bishop Hacket, 1667; suspended for non-residence and scandalous living, 1685; the bishop's palace built as fine for waste of revenues; left £20,000 for hospital for old men, and £14,000 to Oxford University: retired to Astrop-Wells, 1690; d. 1692, aged 85.
77. William Lloyd. 1692; tr. to Worcester, 1699.
78. John Hough, 1699; tr. from Oxford; tr. to Worcester, 1717.
79. Edward Chandler, 1717; tr. to Durham, 1730.
80. Richard Smalbrooke, 1731; tr. from St. David's; charge of, 1746: 'Methodism akin to Romanism'; d. 1749.
81. The Honble. Frederick Cornwallis, 1750; Dean of St. Paul's, 1766-1768; tr. to Canterbury, 1768.
82. John Egerton, 1768; tr. from Bangor; tr. to Durham, 1771.

83. Brownlow North, 1771; tr. to Winchester, 1774.
84. Richard Hurd, 1775; tr. to Worcester. 1781.
85. James, fourth Earl Cornwallis, 1781; Fellow of Merton College, Oxford; Dean of Canterbury, 1775; of Windsor, 1791; of Durham, 1794; d. 1824.
86. Henry Ryder. 1824; tr. from Gloucester; the first Evangelical to receive an English bishopric; great promoter of church work and church building in the diocese; d. 1836.
87. Samuel Butler, 1836; Headmaster of Shrewsbury School, 1798-1836; he carried forward Bishop Ryder's work of organisation; received the title of Bishop of Lichfield; d. 1839.
88. James Bowstead, 1840; tr. from Sodor and Man; fostered Bishop Ryder's work of church extension; drew up rules for rural deans; d. 1843.
89. John Lonsdale, 1843; Canon of St. Paul's; Provost of Eton; Principal of King's College, London; Archdeacon of Middlesex; Theological College at Lichfield founded, 1857; churches restored; the last bishop to reside at Eccleshall Castle; d. 1867.
90. George Augustus Selwyn (*q.v.*), 1867; tr. from New Zealand; d. 1878.
91. William Dalrymple Maclagan, 1878; tr. to York, 1891.
92. Honble. Augustus Legge, 1891; Vicar of Lewisham, 1879.			[T. B.]

Thomas of Chesterfield. *c.* 1350: Harwood. *Hist. and Antiquities of Lichfield*; Beresford, *Dio. Hist.*; Stubbs. *Registrum.*

LIDDON, Henry Parry (1829-90), divine, son of a captain in the Royal Navy, was educated at King's College School, London (where, as his contemporaries remarked, he never was the least like a schoolboy, but was studious, grave, thoughtful, and devout). At Christ Church, Oxford, where he matriculated, June 1846, he was as unlike the ordinary undergraduate as he had been unlike the ordinary schoolboy. He led a secluded and studious life with a handful of like-minded companions, and fell early under the influence of Dr. Pusey (*q.v.*). His early training had been Evangelical; but now he adopted the Catholic position eagerly, and began to regulate his life in accordance with its rules. In 1850, being only twenty-one, and having to compete with men nearly two years his seniors, he gained a Second Class in *Lit. Hum.* In 1851 he was Johnson Theological Scholar. In 1852 he started for Italy, where he was presented to Pope Pius IX., and was plied with all manner of Roman arguments and appeals; but his confidence in the English Church remained unshaken. As Lord Acton said of him in after years, 'he tried and rejected the claim of Rome.' He returned to England in November, and after discussing with Bishop S. Wilberforce (q.v.) the admitted difficulties of Anglicanism, he determined to be ordained without delay. He was made a deacon on the 19th of December 1852, and priest a year later. At first he attempted to work at Wantage, under W. J. Butler; but his health was not strong enough for parochial work, and in 1854 he accepted from Bishop Wilberforce the office of Vice-Principal of Cuddesdon College. [THEOLOGICAL COLLEGES.] There he was exactly in his element, devoting all his fine gifts of spirituality, knowledge, and eloquence to the task of preparing men for the responsibilities of the priesthood. But in 1858 a sudden storm of Protestant misrepresentation burst upon the college. The bishop was frightened by the outcry, and feared that it might damage the institution which he had founded and tended with so much care. Furthermore, he was conscious that there were differences between himself and Liddon on the matter of Eucharistic adoration and the expedient limits of confession, and he 'came with a torn heart to the conclusion' that Liddon must go. So in 1859 Liddon accepted the post of Vice-Principal of St. Edmund Hall, Oxford, and went into residence there in May 1859. His prime care was for the undergraduates of the Hall, many of whom were preparing for holy orders; but his lectures on Sunday evenings were open to all, and very largely attended. His unique powers of preaching were winning general recognition. His sermons were then extempore, extremely long, and elaborately rhetorical. It was obvious that he had studied French models, but the substance of his teaching was what it remained to the end—the Catholic doctrines of sin and repentance, the Church, the Creed, and the Sacraments, as these reach us through the formularies of the English Church. His first book of sermons, called originally *Some Words for God*, but afterwards *University Sermons, Series I.*, was published in 1865.

Liddon resigned the Vice-Principalship of St. Edmund Hall, 1862, and returned to his rooms in 'Tom Quad,' Christ Church, which he retained to his death. Here he passed, even more completely, under the influence of Dr. Pusey. He became examining chaplain to Bishop Hamilton of Salisbury, who made him a prebendary of his cathedral. He under-

took to write a commentary on the book of Leviticus. He helped Bishop Wilberforce in his diocesan missions, he was in great request as a confessor and guide of souls, and he constantly preached at St. Paul's and other London churches. He was appointed at short notice (on the breakdown of A. W. Haddan) to deliver the Bampton Lectures for 1866, and he chose a subject on which he had long thought and reasoned and studied with intense devotion. When the time for delivery came, the lecturer attained the great triumph of his life. The overflowing audiences that heard the lectures, and the wider world outside that read them, now knew that Liddon was the foremost preacher in the English Church, and *The Divinity of our Lord and Saviour Jesus Christ* became a standard work of English theology.

In 1868 Liddon was urged to accept, but finally declined, the Warden-ship of the newly-founded Keble College. In Lent, 1870, he delivered before vast and brilliant congregations at St. James's, Piccadilly, the lectures afterwards published as *Some Elements of Religion*. During the course he was appointed by Mr. Gladstone (q.v.) Canon of St. Paul's, and four months later he was chosen Ireland Professor of Exegesis at Oxford. He was made D.C.L. by Lord Salisbury at the Encaenia of 1870, and became D.D. in the following November.

From this time Liddon's life was almost wholly devoid of incident. Providence had placed him exactly where his singular gifts could be used to the best advantage: he was untrammelled by the duties of executive office, and he remained till the end of his life the chief teacher of the English Church. His power was certainly enhanced, rather than diminished, by the fact that he declined the deanery of Salisbury in 1885, and the bishopric of Edinburgh, to which he was elected in 1886, and refused to be nominated by Lord Salisbury to the see of St. Albans in 1890.

His year was divided between London and Oxford. In both places he was the inspiring preacher and the discreet guide of souls. Every now and then some crisis in the affairs of the Church forced him into prominence of a kind very distasteful to his feelings. He had no love of controversy, but he realised that it is sometimes a duty which cannot be shirked. The 'Purchas Judgment' [RITUAL CASES] of 1871, which prohibited among other things the Eastward Position at the altar, forced Liddon into the disagreeable position of defying his diocesan in his own cathedral. In 1872 the attack on the

Athanasian Creed, fomented by Archbishop Tait (*q.v.*), was repelled in great measure by Liddon's efforts. In 1876 he took a prominent part in opposing Lord Beaconsfield's policy, which aimed at making England the champion of the Turkish power. The prosecutions under the ill-starred Public Worship Regulation Act (*q.v.*) of 1874 prompted the sermons on *Church Troubles* which he preached at St. Paul's in Advent, 1880. In the last year of his life the surrender to Rationalism which he thought he detected in some portions of a book called *Lux Mundi* wrung from him some pathetic protests. The *Life of Dr. Pusey*, which he undertook in 1882 and left unfinished, was a burden too great for his physical resources. He declined in health and vigour, and died (after a terribly painful illness connected with the spine) on 9th September 1890. He is buried in the crypt of St. Paul's Cathedral.

[G. W. E. R.]

Personal recollections: Johnston, *Life and Letters*: G. W. E. Russell, *Life*.

LIGHTFOOT, Joseph Barber (1828-89), Bishop of Durham, was born at Liverpool, and educated at the Royal Institution, Liverpool; King Edward's School, Birmingham (under Prince Lee); and Trinity College, Cambridge (scholar, 1849; senior classic and thirtieth wrangler, 1851; Fellow, 1852; Tutor, 1857). He was ordained deacon, 1854, and priest, 1858, by Prince Lee, then Bishop of Manchester; was Hulsean Professor at Cambridge (*vice* Ellicott), 1861-75; and Lady Margaret Reader (*vice* Selwyn), 1875-9; Canon of St. Paul's, 1871-9; member of the New Testament Revision Company, 1870-80, and of the Universities Commission, 1877-81; Bishop of Durham, 1879-89.

Bishop Lightfoot belongs to the small company of Fathers and scholars whose learning, illuminated by spiritual and critical insight, makes their work a possession not for one century or country but for all. That work was done in two distinct but closely related fields—Biblical and patristic. Within the former fall the commentaries on Galatians (1865), Philippians (1868), and Colossians (1875), with the articles on Acts, Romans, and Thessalonians in Smith's *Dict. Bible*, and the essays reprinted in *Biblical Essays* (1893) and *The Apostolic Age* (1892). To him belongs the credit of bringing home to English students the fact that St. Paul was not an imperfect writer of a debased form of Greek but a master of a living language. Lightfoot's profound learning and 'matchless lucidity of exposi-

tion' ensure that although scholars may not always adopt his conclusions, they will not need to reconstruct the foundations on which these are based. Thus the commentary on Galatians retains its value even for those who accept Sir W. M. Ramsay's arguments for the South Galatian theory. His study for a 'Fresh Revision of the English New Testament' (1871, 1881) is a powerful plea for the work of revision in which he shared. The most keenly debated of his writings, the essay on *The Christian Ministry*, must be studied for itself apart from the inferences and representations of those for whom it says too much or too little.

His patristic works on the Apostolic Fathers—St. Clement of Rome (1869; appendix, 1877; 2nd edit., 1890), St. Ignatius and St. Polycarp (1885; 2nd edit., 1889)—are books from which the student may gain a deeper insight into a scholar's methods of collecting and testing evidence and building surely upon it than from almost any others of the kind. It was this critical and constructive faculty which gave crushing force to the 'examination' (*Contemp. Review*, 1874, 1877; republished, 1889) of Mr. Cassel's anonymous work, entitled *Supernatural Religion*. To the same class belongs the article on 'Eusebius' in *Dict. Christ. Biog.*

Though outwardly shy and undemonstrative, Dr. Lightfoot excited not only veneration but enthusiasm in those who worked with him. His episcopate was marked by the creation of the see of Newcastle (*q.v.*) (1881-2) and an enormous scheme of Church extension (1884 onwards), the division of the archdeaconry of Durham (May 1882), the institution of a canon missioner, the foundation of the White Cross movement (1883), and the gathering round him at Auckland of a body of young graduates, whom he influenced in their training for orders to a remarkable degree. Of his four volumes of sermons, *Leaders of the Northern Church* (1890) is the best known.

[C. J.]

Article 'Bishop Lightfoot' (attributed to Archdeacon Watkins), 1894, reprinted from the *Quarterly Review*: A. Harnack in *Theol. Literaturzeitung*, 14th June 1890; F. J. A. Hort in *D.N.B.*; A. C. Benson, *The Leaves of the Tree*.

LINCOLN, See of. The origin of the bishopric is to be found in Lindsey, a district more or less represented by the present county, where Paulinus (*q.v.*) preached. A separate bishopric was founded for the Lindisfari in 678, the first bishop being Eadhed. A bishopric for the Middle

Anglians was founded at Leicester, and Cuthwin was consecrated to it in 680; and Dorchester having become Mercian (Winchester taking its place as a West Saxon see), the diocese extended to the Thames. In 705 it was united with Lichfield (*q.v.*), but was sundered from it in 737. On the Danish conquest of Mercia, 874, the Bishop of Leicester, Alcheard, fled to Dorchester, and died there in 897, and thus Dorchester became the see of a bishopric which represented the ancient bishoprics of Lindsey and Leicester, and so remained until Bishop Remigius removed his see to Lincoln about 1075.

In 1075 the diocese stretched from the Humber to the Thames, and included roughly the present counties of Lincoln, Leicester, Cambridge, Northampton, Rutland, Huntingdon, Bedford, Buckingham, Oxford, and part of Herts. In 1109 Cambridgeshire was taken from it for the newly founded see of Ely (*q.v.*). In 1541 the establishment of the see of Peterborough (*q.v.*) relieved it of Northamptonshire and Rutland. In 1542 Oxfordshire was put under the new see of Oxford (*q.v.*), and in 1550 the archdeaconry of St. Albans was added to London. In 1837 Bucks was added to Oxford and Leicestershire to Peterborough, in 1837-9 Bedford and Huntingdon to Ely, and in 1845 the portions of Herts still remaining in Lincoln to Rochester. Nottinghamshire, however, except the deanery of Southwell, was transferred from York to Lincoln in 1837, and in 1844 the deanery of Southwell was also added. In 1884, however, Nottinghamshire passed to the new see of Southwell (*q.v.*). With trifling exceptions, the diocese is now (1912) conterminous with the county.

The *Taxatio* of Nicholas IV., 1291, estimates the total value of the bishopric from temporalities and spiritualities at £1000. In the *Valor Ecclesiasticus*, 1534, the net sum of both sources of income is put at £2095, 12s. 5d. Under Edward VI., owing to alienations, it had sunk to £828, 4s. 9d., which is the sum given by Ecton (1711). The income of the see since the foundation of the diocese of Southwell has been £4500.

Bishop Remigius in 1092 created seven archdeaconries; the eighth, that of Stow, seems to have been founded by Bishop Alexander in 1123. The present diocese contains two archdeaconries, Lincoln and Stow, the boundaries of which were rearranged by Orders in Council, 1876 and 1877. The acreage of the diocese (1,775,457) is exceeded only by that of Norwich and St. David's. There are five hundred and sixty benefices.

The population is 564,013. The cathedral church is governed by a chapter, founded by Bishop Remigius in 1092. The constitution was that of Rouen, imitating Bayeux. In its primitive form it consisted of a dean, precentor, chancellor, and treasurer. To these a sub-dean was added in 1145. There were fifty-two prebends. When the treasure was seized by Henry VIII., June 1540, the office of treasurer ceased, and the four residentiaries from that time consisted of the dean and the three remaining officers. By 1660 five prebends had been dissolved and four had lapsed.

BISHOPS OF LINDSEY

1. Eadhed, 678; retired to Ripon on the conquest of Lindsey by the Mercians.
2. Aethelwin, 680; see at Sidnacester (Stow): had studied in Ireland; ruled well.
3. Eadgar, ? 706.   6. Eadulf, 750.
4. Cyneberht, d. 732.   7. Ceolwulf, 767.
5. Alwig, 733.   8. Eadulf, 796.
9. Berhtred, ? 838.
10. Leofwine, ? 953; also Bishop of Dorchester.
11. Sigeferth, ? 997.

The diocese seems then to have been merged in Dorchester.

BISHOPS OF LEICESTER AND DORCHESTER

1. Cuthwine, 680.
2. Wilfrid; administered, 692-705. [702-35 the see was joined to Lichfield.]
3. Torthelm, 737.   6. Werenberht, 802.
4. Eadberht, 764.   7. Hrethun, 816.
5. Unwona, ? 786.   8. Aldred.
9. Ceolred, 840.
10. Alcheard, d. 897-8; on the Danish conquest of Mercia he had fled to Dorchester, which thus became the see of the bishopric.
11. Ceolwulf, 909.   12. Winsige, ? 926.
13. Oskytel, 950.
14. Leofwine, ? 953; also Bishop of Lindsey.
15. Eadnoth, ? 975.   16. Aescwig, ? 979.
17. Aelghelm, 1002.
18. Eadnoth, 1006; Abbot of Ramsey; slain at the battle of Assandun, 1016.
19. Aethelric, 1016; a wise man; influential with Cnut; d. 1034.
20. Eadnoth, 1034; built the minster at Stow; d. 1050.
21. Ulf, 1050; a Norman; ignorant and unworthy; was expelled, 1052.
22. Wulfwig, 1053; Chancellor to Edward the Confessor; d. 1067.
23. Remigius; a monk of Fécamp; cons. 1067 to Dorchester; moved his see to

Lincoln in accordance with the principle laid down at the Council of London, 1075, of removing episcopal sees from villages to cities; he organised his vast diocese under seven archdeacons, and built a noble cathedral; he is said to have preached zealously and to have denounced the slave-trade; d. 6th May 1090. Miracles were believed to be worked at his tomb.

BISHOPS OF LINCOLN

1. Remigius; see above.
2. Robert Bloett, 1094; Chancellor under the Conqueror and under William II., and Justiciar under Henry I.; he was much engaged in secular affairs, magnificent yet humble, and extremely liberal; in later life he was impoverished by law-suits; d. suddenly, 10th January 1123.
3. Alexander, 1123; nephew of Roger, Bishop of Salisbury; a thoroughly secular prelate; was a great builder of fortresses and religious houses; arrested by King Stephen in 1139 and forced to surrender his castles; d. 1148.
4. Robert de Chesney, 1148; foolish and pliable; is accused of wasting the property of his see; d. 26th December 1166. A vacancy of seventeen years, during which Geoffrey, a natural son of Henry II., was elected, 1173, and held the see without consecration until 1182.
5. Walter of Coutances, 1183; learned and liberal; tr. to Rouen, 1184. A vacancy of two years.
6. Hugh of Avalon, St. (*q.v.*), 1186; d. 1200. A vacancy of two years.
7. William of Blois, 1203; kind-hearted and good; d. 10th May 1206. A vacancy of three years.
8. Hugh of Wells, 1209; cons. at Melun during the interdict; organised his diocese by the institution of vicarages; was a vigorous and strict disciplinarian; d. 1235.
9. Robert Grosseteste (*q.v.*), 1235; d. 1253.
10. Henry of Lexington, 1254; of a baronial family; had a dispute with the University of Oxford as to his jurisdiction over it; d. 1258.
11. Richard of Gravesend, 1258; sided with Simon de Montfort during the barons' war; went to Rome for absolution, and remained abroad several years; he is said to have been praiseworthy, and was certainly liberal; d. 18th December 1279.

12. Oliver Sutton, 1280; of the Lexington family; a liberal benefactor to his church; d. 13th November 1299.
13. John Dalderby, 1300; was learned, pious, eloquent, and extremely liberal in his benefactions; d. 12th January 1320. Miracles were said to have been wrought at his tomb, but the attempt of Edward III. to procure his canonisation failed.
14. Henry Burghersh, 1320 (P.); was nephew of the powerful Lord Badlesmere who, against the will of the chapter and by bribes, procured his appointment by papal provision, though not of canonical age; his temporalities were seized by Edward II. on the defeat of the rebels in 1322, but later the King was reconciled to him, and the bishop disgracefully betrayed him; he was Treasurer in 1327 and Chancellor in 1328, and was much employed by Edward III. in secular business; he was an able, bad man; d. 4th December 1340. His ghost is said to have appeared and to have begged that the canons of Lincoln would deliver him from punishment by making restitution to those whom he had wronged.
15. Thomas Bek, 1342 (P.); elected first by the chapter, but appointed by papal Bull of provision; cons. by Clement VI. at Avignon; was brother of Antony, Bishop of Norwich, and kinsman of Antony Bek, Bishop of Durham, and is described as 'a noble and excellent cleric'; d. 2nd February 1347.
16. John Gynwell, 1347 (P.); laid the town of Oxford under an interdict for the riot on St. Scholastica's Day, 1355; he is said to have obtained from the Pope exemption from metropolitan jurisdiction, and he disinterred and caused to be ill treated the body of one of the King's judges, whom he had in life excommunicated by the Pope's order, and who was buried in a church; d. 1362.
17. John Bokyngham, 1363 (P.); pronounced the Lollard preacher Swynderby a heretic, and received his recantation. Boniface IX. translated him to Lichfield in 1397 in order to make room for Henry Beaufort, alleging, what was doubtless true, that Bokyngham's age and infirmities rendered him unfit to rule so large a diocese; he refused the translation, and retired to Canterbury, where he died in the monastery of Christ Church, 1398.

18. Henry Beaufort (*q.v.*), 1398 (P.); tr. to Winchester, 1405.
19. Philip Repingdon, 1405 (P.); had been a prominent Oxford Lollard, but abjured his heresies, 1382; he became an abbot and the friend and confessor of Henry IV.; as bishop he was prominent in putting down Lollardy; he was made cardinal by Gregory XII.; res. 10th October 1419.
20. Richard Fleming, 1420 (P.); cons. at Florence; had defended Lollard doctrines at Oxford in 1409, but had become orthodox: as bishop he was diligent; he attended the council at Pavia and Siena; tr. by Martin V. to York, but the English council would not allow this, and he had to be translated back again; he began to prepare for the foundation of a college (Lincoln) at Oxford for theologians to combat heresy; d. 1431.
21. William Grey, 1431; tr. (P.) from London; had trouble with the dean, John Mackworth, a quarrelsome man; he refused to allow Pope Eugenius IV. to appoint to the archdeaconry of Northampton; d. February 1436.
22. William Alnwick, 1436; tr. (P.) from Norwich; had been tutor to Henry VI., and advised him in founding Eton and King's Colleges, Cambridge; he was able and of high character; he drew up statutes for his Lincoln chapter, but the dean was still recalcitrant; he built the west front of Norwich Cathedral and a fine addition to the palace at Lincoln; d. 1449.
23. Marmaduke Lumley, 1450; tr. (P.) from Carlisle; had been a member of the Council, and in 1447 Treasurer; was one of the Beaufort party, and owed his translation to the Duke of Suffolk; d. December 1450.
24. John Chedworth, 1452; was active against Lollards, who abounded in his diocese; for the most part they abjured, one at least was burned; d. 1471.
25. Thomas Rotherham, or Scott, 1472; tr. (P.) from Rochester; tr. to York, 1480.
26. John Russell, 1480; tr. (P.) from Rochester; was Chancellor under Richard III., 1483-5, and Chancellor of Oxford, 1483; after years of secular business seems to have resided in his diocese, and is described by Sir Thomas More as wise and good, and one of the best learned men in England; d. 1494.

27. William Smith, 1496; tr. (P.) from Lichfield; was much absorbed in business of state; he was Chancellor of Oxford, 1500-3; was extremely liberal; refounded St. John's Hospital, Lichfield, was a benefactor to Oriel and Lincoln Colleges, and co-founder of Brasenose College, Oxford; he was eager and severe in persecuting heretics, especially in Buckinghamshire; d. 2nd January 1514.
28. Thomas Wolsey (*q.v.*), 1514 (P.); tr. to York, 1514.
29. William Atwater, 1514 (P.); had held a large number of valuable benefices; he was about seventy-four when he was made bishop; d. 1521.
30. John Longlands, 1521 (P.); confessor of Henry VIII.; delighted in Erasmus's New Testament, and was called by Sir Thomas More 'a second Colet'; Chancellor of Oxford, 1532; he forwarded the King's divorce from Katherine of Aragon, upheld the Royal Supremacy, and was declared by the rebels of 1536 to be at the bottom of all the trouble; his suffragan, Abbot Mackarel, was hanged, 1537; he appointed two others; he was averse from change in doctrine, and was severe with heretics; d. 1547.
31. Henry Holbeach, Holbeche, or Rands, 1547; tr. from Rochester; cons. 1538 as suffragan to Worcester with title of Bristol; received see of Rochester, 1544; had been a Benedictine monk; held reformed doctrines, and was married; d. 1551.
32. John Taylor, 1552; had been Master of St. John's College, Cambridge, 1538-46; adopted reformed opinions, and was imprisoned, 1540, but soon retracted, and was released; he was deprived, 1554, and died at the end of that year.
33. John White, 1554 (P.); tr. to Winchester, 1556.
34. Thomas Watson, 1557 (P.); Master of St. John's College, Cambridge; obtained restitution of property of which the see had been despoiled by the Crown under Bishops Holbeach and Taylor; was deprived, 1559, and died in prison, 27th September 1584.
35. Nicholas Bullingham, 1560; tr. to Worcester, 1571, the see of Lincoln being much impoverished.
36. Thomas Cooper, 1571; tr. to Winchester, 1584.
37. William Wickham, 1584; tr. to Winchester, 1595.

38. William Chaderton. 1595: tr. from Chester: had through Cecil's influence been President of Queens' College and Regius Professor of Divinity at Cambridge, where he took a leading part against the Puritans; he owed the bishopric of Chester to Leicester's influence, and was kept constantly employed by the Privy Council in carrying out the law against popish recusants; he continued this work at Lincoln; Nonconformity was strong in the diocese; he seems to have been as conciliatory as was possible for him: d. 1608.
39. William Barlow. 1608; tr. from Rochester: wrote the history of the Savoy Conference, and was one of the translators of the Authorised Version; he was an able preacher and controversialist; as Bishop of Lincoln he was mostly non-resident: d. 7th September 1613.
40. Richard Neill, 1614: tr. from Lichfield; tr. to Durham, 1617.
41. George Monteigne, 1617; tr. to London, 1621.
42. John Williams (q.v.), 1621; tr. to York, 1641.
43. Thomas Winniffe. 1642; was made Dean of St. Paul's, 1631, and retained the deanery after his consecration: in spite of the Civil War he remained at his episcopal residence at Buckden until 1646 when, the episcopal estate being confiscated, he retired to Lambourn, Berks; d. 19th September 1654; learned, eloquent, and modest.
44. Robert Sanderson, 1660; had been Regius Professor of Divinity at Oxford; suffered during the Commonwealth and Protectorate; was extremely liberal in repairing the damage done to his cathedral and the episcopal houses; did not cause Nonconformists unnecessary trouble, and in spite of his great age (he was born 1587) was an excellent bishop; d. 29th January 1663.
45. Benjamin Laney, 1663; tr. from Peterborough; tr. to Ely, 1667.
46. William Fuller, 1667; tr. from Limerick; much liked both by Pepys and Evelyn; had suffered during the Civil War; he took 'great pains' to obtain the see of Lincoln; he had a house in the city in which he resided when he visited his diocese; repaired damage done to the cathedral by Puritans: d. 1675.
47. Thomas Barlow, 1675: retained his Fellowship at Queen's College, Oxford, during the Civil War troubles, and be-

came Provost, 1657; a distinguished scholar and controversialist; was a Calvinist, a Low Churchman, and a trimmer; he neglected his diocese; d. 1691.
48. Thomas Tenison. 1692; tr. to Canterbury, 1695.
49. James Gardiner. 1695; a Low Churchman and a Whig; was diligent and conscientious, fully alive to the deplorable state of his diocese and the negligence of many of the clergy; he laboured to bring matters into better order, but he was lacking in resolution; d. 1st March 1705.
50. William Wake (q.v.), 1705; tr. to Canterbury, 1716.
51. Edmund Gibson (q.v.), 1716; tr. to London, 1723.
52. Richard Reynolds, 1723; tr. from Bangor; was a liberal giver, and is described by Doddridge, the Nonconformist, as 'a valuable person'; d. 1744.
53. John Thomas, 1744; tr. to Salisbury, 1761.
54. John Green, 1761; had been Master of Corpus Christi College and Regius Professor of Divinity at Cambridge; was indolent, kindly, and dignified; d. 25th April 1779.
55. Thomas Thurlow, 1779; tr. to Durham, 1787.
56. George Pretyman Tomline, 1787; tr. to Winchester, 1820.
57. George Pelham, 1820; tr. from Exeter; was greedy for preferment, and a pluralist: d. 7th February 1827.
58. John Kaye, 1827: tr. from Bristol; son of a linen-draper: had been Master of Christ's College and Regius Professor of Divinity at Cambridge; in both his dioceses he was a vigorous reformer of abuses of non-residence, plurality, and clerical carelessness; an Evangelical and an admirable bishop; d. 1853.
59. John Jackson, 1853; tr. to London, 1869.
60. Christopher Wordsworth (q.v.), 1869; d. 1885.
61. Edward King (q.v.), 1885; d. 1910.
62. Edward Lee Hicks, 1910; formerly Fellow and Tutor of Corpus Christi College, Oxford, and Canon of Manchester. [W. H.]

V.C.H. Lincoln; G. G. Perry, *Dio. Hist.*

LIVERPOOL, Diocese of. The south-western part of Lancashire, forming the Hundred of West Derby, was originally in the far-stretching diocese of Lichfield (q.v.)

and Coventry, and in the province of Canterbury. In 1542 it was attached, with the rest of the county, to the new diocese of Chester (*q.v.*), and transferred to the province of York. In 1847 the newly formed diocese of Manchester (*q.v.*) took the greater part of Lancashire, including the ancient parish of Leigh in West Derby Hundred; the rest of the Hundred, together with the ancient parish of Wigan, remained in the diocese of Chester as the archdeaconry of Liverpool. The Bishoprics Act, 1878 (41-2 Vic. c. 68), authorised the erection of the diocese of Liverpool and others. £100,000 was raised by voluntary subscription, and after much less delay than in other cases the diocese of Liverpool was constituted by Order in Council, 30th March 1880, and by Order of 28th June 1880 a second archdeaconry, that of Warrington, was created. The parish church of St. Peter, a building of no spaciousness or dignity, was made the pro-cathedral. A scheme was speedily set on foot for the erection of a new cathedral, on the site of St. George's Church in the heart of the city, but Bishop Ryle (*q.v.*) resolved that the parochial work of the diocese should be thoroughly established before money was collected for such a purpose. Great activity in church building ensued, and simultaneously a successful effort was made to provide suitable endowments for the clergy. In 1904 the erection of a new cathedral was at last begun, a fine site, rather far from the heart of the city, being chosen. Considerable progress has been made with a building of remarkable size and dignity. There is as yet no legally constituted dean and chapter, but twenty-four honorary canons form a provisional chapter.

The area of the diocese is 262,829 acres: the population is 1,352,419. There are 12 deaneries, 217 parishes with 230 churches, served by upwards of 400 clergymen. The bishop's income is £4200.

BISHOPS OF LIVERPOOL

1. John Charles Ryle (*q.v.*), 1880.
2. Francis James Chavasse, 1900: formerly Principal of Wycliffe Hall, Oxford.

[T. A. L.]

LLANDAFF, See of, may be said to have originated with St. Dubricius (Dyfrig) and St. Teilo in the sixth century. The Lucius-Christianising legend, which, in its Welsh form, is confined to a small district round Llandaff, and attributes its foundation to King Lucius, in the latter part of the second

century, is now entirely discredited. The real founder of Llandaff—'the monastery on the Taff'—was St. Teilo (died about 580), and in authentic Welsh records his name is always associated with it. St. Dubricius, who lived a generation earlier, was Abbot of Henllan, and afterwards of Mochros, both on the Wye; but Llandaff may rightly be regarded as originally a subordinate settlement to Henllan, being made by Dubricius's disciple, Teilo. Llandaff rapidly grew in importance through princely favour; and it was not long before the archmonastery absorbed the three great Glamorgan monasteries, Llancarfan, Llanilltyd, and Llandocha. [ABBEYS, WELSH.] The extensive ground it covered with settlements or churches, even outside the present diocese (in St. David's (*q.v.*) and Hereford (*q.v.*)), may be seen from the long list of Teilo churches mentioned in its cartulary, the *Liber Landavensis* (compiled c. 1150). Bishop Urban (1107-33), a great upholder of the rights of Llandaff, revived its old claim to thirty-eight Teilo churches and villages in the diocese of St. David's, but unsuccessfully. In his time the Norman barons appropriated a great deal of the diocesan endowments to English abbeys, especially St. Peter's, Gloucester, and Tewkesbury, an action which, since the dissolution, has greatly crippled the work of this diocese.

The diocese is co-extensive with the ancient kingdom or principality of Morganwg, which included several small principalities that had independent existence at an early period. Some unimportant readjustments of boundaries, affecting St. David's and Hereford, were made by Orders in Council in 1844 and 1846. The diocese comprises to-day the whole of Monmouthshire and all Glamorgan, except the Gower Peninsula; and there are portions of a few parishes in the counties of Hereford and Brecon. It has an area of 868,575 acres and a population of 1,003,460.

The *Taxatio* of 1291 assessed the bishop's *Temporalia*, *i.e.* revenues from land, at £93, 9s. 8d., and the *Spiritualia* at £13, 6s. 8d. The *Valor* of 1535 assessed the income at £154, 14s. 1d. It was fixed by Order in Council in 1846 at £4200.

There is mention of a dean (Esni) in 1120, but until 1840 the bishop was *Quasi-Decanus*, and had the decanal as well as the episcopal stall. The Cathedrals Act, 1840 (3-4 Vic. c. 113), joined the deanery with the archdeaconry of Llandaff. The Welsh Cathedrals Act, 1843 (6-7 Vic. c. 77), separated the offices. There are two archdeaconries: Llandaff (dating from 1107) and Monmouth (created 1844). There are four residentiary canons. two being also archdeacons, each receiving £350 per annum. The cathedral, though of the 'Old Foundation,' was wrested into 'New Foundation' in 1843. The chapter now consists of the dean. treasurer (who is the bishop, dating from 1256), precentor (c. 1400), chancellor (1573), four canons residentiary, and six canons non-residentiary—all in the bishop's patronage, as well as the two minor canons. In 1861 the patronage of a number of livings in the dioceses of St. Asaph (*q.v.*) and Bangor (*q.v.*) was transferred to the Bishop of Llandaff to equalise the number of livings in his gift, previously very few. There are twenty-two rural deaneries.

LIST OF BISHOPS

The supposed and early bishops were :—

1. Dubricius; d. c. 546. 2. Teilo: d. c. 580. 3. Oudoceus; d. c. 620. 4. Berthguin. 5. Trichan. 6. Elvog. 7. Catguaret. 8. Edilbiu. 9. Greciclis. 10. Cerenbir. 11. Nobis. 12. Nud. 13. Cimeilliauc. 872; cons. by Ethelred, Archbishop of Canterbury: d. 927. 14. Libiau ; cons. by Archbishop of Canterbury ; d. 929. 15. Marchluid : d. c. 943. 16. Pater: d. c. 961. 17. Culbrit. 18. Gucaun. 982; cons. by Archbishop of Canterbury. 19. Bledri, 983 ; cons. by Archbishop of Canterbury. 20. Joseph. 1022 ; cons. by Archbishop of Canterbury ; d. 1043 at Rome. 21. Herwald. 1056 : cons. by Archbishop of Canterbury at London : d. 1103.

1. Urban, 1107 ; cons. by Archbishop Anselm (*q.v.*) ; probably a Welshman, but a Norman nominee ; d. 1133, at or on his way to Rome ; an active, energetic bishop : to him Llandaff owes its cathedral. See vacant about six years.
2. Uchtryd, 1140 ; a Welshman ; Archdeacon of Llandaff ; d. 1148.
3. Nicholas ab Gwrgant, 1148 ; was in trouble with three Archbishops of Canterbury ; d. 1183.
4. William Saltmarsh, 1186 ; a Norman ; Prior of St. Augustine's, Bristol ; d. 1191.
5. Henry, Prior of Abergavenny, 1193 ; probably began the reconstruction of the cathedral ; d. 1218.
6. William, Prior of Goldcliff, 1219 (P.); d. 1230.
7. Elias of Radnor, 1230 ; Treasurer of Hereford ; d. 1240.

8. William de Burgh. 1245 ; the diocese greatly despoiled through constant wars; d. 1253, blind.
9. John de la Ware, 1254 ; Abbot of Margam, 1237 ; d. 1256.
10. William of Radnor, 1257 ; Treasurer of Llandaff ; d. 1266.
11. William de Braose, or Bruce, 1266 ; Canon of Llandaff ; d. 1287. See vacant ten years.
12. John of Monmouth, 1297 (P.) ; Canon of Lincoln ; d. 1323.
13. John de Eglesclif, 1323 ; tr. (P.) from Connor ; a Dominican ; d. 1347.
14. John Pascal, 1347 (P.) ; a Carmelite Friar ; learned and eloquent ; d. 1361.
15. Roger Cradock, 1361 ; tr. (P.) from Waterford and Lismore ; a Friar Minor ; d. 1382.
16. Thomas Rushook, 1383 (P.) ; the King's confessor ; tr. to Chichester, 1385.
17. William Bottlesham, or Botosham, 1386 (P.) ; titular Bishop of Bethlehem ; tr. to Rochester, 1389.
18. Edmund Bromfield, 1389 (P.) ; a factious man ; d. 1393.
19. Tideman de Winchcomb, 1393 (P.) ; elected first by the chapter; Abbot of Beaulieu ; tr. to Worcester, 1395.
20. Andrew Barrett, 1395 (P.) ; Prebendary of Lincoln ; d. 1396.
21. John Burghill, 1396 (P.) ; the King's confessor ; tr. to Lichfield, 1398.
22. Thomas Peverell, 1398 ; tr. from Ossory ; tr. to Worcester, 1407.
23. John de la Zouche. 1408 (P.) ; a Friar Minor ; d. 1423. With his appointment translations ceased till 1545.
24. John Wells, 1425 (P.) ; cons. at Rome : d. 1440.
25. Nicholas Ashby, 1441 (P.) ; Prior of Westminster : d. 1458.
26. John Hunden (Houden), 1458 (P.) ; Prior of King's Langley, Herts ; res. 1476.
27. John Smith, 1476 (P.) ; d. 1478.
28. John Marshall, 1478 (P.) ; a benefactor to the cathedral ; d. 1496.
29. John Ingleby, 1496 (P.) ; a Carthusian ; Prior of Shene ; d. 1499.
30. Miles Salley, 1500 (P.) ; Abbot of Eynsham ; greatly improved the episcopal palace at Matherne ; d. 1517.
31. George de Athequa, 1517 (P.) ; a Spanish Dominican ; chaplain of Katherine of Aragon ; res. 1537.
32. Robert Holgate (*q.v.*), 1537 ; a Yorkshireman ; Master of the Gilbertines ; tr. to York. 1545. He had a suffragan, John Bird, who was tr. to Bangor, 1539.

33. Anthony Kitchin (*q.v.*) (Kechyn), *alias* Dunstan, 1545; probably the worst bishop of this diocese; d. 1565.

34. Hugh Jones, 1566; the first Welshman appointed for three hundred years (Godwin); d. 1574.

35. William Blethin, or Griffiths, 1575; Archdeacon of Brecon; issued new statutes; d. 1590.

36. Gervase Babington, 1591; Treasurer of Llandaff; tr. to Exeter, 1595.

37. William Morgan, 1595; tr. to St. Asaph, 1601.

38. Francis Godwin, 1601; sub-Dean of Exeter; tr. to Hereford, 1617.

39. George Carleton, 1618; tr. to Chichester, 1619.

40. Theophilus Field, 1619; tr. to St. David's, 1627.

41. William Murray, 1627; tr. from Kilfenora; d. 1640.

42. Morgan Owen, 1640; a friend of Laud (*q.v.*), one of the bishops impeached and imprisoned for promulgating the canons of 1640; d. 1645. The see vacant for over fifteen years.

43. Hugh Lloyd, 1660; Archdeacon of St. David's; d. 1667.

44. Francis Davies, 1667; Archdeacon of Llandaff; d. 1675.

45. William Lloyd, 1675; tr. to Peterborough, 1679.

46. William Beaw, 1679; d. 1706, aged ninety.

47. John Tylor, 1706; Dean of Hereford; d. 1724.

48. Robert Clavering, 1725; Regius Professor of Hebrew at Oxford; tr. to Peterborough, 1728. The diocese was now at its very lowest point. Rapid translations became common.

49. John Harris, 1729; held the deanery of Hereford, and afterwards of Wells *in commendam*; d. 1738.

50. Matthias Mawson, 1739; tr. to Chichester, 1740.

51. John Gilbert, 1740; Dean of Exeter; tr. to Salisbury, 1748.

52. Edward Cressett, 1749; Dean of Hereford; d. 1755.

53. Richard Newcome, 1755; tr. to St. Asaph, 1761.

54. John Ewer, 1761; tr. to Bangor, 1769.

55. Jonathan Shipley, 1769; tr. to St. Asaph within five months from consecration.

56. Shute Barrington, 1769; tr. to Salisbury, 1782.

57. Richard Watson, 1782; Archdeacon of Ely; d. 1816.

58. Herbert Marsh, 1816; established rural deans; tr. to Peterborough, 1819.

59. William Van Mildert, 1819; Regius Professor of Divinity, Oxford; held also deanery of St. Paul's; tr. to Durham, 1826. Bishops again began to reside a part of every year in the diocese.

60. Charles Richard Sumner, 1826; also Dean of St. Paul's; tr. to Winchester, 1827.

61. Edward Copleston, 1828; also Dean of St. Paul's; Provost of Oriel, Oxford; devoted himself to the restoration of churches and building of parsonages; d. 1849.

62. Alfred Ollivant, 1849; a strenuous worker; d. 1882; a residence acquired during his episcopate.

63. Richard Lewis, 1883; d. 1905; a broad-minded, hard-working prelate; he made a great and successful effort, by the erection of churches, to meet the enormous growth of population during this and the previous episcopate; over one hundred and fifty new churches and mission halls were built.

64. Joshua Pritchard Hughes, 1905.

[J. F.]

B. Willis, *Survey of Llandaff*; Newell, *Dioc. Hist.*; Stubbs, *Reg. Sacr.*; Le Neve, *Fasti*

LOLLARDS (name used for Beghards on the Continent, used by Crump at Oxford for Wyclif's (*q.v.*) followers, c. 1382, and soon general; probably applied to street preachers or idlers; the punning derivation from *lolium*, tares, became common). There are two questions: (1) as to the exact connection of Lollardy with Wyclif's teaching, and (2) as to its influence upon the Reformation. Although it is usual to consider Lollardy as the direct result of Wyclif's teaching, there is some discontinuity at the outset between his circle of Oxford disciples (broken up in 1382) and the wider movement. Some well-known Lollards, e.g. Swinderby, had been independent (wholly or partly) of Wyclifite influence, and many later Lollards were merely ordinary instances of earnest men of individual religious feelings. Their revolutionary and Biblical tastes, and sometimes communistic leanings, led to their being called Lollards and considered Wyclif's disciples. Through some of Wyclif's 'Poor Priests' the Oxford academic movement, and the wider general movement independent of Wyclif, were brought into conjunction. The enumeration of Wyclif's heresies and their condemnation — the first serious case of heresy (*q.v.*) in England — gave the bishops a rough test for heretics, and any one condemned for these views would be held a Lollard. With the growth of anti-

Lollard legislation this became commoner. But Lollardy was a result of the general ferment of thought at the close of the fourteenth century. There was a movement of individualism, new social classes were working their way up, new ideas gained ground, and, in default of the Church meeting these new demands, irregular and erratic teachers gained influence. If we take this view of Lollardy it is needless to discuss its exact relation to the Reformation. Cases of religious earnestness joined to disregard of Church order, on the part of men who sought their own salvation in an individualistic way, continued to arise. They were Lollards not because they followed Wyclif, but because they were shaped by the same impulses that shaped the Lollards nearer his day. But the tendency of Lollards to gather in special localities, sometimes those (*e.g.* Leicestershire, Norfolk, and parts of the city of London) where Wyclif or his immediate followers had taught, should be noticed. When persecution revived under Henry VII. and Henry VIII. the victims came largely from the districts which had furnished victims under the Lancastrians.

Among well-known Lollards were William Swinderby, at Leicester and Lincoln and Hereford; John Purvey, generally supposed to be the author or reviser of the second and later Wycliffite version of the Bible, and the writer of *Regimen Ecclesiae* (which is not to be identified with the *Remonstrance* published by Forshall), who laid stress upon preaching above everything, and held the Mass to be a tradition. Purvey was born at Lathbury, and worked near Bristol. In 1401 he recanted, as had done Philip Repingdon (in 1382), afterwards Bishop of Lincoln and cardinal; and (in 1391) Nicholas Hereford, concerned in translating the Old Testament (first Wycliffite version), who had appealed to the Pope and been imprisoned in Rome. John Aston (Ashton), another Oxford disciple of Wyclif, was with Purvey, Hereford, and others inhibited by the Bishop of Worcester (1387). Some of these men were said to be leagued together in an unlicensed (illegal) college. As early as 1382 unlicensed preachers were causing trouble, drawing crowds, and refusing to obey any summons from a bishop. Commissions were issued to sheriffs to arrest persons named by bishops, and to imprison them until the Church was satisfied. But the Commons declared that they had not assented to this, and so the old ecclesiastical procedure went on, but royal letters empowered the bishops to seize and imprison these preachers until the Council decided what to do with them. In 1387-8,

while the excitement and fear due to the rebellion of 1381 still caused anxiety for society and the Church, there was a story of ordinations by certain Lollards in Salisbury diocese, and there were riots in London. The Parliament petitioned the King to act, and he wrote urging the bishops to activity. In the diocese of Norwich Bishop Despenser (*q.v.*) returned from his unfortunate crusade, was stringent. In two ways the Lollards were active: in their schools (cf. the college mentioned above) and in literature. The Rolls of Parliament (1401 and 1414) speak of Lollard schools. In 1424-30 we have cases: Richard Belworth at Ditchingham, John Abraham at Colchester; at Burgh and London; and Thomas Moore at Ludney. The scattering of 'schedules' or pamphlets (as by Aston at his trial, by Benedict Williams (1405), by William Pateshull in the London riots of 1387; in the case of the Conclusions of 1395, of Oldcastle's assertion of his orthodoxy) also tended to spread Lollardy.

The lay party, formerly headed by John of Gaunt, reappeared, and some of the gentry sympathised with Lollards in their attacks upon endowments; among them were the Earl of Salisbury (d. 1400), Sir Thomas Latimer, and Sir Lewis de Clifford. The twelve Conclusions of 1395, attacking endowments, the hierarchy, clerical celibacy, the Mass, prayers for the dead, the immorality of the clergy, presented to the Parliament, illustrate the boldness and the exaggerations of the Lollards. Their denunciation of war and capital punishment is curious. Along with these twelve Conclusions of 1395 should be taken the thirty-seven Conclusions, and the *Remonstrance* published by Forshall. They belong to a cycle of literature which repeated the same material in many forms.

Many Lollard works, such as the *Apology for Lollards*, have been wrongly ascribed to Wyclif. This *Apology* shows the same scope of reading as Purvey's *Remonstrance* and *Prologue* to the New Testament. The addition of prologues strongly Lollard to works (*e.g.* translations of the Canticles, Psalms, etc.) was common, and this spread of Lollard teaching, preaching, and writing made the authorities anxious. Current controversies are often illustrated by political songs. A reaction against the Lollards set in (1401) under the Lancastrians. The sympathy of Richard II. for them has often been exaggerated, and his epitaph describes him as putting down heretics; but the new dynasty was both orthodox and severe, and Archbishop Arundel (1397) was energetic. The Act *De Heretico Comburendo* (1401, 2 Hen. IV. c. 15) spoke of a new sect which usurped the office of preaching, held conventicles and schools, and circulated books and evaded the episcopal jurisdiction. Authority was given to all diocesans to suppress all these. A prisoner was to be held three months until purged or abjured; if obstinate, to be given to the secular courts and burnt. The old lay party presented schemes for confiscating Church property (1404, 1410). The knights of the shires prayed (1410) that convicted clerks should not be placed in bishops' prisons, and that the new statute might be changed. But (1414) new legislation came. Heresy was made an offence at common law; judges were to swear to exterminate it; persons condemned by ordinaries were to be delivered to the secular courts. And by a new provision of great importance justices were to inquire into heresy and to hand the accused over to their ordinaries. There was the same condition of things in England as that abroad under which the Inquisition arose, but it was significant that in England the State took the power to itself. The free action of episcopal jurisdiction was interfered with abroad by the Inquisition, in England by the State. But it may be noted that before this legislation the general principles had been far from clear, as is shown by Sawtre's execution and by Swinderby's appeal to the King, which raised a general principle. The true object of the episcopal courts was to prevent the spread of mischief, not to punish. The claim to punish, or the suggestion from the State that punishment should be inflicted, at once brought in the coercive power of the civil arm. There were many curious cases, such as that of Thorpe (probably much worked up in the pamphlet of his examination, re-edited by George Constantine or Tindal) and that of Richard Wyche. There was also much local support of Lollards (as, 1392, by Henry Fox, Mayor of Northampton). The case of Sir John Oldcastle (by a strange confusion turned into Falstaff) is important. With him Lollardy was more a social or political than a religious matter. He protested his orthodoxy, although in a popular song he was accused of babbling the Bible day and night. He played with rebellion and heresy, and the suppression of his movement threw back Lollardy (1416). Jack Sharpe's rebellion (1431), with its agitation, in London and elsewhere, against the endowed religious and prelates was the last vigorous outbreak. Henceforth Lollardy lived on as a kind of lowly discontent, with a literature of its own, and a rough but localised system of spreading its views. There were

(1420–30) many single cases (*e.g.* William White in Norwich diocese). The north was less troubled by Lollardy than was the south. In Durham the state of religion was backward; neither a wish for reformation nor earnestness had much place. In York there was the case of Thomas Richmond (1426), a Franciscan, who preached against the ministers of the Church (affirming that deadly sin deprived a priest of his priesthood); but the case is remarkable for the able arguments of the authorities that (1) this doctrine of the effect of deadly sin meant anarchy, and (2) that the Church must be left its own control of its own officers (' no man should put his sickle into another's corn'). The provision of instruction in the north did more for the Church than did repression in the south.

In the controversies with the Lollards the victory lay with their opponents. Netter of Walden (a Carmelite, D.D. of Oxford, and present at Pisa and Constance; Provincial of his order, confessor to Henry v.) in his massive *Doctrinale*; William Woodford, an opponent of Wyclif, in his work (see Brown's *Fasciculus*) against the *Trialogus*; Roger Dymok, who wrote against the twelve Conclusions, were all superior to the Lollards in learning and ability. But they failed to see, as Reginald Pecock (*q.v.*) did see, how the movement should be met. Pecock's view was that by understanding Lollard views, and patiently teaching Lollards the truth, they could be won over. It was true that virtuous people were not necessarily, as Lollards taught, the best expounders of Holy Writ — that was a work for learning and wisdom. But the Church must use the vulgar tongue and come down to these earnest men upon their own ground. It was a magnificent ideal. Lollardy was the result of a new stirring of individual life, which without guidance did harm, but if properly met and guided would have lost its danger. It was really a demand upon the Church for new energy, and by Church and State combined was met with repression. Hence its ineffectiveness and its pathos. [HERESY.]

[J. P. W.]

See references under Wyclif; also Gairdner. *Lollardy and the Reformation*; W. H. Wylie. *Hist. of Eng. under Henry IV.*; Foxe. *Book of Martyrs*; Wright, *Political Songs*, R.S.; and for local details *V.C.H.*

LONDON, See of. The bishopric with its see at London was founded for the East Saxons at the consecration of Mellitus (*q.v.*) in 604, and during the Middle Ages the diocese included the city of London, the counties of

Middlesex and Essex, and parts of Hertfordshire. In 1540 was established a bishopric of Westminster, to which Middlesex, with the exception of Fulham, was assigned as diocese, but it was dissolved in 1550. In that year the diocese of London was extended by the transference to it of the archdeaconry of St. Albans from Lincoln. In accordance with the recommendations of the Ecclesiastical Commissioners (1835), carried out by an Order in Council of 1845, the diocese was diminished by its territory in Herts and all Essex except nine suburban parishes, as Barking, East Ham, West Ham, and others. But it was extended by receiving from Rochester eight suburban parishes in Kent, among them Charlton, Lewisham, Greenwich, and Woolwich; and from Winchester the borough of Southwark and thirteen Surrey parishes, as Battersea, Bermondsey, and Camberwell; together with certain peculiars of Canterbury, as Barnes, Mortlake, and Wimbledon. The transfer from Winchester was not to take effect until the next vacancy in that see, and before this occurred the London Diocese Act, 1863 (26-7 Vic. c. 36) repealed that part of the Order. It also provided that the above-mentioned Essex and Kentish parishes should be transferred from London to Rochester. This was done after the death of Bishop Wigram of Rochester in 1867. The diocese now (1912) includes the city of London, the county of Middlesex, and the boroughs of the county of London on the north side of the Thames. Its population is 3,610,000.

The *Taxatio* of Nicholas IV. estimates the total yearly value of the bishopric at £1000. In the *Valor Ecclesiasticus* (q.v.) the net revenue is put at £1119, 8s., which by 1711 had sunk to £1000 (Eeton). The present income is £10,000. There was a suffragan bishop of Bedford (1879-95), and there are now suffragan bishops of Stepney (1895), Islington (1898), Kensington (1901), and Willesden (1911). By the middle of the twelfth century there were four archdeaconries in this diocese; that of London, which must doubtless have existed from the ninth century, and have included the whole diocese—though the more complete organisation introduced by the Normans made it merely the first in dignity among four—appears about 1136, the other three, Middlesex, Essex, and Colchester, all appearing by 1142. In 1550 a fifth archdeaconry, that of St. Albans, was added. In pursuance of an Order in Council of 8th August 1845 the archdeaconries of Essex, Colchester, and St. Albans were transferred to the diocese of

Rochester, and the diocese of London consequently retained only those of London and Middlesex. An archdeaconry of Hampstead was created 1912.

The cathedral church of St. Paul is of the Old Foundation, and is ruled by a dean and four residentiary canons. One canonry is annexed to the archdeaconry of London. There are thirty prebends. The minor canonries are a corporation by Royal Charter. The number was formerly twelve, but under arrangements made by the Ecclesiastical Commissioners will be ultimately reduced to six.

BISHOPS

A British bishop of London named Restitutus attended the Council of Arles, 314, and assented to its decrees.

1. Mellitus (q.v.), 604; d. 624.
2. Cedd (q.v.), 654; d. 664.
3. Wini; cons. in Gaul; Bishop of Winchester, 663 ?; bought the see of London from the Mercian king about 666, and in spite of the scandal caused by this simony, held it till his death in 674 ?
4. Earconwald, 675; a bishop of great sanctity; d. 30th April 693.
5. Waldhere, 693; wrote to Archbishop Bertwald on political matters in 705.
6. Ingwald; d. 745.
7. Ecgwulf; fl. 745-59.
8. Sighere, or Wigheah; fl. 772.
9. Aldberht; fl. 786.   10. Eadgar; fl. 789.
11. Coenwalh; fl. 793.
12. Eadbald, 793; 'left the land,' which may possibly mean died, in 796.
13. Heathoberht; d. 801.
14. Osmund, 802 ?; present at the Councils of Clovesho, 803, and Acle, 805.
15. Aethelnoth; fl. 811-16.
16. Ceolberht; fl. 824-39.
17. Deorwulf; fl. 860.   18. Swithulf.
19. Aelfstan, or Heahstan; d. 898.
20. Wulfsige; fl. 901-10.
21. Heahstan; fl. 910-26.
22. Theodred; in time of King Athelstan; called the Good; caused some robbers to be hanged, and repented all the rest of his life; d. 951 ?
23. Wulfstan.
24. Brithelm; fl. 953-9 ?
25. Dunstan (q.v.), 959.
26. Aelfstan, 961.   27. Wulfstan, 996.
28. Aelfhun, 1004; buried St. Alphege, the martyred Archbishop of Canterbury, in 1012.
29. Aelfwig, or Elfwy; cons. at York by Archbishop Wulfstan, 1014; d. 1035 ?
30. Aelfweard, 1035 ?; held the abbey of

Evesham with the see ; d. of leprosy at Ramsey Abbey, 25th July 1014.

31. Robert of Jumièges, 1044 ; tr. to Canterbury, 1051.

32. William, 1051; deservedly honoured by Englishmen and Normans alike, and specially in London ; d. 1075.

33. Hugh of Orival, 1075 ; d. of leprosy, 12th January 1085.

34. Maurice, 1086 ; began to build Old St. Paul's ; d. 26th September 1107.

35. Richard de Belmeis, 1108; an able statesman and a magnificent prelate : continued building of St. Paul's ; d. 16th January 1127.

36. Gilbert the Universal, 1128 ; a famous scholar ; accused of avarice ; d. 10th August 1134. A vacancy of seven years.

37. Robert de Sigillo ; cons. 1141 ; on the side of the Empress Matilda ; was captured and imprisoned for a while by Geoffrey de Mandeville : he is said to have died from eating poisoned grapes, 1151.

38. Richard de Belmeis II. ; nephew of Bishop Richard (35), 1152 ; lost his speech, probably by paralysis, about 1157 ; d. 4th May 1162.

39. Gilbert Foliot (*q.v.*) : tr. from Hereford, 1163.

40. Richard Fitz-Neal; son of Nigel, Bishop of Ely, 1189 ; like his father, was Treasurer of the Exchequer : wrote the *Dialogus de Scaccario* ; d. 10th September 1198.

41. William of St. Mère l'Église, 1199 ; published the interdict, and fled to France, 1208 ; was reconciled with John, 1213 ; he voluntarily resigned the see in 1221 ; d. 1224.

42. Eustace of Fauconberg, 1221 ; then, and perhaps later, Treasurer ; was employed in political affairs ; he was a liberal benefactor to his church ; d. 2nd November 1228.

43. Roger le Noir, 1229 ; learned and honourable ; was a fearless defender of the rights of the Church ; upheld Hubert de Burgh ; endeavoured vainly to check the proceedings of the foreign usurers, who were a means of papal oppression of the clergy ; d. 29th September 1241. The belief that miracles were wrought at his tomb in St. Paul's is a witness to his character and popularity. A vacancy of three years.

44. Fulk Basset, 1244 ; of noble birth and high character ; actively resisted the oppression of the Church by Inno-

cent IV. ; a prominent member of the baronial and popular party, but went over to the side of Henry III. about 1257 ; d. 25th May 1259.

45. Henry of Wingham, 1260 ; Keeper of the Great Seal, but retired from the Chancery in that year : he held several benefices in plurality; d. 13th July 1262.

46. Henry of Sandwich, 1263 ; a prominent member of the baronial opposition to Henry III. ; suspended in 1266 for neglecting to obey the legate's order to excommunicate Simon de Montfort and his party, and was detained seven years at Rome with small means ; was restored in 1272, and in January 1273 received at St. Paul's with much rejoicing ; d. 15th September 1273.

47. John Chishull, 1274 ; had been Treasurer; was a benefactor to his church : d. 7th February 1280.

48. Richard of Gravesend, 1280 ; a munificent prelate ; benefactor to his church, the poor, and the University of Cambridge ; d. 9th December 1303.

49. Ralph Baldock, 1306 ; appointed Chancellor by Edward I. in 1307, but displaced by Edward II. ; he was one of the Lords Ordainers of 1310, but does not seem to have taken a prominent part in politics ; he wrote a book of annals, not now extant, and was a munificent benefactor to his church ; d. 24th July 1313.

50. Gilbert Segrave, 1313 ; of a baronial family ; d. 18th December 1316.

51. Richard Newport, 1317 ; d. 24th August 1318.

52. Stephen of Gravesend, 1319 ; nephew of Bishop Richard (48) ; as a supporter of the government of Edward II. was in danger of his life from the Londoners in the outbreak of 1326 ; he protested against the election of Edward III. in his father's place, and was implicated in the conspiracy of the Earl of Kent against Mortimer's government ; d. 8th April 1338.

53. Richard Bentworth, 1338 ; was appointed Chancellor ; d. 8th December 1339.

54. Ralph Stratford, 1340 : probably nephew of John Stratford, Archbishop of Canterbury ; had been one of the clerks of Edward III. : upheld his kinsman, the archbishop, in his quarrel with the King : in 1350 Edward recommended him for a cardinalate ; he was a benefactor to Stratford-on-Avon ; d. 7th April 1354.

55. Michael Northburgh, 1354 (P.) ; elected by the chapter, but the election was

annulled by the Pope, and he was provided; had been much employed by the King; was his secretary, and Keeper of the Privy Seal; he wrote, in two letters, an account of Edward's marches in France in 1346, preserved in Avebury's *Chronicle*, and a book on law not now extant; he was probably co-founder with Sir Walter Manny of the London Charterhouse, and left several benefactions; d. 9th September 1361.

56. Simon Sudbury (*q.v.*), 1362 (P.); tr. to Canterbury, 1375.

57. William Courtenay, 1375 (P.); tr. from Hereford; tr. to Canterbury, 1381.

58. Robert Braybrook, 1382 (P.); was Chancellor for six months; he strenuously opposed the Lollards, reformed the chapter of St. Paul's, and was zealous for good order in the Church; d. 28th August 1404.

59. Roger Walden, 1405 (P.); had been consecrated, 1398, to Canterbury on the fall of Archbishop Arundel; was deprived as an intruder on the accession of Henry IV., 1399; spent five years in obscurity, and then received the see of London; d. 6th January 1406.

60. Nicholas Bubwith, 1406 (P.); tr. to Salisbury, 1407.

61. Richard Clifford, 1407; tr. (P.) from Worcester; had been a favourite of Richard II., and Keeper of the Privy Seal; was ambassador to the Council of Constance; is said to have been proposed for the papacy and to have influenced the electors to choose Martin v., 1417; held many benefices in plurality; d. 20th August 1421.

62. John Kemp, 1421; tr. (P.) from Chichester; tr. to York, 1426.

63. William Grey, 1426 (P.); tr. to Lincoln, 1431.

64. Robert Fitzhugh, 1431 (P.); cons. at Foligno; had been Chancellor of the University of Cambridge; was ambassador to Council of Basle, 1434; was popular and of high character; d. 15th January 1436.

65. Robert Gilbert, 1436 (P.); had been Warden of Merton College, Oxford, and Dean of York, and had accompanied Henry V. on his expedition into France: he tried some Lollards, and the condemnation and burning of two of them in 1440 caused much displeasure in London; d. 22nd June 1448.

66. Thomas Kemp, 1450 (P.); nephew of Archbishop John (62); one of the Duke of Somerset's party, but lived peaceably

under the Yorkist kings; he built the pulpit at Paul's Cross and contributed to the building of the Divinity School at Oxford; d. 28th March 1489.

67. Richard Hill, 1489 (P.); in a dispute with the Prior of Christ Church, Aldgate, he came to the priory with an armed force and made the prior prisoner; a controversy with Archbishop Morton on the jurisdiction of their courts ended in his defeat; d. 20th February 1496.

68. Thomas Savage, 1496; tr. (P.) from Rochester; tr. to York, 1501.

69. William Warham (*q.v.*), 1502 (P.); tr. to Canterbury, 1503.

70. William Barons, 1504 (P.); had been Master of the Rolls; d. 10th October 1505.

71. Richard Fitz-James, 1506 (P.); tr. from Chichester; a Churchman of the old school; upheld his Chancellor when accused of the murder of Hunne; a strong opponent of Dean Colet; tried many heretics, but all escaped death; was a man of high character, and much respected; d. 15th January 1522.

72. Cuthbert Tunstall (*q.v.*), 1522 (P.); tr. to Durham, 1530.

73. John Stokesley, 1530 (P.); learned; subservient to Henry VIII., who employed him in his divorce from Katherine of Aragon; a bishop of the old school and a bitter persecutor of heretics; d. 8th September 1539.

74. Edmund Bonner (*q.v.*), 1540; depr. 1549; restored, 1553; depr. 1559.

75. Nicholas Ridley (*q.v.*), 1550; tr. from Rochester; depr. 1553.

76. Edmund Grindal (*q.v.*), 1559; tr. to York, 1570.

77. Edwin Sandys, 1570; tr. from Worcester; tr. to York, 1577; the first married Bishop of London.

78. John Aylmer, 1577; a distinguished scholar and a strenuous upholder of Church order; was severe with Puritans and Nonconformists, who were strong in his diocese; he was hot-tempered, quarrelsome, and bitter-spirited; he made many enemies, who calumniated him, specially in the Martin Marprelate tracts (*q.v.*); d. 3rd June 1594.

79. Richard Fletcher, 1595; tr. from Worcester; had helped in drawing up the Lambeth Articles, and was inclined to Calvinism; he was a self-seeking, subservient courtier; he married a widow for his second wife, for which he was suspended almost directly he

received the see of London; he was restored, but the Queen's displeasure virtually killed him; he died while smoking a pipe, 15th June 1596.

80. Richard Bancroft (*q.v.*), 1597; tr. to Canterbury, 1604.

81. Richard Vaughan, 1604; tr. from Chester; d. 30th March 1607.

82. Thomas Ravis, 1607; tr. from Gloucester; a translator of the Bible; bitter against Nonconformists; d. 14th December 1609.

83. George Abbot (*q.v.*), 1610; tr. from Lichfield; tr. to Canterbury, 1611.

84. John King, 1611; had been Dean of Christ Church; he was a learned theologian, a pious man, an eloquent and diligent preacher, and, as his opposition to the divorce of Lady Essex shows, independent of court favour; d. 30th March 1621. A report that he was reconciled on his death-bed to the Roman Church was proved to be utterly false.

85. George Monteigne, or Mountain, 1621; tr. from Lincoln; tr. to Durham, 1628.

86. William Laud (*q.v.*), 1628; tr. from Bath and Wells; tr. to Canterbury, 1633.

87. William Juxon (*q.v.*), 1633; tr. to Canterbury, 1660.

88. Gilbert Sheldon (*q.v.*), 1660; tr. to Canterbury, 1663.

89. Humfrey Henchman, 1663; tr. from Salisbury; as Canon of Salisbury he had been distinguished by his promotion of reverent ceremonial; he suffered deprivation and spoliation during the rebellion, and dwelt quietly at Salisbury; in 1651 he enabled Charles II. to escape after the battle of Worcester; as Bishop of Salisbury, while an uncompromising High Churchman, he won the respect alike of Churchmen and Nonconformists, specially by his part in the Savoy Conference; in London he gave no trouble to Nonconformists; d. 7th October 1675.

90. Henry Compton, 1675; tr. from Oxford; a younger son of the second Earl of Northampton; had in his youth borne arms for the King, and at the Restoration held a commission in the Horse Guards, but was ordained, 1662; as Bishop of London he opposed the Romanising policy of James II., and was suspended by the Court of High Commission: he signed the invitation to William of Orange, and at the head of a body of volunteers marched into Oxford 'in a blue cloak and with a naked sword'; he tried to promote a union between the

Church and dissenters, and supported the Comprehension Bill, 1689; disappointed of translation to Canterbury, he turned from the Whigs to the Tory party; he was not learned, but was a diligent bishop; his charities were large, and he took much interest in missionary work in North America; d. 7th July 1713.

91. John Robinson, 1714; tr. from Bristol; of humble birth; was employed in diplomacy, 1680-1709; was made Privy Seal, 1711, and was plenipotentiary at the Congress of Utrecht, 1712-13; as Bishop of London he performed his duties regularly, and was charitable, but incompetent; d. 11th April 1723.

92. Edmund Gibson (*q.v.*), 1723; tr. from Lincoln; d. 6th September 1748.

93. Thomas Sherlock (*q.v.*), 1748; tr. from Salisbury; when he accepted the see of London he was seventy, and though an industrious man, could no longer be active; d. 1761.

94. Thomas Hayter, 1761; tr. from Norwich; had been a considerable pluralist and tutor to the sons of Frederick, Prince of Wales; d. 9th January 1762.

95. Richard Osbaldeston, 1762; tr. from Carlisle, which diocese he had neglected; d. 15th May 1764.

96. Richard Terrick, 1764; tr. from Peterborough; had been a pluralist; a good preacher, and generally liberal-minded, except with respect to Roman Catholics, whose chapels he caused to be closed; d. 29th March 1777.

97. Robert Lowth, 1777; tr. from Oxford; an accomplished scholar, specially in Hebrew, as witnessed by his exquisite translation of Isaiah (1778), and an able controversialist; he expressed warm admiration for John Wesley; he declined the primacy, 1783; d. 3rd November 1787.

98. Beilby Porteous, 1787; tr. from Chester; though himself a pluralist while at Chester, and often while Bishop of London absent from his diocese, was for his time an active and reforming bishop; he was fearless and of an independent spirit, and while insisting on church order sympathised with the Evangelical Movement; he supported the abolition of the slave-trade, Sunday schools, and the work of Hannah More (*q.v.*), and urged the better observance of holy days; he was a good preacher and a liberal giver; d. 14th May 1809.

99. John Randolph, 1809; tr. from Bangor; had been Regius Professor of Divinity, and had held other professorships at Oxford; as a bishop he was inconspicuous save for his support of the National Society; d. 1813.
100. William Howley (*q.v.*), 1813; tr. to Canterbury, 1828.
101. Charles James Blomfield (*q.v.*), 1828; tr. from Chester; res. 1856.
102. Archibald Campbell Tait (*q.v.*), 1856; tr. to Canterbury, 1868.
103. John Jackson, 1869; tr. from Lincoln; did much good work at Lincoln, and worked equally well as Bishop of London; a pious and tolerant Evangelical; began the East London Church Fund; d. 6th January 1885.
104. Frederick Temple (*q.v.*), 1885; tr. from Exeter; tr. to Canterbury, 1896.
105. Mandell Creighton (*q.v.*), 1897; tr. from Peterborough; d. 1901.
106. Arthur Foley Winnington-Ingram, 1901; tr. from suffragan bishopric of Stepney, to which he was consecrated in 1897.

[W. H.]

LONGCHAMP, William, d. (1197), Bishop of Ely, was Chancellor of Aquitaine under Richard Cœur de Lion in the time of Henry II. When Richard succeeded his father, he made Longchamp Chancellor of England and Bishop of Ely, and when departing for the Third Crusade further obtained for his favourite a legatine commission, and made him chief justiciar. Longchamp was despised by the barons as a low-born upstart, and courted unpopularity by his arrogant demeanour. Of Norman extraction, he affected to despise the native English, and surrounded himself with a train of foreign knights. He kept an almost royal household, and was served at table by pages of high lineage. When making his progresses he and his servants lived at free quarters on the countryside. But he was loyal to Richard; and his government, though harsh, was guided by the desire to maintain the royal power intact. Unfortunately for himself he preferred autocratic methods, never consulted the Great Council, and put himself in the wrong by chastising without trial those whom he regarded as hostile to his master. Among his victims were Hugh de Puiset (*q.v.*), Bishop of Durham, whom he compelled by force to resign the earldom of Northumberland and justiciarship of the North; Gerard de Camville, a partisan of Prince John, whom he deprived of the shrievalty of Lincoln; and the King's half-brother, Archbishop Geoffrey

of York, whom he arrested for returning to England without leave. John pressed the barons and bishops to impeach Longchamp for misconduct, and carried his point owing to the timely arrival of the Archbishop of Rouen, whom Richard had sent home to investigate the claims against the justiciar. Longchamp attempted to hold the Tower of London against the opposition, but was soon forced to submit. He was condemned to lose his temporal offices and to leave the kingdom. This is the first instance on record of a royal minister impeached in the Great Council; but the precedent is impaired by the irregular character of the proceedings. Richard on his return refused to dismiss Longchamp, and the bishop remained Chancellor of England until his death. The personal character of Longchamp is blackened by the venomous Gerald de Barri (*q.v.*). But there is no doubt that Longchamp was respected by the English bishops so long as he remained the ruler of England; and the Pope dismissed as frivolous the accusations which his political enemies preferred at Rome.

[H. W. C. D.]

Stubbs, preface to *Roger of Hoveden*, iii. (R.S.); Norgate, *Eng. under the Angevin Kings*, vol. ii.: H. W. C. Davis, *Eng. under the Normans and Angevins*.

LOWDER, Charles Fuge (1820-80), born at Bath, eldest son of a banker, was educated at King's College School, London, and Exeter College, Oxford, where he graduated B.A. (Second Class *Lit. Hum.*), 1843, but failed to get a Fellowship. Being ordained, 1843, he worked in the west of England until he became curate of St. Barnabas, Pimlico, 1851-6, during which time that church, with its restored ceremonial, bore the brunt of Protestant attack, both by riot and prosecution. About 1855 a society of clergy for devotion and mission work was founded—the Society of the Holy Cross. Lowder joined it, and began mission preaching in East London on Ash Wednesday, 1856. A settlement was formed in the degraded parish of St. George's in the East, and Lowder took charge of it on 22nd August. In 1858 Lowder and his colleagues were joined by A. H. Mackonochie (*q.v.*). From the first the mission was worked in the spirit of the Oxford Movement. The Eucharistic vestments were used in the mission chapel (and from 1857 in the parish church). This caused some friction with the new bishop, Tait (*q.v.*), who complained of 'dresses and ceremonies,' 'mimicking of popery,' and the like, but did not interfere with the missioners. In 1859 fierce riots broke out in the parish church, 'nominally, and in part really, caused by Mr. Bryan King's ritualistic practices, but largely stimulated by the Jewish sweaters of the East End, whose proceedings the clergy had the unheard-of impertinence to denounce and interfere with.' The riots began, 22nd May 1859, lasted until November 1860, and ended with the rector's resignation. The storm fell partly on Lowder and Mackonochie, who assisted at the parish church, and once at least Lowder's life was in danger. Bishop Tait and the Home Secretary long declined to interfere. The mission churches, served by Lowder and Mackonochie, were not molested after October 1859.

The church of St. Peter's, London Docks, was consecrated on 30th June 1866, and Lowder became first vicar.   In July and August came the cholera, and the heroism of Lowder, the clergy, and sisters of St. Peter's roused wide admiration, and broke down any remaining barrier between him and his neighbours.

In 1868 he was nearly broken by the secession of three of his curates to Rome. In 1869 'the Way of the Cross' was preached through the streets of his parish, 'the *Times* commenting on the folly of such an attempt.' In 1869 and 1878 the Church Association failed to institute prosecutions against him, and in the last instance through Archbishop Tait. 'Father' Lowder (so he was universally known to his people) was deeply beloved by the dock labourers and others for whom he spent his life. His mission produced amazing results far outside its own borders : it began the system of mission districts and settlements. Worn out with work and the begging it involved he died unexpectedly at Zell-am-See, in the Austrian Tyrol, 9th September 1880. His funeral at St. Peter's, with its crowds of weeping men, marked an epoch in the life of the Church in East London. He is buried at Chislehurst.

[S. L. O.]

Charles Lowder : A Biography.

LYNDWOOD, William (1375-1446), canonist, born at Lyndwood, near Market Rasen in Lincolnshire, was educated at Gonville and Caius College, Cambridge, became Fellow of Pembroke Hall, and then removed to Oxford. where he graduated LL.D. He took holy orders, and was preferred to many livings in turn, finally becoming Bishop of St.

Davids in 1442. In 1414 he was appointed by Archbishop Chichele (*q.v.*) his Official Principal, and took part in the trial of the Lollards ; in 1426 he became Dean of the Arches. He seems to have been constantly employed in diplomatic business with Burgundy, Portugal, France, Spain, Scotland, and the Hanseatic League. In March 1432-3 he became Keeper of the Privy Seal. He helped Bekington to promote the foundation of Eton College. He is most famous as the author of the *Provinciale*, a digest in five books of the synodical constitutions of the province of Canterbury from the time of Langton (*q.v.*) to that of Chichele, with explanatory glosses. It was completed in 1433, dedicated to the archbishop, and intended as a text-book for the unlearned, *simpliciter literati et pauca intelligentes*. It is valuable because it gives the opinion of a high ecclesiastical judge on the legislative and jurisdictional powers of the Church of England, and there is no mistaking what Lyndwood's opinion was. He constantly speaks of the archbishop's legislative power and not of that of the provincial council, though he should undertake no *ardua negotia* without the counsel of his brethren. But still he is the legislator. Thus a collision of a provincial constitution and a decretal would not be a collision between two Churches, but simply between a superior and an inferior. And very rarely does he find such collisions. The archbishop may make for his province statutes which are merely declaratory of the *jus commune* of the Church ; he may supplement papal legislation, but he has no power to derogate from, still less to abrogate, the laws made by his superior. Nor can the archbishop override legatine constitutions. Lyndwood is quite clear that the constitutions of Otto and Ottobon are superior to those of any English prelate or council. An English prelate cannot put any statutory interpretation upon them ; his power is merely executive, not authoritative. The constitutions Lyndwood discusses are meagre, and in his opinion merely by-laws, which do very little, and say nothing on more than half the topics of ecclesiastical jurisprudence. [CANON LAW.] Lyndwood is represented in his academic dress on a brass on his father's tomb at Lyndwood (now Linwood) Lincs. [F. M.]

F. W. Maitland, *Canon Law in the Ch. of Eng.* ; W. W. Capes, *Hist. of the Ch. of Eng. in the Fifteenth Century* ; Sir W. Ramsay, *Lancaster and York* ; J. M. Rigg in *D.N.B.*

M

MACKONOCHIE, Alexander Heriot (1825-87), priest, third son of a colonel in the East India Company's service, was born at Fareham, Hants, and educated for a short time at Edinburgh University, whence he removed to Wadham College, Oxford. He worked hard, and gained a Second Class in *Lit. Hum.*, 1848. At Oxford he came to know Charles Marriott (*q.v.*), who deeply influenced his life. He was Curate of Westbury, Wilts, 1849-52, and Wantage (where W. J. Butler was vicar and H. P. Liddon (*q.v.*) one of his colleagues), 1852-8, when he joined the mission at St. George's in the East. [LOWDER, C. F.] He was there during the violent Protestant riots of 1859, and refused the offer of St. Saviour's, Leeds, fearing to desert his post. In 1862 he became first Vicar of St. Alban's, Holborn, a church built and endowed by Mr. Hubbard, afterwards Lord Addington. The parish was a centre of vice, heathenism, and poverty. The first services (which began 11th May 1862) were held over a fish-shop, afterwards in a cellar in Greville Street. Linen Eucharistic vestments were worn in St. Alban's church from its consecration in 1863. In 1864 coloured silk vestments were presented and incense was used. In 1867 the Church Association [SOCIETIES, ECCLESIASTICAL] through a Mr. Martin prosecuted Mackonochie, on the evidence of hired informers, for altar-lights, elevation of the elements, kneeling during the consecration prayer, the mixed chalice, and incense. The first three were pronounced lawful by Sir R. Phillimore (*q.v.*); the Privy Council reversed the decision, and condemned Mackonochie in costs. In 1869 he was prosecuted again for disobeying the judgment, and condemned on one count. In 1870 he was again charged with disobedience, and was condemned in costs and suspended for three months. In 1874 he was prosecuted again, and condemned for using vestments, as on other counts, and suspended for six weeks. The senior curate, A. H. Stanton, refused to celebrate Holy Communion in the manner ordered by the court, and the whole congregation migrated for that service to St. Vedast's, Foster Lane.

March 1878 a fresh attack began before Lord Penzance, and Mackonochie was sentenced to three years' suspension. The Queen's Bench Division granted a prohibition against Lord Penzance, but this was reversed by the Court of Appeal. In 1880 and 1881 came further attempts to enforce suspension,

the House of Lords, to whom appeal was made for a prohibition, upholding Lord Penzance.

February 1882 Mr. Martin appealed for further punishment, and, to avoid more litigation, at the urgent request of Archbishop Tait (*q.v.*) on his death-bed Mackonochie resigned his living, and by exchange became Vicar of St. Peter's, London Docks. Nevertheless, in 1883 the attack was continued. Lord Penzance held the exchange immaterial, and pronounced sentence of deprivation, and his living of St. Peter's was formally sequestrated. He remained in possession of it however until, worn out with the long persecution, he resigned on 31st December 1883. He returned to St. Alban's as curate, but lived much at Wantage and in Scotland. His health was broken and his powers were failing. 15th December 1887, while visiting the Bishop of Argyll, he lost his way, and, overtaken by darkness and storm, was found two days later dead in a snowdrift in the Mamore deer forest, guarded by two dogs who had accompanied his walk.

Though set in the forefront of the ritual movement Mackonochie had no love for ceremonial as such, and was severely unaesthetic and unmusical. Self-disciplined and ascetic, he was a devoted parish priest and a great spiritual guide. He was a firm adherent of the Oxford Movement (*q.v.*) and passionately loyal to the English Church. Tait, though strongly opposed to him, said in 1859: 'I have not a better man in my diocese than Mr. Mackonochie.' His treatment by the Church Association largely helped to detach public sympathy from its cause.   [S. L. O.]

E. A. T., *Memoir*: G. W. E. Russell, *Household of Faith*; E. Ibbotson, *Brief Hist.*

MAGEE, William Connor (1821-91), Archbishop of York, was an example of heredity in the Church, being a grandson of William Magee (1766-1831), Archbishop of Dublin, 1822-31. He was a scholar of Trinity College, Dublin; B.A., 1842; was ordained in 1844 to the curacy of St. Thomas, Dublin, but crossed to England in 1847, becoming Curate of St. Saviour, Bath, and afterwards Minister of the Octagon Chapel, 1851-6, where he made a great reputation as an eloquent preacher. From 1856 to 1864 he was Incumbent of the Quebec Chapel in London,

then returned to Ireland as Rector of Innis-
killen and Canon of Clogher. In 1864 he
became Dean of Cork, and in 1865 Donellan
Lecturer at Trinity College, Dublin, both of
which preferments had been held by his
grandfather. He was also Dean of the
Chapel Royal at Dublin. In 1868 he achieved
fame as the most brilliant oratorical opponent
of the proposed disestablishment of the
Irish Church, and was nominated by Mr.
Disraeli, mainly on that account, to the
bishopric of Peterborough. His credit as
orator and preacher continued to grow, and
he added to it a rather dangerous reputation
for wit, his speeches in the House of Lords
and elsewhere being sometimes more brilliant
than prudent. An epigrammatic remark
made on a Licensing Bill, that he would
rather see England free than sober, secured
a longer notoriety than some wiser sayings.
In his diocese he was an administrator of an
old-fashioned type, not conforming to the
fashion of extreme activity followed by many
of his contemporaries, and his promotion to
the see of York in 1891 was somewhat of a
surprise. He held it for very few weeks,
succumbing to an attack of influenza in the
early summer of that year. He was not
distinguished for theological or other learning,
his only important contribution to science
being a Boyle lecture on the power of prayer,
in answer to Professor Tyndal's presidential
address at the British Association in 1871,
and this was rather popular than strictly
scientific. [T. A. L.]

J. C. Macdonnell, *Life.*

MAGNA CARTA was sealed by King John
at Runnymede, near Windsor, on 15th June
1215. It embodied the chief demands which
the rebel barons had presented to him as
their ultimatum. But it was drafted under
the influence of Archbishop Stephen Langton
(*q.v.*); and like the charter of Henry I., upon
which it was modelled, it concedes benefits to
all classes of the community. Many of its
provisions were temporary in their character, and were omitted from the reissues of
Henry III. and later sovereigns. Some others
express the resentment of the baronial class
against the centralising and levelling policy
of Henry II. The general principles which
the charter enunciates are few and far
between; it is chiefly important as the first
monument of national resistance to autocratic
rule, and as a striking assertion of the principle that the King is under the law. But
almost to our own days it has been extolled
as the palladium of English liberties and the
foundation of our constitutional law.

Four clauses of the original Magna Carta
relate to the Church. The first section
promises that the English Church shall be
free and possess her rights and liberties
unimpaired. This is primarily a confirmation of the special charter to the Church
granted by John on 21st November 1214,
which promises that all elections of prelates
shall be made freely in canonical form, the
King reserving the right to refuse his confirmation, if there be any reasonable cause for
doing so. But the 'freedom' of the Church
had been confirmed in similar terms by
Henry I. and Stephen in their coronation
charters; and there is no doubt that in each
case the 'freedom' claimed was deliverance
from abuses of recent date. In section 14
of Magna Carta the King acknowledges the
right of archbishops, bishops, and abbots to
be summoned individually to the Great
Council, in the same manner as the greater
barons. Under section 22 a special privilege
is accorded to clerks who have rendered
themselves liable to amercement in the royal
courts of justice. They are not to be fined
so heavily that any part of the fine shall fall
upon the revenues which they derive from a
benefice. The principle implied is that
ecclesiastical revenues must be regarded as
wholly devoted to the service of God.
Section 27 recognises the right of the Church
to supervise the distribution of the chattels of
an intestate free man. This reminds us that
the Church claimed a moral right to direct
testators in the disposition of their movables,
which were, speaking broadly, the only form
of property then devisable by will [COURTS].
This clause was omitted from the second issue
of Magna Carta (1216), because it barred the
claim of the King and other lords to appropriate the chattels of their men who died intestate. Magna Carta was revised and reissued
not only in 1216, but also in 1217 and 1225.
In the reissue of 1217 we find one new clause
which imposes an important check upon the
growth of ecclesiastical endowments. It prohibits a form of grant by which the donor
surrenders his land to a church on condition
of being permitted to hold it from the church
for his life. The result of these grants had
been to deprive lay lords of such feudal
incidents as wardship, marriage, and escheat.
This clause is the first of a series of enactments which culminate in the statute of
Edward I. concerning Mortmain (*q.v.*), *De
Viris Religiosis* (1279). They were framed
as much in the interest of the barons as of
the King; but they attest a general conviction that the Church was acquiring a danger-
ously large proportion of landed property.

Magna Carta was annulled by Pope Innocent III. (*q.v.*) on 25th August 1215 at John's request. The Pope stated that the charter had been extorted from the King by force, and that its terms were dishonourable, unlawful, unjust, and derogatory to the royal prerogative. He forbade the King to observe or the barons to enforce it, on pain of anathema. But the revised charter of 1216 was sealed by the legate Gualo, then acting as co-regent with William Marshal. In the preamble to this, and also to the charter of 1217, it is stated that Gualo counselled the reissue. Henceforth Magna Carta was regarded as being ratified and guaranteed by the Church; those who infringed it were frequently punished or threatened with spiritual censures. On one famous occasion Archbishop Peckham (*q.v.*) ordered that a copy of it should be affixed to the door of every parish church (1279), by way of protest against the encroachments which Edward I. had committed upon ecclesiastical 'freedom.' [H. W. C. D.]

The text of Magna Carta in Stubbs, *Select Charters*; see also W. S. McKechnie, *Magna Carta*; H. W. C. Davis, *Eng. under the Normans and Angevins*.

MAN, Isle of, Church in. The Isle of Man is historically no part of our country. Lying between Ireland and Galloway, which was a Gaelic-speaking part of Scotland, Man was originally in much closer contact with them than with England or Wales. The language was Gaelic, and the first Christianity was Irish, as is proved by the dedications of the churches. Of this Christianity, which must date at least from the sixth century, no literary evidence survives.

The continuous history of Man begins with the Norse invasions. Man was the southernmost of a long line of insular settlements. Beginning with Shetland and Orkney, which they called the Northern Isles, their colonies stretched from the Outer Hebrides to Man. The whole, from Lewis to Man, were called the Southern Isles (Suthr-eyar), and this, which passed into the form 'Sodor,' was the original name of the see. 'Sodor and Man' did not come into official use till the seventeenth century, and was due to forgetfulness of the fact that Man was part of Sodor, though it had come to be the only part with which the bishop was concerned. By an unfortunate guess Sodor was given as a name to the little island off Peel, on which the cathedral of Man now stands in ruin.

Man was conquered by the Norsemen before 800, and they were converted by about 1000. The island was at times a dependency of the Scandinavian kingdom of Dublin, at times an independent kingdom, and at other times directly subject to Norway, and this political status determined the position of its Church. In its earlier phases the Christianity of Norway had no diocesan system; the bishops were the King's bishops, exercising jurisdiction from his court. But they were far distant, and it is probable that as Dublin fell under the influence of Canterbury, so Sodor early came under that of York. The first diocesan bishop, according to the *Chronicle of Man*, was one Roolwer (Rolver, *i.e.* Hrolfr, Rolf, Rollo), who must have lived in the time of Edward the Confessor. From Rolf onwards the line can be obscurely traced, with few dates and many contradictions. Probably his successors, like himself, preferred Man to the Scottish islands as a place of residence; though so many even of those whose title was undisputed were buried in England, Ireland, or Scotland that we may assume a certain neglect of episcopal duty.

The connection with York naturally resulted from the want of a definite ecclesiastical status. The last bishop whom we know to have been consecrated there was Gamaliel, about 1160. By this time a constitution had been provided for the Northern Church. In 1151 the King of Man, needing protection against Scotland, did homage to Norway. Thus it was natural that when the English Cardinal Nicolas, afterwards Pope Adrian IV. (*q.v.*), organised the Norwegian Church at the Council of Nidaros in 1152, Sodor should be made one of the suffragan sees in the new province of Nidaros or Trondhjem. The consecration of Gamaliel in defiance of this provision seems to have been the starting-point of a series of conflicts between rival bishops, sometimes the consecrated of York and sometimes he of Trondhjem possessing the see, while his opponent lived in Norway, England, or Scotland, claiming to be bishop, but actually serving as assistant to some diocesan elsewhere.

Canonical order required an electing body as well as a consecrating archbishop. By a very exceptional provision the election to Sodor fell into the hands of a religious house outside the diocese. Furness Abbey, on the coast of Lancashire nearest to Man, was founded in 1127 by Stephen, Count of Boulogne, and afterwards King of England, as a member of the congregation or order of Savigny, a group of strict Benedictine houses which joined the Cistercians in 1147. In

1134 it received from King Olaf I. of Man large grants of land, on which it founded the daughter abbey of Rushen, the only religious house of importance in the island. But Furness not only retained a certain superiority over Rushen; it acted as though no monastery existed in Man, and, as the only ecclesiastical corporation holding (directly or indirectly) a baronial estate in Man, it claimed the right of electing the bishop. The origin of this claim is unknown; it seems to antedate the foundation of the archbishopric of Trondhjem, and may have been exercised before Rushen was established. It was only intermittently enjoyed; though recognised by the Pope in 1244, later popes in 1349 and 1363 asserted that by ancient custom the right belonged to the clergy of the ' city and diocese of Sodor.' Yet once, in 1247, the chapter of St. Germans' cathedral had elected a bishop. No doubt, as elsewhere, the power practically belonged to kings and popes. Iona, which was in the diocese and became a Benedictine house in 1203, never apparently claimed a voice in the election.

The next important event was the cession of Man and the Isles by Norway to Scotland in 1266. Magnus, the last King of Man, had just died in 1265, and Alexander III. of Scotland refused to admit his son to the feudatory kingship. There was some difficulty in making good the new rule, but by 1275 Scotland was in possession. The rights of Trondhjem were secured by the treaty, and five Scottish bishops held the see in succession. All were consecrated in Norway, but as three were buried in Scotland we may assume that they did not devote their whole attention to their diocese. In 1290 Edward I.. in the exercise of his claims over Scotland. took possession, and though Robert Bruce won it back for a short time in 1313, the Scots were quickly expelled, and finally ceded Man to England in 1334. This was but a formality. The English were already in possession, but were not disposed to trouble themselves with a direct rule. After various grants of the kingdom, or lordship, from 1330 onwards, it was finally given in 1406 to Sir John Stanley and his heirs. With him and his descendants, the Earls of Derby, and after the extinction of the direct male line in 1736, with the Dukes of Atholl as representing the heiress, the lordship remained till 1827. The rights of the Lord amounted in practice to a complete internal sovereignty.

The Scots, as soon as Man was lost, annexed their islands, which had formed part of the see, to that of Argyll, which since then has borne the name of Argyll and the Isles. The connection of Man with Norway ceased with that with Scotland, and the see passed under the immediate jurisdiction of Rome, which ignored the rights of Trondhjem. None of the English laws limiting the authority of Rome extended to Man. But in any case of doubt it had come to be usual for immediate recourse to be had to Rome, and a bishop in so dubious a position as an elect of Man could not turn safely to any other source of consecration. Thus in 1349 William Russell was consecrated at Avignon, and his successors till the eve of the Reformation were either consecrated there or else furnished with a provision from Rome. In the fifteenth century the list is very uncertain; at times there seem to have been rival bishops, and usually the bishop was acting as a suffragan somewhere in England, or else was an English abbot, to whom a titular see gave the dignity of a mitre. By whom these bishops were elected, if at all, is unknown. As at least three came from the English neighbourhood of the Earl of Derby, we may assume that they were nominated by him. In no case does the English Crown seem to have exercised its power of rejecting such nomination, either before or after the Reformation. It may be mentioned that three bishops—Simon in 1229, Mark in 1291, and William Russell in 1350—held synods and issued canons of the usual type. Simon also founded the cathedral chapter at St. Germans, or Peel, which disappeared at the Reformation. It had had little history or wealth.

A solitary Bull of Calixtus III. in 1458 speaks of the see as subject to York. This may be an error of the scribe, or it may register, and perhaps by registering confirm, a claim of York. In practice it had no effect, and for another century there was no appeal from the bishop, save to Rome. In 1505 Thomas, Earl of Derby, confirmed to Huan Rufforth, then bishop, and his successors, the lands and liberties of his church, and in 1541 the bishop is officially styled ' Lord Metropolitan.' This liberty was soon to cease. Henry VIII. (*q.v.*) had no respect for rights that could not defend themselves. About 1539, without any pretence of legislation, he confiscated Rushen Abbey and the other religious houses and properties in the island to his own use, without regard to what claims the Lord of the island might possess. In 1542 the see was united by an Act of the English Parliament to the province of York (33 Hen. VIII. c. 31), and in 1546 the King appointed Henry Mann to the see by Letters Patent, with permission to retain the deanery of Chester and other English preferment. Mann held the see through all changes till his death under Mary in 1556, when the Lords resumed their power of appointing the bishop, which was exercised, subject to Letters Patent approving the appointment, till the cession to the Crown in 1827.

The laws of England did not run in the island, and there is no record of any legislation by which ecclesiastical change was introduced. In fact, the Church records of the island are only preserved from the end of the sixteenth century, and its statutes in writing date from 1610. Change in all probability was introduced by the bishops, backed by the Lords, and became gradually complete as old incumbents died out and men of modern sympathies took their place. The process would be the easier that apparently from 1562 to 1568 and certainly from 1576 to 1599 the bishops acted as governors of Man for the absent Lord. But the open practice of some of the older rites continued much longer than in England, and the delay in adapting law to practice is shown by the fact that the children of the clergy were not made legitimate till 1610.

Man had some of the best bishops of the seventeenth and eighteenth centuries, such as Isaac Barrow the elder, Thomas Wilson (*q.v.*), and Mark Hildesley, through whom the Manx Bible and Prayer Book were completed ; and also one at least of the worst. A long and exasperating conflict was happily ended in 1839, when a law was passed commuting the whole tithe of the island and providing for its collection by one public officer, who takes a toll of £525 for the Crown, and distributes the remainder (£5550) among the bishop and the beneficed clergy. This is the chief source of the episcopal income, which is stated at £1500. The bishop has a seat, but no vote, in the English House of Lords.

By the Established Church Act, 1836 (6-7 Will. IV. c. 77), the see was to be united with Carlisle at the next vacancy. This provision was made without the knowledge of the bishop (Ward), who was then almost blind. He at once set to work to save his see, and his efforts hastened his end. The provision was repealed in 1838 (1-2 Vic. c. 30), immediately after his death (*Sixty Years Ago: an Eventful Episcopate*, 1896). In 1875 a proposal to unite the diocese with that of Liverpool came to nothing owing to Manx opposition. The population of the see is 52,034.

The only religious body beside the Church which is of importance is the Wesleyan.

After the death of Bishop Hildesley the Church fell into a laxity which gave an opening to the Methodists, and for two generations they seem to have dominated the religious life of the island. They formally separated from the Church in 1839. Since this Churchmanship, of an Evangelical colour, perhaps derived from Liverpool, has had its due influence.

By the constitution of Man. Church and State have always been closely connected. Bishop, archdeacon, and vicar-general sit in the local Parliament, the Tynwald Court ; ecclesiastical discipline was enforced by the Lord's courts of law till the early nineteenth century ; the mediæval jurisdiction of the vicar-general in probate lasted till 1884, and affiliation cases are still decided by him. The 'convocation' of the island still meets annually, and its power of making canons has never been revoked ; none have, however, been made since 1704, and for their enforcement they would need to pass the Tynwald Court. This court passed an Act in 1880 for the division of the island into rural deaneries, and in 1895 for the constitution of a chapter, with the bishop as dean, and four canons. This chapter does not receive a *congé d'élire* on the vacancy of the see. No change took place in regard to the Church when the Crown purchased from the fourth Duke of Atholl in 1827 the whole of his rights as Lord, including the advowson of the see.

Down to the middle of the nineteenth century many of the clergy used the Manx service on three Sundays in the month, and in some churches the whole service (including the sermon) was said in Manx once a month down to 1875, but English hymns were sung. By that time the generation of clergy to whom Manx was familiar had died out, and the Manx service has not since been used. In recent years the practice of reading the lessons in Manx has been revived. Formerly some of the clergy used to have the English Bible and Prayer Book before them, and translate into Manx as they went along. The first part of the Bible published in Manx was St. Matthew's Gospel under Bishop Wilson in 1748. The Manx Prayer Book was published under Bishop Hildesley in 1765 ; the complete Bible, 1772. The first Manx Hymn Book was published in 1799 ; it included translations of hymns by the Wesleys (*q.v.*) and Watts.

The early lists of bishops are incomplete, confused, and contradictory (see Stubbs, *Registrum Sacrum*, ed. 1897, p. 210). From the time of Henry VIII. they are as follows, but it is not known who was bishop when the see was united to York in 1542:—

1. Henry Mann, also Dean of Chester, 1546; d. 1556.
2. Thomas Stanley, 1555 (P.); d. 1568.
3. John Salisbury, also Dean of Norwich, 1570; d. 1576.
4. John Meyrick, also Governor of Man, 1576; d. 1599.
5. George Lloyd, 1600; tr. to Chester, 1604.
6. John Philips, 1605; also Archdeacon; the first to undertake the translation of Bible and Prayer Book into Manx (1610); as he was a Welshman the Manx clergy refused to have anything to do with his Prayer Book, saying the people would not understand such Manx; d. 1633.
7. William Forster, 1633; d. 1635.
8. Richard Parr, 1635; d. 1644.
9. Samuel Rutter, 1661; d. 1662.
10. Isaac Barrow, 1663; also Governor of Man; tr. to St. Asaph, 1669, but held Sodor and Man *in commendam* till 1671.
11. Henry Bridgman, also Dean of Chester, 1671; d. 1682.
12. John Lake, 1683; tr. to Bristol, 1684; one of the Seven Bishops (*q.v.*).
13. Baptist Levinz, 1685; d. 1693. Vacancy of five years.
14. Thomas Wilson (*q.v.*), 1698; d. 1755.
15. Mark Hildesley, 1755; completed the Bible and Prayer Book in Manx; d. 1772.
16. Richard Richmond, 1773; a peculiarly secular bishop (see Mayor's *History of St. John's College, Cambridge,* iii. p. 561), who destroyed the consistent work of his predecessors since Barrow; d. 1780.
17. George Mason, 1780; d. 1783.
18. Claudius Crigan, 1783; d. 1813.
19. George Murray, 1814; tr. to Rochester, 1827.
20. William Ward, 1828; Rector of Great Horkesley, Essex; saved his see from threatened extinction; d. 1838.
21. James Bowstead, 1838; tr. to Lichfield, 1840.
22. Henry Pepys, 1840; tr. to Worcester, 1841.
23. Thomas Vowler Short, 1841; tr. to St. Asaph, 1846.
24. Walter Augustus Shirley, 1847; d. 1847.
25. Robert John Eden, 1847; tr. to Bath and Wells, 1854.
26. Horace Powys, 1854; d. 1877.
27. Rowley Hill, 1877; d. 1887.
28. John Wareing Bardsley, 1887; tr. to Carlisle, 1892.
29. Norman Dumenil John Straton, 1892; tr. to Newcastle, 1907.
30. Thomas Wortley Drury, 1907; tr. to Ripon, 1911.
31. James Denton Thompson, 1912.

[E. W. W.]

Chronicon Mannine; Dugdale, *Monasticon,* s.v. Furness Abbey and Rushen Abbey; Moore, *Hist. Isle of Man*; *Dio. Hist.*

MANCHESTER, See of. The Ecclesiastical Commissioners of 1835 [COMMISSIONS, ROYAL] recommended that the disproportionately large see of Chester (*q.v.*) should be relieved, and spiritual provision made for the growing population of the towns of Lancashire by the establishment of a bishopric at Manchester. The Established Church Act, 1836 (6-7 Will. IV. c. 77), empowered the Crown to constitute the see by Order in Council, which was issued accordingly, 12th December 1838. It never took effect, and was repealed by the Act which established the see in 1847 (10-11 Vic. c. 108). To avoid increasing the number of bishops in the House of Lords the Commissioners had recommended the fusion of the sees of Bangor (*q.v.*) and St. Asaph (*q.v.*). But this proposal met with much opposition, and the difficulty was overcome by a clause providing that the junior bishop for the time being should always be without a seat in the House. The constitution of a diocese whose bishop was not also a lord of Parliament was a constitutional innovation which caused some misgiving, but the expedient thus introduced has since become the rule on the creation of a new see.

The diocese was established by Order in Council, 10th August 1847, under the Act of that year. It consists of the county of Lancaster, with the exception of Liverpool and the surrounding district, which remained in the Chester diocese until the creation of the see of Liverpool (*q.v.*) and the deaneries of Furness and Cartmel, which were transferred to the see of Carlisle (*q.v.*). It contains 845,904 acres, and in 1847 was divided into the archdeaconries of Manchester and Lancaster. Its population was then 1,123,548. This has now increased to 3,124,296, and archdeaconries of Blackburn (1877) and Rochdale (1910) have been constituted. A suffragan Bishop of Burnley was appointed in 1901, and of Whalley in 1905. The parish church of Manchester, dedicated to St. Mary the Virgin, St. George, and St. Denys, had been a collegiate church since 1422. The college was dissolved in 1547 and refounded in 1578. In 1847 it was constituted the cathedral of the new see, its dean and prebendaries becoming the dean and chapter. The episcopal residence, first fixed at Mauldeth

Hall, five miles from Manchester, was changed under Bishop Fraser to Bishopscourt, a house in the city.

1. James Prince Lee, 1847 ; distinguished Headmaster of King Edward's School, Birmingham ; d. 1869.
2. James Fraser (*q.v.*), 1870.
3. James Moorhouse, 1886 ; tr. from Melbourne ; res. 1903.
4. Edmund Arbuthnott Knox, 1903 ; tr. from suffragan bishopric of Coventry ; formerly Fellow of Merton College, Oxford. [G. C.]

Hansard. *Parl. Debates,* 1847 ; *V.C.H. Lancaster.*

MANNING, Henry Edward (1808-92), Cardinal Archbishop of Westminster, was born at Copped Hall, near Totteridge. His father was William Manning, merchant and M.P. He was educated at Harrow School, 1822-6, playing two years in the cricket eleven, and entered Balliol College, Oxford, in 1827. He soon distinguished himself as a speaker at the Union, and his contemporaries remembered him as a very handsome and smartly-dressed undergraduate, with much self-confidence and lofty ambitions. His father wished him to be a clergyman, but he had set his heart on political life, and was studiously preparing himself for it, when his father became bankrupt, and all hopes of an independent future were dissipated. In order to make a living he accepted a clerkship in the Colonial Office, but the work was distasteful to him and he soon resigned it. He had taken his degree, with a First Class in Classics, at the end of 1830, and he was elected to a Fellowship at Merton College in 1832. He had now made up his mind to seek holy orders. In December 1832 he was ordained deacon by Bishop Bagot of Oxford, and in January 1833 he went to Lavington, Sussex, as curate to a well-known Evangelical, the Rev. John Sargent, who was both squire and rector. On the 3rd of May in the same year Mr. Sargent died, and Manning was appointed to be rector. On the 7th November he married his late rector's daughter, Caroline Sargent, whose eldest sister had married Samuel Wilberforce (*q.v.*). In 1837 Mrs. Manning died. There were no children of the marriage.

Manning was an energetic parish-priest. He had been brought up an Evangelical ; began his work on those lines, and was a frequent and popular speaker on the platforms of Evangelical societies; but gradually the new influences which had been started by the Oxford Movement (*q.v.*) began to affect his

views. He kept aloof from the Tract-writers (though a share in Tract 78, printed 1837, was his), and remained on excellent terms with his diocesan, Bishop Otter ; but he began to realise the authority of the Church, and to maintain the Anglican Rule of Faith as against both popular Protestantism and the claims of Rome. These extremely orthodox views, coupled with his excellence as a preacher and a parish-priest, soon secured him official recognition. He was appointed Archdeacon of Chichester in 1840, and, after the secession of Newman (*q.v.*) and his friends in 1845, he came to be regarded as a leader of the High Church party. But, as years went on and the difficulties of Anglicanism became more apparent, his faith in the Church of England began to decay, and the Gorham Judgment (*q.v.*) of 1850, which seemed to show that the Judicial Committee of the Privy Council was for Anglicans the final authority in matters of faith, completed the process. He resigned his preferments in November 1850, and on the 6th of April 1851 was received into the Church of Rome. He was ordained priest by Cardinal Wiseman two months later, and then went to Rome to prosecute his theological studies, and remained there till 1854. Returning to England he was made Provost of the Chapter of Westminster, and founded and became head of the Congregation of the Oblates of St. Charles at Bayswater. He soon became known as the most ardent of ultramontanes, and so secured the special favour of Pius IX., who made him in 1865 Archbishop of Westminster, and cardinal in 1875. He became one of the most strenuous advocates for the definition of Papal Infallibility, and was a most zealous defender of the Temporal Power. By tact, social skill, and knowledge of the English people, he did much to popularise Romanism in England. He worked hard at social reform, laboured to promote the cause of total abstinence, and served on the Royal Commissions on the housing of the poor, and on elementary education. He died on the 14th of January 1892, and, after lying in state, was buried at St. Mary's Cemetery, Kensal Green. His funeral procession was a striking tribute to the regard and respect in which he was held by the people of London.

[G. W. E. R.]

Personal recollections ; Purcell, *Life.*

MARIAN EXILES, The, were the men and women who fled to the Continent during the reign of Mary to escape persecution [MARIAN REACTION]. Many found their way to Switzerland. Some went to Venice, others to Strasburg and Cracow. The largest body took refuge in Frankfort-on-the-Main. The first party appeared there in June 1554. Their stay was marked by incessant quarrelling. They were allowed the use of the French Protestant Church, and soon formed themselves into parties over the use of the English Prayer Book. William Whittingham (*q.v.*) and John Knox became the extreme anti-Prayer-Book party. They objected principally to the responses, and especially 'the suffrages devised off Pope Gregory,' *i.e.* the Litany; the custom of reading set portions of the Bible as lessons, gospels, and epistles; the observance of holy days; services without a sermon; private communions for the sick; the sign of the cross in baptism; the ring in marriage; the surplice; and the laying on of hands in confirmation. They appealed for help to Calvin, who replied condemning 'sundry leavings of Popish dregges' in the English book, with the result that many waverers were won over, and the anti-Prayer-Book party prevailed. Their triumph was short-lived, as, while they were still disputing, a party arrived, including Richard Cox, Dean of Christ Church and Westminster, and formerly tutor to Edward VI. Cox became a champion of the Prayer Book, and after an unedifying conflict during service time had Knox expelled and the Prayer Book reinstated. Whittingham, John Foxe (*q.v.*), and others then withdrew. Cox was elected minister, but soon resigned. David Whitehead succeeded him, but gave place to Robert Horne, afterwards Bishop of Winchester, in January 1556. A year later an acrimonious controversy arose on a question of Church government and discipline, Horne and Whitehead being protagonists of the two parties. Whitehead was victorious, and Horne withdrew to Strasburg.

Besides the exiles who went to Frankfort a small party, including Peter Martyr (*q.v.*) and Jewel (*q.v.*), afterwards Bishop of Salisbury, took refuge in Zurich, and devoted themselves to study, and, unlike their fellow-exiles, lived in peace and quietness. A small party went to Geneva, and chose for ministers Christopher Goodman (afterwards deprived for Nonconformity) and Knox. Many went to Strasburg, including Grindal (*q.v.*), Sandys, Sir John Cheke (*q.v.*), and Sir Arthur Coke. Troubles arose there also over the use of the Prayer Book: 'While some desire the book of reformation of the Church of England to be set aside altogether, others only deem some things in it objectionable, such as kneeling at the Lord's Supper, the

linen surplice, and other matters of this kind.'

Some went to Basle, and were joined by John Foxe and other dissentients from Frankfort, whose arrival caused an outbreak of strife. Some found their way to Wesel, in Westphalia, but left in a body because the Lutheran magistrates refused to let them celebrate the sacraments in the Genevan manner. In September 1556 they settled in Aarau, with Thomas Lever, Master of St. John's College, Cambridge, as their minister, and adopted a service book drawn up by Bullinger. It is worth noting that Lever two years before had been a champion of the English book at Frankfort.

John Laski, a Polish nobleman and a bishop, with Barlow (*q.v.*), Bishop of Bath and Wells, and a small party visited Poland, and seem to have combined instruction in the art of brewing with an attempt to propagate the principles of the Reformation. In the latter they were quite unsuccessful. The congregation of the Dutch church at Austin Friars founded by Laski underwent many adventures. They originally sailed for Denmark, but were not allowed to land on account of their Calvinistic opinions, and were rejected for the same cause in turn by Lübeck, Weimar, Rostock, and Hamburg. In each place a conference was held, and when their views were known expulsion followed, one Lutheran speaker calling them 'the devil's martyrs.' At last they found a refuge in the cities of East Friesland.

When the news came of the death of Mary in 1558 the great majority of the exiles returned to England. The effect of their sojourn abroad was to add a considerable impulse to the Reforming movement in England, already strengthened by memories of Smithfield. Extreme men like Knox became more determined, and moderate men like Lever and Whitehead became extreme. It is noteworthy that Whitehead, who was a leading supporter of the English Prayer Book at Frankfort, was afterwards deprived for Nonconformity. From one point of view the exile may be regarded as having given birth to English Nonconformity. The five years of freedom the exiles enjoyed, and their liberty to go as far in the Protestant direction as they wished, made it difficult for all, and impossible for most, ever to tolerate contentedly even the *tolerabiles ineptiae* of the English book.

[C. P. S. C.]

A brief discourse off the Troubles begunne at Franceford in Germany 1575; reprinted, Lond., 1908); Utenhove, *Simplex et fidelis Narratio*; *Original Letters* (Parker Soc.).

MARIAN REACTION. The reign of Queen Mary (*q.v.*) is an important era in the history of the English Church. The personal and private affairs of Henry VIII. had precipitated a breach with Rome which had long been preparing, and when the breach was once made it became much wider than Henry intended. The force of protest, when once released, carried the Church under the Edwardian politicians to an extreme, from which there was bound to be some recoil. Consequently at Edward's death there were many who saw no escape from the slippery slope on which the Church had recently seemed to be, except by grasping again the hand of Rome. Accordingly Mary found widespread support for her policy; Pole (*q.v.*) was welcomed, and a solemn reconciliation was made, 30th November 1554. But this reaction also involved more trouble than was at first seen. In some respects easy terms were made for the Edwardines. Married clergy were indeed ejected from their benefices, but in many cases they were put into others. The Edwardine orders were probably condemned in theory, but in practice apparently tolerated, only some supplementary ceremony being added where it was sought. The impropriated Church property was allowed to remain in lay hands, though this was abhorrent to the Queen herself.

But nothing could minimise the antagonism of those who had adopted the new views and those who clung to the old. To the former the old was superstition and idolatry, while to the latter the new was heresy. Consequently the Marian policy became one of acute persecution; and it was only consistent with the mediæval theory to which the prelates and politicians in power were essentially clinging, that that persecution should extend to the rack and the stake, and should involve inquisitorial examination into personal beliefs and private motives. From this procedure the conscience of England revolted; the day of religious toleration had not yet come, nor did it come for many a day, even in theory; but there was a demand for at least that modicum of toleration which soon the Elizabethan policy was to grant, viz. that a man should be judged only by his public action, not upon inquisitorial examination, and that, provided he conformed to certain external requirements of the law, he might believe what he chose. Other circumstances deepened the tragedy of Mary's reign: the hated match with Spain, full of bitterness to a poor, despised, and childless wife; the loss of Calais, the plagues, and agricultural depression. But here, as elsewhere at this period, religion was the chief motive force; and England after five years of the Roman alliance was eager to be rid of it again. The storm of change that swept over the country, as Pole and Mary died, defying governmental restraint, repudiating the leadership of the surviving Marian prelates, and welcoming with open arms the return of those who had been exiles for the reformed faith, shows how spontaneous was the revulsion of 1558, and how essentially short-lived the Marian reaction had been. Nothing had been permanently acquired. The old service-books had been brought back, but only to disappear again; the redecoration of the churches after the Edwardine sacrilege was undone by fresh acts of desecration. The Religious Orders, but momentarily restored, were again scattered. While Mary had perforce perpetuated some of the reforms of her brother and father, such as the increased number of dioceses, Elizabeth perpetuated nothing of her sister's.

But the reaction was valuable because it made a new starting-point for the English Reformation. It broke the entail of many of Henry's worst actions; it interrupted the down-grade tendencies of the rule of Edward's Council; and it showed in how many respects it would be folly, in throwing over the Marian policy, to return to that of Edward or Henry. Thus it prevented a return being made to the Royal Supremacy (*q.v.*), as Henry or Edward understood it, or to the Prayer Book as 1552 had left it, or to the Edwardine degradation of episcopacy, by the practical suppression of Convocation and of all episcopal disciplinary power—to name a few of the chief points. When Parker (*q.v.*) succeeded Pole, he was able to do so with much less of break than when Pole sat waiting for Cranmer (*q.v.*) to be burnt, before he could take possession of his see. And the reaction being over, in consequence of it, even amid the turmoil of controversy and perplexity which filled Western Christendom from end to end, many important things stood out in their true proportion better in England than elsewhere, and were beacon lights for future guidance.   [W. H. F.]

Dixon, *Hist. of the Ch. of Eng.*, vol. iv.; Frere, *Marian Reaction*, C.H.S.

MARPRELATE CONTROVERSY. In 1587 an anonymous pamphlet, *The Epistle to the Terrible Priests of the Confocation House*, written ostensibly by 'Martin Mar-prelate,' appeared on the streets in London. In it and its successors a humorous but ribald attack was made upon the bishops for withstanding the true Reformation. Moreover, said Martin, their mistakes of judgment were so apparent, their ignorance of doctrine so lamentable, and their inefficiency in administration so monumental that any one with half an eye could see that episcopacy was a failure. Martin would carry on war against this 'swinish rabble' and put a 'young Martin in euerie parish. . . . euerie one of them able to mar a prelate.' Martin's identity is still disputed, but the Tracts were the work of various hands, and the most important those of John Penry and William Udall. Their purpose was to render the bishops so ridiculous in the eyes of Elizabeth and her subjects that both would see that episcopacy was a bad form of Church government, because it would not work and because the bishops were fools. Elizabeth would then abolish episcopacy and set up the Book of Discipline for which the Puritans had been petitioning. The Tracts undoubtedly commanded wide attention; Bishop Cooper and the Dean of Salisbury issued ponderous refutations; Dr. Some answered them in kind; while Richard Bancroft (*q.v.*) strained every resource of the State to suppress them, and later preached one of the famous sermons of the century against the authors and their partisans.

There was reason for apprehension. Bancroft had a year or so earlier convinced the leaders of Church and State that the Puritans were few in number and by no means important for their position, wealth, or intelligence, but the reception accorded these Tracts made both ecclesiastics and statesmen wonder whether he had not been mistaken. This was the Armada year, when treason within might mean the loss of England's independence. The Tracts claimed to speak for a large body of men, and Elizabeth, fearful as ever of offending any one influential enough to make himself heard, was inclined to believe that the bishops had disobeyed her strict orders to connive at anything short of disloyalty, and was about to deal harshly with them in consequence. The State feared lest the Tracts portended a discontent so widespread that it might threaten the stability of the government; the Church was apprehensive lest Elizabeth's fright should destroy what independence it had left. The Marprelate Tracts were the climax of the first Puritan assault upon the Church in favour of the Book of Discipline.

But the Tracts had meanwhile opened a rift in the Puritan party itself. The Puritans favouring the Book of Discipline, fully conscious of the fact that the favour of the State was all-important, had decided in 1584 upon a campaign of petitions to Elizabeth and her ministers begging the adoption of their scheme. On its failure they had sanctioned the Tracts which should show the inanity and inefficiency of episcopacy, and in the meantime they had begun secretly to practise the ideas of the Book of Discipline. Classes were already in existence in 1584, and by 1587 provincial and national synods were sitting, and the extension of the scheme was already projected. They believed they had found a loophole in the laws and were comparatively safe. But Penry and Udall went a good deal further in their abuse of the bishops than the majority of the party approved; they roused Elizabeth's fears instead of her sympathies, and found themselves, instead of the bishops, objects of suspicion. The moderates were fearful that the active attempts of Bancroft to find the secret press would uncover the whole Puritan movement; they therefore disowned the Tracts and bitterly regretted their publication.

Their fears were well grounded. Bancroft found the press at Fawsley in Northamptonshire, chased the printers to Coventry and Manchester, where in August 1589 they surrendered. Penry and Udall escaped, but were later caught and executed. The whole Puritan party had by this time been implicated either in the publication of the Tracts or in the attempt to practise the discipline. Several men were arrested in the autumn of 1589 and spring of 1590, but all were finally set free in 1592 from lack of evidence to convict. The Marprelate Tracts, which were to have upset episcopacy, uncovered, and so broke up, the early Puritan movement.

[R. G. U.]

Arber, *Eng. Garner* and *Marprelate Tracts*; Usher, *Presbyterian Movement*, C.S., 1905, and *Reconstruction of the Eng. Ch.*

MARRIAGE, Law of. The Christian Church from the first regarded all marriage as, to quote the Book of Common Prayer, 'an honourable estate instituted of God.' The marriage of Christians, in addition to the divine origin which it shared with all marriage, was a union sanctified by the fact that God had taken human flesh in the Incarnation; that the persons contracting it had been baptized into the Church, whose union with Christ was expressed under the figure of marriage; and that He had approved it and regulated it. Therefore the marriage of Christians is a sacrament (it is so called in the Homilies), and is distinguished by the epithet 'holy.' It retains this character whether solemnised according to the Church's rites or not. For the baptized cannot divest themselves of their position as members of the Church; and in this sacrament the ministers are the parties themselves, the priest being only an appointed witness who gives the Church's blessing. A marriage which lacks that blessing is still a sacrament (unless invalidated by some canonical impediment), though irregular.

JURISDICTION.—It follows that Christian marriage must be subject to the Church's law. In England the Church assumed this jurisdiction from the first. Some of Augustine's (*q.v.*) questions to Gregory (*q.v.*) deal with points of marriage law. Theodore (*q.v.*) in his Penitential laid down rules about marriage. And the Church's law as embodied in these and other enactments was accepted by the State. For instance, Cnut (*q.v.*) gave civil sanction to the Church's rule concerning marriage within the prohibited degrees. An elaborate code of marriage law formed part of the Canon Law (*q.v.*), and Henry II. and his successors did not dispute the Church's right both to enact and to administer the law of marriage. The decisions of the church courts (*q.v.*) on questions of legitimacy were accepted by those of the State. But an attempt to force on the State the Church's rule, by which subsequent marriage of parents legitimatised bastard children, was rejected by the Council of Merton, 1236, the barons declaring *Nolumus leges Angliae mutari.* The civil courts retained control of questions of dower, though Archbishops Boniface and Peckham (*q.v.*) sought to bring them under the Church's jurisdiction.

The papal dispensing power was largely exercised in questions of marriage until 1534, when the Peter Pence Act (25 Hen. VIII. c. 21) ordered that this jurisdiction should be exercised by the Archbishop of Canterbury concurrently with the ordinary dispensing powers of the bishops. [BISHOPS.] The Succession Act, 1534 (25 Hen. VIII. c. 22), forbade the further exercise of the papal dispensing power over marriages within the prohibited degrees. This provision was repeated in 1536 (28 Hen. VIII. c. 7) and 1540 (32 Hen. VIII. c. 38). But apart from the abolition of this power, and of appeals to Rome generally (which in recent times had been largely concerned with marriage cases), Henry VIII.'s statutes did not affect the Church's matrimonial jurisdiction, which its courts continued to exercise until 1857. In 1682 the King's Bench definitely declared

that questions of marriage law fell within the cognisance of the ecclesiastical courts, since 'divines better know how to expound the law of marriages than the common lawyers' (*Watkinson v. Mergatron*, Raym. 464). The first breach in the canon law of marriage was made by Parliament in 1753 (see below). The Act of 1836 transferred the ordinance to 'the bleak and frigid zone of civil contract.' The Church was now administering law the making of which the State had assumed to itself. This circumstance, together with the constant breaches of the Church's law of divorce by private Acts of Parliament, made the matrimonial jurisdiction of the ecclesiastical courts a meaningless survival. By 1830 the time was not ripe for decisive change. The Courts Commission [COMMISSIONS, ROYAL] merely hinted at the desirability of divorce *a vinculo*, and recommended that the church courts should be reformed to enable them to administer the existing marriage laws more efficiently. But reforms came slowly, and the antiquated procedure of the courts, combined with the fact that the Church's law no longer represented the conscience of the nation, to render it imperative that the State should take over the administration of what was becoming an increasingly secular code. A Bill to enable a civil court to grant divorce failed to obtain a second reading in 1843. In 1850 a Royal Commission was appointed to inquire into the law of divorce and its administration. It reported in 1853 that all matrimonial causes should be transferred to a new civil tribunal. Bills founded on the report failed to pass in 1854 and 1856. But in 1857 the Divorce and Matrimonial Causes Act (20-1 Vic. c. 85) abolished the matrimonial jurisdiction of the ecclesiastical courts, and replaced them by a new secular court. The effect of this Act on the law of marriage will be discussed below. As regards jurisdiction, its result was to mark the final separation of the marriage law of the State from that of the Church, which is still binding on the conscience of its members, like any other part of its moral law, but is no longer accepted and enforced as a whole by the civil power. The State has now its own marriage laws (based in part upon the canon law), to which churchmen are subject as citizens except where they conflict with the Church's law. [CHURCH AND STATE.]

WHO MAY MARRY.—The general principle that any baptized man and woman may contract a Christian marriage is naturally subject to considerable limitations. These were reduced by the canonists to fifteen heads.

Some of these, such as *mistaken identity* and the use of *force*, do not require detailed consideration. The intention of the parties to contract marriage with each other was always essential. *Diversity in religion* was also an impediment. Marriage with non-Christians was forbidden by the early councils. The prohibition, though based on Scripture (1 Cor. 7[39]), was frequently disregarded. Prominent examples in English history are the marriages of Aethelbert of Kent [AUGUSTINE] and Edwin of Northumbria [PAULINUS]. In later times marriage with a Jew was felony by English law. By canon law marriage with an unbaptized person, though irregular, is apparently valid. *Physical disabilities* were also grounds of invalidity.

Bigamy.—The fact that either party had a wife living was in general a complete bar to remarriage. In England bigamy was an offence against the ecclesiastical law only, until 1604, when it was made felony except for persons whose husband or wife had been beyond the seas for seven years and were not known to be alive (1 Jac. I. c. 11).

For restrictions imposed by holy orders see MARRIAGE OF THE CLERGY.

By canon law marriage was void by reason of *age* only if the parties were incapable of giving rational consent, *i.e.* under seven years, but it was voidable if the husband were under fourteen or the wife under twelve. Otherwise it was good in spite of the withholding of the consent of parents or guardians. Canon 100 of 1604 forbade but did not invalidate marriage of persons under twenty-one without such consent. By Lord Hardwicke's Marriage Act, 1753 (26 Geo. II. c. 33), marriage by licence was void without such consent if either party (not being a widower or widow) were under twenty-one. This provision was repealed in 1822 (3 Geo. IV. c. 75). And in 1823 4 Geo. IV. c. 76 restored the rule of Canon 100, so that all marriages are now valid if the parties are over fourteen and twelve respectively, though up to twenty-one the consent of parents or guardians should be obtained.

Prohibited Degrees.—Fear of sanctioning incest has caused the Church to prohibit the marriage of near relations. Its law on this subject is based on the Mosaic code (Levit. 18, 20; Deut. 22, 27) and on the Roman civil law, but was much elaborated by the canonists. Its prohibitions were founded on:—

1. Consanguinity, blood relationship either in the direct line, which was an absolute bar, or collaterally through descent from a common ancestor, when the relationship was computed by counting the steps by which each party was separated from that ancestor. Thus brother and sister were related in the first degree, 'first cousins' in the second. If the lines of descent varied in length, the shorter was taken for this purpose. The Lateran Council, 1215, forbade marriage in the fourth degree. Before this it had been forbidden up to the seventh. For this purpose half-blood relationship is equivalent to that of the whole blood.

2. Affinity was based on the text: 'They shall be one flesh' (Gen. 2[21]). The blood relations of either party to a marriage stood in the same relationship to the other; and the rules of consanguinity were applied. This was affinity of the first genus. But the principle was extended so as to make a man related by affinity of the second genus to the husbands and wives of his wife's kindred, and so on. But the council of 1215 declared that only affinity of the first genus was a bar to marriage. Affinity was created by fornication.[1] In 1527 Henry VIII. sought a papal dispensation from the affinity between himself and Anne Boleyn, caused by his illicit relations with her sister (Brewer, *Henry VIII.*, ii. 240). Even a promise to marry was held to create 'quasi-affinity.'

3. Spiritual affinity arose out of the analogy between standing sponsor and actual parenthood. At first the sponsor was only forbidden to marry the godchild or its parent. The rule was afterwards extended to its other kin, and spiritual affinity was held to exist between a person confirmed (and his kin) and the person presenting him for confirmation. This 'maze of flighty fancies and misapplied logic' has been ignored by the English Church since the sixteenth century. Its law no longer knows anything of spiritual affinity as a bar to marriage.

In the Middle Ages the law of prohibited degrees was so far-reaching and complicated that the papal dispensing power had to be freely used as a corrective. This power was abolished in England by the statutes cited above, which reduced the prohibited degrees to those of 'God's law,' meaning the rules contained in Levit. 18 or to be deduced therefrom. A Table on these lines was published by Archbishop Parker (*q.v.*) in 1563, and authorised by Canon 99 of 1604. It is printed at the end of the Prayer Book, and is still the law of the English Church. In practice, however, marriages within these degrees were not held void unless declared so

---

[1] This is apparently still the law of the English Church, though the authorities are not perfectly clear.

by the ecclesiastical court after proceedings taken, and this could not be after the death of either party. Many such marriages were contracted, especially with deceased wives' sisters. But the parties could never be sure that proceedings might not be taken and their children declared illegitimate. In 1834 the seventh Duke of Beaufort contracted such a marriage, and Lord Lyndhurst's Marriage Act, 1835 (5-6 Will. IV. c. 54), was passed primarily to relieve him of this uncertainty. It provided that marriages already contracted within the degrees of affinity should not be annulled, but that for the future all such marriages should be absolutely void. This caused dissatisfaction, and in 1847 a Royal Commission was appointed, with Bishop Lonsdale of Lichfield as chairman. It reported that marriages with a deceased wife's sister were still common, and was in favour of legalising them. Bills with this object were constantly introduced from 1849 to 1907, when 7 Edw. VII. c. 47 enacted that they should not be void or voidable by reason of the affinity, but expressly refrained from altering the position of the clergy of the English Church with regard to them, under the ecclesiastical law, which remains binding on the conscience of churchmen, though that of the State is not in harmony with it in this particular.

It may be added that the canon law divides all impediments to matrimony into two classes: an *impedimentum impediens* does not invalidate the marriage, but renders the parties liable to ecclesiastical censures, *e.g.* if either party is under twenty-one (but over fourteen); an *impedimentum dirimens* nullifies the pretensed marriage altogether, *e.g.* if either party has a spouse living.

CONDITIONS OF MARRIAGE.—It being ascertained that no impediment exists, the essential requisite to constitute the marriage is the mutual *consent* of the parties. From early times this was signified by betrothal, which was of two kinds: *sponsalia per verba de futuro*, a binding contract to marry, which was held to constitute a valid marriage when consummated, and *sponsalia per verba de praesenti*, a declaration that they took one another, then and there, as husband and wife. Such betrothals were hardly distinguishable in effect from actual marriage; they formed a contract which could not be dissolved by one of the parties actually contracting and consummating an otherwise valid marriage with a third person—a fact which shows that the canonists regarded the mutual promise to marry as the essence of the sacrament, not sexual intercourse or the religious cere-

mony. *Consensus facit matrimonium.* The Act of 1540, already cited, forbade marriages solemnised and consummated to be dissolved merely on the ground of pre-contract. But by 1548 it was found that this provision, though 'godly meant,' was 'ungodly abused' by those who wished to break their promises to marry. It was therefore repealed (2-3 Edw. VI. c. 23), and questions of pre-contract left to the church courts to be dealt with according to canon law, until the Marriage Act, 1753, abolished suits for specific performance of contracts to marry.

Betrothal was normally followed by the *marriage ceremony*, which from early times was regarded by Christians as a religious rite. The Church considered it important to prevent any secrecy or uncertainty about marriages. Publicity was a powerful safeguard against violation of the law of canonical impediments. And for these reasons, as well as because it was desirable that it should be hallowed by the Church's blessing, the canon law declared that marriage must be contracted publicly *in facie ecclesiae*. A secret union without any religious ceremony though valid was irregular, and the parties were liable to ecclesiastical censures for violating the Church's discipline.

To prevent such clandestine marriages the custom arose in the twelfth century of publishing *banns*, that is, announcing an intended marriage publicly, and calling on those who knew of any impediment to declare it. In 1200 Archbishop Hubert Walter (*q.v.*) forbade the celebration of marriages until banns had been thrice published in church (*Hoveden*. R.S., iv. 135), and the Lateran Council, 1215, made this the rule of the Western Church.

From at least the early part of the fourteenth century the bishops acquired the power of dispensing with the necessity of banns. This power of granting *licences* was confirmed to the bishops by the Peter Pence Act, 1534 (25 Hen. VIII. c. 21), which also permitted the Archbishop of Canterbury to grant in both provinces such licences and dispensations as had been formerly given by the Pope. The present law of the Church on the subject is contained in the rubrics in the Marriage Service and in Canons 62 and 101. Banns must be published in the parish churches of the parties on three Sundays or holy days, or a licence must be obtained. A common licence, simply dispensing with the necessity of banns, may be granted by any bishop through the Chancellor and his surrogates; a special licence to marry at any convenient time and place only by the Archbishop of Canterbury through his officials. The granting of a licence is a matter of discretion and not of right. The question how far a bishop can control his Chancellor in granting or refusing licences must depend mainly on the wording of the Chancellor's patent. [COURTS.]

The Council of Westminster (1175) had decreed that any priest celebrating a *clandestine marriage* should be suspended for three years. At the close of the seventeenth century Parliament found it necessary to enforce the Church's law on this subject by civil penalties (1695, 6-7 Will. III. c. 6; 1696, 7-8 Will. III. c. 35). In 1711 the clergyman celebrating such a marriage was to be fined £100 (10 An. c. 19). Yet clandestine marriages increased to an alarming extent. 'The vision of a broken-down parson ready, without asking questions, to marry any man to any woman for a crown and a bottle, was an ever-present terror to parents and guardians.' In 1753 this evil induced Parliament for the first time to deal with the principles of the law of marriage by passing Lord Hardwicke's Marriage Act (26 Geo. II. c. 33), enacting that marriages without banns or licence should be void, though by the Church's law they were irregular, indeed, but valid. The Act further required the presence of two witnesses besides the officiating clergyman, and the keeping of a marriage register. This Act being enforced by severe penalties, fourteen years' transportation for a transgressing clergyman, and death for forging an entry in the register, undoubtedly checked clandestine marriages. Eloping couples were obliged to have recourse to Gretna Green, the nearest village over the Scottish border, where the Act did not run. But its stringency in making clandestine marriages void produced evil results, and it was repealed by the Marriage Act, 1823 (4 Geo. IV. c. 76), which re-enacted most of its other provisions but restored the Church's rule as to the validity of clandestine marriages. Thus between 1753 and 1823 a clergyman solemnising such a marriage was liable to transportation, and the marriage was void. Since 1823 the marriage is valid in civil as in canon law, but the clergyman is still guilty of a felony.

Time and Place of Marriage.—By the canon law marriage might not be solemnised between Advent Sunday and the Octave of the Epiphany (exclusive), nor between Septuagesima and Low Sunday, nor between the first Rogation Day and the seventh day after Pentecost (inclusive). In Elizabeth's reign these rules were recognised, and dispensations from them granted by the Archbishops of Canterbury. An attempt to abolish them in part failed in 1562. A canon permitting marriage throughout the year was passed by Convocation in 1575, but did not obtain the royal assent. In practice these prohibitions appear to have lapsed. Canon 62 of 1604 laid down that marriages might only be celebrated between eight and twelve in the forenoon, but a canon of 1888 extended the time to three P.M., to bring the Church's rule into harmony with the Marriage Act, 1886 (49-50 Vic. c. 14). A marriage *in facie ecclesiae* must be celebrated in the parish church of one of the parties, or in some public chapel duly licensed for the purpose. But a special licence may authorise the marriage to be celebrated in any place.

The *form* of marriage is that set out in the Prayer Book, but all that is essential by canon law is the mutual taking of each other as husband and wife. The form of words required by statute for civil validity (Marriage Act, 1898, 61-2 Vic. c. 58) contains a declaration that the parties know no impediment as well as the mutual consent.

Civil Marriage was first permitted in England by the Marriage Act, 1836 (6-7 Will. IV. c. 85). By this and the Acts amending it licences may be granted by a State official, the registrar, the marriage contract entered into in his presence, and in any building registered for the purpose. Such a marriage contracted by members of the Church is valid but irregular, and a breach of discipline.

DIVORCE.—Indissolubility is a characteristic of Christian marriage. From this it follows that though under certain circumstances, such as infidelity or cruelty, it may be advisable to allow the parties to separate, neither of them may marry again during the lifetime of the other; for that would be to break the tie contracted by the original marriage. This rule is based on Holy Scripture (Mt. 5^{32}, $19^{3 \cdot 9}$; [1] Mk. $10^{2 \cdot 12}$; Lk. 16^{18}; Rom. $7^{2 \cdot 3}$; 1 Cor. $7^{10 \cdot 11, \ 39}$). The Western Church has always in theory held the absolute indissolubility of the marriage tie. On marriage as on other subjects the canon law developed and to a great extent became fixed in the twelfth century. Its leading features may thus be summarised :—

1. Marriage was indissoluble; therefore divorce *a vinculo*, from the marriage tie, involving freedom to either party to remarry during the other's life, was absolutely prohibited.

2. This rule was evaded by the practice of declaring marriages null. If impediment could be shown to have existed the marriage

[1] The interpretation of the apparent except in in Mt. 19 is disputed; it has been held to refer to pre-nuptial fornication as nullifying subsequent marriage.

was void *ab initio* ; no tie had ever existed, and therefore both parties were free. This jurisdiction was extensively exercised, especially by the papal court ; so that, in the words of the Act of 1540, already quoted, ' marriages have been brought into such an uncertainty thereby that no marriage could be so surely knit and bounden but it should lie in either of the parties power and arbitre, casting away the fear of God . . . to prove a pre-contract, a kindred, an alliance, or a carnal knowledge to defeat the same.'

3. The distinction was recognised between divorce *a vinculo* and divorce *a mensa et toro*, or separation from board and bed, which was granted by the church courts for adultery or cruelty. This did not break the marriage tie, and so gave no liberty of remarriage ; the possibility of a reconciliation was always borne in mind.

The breach with Rome did not affect this law except by abolishing the papal dispensing power. The *Reformatio Legum* (*q.v.*) proposed, probably under the influence of foreign reformers, to abolish divorce *a mensa et toro*, and to allow divorce *a vinculo* with leave to the innocent party to remarry in cases of adultery, cruelty, desertion, and long absence. This scheme never became law, but is said, apparently on insufficient evidence, to have been acted on by the courts during the remainder of the sixteenth century. In fact, the Church refused to accept the ' wild ideas ' of the foreigners who no longer regarded marriage as a sacrament. The canons of 1597 and 1604 presuppose the older rule against divorce *a vinculo*, deal only with separation and nullity, and specifically forbid remarriage. This prohibition was not always regarded. In 1605 Laud (*q.v.*) married the Earl of Devon to Lady Rich, who was divorced *a mensa et toro* for adultery. His lifelong penitence, and the fact that the legality of the marriage was questioned, show the prevalence of the belief that the marriage tie was indissoluble. Down to 1857 the church courts granted (i) divorce *a mensa et toro* at the suit of either party for adultery or cruelty ; (ii) a decree of nullity on the ground of prohibited degrees, a pre-existing marriage, physical or mental incompetency. This sentence made the marriage void *ab initio*, rendered the issue illegitimate, and the parties free to remarry.

With the church courts thus rigorously administering the canon law it was necessary for those who wished to be free of the marriage tie to have recourse to Parliament. The first private Act was passed in 1552 to legalise the second marriage of the Marquis of Northampton while his first wife was alive. On Mary's accession it was repealed, thus leaving the second marchioness in an equivocal position. More than a century later (1669) an Act dissolving the marriage of Lord de Roos for his wife's adultery passed with difficulty. All the bishops but Cosin (*q.v.*), Reynolds, and Wilkins opposed it. Charles II. (apparently with some idea of obtaining a similar Act for himself) attended the debates in the House of Lords, and found them ' better than a play.' During the eighteenth century the number of private divorce Acts averaged about one a year, and from 1800 to 1852 more than two a year. The party applying for an Act must obtain a sentence of divorce *a mensa et toro* in the church court, and (usually) a verdict and damages for ' criminal conversation ' in a civil court. This was frequently collusive, there being no intention that the damages should be paid. The Standing Orders of the House of Lords required a clause forbidding remarriage of the guilty party to be included in the Bill, but it was always struck out at a later stage. A husband whose own conduct was without reproach could always obtain such an Act for his wife's adultery ; a wife only if the husband's adultery were aggravated by other circumstances. Only four Acts were granted at the wife's instance. An unopposed Act cost in all about £1000 ; the costs were much higher if the proceedings were opposed. This costly, cumbrous, and disingenuous procedure caused general dissatisfaction. Robert Phillimore (*q.v.*) complained of the ' canvassing ' and ' soliciting of support ' in Parliament. And the system of ' granting a private favour by Act of Parliament ' was clearly immoral in itself, as well as in its effect, which was to allow to the rich an exemption from the law which was denied to the poor. There was a growing demand for a readier method of obtaining divorce *a vinculo*. And it was inevitable that the State should refuse to be bound by the Church's marriage law, which no longer harmonised with public opinion. This state of things resulted in the Divorce Act, 1857, which (besides abolishing the ecclesiastical jurisdiction over marriage) allowed divorce *a vinculo* for the wife's adultery or for the husband's adultery with aggravating circumstances. It did not compel a clergyman to remarry a guilty party, but he must allow the use of his church if another clergyman is willing to perform the ceremony. It allowed ' judicial separation,' the equivalent of divorce *a mensa et toro*, for adultery, cruelty, or desertion. The Bill was strongly opposed by Gladstone (*q.v.*) in the Commons and S. Wilberforce (*q.v.*) in the Lords. Tait (*q.v.*), then Bishop of London, supported it. A clause forbidding remarriage of the guilty party was carried by Archbishop Sumner but afterwards struck out. The effect of the Act was to separate the law of Church and State on an essential point of morals and divine revelation. The State has a legal right to consider the marriage tie dissoluble and frame its laws accordingly, but its action cannot affect either the law of the Church or the binding obligation of that law upon churchmen. The indissolubility of Christian marriage was again affirmed by the Convocation of Canterbury in 1896-8.

[G. C.]

W. J. Knox Little, *Holy Matrimony*; *Dict. Chris. Antiq.*, article 'Marriage'; Pollock and Maitland, *Hist. Eng. Law*; Phillimore, *Eccl. Law*; *Reports of Royal Commissions of 1847 and 1850*; *Chron. Conc.*, 1896-8.

MARRIAGE OF THE CLERGY.

In the first three centuries there was no rule of the Church against the ordination of married persons, nor against the use of marriage after ordination. On the other hand, by at least the early years of the third century the rule was established that no bishop, priest, or deacon should marry after ordination; and no instance to the contrary is known, except in so far that for a time in part of the East a deacon could marry if he gave notice of his intention at the time of his ordination; in 451 the Fourth General Council (Canon 14) by implication includes subdeacons in this prohibition, indicating at the same time that in some provinces it had been extended to readers and singers. But at the beginning of the fourth century there was a growing disposition to require the married to discontinue the use of their marriage after ordination. This was checked in the East by the Council of Nicæa (Socr., *H.E.* i. 11), and again at Gangra in 350 (Canon 4). But in the West it was enacted at Elvira in 306 (Canon 33), and at the end of the century in Africa in 390 (II. Carthage, Canon 2); in Spain again in 400 (I. Toledo, Canon 1) and later; and in Gaul in 452 (II. Arles, Canon 44). Meanwhile Pope Siricius urgently enjoined it in his decretal epistle to Himerius of Tarragona in 385; and he was followed by Innocent I. in his letter to Exuperius of Toulouse in 404, and by St. Leo, who extended the prohibition to subdeacons, in 445 (*Ep.* xii. 4); and henceforth abstinence from the use of marriage became the theoretical rule of the Western

Church. The Eastern Church defined its own discipline in the Council in Trullo in 692; it repudiates the Roman tradition, and admits married men to the diaconate and the presbyterate, without their ceasing to cohabit with their wives; but a bishop must separate from his wife before consecration (Canons 13, 48). In his answer to St. Augustine's (*q.v.*) interrogations (Bede, *H.E.* i. 27), St. Gregory the Great (*q.v.*) implies that the major orders in England will be celibate; but elsewhere he allows exceptions in the case of subdeacons in provinces where their celibacy is not customary. How far the rule was strictly carried out in the early Middle Ages is perhaps not very clear. But in England, after the Danish invasions of the ninth century and the desolation and demoralisation that resulted from them, the parish clergy were generally married men living with their wives, and even the monastic and cathedral churches were served by seculars who were generally married and did not live the common life. As a consequence of the monastic revival of the tenth century, in the early years of the eleventh century protests were raised against the married clergy. In the laws made at Aenham (1009) priests are ordered to live in chastity, since it is not lawful for them to use wives; and in the canons written for Wulfsige of Sherborne, and in the pastoral letter written for Wulfstan of York, both by Aelfric (*q.v.*), the unlawfulness of the marriage of priests is urged, while it is confessed that it is impossible to force them to chastity. In the great 'Hildebrandine' reforms, which began with the papacy of Leo IX. (1048-54), along with the uprooting of simony, the enforcement of the celibacy of the clergy was a dominant feature. Leo IX. and Nicolas II. (1059-61) legislated anew on the matter; but a crisis was reached when Hildebrand, now Gregory VII. (1073-86), in a Roman Synod of 1074, following Nicolas II., inhibited married priests, deacons, and subdeacons, and forbade the laity to hear their Masses. This enactment raised a storm of protest in France and Germany. In England it was not at once acted upon. In the Council of Winchester, 1076, canons were forbidden to be married, while parish priests were not required to put away their wives, but the unmarried were forbidden to marry, and bishops to ordain married men to the diaconate or the priesthood. At the Synod of Westminster in 1102, under St. Anselm (*q.v.*), it was ruled that no clerk above a subdeacon might marry, and those who were married must put away their wives; that a married priest might not say Mass, nor the people hear him if he did; and that sons of priests might not inherit their fathers' benefices. It was found impossible to enforce this legislation, and in 1107 Paschal II. in a letter to St. Anselm dispensed with the rule. In 1129 a Synod of London committed it to Henry I. to deal with the recusant clergy, with the result that the King considerably increased his revenue by allowing the clergy to keep their wives on payment of a fine. In the thirteenth century ecclesiastical legislation against the married clergy is repeated over and over again—a proof that the situation persisted; and, in fact, the cohabitation of clergymen with partners, whether after marriage (which however irregular was not void in itself, but only voidable if challenged in an ecclesiastical court during the lifetime of the partners) or in some form of concubinage, continued and was connived at in the fourteenth, fifteenth, and early sixteenth century. On the other hand, there is no ground for the report that a letter of Erasmus implies that Archbishop Warham (*q.v.*) had a wife and family; for the letter has no address, and the insertion of Warham's name is due to the eighteenth-century editor, while the letter was almost certainly meant for Mountjoy.

In the reforming movements on the Continent, both German and Swiss, from the outset (*e.g.* in Luther's *Address to the Nobility* and *The Babylonish Captivity* of 1520) the abolition of the prohibition of clerical marriage was part of the programme. In England even as early as 1521 Henry VIII. had occasion to issue a proclamation inhibiting and depriving those priests, 'few in number,' who had married of their own authority, and threatening with more serious punishment those who should marry hereafter. In 1532, on the eve of his election to Canterbury, Cranmer (*q.v.*) married his second wife; clerical marriage was here also part of the reforming programme; and the *Bishops' Book* of 1537 omitted all reference to any restrictions on the clergy. But this reform made no progress in Henry's reign; on the contrary, the Six Articles Act of 1539 voided all marriages of priests, decreed forfeiture of goods and benefices against those who refused to put away their wives, and made such marriage in future felony; and in the *King's Book* of 1543 the text of the *Bishops' Book* was changed so as to exclude the marriage of priests. On the accession of Edward VI. the situation was at once changed. Convocation in 1547, by fifty-three votes as against twenty-two, resolved that all canons, etc., restricting or condemning clerical marri-

ages should be utterly void; at the beginning of 1549 an Act was passed legalising the marriage of priests (2-3 Edw. VI. c. 21); and in 1552 a further Act aimed at relieving such marriages from the stigma which still attached to them and legitimating the issue of them (5-6 Edw. VI. c. 12). On the accession of Mary, before the repeal of the Edwardine Acts, the married clergy, first in London, then throughout the country, were deprived of their benefices; and the first Act of Repeal in the autumn of 1553 (1 Mar. sess. 2, c. 2) abolished the Acts of 1549 and 1551. These were not restored in Elizabeth's reign, but in 1559 the twenty-ninth of the *Injunctions* recognised clerical marriages, but, in view of offence that had been given through indiscretion on the part of the clergy, the consent of the bishop and two justices of the peace, and the goodwill of the woman's parents, kinsfolk, or master, was required for any such marriage; and the warrant issued to the High Commission empowered it to restore to their benefices those who had been deprived for marriage under Mary. The Millenary Petition presented by the Puritan divines to James I. on his accession in 1603 asked that the Act of 1551 might be revived; and in 1604 both the Edwardine Acts were re-enacted (1 Jac. I. c. 25). Meanwhile in 1563 the Tridentine Council (*Sess.* xxiv. Canon 9) had anathematised any who should say that clergymen in major orders could contract valid marriages.

[F. E. B.]

Thomassinus, *Vet. et nova Eccl. Disciplina.* ii. 60 *sqq.*: J. Wordsworth, *The Ministry of Grace*; E. L. Cutts, *Parish Priests and their People in the Middle Ages in Eng.*; Gee and Hardy, *Documents illustrative of Eng. Ch. Hist.*; Prothero, *Statutes and Constitutional Documents, 1559-1625.*

MARRIOTT, Charles (1811-58), divine, entered Exeter College, Oxford, March 1829, but became scholar of Balliol in November 1832; he won a First Class in Classics and Second Class in Mathematics. Easter, 1833, he was elected Fellow of Oriel (with Rogers, later Lord Blachford), succeeding R. I. Wilberforce (*q.v.*). He was ordained, and, 1838, left Oxford to become first Principal of the Theological College, Chichester, where he began work, February 1839, but resigned, 1841, and returned to Oriel. He had collaborated with Manning (*q.v.*) in compiling No. 78 of the *Tracts for the Times*, 1837, and was a close friend of Newman, Pusey, and Keble (*q.v.*). He became one of the foremost men of the Oxford Movement (*q.v.*), and on Newman's secession, which was a heavy blow to him, he did much to strengthen waverers.

He was associated after 1845 with Keble and Pusey as joint editor of the *Library of the Fathers*, but the real burden of the work fell on Marriott. In 1850 he became Vicar of St. Mary's. Many who were drawn to Rome or unbelief turned to him for help. To his rooms came most foreign ecclesiastics of distinction who visited Oxford, learned Benedictines, American and colonial bishops. When cholera broke out at Oxford, 1854, Marriott was constant in visiting the sick, hearing their confessions, and ministering to them. In a subsequent smallpox epidemic he took the disease, and was seriously ill. In the same year his influence in the University was shown by his election as a member of the Hebdomadal Council, then first constituted. His heavy labours brought on a stroke of paralysis, 1855. He lingered on three years at his brother's house at Bradfield, and died there, 15th September 1858. Marriott was a man of brilliant gifts, a finished scholar, and a thinker. Little remains of his work, since he spent himself so freely on the *Library of the Fathers*. 'No one,' says Church, 'did more than Marriott to persuade those around him of the solid underground religious reality of the Oxford Movement.'   [S. L. O.]

Church, *Oxford Movement* : Burgon, *Lives*.

MARTYR, Peter, properly Peter Martyr Vermigli (1500-62), reformer, was an Italian, born at Florence. He became an Augustinian Canon at the age of sixteen, and studied for eight years in the University of Padua, where he learnt Greek and Hebrew, and became acquainted with Reginald Pole (*q.v.*), who befriended him at Rome when forbidden to preach on suspicion of heresy. He became Abbot of Spoleto about 1530, and Prior of St. Fridian at Lucca, 1534. Here he came to hold Zwinglian views, and in 1543 fled to Zurich to avoid persecution, and thence to Basle, writing to his disciples that he was inspired by God to choose the fit moment for deserting them. At Strasburg he was appointed Professor of Theology, and married Catherine Dammartin, an ex-nun.

In 1547 Cranmer (*q.v.*) invited Martyr and Ochino to England, paid £126, 7s. 6d. for their outfit and journey, and procured pensions of forty marks a year for them. In 1549 Martyr was appointed Regius Professor of Divinity at Oxford, and in 1550 was made Canon of Christ Church, where he shared with the dean, Richard Cox, the distinction of being the first to introduce women as residents in any college or hall in Oxford—a proceeding which was resented by the inhabitants, who broke his windows so often that he was forced to change his lodgings and fortify his garden. He joined with Bucer (*q.v.*) in criticising the Prayer Book of 1549, with which he was imperfectly acquainted, and his exhortations produced their effect in the Prayer Book of 1552. [COMMON PRAYER, BOOK OF.] He was much looked up to by the leading reformers, though his increasing Zwinglianism led to differences with Bucer. In Christ Church he refused to wear a surplice. On Mary's accession he was confined, but allowed to escape to the Continent. Some opposition was made to his reappointment at Strasburg, on the ground that he had given up the Lutheran doctrine of the Eucharist, and though this was unsuccessful at the time he was forced to leave in 1556, and retired to Zurich, where he married again. After the death of Mary he declined to return to Oxford, though he kept up a regular correspondence with Jewel (*q.v.*), Parkhurst, Sandys, and others. His first wife died at Oxford, and was buried in the cathedral, near the tomb of St. Frideswide (*q.v.*). Her body, by Mary's orders, was disinterred and thrown on a dung-heap. After Elizabeth's accession her remains were collected and mingled with the relics of St. Frideswide.   [C. P. S. C.]

Letters (Parker Soc.) ; *D.N.B.*

MARY, Queen (1516-58), the only child of Henry VIII. and Katherine of Aragon who survived infancy, was born on the 18th February 1516. Political matches were proposed for her even in her infant years, and the projects continually changed. She was highly accomplished. Her misfortunes began when she was eleven years old, the time when her father was first known to be seeking a divorce from her mother ; and the way for the great design was paved by a lie, that the French ambassador had questioned the legitimacy of her birth. Six years later the King achieved his purpose by casting off the Pope's authority, marrying Anne Boleyn, and getting from Cranmer (*q.v.*) a sentence declaring the nullity of his marriage with Katherine. Acts were passed in Parliament in accordance with the King's views, and Mary was told that her own father had threatened to take her life if she did not acknowledge herself a bastard. Later, on the birth of Anne Boleyn's daughter, she was more imperatively ordered to give up the name of princess, and was made to act as lady's maid to her half-sister. Her treatment, and that of her mother, grew worse and worse, and they were separated from each other that they might receive no mutual sympathy. Then, after her mother's death, a project was formed by the Imperial ambassador to rescue her from her father's tyranny by carrying her off to Flanders; but she was too well watched. After the fall of Anne Boleyn in 1536 she was once more received into favour, but only after signing, with averted eyes, the repulsive statement that she was the child of an incestuous union. forbidden by God's law and man's. She was then not only relieved from intolerable persecution, but replaced in the succession by her father's will, confirmed by Act of Parliament.

Under the reign of her brother Edward she was again seriously persecuted. Like several of the bishops, she could not acknowledge that the changes in religion made by the Council were constitutional, and she refused to use the new Prayer Book or to discontinue her Mass. The Emperor's ambassador interfered on her behalf, and obtained a promise of toleration to her, which the Council afterwards repudiated as only temporary, Warwick being well aware that the Emperor had troubles enough with the Protestants in Germany to prevent him taking action against England. Finally Warwick, having been created Duke of Northumberland, organised his audacious plot for diverting the succession to the throne from Mary to Lady Jane Grey. Lady Jane, however, only queened it for nine days, and on the 19th July 1553 Mary was proclaimed in London. Bishop Gardiner (*q.v.*) and others were released from prison, and a number of real traitors sent to the Tower. But there was still a dangerous spirit abroad, especially in London. where on the 13th August a dagger was thrown at Dr. Bourne, Bishop Bonner's (*q.v.*) chaplain, while preaching at Paul's Cross, because he said his master's late imprisonment had been unjust. Five days later the Queen issued a proclamation declaring her desire, while maintaining her own religion, to put no undue pressure on her subjects in that matter till a settlement could be reached, and urging mutual toleration. At the same time Northumberland, his son Warwick, the Marquis of Northampton, and three of their confederates were arraigned and received sentence for treason; but only the duke himself and two others were executed. Mary proceeded with cautious lenity. Bishops deprived under Edward were restored to their sees. Gardiner was made Lord Chancellor, and Parliament reversed Edward VI.'s laws about religion.

In November Parliament petitioned the Queen to marry an Englishman; but, un-

happily, she had decided otherwise and promised the Imperial ambassador that she would wed Philip of Spain, the Emperor's son. The Emperor had befriended her hitherto as no one else could do; but politically the choice was most disastrous for England, destroying cordiality with France. Early in 1554 insurrections broke out in various parts against the Spanish marriage, in which, especially in Wyatt's insurrection in Kent, there was a hidden design of restoring the Edwardine religion. But these movements collapsed, even that of Wyatt, after he had reached the gates of London; and, as pardoned rebels had taken up arms again, Mary felt it necessary to be more severe. She now let the sentences passed in November 1553 be executed even upon Lady Jane Grey as well as upon her husband and her father, Suffolk.

In July Philip landed at Southampton, and was married to Mary at Winchester. Then the third Parliament of the reign was summoned, and Cardinal Pole (*q.v.*), whom the Pope had despatched to reconcile the kingdom to Rome, at length arrived in England. He had been kept back more than a year by the Emperor. to whom the marriage was a far more important thing than the reconciliation of England to Rome. He reached Whitehall in November, his attainder having just been reversed by Parliament, and on St. Andrew's Day, the 30th, the Lords and Commons attending at Whitehall, he absolved the realm from schism. Parliament now took steps to repeal antipapal Acts, and, unhappily, to restore the old heresy (*q.v.*) laws which existed before Henry VIII.'s day.

There were misgivings from the first about the effect of reviving these laws in all their severity; and when they began to be put in force Philip's Spanish confessor remonstrated in a sermon at court. But if the old faith and obedience were to be restored they must be guarded, apparently, by the old penalties. And so, early in 1555, began a long course of persecution, intended to root out heresy from a land newly reconciled to the old religion. In January some preachers were examined by Gardiner and the Council, and two or three recanted; but Rogers (*q.v.*) was burned at Smithfield on the 4th February, and Hooper (*q.v.*) and others were sent down to suffer in the country, each at the special scene of his labours. The first layman who suffered was Thomas Tomkins, a weaver, of whose treatment by Bishop Bonner a very distorted account is given by Foxe (*q.v.*). He and five others were condemned by Bonner on the 9th February. He had been long in the bishop's custody at Fulham, not very closely kept, for he was allowed to make hay there, and the bishop, to prevent his rushing on his fate, one day asked him if he thought he could endure flame; on which he held his hand above a lighted candle without flinching. He was burned at Smithfield on the 16th March. Lay victims were now much more numerous than clergymen, and in thick succession there fell, chiefly in London diocese, but elsewhere also, a long array of martyrs, whose principal heresy was the denial of transubstantiation. There were, indeed, spiritual men still among the victims, among whom, besides the three well-known Oxford martyrs, were Bishop Ferrar (*q.v.*), burned at Carmarthen 30th March; John Cardmaker, burned at Smithfield 30th May; John Philpot (*q.v.*), lately Archdeacon of Winchester, burned at Smithfield on the 18th December before the year 1555 was ended. At Oxford Ridley (*q.v.*) and Latimer (*q.v.*) suffered in October, and Cranmer in March 1556. But for the most part the victims were not clergymen. Some were gentlemen, some husbandmen, some artisans, weavers, linen-drapers, and the like, who gloried in the new light of Edwardine religion. The example of martyrdom was contagious, and the bones of a butcher burned in Essex were carried about as relics. Papal religion did not grow in favour by these severities.

The persecution went on as before through that year, and the next, and the next, till Mary's death in November 1558; and the recorded victims number no fewer than two hundred and seventy-six. The martyrdoms, indeed, were mostly in the diocese of London, though there were not a few at Canterbury, Chichester, Coventry, Lichfield, Norwich, and other places. Scarcely one seems to be known in the north of England; but one day at Stratford-le-Bow there were as many as thirteen.

Yet it must be said that heresy and treason often encouraged each other, and Mary thought less of treason against herself than of treason against the Church. The powerful owners of church land had consented to the nation's reconciliation to Rome only on the assurance that they should not be called upon to give up what they had gained from the spoliation of the abbeys. Mary, however, gave freely of her own for the restoration of the monastic system, and set up Westminster (*q.v.*) again as an abbey of monks, and the Charter-house at Sheen, and some houses of friars. Her zeal, nevertheless, met with a poor return from Pope Paul IV., who was an enemy to Spain and to her husband. Her reign, moreover, was still troubled with con-

spiracies, such as that of Sir Henry Dudley in 1556, complicated with French intrigues. Her domestic life, too, was saddened by disappointment of the prospect of having a child by Philip. She was twice deceived about the symptoms. And in her last year came the crowning misfortune of the loss of Calais, taken by the French at the beginning of 1558. She possessed the accomplishments of the learned ladies of her time; she had translated from the Latin the paraphrase of St. John's Gospel by Erasmus, under the editorship of Udall (*q.v.*). Her court was stainless, and she was the first English sovereign to find funds for aged soldiers wounded in the English service, though, unhappily, her will was not attended to. A book of prayers belonging to her is now in the British Museum (*Sloane MSS.*, 1583, f. 15). It opens of itself at a blurred and tear-stained page, on which is a prayer for the unity of the Catholic Church, and another for the safe delivery of a woman with child.   [J. G.]

MAURICE, John Frederick Denison (1805-72), divine, was son of a Unitarian minister, whose family was soon invaded by religious disputes; some members of it becoming Calvinist Baptists, and others conforming to the Church of England.

Amid these controversial voices, Frederick Maurice grew up a silent, meditative, unnatural boy, who cared nothing for games, amusements, or the open air, and 'never knew the note of a single bird.' He passed through a phase of hideous depression, believing himself predestined to hell; and was still in a condition of complete unsettlement when, in 1823, he entered Trinity College, Cambridge. There, under the influence of his tutor, Julius Hare, he gradually emerged from his shyness, and, led by his friend, John Sterling, became a member of the famous 'Apostles' Club.' He was now thinking of going to the Bar, and he migrated to Trinity Hall with a view to studying law. As he neared the close of his University career, he found himself in a position of conscientious difficulty. In order to qualify himself for his B.A., he would have to declare himself a member of the Church of England. If he could do this, his abilities and knowledge seemed to make it certain that he would obtain a Fellowship. But he felt that he could not make the declaration honestly, and he slipped away from Cambridge without a degree. He came up to London with Sterling, and took to journalism, and showed such power with his pen that he was made editor of the

Athenæum, which some of his friends had purchased. But the *Athenæum* failed. His father was ruined. There was illness and death in the home; and he came to the conclusion that, so far, his life had been a failure, and that he was meant after all to be what in his childhood he had wished to be, a minister of the Christian Gospel. He had now decided to join the Church of England. In 1830 he entered Exeter College, Oxford, when he was, of course, much older than other undergraduates, and very poor; but the fame of his high character and intellectual powers got abroad, and he became a member of the famous Essay Club, which was called, after its founder, 'The W.E.G.' He took his degree in 1834, and was ordained to the curacy of Bubbenhall, near Leamington. Here he remained for two years, taking pastoral charge of the parish, and publishing in turn his first (and only completed) experiment in fiction — a kind of veiled autobiography called *Eustace Conway*, and a controversial pamphlet on *Subscription No Bondage*.

In 1836 Maurice was appointed Chaplain at Guy's Hospital. He was a tender and devoted ministrant to the sick and dying; but he found time for thought and for writing. In 1837 he published the one book which, of all the many that he wrote, has had a practical effect and a permanent value. It was called *The Kingdom of Christ, or Hints to a Quaker concerning the Principles, Conceptions, and Ordinances of the Catholic Church*. Here he sets forth the contention of his whole life—that the Catholic Church is the Kingdom of Christ on earth; that the Sacraments are the pledges and guarantees of grace; that the ministry has a real commission from God; and that the Catholic creeds and the English formularies are much nearer the eternal truth of things than the speculations of the sectaries. The book provoked a storm of controversy. Romanists disliked it because it regarded the Roman Church as only a portion of the Catholic whole. Tractarians condemned it because in some points of sacramental theology it differed from Dr. Pusey (*q.v.*). All sectaries agreed in abusing it because of its passionate witness to the claim of the English Church. Only a very small group of intimate disciples accepted it cordially; but through them and their spiritual descendants it has humanised and liberalised the religious movement which sprang from Oxford in 1833. [OXFORD MOVEMENT.] Maurice was now in the way of worldly advancement, not excessive indeed, but valuable as testimony to his increasing

power. In 1840 he was appointed Professor of English Literature at King's College. He was chosen to give the 'Boyle Lectures'; and the 'Warburton Lectures' at Lincoln's Inn; he was made Chaplain of Lincoln's Inn; and in 1846, a theological school being created at King's College, he was appointed Professor of Theology there.

Meanwhile the air was full of industrial unrest. The working classes, bitterly disappointed by the failure of the Reform Act to bring the millennium, were hotly demanding the further reforms which were grouped together in 'The People's Charter.' Maurice had by now gathered round him a group of young disciples, who shared his deep anxiety about the signs of the times, and were even desperately anxious to save the State by applying Christian principles to social and political problems. Hence arose the 'Christian Social' movement, of which Maurice was the prophet and guide. He denounced the creed of Unrestricted Competition, as 'expecting Universal Selfishness to do the work of Universal Love.' He said: 'I seriously believe that Christianity is the only foundation of Socialism, and that a true Socialism is the necessary result of a sound Christianity.' In order to diffuse and enforce these doctrines Maurice, aided by Charles Kingsley (*q.v.*), J. M. Ludlow, E. Vansittart Neale, and Tom Hughes, began to issue in 1848 a little newspaper called *Politics for the People*. It died in the same summer, and Maurice soon replaced it with *The Christian Socialist*, which in turn became *The Journal of Association*, when Maurice became convinced that the way to social salvation lay through Co-operation.

All this social activity, and the enunciation of doctrines which steady-going people regarded as revolutionary, alarmed the Council of King's College. The worldly and the timid and the respectable began to utter warning cries about the strange doings of the Professor of Theology; and in 1851 the principal, Dr. Jelf, felt himself bound to remonstrate with Maurice, who in return flatly refused to unsay his teaching or modify his language. Maurice retained his chair; but, even more than before, he was now a marked and a suspected man. With the quixotic courage which was his truest nature, he soon gave his enemies a fresh ground for attacking him. In 1853 he published a volume of *Theological Essays*, which reaffirmed the main positions taken in *The Kingdom of Christ*, but also contained more disputable matter. He had always been essentially a Platonist. For him all visible phenomena were merely shadows cast by the invisible realities of the Eternal World. Time and Space were words of little meaning. The Eternal Life of God was the only thing which really existed. To have our part in that Life was the unspeakable boon which had been put within our grasp by the Divine Incarnation. 'Eternity has nothing to do with time or duration.' It was not an endless extension of Time but, on the contrary, a condition of timelessness. Eternal Life meant participation in the Eternal Life of God, and Eternal Death was refusal to participate in that Life. 'When I wrote the sentences about Eternal Death,' said Maurice, 'I knew that I was writing my own sentence at King's College.' The event proved him right. As before, Maurice refused to withdraw, to modify, or to capitulate. In 1853, in spite of a vehement protest from Mr. Gladstone (*q.v.*) and some others, the Council dismissed Maurice from his theological chair, and also, in order to make a clean sweep of his pernicious influence, from the chair of English Literature.

This summary act of persecution produced unexpected results. Sympathy flowed in on Maurice like a flood. Soon a fresh sphere of usefulness opened in 'The Working Men's College,' founded in 1854, of which Maurice became Principal. His dismissal from King's College had multiplied his influence tenfold.

In the year 1858 H. L. Mansel, afterwards Dean of St. Paul's, preached the Bampton Lectures, taking as his subject 'Reason and Revelation.' It is difficult at this time of day, looking back through the dense clouds of controversy which those lectures provoked, to discern precisely the points at issue. So far as one can see, Mansel held that man can only know God through Revelation, and regarded 'Revelation' as synonymous with the Bible. From this position it followed that all we know about the attributes of God is derived from the Bible's account of His actions, and that our conception of goodness must be found by a careful collection of all the texts in which the inspired writers in different ages have told us what He did. It is useless to say that this or that is inconsistent with the Divine Love and Goodness. We know that God did it, therefore it must be consistent with His character. If, to take a concrete instance, it is revealed in the Bible that He dooms millions of His creatures to endless torment, such a doom must be just and good. To Maurice all this seemed practical Atheism. He held with passionate tenacity the belief that God has revealed Himself, not

only in the Bible, but in History, in Nature, in Conscience, and, above all, in the Incarnation; that by this combined revelation He has shown us that Moral Beauty which in its perfection is the sum of His divine attributes; and that, if the Bible seems to assign to Him actions or qualities inconsistent with that perfection, we must be misinterpreting the Bible; and our duty is to reread the misinterpreted passages in the light of the divinely enlightened conscience and of all that is implied in the divine Incarnation. Feeling intensely that what Conscience calls good is raised to its highest power in God, and that what Conscience condemns as evil must be evil in God's sight, Maurice attacked Mansel in *Letters to a Student of Theology* with an exceeding great vehemence, which reminded people that, while he resembled St. John in being an Apostle of Love, he resembled him no less in being a Son of Thunder.

By degrees the controversy died out, as all controversies die; and the remainder of Maurice's life was comparatively calm. In 1860 he was appointed to the incumbency of St. Peter's, Vere Street. In 1861 he published his monumental *History of Philosophy*, which is in truth a history of great men in all ages and of all schools, all alike feeling after the knowledge of God, and refusing to be content with any intellectual substitute for Him. In 1866 he was elected Professor of Casuistry and Moral Philosophy at Cambridge. To the end he had to endure the annoyance of being misunderstood and misrepresented. Every one called him a Broad Churchman, some in approval, some in condemnation; but all alike were wrong. Of the Broad Church party he wrote: 'Their breadth appears to me to be narrowness. They include all kinds of opinions. But what message have they for the people who do not live on opinions?' What indeed? That message, in Maurice's belief, was delivered by God to man through the agency of the Catholic Church. He never was, in the usual sense of the word, Protestant. 'He passed from the Unitarian position to the assertion of a kind of Liberal Catholicism; and Catholic he remained to the end.' That his theology should have been persistently misconstrued is due in part to his exceeding vehemence in attacking each sect and schism and 'party' and 'school of thought' in turn; but it is due in greater part to his bewildering style, as obscure as a painting by Turner, and as full of splendid gleams. His old age was calm and honoured, and he died simply of a lifetime of overwork on the 1st of April 1872. He was buried at Highgate. [G. W. E. R.]

Lives by F. Maurice and C. F. G. Masterman.

MAY, William (d. 1560), Dean of St. Paul's and Archbishop-elect of York, elder brother of John May, Bishop of Carlisle, was educated at Cambridge, and became Fellow of Trinity Hall in 1531 and President of Queens', 1537. In 1534 he was appointed Cranmer's (*q.v.*) commissary to visit the see of Norwich, and in 1535, before ordination, was instituted to the rectory of Bishop's Hatfield, Herts, by special dispensation from the archbishop. He was ordained deacon and priest the next year. He signed the Six Articles in common with many others who were to repudiate their doctrine in the next reign. He was one of the commission which drew up the *Bishops' Book*. He received various preferments, culminating in 1545 in the deanery of St. Paul's, which he contrived to retain, in spite of all changes, until the accession of Mary.

He occupied a prominent position under Edward VI., and took a part in most of his ecclesiastical measures. In 1547 he was one of the commissioners who visited St. Paul's to put into force an edict of the Council commanding the destruction of all images in churches. He was dean when Communion was first administered there in both kinds. The altar was pulled down by his command, and he celebrated at a table. In 1547 he was appointed one of the royal visitors to visit the western dioceses. He was perhaps on the commission which drew up the Prayer Book of 1549, and on another which deprived Bonner (*q.v.*), who treated him with scant respect, telling him on one occasion he might speak when his turn came. He was a canonist, and a member of the commission appointed in 1552 to revise the canon law [REFORMATIO LEGUM]. On Mary's accession he lost all preferments, but was otherwise unmolested. When Elizabeth succeeded he was reinstated, and in 1560 elected Archbishop of York, but died the same day. He was buried in St. Paul's. Sir William Petre, who accompanied him on a political mission to France in 1546, described him as ' a man of the most honest sort, wise, discrete and well learnyd and one that shall be very mete to serve his Majestie many wayes'—a not unfair account of him.

[C. P. S. C.]

Strype, *Works*; Foxe, *Acts and Monuments*; Wriothesley, *Chronicle* : *Machyn's Diary*, C.S.

MELLITUS (d. 624), Archbishop of Canterbury, was of noble parentage and a friend of Pope Gregory (*q.v.*), who sent him with others bearing letters to Augustine (*q.v.*) in 601. He converted the East Saxons, and in 604 Augustine consecrated him to be their bishop. Ethelbert of Kent, their superior King, built a church, dedicated to St. Paul, for him in London to be the place of his see. He went to Rome to consult Boniface IV. on matters affecting the English Church, was present at the Pope's council held in 610, and subscribed its decrees. After Ethelbert's death the East Saxons relapsed into heathenism, and their young joint-kings expelled Mellitus from their kingdom, for they were angry because he refused to give them 'the white bread' of the Eucharist without previous baptism. With Justus of Rochester he took refuge in Gaul, and remained there a year. Then Eadbald of Kent recalled him ; but the Londoners would not receive him back, and Eadbald, who was not so powerful as his father Ethelbert had been, could not compel them to do so. On the death of Laurentius in 619 he was made the third Archbishop of Canterbury, and perhaps at this time received a hortatory letter from Boniface V. He suffered much from gout, but his fervent spirit triumphed over his physical infirmity. He died on 24th April 624. [W. H.]

Bede, *H.E.* : Bright, *Early Eng. Ch. Hist.*

MILMAN, Henry Hart (1791-1868), Dean of St. Paul's, a younger son of Sir Francis Milman, Baronet, an eminent physician, was educated at Eton and Brasenose College, Oxford, where he had a distinguished career, winning some University prizes, including the Newdigate in 1812 with a poem on ' the Apollo Belvedere ' ; in 1814 he became Fellow of his college, was ordained in 1816, and in 1818 became Vicar of St. Mary's, Reading, and married in 1824. From 1821 to 1831 he held the professorship of poetry at Oxford, and while ably fulfilling his clerical duties published much poetry, having already written a play, *Fazio, or the Italian Wife*, acted in London in 1818. He studied Sanscrit with success, and later translated some Indian poems. In 1827 he was Bampton Lecturer. A *History of the Jews*, which he published in 1829, treats its subject on the lines of secular history, representing the heroes of the nation as emirs and sheiks, as far as possible eliminating supernatural interposition, and noting the relations between the Jews' religion and other religious systems. The book caused great scandal among churchmen; it was attacked in reviews, and Gladstone (*q.v.*) in his younger days was 'horrified by it.' It exercised a remarkable influence on the progress of religious thought by introducing the application of historical criticism to the Biblical narrative and suggesting the science of comparative religion. His *History of Christianity under the Empire* (1840) is of less importance. In 1835 he was made Canon of Westminster and Rector of St. Margaret's, and in 1849 Dean of St. Paul's, where among other reforms he instituted Sunday evening services. In 1855 he published his great work, *The History of Latin Christianity to the Death of Nicholas V.*, which holds a place among English historical books of the first rank. His *Annals of St. Paul's* was published posthumously. He died on 24th September 1868, leaving four sons and two daughters. Robert Milman, Bishop of Calcutta, 1867-76, was his nephew.	[W. H.]

Ann. Reg., 1868; *Encycl. Brit.*; *B.N.C. Register.*

MISSIONS, Foreign. The English Church has been from the beginning, with a period of lapse from the fourteenth to the seventeenth century, emphatically a missionary Church. In the sixth century Celtic missionaries, among whom St. Columban was prominent, had carried the Gospel from Ireland and Iona to the heathen of the Continent. But the first English Churchman to do so was St. Wilfrid (*q.v.*), who on his way to Rome in 678 was driven by a storm to take refuge among the heathen Frisians, among whom he tarried, preaching and baptizing. A few years later Ecgberht, a Northumbrian priest living in Ireland, desired to carry the faith to the German tribes from whom the Angles and Saxons were sprung. He was prevented, but assisted in sending others to Frisia, Willibrord (*q.v.*) among them. About 693 Switberht, being chosen bishop to assist Willibrord, returned to England, and was consecrated by Wilfrid, the first bishop consecrated in England for work abroad. Among other English missionaries who spread Christianity and civilisation among the Teutonic tribes of Europe were two Anglian priests known as Black and White Hewald, martyred in Saxony (c. 695); Adelbert, a prince of the royal house of Northumbria, who laboured in the north of Holland; and, greatest of all, Wynfrith or Boniface (*q.v.*), 'the Apostle of Germany.' In 883 Alfred (*q.v.*) sent alms to India in fulfilment of a vow made in the Danish

wars. And even during those wars devoted Englishmen were labouring as missionaries in the Scandinavian homes of their enemies. Olaf Tryggvason, King of Norway (995-1000), employed English bishops to convert his people, and Cnut (*q.v.*) sent English missionaries to convert his Scandinavian subjects, and St. Olaf had followed the same policy. St. Sigfrid, a well-known English missionary bishop in Norway and Sweden, lived through most of the eleventh century (Bishop Wordsworth, *National Church of Sweden*, 57-88). But from the eleventh century the missionary spirit was largely overshadowed by the Crusades (*q.v.*). These were in part inspired by missionary zeal, but vitiated by a policy of compulsory conversion by the strong hand. The true missionary spirit, however, survived, notably among the Friars (*q.v.*). About 1230 Adam of Oxford, a famous Franciscan, was sent at his own request by Gregory IX. to preach to the Saracens, and other Franciscan missions to the infidels of the Holy Land followed. The Council of Vienne (1312) ordered that professorships in Arabic, Hebrew, and Chaldæan should be founded at Oxford and other universities to promote the conversion of Jews and Turks. In 1370 William de Prato, a Franciscan who had studied at Oxford, 'was sent to the Tartars by the Pope as Bishop of Peking, and head of the Franciscan Mission in Asia' (A. G. Little, *The Grey Friars in Oxford*). But, as a rule, in the later Middle Ages persecution took the place of evangelisation, and such forays as that of the Teutonic knights in Lithuania, in which the Earl of Derby, afterwards Henry IV., took part, were crusades only in name.

After the breach with Rome foreign mission work with all its machinery had to be begun anew. Yet a keen sense of the duty of Churchmen at home towards non-Christians appears in the records of the Elizabethan adventurers. Sir Walter Raleigh gave the Virginia Company £100 for the propagation of Christianity in its territory. And in 1632 Dr. Donne preached before that company what has been called 'the first missionary sermon printed in the English language.' Archbishop Laud (*q.v.*) recognised the Church's responsibility in regard to the North American colonies, and in 1634 an Order in Council gave the Bishop of London jurisdiction over English congregations abroad. In 1638 a scheme was promoted for establishing the episcopate in North America, but home troubles prevented its realisation. In 1649 the Long Parliament inaugurated the first English missionary

organisation. 'The Society for the Propagation of the Gospel in New England.' £12,000
was collected in English churches by Cromwell's order, the society was refounded by
Charles II. in 1662, and is still at work in
Canada under the name of 'The New
England Company.' After the Restoration
the scheme for a colonial episcopate was
revived, but broke down on Clarendon's fall.
Bishop Compton of London was active in
providing for the spiritual needs of the North
American and West Indian colonies by sending out clergy, and Archbishop Sheldon (q.v.)
was also interested. The Christian Faith
Society for the West Indies was founded in
1691. An attempt at missionary work in
the East Indies was begun in 1682, Robert
Boyle (q.v.) and Burnet (q.v.) being among
its promoters. The S.P.C.K. came into existence in 1698, the S.P.G. in 1701. In 1799 the
Church Missionary Society was born.

Speaking generally, all Anglican missions
throughout the world taken together hardly
form one-seventh of the mission forces of
the world to-day, exclusive of the Church of
Rome. The annual income of the missions
in the world to-day outside Rome amounts
to about £5,070,000. Towards this sum
the Anglican communion does not contribute more than £900,000. The Roman
Church publishes no accounts. The Orthodox
Eastern Church spends about £30,000 upon
its missions exclusive of Japan, which has an
independent income. The Roman Church
claims 10,000,000 adherents. The Roman
Church has among non-Christians about
34,000 European, or American, workers;
the great European and American missions
not in communion with the English, Roman,
or Eastern Churches about 16,500; the
Anglican communion about 2600. It is a
noteworthy fact that any weakening of belief
in full Christian doctrine, whether in connection with the Incarnation or the Resurrection, seems to smite with sterility all mission
work among non-Christians in the rare cases
where it is attempted. There are two other
great organisations, partly Anglican, which
largely aid the mission cause, the British
and Foreign Bible Society and the Religious
Tract Society.

The approximate date which can be taken
as a starting-point for the great revival of
modern missionary work abroad is 1871. In
that year Bishop Patteson (q.v.) was murdered; in 1872 the S.P.G. inaugurated the
Day of Intercession at St. Andrew's tide.
Bishop G. H. Wilkinson being one of the chief
movers. From this time Anglican missions
gained force everywhere. In 1874 Living-

stone died, and the Universities Mission to
Central Africa gained impetus, along with
many other missions, and the C.M.S. entered
Uganda within three years. In 1884 Bishop
Hannington was murdered. The Student
Volunteer Movement arose in 1886, and has
enormously added to the missionary force
within the English Church as well as outside
it. During the last forty years missionary
work has not only advanced by strides, but
has also become much more efficient both
at home and abroad. Within the English
Church distinct advance has been made in
the estimation in which missions are held.
In this respect the newer religious bodies are
still ahead of the Church of England. Among
the Presbyterians and the Methodists the
Church is its own missionary society, as are
the Protestant Episcopal Church in America
and the Church in Canada. In the English
Church proper, however, missionary work is
still done by great societies; but these are
drawing closer together under the influence
of the Central Board of Missions, which
represents the whole Church. This Board
does not collect money for work abroad,
but acts as a regulator and unifier of all
missionary work done by the Church.

Africa.—In 1752 the S.P.G. sent a chaplain
to the Gold Coast. In 1765 the first negro
priest was ordained from that region by
the Bishop of London. This mission was
abandoned, and the C.M.S. began work in
1804. In the same year they went to the Susu
tribes; in 1816 to the liberated slaves sent
from America to Sierra Leone. Except on the
Gold Coast, to which the S.P.G. has returned,
and in Liberia, which is connected with the
Church in America, all Anglican missions in
West Africa are connected with the C.M.S.
By far the largest diocese there is that of
West Equatorial Africa, under a European
bishop with two African suffragans. The
diocese includes Northern and Southern
Nigeria, and extends to Lake Chad, and it has
to confront the advance of Islam from the
north. This advance has been indirectly
aided by British rule. Formerly the Moslem
came as a raider and slave trader; to-day he
comes as a peaceful subject. The African
Christian communities in these regions are
practically self-supporting. English funds
are utilised for the support of European
workers. The Anglican missions in West
Africa must number more than 50,000
adherents, and there are 100 African clergy.
There are six bishops. There is as yet no
organised province of West Africa. In
Nigeria and in Sierra Leone there are fully
organised synods. In 1864 an attempt was

made to create an independent diocese under an African bishop (Bishop Crowther), but the result was disappointing, and there has been no further attempt in this direction.

South Africa.—The first English priest was sent by the S.P.G. in 1820, but it was a feeble mission till the advent of Bishop Gray (*q.v.*) in 1847 at Cape Town. Dioceses followed in quick succession. The S.P.G. has been the chief home agent in supplying funds. Its annual grant to the province is about £22,000. The province of South Africa extends up to the Zambesi, but does not include Madagascar. There are over 1,000,000 Europeans scattered throughout these regions. These have to be shepherded in so far as they will accept the Church's ministrations. Yet they are almost lost among the immense African populations, virile races rapidly increasing in numbers, and the absorbing problem of the future is the colour question. Another element is the large East Indian population, especially in Natal. On the east coast and in Portuguese territory there are serious difficulties with the Government. Portugal fears English influence for political reasons, and English missionaries, though absolutely loyal to the local government, are sorely hindered. The Church of the province of South Africa is an independent daughter Church of the Anglican communion, fully organised, with its archbishop, its general synod, and diocesan synods, and its own ecclesiastical courts. Its European clergy number about 400, its African clergy 75, its adherents about 275,000.

Central Africa.—This region has the Zambesi for its southern boundary, and reaches northward to a point north of the Albert Nyanza. English Church work began at Mombasa in 1844 with Krapf. The Universities Mission at Livingstone's request commenced in the direction of Lake Nyassa in 1859, soon moving to Zanzibar. There are now three dioceses in the U.M.C.A. region. North of it lie the two dioceses of Mombasa and Uganda, under the C.M.S., who entered Uganda by Stanley's request in 1876. Funds from England are used only for the support of European workers, otherwise the Church is self-supporting. There are 50 European clergy and about 35 African clergy, over 2000 catechists, and 60,000 baptized.

Egypt and the Soudan.—These are definitely Moslem lands, with their peculiar difficulties. There is a very efficient band of Anglican clergy and workers in Cairo under the C.M.S. for work among Moslems and the study of Arabic. A weekly paper in English and Arabic is published, and has great influence.

In the Soudan missionary work is steadily advancing among Moslems and heathens, so far as Government restrictions permit. These are gradually being removed. Egypt is under the jurisdiction of the bishop in Jerusalem. In Palestine, under the C.M.S., are missions to Moslems and Jews. [JERUSALEM BISHOPRIC.] Another mission to Moslems under the C.M.S. and of great value is the Persian and Mesopotamian Mission, started in 1869 by Dr. Bruce. Unique in character and effect is the Archbishop's Mission to the Assyrian Christians, inaugurated by Archbishop Benson (*q.v.*) in 1884. Its object is to help the Assyrian Christians to be more worthy and better educated members of their own Church.

India.—The first gift of the English Church for mission work in India was made by the S.P.G. to the Danish Mission in 1709. At that time it was against the charter of that society to undertake work outside the British Empire, and the S.P.C.K. supported the Danish Mission from 1824 to 1834. During the early years of the nineteenth century splendid work was done by the chaplains, such as Martyn, Thomason, Buchanan, Corrie; but caste was in some sense retained, and the missions were weak. Modern missions in strong force in India date from 1813. Middleton was the first bishop, and was followed by Heber. The C.M.S. began its great work in India in 1814, the S.P.G. in 1820. Heber ordained the two first Indians, a Tamil (C. David) and Abdul Masih, a convert from Islam made by Martyn. The missions spread through India from 1811 to 1860, south, north, west, and east as far as Burma. The Zenana Society came in 1861, and the Universities and others have contributed nobly—the Oxford Mission to Calcutta beginning in 1880; the Society of St. John the Evangelist. Cowley, in 1877; the Cambridge Mission to Delhi in 1877; the Dublin University Mission to Chota Nagpur in 1891; and here, as everywhere, the S.P.C.K. has been the handmaid of all. The mass of Anglican Christians is to be found in South India; it is in the Tamil and Telegu countries that we meet with what are called ' mass movements ' at present, and among the lowest castes or no caste. These have so much benefited in every way that it has had a marked effect on other castes. The Indian is not an individualist; tens of thousands probably are believers to-day, who dare not be baptized. One day a whole region may move at once. Women's work, of utmost value everywhere, is probably even more important than men's work in India. Women

2 A   (369)

doctors have here one of the noblest fields in the world.

The see of Madras was founded in 1835, Bombay in 1837. Lahore followed in 1877, then Burma, Travancore, Ceylon, Chota Nagpur, Lucknow, Tinnevelly, Nagpur. The Church has devoted itself equally to all classes. It has spent enormous sums on educational as well as on evangelistic work, on women's work and on medical missions. The Indian Church Aid Association supplies clergy for ministrations to Europeans and Eurasians, who are a great factor in the future of Indian Christianity. A special organisation has lately been created to cope with this work. The organisation of the Church in India is imperfect, but the Indian episcopate is beginning to speak with a united voice. The Bishop of Calcutta is a metropolitan. And an Indian is about to be raised to the episcopate. There are in India 375 European clergy as missionaries, 53 laymen, 200 women, 317 Indian clergy, 6342 lay teachers, including women. But it is America that is converting India. All the forces of all the English missions, Churchmen and Nonconformist combined, do not equal the American forces, which in India are wholly non-episcopal. The English Church may possibly be doing as much as one-tenth of the mission work in India to-day. Meanwhile Indian Christianity is spreading fast.

Eastward from Burma are the Malay States, Singapore, and Borneo, regions of the utmost importance for the Church; they are full of Chinese and Tamils, besides the races indigenous to the country. The foundation of the see of Labuan and Sarawak in 1855 was marked by the first consecration of a bishop of the Church of England outside the British Isles since the Reformation. Singapore was added to it in 1861. In 1909 Borneo and Singapore were made separate sees.

China.—Probably China and Japan, with their enormous populations and races of strong character, are more important for good or for evil in the history of Christendom than any other land at present non-Christian. It is doubtful, however, whether the Anglican communion can claim more than one-twelfth of the Christians in China, even after excluding the Church of Rome. The Church in the United States first entered China in 1837, the first English Churchman in 1844. The C.M.S. is in evidence in South China, with Shanghai, Ningpo, Foochow, and Hong Kong as centres. The S.P.G. helps in the north, with Peking and Tai-an-fu in Shantung as centres. The Canadian Church has com-

menced a mission in Honan, consecrating a bishop and supplying the staff. There is now a newly formed general synod, and periodical meetings are to be held for this purpose. There are eleven Anglican bishops in China, of whom the majority owe allegiance to Canterbury, three to the Church in the United States, one to the Primate of Canada. Women's work and medical missions are a great power in China, and it would seem as though hatred of the foreigner as such were passing away. The Chinese Christians, both in the north and the south, during the last forty years have added a mighty roll of martyrs to the Church's history.

Japan.—The Church in America first entered Japan on the part of the Anglican communion in 1859. The C.M.S. followed in 1869, the S.P.G. in 1872. From Great Britain only the English Church and the Salvation Army are found in Japan. The *Nippon Sei Kokwai* (Holy Catholic Church of Japan) is a portion of the Anglican communion, with its own synod and canons. But the bishops are at present accepted from abroad; 4 are British, 2 American, 1 Canadian, yet all owe definite allegiance to the *Nippon Sei Kokwai* and its jurisdiction. This Church has 7 bishops, the proportion of clergy being 70 foreign and 57 Japanese, while the baptized number about 15,000. The Church in Japan has its own external mission field in Formosa, and also in the Bonin Islands. Here, as elsewhere, the English Church can hardly be one-fourth of the non-Roman and non-Eastern Church Christians. The Roman Church claims 60,000 adherents, the Russian Orthodox Church more than 30,000.

Corea.—America is the chief factor in Corean Christianity, with the exception of Rome. The American missions are non-episcopal. There are some 340 of their workers as against some 30 Anglicans. Excluding Rome, there are probably 200,000 Corean Christians to-day, the fruit of thirty years' work. The English Mission began in 1890 under Bishop Corfe, and is filled to-day with an intense evangelistic spirit, coupled with strong Catholic principles. It is for the most part a celibate mission. In Manchuria the English Church works at present only among Europeans.

The South Pacific.—The province of New Zealand has for its premier mission field the diocese of Melanesia, founded by Bishop Patteson, 1861, but inaugurated by the late Bishop G. A. Selwyn (*q.v.*). The Church in Australia places its New Guinea Mission in the same prominent position. In New Guinea the British region is divided for mission purposes by the Government into three or four portions: Congregational (L.M.S.), Roman, Anglican, Methodist. The Anglican portion is magnificently ordered, and is the pride of the Australian Church. The see of New Guinea was founded in 1896. Within Australia there are strong Anglican missions to aboriginals on reserves and to Chinese. In Melanesia there are, besides the bishop, 12 European clergy, 685 ordained and unordained Melanesian workers, and about 16,000 adherents, mostly baptized. The diocese of Polynesia was founded in 1908. But in Oceania, as elsewhere, the English Church is far surpassed in strength and numbers by the Roman Church and by the other great missions. Excluding Rome, it is probable that only one out of fourteen Christians belongs to the English Church.

Canada.—All along the northern regions of Canada there have been for years strong missions among Indians and Esquimaux under the C.M.S. This society is slowly withdrawing now that the early work of evangelisation is being completed, and the Canadian Church is undertaking the burden.

The West Indies.—In the province of the West Indies there are missions to East Indians and Chinese, who are in large numbers in Trinidad and British Guiana. In the latter diocese there are missions also to the aboriginal Indians with a record of noble work.

South America.—The English Church is represented by three dioceses: British Guiana (1842), the Falkland Islands (1869), and Argentina (1910). The South American Missionary Society has for years done a noble work among races such as those in Terra del Fuego, the Paraguayan, Chaco, and the Araucanian Indians.

The care of scattered Church people must also be mentioned. The white Christian, if he falls away in pioneer lands, becomes worse than a pagan. The S.P.G. made this duty its first responsibility in every part of the earth. The Colonial and Continental Church Society of late years has taken up the problem strongly.   [H. H. M.]

Hunt, *Hist. Eng. Ch. to 1066*; Maclear, *Hist. of Christian Missions in Middle Ages*; Grant, *Missions* (Bampton Lectures); Hutton, *Hist. Eng. Ch., 1625-1714*, xvii.; article 'Foreign Missions,' *Encycl. Brit.*; *First Annual Review of Foreign Missions of the Ch.*, 1908; *Central Boards of Missions*; *Statistical Atlas of Foreign Missions*; *Edinburgh World Missionary Conference*, 1910.

MONASTERIES, Suppression of the. But for its sweeping and tyrannical character the conduct of Henry VIII. (*q.v.*) in putting down monasteries was not unprecedented, nor even quite unjustifiable. These establishments had been long on the decline, many of them were encumbered with debt, and could not keep up their numbers. They failed at times to give exhibitions to the Universities, and there was certainly no small demoralisation in some houses. Yet though in former times alien priories had been suppressed, and even one or two other houses, Wolsey's (*q.v.*) great scheme for the suppression of a number of small monasteries with a view to the promotion of learning by new colleges was not generally popular; and after he had procured at great expense from the Pope and from his sovereign full powers to carry it out, most of the endowments were confiscated at his fall. The Ipswich College was never established, and that which was to have borne his name at Oxford was established on a smaller scale. The King then caused the reduced establishment to bear his own name as 'King Henry VIII.'s College.' It now bears the familiar name of Christ Church.

But Wolsey's beginning suggested to the King ideas which bore further fruit when his repudiation of papal authority committed him to a new church policy. Monasteries were specially dependent on Rome, their whole religious life determined by rules which could only be relaxed by reference to the Roman See; and however easy Henry found it to coerce the bishops, only one of whom earned martyrdom by not acquiescing in his Supremacy, it was a much more serious matter to have hosts of communities all over the country clinging to the old tradition of Rome as a final seat of authority. In 1535, before summer had well begun. Royal Supremacy had fully asserted itself by the trials and executions, under new-made laws, first of four monks and a secular priest, then of Bishop Fisher (*q.v.*), and finally of Sir Thomas More (*q.v.*). In the later summer Dr. Richard Layton (*q.v.*) and Dr. Thomas Legh (*q.v.*), both of whom had been instrumental in getting evidence against More and Fisher in the Tower, having accompanied Thomas Cromwell (*q.v.*) into the west of England, obtained from him, as the King's vicegerent in spiritual matters, powers to make a circuit and visit the monasteries of the kingdom generally. They did traverse a large part of the country, laying down strict rules for the monks, and reporting all that they could find in the way of vice and superstition in the different houses, getting, moreover, the visitatorial power of bishops suspended during their visitation, and rearranging the studies at the Universities, where they abolished that of the canon law. They then met at Lichfield and visited Yorkshire and the northern monasteries together. Their reports for the province of York, and those for the dioceses of Coventry and Lichfield, and of Norwich, still survive, full of disgusting foulness, perhaps current scandals, how far well founded it is difficult to judge; but the rapidity with which the work was done forbids us to believe that the 'comperts,' as they were called, were founded on a really judicial examination. The visitors had made an end by the time Henry VIII.'s 'Long Parliament' had met for its last session in 1536. They had visited less than one-third of the monasteries of all England in about half a year. But they had collected sufficient information for the King's purpose. It is not clear that their actual reports were laid before Parliament. More probably it was an account of their substance that is said to have elicited against the monasteries the cry of 'Down with them!' But as early as the 3rd March we find a rumour that abbeys and priories under the value of £200 a year were to be suppressed, and a visit which the King in person paid to the House of Commons on the 11th, when he delivered them a Bill for consideration, seems certainly to mark the introduction of this particular measure. For by the 18th it had become law as 27 Hen. VIII. c. 28; and, according to a later tradition, the Commons were only induced to pass it by the King threatening to 'have some of their heads' if they refused. The King had simply procured damaging reports of the monasteries with a view to suppressing all that he dared at that time. And in the preamble of the Act itself it was strangely asserted that vice was prevalent in small monasteries which contained fewer than twelve monks, while religion was better kept in some larger ones—a statement not exactly in harmony with the reports of the visitors. There was, indeed, a provision in the Act itself to enable the King to preserve from dissolution such of those smaller houses as he thought fit, and he actually spared more than twenty of them for the time, as neighbours in many cases offered considerable sums for their continuance. The heads of the suppressed monasteries were generally pensioned, while the monks were to be transferred to larger and better ordered houses.

The suppression of these minor monasteries was undoubtedly the main cause of the formidable rebellions which broke out in Lincolnshire and Yorkshire in October 1536, and the prolonged state of uncertainty that lasted in the north of England for months after. [PILGRIMAGE OF GRACE.] Yet it was soon apparent that suppressions were to be carried further even than the Act warranted by a process of surrender. The two first surrenders, indeed, were with a view to a grander foundation. In July 1537 Bishop Barlow, who was Prior of Bisham, surrendered that priory to the King with a view to its being re-erected as a mitred abbey, and the abbot and convent of Chertsey at the same time surrendered their house for the better endowment of the new abbey. Then the Prior of Lewes was intimidated into yielding up his house, which the King had agreed to give to Cromwell and the Duke of Norfolk; and Cromwell, who had the larger share, set an Italian engineer to pull down the priory, a magnificent old Cluniac foundation dating from the Conqueror's day, with massive pillars, which he blew up with gunpowder. Cromwell then gave the prior's house to his son Gregory for a residence. The mitred abbey of Bisham had not lasted six months when it, too, was surrendered, 19th June 1538, by the same Abbot Cordrey who had surrendered Chertsey. The taking of surrenders systematically had already been begun in January by the same worthies Legh and Layton who had visited the monasteries. Legh began with Muchelney in Somerset, and went on by Chester, through Yorkshire, as far as Holm Cultram, an abbey on the very borders of Scotland, and returned through the Midlands. Layton went through Cambridgeshire into Norfolk with a colleague whose presence raised uncomfortable suspicions—Robert Southwell, attorney of the Court of Augmentations. As this court had been recently erected by Parliament to deal with the revenues of suppressed monasteries, people naturally said that they were going to suppress monasteries right and left—rumours which Layton unblushingly denounced as a scandal, lest the monks should convey their property out of the reach of the King's agents. And probably it was to reassure the public generally that the priory of Barnwell, which it was thought they were going to suppress, was spared for ten months longer. They went on, in fact, to Norfolk, where they only suppressed Westacre by virtue of a special commission, the monks confessing in a formal document signed by them and sealed with the convent seal that they had forfeited all right to their house and property by maladministration. This document was certainly drawn up for their signature beforehand; and the next surrender which Layton and Southwell took, that of St. Andrew's, Northampton, a month and a half later, was obtained in the same way by a confession prepared for the signature of the monks, with a preamble verbally the same as that of Westacre, though the confession itself was fuller and more humiliating.

Layton and Southwell seem to have been anxious to proceed with due legal formalities in procuring confessions to justify forfeitures to the King's use. But the work was already being carried on elsewhere by other officers of the Augmentations, and as time went on, at least, these formalities were dropped. Boxley Abbey in Kent was surrendered on the 29th January—in what particular form does not appear; but here was a specious case for exposing what was called an imposture. The celebrated 'Rood of Grace,' which nodded its head, rolled its eyes, and did various other things—always more marvellous when reported afar off—was detached from the wall and found actually to have been worked by wires inside the image! The exposure was a thing that served the King's purpose better than any confession. The image was taken to Maidstone and made to perform on market day before the people. It was then brought to London and exhibited at Paul's Cross, where Bishop Hilsey preached eloquently, explaining all the trickery; after which it was immediately broken up and cast among the crowd. But the abbot and monks, instead of being treated as impostors, were pensioned liberally.

Surrenders were, no doubt, procured with the greater ease when a monastery could be charged with encouraging superstition or imposture. Relics and pilgrimages began now to be discountenanced and put down. In his sermon at Paul's Cross, Bishop Hilsey denounced these things generally, and said idolatry would continue till the images to which men offered were taken away. He also declared some gross scandals about 'the Blood of Hailes'—the supposed blood of Christ contained in a phial in a west-country monastery; and an examination of the relic afterwards took place which certainly disproved that it was the blood of our Lord, but disproved popular scandals about it no less. Still 'Our Lady of Walsingham' and 'pilgrimage saints' generally were put down; and when neither fraud nor superstition could be plausibly alleged to quicken surrenders, fear could be too easily inspired of a charge of treason. For abbots and monks were generally disaffected towards the Royal Supremacy; and where there were one or

two insubordinate monks an abbot could easily get into trouble. The Abbot of Woburn surrendered his house through fear; and yet, after all, he and two of his monks were hanged for treason.

In this suppression of the larger houses we see pretty plainly that gentler influences and the show of legality gradually gave place to pure coercion and tyranny. The whole work was almost completed within the two years 1538 and 1539; and in the former year the houses of friars were also suppressed. Only one order of these—the Observants, the stricter branch of the Franciscans — had been suppressed at an earlier date, 1534, on account of their boldness in opposition to the divorce. In the autumn of 1539 the most conspicuous houses which still remained were the three great Benedictine abbeys of Glastonbury (*q.v.*), Reading, and Colchester, and it was suspected that their heads encouraged each other not to surrender. This was no crime; and yet Cromwell's written memoranda show clearly how their indictments, trials, and executions were arranged beforehand. The Abbot of Glastonbury was hanged (15th November) on Tor Hill, beside his monastery; the Abbot of Reading, also in November, beside Reading; and the Abbot of Colchester on the 1st December at Colchester. There was very little spirit left in any abbot after that to refuse to give up his house. Westminster Abbey (which was to be made a cathedral) surrendered on the 16th January 1540, and before that month's end five more monasteries and a nunnery had also capitulated. Then on the 16th February the drama virtually came to a close with the surrender of Thetford in Norfolk.

Never did tyranny produce such great and lasting effects. The booty was enormous: the distress, even from the first, was acute. Perhaps chiefly at the first; for though at the Parliamentary dissolution in 1536 provision was made for pensions to the dispossessed monks and nuns, we find it stated in that very year that many of them wandered about houseless, not knowing how to live. On the other hand, greedy courtiers enriched themselves by obtaining large grants of monastic property and rack-renting the poor tenants of many an abbey. A reign of avarice and peculation ensued, which called forth the indignation of Latimer (*q.v.*) and other reformers. There was some pretence, no doubt, of bestowing the confiscated endowments on better objects. Ten or twelve new bishoprics were to be erected, and some monasteries were to be turned into collegiate churches. But in the end it came to six new bishoprics, of which one was suppressed in the following reign (Westminster). Nor did the universities benefit greatly by royal bounty out of the plunder, though the King ordered the clergy to tax their incomes for the maintenance of scholars there, and himself took the credit of founder of the one greatest college in each seat of learning. For in Cambridge he erected Trinity College by dissolving three smaller establishments and uniting their endowments, while in Oxford he simply appropriated the work of Wolsey and reduced the scale on which it was carried out. Throughout the country he left great gaunt ruins, which it took centuries to convert even into picturesque objects for artists and photographers.

[J. G.]

Wright, *Suppression of the Monasteries*, C.S.; Gasquet, *Henry VIII. and the Eng. Monasteries*; Dixon, *Hist. Ch. of Eng.*; Gairdner, *Lollardy and the Reformation*, ii.; H. A. L. Fisher, *Pol. Hist. Eng., 1485-1547*, app. ii.

MORE, Hannah (1745-1833), came of a respectable family in Norfolk, which contributed two captains to Cromwell's army. Her father, Jacob More, was master of a grammar school at Stapleton, near Bristol. As a child she displayed quick intelligence and a natural interest in books, which her father fostered by teaching her the elements of Latin and mathematics. She also learned, in the society of some French officers on parole, 'that free and elegant use of the French language for which she was afterwards distinguished.' And when she grew up she took her part in teaching the pupils of a girls' school kept by her sisters at Bristol. She had a precocious fondness for using her pen, and before she was eighteen she published a 'Pastoral Drama,' called *A Search after Happiness*, intended for the use of young ladies' schools. Both at Bristol and in the neighbourhood her vivacity, accomplishments, and agreeable manners secured her admission into local society.

In 1773 she visited London, and so began her entry into the great world. She became acquainted with Garrick, and through him with Dr. Johnson (*q.v.*), Sir Joshua Reynolds, De Lolme, Baretti, Gibbon, Burke, and the band of blue-stockings who gathered round Mrs. Montagu. Her visits to London were annually repeated, and very soon she became the fashion, and was asked to all the great houses and smart parties in town.

London just then was not a very spiritually-minded place, yet it was through this quite mundane experience that she found her way to the fervent piety and entire devotion which marked the remainder of her life. The deaths of her friends Garrick and Johnson had a solemnising effect on her thoughts, and she turned instinctively to the more seriously-minded members of the brilliant society in which she moved. Through Mrs. Boscawen, mother of the Duchess of Beaufort and an Evangelical, Hannah More became acquainted with Beilby Porteous, Bishop of London, and with John Newton, whose *Cardiphonia* produced a deep impression on her mind. The gentler influence of the bishop softened the strictness of Newton's theology; and Hannah, though she now began to feel a quickened interest in higher things, did not find herself constrained to part at once with the society and amusements of the world. But gradually she began to find less satisfaction in social and literary pursuits and an increasing desire to devote her talents—which were now universally admitted—to the service of God and man. 'Lord,' she wrote in her journal, 'I am spared, while others are cut off. Let me now dedicate myself to Thee with a more entire surrender than I have ever made.' Henceforward she wielded, as Newton said, 'a consecrated pen.' In 1785 she acquired a little property called Cowslip Green, near Bristol, and to this she retired, spending most of her year there, and only paying short and occasional visits to London. She passed through a season of retirement and spiritual meditation; took stock of her life, past and future, and laid down the lines on which her energies were henceforth to be spent. In 1788 she published a book called *Thoughts on the Importance of the Manners of the Great to General Society*, and published it anonymously, because 'she hoped it might be attributed to a better person, and so might produce a better effect.' As a matter of fact, it was at first attributed to William Wilberforce (*q.v.*), but the true authorship soon leaked out. It had a tremendous success, seven large editions being sold in five months. But she soon turned her attention from 'the great' to the humble, and issued in 1792 a very clever little volume of *Village Politics by Will Chip*, designed to counteract by plain arguments in easy, colloquial English the spread of revolutionary literature among the English poor. The immense success of *Village Politics* set the author on writing a long series of 'Cheap Repository Tracts,' in which religious truth and civil duty were inculcated with persuasive force.

To all this literary labour she added the establishment, maintenance, and constant superintendence of day schools and Sunday schools for the service of the poor in the Vale of Cheddar, in which neglected district she wrought a moral transformation. In all these good works she was nobly aided by her sister Patty, and backed by the purses of friends in the distance—Wilberforce, Porteous, and Henry Thornton. From first to last she was a loyal Churchwoman, and all the leading Churchmen of the day were her friends and counsellors. Her vogue in the religious world was at least as great as it had been in literary and fashionable circles. She was hailed as 'one of the most illustrious females that ever was in the world,' and 'one of the most truly evangelical writers of any age not apostolical.' Bishop Porteous said of one of her tracts: 'Here you have Bishop Butler's Analogy for a halfpenny.'

In 1805 she published *Cœlebs in Search of a Wife*, a really witty satire on the foibles of irreligious society. The first edition was sold off in a day, and thirty more editions before the author died. Other books followed one another in quick succession. She lived a life of incessant activity, and, though her strength began to fail, her pen never flagged. 'The greatest credit is due to her as the first among the Evangelicals who dared to enlist the novel and the drama on the side of religion and virtue.'

It was while she was residing at Cowslip Green that she gave a copy of her *Sacred Dramas* to a boy called William Ewart Gladstone (*q.v.*), saying: 'You have just come into the world, and I am just going out of it.' She left Cowslip Green in 1827, and established herself at Clifton, where she died on the 7th of September 1833.

'It may be questioned whether any one in modern times has lived so long with less waste of existence, or written so much with less abuse of ability.' [G. W. E. R.]

W. Roberts, *Memoir*.

MORE, Sir Thomas (1478-1535), Lord Chancellor of England, was one of those who first thought of reformation of the English Church according to the ideas of the 'New Learning.' He was son of Sir John More, an eminent lawyer and afterwards judge, who placed him in the household of Cardinal Morton, Archbishop of Canterbury, where he attracted attention for his originality and goodness. He studied at Oxford *c.* 1492, and became intimate with Grocyn and Linacre, advocates of the learning introduced by the Renaissance in Italy. He learnt Greek from Linacre, and studied Latin and French, theology and music. He returned to London to study law in 1494, and became a friend of Lily and of Colet (*q.v.*), and in 1497 was introduced to Erasmus, who became his dearest friend. In 1499 More seriously considered whether he had a vocation to holy orders, and he lived some time under the direction of the brothers of the Charterhouse. He lectured at St. Lawrence Jewry (Grocyn was rector) on St. Augustine's *De civitate Dei*. But in 1503 he gave up the idea of becoming a priest, and devoted himself to law, in which he soon acquired great fame. He opposed Henry VII. in Parliament in 1504, married in 1505, visited Louvain and Paris in 1508. Erasmus visited him twice, and there is no doubt that they shared many views as to the corruptions of the Church, the ignorance of the clergy, and the need of reform. He powerfully advocated the study of Greek as an essential part of a sound education, defended the writings of Erasmus, and threw himself on the side of those who desired to bring all the treasures of sacred learning to the assistance of the Church in her struggle against obscurantism on one side and heresy on the other. In 1516 he published his *Utopia*, a scathing criticism of the political and social evils of the day and a plea for toleration. He enjoyed many appointments under the Crown, and was brought into very close relations with Henry VIII. (*q.v.*), who professed great affection for him, which, however, More never trusted. In 1523 he became Speaker of the House of Commons. It is said that he opposed Wolsey in regard to the subsidy demanded in that year, but the story lacks confirmation. He assisted Henry VIII. in his book on the seven sacraments against Luther, and in 1523 himself wrote a further letter against the German reformer. In 1528 he wrote his *Dialogue*, directed against the English reformers, especially Tyndale (*q.v.*). In 1529 he became Lord Chancellor, and was illustrious for his honourable discharge of his high functions. He was stern in enforcing the laws against heretics; but the responsibility in most cases rested upon the bishops, and More must be acquitted of undue severity, judged by the standard of the age. In controversy he was extremely sharp, and he devoted himself to it on his resignation of the Chancellorship in 1532, which was due to his disagreement with the measures directed by King and Parliament against the Roman jurisdiction. He was for a time deceived by the imposture of the Nun of Kent (1533), but repudiated her when she was exposed, and though at first inserted in the Bill of Attainder against her supporters was struck out by the King at the third reading. On 30th March 1534 a new Act required an oath to the succession of Anne Boleyn's issue. The commissioners added to this requirement that of a renunciation of the Pope, and the oath was offered to More at Lambeth by Cranmer, Audley, Cromwell, and the Abbot of Westminster on 13th April. He declined it, and was committed to the Tower four days later. In prison he wrote a beautiful *Dialogue of Comfort against Tribulation*. After much questioning from Cromwell and Rich, in which he declined to commit himself, he was charged with high treason, and tried at Westminster on 1st July 1535. He declared his political loyalty to the King, but confessed that he did not accept the Act of Supremacy. He was found guilty, and was executed on Tower Hill on 6th July 1535, telling the beholders that he died 'in and for the faith of the Catholic Church.'

More's position in the history of the English Church is one of extreme interest. His theology was based very largely on St. Augustine and the Canon Law. He was thoroughly in sympathy with Erasmus, in favour of a Catholic Reformation of practical abuses, a thorough teaching of the ancient faith purged from late excesses of legends and ignorance, and had a wide sympathy with the New Learning. He stoutly defended the Catholic doctrine of the intermediate state and prayers for the dead, and the utility in practice of images, relics, and pilgrimages. He attacked Luther as a heretic, and his English followers, such as Joye, and Tyndale as garbling the New Testament by incorrect translation and annotation. He took a legal view of the Pope's jurisdiction, basing it on Canon Law (including the forged Decretals, which were not then exposed), and so regarded it as part of Catholic obedience. Thus while his mental outlook was modern and wide, he came to die for the later mediæval theory.

[W. H. H.]

Roper's *Life*, Cresacre More's *Life*, and the Latin and English *Works* of More are the best original authorities. Later biographies are by Sir S. Lee in *D.N.B.*, Fr. Bridgett (1891), and W. H. Hutton (second edition, 1910).

MORGAN, William (*c.* 1541-1604), the author of the first translation of the whole Bible into Welsh, was born at Ty Mawr, Wybernant, near Penmachno in Carnarvonshire. He was educated at St. John's College, Cambridge, of which he was a sizar. His first preferment was in 1575 as Vicar of Welshpool and sinecure Rector of Denbigh. In 1578 he became Vicar of Llanrhaiadr ym Mochnant in Denbighshire, and in 1588 Rector of Llanfyllin and sinecure Rector of Pennant Melangell in Montgomeryshire.

It was at Llanrhaiadr that he finished, if he did not also begin, his translation of the Bible. He had not proceeded very far with it when some complaint was made to the bishop against him by some of his parishioners. Its real nature is not known, but it would appear that it was urged through the vindictiveness of an influential local family whose anger he had incurred. The bishop would not be moved, so the case was brought before the archbishop (Whitgift, *q.v.*), and Morgan was summoned to Lambeth. He had been one of Whitgift's pupils, and on learning that he was engaged in translating the Scriptures into Welsh, and having satisfied himself as to his capacity for the task ('being a good scholar, both a Grecian and a Hebrician'), the archbishop urged him to go on and translate the whole Bible. Moreover, he made him his chaplain, and generously promised to discharge the entire cost of publication. Morgan returned home much encouraged. In 1588 the whole Bible (Apocrypha included) was through the press—an edition of from eight hundred to one thousand copies for Church use. Of these some fifty copies exist, perfect and otherwise. In his Latin dedication to Queen Elizabeth he acknowledges his obligations to many who had assisted him in various ways, among them the Bishops of St. Asaph and Bangor, and Dean Goodman of Westminster—the last especially for hospitality during the twelve months the work was passing through the press.

Morgan was promoted to the bishopric of Llandaff in 1595, and translated to St. Asaph in 1601, where he died, 10th September 1604, and was buried in the choir of the cathedral, without any inscription or monument. However, in 1892 a national monument was erected in the cathedral yard to his memory and that of other Welsh Bible translators (eight statuettes in all).

Morgan's is an independent translation made direct from the original. Many of the changes introduced into the Revised English Version were anticipated by him. His translation infused new life and vigour into the language, and fixed the standard of Welsh prose, as well as providing a rich terminology of religious expression. The present authorised Welsh Version, published in 1620, is a recension of Morgan's text by his successor, Bishop Richard Parry, brought into line with the English Version.

Morgan's correspondence with Sir John Wynn of Gwydir reveals him as a very conscientious man and of an independent character. [J. F.]

MORTMAIN. Land held by a religious corporation was said in the Middle Ages to be held in mortmain, or the dead hand, because it was able to escape payment of the feudal dues to the King or other overlord from whom it was held. Much of the national revenue as well as that of the great lords came from these dues, the chief of which was the ' relief ' paid at the death of the tenant by his heir. The overlord was deprived of this income, as well as of his rights of wardship and other incidents of feudal tenure, when the land was acquired by a religious body which never died, married, or begot children. Moreover, a fraudulent practice grew up by which a man could make over his land to such a body, and receive it back as a fief from the Church, thus depriving the overlord of his rights. By the twelfth century a quarter of the land of the kingdom was estimated to be in the grip of the dead hand. Attempts to check this abuse were made in 1217 by Section 43 of the reissue of the Great Charter, and by the Petition of the Barons, 1258, but were ineffective until the Statute of Mortmain, or *De Viris Religiosis*, 1279 (7 Edw. I. st. 2). It recites the injury done by the accumulation of land by religious houses not only to the lords but to the whole nation in the diminution of the revenue available for its defence, and prohibits the alienation of land in any manner which would bring it *ad manum mortuam*, under pain of its forfeiture to the superior lord, and ultimately to the Crown if the intermediate lords failed to enforce their rights. The clergy resisted this law in vain. But it was evaded by collusive law-suits, by giving land to be held in trust for religious bodies, and by consecrating lands as churchyards under the authority of papal bulls. Attempts to check these devices by later legislation, such as 13 Edw. I. st. 1, and 15 Ric. II. c. 5, were not altogether successful. Nor was the law strictly administered. The right of forfeiture might be waived on payment of a fine. And the Crown was never compelled to exercise its right of forfeiture, but might grant licences for land to be held in mortmain (20 Edw. I.). This power was commonly exercised if an inquiry

in Chancery under the writ *ad quod damnum* showed the proposed grant to be desirable. The Crown's power of granting such licences at its discretion was confirmed in 1696 (7-8 Will. III. c. 37) and in 1888 (see below).

In 1531 conveyances of land for maintaining perpetual obits (*i.e.* commemorations of the departed) and similar purposes, if made for more than twenty years, were declared void. This was the first of the statutes against ' superstitious uses,' which were concerned not with the actual holding of property by religious bodies, but with the purpose to which they devoted it. It became a principle of English law that gifts in favour of any religion but that of the Established Church are against public policy, and will not be enforced by the courts. This rule has been gradually relaxed, but some purposes, such as Masses for the dead, are still held to be within it.

In 1554 the operation of the mortmain statutes was suspended for twenty years, in the hope of inducing those who had acquired the property of the religious houses at the dissolution to return it voluntarily (1-2 Ph. and M. c. 8). Later statutes have from time to time made exceptions in the law of mortmain in favour of objects thought to be specially deserving, such as the augmentation of small livings, the foundation of hospitals and workhouses, and the building of churches and parsonages. Exceptions have also been made in favour of the principal Universities and their colleges, and the colleges of Eton, Winchester, and Westminster. The present law controlling the acquisition of land by religious and charitable bodies is comprised in the Mortmain and Charitable Uses Act, 1888 (51-2 Vic. c. 42), and the Acts amending it. Land assured by will to a charitable use must be sold within a year of the testator's death, and other assurances of interests in land for charitable uses must be made by deed, before two witnesses, at least a year before the assuror's death; must take effect immediately, and be free from any reservation in favour of the assuror or his successors. [G. C.]

Stubbs, *Const. Hist.*, ch. xiv. ; Shelford, *On Mortmain* ; Tudor, *Law of Charitable Trusts*.

MORTON, John (*c.* 1420-1500), Cardinal Archbishop of Canterbury, a subservient ecclesiastical statesman under Henry VII., a great builder, the last of the mediæval primates of all England. Born in Dorset, he went to Balliol College, Oxford, and adopted the law as his study and profession. He practised in the ecclesiastical courts, and recommended himself to Bourchier, Archbishop of Canterbury, under whose influence a steady stream of promotion set in. The Wars of the Roses found him an adherent of the Lancastrians, and after Towton, 1461, he followed their course in the north of England. He made his submission to the Yorkists, and renewed the interrupted tale of preferment. He became Master of the Rolls, and won the confidence of Edward IV., who employed him as an ambassador more than once. In 1479 he became Bishop of Ely. The events of 1483-4 brought him again into trouble, and he had to flee the country until Henry VII. came to the throne. He now came to the full height of his influence. Henry trusted him, and consulted him much in the early troublous days of his reign. In 1486 he became Primate, and next year Lord Chancellor, in which office he became a great force, and his speeches in Parliament were a feature of the time. In 1493 he became cardinal at Henry's request, but was far less ecclesiastic than statesman. As archbishop he strove to reform the clergy and to visit the monasteries in his province. He was alive to some of the abuses of his time, and he also did something to restrict sanctuary rights. As statesman he rendered himself unpopular by the financial exactions of the reign, in which he was thought to have some part. To this fact is due the legend of 'Morton's Fork.' He will, however, be chiefly remembered as a builder. Morton's Tower at Lambeth Palace, and his dyke running from Wisbech to Peterborough, preserve his name. At Oxford he helped to rebuild the church of St. Mary, and elsewhere he was vigorous in repairing the see-houses. He was probably too much the lawyer and business man to feel any strong interest in the revival of learning. [H. G.]

MOZLEY, James Bowling (1813-78), entered Oriel College, Oxford, October 1830 (his elder brother Thomas had been elected Fellow there, 1829), but to the surprise and disappointment of his friends obtained only a Third Class in Classics in 1834. He won the English Essay in 1835. He tried for Fellowships at Oriel (1836) and Lincoln (1837), where he was rejected on account of his Tractarianism. He had been from the first associated with the Oxford Movement (*q.v.*), and in 1836 his brothers John and Thomas had married the two sisters of J. H. Newman (*q.v.*). In 1838 he became member of a house in St. Aldate's, Oxford, taken by Pusey (*q.v.*) for graduates studying divinity, and was ordained deacon Trinity, 1838, Newman sending him the surplice in which he had himself been

ordained deacon and priest. He became Fellow of Magdalen, July 1840. He left Oxford, became Vicar of Old Shoreham, and married, July 1856. He was Bampton Lecturer, 1865, his subject being 'Miracles.' Mr. Gladstone made him Canon of Worcester in 1869, and in 1871 Regius Professor of Divinity at Oxford. In 1875 he had a seizure from which he never quite recovered, and after another attack died, 4th January 1878, at Shoreham.

Dr. Mozley, though he developed late, was one of the greatest minds of his day. In the crisis of the Oxford Movement in 1845 his calm reasoning helped to avert panic. He answered Newman's *Development of Christian Doctrine*. Later, the Gorham case [GORHAM, G. C.] led him to differ from High Churchmen. After four years' reading (1851-5) 'he entertained no doubt of the substantial justice of the Gorham decision'; consequently he severed his connection with the *Christian Remembrancer*, which had lasted ten years, and published three books (1855, 1856, and 1862) on the Baptismal Controversy. Church wrote, 2nd January 1855: 'Mozley's book will no doubt . . . accomplish the break up that J. H. N. began. I am very sorry for the result.' Mozley regarded these as his best work. He still remained in other respects 'in a very real sense a High Churchman.' At Christ Church his friends were the High Church leaders: Pusey, Liddon, and King (*q.v.*). His *University Sermons*, his *Essays, Historical and Theological* (collected and republished after his death), and his Oxford lectures to graduates, *Ruling Ideas in Early Ages*, show his powers at their best. In the judgment of Mr. Gladstone, Mozley combined 'the clear form of Cardinal Newman with the profundity of Bishop Butler,' and Dean Church held a like opinion. Few have equalled him for strength and depth of thought. [S. L. O.]

Letters, ed. A. Mozley; Introd. (by A. Mozley) to *Essays, Historical and Theological*: W. A. Greenhill in *D.N.B.*

MUSIC IN THE ENGLISH CHURCH. 'The Christian Church may be said to have started on its way singing' (Frere). Certainly the conversion of England to Christianity took place at a time of all others the most favourable to music. St. Augustine (*q.v.*) brought with him the Roman chants, which had just been arranged and fixed—practically as we now know them—by the great Pope who sent him, and whose name is for all time enshrined in the words we use to describe the Church's own music. 'Gregorian Chant.' [PLAINSONG.]

Though the *Reading MSS.* (the earliest native music of which we have any record) go back no farther than the early thirteenth century, it cannot be supposed that between the coming of St. Augustine and that date the Church in England produced no composers. But all traces of such musicians and their work have perished, if we except such additions to or modifications of Gregorian Chant as local use may from time to time have sanctioned. The *Reading MSS.* are the first authentic specimens we possess of native music. Besides the well-known secular rota or canon, *Sumer is icumen in*, the volume contains several sacred motets in parts. *Regina clemencie, Dum Maria credidit, Ave Gloriosa Virginum, Ave Gloriosa Mater*, by unknown composers (possibly by the monk John of Fornsete). Another specimen of slightly later date is the volume called by Rockstro the *Chaucer MSS.* (in allusion to the fact that it contains the *Angelus ad Virginem*, mentioned in the Miller's Tale). This also contains music scored in two or three parts, and is believed to be at least as old as the middle of the thirteenth century. The founder of the English school, and the first who has left behind him authentic compositions, is John Dunstable, the date of whose birth is unknown, but who died in 1453, and was buried in the church of St. Stephen, Wallbrook. Very little of his music is preserved. Before and after him come great gaps, and he is the only link between the unknown composers of the *Reading MSS.* and *Chaucer MSS.* and the early sixteenth century, as no trace of the work of Hanboys, Saintwix, or Habington (*temp.* Edward IV.) exist, though they were the first who took degrees in music. Fayrfax and Phelyppes are the most important names of the early sixteenth century, and later came Henry VIII., Thorne, Redford, Johnson, Taverner, Parsons, Edwards, Shepherde, and John Merbecke, organist of St. George's Chapel, Windsor, best known by his work, *The Boke of Common Praier noted.* This precious heritage of our Church is a splendid specimen of late Plainsong, in some cases slightly adapted from earlier forms, and fitted to the English words of the first Liturgy of Edward VI. Dr. Christopher Tye and Robert White are the greatest of the composers before Tallis. The well-known setting of the ' Acts of the Apostles ' by the former, together with anthems, services, masses, and motets, are preserved in various libraries, and some have been recently reprinted. White is less known, but much of his work may be found at Christ Church, Oxford.

We now come to the great names of Thomas Tallis and William Byrd, master and pupil. The better known works of Tallis are his Litany and Responses and his service in the Dorian mode. The *Cantiones Sacrae* (1575), the joint work of Tallis and Byrd, contains thirty-four motets of the highest value and beauty. Archbishop Parker's metrical translation of the Psalms (Day, 1567) has tunes in each of the modes by Tallis. Two of these, known as Tallis's Ordinal and Canon, have been 'adapted' by the editors of modern hymn-books. The Canon in particular has suffered, first at the hands of Ravenscroft (1621), who shortened it by exactly one-half. This, however, it bore well, as the phrases cut out were merely repetitions, and Tallis's harmonies were skilfully reproduced almost unaltered. It might have been thought that later editors would have left it at this, but the detestable habit of wrenching the people's part from the tenor and placing it in the treble has distorted this and many another fine tune. Dr. Vaughan Williams, in the *English Hymnal* (1906), first restored the people's part to its original place in the tenor. The third mode melody is perhaps the noblest hymn tune ever written by an Englishman. Altogether the work of Tallis is the most important that has ever been done for the Church by any musician, and his right to be considered the greatest English Church composer is unassailable.

Imbued with the true spirit of polyphonic music was Richard Farrant. His service in mode X has been reprinted, but his authorship of ' Lord, for Thy tender mercies' sake ' is doubted.

In 1549 appeared the first complete metrical version of the Psalms, by Robert Crowley, which contains the earliest known music to the English version. This consists of one tune, of which the melody (the seventh psalm tone) is in the tenor, and which is the first tentative Anglican double chant. The composer is unknown.

In 1553 Francis Seagar published *Certayne Psalms*, with music in four parts, which, however, is more of the nature of a motet than a tune. The origin of the English harmonised psalm tune, which developed later into the hymn tune as we know it, may be traced to Dr. Tye's ' Acts of the Apostles.'

Sternhold and Hopkins's first *Metrical Psalter* (1549) had no music ; and it is not till the edition of 1560 that tunes (not harmonised) were added. The first harmonised version of Sternhold and Hopkins's translation appeared in 1563, and is known as *Day's*

Psalter. In it are one hundred and forty-one psalm tunes in four parts, of which eighty-one are by W. Parsons, and the rest by T. Causton, J. Hake, R. Brimle, and N. Southerton. This was followed by other Psalters containing tunes in four parts, among which we may note Damon's (1579), Este's (1592), Allison's (1599), in which the tune is set in the treble, and Ravenscroft's (1621). These works contain the earliest and finest English hymn tunes, character-ised by a broad and manly style of melody and harmony too often lacking in modern tunes. Until the publication of the *English Hymnal* (1906) they had invariably been mutilated by compilers. Mention should be made of two short anthems by Ravenscroft, 'O, Jesu meek,' and 'Ah, helpless soul,' of great beauty and tenderness, which have been recently printed for the first time.

The last composer in the grand manner was Orlando Gibbons, who wrote for the Church anthems and services of the highest order, preserving the characteristics of the Golden Age well into the seventeenth century. His two-part tunes for George Wither's *Hymns and Songs of the Church* (1623) are an in-valuable treasury of Church tunes.

Anthems, services, etc., by Bull, Munday, Bevin, E. Gibbons, Hilton, Batten, and Morley will be found in the valued collections of Adrian Batten (1635), J. Barnard (1641), Edward Lowe (1661), J. Clifford (1664), Thomas Tudway (1720), and William Boyce (1778).

The Commonwealth was a disastrous time for Church music. The forces of Puritanism, which culminated in the Great Rebellion, were often actuated by a blind and gross hatred of beauty, stateliness, and tradition. The Refor-mation was responsible for much pillage, but now the stalwarts of the Commonwealth ranged the land like the Destroying Angel, and with pious exhortations burnt, amongst other things, every music-book they could lay hands on. Not content with this, they would not allow children to be taught to sing. Fortunately their reign was short, and the Restoration inaugurated a new school of English Church music, of which the leaders were Lawes, C. Gibbons, Child, Pelham Humphry, John Blow, M. Wise, and Matthew Locke — nearly all choristers in the Chapel Royal.

In the hands of these composers the old pure polyphony of the Golden Age developed into a freer art-form with solos, recitatives, duets, ritornelles, and choruses—all forming part of the same composition. Pelham Humphry was the first exponent of the new style, but it was left to Henry Purcell (1658-95) to carry it to its greatest heights. At first largely influenced by Lulli (in compliance with Charles II.'s gay tastes in sacred music), Purcell speedily became the greatest musician of the age, and may be called our national composer. His Church music consists of anthems, services, hymns, songs, psalms, etc., in many cases with orchestral accompaniment. The Purcell Society has undertaken the com-plete edition of his music, of which sixteen volumes have been published. Foremost among his Church works comes the great *Te Deum* in D, only recently purged of the corruptions of eighteenth-century editors.

The Chapel Royal was the nursery, under Dr. Blow, of other excellent musicians, not-ably Dr. Jeremiah Clarke, Dr. William Croft, Dr. Greene, and Dr. Boyce—still heard in our cathedrals.

St. George's Chapel, Windsor, produced Dr. Benjamin Rogers, whose *Hymnus Eucharisti-cus* is sung annually on 1st May, on the tower of Magdalen College, Oxford. George Wither's *Hymns and Songs of the Church* (mentioned above) was followed by Thomas Harper's un-successful attempt to introduce the Genevan tunes into England in their entirety (1632), and later by George Sandys's (son of the archbishop) *Paraphrase upon the Psalms of David* (1636), with music by Henry Lawes. These beautiful tunes, twenty-four in num-ber, have been unaccountably neglected by modern compilers.

John Playford brought out two Psalters (1671 and 1677), the latter of which, containing the whole of the Church tunes, achieved last-ing popularity, reaching its twentieth edition in 1757.

The seventeenth century was responsible for an innovation which cannot be too greatly deplored. Insensible to the traditions of a thousand years, the Church allowed her ancient music, the Gregorian psalm tunes, to be replaced by the Anglican Chant. At first preserving to some extent the dignity and expressiveness of the old Plainsong, the new form rapidly degenerated into a vehicle for banality, which has done more to alienate people of artistic feeling and culture from the Church than is suspected.

The eighteenth century, if we except Boyce and Greene, saw Church music at its lowest ebb. The ideals of this period were worthily represented by Kent and Nares, in the shape of anthems and services made up of trivial tunes poorly harmonised. Handel's ora-torios, which as a nation we may claim, cannot be said to be the product of the Church.

The nineteenth century opened badly, the only Church musicians worth mentioning being Thomas Attwood and the elder Wesley, whose eight-part antiphon, *In exitu Israel*, was much admired by Gounod. To this eccentric old musician we owe the introduction of Bach's music to England, and he was the first to wish for the restoration of the neglected Gregorian Chant—anticipating, in thought at least, by half a century the musical revival arising from the Oxford Movement (*q.v.*). Attwood (a pupil of Mozart) is justly celebrated for his graceful melody, of which a good example is the well-known tune sung to the words, 'Come, Holy Ghost.'

His godson, Thomas Attwood Walmisley, holds an honoured place in Church music. His service in D minor is one of the few by English composers which have sustained nobility of thought and genuine inspiration not unworthy of the exalted words of the *Magnificat*.

His contemporary, the great Samuel Sebastian Wesley (son of the elder S. Wesley), is the fine flower of the English Cathedral School of Music, which after him ran lamentably to seed. His magnificent service in E, and his anthems, 'The Wilderness,' 'Blessed be the God and Father,' and 'Ascribe unto the Lord,' entitle him to rank as the greatest Church musician since Purcell. He combines, as no other Church composer has done, the grand manner of the antique school with the most striking resources of modern harmony and modulation.

Sir John Goss, though he never rises to the heights of Wesley, is distinguished for the manly, 'clean' style of his Church music, which never descends to the 'sugary' sentiment of later composers. With him the genuine school may be said to have closed, though Henry Smart, Edward Hopkins, and George Garrett are worthy of notice as composers of much popular Church music.

We have now to consider what may be called the sentimental school, which has obtained an enormous vogue, and whose influence is still widespread. With this school are associated the names of Stainer, Dykes, and Barnby. The earnestness of these composers is unquestioned, and Dr. Dykes, whose persecution by Bishop Baring at Durham will be remembered, was a distinguished priest and theologian. But it must be acknowledged that their music is insipid and has nothing behind it but the first obvious appeal, which is so easy to make and so easy to respond to. Unfortunately their successors, the composers of to-day, seem little disposed to aim higher than popular taste demands.

English hymnody by the beginning of the nineteenth century had fallen upon sad days. There was no standard collection of tunes, and it was mostly left to the organist to put forth productions of his own for use in his church. The best tunes of Hayes, Wainwright, Carey, and Tans'ur, however, rise superior to the taste of their age, and find a place in our modern collections. We may mention in passing Vincent Novello's *Surrey Chapel Music*, Hullah's *Psalter with appropriate Tunes* (1843), and Mercer's *Church Psalter and Hymn-Book* (1851). Though these compilations achieved popularity, it was not till the appearance of *Hymns Ancient and Modern* (1861) that the urgent need for a standard book was satisfied. The reaction against Victorian ideals in painting, sculpture, music, and art generally, which is so marked a feature of modern life, makes unprejudiced criticism of the book very difficult. It did as much as was possible at the time to revive the best Church song, and each succeeding edition has been an advance on that preceding it. It is impossible, however, for modern criticism to condone the poverty and sentimentality of many of the specially written hymns and tunes.

The *Bristol Tune-Book* appeared in 1863, the ill-fated *Hymnary* in 1872, and *Church Hymns* in 1874. The *Hymnal Companion* (1870) is also still used. But for nearly fifty years *Hymns Ancient and Modern* has been accepted by the average church-goer as the representative hymn-book of the Church. The 1904 edition was, however, the signal for much discontent, which found practical expression in the publication of the *English Hymnal* (1906).

This is the most satisfactory modern book that has yet appeared. It has wisely avoided as far as possible the "specially composed tune"—that bane of many a hymnal.' In it for the first time the great tunes are treated with respect, and the finest versions—in most cases the earliest—have been printed. National music has been largely drawn upon. Welsh hymn melodies, which are distinguished above those of all other nations by a strange and wild religious fervour, are well represented, and English folk-song is most successfully used. The distinguishing characteristic of the book is its courage, which justifies the hope that the next edition may see the exclusion of the few sentimental tunes still left in. [M. S.]

Mention should also be made of the *Fattendon Hymnal*, 1899; the *Oxford Hymnal*, 1898; and *Songs of Sion*, 1905—the latter a valuable repository of Church tunes.

MUSICIANS OF THE ENGLISH CHURCH.

Attwood, Thomas (1765-1838). A choir boy of the Chapel Royal. Sent to Italy to study music by George IV. (then Prince of Wales). He afterwards became a pupil of Mozart at Vienna (1785-7). Organist of St. Paul's Cathedral, and Composer to the Chapel Royal, 1796. Organist of George IV.'s private chapel at Brighton, 1821. Organist Chapel Royal, 1836. Friend of Mendelssohn, who dedicated his three Preludes and Fugues for the organ to him. Composer of much tuneful Church music.

Barnby, Sir Joseph (1838-96). A chorister in York Minster. Organist St. Andrew's, Wells Street, 1863, and St. Anne's, Soho, 1871. Conductor Royal Choral Society, Precentor and Director of Music at Eton College, and Principal of Guildhall School of Music. Editor of *The Hymnary*, and composer of much popular music, including services, anthems, and hymn tunes.

Boyce, William, Mus. Doc. (1710-79). Chorister of St. Paul's Cathedral, and then articled pupil to Dr. Greene, at that time organist. His articles having expired, he became organist of Oxford Chapel, Vere Street. He also took lessons of the celebrated Dr. Pepusch. While still young his hearing, like that of so many musicians, became impaired. He did not allow this to interfere with his work, though it was a serious drawback. He became organist of St. Michael's, Cornhill, in 1736, and in the same year composer to the Chapel Royal. In 1737 he accepted the appointment of conductor of the meetings of the Three Choirs of Gloucester, Worcester, and Hereford. In 1749 he was chosen organist of Allhallows, Thames Street. He succeeded Dr. Greene in 1755 as Master of the King's Music, and conductor of the annual festivals of the Sons of the Clergy at St. Paul's Cathedral. In 1758 he was appointed one of the organists of the Chapel Royal, resigning his posts at St. Michael's, Cornhill, and Allhallows, Thames Street. His deafness increasing, he occupied his remaining years in collecting and editing his valuable work in three volumes, entitled *Cathedral Music*, a collection of the best work of English composers of the previous two hundred years. He wrote many fine anthems and services.

Byrd, William (1512?-1623). Chorister of St. Paul's Cathedral. Anthony à Wood mentions that he was 'bred up to music under Thomas Tallis.' Appointed organist of Lincoln Cathedral about 1563. In 1569 he was elected a gentleman of the Chapel Royal, though retaining his post at Lincoln. In 1575 Elizabeth granted Tallis and Byrd a monopoly for printing and selling music and music paper, English and foreign, for twenty-one years. In the same year they published their famous collection of motets. Tallis's death in 1585 gave Byrd the sole monopoly of the music printing patent. It is curious that Byrd, whom recent discoveries prove to have been a Roman Catholic, should have held an appointment in the Chapel Royal. His great skill and reputation as a musician must have procured him powerful friends. He wrote many masses, anthems, and services, and left behind him one of the greatest names in English music.

Croft, William, Mus. Doc. (1678-1727). One of the children of the Chapel Royal under Dr. Blow. Organist at St. Anne's, Soho. Gentleman extraordinary of the Chapel Royal, 1700. Organist Chapel Royal, 1707. Organist Westminster Abbey, and master of the children, and composer to the Chapel Royal, 1708. In 1724 he published thirty anthems and a burial service in two finely engraved folio volumes, entitled *Musica Sacra*. He is buried in Westminster Abbey.

Dykes, John Bacchus, Mus. Doc., M.A. (1823-76). Born in Hull. Pupil of Walmisley at Cambridge, where he conducted the University Musical Society. Minor Canon and Precentor of Durham Cathedral, 1849. Vicar of St. Oswald, Durham, 1862. He was one of the principal contributors to *Hymns Ancient and Modern*, of which he was joint editor. His anthems, services, and hymn tunes obtained great popularity. He was a distinguished theologian.

Gibbons, Orlando, Mus. Doc. (1583-1625). The son of William Gibbons, one of the town waits of Cambridge. Probably educated in the college chapel choirs of Cambridge. Admitted organist of the Chapel Royal, 1604. In 1612 he published *The first set of Madrigals and Motets of five parts*. For his beautiful tunes in two parts see George Wither's *Hymns and Songs of the Church*. He was appointed organist of Westminster Abbey in 1623, and died of apoplexy in 1625. Much of his music was printed in the collections of Barnard and Boyce. He has been called the English Palestrina.

Goss, Sir John (1800-80). Chorister of the Chapel Royal, and pupil of Attwood, whom he succeeded as organist of St. Paul's Cathedral in 1838. Composer to the Chapel Royal, 1856. Knighted, 1872. He wrote services, anthems, chants, hymn tunes, distinguished for melodious grace and sound part-writing.

Greene, Maurice, Mus. Doc. (1695-1755). Chorister of St. Paul's Cathedral. Appointed organist of St. Dunstan's in the West, 1716, and St. Andrew's, Holborn, 1717. In 1718 he became organist of St. Paul's Cathedral, and on the death of Dr. Croft in 1727 organist and composer to the Chapel Royal. Friend of Handel. Elected Professor of Music in the University of Cambridge, 1730. Master of the King's band of music, 1735. Published his *Forty select Anthems* in 1743. In 1750 he began to collect, with the idea of publishing in score, the best English cathedral music. This he was unable to complete owing to bad health, and he bequeathed his materials to his friend, Dr. Boyce (see Boyce). He is a representative English cathedral composer.

Merbecke, John (1523 ?-1585 ?). Little is known of the life of the man who occupies so unique a place in the annals of English music. In 1542, while organist of St. George's Chapel, Windsor, he was arrested and condemned to the stake for heresy, but was saved through the intervention of Bishop Gardiner (*q.v.*) and one of the commissioners, Sir Humphrey Foster. In 1550 he published his *Boke of Common Praier noted*, a work which stands absolutely alone. It has suffered much at the hands of later editors. No perversion in modern notation should be countenanced for a moment.

Monk, William Henry (1823-89). Born in London. Organist Eaton Chapel, Pimlico; St. George's Chapel, Albemarle Street; and Portman Chapel, St. Marylebone. Director of choir in King's College, 1847, and organist, 1849. Professor of vocal music at the same college, 1874. Organist St. Matthias, Stoke Newington, 1852. One of the principal musical editors of *Hymns Ancient and Modern*, to which he contributed some well-known tunes.

Purcell, Henry (1658 ?-95). The national English composer. Chorister of the Chapel Royal and pupil of Dr. Blow. Appointed organist of Westminster Abbey, 1680, and of the Chapel Royal, 1682. His music is remarkable for its strength, tenderness, and freshness. His great *Te Deum* and *Jubilate* constitute the finest modern settings of those canticles. His anthems are no less remarkable, and 'Thou knowest, Lord,' 'Jehovah, quam multi sunt,' and the anthems composed for the coronation of James II., are among our greatest treasures. Purcell excelled in all kinds of composition, and is the founder of the later English school.

Smart, Henry (1813-79). Born in London. Organist Blackburn Parish Church, 1831;

St. Philips, London, 1836; St. Luke's, Old Street, 1844; St. Pancras, 1864. Composer of much deservedly popular Church music.

Stainer, Sir John, Mus. Doc. (1840-1901). Born in London. Chorister of St. Paul's Cathedral. Organist SS. Benedict and Peter, Paul's Wharf, 1854; Tenbury, 1856; Magdalen College, Oxford, 1859; St. Paul's Cathedral, 1872. It is due to him that the St. Paul's service reached its present high state of choral efficiency. Composer of much Church music.

Tallis, Thomas (1515 ?-85). The father of modern English music, whose compositions for the Church are unsurpassed. It is supposed that he was a chorister in St. Paul's Cathedral, and later in the Chapel Royal. He was organist of Waltham Abbey until its dissolution in 1540. Soon after this he probably became a gentleman of the Chapel Royal. In 1567 he composed eight tunes for Archbishop Parker's Psalter. Elizabeth granted him a monopoly (see Byrd). The *Cantiones Sacrae* (1575) are the joint work of Tallis and Byrd. Tallis was responsible for sixteen of these. His extraordinary song in forty real parts (eight choirs of five voices) is interesting only as an exercise, and not vocally effective. His Preces, Responses, Litany, and service in the Dorian mode were composed in all probability shortly after the Second Prayer Book of Edward VI. (1552).

Tye, Christopher, Mus. Doc. Born early in the sixteenth century. Chorister and afterwards gentleman of the Chapel Royal. Organist of Ely Cathedral, 1541-61. He made a metrical version of the first fourteen chapters of the Acts of the Apostles, which he set to music. Anthems by him are in Barnard's and Boyce's collections. He taught Edward VI. music. He died about 1580. He was a priest, and rector in turn of Doddington-cum-March, Little Wilbraham, and Newton. His anthem, 'O Lord of Hosts,' is a delightful example of the early cathedral school.

Walmisley, Thomas Attwood, Mus. Doc. (1814-56). Born in London. Studied composition under his godfather, Thomas Attwood. Organist of Croydon Church, 1830. Organist of Trinity and St. John's Colleges, Cambridge, 1833. Elected Professor of Music at Cambridge, 1836. Friend of Mendelssohn. His best music is in the true cathedral style. His services in B♭ and in D minor may be cited as instances.

Wesley, Samuel (1766-1837). One of the most remarkable English Church musicians. The greatest organist of his day, to him belongs the honour of introducing the works of Bach to the English public. He was the first modern musician to call attention to the claims of the Church's traditional music, Plainsong. He was a well-read man and a classical scholar, son of the famous Charles Wesley. [WESLEYS.] He wrote oratorios, masses, antiphons, services, and anthems.

Wesley, Samuel Sebastian. Mus. Doc. (1810-76). Natural son of the preceding S. Wesley. Chorister of the Chapel Royal. Organist St. James, Hampstead Road, 1826; St. Giles, Camberwell, and St. John's, Waterloo Road, 1829; and Hampton-on-Thames, 1830. He held three of these appointments simultaneously. He was appointed organist of Hereford Cathedral in 1832. In 1842 he accepted from Dr. Hook (q.v.) the organist's post at Leeds Parish Church. In 1849 he became organist of Winchester Cathedral, and of Gloucester Cathedral in 1865. He is one of the greatest English Church musicians. His most important works are his anthems, 'The Wilderness.' 'Blessed be the God and Father,' and 'Ascribe unto the Lord,' and his services in E. He was no less famous as an organist, and his extempore playing was a thing to wonder at.   [M. S.]

MYSTICS. Mysticism has constantly suffered through being presented and defined only in its aberrations. Hardly more responsible than the astronomer for the conduct and conclusions of the astrologer is the mystic for the Antinomian and the Ecstatic, with whom he is all too commonly identified. To confound it, on the other hand, as is very frequently done, with what is known as Vital Religion, is to confuse the saints who were mystics with the many who were not, leaving unexplained the perfectly recognisable but elusive quality which it is sought to define. It matters not at all what name is given to this quality; but it is obvious that if it is not called mystical it must be called something else; and it would appear more useful to retain the term in the sense whereby it has for centuries indicated the difference between, for example, the Epistles of St. James and of St. John, rather than import into it a new connotation, making it express essentially that which they have in common. The mystic, then, is one to whom a certain attitude of mind is natural; and mysticism may be considered as being less the things regarded than the manner of regarding them. That there is a considerable body of mystical doctrines, as such, no one would deny; but its three most salient examples rather illustrate than tra-

verse the above statement. The mystical paradox (as it is often called) of the absolute necessity for self-suppression, self-dying, since only by this means, and in direct proportion as it is attained, will the life of God penetrate and govern the soul, is the mystic's amplification of the Lord's statement: '*Whosoever would save his life shall lose it; but whosoever shall lose his life for My sake, the same shall save it.*' The 'process of Christ' is the apprehension of St. Paul's words: '*If we have become united with Him by the likeness of His death, we shall be also by the likeness of His resurrection.*' And even 'deification' itself, far from tending necessarily to an unbridled pantheism, should be understood as the translation into character of *becoming partakers of the divine nature.*

It will be most profitable to confine ourselves to the consideration of Christian mystics alone, and to leave on one side the mystics of India and the East; even Plato also, and his great follower, Plotinus, except as they are traceable in the influence exercised through the Alexandrines upon the Cambridge Platonists (q.v.). The Greek Fathers were far more mystically minded than the Latin, with the notable exception of St. Augustine; and it was the Greek writings, especially those of the pseudo-Dionysius the Areopagite, that guided mystical thought and speculation in the Middle Ages. The effect of these latter writings upon Western thought was the result of their translation into Latin by an Irishman, Scotus Eriugena, at the express command of the Frankish King, Charles the Bald. About the same time King Alfred (q.v.) was preparing the way for England's prominence in mystical expression by translating Boethius into the vulgar tongue, his *Consolation of Philosophy* being termed the *vade mecum* of the Middle Ages. It is little known, and less believed, that England possesses a longer roll of famous mystics, in prose and poetry, than any other country; and although the Scotsman or Irishman, Richard of St. Victor (d. 1173), prior of the celebrated abbey of St. Victor, near Paris, achieved his fame apart from his native island, an English school was arising which, a century later, contributed some of the earliest writings in the vernacular, those of Richard Rolle of Hampole (q.v.), and Walter Hilton (d. 1396), an Augustinian Canon of Thurgarton. Hilton's treatise, *The Scale of Perfection*, was the favourite reading of Margaret, Countess of Richmond, mother of Henry VII. Another early English mystic whose works, entitled *The Revelations of*

Divine Love, have lately been recovered, and have achieved a wide popularity, is the anchoress, Dame Julian of Norwich (1342-1442). It will be seen, in the course of this brief review, that of the three classes into which mystics are roughly divided, the philosophical, the devotional, and the Nature mystics, the first is less largely represented in England than the others. Though this country is not lacking in philosophers of distinction, it yet remains that a tendency to abstract speculation is not generally distinctive of the English mind; and it is possible that this circumstance is still further accentuated among English theologians by the absence of what makes so large a feature of the Roman curriculum for holy orders, the training in patristic and scholastic writings. It is apparent that the early English mystics took the line we should expect, of sincere practical piety, and did much to make religion a living thing among the poorer people. This sincere devotional note remains a characteristic of English mysticism throughout its history, even when blended, as in the Cambridge Platonists (*q.v.*), with philosophical thought. While it is characteristic of the mystic that he should always exalt the value of the inner light, and the kernel rather than the shell of true religion, thereby appearing at times to be the champion of individualism and revolt against external authority, nothing is more misleading than to claim him, as is often done by modern American writers, as the essential heretic. Many mystical writers have, it is true, been condemned by Councils, Synods, and Popes, notably Origen, Eriugena, Eckhart, and Molinos; but quite as many bore the imprimatur of the Church they loyally served, to their dying day: among whom we may reckon Richard Rolle and his successors—in fact, by far the greater number of English mystics down to modern times; and on the Continent such great figures as St. Catherine of Siena, St. Francis de Sales, Thomas à Kempis, and St. Teresa. That the gap in mystical writers occurring at the death of Dame Julian should be the longest traceable since Richard Rolle up to our own days, shows the unparalleled continuity of English thought on these lines. It is closed by two great laymen, Sir Thomas Browne (1605-82), author of the *Religio Medici*; and Henry Montagu, Earl of Manchester (1563-1642), Chief Justice of England and Lord Privy Seal, writer of the little treatise called *Manchester al Mondo.* A group of divines leads us on to the Cambridge Platonists: Joseph Hall, Bishop of Norwich

(1574-1656), Giles Fletcher (1584-1623), and George Herbert (*q.v.*) (1593-1633). The saintly Bishop Hall, writer of *Christ Mystical,* and an earnest defender of the Apostolical Succession, was greatly persecuted by the Puritans, and was one of the eleven bishops imprisoned in the Tower under the Long Parliament. To Giles Fletcher, author of *Christ's Victory and Triumph,* etc., and George Herbert, one of the most widely famous of the English mystics, must be added three other poets: the chivalrous and adventurous Francis Quarles (1592-1644), who served first the Queen of Bohemia, and later became secretary of Archbishop Ussher (*q.v.*), but lost everything in the royal cause; and Richard Crashaw (1613-50), who himself, the son of a fierce antipapist, was turned out of Peterhouse for his Roman Catholic leanings, and died a canon of Loretto. Henry Vaughan, the third (1621-95), was imprisoned as a Royalist; and after his release, practised as a physician in Wales. His collection of poems, *Silex Scintillans,* is as widely known as those of George Herbert. Simultaneous with the rise of the Cambridge Platonists were two other mystical movements, each of the three, as far as can be traced, keeping perfectly clear and distinct from the others. The more famous of these two movements was Quakerism, possessing both in its tendencies and in the writings of its prophets, Isaac Penington (1616-79), George Fox (1624-90), and William Penn (1644-1718), undoubted affinities with mysticism, though not in itself of so avowedly mystical a tendency as the other movement, known as that of the Philadelphians. In 1652 a certain Dr. Pordage held meetings for the study of the great German mystic, Jacob Böhme. Out of these gatherings was formed in 1670 the Philadelphian Society by Mrs. Jane Leade—the whole inspired with a high mystical purpose and the avowed intention of giving practical expression to the doctrine of universal brotherhood. They established relations with German and Dutch mystics of the time; but were forbidden to meet together, and gradually died out. A singular feature in English mysticism is Cromwell's chaplain, Peter Sterry (d. 1672). One of the fourteen Puritan divines sent by the Lords to the Westminster Assembly, he sat in it almost from the beginning. Thomas Traherne (1637-74), the greatest English Nature mystic, whose prose and poetical works have only recently been reissued, was a worthy follower of the great seventeenth-century group of poets, and has many links also with the Cambridge Platonists.

The next outstanding figure is that of William Law (*q.v.*); and from his days onwards the torch of mysticism, grasped in turn by Blake, Coleridge and Wordsworth, has not suffered extinction. In no age, in spite of all its perversions and imitations, has there been a keener appreciation of its spirit than in our own.

[E. C. G.]

N

NEALE, John Mason (1818-66), divine, only son of a distinguished Cambridge scholar who became an Evangelical clergyman, was educated at Sherborne, and in 1836 became scholar of Trinity, Cambridge. His dislike of mathematics prevented his gaining classical honours, which, before 1841, it was impossible to take without previous mathematical honours. He took a Pass degree, 1840. He then became assistant tutor, and after his ordination in 1841 chaplain at Downing College. He won the Seatonian prize poem in 1845, and on ten occasions afterwards. He founded the famous Cambridge Camden Society for Archæological and Ecclesiological Studies. Evangelicals and Low Churchmen feared it, and Bishop Sumner refused to licence Neale to St. Nicholas, Guildford, in 1841. Bishop Monk of Gloucester ordained him priest, Trinity, 1842, and next day he became Vicar of Crawley, Sussex. Here his health, always delicate, failed, and he resigned the living. He married, July 1842, and, 1843-6, lived chiefly in Madeira. He then accepted the Wardenship of Sackville College, East Grinstead—a small seventeenth-century almshouse—a post worth £28 a year. He received no further offers of preferment, save the provostship (deanery) of Perth in 1850 and a small living in 1856. He declined them.

He was created D.D. by Trinity College, Hartford, Conn., 1860. At Sackville College Neale was much persecuted. He had rebuilt the chapel, and used the ordinary altar ornaments—cross, candles, and flowers. Bishop Gilbert of Chichester attacked him for this, and finally inhibited him in the diocese, 1847. The mob took up the tale. There were riots in 1848, in 1851, and later in 1856. In 1857 there was a disgraceful scene at the funeral of a Sister at Lewes. Neale was knocked down, and the Sisters with difficulty rescued. In 1866, a few months before his death, he was mobbed in the streets of Liverpool. Bishop Gilbert removed his inhibition and became reconciled to Neale in 1861.

Neale's work was manifold. He was a Church historian, theologian, controversialist, preacher, spiritual guide, poet, story-writer, and a marvellous linguist, speaking twenty languages. He founded the sisterhood of St. Margaret, East Grinstead (1854), and his hymns (chiefly translations from Greek or Latin), 'Art thou weary,' 'Jerusalem the golden,' and many more, are in all collections. His learning did much to promote a better understanding with the Eastern churches. His stories, *The Farm of Aptonga, Theodora Phranza*, and others had before his death been translated into the chief European languages, and are widely known. He was a traveller, and wrote on Portugal and Dalmatia. Through all the crises in the English Church, 1845-51, Neale was unshaken, and did much to steady the unsettled. In private life he was gentle and sensitive, with strong affections and a great sense of humour. He died, worn out with labours, at Sackville College, 6th August 1866.

[S. L. O.]

Memoir; Letters; Memoirs of a Sister of St. Saviour's Priory; Huntingdon. *Random Recollections.*

NELSON, Robert (1656-1715), religious writer and philanthropist, son of a rich London merchant, was educated at St. Paul's School, and then by George Bull, afterwards Bishop of St. David's, from whom he learnt his strong Church principles. Early in life he contracted a warm friendship with Tillotson (*q.v.*). In 1682 he married the Lady Theophila Lucy, who, to his great grief, became a Romanist, but this did not prevent the union being very happy. He disapproved of the Revolution of 1688, retiring to the Continent during its course. He returned in 1691, firmly resolved never to acknowledge William and Mary, and therefore joined the Nonjurors (*q.v.*), mainly because he did not wish to join in the prayers for the royal family. On these grounds Tillotson approved of his secession. In 1710, before the death of William Lloyd, the last of the deprived bishops except Ken, Nelson, together with Dodwell and others, returned to the national Church, but did not join in the prayers for the royal family. This defection was perhaps the greatest blow the Nonjuring cause received. On Easter Day

Nelson received the Blessed Sacrament from Archbishop Sharp (*q.v.*) of York. In 1713 he assisted in the publication of *The Hereditary Right Asserted*, by George Harbin.

During his Nonjuring days Nelson remained on good terms with many of the conforming clergy, and supported nearly all the various charitable and philanthropic institutions of the age. He was an enthusiastic patron of the Religious Societies (*q.v.*) and of the Societies for the Reformation of Manners (*q.v.*), and an influential member of the S.P.C.K. and the S.P.G. He gave valuable assistance to Dr. Bray's (*q.v.*) scheme for providing parochial libraries in England, to the Corporation of the Sons of the Clergy, and to the Charity School Movement. In 1710 he was appointed to the Commission for building fifty new churches in London. In Anne's reign he became celebrated for his religious writings. His best known works are his *Companion to the Fasts and Festivals of the Church of England* (1704), of which a thirty-sixth edition appeared in 1836; a *Life of Bishop Bull* (1713), his old tutor; and his *Address to Persons of Quality* (1715). Nelson spent and bequeathed his own fortune in charitable works, and has been well called the 'pious Robert Nelson.' [G. V. P.]

C. F. Secretan, *Life and Times of the Pious Robert Nelson*; Overton, *The Nonjurors*.

NEVILLE, Ralph (d. 1244), Bishop of Chichester, was an illegitimate cadet of the noble house of his name. Honorius III. by Bull, 25th January 1220, removed this canonical disability to his ordination. He early entered the Government service as a clerk in the Chancery. King John was his patron, and in 1214 he received the deanery of Lichfield, and within the next two years some six livings in various parts of England, and a prebend in St. Paul's. October 1222 he was elected Chancellor of Chichester, and immediately afterwards bishop, but was not consecrated until April 1224. 1226 he became Chancellor of England, and in 1227 the appointment was made for life. He was chosen archbishop by the Canterbury monks, 1231, but Gregory IX. quashed the election, fearing, it is said, Neville's independent spirit. 1238 he was elected Bishop of Winchester, but Henry III. refused his assent, and called all who voted for Neville 'fools.' The bishop had been the colleague and friend of Hubert de Burgh, and was opposed to the foreign influences which dominated the court. In 1236 he refused to resign his chancellorship at Henry's request. In 1238 the King forced him to give up the Seal, but he retained the title and emoluments of Chancellor. In 1242 the office was restored to him. His house in London was opposite the Temple, and its site, Chancery Lane, owes its name to his residence there. Bishop Neville was an excellent public servant, and a loyal official, who helped to preserve the throne during the minority of Henry III. He was a just and merciful judge, a generous benefactor to his cathedral church, and a careful husband of his episcopal property. The letters from his steward in Sussex throw much interesting light on thirteenth-century farming. By his refusal to resign the chancellorship save to the Council which had conferred it on him, Bishop Stubbs holds that Neville anticipated the later constitutional doctrine of the responsibility of ministers. [S. L. O.]

D.N.B.; *Royal Letters Henry III.*, R.S.; *Sussex Archæol. Collections*, iii.; Stephens, *Memorials of See of Chichester.*

NEWCASTLE, See of. The earliest Northumbrian see was that of Lindisfarne, founded by Aidan (*q.v.*) in 635. There was also a see of Hexham, 678-821. In 881 Eardulf, the last Bishop of Lindisfarne, was driven thence by the Danes, and fixed his see at Chester-le-Street. In 991 his successor, Aldhun, was again driven out by the Danes, and settled at Durham, from whence the church of Northumberland was governed for nearly nine hundred years. [DURHAM, SEE OF.]

A separate bishopric for Northumberland was discussed under Edward VI., but nothing was done. In 1854 the corporation of Newcastle-on-Tyne, supported by other local bodies, petitioned the Home Secretary for a separate diocese, pleading that proper administration of the Church in their county was impossible while it remained a distant part of the immense Durham diocese. In 1876 Bishop Baring took the matter up, and supported the inclusion of Newcastle in the Bishoprics Act of 1878 (41-2 Vic. c. 68), under which the see of Newcastle was founded by Order in Council published 23rd May 1882. Its income was fixed at £3500, £1000 a year being taken from that of Durham, and over £75,000 raised by voluntary contributions. Benwell Tower, two miles from Newcastle, was presented to the see as an episcopal residence by Mr. J. W. Pease, a member of the Society of Friends. The parish church of St. Nicholas, Newcastle, dating chiefly from the fourteenth century, became the cathedral church. Though there are four endowed canonries the chapter has not yet been legally constituted, and the bishop is appointed by Letters Patent from the Crown. The diocese consists of the county of Northumberland, with Berwick-upon-Tweed, and the ancient civil parish of Alston, with its chapelries in Cumberland. It contains 1,290,312 acres, has a population of 700,014, and is divided into the archdeaconries of Northumberland (first mentioned, 1140) and Lindisfarne (separated from it in 1882).

BISHOPS

1. Ernest Roland Wilberforce, 1882 ; tr. to Chichester, 1895.
2. Edgar Jacob, 1895 ; tr. to St. Albans, 1903.
3. Arthur Thomas Lloyd, 1903 ; tr. from Thetford ; formerly Vicar of Newcastle ; a most active and saintly bishop ; d. 1907.
4. Norman Dumenil John Straton, 1907 ; tr. from Sodor and Man.

[G. C.]

NEWMAN, John Henry (1801-90), cardinal, son of a London banker, was brought up under Calvinistic influences, went through the process of conversion in 1816, which he ever after regarded as a turning-point in his life ; was sent up to Trinity College, Oxford, very young, did not highly distinguish himself in the schools, but in 1822 was elected, after examination, a Fellow of Oriel, then the leading college in the intellectual life of Oxford. He became a Tutor of the college in 1826. Hurrell Froude (*q.v.*) was elected a Fellow in the same year. Newman had united with Froude to vote for Hawkins as Provost against Keble (*q.v.*). For this he was rewarded in 1829 by Hawkins turning him out of his tutorship, because he insisted on construing strictly the tutor's function *in loco parentis* to have regard to the moral and spiritual welfare of his pupils. In 1832 he went abroad with Froude and his father, the archdeacon. The journey in which Newman saw Rome for the first time was undertaken for the sake of Froude's health, which it did not permanently re-establish. Newman himself towards the close was alone, and nearly died of fever in Sicily. It was on the voyage back from Marseilles that he wrote ' Lead, kindly Light.' So far as Newman was concerned it was chiefly during the long dream time of this interlude that the thoughts gathered which were to take shape in the Oxford Movement (*q.v.*). The year of the great Reform Bill was one which foreboded great danger to the Establishment. And the Movement avowedly took its origin in the endeavour to find some defence for the Church of England deeper than that of mere political conservatism. Newman resolved to proceed by the method of short tracts, and becoming the editor, wrote the first with its call to battle, ' I am but one of your-selves, a presbyter.' And the circulation, which was conducted in somewhat primitive fashion, began shortly to affect the country parsonages. Newman had been presented by his college in 1828 to the living of St. Mary's, Oxford. This was to prove his widest source of influence in the English Church. His sermons, though not definitely propagandist, attracted all those undergraduates who listened to sermons at all, and moulded a whole generation of clergy. In 1833 he also published his first volume, *The Arians of the Fourth Century*, which as an exposition of Catholic doctrine is unrivalled, and as history is far less unsatisfactory than is often sup-posed, due regard being had to the date of its publication. In 1834 the Movement, which had been proceeding by rapid strides, received a great accession of strength in the person of Pusey (*q.v.*).

In 1836 came the controversy over Hamp-den's (*q.v.*) Bampton Lectures. In this Newman was the main assailant. The same year began the connection with the *British Critic* (a magazine started in 1814), which was to contain so many solid contributions to theology and some of Newman's best writing. In 1839 the downgrade began. Newman read an article of Wiseman's on 'The Anglican Claim,' and declared that it was the first serious blow he had received from the Roman side. From this ' stomach-ache ' he never recovered. He began to fear that the English Church was no better off than the Donatists or the Monophysites, and although he buoyed himself up with fresh arguments, such as the essay on *The Catholicity of the Anglican Church*, he was never more a whole-hearted defender of the *Via Media*. Influ-enced partly by Ward and others of the more extreme men who had come late into the Movement, he wrote in 1841 Tract 90, designed to prove that the Protestant interpretation which custom had affixed to the Thirty-nine Articles was not binding, but that they might be construed in a Catholic sense. In the course of this tract he lays down the principles of the ethics of conformity, as they are now almost univers-ally received. The tract provoked an outcry. Four Oxford Tutors, of whom Tait (*q.v.*) was one, protested against its alleged immorality, and the bishops after some delay began to charge against its author. In obedience to his own bishop Newman stopped the further issue of the Tracts. He had fitted up a few cottages at Littlemore as a sort of refuge for men desiring to live in community. There he retired with a few others. In 1843 he published a retractation of all the hard things he had said of the Roman Church, and resigned St. Mary's. One further event greatly moved him, and this was the establishment of the Jerusalem Bishopric (*q.v.*), the ill-fated project of Bunsen. He wrote a letter to the archbishop publicly protesting against this. But though it may be thought to have intensified his feeling, this incident did not originate or even accelerate his action. In 1845 a successful attempt was made to censure W. G. Ward for the *Ideal of a Christian Church*, but the proctors' veto (exercised by Church (*q.v.*) and Guillemard) saved Newman from insult. He was engaged on that essay, afterwards published, *On the Development of Christian Doctrine*, which is in some ways the most original of all his works. Before the book was really completed he took the final step, and was received into the Roman Church on 9th October by the Passionist, Father Dominic.

After an interlude at various places in England, Newman was sent to Rome for a year. In 1847 he founded the congregation of the Oratory of St. Philip Neri in Birmingham, which in 1852 was removed to the suburb of Edgbaston. This remained his home for the rest of his life, except for the short and intermittent sojourn in Dublin. In 1850 he delivered the lectures on *The Difficulties of Anglicans*. The course was designed to show that Rome was the logical outcome of Tractarianism, and that the difficulties felt by many were not vital objections to the Roman system. At this time, 1851, there took place the famous papal aggression. At the inauguration of the 'revived' Roman hierarchy Newman preached that sermon on 'The Second Spring' which Macaulay was declared to have by heart. In view of the outcry provoked by the unwise phraseology of Cardinal Wiseman Newman was induced to deliver the course of lectures on *The Present Position of Catholics in England*. This volume contains some of the best specimens of his irony. Unfortunately, however, he alluded, in terms entirely justified, to the character of an ex-Dominican, Dr. Achilli, who had been greatly advertised by the ultra-Protestant party. Achilli prosecuted Newman for criminal libel. In the existing state of the public mind, with a judge manifestly prejudiced, it was not surprising that Newman was condemned. This was directly in the teeth of the evidence; but a motion for a new trial failed, and New-

man was sentenced to a fine of £100, in a case of which the costs were £14,000. On the whole, however, he had gained; the money was subscribed for him, and the manifest injustice of the verdict turned feeling in his favour. In 1854, at the request of Cardinal Cullen, Newman became the Rector of the Roman Catholic University in Dublin. His position was hopeless from the first. The bishops wanted nothing of Newman but his name; they hampered and insulted him; their ideal was merely a superior sort of seminary; and after three years' disappointing efforts Newman retired. One good result had come of the ill-fated project, the lectures on *The Idea of a University*. From 1857-61 Newman was also much occupied with another difficult matter. Sir John (later Lord) Acton and others had been for some time endeavouring to raise the standard of culture among Roman Catholics, and as a means to this end they had chosen a magazine. *The Rambler*, however, became so extravagant in theological liberalism that the authorities were set against it. Eventually, after much negotiation, Newman consented to take over the editorship. He retained it, however, for a very few months. An article of his own on 'Consulting the Laity in matters of Faith,' though it contains one of the best possible expositions of the true principles of authority, was denounced to Rome, and could not but be offensive to strict ultramontanes. After this, the review was bought by Acton, and Newman was invited sometimes to give advice. But the net result of his intervention was that he had awakened the distrust of both sides, and left the breaches unhealed. Probably, however, if it had not been for Newman, Acton and Simpson would not have been able to continue the *Home and Foreign Review* as long as they did. It should be said that the Oratory School at Edgbaston was founded in 1859. Newman was not headmaster, but exercised a general supervision, and his name had much to do with the success of the school. At this time his position was at its *nadir*. Distrusted by the authorities of his own Church, openly attacked in the *Dublin Review* by W. G. Ward, with the influence of Manning (*q.v.*) on the increase and incurably hostile, Newman had fallen out of public notice; his books had ceased to sell, and his work appeared to be over.

In 1864 came the chance of his life. He took it, and after the publication of the *Apologia pro Vita Sua* his place in English life was secure. Kingsley (*q.v.*) began by making a charge of deliberate approval of falsehood against Newman. Invited to give his authorities, he was unable to do more than allude to the general trend of a sermon. Pressed still further, he still refused to withdraw his charge, and made even baser insinuations in a rejoinder entitled *What then does Dr. Newman mean?* Newman discerned that here was the true point at issue –the meaning and spirit of his whole life; and the *Apologia*, written at white heat and coming out in weekly parts, was the consequence. A public assurance of the sympathy of his co-religionists made him more than ever dangerous to the extreme ultramontanes, like Manning, Ward, and Vaughan, styled by Newman 'the three tailors of Tooley Street.' A suggestion that he should go to Oxford to preside over a Roman Catholic college or hostel was bitterly opposed by his enemies. In the year 1870 he issued his *Grammar of Assent*. This with the *Development* and the *University Sermons* is Newman's most important contribution to the philosophy of religion, and anticipates much that has been recently written from the philosophic side on the nature of belief. The book was approved by Ward, but its strong anti-scholastic tendency made it unpopular with the exponents of the prevailing scholastic orthodoxy. This was the time of the Vatican Council. Newman, though he believed the doctrine of 'Papal Infallibility,' was opposed to its promulgation, and to the influence of Manning and the Jesuits who pressed for it. Thus he was in the strictest sense an inopportunist. Though invited, as one of the theological assessors, by Archbishop Dupanloup, Newman refused to attend the Council. But his views were known, and the unauthorised publication of a private letter gave them more pronounced expression than he would have desired. Despite this, when in 1874 Mr. Gladstone (*q.v.*) published his pamphlet on *The Vatican Decrees in their bearing on Civil Allegiance*, all turned to Newman for help. His *Letter to the Duke of Norfolk* forms not merely a most effective answer to Mr. Gladstone, but is also a very adroit blow delivered at the extreme ultramontanes. Even Acton could say that he might accept the decree with Newman's explanations. The only other event of importance in Newman's life is the offer of the cardinalate. When Pius IX. was succeeded in 1876 by the more liberal Leo XIII., Newman's admirers felt that it was opportune to ask for some recognition. After some difficulty, created by Manning, the honour was conferred in 1878, and Newman lived the last twelve years of his life honoured alike within and without his own communion. He wrote no more books, but in 1881 published an article of liberal tendency on the object of Biblical criticism, and spent much time in arranging his correspondence. After growing gradually more and more feeble, he died on 11th August 1890. The chorus of eulogy which followed his death provoked hostile critics. In *Philomythus, Newmanianism*, and his two volumes on the *Anglican Life of Cardinal Newman*, Dr. E. A. Abbott set himself to besmirch his reputation, and employed arguments on a lower level than those of Kingsley.

The personal charm and extraordinary subtlety of Newman's character render him one of the most intimate and alluring of writers. His contribution to the life of his time may be summed up as follows:—He discerned earlier than most men the terrific strength of the forces that threatened to engulf the Christian faith; he saw that the existing bulwarks, alike intellectual and political, were of little value; and that the true conflict was between rationalism as an accepted principle and the religious sense of men. He saw that those who decide for the religious sense have decided for a power super-individual, and that the collective consciousness of the religious community must be their authority rather than the individual reason. Further he saw that all beliefs must be ultimately determined by their relation to life, and that real assent would be no merely mechanical result. Man is not merely a sort of super-Babbage, grinding out conclusions like a calculating machine. Thus all his religious philosophy arises from the denial to the individual of the power to form entirely valid conclusions *once he has accepted the postulate of religion*; while in his view of the social consciousness, as incarnate in the Church, he is led to develop the doctrine of organic evolution in the spiritual just as Darwin did in the natural world. It is sometimes a question how far the development allowed by Newman is truly organic, and how far it is a mere logical explication. On the whole, however, the better opinion appears to be that it was the former, or at least that he was feeling his way to it. This seems clear from the famous passage about the Church 'changing that she may remain the same.' It is the viewing of all religious philosophy under the category of life that is Newman's main contribution. Its value is permanent, and his influence is in some ways on the increase.

This he foresaw. In his darkest moments he seems to have felt that he would be appreciated after his death, and the interest in him in France and Germany has developed in him in the last ten years. This is testified by works like those of Henri Brémond in France, and Lady Blennerhassett in Germany.

Of the style so much has been said that it is idle to add a word. Mr. Gladstone described it well as 'transporting.' Its mingling of sweetness and austerity and the depth of its *intimité* make it unlike all else.

[J. N. F.]

Life and Correspondence, ed. A. Mozley ; *Life* by Wilfrid Ward ; *Apologia pro Vita Sua.*

NONCONFORMITY. It is needless to carry the history of Nonconformity in England beyond the reign of Elizabeth. In earlier days a resemblance of ideas can be discovered but no continuity of organisation. The prime motive of Nonconformity, as we know it, was antagonism to tradition as embodied in Rome. At the beginning of Elizabeth's reign, though there was a widespread survival of sympathy with the old order, it was mute and passive. The governing and thinking classes were eager for change ; repugnance excited by the horrors of Mary's reign, hatred of Spain, and the example of the most enlightened and progressive parts of Europe worked together to stimulate the desire. The Roman communion was not as yet effectually reformed and disciplined, nor was it clear that the progress of the Protestant Reformation was to be stayed at the point it had already reached. The future seemed to belong to the new Churches ; even in France, till Henry IV. bought Paris by a change of creed, it was quite possible that Protestantism might at least share the nation with Rome. It was natural, then, that in England the ardent spirits should strive to complete the breach with the past, and should cherish resentment against what seemed the half-hearted compromise established as the national Church. And in excuse for them it must be borne in mind that till the rise of Bancroft (*q.v.*) and Hooker (*q.v.*) the Church of England held no obviously consistent position, either in theory or practice, by which it could be discriminated from its foreign allies. Its tone was apologetic on the side of argument ; it pleaded that the practices it retained from the past were pardonable, and at the worst were no sufficient reason for a schism, or for a revolutionary change in usages and constitution. But what was wanting in resolute maintenance of the ecclesiastical position was supplied by a vigorous policy of suppression, the victims of which could not distinguish between the

share of the Church and that of the State in their sufferings.

The danger to the Church from this movement was that its promoters professed themselves to be, and in eyes of many were, the foremost champions against Rome. We are apt to think of their protest as directed primarily against our own Church's peculiarities ; statesmen like Burghley regarded their domestic sallies as pardonable because they seemed the most consistent, and therefore the most formidable, opponents of the alien. But we may leave out of account, as having had no permanent results, such separatism as was merely a protest against ancient observances, without a definite Church theory of its own. The agitation was only dangerous when it became logical : and the French reformers were ready to supply a reasoned and consistent scheme. By this time the German reformation had fallen into the background. Its strength had been in inward feeling and in the support of the State, and as feeling grew less intense it was replaced by an orthodoxy which became as scholastic as the mediæval, while the support of the local government grew into a domination. But if Lutheranism was unattractive, it was also remote. The Lutheran regions were severed from Britain by a screen of Churches which may, for all practical purposes, be called Calvinist. From the North Sea to the Alps, Western Europe, where it was not Roman, was Calvinist, and it was among Calvinists of varying shades that the Marian Exiles (*q.v.*) had resided, and had learned that a national Church, to include all the members of the nation, is a necessary part of the divine order ; they had also learned that the Scripture reveals the right constitution of this Church, and that existing Churches must, as a matter of duty, be reconstructed after this pattern. The wisest leaders of Continental reform pressed, indeed, for unity in England, lest the nation should be lost through internal disputes to the common cause ; but logic and passion were too strong. It passed for nothing that the English Church, or at least its leaders, had no quarrel with the doctrines of the extreme reformers, and was hostile to Rome. There was an appearance of compromise, a retention of historical institutions which seemed unscriptural to men who had reached the conclusion that bishop and presbyter were at first, and therefore were designed always to be, names for the same office. There was also—and here they were justified in their complaints—a notorious inefficiency in the working ministers of the Church, and a failure of the bishops to raise the standard. And so in the first great manifesto, *The Admonition to the Parliament* of 1571, the practical failure is used to enforce the need of new principles of government. It is useless to ' patch and piece,' as hitherto. The English Church must ' altogether remove whole Antichrist, both head and tail, and perfectly plant that purity of the word, that simplicity of the sacraments and severity of discipline, which Christ hath commanded and commended to His Church.' This result was to be attained by the establishment of a ministry with coercive powers, in the enjoyment of the existing church revenues, all the members of which were to be on a parity with one another, while they were to be organised in an elaborate system of courts that should culminate in a national assembly. The scheme was based on the assumption that the character of a Church is not affected by its constitution. Before and after this revolution the Church of England would retain its identity as an orthodox, anti-Roman communion ; and the innovators held that they were not quarrelling with it but with certain accidental peculiarities that disfigured it. They could not sanction these defects by conforming to its existing rules, but they claimed that their loyalty was shown by the very fact of their zeal for its improvement. For this improvement they laboured by controversy and by attempts at organisation. We are only concerned with the latter.

I. Presbyterians

At Wandsworth in 1572 was established a definitely Presbyterian Church, which was promptly suppressed. But the founders were not discouraged. They believed that the future was theirs, and prophesied that Matthew Parker (*q.v.*) would be the last Archbishop of Canterbury. A more comprehensive scheme was quickly started. Like-minded clergy were to form voluntary associations, either for mutual improvement in preaching and in spiritual exercises, or else for mutual discipline ; and though they held their benefices by patronage and episcopal institution they were to regard this private membership as their true right to exercise their ministry. They were to admit such others as they thought fit, and gradually to extend both the membership and the authority of these private societies till they became the actual government of the Church. When a federation of such local organisations sent representatives to a national assembly the work would be accomplished ; and though the higher officers, such as bishops and arch-

deacons, might still survive, they would be of merely antiquarian interest without administrative power. In parishes, especially in towns, where the clergy were out of sympathy with the movement, and there was little hope of more amenable successors being appointed, wealthy laymen subscribed to buy up impropriate tithe as an endowment for lectureships to be held by Puritan clergy. The churchwardens would see that they had access to the pulpit, and they would be regarded by their adherents as the true ministers of the parish and accepted as such in the ' class,' or association of neighbouring clergy. There was, in fact, the beginning of such a government as existed in the Presbyterian Church of Scotland. Under the weak rule of Grindal (*q.v.*) and with the support of many leading laymen, who protected the innovators by giving them the post of chaplain, the plan seemed likely to succeed. When Bancroft brought method into the government of the Church, and churchmen came to be conscious of distinctive principles of their own, the attempt to create an *imperium in imperio* was abandoned. Meanwhile a new danger, that of Independency, was rising, whose negation of the principle of national Churches was repugnant to the Presbyterians, and drove them into closer sympathy with Anglicans, as maintainers equally with themselves of the threatened principle. There was also the obvious consideration that a benefice in the Established Church did actually confer upon the minister much of the authority he desired, and also gave him power to work for its increase ; while the natural tendency to acquiesce in a familiar position made submission to the pressure of authority and tolerance of the new arguments of the Anglican school seem comparatively easy. Thus the successors of stern and consistent champions of the Presbyterian principle, such as Cartwright (*q.v.*) and Travers (*q.v.*), were men content to live and let live. Their protests grew steadily fainter, though their principles were cherished in their hearts, ready to emerge in protest against Laudianism, which itself was not an arbitrary innovation but the inevitable and normal outcome of the Anglican mode of thought. But the fact that the Westminster Assembly of 1643 was composed of elderly beneficed clergy, episcopally ordained under Elizabeth or James I., and quite satisfied as to the validity of their position, shows how thoroughly at home Presbyterianism had come to be in the Church. Latent it had been, but its advocates felt no incongruity in their task of rendering it explicit as the discipline and doctrine of England. The Church, in their judgment, was not essentially changed, but only practically improved, by the innovation.

For a moment it seemed that they had won a lasting triumph. To the merchants of London and Bristol, to a large proportion of the trading and landed classes throughout the country, it appeared that the interests of civil liberty were bound up with those of a rigorous ecclesiastical discipline. The Puritan clergy were eager to undertake their share of the work; excommunication was to be a power in constant exercise. But the laity flinched from the prospect, and the Presbyterian system was effectually set in motion only in London and the neighbourhood of Manchester. The failure was due quite as much to the unwillingness of the average Englishman to submit to a Genevan regime as to the rival enthusiasm of Independency. In the curiously anarchical system which subsisted under the Commonwealth any one who could obtain a presentation and pass the ' Triers ' might enjoy a benefice were he Presbyterian, Anglican (provided he did not use the Prayer-Book), Independent, or Baptist. Probably a majority were in general sympathy with the Westminster Assembly, but though they could enforce payment of their income from endowment, they could not silence those whom they denounced as ' sectaries.' Any one might form a separate congregation, and the Presbyterian ideal of a coercive and uniform Church was as distant as ever.

We cannot wonder that the Presbyterians worked for, and welcomed, the Restoration. They valued highly their own share in bringing it about, and expected to be rewarded by such a modification of the national Church as should make it equally agreeable to themselves and to the Anglicans. They were prepared to make considerable concessions, for they recognised that the Church must be a home for their old adversaries as well as for themselves; and they were bitterly disappointed when they found that no concessions would be made by the other side. They had, in fact, totally failed to realise the reaction of public opinion to royalism and episcopacy. Still, for more than a generation they clung to the hope of comprehension, and were encouraged in the hope by an important element within the Church. [REUNION, IV.] This longing for unity persisted in spite of a persecution, which was singularly impolitic. Baxter (*q.v.*) was steady, if not always practical, in his advocacy of reunion on terms which, he thought, might easily be arranged without dishonour to either side. Among Anglicans, Tillotson

(*q.v.*) pleaded for comprehension, and Stillingfleet (*q.v.*) showed, by his efforts to make peace among conflicting Presbyterians, that he did not consider them as aliens. But such sympathy and such efforts were vain, and the Presbyterians sank into the state of a number of detached congregations. This was fatal to them. Their principles required that they should be an organised national Church; they were now in the position of the Independents. If a chapel were vacant its lay officers could only, as a separate corporation, enter into agreement with an individual minister to fill the charge; such a transaction, perfectly satisfactory to Independents, contradicted the very root principle of Presbyterianism. Still they retained, at least into the reign of George I., a large proportion of the mercantile wealth of England; and perhaps under Anne the number of Presbyterian peers was not much smaller than that of Roman Catholic peers to-day.

But a great and fatal doctrinal change was impending. While the Independents, for the most part of humbler status and less exposed to the social and intellectual spirit of the eighteenth century, usually maintained the old Puritan Calvinism, it was rapidly softened among the Presbyterians after the Restoration. The orthodox Baxter took the lead in this movement of thought, and those who followed him were often called Baxterians. But this reaction against rigorous doctrine coincided in time and soon coalesced with the tendency that became Unitarianism.

II. UNITARIANS

This was a mode of thought that sprang up in the early years of the Reformation, and had never been suppressed, though its adherents had been systematically persecuted in England as elsewhere. The last to suffer at the stake in England were two Arians, burnt in 1612; and John Biddle, the first minister avowedly to teach Unitarianism in England, suffered repeated imprisonment under the government of Cromwell and Charles II. The Westminster Assembly, indeed, was eager for his execution. In the ferment of thought during the Commonwealth the hated doctrine gained many adherents. Milton, in his later years, was affected by it. And it had a strong attraction for the mind of the eighteenth century. Sir Isaac Newton was its most distinguished lay convert, while some of the most talented of the clergy, in the early part of the century, such as Samuel Clarke, Rector of St. James's, Westminster, and the Cambridge Professor

Whiston (*q.v.*), were its advocates, without feeling it necessary to leave their Church.

More causes than one influenced the Presbyterians in the same direction. Their desire for a comprehension that should admit them to the Church led them to minimise points of difference in one direction, so that it was natural for them to minimise them in others. It was they who especially practised occasional conformity, *i.e.* the reception of the Communion at their parish church as a preliminary to the assumption of civil office ; and the party in the Church that sympathised with this proceeding on their part was that which was most inclined to theological indifference. And the reaction of the age against the precise doctrines, faith in which had been urged as essential on every side for a century and a half, led to an estimate of benevolence, in God and man, as the highest of qualities. Tolerance and generosity seemed nobler than orthodoxy, especially to men for whom orthodoxy was apt to mean a crude doctrine of predestination. These were among the causes which led to the prevalence of this new teaching among the English Presbyterians, in spite of the fact that it was dangerous to hold it. Unitarians were expressly excluded from the benefit of the Toleration Act of 1689, and their faith was a criminal offence.

We may now trace the growth of the innovation among them. Since Thomas Emlyn (1663-1741) the line of Unitarian ministers has been continuous. He suffered much both from the hostility of orthodox dissenters and from the law ; his final release from prison was in 1705. But allies were springing up in many quarters, especially in London and Exeter, whence the Presbyterian ministers were ejected in 1719 by their laity, who were not yet in sympathy with the movement. Both parties appealed for support to the dissenters of London, who since 1691 had been united by a treaty, called the 'Heads of Agreement,' in a loose federation. A memorable meeting was held at Salters' Hall in February 1719, just before the Exeter ejectment, at which a resolution in favour of the exclusion of the Unitarians was carried by the vote of fifty-seven ministers and delegates against fifty-three. If the Presbyterians had been alone there would have been a large majority for comprehension. Not that all those who were in favour of toleration were unorthodox, but that there was in the whole communion a general dislike for non-Scriptural terms of communion. The trust deeds of most of the Presbyterian chapels had been deliberately drawn in vague terms,

without specification of the doctrine to be taught ; and now, in spite of the danger, good men regarded the admission of Unitarianism as a lesser evil than the definition of doctrine. The consequence was a large secession to Independency, so that among the Presbyterians, even where the trusts were definitely orthodox, Unitarian teaching became general. The movement, which was from one point of view a natural reaction from rigorism, swept all before it. There was a great outburst of intellectual life, in which Chandler, Lardner, and Priestley were conspicuous ; both historical theology and philosophy, moral and natural, were advanced by Unitarian scholars. At the same time the movement exerted an attractive force. Not only among Nonconformists, and especially (as we shall see) Baptists, but also among Churchmen it had a serious vogue. It is no secret that several bishops, both English and Irish, were in sympathy with it ; and there was a strong agitation for the relief of the clergy from the subscription to the Articles. It was led by Francis Blackburne, Archdeacon of Cleveland, and was defeated in Parliament in 1772, after a famous speech by Burke, in which he denounced the proposal that the subscription should be to the Scriptures, to be interpreted by each as he would. Though Blackburne retained his position, Theophilus Lindsey, John Disney, and other men of some mark entered the Unitarian ministry. Much feeling was excited by the ejection of William Frend from his Fellowship at Jesus College, Cambridge, for the same cause in 1787. And similar secessions followed for the next generation ; that of S. T. Coleridge, who was candidate for the Unitarian chapel at Shrewsbury in 1798, but left the creed by 1807, is especially noteworthy.

But the movement had its obviously weak sides. This extraordinary change of doctrine seems to have taken place almost, or quite, unconsciously in most cases. It was at first little more than a shifting of sympathies, as in the case of Isaac Watts, the hymn-writer ; but gradually such names as Eusebian, semi-Arian, Arian, Socinian came to be used as terms of praise, and latterly Unitarian, which was late in coming into general use, though it was devised before 1700, and is used for the sake of clearness throughout this article. The change may be well traced in the lives of the Calamy family, extending from 1600 to 1876, in the *Dictionary of National Biography.* It may also be seen in the history of the valuable trust of Lady Hewley, founded in 1705, for the support of 'poor and godly preachers.' Lady Hewley was a Presbyterian, but the trustees and beneficiaries came to be Unitarian, and astonishment as well as resentment was felt when in 1842 the charge of the trust was restored by the Court of Chancery to orthodox hands (*Shore v. Wilson*, 9 C. and F. 355). But if the change of spirit had come quietly, and with no sense of revolt against the past, it was none the less an effective barrier against the rising tide of the Evangelical movement. The Presbyterians could not be vivified by it, and lost seriously by the secession of members touched by the new enthusiasm.

But at the same time a new spirit of pugnacity, political and religious, was awakened in them. The old spirit had been one of placid tolerance; the new Unitarians, who rejoiced in the name, were aggressive. They took an active part in agitation against the abuses of the eighteenth century; the tendency of the revivalists was conservative, while theirs was radical. Priestley may be regarded as typical; when the Tory mob of Birmingham destroyed his chapel it was to the cry of 'No Presbyterians.' As the day of triumph for the political reformers drew near, the Unitarians, and especially their ministers, enjoyed the confidence and influenced the policy of the Whig leaders to an extent that was out of all proportion to their numbers. Their vigour was naturally shown in religious controversy. They spoke contemptuously of the old beliefs and carried on a vigorous polemic against them. Public debates between champions of Unitarianism and of orthodoxy, the latter often Anglican, were favourite intellectual exercises in the early nineteenth century. Hence an active hostility on the other side, which lost to the Presbyterians the trust of Lady Hewley, and would have lost the Unitarians almost all their chapels, as having been built for Trinitarian worship, had not Lord John Russell in 1845 passed an Act which made possession for twenty-five years a sufficient title. In fact, the 'old chapel' of practically every town in England was Unitarian at the end of the eighteenth century, though many were almost extinct. At the date of Russell's Act the number had again greatly diminished, and it is still smaller now. In fact, save in some of the northern and midland manufacturing towns, e.g. Birmingham, Unitarianism is simply a hereditary creed, held by the descendants of the English Presbyterians, who are still, by wealth and education, though not by numbers, an influential body. It is said that their tendency is to pass over to Independency as a larger society and with a more vigorous corporate life. It may be that they are exerting an influence upon Independent thought. The old English Presbyterianism has no orthodox descendants. Orthodox minorities of chapels which became Unitarian joined the Independents; sometimes whole congregations did so, as a protest against the new theology of their fellow-Presbyterians, or again an orthodox minister who obtained election as successor to a Unitarian (a not uncommon case) would carry his chapel and flock to Independency. There are probably no chapels, there is certainly no organised society, called Presbyterian and claiming a continuous and orthodox succession from the original English Presbyterians. Their historical heirs are the Unitarians; the 'English Presbyterian Church' of the present day is a Scottish colony, organised within the nineteenth century, whose whole antecedents lie beyond the Border.

III. CONGREGATIONALISTS

The second of the two great types of Nonconformity is the Congregational, which itself has two branches, the Baptist and the Independent. Like the other, it had its origin at the Reformation. Besides the successful reformers, who stamped their systems upon nations or states, there were many others, not less earnest, and often quite as reasonable, who failed to make any public impression. Their teaching varied, but the most important were men who denied the validity of infant baptism, because it was not the profession of a personal faith. If religion was a personal matter, the Christian Church must consist of believers only; the indifferent and the unworthy had no place in it. Thus a local Church, embracing all the inhabitants of a district, whatever their spiritual state, did not fulfil the conditions laid down in the New Testament; whether it were Roman, Lutheran, Zwinglian, it was no true Church. And further, the Church for the believer meant no wider association than those persons with whom he personally was in communion. There might be, and should be, alliances of like-minded Churches, but these could not, without sacrifice of their essential character, give up their independence. Thus the number of Churches was indefinitely large, and no smallness of membership impaired the completeness even of the least. Christ was the Head of each, and therefore it was perfect in itself. Men who held such views penetrated everywhere, and everywhere raised antagonism. The Reformers were as hostile as the Romanists, for they, too, had accepted the idea of a national Church. If Balthazar Hübmaier was burned at Vienna in 1528, Felix Manz was drowned with Zwingli's approval in the Lake of Zurich in 1527. Both were evangelically orthodox, and advocates of tolerance before the time. Their crime was that they broke up local Churches; and in the presence of the concentrated force of Rome this was a real danger for the Protestants. And soon the cause of the Separatists was discredited by the excesses of a minority, the worst being the scandalous Anabaptists of Münster. Thus they came to have a bad name as men of doubtful character, as well as disturbers of unity, although most were blameless in life and orthodox in creed. Hence they were driven in self-defence to elaborate a doctrine of toleration, or rather of neutrality on the part of the State; a doctrine which was, in fact, a necessary part of their position, though in less stormy circumstances they might have emphasised it less.

Those who first propagated their doctrine in England were of the least offensive type. They practised infant baptism, holding that the faith of the parents justified the admission of the children. Not later than 1568 one Richard Fitz had founded, and was minister of, a 'privy Church' in London. He was a teacher of the common Calvinism of the day, and had all the Puritan hatred for historical religion. But, unlike the normal Puritans, he did not wish to gain possession of the organisation of the Church, and complete the Reformation by reducing it to what seemed the Scriptural pattern. It could not be purified, just because it was national; it must be abandoned. He described his own as 'a poor congregation whom God hath separated from the Church of England'; and the divine purpose was to be fulfilled by a process of disintegration. There was not to be one Church; there was to be a multitude. We cannot wonder that this doctrine met with general hostility. Fitz soon disappeared, and his Church with him, but from Robert Browne onwards the line is unbroken. Browne became enamoured of the Genevan discipline, and had his full share of the troubles of those who tried to introduce it into England. But about 1580, being about thirty years of age, he revolted from Presbyterianism, and founded a Congregational society at Norwich. He had the advantage not only of eloquence but of a logical mind, and was able to present his theory at its best. 'The Church planted or gathered,' he said, 'is a company or number of Christians or believers, which, by a willing covenant made with their God, are under the government of God and Christ, and keep His laws in one holy communion.' But the people so associated are not a democracy. Browne had a very high conception of authority, both civil and religious. The former is ordained by God; and as for the latter, 'Church governors are persons receiving their authority and office of God for the guiding of His people the Church, received and called thereto by due consent and agreement of the Church.' The pastor's power is derived from God, not from the people; the Church's duty is to discover to whom God has entrusted this power, and then to obey him. This theory was strongly advanced by the late Dr. Dale of Birmingham in his standard *History of English Congregationalism* (1907). In practice the minister has too often been the hired servant of the congregation. Browne himself, from motives that cannot be discovered, seceded from his own society, and spent the latter half of his life in conformity as master of Stamford Grammar School and as Rector of Achurch, Northants, till his death in 1633. The cause he had advocated did not suffer by his desertion, and its new leaders exhibited a spirit as bitter as his. Their most striking achievement was the raising of the 'Martin Marprelate' controversy (*q.v.*) by John Penry, a young Welshman who had graduated at Cambridge in 1584 but had not accepted orders, holding that ordination was invalid unless accompanied by, or consisting in election to the ministry over a particular congregation. He was an earnest and able man, and soon came into collision with Whitgift (*q.v.*), not only as an irregular preacher, but also through his denunciations (doubtless in many cases well grounded) of the clergy in Wales. He was treated with severity, and retaliated by publications printed at his secret press, with which he moved about England. For two years he avoided his pursuers, and poured out a succession of scurrilous pamphlets against the bishops and also against Elizabeth, branding her as a worse tyrant than Mary. In 1590 Penry escaped to Scotland, but presently returned, joined a Separatist congregation at Stepney, was quickly recognised, arrested, tried, and hanged in 1593. He had deliberately taken the risk; and we cannot pity him as we do the equally rigid Separatists, such as Barrow and Greenwood, whose death (1593) was made inevitable by Penry's aggressiveness.

Congregationalism made little headway during the next generation. Its most earnest advocates took refuge in Holland, where they quarrelled much among themselves, and printed many books and formed many schemes for the conversion of England. Under James I. they began to form private congregations in England; in 1616 was established one, now calling itself the ' Church of the Pilgrim Fathers,' which has had a continuous existence in South London till the present day. Soon after this the thought of emigration began to attack the Separatists. It is true that the most prominent of the settlers in New England, the first of whom left England in 1628, were Puritans of the normal kind, who believed in a State Church. But in their new circumstances they established their churches on Separatist lines of voluntary adhesion. Yet since it was necessary that there should be churches throughout the settlements at a reasonable distance apart, so that each citizen—citizenship was confined to members of these churches till 1664—might have one within his reach, the result was the *de facto* establishment of a parochial system. Soon all New England had voted the support of the ministry out of taxation, and dissenters from this Congregational establishment were not relieved from the payment till 1729, while the connection with the State continued much longer, lasting in Massachusetts till 1834.

When New England was settled there was no token of an approaching victory for Congregationalism. The cause was unpopular. In 1641, when the Long Parliament issued its Grand Remonstrance, the manifesto which was designed to win public favour in the approaching conflict with the King, the promise to suppress the exorbitance of prelacy was balanced by another, that ' private persons and particular congregations ' should not be allowed ' to take up what form of divine service they please; for we hold it requisite that there should be throughout the whole realm a conformity to that order which the laws enjoin according to the Word of God.' And in the Westminster Assembly, which consisted for the most part of clerical delegates, two from each county, selected by its members of Parliament, there were but five Independents, and these were not whole-hearted Separatists, like their Elizabethan predecessors. They admitted that the State must compel its members to attend church, and therefore sanctioned the practical continuance of a parochial system. Unless there were churches in every parish, coercion could not be applied. But they stipulated that the churches should be organised on Con-

gregational lines; though they also insisted that those who were forced to attend should not be forced to become members of the ' Church,' in their sense, and that the ' Church ' should not be compelled to receive them as members. There were to be an outer and an inner circle. In effect, they had their way. The attempt to enforce Presbyterianism, as we have seen, broke down, and every parochial clergyman, whatever his sympathies, had in practice to be an Independent. For the parish system, with its endowments, was maintained, and for want of any higher organisation the incumbent was concerned only with his own congregation. And among these incumbents many were Congregationalists, who had no scruples, here or in America, over the acceptance of a secure financial position. But there is no doubt that, in parishes where the minister was not of their school, the Congregationalists took advantage of the liberty allowed under the Commonwealth to form a local society after their own mind.

At the Restoration such informal assemblies were suppressed, and in 1662 the Congregational occupants of benefices had to conform or secede. This blow had no such disastrous effects in their case as in that of the Presbyterians. They returned at once to what was, in theory, their right position; their principles made it impossible to cherish any keen regret for the loss of an official position. In one respect only did they fall short of their original standard. They seem to have lost their ideal of the divine right of the single Church, and to have made the engagement of a minister a mere matter of business between him and the officers of the congregation. It was not their circumstances, but rather the example of the Presbyterians, who could do nothing better now that their dream of a national position had passed, that led to this declension. But the general lassitude after a century and more of denominational conflicts is sufficient to explain any indifference to original standards.

From the Revolution onward they lived a quiet life, like other dissenters. Attempts to coalesce with the Presbyterians were as fruitless as those of the latter to combine with the national Church. Soon, as we have seen, doctrinal divergence began. The Independents were rigorous in their Calvinistic orthodoxy; till the end of the eighteenth century, and even later, their standard was the Westminster Confession. Though some of their leaders were affected by the prevalent Arian thought, it never became dominant among them, as among the Presbyterians. In fact, orthodoxy became the paramount consideration, and the doctrine of the ministry fell into the background. Thus they were drawn towards the Church of England, which, on its side, did not lay great stress in the eighteenth century on the historical claims of its ministry. And the Congregationalists, though dwindling in numbers, were a weighty and scholarly body, taking an important part, at the Church's side, in the conflict with Deism and in Scriptural research.

When the great Methodist revival took place the Independents threw themselves decisively on the Calvinist side. (See below.) The Arminianism (*q.v.*) of the Wesleyans revolted them, and they were often irritated by the loss of zealous adherents, who were drawn away by the attraction of a more vivid life in the new community. On the other hand, the most vigorous element in the English Church was that of the Calvinist Evangelicals. They, too, were at daggers-drawn with Arminianism, and in their eagerness to promote their cause were ready to enlist Congregational help. In fact, the languishing Congregational society was revived by Evangelical members of our communion. They preached far and wide outside their own parishes; how were they to retain their converts where the parish clergy were unsympathetic? What would now be the obvious resource, the building of a new church, was not available. Till the nineteenth century it required an Act of Parliament and the establishment of a new civil, as well as ecclesiastical, organisation, and it was not likely that consent would be given. The plan frequently adopted was the foundation of a Congregational chapel. Henry Venn (*q.v.*) promoted more than one in the district round his parish of Huddersfield, and when he left that place, and was dissatisfied with his successor, he headed the subscription list for a chapel that should perpetuate his doctrine. The same result followed the teaching of such men as Grimshaw of Haworth and Berridge of Everton. In these chapels the use of the Prayer Book was not uncommon, and the teaching was exactly that of Anglican Calvinists. But a further step was taken. Churchmen found the funds for the education of Congregational ministers of poor and pious men, whose work should be essentially undenominational revivalism, and only incidentally that of the Independent minister. Thus a great impetus was given to Congregationalism, which soon in consequence regained self-confidence and the sense

of a corporate life, and of the difference between itself and Anglicanism. Yet for a while this practical subordination produced remarkable results. Such men as Rowland Hill were of this spirit; and the London Missionary Society was founded in 1795, and maintained till about 1815, on the principle that no system of association is binding upon Christian people. The very basis of Independency, for which its founders had been content to die, was explicitly rejected; and though that excellent Missionary Society is now in practice Congregational, in theory it still allows members of other communions to work in its ranks, and to organise their converts after their own principles.

But this phase passed away. Side by side with the protégés of the Anglican Evangelicals there were working prominent and successful ministers, whose horizon was that of their own denomination, and to these the former class was inevitably attracted, as they grew conscious of their own usefulness and of the difference in practical status between themselves and those under whose protection they had gained their position. Thus the link grew gradually weaker, yet the character of Congregationalism long remained one of serious Evangelicanism, detached from politics, and indeed animated by dislike for those agitations in which the Unitarians took the lead, and which seemed to be tinged with their spirit. This temper might have continued—as late as 1880 Mr. Paxton Hood was forced to resign his charge at Manchester on account of his strong Liberal opinions (*D.N.B.*, *s.v.*)—but for two causes. One was the foolish policy of Lord Liverpool's government in attempting to depress dissent in the supposed interests of the Church—a policy which was supported by too many of the bishops. This drove dissenters together, and diffused among them a general hostility to the Church. The other was the change wrought within the Church by the Oxford Movement (*q.v.*), which rendered conspicuous points of difference which hitherto Evangelicals, both Anglican and Congregational, had been able to ignore. It was not by accident that the new spirit reached its climax of violence in 1841, when the Church of England was described as a ' life-destroying upas.' Such exaggeration has in recent times disappeared; but perhaps the competitive spirit, engendered in business circles of the north, has not ceased to influence the attitude taken up by Congregationalists towards the Church. Meanwhile their tendency is away from Separatism and towards organisation. It must also be said that Congregational thought has been peculiarly open to modern influences from Germany and elsewhere, and is now often quite as 'emancipated' as that of the Unitarians, for whom their forefathers felt such repugnance. The denomination is the most insular of all our large religious bodies. It has never taken root on the Continent of Europe. In great Britain it has some 495,000 Church members, in Canada only some 11,000, and in Australasia about 20,000. In the United States are 730,000. Converts in various mission fields number 120,000 members (*Dict. Religion and Ethics*, 1911, iv. p. 24).

IV. BAPTISTS

The second branch of the Separatists or Independents, the Baptists or Anabaptists, as their opponents of the sixteenth century called them, are certainly, though obscurely, connected with mediæval movements of rebellion in thought. A revival of that old desire for Biblical simplicity in faith and worship and for separation of the Church from the world that had often arisen and never been wholly suppressed in the Middle Ages was stimulated by the protests of Luther, but the seed from which it sprang was not of his sowing. In 1525 the rebaptism of adults on profession of faith was publicly performed at Zurich and at Waldshut in Southern Germany, and from that time onward the movement grew rapidly, in spite of terrible slaughter perpetrated both by Protestants and Romanists. Fugitives from the Netherlands reached England under Henry VIII., and found sympathisers, in whose minds, it is practically certain, the teaching of the Lollards (*q.v.*) was lingering. The little societies which sprang up here and there were of blameless people, holding no such wild doctrines as were exemplified at Münster; but after the outbreak in that city (1534-5) it was inevitable that they should be suspected of sharing Anabaptist principles at their worst. All English parties were equally hostile to them, and their divergence from current theology was quite as fatal as their ecclesiastical system. They were Arminian (to use a later term), and so were at issue with the Augustinianism of the day, and they allowed themselves such liberty of Christological speculation as to incur the suspicion of Arianism. Arianism was one of the grounds on which Joan Bocher was burnt in 1549 in Kent; Kent was to be the stronghold of the General Baptists in the next century. But in spite of violent though spasmodic persecution obscure congregations of Anabaptists seem to have survived till the end of Elizabeth's reign in various parts of England.

But these were not to be the origin of the English Baptists, as we know them, though doubtless the survivors were ready to join the new congregations as soon as they were formed. The continuous history begins with a congregation of Separatists at Amsterdam, founded by English exiles in 1592 and increased by later accessions. They were Independents, and practised infant baptism, but some of them came to have scruples by contact with the *Mennonites*, a body of gentle and orthodox Baptists, founded by Menno Simons, a priest of Friesland, who had been drawn to the persecuted Anabaptists by sympathy with their sufferings, and was converted to their doctrine in 1535. He became its fearless and effective advocate, and when Holland became free and Protestant his church flourished in that country. Among the English exiles who were attracted by this teaching was John Smith, a Fellow of Christ's College, Cambridge, and an unbeneficed clergyman, who had renounced his orders and become an Independent. On Dutch soil he renounced his Calvinism, and became convinced that Scripture requires the baptism of believers. He therefore baptized himself in a meeting of his followers, and afterwards baptized them, all professing their faith. This act, which gained him the title of the 'Se-Baptist,' was performed about 1608, and broke up the unity (such as it was) of the English Separatists of Amsterdam. For a while the little body of Baptists held together, but presently Smith became doubtful of the regularity of his proceeding, and applied to the Mennonites for admission by baptism into their church. They were slow to decide, and Smith died at Amsterdam in 1612, before their answer came. It was favourable, and Smith's followers (a minority of his own little flock) were admitted, and were lost among the Mennonites. But while they disappear from history, the majority of these first English Baptists, from whom their leader had parted, were to be the founders of their denomination in England. They were satisfied with their position and resented Smith's doubts; they therefore formed themselves into a separate church under Thomas Helwys, who had the courage to return with his people to England in 1611. He established himself in London, was successful as a preacher, and suffered less persecution than might have been expected, being protected by family influence. The denomination rapidly spread, especially in London, Leicestershire, and Kent.

Such was the beginning of the *General Baptists*, or 'baptized believers who own universal redemption.' In their eyes baptism was chiefly 'a sign of profession and mark of difference, whereby Christian men are discerned from others that be not christened,' as our Article xxvii. puts it; and the distinction was made as broad as possible. For instance, marriage outside their Church was punished by exclusion. For infants, in their eyes, baptism could have no value, for they held that children inherited no guilt, and attached no importance to Christian parentage as conferring upon the offspring a right to baptism. As one of their 'six principles,' which they derived from Hebrews 6, they practised the laying on of hands after baptism. Feet-washing also was among their religious customs. In their ministry, which was elective, it was not uncommon for several preachers to be attached to one congregation; the ministers usually maintained themselves by some handicraft. A peculiarity of their ministry was that of a special class of 'messengers,' or apostles, who were, and are, called in for the setting apart of a minister. But there is no thought of succession or of an authority other than that which is derived from the congregation. For their higher organisation there were from the first local associations, and from 1654 a General Assembly, which still continues, and has the longest and most perfect series of records of any Nonconformist body in England.

Before passing on to the later history of the General Baptists it will be well to trace the beginnings of their brethren and rivals, the *Particular Baptists*. Henry Jacob, a clergyman who had become a Separatist and established a congregation at Middelburg in Holland, returned with his flock to London in 1616. They were strict Calvinists, but among them were some, including Jacob himself, who could find no warrant of Scripture for the baptism of infants. But Jacob held that parish churches might be true churches, and did not make the question of baptism crucial. The consequence was a succession of separations, more or less amicable, by one of which in 1633 the first congregation of strict Calvinistic Baptists was formed. This body in 1642 added immersion to its principles, a triple effusion of water over the head of the kneeling recipient having been practised hitherto. But though strict Baptists spread more rapidly, there were also congregations with open or mixed communion, of which Bunyan's at Bedford was one. Such societies required

a Calvinistic confession of faith from their members, and were in all respects, save that of indifference on the point of baptism, similar to the strict or Particular Baptists and to the Independents. They did not, however, attain to any great numbers or importance. At the present day it seems to be not unusual for a minister of the one communion to be chosen as its pastor by a congregation of the other, though probably, if the congregation be Baptist, it is one that is loosely attached to the system of its denomination. It may also be mentioned here that very early in the movement Sabbatarian or Seventh-day Baptists appeared in England, teaching the obligation of the Jewish Sabbath —a doctrine which they had learnt from Germany. Though now almost extinct here, they survive in some numbers in the United States.

The Civil War gave the Baptists the opportunity of expansion. They had been among the first and most consistent advocates of the liberty of conscience, and they were not slow to fight for it. Unlike their Continental fellows, they had no scruple about bearing arms. Among the leading officers of the Parliamentary army were many Baptists, and also among the conspirators against the restored monarchy. The latest estimate of the number of congregations formed by the end of the Commonwealth gives one hundred and fifteen to the General and one hundred and thirty-one to the Particular Baptists (*Transactions of the Baptist Hist. Soc.*, ii. 236), and among their pastors were a fair number who had, more or less inconsistently, accepted a parochial position. Perhaps forty were ejected in 1662, and a certain number must have had to surrender their benefices to the lawful holders on their return, 1660. Many, however, disapproved of such a departure from principle as the acceptance of an ecclesiastical living.

From the Restoration the story is one of growth of the Particular and of decay of the General Baptists. The former, who had formed a General Assembly of their own in 1689, clave, like the Independents, to the Westminster Confession and Calvinist principles. The latter were affected by the same mode of thought as the English Presbyterians, though their adoption of Arian and afterwards of Unitarian views was neither so rapid nor so complete. Occasionally a Particular congregation, touched by the new mode of thought, would secede to the Assembly of the General Baptists; more often an orthodox body of the latter would find refuge with the Particular

Baptists from the novel teaching. Sometimes a congregation of the General Baptists would oscillate between Trinitarianism and Unitarianism, according to the views of its minister for the time being. But the tendency of the General Baptists as a whole was towards Unitarianism. Sometimes a congregation professed that doctrine, and simultaneously forsook the membership of their General Assembly; more often they combined the old membership with the new teaching.

The great revival of the eighteenth century affected both the Particular and the General Baptists. The Calvinist teaching of Whitefield (*q.v.*) was as acceptable to the former as the Arminianism of Wesley (*q.v.*) to the latter, and in the wide outburst of feeling old religious associations were less regarded than is often supposed. Evangelical fervour was to be found among Particular Baptists, and so they won recruits. It was also found among those General Baptists who had retained their orthodoxy, but the converts who joined them through Methodism were not content with the ambiguous position of their new denomination. The orthodox element seceded, and in 1770 formed the *New Connection of General Baptists,* which held no communion with the old General Assembly. The latter retained only the Latitudinarian congregations, and under the influence of William Vidler (about 1800) became aggressively Unitarian. At the present day the denomination survives as a small inner circle within the decayed Unitarian body, still preserving its legal and historical continuity, and meeting annually in its old General Assembly. The New Connection of the General Baptists, being Arminian, could not coalesce with the Particular Baptists, who were, in their turn, prevented by their peculiar rite from such association with the Anglican Evangelicals as was possible for the Independents. Thus the effect of the Methodist revival was both to vivify the orthodox element among the Baptists, and also to heighten their corporate sense.

When the interest in predestination died down there was nothing to hinder a coalition between the Particular Baptists and the orthodox wing, the New Connection, of the General Baptists. But before this was possible the Particular school was to pass through a phase of high Calvinism, which in many cases verged upon fatalism and Antinomianism. From this unhealthy state the denomination was rescued by the novel interest in foreign missions which spread through all Evangelical communions towards the end of the eighteenth century. William Carey (1761-1834), a self-taught scholar with a gift for languages, was minister of a congregation at Leicester, and was deeply impressed with a sense of the duty of Christians to the heathen. After a struggle of three years with the strict Calvinists, who believed that God would save those who were to be saved, and that human effort was presumptuous and futile, he and others of like mind founded in 1792 the 'Particular Baptist Society for the Propagation of the Gospel among the Heathen.' Carey himself went out to Bengal in 1794, and is one of the heroes of missionary enterprise. He died at his post after forty years' service. From the date of the institution of the mission strict Calvinism grew weaker among the Baptists; their greatest preacher, Robert Hall (1764-1831), exerted his influence against it. The *Baptist Union,* designed to be comprehensive, was founded in 1813, and has by degrees come to include everything that is influential in the denomination. The final merging of diverse interests may be said to have taken place in 1891, when the Missionary Society of the New Connection of General Baptists was amalgamated with that of the Particular Baptists. The historical difference now counts for nothing; and all Baptists, save some surviving Calvinists, are at one in doctrine and sympathy.

The Baptists, though in their earlier days they had men of learning for their ministers and among their laity many members of wealth and position, have never rivalled the intellectual eminence of the Independents, and have perhaps ministered in later times to a less educated class. In their earliest days they were among the most courageous advocates of tolerance, or rather of the neutrality of the State; and it seems that, except in their days of strict Calvinism, there has been among them a political sense as definite as their religious creed. They were the first orthodox denomination that, as a whole, was in sympathy with the wave of democratic feeling excited by the French Revolution; and in spite of the prominence of Unitarians on the Whig side their repugnance to that doctrine did not inspire them with indifference, such as was felt by many other dissenters, to the reform of Parliament. It is needless to say that this adherence to one political party has continued to the present day.

In England the Baptists are now a somewhat smaller body than the Congregationalists. On the Continent of Europe they are few. On the other hand, in the United States they are, next to the Roman Catholics and the Methodists, the largest denomination, or rather group of denominations, for they are split into at least ten important and many smaller communions. A large proportion of their members are of negro race. The Baptist missions in India have been very fruitful.

V. METHODISM

The latest important separation from the English Church is that of the Methodists. From the first the idea of mutual influence for good exercised by Christian people in close association was dominant among those who were to be the leaders in the movement. Charles Wesley [WESLEYS] of Christ Church joined with two or three other Oxford undergraduates early in 1729 to form a society with strict rules of life, work, and religious observance, to which the nickname of ' the Methodists ' was quickly given. In the autumn of 1729 John Wesley (*q.v.*), brother of Charles, returned to Oxford and became the leader of the movement, which gained a number of adherents in Oxford during his residence, which lasted till 1735. Among the latest, joining in 1735, was George Whitefield (*q.v.*). When John Wesley left Oxford that city ceased to be the centre of Methodism ; its adherents for the most part entered into holy orders, and began spiritual work in different parts of the country. There had been little sympathy among the teachers in the University, and few, if any, of the Methodist graduates remained in Oxford.

From this time the Methodists were a power in England at large, the young clergy in their various parishes spreading the cause. But for a while the leaders left them. The two Wesleys and Whitefield went to the American colonies, where John Wesley founded a society after the Oxford pattern in Georgia ; while Whitefield had wonderful success as a revivalist, and stamped upon American religion its characteristic excitement. In America also the Wesleys came into close contact with the Moravians, though they were never at home in their peculiar mysticism. We must bear in mind that Moravians were not regarded by English Churchmen exactly as other dissenters. Archbishop Potter in 1737 gave them his informal recognition, Bishop Wilson (*q.v.*) of Sodor and Man was their friend, and in 1749 they were placed by Parliament in a specially favoured position, and declared to be a Protestant Episcopal Church. To this day the Moravians attach great importance to this solemn attestation

of the character of their Church. In 1738, after his return from Georgia, John Wesley experienced a conversion, under Moravian influence, which marks a fourth stage in his development ; and though he was to part, somewhat ungraciously, from them as from others who had been his teachers, their organisation and their spirit were to leave a permanent mark upon Methodism. Meanwhile the evangelistic work went happily on ; there was hostility, but there was also support from high quarters. Wesley's English society, in alliance with the Moravians, was started in 1739 in London ; Whitefield, before his departure for America, had founded one on the Oxford model at Gloucester. There was no sign as yet of any breach in the ranks of the Methodists, still less any symptom of departure from the Church of England.

But in 1740 two important disputes arose. John Wesley parted from the Moravians and founded a special society of his own followers in London ; and a decisive turn was given to the fortunes of Methodism by the doctrinal dispute between him and Whitefield. The inevitable cleavage between Arminians and Calvinists appeared. We have seen how it affected other bodies ; it was to be as disastrous to the Methodist cause. The Wesleys were brought up in a Laudian home. Both their parents represented a violent reaction from a Puritan ancestry. The mother had actually passed through a Socinian phase in her transition from the Calvinism of her father to the Arminianism of her husband ; as we have seen, the Socinian insistence on divine benevolence was a protest against the stern predestinarian doctrine of Calvinism. As strict churchmen, the Wesleys had little or no contact with the orthodox dissenters, among whom Calvinism prevailed. In fact, the only dissenter with whom John Wesley ever seems to have had any intimacy was the curiously neutral Philip Doddridge, in whom personal orthodoxy was combined with a tolerance that embraced Socinians. On the other hand, Whitefield, though ordained, was from the first indifferent to distinctions of church and chapel. His wonderful rhetorical gifts were nowhere more powerfully exercised than among the Presbyterians of Scotland and the dissenters of every school in America, where he ignored his own communion, and at last was buried in a Presbyterian church in Massachusetts. Not that he preferred the chapel ; rather he accepted without criticism that great mass of Calvinist exegesis which was common to orthodox Protestantism, and regarded agreement with its teaching as the one essential. Within the Church the same doctrine was soon to be dominant, and was to make the position of Arminian Churchmen uncomfortable, if not untenable.

The breach came in 1740, when Wesley preached at Bristol, and afterwards published, a sermon on 'Free Grace.' It was meant as a protest, if not a challenge, and Whitefield promptly replied. The leaders had a nobler spirit than their followers; they were soon personally reconciled, and occasionally worked together; and by Whitefield's request Wesley preached the sermon at the English commemoration of his death. But serious cooperation was impossible when the rank and file on both sides were embittered, when partisans flung scurrilities, and when, especially on the Calvinist side, every effort was made to win deserters from the other camp. The weary controversy came to be conducted by the *Arminian Magazine* on the one side and the *Gospel Magazine* (which has but lately expired) on the other; and though the temper and the arguments be equally unattractive, it must have had an educative influence in its day.

By this time both the great leaders were organising their scattered societies into larger unities. Whitefield was the first to take this step. In 1743 he presided at the first conference, held at Watford, near Cardiff, of his Calvinistic Methodist followers. Five clergy and ten lay preachers formed the assembly; and it is a sign of Presbyterian sympathies that the president—an office bestowed upon Whitefield whenever he might be in England—was styled 'Moderator,' as in Scotland. Whitefield had no gift or taste for administration, and soon resigned the office. By this renunciation the success of the 'Welsh Calvinistic Methodist Church' may be explained—a success which contrasts strikingly with the failure of his English organisation. The associated societies in Wales spread rapidly, the chief leaders coming to be David Jones (1735-1810), Vicar of Llangan, Glamorganshire, and Thomas Charles (1755-1814), who, like Whitefield, was never beneficed. Their Calvinist principles rendered it easier for the Welsh revivalists than for the followers of Wesley to associate with the more serious clergy of the Church, and the patronage of the Countess of Huntingdon (*q.v.*) had a like effect. But practical difficulties, caused as much by their rejection of the Church's discipline as by the frequent persecutions which forced them, in self-defence, to register their meeting-houses as dissenting chapels, gradually weakened the

bond. Yet till the death of David Jones Communion was only celebrated by priests, and usually received in the parish churches. The decisive step was taken as soon as the death of Jones gave undisputed control to Charles. In 1811, twenty-seven years after Wesley had taken the same step, Charles ordained several of the lay preachers, and the Welsh Calvinistic Methodists, whose organisation was already complete in every other respect, began their separate course. It was not for another generation that they fell under political influences which made them hostile to the Church from which they sprang. They are not less completely separate from the Wesleyans, though the old strife of Calvinist and Arminian is extinct. In the *New History of Methodism*, which gives the fullest account of Methodist organisation throughout the world, they are ignored; their actual association, like their system of government, is Presbyterian, and they are in full alliance with the United Free Church of Scotland and the Presbyterian Church of England. Next to our own communion, they are the largest religious body in the Principality of Wales, where Arminian Methodism, in spite of Wesleyan efforts, has struck no deep roots.

Whitefield's conference was quickly copied by Wesley. As yet there seemed no sign that his movement was to be more important than the other, though his extraordinary gift of government was already developed, and he was keeping the societies that he founded under a strict supervision, maintained by a visitation that was directed at least as much to the welfare of his converts as to their increase in numbers. For instance, in 1743 he visited his people at Newcastle-upon-Tyne, and after he had ejected fifty as unworthy, he records that eight hundred remained, though a number of dissenters had withdrawn because three leading ministers of the town had refused communion to his adherents. We must notice that though Wesley required converts from indifference to communicate with his own church, it was not he but the ministers who made Methodism incompatible with the older forms of dissent. In the same year he issued the first rules, religious rather than governmental, for the 'United Societies.' That they should be united was a necessity of administration. In 1744 his first conference was held; it was attended by six clergy, including the two Wesleys, and four lay preachers, and has been held annually ever since.

We must now consider what was the actual relation of the Wesleyan Methodist body, thus increasingly conscious of its own coherence, towards the English Church. The most important point was that of Communion. It was usually possible for the Methodists to attend in a body at some parish church at a stated service, or to arrange for a special corporate Communion from time to time. When this was difficult, John Wesley took the opportunity of the sickness of a convert to hold a large private celebration; Charles Wesley, less scrupulous, would assemble his people in a school or other unconsecrated building. But a strong desire arose among Methodists for a Communion of their own. Not many of the preachers had been devout members of the Church; most had been quite indifferent before their conversion, but a good number had been Nonconformists. Such men had no tie to the Church except their periodical Communion; and the mass of the Methodist people had no religious associations outside the society. Preachers and people wished their system to be complete, and as the number of itinerant clergy dwindled their urgency increased. Charles Wesley ministered regularly in London from 1756, and his brother found few recruits for the travelling work. We find, as a startling novelty, that preachers at Norwich celebrated in 1760. Even before this there had been symptoms of a desire for separation in the annual conference; and John Wesley's reading had led him to the conclusion that ordination by bishops was a matter of discipline, not of principle. Stillingfleet (*q.v.*) and Lord Chancellor King were the authorities he trusted for the view that the office of priest is identical with that of bishop. But it was long before he acted. Though he asserted in 1780 that he had as good a right to ordain as to administer the Lord's Supper, it was not till 1784 that he exercised the right, and then only for America or Scotland; and to the last he asserted that his action, not affecting England, made no change in his relation or that of his people to the English Church. Yet as early as 1747 he had put the New Testament into the hands of a kneeling preacher with the words: 'Take thou authority to preach the Gospel,' but without imposition of hands. His chief prompter was Thomas Coke (1747-1814), a wealthy and ambitious unbeneficed clergyman, who was one of the three priests who laid their hands on the first candidates. Later in 1784 he was himself set apart, with laying on of hands, as 'superintendent' of the work in America—a title which he at once changed, to Wesley's indignation, into 'bishop.' The largest Methodist bodies in

the United States retain the title of bishop for their chief officers, and distinguish themselves as 'Episcopal Methodists.' In that country Methodism has enormously increased. The great majority of the eighteen million people now under Methodist instruction, according to Whitaker's *Almanack*, are in the United States.

Though Wesley refused to recognise the fact, separation in England was inevitable. He must himself be regarded as the chief cause of it. He had promoted with all his force a corporate feeling in his society, and in 1784 provided by deed for its continuance, under the government of the 'legal hundred' of co-opted senior ministers. Before his death the chapels (there were three hundred and fifty-nine in England in 1784) were generally licensed as dissenting places of worship, though their purpose was specified simply as that of places for preaching the Gospel. Thus the machinery was ready, and also the men. For Wesley had been quite indifferent to Church sympathies in his choice of preachers. Provided they were earnest and able and free from the taint of Calvinism, he had cared nothing for their ecclesiastical antecedents. Many, in fact, had joined him from dissent; he had excited much hostility among dissenters by enticing away, as they thought, their rising hopes. And when he had secured his preachers, either from irreligion or dissent, he did nothing to train them in Churchmanship. Their whole interest was in their own society, and it was inevitable that they should desire to make it complete and self-sufficing; in other words, to separate altogether from the Church.

The state of the Church, after the revival had gained a firm hold upon it, was not such as to attract the Methodists. The serious men were all, or almost all, Calvinists, and only the more moderate Calvinists, such as Charles Simeon (*q.v.*), would tolerate the errors of 'free grace.' We have seen how Congregationalism, as an evangelistic agency, was fostered by the Calvinists within the Church, and the second branch of the revival, that led by Whitefield, was for some time to dwell on the border-line between the Church and Independency. Whitefield founded his English organisation, which was to be a failure, in 1756; or rather Selina, Countess of Huntingdon, the great patroness of the Calvinist movement, took the lead in government, while Whitefield furnished the inspiration. Far more clergy were enlisted under their banner than under Wesley's, and her right as a peeress to appoint chaplains saved many of them from the charge of irregularity. Her position was frankly undenominational; her chief foundation, Trevecca College, was to be for the training of ministers, either for the Church or for dissent. The one essential was that they should be in earnest, and be Calvinists. She was also liberal in building chapels, of which she retained the freehold. When her preachers, following the Wesleyan example, recognised the practical convenience of registering the buildings as places of dissenting worship, her chaplains who held parishes, such as Romaine, withdrew from her organisation. The natural consequences swiftly followed. Two of her unbeneficed chaplains anticipated Wesley by holding an ordination in 1783, and when Lady Huntingdon, before her death, vested her chapels in trustees she established a dissenting body which is still called her 'Connexion.' It is simply an inner circle among Congregationalists, maintained in existence by legal requirements. Her college also is purely Congregational. The results of Whitefield's work and of that of his supporters, other than such as were under the control of the countess, have had the same history. The most remarkable of his school was Rowland Hill, who did not proceed beyond deacon's orders. He was equally critical of Church and dissent, pursuing his own line of earnest revivalism and hostility to the Arminians. The 'Surrey Chapel,' which he founded, is now one of the chief fortresses of Congregationalism in London. In fact, the want of any characteristic doctrine of the Church, or rather the positive assertion that there is no such doctrine, marked both the Anglican and the Congregational sides in this alliance. Its lasting result has been three great societies: the London Missionary Society, which in defiance of its foundation principle has become Congregational; the British and Foreign Bible Society, which is now wider in its sympathies than its founders might have approved; and the Religious Tract Society, which has succeeded in maintaining its neutrality.

While the Calvinist revival had no special doctrine to hold its adherents together, the Arminian school were driven back upon themselves. Nowhere, within or without the Church, had they any considerable support; if they had remained there would probably have been a great Calvinist secession.

We must conclude by tracing the development of Wesleyan Methodism in its various branches. After John Wesley's death things remained for a while as they were; his influence checked the impulse of separation.

But it was proposed at each annual conference, and agitation in the congregations increased. In 1792 resort was had to the lot, whether or no the general administration of the sacraments should be undertaken. The lot fell against it; but in 1795 the conference resolved to leave it open to the congregations to choose for themselves; and except in Ireland they chose to separate, though many individuals, Methodists in all other respects, continued to receive the Holy Communion in their parish churches. This compromise found no supporters in the younger generation, and is now extinct. But in Ireland it was retained by the main body till 1870, when the Methodists decided that the disestablished Church was not that to which they had adhered hitherto. They then severed a connection which does not appear to have been satisfactory to either party. In England separation was emphasised by the assumption of the title of ' Reverend ' for the ministers in 1818; and the laying on of hands, not exercised since Wesley's death, was resumed in 1836. It was carefully stated that the rite is not essential; and the Methodists, unlike their founder, hold no doctrine of a Presbyterian transmission of the ministry.

The later history of Wesleyan Methodism is largely that of a conflict between conservative and ' liberal ' tendencies, leading to division, which now is tending to heal itself. The autocracy of Wesley, who had kept his preachers under his own control, was followed by the oligarchy of the Legal Hundred. The spirit of Methodism was very conservative. It supported Pitt against the revolutionary movement, and in the next generation brought upon itself the scurrility of Cobbett, who saw in each of its chapels a bulwark of the unreformed Parliament. But from the first there was a democratic party, which agitated for popular government of the denomination. Its leader was Alexander Kilham; he and his followers were expelled in 1796, and founded the Methodist New Connexion, which rapidly gained importance, and has in later times been the branch of Methodism that has continued to draw the largest proportion of its membership from the working classes. Many of the leaders of the Labour Movement have sprung from its ranks and learned the art of speaking in its pulpits. But its most important result has been the Salvation Army. ' General ' Booth (1829-1912) seceded from the ministry of the New Connexion in 1861 to undertake independent evangelistic work. He established a great philanthropic organisation, based as it seems, like an inverted pyramid, upon a small and stationary membership, and supported by external subscriptions. He disused the sacraments, though his teaching was otherwise the evangelicalism usual among Methodists, and he kept entire control of the army in his own hands.

The next democratic revolt was against the discipline enforced by the Legal Hundred. William O'Bryan, a Cornish preacher, awoke much excitement and made many converts. He and they would not submit to the rules of the denomination, which were imperiously pressed. The result was his expulsion and the establishment of the 'Bible Christians' as an independent and democratically governed community in 1815. It had much success in the west of England. But in spite of these warnings the central government of the Wesleyan Methodists remained repressive, and no concessions were made to popular demands. At the same time Wesleyans were rising in the social scale, and with education there came the demand for an educated ministry. Hence indignation among those who regarded the untutored pleadings of the earlier preachers as the true eloquence for Methodists when it was resolved to found a 'Theological Institution' in 1834. This was the occasion of one of a succession of schisms, the most serious of which was caused by the expulsion of a number of ministers in 1849 for carrying on, not always courteously or candidly, a 'reform agitation.' They were followed, it is said, by one hundred thousand people, and founded a separate denomination, which in 1857 was merged with other seceders in the 'United Methodist Free Church.' This united in 1907 with the Methodist New Connexion and the Bible Christians to form the 'United Methodist Church,' which has now one hundred and forty-four thousand members. The lesson of the need of concession was not lost upon the parent denomination. The system of suppression came to an end with the death of Jabez Bunting (1779-1858), and by successive acts of legislation the constitution of the Wesleyan Methodists has become as democratic and as flexible as that of their rivals.

Omitting two small bodies which arose in the strife that has been mentioned, and have refused to join any of the larger bodies, we must turn to the last of the Methodist denominations. By the year 1800 Methodism, at least among its leaders, had become staid and decorous. But there was an outburst of the old revivalism in that year, led by Hugh Bourne, a carpenter, and lay preacher of great spiritual force, in North Staffordshire, which spread over the potteries and the adjacent parts of Cheshire in the following

years. It was inflamed by the arrival in England of Lorenzo Dow, an American enthusiast, expert in the novel methods of the 'camp meeting.' Bourne and his following welcomed the device, and a great camp meeting was held on a hill named Mow Cop, with the expected success in regard to excitement, but also, as the Methodist leaders thought, with results of moral mischief. The conference decided that such meetings in future were not to be held. Bourne defied them, and was expelled in 1808. By 1810 he and his people had formed a community called 'Camp-Meeting Methodists'; other dissidents joined them, and the enlarged body took the name 'Primitive Methodists' in 1812. Those who did not sympathise with their fervour preferred to call them 'Ranters.' The denomination had many difficulties, largely internal, to contend with. It has now 210,000 members, while the Wesleyans have 514,000 (Whitaker's *Almanack*, 1912).

All the Methodist bodies have the same government, the same circuit system, by which one or two ministers are for about three years responsible for all the chapels of a district, the services being largely conducted, under their superintendence, by local preachers according to an elaborate quarterly 'plan.' The ministers are paid and pensioned from a central fund, which assures a modest competence to all. Thus there are no prizes in the calling; and influence in the denomination means influence not through the weight of an important congregation, but through the power of attractive speech on many platforms or the gift of counsel in the central government. But, speaking generally, the characteristic of the Wesleyan ministry, and no doubt of that among other Methodists, is a high average of efficiency rather than the eminence of individuals; and the laity, as preachers and as governors, hold so large a place in the public life of the various bodies that the particular ministers cannot gain such prominence as in other dissenting societies. Nor have the ministers, with some exceptions, attained much eminence in the fields of knowledge or thought. Methodism has shown itself, in all its branches, peculiarly conservative in theology. While doubtless different strata of education are predominant in different denominations, the tendency in all is steadily upwards, and Methodism seems to be ceasing to appeal to any class socially lower than the intelligent artisan. Thus old barriers between the humbler and the more refined types of Methodism must be tending to disappear, and probably there will before long be a fusion of all English Methodists into one body, such as has already taken place in Canada and Australia.   [E. W. W.]

VI. THE SOCIETY OF FRIENDS, COMMONLY CALLED QUAKERS

How is it possible that a sect, numerically small, for generations despised, appealing to the nation neither through its literature nor through its pulpits, could have exercised that purifying influence upon religious life, far beyond its own borders, which is rightly ascribed to the Society of Friends ?

Not through fictitious external claims, as a world-embracing Church, but through quiet, insistent, moral influence ; not through the intellectual appeal of a theological system, infallible and complete, but through unflinching assertion of its mystical views rather than its dogmas ; not through an elaborate and technically perfect system of Church organisation, but through a peace-loving, loyal attachment to a very practical constitution has the Society of Friends exerted a persistent and purifying influence for two hundred and fifty years, not merely on the religious life of England, but also upon that of the United States of America.

That influence has not been uniformly exerted throughout that period. The latter half of the seventeenth century, the period of persecution, saw the expression of the distinctive opinions held by the Society in their most vigorous and, because so little understood, in their most objectionable form. During the eighteenth century and the first half of the nineteenth, the period of quiescence, it ceased to be aggressive. In the latter half of the nineteenth century it assumed an influence in political and social life out of all proportion to its numerical strength ; it exercised a permanent stimulus upon philanthropic effort, springing from the sterling character of its members and their firm adherence to their distinctive tenets.

The origin of these ' peculiar views '—at the present time by no means ' peculiar '—must undoubtedly be sought amongst the mystical speculations both on the Continent and also in England, both in the Catholic Church itself and in the turbulent religious atmosphere of the Puritan revolution. It is not possible to trace at present the exact connection, still less any direct contact, with these mystics in order to explain the remarkable rapidity of the propagation and the whole-hearted devotion of the ' First Publishers of Truth,' or those who received their direct inspiration from the life and teaching of George Fox. But it is unwise to regard George Fox as an isolated phenomenon.

His views, or, as he preferred to call them, his ' openings,' are in the main traceable amongst the German and English mystics. From the ' Friends of God of the Oberland ' in the fourteenth century is derived the separatist leaning towards the small group, and from the ' Brethren of the Common Life ' his absolute dependence upon the direct guidance of the Holy Spirit. In fact, no spiritual expression is of any value in his eyes except what is derived by direct inspiration or ' opening.' Dogma, or crystallised theological opinion, or as he called it ' notions,' he distrusted. His view of the importance of direct inspiration runs directly counter even to the views of the Lollards and the Anabaptists upon the Bible as the supreme and all-sufficient rule of life. Still more vigorously he opposed all institutional Christianity, which had become jejune and barren, because separate from and uninspired by the life-giving Spirit. The Anabaptists, with whom Fox was brought into contact through his uncle, Pickering, ' suggested,' doubtless, the negation of infant baptism and the sacraments generally, except in their spiritual sense. His tenets about oaths, war, capital punishment, ' set services,' and ' quiet waiting ' are found fully expressed in the ' Family of Love,' as founded by Niklaes of Münster in the sixteenth century. The term ' seeker ' had since 1617 come to be applied to those Anabaptists, Familists, and Brownists who were dissatisfied both with the Church of England and the Presbyterian communions. These were not a homogeneous body, but rather represent residuals of various movements ; some are sporadic and are assimilated into larger movements. Their character is appositely expressed by William Penn in his preface to G. Fox's *Journal* as ' Like doves without their mates.' Without assuming that all the seekers were converted *en masse* by Fox, their existence explains in part the rapidity of the increase of Fox's disciples.

The personality of Fox is, however, the dominating factor of the movement. He was born at Fenny Drayton in Leicestershire in 1624 ; his father, Christopher Fox, ' righteous Christer,' was a Puritan weaver, and his mother, Mary Lago, came of the ' stock of the martyrs.' He was intended for holy orders, and evidently showed no disinclination towards that profession. He explains, however, that he was ' persuaded by others to the contrary,' and was apprenticed instead to a shoemaker. His sterling honesty of character and love of plain dealing, even though still an apprentice, is shown by his general reputation, that 'if George says "Verily" there is no altering him.' It was not, however, until the early summer of 1643, when invited by his cousin, Bradford, and another 'professor,' who were with him on business at a fair, to drink healths that he felt the inconsistency of that practice, paid down his groat, went away, spent the night praying and crying to the Lord, and heard a voice speaking to him: 'Thou seest how young people go together unto vanity, and old people into the earth, and thou must forsake all, both young and old, and keep out of all, and be as a stranger unto all.' 'Then,' says Fox, 'at the command of God, on the ninth day of the seventh month 1643, I left my relations and brake off all familiarity or friendship with young or old.' 'I had wherewith,' he says, 'both to keep myself from being chargeable to others and to administer something to the necessity of others.' He spent nine months at Lutterworth, Northampton, and Newport Pagnel, but being in doubt whether he was doing right, and hearing that his parents desired it, he returned home in 1644. He was still far from clear about what he must do, and was advised by his relations to marry; others wished him to join an auxiliary band of the Parliamentary army; a clergyman recommended him 'to smoke tobacco and sing psalms'; another suggested blood-letting, but though this was tried no blood would flow. He had much intercourse at this time with Nathaniel Stephens, the Rector of Fenny Drayton, a kind, patient Calvinist, who discussed infant baptism and other doctrines with Fox, but annoyed him by a reference to the conversations in the pulpit. Thus he expresses himself: 'The Lord opened to me that being bred at Oxford or Cambridge was not enough to fit and qualify men to be ministers of Christ.' He left off attending church, and preferred on Sundays to walk in the fields with Bible in hand, and when reproached by his friends answered: 'There is an anointing in man to teach him, and the Lord will teach His people Himself.'

Thus the contact with the religious opinions of those able to teach him had only served to repel him, and William Penn's statement in the preface to the *Journal* is substantially true: 'As to man, he was an original, being no man's copy.'

Probably in 1647, his ministry began at a time when Fox was following his trade at Mansfield. It seems to have consisted chiefly in visits to 'shattered baptists' in Dukinfield, Manchester, in Nottinghamshire and Leices-

tershire. His preaching consisted of a 'few but powerful and piercing words.' Among these 'tender' separatists he found his first woman preacher, Elizabeth Hooton of Skegby, near Mansfield. They seem to have formed a group and called themselves 'Children of the Light,' thus emphasising Fox's chief message, the Light of Christ as the Guide to Eternal Life. The traces of this early preaching bear a close resemblance to the *innere Erleuchtung* of Jacob Böhme; in fact, his books seem to have been read by Fox's early followers. Fox was by no means a visionary, but, on the contrary, his mind was strongly set on realities. He strongly discountenanced 'doubtful disputations,' and strove rather by means of a pointed phrase to strike at the core of things. He had much to do to calm the 'dark imaginations,' 'the exalted spirits,' and the 'whimseys' of those of his hearers who belonged rather to the 'Ranters' than to the Quakers. He attacked all insincerities of convention, 'their images and crosses and sprinkling of infants, with all their holy days.' 'When the Lord,' he adds, 'sent me forth into the world He forbad me to put off my hat to any, high or low, and I was required to Thee and Thou all men. . . . I was not to bid people "Good Morrow" or "Good Evening."'

His itinerant preaching journeys continue incessantly from 1649 to 1691, and close practically with his death, and throughout this period not simply Fox himself but his followers both men and women had to suffer countless and indescribable persecution. George Fox was convicted and imprisoned at Derby in 1650 and at Carlisle in 1653 under the Blasphemy Act of 1650. His followers were frequently committed under the Brawling Act of 1553 (1 Mar. st. 2, c. 3) for disturbing the preacher or for wearing the hat during a proclamation. During the Commonwealth period three thousand one hundred and seventy Friends suffered for conscience' sake. Throughout the Restoration period the persecution was much more stringent when charges were brought against them for refusing the oaths of Supremacy and Allegiance they refused on principle to swear in a law court or elsewhere and for non-attendance at church, especially under the Quaker Act of 1662 (13-14 Car. II. c. 1), directed against those who maintained that the taking of an oath was illegal, and also under the Conventicle Acts of 1664 and 1670 (16 Car. II. c. 4 ; 22 Car. II. c. 1). Baxter's shrewd remark that Quakers are 'Ranters reversed,' implies that Fox's calm spirit and his teaching of religious silence, just at a time when talk was the besetting malady of Presbyterianism, had sobered faction and disciplined fervour amongst his followers, and his quiet genius for organisation had crystallised an unmanageable mass into a systematic network of meetings, and imbued the individual Friend with an exalted sense of corporate responsibility and a co-operative spirit that has gradually developed a true citizen character throughout the Society.

Probably the most charming and brilliant of the itinerating preachers first influenced by Fox and others was James Nayler. It is reported that lords, ladies, officers, and ministers listened to him at a meeting in Lady Darcy's house, 'behind a ceiling.' The adulation of two women, Martha Simmonds and Hannah Stranger, combined with the rigour of his imprisonment in Exeter, though George Fox visited him there when released from Launceston and found him 'dark and much out,' had brought him to imagine that he was the Messiah. Thus on 24th October 1656 Nayler was led in procession through the Redcliffe Gate of Bristol into the centre of the city, preceded by women, who threw their garments in the way and cried, 'Holy, holy, holy, Lord God of Israel.' This demonstration was not participated in by Bristol Friends. Being asked by the magistrates, 'Art thou the only Son of God?' he replied, 'I am the Son of God, but I have many brethren.' The case was reported to their town-clerk, who was in Parliament, and thus reported to the House. A Committee was appointed to examine and report. Nayler was summoned to London, and after lengthy debate sentenced by the House, evidently without any legal authority, to be pilloried in Palace Yard, whipped by the hangman to the Old Exchange, have his tongue bored, and to be branded on the forehead with the letter B. He was then ordered to Bristol, where the whipping was repeated in a more lenient form on 27th January 1657. After being taken back to London, in three months' time he was reported to be 'loving and much nearer the truth than he was.' This episode had a momentarily disastrous effect upon the Quaker movement, particularly in the West of England. Probably nowhere was the Restoration persecution more extensive and cruel than in Bristol. In 1682 nearly all the adult Quakers were in prison.

Fox, however, continued his missionary journeys unmoved by Nayler's fate. He visited every county in England and Wales, Scotland in 1657, Ireland in 1669, the West Indies and North America in 1671-3, and Holland both in 1677 and 1684. He suffered eight imprisonments. He wrote and complained about the condition of the gaols, and used the press as an agency for the dissemination of his opinions, though he dissuaded his followers from overmuch printing. At Swarthmoor, near Ulverston, Fox 'convinced' Margaret Fell, wife of Judge Fell, M.P. and Judge of Assize of the Chester and North Wales Circuit, and from this time forward this old Elizabethan manor-house, still standing, served as the nucleus and focus of the Society. Judge Fell died in 1658, and eleven years later Margaret Fell married George Fox. Their married life, disturbed by George Fox's constant absence on missionary journeys, was terminated by the death of Fox on 13th January 1691.

Toleration can hardly be expected on either side in Puritan controversy; but it can be fairly asserted of Fox and his followers that their polemical writings show less personal rancour and scandal than those of their opponents. In 1653 and 1654 Fox published *Unmasking and Discovering of Antichrist*, directed chiefly against the theories of Puritan 'Professors,' and *The Vials of the Wrath of God Poured forth upon the Seat of the Man of Sin*, in which he attacked Original Sin. In 1659 he replied to over a hundred pamphlets issued against Quakers in *The Great Mistery*. Of his followers, Edward Burrough answered John Bunyan's *Some Gospel Truths*, and Samuel Fisher in a more scholarly treatise, *Rusticus ad Academicos* (1660), replied to Richard Baxter. Owen, and others on the question of the foundations of faith whether upon the *Inner Light* or upon the letter of Scripture.

The organisation of the Society grew up naturally, beginning in November 1656 by a meeting of elders at Balby, near Doncaster. These meetings exercised a wise and gentle restraint upon promiscuous preaching, and issued letters of counsel and advice to the members concerned. In 1656 there is an entry in Fox's *Journal*. 'I was moved by the Lord to send for one or two out of a county to Swarthmore and to set up the men's meetings where they was not. . . . And about this time I was moved to set up the Men's Quarterly Meetings throughout the nation, though in the North they was settled before.' This was probably the first General Meeting, and was continued at Skipton in subsequent years. The main object of these gatherings was to provide funds by collections for ministering and persecuted Friends. In 1658 it is evident that monthly meetings were held to discharge the local business of each smaller group of Friends, to register births, marriages, and burials. The county was in the main the unit of administration, but groupings of counties occur. In no case did the superior general meeting supersede the individual congregation. They do not attempt to exercise authority. The hierarchy of bishops, priests, and deacons has its threefold counterpart among Friends—ministers, elders, and overseers. Their religious meetings were held without prearranged ritual or ceremony, and often in silence. This organisation was overhauled in 1667, and henceforth wherever Fox went, he was careful to organise as he proceeded. At the same time marriages are celebrated in meeting and not before a civil magistrate. But there were not wanting individualists in the society who strongly opposed this organisation.

Of the subsequent works to establish the society, the chief are Robert Barclay's *Apology for the True Christian Divinity, as the same is held forth and preached by the people, called in scorn Quakers* (1676); William Penn's *No Cross, no Crown*, written in prison. Penn's successful foundation of Philadelphia in 1682, and the establishment of a colony in Pennsylvania, in the constitution of which Quaker principles play a large part, formed a new departure in colonisation, by which the rights of the aborigines were respected.

Having already acquired the liberties they desired, throughout the eighteenth and nineteenth centuries the Quakers spent their energy in efforts for their own consolidation and equipment as an independent sect. Following the lead of Wesley, education was provided for all members by the establishment in 1779 of Ackworth School, near Pontefract, for boys and girls, and subsequently similar boarding-schools were partly endowed throughout England, Ireland, and America. Their aim was to afford a simple, cheap yet thorough commercial education. Thus Quakers grew in respect, both for their integrity and their business intelligence. This led directly to the accumulation of wealth, though John Dalton, educated at the Lancaster School, as founder of the Atomic Theory in chemistry, is a proof that the school also produced original thinkers. Their labours external to their own society were directed towards improvements in the treatment of prisoners. Elizabeth Fry (1813) did much valuable and permanent work. Though numerically small—the total number of Quakers in Great Britain at the present time is under 20,000—yet they have shared largely in obtaining freedom for slaves and respect for the rights of aborigines; in the

organisation of Sunday schools, especially for adults; in agitation against war, particularly during the Crimean War; against the Opium Trade, and in the solution of social problems.

Special provision was made for Quakers by the Toleration Act, 1688 (1 W. and M. c. 18). They were not required to take the oaths imposed upon other Nonconformists, but a special declaration was provided for them, and in 1696 they were allowed to make affirmation in any case where by law an oath is required (7-8 Will. III. c. 34; continued in 1714 by 1 Geo. I. st. 1, c. 6). In 1833 the House of Commons unanimously decided that Joseph Pease, the first Quaker to take his seat, might make affirmation in place of taking the usual oaths. The special treatment accorded by the Toleration Act led to the exclusion of Quakers from later Acts relating to other Protestant Nonconformists. Marriages contracted and solemnised according to their usage are expressly recognised as valid by the Marriage Act, 1836 (7 Will. IV. c. 85). Special provision was made for the recovery of tithes (*q.v.*) and church rates (*q.v.*) from Quakers. [C. O.]

NONJURORS, The. This name belongs to the clergy and laity who scrupled to take the oath of allegiance to William and Mary, 1689, on the ground that they were still bound by their former oath to James II., 'his heirs and lawful successors.' If it had been possible to constitute William and Mary regents there need have been no Nonjurors, but. 7th February 1689, the Convention recognised the Prince and Princess of Orange as sovereigns of England, and the first means taken to secure the stability of this settlement was the imposition of an oath of allegiance. This was ordered to be taken before 1st August by all ecclesiastics, under pain of suspension. Six months' grace was allowed before deprivation. Nine English bishops, fearing to violate their consciences, refused the oath; they were Archbishop Sancroft (*q.v.*), Bishops Ken (*q.v.*), Turner (Ely), Lake (Chichester), White (Peterborough)—who had all been among those sent to the Tower by James II. [SEVEN BISHOPS]—Cartwright (*q.v.*), Frampton (Gloucester), Lloyd (Norwich). and Thomas (Worcester). One Irish bishop, Sheridan of Kilmore and Ardagh, and practically the whole Scots clergy, bishops, and priests, were in the same case. Three of the English bishops—Cartwright, Thomas, and Lake—died before their deprivation, the last two each making solemn dying declarations of their reasons for refusing the oath. With these bishops were about four hundred clergy and some eminent laymen.

The separation of the Nonjurors thus appears at first political, yet for a century past the English Church had taught so insistently the complementary doctrines of Non-resistance and Passive Obedience that politics and churchmanship were inextricably mixed. Bishop Lake in his dying declaration (27th August 1689) says that he took these doctrines (Non-resistance and Passive Obedience) 'to be the distinguishing character of the Church of England'; and Ken in his will declares 'that he dies in the communion of the Church of England . . . as it adheres to the doctrine of the Cross,' by which he meant the doctrine of Passive Obedience, following Kettlewell (see Kettlewell, *Complete Works*, i. 167 ; ii. 143-4).

Non-resistance was taught in the Homily on Wilful Disobedience (1569), and was the doctrine that rebellion of subjects against their prince was in every conceivable instance a grievous sin. Passive Obedience was the attitude to be adopted by the subject towards unlawful commands of his prince. No one was bound to concur in their execution, but no subject must resist them by arms. These doctrines, which involved further the Divine Right of Kings, 'were held as against "Papists" who set the Pope, and " plebists " who set the people, above the Lord's Anointed.'

But to 'the State point' was soon added a 'Church point.' The bishops and clergy deprived in 1690 were deprived solely by Act of Parliament. There was no attempt at any canonical sentence, and whatever may be said for the necessities of the time, this was a grave violation of Church order. Many of the best churchmen who had taken the oaths refused sees thus irregularly declared vacant, as South (*q.v.*), Sharp (*q.v.*), and Beveridge. The sees were kept open for a time in the hope that the deprived bishops might return, and no bishops were consecrated to fill them until the summer of 1691.

Meanwhile the deprived bishops considered they held their canonical rights to the obedience of their clergy. Sancroft, urged by Bishops Lloyd and Turner, determined to continue the succession of bishops, since many of the English prelates were, in the Nonjuring view, schismatical intruders. The old archbishop delegated all his archiepiscopal powers to Lloyd, 9th February 1692. The question of the new consecrations divided the moderate from the more thoroughgoing party. Frampton stood apart from it, and Ken, though reluctantly giving his consent

to the act, frankly disliked it. Great pains were taken to act constitutionally. The Suffragan Bishops Act (26 Hen. VIII. c. 14) was relied on since no 'election' was possible. Dr. Hickes (*q.v.*) was sent, May 1693, to James II. with a list of names. The King selected Hickes and Wagstaffe (*q.v.*), who were consecrated with great secrecy, 24th February 1694, by Lloyd, Turner, and White.

The accession of Anne might have done something to heal the schism, for James II. had died, 1701, but for an 'Abjuration Oath' ordered by one of the last Acts of William III., 1701 (13 Will. III. c. 6), which required as a qualification for all office in Church or State an abjuration of 'the pretended Prince of Wales.' In 1714 another Act (1 Geo. I. st. 2, c. 13) imposed on all who held a public post of more than £5 annual value an oath that 'George I. was rightful and lawful King, and that the person pretending to be Prince of Wales had not any right or title whatsoever.'

These later oaths were a blunder, since they prevented the return of many. The deprived clergy were by no means political Jacobites ; they were not as a body engaged in plots for the return of the exiled family. They were scrupulous churchmen, who gave up income and position rather than violate the sanctity of their oaths. Queen Anne's churchmanship, the death of Ken, the last of the 'Deprived Fathers,' 1711, with his known wish to heal the schism, induced the more moderate Nonjurors to return to the English Church. Hickes and the stricter sort remained uncompromising, and in 1713, with the assistance of two Scots bishops, he consecrated Jeremy Collier (*q.v.*), Spinckes, and Hawes to the episcopate. These bishops took no territorial titles, and were consecrated 'not as Diocesan but as Catholic successors' to the bishops originally deprived. In 1716 two important movements took place. The Nonjurors attempted to establish communion with the Eastern Church by negotiations which lasted over nine years. [REUNION, II.] If some of their suggestions were fanciful, yet the Nonjuring bishops were uncompromising in their firmness to what they held to be the truth. In the same year the controversy on 'the Usages' began. Bishop Hickes, like other Anglican divines before and after him, had preferred the Communion Office in the 1549 Prayer Book to that of 1662. He had used the 1549 Office in his oratory in Scroope's Court, and had reprinted it in an appendix to his *Christian Priesthood*. In July 1716 it was proposed among the Nonjurors to use the

Liturgy of 1549. Meetings and discussions followed. The majority were against change. Collier with the most learned liturgiologists, Brett, and the Scots bishop Campbell, urged the addition to the 1662 book of what were termed ' the Usages.' These were (1) the Mixed Chalice at the Eucharist ; (2) public prayer for the Faithful Departed : (3) prayer for the descent of the Holy Ghost on the Oblations ; (4) the Prayer of Oblation of the Consecrated Sacrament, from the Book of 1549.

Thomas Deacon, later a bishop, then a very young priest, took an active part in favour of the Usages. Some Nonjurors, indeed, considered the Usages essential. Finally, in 1718, a new service-book, the work of Collier, Brett, and Deacon, was composed and published. It was largely the Liturgy of 1549, with additions and alterations from primitive Eastern sources. It contained further Offices for Confirmation (in which the Chrism and Sign of the Cross were restored) and the Visitation of the Sick (where Unction is prescribed). It was formally authorised for use by Collier, 11th March 1719. Meanwhile more consecrations had taken place. Dr. T. Brett and Henry Gandy, consecrated on 25th January 1716 in Mr. Gandy's chapel, were both men of learning and distinction. Brett was a member of an old Kent family, wealthy, and had been a country rector. Gandy had been a well-known Fellow of Oriel, Oxford, but had lost his preferment at the Revolution. He had succeeded Hickes at the oratory in Scroope's Court. After 1719 the ' Usagers ' and ' Non-usagers ' remained apart, each side consecrating bishops. On the Non-usager side Hilkiah Bedford and Ralph Taylor were consecrated, 25th January 1721, in Dr. R. Rawlinson's chapel at Gray's Inn. Taylor had been chaplain to the English churchmen at St. Germans. He consecrated two bishops alone and on his own authority. On the Non-usager side were also consecrated Henry Doughty (by four Scots bishops at Edinburgh, 30th March 1725, at the request, however, of Collier and Spinckes), John Blackbourne (Ascension Day, 6th May 1725, at Gray's Inn), Henry Hall (11th June 1725 at Gray's Inn), and Richard Rawlinson, the famous antiquary, 25th March 1728, at the chapel in Scroope's Court, Holborn. On the Usager side there had been consecrated John Griffin (25th November 1722) and Thomas Brett, junior (9th April 1727). George Smith was consecrated by Non-usager bishops, 26th December 1728, and to his good offices and those of Dr. Brett on the other side, is chiefly due

the healing of the division, for bishops of both sides united in consecrating Timothy Mawman, 17th July 1731. A year later the separation, as far as the main body went, was formally healed. An ' Instrument of Union ' was signed in London, 17th April 1732, by both the Bretts on behalf of the Usagers, and by Gandy and Rawlinson (for himself and for G. Smith) for the Non-usagers, by which the Usagers agreed to give up their ' New Office ' after the following 1st September and to celebrate according to the form used in the ' Established Liturgy.' Phrases in that Office were stated, however, to be understood in the sense of the Usagers (Prayers for the Dead and Invocation of the Holy Spirit), and a little water was ' always to be privately mix'd with the Sacramental Wine before it be placed upon the Altar.' Further, it was agreed ' to consecrate at first rather more than sufficient for all the Communicants that there may never be any need of a Second Consecration.' (The documents printed in *Athenæum*, No. 4254, 8th May 1909.) Bishop Blackbourne is said to have stood apart from this union till his death, 1741. He was a saintly old man, and lived in London, ' almost lost to the world, and hid among old books.' He answered one who inquired if he belonged to Blackbourne's diocese. ' Dear friend, we leave the sees open, that the gentlemen who now unjustly possess them, upon the restoration, may, if they please, return to their duty, and be continued. We content ourselves with full episcopal power as suffragans.' It is an exact illustration of the position claimed by the later Nonjuring bishops. The last of the regular line was Robert Gordon, or Gordoun, consecrated 11th June 1741. He ministered at an oratory in or near Theobald's Road, London, and from an account of his services in 1764 appears to have returned to some of the Usages. In 1777 he commended his flock to the Scots bishops after his death, which occurred in November 1779. Their bishops were not the only distinguished Nonjurors. Among the priests were John Kettlewell (1653-95), a master among English devotional writers ; Charles Leslie (1650-1722), the deprived Chancellor of Connor, whose brilliant gifts were used in defence of the Christian faith specially against the Deists, but who dealt with almost all the opponents of the Anglican position in turn (the publication of a complete edition of his works at Oxford, 1832, was the herald of the Oxford Movement, *q.v.*) ; William Law (*q.v.*) (1686-1761) ; Thomas Carte (1686-1754), a distinguished historian : and Thomas Baker (1656-1740), a Nonjuror of the type of

Ken, and one of the most learned antiquaries of the University of Cambridge. Among lay Nonjurors: Robert Nelson (*q.v.*); Francis Cherry (1665-1713), the cultivated Berkshire squire, and patron of Hearne; and Henry Dodwell (1641-1711), the learned Camden Reader in Ancient History at Oxford, returned to the National Church in 1710; Thomas Hearne (1678-1735), most famous of English antiquaries; Samuel Jebb (1694-1772) and his son, Sir Richard Jebb (1729-89), were among Nonjuring physicians. John Byrom (1692-1763), the poet (and author of 'Christians, awake'), though not strictly a Nonjuror, for he never refused the oaths, was both in theology and politics really of their body.

Two irregular successions of Nonjuring bishops demand notice. Bishop Ralph Taylor in 1722 (the year of his own consecration and death) consecrated Dr. Richard Welton and a Mr. Talbot as bishops for the American colonies. The act was irregular and uncanonical, since by Church law three bishops are required for a regular consecration. Necessity in this case may have been held to justify the act. Welton (who had been a well-known London rector) died in 1726, and Talbot probably in 1727. Dr. Timothy Newmarsh is said, on the strength of a MS. note in the possession of the late Dr. F. G. Lee, to have been consecrated by Hall and Welton in the oratory in Gray's Inn, 29th May 1726. Nothing is known of this consecration, and at the date given Welton was on his way from America to Lisbon, where he died in August. Recent investigation has made it practically certain that no such person as 'Bishop Timothy Newmarsh' ever existed, save as the picturesque figment of some imaginative brain, though Dr. Lee believed that he possessed the morse of a cope of this shadowy prelate.

The settlement between Usagers and Nonusagers in 1732 had not been accepted by the Scots bishop Campbell, or by two other learned priests, both friends of Collier, Roger Laurence and Thomas Deacon. Laurence was already famous before he joined the Nonjurors by his treatise, *Lay Baptism Invalid*, published 1708. It had roused a fierce controversy, in which Bingham (*q.v.*), Hickes, and many others took part. He was a strong Usager, and in 1733 Bishop Archibald Campbell consecrated him bishop, and Laurence then joined Campbell in consecrating Deacon.

Thomas Deacon (1697-1753), a man of many gifts, was born at Limehouse, the son of a sea-captain, and was ordained deacon, 12th March, and priest, 19th March 1716, in the Scroope's Court oratory by Collier when he was not yet nineteen years old. He was certainly learned and cultivated, and besides his part in the Usages controversy studied medicine under the well-known physician, Richard Meade. He removed to Manchester to practise medicine between 1719-21. He was much respected there as a physician, and he ministered also as a Nonjuring priest. After his consecration in 1733 he put forth a *Compleat Collection of Devotions*, 1734, which restored many primitive usages, such as Infant Communion, the draught of Milk and Honey after Baptism, and Exorcism of the Possessed. John Wesley (*q.v.*) gave him suggestions for arranging the Proper Psalms for fast and feast days in his Offices.

Deacon thus became the representative of the old Usager body, and when Bishop Campbell died, 1744, took over the superintendence of the London clergy and laity who had been in communion with Campbell. Deacon's family were deeply involved in the Forty-five. Three of his sons were taken prisoners, one was executed, one died in prison, and the third was transported for life. Deacon himself died at Manchester, 1753, where his tombstone describes him as 'the greatest of sinners and the most unworthy of primitive bishops,' and contains a prayer for his soul and that of his wife. He was a man of wide and deep learning, and was to the end a friend of William Law. Before his death Deacon had consecrated Kenrick Price bishop (8th March 1752). Price was a grocer, but for more than thirty-seven years he presided 'over the remnant of the ancient British Church in Manchester, without the least worldly profit.' Bishop Price died in Liverpool, September 1790, and either he or Bishop Deacon had consecrated to the episcopate a very shadowy but interesting figure, P. J. Browne, M.D., who is said to have been in reality Lord John Johnstone, younger son of the Marquis of Annandale. A letter from him occurs in Byrom's *Remains*. Bishop Browne, dying 17th June 1779, predeceased Bishop Price, who continued the succession, however, by consecrating in 1780 William Cartwright, a son-in-law of Bishop Deacon, an apothecary first in London and after 1769 in Shrewsbury. Bishop Cartwright was a very dignified and benevolent gentleman who ministered to the scattered remnant in Lancashire, and a record exists of a baptism with trine immersion, Chrism, and Communion administered by him, 7th May 1797. In 1761 he issued a book of the Day Hours, 'to be used by all religious Societies where there is a Priest and in the Houses of all the Clergy.' Bishop Horsley of St. Asaph, when visiting Shrewsbury, surprised his hearers by maintaining that Bishop Cartwright was as much a bishop as himself. It is recorded that Cartwright used to dress in purple cloth. He died and was buried at Shrewsbury, 14th October 1799. Dr. Seabury, the first bishop of the American Church. seems to have applied indirectly to Bishops Cartwright and Price to know whether he could receive consecration from them. In 1795 Cartwright consecrated Thomas Garnett, who is said to have been ' keeper of the Communion Plate ' of the congregation in Manchester. Bishop Garnett consecrated Charles Booth, a watchmaker in Long Millgate, Manchester, who removed to Ireland, where he died in 1805. With him the irregular line ended.

There are vague reports of Nonjuring congregations lingering on in the early nineteenth century in the west of England, and Lathbury had been told that a Nonjuring clergyman ' was living so late as the year 1815.' But the term ' Nonjuror ' was later often loosely used to describe a strict High Churchman.

Little can be gleaned as to the worship of the Nonjurors. The Non-usagers would not differ from the contemporary practice of the Established Church. The Usagers, however, in 1718, and again after 1734, went further. Bishop Deacon in his portrait in episcopal dress wears a pectoral cross and carries a pastoral staff. The head of the pastoral staff of Bishop Kenrick Price was preserved as late as 1844. and is probably that now in possession of the Society of St. John the Evangelist. Cowley. A MS. in the Bodleian Library (Add. D. 30) asserts ' on information derived from Mr. Seddon ' that the Nonjurors of Dr. Deacon's congregation ' had vestments, candles, etc., same as Catholics, dipped infants, and did not believe in Transubstantiation.' An extract from the *New Manchester Guide*, 1815, records that in 1815 the Nonjurors had no place of worship, says that Bishop Thomas Garnett ' sold the plate ' at Halifax, and that his successor, Bishop Booth, ' burned his books in the street.' A small box containing a glass chalice, paten, flagon, and a corporal, probably belonging to Bishop Deacon, was given to the Society of St. John the Evangelist, Cowley, in 1906. Described as ' a medicine chest, together with two Nonjuring Devotional books,' it had been bought in Manchester by Dr. Sedgwick in the nineteenth century.

The Nonjuring secession was a grievous blow to the English Church. Eminent alike for their piety and learning, these men, who preferred poverty to perjury, were the type of clergy and laity who are the glory of the Church in every age. Posterity has dealt unjustly by them. Even Dr. Johnson repeated the unworthy slander of Colley Cibber, who in his adaptation of Molière's *Tartuffe* changed the title to *The Nonjuror*. More recent research has done them truer justice. Harassed by penal laws made by Whig governments. the Nonjurors meekly accepted their lot; they were, for the most part, scholars and gentlemen, and they carried on in their theology the tradition of the Caroline Divines (*q.v.*), and by preserving the Catholic tradition they were the precursors of the Oxford Movement. The supposed resemblance of the Tractarians to the Nonjurors indeed provoked the fierce invective of Dr. Arnold (*q.v.*) and the *obiter dicta* of various bishops, and led to a belief, current in the 'fifties, that the Tractarians were about to form a Nonjuring Church.   [S. L. O.]

Lathbury, *Hist. of the Nonjurors* ; Overton, *The Nonjurors* ; H. Broxap, *Biography of Thomas Deacon.*

NORMAN CONQUEST, The, is sometimes said to have begun with the reign of Edward the Confessor ; but this is only a fanciful way of expressing the truth that the personal connection of that sovereign with Normandy led to a considerable immigration of Norman favourites, and suggested hopes of the English succession to Duke William. The Conquest, in the literal sense, began with the battle of Senlac, or Hastings (14th October 1066), and was rendered complete by the Harrying of the North (1069), which crushed the last considerable revolt of the English. The general effects of the Conquest upon English society and institutions must be studied in such works as Freeman's *Norman Conquest* ; we are here concerned with this great revolution only in so far as it affected the English Church. After Senlac there was a party among the English clergy who would have welcomed the election of Eadgar Aetheling, the legitimate representative of the House of Cerdic. But they were deserted by the English earls ; and accordingly the advance of William upon London was followed by the submission of the leading bishops. The example was set by Stigand of Canterbury, whose irregular appointment and recognition of a schismatic antipope had enabled William to represent his expedition as a holy war, and to obtain for it the blessing of Alexander II. Ealdred (*q.v.*), the patriot Archbishop of York, consented to crown the Conqueror, and thus gave the semblance of a legal title to the new dynasty. Throughout the troubles of the next few years the Norman was loyally supported by the native clergy. He showed his gratitude by respecting the endowments and privileges of the principal churches. The Domesday survey proves that this forbearance was not invariably maintained. But there are cases on record in which the King allowed the English shire-moots to adjudicate, in accordance with English law, on the claims of aggrieved bishops and abbots. He was less conservative in dealing with the personnel and the discipline of the clergy; for here he was influenced by political and religious considerations, which made him indifferent to English sensibilities. It was clearly desirable that the immense estates and territorial influence of the English churches should be controlled by Normans. By the close of the reign there was left but one English bishop, Wulfstan (*q.v.*) of Worcester, and the leading religious houses were also ruled by foreigners. For this policy there was some excuse in the low *morale* of the English clergy and the relaxed discipline of English monasticism. The ecclesiastical policy of William was inspired by Lanfranc (*q.v.*), a sincere supporter of the Hildebrandine programme of reform; and the King was religious after a fashion. Moreover, he came to England as the soldier of the Pope, and was sufficiently acquainted with the efficacy of papal censures to realise the importance of redeeming his pledges. His relations with Alexander II. were cordial, and his first attack on the English bishops was made with the co-operation of papal legates, who sanctioned the deposition of Stigand and other prelates and approved the appointment of Lanfranc to Canterbury (1070). Gregory VII., who was more exacting, found the King by no means submissive. William refused in decided terms to acknowledge himself the vassal of the Holy See (*c.* 1080); he persistently disregarded the papal decrees against lay investiture (*q.v.*); he imprisoned Odo of Bayeux for preparing an expedition to assist Gregory in his wars with the Empire (1082); and he enacted that no Pope should be recognised, no papal letters received, in England without the sanction of the Crown. But, even in Gregory's time, the King acknowledged the right of the Pope to receive Peter's Pence (*q.v.*) and other accustomed dues. In spite of some mistaken choices, the nominations to English prelacies were usually so good that Gregory condoned William's irregular methods of

appointment, and spoke of him as more deserving of honour than other princes. This judgment may be justified by reference to measures of reform which truly expressed the Hildebrandine ideal. First in importance was the revival of the national Church Council for purposes of legislation [COUNCILS]. In the later Anglo-Saxon period the Witan, composed of both lay and spiritual magnates, had made laws indifferently for Church and State. Under William I. a council of the clergy met at the same time as the *Magnum Concilium* of feudal tenants in chief, but deliberated apart, and passed ecclesiastical canons which were subject only to the King's approval. The King occasionally took part in these assemblies, but there is no suggestion of undue influence on his part. Next comes the separation of the spiritual and temporal law-courts, which was effected by a royal ordinance about 1072 [COURTS]. It is possible that bishops retained the right of assisting the sheriffs in secular justice and tempering the law with mercy. At all events they possessed, under this ordinance, the exclusive right of supervising judgments by ordeal (*q.v.*). But the importance of the bishop in the popular law-courts rapidly dwindled; while the claims of the reformed episcopal jurisdiction were as rapidly enlarged. This measure gave to the clerical estate a new sense of corporate unity, and led inevitably to the conflict of lay with ecclesiastical jurisdictions under Henry II. Thirdly must be mentioned the canon, passed by the Council of Winchester in 1076, which to some extent enforced the recent Lateran decrees (1074) on the subject of clerical celibacy. The English canon made, however, an important concession by recognising the marriages of parish priests, if contracted before 1076. The Hildebrandine rule, with its uncompromising severity, was only adopted under Anselm's (*q.v.*) primacy in 1102. While thus enforcing the separation of the clergy from the laity, the Conqueror did not hesitate to employ ecclesiastics as political functionaries. Bishop Walcher of Durham held the earldom of Northumbria from 1076 to 1080; Odo of Bayeux (*q.v.*) was Earl of Kent from 1067 to 1082; both Odo and Lanfranc acted as regents (justiciars) during the absences of the King from England. The trial and punishment of Odo show the King's determination to keep a tight hand on his bishops in their secular capacity as tenants-in-chief. And their spiritual powers were limited by the rule that no tenant-in-chief might be excommunicated without the King's consent. Some other ecclesiastical changes of the period, though striking and important, must be briefly summarised. The unity of the English Church was reasserted by Lanfranc, who demanded a profession of obedience from Archbishop Thomas of York, and justified his claim before an English council (1072), to which the dispute had been referred by Alexander II. A council of 1075 ordered the removal of bishops' sees from villages to towns; with the result that Old Sarum took the place of Sherborne, Chichester of Selsey, Chester (afterwards Coventry) of Lichfield, Thetford (afterwards Norwich) of Elmham, Lincoln of Dorchester-on-Thames, Bath of Wells. The new race of prelates showed extraordinary zeal in building new churches, as for instance at Canterbury, Rochester, Winchester, St. Albans, Hereford, York; and a new style of ecclesiastical architecture, modelled on that of Normandy, penetrated every English shire [ARCHITECTURE]. The Cluniac ideal of monasticism was popularised; at Canterbury, Durham, Rochester and elsewhere, the canons of the cathedral chapters were expelled to make way for monks.

[H. W. C. D.]

W. R. W. Stephens, *The Eng. Ch., 1066-1272*; Stubbs, *Lectures on Early Eng. Hist.*, pp. 89-107; H. W. C. Davis, *Eng. under the Normans and Angevins*.

NORWICH, See of. The conversion of East Anglia took place about the year 628, when Earpwald the King and his people accepted the faith and were baptized. Shortly after his succession he was killed, and the East Anglians lapsed into idolatry. In 631 his half-brother, Sigbert, made himself King. He was a Christian who had been converted during an exile in Gaul, and he was determined to re-establish Christianity in East Anglia. At this time a Burgundian, named Felix, had offered himself to Honorius, Archbishop of Canterbury, for missionary work in this land. Whether he was a bishop or received consecration at the hands of Honorius is not clear, but it is certain that Honorius appointed him Bishop of East Anglia, and sent him to Sigbert. The seaport town of Dunwich—not the present town of that name—was given him as his see city. Dunwich remained the title of the see until 673, when Archbishop Theodore caused the diocese to be divided. The South Folk continued under the bishops of Dunwich, while for the North Folk the new diocese of Elmham was formed.

At the time of the Danish invasions there appear to have been no bishops in East Anglia for many years. When they reappear they

are bishops of Elmham alone, and the whole of that country has become one diocese as at the first. In 1078 Bishop Herfast removed the see to Thetford, then an important town. But it was soon overshadowed by Norwich, whither the see was once more removed in 1094 by Bishop Herbert Losinga. Losinga will always be famous for having built the cathedral, the greater part of which still remains. Himself a monk of Fécamp, he introduced the Benedictines into Norwich, and caused his new cathedral to be also a monastic church. At the Dissolution in 1538 the prior became the first dean, and six prebendal stalls were created. One of these was annexed to the mastership of St. Catherine's Hall, Cambridge, under 12 An. 2, c. 6 (1713), and two were suspended by the Cathedrals Act, 1840 (3-4 Vic. c. 113). The diocese to-day includes six hundred and three of the six hundred and seven ecclesiastical parishes or districts of the ancient county of Norfolk (three being in the diocese of Ely and one in that of Lincoln); and the ancient county of Suffolk, with the exception of the rural deaneries of Blackburn (except Ricklinghall inferior), Clare, Fordham, Sudbury, Thingo, Thedwaster —all in the archdeaconry of Sudbury. These were transferred in 1837 to the diocese of Ely.[1] It was formerly divided into four archdeaconries: Norwich (first mentioned, 1124), Norfolk (first mentioned, c. 1200), Suffolk (first mentioned, c. 1126), and Sudbury (first mentioned, c. 1126, but the list is not successive till c. 1225), since 1837 in the diocese of Ely. The archdeaconry of Lynn was constituted in 1894. The acreage of the diocese is 1,994,525, and the population 733,307 (est.). The income of the see is given in the *Taxatio* of 1291 as £666, 13s. 4d. for *Temporalia*; no *Spiritualia* are recorded in 1291, but under Henry VI. they amounted to £28; in the *Valor Ecclesiasticus* (1535) the income is £978, 19s. 4½d. The value for first-fruits is given by Ecton (1711) as £834, 11s. 7½d.; it is now £4500. There were seven bishops suffragan between the years 1263 and 1531. Suffragan bishops of Thetford and Ipswich were appointed in 1894 and 1899 respectively.

BISHOPS OF DUNWICH

Felix, 630. Thomas, 647. Boniface, 652. Bisi, 669. Accci, 673. Aesewulf. Eadulf,

[1] Up to 1837 one parish in Norfolk (Emneth) was in the diocese of Ely, one in Suffolk (Freckenham) was in Rochester, and three churches were peculiars of the Archbishop of Canterbury. It included sixteen churches and chapels in Cambridgeshire. The peculiars were abolished in May 1847.

? 747. Cuthwine. Aldberht. Eeglaf. Heardred, ? 781. Aethun, 790. Tidferth, 798. Waeremund, ? 824. Wilred, 825. Aethelwulf.

BISHOPS OF ELMHAM

Baduvine, 673. Nothbert, ? 706. Heatholac. Aethelfrith, 736. Eanferth, ? 758. Aethelwulf, ? 781. Alcheard, ? 786. Sibba, ? 814. Hunferth. Humbert, d. 870. Eadulf, ? 956. Aelfric. Theodred, ? 975. Theodred, d. 995. Aelfstan, 995. Aelfgar, 1001; res. 1016, 1021. Alfwine, or Alwin, 1016. Aelfric, d. 1038. Alfric, 1038. Stigand, 1043; tr. to Winchester. Aethelmar, 1047; brother to Archbishop Stigand, who procured him the see; depr. at Council of Winchester, 1070. Herfast, 1070; removed the see to Thetford, 1075; d. 1085? William of Beaufeu, 1086; d. 1091.

BISHOPS OF NORWICH

1. Herbert Losinga, 1091 (Thetford); Abbot of Ramsey; obtained the see (Thetford) by purchase; d. 1119.
2. Everard of Montgomery, 1121; Archdeacon of Salisbury; aroused the hostility of the monks of Norwich; vacated the see, probably under compulsion; retired to Fontenay; became a Cistercian; d. 1150.
3. William de Turbe, 1146; a monk who had spent all his life from boyhood in the monastery of Norwich; consistently and openly opposed Henry II. and supported Becket; d. 1174.
4. John of Oxford, 1175; scholar, lawyer, politician; supported the King during the quarrel with Becket; presided over Council of Clarendon, 1164; Dean of Salisbury, 1165; excommunicated by Becket, 1166; d. 1200.
5. John de Gray, 1200; a native of Norfolk; favourite of King John, who obtained his nomination to Canterbury in 1205; d. 1214.
6. Pandulf (q.v.), 1222; Papal Nuncio; described as Bishop of Norwich in 1215, though still in minor orders; not cons. until 1222.
7. Thomas Blunville, 1226; during his episcopate the friars settled in Lynn and Norwich; d. 1236.
8. William de Ralegh, 1239; elected in succession by the monks of Winchester, canons of Lichfield, and monks of Norwich to those sees respectively; Henry III. refused him Winchester, so he chose Norwich; again elected to Winchester, 1244, to which election the King this time agreed.

9. Walter de Suffield, or Walter Calthorp, 1245; saintly and wealthy; built a new Lady Chapel, in which he was buried; left large bequests; it was believed that miracles were worked at his tomb; d. 1257.
10. Simon de Wanton, or Watton, 1258; a distinguished lawyer; held no clerical appointment, and perhaps was not ordained before his election to Norwich; changed sides in 1262 from the Barons to the King; d. 1266.
11. Roger de Skerwyng, 1266; monk of Norwich; Prior since 1257; d. 1278.
12. William Middleton, 1278; Dean of Arches; Archdeacon of Canterbury; during his episcopate the monastery of Norwich began the support of scholars at Oxford; d. 1288.
13. Ralph Walpole, 1289; tr. to Ely, 1299.
14. John Salmon, 1299 (P.); Prior of Ely; career political rather than ecclesiastical; Chancellor of England; enlarged the bishop's palace, and began building the cloisters; d. 1325.
    [Robert Baldok; elected to the see, 1325; Chancellor of England; never bishop of the diocese, as the Pope refused him consecration; died in Newgate Prison.]
15. William Ayermin, 1325 (P.); obtained the see through the influence with the Pope of Isabella, to whose side he deserted from Edward II.; did not receive the temporalities of the see until after the fall of the Despensers; d. 1336.
16. Antony Bek, 1337 (P.); Dean of Lincoln; frequently at strife with the monks of Norwich; d. 1343.
17. William Bateman, 1344 (P.); son of a Norwich citizen; official at the court of Avignon; a distinguished lawyer; founded Trinity Hall, Cambridge, as a school of civil and canon law; d. 1355.
18. Thomas Percy, 1356 (P.); only twenty-two years old when appointed; restored the cathedral, which had suffered in the gale of 1362; built the clerestory of the choir; d. 1369.
19. Henry Despenser (q.v.), 1370 (P.).
20. Alexander Tollington, or Tottington, 1407 (P.); Prior of Norwich; d. 1413.
21. Richard Courtenay, 1413 (P.); never enthroned in the cathedral; four times Chancellor of Oxford; repudiated right of primate to hold a visitation at Oxford concerning Lollardy, 1411; d. 1415.
22. John Wakering, 1416; Archdeacon of Canterbury; Master of the Rolls,

1405-1415; began persecution against Lollards; d. 1425.

23. William Alnwick, 1426 (P.); Archdeacon of Salisbury; summoned White, the Lollard, to trial, and pronounced his condemnation; tr. to Lincoln.

24. Thomas Brown, 1436; tr. (P.) from Rochester; d. 1446.

25. Walter Le Hart, 1446 (P.); Provost of Oriel College, Oxford; built the vaulted roof of the cathedral nave.

26. James Goldwell, 1472 (P.); d. 1499.

27. Thomas Jane, or Janne, 1499 (P.); purchased the see by payment to the Pope of 7300 golden florins; d. 1500.

28. Richard Nix, or Nykke, 1501 (P.); prominent in opposition to heresy, and specially in attempts to suppress heretical literature; at his death the estates of the abbey of St. Benet's Hulme and the priory of Hickling became the endowment of the bishopric, of which the original revenues were confiscated by the Crown; d. 1536.

29. William Rugg, or Repps, 1536; Abbot of St. Benet's Hulme; res. the see, 1550.

30. Thomas Thirlby, 1550; tr. from Westminster; tr. to Ely, 1554.

31. John Hopton, 1554; a Dominican; confessor to Queen Mary; d. 1558.

32. John Parkhurst, 1560; encouraged Nonconformist practices; indolent, lax, unspiritual; d. 1575.

33. Edmund Freke, 1575; an Augustinian canon; tr. from Rochester; strong opponent of Puritans; tr. to Worcester.

34. Edmund Scambler, 1585; tr. from Peterborough; d. 1592.

35. William Redman, 1595; Archdeacon of Canterbury; d. 1602.

36. John Jegon, 1603; Master of C.C.C., Cambridge; Vice-Chancellor of the University; Dean of Norwich; d. 1618.

37. John Overall (*q.v.*), 1618.

38. Samuel Harsnet, 1619; Master of Pembroke College, Cambridge; tr. from Chichester; tr. to York, 1628.

39. Francis White, 1629; distinguished controversialist; tr. from Carlisle; tr. to Ely, 1631.

40. Richard Corbet, 1632; Dean of Christ Church; tr. from Oxford; d. 1635.

41. Matthew Wren (*q.v.*), 1635.

42. Richard Mountague, 1638; tr. from Chichester; friend and disciple of Laud; voluminous writer of Anglican pamphlets; attacked by House of Commons, 1625; d. 1641.

43. Joseph Hall, 1641; tr. from Exeter; High Churchman, able controversialist;

suffered during Commonwealth; never left his diocese; d. 1656.

44. Edward Reynolds, 1661; Dean of Christ Church, from which ejected in 1650; friend of Baxter, by whom recommended for a bishopric, and, like whom, was 'known to be for moderate Episcopacy'; author of 'General Thanksgiving' in Prayer Book; d. 1676.

45. Antony Sparrow, 1676; Fellow of Queens' College, Cambridge; ejected thence during the Commonwealth; tr. from Exeter; author of *Rationale upon the Book of Common Prayer*; d. 1685.

46. William Lloyd, 1685; tr. from Peterborough; Nonjuror; deprived of his see; d. 1709. [NONJURORS. SEVEN BISHOPS.]

47. John Moore, 1691; a great collector of books; at his death his library was bought by George I. and given to the University of Cambridge; tr. to Ely, 1707.

48. Charles Trimnell, 1708; Prebendary of Norwich; Archdeacon of Norfolk; an Erastian; tr. to Winchester, 1721.

49. Thomas Greene, 1721; Master of C.C.C., Cambridge; domestic chaplain to George I.; tr. to Ely, 1723.

50. John Leng, 1723; chaplain to George I.; d. of smallpox caught at coronation of George II., 1727.

51. William Baker, 1727; tr. from Bangor; d. 1732.

52. Robert Butts, 1733; Dean of Norwich; tr. to Ely, 1738.

53. Sir Thomas Gooch, Bart., 1738; tr. from Bristol; founded society for the support of the widows and orphans of the clergy of the diocese; tr. to Ely, 1748.

54. Samuel Lisle, 1748; tr. from St. Asaph; d. 1749.

55. Thomas Hayter, 1749; Archdeacon of York; chaplain to George II.; tutor to George III.; tr. to London, 1761.

56. Philip Yonge, or Young, 1761-1783; Fellow of Trinity College, Cambridge; Public Orator of the University; Master of Jesus College; Canon of St. Paul's; tr. from Bristol; d. 1783.

57. Lewis Bagot, 1783; tr. from Bristol; tr. to St. Asaph, 1790.

58. George Horne (*q.v.*), 1790.

59. Charles Manners Sutton, 1792; Dean of Peterborough; tr. to Canterbury, 1805.

60. Henry Bathurst, 1805; supported Roman Catholic Emancipation and the Reform Bill; said to be unorthodox; d. 1837.

61. Edward Stanley, 1837; did much to revive Church life in the diocese; father of Dean Stanley (*q.v.*); d. 1849.

62. Samuel Hinds, 1849; Dean of Carlisle; owed his promotion to his friendship with Archbishop Whately; res.. after marrying his cook. 1857.

63. The Honble. John Thomas Pelham, 1857; member of the family of the Earls of Chichester; an old-fashioned Evangelical; d. 1893.

64. John Sheepshanks, 1893; did much to revive Church life in the diocese; res. 1910; d. 1912.

65. Bertram Pollock, 1910; formerly Headmaster of Wellington.   [E. M. B.]

V.C.H., Norfolk, ii. : Jessop, *Dio. Hist.*

NOWELL, or **NOEL,** Alexander (1507?-1602), Dean of St. Paul's, the reputed author of much of the Prayer Book Catechism, was educated at Brasenose College, Oxford, and is said to have shared rooms with John Foxe (*q.v.*). He became Fellow of his College and Public Reader of Logic in the University, and after being ordained was appointed Master of Westminster School and Prebendary of the Abbey. In Edward's time he became known as a preacher, and ' preached in some of the notablest places and auditories in the realm.' He was returned as Member of Parliament for Looe in Mary's first Parliament, but was not allowed to sit as 'having a voice in' Convocation [PARLIAMENT, CLERGY IN]. He then went abroad, and took a leading position among the exiles at Frankfort, and in their disputes joined the Presbyterian side [MARIAN EXILES]. On Mary's death he returned to England, became Archdeacon of Middlesex, Rector of Saltwood, Canon of Canterbury, and Prebendary of Westminster.

In November 1560, in recognition of ' his godly zeal and special good learning and the singular gifts and virtues,' he was elected Dean of St. Paul's. He preached constantly before the Queen, but was nearly disgraced by putting a richly bound Prayer Book with pictures of the saints and martyrs in her place at St. Paul's, which she ordered the verger to remove. After service she went into the vestry, and rated the dean for having infringed her proclamation against ' pictures, images, and Romish relics.' Two years later, with some inconsistency, she interrupted him in a sermon in which he spoke slightingly of the crucifix, and called aloud from her seat: ' To your text, Mr. Dean. Leave that; we have heard enough of that.' to the complete discomfiture of the preacher, who was unable to proceed.

In 1562 he became Rector of Much Hadham, Canon of Windsor in 1594, and Principal of Brasenose, 1595. He died in 1602, and was buried in St. Mary's Chapel, behind the high altar, in St. Paul's. He was twice married, but had no children. He was considered an authority on educational matters, and endowed a free school at Middleton, but will be chiefly remembered as the author of three Catechisms. (1) The ' Large Catechism,' approved by Convocation in 1563, and first printed in 1572 with a dedication to the archbishops and bishops. (2) An abridged edition of it, called the ' Middle Catechism.' (3) The ' Small Catechism ' of 1572, which is nearly identical with that in the 1549 Prayer Book, of which Nowell was probably the author as well as of the first part of our present Catechism, the second part being added in 1604, reduced and altered from Nowell's. [COMMON PRAYER, BOOK OF.]

         [C. P. S. C.]

Foxe, *Acts and Monuments* ; Strype, *Annals* and *Memorials* ; *Troubles at Frankfort.*

O

OCKHAM, **William of** (d. 1349), *Doctor Invincibilis*; a Franciscan and one of the most notable of the later scholastics. After graduating B.D. at Oxford he migrated to Paris for his D.D., and there made his reputation. He became with Marsiglio of Padua, also in Paris, a pronounced supporter of the stricter school of Franciscans, and justified the extreme interpretation of the vow of evangelical poverty, as against Pope John XXII. Both on this ground and on that of his views on the rights of the secular power, Ockham and Marsiglio became a mark for the hostility of the Pope, at that time absorbed in the throes of the controversy with Lewis of Bavaria. Summoned to Avignon in 1333, he was condemned by the Pope; but Ockham escaped, and fled to King Lewis. He remained at his court, and accompanied him back from Italy to Bavaria. In spite of the Pope's constant attacks and Bulls of excommunication, the little party of Imperialists lived quietly at Munich under the King's protection. With Michael de Cesena Ockham may be regarded as the leader of the *fraticelli* in what was to be the death struggle of the party with the Conventuals. In the *Opus Nonaginta Dierum*, printed in

Goldast's great collection, vol. ii.. Oekham replied to the Pope's attack on the Franciscan ideal. John XXII.. however. had given to his opponents a chance of revenge by his views on the Beatific Vision. Oekham was secure of orthodox support in accusing the Pope of heresy in his *De dogmatibus Papae Johannis XXII*. His best known and most important works. however. are those which relate to the final phase of the long mediæval conflict for supremacy between the *sacerdotium* and the *imperium*. The actual course of the dispute between John XXII. and Lewis of Bavaria is of far less interest than those which preceded it. There are no incidents like that of Canossa. and no characters of such universal interest as Frederic II. or Barbarossa. The literature, however. of this the final phase of the conflict is of far greater value. Partly this is due to the fact that it is post-Aristotelian. and the *Politics* had had time to filter into the educated mind of Europe. The first phase of the controversy was largely Scriptural, and the theocratic mysticism of Gregory VII. intensified this tendency. The second was largely *legal* ; the revived study of the Roman law furnished the atmosphere in which the struggle between the Popes and the Hohenstauffen was carried on. The final phase. however, was definitely political, and there is evidence of a distinct effort to find some general philosophy of the State, and in that scheme to find the true place for the clerical power. The most notable work in the controversy is not that of Oekham but of Marsiglio, the famous *Defensor Pacis*. Yet the great dialogue of William of Oekham, filling six hundred pages of Goldast, is a mine of interest and suggestion for those who desire to see how the mediæval mind in its final efflorescence envisaged the problem. It is also very important, as heralding the modern view of the State. Oekham, who had made his submission, died as an orthodox friar in 1349.

His position in the history of philosophy is also important. An extreme Nominalist, he divided in the sharpest manner the spheres of faith and reason, and appears to have held a view of the nature of religious belief not dissimilar altogether from modern Pragmatism. His attitude to reason had a good deal to do with that of the reformers, more especially Luther ; and he is remembered for some acute maxims, such as the famous *entia non sunt multiplicanda praeter necessitatem*.   [J. N. F.]

ODO (d. 1097), Bishop of Bayeux and Earl of Kent, was the uterine half-brother of William

the Conqueror. from whom he received the see of Bayeux in 1049 or 1050. when fourteen or fifteen years of age. Though secular in his life and interests, he was a liberal benefactor to his cathedral church, which he entirely rebuilt, and even became a patron of learning. He sent some of his clerks to study at Liège and other centres of learning ; among them Thomas. afterwards Archbishop of York ; Samson. brother of Thomas, afterwards Bishop of Worcester ; and Turstan, who became Abbot of Glastonbury in 1081. In 1066 Odo founded the priory of St. Vigor at Bayeux, which he colonised from the abbey of Mont St. Michel. In the conquest of England he took a prominent part. He contributed forty ships to the fleet, and fought in person at Senlac, armed with a mace instead of a sword that he might not be guilty of shedding blood. He received as his share of the spoil a number of estates in many shires, together with the earldom of Kent. He is called *Comes Palatinus* by Orderic Vitalis, but simply *comes Cantiae* in charters ; and it is doubtful whether he held Kent as a palatine earldom in the modern sense. He acted as regent for William I. in 1067, and was of great importance in English administration till 1082. On at least two occasions he led a royal' army against rebels in England. He was detested for his harshness and avarice ; even the church of Canterbury suffered at his hands. In 1082 he was preparing an expedition to Italy, probably not. as Orderic states,. to secure the papacy, but rather to assist Gregory VII. He was arrested by William I., and impeached before the Great Council for breach of feudal loyalty. He pleaded that, as a bishop. he could not be tried by laymen, but was told that the Council dealt with him only in his secular capacity, as Earl of Kent,. and was adjudged guilty. William kept him in close confinement at Rouen despite the remonstrances of Gregory VII., but reluctantly granted a pardon when on his death-bed. Returning to England, Odo recovered his earldom from William II., but immediately organised a baronial revolt in favour of Duke Robert (1088). The revolt was suppressed, and Odo was banished from England, the English troops of Rufus clamouring in vain for his execution. Henceforth Odo was the right-hand man of Duke Robert in Normandy, and was active in defending the duchy against Rufus. The duke and the bishop departed together on the First Crusade (September 1096) [CRUSADES], but Odo sickened on the way, and died at Palermo (February 1097). He left an illegitimate son, John, who entered the service of Henry I. [H. W. C. D.]

Freeman, *Norman Conquest* and *William Rufus*; H. W. C. Davis, *Eng. under the Normans and Angevins.*

ORDEAL (Ordal) is an Anglo-Saxon word meaning 'judgment,' which was early confined to the special sense of 'God's judgment,' which in German still has to be expressed by the full form, *Gottesurtheil.* In the *New English Dictionary* it is defined as ' an ancient mode of trial among the Teutonic peoples, retained till after the Norman period, in which an accused or suspected person was subjected to some physical test fraught with danger, . . . the result being regarded as the immediate judgment of the Deity.' The usage had passed over from paganism without any change save in its religious sanction, and has parallels in many races and ages. Our ancestors before the Norman Conquest, if charged with a crime of which they had not been caught in the act, were allowed to purge themselves by oath-helpers, afterwards called compurgators, the number of whom varied according to the dignity of the accused and the gravity of the charge. They were to profess their belief, based on personal knowledge, of the good character of the accused. In a very simple age it was probably a satisfactory test that a man's neighbours should be willing to do this. If they refused his only chance of escaping conviction was by the ordeal. Unfortunately none of the earlier forms of ordeal have survived, though that of hot water is mentioned in the 37th law of Ine (688-95). But no less than sixteen later formulæ are collected in Liebermann's *Gesetze der Angelsachsen,* and the editor believes that more may be discovered. He holds that the existing forms were introduced from the Continent between A.D. 850 and 975, though they have been altered in England. Combining, for the sake of brevity, the features of the various rituals, we find that the ordeal is always under the direction of the clergy. The accused must fast for three days, and at the appointed time a Mass is said, at which he communicates, being warned by the priest to abstain if he is guilty. Such abstention would be a confession of guilt. After the Mass a litany is sung, and the ' creature ' of water or iron is exorcised, blessed, and adjured to reveal the truth. If cold water is chosen the man is thrown in; in case of innocence he sinks. If hot iron, he has to carry a ball, of triple weight in more serious cases, for a distance of nine feet; if hot water, according to the

case, he lifts a stone from the cauldron at the depth either of his wrist or of his elbow. In both ordeals the member is swathed up and sealed for three days. Then the priest examines it, and if he finds an open wound, from which matter is proceeding, he pronounces the man guilty. The remaining ordeal for which the rite has survived is that of swallowing. The exorcism, blessing, and adjuration of the ' creatures ' is as before; the accused is given a mouthful of barley bread and goat's milk cheese, and if he fails to swallow them he is guilty. Another ordeal —for which the rite is lost—was that of walking blindfold between hot ploughshares, but apparently cold water and hot iron were those most commonly applied. They were used with great seriousness, at least in the earlier times; human life was too sacred to be forfeited on merely human testimony. They were part, therefore, not of secular but of ecclesiastical law, and so remained till their disuse. Partial disuse came in with the Conquest. Unlike the English, the Normans employed the other Teutonic test of guilt or innocence, that by battle, and though ordeal remained open to the conquered race they were allowed their choice between it and fighting. The ordeal seems to have been preferred, perhaps because collusion was easy. William Rufus flatly denounced it as dishonest; and the temptation to be merciful must have been strong. But it was a pope who suppressed it. Innocent III. (*q.v.*), at the great Fourth Lateran Council of 1215, Canon 18, commanded the clergy to take no part in ordeal proceedings, and as their active participation was necessary for this mode of trial, it fell at once into desuetude.

[E. W. W.]

Pollock and Maitland, *Hist. Eng. Law,* especially chap. ix., sec. 4. The texts are in Liebermann, *op. cit.,* 401-29.

ORDINATIONS, Anglican. Since the beginning of the seventeenth century the validity of the orders conferred in the English Church has been assailed from time to time by Roman Catholic writers; Anglican ecclesiastics conforming to the Roman Church have been reordained; and in 1896 Leo XIII. determined that orders conferred by the English rite are, and always have been, null and void. There was some preliminary skirmishing on the part of the controversialists of Elizabeth's reign; but the grounds of their attack were vague, and it is at least uncertain whether it was directed against the validity, and not merely against the regularity, of the ordinations assailed. In

1603, perhaps in consequence of the clearer statements of Bancroft (1589), Bilson (1593), and Hooker (*q.v.*) (1597) on the subject of holy order, a definite attack on the reality and validity of the English succession was opened by Kellison, and he was followed up by the Jesuits Holywood (1604), Fitzherbert (1613), and Fitzsimons (1614). This attack called forth the reply of Francis Mason, *Of the consecration of bishops in the Church of England* (1613), which was answered by Champney in 1616, in reply to whom Mason's book was republished in an enlarged form in 1625 as *Vindiciae Ecclesiae Anglicanae*. The dispute was renewed in 1645 in a correspondence between J. Cosin (*q.v.*), during his exile, and Robinson, Prior of the English Benedictines in Paris (Cosin, *Works*, iv. 241). In 1657 the Jesuit Peter Talbot shifted the ground of attack in consequence of the publication of J. Morin's great work, *De sacris ordinationibus*, in which current opinions as to the 'matter' of the sacrament of order were corrected by an investigation of the history of rites of ordination. In 1658 J. Bramhall replied to Talbot (Bramhall, *Works*, iii. 5), and Lewgar replied to Bramhall (1662); and the controversy was continued, G. Burnet (*q.v.*) (1677) and H. Prideaux (1688) replying to other assailants. In 1720 Eusèbe Renaudot, author of *Liturgiarum orientalium collectio*, and the collaborator of Nicole and Arnauld in *La perpétuité de la foi*, contributed to a second edition of Tho. Gould's *La véritable croyance de l'Eglise catholique*, an adverse memoir on Anglican ordinations, on which he had already been consulted by Bossuet. He was replied to by Le Courayer in his *Dissertation* (1723) and *Défense de la Dissertation* (1726); and the Dominican Le Quien (1725) replied to Le Courayer, and the Jesuit J. Constable (1727) borrowed Le Quien's argument. The first and the fourth of the *Tracts for the Times* (1833) were a call to clergy and laity to consider afresh the apostolic succession, and, as was natural, interest in the question was revived. H. J. Rose (*q.v.*) had already given an abstract of Le Courayer's argument in App. vi. to the 2nd ed. of his *Commission and Consequent Duties of the Clergy* (1831); Sir W. Palmer summarised the controversy in his treatise *On the Church* (1838); A. W. Haddan re-edited Bramhall, with notes and corrections, in the *Library of Anglo-Catholic Theology* (1842), and later discussed the whole matter afresh in *Apostolical Succession* (1869); and Le Courayer was republished in English in 1844. On the Roman side, Lingard had refuted part of the current Roman argument

as unhistorical (1829, 1834); the general assault was again delivered by Kenrick in America (1841); in 1873 the whole contention was restated, if captiously and sceptically, yet with great ability, exhaustiveness, and candour, by E. E. Estcourt in *The Question of Anglican Ordinations discussed*; and in 1879 appeared A. W. Hutton's *Anglican Ministry*, with a preface by J. H. Newman. As the upshot of some discussions in 1893 between Lord Halifax and the Abbé Portal on possibilities of reunion, it was thought that a reconsideration of English ordinations would form a convenient point of departure for some attempt to further better relations; and a discussion was initiated by M. Portal, and continued by MM. Gasparri and Boudinhon and others, who concluded in favour of the validity of the ordinations, while the Anglican contention was ably restated by Messrs. Denny and Lacey in *Dissertatio apologetica de Hierarchia Anglicana* (1895). The French divines pressed the matter on the attention of Leo XIII., who was at that time exerting his influence to promote the union of Christendom, and in consequence he determined to have the question re-examined, and appointed a commission of eight for the purpose. After sessions lasting for six weeks the commission submitted their results to a committee of cardinals, who in two months reported to the Pope against the validity of English orders, and on 18th September 1896 Leo XIII. issued the Bull *Apostolicae curae*, which pronounced that 'ordinations performed by the Anglican rite have been and are utterly invalid and altogether null.' The English archbishops (Temple and Maclagan) issued a *Responsio* to the Bull (19th February 1897), addressed to all the bishops of the Catholic Church, which was issued also in English, French, and Greek. Leo XIII. sent a short letter in answer (20th June); and Cardinal H. Vaughan and the English Roman Catholic bishops replied to the archbishops (29th December) in *A vindication of the Bull 'Apostolicae curae.'*

Here it is impossible to do more than indicate shortly the objections that have been made, and the answers that have been given, in a discussion which has involved an immense amount of minute detail.

Since the English succession, at least for some forty years, derived exclusively from Parker (*q.v.*) and his consecrators, the discussion has largely been concentrated upon his consecration. It will be convenient, therefore, to refer to the particular objections raised to Parker's consecration, and to combine with them as we go the parallel objections which apply more generally. Matthew Parker was elected by the chapter of Canterbury on 1st August 1559, confirmed on 9th December, and consecrated in Lambeth Chapel 17th December, by Barlow (*q.v.*), late Bishop of Bath and Wells, now elect of Chichester; Scory, late of Chichester; Coverdale (*q.v.*), late of Exeter; and Hodgkin, suffragan of Bedford; according to the rite of 1552 [COMMON PRAYER, BOOK OF], except in one particular, viz. that all the bishops recited the formula *Take the Holy Ghost*, etc.; and the whole procedure is described in the Lambeth Register. This description is exceptionally minute, no doubt because, while the Book of Common Prayer had been restored to its legal status by the Act of Uniformity, the Ordinal had not been so restored, and it remained without legal recognition till 1566—an omission which gave the Roman controversialists of Elizabeth's reign the ground for their attacks on the *legal* status of the bishops. This consecration has been assailed on various grounds.

1. *The Nag's Head Fable.*—In 1604 a story was set afloat by Holywood, and was subsequently repeated by controversialists down till the nineteenth century, which implied that no such consecration had taken place; to the effect that the Anglican succession originated at the Nag's Head Tavern in Cheapside, where Scory, described as himself unconsecrated, laid a Bible on the heads of the kneeling nominees for several sees, saying to each: 'Take thou authority to preach the Word of God sincerely'; and this is all the consecration they received. This absurd story, which was unknown even to controversialists for forty-five years, and is inconsistent with facts other than those of Parker's consecration, has been abandoned by all.

2. *The Lambeth Register.*—The legend was confuted by appeal to the normal evidence for the facts, Parker's Register at Lambeth. Immediately the genuineness of the Register was denied, and Mason was charged with forging it. The charge was quite groundless; and even if it had been otherwise, the evidence for the consecration would scarcely have been affected. For the process of the promotion of a bishop involves a long and intricate series of necessary documents, and all these are preserved in Parker's case, in due form and in their right places. Nor is the Register otherwise the only evidence for the fact of the consecration, which is described or alluded to in all sorts of contemporary documents; and no question is now made that what is recorded in the Register took place as there described.

3. *Barlow's Episcopal Character.*—In 1616, *i.e.* not till forty-eight years after Barlow's death, the objection was raised that Barlow, Parker's principal consecrator, had never himself been consecrated, chiefly on the grounds that there is no record of his consecration in Cranmer's Register at Lambeth, and that he and Cranmer held and expressed the view that consecration was unnecessary. To this it is replied (*a*) that it is neither wonderful nor exceptional that a document should be missing, especially in Registers so carelessly kept as those of the archbishops of this period, Warham, Cranmer, and Pole, where numbers of documents are missing which ought to be found, including the certificate of the consecration of S. Gardiner (*q.v.*) himself; (*b*) that, whatever personal opinions Cranmer and Barlow expressed four years later, and in spite of the ribald remark charged against Barlow in the year of his promotion (1536) to the effect that the king's nomination could make as good a bishop as Barlow himself, there is no reason to suppose that either of them ever acted officially on these opinions: while Cranmer signed the official *Declaration of the functions and divine institution of bishops and priests* in 1536 or 1537, and both Cranmer and Barlow signed the *Bishops' Book* of 1537 and the *King's Book* of 1543; while within a week or two of the date at which Barlow must have been consecrated Cranmer certainly consecrated two bishops, and in 1548 he issued a *Catechism* in which the doctrine of the Apostolic Succession is expressed with even naïve crudity: and Barlow acted always as a bishop in all respects, taking part in the consecration of other bishops, without challenge or suspicion on anybody's part—for it is not pretended that even his colleagues knew the alleged facts, and this though he was involved in a struggle with his own chapter at St. David's, and though Cranmer, had he failed to consecrate him, would have subjected himself and his officials to the penalties of *praemunire* by a statute passed only two years before; (*c*) and that even if Barlow had never been consecrated, Parker's consecration would be unaffected, for neither the doctrine of the Church nor a consensus of theologians enforces the view that only one of the three bishops required, as a matter of regularity, to co-operate in the consecration of a bishop is the real consecrator, and the others contribute nothing but their witness; the other three of Parker's consecrators were sufficient, or if two of them are challenged as consecrated by the English rite (on grounds noticed below), Hodgkin alone, who was consecrated by the

Latin Pontifical in 1537, was sufficient for validity.

4. *The Rite.*—Next, the sufficiency of the Edwardine rite has been questioned, mainly on two grounds. (*a*) That in the 'form' of ordination—the 'Take the Holy Ghost,' etc.—in the case of both bishops and priests, the order conferred is not specified—for the defining words of the present form were not added till 1662 (though, in fact, then only in view of Presbyterian arguments) ; and hence the form was indeterminate and applicable to other conditions. To this it is replied that in other 'forms' of which the validity has not been questioned, there is no specification of the order conferred : while in fact the Edwardine forms were not indeterminate, since they were determined, in the case of bishops, by the words of 2 Tim. 1[6], which follow and by common consent refer to the episcopate, and in the case of priests, by the rest of Jn. 20[23], which is taken over from the Latin Pontifical ; and also, by the whole context of the rite in which they occur, which is explicitly the consecration of a bishop or the ordination of a priest as the case may be. (*b*) That, in the ordination of presbyters, the delivery to the ordinand of the paten with the bread and the chalice with wine and water, with the words ' Receive authority to offer sacrifice to God and to celebrate Masses as well for the quick and the dead,' which was regarded as the 'form' and 'matter' of ordination to the priesthood, and had so been defined by the Pope, Eugenius IV., in the fifteenth century, was omitted in the Edwardine rite. To this it is only necessary to reply, at the moment, that the researches of J. Morin in *De sacris ordinationibus*, before referred to, showed that this is a comparatively modern ceremony, unknown to the East and for a thousand years to the West, and is not the ' form ' and ' matter ' of ordination to the priesthood, and the view that it is so has now been abandoned.

5. *Intention.*—It was objected, on the ground of the private opinions of Barlow, mentioned above, that he did not intend to confer the orders of the Church. Now it is obvious that a minister of the Church must have a serious intention of doing what he is about ; that he must not merely ' play church.' But it seems also obvious that a minister, who as such only exists as the organ of the Church, cannot by a mere inward determination, of which he gives no outward sign, evacuate of all meaning the acts which he does only as authorised by the Church. ' The minister of a sacrament acts in the person of the whole Church, whose minister he is ; and in the words he utters it is the intention of the Church that is expressed, and this suffices for the perfection of the sacrament unless the contrary is outwardly expressed on the part of the minister or the recipient ' (St. Thomas Aquinas, *Summa*, iii. 68 § 8 ad. 2). Hence all that is required of a minister is, in the words of the Council of Trent, that he must have ' the general intention of doing what the Church does ' ; and the evidence of this intention is that, without protest, he solemnly uses the rite of the Church. In the case of Parker's consecration there is no ground for suggesting that the ministers did not seriously mean to do what they were about, *i.e.* to carry out the rite of the Church and to ' do what the Church does.' And as to what the Church not only does but intends, this is obvious from the Preface to the *Ordinal*, viz. she intends to continue the orders that have been in the Church since the Apostles' time ; and this cannot be affected by any opinions that individuals may have held in the sixteenth century; while if any one's opinion is relevant to the questions it is Cranmer's, and he, in the Catechism of 1548, already mentioned, unequivocally asserts the Apostolic Succession by communication of the Holy Ghost continuously all down the ages. But finally it is objected—and this no longer with special reference to Parker's consecration—that the intention of the Anglican Church itself, as expressed in the *Ordinal*, is defective ; for not only does the rite contain no acts or words explicitly conferring the authority to consecrate and offer the Body and Blood of the Lord, which is the essence of priesthood, but the acts and words (*e.g.* the delivery of paten and chalice, etc.), in which for centuries the conveyance of this authority had been expressed and symbolised, had been rejected ; and the atmosphere in which the rite was compiled shows that this rejection was deliberate and significant. To this it is replied that holy order can mean and contain nothing more than what our Lord instituted and the Apostles conferred, and the Anglican Church makes it abundantly clear that she intends to confer this ; that the Church ordains to an order and an office and all that it contains, and it is not necessary to specify or even explicitly to intend the particular contents of the authority conveyed ; that even if it were granted that the doctrine of the Anglican Church is erroneous, yet even heresy, and heresy affecting the substance of the sacraments, has not been held to affect the validity of sacraments celebrated and conferred ; that forms of ordination of unquestioned

validity contain no explicit reference to sacrifice or even (as in the ancient parts of the Roman rite itself) to the Eucharist at all, while St. Thomas in his discussion of order does not even allude to sacrifice (*Summa*, iii. 38) ; that the sacrifice of the Eucharist is not something over and above the sacrament itself, and in conferring the authority to minister and dispense the sacraments, the Church confers and intends to confer all that is included in ministering the sacraments, and therefore of necessity, along with the authority to consecrate, the authority also to sacrifice ; and finally the Anglican Church has never questioned any doctrine of sacrifice defined before the Council of Trent (and the Tridentine definition is later than the compilation of the Ordinal) or such a doctrine as satisfied Peter Lombard and St. Thomas Aquinas, or indeed any such doctrine as is in itself really intelligible.

The *Apostolicae curae* ignored all the particular questions relating to the consecrations of Barlow and Parker, and confined itself to a criticism of the English rite and the intention expressed in it ; and this only in the second place and out of ' consideration and charity ' ; since the question was no longer an open one, but had been decided by the Roman see from the first, and the original decision had been carried out consistently in practice ever since, orders conferred under the English rite being treated as null, and the recipients of them, on occasion, reordained. To this it is replied, that while no instance is forthcoming of an Edwardine clerk being deprived for lack of order under Mary, and many continued to hold their benefices or were promoted to new ones, the assertion that the Roman See had already rejected Edwardine ordinations rests upon a dubious interpretation of the papal documents issued to Pole and of Pole's own *General Indulgence* ; and that the point is, not what has been the subsequent Roman practice, as to which there is no question, but whether the practice has been based on adequate knowledge of the facts ; and this question the Bull does not clear up.

[F. E. B.]

Haddan, *Apostolical Succession* : Estcourt, *The Question of Anglican Ordination Discussed* ; Denny and Lacey, *Dissertatio apologetica de Hierarchia Anglicana* ; Lacey, *A Roman Diary* ; Lord Halifax, *Leo XIII. and Anglican Orders.*

ORNAMENTS RUBRIC. When the English Prayer Book was issued to supersede the Latin service-books, the question naturally arose as to the ceremonies which were to accompany the new rite, and as to the ' Ornaments ' of the Church and the Minister. The First Prayer Book of 1549 continued the existing custom for the most part as to the Ornaments of the Minister so far as parish churches were concerned. It expressly ordered the Celebrant to wear an alb with a vestment or cope, and the Sacred Ministers to wear albs with tunicles. For the Ante-Communion service, when no celebration followed, the officiant was to wear an alb or surplice, with a cope ; for matins and evensong, at baptisms and burials, a surplice. In cathedrals and colleges, but not of necessity in other places, the clergy in quire were to wear surplice and hood ; and the hood also was recommended to be worn by preachers. For a bishop too the old use was retained ; over his rochet (which he wore out of church) he was to put on a surplice or alb with a cope or vestment, and his pastoral staff was to be carried either by himself or by his chaplain.

The term vestment here used denotes not a garment but a set of garments, usually made in suit of the same material ; it comprised normally at least (1) chasuble, (2) stole, and (3) fanon or maniple, but it was capable, especially in certain connections, of comprising a much larger series of required ornaments. With the alb the girdle and amice were universally worn ; indeed, the alb without them was incomplete. The rubric therefore is in a sense ambiguous, just as it would be to describe a man as wearing a plain white shirt and a tweed suit : the description is adequate to any one who knows the customs of the day, but it is not exhaustive.

At this stage there was no controversy as to the dress of the minister, and no change was made by the book of 1549. Bucer noted at the time that, as a concession to the conservatives, the vestments commonly used in the sacrament of the Eucharist are being retained. There is nowhere any justification for a theory which the *Encyclopædia Britannica* has borrowed from a German Jesuit, that the stole and girdle were abolished in England in 1549.

Three years later the concession was withdrawn, for the Second Book restricted the archbishop or bishop to his rochet and the priest or deacon to a surplice only. The vestiarian controversy began, however, with the Elizabethan book of 1559, which is the immediate source of the present Ornaments Rubric. The compromise then adopted was that the book should be that of 1552 (with a few changes), not that of 1549, but with a proviso that the ornaments of 1549 should be retained until other order should be taken. Consequently the older Ornaments Rubric of 1552 did not appear in 1559, but in its place a rubric framed as the equivalent of the proviso in the Act of Uniformity. The clause stating that other order might be taken in the matter was omitted, but a reference was made to the Act itself, which was printed in full at the beginning of the book.

There have been three questions raised as to the rubric. First, whether the words ' such ornaments in the church as were in use by authority of Parliament in the second year of the reign of King Edward the VI.' refer to the First Prayer Book or to the months preceding its issue. It is now generally agreed that the reference is to the former.

Secondly, it is questioned whether the rubric was ever superseded by ' other order ' taken in the matter; and thirdly, whether if this was the case in Elizabeth's reign, the present rubric (which is not that of 1559 but of 1662) is affected by it or is independent of it and supersedes it. The present rubric only differs from that of 1559 by deserting the phraseology of 1552 in order to follow more exactly the Proviso.

With regard to these questions, it must be remembered that the rubric was never fully complied with either between 1559 and 1661 or in the century and a half following the issue of the new rubric of 1662. There is no clearly proved instance of the wearing of chasuble or stole all through these periods. Already, before the Act was passed in 1559, such ornaments were being destroyed up and down the country; more perished, and with some better show of authority, during the Royal Visitation in the summer of 1559; and thenceforward the destruction slowly continued as it became more and more evident that (to use a phrase of Parker's, *q.v.*) they ' serve not to use at these days.' The difficulty of the time was to obtain obedience to the rubric in any degree. In 1560 the bishops attempted to secure a cope at the Eucharist and a surplice at other services, but without much success. In 1566 they reduced their demand still further to a surplice in parish churches, and copes at the Eucharist only in cathedral and collegiate churches. But still disobedience prevailed, and after this minimum demand was strengthened by being formulated in Canons 24 and 25 of 1604, there were few cathedrals that set the example of conformity and many incumbents who disliked or refused the surplice.

As to the question whether the Crown took other order there are two suggestions in the affirmative. Some have treated the Injunctions (*q.v.*) of 1559 as being such action. It was undoubtedly royal action, but so vague is the thirtieth Injunction that it probably refers only to the outdoor clerical dress; and if it be supposed, as it has been by some, to be a return to the rubric of the book of 1552, there is no accounting for the insistence on the cope, which that rubric forbad, in 1560, 1566, and 1604.

Others have seen a taking of other order in the Advertisements (*q.v.*) of 1566, and it was on this ground that the Privy Council decided against the legality of the Edwardine vestments (*Ridsdale v. Clifton*, 1877, 2 P.D. 276). But further investigation has justified those who maintained the contrary; for historically it seems certain that the Advertisements had no royal authority accorded to them; and, if that is so, the Privy Council decision rests upon a misapprehension. The whole question is intricate, but it has recently been reinvestigated by a series of historians, and following in their wake by a committee of bishops of the Convocation of Canterbury, who conclude ' that the Ornaments Rubric cannot rightly be interpreted as excluding the use of all vestments for the clergy other than the surplice in parish churches, and, in cathedral and collegiate churches, the surplice hood and cope.'

This conclusion is reached by the bishops only after the study of the third question, viz. the effect of the action taken in 1661 and 1662. The Privy Council judgment took the rubric of 1662 to be a mere continuance of the existing state of things, and therefore to be qualified by the Advertisements, and authorise only surplice and cope. But it is to be observed that the bishops refused the petition of the Puritans, who demanded to have the rubric excluded or altered, on the ground that ' it seemeth to bring back the cope, alb, etc., and other vestments,' which they also described as obsolete ceremonies. It is clear therefore as a matter of history that they had this point before them when they decided to remodel the rubric, and renew the reference to the book of 1549 as the authority to be followed in this respect.

Further investigation has therefore cut away the ground from under the Privy Council decision of 1877. The historians have discredited it increasingly, and an eminent lawyer at the time (Chief Baron Kelly) described it as a judgment of policy, not of law. [RITUAL CASES.]

The Ornaments Rubric is now generally recognised as authorising in its true interpretation the ornaments of 1549. It may seem even to enforce them ; but other ceremonial rubrics are, as a rule, not necessarily to be carried out in the fullest degree everywhere : and if this one in its present form seems to demand too uncompromisingly, a simple change of 'shall' to 'may' would give room for discretion and authorise the two usages now prevailing, and justified, the one by enactment and the other by tradition. [VESTMENTS.]   [W. H. F.]

The Ornaments of the Ch. and its Ministers, Convocation Report, No. 116 (1908) ; Frere, *Principles of Religious Ceremonial,* c. xiv.

OSMUND, St. (d. 1099), Bishop of Sarum, is described in the Commemoration Service in use in Salisbury Cathedral as 'builder of the Cathedral Church of Old Sarum, founder of the Cathedral Chapter, and giving lustre to the Church by the "Use of Sarum." '

St. Osmund was 'probably an earl' (Bishop J. Wordsworth), son of Henry, Count of Séez, by Isabella, daughter of Robert, Duke of Normandy. He came over as a chaplain to his uncle, the Conqueror, and became Chancellor, *c.* 1072-8. He was employed on the Domesday survey at Grantham, and was present at the Council of Sarum in April 1086 when the results of the valuation were laid before William. Osmund's own labours are said to have extended through the north of England, while he is believed to have held the earldom of Dorset.

In 1078 he became Bishop of Sarum. [SALISBURY, SEE OF.] The cathedral of Old Sarum may have been begun by his predecessor, but Osmund may justly claim to have built the greater part. In one of his two undoubted charters he claims to have ' constructed the church of Sarum and to have constituted canons in it.' He founded a chapter on a model which H. Bradshaw discovered to be peculiar (in Normandy) to Bayeux, but which served as a model for England [CHAPTERS, CATHEDRAL], and was introduced into Scotland and Ireland. He attracted to himself a number of learned and musical clergy, worked with his own hand at writing and binding books for their library, made (so tradition testifies) an ordinal of divine service [SARUM USE], and endowed canonries with a generosity so businesslike that he was slanderously reported to be covetous and grasping. Besides lands the endowments consisted of half the oblations (excepting the ornaments) laid upon the high altar, and

the whole of the offerings on the other altars ; burial fees and half the offerings made at funerals when the bishop himself was celebrating, excepting half the gold offered in church. When any canon died two-thirds of that year's income of the vacated prebend was to go into a common fund for the surviving canons, and the other third of it to the poor (Bradshaw and Wordsworth, *Cathedral Statutes,* iii. 870). These endowments of St. Osmund continued until the prebendal stalls were disendowed on the recommendation of the Cathedral Commissioners.

According to William of Malmesbury, Osmund officiated at the retranslation of St. Aldhelm's remains in 1078, and procured from the Abbot of Malmesbury a bone of St. Aldhelm's left arm, which he placed in a silver coffer. With this relic he cured the severe illness of Archdeacon Everard, and enabled Hubald, another of his acting archdeacons, to sing the *Alleluia* at Mass on All Saints' Day. He was present at the consecration of Battle Abbey Church, 11th February 1094 (*Chron. de Bello*), and in 1095 he opposed Anselm (*q.v.*) at Rockingham, but in the May following asked his forgiveness, and was reconciled. He expiated (says William of Malmesbury) whatever faults he may have had by patiently enduring a painful disease, of which he died on the 4th of December 1099. He was buried at Old Sarum. The *Carta Osmundi de prima Institutione ecclesie* is printed in Bradshaw and Wordsworth's *Cathedral Statutes,* iii. pp. 869-71, cf. ii. p. lxxxiii *n.* and *Altera Constitutio* or *Aliae Ordinationes,* probably of the same year (1091). *ibid.,* ii. pp. 7-10. To St. Osmund, as the late Bishop J. Wordsworth declared in his commemoration sermon on 5th November 1889, those who followed him have always looked 'not only as to the founder of a cathedral body, but as to the giver to it of a ritual which made Salisbury in both respects an example to other churches.' In 1228 Bishop Richard Poore, who embodied as much as possible of Osmund's two charters in the Sarum Ordinal and Consuetudinary of his day, and to whom the fuller development of Sarum use is mainly to be attributed, procured a Bull from Gregory IX. for holding an inquiry into the grounds for allowing his great predecessor's canonisation. Successive bishops and chapters and kings of England repeated the petition, but not until 1457, after the canons of Salisbury had contributed £700 and carried on negotiations for upwards of four years, was the request granted. Osmund's remains were removed from Old Sarum to the Lady Chapel at Salisbury, and were buried there. His relics were translated to the shrine in July 1457.

Three Dorset churches—Evershot, Melbury Osmond, and Osmington—bear ancient dedications in St. Osmund's honour. Remains of his shrine, with six apertures, are now in Sarum Cathedral nave.

In 1472 Sixtus IV. granted an indulgence to all who visited Salisbury Cathedral on St. Osmund's feast, and on 21st March 1481 an assembly at St. Paul's, London, ordered 4th December to be observed in his honour.

[c. w.]

Authorities quoted in text: Rich Jones, *Fasti Sarisb.*; C. Wordsworth, *Continuation of Lincoln Black Book* and *Cathedral Statutes*; C. L. Kingsford in *D.N.B.*; an account of the canonisation proceedings, ed. A. R. Malden for Wilts Record Soc., 1901.

OSWALD, ST. (604 ?-42), King of Northumbria, son of Ethelfrid of Bernicia by Acha, sister of Edwin of the rival house of Deira, on the defeat and death of his father in 617 took shelter, together with his brothers, with the Scots of Dalriada, among whom he received baptism, dwelling for a time with the monks of Iona, and perhaps also in Ireland. When his elder brother Eanfrid, who had apostatised, was slain by the British King Cadwalla in 634, Oswald, encouraged by a vision of St. Columba, defeated and slew Cadwalla at Heavenfield, near Hexham. His victory made him King of Bernicia, to which, as Edwin's nephew, he reunited Deira ; he added Lindsey, and gained supreme influence over other kingdoms of English, Britons, Picts, and Scots, was termed *totius Britanniae imperator*, and became reckoned among the kings called Bretwaldas. He stood godfather to the West Saxon King Cynegils, married his daughter, said to be named Cyneburga, and joined him, apparently as his superior, in granting Dorchester to Birinus (*q.v.*). Anxious for the evangelisation of his people, he applied to the monks of Iona for a bishop ; one was sent, but resigned his mission, and Aidan (*q.v.*) was sent in his place. Oswald forwarded Aidan's work in all possible ways, and at first acted as his interpreter. Profuse in charity, at one Easter feast he gave the food prepared for him to the poor, and ordered the silver dish on which it was served to be broken up and distributed among them. On this Aidan prayed that his hand might never decay. He was defeated and slain by Penda, the heathen King of Mercia, at Maserfield, identified with Oswestry (Oswald's Cross), Shropshire, on 5th August 642. As he fell he prayed for the souls of his men

fighting round him. His head and hands were fixed on poles, and the next year were removed to Northumbria ; the right hand was believed to be undecayed five centuries later. In 875 his head was placed in St. Cuthbert's coffin, where it still was at Durham in 1828. Many miracles were ascribed to his relics. He left a son Ethelwald [see under Oswy]. [w. h.]

Bede, *H.E.*; Reginald, *Vita S. Oswaldi* (twelfth century), *ap.* Sym. Dunelm. *Opp.*; Adamnan, *Vita S. Columbae.*

OSWY, or **OSWIN** (612 ?-71), King of Northumbria, brother of Oswald (*q.v.*), was, like him, brought up and received baptism among the Scots. After Oswald's death in 642, and a hard struggle with Penda of Mercia, he established himself as King in Bernicia, while in 644 Oswin, a cousin of Edwin, became King in Deira. Oswy married Eanflaed, the daughter of Edwin. As his power increased he made war on Oswin, who fled before him, was betrayed and murdered by his command in 651 at Gilling, where at Eanflaed's request and in atonement he gave land for a monastery, in which prayers should be said for Oswin's soul. Deira, however, accepted Ethelwald, Oswald's son, as King. Oswy persuaded Penda's son Peada, under-king of the Mid-Angles, to be baptized and receive Christian teachers as a condition of marrying his daughter, and converted Sigeberht, the East Saxon King, and sent Cedd (*q.v.*) to evangelise that people. In 655 Penda, who had slain five Christian kings, pressed him hard, but Oswy defeated and slew him on the Winwaed, apparently in the Leeds district. In fulfilment of a vow made before the battle he gave lands for the foundation of twelve monasteries. This victory enabled him to reunite Deira with the northern kingdom, and he made his son Alchfrid under-king over it. He warred successfully against the Britons, had power over the Scots, and probably even greater dominance over other English kings than Oswald, and he also came to be reckoned as a Bretwalda. His wife Eanflaed, Alchfrid, and Wilfrid (*q.v.*) urged him to accept the Roman ecclesiastical usages, favoured by the Deiran party in his kingdom, in place of the Scotic, which were observed in Bernicia. He presided over a conference on this question at Whitby in 664, and decided in favour of the Catholic Easter, and the Scotic clergy either left England or conformed. His decision was probably due to political rather than ecclesiastical reasons. When Wilfrid, who had become Bishop of Northumbria, stayed long abroad, he gave his bishopric to Chad (*q.v.*), and perhaps in connection with this change Alchfrid rebelled against him, and he made another son, Egfrid, under-king in his stead. In 667, acting as superior King, he joined Egbert of Kent in asking Pope Vitalian to consecrate Wighard to Canterbury. At Archbishop Theodore's request he sent Chad to be bishop of the Mercians, and he received Wilfrid as Bishop of York. Wilfrid gained great influence over him, and Oswy hoped to make a pilgrimage to Rome in his company; but he died on 15th February 671, and was buried at Whitby. He had a natural son, Aldfrid, King of Northumbria, 685-705 ?

[W. H.]

OVERALL, John (1560-1619), Bishop of Norwich, was born at Hadleigh, educated at the Grammar School there and at St. John's, Cambridge. In 1578 entered Trinity College as a scholar, became Minor Fellow, 1581, and in 1596 Senior Fellow, and then Master of Catherine Hall and Regius Professor of Divinity, holding both offices till 1607. He had been ordained in 1592, and held the vicarage of Epping. At Cambridge he opposed the prevailing Calvinism, and his appointment to the professorship was a sign that strict Genevan doctrine was on the wane, for Dr. Whitaker, his predecessor, had had a share in framing the Lambeth Articles (1595). [CALVINISM.]

In 1602 he succeeded Nowell (*q.v.*) as Dean of St. Paul's, and during his tenure of this office held two rectories in Hertfordshire, one of them for a year after his acceptance of a bishopric. At the Hampton Court Conference (*q.v.*) in 1604 he took a prominent part in the discussion on Predestination, and gave satisfaction to James I.; and when Dr. Reynold's request for an addition to the Church Catechism was granted Overall amended and abbreviated a form prepared by Nowell.

The present questions and answers on the Sacraments are, with a few verbal alterations made in 1661, due to him. Overall also took part in another result of the conference, the revision of the Bible, being on the Westminster Committee which took in hand Genesis to 2 Kings, under Andrewes (*q.v.*) as president (1611). In 1605 he became Prolocutor of the Lower House of Convocation of Canterbury. The King had been anxious to obtain Church opinion on his support of the Dutch against Spain. Convocation agreed upon a book with a number of canons, so-called, on the subject. The title was *Concerning the Government of God's*

Catholic Church and the Kingdom of the World. Its authors have been condemned as advocates of arbitrary government. As a matter of fact, they were attempting to defend the position of national sovereigns against papal attacks. James, however, refused to sanction Canon 28, which allowed a 'new form of government' which had originated in successful rebellion. The book would probably have been forgotten had not Sancroft (*q.v.*) published it, a few days before his suspension, as *Bishop Overall's Convocation Book*, obviously overlooking the force of Canon 28. Sherlock (*q.v.*) took advantage of Overall's authority to make his peace with the *de facto* King William III.

In 1614 Overall became Bishop of Coventry and Lichfield, and was translated to Norwich, 1618. His pupil, Cosin (*q.v.*), tells us that he used the Prayer of Oblation immediately after Consecration and before Communion (*Works*, v. 114), and Fuller (*q.v.*) that as bishop he was 'a discreet presser of conformity.' Although he has left no great works of his own, he gave Voss much material for his *History of the Pelagian Controversy*, and had much influence on Laud (*q.v.*) and Cosin. The latter erected a monument and wrote his epitaph (1669) in Norwich Cathedral.

[B. B.]

OXFORD MOVEMENT is the name generally given to the religious movement which began in 1833, since its chief agents were members of the University of Oxford, and Oxford was its centre until 1845.

The Church in England had become by 1833 bitterly unpopular. Its bishops, in the House of Lords, had taken considerable part in rejecting the Reform Bill of 1831 (twenty-one of the majority of forty-one were bishops). Its beneficed clergy, to a large extent squires and country gentlemen, were members of the unpopular Tory party. There was, in the words of a political opponent, 'a black recruiting sergeant in every village.' The riots at Bristol in 1831 had resulted in the burning of the bishop's palace, and when the Reform Bill of 1832 had passed it was believed that the triumphant Whig ministers would treat the Church as they had treated the un-reformed House of Commons and improve it away. Spiritually the Church was weak. The Evangelical Movement had spent much of its force, and was confined principally to fashionable watering-places, as Bath, Cheltenham, and Tunbridge Wells, and to proprietary chapels in the large towns. Its influence on the people at large was being exercised chiefly through the dissenters.

The old High Church party was small and select, but timid and cautious. It included such men as Joshua Watson (*q.v.*), Bishops Blomfield (*q.v.*), Phillpotts (*q.v.*), and Archbishop Howley (*q.v.*), but its influence did not reach beyond a limited circle of dignified churchmen, and was more confined than that of the Evangelicals. The bulk of the clergy and laity seem to have been outside both spheres of influence, and quiet worldliness was the distinguishing feature of Church life. A small band of 'Liberals' (called earlier the 'Noetics') existed: their centre had been originally at Oriel College, Oxford. Whigs in politics, their aims were chiefly to relax subscription to creeds and formularies in favour of comprehension. Their influence was as limited as that of the High Churchmen. They were aghast at the state of affairs, and the most prominent among them, Dr. Arnold (*q.v.*), wrote in 1832 : 'The Church as it now stands no human power can save.' His project and that of his school was to break down all barriers between the Church and dissenters and to form one federated National Protestant Establishment, loosing the ties which bound the English Church to the One Holy Catholic and Apostolic Church.

But the Movement was called forth not only by the political dangers of the Reform time. Charles Lloyd, Bishop of Oxford and Regius Professor of Divinity, had in 1823 begun private lectures to the younger Fellows of colleges, and his course on the history of the Prayer Book had taught them that its sources were primitive and mediæval, and had set them to study sympathetically the devotions of the pre-Reformation Church. W. Palmer's *Origines Liturgicae*, published in 1832, turned men's eyes in the same direction.

The struggle over Roman Catholic Emancipation was another active cause. The victorious Roman Catholics under Daniel O'Connell were allied with the Whigs against the English Church, and the Oxford Movement was born partly 'out of the anti-Roman feelings of the Emancipation time. . . . It was to avert the danger of people becoming Romanists from ignorance of Church principles.' This is witnessed to in the preface to Mr. Keble's famous sermon on 'National Apostasy' (see below), and the earliest advertisement for the *Tracts for the Times* (see below) describes them as 'Tracts . . . against Popery and Dissent.' But over and above these causes there was the hatred of 'Liberalism' in religion, by which was meant 'the tendencies of modern thought to destroy the basis of revealed religion, and ultimately of all that can be called religion

at all' (Church). It was the spirit which, released at the French Revolution, had got to work in the lecture-rooms of German universities and was beginning to influence thought in England in the doctrine that education, civilisation, rational intelligence, 'the march of mind,' would cure the evils and sorrows of mankind.

In 1832 it seemed as if, in Arnold's phrase, no human power could save the Church. Yet that supreme work was reserved for a devoted and brilliant band who were united in membership of the most distinguished Oxford college of the day, Oriel, and in a passionate loyalty to the English Church. They had studied and cared for its past, they deplored its present, but they hoped high for its future. Their senior and leader was John Keble (*q.v.*), who had learnt the old Catholic truths from his father, a Gloucestershire vicar. A sermon on 'National Apostasy,' preached by him in the university pulpit on Sunday, 14th July 1833, was the formal beginning of the Movement. The sermon was evoked by a Bill, then before Parliament, for suppressing ten Irish bishoprics. Men saw in this the prelude of spoliation, and felt that a crisis had come. Following this sermon, on 25th July, four clergy met in conference at Hadleigh Rectory, Suffolk, to concert practical measures. They were the rector, Hugh James Rose (*q.v.*), a Cambridge man ; the Rev. William Palmer, a learned Dublin graduate, living in Oxford; the Rev. the Honble. A. P. Perceval, a dignified country clergyman; and the Rev. R. H. Froude (*q.v.*), the intimate friend of Keble and Newman (*q.v.*). The conference lasted four days, and two points were agreed on to fight for, the doctrine of the Apostolical Succession and the integrity of the Prayer Book. There was a further idea of founding an 'Association,' which the Oriel men disliked and which was never realised, but two addresses to Archbishop Howley, one from seven thousand clergy, the other from two hundred and thirty thousand heads of families (in drafting which Joshua Watson took part), were signed and presented during 1834 ; they were results of the Hadleigh Conference. Far more important and far-reaching were the *Tracts for the Times, written by Members of the University of Oxford*, the first three of which were issued on 9th September 1833. These were begun 'out of his own head' by John Henry Newman (*q.v.*), the other great leader of the Movement, and Fellow of Oriel. These early Tracts (which furnished a nickname for the Movement : its adherents were called 'Tractarians') are unique. 'Clear, brief, stern in their appeal to conscience and reason, they are like the short, sharp, rapid utterances of men in pain and danger and pressing emergency.' They were the first public utterances of the Movement as a whole, and ' they rang out like pistol shots.' No wonder, since their authors were among the ablest men of the day: Keble, Newman, Froude, and later Pusey (*q.v.*). At first the older and more dignified men, W. Palmer and A. P. Perceval, were alarmed by the Tracts; later on both wrote in the series. The accession of Dr. Pusey to the Tract-writers in 1834 gave a fresh basis to the Movement. He gave it 'a position and a name,' for he was profoundly learned, of great weight in Oxford, and from his family connections well known outside it. And he was 'a man of large designs,' and soon took his place with Keble and Newman as one of the leaders.

The object of the Tracts, as of the Movement as a whole, was to recall men to the foundations on which churchmanship rested. They defended the Church not as a State establishment, but as the Divine Society founded by the Lord Jesus Christ, endowed with supernatural powers, the trustee of the revealed Catholic faith, and the possessor of a ministry which descended directly from the apostles. This teaching, which had been that of the Caroline Divines (*q.v.*) and the Non-jurors (*q.v.*), had been largely obscured in the previous century, though it was still held, at least in its main outlines, by the older High Churchmen, like Joshua Watson, and by the suffering remnant of the Church in Scotland. The Movement quickly gathered force, partly from the intellectual brilliance of its members, partly from the holiness of their lives. Besides Keble, Newman, and Pusey, they included R. I. Wilberforce (*q.v.*), R. H. Froude, R. W. Church (*q.v.*), C. Marriott (*q.v.*). I. Williams (*q.v.*), J. B. Mozley (*q.v.*), and among their sympathisers were M. J. Routh (*q.v.*), Dean Hook (*q.v.*), H. E. Manning (*q.v.*), and Gladstone (*q.v.*). But the revival provoked bitter opposition. Archbishop Whateley (*q.v.*) and Dr. Arnold attacked it savagely, while some Evangelicals, as Bishop D. Wilson (*q.v.*), regarded it as the work of Satan. The English bishops were at the best, as Phillpotts and Blomfield, timid and cautious, and denounced extravagances warmly. Until 1843 one of the greatest forces of the Movement in Oxford was Newman's sermons, preached in his place as Vicar of St. Mary's. 'Without them,' says Dean Church, 'the Movement would never have been what it was. The sermons created

a moral atmosphere in which men judged the questions in debate.' The English Church has ever been strong in preachers, but rarely have sermons like those of Newman at St. Mary's been preached and listened to.

Attacks on the Movement came not only from Broad Churchmen and Evangelicals, but from Roman Catholics and the University authorities. The Roman Catholics were led by Cardinal Wiseman, who began his attack on the position claimed for the English Church in Lent, 1836. The University authorities, for the most part complacent, unlearned, and pompous folk, given chiefly to politics and the pleasures of the table, at first regarded the Movement with smiles and jokes, or with contemptuous indifference. Later this attitude changed into one of 'helpless and passionate hostility.' 'Blind and dull as tea-table gossips,' they failed to see that the Movement which they disliked was one 'for deeper religion, for a loftier morality, for more genuine self-devotion . . . .' and they treated it as a mere revival of popery. From 1836 onwards there were unceasing attacks by the Latitudinarians and Evangelicals, the Oxford authorities and the Roman Catholics. Further difficulties arose from a new party in the Movement itself. These ' cut into it at an angle ' and tried to deflect its course in their own direction. Able and brilliant to a man, they despised the solid Anglican foundations on which the older men had built. Among them were W. G. Ward, F. W. Faber, F. Oakeley, all of whom went to Rome: indeed, 'their direction was unquestionably Romeward almost from the beginning of their connection with the Movement.' In 1839 doubts as to his position crossed Newman's mind, and early in 1841, with a view to meeting them and to answering the difficulties raised by the extreme men, he published Tract No. 90, *Remarks on certain Passages in the Thirty-nine Articles.* The Heads of Houses at Oxford (with two exceptions) hastily branded it as dishonest, though many of the old High Churchmen, as Hook and Palmer, defended it.

The condemnation of this Tract by many English bishops, the Jerusalem Bishopric (*q.v.*), and further doubts raised by his study of Church history, ' broke' Newman by the end of the year. In February 1842 he retired to Littlemore, and resigned his living, 18th September 1843. May 1843 Dr. Pusey was suspended by the Vice-Chancellor from preaching before the University for two years on account of a sermon on the Holy Eucharist. 1844 W. G. Ward published *The Ideal of a*

Christian Church—a Romanising book. The Oxford Heads seized their chance. In February 1845 in Convocation at Oxford the book was censured and Ward deprived of his degrees, but a proposal to condemn Tract No. 90 was vetoed by the proctors. Guillemard and Church. After this the Romeward drift began. Ward and his friends went first. Newman was received at Littlemore, 9th October 1845. The main body, under Keble, Pusey, and Marriott, stood firm; but for years to be a ' Tractarian ' or a ' Puseyite ' was to be a man proscribed, and the victorious authorities did their best to extirpate the Movement in Oxford. It spread to the country and the great towns. Although from 1836 to 1845 the Tractarians were ' fighting for their lives,' they did much amid the storm of controversy to justify their appeal to the Anglican divines and to the Fathers of the Church. In 1836 a *Library of the Fathers* was begun, under the joint editorship of Keble, Newman, and Pusey—a series of scholarly translations—the main burden of which after 1845 fell on Charles Marriott and broke him down. The *Anglo-Catholic Library*, begun about the same time, reprinting the works of the Caroline divines, was another splendid witness to the sound learning and scholarship of the men of the Movement. The wonder is that in so brief a time they accomplished so much. ' There were giants in the earth in those days.' In 1850 the Gorham judgment [GORHAM, G. C.] caused a further crisis and a large secession. Manning, R. I. Wilberforce, and many more joined the Roman Catholic Church, but the leaders again stood firm. The principles of the Movement, as carried out in practice in the large towns, at first roused much opposition. There were riots in London, at St. Barnabas, Pimlico, 1850, and at St. George's in the East, 1859-60. [LOWDER, C. F.; MACKONOCHIE, A. H.] Dr. J. M. Neale (*q.v.*) experienced much mob violence. The press from 1850-70 bitterly ridiculed the revival, and the Court was also hostile. The bishops, with few exceptions, as S. Wilberforce (*q.v.*) and W. K. Hamilton of Salisbury, were chosen from opponents of the Movement. The ability and religious force of the leaders triumphed over these difficulties, and the power of the younger men, Dr. Liddon (*q.v.*) and Dr. King (*q.v.*), together with wider knowledge of history and theology, modified the old hatred. The leaders of both political parties from 1880-1900, Mr. Gladstone and Lord Salisbury, sympathised with the Movement, and from the primacy of Archbishop Benson (*q.v.*) the

era of persecution ceased. The truth and force of the revival made itself felt on all hands, it began a fresh period of Church life and energy, and hardly a church in communion with the see of Canterbury fails to show trace of the Movement which began at Oxford in 1833.   [S. L. O.]

R. W. Church, *Oxford Movement*; Newman, *Apologia* and *Letters and Correspondence*; *Lives* of Pusey, Keble, Church.

OXFORD, See of, was formed by Henry VIII. out of that of Lincoln (*q.v.*). In a list of proposed new bishoprics drawn up in 1539 occurs ' Oseney cum Thame,' and on 1st September 1542 were issued the Letters Patent of erection of ' the late monastery of Oseney to be the cathedral church of a bishop, dean, and six prebendaries, with the King's chaplain, Robert King, Bishop " Ronensis " *in partibus* (and late Abbot of Oseney and Thame), as its first bishop, having for his palace the college or mansion called Gloucester College . . . the office not to prejudice the University of Oxon '; while to the dean and chapter of Oxford were given the site, church, and furniture of the late abbey of Oseney. At the same time the town of Oxford was created a city. The new see thus obtained a considerable share of monastic property, for besides the grant of most of the possessions of Oseney and Thame, the palace designed for the bishop was simply the old Benedictine college. The diocese was a small one, consisting merely of the city and county of Oxford. For three years it possessed two deans and chapters—that of Oxford, with its seat at Oseney, and that of Christ Church, with its seat at St. Frideswide's. But in 1545 the King resumed possession of the lands of both, and in 1546 they were amalgamated, and St. Frideswide's was constituted as the cathedral church with a dean and eight canons. In 1858 the University Commission suppressed two canonries, and annexed five to professorships in the University and one to the archdeaconry of Oxford. After 1546 Oseney fell rapidly into decay, and to-day not a stone of the abbey church is visible. The bishops, too, lost their palace (which eventually became Worcester College), and were forced to live on one or other of their scattered estates, until Bishop Bancroft built the palace at Cuddesdon early in the next century. The earlier history of the see of Oxford is not very inspiring. The diocese was the smallest in England ; the cathedral was also a college chapel; during the first sixty years of its existence the see was vacant no less than forty.

Few of the bishops before Wilberforce were men of distinction. Many of the seventeenth and eighteenth-century prelates were academic pedants immersed in the pettinesses of University business, and ignorant both of the world and of themselves. With the seventeenth century a proper succession of bishops began, but the outbreak of the Civil War brought new disasters. The Royalist garrison of Oxford burned the newly erected palace of Cuddesdon, and Bishop Skinner was forced to live in retirement at Launton, carrying on the succession of the clergy by numerous and secret ordinations. After the Restoration Bishop Fell (*q.v.*) began the rebuilding of Cuddesdon, which remains much as he left it. The difficulties in which the University and diocese were placed by the arbitrary acts of James II. can be best understood by the King's dealings with Oxford through his various tools, of whom Bishop Parker (*q.v.*) was one of the basest. In the eighteenth century the chief interest lies in the growth of Methodism [NONCONFORMITY : Methodism] in the University and in the cordial relations which subsisted between John Wesley (*q.v.*) and Bishop Potter ; so in the early nineteenth century between the early Tractarians and Bishops Lloyd and Bagot. Under Bishop Bagot the see attained an accession of territory and dignity. Ecton (1711) gives the value as £381, 11s. 0½d. Berkshire was transferred from the diocese of Salisbury by Order in Council of 10th October 1836, and with it the chancellorship of the Order of the Garter. The county of Buckingham was transferred from the diocese of Lincoln by Order in Council of 19th July 1837, and the diocese became from the smallest one of the largest in England. It now contains 648 parishes, with a population in 1911 of 695,878. Of the three archdeaconries Oxford and Bucks both date from about 1078, and Berks from the twelfth century.

BISHOPS

1. Robert King, 1542, College of Bernardines, Oxford ; Abbot of Brewerne. Thame, and Oseney ; suffragan of Lincoln under the title *Reonensis in partibus* (perhaps Oreos in the island of Eubœa and province of Athens) : a man of exceedingly accommodating disposition ; accepted the post of Abbot of Oseney, while still holding Thame, for the express purpose of surrendering both abbeys ; retained his see uninterruptedly till the end of Mary's reign, and sat at Cranmer's trial ; the fine old house, known as Bishop King's house, in St. Aldate's, Oxford, is unanimously attributed to him by the Oxford handbooks, but there is no real evidence that it was built by him ; d. 1557 ; buried in the cathedral.

Thomas Goldwell, 1558 ; All Souls, Oxford ; chaplain to Cardinal Pole (*q.v.*) ; a violent papalist ; Bishop of St. Asaph, 1555 ; nominated Bishop of Oxford, November 1558, but as he was not yet in possession of the see at Mary's death it is doubtful if he should be placed in the succession ; he fled to the Continent, and spent the rest of his life chiefly in Italy ; d. 1585. See vacant more than nine years.

2. Hugh Curwen, or Coren, 1567 ; possessed a conscience which never acted to the detriment of its owner's interests ; he was educated both at Cambridge and Oxford ; was Dean of Hereford in the reign of Edward VI., and Archbishop of Dublin, 1555-67, when this 'old unprofitable workman,' whose morals were as suspect as his language was notorious, was nominated to Oxford : d. 1568. See vacant twenty-one years.

3. John Underhill, 1589 ; New College ; Rector of Lincoln College, 1576 ; was persuaded to take the see 'in a way to a better,' but 'ere the first-fruits were paid he died in much discontent and poverty,' 1592. See vacant eleven years, ' a prey to the Earl of Essex.'

4. John Bridges, 1604 ; Fellow of Pembroke College, Cambridge ; Dean of Salisbury, 1577 ; ranks high as an Anglican controversialist, both against the Roman party as represented by Sanders and Campion and against the Puritans : his vast *Defence of the Government Established in the Church of Englande for Ecclesiasticall Matters* (1587) was the immediate cause of the first Marprelate Tracts, the first of which assails Bridges both as a bore and as a defender of ' the proud popish, presumptuous, profane, paultrie, pestilent, and pernicious prelates, bishop of Hereforde and all ': d. 1618.

5. John Howson, 1618 ; Christ Church : earned the favour of James I. by his ' sound preaching and ready penning of theologicall treatises' against Roman and Puritan opponents of the Church : tr. to Durham, 1632.

6. Richard Corbet, 1628 ; Dean of Christ Church ; poet, wit, and practical joker ; ' One time as he was confirming,' says Aubrey, ' the country people pressing

in to see the ceremonie, sayd he. "Beare off then, or I 'll confirme yee with my staffe." Another time being to lay his hand on the head of a man very bald, he turnes to his chaplayne and sayd, " Some dust, Lushington," to keepe his hand from slipping ' : tr. to Norwich 1632.

7. John Bancroft, 1632 ; nephew to Archbishop Bancroft (*q.v.*) ; Master of University College ; styled by Prynne ' a corrupt unpreaching popish prelate ' ; builder of the palace at Cuddesdon (1635), and was buried there; d. 1641.

8. Robert Skinner, 1641 : Trinity College ; tr. from Bristol ; one of the bishops committed by Parliament to the Tower, 1642 ; tr. to Worcester, 1663.

9. William Paul, 1663 ; All Souls ; Dean of Lichfield, 1661 ; d. 1665.

10. Walter Blandford, 1665 ; Warden of Wadham ; tr. to Worcester, 1671.

11. Nathaniel Crewe, 1671 ; Rector of Lincoln College ; favoured by James II. as Duke of York, by whose influence he was tr. to Durham, 1674 ; a sycophant and time-server, but extremely munificent.

12. Henry Compton, 1674 ; Canon of Christ Church ; tr. to London, 1675.

13. John Fell (*q.v.*), 1676 ; Dean of Christ Church ; d. 1686.

14. Samuel Parker (*q.v.*), 1686 ; Archdeacon of Canterbury ; d. 1688.

15. Timothy Hall, 1688 ; an obscure B.A. of Pembroke College ; rewarded with this bishopric by James II. for reading the Declaration of Indulgence, but was never in actual possession of the see ; d. 1690.

16. John Hough, 1690-9 ; President of Magdalen College after a prolonged struggle with James II. ; tr. to Coventry and Lichfield, 1699.

17. William Talbot, Oriel College ; Dean of Worcester, 1691 ; Latitudinarian ; tr. to Salisbury, 1715.

18. John Potter, 1715 ; University College ; Canon of Christ Church and Regius Professor of Divinity ; tr. to Canterbury, 1737.

19. Thomas Secker, 1737 ; Exeter College ; tr. from Bristol : tr. to Canterbury, 1758.

20. John Hume, 1758 ; tr. from Bristol ; tr. to Salisbury, 1766.

21. Robert Lowth, 1766 ; New College ; tr. from St. David's ; tr. to London, 1777.

22. John Butler, 1777 ; educated in Germany ; Sir R. Hill (*Piet. Oxon.*, 1768 ed., ii. p. 34) says that he was familiarly known as ' Dr. Pig and Castle,' from an inn at Bridgnorth, whose wealthy hostess he married, 1768 ; a Tory pamphleteer ; tr. to Hereford, 1788.

23. Edward Smallwell, 1788 ; tr. from St. David's ; d. 1799.

24. John Randolph, 1799 ; Canon of Christ Church and Regius Professor of Divinity ; tr. to Bangor, 1807.

25. Charles Moss, 1807 ; Christ Church ; owed his fortune, ecclesiastical and financial, to his father, Charles Moss, Bishop of Bath and Wells ; d. 1811.

26. William Jackson, 1811 ; Canon of Christ Church and Regius Professor of Greek ; appointed to the see by the Prince Regent only because his elder brother, Dean Cyril Jackson, had already refused it ; is described as ' very self-indulgent,' as indeed his portrait displays him ; d. 1815.

27. Edward Legge, 1815 ; Dean of Windsor ; d. 1827.

28. Charles Lloyd, 1827 ; Canon of Christ Church and Regius Professor of Divinity, in which office he exercised considerable influence on the future leaders of the Oxford Movement ; d. 1829.

29. Richard Bagot, 1829 ; Christ Church, Oxford ; Fellow of All Souls ; Dean of Canterbury ; sympathised generally with the Tractarians ; tr. to Bath and Wells, 1846.

30. Samuel Wilberforce (*q.v.*), 1846 ; Dean of Westminster ; tr. to Winchester, 1869.

31. John Fielder Mackarness, 1869 ; Merton College ; Prebendary of Exeter ; eminent Liberal High Churchman ; d. 1889.

32. William Stubbs (*q.v.*), 1889 ; tr. from Chester ; d. 1901.

33. Francis Paget, 1901 ; Canon, 1884, and Dean, 1892, of Christ Church ; through his learning, piety, and power he will be ranked as one of the greatest bishops of the see ; d. 1911.

34. Charles Gore, 1911 ; Fellow of Trinity College ; tr. from Birmingham.

[G. B.]

Marshall, *Dio. Hist.*: *V.C.H.*, Oxford, Berks, Bucks.

P

PACE, Richard (1482 ?-1536), scholar, diplomatist, and Dean of St. Paul's, was born in or near Winchester and educated in the Bishop's School there, at Queen's College, Oxford, and at Padua, where he became acquainted with Erasmus. He was a distinguished scholar, who amused himself by translating Plutarch into Latin, and did much for the study of Greek at Oxford and Cambridge, but the best part of his active life was spent as a diplomatist.

He accompanied Archbishop Bainbridge to York to Rome. Bainbridge was murdered, and Silvestro dei Gigli, Bishop of Worcester, was suspected. Pace did his best to bring the crime to light, and Pope Leo x., attracted by his faithfulness to his employer, recommended him to Henry VIII. (*q.v.*), to whom he became secretary on his return to England in 1515. In the same year he went as ambassador to Switzerland to counteract the growing French power. In 1518 he went to Germany to endeavour to procure the election of Henry as Emperor, and though unsuccessful was made Dean of St. Paul's on his return. In 1520 he attended Henry at the Field of the Cloth of Gold, and preached a sermon on the blessings of peace. In 1521 he translated into Latin Fisher's sermon on the papal bull against Luther, and went to Italy to procure Wolsey's election as Pope, and again on the same errand in 1523 on the death of Adrian VI. Returning home on the election of Clement VII., he was soon sent on a mission to Venice. While there he failed in mind and body, became incapable of discharging his public duties, and was under some form of restraint until his death. His benefices and preferments were many, but he can have spent little time in the discharge of the duties attached to any of them. He seems to have held simultaneously with the deanery of St. Paul's the deaneries of Salisbury and Exeter, the archdeaconry of Dorset, four prebends, two vicarages, and two rectories, besides being Reader in Greek at Cambridge.

He was in many respects a typical divine of the Renaissance, an accomplished scholar, and cultivated man of the world, amiable and of moral life, who used the Church as a means of worldly advancement and its offices as sources of revenue and dignity.

[C. P. S. C.]

Strype, *Memorials*; *D.N.B.*

PALEY, William (1743-1805), Archdeacon of Carlisle, son of the Rev. W. Paley, who was for fifty-five years headmaster of Giggleswick school, was born at Peterborough, entered Christ's College, Cambridge, in 1759, graduated as Senior Wrangler in 1763, was elected Fellow in 1766, and worked industriously as Tutor till 1776, when he was collated by the Bishop of Carlisle to the rectory of Musgrove. He held various benefices in that diocese until 1794, when he became Prebendary of St. Paul's and Sub-Dean of Lincoln, and in 1795 was collated to the valuable rectory of Monk-Wearmouth in the diocese of Durham. After he left Cambridge his life was chiefly spent in the composition of works, avowedly constructed out of materials accumulated in the course of his tutorial work, and evincing little originality or profundity, but characterised by good sense and usually by clear thinking. His chief productions are :—

1. *The Principles of Moral and Political Philosophy*, 1785; a work of much pretension and mediocre performance which won a reputation far exceeding its deserts, chiefly because of its combination of severe utilitarianism — his canon being ' Whatever is expedient is right ' — and the strictest theological orthodoxy. He effected this combination by referring ultimate human happiness to a state of future reward and punishment, awarded on the measure of obedience to arbitrary commands of the Creator. The treatise contains three good things : a contention that the will of God, and consequent moral obligations, can be ascertained no less by an inquiry into the natural consequences of human action than from the revealed declarations of Holy Scripture ; a polemic against the notion of a special ' moral sense ' by which good and evil actions may be directly discerned ; and a destructive criticism of the political theory of social contract.

2. *Horae Paulinae*, 1790 ; his ablest and most useful as well as most original work, though he himself held it cheap. It consists of an ingenious and convincing argument, showing by an examination of ' undesigned coincidences ' that neither could the Acts of the Apostles have been founded on the extant Epistles of St. Paul, nor the Epistles forged out of the information afforded by the Acts ; thus the documents mutually corro-

borate each other. It is a piece of genuine though narrow criticism, utilising all the materials available at the time. It has been well said that the most suspicious counsel at the Old Bailey could not put two witnesses through a stricter cross-examination than that to which Paley subjected the two writers. This work was speedily translated into French and German.

3. *A View of the Evidences of Christianity,* 1794; a work long overrated but now almost forgotten. It is based on a crude conception of miracles as attesting the truth of a divine revelation, the miracles themselves being attested by trustworthy witnesses. The best thing in the book is the vindication of the subjective honesty of the witnesses, based on the fact that the profession of Christianity brought them nothing but persecution and contempt. The attempted proof of the objective truth of the revelation thus attested is spoilt by the implication of the writer in a vicious circle—a curious fault in so clear-headed a man. Revelation is attested by miracles; a miracle is defined as a work of power which God alone can do; but the fact that the extraordinary events relied on are miraculous in this sense is attested only by the revelation itself.

4. *Natural Theology,* 1802; by far his best work, regarded from a literary point of view, and containing some things of permanent value. It successfully establishes the reasonableness and probability of a theistic interpretation of the universe, and fails chiefly because of his persistent attempt to make the proof demonstrative.

In the *Athenæum* of 1848 it was shown that Paley borrowed almost the whole argument of this last work, without acknowledgment, from the Cartesian Nieuwentyt's treatise on the works of the Creator, an English translation of which, *The Religious Philosopher,* appeared in 1718. The plagiarism has been defended on the ground of Paley's habitual use of his old note-books, in which he had amassed materials without indication of their source, but the borrowing here is too systematic to be covered by that explanation. It is more fully accounted for by his own defence of the lack of citations in the *Moral Philosophy,* where he contended in effect that what is published is public property, and that authors need not be cited except when they are put forward as authorities. He claimed to be 'something more than a mere compiler,' and it must be allowed that he improved at least the presentment of Nieuwentyt's argument. He

died at Lincoln, where he was keeping his annual residence as sub-dean, May 1805, and was buried at Carlisle, where he was archdeacon. [T. A. L.]

PALL (*pallium,* ὠμοφόριον). In the earliest representations, in the mosaics of the sixth century, the pallium is a scarf, woven of white wool, four or five inches broad and some twelve feet long, adorned with a fringe and a small black or red cross at each end, worn over the chasuble, looped round the shoulders so as to fall in a V shape back and front, the ends crossing, and presumably pinned, on the left shoulder and hanging down back and front. In the eighth century the pendants were drawn in and pinned to the points of the loops, so that the pallium presented a Y shape before and behind; in the course of the ninth century it was sewn into this form, so that the pins, though retained, became useless. By the eleventh century it had begun to be cut out in the shape of a circular collar, with pendants back and front (as in the arms of the see of Canterbury); but the stuff continued to be doubled on the left shoulder, a survival of the original crossing of the pendants. It was not till in and after the ninth century that the crosses were multiplied, and in particular they came to be attached to the shoulders and to the points at which the pendants were pinned to the collar; but there was no rule as to the number of them. The pall has tended to diminish in size; to-day it is only about two inches wide, and the pendants about twelve inches long, and the collar lies rather closely round the neck.

Its origin is obscure. The Græco-Roman pallium was a large quadrangular woollen wrapper—a garment which was a favourite one with Christians (see *e.g.* Tertullian, *de Pallio*), and was for long in pictorial representations the conventional dress of apostles and of early martyrs and saints (see *e.g.* the sixth-century mosaics in S. Apollinare Nuovo at Ravenna). A probable view is that in origin the ecclesiastical pallium was this garment 'contabulated,' *i.e.* folded into a strip. The eighth-century forger of the Donation of Constantine regarded the Roman pallium as the *loros* worn by the Emperor and the consuls, and as conferred by the Emperor on the Pope; and the Imperial origin of the pallium is suggested by the fact that in the sixth century the Popes asked permission of the Emperor at Constantinople before conferring the pallium on bishops outside the Imperial frontiers; while the Archbishop Maurus of Ravenna asked for and obtained the pallium direct from the Emperor. Now the

Imperial *loros* is a 'contabulate' *toga picta*; and it may well be that the pallium was originally conferred by the Emperor on prelates as parallel to the consular *loros*, but as, in its austerity, more congruous to the ecclesiastical character than its gorgeous secular counterpart.

The pallium was worn by all bishops in Merovingian Gaul, probably in Spain and Africa, and certainly, as now, in the East, where there is evidence for its use in about 400 (S. Isid. Pelus., *Epp.* i. 136). In peninsular Italy it was otherwise; there only the Pope and the Bishop of Ostia, the ordinary consecrator of the Pope, used the pallium of right at the end of the fifth century. But the Roman pallium gradually obtained a special significance. The Popes began to confer it on bishops, whether within or without their own immediate sphere, as a mark of personal distinction; first to be used only at Mass, and later on certain specified occasions; especially on their vicars, like the Bishops of Thessalonica, Justiniana Prima, and Arles— and the grant made to St. Cæsarius of Arles in 516 by Symmachus is the first certain instance recorded of the papal grant of the pallium—or on specially eminent prelates, and in course of time on all metropolitans; *e.g.* palliums were sent to several metropolitans in Gaul in the time of St. Boniface (*q.v.*), and metropolitans were required to receive them throughout the Frankish dominions under Charles the Great; while in 866 Nicolas I. lays it down that no metropolitan may be enthroned or celebrate before receiving the pallium. Consequently it comes to be interpreted as signifying the *plenitudo pontificalis officii*; while the fact that the palliums were before distribution laid for a night on the tomb of St. Peter signified that the receiver had a special share in the prerogative of the Prince of the Apostles.

In England the pallium was conferred by St. Gregory the Great (*q.v.*) on St. Augustine (*q.v.*). Laurentius and Mellitus (*q.v.*) did not receive it; but from Justus down to Reginald Pole (*q.v.*) it was regularly conferred on the metropolitans of Canterbury, except in the case of Aelfsige, who died on his way to fetch his pallium from Rome, and of Stigand, one of whose offences was that he appropriated the pallium of his extruded predecessor, Robert of Jumièges, which he used for six years before receiving one of his own from the irregular Pope, Benedict IX. Honorius I. in 734 sent a pallium for St. Paulinus (*q.v.*) of York, but he had fled south before it reached him; and the first metropolitan of York was Egbert, who received the pallium from Gregory III.

in 734, and it was granted to his successors down to Edward Lee (1531-45). The Annates Act, 1534 (25 Hen. VIII. c. 20), provided that on the election of an archbishop the Crown should signify the election to one archbishop and two bishops or to four bishops, requiring them to invest and consecrate the elect, ' and to give and use to him such *pall*, benedictions, ceremonies, and all other things requisite for the same, without suing, procuring, or obtaining any bulls, briefs, or other things at the said see of Rome, or by the authority thereof in any behalf.' Accordingly, on the elevation of Holgate (*q.v.*) to York in 1545, Cranmer (*q.v.*) blessed a pallium and conferred it on him (Cranmer's *Register*, 309*b* *sq.*). Henceforward, except in the case of Pole, the pallium was disused. [F. E. B.]

De Marca, *de Concordia*, vi. 6 *sq.*; Thomassinus, *Vet. et nova Discipl.*, i. ii. 53 *sqq.*; Duchesne, *Origines du Culte Chrétien*; W. E. Collins, *Beginnings of Eng. Christianity*; J. W. Legg, *The Blessing of the Episcopal Ornament called the Pall* (*Yorkshire Archaeol. Journal*, xv.); Braun, *Die Liturgische Gewandung* (abbreviated in *Catholic Encyclopedia*, xi.).

PANDULF (d. 1226), papal legate and Bishop of Norwich, first visited England in 1211 as the nuncio of Innocent III. (*q.v.*) to negotiate for John's submission. He was of Roman origin, and at that time a sub-deacon employed in the papal household. Nothing came of his first mission; but, according to a late authority (*Burton Annals*), he threatened to absolve the English from their allegiance, and to enforce the sentence of excommunication against John, which had been already issued but was then suspended. Pandulf came again in 1213, when John had offered submission, to present the conditions imposed by the Pope. He met the King at Dover, and received John's written promise to abide by the judgment of a legate in the matters for which he had been excommunicated (13th May). On 15th May John surrendered the realms of England and Ireland to Pandulf as the Pope's representative, promising that he and his heirs would hold them from the Roman Church, would render liege homage to the Pope, and would pay a tribute of a thousand marks. Wendover says that this surrender was exacted by the Pope. The Barnwell annalist describes it, with more probability, as the spontaneous act of John, who certainly could not have found a better method of eluding the English opposition. The further work of settlement was entrusted to a legate, Nicholas of Tusculum. But Pandulf was much employed in England during the stay of Nicholas, and after his departure, on the business of the Pope and the King. In Magna Carta (*q.v.*) Pandulf appears as one of John's counsellors and as surety for his good faith. But when Innocent quashed the Charter Pandulf excommunicated the leading barons and suspended Stephen Langton (*q.v.*). His action was upheld at Rome, but in 1216 he was superseded by the legate Gualo, and returned to Rome. In 1218 he returned to England as Gualo's successor, and for three years played a leading part in secular and ecclesiastical affairs. Both he and Honorius III., by whom his actions were minutely controlled, showed a sincere anxiety to benefit the cause of the young Henry. But Pandulf's autocratic behaviour was resented both by Langton and by Hubert de Burgh. Though bishop-elect of Norwich, the legate was exempted from Langton's jurisdiction, and made ecclesiastical appointments without reference to the archbishop. To the royal ministers and council he issued peremptory orders on the smallest of administrative questions; he supervised diplomatic negotiations, interfered in judicial business, and disposed of royal patronage. His recall was at last demanded and obtained by Langton. He resigned his legateship in July 1221, and left England; but he kept the see of Norwich, to which he was consecrated at Rome in 1222. He died in 1226, and was buried in Norwich Cathedral.

[H. W. C. D.]

Norgate, *John Lackland*; Shirley, *Royal Letters*, vol. i., Introduction; H. W. C. Davis, *Eng. under the Normans and Angevins.*

PAPACY, THE, AND ITS RELATIONS WITH THE ENGLISH CHURCH. The

history of the Papacy, both in itself and in its relations with England, falls into strongly marked periods.

1. The primitive period left Rome with a precedence of honour, with a jurisdiction, limited but definite, as a court of appeal, and with a traditional claim to great respect. The claim to succeed to the power of St. Peter, taken to imply government over the other Apostles, intensified this authority, and the Popes spoke as representing St. Peter. Amid the political disorder of the earlier Middle Ages the Papacy was able to be a real centre of unity; and its interest in missions (St. Gregory the Great (*q.v.*), St. Boniface (*q.v.*)). joined to a sense of responsibility for the new races of Europe, raised its power. With Gregory the Great a new period begins; but a word should be said as to the British

Church, partly belonging to the first period. There is little ground for asserting any special British independence of the Papacy. The British Church inherited the traditions of the period when the papal power was beginning to grow. Hence the differences between the missionaries from Rome and the Celtic Christians, which, however, gradually disappeared as Britons and English grew into unity.

2. The mission of St. Augustine (*q.v.*) came definitely from Rome, and hence England, unlike the Continent, was unaffected by the politics and traditions of the Roman Empire. Gregory the Great was definitely our 'Apostle,' and a peculiarly close connection with Rome thus began. Rome stood for a larger civilisation and a wider Christian unity. The best of the English kings and ecclesiastics felt this, and it is seen in (*a*) the definite adoption (Synod of Whitby, 664) of Roman customs; (*b*) the frequent pilgrimages to Rome; (*c*) the early institution—when exactly is doubtful—of Peter's Pence (*q.v.*) (afterwards applied to the support of the English school at Rome); (*d*) the sending to Rome for consecration of Wighard, chosen as Archbishop of Canterbury. On his death there Vitalian, the Pope, chose, although possibly not asked to do so, with great care and excellent results Theodore as archbishop. With him the Roman gift for organisation came to England: Wilfrid (*q.v.*) and Benedict Biscop (*q.v.*) are types of men who understood this side of the Roman connection. But Wilfrid's appeals to Rome against Canterbury showed another side, and the disregard of the Roman decision by the civil and ecclesiastical authorities may be noted, although it is not to be exaggerated into a repudiation of Roman authority, nor are the appeals to be regarded as precedents. [For the case of Dunstan refusing to obey the Pope in recalling an excommunication see Makower, *Const. Hist. of Ch. of Eng.*, sec. 23.]

3. With the Norman Conquest a third period begins. The Normans both in Normandy and in Sicily were allies of the Papacy, and appreciated the order and unity for which the Papacy stood. They agreed with the ideas of reform, which began to be powerful with the Pope Leo IX. and under the Emperor Henry III. in Germany. Simony was prevalent, with a low idea of the Church's responsibility. Against this appeared the conception of a Church purified, compact, and organised under the Papacy: this resulted in the struggle over Investitures (*q.v.*). The English Church was backward,

isolated, and needed reform. Stigand's position was significant. The Norman Conquest, blessed by Alexander II., who declared William I. the rightful king, made a change. Lanfranc (q.v.), too, was a reformer, and thus after his accession (1070) the English Church was governed in strict alliance with the Papacy and its ideas of reform. At the Council of 1070 (when Stigand was deposed) three legates were present, and from this time legates (now beginning to be widely used) often visited England. They worked with the revival of synods and councils, which had for some time been almost disused in England. The policy of William I. towards the Papacy must be noted : while keeping to the limits of custom, of the English State and of the Western Church, he refused to regard himself as a vassal of the Pope. Lanfranc, too, was rebuked by Gregory VII. for not visiting Rome at a time when frequent visits thither by bishops and attendance at the yearly councils there were the rule. But as William and Lanfranc kept the Church free from abuses, Gregory, glad to gain this, did not urge his demands. (See Böhmer, *Kirche und Staat in England und in der Normandie im XI. und XII. Jahrhundert.*) Anselm's appeal to Rome (1095), although the best known, was not the first case : William of St. Calais had previously appealed (1088). The cases illustrate both the growing tendency to appeals, and the royal claim to restrict them : this claim, however, was not always pressed, since it was easy to arrange matters with the curia.

The canon law, revived first in Germany and then in Italy, was now developing, and the best ecclesiastical ideas of the day were based upon it. William I. had separated the civil and the Church courts in England, and the new system began just when the canon law was having great effect. Under Archbishop Theobald the new system was more fully organised, and the canon law, besides its general Roman connections, made appeals to Rome and the ultimate jurisdiction of the Papacy an essential part of Church order. But the working of this system was interfered with sometimes by royal power, sometimes by political causes. A controversy has been raised as to the exact force of the Roman Canon Law in England before the Reformation. Stubbs accurately and cautiously defined the Roman Canon Law as having great authority, but he also knew that it was inoperative sometimes against the royal power, sometimes against local ecclesiastical custom. It is incorrect to say (as in a statement which

Maitland attacked) that Roman Canon Law needed for validity in England reception by the English Church ; it is equally incorrect to regard it as absolutely binding and accepted in spite of all conditions. To Lyndwood (q.v.) —the great fifteenth-century lawyer and Official of Canterbury—the Church of England was *quædam universitas* (i.e. a corporation with an independent life). The mediæval mind did not distinguish as we do between two societies, the Church and the State, although it did distinguish between two classes of officials, those of the King and those of the Church ; it mattered little that the restrictions which hindered the perfect working of the Roman Canon Law came sometimes from the royal law, sometimes from local ecclesiastical use. The contention made by Standish (q.v.) before Convocation (1514), that a constitution ordained by Pope and clergy was not binding in a territory where the use is always otherwise, could be justified by mediæval practice, although possibly not by the rigid theory of the canon law. But it should be remembered that the papal power was constantly growing both in theory and in practice. The tendency which in civil politics produced centralised governments was seen in the Church also, and hence the papal jurisdiction and right of control steadily grew, with some advantages and with some disadvantages. It was at times convenient for the Crown to make use of the papal power ; it was at times convenient for ecclesiastics to have in the Pope a defence against the Crown. And the papal control over bishops steadily grew : (a) the changing interpretation of the pall (q.v.), at first a mark of honour, then regarded as a mark of jurisdiction conferred, and (b) the oath taken by metropolitans to the Pope, are illustrations of this growth.

William I. had made a rule not to admit any legate into England unless appointed at the request of King and Church. Anselm protested against the visit of a legate, as interfering with his own prescriptive rights. (For the consecutive history see Makower, sec. 24.) When a legate held a council at London (1125) the archbishop, William of Corbeil, obtained a commission for himself as legate to avoid this interference, and after a period in which this union of offices was intermittent it became permanent when Langton obtained the legateship (1221). Thus the archbishops of Canterbury were *legati nati*, and it was only occasionally and for special purposes that legates *a latere* visited England. The legateship of Henry of Blois (q.v.) under

Stephen; the interference with the archbishop's power by the presence of Gualo and Pandulf (*q.v.*) under Henry III., as well as the visits of Otho and Ottobon; and the struggle caused by the legatine commission of Henry Beaufort, Bishop of Winchester, should be noted. Finally, the commission given to Wolsey (*q.v.*) was specially wide, and after his fall it was difficult to distinguish between the powers inherent in the archbishop and those held by him as legate representing the visitatorial power of the Pope. The mixture of them had led to greater dependence upon Rome and acquiescence in papal claims. The Archbishops of York had received a legatine commission from 1352 onwards, and were sometimes used to depress the power of Canterbury.

4. The struggle between John and the Papacy—which in the thirteenth century was held by a succession of its ablest rulers—led to a change in relation. John resigned England and Ireland to the Pope, to receive them back as a Papal fief on a yearly tribute of a thousand marks. Sicily was now governed by Innocent III., as guardian of Frederic II., and after John's death Papal legates really bore a chief part in the government of England. The connection with Rome thus took on a new form. (Luard, *Relations between England and Rome*; and Gasquet, *Henry III. and the Church*.) From the reign of the Confessor up to the reign of John, the Popes had interfered at times in the appointment of Bishops (*q.v.*), and disputed appointments had been referred to Rome. When capitular elections became the rule disputes were commoner, and were so referred. In these appointments the interests of the Crown, which we must now begin to distinguish from those of the Church, came into conflict with those of the Pope; but the papal confirmation of appointments (sometimes a mere form, but also capable of being more) was fixed by custom. Paschal II. (1099-1118) claimed this right (which resulted from the claim to control all bishops) in respect of all sees, although it had hitherto usually belonged to the metropolitan, in respect of his own province. Innocent III. (*q.v.*) claimed the right to appoint a bishop where an unworthy person had been elected; in the case of Langton he actually appointed on his own authority. This went beyond confirmation. Appeals in disputed elections became commoner, and gradually chapters lost their right of election, while the appointment became a matter of arrangement between King and Pope. But the system of provisions (1226 onwards, by which the Pope interfered

with the rights of patrons) was soon extended to bishoprics (fourteenth century). The Statute of Provisors (*q.v.*) was an attempt to check this interference (the evils of which are plentifully illustrated by the papal registers for England), but the statute was often evaded by Pope and King working together; and although capitular elections were free for a short time under Henry V., before the reign of Henry VIII. the King, through the connivance of the Pope, really regulated all episcopal appointments. [BISHOPS, PROVISORS.] Thus at the very time when legislation against papal power began, the freedom of the Church was sacrificed to arrangement between King and Pope. The history of the French Church illustrates this side of our history. The Universities approved of the papal provisions because they were often used for the promotion of their members.

Papal 'taxation' or 'exactions' was based on the right of the Pope first to ask and then to command help from the Church; its gradual growth out of the earlier requests for grants to crusades should be traced in detail. There was a mixture of demands forced upon the clergy, in which the Pope was aided by the King, and of voluntary contributions, and the whole was supervised by a collector, who was bound by oath. (Stubbs, *C.H.*, iii. p. 336.) Under Henry III. the regular papal taxation fell heavily upon the clergy, but although the King was allowed to share in it, other modes of raising money superseded this. The claim to first-fruits, which began in the thirteenth century and was enlarged afterwards, was held to be very oppressive, and in spite of national feeling, expressed by Grosseteste and by the outspoken Matthew Paris, the oppression continued.

5. The claim of the Pope to be the 'Universal Ordinary' and to supersede local authority showed itself in many ways, as *e.g.* in the control of indulgences. Archbishop Chichele (*q.v.*) in 1423 issued an indulgence for his province, following the old custom by which indulgences had been under episcopal control; but Martin V., insisting upon the papal claim to supersede local jurisdiction, rebuked this as presumption. This is one illustration of the process of papal interference with episcopal authority which developed throughout the Middle Ages, and is further illustrated by the discussions and regulations at Trent. The same process is seen in jurisdiction over heresy when the Inquisition, allied to the Papacy, superseded the old episcopal control. In England the peculiar course taken, excluding the Inqui-

sition but making use of the power of the State, should be noted. [LOLLARDS.] This advance of papal claims came to a crisis with Boniface VIII. and his Bull *Clericis Laicos* (1296). Between the Pope and the King the position of Archbishop Winchelsey was difficult. Here again French history helps to explain English. The policy of Boniface led, through his struggle with the French crown, to the papal sojourn at Avignon, during which the steadily growing exactions and exercise of power were made more unpopular by their coincidence with the English wars against France. A Papacy under French control did not recommend itself. (Creighton, *Papacy,* chaps. i. and ii.) The alliance of King and Pope weighed still more heavily upon the Church. The sojourn at Avignon was followed by the papal schism under Urban VI. (1378), which directly led to a criticism of papal authority just when the exactions had caused a demand for reform. (Funk, *Manual of Ch. Hist.,* ii.: Salembier, *Le Grand Schisme d'Occident,* Paris, 1902; Workman, *Age of Wyclif* and *Age of Hus*; and Creighton as above.)

6. **The Great Councils of the West.** In papal history these councils mark an epoch of great importance. The independence of national Churches, the rights of the episcopate and of the college of cardinals, the demands for reform 'of head and members,' all press for recognition and settlement. In England the anti-Lollard legislation illustrates the exercise of papal authority, but insular troubles somewhat hampered England in international matters; yet we should note the part played by the English delegates at Pisa (1409)—Hallam, Bishop of Salisbury, Chichele of St. David's, and Chillenden, Prior of Christ Church, Canterbury; and at Constance (1414) by Hallam with others. But in spite of the agitation and criticism, and of the demands made, the Papacy came out of the conciliar period stronger than before. It was enabled to do this by its concordats with the national churches. (Creighton, *Papacy,* Bk. II. chap. viii.) By these some reforms demanded by the nations were conceded in return for recognition of papal claims; but the English concordat was short and comparatively insignificant, although by its very shortness it illustrates the national claim to independence. Thus at the close of the Middle Ages all other relations of the Papacy with England were really obscured by its relation with the Crown (now becoming stronger than ever, and acting along with the nation). Hence in the Reformation (*q.v.*) period this special

relation is of fundamental importance. But the explanation of that importance is found in the many-sided growths and theories of the Middle Ages. Incidents such as took place under Archbishop Chichele (a series reaching from 1421 to 1428), showed the difficulties of the position: he was commanded to procure the repeal of the Statutes of Provisors and *Praemunire,* was suspended by a Bull which the protector, the Duke of Gloucester, refused to have opened, and appealed to a General Council. The archbishop was humiliated, the Pope persisted in his demands, but the Government while maintaining its statutes quieted the Pope in other ways.

7. A discussion of the relations of the Papacy with England during the Reformation period would involve a detailed history of events. They can only be properly understood by a comparison with (*a*) the cases of France and Germany, and (*b*) the history of the Council of Trent. For the later periods these relations are mainly diplomatic and political. The negotiations under James I. and Charles I. have not yet been fully studied. (See, however, Meyer as before in the continuation of the work.) The relations of Roman Catholics to the State became widely separated from those between the State and the Papacy. The relations between the English Church and the Papacy arise mainly in the controversy as to Anglican ordinations (*q.v.*) and the question of Reunion (*q.v.*). The great change of relations at the Reformation needs for its full justification a view of the growth of the Papacy in later times. (Nielsen, *History of Papacy in Nineteenth Century.*) The tendency, seen before the Reformation, to excessive interference with episcopal and local independence, has greatly developed. [J. P. W.]

See the books already mentioned, and for the Papacy, Mirbt, *Quellen zur Geschichte der Papsttum und dem römischen Katholismus.* Leipzig, new edition, 1912; Pastor, *Hist. of the Popes,* trans. by Antrobus, 1899, etc.; and the general Church histories, Funk, Gieseler, Moeller, and Kurtz. The controversies on Papal power and its nature are not referred to, but are instructive.

PARISH, for the purposes of this article, means a definite area of land, the inhabitants of which have a right to the religious offices of an incumbent who is normally in priest's orders, and the duty of accepting his services. He receives a specified and permanent income, and is nominated by a patron to the benefice.

While the episcopal government of the

Church, in the manner to which we are accustomed, was imitated from the bureaucratic system of the Roman Empire, as it was devised by Diocletian and perfected by Constantine the Great, the parochial system, with its 'freehold of the clergy,' is of Teutonic origin, and the adjustment of the two forms a great part of Church history. The system of ecclesiastical patronage is universal, in the past and often in the present, in the lands which have been or are under Teutonic rule. It was equally prevalent, in the first age of their Christianity, among the Arian and the Catholic Germans, and is so uniform in character that it must be an institution of the time before the tribes dispersed to settle in the conquered provinces of the Empire. In other words, it is older than their conversion. Patron and priest must represent the primitive lord of land in his religious capacity, whose right and duty it is to provide worship for the benefit of his family, his dependents, and those who hold land under him, and the delegate whom he appoints to perform this worship for him. This is the thesis of Ulrich Stutz, now widely accepted. Such a lord—the old doctrine of the free Teutonic village community is no longer tenable—was owner of the place of worship and master of his agent for the purpose of worship, and he made a profit for himself, beyond what he paid his priest or allowed that priest to accept from worshippers, out of the receipts of his temple.

When the Germans became Christian it was impossible to root out this conception of the relation between lord and priest. The church fabric was the property of the landlord; according to the theory of English law, it so remained till the fifteenth or sixteenth century (F. W. Maitland, *Collected Papers*, iii. 231 f.). He gave it as a *beneficium* to what man he would, though the authorities of the Church strove, and ultimately with success, to secure that the person beneficed should not be a serf. In that case his dependence upon his patron would have been absolute. The recipient was bound to perform his duties, and to accept such stipend as the owner might give. On such terms he was presented to the bishop for ordination, was ordained on the title of his benefice (to use later terms), and normally held it till his death.

We may wonder that the bishop should have had so small a share in the business, and should have consented to such derogation from his office. The only plausible explanation is that there was property annexed to the priesthood, which passed from the last

pagan to the first Christian occupant, and could only be obtained by submission to the old conditions of grant and tenure. And the bishops among the Teutons had no large staff of clergy at their own disposal; if local worship was to be maintained it could only be by the permission of the lord, and out of the existing revenue. This was from what we call the glebe land, which has peculiarities attaching to it that in no wise savour of a Christian origin.

The normal glebe of an English benefice is two yard-lands, *i.e.* twice as many strips of land in the common fields as were held by the normal member of the village community, together with a double share in the other rights of the community. Sometimes, indeed, the priest had the pasture rights of two yard-lands and a half, though he had not the same excess in other respects. In an enclosed parish this holding would amount to from forty to sixty acres, an extent which is very common. Where there is, at the present day, a large glebe, it will almost always be found to have been received in lieu of tithe, at an enclosure of the eighteenth or early nineteenth century. With his two yard-lands the priest was a member for all purposes of the community, ploughing and reaping with them, his cattle pasturing with theirs. He was, however, free from any servile duties that were laid upon his fellow-members, such as that of labouring on the lord's demesne. His interests, however, were bound up, in respect of his glebe, with those of his humbler parishioners, and detached from those of the lord. The glebe was burdened with the duty of supplying a bull and a boar for the service of the animals, not of the lord but of the members of the community. This is attested for all parts of England, and survived in some places to very recent times. In Germany it prevailed everywhere, from the North Sea to Styria, though there the duty often extended to the further provision of a stallion and a ram, or one or more of these four animals according to the custom of particular villages (F. X. Künstle, *Die deutsche Pfarrei*, 88). So strange and so widely prevalent a custom must be anterior to Christianity. As in Ireland and Armenia (though in both the circumstances were quite different from those of Teutonic lands) there was religious property waiting for an occupant, and the Christian stepped in, accepting the same conditions of tenure as his pagan predecessor. It must be borne in mind that all this took place before the institution of compulsory Tithe (*q.v.*).

Since the owner of the church expected

to derive profit from it, his interest required that it should have a congregation, whose fees and offerings would form a considerable part of the revenue to be divided between himself and the priest. Hence compulsory attendance on the part of those dependent on the lord. As they had to grind their corn at his mill, so they had to perform their religious duties at his church. We must bear in mind that religion meant, in practice, the ordinances of religion, and Bede (*q.v.*) has told how illiterate priests sometimes were (*Ep. ad Egbertum*, sec. 5). As the country became more populous such private churches spread. A well-known piece of alliterative verse of the ninth century explains some of the growth. If a free man (ceorl) in the King's service thrives till he gain five hides of land (the many parishes called Fifield, Fyfield, Fifehead all mean 'five hides,' and show what the estate was), and have church and kitchen, bell-house and mansion, seat and office in the King's hall, then he is to rank as a thegn. We must not suppose that he buys out some proprietor of cultivated land. He collects twenty of what were afterwards called copyholders—or rather nineteen, for the priest of his church will take the place of two—and establishes a new village community in the waste. We see that the possession of a church is one of the conditions of his gentility. But we must also recognise the possibility of a lordless village subscribing lands to secure itself a priest, at least in the period just before the Conquest (Maitland, *Domesday and Beyond*, 144). The process went on even after the Norman Conquest, for the Domesday picture of England shows that in many districts there were fewer villages than in later times, especially in the eastern counties. In the towns, also, it seems that the period after the Conquest was fertile in the foundation of proprietary churches, especially in London.

Since there was no system of ecclesiastical control over these churches so long as they remained in lay hands, great efforts were made to obtain the churches for bishops or ecclesiastical bodies. This would not diminish the authority of the owner, but the owner would be a Churchman or body of Churchmen. In the case of the chapter of St. Paul's, which was peculiarly successful in acquiring churches, we are well informed as to the way in which the power was used. Their churches in the city of London were regularly rented out in the eleventh century, the rent in some cases reaching £1 ; the Domesday price of an ox is 2s. or 2s. 6d. The tenant was often the priest who did the duty ;

but often a third person, perhaps a layman or a woman, paid the rent and was responsible for the services, hiring a priest to conduct them. The churches were, in fact, property and a source of income, even when they were held by ecclesiastics ; and on the episcopal estates the same process was carried out, the archbishops and bishops establishing priests in the position that has been described, instead of keeping in their own hands the superintendence of the spiritual work.

Thus, with glebe land as its financial basis and the actual ownership of the church building as its outward symbol, the system was established with which we are familiar. It was anterior to tithe, as a compulsory payment, and was not affected by it. From this original ownership has sprung the undisputed claim of the King's courts to decide in all disputes concerning property in advowsons, the form which the old ownership of churches finally took. From it also sprang such acts of ownership as the division of advowsons among heirs, which might result either in alternate presentation or the ultimate division of the parish. From it, again, came the separation of advowson from estate. In such case as that of co-heiresses an equalisation of the shares was effected in this way, a church being thrown in to balance a deficiency of land, *e.g.* Graveley and Watton, both in the fourteenth century (Cussans, *Hertfordshire*). But the process began earlier, for in the thirteenth century the famous Abbot Samson of St. Edmund's Bury was busily investing the surplus funds of his abbey in churches and half-churches, while there is ample evidence that the clergy themselves were often their own patrons, and the extraordinary prevalence of exchanges in the centuries before the Reformation shows that their hold upon their rights was a strong one.

Things might have remained as they were in England had not the great struggle over Investitures (*q.v.*) arisen on the Continent. The idea was there prevalent, about the year 1000 and earlier, that even bishoprics were benefices, and there were cases in Southern France of their being bequeathed and sold. In Germany, especially, the stronger emperors treated them as proprietary churches, as we have seen that English lords did the churches of their villages; and finally Rome itself came to be so regarded. But the emperors, in reforming Rome, had raised Roman self-respect, and the Imperial claim to be the ultimate and divinely constituted authority was confronted by the similar papal claim. As regards the parish churches, the result of prolonged conflict was something of a compromise. By Alexander III. in the Third Lateran Council of 1179 it was made the common law of the Church, so far as Roman authority extended, that the bishop should institute to livings and the patron (no longer the proprietor) should present and not collate. Only the bishop could, and in England can, collate to a living, *i.e.* to one in his own gift, collation being the giving of a church to a clerk by the ordinary in whose gift it is. In course of time the theory was invented that the Church, in recognition of the generosity of a founder, allows his successors in title to nominate to the benefice he endowed. The theory, historically false in regard to all earlier benefices, served to justify the change, and was itself true of later foundations.

Thus the doctrine of patronage took its present form. The position of the incumbent was strengthened as against the patron. while in face of the bishop he maintained his 'freehold' position—a security of tenure which in later times was to save both the Evangelical and the Oxford Movements from episcopal suppression. For the bishop gained no further powers over the incumbent, when once instituted ; there was not the Continental idea that the bishop has a general control over ecclesiastical property in his diocese. By a peculiarity of English legal thought the holder of a benefice is a 'corporation sole,' the freeholder of his house and sources of income.

His parish was originally a purely ecclesiastical unit of administration ; in the northern half of England it often contained several, even many, civil units or townships, though elsewhere parish and vill usually coincided in area. The area, for both purposes, would become more precise as considerations of tithe compelled attention to its limits. The position of the incumbent towards his parishioners was a strong one. He had the law both of Church and State to support him ; and in the Middle Ages, when every one thought as much of rights as of duties, he often had successful litigation with his parishioners. Upon them the custom of England, departing from general canon law, cast the maintenance, and the rebuilding if need be, of every part of the church except the chancel. It was ruled that even a sacristy opening out of the latter must be repaired by the parish. England also laid upon the parish the provision of ecclesiastical vestments and ornaments ; and hence. when the idea of representation spread from Parliament to local affairs, came the election of churchwardens. They seem not to have been general before the fourteenth century, and the moneys which they handled were as a rule voluntarily collected. It was not till Tudor times that Church Rates (*q.v.*) were regularly voted and levied. Then. also, the new necessity for systematic relief of the poor cast upon the existing parochial machinery, with the incumbent at its head, fresh and important duties of raising and spending money. There was no existing local machinery that could do the work, and it seemed better to enlist the parochial organisation than to devise a new one. As society grew more complex new rates were ordered by Parliament, but still under the same parochial authority. It was an ecclesiastical authority, and had to enforce payment by the ecclesiastical penalty of excommunication, which had serious consequences, *e.g.* a tradesman labouring under it could not sue for debt. These civil disqualifications of excommunication were not removed till 1813, after which year parochial rates could be claimed through ordinary legal process. The parish under its rector also assumed in different places various functions for which no other organ could be found. Where a parish contained only freeholders, the lord having been bought out by them, it could take the place of his court, and lay down and enforce rules for common fields and pasturage and elect officers for such purposes. And generally the parish was so useful that Parliament found it necessary to create the 'civil parish' as a unit of organisation, by a series of Acts from 1663 onwards. Such a civil parish is a district for which a separate poor rate is made ; in many places, especially in the north of England, the townships of a large parish had established their independence in this respect. The modern parish council as an incident of local government is a development of the civil parish.

Till recent times the creation of new parishes could only be effected by a special Act of Parliament, since a new area for civil as well as ecclesiastical purposes was thus established. Such Acts were costly and rare ; the only large provisions of this kind ever made were that for fifty parishes in London under Anne (1710, 9 An. c. 22), and the Church Building Act of 1818 (58 Geo. III. c. 45) with its grant of £1,000,000, followed by £500,000 in 1824 (5 Geo. IV. c. 103). By these Acts not only were churches built, but parishes were assigned to them. Previously a remedy had been sought in chapels of ease, perpetual curacies without cure of souls. or proprietary chapels—all of which were fairly numerous. Of actual parish churches it is said that only a dozen were built in London between 1760 and 1818. The state of Leeds before Hook's (*q.v.*) generous renunciation in 1844 is well known (Stephens, *Life of Hook*, ii. 159). From 1843 (6-7 Vic. c. 37) onwards a succession of Acts has made the creation of new parishes, for ecclesiastical purposes only, easy and cheap. They are established, under various titles, by an Order in Council on the recommendation of the Ecclesiastical Commissioners, and by a similar procedure small parishes can be combined.   [E. W. W.]

PARKER, Matthew (1504-75), succeeded Pole (*q.v.*) as Archbishop of Canterbury, being elected 1st August 1559, and consecrated at Lambeth on 17th December following. No archbishop ever less desired the post or resisted his appointment longer. But Elizabeth and Cecil were convinced that he was the one man available for the office, and the event justified their choice. Previous experiences had prepared Parker for his task. He came from the conservative East Anglia, and on being thrown in with the leading reformers at Cambridge (1521) he learnt to go a long way with them but to refrain from their extremer courses. Deep study of the Bible and the Fathers strengthened a mind that was naturally mediating and judicial. He reluctantly accepted the post of chaplain to Anne Boleyn, who in 1535 presented him to the deanery of Stoke (Suffolk), a collegiate church of secular priests. He also won academic distinction at Cambridge as Master of Corpus Christi (1544) and Vice-Chancellor, and later he became Dean of Lincoln; but he refrained from any prominent part in ecclesiastical politics. At Mary's accession he could not cast in his lot either with those in authority or with the exiles abroad [MARIAN EXILES]; so as a deprived married priest he spent the time in obscurity and in study, with dangers ever impending, but never actually reaching him. Thus he learnt to form a sound judgment of his own in the midst of conflicting tongues, and to maintain it with gentleness and conviction.

Elizabeth had already reigned nine months before Parker was drawn out from his retirement, so he had little part in the momentous events of those days. Many difficulties arose about his consecration, since the Marian bishops refused to act; and hence arose the extravagant Nag's Head fable, asserting that no consecration ever took place, but only a mock ceremony in a Fleet Street tavern. In fact, the evidence of his consecration is abundant; both the ceremony and the record of it were provided

for with exceptional care. The fable is the earliest of a long series of ineptitudes that has characterised the Roman view of English orders. [ORDINATIONS, ANGLICAN.] Consecrated himself by Bishops Barlow (*q.v.*), Scory, Hodgkin, and Coverdale (*q.v.*), the new archbishop was soon busy with further consecrations; most of the vacant sees were filled again, and episcopal government was restored after a year's turbulent interlude.

It was Parker's task to steer the bark of the Church between Scylla and Charybdis. While every one else vacillated, from the Queen downwards, and no one more than she, he alone knew his course and kept it. This tenacity was characterised, however, by great forbearance and gentleness. He shielded the Marian prelates from the worst rigours of the penal laws, and in countless ways mitigated their hard lot. He bore long and patiently with the tiresomeness of those who would not wear a surplice because it was white, or a college cap because it was square; and when at last he felt himself compelled to proceed against their rebellion he did so reluctantly and mercifully. Living in an atmosphere of corruption and venality, he was one of the few great people in Church or State who were untouched by it; and he maintained the property of the Church and a high standard of administrative integrity against powerful courtiers and against the Queen herself. His maintenance of the Prayer Book in face of the attack of the Genevan party would of itself win for him the perpetual gratitude of churchmen; but we owe to him further the revision of the Edwardine Articles of Religion (*q.v.*), the New Calendar of 1561, which recovered the Black Letter Saints' Days, the definition of the Church's marriage rules with the Table of Degrees [MARRIAGE, LAW OF], the Second Book of Homilies, and the Canons of 1571. While documents such as these secured the position of the Church on paper, the archbishop was in practice carrying the traditional administration and discipline in the face of hostility from friend as well as foe. It is easy to criticise what was done, to complain that more was not done to reform mediæval abuses in the clergy, in patronage, in ecclesiastical suits, and so forth; it is easy to regret some of the methods employed, to note the unsatisfactory character of the Ecclesiastical Commission [COMMISSION, COURT OF HIGH] in itself and in its working, or to deplore the over-reliance upon the secular arm. Parker was a man of his own time, and worked along the lines of the day: so, while striking a better balance than most people between conservatism and innovation, he failed where the age failed, was blind where it was blind. And when he was gone, and Grindal (*q.v.*) took his place, the mass of blundering that ensued showed more clearly than anything previous how great had been the wisdom of Parker.

His closing years were much saddened by the accumulating difficulties of the situation. As the position of the Church and its refusal of Rome and Geneva became more explicit, so the hostility increased on either hand. A more fighting policy was required, and Parker's delicately adjusted edifice needed to be handed over to a Whitgift (*q.v.*) —a man incapable of erecting it but better capable of defending it. The transition begins already in 1572, when Parker entrusts to Whitgift the reply to the Puritan attack made on the Church by the *Admonition to the Parliament*, and the remaining three years of his life were greatly saddened by the unfair treatment which the archbishop received from great courtiers such as Leicester, and from the Queen herself.

His solace, now as ever, lay in study and literary work. He was a great collector and lover of books, as the treasures testify which he left to the library of his old college at Cambridge; but he was a student, even more than a collector, and an encourager and patron of the studies of others. His translation of the Psalter, published in 1567, was the work of his Marian retirement. History, and especially Anglo-Saxon antiquities, occupied his leisure during his primacy. His *De Antiquitate Britannicae Ecclesiae*, printed in 1575, is an account of the archbishops from St. Augustine—'my first predecessor'—down to his own time, and it closed with a brief autobiography. His course was then nearly run, and on 17th May 1575 he died. He was buried in Lambeth Church, where his tomb was desecrated by Puritans in 1648. Under Sancroft's (*q.v.*) primacy his bones were recovered, and reburied with the epitaph, *Corpus Matthaei Archiepiscopi hic tandem quiescit.* [W. H. F.]

Strype, *Life of Archbishop Parker*; Kennedy, *Archbishop Parker*.

PARKER, Samuel (1640-88), Bishop of Oxford, is one of the most interesting characters in the political and religious controversies of the reigns of the last two Stuart kings. A study of his career reveals, in great measure, both the objects of James II.'s religious policy and the difficulties which stood in that King's way. Parker was at Oxford during the Commonwealth, and posed as a Presbyterian of the straitest sort, but the Restoration produced a change in his views. He deserted Wadham and Presbyterianism for Trinity and the Church of England. He next became chaplain to a nobleman, where 'he gained a great authority among the domestics; they all listened to him as an oracle'—a courtship which only made him still more in love with himself. He amassed some Church preferments, including the archdeaconry of Canterbury, and wrote numerous philosophical works. But he was chiefly known through his controversy with Andrew Marvell. Parker had made himself the protagonist of those who regarded ecclesiastical divisions as a danger to the unity of the state. In 1670 he published his *Discourse of Ecclesiastical Politie*, which for railing, his 'best, nay his only talent,' would be hard to surpass, though Parker professed to look upon himself as a person of 'tame and softly humour.' The object of the book is to assert the authority of the chief magistrate over the consciences of subjects in matters of religion. 'Why,' it asks, 'should the Church be so salvagely worried by a wild and fanatique rabble; why should the pride and insolence of a few peevish, ignorant and malapert preachers once more involve the kingdom in blood and confusion?' 'when people separate and rendevouz themselves into distinct sects and parties . . . their minds (like the salvage Americans) are as contracted as their heads, and all that are not within the fold of their Church are without the sphere of their charity.' The only cure is absolute submission of conscience to the State. 'If my conscience be really weak and tender, what can become it more than humble obedience and submission to authority?' The book naturally evoked a furious controversy. Though it made some good points it had on the whole the misfortune to be stupid, with its 'abundance of ranting, raving, reviling expressions, insomuch that the Arch-Angel was more civil to the devil than the archdeacon to the dissenters, and yet all to no purpose.' It had the misfortune, too, of being answered by the greatest satirist of that day, and very nearly the greatest of any day. Marvell's *Rehearsal Transposed* is, perhaps, the most splendid example of his satirical powers. It savagely exposes the violence and the aims of his opponent. 'Though it hath been long practised, I never observed any great success by reviling men into conformity.' Grant the King the authority that Parker allows him and 'His Majesty may lay by his Dieu and make use only of his Mon Droit.' Marvell's attack was so peculiar and so entertaining 'that from the King down to the tradesman his book was read with great pleasure.' Burnet (*q.v.*) is probably right in saying that the result of the controversy was the humiliation of Parker and his party. He next became an apostle of Toleration. At the end of 1686 James II. thrust him into the bishopric of Oxford. His tenure of the see, though short, is important in two ways: his efforts first to force the King's doctrines of toleration on the diocese; and secondly, to secure the King's supremacy in the University. He early came into conflict with his clergy, publishing a pamphlet, *Reasons for abrogating the Test*, in which he urged the abolition of the oath of office against Transubstantiation imposed by the Test Act of 1678. So far as they go his arguments are sound enough, *e.g.* when he objects that the ordinary member of Parliament is too stupid to understand the meaning of the abstruse terms of such an oath. But he laid himself open to the charge of self-seeking, and it was openly asserted that the pamphlet was written with the object of exchanging a poor for a rich bishopric. His quarrel with his clergy arose over his endeavour to make them subscribe to an address thanking the King for his Declaration in favour of Liberty of Worship, or rather for his promises to maintain the Church of England which the declaration contained. The clergy, with one exception, refused, alleging that the legal rights of the Church of England required no further guarantees, and that the bishop had no right to impose his arbitrary will upon them independently of the metropolitan. The incident sufficiently unveils Parker's character. Like many men of low birth, he had an exclusive sense of his own petty dignity, and he was obsessed with the idea that the clergy ought not to make the interests of the Church their primary consideration, but rather *his* authority. Parker's end was sad. The King's efforts to establish his religion in Oxford had been checked by the refusal of the Fellows of Magdalen to elect as President his Roman Catholic nominee. James (August 1687) ordered them to elect Parker. They refused, and chose Hough; the King came to Oxford in person, yet with all his browbeating could not attain his end. The resistance of the Fellows was eventually overcome by force, and Parker was installed, at first by proxy. His residence lasted less than five months, a period which was spent in admitting popish Fellows and expelling 'waggish, quarrelsome scholars.' It was the

general expectation that he would openly declare himself of the King's religion, as the Master of University had already done. 'The great obstacle,' said a contemporary pamphlet, 'is his wife, whom he cannot rid himself of.' But he refused to allow the Roman Catholic services in chapel, and when one day he received royal orders to admit yet more popish Fellows, he 'walked up and down the room, and smote his breast, and said: " There is no trust in princes. Is this the kindness the King promised me ? To set me here to make me his tool and his prop ! To place me with a company of men, which he knows I hate the conversation of ! " So he sat down in his chair, and fell into a convulsion fit, and never went downstairs more till he was carried down' (20th March 1688).

[G. B.]

Wood, *Athen. Oxon.*; Burnet, *Hist. Own Time*.

PARLIAMENT, Clergy in. From the Conversion (*q.v.*) the bishops sat in the Witenagemots of the separate kingdoms, and afterwards of the whole country, by virtue of their spiritual office, which gave them the position of advisers of the Crown. Before the Norman Conquest some abbots also sat in the Witenagemot, and after it in the Great Council, as did all the bishops. When, in the development of Parliament during the thirteenth and following centuries, the Great Council was replaced by the House of Lords, the bishops of all the English and Welsh sees (except Sodor and Man (*q.v.*), which was not part of the province of York till 1542) and as many abbots and priors as had acquired the right of personal summons were included in it as the estate of Lords Spiritual. But they were now held to be summoned, like the temporal peers, by virtue of their tenure of their baronies from the Crown. During the vacancy of a see the Guardian of the Spiritualities was summoned, though he held no barony, because he alone could call the inferior clergy to Parliament (see below). The abbots and priors, finding attendance a burden, insisted that they need only come if they held their lands by military tenure, and their number in Parliament, as high as seventy-five early in the fourteenth century, sank during its course to twenty-eight. Even so, the archbishops and bishops numbering twenty-one, the spiritual peers formed more than half of the mediæval House of Lords. Between 1509 and 1534 Henry VIII. appears to have deliberately increased the lay peers from thirty-six to fifty-four, in order to secure a majority for his anti-clerical legislation. At the dissolution of the monasteries the abbots and priors disappeared from Parliament, but by an Act of 1536 (27 Hen. VIII. c. 45) the bishops of Norwich were made abbots of St. Benet's Hulme, and it has been urged that they retained the right to sit in this capacity. Under the statute 31 Hen. VIII. c. 9 (1539) six new sees were created, and their occupants summoned to the House of Lords, though they had no baronial tenure. That of Westminster only lasted till 1550, since when the number of English spiritual peers has stood at twenty-six ; except from 1642, when they were excluded by 16 Car. I. c. 27, until they were restored in 1661 (13 Car. II. c. 2). The foundation of the see of Manchester (*q.v.*) in 1847 produced the constitutional innovation of an English diocesan bishop without a seat in the House of Lords. Subsequent creations of new sees have always been accompanied by the proviso that the number of bishops in Parliament should not be increased. It is laid down that these shall always be the two archbishops, the bishops of London, Winchester, and Durham, and twenty-one others, in order of seniority irrespective of the sees they occupy. A somewhat similar rule was in force for Ireland from the Act of Union (1801) to the disestablishment of the Irish Church (1869), when one archbishop and three bishops of that Church sat in the House of Lords under a scheme of rotation.

The claim that the bishops sit by virtue of baronial tenure, which was commonly accepted in the Middle Ages, and was advanced by themselves in 1388, has now disappeared. It could never have been valid for the sees created in the sixteenth century and later, and since 1860 (23-4 Vic. c. 124) all episcopal estates, with unimportant exceptions, are vested not in the bishops but in the Ecclesiastical Commissioners. The bishops now sit in the House of Lords, of which they form the oldest portion, by virtue of their spiritual office, as they did in the Witenagemot. The distinction is expressed in the words of the writ. They are summoned on their ' faith and love ' to the Crown, the temporal peers on their ' faith and allegiance.'

In the Middle Ages the bishops sometimes claimed that, as they were a separate estate from the temporal peers, their separate consent was necessary to legislation. In 1515 the judges held that a valid Parliament could be held without them (Keilwey, *Reports*, 184). The Act of Uniformity (*q.v.*), 1559, was passed, although all the bishops present voted against it. The law as finally settled is as stated by Coke (Insts., ii. 585). The bishops have a right to be summoned to Parliament, but their actual presence and separate assent are not essential. It is noteworthy that laws passed before their restoration in 1661 are valid. The temporal peers have frequently regarded them with jealousy, and in 1692 resolved that though Lords of Parliament they were not peers. This opinion, which first appears about 1625, though historically questionable, is now the doctrine of the constitution. Therefore a bishop apparently has not the privilege of being tried by the peers for treason or felony. Soon after the Reform Act of 1832 efforts towards excluding the bishops from Parliament were made in the House of Commons, but without result (1834, 1836, 1837).

Representatives of the clergy were occasionally summoned to the secular councils of the twelfth and thirteenth centuries. In 1295 Edward I. issued writs to the archbishops and bishops commanding them to attend Parliament, and to forewarn (*praemunientes*) the deans and archdeacons to be present in person, each chapter by one proctor and the parochial clergy of each diocese by two. The clerical estate of Parliament thus formed must be distinguished from the Lower Houses of Convocation (*q.v.*). These are two separate spiritual assemblies, parts of the provincial synods of the English Church. The clerical estate was to be a single body, an integral part of Parliament, in which it was to represent the temporal interests of the clergy.

Edward designed that it should vote the taxes to be paid by them, but to this they objected, preferring to maintain the right they had established to tax themselves in Convocation. Their wish was respected, and the chief reason for the clerical estate in Parliament was thus removed. The proctors seldom attended, and took little part in the proceedings. In the first half of the fourteenth century the kings were wont to send a separate mandate enjoining the archbishops to compel their attendance, which, however, seems to have ceased altogether soon after the end of that century. From about 1377 the wording of the writ was changed from *ad faciendum et consentiendum* to *ad consentiendum*. The consent only of the clergy was asked, and this they might be supposed to give by their absence. That they sometimes took part in the proceedings even after this date is shown by the case of Haxey, Canon of Lichfield, Lincoln, Howden, and Southwell, and clerical proctor in Parliament in 1397, when he attacked abuses of administration, and especially the expense of maintaining many bishops and ladies at court. For this he was condemned to death as a traitor, but was saved by his privilege of clergy. In September 1397 the spiritual estates in both Houses of Parliament chose Sir Thomas Percy, Knight, to give assent on their behalf to the actions of Parliament.

In 1547 the Lower House of Canterbury Convocation petitioned, but without result, that ' according to the antient custom of this realm, and the tenor of the king's writs for the summoning of the parliament,' they ' may be adjoyned and associated with the lower house of parliament,' and that if this were not done no laws affecting the Church might be passed. The *praemunientes* clause, summoning the clerical proctors to Parliament, is still retained in the writs, and instances of elections under it are found down to the latter part of the seventeenth century.

In 1553 Nowell (*q.v.*) was not allowed to sit in the House of Commons because as a prebendary of Westminster he had ' a voice in the convocation house.' The presence of Sir John Tregonwell, a lay prebendary on the committee which thus reported, shows that holy orders, not the holding of preferments, were considered the real bar. Until the Act of Uniformity (*q.v.*), 1662, made episcopal ordination obligatory, deaneries and prebends, being *sine cura animarum*, were considered appropriate rewards for lay civil servants. Instances of lay deans [WHITTINGHAM] sitting in the House of Commons are Sir John Wolley (d. 1592), Elizabeth's Latin secretary, and Sir Christopher Perkins (d. 1622), a diplomatist, both Deans of Carlisle. Dr. French Laurence sat in Parliament, 1796-1809, while holding the lay prebend of Salisbury attached to the Regius Professorship of Civil Law at Oxford. Since Convocation gave up the right of taxation in 1664 the clergy have voted in Parliamentary elections ; but the question of their right to sit in the Commons was not finally settled till 1801, when Horne Tooke, who was in priest's orders, having been elected for Old Sarum, an Act was passed declaring the clergy ineligible (41 Geo. III. c. 63).

The Clerical Disabilities Act, 1870 (33-4 Vic. c. 91), provided that a clergyman of the English Church can render himself eligible to sit in the House of Commons by resigning his preferments and executing a deed relinquishing all the rights and privileges of holy orders. Canon 76 enacts that no clergyman shall give up his orders, or ' use himself as a layman,' on pain of excommunication. But a temporal peer who is in holy orders may sit in the House of Lords. [G. C.]

Stubbs, *C.H.*, vi., xi., xv., xx., and *Sel. Charters*; Anson, *Law of the Constitution*; Freeman, *The House of Lords* (' Hist. Essays,' 4th ser.); Pike, *Const. Hist. of the House of Lords*; Atterbury, *Rights of Convocation*; Hansard, *Parl. Hist.*, xxxv.; *Parl. Debates*, xxiii., xxxiii., xxxvi.

PATRICK, Simon (1626-1707), Bishop of Ely, eldest son of Henry Patrick, a pious mercer of Gainsborough, was educated at the Grammar School there, and at Queens' College, Cambridge, where, as he was poor, the master helped him by giving him work as a transcriber, and he soon obtained a scholarship. He graduated B.A. in 1648, was ordained by a Presbyterian *classis*, and began to preach; but having learnt from the works of Hammond and Thorndike the necessity of episcopal ordination, he received it privately in 1654 from the ejected Bishop of Norwich, Joseph Hall. He became chaplain to Sir Walter St. John at Battersea, and in 1658 was appointed to the vicarage there. At the Restoration he gladly conformed to the Church order. In 1661 he was elected Master of his college, but a mandate from Charles II. led to the appointment of another. In 1662 he was presented to the rectory of St. Paul's, Covent Garden, and was recognised as distinguished among the great London preachers of the time. Throughout the plague of 1665-6 he remained at his post; he was diligent, and caused prayers to be read in his church twice daily. Having graduated D.D., he was incorporated of Christ Church, Oxford, in 1666. He was a friend of Tenison, afterwards archbishop, and at a later date co-operated with him in founding a school for the education of the poor in the parish of St. Martin-in-the-Fields. He was made one of the King's chaplains, and in 1672 was appointed a prebendary of Westminster, where he became sub-dean. In 1679 he received the deanery of Peterborough, which he held along with his London benefice. Together with Dr. Jane he represented the English Church in a conference with Romanist divines arranged by James II. in 1686. He was the first to sign the resolution of the London clergy in May 1688 not to read the Declaration of Indulgence. [SEVEN BISHOPS.] He took the oath at the Revolution, and was one of the commissioners appointed by William III. in 1689 to examine the liturgy with a view to the comprehension of Nonconformists. He was consecrated Bishop of Chichester, 1689. In 1691 he was translated to Ely. As bishop he upheld the principles of the Church, and made it efficient in his diocese. He was one of the founders of the Society for Promoting Christian Knowledge, and warmly supported the Society for the Propagation of the Gospel. He was devout, learned, and of an eminently practical cast of mind. Patrick was a prolific author. His *Parable of the Pilgrim*, published in 1664, fourteen years before Bunyan's famous allegory, and vastly inferior to it as literature, soon ran through six editions; an abridged edition was published in 1840. He also wrote *Commentaries on the Old Testament*, which were long held in high esteem ; controversial treatises against both Roman Catholic doctrines and Nonconformity; many books of devotion and on religious subjects, and poems ; and he left an *Autobiography*, which was first published in 1839. His principal works, excluding the *Commentaries* but including the *Autobiography*, were collected and published in nine volumes in 1858.

[W. H.]

Autobiography: Chamberlayne. *Memoir* in *Parable of the Pilgrim* ; *D.N.B.* : Hutton, *Hist. Eng. Ch.*, 1603-1714.

PATTESON, John Coleridge (1827-1871), Bishop of Melanesia, was son of a Justice of the King's Bench ; his mother was one of the remarkable Coleridge family. At Eton, where he was more noted for purity of character than for ability, he became Captain of the Eleven. His mind turned early towards a missionary vocation. At Oxford he became a Fellow of Merton College, and then went to Dresden to learn Hebrew. There he formed a lifelong friendship with Max Müller, and found that he had an unusual faculty for learning and speaking languages. With this further sense of qualification for missionary work he became curate of Alfington, near his father's house in Devonshire. In 1854 Bishop Selwyn (*q.v.*) came to England. He had asked Lady Patteson for Coleridge as a boy, and now gave him an invitation, which Patteson without reserve accepted. Never was a more complete surrender. The old judge gave up the stay of his old age, the son gave up home, friends, the art and music that he loved, determined never to return. By the indulgence of his college he retained his Fellowship. He accompanied Selwyn to New Zealand, with the intention that he should take special charge of the Melanesians. In the first year he visited the New Hebrides. He loved the natives as soon as he knew them, and declared that he would not change his life with them

for any other. They being now taught in their own tongues expanded with delight ; and moving down with him to the sunny beach at Kohimarama they formed the nucleus of the native teaching body who were, it was hoped, to evangelise the islands. The place of Bishop Patteson in history is not fixed by enterprise or wise plans, though these were not wanting, but by his extraordinary command of native languages, and his power of living with young savages, understanding them, and drawing them upwards by his personal influence. The Melanesian portion of the Pacific, with its multitude of islands, is divided by a strange multiplicity of languages. Patteson, before he died, could speak in about thirty ; with five or six he was thoroughly conversant ; he spoke all these like a native, but he did not live to print or write much of what he knew. It is hard to conceive how the Melanesian Mission could have advanced without him.

His fitness for the charge of Melanesia being proved he was consecrated Bishop of the Mission on St. Matthias's Day, 1861, by the bishops of New Zealand, acting without patent or other authority than that inherent in their episcopate. He soon had a new vessel, the *Southern Cross*, and a few young men in training, and thought the time had come to appeal for assistance in Australia. This he did in 1864 with persuasive and pathetic eloquence.

In the next island voyage his boat was attacked, and two young Pitcairners killed by arrow wounds—a lasting grief to the bishop. In the next year he spent some time at Mota, establishing the first of the native schools with which he hoped to furnish all the groups. But now the distance of New Zealand from the Melanesian Islands, the cold of the winter, the constant occupation of the bishop in matters apart from his mission, made it necessary to move the headquarters to Norfolk Island, the only place available. There, when not in the islands, the last years of his life were spent, with his room opening into the chapel, in freest intercourse with expanding native minds, reading Hebrew and theology with the young clergy, discussing principles and methods of missionary and linguistic work, and in the nursing of the sick. This happy life was interrupted by sickness ; and then came his last voyage. The troubles of the labour trade had begun—a scourge to the islands and a serious danger to the mission. In 1871 the bishop spent some time at Mota, baptizing many natives. It was on the little island of Nukapu that his life was taken by natives enraged by the kidnapping of five of their number by a labour vessel from Fiji. One of the mission clergy, Joseph Atkin, and a native teacher were killed by arrows. The bishop's body was restored, with five wounds, covered with a palm leaf in which five knots were tied. It was sunk in the sea as the vessel hung off the island in a calm, and the near volcano sounded like funeral guns.

Miss Yonge (*q.v.*), in her *Memoir*, has made Bishop Patteson's life and work widely known. What he gave to English people in example can be understood; to those who lived with him he seemed to move on holy ground; the first generation of Melanesians who heard the Gospel had in him their pattern of a Christian.   [R. H. C.]

C. M. Yonge, *Life*; personal recollections.

PAULINUS (d. 644). Bishop of York, a Roman, was sent by Pope Gregory (*q.v.*) to Augustine (*q.v.*) in 601. He was consecrated bishop in 625 that he might accompany Ethelburga, daughter of Eadbald, King of Kent, who was going north to marry Edwin, the Northumbrian King. When in 626 Edwin was hesitating whether to receive baptism, Paulinus reminded him that, when an exile at the court of Raedwald, the East Anglian King, and in peril of his life, he had appeared to him and foretold his future greatness, and that Edwin had promised that if his prophecy were fulfilled he would accept his teaching. Paulinus may have been in East Anglia at the time, perhaps about 616. Edwin acknowledged the promise; the Northumbrian witan decided to accept Christianity, and Edwin was baptized by Paulinus, together with many of his house and his nobles, on Easter-eve, 11th April 627, in a wooden church hastily erected at York and dedicated to St. Peter. At the instigation of Paulinus the King raised a stone church over this wooden building and made York the place of his see. Paulinus, for the most part, dwelt with the King, and the whole of Edwin's wide dominions were his mission field. He baptized many in the Swale at Catterick; for there were no churches, and we read only of one, besides that at York, being built in Deira, at Campodunum (perhaps Doncaster), though there probably were others. He visited Bernicia with the King and Queen, and for thirty-six days at Yeavering catechised and baptized a multitude of people in the glen; so, too, he did in the Trent Valley; and he also visited Lindsey, where he converted the reeve of Lincoln, who built a stone church there.

In that church he consecrated Honorius to the see of Canterbury, probably in 627. When in 633 Edwin was defeated and slain at Hatfield by Penda of Mercia and the Briton Cadwalla, Ethelburga fled to Kent, and Paulinus accompanied her. His faithful deacon James, however, remained in Northumbria preaching and baptizing. Paulinus received the bishopric of Rochester, and a pallium [PALL], sent in 634 by Pope Honorius, which would have given him archiepiscopal dignity, but as it was not granted until after he had left York he cannot strictly be called archbishop; indeed, the line of archbishops of York did not begin until a century later. He died at Rochester on 10th October 644. He was a tall man, a little bent, with black hair, a thin face, and an aquiline nose, and of a venerable and awe-inspiring aspect.   [W. H.]

Life of Pope Gregory the Great (the oldest), ed. Gasquet; Bede, *H.E.*

PEARSON, John (1612-86), Bishop of Chester, was a native of Great Snoring in Norfolk. He was educated at Eton and Queens' College, Cambridge, was elected Scholar (1632) and Fellow (1634) of King's, was Prebendary of Nether-Avon, Salisbury (1640-61), Rector of Thorington in Suffolk (1640), weekly preacher at St. Clement's, Eastcheap (1654). In 1660 he became Rector of St. Christopher-le-Stocks, Prebendary of Ely, Archdeacon of Surrey, and Master of Jesus College, Cambridge; in 1661 Lady Margaret Reader in Divinity, in 1662 Master of Trinity College, Cambridge, and in 1673 Bishop of Chester. His most important writings were *An Exposition of the Creed*, published in 1659; *Vindiciae Epistolarum S. Ignatii*, 1672; *Annales Cyprianici*, 1682; *Dissertationes de serie et successione primorum Romae Episcoporum*, published in a posthumous collection of some of his writings in 1688, and some of the treatises included in the edition of his *Minor Works*, published from MSS. by Archdeacon Edward Churton in 1844. A good idea of his thought and methods may be formed by comparing the *Exposition of the Creed*, written for ordinary readers, with the *Minor Works*, written for scholars. A very incomplete impression would be formed from either studied separately. The most valuable part of the *Exposition of the Creed* is in the elaborate notes, consisting largely of quotations from patristic literature, in which he was extraordinarily learned. His theology is marked by his clear grasp on the truths concerning the Being of God, the Holy Trinity, and the

Incarnation. In some respects his *Exposition of the Creed* is open to criticism, as in the omission of a sufficient treatment of any other than the intellectual elements of faith ; in his emphasis on the supposed fact that the world was made ' most certainly within not more than six, or at furthest seven, thousand years' (in the first edition he wrote, ' most certainly within much less than six thousand years ') ; in his completely ignoring, probably as part of a revolt against some mediæval ideas about Purgatory, the intermediate state ; in his apparent view that the material particles of our present bodies will be restored and reunited in the resurrection ; and in the extent to which he associates local movements ' through all the regions of the air, through all the celestial orbs,' with the Ascension of our Lord. But when all such qualifications are made, it remains a splendid example of strong and solid treatment of fundamental theology and a permanently valuable exposition of orthodox belief. In his other writings much of his historical and critical work is of a very high order, and exhibits an interesting combination of scholastic method with such knowledge as was possible in his day. His ecclesiastical position is well shown by his contentions that the papal claims are to be rejected as destructive of that true idea of the ministry which regards all the bishops as successors of all the apostles, and that bishops alone can ordain.　　　　　[D. S.]

PECKHAM, John (*c.* 1240-92). Archbishop of Canterbury, was a Yorkshireman, a student of Paris and apparently of Oxford, and entered the Franciscan Order. He returned to Oxford about 1270 and became a leader of the Franciscan movement, and finally the Provincial of the Order in England. He was famous for his austerities, ' fasting as it were for seven Lents a year,' and travelled on foot to attend a general chapter of his Order at Padua. He was summoned to Rome by Pope Nicholas III. (himself a Franciscan, and known as the Sun of the Order, of which Peckham was the Moon), and was made *Lector Sacri Palatii.* He was in Rome when Robert Kilwardby, Archbishop of Canterbury, resigned his office in 1278. Robert Burnell, Bishop of Bath and Wells, the Chancellor of England, was elected to succeed him, but the election was quashed by Nicholas III., who nominated Peckham, 1278, and urged him to stamp out the scandal of pluralism in his province. To this end Peckham summoned a provincial synod at Reading in 1279, in which,

finding the decretal *Ordinarii Locorum* of the Council of Lyons of 1274 too severe, he promulgated a constitution of his own founded on that of the Lateran Council of 1215. He also published articles directing the clergy to explain the excommunications issued against impugners of Magna Carta and those who interfered with the Church courts. These he was compelled by Edward I. to withdraw, and the King in return caused Parliament to pass the Statute of Mortmain (*q.v.*). His intervention in the Welsh war of Edward I. was due to his desire to put down what were said to be abuses in the Welsh Church, to bring it more closely under the control of Canterbury, and into greater conformity with English customs. He seems to have meant well, and tried to arrange some settlement, but was not always judicious in his treatment of Welsh national feeling.

Peckham was greatest as a theologian and physicist. As archbishop he was energetic and zealous for Church reform ; he sincerely loved justice and hated oppression, but his want of tact and insistence on the rights of his office brought him into frequent quarrels, and to a great extent frustrated his good intentions. In personal character he was humble, kindly, and devout. He died at Mortlake in 1292 after a long illness, and is buried in Canterbury Cathedral.
　　　　　[G. C.]

Registrum Epistolarum Fratris Johannis Peckham, R.S. ; *D.N.B.* ; Ogle, *Canon Law in Mediæval England.*

PECOCK, Reginald (1395?-1460?), was born in Wales, and after a career of some distinction at Oxford, during which he was made a Fellow of his college (Oriel), was summoned to court, where his learning won him approval. Probably to Humphrey, Duke of Gloucester, he owed more than one preferment. In 1431 he was appointed Master of Whittington College in London. In 1444 he was consecrated Bishop of St. Asaph, and in 1450, through the influence of William de la Pole, Duke of Suffolk, was translated to Chichester. He wielded the pen of a ready writer, and in 1457 he was charged with having uttered heretical opinions in many of his books. His trial, or rather trials, before Archbishop Bouchier culminated in his downfall. He was offered the choice of either recanting his opinions and publicly burning his books, or else becoming himself fuel for the fire. He chose the former alternative. Fortunately copies were kept of some of the offending volumes. He ended his days in captivity in the abbey of Thorney under cruel conditions, for he was deprived of all books, save a missal and a breviary, and he had 'nothing to write with ; no stuff to write upon.'

He appears to have been a man of complex temper—conservative in his relation to the practices of the Church, radical in his treatment of theological questions. In matters of practice he was always ready to defend the *status quo* and to minimise the evils of the time, which were a scandal not only to the Lollards, but to many orthodox churchmen.

In a sermon preached at Paul's Cross in 1447 he defended the non-resident and non-preaching bishops of the day, and in his greatest work (*The Repressor*) may be found an ingenious and subtle defence of such matters as the wealth of the clergy, pilgrimages, the multiplication of monastic houses, in which he assumed that any abuses connected with these were the creation of uninformed imagination. He was an ardent supporter of the temporal as well as of the spiritual power of Rome.

But it is as a thinker that Pecock stands out as a man of original mind, and the one intellectually remarkable figure of his day. He was entirely opposed to the narrow view of the Lollards as to the verbal inspiration of Holy Scripture, and this fact led him to develop views concerning the supremacy of natural reason which excited the antagonism of Churchman and Lollard alike. The contention of the latter was that 'no ordinance is to be esteemed a law of God, unless it be grounded in Holy Scripture.' The fallacy of such a proposition was the occasion for Pecock to adopt a line of reasoning that revealed his mental vigour and helped to cause his own undoing. This is contained in *The Repressor*. To the contention of the Biblemen, he replied that 'it belongeth not to Holy Scripture to ground any governance, or deed, or service, or any law of God, or any truth of God which man's reason by nature may find, learn, and know.' He applied this statement to the moral law, which, he urged, can be known apart from any help of Scripture, and which, indeed, was known before the books of the Bible were written. His conclusion is that the purpose of Scripture is to encourage men to keep the moral law, but that that law itself is taught by man's reason. If reason and Scripture come into conflict, the former must be obeyed, for that which is written in the heart is superior to any outward words.

His *Book of Faith* is a characteristic example of the two sides of his mind. On the one

hand there are passages which, taken by themselves, could have excited no suspicion even in the fifteenth century. But in his discussion of the nature of faith, and the authority of the Church and of Scripture, a great deal of a very different character may be discovered below the surface ; and when, in the prologue to the book, he affirmed that 'no clerk ought to be displeased' with what was to follow, he must have had a shrewd suspicion that he was about to stir up a considerable amount of clerical displeasure. In Chapter iv., Part II., he has a striking contrast between *Credo* and *Credo in* as relating to the Catholic Church, and he announces his intention of applying the same treatment to the one baptism, the forgiveness of sins, and the life everlasting. It is to be regretted that the chapters containing this further matter are missing.

In his discussion of the authorship of Genesis he displayed a critical temper which even to-day is modern. It should be added that his overweening conceit must have increased the bitterness of his opponents, and there is something to be said for the opinion that political enmity contributed to his misfortunes. Moreover, his frank opposition to the war with France could not have increased his popularity.   [E. M. B.]

The Repressor, ed. Babington, R.S., 1860 ; *The Book of Faith*, ed. Morison ; J. Gairdner, *Lollardy and the Reformation in Eng.*, vol. i.

PECULIARS. The word is used to denote a parish or group of parishes 'exempt from the jurisdiction of the Ordinary of the diocese,' *i.e.* the bishop, and in which some other authority than he instituted, and, when necessary, tried the clergy, and proved the wills. [COURTS.] In mediæval England the dioceses were honeycombed with these jurisdictions. They fall into these classes :—

1. *Monastic Peculiars.*—The very great abbeys secured exemption from the diocesan jurisdiction of the bishop and his archdeacon, and this privilege was extended to the churches on their estates all over England. Westminster (*q.v.*), St. Albans (*q.v.*), Bury St. Edmunds (*q.v.*), Glastonbury (*q.v.*), and Evesham were in this position. They were exceptions from the Benedictine houses owing to their immemorial antiquity. In some of them the ordinary jurisdiction of the abbey was exercised by its own archdeacon, as at Westminster and St. Albans.

2. *Peculiars belonging to whole Orders.*—The Gilbertines and Præmonstratensians were exempt from diocesan jurisdiction, and

though they held little land they held many parishes.

3. *Royal Peculiars, i.e.* the churches on lands surrounding a royal castle, as Shrewsbury, Bridgnorth, and Hastings. These were liable to archiepiscopal visitation. Windsor and Westminster Abbey are of this class where the Ordinary is the Crown. In 1832 there were eleven of these.

4. *Archiepiscopal Peculiars*: springing from their right to execute jurisdiction where their seats or palaces were. Of these the Archbishop of Canterbury had very many and the jurisdiction over them was exercised by commissaries. These still survive nominally in the titles of the Deans of Bocking, Hadleigh and Stamford. The Deanery of the Arches in London was another Archiepiscopal Peculiar.

5. *Episcopal Peculiars*: situated in one diocese, but under the jurisdiction of the bishop of another. *e.g.* the Bishop of London had four parishes in the diocese of Lincoln. If a bishop had a residence in another diocese it was a Peculiar of this kind. Bishops might also have Peculiars in their own dioceses, *i.e.* places subject immediately to their jurisdiction to the exclusion of that of the archdeacon.

6. *Cathedral Peculiars.*—These arose from the division of the cathedral property between the bishop and the chapter, which took place usually in the twelfth century. [CATHEDRAL CHAPTERS.] In these the chapter exercised ordinary jurisdiction over their property, and instituted clerks. The jurisdiction varied. At Lichfield each prebendary was Ordinary in his own church : at Salisbury and elsewhere the whole chapter collectively was the Ordinary ; sometimes the Dean had his own Peculiar jurisdiction as well as that held with his Chapter, and well into the nineteenth century Deans of Salisbury held Visitations of their Peculiars and delivered charges (*e.g.* Dean Pearson in 1839 and 1842).

A complete and clear list of the various Peculiars in England is printed in the appendix to the first five volumes of the *Valor Ecclesiasticus* (*q.v.*) 1810-1825. These are given under the hands of the various diocesan bishops in answer to inquiries sent out by the Commission on the Public Records. Canterbury, Bangor, St. Asaph, and Llandaff had none, nor had Durham and Carlisle in the northern province. They are given as under :—

Vol. i. Rochester, Bath and Wells, Bristol, Chichester and London.
Vol. ii. Winchester, Salisbury, Exeter, Oxford and Gloucester.

Vol. iii. Hereford, Lichfield, Worcester, Norwich, Ely.
Vol. iv. Lincoln, Peterborough, St. David's.
Vol. v. York and Chester.

A further list of such courts with much information is in App. D, No. 8 of the *Eccles. Courts Commission Report*, 1832 (pp. 554 *seq.*). By that time the four Welsh dioceses and Chester had no courts below the Diocesan. Durham had, however, a Peculiar of the Dean and Chapter.

From 1559 the power of the bishops over Peculiars had begun to develop. The Act of Supremacy, 1559 (1 Eliz. c. 1), gave them jurisdiction for purposes of the Act over all exempt places. A proposal to subject Peculiars and exempt places to the diocesan was made later in the reign. Bishop Randolph at Oxford laboured with the same design and charged on the subject in 1802 and 1805. Peculiars, he said, were due ' to the usurpations of Papacy in the very worst times of its prevalence.'

Peculiars were brought under the jurisdiction of the diocesan by the Act for enforcing residence, 1803 (43 Geo. III. c. 84), but only for the purposes of that Act. A Bill to transfer their jurisdiction altogether to the diocesan courts failed to pass in 1812. In 1832 the Ecclesiastical Courts Commission [COMMISSIONS, ROYAL] reported that there were nearly three hundred such jurisdictions, and recommended their abolition. The Act 6-7 Will. IV. c. 77 gave the Ecclesiastical Commissioners power to prepare schemes, to be carried into effect by Order in Council, transferring Peculiars to the jurisdiction of the diocesan. This power was extended in 1850 (13-14 Vic. c. 94). Peculiar jurisdiction was gradually abolished by 1-2 Vic. c. 106 (1838), by the Church Discipline Act, 1840 (3-4 Vic. c. 86), and by 10-11 Vic. c. 98 (1847) and subsequent Acts. Many Peculiars were abolished for all purposes by Order in Council of 8th August 1845 ; but the Peculiars of cathedral churches and royal residences, including Westminster Abbey, were excepted. Some Peculiars were abolished by special Acts of Parliament, as St. Burian's, Cornwall, by 13-14 Vic. c. 76 (1850), and a few still exist.

Donatives were livings once in the gift of an ecclesiastical body, which had ordinary jurisdiction over them, which when the corporation to which they belonged was dissolved, passed to the grantees of the land. The owner of the living was also the Ordinary, and could institute irrespective of the bishop. This led to grave abuses. Donatives augmented by Queen Anne's Bounty (*q.v.*)

became thereby subject to the diocesan. All Donatives were gradually brought under episcopal jurisdiction in the same way as Peculiars, and were finally abolished by the Benefices Act, 1898 (61-2 Vic. c. 48). A bishop now has sole ordinary jurisdiction in his diocese. [s. l. o.]

Burn, *Eccl. Law*; Phillimore, *Eccl. Law*; and authorities in the text.

PENTECOSTALS, or Whitsun - farthings, were offerings made to the cathedral church at Pentecost. They grew from voluntary offerings from those who according to custom (mentioned 1396, see Gibson, *Codex*, p. 1017) visited the mother church of the diocese at that season, into a fixed payment from every parish to the bishop, recoverable in the ecclesiastical court. In Phillimore's *Eccl. Law* (2nd ed., 1895, p. 1245) they are said to be still paid by particular churches in a few dioceses. [g. c.]

PETERBOROUGH, See of. It is supposed that Peada, eldest son of Penda, fourth King of Mercia, founded a monastery at Medehamstede, the modern Peterborough, about the year 655, but did not live to finish his work. He was succeeded by his brother Wulfhere, who completed the minster. Aethelred, his brother, was an even more munificent benefactor, and is said, though much doubt has been thrown upon the story, to have obtained through St. Wilfrid (*q.v.*) many extraordinary privileges from Rome. Under Abbot Hedda the monastery was raided by the Danes (870) and burnt, when the archives were destroyed. Beorred, King of the Mercians, seized all the lands belonging to it between Stamford, Huntingdon, and Wisbech, and divided them amongst his soldiers. The rebuilding probably commenced in 966, chiefly through the efforts of Aethelwold, Bishop of Winchester, who dedicated it to St. Peter, whence the adjacent village took the name of Peterborough. The first abbot of the new monastery was Adulf, Chancellor of King Eadgar, who, having accidentally caused the death of his only son, forsook the court and became a monk; afterwards Archbishop of York. Other abbots of note were Kenulf, who augmented the revenues and obtained a confirmation of the charters from Aethelred II., and afterwards became Bishop of Winchester. Brand, being abbot under the Conqueror, offended him by applying to Eadgar the Atheling for confirmation, and was compelled to pay a fine of forty marks of gold before either his own election or the privileges

of the monastery were secured. Under the next abbot, the Norman Thorold, Hereward the Wake, joining a Danish force, proceeded to Peterborough and robbed the monastery of some of its chief treasures, including the uncorrupted right arm of St. Oswald (*q.v.*). This, however, was regained by the Prior. Later the monks paid the King three hundred marks of silver for the privilege of electing their own abbot, and elected Godric. During the abbacy of John de Seez a fire occurred (1116) which nearly destroyed the monastery—said to be a divine judgment on the blasphemy of the abbot, who, on some trivial annoyance, 'fell a-cursing.' In 1117 he laid the foundation of a new church, the origin of the present cathedral. Martin de Bec, appointed in 1133, was assiduous in the work of rebuilding. Other famous abbots were Benedict, who completed the nave; he was Keeper of the Great Seal to Richard I. Robert de Sutton, who first joined the side of the Barons and then that of Henry III., and was heavily fined in consequence. At the dissolution (1539) Peterborough had become one of the richest and most famous monasteries in England. According to Paley, the church was spared owing to its containing the remains of Katherine of Aragon.

In 1541 Letters Patent were issued converting the monastic church into the cathedral of a new diocese, which consisted of the counties of Northampton and Rutland (except three parishes in each), hitherto in that of Lincoln. It was endowed with one-third of the property of the abbey, amounting to £733 yearly value; the other two-thirds were assigned to the King and to the new chapter. The income of the abbey in 1534 was £1721, 14s., according to Dugdale; Speed values it at £1972, 7s. Ecton (1711) gives the income of the see as £414, 17s. 8½d. It is now £4500.

The chapter as founded, 1541, consisted of a dean and six prebendaries or major canons, six minor canons, a deacon, sub-deacon, eight singing men, eight choristers, two schoolmasters, twenty scholars, six almsmen, and others—in all, about seventy. Queen Mary gave the bishop the presentation to the canonries. Two of the major canonries were suspended in 1840 (3-4 Vic. c. 113).

Until 1837 the diocese consisted of the single archdeaconry of Northampton (first mentioned, c. 1078). In that year the county of Leicester, forming the archdeaconry of Leicester (first mentioned, c. 1078), in the diocese of Lincoln, was added to Peterborough. In 1875 the archdeaconry of Oakham was formed out of that of Northampton. A bishop suffragan of Leicester was appointed, 1888. The population is 792,827.

Bishops

1. John Chambers, 1541; last abbot of the monastery. ' He loved to sleep in a whole skin and desired to die in his nest'; so, finding he could not avert the dissolution by bribery, surrendered the monastery to the Crown, 1539. and became bishop of the new see, 1541; d. 1556.
2. David Pole, 1557 (P.); LL.D.: Fellow of All Souls, Oxford; depr. by Elizabeth, but left at liberty; d. 1568, leaving his books to All Souls College, desiring them to send and fetch the same ' on account of my poverty at my latter end' (*Fenland Notes and Queries*, ii. 112).
3. Edmund Scambler, 1561; tr. to Norwich.
4. Richard Howland, 1585; Master of St. John's, Cambridge; recommended in 1594 for the archbishopric of York, ' which he much endeavoured after but was put by'; d. 1600. In 1587 Mary Queen of Scots was buried in the cathedral church, but was removed to Westminster, 1603.
5. Thomas Dove, 1601; chaplain to Queen Elizabeth: d. 1630.
6. William Piers, 1630; tr. to Wells.
7. Augustine Lindsell, 1633; tr. to Hereford.
8. Francis Dee. 1634; d. 1638.
9. John Towers, 1639; formerly dean; ' succeeded to the bishopric through his own great solicitations.' During his episcopate the cathedral suffered greatly from the excesses of the soldiery. It was used as a parish church for Presbyterians. Bishop Towers d. 1649. ' having been outed of all by the iniquity of the times,' and the see was vacant twelve years.
10. Benjamin Laney, 1660; tr. to Lincoln.
11. Joseph Henshaw, 1663; Dean of Chichester; ' lived not very hospitably in his diocese '; author of a book famous at the time, *Horae Succisivae*: d. 1679.
12. William Lloyd, 1679; tr. to Norwich.
13. Thomas White, 1685; the lifelong friend of Ken (*q.v.*) and a devout scholar; one of the Seven Bishops (*q.v.*); ' being a single man distributed a good deal in charity'; depr. in 1690 for refusing to take the oath of allegiance to William and Mary, and became a leading Nonjuror: d. 1698.
14. Richard Cumberland, 1691; a learned author who wrote a refutation of the ' free principles ' of Hobbes's *De legibus Naturae disquisitio philosophica* widely circulated in England and abroad; d. 1718.
15. White Kennett, 1718; b. 1660; educated at Westminster and St. Edmund Hall. Oxford, of which he was Vice-Principal. 1690-1695. In early life a Tory and High Churchman, he became after the Revolution a strong Whig. He was a popular London rector, and became Dean of Peterborough, 1707. He wrote against Atterbury (*q.v.*) on the history and rights of Convocation. He was a distinguished antiquary, and in earlier life a patron of Thomas Hearne. At Peterborough he greatly enriched the chapter library, gathering a collection of fifteen hundred volumes and tracts. Dr. Welton [Nonjurors], Rector of Whitechapel, when placing in his church a new altar-piece, a picture of the Last Supper, bade the artist give to Judas Iscariot the features of Bishop Burnet (*q.v.*). The artist, fearing the consequences, substituted Kennett. Among the crowds who came to see the picture was Mrs. Kennett, who ' recognised her husband with indignant astonishment.' Kennett obtained from the consistory court an order for the removal of the picture; d. 1728.
16. Robert Clavering, 1729; tr. from Llandaff: d. 1749.
17. John Thomas, 1747; tr. to Winchester.
18. Richard Terrick, 1757; tr. to London.
19. Robert Lambe, 1764; d. 1769.
20. John Hinchcliffe, 1769; son of a London stable-keeper; Headmaster of Westminster; Master of Trinity College, Cambridge, which position he retained after becoming Bishop of Peterborough, until in 1789 he was appointed Dean of Durham, which he held with his bishopric till his death in 1794.
21. Spencer Madan, 1794; tr. from Bristol: d. 1813.
22. John Parsons, 1813; Master of Balliol; introduced many reforms there; retained the Mastership till his death in 1819; buried in Balliol College Chapel.
23. Herbert Marsh, 1819; tr. from Llandaff: had been Lady Margaret Professor of Divinity at Cambridge. Pitt settled £500 a year on him to mark his approval of his *History of the Politics of Great Britain and France*: d. 1839.
24. George Davys, 1839; Fellow of Christ College, Cambridge; tutor to Princess —afterwards Queen—Victoria; Dean of Chester; d. 1864.

25. Francis Jeune. 1864 ; Fellow and later Master of Pembroke College, Oxford ; Headmaster of King Edward's School, Birmingham ; Dean of Jersey and Dean of Lincoln : a strong opponent of the Oxford Movement : d. 1868.
26. William Connor Magee (*q.v.*), 1868 ; tr. to York.
27. Mandell Creighton (*q.v.*), 1891 ; tr. to London.
28. Honble. Edward Henry Carr Glyn, 1897 ; formerly Vicar of St. Mary Abbotts, Kensington.   [G. F. A.]

Gunton. *Hist. of the Ch. of Peterborough* (1686) ; Poole, *Dio. Hist.* ; Browne Willis, *Surrey.*

PETER'S PENCE. The early history of this impost is obscure. There is evidence throughout the tenth century that it was being collected, but the iteration of the command, and the magnitude of the fines threatened in case of disobedience, make it probable that payment was often refused. Before the tenth century there is only one piece of clear evidence, viz. Asser's assertion that Aethelwulf, Alfred's father, sent every year three hundred mancuses (a mancus equals 2s. 6d.) to Rome for his soul's good, one hundred for lights at St. Peter's, one hundred for lights at St. Paul's, and one hundred for the Pope personally. There is no hint that Aethelwulf was following a precedent or that his successors continued the contribution. In fact, Asser (sec. 99 ff.) in his long account of the way in which Alfred (*q.v.*) distributed half his revenue to charities and churches, at home and abroad, does not name Rome as one of the recipients, though his alms to Rome are several times named in the A.-S. Chronicle. Thus we cannot find the origin of Peter's Pence in a direct royal gift: in fact, no king could have bound his heirs in such a way. Yet there is no reason to doubt that as a tax, not a gift, the ' Romescot,' ' Rome fee,' ' Rome penny,' ' Hearthpenny' was levied in England before Alfred's day. Historians later than the Norman Conquest, yet doubtless using old tradition, assign its origin to Ine of Wessex (d. 726) or Offa of Mercia (d. 796), stating in both cases that an annual penny was charged upon each hearth, *i.e.* inhabited house. The object of the charity is said to have been poor English pilgrims at Rome, resident in the *Schola Saxonum*, which is regarded as an almshouse—an anachronism which discredits the story, as Mr. W. H. Stevenson has shown (*Asser*, p. 244). But a mistaken guess as to motive does not lessen the probability that

one of these kings, perhaps Offa, established the tax ; and refusal to pay came to be regarded as an insult not only to God but to the King, for it was ' royal alms.' Farther north we have ample evidence in the ' Northumbrian Priests' Law,' which is earlier than the Conquest, for the mode of collection. Three collectors were appointed for each wapentake, and the sum received was delivered to the bishop, who shared with the King, according to the Laws of Cnut (*q.v.*), the fines inflicted for non-payment. In spite of stringent laws the tax was ill paid, and seems to have fallen into desuetude under Edward the Confessor. This was one of the grievances that led Alexander II. to encourage William's invasion : and it was natural, in the thought of that age, that the Pope should have regarded the payment as a tribute, and have made the claim, rejected by the Conqueror, of a superiority over England. However, from William I. onwards the payment was made, and though Alexander had said that it had been formerly divided between Pope and *Schola*, it now passed as a whole into the Pope's treasury. It seems that after the Conquest the poorest householders, whose property did not exceed 2s. 6d. (the Domesday price of an ox), were excused, but from others the impost was systematically levied. But in the twelfth century an agreement was made, at an unknown date, by which the bishops paid a fixed sum of three hundred marks (£200) to the Pope, from which a deduction of one mark was allowed, making the annual payment £199, 6s. 8d. It was assessed in fixed proportions on the different bishops, Lincoln paying the largest share, £42, nearly double as much as London and Norwich, which followed it. The smallest charges were on Rochester, £5, 10s., and Ely, £5. Durham, Carlisle, and the Welsh sees contributed nothing. The collection was profitable to the bishops ; in 1214 Innocent III. complained that they levied one thousand marks from their dioceses and only paid him three hundred. He tried, and failed, to raise the assessment, which remained unaltered till payments to the Pope ceased. By that time Peter's Pence were but a small part of the great revenue collected by the Pope's agent in England, and no provision was made by Henry VIII. to retain this source of income, as he retained first-fruits and tenths, for himself. With the rejection of papal authority Peter's Pence disappeared. It was abolished by the Act 25 Hen. VIII. c. 21. It is worthy of mention that nowhere, save in England and the Scandinavian countries, was there this systematic contribution to Rome. Probably it was through English influence, either from the time of Cnut or from that of the English Cardinal Nicolas, afterwards Adrian IV. (*q.v.*), who settled the ecclesiastical state of the northern countries, that the payment spread to Scandinavia. [E. W. W.]

PHILLIMORE, Sir Robert Joseph (1810-85), Dean of the Arches, son of Joseph Phillimore, himself a distinguished civilian, was educated at Westminster and Christ Church, of which he was a Student. There he formed life-long friendships with W. E. Gladstone (*q.v.*) and G. A. Denison (*q.v.*), whose sister he married in 1844. As an advocate he rapidly attained success, and became Chancellor of the dioceses of Chichester, Salisbury, and Oxford. As member of Parliament for Tavistock (1852-7) he promoted legislation to reform the ecclesiastical courts. In 1862 he was made Queen's Advocate and knighted, and was a leading adviser of the Government upon questions of international law. But his chief interests lay in the church courts, where he was 'looked upon by Churchmen as their natural advocate.' In 1867 he was appointed Judge of the Admiralty Court and Dean of the Arches in succession to Dr. Lushington, who retained, however, the Mastership of the Faculties, the lucrative office which furnished the salary for the deanery. In 1873, on Lushington's death, Phillimore reunited the salary with the work. He tried a number of important cases, including *Martin* v. *Mackonochie* and *Sheppard* v. *Bennett*. His judgments were marked by wide learning and by an appreciation of the true functions of an ecclesiastical court. His interpretation of Prayer Book and Articles by the light of history, and by the mind of the Church as shown in the writings of divines of acknowledged eminence, was a welcome contrast to the harsh Erastianism of the Privy Council, which told him he should confine himself to 'the plain meaning' of the Formularies. He has been justified, however, by the admission of his methods of interpretation by the Privy Council itself in *Read* v. *Bishop of Lincoln*. He resigned the Deanery of the Arches in 1875, but continued to sit as a judge of the Probate Division till 1883. In 1881 he was created a baronet.

Phillimore was 'before all things a devoted and warm-hearted Churchman.' 'No one who knows him,' said Dr. Pusey, 'can doubt what he has done for religion.' He served the Church not only as an erudite lawyer, but also as a member of the Ritual and Ecclesiastical Courts Commissions. His published works were by no means confined to legal

subjects, for he was a scholar of culture and refinement. [G. C.]

D.N.B.; article by Dr. Liddon in *Guardian*, 11th February 1885; *Eccl. Judgments*, with preface by himself.

PHILLPOTTS, Henry (1778-1869), Bishop of Exeter, son of a Gloucester innkeeper, won a scholarship at C.C.C., Oxford, at the age of thirteen, and a Fellowship at Magdalen four years later. As Rector of Stainton-le-Street, Durham, he was a diligent parish priest, at the same time gratifying his legal tastes by active work as a magistrate. He came into notice as a vigorous Tory controversialist and an opponent of Roman Catholicism. On becoming Dean of Chester in 1828 he was unjustly accused of changing his opinions on Roman Catholic Emancipation for the sake of preferment. His appointment as Bishop of Exeter in 1830 was unpopular in the diocese, where the prevailing tone was Evangelical, while Phillpotts was a sacramentalist and a High Churchman of the old school. Moreover, he had a reputation for nepotism, time-serving, and pluralism. His zeal for church discipline, combined with a natural love of litigation, involved him during his episcopate in more than fifty law-suits, which cost him in all between £20,000 and £30,000. Most of them were concerned with questions of church patronage and discipline. After the most famous of them [GORHAM] he published a denunciation of Archbishop Sumner (*q.v.*) as 'a favourer and supporter' of heresy, and protesting against the institution of Gorham by the archbishop, said: 'I cannot, without sin—and by God's grace I will not—hold communion with him, be he who he may, who shall so abuse the high commission which he bears.' He also accused the judges of being 'swayed by other motives besides justice and truth,' and assembled a diocesan synod at Exeter, the first held in England for many years [COUNCILS], to reaffirm the doctrine impugned.

In the House of Lords he was soon recognised as an orator of the first rank. For over thirty years he took a leading part in debate as an independent Tory and High Churchman, vigorously resisting any encroachment on the rights and privileges of the Church, and interesting himself in measures which concerned the moral and social welfare of the people. His opposition to the Reform Bill increased his unpopularity in his diocese. Lord Grey 'never could endure him,' and he answered that minister's advice to the bishops to 'set their house in order' by a violent counter-attack. He opposed the Poor Law Amendment Act of 1834, especially protesting against its injustice to the mothers of illegitimate children. In 1844 he introduced a Bill for the suppression of brothels and of trading in seduction and prostitution. He attacked with equal vigour the Dissenters' Chapel Bill, 'that horrid system,' the socialism of Robert Owen, and the proposal to allow marriage with a deceased wife's sister, which formed the subject of one of his latest speeches in the House.

Phillpotts's love of controversy, his intemperate methods of conducting it, and his high-handed rule at Exeter made him many enemies, who denounced him as a 'turbulent prelate,' 'domineering,' and 'the pest of his diocese.' But while freely accusing him of ambition and love of intrigue, they could not deny him the possession of great talents and a personality of remarkable force, which enabled him to fill, not unworthily, a large space in the church history of his time. A conscientious and hard-working bishop, he did much to restore church life in a stagnant diocese where firm discipline was needed. Though he condemned Tract 90 he recognised the value of the Oxford Movement (*q.v.*) and the devotion of its adherents, and showed courage in defending them. In 1848 he sanctioned a community of Sisters of Mercy under Miss Sellon for work among the poor of Devonport, and supported them against strong opposition. He took a keen interest in the proposed see of Truro (*q.v.*), and contributed liberally to its endowment, as well as to the restoration of Exeter Cathedral and other objects. From 1863 he lived in seclusion, being physically infirm, though 'in full force intellectually,' as Bishop S. Wilberforce wrote of him in 1867, adding: 'It is very striking to see the taming of the Old Lion.' He was in process of resigning his see when he died. [G. C.]

Shutte, *Life* (to 1832); Hansard, *Parl. Debates*, 1831-63; *Edinburgh Review*, July 1850; A. C. Kelway, *George Rundle Prynne*.

PHILPOT, John (1516-1555), Archdeacon of Winchester and Protestant martyr, third son of Sir Peter Philpot, was born at Compton, Hants, in 1516. He was educated at Winchester and New College, Oxford, where he was Fellow, 1534-1541. He became a convert to the Reformed opinions, and went abroad when the Act of the Six Articles was passed in 1539. He was ever contentious, and through disputing with a Franciscan on the road from Venice to Padua nearly fell into the clutches of the Inquisition. Return-

ing to England, he went to Winchester, 'and as the time ministered more boldness to him he had divers conflicts with Gardiner the Bishop' (*q.v.*). Gardiner complained: 'One Philpot in Westminster whom I accounted altered in his wits devised tales of me the specialities whereof I was never called to answer to.' Afterwards he quarrelled bitterly with Poynet (*q.v.*), Gardiner's successor, who claimed a yearly pension from him. 'This causing contention between them, intolerable troubles arose and slanders in that diocese to them both'; the bishop's registrar, who seems to have fomented the quarrel, then waylaid him, and set his men to beat him. But though severely beaten he could get no remedy in the spiritual court, as the bishop and registrar were against him.

When Mary succeeded he took part in a debate in Convocation on the Catechism and the Presence in the Mass, and soon showed himself the protagonist of the half-dozen who took the Protestant side. According to his own account, he could more than hold his own with his antagonists, and adopted an aggressive and somewhat contemptuous tone, which provoked more than one rebuke from Weston, the prolocutor. The debate chiefly turned on the corporal presence in the Eucharist, which Philpot hotly denied. 'That sacrament of the altar, which ye reckon to be all one with the mass, is no sacrament at all, neither is Christ in anywise present in it.' He was soon afterwards committed to prison, and after remaining there a year was handed over to Bonner (*q.v.*), who tried hard to persuade him to recant, and seems to have done his best for him; but he maintained the same defiant attitude, and was at length condemned and burnt in Smithfield in December 1555. He met his death with great courage and resolution, kissing the stake, and saying: 'Shall I disdain to suffer at this stake seeing my Redeemer did not refuse to suffer a most vile death upon the Cross for me ?'

He was a man of much learning and wholehearted devotion to what he believed to be the truth, but obstinate and quarrelsome, and as relentless to his opponents as they were to him. He approved of the burning of Anabaptists, and on one occasion having spat on an Arian wrote a tract to justify his action. [C. P. S. C.]

Foxe, *Acts and Monuments*; Strype, *Memorials*; *Machyn's Diary*.

PILGRIMAGE OF GRACE, The, was a rising in Yorkshire, preceded by one in

Lincolnshire, which had broken out mainly in consequence of the first attempt to put down the smaller monasteries under the Act of 1536 [MONASTERIES, SUPPRESSION OF]. Commissioners for a subsidy visited Lincolnshire in the end of September just after the suppression of the abbey of Louth Park and the nunnery of Legbourne, and rumours were spread of new and excessive taxation, with the suppression of many parish churches and diminution of holidays. The insurgents, with entire loyalty, sent two deputies to the King, and compelled the country gentlemen to take an oath to stand by them. The King was for some days in serious anxiety about the issue, and was much relieved to find that Lincolnshire was pacified by a message from the Earl of Shrewsbury. Before this trouble was over Yorkshire was up in arms, and the movement soon spread over all the north of England. Robert Aske, a lawyer, ordered a muster on Skipwith Moor, and by the middle of October he had easily obtained possession of the city of York. He issued a proclamation denying that they had assembled on account of taxation, but because ill-disposed persons in the King's council sought to destroy the Church and rob the whole body of the realm. And his followers, entering on a ' pilgrimage of grace,' swore that their only objects were the maintenance of God's faith and Church militant, preservation of the King's person and issue, and purifying the nobility of all villains' blood and evil counsellors. They must restore Christ's Church in its purity and put down heretical opinions.

The Archbishop of York and others who were afraid to countenance the movement retreated into Pomfret Castle, which held out for the King for a short time under Lord Darcy, while the Earl of Cumberland, on his way to Hexham, returned to Skipton Castle, where he was besieged. But Darcy surrendered Pomfret Castle to Aske. Thither the Earl of Shrewsbury, the King's lieutenant for the north, despatched Lancaster herald with a royal proclamation ; but Aske refused to let him read it, saying they were all going up to London on pilgrimage to obtain an answer to their articles. The Duke of Norfolk, marching northwards, found it needful to make a truce with the rebels (27th October), with declaration of the King's pardon, while Sir Ralph Ellerker and Robert Bowes went up with him to set forth their demands to the King. The King detained them more than a fortnight at Windsor, while their comrades in the north were impatient, and sent them back with a carefully worded reply, on which a council

was held at York. They had to consider that Norfolk was coming down again to meet the northern gentry at Doncaster on the 5th December, and issues of peace and war still hung in the balance. It was arranged that there should first be a meeting of the commons at Pomfret, where the northern clergy should also assemble under Archbishop Lee, to give their advice whether there were just cause for fighting. The archbishop was alarmed, having already yielded to the commons when Darcy surrendered Pomfret ; and he preached there on Sunday, the 3rd, a sermon with which his hearers were disappointed, declaring that there was no cause to fight for the faith, as the King had provided sufficient safeguard for it by the Ten Articles lately set forth. But the Convocation passed resolutions in favour of papal jurisdiction and the old order of the Church. Norfolk was perplexed, and made an interim arrangement, promising a free Parliament in the north of England, which the King had agreed to for complete settlement of differences. The ' pilgrims ' then tore off their badges of the Five Wounds of Christ, saying: ' We will wear no badge or sign but the badge of our Sovereign Lord.'

But good faith was not kept by the King. He called Aske up to a private conference, and treated him with so much urbanity that on his return to the north at the New Year (1537) he tried to assure everybody that the King was very gracious. The King, he said, had approved the general pardon, Norfolk was coming again to the north, and all grievances would be heard in a Parliament at York, at which the Queen would be crowned. But in spite of these assurances there were grave misgivings. Many said they wanted no pardon, as they had done no wrong. The King seemed to be fortifying Hull and Scarborough. One John Hallom was caught in an attempt to surprise Hull. Sir Francis Bigod failed in an attempt on Scarborough, but fled to the West Borders, where there was a new rising owing to the King's use of border thieves to keep the country down. Norfolk did come, but not as a peacemaker. He went first to Carlisle, punishing the insurgents with martial law, and terrifying the country with savage executions. Then going on to Durham and York he endeavoured to find who were responsible for the demands made at Doncaster. He got Aske into his hands, and sent him up to the King, who sent him down again to suffer for treason in Yorkshire, while a number of Lincolnshire and Yorkshire rebels were tried, hanged, and quartered in London.

In Lancashire the Abbots of Sawley and Whalley were hanged, and the Abbot of Furness felt it prudent to surrender his house.   [J. G.]

PLAINSONG IN THE ENGLISH CHURCH.

Plainsong (*Cantus Planus*), Even or Level Song, *i.e.* having all notes of an even and indefinite time value, is the Church's own music, proceeding from the Church's prayers, 'born at the Altar, grown to greatness with the Church itself, and ordered together with its worship' (Wagner).

England was perhaps the first country to receive the Gregorian Chant, and the earliest copies of Gregory's *Antiphoner* were perhaps brought here by St. Augustine (*q.v.*) (596). The antiphon *Deprecamur Te*, chanted by the great missionary and his companions as they advanced to greet King Ethelbert, was the first Gregorian music ever heard in England. Augustine organised the Church music after the Gregorian pattern. James, one of his band, was, as Bede (*q.v.*) relates, a noted teacher of the chant, which soon spread over the island. The position of cantor became one of great importance, and was held by many distinguished priests.

The Council of Clovesho (747) ordained that the liturgical chant should be carefully studied according to the Gregorian *Antiphoner*. 'The time of working and planting had lasted for a century and a half; from 750 onwards the Liturgy and liturgical chant in England continued in a quiet and steady course. The numerous monasteries faithfully guarded the rites and music which had been entrusted to them.' An attempt at innovation, soon ended, took place in the eleventh century, and it was not till the ecclesiastical disturbances of the sixteenth century that the chant began to die out in the country which had first received it from Rome. There were three principal 'Uses,' viz. Sarum, York, and Hereford, of which perhaps that of Sarum (*q.v.*), as given in the old MSS. of the thirteenth and fourteenth centuries, is the finest.

Plainsong never completely died out in England except during the Commonwealth, when there was very little music at all. The versicles and responses at least—which are just as much Plainsong as the Mass chants—have always been sung, though more often than not corruptly, in our cathedral and parish churches.

The Reformation did not abolish Plainsong, or introduce what is called 'Anglican' music. The great settings of Canticles and Communion service of Tallis, Byrd,

Gibbons, Farrant, and others were musical developments independent of the Reformation. The first and most celebrated product of the Reformation was a little volume called Merbecke's *Boke of Common Praier noted*, which is entirely Plainsong. The first 'Anglican' chant did not make its appearance till more than one hundred years after the breach with Rome.

If we except the versicles and responses, Plainsong fell into disuse in England from the Commonwealth till 1843, when Mr. W. Dyce published his *Book of Common Prayer noted* (after Merbecke's system). This was soon followed by Oakley's *Laudes Diurnae*, in which the Psalms and Canticles were adapted to Gregorian tones for the use of Margaret Chapel (now All Saints, Margaret Street). In 1850 the Rev. Thomas Helmore issued his *Psalter and Canticles noted*, which, with his *Brief Directory of Plainsong* (1850) and his *Hymnal Noted* (1851), have been the standard text-books of the English Plainsong revival till recently. The names of these reformers must ever be honoured. They did excellent and much-needed work. But they were handicapped by want of knowledge. They never quite grasped the first principles of Plainsong, *i.e.* that the time value of the notes depends entirely on that of the syllables to which they are sung. There is always in Helmore's work the feeling that he is trying to set up an arbitrary rhythm in order that the time may be beaten out if need be. Their versions of the chant were mostly taken from debased French sources, and are very corrupt. The outcome of this revival was the foundation in 1870 of the London Gregorian Choral Association. Their festivals at St. Paul's Cathedral were for forty years conducted on the principles of Helmore. In 1910, however, the association courageously reformed itself, and its future on Solesmes lines seems settled.

In the last two decades of the nineteenth century the labours of the monks of Solesmes have brought to light much that was unknown concerning the chant and its performance. The following extract from the preface to *A Manual of Gregorian Chant* (1903) lays down the right methods:—

'Of all the elements which compose rhythm, strength, duration, pitch, movement, the last is the most important. . . . The progress of the voice in singing may very well be compared to a man's walk, or rather to the flight of a bird. When the bird soars up, it seems that the first impulse will carry it very far; however, it soon dies away, and a new flap of the wings is necessary to give a fresh impulse and keep up the bird in its flight.

'The same must be said of the voice: the first impulse cannot last for ever, and it is necessary that the voice should soon find a support on which it may alight, as it were, and receive a fresh impulse. Thus the voice moves in a succession of ups and downs, which were called by the ancients "arsis" and "thesis," and are represented by the successive rise and fall of the hand or foot of the singer.

'This, of course, is not peculiar to Plain Chant, but is found also in all kinds of music, so that the rhythm of Gregorian Chant is not essentially different from the rhythm of modern music, in which the successive impulses of the voice are marked by the bars which separate the measures.

'The use of these bars, however, in Plain Chant, would be a great mistake, as it would lead to a confusion of the two kinds of music, which might again cause the destruction of Plain Chant.

'Measure, in modern music, is based on the division of time into equal parts, so that the syllables, whether long or short, must adapt themselves to the notes to which they are sung; whilst in Plain Chant the value of the notes in syllabic passages depends entirely on the value of the syllables and on their place in the sentence.

'Moreover, in modern music, the *thesis* or stress of the voice marked by the bars is regularly strong, while in Plain Chant it may be strong or weak indifferently; all depends on the value of the syllable on which the voice finds support for a fresh impulse.

'This shows that, strictly speaking, the rhythm of Plain Chant is not measured rhythm, but there is something in it more immaterial and less mechanical than in modern music.' [MUSIC IN THE CHURCH.]

[M. S.]

For a comprehensive history Professor Peter Wagner's great work, *Introduction to the Gregorian Melodies*, Part I., has been translated into English; Dr. Frere's article in Grove's *Dictionary* and *Elements of Plainsong* (P. and M.M. Soc.).

POETRY IN THE ENGLISH CHURCH.

The periods in which religious poetry has most flourished in England have not been the great periods of secular poetry—the age of Chaucer, the age of Shakespeare, the age of Byron and Shelley and Wordsworth and Keats. The impulse to the poetic art in general comes usually from the widening of horizons, produced by a great addition to

human knowledge, or by a new point of view from which knowledge is regarded; such as were, in their several ages, the discovery of Italian literature, the discovery of the new and the rediscovery of the old world, and the discovery of the 'rights of man.' Such additions to knowledge tend for the moment to damp religion down. On the other hand, religious poetry does not flourish in times of religious controversy when pamphlets are flying. We have no religious poets during the Reformation period, or during the reaction under Mary; nor, again, during the controversies of the eighteenth century. A revival of religious poetry implies a revival of religion, and we find that the periods when religious poetry has most flourished in England since the Norman Conquest have been certain periods of religious enthusiasm: (1) the thirteenth century, when religious emotion had been rekindled by the friars, and they and the monks were at the height of their influence for good; (2) the seventeenth century, when the revived study of antiquity had rekindled the saintly ideal in the hearts of churchmen like Bishop Andrewes (*q.v.*); (3) the middle of the eighteenth century, under the influence of the Evangelical revival; (4) the Tractarian revival in the early nineteenth century; (5) a mid-Victorian period of speculative theology.

1. *The Thirteenth Century.*—In the great cathedrals of Salisbury and Lincoln and the abbey church of Westminster, which were built in this century, we can trace the development of the new architecture from what preceded it. What models had the religious poet? There were (*a*) the Latin hymns of St. Bernard and others; and accordingly we find English lyrics written after this pattern, which have passion and dignity and are free from the mawkish taint that hangs about many of our modern imitations. There were also (*b*) the Norman-French poems of the *trouvères*, which were being imitated by the court poets with success; and we find these new lyrical forms, of all varieties, put to the service of sacred poetry, and used with a freshness and vividness that are admirable. Here, for example, is a singularly vivid picture of the crucifixion :—

'High upon a down
  Where all folk see it may,
A mile from the town,
  About the mid-day,
The Cross is up areared :
His friends are afeared,
  And clingeth as the clay :
The rood stands in stone,
Mary stands alone
  And saith *well-away*.

'The nailës be too strong,
The smithës are too sly,
Thou bleddest all too long,
The tree is all too high :
The stonës be all wet :
Alas, Jesu the sweet,
For now friend hast thou none.
But Saint Johan to-mourning
And Mary weeping
For pine that thee is on.'[1]

A great deal of this early poetry is more in the vein of Ecclesiastes than of the Gospel. The line between the monastic contempt of the world and the old Preacher's doctrine of vanity was a fine one, and the natural English melancholy expressed itself characteristically upon the transitoriness of everything human without always an equally complete recognition of the eternity of what is divine. There is a remarkable poem by a Franciscan, Brother Thomas of Hales, written before 1250 for a young lady who asked him for a love-song, one verse of which anticipates a famous *ballade* of Villon :—

'Where is Paris and Heleyn
That were so bright and fair of blee,[2]
Amadas, Tristram, and Dideyne,
Isoude and allë they,
Hector with his sharpë main.
And Cæsar rich of worldës fee ?
They be iglyden out of the reyne,
So the shaft is of the clee.'[3]

Old English Miscellany (E.E.T.S., 1872).

The lyrical religious poetry of the fourteenth and fifteenth centuries does not differ greatly from that of the thirteenth in its general character. The best of all the religious verse that has survived from the fifteenth century is the beautiful allegory with the refrain, taken from Canticles, *Quia amore langueo.* To this century also belong the many Christmas carols preserved in the Sloane MS. 2593 (Brit. Mus.), edited by Thomas Wright for the Warton Club. But the fourteenth century, which produced Wyclif, produced also that most interesting allegorical and satirical poem or group of poems in the old alliterative measure known as ' Piers the Plowman.' It is impossible in a few words to give a summary of its contents or estimate of its merit. The best account of it is the essay contributed by Professor Manly of Chicago to the *Cam. Hist. Eng. Lit.* (ii. 1-42).

Before passing to the second great period of religious poetry we may notice one or two names in the sixteenth century. Spenser's

---

Faery Queene is in intention a religious allegory, describing the conflict of a Christian with the temptations of world, flesh, and devil. But as the poet wrote it in the manner of Ariosto, as a cycle of romantic adventures, it is possible for the reader almost to ignore its moral significance, the interest of the story and the beauty of the writing being independent of the allegory. Hence it is only in occasional passages, such as the stanzas on the ' Ministry of Angels ' (ii. 8), that we find what can strictly be called sacred poetry. More simply religious is the ' Hymn of Heavenly Love,' which appeals to us as directly as to Spenser's contemporaries except in passages dealing with the cosmogony. The ' Hymn of Heavenly Beauty ' is a piece of poetical Platonism, which would have shocked Plato by its Puritan conclusion. In the next generation Spenser had a devoted disciple in Giles Fletcher, who wrote on the Nativity and the Passion, sometimes very beautifully. But for the most part the religious verse of the sixteenth and early seventeenth centuries consists of occasional poems by writers who put their strength into secular poetry, or by private gentlemen like Sir Henry Wotton and Sir Walter Ralegh. Campion, the song-writer, and Ben Jonson have left us several pieces of great beauty. Herrick's ' Noble Numbers ' have all the rhythmical skill that distinguishes his secular poems, and not a little of their quaintness. They are not deeply spiritual, but they have the air of sincerity. Some of the best of these occasional poems are anonymous, such as ' Hierusalem, my happy home ' and ' Yet if his majesty our sovereign lord.'

2. *The Seventeenth Century.*—The new movement of the seventeenth century was inaugurated by John Donne, Dean of St. Paul's, and from him it passed to his young friend, George Herbert (*q.v.*), and to Richard Crashaw, and through Herbert to Henry Vaughan. The imaginative intensity of Donne takes in each of his successors a different shape : in Herbert of devout submission, in Crashaw of ecstatic adoration, in Vaughan of mystical contemplation. Donne's religious verse, though less crabbed than his satires, is often obscure, but the thought is always worth digging for. A worse fault is the morbid strain which infects this, as all his writing, and appears in the design of his monument at St. Paul's. The four sonnets on ' Death ' are perhaps the greatest of his religious pieces, but the simplest and most beautiful is the ' Hymn to God the Father,' which he wrote for the choristers at St. Paul's, and so took pains to

make smooth. The best introduction to the religious verse of Donne is his Life by Izaak Walton; and that Life and the Life of Herbert afford the best commentary on this school of poetry. Herbert's poetry, indeed, is unintelligible apart from the story of his life. He handed the manuscript on his deathbed to the clergyman who attended him, with these instructions : ' Sir, I pray you deliver this book to my dear brother Ferrar, and tell him he shall find in it a picture of the many spiritual conflicts that have passed between God and my soul, before I could subject mine to the will of Jesus my Master ; in whose service I have now found perfect freedom : desire him to read it, and then, if he can think it may turn to the advantage of any dejected poor soul, let it be made public ; if not, let him burn it, for I and it are less than the least of God's mercies.' Herbert's biography shows of what nature those conflicts were. The original disturbing cause was the desire to rise at court. In early life his prospects were brilliant ; but the death of King James and his patrons disappointed him of his hopes. This disappointment led him to reconsider his way of life, and it supplies occasion for some of his most interesting poems, *e.g.* ' The Quip.' The enemy he encounters is not the flesh, but the world. In Herbert's poetry two or three things are especially striking : (1) The high merit of the ordinary level of his style, that of a scholar and a gentleman ; always dignified, with a calm and sustained equableness. (2) The mastery of metre. The particular form of stanza is always happily chosen to meet the character of the mood to be expressed. (3) The wisdom of the sentiment. The *Church Porch*, a body of rules of common morality and good manners, must strike every reader as full of wisdom ; but the wisdom is as conspicuous in matters of religion. No better example could be given than the famous ' Elixir.' (4) But beyond the poet's skill and wisdom there is in Herbert at his best an intimacy and touching sweetness that brings what he has to say home to his reader. Sometimes a whole poem is written in this delicate vein, sometimes it breaks out suddenly in a dry place. Examples are ' Discipline' (' Throw away thy rod '), which for its simplicity and restrained passion might stand as the perfection of the religious lyric ; ' The Flower' (' How fresh, O Lord '), and the exquisite quatrain in ' Easter' :—

' I got me flowers to strew Thy way ;
   I got me boughs off many a tree :
But Thou wast up by break of day,
   And broughtst Thy sweets along with Thee.'

Henry Vaughan was a disciple of Herbert, and borrowed from him one of his least happy qualities, the trick of curious metaphor, as well as many of his metres and topics. But what Vaughan has of the best is his own. Constitutionally he was a very different person from Herbert. The one was an ascetic, the other a mystic. Vaughan has a passion for nature ; he observes her moods ; to him the world is but a veil for the Eternal Spirit, whose presence may be felt even in the smallest part. He makes us feel, as Frederick Myers said of Wordsworth, that ' Nature is no mere collection of phenomena, but infuses into her least approaches some sense of her mysterious whole.' Hence to Vaughan, as to Wordsworth, everything in nature is interesting. There are ' surprises' laid by God ' in each element to catch man's heart.' The wind is a true type of the Spirit ; the streams are a type of man's pilgrimage. Naturally many of the poems deal with the contrast between the ' toil unsever'd from tranquillity ' of the rest of the universe, and man's restless waywardness. The world, says Vaughan, would be Paradise if man would but open his eyes and look about him intelligently. As it is, he too often loses wonder as he grows up. The ' Retreat ' is well known to be the germ of Wordsworth's great ' Ode on the Intimations of Immortality from Childhood.' It is not often that Vaughan gets his voice as clear as in that poem. Often his pieces begin well, and then lose themselves in the sand. But there are one or two in his own characteristic vein, in which the inspiration is maintained throughout. The finest is that on ' Departed Friends.'

With Vaughan may be associated Thomas Traherne, who has much in common with him, notably the doctrine that earth would be Paradise if men did not lose the spirit of wonder. His central idea is that the world was created for man's delight, and fails of its purpose if man is not delighted.

Crashaw is a poet of a very different stamp from these. He is fluent, fervent, ecstatic ; at his worst sinking to ineptitudes of extravagance, and at his best rising into raptures, of which neither Herbert nor Vaughan was capable. A Fellow of Peterhouse when that was the ' ritualistic ' college at Cambridge, he joined the Roman communion when the commissioners appointed by the Long Parliament purged that society, and died a Canon of Loretto not without a suspicion of poison. The best measure of his accomplishment as a master of language is the version of Strada's poem on the Nightingale who had a singing match with a Musician ; but some of his religious verse is almost as wonderful in execution. The finest, on the whole, is the poem, 'To the Name above every Name.' But that poem also exhibits Crashaw's characteristic defect. There are repetitions both of words and sentiments; and there is not enough substance in the thought to bear being hammered out into two hundred and forty verses. Fluency and carelessness and thinness of idea being his besetting faults, he is at his best when his subject is definite and ample, and his metre fixed, as in the 'Hymn to St. Teresa,' and the lines to the Countess of Denbigh, which should be read in the corrected version. The best example of his florid manner is the 'Hymn of the Nativity'; of his passion, the appendix to 'The Flaming Heart' ('O thou undaunted daughter of desires').

More popular than any other seventeenth-century poet in his own day was Francis Quarles, who was born a year before George Herbert. He has an easy mastery of rhyme and rhythm, but his thought is commonplace. One stanza in the *Emblems* is still remembered for a *hapax legomenon* :—

'What mean dull souls, in this high measure
To *haberdash*
In earth's base wares, whose greatest treasure
Is dross and trash:
The height of whose enchanting pleasure
Is but a flash?
Are these the goods that thou supply'st
Us mortals with? are these the high'st?
Can these bring cordial peace? False world,
thou liest.'

There are two great names in the seventeenth century which must not be passed over in the most summary survey of religious poetry, though they were both outside the main movement. It is not easy to speak of Milton as a religious poet without seeming to disparage him, because although in his case, as in Spenser's, the greatest of his poems is on a religious subject, its interest is not chiefly a religious interest. *Paradise Lost* is beyond question the most magnificent poem in the English language, but it would be difficult to conceive of it as exercising any religious effect upon its readers. And the same thing is true of the 'Ode on the Nativity'; that, too, in its special way is magnificent, but it is not religious. Milton is most religious when he is putting into his verse his own personal thoughts about life and goodness and God, as in certain well-known passages of *Comus* and *Samson Agonistes*, the Sonnet on his blindness, and the 'Ode at a Solemn Music.' With Milton may be mentioned his friend Andrew Marvell,

a curiously ambiguous personality, both in life and art. Many of his pieces cannot be taken seriously — they may be the experiments of a young scholar—but the 'Dialogue between the Resolved Soul and Created Pleasure' and the 'Ode on a Drop of Dew,' while they have all the 'witty delicacy' that distinguishes Marvell at his best, are genuinely religious.

3. *The Evangelical Revival.* —The third period of religious poetry was marked by a development of hymnody, in which the experiences of the Christian believer were generalised for use in the congregation on the model of the Hebrew Psalter. This movement began quite early in the eighteenth century with the *Hymns and Spiritual Songs* of Isaac Watts (1707, 2nd ed. 1709), followed by his *Psalms of David* (1719), both of which enjoyed immense popularity among the Dissenters. The best of them, 'Jesus shall reign where'er the sun' and 'O God, our help in ages past,' from the Psalter, and 'Come, let us join our cheerful songs' and 'When I survey the wondrous cross,' from the Hymns, are still among the very best of their kind. Addison enriched the language of devotion with some fine pieces after Watts's model, printed in the Saturday *Spectator* (1712), three of which are still popular: 'The Lord my pasture shall prepare,' 'When all Thy mercies, O my God,' and 'The spacious firmament on high.' Consequently when the Wesleys (*q.v.*) began their evangelistic work in the Church of England they had an admirable instrument ready to their hand of which Charles Wesley made an unexampled use. He wrote hymns to the number, it is said, of six thousand five hundred, which appeared in various volumes from 1737 to 1762; and some have an exquisite lyrical accent. It was his brother John, however, who wrote the only religious verse of the movement which takes rank not as a hymn but as a poem, the 'Jacob wrestling.' Through Wesley and Whitefield the impulse to sacred song reached John Newton, and through him it inspired William Cowper. The *Olney Hymns*, published in 1779, contained Newton's 'Glorious things of Thee are spoken,' one of the most grand and jubilant of hymns, and Cowper's 'Hark, my soul, it is the Lord,' one of the most tender. Three years before, Toplady had issued the volume of *Psalms and Hymns* which gave to English Christianity perhaps its most popular hymn, 'Rock of Ages'; and in 1773 a posthumous volume of *Poems* by John Byrom appeared, which among much mere paraphrasing

of passages from his master, William Law, contained the beautiful lyric, ' My spirit longeth for thee,' which appears in a mangled form in modern hymn-books.

4. *The Romantic and Tractarian Revivals.*—Before proceeding to speak of the poets of the Tractarian revival, it is necessary to call attention to a religious side of the Romantic revival which preceded it. No one will dispute that both Wordsworth and Coleridge were religious men, and that the poetry of the one and the prose writings of the other have exerted a deep influence upon the religious thought of the century. But it would be true to say that Wordsworth's influence has been felt in the more fundamental region of natural religion rather than in any imaginative representation of Christian doctrine. The *Ecclesiastical Sonnets* are not inferior in merit to the bulk of the *Christian Year,* and if they have escaped popularity it is because English Churchmen are as a rule uninterested in their own past history ; but no one would call them inspired, and on Englishmen generally they have left no mark. The religious poetry of Wordsworth is to be sought in his great ' Ode on the Intimations of Immortality ' and the ' Ode to Duty,' and also in passages of the *Excursion.* The first principle of his theology, that the spirit of intelligence and love which we find in simple and innocent human nature also animates the external world, is expressed with special beauty and power in the ' Lines written near Tintern Abbey.' The transcendence of God, no less than His immanence, is asserted in such poems as ' An Evening Voluntary.' In reply to the charge that he ' averted his eyes from half of human fate,' it is sufficient to point to ' Resolution and Independence ' and ' The Afflictions of Margaret,' and the fine lines prefixed to 'The White Doe of Rylstone' (' Action is transitory,' etc.). The name of Coleridge among sacred poets is best represented by his son Hartley, who wrote many excellent sonnets, the best known being that which concludes with the lines :—

' Think not the faith by which the just shall live
Is a dead creed, a map correct of heaven,
Far less a feeling fond and fugitive,
A thoughtless gift withdrawn as soon as given.
It is an affirmation and an act
That bids eternal truth be present fact.'

Earlier, however, than Wordsworth and Coleridge, William Blake, the harbinger of the Romantic revival, had enriched sacred poetry with a few pieces of marked power and originality. Much of Blake's religious verse is marred by the antinomian tendency which he had imbibed from William Godwin ; but in the *Songs of Innocence* and *Songs of Experience* he has supplied an almost startling imaginative commentary on the social problem. It would be difficult to find a parallel to the two poems on ' Holy Thursday ' without going back to the eighth-century Jewish prophets; and every social reformer since has found inspiration in the poems on the New Jerusalem, ' England, awake, awake, awake ! ' and ' And did those feet in ancient times.' No other Christian poet has so insistently urged the Christian duty of forgiveness.

The *differentia* of the poems to which the Tractarian revival gave rise may be found in a certain didactic strain. This is true even of those poems in the *Christian Year* (1827) which were written before Keble (*q.v.*) conceived the idea of making that very popular collection. The earliest poems in the book, composed in 1819, are ' Blest are the pure in heart,' ' Lord, and what shall this man do?' ' When God of old came down from heaven,' ' There is a book, who runs may read,' which are all doctrinal, and these together with the Morning and Evening poems have long taken their place, in whole or part, among the hymns of the English Church. This didactic character partly accounts for their popularity. Parents taught them to their children on the Sunday, and the children again to their children, so that the *Christian Year* became a tradition in many households.

The consequent debt owed by English Churchmanship to the *Christian Year* is very great; for, as has been well said, 'it has a real openness of mind for the whole large view of the Church and the world.' The same didactic quality, but in a sterner mood, is characteristic of the *Lyra Apostolica,* an anthology consisting of pieces written by Newman (*q.v.*) and R. H. Froude (*q.v.*) during a voyage to the Mediterranean in 1833, with others by Keble, Isaac Williams, Bowden, and R. I. Wilberforce. Of the 179 pieces in the volume Newman contributed 109 and Keble 46. Though Newman wrote verse, only, as it were, with his left hand, not a few of his contributions to the *Lyra Apostolica* take a high place among English sacred poems. ' Lead, kindly Light,' written when its author was becalmed in the Strait of Bonifazio, and ' aching to get home,' has become as popular a hymn, from its exquisite rendering of a mood of depression overcome by faith, as the angels' song in the ' Dream of Gerontius ' (' Praise to the Holiest in the height '). No less beautiful are two

poems on the blessed dead, called ' Rest ' and
' Knowledge.' More directly didactic are
such verses as the 'Zeal of Jehu' and
' Deeds, not Words,' which make their point
with remarkable trenchancy. Keble's most
beautiful contributions to the *Lyra Apostolica*
are ' The Winter Thrush,' an unrhymed ode
called ' Burial of the Dead,' inspired by the
loss of his favourite sister, and ' The Watch
by Night.' But of the *Lyra Apostolica* it is
true to say that the whole was greater than
any single part, because it recalled and impressed the idea of the Church as a spiritual
society with a history and standards and
discipline of its own. Of the poetry of Isaac
Williams (*q.v.*), which was pre-eminently
' of an age,' it will be sufficient to say with
Dean Church that ' it was in a lower and
sadder key than the *Christian Year*, which
no doubt first inspired it ' ; that ' it wanted
the elasticity and freshness and variety of
Keble's verse ' ; but that ' it was the out-
pouring of a very beautiful mind.'

The direct heir of the tradition of scholarly
poetry that originated with the Tractarians
was Richard Chenevix Trench (*q.v.*) (1807-
1886), afterwards Archbishop of Dublin.
With much of Newman's gnomic force he
has greater facility in expression, and on
another side he has much of Keble's mystical
delight in natural beauty. F. W. Faber
(1814-1863) wrote a few memorable pieces,
but is chiefly remembered as a hymn-writer.
Later in the century came two gifted women,
Dora Greenwell (1821-1882) and Christina
Rossetti (1830-1894), the former teaching
gentle lessons of patience and hope, the latter
crying with passion against a vain world.
Both poetesses had learned in suffering,
physical and mental, what they taught in
song. The former has the advantage in
the bracing quality of her message, the latter
in original genius. Few sacred poems reach
the level of Miss Rossetti's ' From House to
Home ' and ' A New and Old Year Song,'
and most of her religious lyrics display some
touch of imaginative or rhythmical' beauty,
though there is too little variety in the
thought.

5. *The Theological Revival.*—The religious
movement of the mid-Victorian age was, in
the main, a theological apologetic against a
new materialism in society due to a rapid
development of the natural sciences, and a
new disquietude among the faithful due to
what seemed to be the possible results of
Biblical criticism. The sense of these dangers
is felt in many poems by A. H. Clough
(1819-1861) and Matthew Arnold (1822-1888),
and each in his own way made an endeavour

to minister to the needs of the time. But
the chief religious poets of this era are its
two greatest poets, Tennyson and Browning.
Tennyson was much impressed by the doctrine
of the evolution of species, and he met the
current materialistic deduction from it by
the passionate affirmation of two deep
convictions : (1) that such a process
must extend beyond death and be a progress
to some ' far-off divine event to which the
whole creation moves ' ; (2) that if Nature
is to be interpreted by Man, and not Man by
Nature, we have in man's highest powers and
thoughts and feelings the best evidence of the
Creator. The welcome thus given to the
bright side of evolutionary doctrine, as
supplying new evidence to the heart and
imagination of the Being of God, the truth of
immortality, and the perfectibility of the
human race is one of the great debts that the
age owes to Tennyson. He has treated this
and kindred questions in ' In Memoriam,'
' The Making of Man,' ' By an Evolutionist,'
and ' The Ancient Sage.' In Browning there
is a great deal of mere argumentation,
philosophical and theological, which is not
poetry at all. But now and again, as he
muses, the fire kindles. Of the three great
attributes of God—power, wisdom, love—it
is the last that especially needs establishing
in face of evidence that seems to conflict
with it ; and it is to the establishment of this
truth that Browning devotes himself, making affirmation of his own beliefs through
the mouth of the Pope in ' The Ring and the
Book,' Saul, Paracelsus, Rabbi ben Ezra, and
many another dramatic character. The peculiar value of Browning's religious poetry to the
churchman is that from the ideal of his own
heart he asserts not only, like Tennyson, the
benevolence of God to His creatures, but the
self-sacrifice of God, and so the special doctrine of Christianity. From this profound
conviction of the perfect love of God he
pronounces on all the great problems of life,
sin, pain, and death. Among the writers of
religious poetry in the latter half of the
nineteenth century must be mentioned three
Roman Catholics—Coventry Patmore, Francis
Thompson, and Gerard Hopkins, who to a
certain exuberance characteristic of their
Church joined a genuine religious ardour.

[H. C. B.]

POLE, Reginald, Cardinal (1500-58), Archbishop of Canterbury, a younger son of Sir
Richard Pole by his wife Margaret, daughter
of the Duke of Clarence, was born at Stourton Castle in Staffordshire. Educated at
Sheen Charter-house and Oxford, as a youth

of the blood royal. Henry VIII. (*q.v.*) took much interest in his upbringing, and gave him several pieces of church preferment even as a layman in his teens. In 1521 he went to Padua, and made many friendships with scholars. He visited Rome at the Jubilee in 1525, and returned to England in 1527. But in 1529 he obtained leave of the King to go abroad again to study at Paris. He was really afraid of being entangled in Henry's project for a divorce, but found he had not escaped the danger at Paris, where the King required him to obtain University opinions in his favour. This he did, and returned again to England. After Wolsey's death in 1530 the King offered him the choice either of the archbishopric of York or the bishopric of Winchester to secure his favour in promoting the divorce, and his real regard for Henry at that time made it embarrassing to refuse. Pole, however, drew up a paper to dissuade the King from his object, in which Cranmer (*q.v.*) admitted the arguments would to most people appear convincing; and he obtained leave of the King in January 1532 once more to go abroad. Henry even continued his pensions. He went first to Avignon, but, not liking the climate, removed to Italy again, and spent some years between Padua and Venice.

Meanwhile the news from home was distressing. The King divorced Katherine and married Anne Boleyn in 1533. Pole's mother, whom Henry had made Countess of Salisbury early in the reign, was governess to the Princess Mary, and Mary (*q.v.*) was now disinherited. Popular feeling was strong against the King, and some politicians even hoped that Pole might marry the Princess and combine Yorkist and Tudor claims to the Crown. That was too dangerous a project, and nothing was said of it to Pole himself. But in 1535 it was suggested to him in the Emperor's name that it lay with him by virtue of his birth and abilities to redress the wrongs of Katherine and pacify discontent in England—a message to which he sent an oral reply by a confidential messenger. Certainly he was most anxious to avoid rash movements. At this time he was solicited on the King's behalf by Thomas Starkey, who had been his chaplain at Padua and was now in England in the King's service, to write out his carefully considered opinion, not on the divorce, on which he had already given it, but on two academic questions: (1) whether marriage with a deceased brother's wife was permissible by divine law, and (2) whether papal supremacy was of divine institution. These points, it was intimated, he might still be able to decide in the King's favour, as what he had previously written was only against the policy of the King's acts; but there was no desire, he was assured, to control his judgment.

Starkey had been trying to persuade the King, though he confessed Pole had always been very reticent on these subjects, that fuller study had inclined him to the King's own views; and by letters to Pole himself he endeavoured to lead him in that direction. Pole made him no direct answer, seeming as if he required further time to consider the matter; and indeed he was composing a long treatise in reply, which he only finished in May 1536. It was meant merely for the King's own eye; but it did not at all coincide with his inclinations. In fact, it was a very severe censure of Henry's conduct, written, as he said, not without tears, owing to his old regard for him. Henry dissembled his indignation and urged Pole to come and discuss matters with him in conference; but the severe laws he had himself got enacted were a sufficient excuse for non-compliance. Still, after the fall of Anne Boleyn he had hopes of the King's return to the Church. His friends in Italy feared that the entreaties of his family at home might prevail with him to go back to England, and the Pope summoned him to Rome to a consultation with reference to the proposed General Council. He accordingly went thither and, not a little to his dismay, was made a Cardinal in December 1536. He also took an active part in the *Consilium Delectorum Cardinalium*, published two years later, for reforming abuses in the Church.

The King was intensely angry at his being made Cardinal, but avoided showing it. Two great insurrections had just taken place in the north of England, and he had much cause for anxiety. The Pope, moreover, in February 1537 made his new cardinal a legate (*q.v.*), with instructions to go through France or Germany towards England, and perhaps to Scotland, where his presence would have had a most disturbing influence. But commotions had already been allayed by smooth words, and Pole's mission was too late. Accompanied by Giberti, a known friend of England, he only reached Lyons on the 24th March. There was war between the Emperor and Francis, each of whom feared to affront Henry, and Henry as the legate passed through France demanded his extradition as a traitor. Such a demand was outrageous; nevertheless, it was only evaded. Francis promised not to receive Pole as legate, and though the cardinal made a public entry into Paris he was told that his presence in France was inconvenient. So he withdrew to Cambray, a neutral place, leaving Giberti to discharge his mission to Francis I., while he awaited a safe-conduct from Mary of Hungary, Regent of the Netherlands. But through his ambassador at her court Henry had insisted, as he had done with Francis, that Pole should be delivered up to him if he entered the Emperor's dominions; and though she protested at first that she must receive a legate, she excused herself from seeing him, and sent him an escort to conduct him to Liège, where he was safe under the protection of the Cardinal of Liège, with whom he remained three months, till licensed by the Pope to return from his abortive mission.

In the end of 1538 Pole's brother, Lord Montague, and the Marquis of Exeter were beheaded in England on a charge of treason, in which his whole family were involved. At the same time new indignation was awakened against Henry at Rome by the spoliation of Becket's shrine and the burning of his bones. So in December Pole was despatched once more with a legatine commission to visit first the Emperor in Spain and afterwards Francis (for they had made peace by this time) to persuade them to break off intercourse with England. But though the Emperor would not listen this time to Henry's demand for his extradition, he declined to take such a step without being sure of Francis, and as Francis had the like jealousy of the Emperor, this second mission of Pole's turned out as fruitless as the first. Moreover, he was in continual danger from assassins willing to do Henry service. In 1539 Parliament passed an Act of Attainder against Pole and many others, including his mother and his deceased brother, Lord Montague. Pole was then at Carpentras staying with his friend Sadolet, whose sympathy was his best consolation. But the Pope required his presence in Rome once more, and gave him a bodyguard for surety against assassins. In 1541 Contarini, on being sent to the Diet at Ratisbon, took counsel with Pole how to conciliate the Protestants, and there was a nearer approach to agreement then than at any other time. Pole was, however, in want of means, and the Pope gave him 'the legation of the Patrimony'—that is, the secular government of a district, of which Viterbo was the capital. At this time news came of his mother's barbarous execution, which horrified every one. 'I am now,' said he, 'the son of a martyr, and we have one patron more in heaven.'

In 1542, when a premature attempt was made to open the Council at Trent, Pole was one of the three legates sent thither for the purpose. He had a similar commission in 1545, but his two colleagues reached the place without him, as there was a plot against his life. He was, however, at the actual commencement in December, and continued there till, in June next year, his state of health compelled him to leave for Padua. There he kept up correspondence with the Council till, with the Pope's permission, he returned to Rome in November. In January 1547 Henry VIII. died, and Pole, not knowing what would happen, wrote to the council of Edward VI. of the necessity of redressing the wrongs done during the late reign. He sent frequent messages, but they were not listened to, he being excepted from the general pardon at Edward's accession. On the death of Paul III. in 1549 Pole was nearly elected Pope. In 1550 Julius III. issued a Bull for the resumption of the Council at Trent, but in April 1552 it had to be again suspended owing to the war waged by the Lutherans in the Tyrol. This time Pole was not a legate, and had taken no part in its proceedings. In the spring of 1553 he withdrew to a monastery on the Lake of Garda, where news reached him of the death of Edward VI. He at once received a commission as papal legate not only to Queen Mary (q.v.), but to the Emperor and to Henry II. of France. But much had to be done before he could set foot in England, partly owing to the state of the country and partly to the Emperor's jealousy lest he should be an obstacle to the match with his son Philip. So Pole was detained on the Continent with idle efforts to make peace between the French King and Charles V., while in England Mary was crowned, Parliament reversed the Edwardine legislation, and Philip landed and was married to her. But there was still one point on which great people required assurance before they would welcome a legate come to reconcile England to Rome. The grantees of church lands had no mind to restore them. Pole obtained powers of dispensation that their rights should not be questioned. But these were not enough, and Rome itself felt the necessity of dropping the claims of the Church. So in November 1554 Mary's third Parliament reversed Pole's attainder, and two noblemen were sent to the Low Countries to conduct him into England. In coming he forbore to assume the character of legate till he received a message from the Queen at Rochester requesting him to do so. A patent had just been issued to enable him to exercise legatine functions, and next day he received letters under the Great Seal notifying that all laws passed against him had been repealed. He reached Whitehall by river on Saturday, 24th November, and had a most cordial reception both from Philip and Mary. On Tuesday following the two Houses of Parliament were summoned to hear him declare the object of his mission; and on the 30th they came before him at the palace, where, at the Queen's supplication, he absolved a penitent nation from the sin of schism. Convocation next day drew up an address to the King and Queen acknowledging that it was a natural duty to restore alienated property to the Church, but begging their intercession with the legate to confirm existing titles, otherwise it might be dangerous.

Shortly after this Pope Julius III. died, and his successor, Marcellus II., died three weeks after being elected. Then Cardinal Caraffa was chosen, who took the title of Paul IV. At both the conclaves Pole had been again spoken of as likely; and on the second occasion not only Mary but the French court did what they could for him, but they were too far off. Pole, however, presided over some ineffectual conferences near Calais for peace between the Emperor and France. Meanwhile Paul IV. expressed to an English embassy the highest approval of what Pole had done in the restoration of England to the Church, and gave them certain Bulls, one of which, however, touched in a general way the delicate question of the restoration of church property. In spite of past assurances this caused uneasiness, which another Bull was issued afterwards to relieve. Restitution was not to be asked; but the Queen, for her part, avowed that she would give up tithes and first-fruits and do her best to restore what else she had of the Church's property.

In 1555 Pole held a legatine synod, which enacted a code of constitutions and contemplated a number of reforms. On the deprivation of Cranmer the administration of the see of Canterbury was committed to Pole (11th December). As yet he was no priest, but he was so ordained at the Grey Friars, Greenwich, on the 20th March 1556, and he celebrated his first Mass next day—the day Cranmer was burned at Oxford. Then on Sunday, the 22nd, he was consecrated Archbishop of Canterbury. About the same time he was elected Chancellor of the University of Cambridge in succession to Bishop Gardiner (q.v.), and in October following Oxford paid him the same honour.

Of the Marian persecution it does not appear that Pole was a great instigator, or that he had much to do with it. Three penitent heretics who had been condemned once obtained pardon on appeal to him as legate; but no doubt he did not interfere with the ordinary course of what were simply legal executions. A strange thing at the end of his career was that he somehow incurred the displeasure of Paul IV., who had not long before extolled his conduct to the utmost. This was doubtless connected with that Pope's hatred of Spanish rule in Naples: and when after the abdication of Charles V. Philip II. became King of Spain and Naples as well as of England, matters did not improve. There was war in Italy between the Pope and Philip, and renewed war between Spain and France, as Henry II. became the Pope's ally. In April 1557 the Pope withdrew all his legates from Philip's dominions generally, and cancelled Pole's legation, though England was neutral at the time.

Philip and Mary wrote joint letters to the Pope for the restoration of Pole's legateship, as his services could not be dispensed with. For Mary's sake, but not for her husband's, since a legate in England was required, Paul promised to appoint one, but would not revoke what he had done. He made the Queen's confessor, Friar William Peto, a cardinal, and wrote to Pole requiring his presence at Rome. But Mary, learning from her ambassador, Carne, what was done, stopped the Pope's messenger at Calais to await the return of one whom she herself sent to Rome. Pole begged her to let the Pope's messenger come, and said his own legatine functions were at an end; but he sent a messenger to the Pope to show how ill His Holiness had rewarded his zealous services. Never had Pope so treated a legate before, replacing him by another without calling him to justify himself from suspicions. The Pope was strangely prejudiced against Pole and all who favoured him, hinting that he was a heretic—a strange imputation, as Pole himself wrote, on one whose trials and hardships had been entirely due to heretics.

Queen Mary died in the morning of the 17th November 1558 and Pole in the evening of the same day. He was buried in Canterbury Cathedral. [J. G.]

Phillips, *Life of Pole*; *Venetian Calendar*, vols. v., vi.

POPISH PLOT, The, was a pretended plot for assassinating Charles II., massacring Protestants, and establishing Romanism, which Titus Oates professed to have discovered in 1678.

Oates (1649-1705), the chief perjurer, was a man of the vilest character. He was expelled from Merchant Taylors' School in 1665, and afterwards went to Sedlescombe school, near Hastings, and thence to Gonville and Caius College, Cambridge. His tutor, Dr. Thomas Watson, said of him: 'He was a great dunce, ran into debt, and being sent away for want of money, never took a degree.' He managed, however, to get ordained, and became Vicar of Bobbing, 1673. Soon afterwards, 1674, he got into trouble for a false charge against a Hastings schoolmaster, and was put in prison and condemned to pay £1000 damages and charged with perjury, 1675. He escaped from gaol, and obtained a post as a naval chaplain, but was expelled within a few months. He then became chaplain to the Protestant members of the Duke of Norfolk's household, 1676, and this gave him his opportunity of knowing something of the hopes and designs of Roman Catholics. Becoming acquainted with Dr. Israel Tonge, a well-known Protestant controversialist, he joined him first in denunciation of papists and then in concocting details of an alleged plot. To acquire sufficient local and personal knowledge Oates in April 1677 formally professed conversion to the Church of Rome, consorted with the Jesuits, and sought admission to their order. He was actually sent to their college at Valladolid in June, but was expelled after five months, and returned to London. In December he was admitted to the seminary of St. Omer, but was expelled from it in June 1678.

On his return he and Tonge fabricated the details of the plot. By the instrumentality of one Kirkby it was brought to the King's notice, and Kirkby's statement was supported by a paper drawn up by Oates and given by Tonge to Danby. Oates and Tonge also appeared before Sir Edmund Berry Godfrey, a justice of the peace, and deposed to the truth of forty-three written articles giving particulars of the plot. The chief points were: that the Pope, Innocent XI., had appointed the Jesuits to have supreme power in the kingdom; that the King was to be assassinated, and that Père la Chaise had lodged £10,000 in London as a reward for the murder; that Sir George Wakeman had been paid £8000 to poison him; that four Irish cut-throats had been hired to stab him in his coach at Windsor; and two Jesuits, Grove and Pickering, were to be paid £15,000 to shoot him with silver bullets. His death was to be followed by a French invasion of Ireland and a general massacre of Protestants.

This had been settled, according to Oates, at a general 'consult' of the Jesuits held at the White Horse Tavern in Fleet Street, at which he said he had been present. The consult had, in fact, been held at the Duke of York's house, and Oates would not in any case have been admitted.

Oates was summoned before the Council, and his tale eagerly accepted—the King alone remaining incredulous. He was granted a salary of £40 a month. A number of Jesuits were apprehended, including Coleman, the Duke of York's secretary. Public feeling had begun to be aroused when an event occurred which fanned the flame of Protestant frenzy into a blaze. On 17th October 1678 Sir Edmund Berry Godfrey was found strangled in a ditch at the foot of Primrose Hill. The Jesuits were credited with the murder. It has long been regarded as one of the undiscovered crimes of history; but Mr. Pollock, the latest historian of the plot, believes that Prance, the informer, by whose word three men were executed, was one of the murderers, and the others were the Jesuits, Walsh, Pritchard, and Le Fevre—the motive for the murder being that Coleman had disclosed to Godfrey that the Jesuit consult had taken place at the house of the Duke of York, who would have been ruined if this had come out, and it was necessary therefore to get him out of the way.

Whoever perpetrated the crime its effect was undeniable. A reign of terror for Roman Catholics began. Informers and false witnesses appeared on every side, of whom one, William Bedloe, almost as magnificent a perjurer as Oates, was chief. They were encouraged by the Whigs, who made considerable party capital out of it. In November Parliament passed a resolution that 'there hath been and still is a damnable and hellish plot contrived and carried out by Popish recusants for the assassinating the King and rooting out the Protestant religion,' and had the vaults under Westminster Hall searched for gunpowder. For the first time a real attempt was made to put the laws against popish recusants into force. All over the country the houses of Roman Catholic gentry were searched for arms, prisons were filled, and estates confiscated. Besides the three executed for Godfrey's murder, fourteen were put to death for high treason. Eight priests were executed on account of their orders under a statute of 1585 (27 Eliz. c. 2). Five more died in prison. Thirty more persons were condemned to death, but were reprieved, of whom sixteen died in prison. Roman Catholics in London were banished to the country. Thirty thousand were said to have fled. Their books, relics, and vestments were burnt. Houses were ransacked. Those in prison were not provided with food, and being sometimes arrested at inns, on sick-beds, or in hiding-places were often hurried away without money, and depended for subsistence on the charity of their friends. Many abjured. The Jesuit Warner wrote: 'Hope itself is scarce left us.'

Oates even ventured to accuse the Queen of complicity in the plot against her husband's life. Five Roman Catholic peers were impeached, but only one, Lord Strafford, was executed. The persecution received its first check by the acquittal of Sir George Wakeman, the Queen's physician, and four others in July 1679, when the untrustworthiness of the witnesses became evident to the less violently prejudiced. But the last execution did not take place until July 1681, when Archbishop Plunket of Dublin and Edward Fitzharris were executed for high treason.

The question arises, Was there any plot at all ? Was there any fire concealed as much as revealed by the smoke of Oates's perjuries ? In all probability there was.

For the first thirteen years of his reign the Roman Catholics looked for help to Charles II. In 1662 he issued a Declaration of Indulgence, suspending all penal laws against dissenters, both Roman Catholic and Protestant, but was powerless to enforce it in face of the opposition in both Houses of Parliament. Failing in this, his next plan seems to have been to use the help of Louis XIV. to establish Roman Catholicism as the state religion and make himself independent of Parliament. This scheme was proposed to the Pope through Richard Bellings. It was the object of the secret treaty of Dover of 1670, when Charles was promised £150,000 and six thousand men if required. As part of the programme, he declared war against the Dutch in 1672, and two days before issued a second Declaration of Indulgence. But the war was comparatively unsuccessful. The Declaration was revoked in 1673, and when he made peace with the Dutch in February 1674 he may be said to have finally abandoned the policy of establishing Roman Catholicism. Henceforward he looked to secure his power by other means, and English Roman Catholics knew that they must look elsewhere both for relief and dominance, and their hopes were now centred on the Duke of York.

Coleman, the Duke's secretary, formerly a pupil of the Jesuits, became the centre of a new series of intrigues, upon which his letters down to 1675 throw considerable light. He corresponded with the papal court and with Père la Chaise and other Jesuits in France. His intentions are reasonably plain. 'We have here a mighty work upon our hands, no less than the conversion of three kingdoms . . . and there were never such hopes of success since the death of Queen Mary as now in our days when God has given us a prince who is become zealous of being the author and instrument of so glorious a work. . . . That which we rely on most next to God Almighty's Providence and the favour of my master the duke is the mighty mind of his most Christian Majesty.' His first idea seems to have been to bribe Charles—with French or papal gold—to dissolve Parliament, issue a Declaration of Indulgence, and leave the main business of government in the hands of the Duke of York. Finding that this scheme would not work, his next plan was to bribe Parliament to petition the King to restore the duke and to pass an Act for liberty of conscience. £20,000 he thought would be enough. But he was speedily undeceived, and had to abandon this project also.

It was by now clear that the King was an impediment in the way of the realisation of these aims, as he had definitely engaged in a policy of Anglican predominance. He must either be thrust aside, and the matter concluded without him, or forced into action. The intrigues of 1675-9 are obscure, as Coleman's correspondence ceases. But there is good reason to suppose that he and the Jesuits were as busy as ever. It seems unlikely that they should have continued to indulge hopes of the conversion of England in the near future as they undoubtedly did if they did not contemplate some bold stroke. What this was to be we cannot tell. It is at least likely that nothing definite had been decided on when Oates appeared on the scene. Oates was undoubtedly a liar, and all, or nearly all, his sworn statements were perjuries. The sources from which he borrowed the literary form of his fabrication can be traced. Plots were common in his day, and a tract survives describing the trial and execution of several men in 1662 for a plot not unlike that outlined by him. He must also have been cognisant of the narratives of the Gunpowder Plot and the Havernfield Plot, and both of them disclose points of close resemblance with the Popish Plot. In William Prynne's account of the Havernfield Plot, under the title of *Rome's Master-piece*, there is even the device of drawing out the plot in articles. But for all that he knew a little and guessed more of what was going on, and reared his clumsy super-structure of lies on a foundation of fact of which he guessed rather than knew the truth.

In April 1682 his pension was reduced to £2 a week, and in August it was withdrawn altogether. In 1684 he was arrested for calling the Duke of York a traitor, condemned to pay £100,000, and in default imprisoned. After the accession of James II. he was tried for perjury, condemned to pay a fine of 2000 marks, to be stripped of his canonical habits, to be whipped from Aldgate to New-gate and two days later from Newgate to Tyburn, and to be imprisoned for life. Soon after the accession of William and Mary he was released, and at the request of the Commons given a pension of £5 a week. In 1693 this was suspended at the instance of Queen Mary on account of his published libels on her father, but after her death he was granted in 1698 £500 to pay his debts and a pension of £300 a year. He became a Baptist, and used to preach in Wapping Chapel, but was expelled from that sect ' as a disorderly person and a hypocrite.' He died in 1705. In person he was hideous. He was short, bull-necked, and bow-legged. His forehead was low and eyes small and very deep-set. His face very large and red, and his chin so long that the mouth seemed to come in the middle. [c. p. s. c.]

Titus Oates, *D.N.B.*; Pollock, *Popish Plot*; articles by W. C. Abbott in *E.H.R.*, January 1910, and *American Hist. Rev.*, April and July 1909.

POYNET, or **PONET**, John (1514-1556), Bishop of Winchester, was educated at Queens' College, Cambridge, where he became Fellow, Bursar, and Dean. He was an ex-cellent classical scholar and a very learned man, knowing mathematics, astronomy, and Italian. He adopted Reformed opinions, became chaplain to Cranmer (*q.v.*), and held several preferments. The Act of the Six Articles does not appear to have troubled him. After the accession of Edward VI. he preached before the King on Fridays in Lent, 1550, Hooper (*q.v.*) preaching on Wednesdays. Both were rewarded with bishoprics; Poynet with Rochester. He was the first bishop consecrated under the new Ordinal. In the following year he was nominated to succeed Gardiner (*q.v.*) at Winchester.

He had first to surrender the lands and revenues of the see, then enormously rich,

and received in exchange a fixed sum, derived from certain rectories, of the value of two thousand marks a year. He was also allowed a large remission of tenths and first-fruits— an allowance to himself and not his successors, which can only be regarded as a bribe. The alienated lands were given to courtiers. His chief work was his *Short Treatise of Politique Power*, a work of some importance for the history of the time, and one of the earliest statements of the doctrine of tyranni-cide. He also engaged in an acrid contro-versy with Dr. Martin in defence of the marriage of the clergy. His own matrimonial experiences were curious and unedifying. He seems to have gone through the form of marriage with a butcher's wife at Nottingham during the life of her husband, and Machyn in his *Diary*, 1551, states: ' The 27th day of July was the new Bishop of Winchester divorced from the butcher's wife with shame enough.' He was also ordered to pay the husband a yearly pension as compensation. He then married again. On the death of Edward he was deprived as being married and intruded. He joined Wyatt, and when the rebels were delayed at Brentford he counselled some of the officers ' to shift for themselves as he intended to do,' and made his escape to Strasburg, where he died. He was a man of considerable abilities but indifferent character, and a scurrilous writer. [c. p. s. c.]

Foxe, *Acts and Monuments*; Strype, *Memorials*; S. R. Maitland, *Essays on the Reformation*, p. 54.

PRAEMUNIRE. The mediæval church system produced in the English Church a tendency to look on itself as a separate body, standing apart from the general life of the nation, and dependent on a foreign power, the Pope, rather than on the English Crown. As the consciousness of united national life increased kings and parliaments sought to resist this tendency in the Church. The statutes of Provisors (*q.v.*) show the opposition to the papal encroachments on patronage in the English Church. The statutes of *Prae-munire* form another incident in the same struggle to assert the supremacy of the Crown over the Church, whose members are also the Crown's subjects, and to control their communications with a foreign power. They are especially aimed at the encroachments of that power on the jurisdiction of the English courts.

The first of the statutes (1353, 27 Edw. III. st. 1, c. 1) enacts that any one drawing the King's subjects out of the realm on pleas the cognisance whereof belongs to the King's courts, or impeaching the judgments given in those courts, shall have a day appointed to answer his contempt, and if he fail to do so shall be put out of the King's protection, his lands and goods forfeited, and his body imprisoned at the King's pleasure. This statute, though directed at the court of Rome, is general in its terms and names no names. The next (1365, 38 Edw. III. st. 2) specifically mentions citations from Rome as causing injury to the King and realm, and also deals with the evil of provision. The principal statute of *Praemunire* was passed in 1393 (16 Ric. II. c. 5), and is even more outspoken. It declares that by the Pope's usurpations the laws of the realm are 'defeated and avoided at his will, in perpetual destruction of the sovereignty of the King.' It gives the offender no *locus poenitentiae*, or opportunity to explain his action, and re-enacts the former penalties against any who should procure, bring into the realm, receive, or execute any bulls, excommunications, or other instruments from Rome. The name *praemunire*, which came to be applied indifferently to the statutes, the offence, the writ, and the severe and comprehensive punishment, was taken from the word in the writ which bids the sheriff warn (*praemunire*) the accused to appear and answer to the charge.

This legislation was not altogether effective in checking appeals to Rome. Some cases had to be taken thither because the local courts were not competent to deal with them. In others the kings gave leave to appeal, or connived at breaches of the law. But the diminution in the number of appeals to Rome in the fifteenth century was in part due to these statutes. In 1439, and again in 1447, Convocation complained that they were being used against the English Church courts, for whose protection they had been devised. Apparently then, as in the seventeenth century, the civil lawyers found them a useful weapon in the perennial warfare between the two jurisdictions, though in 1514 Richard Hunne was unsuccessful in an attempt to sue *praemunire* against a priest who had cited him in the church court. But in 1515 the judges determined that Convocation had been guilty of *praemunire* in proceeding against Standish (*q.v.*), a friar who had defended the Act restricting benefit of clergy (*q.v.*). This was but a slight foretaste of what was to follow. In 1529 Henry VIII., with barefaced injustice, declared that Wolsey's (*q.v.*) acts as legate constituted an offence of *praemunire*, though they had been done with

the acquiescence, and even at the orders of, the King; and in 1530 that the recognition of the legate's authority by the whole body of the clergy and laity involved them in his guilt. By this threat he extracted the Submission of the Clergy from Convocation (*q.v.*) in 1531. Having proved the value of his weapon, he used it freely to enforce his ecclesiastical legislation of 1533 and 1534. The statutes 24 Hen. VIII. c. 12, 25 Hen. VIII. cc. 19 and 21 apply its penalties to all who are concerned in appeals to Rome or in bringing licences or dispensations from thence; and 25 Hen. VIII. c. 20 makes it the penalty for refusing to elect or consecrate the King's nominee to a bishopric. In 1553 these extensions of *praemunire* were abolished, and it was restricted to the offences to which it had been applicable at the accession of Henry VIII. (1 Mar. st. 1, c. 1). In 1554 it was made the penalty for those who should molest the possessors of the abbey lands (1-2 Ph. and M. c. 8). This was confirmed by Elizabeth, who also revived Henry's statutes, and used *praemunire* to enforce her ecclesiastical supremacy (1559, 1 Eliz. c. 1) and to harry the Roman Catholic recusants. It was made the penalty for maintaining the Pope's authority, being reconciled or reconciling others to him, helping to maintain Jesuits or priests, bringing into the realm bulls, 'crosses, pictures, beads, or such like vain and superstitious things from the bishop or see of Rome,' and similar offences (1563, 5 Eliz. c. 1; 1571, 13 Eliz. c. 2; 1585, 27 Eliz. c. 2). After the discovery of the Gunpowder Plot the refusal to take the oath of allegiance was added to the list (1606, 3 Jac. I. c. 4). The statute of 1563, however, declared that persons attainted of *praemunire* might not be slain at sight with impunity, a point which had previously been considered doubtful. Under James I. *praemunire* formed part of the quarrel between the temporal and ecclesiastical courts. It was asserted that since the church courts were definitely acknowledged to be under the Royal Supremacy, and were regulated by statute, it was no longer possible for them to encroach on the rights of the Crown, and therefore *praemunire* could not lie against them. Coke and the judges, however, maintained that the bishop might still act to the prejudice of the Crown by assuming jurisdiction over cases cognisable in the King's temporal courts, and in such case *praemunire* would lie.

Down to the reign of Henry VIII. *praemunire* had been a weapon with which the State resisted the encroachments of the papacy and enforced the Royal Supremacy over the

English Church. Elizabeth diverted it from its original use to the repression of Roman Catholic recusancy, and in her reign it was also extended to purely civil offences. In 1571 it was applied to those who took interest at a higher rate than ten per cent. per annum (13 Eliz. c. 8), and was afterwards adopted by the criminal law as the penalty for various offences, including the promotion of bubble companies (1719, 6 Geo. I. c. 18), down to 1772, when those who assisted at breaches of the Royal Marriage Act (12 Geo. III. c. 11) were made liable to *praemunire*. In the nineteenth century it was twice the subject of rather academic discussion in the House of Lords. After the Hampden (*q.v.*) case in 1848 Bishop Phillpotts (*q.v.*) presented a petition for the repeal of those provisions of 25 Hen. VIII. c. 20 which make *praemunire* the penalty for refusing to elect or consecrate a bishop designate. Lord Denman then said that such a penalty was 'objectionable and unworthy of a civilised country,' and he would be glad to see it abolished. No action was taken, however, either then or in 1864, when Lord Westbury alleged that by condemning *Essays and Reviews* (*q.v.*) without a licence from the Crown, Convocation had made itself liable to *praemunire*. But this was scarcely a correct exposition of the law, the better opinion being that the royal licence is only required for the formal enactment of canons. [PAPACY AND THE ENGLISH CHURCH.]

[G. C.]

Statutes; Stubbs, *C.H.*, xix.: Wilkins, *Concilia*; Blackstone. *Commentaries*, IV. viii.; Coke, *Insts.*, iii. 119; *Reports*, xii. 37; Hansard, *Parl. Debates*, 1848 and 1864.

PROCTORS. The growth of an ordered system of Canon Law (*q.v.*) and Courts (*q.v.*) administering it involved the appearance of a body of professional canon lawyers. In 1237 the legate Otho laid down rules which illustrate the formation of a close corporation of such lawyers, formally appointed and bound by oath to respect professional etiquette. Already the distinction between advocates and proctors roughly corresponds to that between barristers and solicitors, and can be summed up in the words of Ayliffe, the eighteenth-century canonist, that advocates or 'persons of the long robe' should be skilled in knowledge of the law and proctors in the practice thereof; and he adds that the office of the one is difficult and honourable, and of the other easy and of no honour at all. In 1281 Archbishop Peckham (*q.v.*) decreed that no one should practise as an advocate until he had studied civil and

canon law for three years at least. In 1567 some of the advocates bought the site of Doctors' Commons, to the south of St. Paul's Churchyard, and at their own expense built courts, a hall and library, and houses for the judges and advocates. Here the provincial courts of Canterbury and the consistory of London were held for three centuries. The Court of Admiralty was added in 1666, and in 1672 the buildings, which had suffered in the Great Fire, were restored. In 1768 the advocates were incorporated under royal charter into 'The College of Doctors of Laws,' consisting of a President (the Dean of the Arches for the time being), and Fellows, who must have taken the degree of Doctor of Laws at Oxford or Cambridge, and have been admitted advocates under a rescript from the Archbishop of Canterbury. No advocate might practise for a year after admission. The judges in the provincial courts were chosen from among the advocates. Thirty-four proctors, licensed by the archbishop, were also attached to the college. No proctor could be admitted to practice until he had served seven years as articled clerk to one of these thirty-four. In 1536 the proctors of the Court of Arches had tried to induce Archbishop Cranmer (*q.v.*) to restrict their number to ten in order that this close corporation might enjoy a more lucrative practice; but this attempt failed, for even when there were twenty or more they were 'so overladde with causes that they were driven to take oft and many delayes and prorogations.' The inconveniences resulting from Warham's restriction of the number to ten had been one of the complaints of the Commons against the church courts in their petition of 1532. The canons of 1604 lay down rules for the conduct of proctors, forbidding them to act without the counsel of an advocate, or 'to be clamorous in court,' where their 'loud and confused cries' were 'troublesome and offensive to the judges and advocates' (Canons 129-33). Proctors and advocates as officers of the ecclesiastical courts were under their control, with which the temporal courts could not interfere.

In modern times the bulk of ecclesiastical practice consisted of matrimonial and testamentary cases, which were taken from the church courts by the Probate and Divorce Acts, 1857 (21-2 Vic. cc. 77 and 85). Under the Probate Act the College of Doctors of Law was dissolved, and its property handed over to the existing members for their own benefit. The ecclesiastical courts were now thrown open to the whole bar. And by the combined effect of these Acts and the Legal

Practitioners Act, 1876 (39-40 Vic. c. 66), and the Solicitors Act, 1877 (40-1 Vic. c. 25), the distinction between proctors and solicitors was similarly obliterated. The ecclesiastical courts under the old system had the reputation of providing a number of somnolent and comfortable posts, for the loss of which their possessors were handsomely compensated. On the other hand, these reforms resulted in the disappearance of the race of ecclesiastical lawyers, and practically put an end to the study of canon law, which had been 'languidly pursued' so long as the ecclesiastical bar provided a separate career with lucrative prizes of its own. There is now little inducement for any lawyer to pay special attention to the Church's law, the study of which therefore tends to fall into desuetude.

The word proctor, a form of 'procurator,' is also used to denote the representatives of the clergy in Convocation (*q.v.*), and the principal executive officers in the older Universities.

[G. C.]

Gibson, *Codex*; Ayliffe, *Parergon*; Burn, *Eccl. Law*; Strype, *Memorials of Cranmer*, app. xviii.; *Report of Eccl. Courts Commission*, 1832.

PROCURATIONS. At Bishops' (*q.v.*) or Archdeacons' (*q.v.*) visitations the provision of necessary entertainment for the visitor and his retinue was a charge upon the parish or religious house visited. It was at first paid in kind, the amount being fixed by local custom. Before the end of the Middle Ages these 'procurations' were commuted for a money payment, which formed part of the regular income of the bishop or archdeacon, and was recoverable in the ecclesiastical court. In England the procuration payable to an archdeacon was 7s. 6d.; 1s. 6d. for himself and his horse, and 1s. for each of six followers; and this customary pay overrode the decretal *Vas Electionis* of Benedict XII., which fixed a larger sum. At the Suppression of the Monasteries (*q.v.*) provision was made for the payment of their procurations by the new owners of their lands (see 27 Hen. VIII. c. 28; 31 Hen. VIII. c. 13; 32 Hen. VIII. c. 22; 34 Hen. VIII. c. 19). Since the revenues of archdeacons and bishops have been vested in the Ecclesiastical Commissioners under 3-4 Vic. c. 113, 23-4 Vic. c. 124, and 31-2 Vic. c. 113, bishops' procurations have been allowed to lapse, and in some cases those of archdeacons also; but some are still payable, irrespective of visitation. (*Archd. of Exeter v. Green*, *Times*, 17th Aug. 1912.)

A procuration was also due at the consecration of a church for the refreshment of the bishop and his train. At the consecration of Elsfield Church in 1273 two marks were paid for this purpose. [G. C.]

Gibson, *Codex*; Phillimore, *Eccl. Law*; J. S[tephens], *Procurations*, 1661.

PROVISORS were persons appointed by the Pope to benefices not yet vacant, the appointment taking effect on the next vacancy. The papal claim to override the rights of patrons by this system of provision first appears in England early in the thirteenth century. In 1226 the legate Otho asked that two prebends in each cathedral should be reserved for the Roman See. The request was refused, but others followed, culminating in 1240 in the demand that the Bishops of Lincoln and Salisbury should find benefices for three hundred Italian clerks. Such demands roused public opinion in England to strong opposition, and the intruded foreigners were sometimes mobbed, with the connivance of the sheriffs. The popes, however, continued the practice in spite of the remonstrances of Grosseteste (*q.v.*) and other English bishops. In 1307 the Parliament of Carlisle petitioned against the unbridled multitude (*effrenatam multitudinem*) of provisions, reciting the injuries suffered by patrons in the loss of their rights, and by the whole realm in the accumulation of benefices in the hands of aliens and absentees. At that time no statute was passed. The success of the temporal courts in asserting their jurisdiction over suits arising out of presentations to benefices did much to preserve the rights of lay patrons, and to check the papal encroachments in this direction [COURTS]. But the popes continued to provide to positions in the gift of churchmen and religious houses, who could not well seek the assistance of the lay courts against their spiritual overlord.

Matters became more serious when the popes began to reserve to themselves appointments to bishoprics. This was an extension of the power they had previously enjoyed of deciding between rival candidates, a decision which sometimes took the form of setting aside both and appointing their own nominee. The first case of such provision was the appointment of Langton (*q.v.*) to Canterbury, 1206. On the death of Archbishop Winchelsey of Canterbury (1313) Clement V. reserved to himself the appointment of a successor, and between 1317 and 1334 no fewer than eighteen appointments to English sees were reserved by John XXII., who in 1328 asserted a claim to appoint to all vacancies caused by translation. Such encroachment would have been impossible without the connivance of the

Crown, and it is significant that the bishop appointed to Canterbury in 1313 was the candidate favoured by the King. Edward III. remonstrated against the papal claims, but he allowed them in practice, on the understanding that they were frequently exercised in favour of his own nominees, an arrangement which caused Clement VI. to observe in 1345: 'If the King of England were to petition for an ass to be made bishop we must not say him nay.' This remark led to an unseemly jest at the banquet which followed the consecration of Bradwardine to Canterbury at Avignon in 1349. A clown was brought into the hall riding an ass, and bearing a petition that he might be made Archbishop of Canterbury. In England the system was not regarded as a joke. The Pope was seen to use his privilege not merely to reward his friends, but as a lucrative source of income by the open sale of benefices and dignities. Disgust was heightened by the fact that England, 'the milch cow of the papacy,' suffered more by this traffic than any other country, and that many of those who profited by it were Frenchmen, with whom England was then at war. In 1343 and the following years Parliament petitioned in strong terms against the practice, with the result that the first statute of Provisors was passed in 1351 (25 Edw. III. st. 4, sometimes cited as st. 6). It enacts that elections and presentations shall be free ; that appointments to which the Pope provides shall be forfeited for that turn to the Crown ; and that if the provisor disturbs the lawful holder he shall be imprisoned and fined at the King's will. This was re-enacted by later statutes of Provisors in 1365 (38 Edw. III. st. 2) and 1390 (13 Ric. II. st. 2, c. 2). The weakness of this legislation was that it left the remedy in the hands of the King, who, as a rule, had no wish to quarrel with the Pope, or to enforce his own rights if a satisfactory compromise could be found. A system of collusion grew up. The popes retained complete rights over sees vacated by translation, and a rule of give and take was followed, neither party opposing the nominees of the other. When they were agreed upon a candidate the King sent a letter to the chapter nominating him, and the Pope provided him. Thus both were satisfied. The kings retained a cheap and easy method of rewarding their friends and servants, and the popes their source of income together with the recognition, in theory, of their right to appoint to all bishoprics. The sufferers were the chapters, who lost their right of election. [BISHOPS.]

That the statute of Provisors was not con-

sidered altogether ineffective is shown by the fact that in 1391 the House of Commons successfully resisted an attempt to repeal it. The statute of *Praemunire* (*q.v.*) of 1393 supplied the machinery for enforcing it. It was supplemented and strengthened by statutes against the purchase and tenure of benefices by aliens, and similar legislation, and for a time the flow of provisions was checked. Martin v. strongly urged Archbishop Chichele (*q.v.*) to secure the repeal of the 'execrable' statute of Provisors, but in vain. Under Henry VI. the papal claims were again admitted. But by the beginning of the sixteenth century the kings had got the real power in the matter into their hands. Their nominees were accepted as a matter of course, and when in 1534 Henry VIII. abolished the Pope's share in appointment to bishoprics (25 Hen. VIII. c. 20) he did little more than give statutory sanction to the system already in existence. Mary (*q.v.*) revived the form of provision. In 1554 she petitioned Pope Julius III., 'according to the custom of the realm' of England, that he would provide seven bishops to the sees to which she had appointed them. This was done at a consistory held at Rome, 6th July (Raynaldus, *Annales*, sec. 5). The abolition of the papal authority in the English Church naturally put an end to provision to minor dignities and benefices, in which the popes had in a great measure succeeded in evading the law. Bishop Morteval of Salisbury, for instance, complained that of fifty offices to which he had the right of collation, twenty-eight were held by papal provision in 1315. After 1534 the statutes, being no longer required, became entirely obsolete, the only allusion made to them by so exhaustive a legal writer as Blackstone being a warning to his readers that in prohibiting the purchase of provisions at Rome they did not forbid the buying of grain and other victual there. [PAPACY AND ENGLISH CHURCH.]

[G. C.]

Stubbs, *C.H.*, xiv. and xix. ; Wilkins, *Concilia* ; Statutes.

PUBLIC WORSHIP REGULATION ACT, 1874

(37-8 Vic. c. 85), was the result of the spread of ceremonial in the 'sixties, the common prejudice against it, and the unsatisfactory results of litigation on the subject. Lord Shaftesbury, the leader of the opposition to ceremonial, introduced various Bills to reform the church courts. Eventually Archbishop Tait (*q.v.*), convinced that legislation was inevitable, determined to undertake it himself, and, with the assent of the bishops, drafted a Bill for the session of 1874. Ill-luck pursued it. The dissolution of Parliament necessitated a new Convocation, which did not meet until the Bill was already before Parliament, and had no opportunity of discussing it. And through some indiscretion the press was enabled to publish its outline prematurely, so that the clergy first learned the intentions of the archbishop from their daily newspaper. Tait, in vain, assured High Churchmen that the Bill dealt only with procedure and would not alter the Church's law. As introduced by him into the House of Lords, it proposed to create in each diocese a Board of Assessors (clerical and lay), to whom the bishop should refer complaints, and on whose advice he should act; an appeal was allowed to the archbishop, whose judgment should be final. When Convocation met, the Lower House refused to approve these proposals, and suggested an alternative scheme. Opposition was intensified by the action of Lord Shaftesbury. Tait's intention to revive and strengthen the bishop's *forum domesticum* was not what Shaftesbury required, and he proposed amendments entirely altering the character of the Bill, ignoring diocesan courts, introducing a lay judge, and giving an appeal to the Privy Council. Tait and nearly all the bishops reluctantly accepted these amendments rather than lose the Bill, which thus became mainly the work of Shaftesbury, who took advantage of Tait's desire for legislation and the anti-High-Church feeling to carry out designs which had hitherto failed. In the House of Commons Disraeli, amid a storm of cheers, described it as 'a Bill to put down ritualism' and 'mass in masquerade.' Sir William Harcourt, leader of the extreme Erastians, claimed that Parliament could deal with all church matters, and denied the spiritual jurisdiction of the bishops, on the ground that no bishop 'enforced his behests by a *posse comitatus* of angels.' Gladstone (*q.v.*) pleaded for a reasonable diversity of use, deprecated the ill-advised interference of Parliament, and brought forward six resolutions against the Bill. But his influence and eloquence were powerless. On one point, the bishop's veto, Tait had stood firm against Shaftesbury. The Commons inserted an appeal from this to the archbishop. The Lords rejected this amendment, and, largely through Tait's personal influence, the Commons gave way.

The Act provides for the appointment by the two archbishops, jointly, of a barrister or ex-judge, who must sign a declaration that he is a member of the Church of England, as

judge of the provincial courts of Canterbury and York. If they fail to appoint the Crown shall do so. The bishop, on representation by an archdeacon or churchwarden or three parishioners, of any illegality, may either veto proceedings, or with the consent of the parties decide the case himself, or transmit it to the judge, from whom an appeal shall lie to the Privy Council. Obedience to the judge's order shall be enforced by inhibition, and eventually by voidance of the benefice. Many churchmen at once repudiated the Act as possessing no spiritual authority. It had been passed by Parliament in the teeth of Convocation backed by a strong body of church opinion; it overrode the constitution of the church courts, and the requirements of the Church's law as to the appointment and qualifications of ecclesiastical judges; it ignored the diocesan court, and it recognised the disputed jurisdiction of the Privy Council. Lord Penzance, an ex-judge of divorce, was appointed by the archbishops, and his refusal to qualify himself as an ecclesiastical judge emphasised the fact that his jurisdiction was derived solely from Parliament. Therefore it was consistently disregarded by the great majority of clergy. Attempts were made to hamper it by applying, whenever opportunity offered, to the temporal courts for a prohibition. These applications met with varying success, and on one occasion led to a sharp controversy between Penzance and Lord Chief-Justice Cockburn as to the jurisdiction of the new court. Between 1877 and 1882 four clergy were imprisoned for contumacy, an unforeseen result which did much to bring the Act into odium, and strengthened the hands of the bishops in vetoing prosecutions. Down to 1882 eighteen suits had been initiated under the Act, of which eight had been vetoed. After that time prosecutions became still less frequent, and for several years before Penzance's retirement in 1899 his court had been practically deserted. He has been succeeded by properly qualified ecclesiastical judges. But though both the Courts Commission, 1883, and the Discipline Commission, 1906 [COMMISSIONS, ROYAL], recommended its repeal, the discredited Act still exists, and is sometimes thought to taint the provincial courts with Erastianism [COURTS, RITUAL CASES].   [G. C.]

Hansard, *Parl. Debates*, 1874; *Chronicle of Convocation*; *Life of Abp. Tait*, xxiv.; Law Reports; Proceedings of *Eccl. Courts Commission*, 1883, and *Eccl. Discipline Commission*, 1906.

PUISET, Hugh de (1125-95), Bishop of Durham, was a nephew of King Stephen, and owed his rapid promotion in the Church to that relationship. In 1142 he was made Archdeacon of Winchester by his uncle, Henry of Blois (*q.v.*); in 1143 received the treasurership of York from his cousin, Archbishop William: and in 1153 was elected to the see of Durham, though under the canonical age, at the instance of the King. Archbishop Henry Murdac refused to consecrate him, on the ground of his youth, his secular tastes, and his loose morals. But he obtained support from Henry of Blois and even from Theobald of Canterbury: and Anastasius IV. was persuaded to consecrate him at Rome. As Bishop of Durham he ruled his monks, his clergy, and his barons with an iron hand, riding rough-shod over privilege and custom. He defended the liberties of Durham with success against the see of York; and Henry II. showed him a remarkable degree of indulgence, in consideration of the importance of his palatinate as a bulwark against the Scots. This favour was ill repaid by Puiset, who in 1173 made a truce with William the Lion, and gave the Scots free passage through his lands. In consequence he lost for a time his chief castles, but he recovered the King's grace by paying a fine of two thousand marks. His energies were chiefly devoted to the aggrandisement of his see. He added largely to the episcopal estates, and compiled the famous survey of them which is known as the Boldon Book; he reorganised the administration of the palatinate, restored the castles of Durham and Northallerton, and completed the city wall at Durham. His life was secular; but he observed a certain decorum, and spent his wealth lavishly on such pious works as the Galilee of Durham Cathedral and the leper hospital of Sherburn. On the accession of Richard I. the bishop made haste to purchase from the King the earldom of Northumberland and the justiciarship of England beyond the Humber—a transaction which scandalised strict churchmen, and placed Puiset in a position resembling that of a German prince-bishop. The bargain was the more scandalous as the bishop used the funds which he had raised for the crusade to pay the heavy price demanded by the King, and begged or bought a papal dispensation from his crusading vow. Longchamp (*q.v.*), the Chief Justiciar, soon picked a quarrel with him, and compelled him to resign his new dignities; but Puiset appealed to the King, and obtained restitution of the earldom. This he held until 1194, when it was given to Hugh Bardulf by Richard, in spite of Puiset's offer to pay for a renewal of his grant.

Puiset attempted, between 1190 and 1192, to make his see independent of York, and actually obtained a grant of exemption from Clement III.; but this was cancelled by Clement's successor, Celestine III. Puiset died in March 1195, absorbed to the last in plans for recovering his earldom.

[H. W. C. D.]

Stubbs, prefaces to *Roger of Hoveden*, i. and ii., R.S.; Norgate, *Eng. under the Angevin Kings*.

PURITANISM. The term is exclusively used of an English variety of extreme Protestantism existing both within and without the English Church. Its meaning and spirit are, however, not confined to England or to any one phase of Church history. Apart from the special doctrines associated with it historically, Puritanism has always signified a certain view of spirituality and the means of attaining thereto. The Puritan spirit is a 'world-renouncing' spirit, and seeks God by way of denying all external means; thus it is closely akin to Manichæism in its view of the material world as essentially evil, and is ascetic in the Oriental as opposed to the Catholic sense. With a denial of all external means, Puritanism also tends to individualism in religion, although that tendency does not manifest itself at first.

Wyclif (*q.v.*) is justly regarded as the forerunner of English Puritanism. His whole attitude to Catholic doctrine and life is essentially that of the Puritans, and he seems to have shared fully their dislike of art and all amusement. Indeed, he was far more closely akin to the Puritans than was Luther with his expansive geniality. But the Puritans proper can hardly be said to have appeared in England before the reign of Elizabeth.

The situation in the reign of Elizabeth was of the nature of a reaction. Mary's government had made her religion unpopular. Tired of the Spanish alliance, humiliated by the loss of Calais, and deeply moved by the policy of persecution, the nation was prepared for change. It was not Protestant in spirit (in the ordinary sense), but it desired something like the Henrician system. That desire to a large extent was fulfilled by Queen Elizabeth and her advisers in the new settlement. [ELIZABETHAN SETTLEMENT.] The Act of Supremacy secured the nation against further encroachments on the part of the papal monarchy, and the Act of Uniformity (*q.v.*) gave them a form of service, tolerable if not popular. For many, however, the Book of Common Prayer did not go far enough. The moment it had become clear that no such dangers as those of the previous reign were before them, large numbers of the English Churchmen who had been in voluntary exile returned to this country. In Geneva and Heidelberg they had learned to love the bare services and elaborate preachments of the prevailing fashion. Europe, or a large part of it, owned in Calvin an intellectual and spiritual master, and his authority was more absolute than that of most of the popes. Swayed by these notions such men came back hoping for a ' root-and-branch ' revolution, and anxious to reform the Church on the Calvinist Presbyterian model. Thus when it appeared that the new order would not only continue episcopacy, but would enjoin set prayers, sacerdotal vestments, and outward sacramental signs, there was a great outcry. The first few years of Elizabeth's reign were filled with the ' Vestiarian ' controversy. Those who had looked for a church entirely purified bitterly complained of the rags of popery, and there was in some cases great difficulty (as there had been in the case of Bishop Hooper, *q.v.*), in others impossibility, in securing even a *minimum* of discipline. It was to achieve this *minimum* of decorum that Parker (*q.v.*) issued his famous ' Advertisements ' (*q.v.*) in 1566. They had the archiepiscopal not the royal authority, and they were ineffectual at the moment. The bishops were largely Puritan in sympathy, though prepared to enforce order to a limited extent.

Later on in the reign, in the 'seventies, there was a definite and determined attempt to remodel the Church on the Presbyterian lines. This took two forms. First, there was an appeal to Parliament to do what was needful by legislation. Many were the conflicts on the matter between the Queen, who upheld the authority of bishops and Convocation, and the narrow Puritan laymen, *e.g.* Wentworth and Strickland, who were endeavouring to force a reform over the heads of the clergy. To the Queen's firmness, however, more than to any other cause, it was due that that attempt failed and only came to maturity in the Long Parliament. Apart from this, however, under the influence of Thomas Cartwright (*q.v.*), the author of the *Admonition to Parliament*, attempts were made to introduce the Presbyterian form of government as a voluntary system, while complying with the law in the matters of patronage and conformity.

This, however, was defeated largely through the resolution of Whitgift (*q.v.*), whose tenure of the primacy is of capital importance. It is true that before this time both Brownists and Baptists [NONCONFORMITY, III., IV.] had become definitely organised as separatist bodies. But by the end of the sixteenth century it appeared that the effort to Puritanise the English Church was unlikely to succeed; while Bancroft (*q.v.*) had already in his famous sermon taken up that line on the divine right of episcopacy, which was ultimately to mean so much more.

When James I. became king the Millenary Petition set forth the state of feeling. It witnessed to the strength of the Puritan clergy in numbers, and to their desire for no more than a toleration. The point made then and at other times was that it was unwise and unchristian to insist on compliance in matters of ceremony, and that toleration within the limits of the Establishment would be but right. Bacon was for indulgence of these ' nonconforming ' clergy. Not so, however, the King, whose experience in Scotland had not led him to love the Puritan *ethos*. The Government took the course of imprisoning some of the petitioners, and in the Hampton Court Conference (*q.v.*) which followed it was made abundantly clear that conformity would be enforced as far as possible, and that James was in no mind to weaken the Elizabethan settlement (*q.v.*). From this time till the Restoration, and indeed till 1688, the relations of the Puritan party to the authorities form the pivot on which all politics revolve. From the very beginning of the reign, in the *Apology of Parliament*, and right on till its close, the Puritan difficulty is one of the main causes of misunderstanding between James and his Parliament.

All this was accentuated in the reign of Charles I. (*q.v.*). This was due to two causes. The King himself was brought up as an English Churchman, and had to the Prayer Book a romantic attachment which was to cost him his life. Thus on his side there were elements of religion and passion added to his regard for the episcopal system and liturgy which were entirely foreign to the mind of James, essentially a foreigner. Secondly, by the beginning of the reign of Charles a new group of clergy had risen into prominence, whose opposition to the Puritans was far deeper than that of the time-serving prelates of Queen Elizabeth, and more conscious, if not logically more real, than that of Matthew Parker. Most of the bishops, and still more of the clergy, of the first fifty years of the Elizabethan settlement, were divided from the Puritans by no very deep or discernible distinction. They differed on matters of Church government, on their notions of their relation to the civil power, on the extent of their dislike to outward forms; but in essentials they were agreed. Above all, they held without qualification that complex of doctrines known as Calvinism (*q.v.*). This is shown by the readiness of Whitgift to adopt the Lambeth Articles. This, however, was no longer to be the case. The case of Arminius and the Remonstrants had opened men's minds. [ARMINIANISM.] The specula- tions which it evolved were far-reaching. There grew up a school of divines who were convinced that the whole doctrine of the relation of God's Providence to man's freedom was a mystery; that in regard to many matters the only wise or Christian attitude is a reverent agnosticism; and that, in particular, the explicit statements of Calvin- ism are revolting and incompatible with the belief that God is Love. On these matters they were willing to adopt a non-committal attitude; while, on the other hand, they were wedded to the notion of decorum of cere- monial observance and a uniform standard of worship, enforced by authority, and to a high view of the sacraments, not common among the Puritan clergy. Laud (*q.v.*), their leader, was the personal friend and adviser of the King; and the favour of the Government was consistently shown to those stigmatised as lax or Arminian clergy. The Puritan spirit grew more violent with opposition. It proceeded to attack Richard Mountague [CAROLINE DIVINES] for his alleged anti-Calvinist opinions, and was seeking in every way to make a Calvinistic interpreta- tion of the Articles compulsory, when Charles interposed with the declaration, still prefixed to the Prayer Book, which asserts that no 'gloss' is needed, and is plainly framed to admit freedom inside the limits of subscrip- tion. The Laudian rule, coupled with the personal government of Charles, drove every one with a grievance into the Puritan camp. This was interrupted by the attempt, and then the failure of the attempt, to introduce the new Prayer Book into Scotland. Charles faced the Long Parliament (after the brief futility of the Short Parliament) with the knowledge that he would have to yield many points. The unwise canons of 1640 had further aroused opposition, and there was no doubt that the Parliament was deter- mined to put a stop to the tyrannies of the last ten years, and in that sense to put an end to prelacy. Both the Star Chamber and the Court of High Commission (*q.v.*) were

abolished. But there was no general desire to alter the form of the Church as by law established.

The history of the months between the opening of the Long Parliament and the outbreak of the Civil War is the history of the way in which episcopacy became the rallying war-cry on either side. At first it appeared that there were only a few members in favour of the 'root-and-branch petition,' but by the time Charles returned from Scotland it was clear that there was a strong party in favour of an entire remodelling of the Church. When Charles wrote the letter to the Lords which announced his resolve to abide by the Book of Common Prayer, he took the step which created the royalist party. He had faced the angry squires and resolute lawyers in 1640 with no support but among a small band of courtiers and officials. Now he had the bulk of the nation on his side. The Civil War was not a war for political power nor for religious liberty. It was a war between two sets of ideas, each of them with a footing within the Church, and each claiming an exclusive right to be enforced by persecution. The Solemn League and Covenant, 1643, which Pym negotiated, drove the Parliamentarians still further in the direction of enforced Puritanism. The Westminster Assembly met in consequence, and after great difficulties there was issued in August 1645 the new Directory of Public Worship and ordinances passed for the introduction of the Discipline. This, however, was never really enforced except locally; England was never in any real sense Presbyterian. With the victory of the army, she ceased to be so even nominally. The Cromwellian rule was an Independent government, during which, in the name of liberty, toleration was denied to the Prayer Book, and in the name of religion the Quakers were harried. With the Restoration, the most popular event in English history, there vanished the last hopes of Puritan rule. The nation showed plainly enough that it would never endure another 'reign of the saints,' and the only question was how much of toleration the Puritan party could secure. The Act of Uniformity barred, and was intended to bar, the retention of their livings by the bulk of the Puritan clergy. The Clarendon Code was an attempt, no less stupid than barbarous, to stamp them out by persecution. The rest of the subject is better studied under the heading of Tolera- tion (*q.v.*). But Puritanism was indeed de- caying through other causes. The writings of Richard Baxter (*q.v.*) mark the change.

His attitude is that of the liberal rationalising spirit of the era of Descartes, and his *Reasonableness of the Christian Religion* prepared the way for Locke. In Church matters he heralded modern undenominationalism. The Restoration witnessed the gradual secularising of politics; and during the next fifty years the Puritan and Laudian schools alike give way to the Latitudinarian (*q.v.*), and the forces that made eighteenth-century Deism (*q.v.*) and Establishmentarianism are seen at work. Until both Church and Dissent were revived by Wesley (*q.v.*), the old spirit had largely decayed. Although Puritanism represents certain permanent tendencies in human nature, and can be discerned to-day in many ethical and social movements, even apart from religion, English Puritanism in its distinct form can hardly be said to have outlasted the reign of Charles II.

Puritanism, alike within and without the English Church, has had a very strong effect in moulding the English character. It has intensified all those characteristics hostile to art, and by forbidding all other outlets to energy, concentrated on money-making the energies of the middle class. On the other hand, it led to a strong sense of duty, a high level of personal morality, a rigid if unsympathetic integrity, and an austere simplicity. These elements seem to be decaying with the breaking up of the intellectual foundations on which Puritanism was reared; above all, the literal infallibility of the Bible. In some of the great writers of the Victorian Age there can be traced the process of this 'exodus from Houndsditch,' in the phrase of Carlyle, who himself exhibits the retention of the characteristics of English or rather Lowland Scotch Calvinism with the repudiation of its Christian basis. In Matthew Arnold's writings a vigorous polemic was conducted against the literary and artistic ideals which Puritanism had fostered in the middle class; and probably the better educated modern dissenters have been more affected by his influence than they would care to admit. In the novels of Mark Rutherford can be seen depicted the breakdown of provincial Puritanism under the stress of modern knowledge; and Mr. Arnold Bennett's *Clayhanger*, with his other stories, displays sides of the same process.   [J. N. F.]

PUSEY, Edward Bouverie (1800-82), divine, son of the Honble. Philip Bouverie (son of the first Lord Folkestone), who took the name of Pusey on inheriting the estate of Pusey in the Vale of White Horse. His mother was Lady Lucy Cave, daughter of Lord Harborough. He early became a good horseman and a good shot, a strong swimmer and an excellent whip. In 1807 he went to a private school at Mitcham, where he was severely disciplined, and so well taught that he could have passed the Oxford 'Smalls' before he left the school. In January 1812 he went to Eton, where he is said to have been the last boy who learned dancing. After Eton he spent fifteen months of hard study as a private pupil of Dr. Maltby, afterwards Bishop of Durham; and in 1819 he went up to Christ Church. For his first two years he mixed his reading with a good deal of hunting, but in 1822 he obtained his First Class in Classics. 1823 he was elected Fellow of Oriel, and in 1824 won the Latin Essay; but his mind was already set on a more exhaustive scheme of study, bearing especially on the criticism of the Old Testament. His attention was first turned in this direction by his friendship with Julian Hibbert, who, while still a schoolboy, had begun to question the foundations of the Christian faith, and who developed into a bitter and pugnacious atheist. Through his attempts to convince his friend, Pusey first learned the virulence of anti-Christian thought, and became convinced of the necessity of investigating the systems, philosophical and literary, on which the foes of faith relied. He went to Göttingen in 1825, and thence to Berlin. In both places he put himself in close communication with the professors of the most advanced criticism. He went into residence at Oriel in 1826, and after studying Hebrew, Arabic, and the cognate languages, returned to Germany, and 'toiled terribly,' working at Oriental languages for fifteen or sixteen hours daily. When he returned to Oxford in 1827, he was what very few men in England then were, a Semitic scholar. H. J. Rose (*q.v.*) had preached before the University of Cambridge a series of 'Discourses on the State of the Protestant Religion in Germany,' in which he showed that the popular Protestantism of Germany had gone very near to losing its hold on the fundamental truths of Christianity. Some of the German teachers whom Rose attacked had become Pusey's personal friends, and they asked him to vindicate their teaching against what they, and he, considered to be Rose's uncharitable misstatements. Circumstances deferred the task of vindication until 1828, when he published *An Historical Enquiry into the Probable Causes of the Rationalist Character lately predominant in the Theology of Germany*. His defence of his German friends was remarkable. So far as he admitted the decay of faith among them he attributed it to reliance, in the seventeenth and eighteenth centuries, on the mere forms and phrases of orthodox religion, without care for the spiritual realities which they are intended to convey. But he afterwards came to see that he had judged some of the German theologians too leniently, and he realised the fatal tendency of their destructive criticism. He made all the amends in his power, and withdrew from circulation his two defences of German theology, and ordained in his will that they should not be republished. On Trinity Sunday, 1828, he was ordained deacon, and on the 12th of June he was married to Maria Catherine Barker, with whom he had fallen in love before he went to Oxford. In the following September he was appointed Regius Professor of Hebrew and Canon of Christ Church. He was ordained priest on the 23rd of November; on Christmas Day he celebrated the Holy Communion for the first time. His official house in the 'Tom' Quadrangle of Christ Church was his first and last independent home, the birthplace of his children, and the scene of his long life's work.

At first the leaders of the Oxford Movement (*q.v.*) left Pusey on one side. In a casual conversation Pusey told Newman (*q.v.*) that he had been too hard on the Evangelicals[1] (*q.v.*). It would be better to conciliate them. Pusey had thoughts of writing something with that purpose. 'Well,' said Newman, 'suppose you let us have it for one of the Tracts'; and Pusey consented. The 'something' turned out to be a Tract on the 'Uses of Fasting,' which was published in 1834; and its appeal to the Evangelical school lay in its clear and earnest recognition of the personal relation of the individual soul to God. By this publication Pusey became publicly and formally identified with the Oxford Movement. 'Dr. Pusey,' wrote Newman in 1864, 'gave us at once a position and a name. . . . He was a Professor, and Canon of Christ Church; he had a vast influence in consequence of his deep religious seriousness, the munificence of his charities, his Professorship, his family connections, and his easy relations with the University authorities. . . . There was henceforth a man who could be the head and centre of the zealous people in every part of the country who were adopting the new opinions.' Meanwhile Pusey had been sedulously cataloguing the Arabic manuscripts in the Bodleian Library. He completed this task in 1835, and

[1] In later years Pusey said: 'I loved the Evangelicals because they loved our Lord,' and 'I loved them for their zeal for souls.'

now turned to the 'Tracts,' for which he had promised to write on the doctrine of Baptism. On this subject he wrote three Tracts, which taken together amount to a treatise. Their appearance was 'like the advance of a battery of heavy artillery on a field where the battle has been hitherto carried on by skirmishing and musketry. It altered the look of things and the conditions of the fighting' (Church). 'After No. 67 the earlier form of the Tracts appeared no more.' Henceforth the official chief of the Movement, as it was seen by the world outside Oxford, was Pusey. 'Its enemies fastened on it a nickname from his name,' which was recognised all over England as the name of the party, and found its way into foreign languages (*e.g. Puseista*, used by Pius IX.).

Mrs. Pusey died on 26th of May 1839; and she had been, as Newman said, 'the one object on earth in which his thoughts have centred for the greater part of his life.' It was inevitable that such a cross as this, so heavy and so sharp-edged, should leave a permanent impress on Pusey's heart and life; but it was not permitted for a single week to impede his work for God and souls. The work, however, was resumed under altered conditions. Pusey retired absolutely from the world. He even declined to attend the official dinners of the chapter of Christ Church. He henceforth refused to enter his own drawing-room, because his wife and he had used it so much together. He never passed her grave without a prayer. He kept in daily remembrance the hour of her departure. He insisted on regarding her early death as a special punishment for his sins. As years went on he dwelt increasingly on this thought, and multiplied the practices of austerity which seemed to drive it home. He laid stripes on himself; he wore haircloth next his skin; he ate by preference unpleasant food. He never 'looked at beauty of nature without inward confession of unworthiness.' He made mental acts of being inferior to every one he saw, especially the poor and the neglected, or the very degraded, or children.' He drank cold water, remembering that he was 'only fit to be where there is not a drop to cool the flame.' He made 'acts of internal humiliation' when undergraduates or college servants saluted him. To crown all, he made it a rule 'always to lie down in bed, confessing that I am unworthy to lie down except in Hell, but so praying to lie down in the Everlasting Arms.'

In March 1841 Newman resigned his place

in the Movement. The leadership, which he had shared with Pusey, passed wholly into Pusey's hands. Referring to this time, Pusey wrote in after years : ' Dear J. H. N. said to me one day at Littlemore : " Pusey, we have leant on the bishops, and they have given way under us." Dear J. K. and I never did lean on the bishops, but on the Church.' Surely the diverse fates of Newman and Pusey can be read in that one sentence. Henceforward Pusey (always with ' J. K.' in the background) had to encourage the hopeless, and rally the downhearted, and reassure the cowardly, and guide the perplexed. He had to think, and plan, and negotiate, and, when necessary, fight for all the rest.

The great sorrow of his wife's death, which in 1839 sundered Pusey for ever from the world, seems to have given a practical turn to an idea already present to his mind. In December 1839 he wrote to Keble : ' Newman and I have separately come to think it necessary to have some " Sœurs de Charité " in the Anglo-Catholic Church ' ; and he wrote in the same sense to Dr. Hook (*q.v.*). The first community of sisters was founded in 1845. [RELIGIOUS ORDERS, MODERN.] Pusey superintended it and did more than any other one man to lay the basis of the Common Life for Women in the English Church.

In his treatise on Baptism he had laid great stress on the serious import which inspired writers attach to post-baptismal sin. His language may have been too unguarded and unqualified ; certainly he was misunderstood and misrepresented. S. Wilberforce (*q.v.*) accused him of ' Novatian hardness.' Others said that he had ' scared ' them with the ghastly notion that post-baptismal sin is unforgivable. J. B. Mozley (*q.v.*), though defending the substance of Pusey's teaching, saw something ' harsh ' in his way of stating it. Pusey was always willing to take advice from friends, and these considerations led him to plan a course of sermons on ' Comforts to the Penitent.' He originally thought of taking Absolution as the first of these ; but, having regard to the highly uninformed state of the public mind, he chose instead the Holy Eucharist, as ' a subject at which they would be less likely to take offence.' The sermon was preached before the University on the 14th May 1843, and did not invite or suggest controversy. It was a plain restatement, in language venerated all over Christendom, of the Eucharistic truth which has been held from the beginning.

But 1843 was an electrical time. The University was the centre of disturbance, and Pusey was delated to the vice-chancellor as having preached false doctrine. The vice-chancellor called to his aid six doctors of divinity. Sitting in secret conclave they examined the incriminated sermon, but gave Pusey no opportunity for defence. They condemned his teaching as erroneous, and suspended him from preaching before the University for two years. Whatever this strange performance was intended to effect, what it actually effected is certain. It called the attention of churchmen to a truth of the Catholic faith which had been strangely overlooked. It gave Pusey an unequalled opportunity of demonstrating (by the publication of the sermon, with an appendix of authorities) the soundness of his doctrine ; and it helped to make him for the rest of his life the special champion and the most insistent teacher of the Real Objective Presence, and all that it involves.

On 1st February 1846 Pusey, whose term of suspension had expired, preached again before the University. Pursuing his plan of showing the various means of grace appointed for the restoration of the repentant sinner, he chose for his subject, ' The Entire Absolution of the Penitent,' and began by a reference to the circumstances under which he had been suspended. ' I was endeavouring to mitigate the stern doctrine of the heavy character of a Christian's sins, by pointing out the mercies of God which might reassure the penitent.' In the condemned sermon, which he now reasserted to the very height of its doctrinal position, he had shown the supreme blessing conveyed through the Holy Eucharist. He now continued the same line of thought. All forgiveness is of God. The Church and her ministers are not substitutes for but instruments of Christ, the one Absolver. But that the one Absolver had delegated to His Church the absolving power was plain from the words of the text (Jn. 20²¹·³) ; and that the Church of England claims the right to exercise this awful gift is plain from the formula of absolution in the Visitation of the Sick, when read in connection with the Ordinal. ' The Church of England teaches the reality of Priestly Absolution as explicitly as it has ever been taught, or is taught to-day, in any part of Christendom.' Against this sermon no public or official objection was raised. The Doctrine of the Keys was triumphantly vindicated, and a great part of Pusey's subsequent life was spent in applying it practically. Probably no priest in the Church of England has ever heard so many confessions or directed so many consciences, but he had not yet made his own confession. He now wisely placed himself under Keble's guidance, and made his first confession at Hursley in December 1846.

From the way of life which he would have chosen for himself—retirement, study, prayer, and private ministry to souls—Pusey was constantly recalled by the duty of publicly championing imperilled truth. In 1850 he addressed a great meeting in London, called to protest against the 'Gorham Judgment.' His speech was a rallying voice of encouragement and hope in a day of terror and defeat and flight. 'The Judicial Committee,' he said, 'of five persons have not power to commit the Church of England to heresy.'

Newman, while an Anglican, had written : 'The Heads of Houses may crush Tractarianism; they will then have to do with Germanism.' In the early 'fifties his prophecy began to be made good. The 'Liberal' school in theology (so termed by a curious misnomer, for nothing on earth can be less Liberal than the attitude of Latitudinarians towards Catholicism) had of late made great advances. *Essays and Reviews* (*q.v.*), the work mainly of this school, published in 1860, disturbed the faith of some, and its writers were upheld by the Judicial Committee. Throughout these commotions, which extended, roughly, over ten years, Pusey, though deeply distressed and worried on all hands, kept his head, his justice, and his charity. He responded warmly to an appeal from Lord Shaftesbury (who before this had bitterly attacked him) for co-operation with Evangelicals in the battle against unbelief.

This conflict with unbelief led Pusey, by a way wholly unforeseen, into conflict with Rome. In 1864 he published a pamphlet on the legal force of the judgment on *Essays and Reviews*, and in his preface he had said that some Roman Catholics seemed to be in an 'ecstasy of triumph at the victory of Satan,' though others were 'saddened' by anything which weakened 'the great bulwark against Infidelity in this land.' To this rather provocative language Manning promptly replied in an open letter to Pusey on 'The Workings of the Holy Spirit in the Church of England.' In this letter he disclaimed all sympathy with Satan, but was at great pains to show that the English Church was not, and could not be, a 'bulwark against Infidelity.' Contrariwise, he maintained that she was 'a cause and spring of Unbelief,' by reason of the fact that she herself had rejected divine truth. To this railing accusa-

tion Pusey rejoined in *The Truth and Office of the English Church.*

Some attempts, very mild at first, to promote order and comeliness in divine worship had marked the whole course of the Catholic revival. Such attempts came to be called 'Ritualism'; and in the autumn of 1866 there was an outbreak of anti-Ritualist passion in the *Times*. In February 1867 the bishops endeavoured to conciliate public opinion by passing a Resolution on Ritualism, which seemed to imply censure of the doctrine which ceremonial is meant to express. This brought Pusey into the field. He published, under the title *Will ye also go away?* a sermon with a preface and appendix. In this sermon he reaffirms, in simple words but with unabated force, the doctrine of the Real Objective Presence. In the preface he refers to the episcopal manifesto, and gives his opinion on ceremonial. 'The so-called Ritualist movement was eminently a lay movement. We, the clergy, had taught the truth ; the people had said : "Set it before our eyes." Although I have never taken part in the Ritualist movement, I believed and believe that the object of that movement has been to set before the eyes Catholic truths in regard to the Holy Eucharist which have ever been received in the Church.'

The fourth report of the Ritual Commission [COMMISSIONS, ROYAL] in 1870, with its suggestions as to the Athanasian Creed, stirred Pusey's indignation, and he plunged into the fight. He averred that, if the Creed were touched, he should resign his preferments. 'It would not be the same Church for which I have fought hitherto. . . . We have endured much, but we cannot endure having one of our creeds rent from us.' The fight raged all through 1871 and 1872, and the victory was not won till May 1873, when it was agreed in Convocation that the Athanasian Creed should be retained unmutilated, and should be used in public worship as before. The battle had been won by Pusey, and his right-hand man had been his devoted disciple, H. P. Liddon (*q.v.*).

In the winter of 1872-3 Pusey had a severe illness, and from henceforward was an altered man. His mental powers and his habits of diligence remained unimpaired, but his bodily health declined. He was specially liable to attacks of bronchitis, and he took to living almost entirely indoors. The greater part of the year he spent in Christ Church, but went occasionally for change of scene to the 'Hermitage' at Ascot, near the convent occupied by the Devonport Sisterhood. He became almost stone deaf, and, when hearing confessions, he asked the penitent to aid him by putting on paper what he wished to say. His voice became so husky that he could not preach, and his last two University sermons were read for him by others. As a younger man he had often worked all night as well as all day. Even at seventy years of age he would make appointments for seven A.M., and continue working till twelve at night. Until declining strength made it impossible, he used to celebrate the Holy Communion in his study every day, generally at four in the morning (he had received special permission from Bishop Wilberforce so to do), and to the end he thus celebrated in this way on Sundays and saints' days. When celebrating in his own house he wore a surplice and a crape scarf : but in a church where the Eucharistic vestments were used he wore them. In June 1882 he went to his 'Hermitage' at Ascot. Towards the end of July he began to flag. The sisters, whose confessions he heard,

thought that he was not quite equal to himself. Still, on his eighty-second birthday (22nd August) he was quite bright. Two days later he was less well ; but he gathered strength to write to the *Times* two pathetic appeals on behalf of the Rev. S. F. Green, imprisoned under the P.W.R. Act. On the 4th of September he took to his bed. In the mental wanderings which prevailed through the night of 13th September he thought that he was performing the priestly acts which had been the occupation and glory of his life. On Saturday, 16th, he seemed to be murmuring the *Te Deum*, and he passed away at three in the afternoon, with the words on his lips: 'My Lord and my God.' On the 21st of September he was laid in the nave of Christ Church Cathedral, beside his wife and his two elder daughters. The list of his published works fills an appendix of fifty pages in the fourth volume of his *Life*.

[G. W. E. R.]

Lives by Liddon and G. W. E. Russell.

Q

QUEEN ANNE'S BOUNTY. In 1704 Queen Anne announced to the House of Commons her intention of giving up for the benefit of the Church the revenue from first-fruits and tenths appropriated to the Crown in 1534. [VALOR ECCLESIASTICUS.] She proposed that this revenue, amounting to £16,000 or £17,000 a year, should be devoted to the augmentation of small livings, of which Burnet (*q.v.*), who claims to have suggested the design, says there were some hundreds 'that had not of certain provision £20 a year, and some thousands that had not £50.' Marlborough, who was all-powerful with the Queen, was willing to purchase Tory support for the French war by allowing her to make this gift to the Church. Accordingly the Act 2-3 An. c. 20 (commonly cited as c. 11) was passed 'for making more effectual Her Majesty's gracious intentions.' It recites the evils that follow from the clergy 'depending for their necessary maintenance upon the good will and liking of their hearers,' which places them 'under temptation of too much complying and suiting their doctrines and teaching to the humours rather than the good of their hearers.' It provides for the erection of a corporation to hold and administer for the purpose proposed the revenue surrendered by the Crown and any other grants that might be made. On 3rd

November 1704 Letters Patent were issued appointing some two hundred 'Governors of the Bounty of Queen Anne'; 'a numerous body of men selected from those already overworked. Such was the idea then to secure efficient administration.' They included all the bishops (except Sodor and Man), deans, lord-lieutenants, privy councillors, serjeants-at-law, and the mayors of all the cities in England.

The governors found their revenue greatly in arrears and much encumbered. At their instance Acts were passed in 1706 and 1707 discharging all livings of less than £50 a year from payment of first-fruits and tenths (5-6 An. c. 24, 6 An. c. 54, commonly cited as c. 27). This affected about three thousand nine hundred livings, and reduced the revenue by about £3000. By 1713 they had cleared away preliminary obstacles, and could begin their proper work by awarding twenty-eight poor livings £200 each. Further Letters Patent were issued creating additional governors, including all the Queen's Counsel, and laying down the rule that all augmentations should be 'by the way of purchase, and not by the way of pension,' *i.e.* they were to grant capital sums, not annuities. An Act of 1714 (1 Geo. I. st. 2, c. 10) enabled them, with the approval of the Crown, to make rules under which to work. They employed strange and unfortunate methods. All eligible parishes claiming aid went into the ballot-box, and as many were drawn out as there were grants of £200 to distribute. Thus (though no cure exceeding £10 a year might be augmented until all under that amount had received £200) many livings had five or six grants in the course of a century, while others as deserving had no grant at all. The number of claims was so great that livings of over £35 did not become entitled to a grant till 1788. Unhappily for the Church, practically the only investment then allowed by public opinion was freehold land. When no land in the parish was to be had the nearest land obtainable was bought. Hence difficulties have arisen, many parishes possessing small estates twenty or thirty miles away.

Livings not exceeding £35 might be augmented by grants of not more than £600 on a benefactor contributing an equal or greater sum. The limit of £35 was raised to £60 in 1804, and to £200 in 1820. Since 1836 nearly the whole of the funds have been applied to meeting benefactions, and the ballot has been practically abandoned.

In 1777 the governors were empowered to lend money on mortgage to incumbents for building or repairing parsonages (17 Geo. III. c. 53), and in 1803 to make grants for the purchase or building of parsonages (43 Geo. III. c. 107). Later statutes have extended their powers and duties in receiving and advancing money. In 1838 the separate collection of first-fruits and tenths was abolished, and the Treasurer of Queen Anne's Bounty appointed sole collector (1-2 Vic. c. 20). And by Order in Council,

27th November 1852, they were commuted for fixed annual payments.

Between 1809 and 1820 Parliament, under the influence of Tory governments, made eleven grants of £100,000 each to the fund. These additions to taxation were made at the height of the popular distress. The first private benefaction was £600, given in 1708. By 1867 the total received from private benefactors was over £2,000,000, and the grants awarded from the governors' own funds had reached £3,500,000. From 1836 to 1868 the amount awarded in grants was about £11,600 a year, and from 1880 to 1899 £28,300 a year. By 1899 the total grants (including private benefactions) had exceeded £7,500,000. In 1898 the minimum grant was reduced from £200 to £100.

In 1868 a Select Committee of the House of Commons recommended that the number of governors should be reduced. It was then about five hundred and eighty, and by 1900 had reached six hundred and fifty, owing chiefly to the increase in the number of Queen's Counsel. Only fifty-two governors were ever summoned to the meetings. In 1901 a joint Select Committee of both Houses recommended that, to avoid duplication of work, the governors should be amalgamated with the Ecclesiastical Commission. [COMMISSIONS, ROYAL.] The governors expressed disapproval of this proposal, maintaining that their administration compared favourably with that of the Commissioners. No action has yet been taken, though a Bill to effect the amalgamation was introduced in 1902. [G. C.]

Hodgson, *Account of the Augmentations of Small Livings*, 1826: *Proceedings of the Select Committees*, 1868, 1900, 1901.

R

REFORMATIO LEGUM ECCLESIASTICARUM. The document which goes by this name was a scheme of order and discipline for the Reformed Church of England which was never allowed to take effect. 'The Submission of the Clergy' in 1532 was a sequel to the recognition of Royal Supremacy extorted from Convocation in the previous year. It virtually abrogated the canon law (*q.v.*). For by it the clergy engaged not only to enact no new canons without the King's consent, but to submit the old ones to the examination of a royal commission of thirty-two persons, half laymen and half clergy,

that only those canons should remain binding which were found consistent with God's laws and those of the realm. This proposed commission was never constituted in Henry VIII.'s days, though repeated Acts of Parliament were passed to give effect to the intended revision : and the like efforts continued under Edward VI., till in 1551 there was actually issued not only a commission of thirty-two, as promised, but a select commission of eight to rough-hew the work of forming a new body of canon law. Just at this time preparations were making for a new Prayer Book more agreeable than the first to Calvin and the Swiss reformers, who were consulted with a view to the establishment of a common religion independent of Rome—an object to which the commission on the canon law seemed a natural supplement. The result of their labours was presented by Cranmer (*q.v.*) to Parliament in March 1553, but the Duke of Northumberland would not allow the matter to be discussed. Little more than three months later Edward VI. died, and the work remained in MS. till 1571, when it was printed by Foxe (*q.v.*), the martyrologist, with a preface in which it was surmised, with no small assurance, that it would have been issued for public use by Parliamentary authority if Edward's life had been spared. Such a suggestion, however, is against all appearances. The work was simply a new system of canon law drawn up very much in the style of the old decretals and constitutions, but adapted, with some doctrinal modifications, to a Church under Royal Supremacy. Transubstantiation was repudiated, and, strange to say, reception in a sitting posture was virtually sanctioned, a fact which seems to show that Cranmer did not have his own way in the commission. Like the old pontifical compilations, the book is divided into titles. There are fifty-one titles (not numbered, unfortunately, for reference), and all but the last (which is only a schedule of rules of law) are divided again into chapters. The whole work is set forth as proceeding from the King's mouth, and the subjects range from the Holy Trinity and the Catholic faith (tit. i.) to such matters as dilapidations of churches and vicarages (tit. xv.). There is, however, no surrender of ecclesiastical jurisdiction to the civil power. In tit. xliv., for example, violence used towards a clergyman is treated as an atrocious crime, involving excommunication of the offender ; from which he can only be relieved by full discharge of such penance as the ordinary shall think fit to impose.

The authority on which the whole is set forth is curiously indicated in Chapter I. of the very first title : *De fide Christiana ab omnibus amplectenda et profitenda.* The language, translated from the Latin, is as follows :—' As all royal power and administration of laws is derived from God, we must take our beginning from God, whose nature being first set forth truly, it will be easier to foresee the rest of those laws which we have procured to be enacted for the conservation of the state of the Church. Wherefore we will and order all men who are any way under our rule to accept and profess the Christian religion ; against which whoever begin any

cogitations or actions alienate God from themselves by their impiety. We, moreover, who are ministers of the divine Majesty, have determined that all their powers, and even life itself, are to be forfeited by whoever have involved themselves in such outrageous wickedness. And let this be valid among all our subjects of whatever name, place, or condition they be.'

This was drawn up by divines in the King's name, and no doubt sounded too high a note for mere secular statesmen.   [J. G.]

Reformatio Legum, ed. Cardwell.

REFORMATION IN ENGLAND, The,

should always be studied over the whole period 1509-1662, not in isolated reigns or periods which give a false impression of its course and results ; it should not be separated from the preceding mediæval history or from the Continental history of the period, with which it has many resemblances and many differences, both equally instructive. And the study of the Middle Ages in England forms a necessary introduction. Broadly speaking, at the close of the Middle Ages we can see five great forces at work. These are : (1) national life ; (2) individualism ; (3) a new vigour of learning and inquiry ; (4) a renewed study of the Scriptures ; (5) a spirit of questioning and criticising authority, seeking to know its utility and not accepting it on trust or from the mere fact of its existence.

1. The Middle Ages had developed the great nations, and given some of them great national institutions, monarchies, parliaments, and so forth. The growth of these nations had been accompanied by some friction and jealousies against other bodies, notably the Western Church and the Papacy. If these had sometimes helped the national life their aims had been different ; questions of Church and State, of Papacy and Monarchy, of the Curia and national Churches, had arisen from time to time and in many ways. But the Middle Ages had never drawn the sharp distinction which we do between Church and State ; their view (which is seen clearly in the Investiture contest and its literature) was rather that of one society organised in different ways, which sometimes agreed, sometimes crossed, each other. And the Middle Ages had never cared to reconcile, had indeed hardly faced, the contradictions which were inherent in such a system. But these contradictions and the problems arising out of them really underlay the rich and varied development of mediæval society ; their emergence was only a matter of time, and would inevitably give rise to strife. If the

great nations had formed central institutions and strong powers, the Papacy had done the same; its central courts had grown greatly, as a matter of convenience more than of ambition, especially in the fourteenth and fifteenth centuries. And inside the different nations the Church, with its fundamental idea of an international Christian Society, and with its developed courts and organisation, represented an ideal very different from that of the great national States. When stress was laid upon the latter men would have to reconsider questions of great importance; all sorts of difficulties, all sorts of solutions, were sure to appear. A change of society and social ideals, which had been slowly forming throughout the Middle Ages, came to a crisis in the sixteenth century, and affected both political and religious history. This is the significance of the strong national feelings, strong monarchies, and conflicting national policies which form the background of the Reformation. Differences between Church and State, difficulties between the Papacy and the Monarchy in England, had appeared throughout the Middle Ages. [PRO-VISORS, PRAEMUNIRE.] Their more emphatic appearance at the Reformation [SUPREMACY, ROYAL] was a result of the general movement indicated here. Not only under Henry VIII. and Elizabeth in England, but also under Mary, and in France, Germany, and Spain, we see the same problems arising.

2. The Middle Ages in their strong instinct for society, for corporations and gilds (giving rise to institutions national, local, and social), had tended to depress individuality, to produce types, and restrain individual activity. In politics and commerce there were signs at the end of the Middle Ages that the old corporate ideals were losing force; individual enterprise became the great factor in an age of growing competition. In the history of thought, too, individuals rather than schools were becoming important. In ecclesiastical and religious matters the same change took place. Individual religion—never, of course, forgotten—became relatively more urgent; individual more than social needs pressed for attention. Just as with the vigour of national life the use of national languages for religious purposes appeared—it may be noted that France and Germany (in their *Libels of Reformation* at Trent) both favoured the use of the vernacular in the Mass and divine service—so books of private prayer and personal instruction became more common. Individualism was a religious force capable of great things, but above all needing instruction; it was likely to run

into excesses, and it needed guidance. It was a problem for the Church and its teachers; the wisdom or the lack of wisdom shown in the treatment of this new force greatly affected the history of the Reformation. Many of the phenomena of the Reformation period in England and on the Continent, much of its power and many of its defects, may be explained by this rise of individualism and the difficulty of treating it.

3. The Revival of Learning, closely connected with the new spirit of inquiry, was a direct result of mediæval teaching; it was quickened by many events and processes of the late fifteenth and early sixteenth centuries, and it worked along with the power of individualism; thought, inquiry, personal peculiarities were all quickened. There was, as shown by Erasmus, Colet (*q.v.*), and others, a wish for reform of abuses and better instruction. A reformation on conservative lines should have been possible; the English Convocation in 1532 (like the too timid Lateran Council of 1512 and the too long-delayed Council of Trent) did attempt the task. But the struggle between Pope and Monarch, and the appearance of more drastic reformers, made this conservative reform difficult. In England, as in Germany after Luther, many supporters of the New Learning eventually became strong supporters of what was in existence. The strong measures of Henry VIII. and the violent changes under Edward VI. alienated some moderate reformers; others, like Gardiner (*q.v.*), who under Henry VIII. had supported Royal Supremacy, became under Mary opponents of change, when under Edward VI. they had seen it too rapid and destructive.

4. It should not be forgotten that the Reformation was not purely destructive. A deep revival of religious earnestness, showing itself mainly on the side of individuality, began towards the end of the fifteenth century. This was the positive side of the Revival of Learning, of the Lutheran and Zwinglian and Calvinistic movements, of the Oratory of Divine Love in Italy and of the Jesuit Society; it showed itself on the Continent in widespread reform of existing Religious Orders and of Friars—such as helped to form the mind of Luther. In England we see it in the Oxford Reformers, and in the movement at Cambridge which followed the teaching of Erasmus (1511) and was fostered by Bishop Fisher (*q.v.*) and his foundations. One of its manifestations was a study of Scripture and an appeal to its authority. The study of Hebrew and Greek and the invention of print-

ing made this study more fruitful and popular, but its novelty is often overstated. The Scriptures were better known in the Middle Ages, and versions of them were commoner than is often allowed in popular statements. It is a mistake to suppose that the mediæval Church was hostile to the study or spread of the Scriptures either in learned languages or in the vernacular. [LOLLARDS; WYCLIF; BIBLE, ENGLISH.] But the *Novum Testamentum* of Erasmus and his comments upon the Scriptures had great influence. This was particularly the case at Cambridge, where a number of young scholars took up the study of the Scriptures and of writings upon them. [CRANMER, LATIMER, RIDLEY, TYNDALE.] This movement was not interfered with until Robert Barnes (Christmas Eve, 1525) made his celebrated attack upon Wolsey in a sermon, which led to the break up of the party. Many of the Cambridge men taken over by Wolsey to his new foundation of Cardinal's College had belonged to it. But there was another side of the movement. Tyndale, besides his work at the Scriptures, was a writer of pamphlets extreme in their theological views and politically dangerous, and his life illustrates the mixed tendencies at work in the Reformation. But the appeal to the Scriptures (always recognised by the Church) became with some of these reformers the sole test of doctrine and practice; it was a principle adapted by many of the Puritans and contended against by Hooker (*q.v.*). Its influence with Cartwright (*q.v.*) and the Presbyterians as well as with others should be noted. And many individuals took their own interpretation as authoritative, so that religious life became decentralised. It was an exaggeration of the sound principle of the Revival of Learning, and in the hands of unlearned or undisciplined men it did much harm. The rise of various, sometimes small, religious bodies was a result of it. The working of this appeal to the Scriptures should be studied in the recognition of it by the English Church as seen in the Prayer Book [COMMON PRAYER, BOOK OF] and elsewhere (Ten Articles of 1536; the *Bishops' Book*, 1537; and the *King's Book*, 1543), as well as in the exaggeration of it by the Puritans. A positive result of the English Reformation was the place given to the Scriptures in the vernacular together with the Prayer Book. The attainment of this positive result was in danger both from those who disliked its freedom and from those who, like some Reformers and the Puritans, abused the principle itself.

5. The great councils of the West and the controversial literature of the Middle Ages had raised, and left unsettled, many questions as to the nature of the Church, its organisation and government. Questions of the relation of the State to the Papacy, of the Episcopate to the Papacy, and so on, had been raised. When in the course of the Reformation the course of events raised the question of papal power—which Sir Thomas More (*q.v.*) had foreseen would become critical—these earlier works were studied afresh. Debates have been raised as to the feeling in England towards the Papacy. On the whole, it seems that then the papal claims were generally accepted, although the discussion and final disproof of the forgeries of the False Decretals and the Donation of Constantine disturbed opinion; complaints about jurisdiction and irritation at its abuse were another matter. Complaints were also made against the Church courts (*q.v.*) in England itself. Warham (*q.v.*) attempted a reform of them, the Reformation Parliament dealt with them, and the case of Richard Hunne caused much discussion. The 'King's Matter' or 'Divorce' under Henry VIII. raised issues of papal power and also of ecclesiastical jurisdiction; it was the occasion, although not the cause, of the 'Reformation' so far as it went under Henry VIII. The abolition of papal power—which Henry did not probably think irrevocable until late in his reign—took place under the conditions of the other movements we have spoken of. This question was raised on the Continent also.

As to the course of the Reformation in successive reigns, under Henry VIII. papal jurisdiction was abolished, the national sovereignty was asserted more vigorously than before, and the Royal Supremacy—especially under Cromwell (*q.v.*) as Vicar-General—was used with great tyranny. The fall of Wolsey made this assertion possible, and the Submission of the Clergy enforced it. The Suppression of the Monasteries (*q.v.*) wrought a great change in society. For a time it enriched the King, and it removed in Parliament and in the Church obstacles to the carrying out of his will. But, in a sense, it was independent of the Reformation, and thus the legislation of Mary's reign, while restoring old conditions, left the Suppression still effective. Doctrinally little change was made under Henry, although the process of liturgical revision, and encouragement of the vernacular in worship, was begun. The King—politically in his negotiations with the Lutherans, and religiously in his conniving at the circulation of extreme reforming tracts—played with these popular forces. His reign, therefore, is one in which various and opposed tendencies of thought and action are mingled. Under Edward VI. the effect of politics is strongly marked ; plunder of the Church increased, and, more for convenience than from conviction, extreme tendencies were encouraged, as may be seen in popular sermons and in the differences between the First and Second Prayer Books of Edward VI. Cranmer's (q.v.) plans included not only the prayers in English, but (in accordance with primitive practice and Continental reforming usage) frequent meetings of synods and a codification of English Canon Law (q.v.). The removal of Papal power had made the church law chaotic ; such parts of it as were not contradictory to the law of the land were still authoritative by statute. A Commission had been appointed under Henry to codify it, and the *Reformatio Legum* (q.v.), produced in MS. by Parker under Elizabeth when the question of codification came up, represents Cranmer's views, greatly influenced by the foreign divines who under Edward VI. visited England. But, happily, this scheme was not adopted, and although successive canons (the history of their formation is instructive) partly supplied its place, some disorder was due to the chaotic state of church law. The difficulties felt by Parker (q.v.) and even his successors were largely due to this, and the arbitrary Court of High Commission (q.v.) set up under Elizabeth, and used under the Stuarts, badly supplied its place. But the control of morals by the ordinary courts, episcopal and other, still went on, and only gradually disappeared after the Civil War. It is hard to say what might have taken place in England under the rule of self-seeking politicians and the influence of foreign reformers had not Edward's death and the accession of Mary caused a break. Under Mary (q.v.) England was reconciled to the Papacy, and so far as possible the old state of things restored. [MARIAN REACTION.] Gardiner and others, who had under Henry supported the Royal Supremacy, now supported the Papacy as the only efficient barrier against revolution. But the unpopularity of the Spanish marriage and the severe persecutions, due mainly to the Queen herself in her wish to enforce her own religion, caused some change in public opinion. On her death Elizabeth's accession was popular, although it is probable that on the purely religious side the Elizabethan Settlement (q.v.) only gradually commended itself. Naturally the bishops and Convocation did not welcome

the reaction which took place. From the first the rejection of papal power, and a return to the conditions of Henry's reign (although the title of Supreme Governor, at the Queen's wish, replaced that of Supreme Head), was determined on. Archbishop Parker was called upon to rule the Church, and his moderation and wisdom were effective, although hampered by the statesmen who were puritanically inclined, and by the exiles of Mary's reign, who returned from the Continent strongly tinged with Calvinism and with a dislike of even moderate ceremonial. Parker's main tasks were the enforcement of discipline and the provision of clergy. The Vestiarian controversy soon gave way to larger controversies as to the nature of Church government. The excommunication of the Queen by Pius V. (1570) and the influence of Cartwright at Cambridge marked the failure of the Government's attempt to include all sections of the nation in the Church. Presbyterianism —which in England led to the assertion of the sinfulness of episcopacy—attempted secretly to undermine the Church. It was an attempt to reproduce in England the model of ' the best reformed churches abroad.' It was this movement which Whitgift (q.v.) with the help of Bancroft (q.v.) put down. But although suppressed in this form, another type of Presbyterianism was introduced later on from Scotland, and became of great importance in the Civil War and under the Commonwealth.

Under Elizabeth Puritan tendencies maintained their power inside the Church, as Nonconformity (q.v.), scrupling at ceremonies or doctrine or ritual, and outside the Church, gave rise to separate bodies—Independents and Baptists. [NONCONFORMITY.] On the other hand, the Roman Catholics, who early in the reign had sought papal leave to worship in their parish churches and under the Prayer Book, also formed a separate body. [ROMAN CATHOLICS.] The zeal of the Jesuit mission, aiming at the reconversion of England, and connected through some of its members with political plots, led to a quarrel between the older Roman clergy and the new missionaries (the Archpriest controversy) and an appeal to Rome. The formation of an organisation for the Roman Catholics was the result, and thus the English Church was confronted by other religious bodies on two opposite sides. The close connection between questions of politics and religion, as seen in the French religious wars, the revolts of the Netherlands, and later on the Thirty Years War, made these internal differences more difficult. Henceforth the history of religious Toleration (*q.v.*) and the penal laws as to religion has to be followed. At times of excitement the House of Commons, supported by the nation, clamoured for the strict observance of these laws, and after the Restoration the Commons were more vindictive than either Crown or Church.

The peculiar character of the English Reformation, seen in its preservation of episcopacy and its deliberate appeal to the primitive Church as well as to the Scriptures, and testified to by the criticisms of foreign reformers as well as by English theologians under Elizabeth (see especially the Zurich Letters), was shown more plainly as the reign of Elizabeth went on. Externally it led to long controversies, in which the works of Bishop Jewel (*q.v.*) are specially significant, against the Church of Rome. These go on under the Stuarts, and Laud's controversy with Fisher is specially noteworthy. On the other side is the great struggle against the Puritans, in which Hooker defined the Anglican position. It was sometimes convenient for the government to misrepresent its position with a view to political alliances abroad. But the basis nevertheless laid down in theory was gradually worked out in fact, and by its practical efficiency the English Church had by the end of Elizabeth's reign greatly strengthened its hold upon the nation. And it should not be forgotten that much in the Elizabethan Settlement was only intended as an 'Interim': bishops, on the one side, hoped to be able later on to enforce the Ornaments Rubric (*q.v.*) and to stiffen up discipline; the returned exiles, on the other hand, always hoped to carry the Reformation a stage further. Future difficulties were therefore certain. On one important matter, the recognition of foreign and non-episcopal orders, the opinions of individuals have less weight than the regulation and practice of the Church: Whitgift's declaration that he knew no cases in his province in which ministers without episcopal ordination held benefices is decisive when taken along with the practice. In spite of friendliness towards other Christians, there is absolutely no evidence from the Elizabethan or Stuart period for the recognition of non-episcopal orders by the English Church. [REUNION, IV.] The necessity of episcopal ordination was a generally accepted fact up to the time of the Reformation; its assertion and proof were made necessary when its truth was questioned. Thus from the time of Elizabeth onwards it was defended: argument and the practice of the Church went together.

The strong Calvinistic tone of English theologians under Elizabeth gradually gave way to so-called Arminianism (*q.v.*) under James I. The Lambeth Articles (never authoritative) had represented a compromise between extreme Calvinists and their opponents, but even the doctrine of these Articles was too Calvinistic for a later day. The growing theology of Laud's school was very different, and it was accompanied by new stress upon Church discipline, and upon Catholic as opposed to Puritan practice. There had been much laxity in discipline, and many ministers had not conformed strictly to the Prayer Book. The attempt to enforce this conformity, to make the system of the English Church as laid down by the Prayer Book effective in practice, was the work of Laud. Throughout Europe there was a strong Catholic reaction, and it was the Catholic, as distinct from the reformed, side of the English Church upon which Laud laid emphasis. But he had to reckon with views and practices which were the result of many varying tendencies and periods in the English Church. The dislike of the church courts, the dread of Romanism, the opposition to his revival of canonical legislation, all worked against him. Further, he depended too much upon royal help and upon the arbitrary ecclesiastical Court of High Commission (*q.v.*), and this association of his ecclesiastical principles with the assertion of absolute royal power brought disaster upon the Church. The Civil War and the Commonwealth represent the triumph in ecclesiastical matters of the extreme Reforming school, which had tried to evade, to transform, and finally to overcome, the settlement of the Church. Hence the true issue of the Reformation is to be seen when at the Restoration the Church of England returns to its former position, with its formularies and organisation. The final struggle with tendencies, seen again and again during the period, had taken place. There were some changes, due to lapse of Church usage during the civil wars; the growing disuse of confession, of ecclesiastical discipline, etc., which is often ascribed to the Reformation, is really due to the period just after the Restoration; the struggle as to whether ecclesiastical supremacy was only to be exercised by the Crown or whether it was not also shared by Parliament had been seen beginning under Elizabeth. Under Charles I. and the Commonwealth Parliament had interfered largely in Church matters. Thus after the Restoration the Church of England had in practice lost something of the independence which in theory and constitution belonged to it. The Reformation, emphatic enough in some of its work, positive enough in its repudiation of the Papacy, in its appeal to Scripture and the Primitive Church, had left many difficulties behind. There was justice in the Puritan criticism that its discipline was imperfectly administered, and in the other criticism that it had not asserted sufficiently its freedom against the Civil Power. These difficulties were legacies of the Reformation. On the other hand, the Reformation had also left it in close touch with the whole national life, which would have been doubtful under papal control; it had also inherited the Reformation appeal to the Primitive Church and to the Scriptures— an appeal made clear in its Prayer Book and all its ecclesiastical documents; it had also inherited a love of learning and intellectual freedom, which it would have been difficult to preserve had it committed itself more completely to either side in the Reformation struggles. These were great results, but even greater was that preservation of continuous life which was to show itself in future days. The Reformation had thus left many difficulties and caused others, but for its justification, on the conservative and on the reformative side, the Church of England can appeal to its later history. [CONTINUITY OF THE CHURCH OF ENGLAND.] [J. P. W.]

For illustrations from the Continental Reformation see Kidd, *Documents of the Continental Reformation*; Ranke, *Hist. of the Popes* and *The Reformation in Germany*; *C.M.H.*, vols. ii. and iii.; Whitney, *The Reformation* in *Hist. of the Church Universal*. For the English Reformation, Dixon, *Hist. of the Ch. of Eng.*: J. Gairdner, *Lollardy and the Reformation*. Volumes in the *Pol. Hist. of Eng.* by Fisher, Pollard, and Montague: volumes in *Hist. of the Eng. Ch.* by Gairdner, Frere, and Hutton. In most of these works references to original documents and bibliographies will be found.

RELIGIOUS ORDERS.—I. Monasticism had in early times more claim perhaps to the gratitude of England than to that of any other country, for to its influence was mainly due the revival of the Christian Church, which had been swept away, save in the west, by the paganism that ensued upon the Saxon conquest. By the companions of St. Augustine (*q.v.*) and their successors in the south, by the enthusiasm of the Irish monks in the north of England the reconquest was gradually accomplished. For a century every monastic settlement was a missionary agency, and the regular clergy formed for the most part the staff of every mission church. On their ministrations and counsel the bishops leaned in the first sees that were founded, though the secular clergy acted with them or replaced them in the subdivided bishoprics of later days. But the debt was far greater than this. The rule which St. Benedict drew up among the hills of Subiaco and at Monte Cassino early in the sixth century determined for ages the spirit and details of cloistered life in Western Europe. Besides the vows of humility, chastity, and obedience he insisted on the daily discipline of manual labour, which, like prayer, was an effort to conform to the Divine Will. The inmates of the early Benedictine houses assembled in the morning hours; each had his daily task and the needful tools assigned him, and went forth to his unquestioned labour. There he and his brethren drained the marshes, felled the forests, and made a garden of many a dreary waste; while their example gradually taught its lesson to rude races that loved the excitement of the chase and war, but scorned the drudgery of common labour.

Their influence in later days took many other social forms. Their libraries preserved the literary treasures of the old world, while they wrote out the history that was being made around them, and trained within their walls the schoolmasters of the future. Amid unceasing vicissitudes of turmoil and strife the convent walls constantly appealed to the high ideals of peace and order; their privilege of sanctuary sheltered the fugitives from the blood feud and arrested the pursuit of vengeance, while in quiet times the many victims in life's struggles turned to them for sympathy and succour, travellers found a resting-place, and the asperities of class distinctions in the society around were softened by the fusion of ranks within the walls, where kings became monks, and monks like Dunstan (*q.v.*) and Anselm (*q.v.*) became archbishops and ruled kingdoms.

The influence of the Benedictine rule in Saxon England naturally followed on the arrival of the Benedictine Augustine (*q.v.*) and his missionary band and the spread of the movement which they began. The monks who had been driven by the Lombards from their home on Monte Cassino were welcomed by St. Gregory (*q.v.*) in his foundation on the Cœlian hill in honour of St. Andrew. The Prior of St. Andrew was chosen by him as the leader of the missionary enterprise, and the rule which had thus been carried in repeated wanderings was, of course, accepted in all the settlements they planted. Celtic monasteries indeed lived on in Wales and Ireland with austerer forms and peculiar relations in some cases to the bishops who resided in their cloisters. It is impossible to read without a thrill of admiration of the energy of self-devotion with which the Irish monks streamed forth to plant the Cross in so many lands of northern heathendom, and for a time St. Aidan (*q.v.*) and the Celtic missionaries successfully contended with the Italian teachers for the honour of evangelising a great part of England. But finally that fine school of apostolic influence with its special traditions and narrower range of culture gave place to the more flexible and less ascetic spirit of the great order, and with its predominance the disputed territory passed from the backwaters of secluded piety into the main stream of general Church life. Thenceforth through the Saxon period the Benedictine Rule prevailed almost without a rival in the cloisters. To it belonged the religious houses to which half the cathedral churches were attached, and the old abbeys with their widespread manors and great historic names, like Bury (*q.v.*) and Glastonbury (*q.v.*), Westminster (*q.v.*) and St. Albans (*q.v.*). They passed through great vicissitudes and saw many of their weaker neighbours fall before the storms; they had sad periods of self-indulgence and decline, but in the main they adhered to their leading principles of duty. They did not lapse so far from the original ideal as did many of the like societies in other lands, and therefore perhaps England did not experience the great revivals which from time to time called new orders into being on the Continent to correct the slumbering devotion of the old. No important order originated here, for the Gilbertines were never very numerous or strong, perhaps from the absence of the evils that roused the reforming spirit elsewhere. There had been indeed in earlier days a dismal period of demoralised and ruinous conditions, when the genuine spirit of the Benedictine rule languished and seemed nigh to death. The Danes swept over the land, attacking the religious houses with special fury; the few that survived lost heart and energy to strengthen the weakened traditions of cloistered discipline; schools and learning faded out of sight; Church life seemed to sad eyes faint and sick. Then came the vigorous revival of Dunstan (*q.v.*) and Aethelwold and Oswald, who sought perhaps the knowledge of the old discipline at Fleury. The restored monasticism was self-assertive and aggressive. It turned the secular clergy out of the stalls which they were beginning to claim by right of family succession in the churches which they had invaded as at Winchester, or held of old as at Rochester and Worcester. The new colonies became

nurseries of spiritual independence and patriotic spirit, and as such were regarded with mistrust by the first Norman monarchs. There was indeed no lack of religious susceptibility in the conquering dynasty and race. They showered their bounties with an ungrudging hand at times when they were stirred to reverence or thrilled with shame. But at first after the Conquest, in their gratitude for victory won, they gave largely of the spoils of war to the abbeys and the priories of their Norman homes, whose prayers had followed them to the battlefield. Manors and advowsons fell into the hands of foreign monks, who felt ere long their tenure insecure unless a daughter priory or cell were planted to guard the new possessions. The parishes that had been transferred to them they could charge with a pension in their favour, but there was grave risk of forfeiture of this when England was at war with France and alien priories passed into the King's hands. In many cases, therefore, foreign abbeys made the best terms they could with English bishops or cathedral chapters, and gave away to them advowsons, as of free grace, to gain an influential patron for other interests at stake. So much at least may be read between the lines of many a pious charter.

The patriotic spirit that the Conqueror found in the English monasteries did not long continue. In fear of pressure from the heads of Church and State they looked abroad for permanent support, and in payment for the privileges which they thus obtained they became in spirit colonies of papal Rome. Their annalists indeed in later days groaned under the exactions to which the land was subjected by the insatiable cupidity of the Roman court, when its agents were quartered on their churches and enormous tributes levied, but they could not venture to renounce the aid of so powerful a protector, with whose help bishops and even kings might be at times defied. It was their pride to gather in their archives the series of papal Bulls which had been granted to their prayers: the ancient charters—forgeries sometimes—which were prized as the evidences of privileges and exemptions bestowed on the whole order, or on its members, which defined their rights and secured them from episcopal control.

The general government of a monastery depended on the abbot, who had been elected by the monks after the royal licence had been gained, and had received confirmation from the bishop or Pope, his special deputies being the prior and sub-prior appointed by him. In cathedrals and the smaller monasteries, as in the Cluniac, the prior elected by the monks acted like the abbot in the larger, and he with the second or third prior was assisted by the *circatores claustri*, or *circas*, who watched over the discipline without authority to do more than report. Below these in rank were certain office-bearers, named *obedientiarii*, each of whom provided for a special department of the common cloister life. For the expenses of each of the more important, separate estates, or charges on dependent parishes, were commonly set apart, and the accounts of these were drawn up year by year at their direction, and presented at the general audit. Many such rolls have been preserved from early ages, and exhibit in minute detail the whole system of administration. These officers were :—

1. The *precentor*, the officer who had the highest authority in the management of the church services, in the choice of the music, and the regulation of the singing. He had a succentor under him, and acted also as librarian and archivist. He drew up the mortuary roll, and kept one of the keys of the common chest.

2. The *sacristan*, with sub-sacrists under him, who were called by various names, had the general care of the church, its cleaning, lighting, furniture, incense, and wine.

3. The *anniversarian* was charged with the commemoration of the special benefactors of the monastery.

4. The *cellarer*, who ranked commonly next after the precentor, had, in the language of the rule, 'to care for all things necessary for the brethren in bread and drink and divers kinds of food.' He had also to provide all the vessels required for the refectory, cellar, and kitchen, and for the fuel and all materials required. To assist him he had a sub-cellarer and steward of the grain (*granatarius*). Part of his duties was in some houses taken over by a *hordarian* set over the hoard, or the supplies of food in the larder, as also by a *curtarian*, a kind of manciple who gave out the bread and beer for the table.

5. The *refectorian* had the charge of the dining hall or frater, with that of the benches, tables, cloths, napkins, and straw, as also for the lavatory annexed.

6. The *kitchener*, with assistant cooks and servants, had the care of the whole kitchen department.

7. The *chamberlain* had charge of the wardrobe and the bedding of the brethren, defrayed the cost of the laundry, prepared for the baths and general shaving, and once a year had the dormitory cleaned out.

8. The *infirmarian* was appointed to take care of the infirm and sick, to bring from the aumbrey books for them to read, and to regulate the practice of periodical blood-letting.

9. The *almoner* by Lanfranc's rule should 'find out where in the neighbourhood the sick are lying, and before entering the house turn out all women into the street, and then going in console the sick person kindly, offering him what he can.' He distributed the remnants of the meals and gave the customary doles, and provided mats for the monks' feet in church.

10. The *guest-master* received and cared for travellers and visitors to the monastery, a charge which was often a heavy burden when the house lay near to any of the great highroads.

11. The *custos operum*, master of the fabric, superintended necessary repairs.

12. The *master of the novices* was to be 'a person fitted for winning souls,' having the general care and instruction of the novices during their period of probation.

13. The *hostiarius* kept the gate as porter, and had a horse to attend the superior on his journeys when required, leaving a deputy in his place.

As regards the daily life: a large part of the day was occupied by the regular services, which began soon after midnight and ended only just before bedtime. Matins and Lauds during the night were followed by a return to bed, after which came Prime and the early Mass of the Blessed Virgin; then the chapter Mass, followed by the daily meeting in the chapter-room for purposes of discipline and matters of public business. Then came High Mass, followed directly by the dinner, during which some passage of a good book was read aloud by the conventual reader who was on duty for the week. The working hours were in the afternoon—the work in earlier ages including manual labours in the fields and all forms of domestic duty within the house; but in the later Middle Ages menial labours were found irksome: the venerable maxim, *laborare est orare*, was forgotten, and a large number of servants in the wealthier houses performed the necessary tasks, leaving little opportunity for work except the study of the books borrowed from the library, any literary work or transcription and illumination of MSS., and the accounts of the Obedientiaries. In the evening came Vespers, followed by supper when it was allowed, and by Compline finally to close the day. Interspersed or variously combined with the other offices were sung the prayers of the canonical hours of Tierce Sext, and None.

To pass on to the other congregations : the Cluniac, a modification of the Benedictine, great as was its reputation and widespread as was its influence on the Continent of Europe, was never very popular in England. It began A.D. 912 with Berno, Abbot of Gigny, who built a monastery at Cluny, near Macon, from which grew what became the fashionable order of the day, whose houses were centres of education and learning. Its ideal was that of a great central convent with dependent societies widely scattered, all in close relations and ties of obedience to the mother house. The vast confederacy thus established, with its imperial government, became a notable power in Europe, and continued for two hundred years as a source of piety and learning. The superior of each house was the nominee of the Abbot of Cluny, and ranked therefore only as his prior, subject to his visitation and dependent on his orders. For more than a century there was no sign of it in England ; under the Conqueror came Barnstaple, and Lewes soon after. These and others, of which the more eminent were Wenlock, Bermondsey, Pontefract, and Montacute, ranked only as alien priories, with no national status, as they held their property only by the grace of Cluny. In times of war with France—which covered long periods—their possessions might be confiscated, and the benefices of which they held advowsons filled by presentation of the Crown. Many of them were in course of time entirely suppressed, while others managed to free themselves from alien dependence, and no large number survived to perish at the general suppression.

As the Cluniacs had originated from the Benedictines, so the Cistercians went forth from the Cluniacs, each order adding more rigour to the original rule, the lax observance of which was the cause of the reform. In 1098 a little band of monks, with their abbot and prior at their head, passed through the abbey gateway of Molesme, in the diocese of Langres, journeying on through a wild and rugged country till they reached the forest of Citeaux, in the province of Burgundy. Here, in the solitude which they desired, with the sanction of the Lord of Beaune and of the legate of the Holy See, they chose a spot for the new foundation from which the multitude of Cistercian houses were to take their name. The main features of the distinctive system which was adopted by the new order were ascribed to Stephen Harding, an Englishman, who had been the leading spirit among the malcontents at Molesme and was himself abbot of Citeaux. St. Benedict had enjoined

no marked austerity in food or dress, and the manual labours which he prescribed had been disused when the rents of the monks' estates sufficed for all their wants. The Cistercians abstained from flesh diet, wore only white woollen clothing, and insisted on hard work. As Gerald de Barri (*q.v.*) wrote of them, 'seeking out the desert places of the wilderness and shunning the haunts and hum of crowds, earning their daily bread by manual labour, and preferring uninhabited solitudes, they seem to bring back to one's eyes the primitive life and ancient discipline of the monastic religion, its poverty, its parsimony in food, the roughness and meanness of its dress, its abstinence and austerities' (*Speculum Ecclesiae*, Brewer's transl.). He adds that they were conspicuous for their charity and hospitality ; for their gate is never closed—at morning, noon, and evening it stands open to all comers. Unlike the Cluniacs, they maintained the independence of the separate houses, but organised their union by the presiding influence of the Abbot of Citeaux, under whom the superiors of all were bound to meet in yearly chapters. The fundamental statutes were drawn up by the founder, Stephen, under the name of the *Carta caritatis*, to be constantly observed in all their houses. St. Bernard, the renowned champion of the Church, was one of the first to join the little band at Citeaux, to pass on thence to plant a daughter house at Clairvaux, and spread the influence of the order far and wide, for within fifty years the abbeys grew to the number of five hundred. In England the first abbey was founded at Waverley in 1129, and the number grew rapidly up to the hundred which existed at the close. A refined simplicity in the main lines and a sparing use of decorative details are distinctive features of Cistercian buildings, which are even in their ruined state, in their setting of green fields and wooded hills, among the loveliest features of our rural scenes. The Cistercians did not indeed long retain their early reputation. Walter Map, the satirist, at the end of the twelfth century, paints them in much coarser colours, and Gerald de Barri, whose high praises have been quoted, tells many a story of their life on the Welsh borders in which covetous worldliness bulks largely. There was much, it has been urged, to account for these unfavourable pictures. The older monasteries were living freely on the bounty of an earlier age in their rich lands in the south. There was left for the Cistercians ' the rocky highlands of Yorkshire or the gleaning of grapes in the dismal flats and unreclaimed swamps of Lincolnshire.'

It needed industry and thrift to make progress under such conditions. They became great sheep-masters, making England famous for fine wool; they improved the breed of horses and deforested their lands. Frequenting markets, driving hard bargains, they faced the risk of mingling the guile of the serpent with the innocence of Eden. Left in twos or threes in remote cells as overseers, some lapsed into discreditable courses, and sullied the fair fame of the whole order which did so much for the country life of England.

The Carthusian Order took its name from the Chartreuse in the mountains near Grenoble, where in 1086 St. Bruno built for himself and a few companions an oratory with separate cells, where they lived in the most austere asceticism, with scanty dress and coarse hair shirts, on a diet of bean bread and pulse and herbs, with no addition of flesh meat, saying in their cells the prayers of the Lesser Hours, and only assembling together for Matins and Vespers. For a hundred years this rigorous system attracted no votaries in England, and at the suppression there were few houses which had accepted a rule of such excessive hardship, the last founded being the well-known Charterhouse of Shene.

There was a distinct group whose members were called Canons, like the clergy of cathedrals for whom Chrodegang had framed a rule of common life, but whose system was conventual or practically monastic. Their profession was to a special house, though, unlike the monks, they were allowed to serve impropriated parishes. Of these the Austin or Black Canons came into England soon after A.D. 1100 to St. Botolph's, Colchester, and numbered about a hundred and seventy houses at the time of the dissolution. Many of these were of no great importance, but Waltham Cross and Cirencester had mitred abbots at their head. Speaking generally, there were no very distinctive features in their rule.

Another set of like societies were the Premonstratensian Canons, settled first by St. Norbert at Prémontré, near Laon, who were also called White Canons from their dress. Their rule was like that of the Austins, with the distinctive feature that the abbot of the mother house of Prémontré was abbot-general of the whole order, with the right to visit all the communities, by himself or by deputy, and to hold a general chapter of the whole. There was therefore an adequate supervision of all the English houses, and from the extant reports of the visitations there appears to have been little ground for censure among their thirty-four houses in England.

The Gilbertine Canons took their name and rule from St. Gilbert of Sempringham (*q.v.*), whose order included both men and women in the same sets of buildings.

The Military Orders were connected with the practice of pilgrimage and the crusading movement. [CRUSADES.]

The Hospitallers of St. John of Jerusalem, instituted in 1092, ministered to the needs of pilgrims, who visited the Holy Land, in cases of sickness or destitution. They soon began in England, being established in 1100 near Clerkenwell, and the commanderies on their estates were widely scattered throughout the land. Their rule, except as to military duties, followed the practice of the Austin Canons.

The Knights Templars, so called because their abode at first was in rooms near the Temple at Jerusalem, were founded about A.D. 1118 to protect the roads traversed by pilgrims and to guard the holy places. Richly endowed by noble benefactors in all parts of Christendom, they soon settled in England, and in 1185 found a central home in Fleet Street, called the New Temple, where their church still stands. Dependent as cells on the London house were the preceptories which were built on their estates. Their story is memorable beyond that of others on account of their sudden downfall and their tragic fate. As to the real cause of their ruin there is little doubt. Philip the Fair of France coveted their wealth, was jealous of their military power and strongholds, and was determined to crush a rival influence that even a king might find too strong. He found a supple tool in a crafty Pope, Clement V., who owed the King his papal crown and dared not thwart his aims. In one day the whole brotherhood in France was hurried off, to wait in prison for trial for the blasphemy and obscene rites of which they were accused. The Grand-Master and his comrades were tortured in their dungeons, and at last given to the flames; but the trial was a mockery of justice. In England the charges were not credited at first, but urgent pressure was applied, and the chiefs of Church and State decided to arrest the Templars. The accused in their despair submitted to abjure their errors and do penance; their houses were broken up, the inmates distributed among other communities, and the whole order formally dissolved by the authority of Clement V. in 1312. Their estates were given finally to the Hospitallers. The tragedy gave a shock to the religious world, but its infamy could not be fully realised at

2 I

first; and the order itself was little loved, though feared and honoured, for its privileges were odious and had ceased to have a meaning when Acre had fallen, and the Holy Land was abandoned to unbelievers.

There were numerous nunneries belonging to all the orders which have been specified, excepting the Carthusian and the Military Orders. In addition to these we may note the Bridgettines, for whom St. Austin's rule was modified by St. Bridget, Queen of Sweden. Their one house in England was at Syon, near Isleworth, founded in 1414; dissolved with all the rest, it was restored by Mary, only to be suppressed again under Elizabeth. But after various wanderings the community returned again, settling itself in Chudleigh—a unique case of survival.

Some few of the nunneries were wealthy and important, like Shaftesbury (*q.v.*), Dartford, Amesbury, and St. Clement's of York: but for the most part they were little families of modest means, making no great stir in the social world. To some of them the neighbouring gentry sent their daughters for their schooling, as there was so little educational provision for the girls elsewhere; others enjoyed more freedom of intercourse with the outside world than was allowed commonly to monks. In general, they offered shelter to the homeless from the storms of troubled times, and their presence made for peace and kindly charities as well as for devotion. On the whole, the evidence presents favourable pictures of their home life, with occasional frailties sharply corrected by a bishop's hand, with natural bickerings of uncongenial tempers living too closely and too long together, but with little grave disorder.

By the end of the thirteenth century many of the less important and younger monasteries began to feel the pressure of hard times. Ambitious superiors had built on too large a scale or spent extravagantly; the streams of new endowments ceased to flow; the produce of their lands diminished, and they were in debt to moneylenders. With one accord they cast longing eyes upon the tithes of the parishes where they had—as frequently —advowsons, and petitioned their bishops for licence to appropriate them. The answer commonly was gracious, though a Swinfield repeatedly refused the request of Edward I. that the priory of Worcester might have Lindridge, and a scrupulous Pope scoffed indignantly at a like request from the wealthy priory of Durham. The episcopal registers abound in answers to such appeals, and the form seems almost stereotyped for common use. The bishop hears that the endowments are but scanty; hospitality to wayfarers and charity to the poor exhaust their funds; fire or flood has done havoc in their buildings, or a murrain carried off their cattle. He accedes to their request on the condition that adequate provision for a vicar shall be made, and this he will himself apportion. Sometimes he interposed with help to ward off imminent ruin, or bought up the property of alien priories for some larger scheme of social usefulness. In other cases the Crown might interpose to appoint an official guardian to deal with creditors, and feed the monks till by better management readjustment could be made.

Meantime the bounty of benefactors turned steadily away from the monastic houses. There were very few new foundations, fewer enrichments of the old. Generous piety gave its wealth to charities, hospitals, schools, and colleges, which now stood higher in the popular favour. That there was much to account for this in the conditions of cloistered life cannot be reasonably doubted. The episcopal registers lie open with the records of laxity and disorders which called for the censure of the bishops at their visitations. These might have been more numerous if papal exemptions had not withdrawn whole orders and important houses from such official scrutiny, while it was a far cry to Rome, which alone could interpose.

It is fair to note that in a great Benedictine monastery thus exempted the long traditions of reverence and order were probably maintained; there was no marked departure from the old ideal of cloistered life; while in an order like the Premonstratensian visitations were constantly repeated, and the reports were good. But it must be owned that the traditions of learned industry, which took the place of the manual labour of earlier ages, seemed to die away; the annals, which are of such value for the history of remoter times, as published in the Rolls Series, fail almost completely in the later period; the interests of education owed them little, for we read complaints that the schools for the novices and younger monks are much neglected, while there is scant evidence that they did much to teach the childhood of the outer world; they might still entertain the wayfarer as of old, but actual charity for local needs consisted in the distribution of trust funds in form of doles.

It may be urged indeed with truth that in these respects the language of disparagement, like that of praise of their influence in earlier times, appeals to a standard which the admirers of ascetic virtue cannot recognise.

The monks entered their cells to save their own souls, not for directly pastoral work ; for they were monks, not friars, and bound by no utilitarian rule. Their founders gave endowments for the benefit of their prayers and the sanctity of their example. In that case the question may be narrowed to the doubt if they were really maintaining in general a high level of spiritual life, and if they were not far too many, in proportion to the population round them, to be seriously engaged in the pursuit of their professed ideal.

It may be hard, however, to form a dispassionate judgment on this subject when we read of what was done by Henry VIII. and his unscrupulous agents when the suppression was resolved on. It was an infamy to send out such unworthy instruments to gather evidence in hot haste from any quarter on such a multitude of religious houses. The reports sent in are utterly worthless ; no one can detect the modicum of truth which they may contain, for the object was not to prove facts but to condemn outright. [MONASTERIES, SUPPRESSION OF ; LEGH : LAYTON.]

[W. W. C.]

The *Obedientiary Rolls of St. Swithun*, ed. Dean Kitchin (Winchester Record Soc.) ; *Accounts of the Obedientiaries of Abingdon*, ed. B. E. G. Kirk (C.S.) ; *Chronicon Monast. de Abingdon*, ed. J. Stevenson (R.S.) ; Abbot Gasquet, *Eng. Monastic Life* ; Canon W. W. Capes, *Hist. of Ch. of Eng. in Fourteenth and Fifteenth Centuries*.

RELIGIOUS ORDERS. II. Modern.—

The Act of Elizabeth dissolving the Religious Houses refounded by Mary (1 Eliz. c. 24, *al.* 39), ended the formal expression of the Religious Life, technically so called, in England, with two exceptions, until the nineteenth century. The idea, however, never died down, and attempts were made to realise it. The house of Nicholas Ferrar (*q.v.*) in 1625 at Little Gidding, although not strictly conventual, for the inmates had taken no vows, was yet a harking back to the idea of the community life, and as such it was disliked by the Puritans, who called it ' The Arminian Nunnery.' After the Restoration a community of some twelve ladies of gentle birth was begun in London, Sancroft (*q.v.*), then Dean of St. Paul's, acting as their director. One lady, elected abbess, went to Flanders to study the rule of St. Benedict in one of the English Benedictine houses there. The project, however, came to nothing, the abbess marrying and seceding to Rome. This community is known only from an account in the autobiography of

' Father Bede of St. Simon Stock,' one Walter Joseph Travers, a Discalced Carmelite (Fr. B. Zimmermann, *Carmel in England*, 1899). Later on, however, the idea gained ground. Archbishop Leighton (1611-84) regretted that ' retreats for men of mortified tempers ' had been lost in the English Church, while Fuller (*q.v.*) would have been glad if nunneries had continued ' those good shee-schools,' but without vows. In 1694 Mary Astell (1668-1731), daughter of a Newcastle merchant, published *A Serious Proposal to the Ladies*, which was ' to erect a monastery, or if you will (to avoid giving offence . . .) we will call it a *Religious Retirement*.' There were, however, to be no vows or irrevocable obligations. Daily services ordered ' after the cathedral manner, in the most affecting and elevating way,' frequent Eucharists, ' a course of solid instructive preaching,' and special carefulness about the fast days of the Church were part of the scheme. The *Proposal* was favourably received, and in 1697 a Second Part appeared, dedicated to the Princess Anne of Denmark (Queen Anne). ' A certain great lady,' either Queen Anne or Lady E. Hastings, proposed to give £10,000 towards erecting such a college. Bishop Burnet (*q.v.*) remonstrated warmly, saying it would appear ' to be preparing the way for Popish Orders, and would be reputed a nunnery ' (Ballard, *Mem. of British Ladies*). The *Tatler*, Nos. 32, 59, and 63, attacked and shamefully misrepresented the project, which was, as its author said, ' rather *academical* than monastic.'

Edward Stephens (*q.v.*) printed about 1696-7 a *Letter to a Lady*, which contains with it *The more Excellent Way; or a Proposal of a Compleat Work of Charity*. The two papers are complementary. The *Letter* describes the *Proposal*, which is to found a religious house for men and another for women—that for women first, ' because of that sex we find most devout people, and because their employments better admit of intermission,' and so make regular daily churchgoing more possible. The *Proposal* says in a note that ' a Religious Society of Single Women,' according to this design, has begun, and the *Letter* adds that the author has for that purpose ' procured a Friend to take a Lease of a convenient House of near £40 per annum.' There seem to have been at the time twenty-one women in this Order.

In 1698 Sir Geo. Wheeler (1650-1723) published *The Protestant Monastery*, a book of devotion for the Christian home, which illustrates views current among High Churchmen as to the monastic life. He defends the term monastery used by Bishop Duppa, and praises the monasteries he had seen in Greece. In Chapters III. and IV. he discusses the possibilities of monasteries for men and for women. He doubts as to the former; the latter he considers 'more convenient, if not very necessary, for all times and countries.' He hopes for more 'unprejudiced times,' in which such projects may be realised.

In 1737 Sir Wm. Cunninghame of Prestonfield, Edinburgh (1663-1740), 2nd Baronet of the family of Cunninghame of Caprington. approached Archdeacon Thomas Sharp (1693-1758), son of Archbishop Sharp (*q.v.*), with a proposal for 'a Nunnery of Protestant religious and virtuous persons, well born, of the female sex, conforming themselves to the worship of the Church of England.' Sedgefield, Durham, was suggested as the place for the foundation. The scheme is given in detail. There were to be a prioress and sub-prioress, but no vows. The archdeacon deprecated the proposal at great length (*Life of Archbishop Sharp*, II. app. iii. 281-302).

The eighteenth century was not likely to produce such foundations, yet Richardson in *Sir Charles Grandison* (1753) wishes there could be a Protestant nunnery in every county 'with a truly worthy divine, at the appointment of the bishop of the diocese, to direct and animate the devotion of such a society'; and W. Law (*q.v.*) at Kingscliffe and Lady E. Hastings both lived lives devoted to prayer and almsgiving on the lines of the Religious Life; and John Wesley (*q.v.*) records (*Life of Fletcher of Madeley*, 1786) that when he was young he was 'exceedingly affected with an account of Mr. Ferrar at Little Gidding, . . . and longed to see such another family.' English philanthropists, as John Howard in 1776, were struck by the Béguines of Belgium; and more emphatic expression of admiration for such Sisters and of the need for them in England is borne by Southey in his *Colloquies*, ii. 330 (1829), and by Dr. Gooch in the letters of 1825.

The modern revival, however, is due to the Oxford Movement (*q.v.*). The project of a sisterhood suggested itself independently to Newman (*q.v.*) and Pusey (*q.v.*) in 1839. Letters of 1840 between Newman, Pusey, and Keble (*q.v.*) refer to the question. Newman 'despaired of' the project at first (*Anglican Letters and Correspondence*, ii. 295, 298, 311, 315); he had written in 1836 to F. Rogers urging him to find a substitute in parishes for 'Parsons' wives.'

The first Sister to dedicate herself to the Religious Life was Miss Marian Hughes on Trinity Sunday, 5th June 1841, in St. Mary's, Oxford, and she shortly after went abroad to study the Religious Life among women in France. She did not actually enter a community until her father's death in 1849. She was professed in 1841 by Dr. Pusey, who hesitated to receive such a profession, since he had no authority from the bishop to do so. Later he received such authority. Miss Hughes lived as the Mother Superior of the Convent of the Holy Trinity at Oxford until May 1912.

In April 1844 other churchmen were at work, and meetings were held in London. Lord John Manners, Mr. Gladstone (*q.v.*), and Dr. Hook (*q.v.*) were resolved to establish a sisterhood in part as a memorial to Southey, and the first revived sisterhood began at 17 Park Village West, N.W., on Wednesday in Easter week, 26th March 1845.

Another community was founded in 1848 at Devonport under Miss Priscilla Lydia Sellon (1821-76), with the direct approval of the bishop, Phillpotts (*q.v.*). It was called 'The Society of the Holy Trinity of Devonport.' It early provoked attack from Protestant quarters, partly because the view of holy obedience held by Miss Sellon was of an abnormal description. A vivid pamphlet literature exists on the subject; and alleged eccentricities of the early days at Devonport have been the basis of later attacks on sisterhoods in general, *e.g. Sisterhoods in the Church of England*, 2nd ed., 1863 ; *The Anglican Sister of Mercy*, etc. The sisterhood in Park Village, whose Superior and other sisters went out to the Crimean War as nurses with Florence Nightingale in 1854, was broken up, and the surviving members joined the Devonport Society. The Society of the Holy Trinity began a Home at Ascot in 1861, and finally withdrew from Devonport *c.* 1902.

The community of St. Thomas the Martyr, Oxford, was founded in 1847 by Canon Chamberlain. Other communities followed, chiefly in the diocese of Oxford, where Bishop S. Wilberforce (*q.v.*) was sympathetic, or they grew up round churches which were centres of revived life. Thus in 1848 began the famous Sisterhood of St. Mary the Virgin, Wantage, under the guidance of the vicar, W. J. Butler. On 23rd December 1849 was founded the Society of the Holy and Undivided Trinity at Oxford under Miss Hughes, professed in 1841 ; in 1852 the Society of St. John the Baptist, Clewer, under Harriet Monsell (professed, St. Andrew's Day, 1852), inspired by

Canon T. T. Carter. The Community of All Saints was founded in 1851 by W. Upton Richards, Vicar of All Saints, Margaret Street, London, a famous Tractarian sanctuary. In 1855 the Community of St. Margaret, East Grinstead, was founded by Dr. J. M. Neale (*q.v.*) on lines suggested by the Order of the Visitation founded by St. François de Sales and by the principles of the Society of St. Vincent de Paul. In June 1856 the sisters began to occupy their first house at East Grinstead. In 1855 the Community of the Blessed Virgin Mary was founded at Brighton by A. D. Wagner, Vicar of St. Paul's —the approval of the Bishop of Chichester, in whose diocese these last communities were situated, being doubtless secured by the influence of Bishop S. Wilberforce (Neale, *Letters*, 277), whose country house was at Lavington in Sussex. In 1856 Lavinia Crosse founded the Community of All Hallows at Ditchingham, Norfolk; and in 1857 the Community of the Holy Cross (now at Hayward's Heath, Sussex) was founded for work in St. George's in the East, London, by C. F. Lowder (*q.v.*) and Miss E. Neale, sister of Dr. J. M. Neale.

Other Sisterhoods founded since then are the Community of St. Peter, Horbury, Yorks, founded by Canon John Sharp and Mrs. Sidney Lear, 1858; the Community of St. Peter, Kilburn, founded by Rosamira Lancaster, 1861; that of the Holy Name of Jesus at Malvern Link, founded in connection with St. Peter's, Vauxhall, 1865, by its first vicar, G. Herbert; the Sisters of Bethany, Lloyd Square, W.C., founded by Miss Etheldreda Anna Benett in October 1866; the Holy Rood at North Ormesby, Middlesborough, founded 1867; St. Mary and St. John, Chiswick, 1868, united 1910 with St. Margaret's, East Grinstead; the Community of the Paraclete, founded by Arthur Tooth, Vicar of St. James's, Hatcham, 1873, removed to Woodside, Croydon, 1877; St. Lawrence, Belper, 1874; St. Denys, Warminster, founded by Canon Sir J. Erasmus Philipps, Bart., 1879; St. Katherine of Egypt, Fulham, 1879; the Sisters of the Church, founded by Emily Ayckboum, 1870, recognised by the Bishop of London, who became Visitor, 1903; the Sisters of Charity, Servants of the Poor, founded 1868 by A. H. Ward, Warden of St. Raphael's, Bristol; the Community of the Epiphany at Truro, founded by Bishop G. H. Wilkinson, 1883; the Holy Comforter, Upper Edmonton, 1891, now of Baltonsborough, Glastonbury; Sisterhood of the Ascension, 1894, founded with the special approval of

Bishop Temple (*q.v.*) in the parish of the Annunciation, Bryanston Street, W.; St. Michael and All Angels, Hammersmith, founded under Bishop Temple, 1895; the Holy Family, 1896; the Community of the Servants of Christ, founded in the parish of St. Stephen, Upton Park, 1897, now at Pleshey, Chelmsford; and an enclosed Order of the Love of God founded at Cowley, Oxford, in 1907.

Other sisterhoods are the Sisters of the Poor at St. Michael's, Shoreditch, founded by the vicar, H. D. Nihill, and Hannah Skinner, 1866; the Community of St. Mary and St. Scholastica, founded by Father Ignatius in 1868 to observe the strict rule of St. Benedict, but separated from his community later, moved in 1893 to Malling Abbey and 1911 to St. Bride's Abbey, Milford Haven, affiliated 1907 to the Benedictines of Caldey Island; and a Community of St. Mary the Virgin, founded by G. Nugee, then Vicar of Wymering, Hants, *c.* 1866. The Nursing Sisters of St. John the Divine, founded in 1848 to improve the nursing in hospitals, in 1850 began to nurse in the London hospitals. In 1868 the late Mr. J. G. Talbot founded at Tenterden the Kent Penitentiary. This was moved in 1865 to Stone, near Dartford, and in 1877 the ladies who worked in it formed themselves into the Community of the Blessed Virgin Mary, under Miss Harriet Nokes as Superior. In 1910 the work was taken over by the Clewer Sisters, and the original community ceased. A Sisterhood of the Divine Compassion begun at Plaistow at the same time as the Brotherhood, 1894, became in 1897 the Society of the Incarnation of the Eternal Son, and works at Saltley, Birmingham.

The growth of communities for men since the Oxford Movement has been slower, and there have been various experiments. Mr. Newman retired to live at Littlemore, February 1842, and proposed to build a monastic house and form a community there. From 25th April 1842 (Bloxam MSS., 457) the inmates began to say the Breviary offices, and they lived a strict community life until they left the English Church in 1845. But there were no vows, and it can scarcely be ranked as a religious order, though it was the tentative beginning of what might have become an order. F. W. Faber when Rector of Elton, Hunts (1843-5), formed a small community of some seven young men and a Society of St. Joseph. Their devotions were interrupted, it was believed, by supernatural noises (*Life and Letters*, 216-38).

In 1849 G. R. Prynne endeavoured to

establish a brotherhood at St. Peter's, Plymouth.

In May 1855 Edward Steere (*q.v.*), later the famous bishop of Zanzibar, began a community for men, the Brotherhood of St. James, at Tamworth, but the experiment seems to have failed within a year.

In 1863 Joseph Leycester Lyne, better known as Father Ignatius, O.S.B., sought to revive the Order of St. Benedict in England. After living at Ipswich (1862), Norwich (1863). and Laleham (1867) the community was established at Llanthony, July 1870, where a modern abbey was built. The community was never large, and the English bishops never recognised it; on the death of Father Ignatius, 1908 (a remarkable mission preacher and a man of great devotion, though wilful and eccentric), the buildings of Llanthony passed to the Benedictine community at Caldey. Miss Goodman, a former Devonport sister, describes an earlier attempt of Father Ignatius (1861) to form a brotherhood (*Sisterhoods*, 2nd ed., 128-31), and alludes to some attempt to found a community for men in 1844 ' at an obscure village in Suffolk.' Her reference is probably to F. W. Faber at Elton.

Most famous, with branch houses in three continents, is the Society of St. John the Evangelist, Cowley, founded by R. M. Benson, Vicar of Cowley and Student of Christ Church, Oxford, 6th May 1866, when he. with Father O'Neill (an Eton tutor) and Father Grafton (Bishop of Fond du Lac, 1889), made their professions together. The impulse to found the Society came from a sermon by Mr. Keble preached at Wantage, 22nd July 1863.

On St. James's Day, 25th July 1892, the Community of the Resurrection was begun by Bishop Gore, then Principal of Pusey House, Oxford. The community ' consists of priests occupied in various works—pastoral, evangelistic, literary, and educational.' It arose from the drawing together of the clergy living at Pusey House and those of the Oxford Mission in Calcutta. Established first at Pusey House, then, September 1893, at Radley, the community moved to Mirfield in 1898. One of its chief works is the College of the Resurrection for training ordinands.

The Society of the Sacred Mission, begun in 1891 in Brixton with a view to training men for service abroad, moved in 1897 to Mildenhall, and was established at Kelham, 1903. Its house is a recognised theological college, and trains many men for the priesthood. The Order was founded by H. H. Kelly.

The Society of the Divine Compassion was founded, 20th January 1894, at Plaistow by the Honble. J. G. Adderley and others. It is dedicated to the Sacred Heart of Jesus and in honour of St. Francis.

The strict rule of St. Benedict was revived in 1898, when a community was founded by Aelred Carlyle under the special sanction of Archbishop Temple. The community, which began in the Isle of Dogs, moved later to Painsthorpe, and finally to Caldey.

Other attempts at brotherhoods were the Order of St. Augustine, begun by G. Nugee at Cosham and then at Wymering, Hants, *c.* 1870, removed to Walworth 1877.

A Brotherhood of the Holy Redeemer, founded 1866 at Torrington, Lincs, by the rector, T. W. Mossman, for poor students wishing to be ordained. It was disliked by the bishop (Jackson), and removed to Newcastle-on-Tyne, where it collapsed.

An Order of St. Joseph was founded by R. Tuke, A.K.C., Curate of St. John's, Hackney, *c.* 1865. The community—a very small one—called themselves Augustinians. After a short time they seceded.

A Brotherhood of the Holy Spirit was founded at Stoke-on-Tern, Shropshire, by the rector, R. W. Corbet, in 1869. The community, which was for priests, ended in 1879. During its existence it received the special benediction of Pope Pius IX., on the stipulation that the Hours were said in common.

A Brotherhood of St. Paul, founded in 1891 by W. Moultrie Robbins, was a direct result of the Resolutions of Convocation in 1890, and was specially favoured by Bishop Temple. Its headquarters were in Lisson Grove, London, and its work was street preaching and visiting. After a few members had joined it the community came to an end.

This revived Religious Life has from time to time been sealed with the formal approval of the English Church. The question of Rules was discussed in the Canterbury Convocation in 1861 and 1863, when on 14th February an address sympathetic towards the communities from the Lower House was approved by the Upper, and the bishops commended sisterhoods and their work to the prayers of the Church.

In July 1875 a Committee of the Lower House of Canterbury Convocation was appointed ' to consider the rise, progress, and present condition' of sisterhoods and brotherhoods. The Report was presented, May 1878, and strong resolutions were passed expressing thankfulness for their work, as well as for the episcopal recognition accorded to them. (The Report was based on returns made only by communities in the Canterbury province.)

In July 1889, in the same Convocation, Archdeacon (later Dean) Farrar, in a speech of great eloquence, proposed resolutions in favour of brotherhoods, clerical and lay. They were debated and carried with much enthusiasm, February 1890, and were passed by the Upper House. The chief result of the discussion was to bring out the wide sympathy felt for the revival.

The growth of Religious Orders in the English Church in the period 1845-1900 is almost without parallel in Christian history, and there are far more women in Religious Orders in England in 1912 than there were when the Religious Houses were dissolved by Henry VIII.

The number of sisters at the Dissolution is calculated at 745; from tables prepared in 1909 there were then some 1300 (Bishop Weller's *Hale Mem. Sermon*, 1909, app. ii.).

[S. L. O.]

Bishop H. R. Weller, *Religious Orders in the Anglican Communion*, Milwaukee, 1909 ; article in *Encyc. Brit.*, 'Sisterhoods,' but both need correction and are incomplete.

REPRESENTATIVE CHURCH COUNCIL, The,

was formed to meet the desire for a national council [COUNCILS] which found expression shortly after the revival of Convocation (*q.v.*). Every subject on which the judgment of the Church was desired had to be considered by the two Convocations separately, which led in practice to inconvenience and delay. It appeared, however, that the archbishops had no power to summon a national synod without the consent of the Crown. The Convocations could only hold joint meetings informally, and this they did in 1896, and again in 1899 and the following years. A Bill to enable the two Convocations to sit together failed to pass through Parliament in 1901. In 1904 resolutions were passed by both Convocations separately, and also by the Houses of Laymen, requesting the archbishops to summon a 'Representative Church Council' of bishops, clergy, and laity, which met for the first time under that name in July of the same year. In 1905 it agreed upon its constitution, the first article of which provides that it shall consist of three Houses. The members of the Upper Houses of the Convocations of the two Provinces of Canterbury and York constitute the first House, or House of Bishops; the members of the Lower Houses of the Con-

vocations of both Provinces constitute the second, or House of Clergy; and the members of the Houses of Laymen of both Provinces constitute the third, or Lay House. The two archbishops are joint presidents of the Council. Provision is made for the three Houses to sit together or separately. In any case, its acts must receive the assent of all three Houses. Article 10 of the constitution defines the relations of the Council to the episcopate and to Convocation, and guards it from the imputation of seeking to usurp the functions of either in the Church's constitution : 'Nothing in this Constitution nor in any proceeding of the Council shall interfere with the exercise by the Episcopate of the powers and functions inherent in them, or with the several powers and functions of the Houses of Convocation of the two Provinces.' Article 11 forbids it ' to issue any statement purporting to declare the doctrine of the Church on any question of theology.' A scheme was also drawn up for the representation of the laity by indirect election on a communicant's franchise. It was hoped that the assembly thus constituted would be able to formulate and express the opinions of churchmen upon questions of importance in Church and State, and so assist Convocation and Parliament in ascertaining the mind of the Church ; and also that legislative powers might be conferred upon it at some future time when it should have proved itself capable of exercising them. The Council has met annually since then (the three Houses sitting together), and has passed resolutions on various subjects. But the advantages which might be expected to follow from the existence of a single assembly speaking for the whole national Church have been to a great extent nullified by its unrepresentative character and the seeming unreality of its proceedings. It is no more representative of the clergy than the Convocations are, and it lacks the weight which they derive from their historical and constitutional position. The presence of laymen as constituent members effectually debars it from ever becoming a constitutional synod of the Church. Whatever position it may attain in the future, it has at present failed either to gain the confidence of Churchmen, or ' to appeal,' as was hoped at its inception, ' to the mind and conscience of the nation.'

[G. C.]

Chronicle of Convocation ; *Times* ; Reports of the Council's proceedings (S.P.C.K.).

REUNION.

(1) With the Roman Church. The breach with Rome took place, 1538-9, and although Henry VIII. twice, according to Bishop S. Gardiner (*q.v.*), was about to attempt to heal the division, in fact no such attempt was made. The English Church returned formally to the obedience of and communion with Rome in the second year of Mary, 30th November 1554. The breach with Rome was reopened when the Elizabethan Acts of Supremacy and Uniformity became law, 1559. For some time, however, it seemed capable of being closed. English diplomatists asserted that the Pope was willing to accept the Prayer Book if Elizabeth would acknowledge his supremacy. The Bishop de Quadra, the Spanish ambassador in 1562, defending English Romanists who attended the Church services to avoid the penal laws, said that those services contained no impiety or false doctrine. The excommunication of Elizabeth by Paul V. in his Bull *Regnans in excelsis*, 25th March 1570, effected the breach begun in 1559, and the idea of Rome became in England linked with that of treason, and later of assassination.

Under James I. the rise of the theologians of the school of Hooker (*q.v.*), and the consequent reaction from Calvinism, while it produced the great Anglican controversialists against Rome, Andrewes (*q.v.*), Laud (*q.v.*), Mountague [CAROLINE DIVINES], and others, yet did something towards Reunion by clearing the issues and illustrating the great amount of ground common to both communions.

Under Charles I. (*q.v.*) direct negotiations were carried on between the Roman See and the English Government with regard to the oath of allegiance to be taken by English Roman Catholics. An English Benedictine, Dom Leander, was sent by Urban VIII., 1632, as agent from the Roman court, and Panzani, an Oratorian, in 1634. Leander thought reunion 'seemeth possible enough, if the points were discussed in an assembly of moderate men, without contention or desire of victory, but out of a sincere desire of Christian union.' Panzani thrice discussed reunion with Bishop Mountague, who assured him that both archbishops and the Bishop of London (Juxon, *q.v.*), and many others, were favourable to it and ready to concede 'a supremacy, purely spiritual,' to Rome. The Jesuits and the Puritans in England were regarded as the chief obstacles to an understanding. Panzani was succeeded by Cuneo (*i.e.* Con, a Scot), who was in England 1636-9. Cuneo disliked Laud, and regarded him as an obstacle to reunion. Laud was apparently offered the cardinalate

after he became primate, and refused at once, as he would not think of reunion 'till Rome be other than she is.' Like Andrewes, he prayed daily for the reunion of Christendom, but would not consent to unconditional submission to Rome.

Reunion was advanced by the publication in 1633 of a learned *Paraphrastica Expositio* of the Thirty-nine Articles by Sancta Clara (Christopher Davenport), a Franciscan, and chaplain to Queen Henrietta Maria. He held eighteen of the Articles to be orthodox, two mere logomachies, and the remaining nineteen 'patient, but not ambitious, of a Catholic interpretation.' He defended the sufficiency of the Edwardine Ordinal, and believed Anglican Ordinations (*q.v.*) to be valid. The Jesuits failed to secure the condemnation of his book. It is supposed to have formed the basis of Tract No. 90. [OXFORD MOVEMENT.]

During his exile and after his accession Charles II. desired the help of the Roman See in return for the full toleration of Roman Catholics. In 1663 remarkable terms for reunion were drawn up. While accepting the decrees of the Council of Trent, the English Church was to remain largely national, the Archbishop of Canterbury to be Patriarch of the three kingdoms. Only a few rights were reserved to the Roman See. Existing bishops were to remain, but to be reconsecrated by three legates specially appointed. The King was to nominate to bishoprics, and the existing rights over former Church property respected. Protestants were to enjoy complete toleration. Communion was to be in both kinds to those who wished it; the Eucharist was to be in Latin, but with English hymns; married clergy should retain their wives; celibacy was not to be introduced till later ; some of the Religious Orders were to be revived. 'It is not clear how far the King was privy to this scheme . . . it agrees, however, both with his views and with his position. . . . We can as little imagine that the Anglican episcopate had approved these projects ' (Ranke, iii. 400). The so-called Popish Plot (*q.v.*), 1678, fanned into flame the old political hatred of Roman Catholics, and Charles II.'s reception into that Church on his death-bed, and the attacks of James II. upon the English Church, roused churchmen to controversy and to emphasise points of difference rather than of agreement with Rome.

In 1704 appeared a remarkable *Essay towards a Proposal for Catholic Communion . . . by a Minister of the Church of England*. The author is unknown, but was possibly

W. Bassett, Rector of St. Swithin's, London. It is an appeal by a man of 'moderate' rather than extreme views, and in the interest of general reunion endeavours to show how and where it is possible with Rome.

In 1717 William Wake (*q.v.*), Archbishop of Canterbury, was engaged in correspondence by some doctors of the Sorbonne, acting with the concurrence of Cardinal de Noailles, Archbishop of Paris, as to the possibility of reunion. Du Pin was the principal agent on the French side, and in his *Commonitorium* on the XXXIX. Articles approved twenty-three absolutely; the remainder could be admitted with explanations. Wake satisfied the French divines as to Anglican orders, and did not consider Transubstantiation an insuperable difficulty. The death of Du Pin, 1719, the changed attitude of the French Government, the power of the French Jesuits, and especially the opposition of Dubois, Archbishop of Cambrai, brought the negotiations to an end. Wake in his last letter to Du Pin, 1st May 1719, says:

In dogmas, as you have candidly proposed them, we do not much differ; in Church government less; in fundamentals, whether regarding doctrine or discipline, hardly at all. From these beginnings how easy was the advance to concord, if only our minds were disposed to peace.'

In 1723 Pierre François le Courayer, a Canon Regular of the Augustinian abbey of St. Geneviève at Paris, published a *Vindication of Anglican Orders*. He was created D.D. at Oxford, 1727. In 1728 he settled in England, where he was much patronised, and amassed a fortune. He seems to have remained externally a Roman Catholic though excommunicate, and sometimes he dressed as a layman. On his death, at the age of ninety-five in 1776, he was buried in the cloisters of Westminster Abbey. Two works, published posthumously, showed him to have lapsed in later years into views akin to Unitarianism.

The eighteenth century was not likely to be fruitful in projects of reunion. Isolated churchmen, specially well informed, like Dr. Johnson (*q.v.*), were free from the conventional prejudices against Rome. Johnson when in Paris was sympathetic with and appreciative of much that he saw in French religious life. The horrors of the Revolution, 1789, did more to stir English sympathies with the French Roman Catholics. Shute Barrington, Bishop successively of Llandaff (1769), Salisbury (1782), Durham (1791-1826), in a charge urged the attempt at reuniting the Churches of England and

Rome as a public duty of the greatest magnitude. That reunion he considered 'not very remote.' The charge is printed as a preface to a *Book of Common Prayer*, by P. Gandolphy, London, 1815.

The matter of Roman Catholic emancipation brought the question of reunion forward. In the House of Commons in 1824 a Mr. Robertson spoke strongly in favour of reuniting the two churches, and Dr. J. Doyle, Roman Catholic Bishop of Kildare and Leighlin, wrote (13th May 1824) urging such reunion, referring to the efforts of Archbishop Wake, and proposing a conference of divines. The time was unfavourable. Various pamphlets and sermons on the same side followed as in 1842, *A Union between the Roman Catholic and Protestant Churches rendered Practicable*, and *The Roman Catholic and Anglican Churches proved to be nearer to each other than most men imagine.*

The Oxford Movement (*q.v.*), on the spiritual side, made for reunion by clearing the air of prejudice and emphasising the points of agreement between the Churches. But it was in origin anti-Roman, and J. H. Newman (*q.v.*) was for long bitter in his denunciations of Rome. In conversation with Dr. Wiseman at Rome (in 1832) R. H. Froude (*q.v.*) and Newman spoke of reunion, and were surprised to learn that it involved 'swallowing the Council of Trent as a whole.' The leaders of the Movement after 1836 were too much occupied in defending the English Church against Roman Catholic attacks to engage in schemes for reunion. The more extreme wing of the school who were drawn towards Rome went further, and early in 1841 W. G. Ward, in a letter to the *Univers* which roused some excitement, expressed ardent desire for reunion with Rome. These were met from the Roman side by Ambrose Phillipps de Lisle, a Leicestershire gentleman (1809-78), who had become a Roman Catholic, 1825, but cherished great affection for the English Church.

The secessions to Rome in 1845 and 1850-1 naturally hindered plans for reunion, some of the recent converts, especially Manning (*q.v.*), being unwilling to consider any plan save that of absolute submission by Anglicans. Cardinal Wiseman, however, in a *Letter to Lord Shrewsbury*, 1841, had appeared to take a less uncompromising view, and pleaded for mutual explanation.

In 1857 Mr. Phillipps de Lisle printed his *Future Unity of Christendom*, and in the same year was founded, 8th September, 'The Association for the Promotion of the Unity of Christendom,' which included clergy and laity of the Roman Catholic, Greek, and Anglican communions. Its only obligation lay in a common daily prayer for unity. English Roman Catholic bishops secured the condemnation of the Association at Rome, September 1864, largely through the action of Manning, and Roman Catholics were ordered to withdraw from it. The Association, however, continues. At the end of 1864 Manning published an attack on the English Church in a letter to Dr. Pusey (*q.v.*), who replied in a learned *Eirenicon*, published September 1865. Pusey pleaded for reunion between the Churches and for mutual explanations, and in October presented the book in person to several French bishops. Two English bishops, Hamilton of Salisbury and Ellicot of Gloucester, warmly approved it, but it roused the indignation of most English Roman Catholics, especially Newman, who replied to it in a famous *Letter*, January 1866. 'There was,' he said, 'one of old time who wreathed his sword in myrtle ; excuse me—you discharge your olive branch as if from a catapult.'

From 1865 Pusey was in friendly conversation with great French ecclesiastics. In 1869 he published a second and in 1870 a third *Eirenicon* in the form of letters to Dr. Newman, and had hopes of the case of England being brought before the Vatican Council of 1870 through Mgr. Dupanloup. Bishop A. P. Forbes of Brechin was an eager assistant of Pusey in this work, but the triumph of Ultramontanes at the Council put an end to any hope of immediate action. In 1867 an English layman, G. F. Cobb, published a learned work, *The Kiss of Peace, or England and Rome at one on the Doctrine of the Eucharist*, in the interest of reunion.

In 1877 began a stranger effort, the Order of Corporate Reunion. Its history is still shrouded in mystery. The Order was 'instituted,' 2nd July 1877, and the first Pastoral of its Rulers, formally promulgated on 8th September, 'being read in the presence of witnesses on the steps of St. Paul's Cathedral and in other places throughout the land.' The object of the Order was apparently to bring about reunion by reordaining English clergy *sub conditione*, and thus supplying the English Church with orders which Rome would recognise. For this purpose the founder, Dr. F. G. Lee, Vicar of All Saints, Lambeth, had been secretly consecrated bishop in or near Venice (report said by bishops of the Roman and Eastern communions on the high seas, to avoid interference with other jurisdictions), and himself consecrated as bishops T. W. Mossman, Rector of

West Torrington, Lincs, and a learned layman, Thomas Seccombe of Terrington, Norfolk. There is evidence that they consecrated other bishops. The Order promulgated orders of service to be used in its oratories, but was never an important or large body, and was from the first repudiated by High Churchmen. The mystery surrounding it invested it with romance. It failed to promote the object at which it aimed, for two of its bishops were received on their death-beds into the Roman Church : Dr. Mossman in 1885 and Dr. Lee in 1901.

In 1894 some learned French clergy began to study afresh the question of Anglican ordinations, and a remarkable pamphlet of that year, by 'Fernand Dalbus' (the pseudonym of the Abbé Portal), concluded that the English rite was adequate, although for reasons not generally admitted by Roman theologians, it considered the orders invalid. A distinguished scholar, the Abbé Duchesne, in July 1894 set these reasons aside, and concluded that English ordinations ' *might be recognised* as valid.' Eventually the Pope, Leo XIII., appointed a commission to report. Much interest was taken in the matter. Mr. Gladstone, May 1896, wrote a letter to the Archbishop of York emphasising the friendly action of the Pope. The English Roman Catholics, as represented by Cardinal Vaughan, were anxious that Anglican orders should not be recognised ; and their party ultimately prevailed, and in September 1896 the Bull *Apostolicae Curae* declared that the question of Anglican ordinations had already been determined adversely from the first. This decision was a serious blow to hopes of reunion for the time, for friendly intercourse had begun with the French clergy, and a review, published weekly, *La Revue Anglo-Romaine*, begun in November 1895, was brought to an end, after fifty-one numbers, in November 1896 in consequence of the decision.   [S. L. O.]

Sancta Clara, *Paraphrastica Expositio*, republished, with a translation, 1865. The *Essay towards a Proposal for Catholic Communion*, 1704, was republished as *An Eirenicon of the Eighteenth Century*, with valuable Introduction by H. N. Oxenham, 1879. For negotiations between Wake and Du Pin. Lupton, *Archbishop Wake and the Project of Union*, 1896. Courayer's book was reprinted, Oxford, 1844. Bishop Shute Barrington's charge is quoted in *Reunion Magazine* (1879), i. 15. For the period 1864-70, Liddon, *Life of Pusey*, iii. 106-94. For the Order of Corporate Reunion, the *Reunion Magazine*, 1879, prints the formal documents. See Correspondence in the *Tablet*, 1902, pp. 216-17. 298, and 28th November 1908 to 13th March 1909 : Walsh, *Secret Hist. of the Oxford Movement*, chap. v., otherwise usually an untrustworthy book. For the events 1894-6, Moberly, *Ministerial Priesthood*, app., gives an account of the French works: T. A. Lacey, *A Roman Diary*; Snead-Cox, *Life of Cardinal Vaughan*; Purcell, *Life of A. P. de Lisle*; Lord Halifax, *Leo XIII. and Anglican Orders*; and a volume lettered 'Reunion' among the MSS. of Dr. J. R. Bloxam at Magdalen College, Oxford, gives much information.

(2) **With the Orthodox Eastern Churches.**— A theory once popular, but now discredited, sought to find an Asian origin for Christianity in Britain, but the fact that a Greek monk, Theodore of Tarsus (*q.v.*), was one of the most important of the early archbishops of Canterbury, forms a link between the English and Eastern Churches. When the division between East and West was thought to have been healed at the Council of Florence (1439), Henry VI. sent envoys with letters of congratulation, written in no formal terms, to express his joy at the reunion, and public thanksgivings, processions, and litanies were celebrated throughout England. The attempted reunion at Florence failed, and during the troubles which succeeded in Western Christendom, and especially in England, the Eastern Churches seem to have been forgotten. The English Reformers of the sixteenth century paid little attention to the East. They appealed on controverted points to Greek customs and Greek opinions, but Bishop Jewel (*q.v.*) in his *Defence of the Apology* says: 'What the Grecians this day think of us I cannot tell.' The Church of Constantinople was expressly omitted from the charge of error brought against the other four patriarchates (Jerusalem, Alexandria, Antioch, and Rome) in Article XIX., but direct intercourse between England and the Eastern Churches was hardly practicable until 1579, when a commercial treaty with Turkey was made and the Levant Company founded. Bishop Andrewes (*q.v.*) prayed daily for reunion, 'for the Eastern Church, its deliverance and union,' and his devotions themselves owe a good deal to Eastern service-books.

In 1611 George Sandys (son of an archbishop of York) visited Alexandria, and became acquainted with the remarkable Cyril Lucar, Patriarch of that see (1602-21) and Patriarch of Constantinople (1621-38). Sandys reports him as saying 'that the differences between us and the Greeks are but shells.' In 1616 Cyril began to correspond with Archbishop Abbot (*q.v.*), and in that year, at James I.'s request, sent a Greek priest, Critopoulos, afterwards Patriarch of Alexandria, to study for five years at Balliol College, Oxford, where Abbot seems

to have supported him. Sir Thomas Roe, ambassador at Constantinople (1621-8), protected Cyril, and through Roe the Patriarch presented Charles I. with the splendid MS., the Codex A. (Alexandrinus). Cyril was murdered, through Jesuit intrigues, in 1638.

Friendly intercourse between Anglicans and Easterns continued throughout the seventeenth century, partly through the succession of distinguished chaplains to the English community at Aleppo and partly through the clergy and laity connected with the embassy at Constantinople. Dr. Isaac Basire, who travelled in Greece (1650-78), at the request of the Metropolitan of Achaia preached twice to his assembled suffragans and clergy; and Païsius, Patriarch of Jerusalem, 'the better to express his desire of communion with our old Church of England,' gave Basire 'his bull or patriarchal seal in blank (which is their way of credence) besides many other respects.' With a view to a better understanding between the Churches, Dr. Basire circulated a Greek translation of the Church Catechism. After the Restoration the interest in the Eastern Churches quickened. Successive chaplains at Constantinople—Dr. Thomas Smith (chaplain, 1668-71), Fellow of Magdalen, Oxford, and later a Nonjuror; Dr. John Covel (1671-8), afterwards Master of Christ's, Cambridge; and Edward Brown (1678)—were learned and sympathetic. Dr. Smith published in 1676, under the special sanction of the Bishop of Oxford, a Latin work on the Greek Church (second edition, 1678, and English, 1680). Dr. Covel printed a somewhat similar treatise in 1722, in which he relates that Gunning, Pearson (*q.v.*), and Sancroft (*q.v.*) in 1670 asked him to inquire carefully into the teaching of the Easterns on the Real Presence. To them was addressed, presumably, a synodical answer 'sent to the lovers of the Greek Church in Britain' (1672), a copy of which was among the documents sent to the Nonjurors in 1721 (see below). Sir Paul Ricaut, an able and devout layman, secretary to Lord Winchilsea at Constantinople (1661-9) and consul at Smyrna (1669-78), was eager in the cause, and printed a book on the Greek and Armenian Churches (1678). The project of Archbishop Abbot and Cyril Lucar had not wholly failed, for after the Patriarch's death a trusted official of his, Nathanael Conopius, was befriended by Archbishop Laud (*q.v.*), and sent by him to Balliol, Oxford. He became Minor Canon of Christ Church, where he remained until expelled by the Parliamentary visitors. He then returned to the East, and became Bishop of Smyrna (1651).

From 1677 onward a project of founding a college for Greeks at Oxford was afoot. It was not realised until 1698, when it was arranged that twenty students, five from each patriarchate, should reside at Gloucester Hall (later Worcester College). A number of Greeks came, but ' the scheme, after a hopeful beginning, came to an unhappy end,' in spite of the efforts of Edward Stephens (*q.v.*). ' The college was mismanaged, and the students were drawn off elsewhere ; some led an irregular life, and others were (it is said) lured away by Roman intrigue.' In 1677, largely through the efforts of Compton, Bishop of London, a Greek Church was built in the then fashionable district of Soho, which was served by the exiled Metropolitan of Samos, Joseph Georgirenes. This building in the eighteenth century fell into disuse, and after many years of desecration was reconciled and restored to Christian worship in 1850 as St. Mary's, Crown Street, Soho.

The influence of the desire for an understanding with the East is seen in the recommendation of the Royal Commission to revise the Prayer Book (1689-90) as to the *Filioque* clause in the Nicene Creed. ' It is humbly submitted to the Convocation whether a Note ought not here to be added with relation to the Greek Church, in order to our maintaining Catholic Communion.'

In 1701 the friendly relations were further emphasised by the respect paid to Neophytus, Archbishop of Philippopolis, and his attendants then visiting England. Oxford and Cambridge conferred on the archbishop the D.D. degree ; at Oxford his suite were created M.A., and his physician M.D.

In 1714 the persecuted Church of Alexandria sent to England Arsenius, Archbishop of the Thebaid, with an archimandrite, four deacons, and others ' to crave the assistance of good Christians.' They received £200 from Queen Anne, £100 from George I., and other help ; but they outstayed their welcome, and the authorities were anxious to get rid of them. They remained, reduced to great poverty, until 1716. In July of that year the Scots bishop, the Honble. Archibald Campbell, proposed to the English Nonjurors (*q.v.*) that they should ' endeavour a union with the Greek Church.' Bishops Collier (*q.v.*), Campbell, and Spinckes drew up proposals ; Spinckes put them into Greek, and the three bishops ' delivered them to the Archbishop of Thebais, who carried them to Muscovy, and engaged the Czar (Peter the Great) in the affair.' The Czar ' heartily espoused the matter,' and sent the proposals ' to the Patriarch of Alexandria to be communicated to the four Eastern

Patriarchs.' Meanwhile the question of the Usages had divided the Nonjurors, and when the Patriarchs' answer came in 1722 Bishop Spinckes, as leader of the Non-usagers, declined to go further in the matter. The Usager bishops, however, replied to the Patriarchs (29th May 1722), and at the same time wrote to the Holy Synod of the Russian Church. The Patriarchs rejoined in September 1723, and there negotiations with them ended. But negotiations with the Russian Church, which seemed far more promising, were only broken by the death of Peter the Great in 1725. The suggested basis for reunion, the *Proposal for a Concordate*, etc., of 1716, is learned but at times odd. It suggests a rearrangement of the patriarchal thrones, (settled by general councils for nearly fourteen centuries), and proposes to transfer the primacy of the Universal Church to Jerusalem. It mentions twelve points on which the Nonjurors and Easterns were agreed, but adds five ' wherein at present they cannot so perfectly agree.' (1) The Nonjurors do not give to œcumenical canons authority equal to that of Holy Scripture. (2) They fear undue honour paid to the Blessed Virgin. (3) They cannot invoke saints and angels. (4) They hesitate to worship the sacred symbols in the Eucharist. (5) They fear the Eastern use of sacred pictures. They suggest finally that a church, ' called the Concordia,' shall be built ' in or about London, which may be under the jurisdiction of the Patriarch of Alexandria,' where the English service shall at times be used, and ' that if it shall please God to restore the suffering Church of this island and her bishops to her and their just rights,' then on certain days divine service according to the Greek rites shall be celebrated ' in the Cathedral Church of St. Paul.' The answer of the Patriarchs is a document of portentous length, and the sum of it is that the Easterns could alter nothing. The reply of the Nonjurors shows ability and profound learning. Though their explanation of their views on the Holy Eucharist seems to prove them Virtualists [HOLY EUCHARIST], they ask for liberty as to ' Invocation of Saints, the worship of images, the Adoration of the Host.' The Patriarchs in return declined to change their attitude, though they wrote with great courtesy and friendliness, and sent copies of the decrees of the Synod of Jerusalem of 1672.

In 1724 Archbishop Wake (*q.v.*) had become aware of these negotiations, and addressed a dignified letter to the Patriarch of Jerusalem dated September 1725. He urged the Patriarch to beware of the Nonjurors as schismatics under fictitious titles. 'Meanwhile,' he wrote, 'we, the true Bishops and Clergy of the Church of England, as, in every fundamental article, we profess the same Faith with you, shall not cease in spirit and effect (since otherwise owing to our distance from you we cannot) to hold communion with you, and to pray for your peace and happiness.' And he entreated the Patriarch 'to remember him in his prayers and sacrifices at the Holy Altar of God.' In the opinion of Bishop Wordsworth of Salisbury, it was due to Archbishop Wake's intervention 'that the action of the Nonjurors did not compromise the relations of the English with the Eastern Church more than it seemed likely to do.' Mr. G. Williams suggested that the uncompromising attitude of the Patriarchs was due to their discovery that the Nonjurors were not the official representatives of the English Church. From 1725 for more than a century there is no record of any intercourse between the Churches, though 'research into the archives of the S.P.C.K. and other similar repositories would probably yield fruit' (Bishop J. Wordsworth).

Official intercourse was renewed by the ill-fated Jerusalem Bishopric scheme (*q.v.*), which in 1841 was designed, according to G. Williams, 'as an embassy of peace and good will to the Eastern Church.' The first bishop, Dr. Alexander, bore a commendatory letter to the Patriarchs from Archbishop Howley (*q.v.*), which stated that Alexander was forbidden to intermeddle in any way with the prelates of the East, and was to show them due reverence, and the letter avowed 'our hearty desire to renew that amicable intercourse with the ancient Churches of the East, which has been suspended for ages; and which, if restored, may have the effect, with the blessing of God, of putting an end to divisions.' As a further proof of this, the learned G. Williams (1814-78), Fellow of King's, Cambridge, who was deeply interested in restoring communion with the Eastern Church, accompanied him, at Archbishop Howley's request, as chaplain.

The Oxford Movement (*q.v.*) had stirred the longing for unity with the Eastern as well as the Roman Church, and in 1839 William Palmer (1811-79), Fellow of Magdalen, Oxford, a deacon, petitioned the Grand Duke Alexander of Russia, then visiting Oxford, to take means to bring about an understanding between the English and Russian Churches. Dr. Routh (*q.v.*) aided Palmer, and when in 1840 Palmer visited Russia with a view to explaining the position of the English Church, Dr. Routh gave him a letter to the Russian bishops, asking them if, after examination, they considered his faith orthodox, to admit him to communion. Mr. Palmer was aided in his endeavours by a gifted and fair-minded bishop, Dr. Luscombe, who had been consecrated by the Scots bishops in 1825, at the request of the English hierarchy, to minister to the English churchmen in Europe, and who lived in Paris till his death in 1846. The venerable Bishop Torry of St. Andrews also gave Mr. Palmer counsel and credentials. But Palmer's efforts, though thorough and earnest, met with little immediate response, and were in part counteracted by his secession to Rome in 1855.

The action of Bishop Gobat of Jerusalem in proselytising from Greek Christians might have caused serious friction, but it was met by a strong formal protest largely organised by Neale (*q.v.*) and sent to the Patriarchs in 1854. The Crimean War for a time checked hopes of mutual understanding, but in July 1863 the Lower House of the Canterbury Convocation appointed a committee 'to communicate with the committee' of the General Convention of the American Church (appointed in 1862) 'as to intercommunion with the Russo-Greek Church.' Later it was suggested that overtures towards intercommunion 'should be extended to the other Eastern patriarchates,' and this was done in 1866. The committee reported annually from 1865-72, and from 1874-6, the Lower House unanimously resolving in 1868 that the archbishop and bishops take steps towards opening direct negotiations with the Eastern Patriarchs.

Voluntary associations of churchmen have been formed for the same object. The Association for Promoting the Unity of Christendom, founded in 1857, includes Eastern as well as Anglican churchmen; the Eastern Church Association, first founded in April 1864, by the untiring efforts of George Williams gained much episcopal support, the Metropolitan of Servia (Archbishop of Belgrade), Bishops S. Wilberforce (*q.v.*) and Hamilton of Salisbury being among its patrons. The Association was refounded in 1893 under Bishop Wordsworth of Salisbury.

Conferences for reunion met at Bonn in 1874 and 1875, when representatives came from the Eastern, the Old Catholic, and the English Churches, and Dr. Döllinger presided. The question of the *Filioque* was discussed in 1875, and a formula of concord was reached. Among the English representatives were in

1874 Bishop Harold Browne of Winchester, and in 1875 Dr. Liddon (*q.v.*). Though without immediate result, these conferences undoubtedly did much for the cause of reunion; while the Anglican and Eastern Orthodox Churches Union, founded in 1906, has distinguished Eastern as well as English bishops among its members, and publishes a magazine (*Eirene*) in English and Greek.

The Lambeth Conferences [COUNCILS] have each in turn been followed by official intercourse with the Orthodox East. Archbishop Longley on 28th November 1867 sent a formal letter to the Patriarchs with a copy of the encyclical issued by the assembled bishops, and the same course has been followed on each occasion, save that in 1897 the Bishop of Salisbury was commissioned to deliver in person to each of the Eastern Patriarchs the resolutions on unity. The Conference of 1888 appointed a committee ' to consider the relation of the Anglican communion to the Eastern Church,' and its report expressed the hope ' that at no distant time closer relations may be established between the two Churches.' The 1897 Conference desired the two English archbishops with a committee to confer with the Orthodox Eastern Patriarchs, ' with a view to . . . establishing closer relations ' with them (Resolution 36), while the committee on reunion of the 1907 conference ' recorded with thankfulness the steady growth of friendly intercourse between the two communions since 1897, and the Conference sent a letter of greeting to a National Council of the Russian Church, which seemed at the time to be on the point of meeting, and requested that the 1897 committee should be made permanent (Resolutions 60, 61).

Acts of personal civility between ecclesiastics of both Churches have been frequent since 1870, when Archbishop Lycurgus of Syra and Tenos, visiting England, received an honorary degree of D.D. at Oxford, and was present at the consecrations of Dr. Mackenzie as Bishop of Nottingham and Dr. Mackarness as Bishop of Oxford. English bishops have been received with marked honour by the Russian Church, *e.g.* Archbishop Maclagan in 1897, and Bishop Creighton (*q.v.*) in 1896 when he attended the coronation of the Czar.

The English and Eastern Churches are on terms of official friendship, but intercommunion is not yet accomplished, nor are English Orders and sacraments as yet recognised officially by the Eastern Churches,

though individual divines among them have declared themselves in their favour.

[S. L. O.]

G. Williams, *The Orthodox and the Nonjurors*, London, 1868. The original text of the ' Proposals ' of the Nonjurors was discovered by Bishop Dowden of Edinburgh, and an account of it was published in the *J.T.S.*, vol. i. 562. They are printed in Martin and Petit's *Collectio Conciliorum* (Paris, 1905), vol. i., cols. 370-624 ; Bishop J. Wordsworth, *The Ch. of Eng. and the Eastern Patriarchates* ; *Reports of the Committee on Intercommunion, 1865-76*, printed as *Occasional Papers of the Eastern Ch. Association*, New Series, viii., ix., and x. For the Greek College at Oxford, *Union Review*, vol. i. 490, 1863 ; W. J. Birkbeck, *Russia and the Eng. Ch.*, vol. i. ; *A Visit to the Russian Ch.*, ed. J. H. Newman ; Dr. A. C. Headlam, ' Relations with the Eastern Churches ' in *Ch. Problems*, 1900 ; Dr. J. M. Neale, *Life and Times of Bishop Patrick Torry*, chap. vi.

(3) **With the Foreign Reformed.**—The breach with Rome in 1534 led almost of necessity to attempts at union with the reformed abroad, and in December 1535 negotiations were opened with ' the Princes of the Augsburg Confession,' *i.e.* the Lutheran princes of the Empire who adhered to the Confession presented to the Emperor at Augsburg, 25th June 1530. Foxe, Bishop of Hereford, with Heath (*q.v.*), afterwards Archbishop of York, and Dr. Barnes (burnt as a heretic, 1540) were sent to the princes at Smalcald to urge them to refuse a General Council offered by the new Pope, Paul III., and instead to come to a unity of doctrine with the English Church. This proposition by Henry VIII. ' may claim the eminence of having hindered the last chance of the reconciliation of the world ' (Dixon, *Hist.*, i. 309). The English divines made an unfavourable impression. ' Nicolas Heath the Archdeacon alone excels in Humanity and Learning. As for the rest of them they have no relish of our Philosophy and Sweetness.' The Germans insisted that Henry must approve the Augsburg Confession. Bishop S. Gardiner (*q.v.*), who saw the proposed Articles, advised against them. In 1536 the conferences with the Lutherans proceeded slowly, and ended without result in April. In 1538 Henry, from political motives, was even more eager for alliance with the Lutheran princes, and a distinguished Lutheran embassy, led by Burckhardt, arrived and conferred with an English committee of three bishops (including Cranmer, *q.v.*, and Tunstall, *q.v.*) and four doctors. The negotiations broke down in August, since the English divines ' would not let go their Communion in one kind, their private Mass, and their

Celibacy of Priests.' In 1539 the Lutheran ambassadors returned, and were willing to make great doctrinal concessions to the conservative bishops, but the Act of Six Articles (31 Hen. VIII. c. 14) marks the complete breakdown of the attempt at union. Thirteen Articles, however, agreed upon apparently at the conferences of 1538 (and discovered among the Cranmer MSS. in the nineteenth century) had a considerable influence on the later XXXIX. Articles (*q.v.*). Archbishop Cranmer long cherished a scheme for uniting the Foreign Reformed with the English Church in one communion, an idea which had originated with Melanchthon, and with this in view he invited various distinguished foreigners to England to prepare 'one common harmony of faith and doctrine.' For this he laboured from Henry VIII.'s death, 1547, to 1553, but the project was frustrated partly by the lukewarmness of Melanchthon and partly by the difficulties of England itself. This conference was to have been attended not only by Lutherans, but by 'the different shades of Swiss reformers.' This dream was shared only by the archbishop and his immediate friends, and there can be no doubt that the larger body of the English bishops would have been opposed to it.

Throughout the greater part of the reign of Elizabeth the bond between the English Church and the Swiss reformers was close, Beza, Calvin, and Bullinger exercising the greatest influence over English theology. But notwithstanding this pressure the orders of these Presbyterian bodies seem always to have been reckoned irregular and invalid, and it was objected to Dean Whittingham (*q.v.*) of Durham in 1578 that he 'was not made minister after the Orders of the Church of England, but after the Form of Geneva.'

No further schemes of reunion with the Foreign Reformed seem to have been proposed until the reign of James I. In 1618 four Anglican divines attended the Synod of Dort in Holland: Bishop Carleton of Llandaff; Dr. Hall, later Bishop of Norwich; Dr. Davenant (*q.v.*), later Bishop of Salisbury; and Dr. Samuel Ward. They protested against Article 31 of the Belgic Confession, which denied episcopal government when it was proposed for the approval of the foreign divines, and Bishop Carleton made a strong defence of the Apostolic Succession of bishops. These English were, in Collier's words, 'no more than four court divines; their commission and instructions were only from the King . . . they had no

delegation from the bishops, and by consequence were no representatives of the British Church.' Individual Churchmen, however, especially Bishop Davenant and John Durie (1596-1680), laboured to reunite the Foreign Reformed among themselves, especially 'the Calvinists to the Lutherans,' a work aided by Archbishops Abbot (*q.v.*) and Laud (*q.v.*).

After the death of Charles I. (*q.v.*) and the proscription of the English Church [COMMONWEALTH, CHURCH UNDER] friendly relations with the Foreign Reformed took place in France, and Cosin (*q.v.*) and others attended their ministrations. Others, however, as Clarendon, refused to do this; but, owing to the still lively fear of the political power of Rome, many Churchmen emphasised eagerly their belief in the 'Reformed Churches' and communicated with them. But the ministry of these Churches was never recognised officially by the English Church, although in individual cases under Queen Elizabeth, and once, it is said, after 1662, men ordained by them have held English benefices.

While among High Churchmen in the seventeenth century there are to be found great names, as Cosin and Denis Granville (*q.v.*), who appear to have reckoned the Foreign Reformed as 'true' though imperfect Churches, and were disposed to recognise their ministry as valid though irregular, yet these were only the opinions of individual divines, and the English Church has never deflected from the view expressed in the preface to the Ordinal, that episcopal consecration or Ordination is necessary to constitute a Bishop, Priest, or Deacon; and while the fear of Rome in the seventeenth century very largely accounts for the attitude of some of the divines, the official view of the English Church was expressed by the Lower House of the Convocation of Canterbury in 1689, when (in an address to the Crown) it vetoed the words 'the Protestant Religion in General' lest 'it should own the Presbyterian Churches of the Continent'; and great names at the same period are on this side, as Dr. Hickes (*q.v.*) in his *Answer to the Rights*, etc., 1707. The practice of the English Church has been to reordain ministers of the Foreign Reformed while recognising at once the orders of Rome.

In 1708 Frederick, King of Prussia, desired to unite the Lutherans and Calvinists in his dominions, and at the same time to obtain for them a liturgy and the Apostolical Succession, for which purpose he sought a union with the English Church. The attempt was renewed in 1710, when Archbishop Sharp (*q.v.*), and through him Queen Anne, became interested. The Prussian Ambassador (M. Bonet), in a long account of the negotiations to his King, 17th March 1710-11, alleges that the English clergy are ' possessed with ' a belief in the Apostolical Succession, ' and upon this supposition they allege there can be no true ecclesiastical *government* but under bishops of this order ; nor true *ministers* of the Gospel but such as have been ordained by bishops ; and if there be others that do not go so far, yet they all make a great difference between the ministers that have received imposition of hands by bishops and those that have been ordained by a synod of presbyters.' The negotiations were ended by the death of the Prussian king, 1713.

Earl Stanhope, in introducing a Bill for the relief of Protestant dissenters, 13th December 1718, ' argued that by the union of all true Protestants, the Church of England would still be the head of all the Protestant churches, and the Archbishop of Canterbury become the patriarch of all the Protestant clergy.'

For the rest of the century interest in and intercourse with the Foreign Reformed bodies waned in England. The Moravian Brotherhood, as a society in the English Church, elected Bishop T. Wilson (*q.v.*) one of ' the Antecessors of the General Synod of the brethren of the Anatolic Unity,' 1749, an office which he accepted with pleasure.

In the cause of Foreign Missions English Churchmen and Lutherans worked together in India throughout the eighteenth century, the S.P.C.K. subsidised the Danish and German Lutheran Missions in the Madras Presidency, and these relations ceased only in 1824 when the missions were taken over by the S.P.G. The C.M.S. also in its earliest years employed Lutheran agents in India in default of English clergy, but the fact remains that Lutheran orders have never been recognised officially by the English Church.

The scheme for a Bishopric in Jerusalem (*q.v.*) to be managed jointly by England and Prussia, carried through in 1841, was in reality an indirect attempt to unite the English Church with the State Church of Prussia, or to lead the way to such a union by giving the Prussian clergy valid orders. The scheme failed of its object.

The question of Moravian ' orders ' came before the Lambeth Conference in 1878, and again in 1888. In 1888 the Conference decided that efforts should be made to establish more friendly relations with the Swedish Church. A previous effort towards negotia-

tion with the Scandinavian Churches had been made by the Aberdeen Diocesan Synod in 1863. The Conference of 1897, while avowing its insufficient information as to the orders of the Moravians, expressed ' a hearty desire for such relations with them as will aid the cause of Christian unity,' recommended ' further discussion,' and asked for committees to consider both Moravian and Swedish orders. In the Conference of 1908 a Swedish bishop (Dr. Tottie) attended with a letter to the bishops, and a committee reported that Swedish orders ' were a matter for friendly conference and explanation.' A committee in 1906 had found the claim to episcopal succession among the Moravians ' not proven,' and the Conference of 1908 laid down precise regulations as to alliance with the Moravian body. The General Synod of the Moravian Church in June 1909 at Herrnhutt welcomed the Lambeth decrees warmly; and Bishop J. Wordsworth in his last work, *The National Church of Sweden*, looked forward to an alliance with the Swedish Church, which should unite with the English Church the estimated seventy millions of Lutherans.

Projects for reunion with the Old Catholics were adumbrated by the Conferences held at Bonn, 1874 and 1875, and a message of sympathy with them was contained in the official ' letter ' of the Lambeth Conference of 1878. Desire for friendly relations with the Old Catholics of Holland, Germany, Switzerland, and Austria was expressed in the Conference of 1888, though the Conference believed that ' the time had not come for any direct alliance.' In 1897 the desire for friendly relations was renewed, and the offer of Communion to their members was repeated. Similar resolves ' to maintain and strengthen the friendly relations which already exist ' were passed in 1908. Strong sympathy between members of the English Church and the so-called Jansenist Church of Holland began with the *History* by Dr. J. M. Neale (*q.v.*), published in 1858, before any Old Catholics existed and the Society of St. Willibrord (the Anglican and Old Catholic Union), of which Dr. Collins, Bishop of Gibraltar, was the first Anglican president, and which bishops of both Churches have joined, was founded in 1908, ' to promote a closer intercommunion ' between the English Church and the Old Catholics abroad.

[s. l. o.]

For the movement, 1535-9, Strype, *Eccl. Mem.* (fol. ed.), i. 228-32, 341-3, and app. 157-63 ; Hardwick, *Hist. of the Articles*, c. 4. For Cranmer see *Remains*, P.S., 420, n. 4 ; *Original Letters*, P.S., 24 ; Hardwick, *op. cit.*, 70-3.

For Synod of Dort see Collier, *Eccles. Hist.*, ed. 1840, vii. 111, and for John Drurie, Wordsworth, *Nat. Ch. of Sweden*, 290-8. For the question of the Ministry of the Foreign Reformed see Goode, *Brotherly Communion with the Foreign Protestant Churches desired*, etc. (1859), and Henson, *Relation of the Ch. of Eng. to the other Reformed Churches*, 1911. As to alleged cases in which the English Church officially recognised persons in the ministry of the Reformed Churches as competent to minister without episcopal ordination, see Denny, *Eng. Ch. and the Ministry of the Reformed Churches* (Ch. Hist. Soc., 1902), which by anticipation answers statements of Dr. Henson in his *Relation*, etc. For the eighteenth century see *Life of Archbishop Sharp*, i. 403 seq., ii. app. ii., 153-215; Lord Mahon, *History*, i. 191. *Reports of the Lambeth Conferences*.

(4) **Home Reunion.**—This question arose for the first time in the reign of Elizabeth. [NONCONFORMITY.] Earlier separatists from the English Church [LOLLARDS] were dealt with as heretics [HERESY], and under Elizabeth the Act of Uniformity (*q.v.*) was a measure of coercion. The Puritans (*q.v.*), who desired the formularies to be changed in their interests, were rebuffed at the Hampton Court Conference (*q.v.*), and toleration (*q.v.*) was of slow growth. In 1667 a scheme for ' comprehension ' of Presbyterians (*q.v.*) was put forward, and such schemes were frequent throughout the reign of Charles II. The movement was partly political, and was supported by those who were later called ' Low Church ' (*q.v.*). Tillotson (*q.v.*) and Stillingfleet (*q.v.*) sympathised, and Bishop Croft of Hereford in *The Naked Truth*, 1675, advocated concessions. Burnet (*q.v.*) then zealously opposed the movement in his *Modest Survey . . . of Naked Truth*, 1676. Dr. Whitby in *The Protestant Reconciler*, 1682, pleaded for further concessions. In practice, however, the more Puritan bishops, as Seth Ward (*q.v.*), were most vigorous with dissenters, while churchmen of the school of Juxon (*q.v.*), Sanderson, and Sancroft (*q.v.*) were mild and gentle.

The Revolution of 1688 led to further schemes of comprehension, and the commission of 1689 [COMMISSIONS, ROYAL] proposed terms of reunion which would have compromised the question of the apostolic ministry. Convocation rejected the proposals. Burnet was eager in the cause, yet was active in winning over dissenters to the Church, and greatly lessened, he says, their number and influence in Salisbury. The schemes of comprehension concerned principally the Presbyterians: many of the Independents were wholly irreconcilable. The Baptists showed no disposition to come to

an agreement with the Church, nor did members of the Society of Friends. [NONCONFORMITY.]

The removal of the fear of Rome in 1689 broke up the alliance between Churchmen and dissenters in England, and although comprehension was debated in Convocation in 1702, the tide of feeling in Queen Anne's reign was entirely against it. In 1718 a correspondence on reunion was begun between Dr. Samuel Chandler (1693-1766), the eminent Presbyterian, and Bishop Gooch of Norwich, in which Bishop Sherlock (*q.v.*) and Archbishop Herring, as well as Dr. Philip Doddridge, the Presbyterian (1702-51), took part. No practical results followed.

The rise of the Methodists, while it led to sympathy between Evangelicals within and without the English Church, brought no proposal for home reunion or comprehension, and the subject did not again arise until Dr. Arnold (*q.v.*), alarmed at the dangers which threatened the Church in 1832, published his *Principles of Church Reform*, which proposed the union of all sects with the Church by Act of Parliament, *i.e.* that all Christian bodies should be recognised as belonging to the National Church, a proposal which was rather federation than reunion, and which Arnold considered ' comprehension without compromise.' The proposal had been in part dictated by exaggerated fears. ' Nothing can save the Church but a union with the dissenters,' he wrote (January 1833). The proposal roused a storm of protest, and was answered by the Oxford Movement (*q.v.*).

Movements for home reunion came next from the adherents of that Movement. In 1869 a committee was formed at the Wolverhampton Church Congress to form a society for the reunion of Christendom on the basis of the national Church. Its method was to win back dissenters by way of compromise. The society was a complete failure, and in 1878 its members joined the Home Reunion Society, which was founded by a devoted layman, William Thomas Mowbray, in 1873. Its constitution was finally settled (January 1875) under its first president, Bishop Harold Browne of Winchester. The society is pledged to support no scheme that can compromise the teaching of the Three Creeds or the episcopal constitution of the Church. It has done much by prayer, conference, and social intercourse between churchmen and dissenters to bring about a better understanding. At successive Lambeth Conferences since 1888 the subject has been considered, that of 1888 laying down the four principles on which such reunion must proceed, viz.: (1) the Holy Scriptures as the rule of Faith; (2) the Apostles' and Nicene Creeds; (3) the two Sacraments of the Gospel; (4) the Historic Episcopate. This was reaffirmed by a committee of the Conference of 1897, and Resolutions 75-8 of the Conference of 1908 conceived that under certain conditions 'it might be possible to make an approach to reunion on the basis of consecrations to the episcopate on lines suggested by such precedents as those of 1610.'

Individual clergy have gone further. A series of sermons by Dr. Henson on *Godly Union and Concord*, 1902, advocated a more complete surrender of the Church's practice, and Bishop Percival of Hereford invited and admitted dissenters to Communion in his cathedral in June 1911. The bishop's action was disclaimed in Convocation, and such endeavours have seemed less attempts at reunion than demonstrations against the Oxford Movement and the Church principles for which it stood, just as in the seventeenth and eighteenth centuries the desire to comprehend Presbyterians was in great measure dictated by a desire to relax the formularies. The Established Church in Scotland has stood on a somewhat different footing. In 1610 James I. and VI. induced three Scottish titular bishops to accept consecration from the English episcopate, and they, returning home, consecrated the rest of their brethren. (From 1572 there had been bishops who were, in fact, Presbyterian ministers.) Until 1689 the Church, under regularly consecrated bishops, continued in Scotland in full communion with the English Church. After 1689, when the Presbyterian Establishment was set up, communion between the Established Church of Scotland and the English Church ceased, though efforts were made, especially by Bishop C. Wordsworth of St. Andrews, to bring about intercommunion.

[S. L. O.]

Abbey and Overton, *Eng. Ch. in Eighteenth Century*, i. 386-410; *Reunion Magazine*, December 1910, 'Home Reunion': *Lambeth Conference Reports*, 1888, 1897, 1908.

RICHARD OF WYCH, St. (? 1197-1253), Bishop of Chichester, was born at Wych (now Droitwich), near Worcester, son of well-to-do parents, who seem to have been landowners. The family name was apparently Chandos, for his brother is so named in the bishop's will. On the death of Richard's father the family became extremely poor, and Richard, though the younger son, undertook the management of the property, and after several years of strenuous labour restored the family fortunes. His brother in gratitude offered to make over the lands to him (the estate seems to have been named Burford: no trace of the name now survives in the neighbourhood), and urged him to marry 'a certain noble lady.' Richard declined these suggestions, and went to Oxford to prepare for holy orders. He lived very poorly, since a priest, to whom he had entrusted his capital, wasted it. Richard shared a lodging with two undergraduates as poor as himself. They had but one warm tunic and one hooded gown between them, and in this they attended lectures in turns. Their ordinary food was bread and vegetables with a very little wine. They had fish or meat only on great festivals or when entertaining guests. After his course at Oxford, Richard went to Paris. He seems then to have taken his M.A. at Oxford, and to have spent seven years in the study of Canon Law at Bologna, where he was greatly distinguished. His tutor there offered him his daughter in marriage; but his heart was set on the priesthood, and in 1235 he returned to Oxford, where he became Chancellor of the University. The two best churchmen of the day had meanwhile marked him: Archbishop Edmund Rich (*q.v.*) and Bishop Grosseteste (*q.v.*), and each invited him to become his Chancellor. Richard accepted the offer of the archbishop, and became his devoted follower, accompanying him in his exile, and continuing with him till his death at Soissy, 1242. He was of great assistance to the archbishop's biographer, to whom he gave much material. Overcome with grief at his master's death, he retired to a Dominican house at Orleans, where he studied theology, was ordained priest, and wished to enter the order. He was recalled to England by the new primate, Boniface of Savoy, and induced to resume his Chancellorship. At the same time he became Vicar of Deal and Rector of Charing, Kent.

Richard Passelew had been elected bishop by his fellow canons of Chichester, 1244. Archbishop Boniface caused him to be examined formally by Grosseteste, and then quashed the election. He recommended Richard of Wych to the canons, who elected him unanimously. Henry III. was furious, and refused to surrender the temporalities of the see, objecting that Boniface had 'provided' Richard. The Pope, Innocent IV., heard the case at Lyons, confirmed the election, and consecrated Richard, 21st July 1245. For two years Henry kept the temporalities, and Richard was a homeless wanderer in his own diocese, living chiefly with a poor priest—one Simon of Tarring—but working most actively, traversing the downs and woods on foot. He won the hearts of the Sussex folk in an astonishing degree, and was a model bishop. His statutes for the diocese regulate conduct and ceremonial alike, and show Richard a wise ruler as well as a good parish priest. (They are in Wilkins, *Conc.*, i. 688-93.) He instituted contributions, later called St. Richard's pence, from each church in the diocese, to be offered for the upkeep of the cathedral church on Easter Day or Whit Sunday. In 1246, threatened with excommunication, Henry III. restored the temporalities.

Details of Richard's personal life are full and vivid in his earliest biographies. He never ate meat, on humanitarian grounds, and when lamb or chicken was served at his table he would exclaim: 'O if you were rational and could speak, how you would curse our gluttony. We indeed have caused your death, and you, innocents, what have you done worthy of death?' Though he lived with extreme simplicity his dress showed his good breeding and good taste, 'neither too smart nor too shabby' (*nec nitida nimium nec abjecta plurimum sed ex moderato et competenti habitu*). In his name is found by his biographer, Ralph of Bocking, the memory of his beautiful manners (Ricardus = *Ridens. Carus, et Dulcis*).

'His very name the record of his smile
And of his sweetness and his charm.'
(WARREN.)

In politics Richard was of the school of Grosseteste, and strongly opposed to royal absolutism, and is reckoned by Stubbs among the political heroes of the century (*C.H.*, ii. 314). He was an ardent Crusader, and preached the Crusade throughout his diocese and in Kent. While preaching it his strength gave way. He was carried to Dover, consecrated a church there to the memory of his master and friend, St. Edmund, and died about midnight, 3rd April 1253.

'The gentle confessor, Bishop Richard,' was buried in his cathedral church, near the altar of St. Edmund, by his direction. He was canonised by Urban IV., 22nd January 1262, in the Franciscan church at Viterbo. His memory lingered long in Sussex (there was a Guild of St. Richard at Eastbourne in the fifteenth century), and at Droitwich, where the omission of his festival, 1616, was followed by the drying up of a well, which reflowed when the observance was resumed. His festival was kept in Droitwich in 1680,

and the wakes which were its modern development flourished until the nineteenth century. More strange was an Italian devotion to him, illustrated by a *Life* published at Milan in 1706, in which St. Richard appears as the protector of the Coachmen's Union of Milan. It exhibits him (in a frontispiece) distinguished by a nimbus, driving a coach and four. The origin of this devotion is 'beyond conjecture.'

Henry VIII. ordered his shrine to be destroyed, 4th December 1538; the directions were very precise (Wilkins, *Conc.*, iii. 810); it has been in part restored. The barons of the western Cinque Ports (Hastings and her members) were accustomed to present their share of the coronation canopy to St. Richard's tomb. He is still commemorated in the calendar of the English Church on 4th April. [S. L. O.]

Lives in *Acta Sanctorum* (April), i. 277 *seq.*, and by Stephens in *Memorials of the See of Chichester*. A very excellent *Life* is in Newman's series, probably by R. Ornsby; others are in *D.N.B.* by Mrs. Tout, and by Canon Cooper in *Sussex Arch. Coll.*, xliv. His will is printed in *Sussex Arch. Coll.*, i. 167 *seq.*

RIDLEY, Nicholas (1500?-1555), Bishop of London, second son of Christopher Ridley of Unthank Hall, belonged to an old Northumberland family; 'being a child, learned his grammar with great dexterity at Newcastle,' and then went to Pembroke Hall, Cambridge, of which he afterwards became Fellow. After graduating M.A. he pursued his studies at the Sorbonne and at Louvain, and returned to Cambridge about 1530. He was active in securing the official recognition of the Royal Supremacy (*q.v.*) by the university, but it does not appear when he first became a convert to reformed views. He seems to have owed his change to his own studies, especially to Bertram's book on the Eucharist. 'This Bertram was the first that pulled me by the ear and that first brought me from the common error of the Romish Church and that caused me to search more diligently and exactly the Scriptures and the writings of the old ecclesiastical fathers,' and to conversations with Cranmer (*q.v.*) and Peter Martyr (*q.v.*). He preached in 1539 against the Six Articles, but seems even then to have accepted the doctrine of the corporal presence in the sacrament, and did not finally reject it before the end of the reign.

He became chaplain to Cranmer in 1537; Vicar of Herne, 1538; Master of Pembroke Hall, 1540; chaplain to the King and Canon of Canterbury, 1541; and though suspected of heresy and examined by commissioners succeeded in holding all these preferments during the rest of the reign. On the accession of Edward VI. he became Vicar of Soham in Cambs., and Bishop of Rochester in September 1547, and obtained permission to hold *in commendam* his two vicarages and two canonries until Christmas, 1552, and he also retained the Mastership of Pembroke Hall. He went with Cranmer as a deputation from the Council to Edward VI. to ask permission for Mary (*q.v.*) to hear Mass at the request of Charles V. At which request the King burst into such bitter weeping and sobbing that the bishops, 'seeing the King's zeal and constancy, wept as fast as he,' and gave up their purpose.

At the beginning of the reign he accompanied as preacher the visitors sent to enforce Reformation doctrines in the dioceses of York, Durham, Carlisle, and Chester, and later, in 1549, he was one of the visitors at Cambridge. He presided over three disputations concerning the Eucharist, and summed up in favour of the Protestants. He rejected transubstantiation, and equally disclaimed holding the view that the sacrament was 'a bare sign.' His theory was that the faithful receive not Christ's Body, but the 'power and inward might' of His Body. And he would have forbidden any honour being paid to the outward sign, but only to the Body of Christ in heaven. His argument was learned, and he attached much importance to the opinion of the 'old ancient fathers.' He became Bishop of London when Bonner (*q.v.*) was deprived in 1549.

As bishop, Foxe (*q.v.*), a partial authority, tells us that 'he so travailed and occupied himself by preaching and teaching the true and wholesome doctrine of Christ that never good child was more singularly loved of his dear parents than he of his flock and diocese. Every Sunday and holiday he lightly preached in some one place or other, except he was otherwise letted by weighty affairs and business, to whose sermons the people resorted, swarming about him like bees.' He ordered the altars in his diocese to be replaced by communion tables, but laboured earnestly to induce Hooper (*q.v.*) to wear the episcopal vestments required by law, as being 'things indifferent.' He was perhaps one of the committee which drew up the Prayer Book of 1549. A sermon he preached before the King was in part responsible for the founding of Christ's Hospital, St. Thomas's Hospital, and the Bethlehem Hospital. Like Latimer (*q.v.*), he remonstrated against the rapacity of the courtiers and great nobles and their seizure of Church property. In 1552 he

visited Mary, who received him courteously, but declined his offer to preach to her—a refusal of which he made a good deal later. He was persuaded by Northumberland to sign the document which acknowledged the title of Lady Jane Grey to the throne, and was promised the bishopric of Durham. Immediately after the King's death, by command of the Council, in a sermon at Paul's Cross before the Lord Mayor and corporation, he declared Mary and Elizabeth to be illegitimate, and denounced Mary's religious opinions.

When all hope of establishing Lady Jane Grey on the throne was over, 'he speedily repairing to Framlingham to salute the Queen had such cold welcome there that being despoiled of all his dignitie he was sent back on a lame halting horse to the Tower.' He was excepted from the Queen's amnesty, and Bonner was reinstated Bishop of London. In March 1554 he was sent to Oxford with Cranmer and Latimer to dispute with learned divines of both Universities about the Presence in the Eucharist.

When the three articles were read to him : (1) affirming that Christ's natural Body was in the sacrament ; (2) denying that the substance of bread and wine remained after consecration ; (3) affirming that the Mass was a sacrifice propitiatory for the sins of the quick and dead, he said : 'They were all false and that they sprang out of a bitter and sour root. His answers were sharp, witty, and learned.' He denied the presence of Christ's natural Body, but admitted a spiritual presence. 'I confess that Christ's Body is in the sacrament in this respect ; because there is in it the Spirit of Christ, that is the power of the Word of God, which not only feedeth the soul but cleanseth it.'

As a result, he was declared a heretic, but it was not until September 1555, when Parliament had re-enacted the penal laws, that he was tried under the new statutes. He was sentenced and then formally degraded by Bishop Brooks and the vice-chancellor. During his degradation 'Dr. Ridley did vehemently inveigh against the Romish bishop and all that foolish apparel [the Mass vestments], calling him antichrist and the apparel foolish and abominable, yea too fond for a Vice in a play.' He was then handed over to the mayor, and the next day was brought to execution with Latimer. His brother-in-law, Shipside, fastened bags of gunpowder round his neck; but in spite of this death was long in coming, as the fire only burnt his feet and legs, and he suffered horribly, crying out continually: 'Lord, have mercy on me. Let the fire come unto me. I cannot burn.' At last the fire touched the gunpowder, and death released him.

Foxe tells us that he was 'a man right comely and well proportioned in all points'; 'learned, wise of counsel, deep of wit and very politic in all his doings.' He seems to have been gentle and void of rancour, and treated Bonner's mother with great kindness when he succeeded Bonner as Bishop of London. He was much given to prayer and contemplation; his chief relaxation was playing chess. He was a man of independent judgment, and perhaps the master-spirit among the Reformers. 'Latimer leaneth to Cranmer, Cranmer leaneth to Ridley, and Ridley to the singularity of his own wit.'

He had the austere mind of the Puritan, which objected to all sensible objects as aids to devotion. He would have banished all images, including presumably pictures and stained-glass windows, on the ground that if they did not lead to superstitious abuse, they were liable to distract the mind from prayer.

He seems to have realised the failure of himself and his fellow-reformers to stem the tide of immorality, which prevailed after even more than before the changes were begun. 'It was great pity and a lamentable thing to have seen in many places the people so loathsomely and unreligiously to come to the Holy Communion and to the Common Prayers . . . in comparison of that blind zeal and undiscreet devotion which they had aforetime to those things whereof they understood never one whit.'

[C. P. S. C.]

Strype, *Memorials*; Foxe, *Acts and Monuments*; Ridley, *A Brief Declaration of the Lord's Supper*, with a memoir by Bishop Moule; *Works* (Parker Soc.).

RIPON, See of. Ripon was apparently the seat of a bishop for a short time in the seventh century, when Wilfrid (*q.v.*), finding his see of York occupied, resided there from 666 to 669, and Eadhed, Bishop of Lindsey, retired there on the conquest of his diocese by Mercia (c. 678). But after his death no bishop had his seat at Ripon until 1836. In 1835 the Ecclesiastical Commissioners [COMMISSIONS, ROYAL], desiring to bring the great dioceses of the north to a more manageable size, recommended the erection of a see there, to be endowed by the reduction of the larger episcopal incomes. The Established Church Act, 1836 (6-7 Will. IV. c. 77), empowered the Crown to carry this out by Order in Council, and the see was established, 5th October 1836. An increase in the number of bishops in the

House of Lords was avoided by the fusion of the sees of Gloucester (*q.v.*) and Bristol (*q.v.*). The new diocese consisted of that part of the county of York which was formerly in the diocese of Chester, and also of part of the diocese of York. The boundary between Ripon and York was rearranged by Order in Council, 1st February 1838, but in 1888 part of the diocese of Ripon was transferred to Wakefield (*q.v.*). The diocese consists of a great part of the North and West Ridings, with a few parishes in Lancashire, and has a population of 1,136,045. The income of the see is £1200. It was originally divided into the archdeaconries of Richmond (first mentioned, as part of York diocese, 1088) and Craven (created 1836). An archdeaconry of Ripon was formed in 1894. A bishop suffragan was appointed in 1888 with the title of Bishop of Penrith, which in 1889 was changed to Richmond, and in 1905 a bishop suffragan of Knaresborough was appointed. A bishop's palace was built near Ripon, 1838-41. The church of SS. Peter and Wilfrid, Ripon, whose crypt dates back to the seventh century, had belonged to the Augustinian Canons from the eleventh century until the Dissolution under Henry VIII. It was refounded as a collegiate church by James I. in 1604, and in 1836 it became the cathedral church of the new see, and its dean and prebendaries became dean and canons.

1. Charles Thomas Longley, 1836; administered the diocese successfully. Sir Robert Peel, in the House of Commons, commended his 'unremitting activity, zeal, and piety'; tr. to Durham, 1856.
2. Robert Bickersteth, 1856; Evangelical; advocated legalisation of marriage with a deceased wife's sister; d. 1884.
3. William Boyd Carpenter, 1884; res. 1911.
4. Thomas Wortley Drury, 1912; tr. from Sodor and Man. [G. C.]

RITUAL CASES. The revival of ceremonial which was a development of the Oxford Movement (*q.v.*) met with considerable opposition from the first, although the 'ritualists,' as they were vulgarly and inaccurately called, contended that they were restoring lawful practices which had fallen into disuse. *Westerton v. Liddell*, the first suit in which these questions were brought before the courts, was begun in 1855 after communications of both parties with Bishop Blomfield (*q.v.*), who censured the 'disrespectful and menacing tone' adopted by Westerton, the churchwarden. The action was brought in the consistory court of London against Liddell, Vicar of St. Paul's, Knightsbridge, for the removal of the high altar and its cross, candlesticks, coloured altar-cloths, and the credence table. A parallel suit (*Beal* v. *Liddell*) was brought in respect of the district church of St. Barnabas, Pimlico. The decision was in Westerton's favour on all points except the candlesticks (which were held to be legal if the candles were only lit when necessary for giving light), and was confirmed by the Court of Arches on appeal. Liddell appealed to the Privy Council, which thus had a question of ceremonial before it for the first time. It upheld the 'ritualist' view of the Ornaments Rubric, and pronounced the altar-cloths, credence, and cross on the screen legal, confirming the courts below in other respects, 1857.

After this the ceremonial revival spread rapidly. In 1868 began the famous suits of *Martin* v. *Mackonochie* [MACKONOCHIE, A. H.], the last judgment in which was not delivered till 1883. In the Court of Arches Sir Robert Phillimore (*q.v.*), in an elaborate judgment, decided that altar-lights were legal, that incense, the mixed chalice, and elevation of paten and chalice were not, and that 'excessive kneeling' during the prayer of consecration was one of a class of practices neither ordered nor forbidden by the Prayer Book, but intended to be governed by the discretion of the bishop. The Privy Council held that lights and 'excessive kneeling' were illegal, and in 1870 suspended Mackonochie for three months for disobeying its judgment, thus assuming a power to inflict a purely spiritual penalty. The next important case was *Elphinstone*, afterwards *Hebbert*, v. *Purchas*, 1869-71 (the original promoter, a colonel, dying during the suit and being replaced by a retired Indian judge). The defendant, perpetual curate of St. James's Chapel, Brighton, was charged with some thirty-five alleged illegal practices, including the hanging of a stuffed dove over the Holy Table on Whitsunday. From many of them he was admonished to abstain by the Dean of the Arches, who decided, however, that the eucharistic vestments (*q.v.*), the eastward position, wafer bread, and the mixed chalice were legal. In these points the Privy Council reversed the judgment and declared them illegal. It decided that 'the cope is to be worn in ministering the Holy Communion on high feast days in Cathedrals and Collegiate Churches, and the surplice in all other ministrations.' Mr. Purchas did not appear in either court owing to poverty and ill-health. Although the suit

was undefended, the taxed costs amounted to £7661, 18s. 7d. *Clifton* v. *Ridsdale* was the first case brought under the Public Worship Regulation Act (*q.v.*). The Rev. C. J. Ridsdale was incumbent of the district chapelry of St. Peter, Folkestone. The charges against him were the use of vestments, wafers, and similar matters. Lord Penzance gave judgment in accordance with the Privy Council's decision in *Hebbert* v. *Purchas*. Ridsdale appealed to the Privy Council, recently reconstituted under the Act of 1876. Hopes were entertained that thus reconstituted that court would cut itself off from its questionable past and prove a more suitable tribunal for the decision of Church cases. It allowed the questions decided in *Hebbert* v. *Purchas* to be reopened and reargued, but eventually dismissed the appeal on all points, though it apparently extended the Purchas decision as to the cope so as to make it apply to all Eucharists in cathedral and collegiate churches. The combined effect of this and the Purchas judgment was utterly to discredit the Privy Council in the eyes of a very large number of churchmen. They were accused of inconsistency in admitting and even appealing to its jurisdiction as long as it seemed likely to decide in their favour, and repudiating its authority when the judgments went against them. But it must be remembered that the Privy Council was in possession of the field. There was no other tribunal to which those who were dissatisfied with the decisions of the provincial court could turn. And although its claim to adjudicate upon doctrine had already been questioned, it was not easy to realise all at once that it had no right to the jurisdiction which it claimed in the less vital matters of ceremony until it stultified itself by the nature of its decisions. Discontent centred mainly round two points. The judgment in *Martin* v. *Mackonochie* had seemed to sanction the eastward position, and many clergymen, among them Bishop S. Wilberforce (*q.v.*), had in consequence adopted that position instead of the 'north end.' Much astonishment and indignation ensued when in the Purchas case the Privy Council, ignoring, as it seemed, its previous ruling, held that the north end position was compulsory throughout the Communion service. The two senior canons of St. Paul's Cathedral, Dr. Liddon (*q.v.*) and Mr. Gregory, openly disregarded the judgment in this respect and published their reasons. The decision against eucharistic vestments was even more vehemently disputed. For the Privy Council both in *Westerton* v. *Liddell* and *Martin* v. *Mackonochie* had taken a view of the Ornaments Rubric which sanctioned them, and it was held by weighty authorities that that view can only be avoided by a misunderstanding (some even said a falsification) of the historical evidence. A strong minority of the court disapproved of the judgment in *Clifton* v. *Ridsdale*. Lord Chancellor Cairns, by unexpectedly reviving an Order in Council of 1627, prevented them from officially publishing their dissent, but the existence of this minority (which included Sir R. Phillimore, the first ecclesiastical lawyer of the day), leaked out and added to the dissatisfaction. Chief Baron Kelly, another member of the court, was known to have declared that the judgment was one of 'policy, not law.' And a third member of the minority, Lord Justice Amphlett, spoke of it as 'a flagitious judgment.' From this time dates the complete repudiation by High Churchmen of the authority of the Privy Council. Its incompetence, and the one-sided nature of its decisions, led to investigations into its origin which revealed its complete lack of jurisdiction. The next period is one of undefended ritual prosecutions. The court of first instance also was one which churchmen could not recognise, as being set up only by Parliament in the Public Worship Regulation Act. After the Purchas judgment the Church Association called on its members for an 'abundance of complaints.' A large proportion of those which resulted were vetoed by the bishops, but some reached the courts. Five of the clergy prosecuted were imprisoned for periods varying from a fortnight to nineteen months, namely, A. Tooth, Vicar of St. James's, Hatcham, in 1877; T. P. Dale, Rector of St. Vedast and St. Michael le Querne, city of London, in 1880; R. W. Enraght, Vicar of Holy Trinity, Bordesley, in 1880; S. F. Green, Rector of St. John's, Miles Platting, in 1881-2 [FRASER, JAMES]; and J. Bell Cox, perpetual Curate of St. Margaret's, Toxteth Park, Liverpool, in 1887. In *Perkins* v. *Enraght* a consecrated wafer was produced in court, and Archbishop Tait (*q.v.*) with difficulty secured its return.

In 1888 the suit of *Read* v. *Bishop of Lincoln* was brought on behalf of the Church Association against Bishop King (*q.v.*) for alleged illegal practices. After some uncertainty as to jurisdiction the case was heard by Archbishop Benson (*q.v.*) with five episcopal assessors. The court decided that the sign of the cross in absolution and benediction was illegal, but that the following were not illegal:—the eastward position (provided that the manual acts were not hidden), the mixed

chalice (provided that it were not ceremonially mixed as a part of the service), the ablutions, altar-lights, and the singing of the *Agnus Dei*. On appeal the Privy Council upheld the archbishop's decision, except that it left the question of altar-lights undecided, finding that the bishop was not responsible for their lighting. The bishop appeared by counsel before the archbishop, but not before the Privy Council, as he declined to recognise its jurisdiction. This case broke the spell of the Privy Council by showing that its previous decisions were not infallible or irrevocable, but could be reconsidered in the light of history and liturgiology. Though some doubt was expressed as to the jurisdiction of the archbishop's court, its spiritual character and moral authority were unquestionable. Without violation of conscience or principle, the clergy could yield to it an obedience which they were obliged to deny to Lord Penzance and the Privy Council, and even to bishops when, instead of relying on their spiritual authority, they aspired only to enforce the decrees of those tribunals. Its practical effect was to bring to a close the epoch of ritual prosecutions. Later suits dealing with ceremonial matters have been few and unimportant. Irregularities of ceremonial, real or supposed, no longer occupy so disproportionately large a place in the affairs of the Church as they did before the Lincoln Case, and the bishops have been left to deal with them by the exercise of their spiritual authority, and in accordance with the laws of the Church, unhampered by interference from without. [COURTS.]

TABLE OF PRINCIPAL CASES

Westerton v. *Liddell* and *Beal* v. *Liddell*,[1] 1855-7, 4 W.R. 167, 5 W.R. 470. See above.

Flamank v. *Simpson*, 1866-8, 1 Adm. and Eccl. 276, 2 Adm. and Eccl. 116. Heard with *Martin* v. *Mackonochie* in Court of Arches, the charges being substantially the same. No appeal.

Martin v. *Mackonochie* I., 1868-70, 2 Adm. and Eccl. 116, 2 P.C. 365, 3 P.C. 52, 409. See above.

Sumner v. *Wix*, 1870, 3 Adm. and Eccl. 58. Lights at the gospel, lights on either side of the holy table or on a ledge over it, not required for giving light, and incense preparatory to Holy Communion held unlawful by Court of Arches.

Elphinstone v. *Purchas* and *Hebbert* v. *Purchas*,[1] 1869-71, 3 Adm. and Eccl. 66, 3 P.C. 605. See above.

Martin v. *Mackonochie* II., 1874, 4 Adm.

[1] Report also published in volume form.

and Eccl. 279. Lights at morning prayer, *Agnus Dei*. sign of the cross, held unlawful by Court of Arches; other charges, vestments, etc., covered by previous decisions. Mackonochie suspended for six weeks by Sir R. Phillimore.

Combe v. Edwards (afterwards De la Bere), 1874-8, 4 Adm. and Eccl. 390, 2 P.D. 354, 3 P.D. 103. Charges, vestments, lights, mixed chalice, etc. Plea that promoter held a pew in an Independent chapel held irrelevant. In his judgment Lord Penzance vigorously criticised Lord Chief-Justice Cockburn for prohibiting him.

Durst v. Masters, 1875-6, 1 P.D. 123, 377. Movable cross on retable held illegal.

Clifton v. Ridsdale,[1] 1875-7, 1 P.D. 316, 2 P.D. 376. See above.

Hudson v. Tooth, 1876-7, 2 P.D. 125, 3 Q.B.D. 46. Lights and incense in procession held unlawful. In this and the three following cases the stock charges were brought, vestments, eastward position, altar lights, mixed chalice, etc., and in each the defendant was imprisoned for contumacy.

Serjeant v. Dale, 1878-81, 2 Q.B.D. 558, 8 Q.B.D. 376.

Perkins v. Enraght, 1879-81, 43 L.T.N.S. 770, 6 Q.B.D. 376.

Dean v. Green, 1879-82, 8 P.D. 79.

Martin v. Mackonochie III., 1880-3, 6 P.D. 87, 7 P.D. 94, 8 P.D. 191. Same charges as before. Sentence of deprivation pronounced by Lord Penzance.

Combe v. De la Bere II., 1880-1, 6 P.D. 157, 22 Ch.D. 316. Same charges as before. Lord Penzance pronounced sentence of deprivation.

Hakes v. Cox, 1885-92, 19 Q.B.D. 307, 20 Q.B.D. 1, 15 A.C. 506. 1892 P. 110. Vestments and other usual charges. Defendant's imprisonment for contumacy led to decision of an important point of *habeas corpus* law by civil courts.

Read v. Bishop of Lincoln,[1] 1888-92, 13 P.D. 221, 14 P.D. 88, 1891 P. 9, 1892 A.C. 644. See above.

Davey v. Hinde, 1899-1903, 1901 P. 95, 1903 P. 221. Faculty granted for removal of stations of cross, images, and other ornaments placed in church without a faculty.

Bishop of Oxford v. Henly, 1906-9, 1907 P. 88, 1909 P. 319. Reservation of the blessed sacrament and service of benediction held unlawful. Defendant did not appear, and was deprived.   [G. C.]

Law Reports; Paul, *Hist. Mod. Eng.*; Cornish, *Eng. Ch. in Nineteenth Century*; contemporary memoirs and biographies.

_____
[1] Report also published in volume form.

ROCHESTER, See of, owes its foundation to St. Augustine's desire to extend the operations of the Church. In 604 he consecrated Justus Bishop of Rochester. Bede (*q.v.*) shows that the share of King Aethelberht in the foundation of the see was considerable. 'As for Justus, Augustine ordained him bishop in Kent, in the city of Durobreve (Rochester), in which King Aethelberht made the church of the blessed apostle Andrew'; he also presented many gifts to the bishop, and added lands and possessions for the use of those who were with him.

Portions of the foundations of the church here mentioned still remain beneath the soil, and the position of its eastern apse is shown by lines that have been cut in the floor of the nave of the present cathedral.

The cathedral was at first served by a college of secular canons, an arrangement which continued until 1082, when Bishop Gundulf replaced them by Benedictine monks, who were in turn dispossessed at the Dissolution (*c.* 1541) by a dean and six canons. Under the Cathedrals Act, 1840 (3-4 Vic. c. 113) the number of canons was reduced to four. In 1713 one canonry was annexed to the Provostship of Oriel College, Oxford, but was severed from it in 1882 and annexed to the Oriel Professorship of the Interpretation of Holy Scripture.

Rochester for many centuries occupied an intimate and dependent position in relation to Canterbury. When, *e.g.*, the latter see was vacant, its affairs were administered by the bishops of Rochester and *vice versa*. The bishops of Rochester were for a considerable time appointed directly by the archbishops, though occasionally this rule was broken by royal interference. The privilege of appointing to the see of Rochester was confirmed to the archbishop by a royal charter of the thirteenth year of King John. The developments after the Norman Conquest did not involve any immediate weakening of the hold of Canterbury upon Rochester, and Lanfranc (*q.v.*) not only appointed Gundulf bishop, but also caused him to build a new cathedral and to found the monastery If the *Martiloge* of Canterbury is to be trusted, the new order of things was entirely due to Lanfranc. 'He also began the church of Rochester from the foundations. He honestly finished that which was begun, and adorned it with many and decent ornaments. Above all, he instituted there the holy religion of monks.'

Since Gundulf was both a monk and a distinguished architect, it is clear that he was chosen to be bishop to superintend the introduction of these changes. Such a position of dependence could be neither permanent nor peaceful, and by the twelfth century, though the archbishop still nominated in the case of a vacancy, there was a formal election of his nominee on the part of the chapter. Naturally this caused disputes, in which it appears that not only the archbishops but the monks of Christ Church, Canterbury, were eager to assert their rights over Rochester. They claimed, *e.g.*, that on the death of a bishop his pastoral staff should be carried to Canterbury Cathedral, and kept there until the new bishop had been consecrated. On one occasion, at least, the monks of Rochester evaded meeting the claim by burying the staff in the coffin of the bishop.

After the dispute concerning the choice of Richard of Wendover in 1235, in which the monks of Rochester won, the part played by the archbishop in the elections amounted only to a formal assertion of a right which had ceased to exist in fact. However, apart from such differences, the archbishops were always zealous for the rights of Rochester. The Bishop of Rochester to this day remains provincial chaplain of Canterbury, an office he held from at least the twelfth century : from the thirteenth he was also the Primate's cross-bearer.

The temporalities of the see were assessed in the *Taxatio* of 1291 at £143, 12s. 3d., and the spiritualities at £46, 13s. 4d., which by Henry VI.'s reign had increased to £116. 13s. 4d. In the *Valor Ecclesiasticus* (1534) it was worth £369, 18s. 10½d. Ecton (1711) gives the value as £358, 4s. 9½d. The Act of 1905 provided that the income should be £4000, and that the sum of £15,000 should be set aside from the proceeds of the sale of Addington 'for the provision and maintenance of a residence for the Bishop of Rochester.'

Rochester has specially suffered in the matter of frequent alterations in its diocesan boundaries, which have been changed without any regard to antiquity or history, and this venerable diocese has been more than once treated as the dumping-ground for territory that no one else desired to possess.

1. From 604-1846 the diocese consisted of the western part of Kent, which has been thought to have been a separate sub-kingdom. Towards the end of the thirteenth century the original diocese of Rochester was subdivided into the rural deaneries of Rochester, Dartford, Malling, and Shoreham. Shoreham was a peculiar of Canterbury.

2. In 1846 the deaneries of Dartford, Malling, and Shoreham were transferred to Canterbury, and the diocese of Rochester was made to include the deanery of Rochester

(including the present deaneries of Cobham and Gravesend) and the counties of Hertford and Essex (with the exception of Barking, East Ham, West Ham, Little Ilford, Low Leyton, Walthamstow, Wanstead, Woodford, and Chingford).

3. From 1867-1877 the diocese comprised the deaneries of Rochester, Greenwich, and Woolwich in Kent, and the entire counties of Essex and Hertford.

4. In 1877 Essex and Hertford became the diocese of St. Albans (*q.v.*), and the Parliamentary divisions of East and Mid-Surrey, *i.e.* South London, were added to Rochester.

5. In 1905 the diocese of Southwark (*q.v.*) was created. This comprised East and Mid-Surrey, as well as that part of West Kent which is included in the county of London. With this latter exception Rochester received back its original territory, and its boundaries were once more what they had been for the first twelve hundred years of its existence. The population is 497,434.

The diocese is now divided into two archdeaconries : Rochester (occurs, 1089) and Tonbridge (created, 1906).

LIST OF BISHOPS

1. Justus, 604 ; tr. to Canterbury, 624.
2. Romanus, 624.
3. Paulinus, St. (*q.v.*), 633.
4. Ithamar, 644.   5. Damian, 655.
6. Putta, 669 ; tr. to Hereford. 676.
7. Cuichelm, 676.   8. Gebmund, 678.
9. Tobias, 693.
10. Eadulf, or Aldful, 727.
11. Dunn, or Dunno, 741.
12. Eardulf, 747.   13. Diora, before 775.
14. Weremund I., before 785.
15. Beornod, or Beormund, about 803.
16. Tatnoth, 844.
17. Bedenoth, or Badenoth.
18. Weremund II., before 860.
19. Cuthwulf, 868.
20. Swithulf, or Swithwulf, 880.
21. Ceolmund, 897.   23. Burrhric, 934.
22. Cyneferth, 926.   24. Aelfstan, 955.
25. Godwine I., 995.
26. Godwine II., 1046.
27. Siward, 1058.   28. Arnost, 1076.
29. Gundulf, 1077 ; a monk of Bec. ; architect of the first Norman cathedral, of the keep of Rochester Castle, and of the White Tower of London : d. 1108.
30. Ralph d'Escures, 1108 ; tr. to Canterbury. 1114.
31. Ernulf, 1115 ;   Prior of Canterbury ; Abbot of Peterborough ; made many additions to the cathedral ; compiler of *Textus Roffensis*; d. 1124.

32. John, 1125; Archdeacon of Canterbury; d. 1137.
33. John de Seez, 1137; d. 1142.
34. Ascelin, 1142; Prior of Dover; engaged in controversy with the monks; d. 1148.
35. Walter, 1148; Archdeacon of Canterbury; brother of Archbishop Theodore; d. 1182.
36. Waleran, 1182; Archdeacon of Bayeux; elected by the chapter; d. 1184.
37. Gilbert Glanville, 1185; treated the monks harshly, and excommunicated King John; d. 1214.
38. Benedict de Sansetun, 1215; freely elected by the chapter; d. 1226.
39. Henry Sandford, 1227; Archdeacon of Canterbury; the existing choir first used; d. 1235.
40. Richard Wendover, or Wendene, 1238; d. 1250.
41. Laurence of St. Martin, 1251; under him St. William of Perth was canonised— a Scottish baker murdered on pilgrimage near Rochester; the gifts at his shrine paid for the building of the choir; d. 1274.
42. Walter of Merton, 1274; founder of Merton College, Oxford; Chancellor of England; d. 1277.
43. John Bradfield, 1278; d. 1283.
44. Thomas Inguldsthorpe, 1283; d. 1291.
45. Thomas of Wouldham, 1292; d. 1317.
46. Haymo Heath, or Hythe, 1319 (P.); built a central tower and spire of the cathedral; d. 1352.
47. John Sheppey, 1353 (P.); Prior of Rochester; Chancellor of England; d. 1360.
48. William Whittlesey, 1362 (P.); tr. to Worcester, 1369.
49. Thomas Trilleck, 1364 (P.); Dean of St. Paul's; d. 1372.
50. Thomas Brinton, 1373 (P.); d. 1389.
51. William Bottlesham, 1389; tr. (P.) from Llandaff; d. 1400.
52. John Bottlesham, 1400; d. 1404.
53. Richard Yonge, 1404; tr. (P.) from Bangor; d. 1418.
54. John Kempe, 1419; (P.) tr. to London, 1422.
55. John Langdon, 1422 (P.); d. 1434.
56. Thomas Brown, 1435 (P.); Dean of Salisbury; tr. to Norwich, 1436.
57. William Wells, or Wellys, 1437 (P.); d. 1444.
58. John Lowe, 1444; tr. (P.) from St. Asaph; d. 1467.
59. Thomas Scott de Rotherham, 1468; tr. to Lincoln, 1472.

60. John Alcock, 1472; Dean of Westminster; tr. to Worcester, 1476.
61. John Russell, 1476 (P.); tr. to Lincoln, 1480.
62. Edmund Audley, 1480; tr. to Hereford, 1492.
63. Thomas Savage, 1493; (P.) Dean of Westminster; tr. to London, 1496.
64. Richard Fitzjames, 1497; tr. to Chichester, 1503.
65. John Fisher (*q.v.*), 1504 (P.); d. 1535.
66. John Hilsey, 1535; author of a Primer; a supporter of T. Cromwell; d. 1539.
67. Nicholas Heath (*q.v.*), 1540.
68. Henry Holbeach, or Holbeche, 1544; tr. from Bristol; tr. to Lincoln, 1547.
69. Nicholas Ridley (*q.v.*), 1547; tr. to London, 1550.
70. John Poynet (*q.v.*), 1550; tr. to Winchester, 1551.
71. John Scory, 1551; tr. to Chichester, 1552.
72. Maurice Griffin, 1554 (P.); d. 1558.
73. Edmund Guest (*q.v.*), 1560; tr. to Salisbury, 1571.
74. Edmund Freke, 1572; tr. to Norwich, 1575.
75. John Piers, 1576; tr. to Salisbury, 1577.
76. John Yonge, 1578; d. 1605.
77. William Barlow, 1605; tr. to Lincoln, 1608.
78. Richard Neile, 1608; Dean of Westminster; tr. to Lichfield, 1610.
79. John Buckeridge, 1611; tr. to Ely, 1628.
80. Walter Curll, 1628; tr. to Bath and Wells, 1629.
81. John Bowle, 1630; d. 1637.
82. John Warner, 1638; d. 1666.
83. John Dolben, 1666; tr. to York, 1683.
84. Francis Turner, 1683; tr. to Ely, 1684; one of the Seven Bishops (*q.v.*).
85. Thomas Sprat, 1684; man of letters, tolerant; sat on James II.'s Ecclesiastical Commission, but joined in crowning William and Mary; held the deanery of Westminster with the bishopric, as did the next six bishops; d. 1713.
86. Francis Atterbury (*q.v.*), 1713; depr. 1723.
87. Samuel Bradford, 1723; tr. from Carlisle; d. 1731.
88. Joseph Wilcocks, 1731; tr. from Gloucester; d. 1756.
89. Zachary Pearce, 1756; tr. from Bangor; a classical scholar; d. 1774.
90. John Thomas, 1774; d. 1793.
91. Samuel Horsley, 1793; tr. from St. David's; tr. to St. Asaph, 1802.

92. Thomas Dampier, 1802; Dean of Rochester; tr. to Ely, 1808.
93. Walter King, 1809; d. 1827.
94. Hugh Percy, 1827; tr. to Carlisle. 1827.
95. Lord George Murray, 1827; tr. from Sodor and Man; the last bishop to wear his wig in the House of Lords; d. 1860.
96. Joseph Cotton Wigram, 1860; d. 1867.
97. Thomas Legh Claughton, 1867; tr. to St. Albans, 1877, which see he largely helped to found.
98. Anthony Wilson Thorold, 1877; tr. to Winchester, 1890.
99. Randall Thomas Davidson, 1891; tr. to Winchester, 1895.
100. Edward Stuart Talbot, 1895; Warden of Keble College, Oxford; Vicar of Leeds; tr. to Southwark, 1905, which see he helped to found.
101. John Reginald Harmer, 1905; tr. from Adelaide. [E. M. B.]

Pearman, *Dio. Hist.*; W. H. St. John Hope, *Cathedral Church and Monastery of St. Andrew at Rochester.*

ROGER LE POER, d. (1139), Bishop of Salisbury, was at first a poor priest of Caen, who in the time of William Rufus commended himself to the future Henry I. by the celerity with which he said Mass. Taken into the prince's household, he proved a loyal servant in adversity; and such was his native shrewdness that, although illiterate, he became a confidential minister. Soon after the accession of Henry to the English throne Roger was appointed Chancellor (1101) in succession to William Gifford. Next year he was nominated to the see of Salisbury (September 1102). His canonical election followed in 1103; but Anselm (*q.v.*) refused to consecrate him on the ground that he had accepted investiture (*q.v.*) from the King's hands. Roger remained a bishop-elect until the King had adjusted his differences with Anselm and Paschal II. (1107). Immediately afterwards he was consecrated by Anselm. On being elected to Salisbury, Roger had resigned the chancellorship; but within the next six years he accepted the more onerous office of Chief Justiciar. In this capacity he was *secundus a rege.* He presided over the royal court of justice, and acted as regent of England when Henry was absent in Normandy. For some years he added to his other duties the supervision of the exchequer. His knowledge of finance was unrivalled, and he appears to have placed the fiscal system

of the kingdom on a sounder basis by his close attention to detail. Such activities were inconsistent with the ordinary standard of episcopal duty. But Roger was encouraged by Anselm, and even by the Pope, to continue in a position where he could render eminent services to the Church. As a royal lieutenant, the justiciar seems to have served his master honestly. He was trusted by Henry I., who heaped estates and preferments upon him. But he took presents without scruple from all who had business with him. As a bishop he was little to be commended. He heard Mass with regularity, and he rebuilt his cathedral. But he was grasping and ostentatious. He lived openly with a concubine, and acknowledged the son whom she bore to him. He used his influence with the King to obtain for his nephews, Alexander and Nigel, the rich sees of Lincoln and Ely. On the death of Henry I. (1135) Roger declared for Stephen, in spite of the fact that he had already sworn allegiance to the Empress Matilda (1126). Matilda's Angevin marriage was unpopular in England, and Roger affirmed that he considered himself released from his oath when she was given to a foreign husband. But he drove a profitable bargain with Stephen, who could not dispense with his assistance. His son, Roger le Poer, became chancellor; the treasury was given to Nigel of Ely; and Roger received for himself the royal borough of Malmesbury. He held no definite offices, but behaved as though still justiciar, and irritated the King's followers by his arrogance. He and his kinsmen were soon accused of conspiring in favour of the Empress—a charge to which some colour was lent by the fact that they were strengthening the defences and adding to the garrisons of their castles. Stephen accordingly arrested the old bishop, his son, and Nigel of Ely, and demanded the surrender of their castles as the price of their release. These terms were accepted, but not until Stephen had threatened to hang the Chancellor before the walls of Devizes Castle, into which Bishop Alexander had thrown himself. Alexander lost his temporalities, but the rest of the family suffered no further punishment. Their cause was taken up by the legatine council of Winchester (1139). Stephen attempted to meet the charge of sacrilege by stating his grievances against Roger; but Stephen finally defied the council, and appealed to Rome against its decisions. This was the beginning of his ruin: Bishop Roger was shortly to be avenged by the Empress and the offended legate, Henry of Blois (*q.v.*). But Roger died at the end of

1139, worn out by chagrin and the shock of his disgrace. **[H. W. C. D.]**

Stubbs, *C.H.*, vol. i.; Norgate, *Eng. under the Angevin Kings*; J. H. Round, *Geoffrey de Mandeville*; H. W. C. Davis, *Eng. under the Normans and Angevins*.

ROGERS, John (1500 ?-1555), Protestant divine and first martyr under Mary, a native of Aston, near Birmingham, was educated at Pembroke Hall, Cambridge, and became Rector of Holy Trinity in the City of London, 1532. In 1536 he resigned, and became chaplain to a company of Merchant Venturers at Antwerp. There he met Tyndale (*q.v.*), and became a convert to the new views. Before his arrest in 1535 Tyndale seems to have handed over to him his incomplete translation of the Old Testament, which Rogers prepared for the press, completing the Old Testament by adding the rendering of Miles Coverdale (*q.v.*) when Tyndale's stopped, added Tyndale's own translation of the New Testament already published, and a preface, marginal notes, and calendar by himself, and a list of 'commune places' in a table of contents, which included most of the passages which were supposed to confute Roman doctrine.

The Bible was dedicated to Henry VIII. and printed at Antwerp in 1537; fifteen hundred copies were sent to England to be sold by permission. The translator's name was given as Thomas Matthew—Tyndale's fate having taught a lesson of prudence to translators and editors. While at Antwerp he married, 'knowing the Scriptures and that unlawful vows may lawfully be broken,' and soon afterwards became head of a Protestant community in Saxony.

On the accession of Edward VI. he returned to England, and was presented to the rectory of St. Margaret Moyses, the vicarage of St. Sepulchre in London, the prebend of St. Pancras with the rectory of Chigwell, and was afterwards made Divinity Lecturer at St. Paul's. According to Foxe, he refused to intercede with Cranmer to save the crazy Anabaptist Joan Bocher from burning, remarking that it was a 'gentle punishment.'

After the death of Edward he preached a sermon at Paul's Cross, warning the people to beware of pestilent popery, idolatry, and superstition, for which he was called to account before the Council. Though dismissed at the time he was soon brought before the Council again, and commanded to keep his house, whence he was removed to Newgate, January 1554. While there he drew up with Hooper (*q.v.*), Bradford, and others a document professing the extremest form of Protestant doctrine. After further examinations before the Council he was condemned by a commission presided over by Gardiner (*q.v.*) at St. Saviour's, Southwark.

He asked for permission to see his wife before he died, but it was refused. He is said to have met her with his eleven children on his way to execution. He refused a pardon at the stake, and was burnt at Smithfield, 4th February 1555. The family of Frederic Rogers, afterwards Lord Blachford, claims descent from him. **[C. P. S. C.]**

Foxe, *Acts and Monuments*; Strype, *Memorials*.

ROLLE, Richard, of Hampole (1290-1349). The only authentic account of this, the earliest English mystical writer known to have written in the vernacular, comes from the very unusual source of an Office compiled for use after his canonisation, which, however, never took place. This shows that Richard was born near Pickering in Yorkshire, and was sent to Oxford by an ecclesiastical patron. When he was nineteen he experienced so overwhelming a sense of sin, and desire for complete spiritual surrender, that he left the University, where the intellectual revival from Paris was in full force, under the purely scholastic influence of Duns Scotus (*q.v.*). The ardent and contemplative spirit of Richard Rolle reacted against the subtleties of the schools, so often without either practical or devotional issue; and sent him, having begged tunics and a hood from his sister, to embrace the life of a hermit. John of Dalton, father of an Oxford friend, granted him a cell on his estate at Topcliffe, and supplied his few wants. Persecution obliged him to wander, till he became chaplain to the Cistercian nunnery of Hampole, near Doncaster, where he died. His influence was very wide, and his numerous writings were known to a large number of followers, including Walter Hilton, and later, to John Wyclif (*q.v.*). Even in life his reputation for holiness was almost as great as after death, when miracles were alleged to have been worked at his grave. *The Form of Perfect Living* is his best known work. He also wrote little treatises on *Our Daily Work*, on *Prayer*, on *Grace*, together with Meditations, Epistles, and Poems. The treatise known as *The Prick of Conscience*, for long ascribed to him, has lately been shown to bear no trace whatever of his style or his fervent ecstatic manner of thought. **[E. C. G.]**

Works; Horstman, *Richard Rolle of Hampole*, Radcliffe College Monographs, No. 15; R. H. Benson, *A Book of the Love of Jesus*.

ROMAN CATHOLICS. Roman Catholic is the official title in England of the body of Christians which is in communion with Rome. They themselves prefer to be called simply 'Catholics,' because they are not yet able to see how it is possible to be catholic without being in communion with Rome. The English Church, or *Ecclesia Anglicana*, from the time of its foundation by St. Augustine (*q.v.*) acknowledged the current claims of the papacy, and, as they grew, it continued to do so down till the sixteenth century. The Celtic Christianity, which had grown up in a condition of much greater detachment from Rome, had been defeated on this point at the Council of Whitby in 664 by King Oswy's (*q.v.*) approval of a somewhat risky argument of St. Wilfrid (*q.v.*). Thenceforward the English Church was Roman in the sense that it was in communion with Rome, but its title was *Ecclesia Anglicana*, or English Church.

In the sixteenth century it broke from Rome under the influence of the revival of learning and a renewed study of the Bible and patristic literature. Henry VIII.'s (*q.v.*) personal quarrel with the Pope facilitated this at the time, just as Mary's (*q.v.*) Spanish feeling facilitated the reconciliation of her day. But when the breach was renewed under Elizabeth it became necessary to find some name for those who, finding that they could not by the Pope's direction be in communion both with Rome and with the English Church, elected to adhere to the former. It was a new situation, and a new nomenclature was required. In practice the contemporary name soon came to be 'Recusant' (where it was not a mere quarrelsome nickname such as 'Papist'), that is, a person who refuses to attend the English services. Queen Mary's first proclamation (1553) bade her subjects 'live together in quiet sort, and Christian charity, leaving those new-found devilish terms of papist and heretic and such like.' There had already been some sparring as to the right to the title 'Catholic,' for the reformers claimed to be the true Catholics on the ground of their adherence to Biblical and patristic doctrines; but it was in Elizabethan controversy that the term 'Roman' was adopted as the qualifying adjective suitable to 'Recusant' Catholics. The accurate antithesis to Roman Catholics was 'Protestant Catholics,' and this phrase was used for a time by controversialists of the English Church to describe their own position. Unfortunately the bitterness that prevailed on both sides spoilt the nomenclature, and tended to popularise on the one side the terms Protestant (as a noun not an adjective) and papist, and on the other side Catholic and heretic. But in less heated areas the name Roman Catholic won its way as being accurate and conciliatory; for the Recusants never objected to the adjective Roman in itself, and it is only in recent days that they have objected to its use in conjunction with the term Catholic. In numberless cases, when they have wished to be conciliatory, they have used the term Roman Catholic of themselves.

The Act of Supremacy, 1559 (1 Eliz. c. 1), compelled all office-holders in Church and State to abjure all foreign ecclesiastical jurisdiction, and laid heavy penalties on all who maintained such jurisdiction. In 1563 the offence was expressly defined as maintaining the authority of the Bishop of Rome or of his see, and was subjected to the penalties of *praemunire* (*q.v.*) (5 Eliz. c. 1). In 1571 bringing in or being in possession of Bulls or other instruments from Rome was made treason (13 Eliz. c. 2). This was in answer to 'that roaring Bull,' *Regnans in excelsis* (1570), in which Pius V. excommunicated and deposed the Queen. In 1581 to say or hear Mass was made punishable by fine and imprisonment (23 Eliz. c. 1). In 1584 Jesuits and seminary priests were ordered to leave the realm or suffer the penalties of treason (27 Eliz. c. 2). And in 1593 all Recusants were put under severe restrictions (35 Eliz. c. 2). Under these cruel persecution laws the Recusants were prevented from forming into any organisation; they carried on no episcopal succession, and it was not until 1568 that they founded seminaries abroad at Douai and elsewhere in order to keep up a supply of clergy to minister in secret to their adherents in England, and missioners to work for the reconversion of the country. Some organisation began in 1598 with the appointment of an archpriest; but internal quarrels marred the work, and all proposals for re-establishing an episcopal government were defeated, perhaps by Jesuit influence. It was not until 1623 that a bishop was appointed for England.

After the Gunpowder Plot still harsher restrictions were placed on Recusants, including the necessity of receiving communion in the English Church thrice a year (3 Jac. I. cc. 4-5). The weight of persecution pressed heavily through the greater part of the seventeenth century in spite of the efforts of Charles II. and James II. to lighten it. In 1678 they were prohibited from sitting in either House of Parliament (30 Car. II. st. 2). After the Revolution Roman priests saying Mass or keeping school were made liable to imprisonment for life. And all papists were made incapable of purchasing lands, or even, unless they took the oaths of allegiance and supremacy, of inheriting them (1700, 11 Will. III. c. 4). The repeal of these provisions in 1778 (18 Geo. III. c. 60) led to the ' Gordon Riots ' of 1780. A larger measure of toleration followed in 1791. Roman Catholics who took an oath abjuring the Pope's deposing power were freed from persecution, and the teaching professions and some others were opened to them ; and Roman Catholic worship was legalised under restrictions (31 Geo. III. c. 32). By the Roman Catholic Relief Act, 1829 (10 Geo. IV. c. 7), the Declaration against Transubstantiation imposed in 1678 was abolished for some purposes, but not entirely till 1867 (30-1 Vic. c. 67). Roman Catholics were allowed to sit in Parliament and vote at elections, all restrictions on their possession of property were removed, and all offices in the state were opened to them except a few, of which the Lord Chancellorship and the Lord Lieutenancy of Ireland are the most important. By 12-13 Will. III. c. 2 the sovereign may not be a Roman Catholic nor marry one.

Until Emancipation was secured in 1829 the proper organisation of the body could hardly be effected. Since then the old system of government by vicars - apostolic has been altered by the establishment in 1850 of a new hierarchy, with an archbishopric at Westminster and a number of suffragan sees ; and further developments were announced (1912) which created three provinces, with archbishops at Liverpool and Birmingham. The setting up of a territorial hierarchy in 1850 was at the time greatly resented by the English public, but the resentment has for the most part died down. The English Church has nothing to fear from the Roman Catholic body ; it has much to learn and much to teach ; it does not set much store either on those clergy and laity whom it accepts back from Roman Catholicism, nor on the much advertised secessions from its own numbers to the Roman obedience. In view of the present fight of Christianity against gathering foes, no less than in the hope of future reunion, it is desirable that the body should be as strong and as well organised as its relative smallness in this country allows it to be. [PAPACY AND THE ENGLISH CHURCH, REUNION.]   [W. H. F. and G. C.]

ROSE, Hugh James (1795-1838), divine, came of an ancient Scottish Jacobite family, and was educated at Uckfield and Trinity

College, Cambridge, where he won great distinctions, but missed a Fellowship. Travelling in Germany (1824-5) he became acquainted with the rationalistic theology, and on his return preached and wrote against it. Pusey (*q.v.*) replied, defending the Germans.

In 1826 Rose, as Christian Advocate at Cambridge, preached a course on ' The Commission and consequent Duties of the Clergy,' in which he insisted on the Apostolical Succession, and taught clearly the Catholic doctrine of the Christian ministry. A second edition of these sermons, called for in 1831, was justly regarded by Rose as a sign that his ' old-fashioned opinions ' were popular. In 1830 he became Rector of Hadleigh, Suffolk, where, 25th to 29th July 1833, an informal conference was held to organise a scheme for defence of the Church. Those present, besides Rose, were R. H. Froude (*q.v.*), William Palmer, a distinguished scholar, and the Honble. A. Perceval. It was agreed to fight for two points, the doctrine of the Apostolical Succession and the integrity of the Prayer Book. Rose founded in 1832 the *British Magazine*, an organ of Church principles. In 1833 he became Divinity Professor at Durham, but resigned from ill-health next year, when he became domestic chaplain to Archbishop Howley (*q.v.*). In 1836 he was made Principal of King's College, London, but his delicate health interfered with his work. He went to Italy, October 1838, and died at Florence, 22nd December.

He was a devoted friend of J. H. Newman, who thus dedicated the fourth volume of his famous *Sermons*: ' To Hugh James Rose . . . who, when hearts were failing, bade us stir up the strength that was in us, and betake ourselves to our true Mother.'

Rose at first warmly approved of the *Tracts for the Times*, though he did not write for them. Later he became critical of certain tendencies in them. By Burgon (*q.v.*) he has been held the true author of the Movement of 1833 ; a mistaken view, for Rose had neither the genius nor the power of a leader, but he was a most valuable ally, trusted by the old-fashioned and dignified High Churchmen of the day, and a man of singular holiness, and of great personal charm.   [S. L. O.]

Burgon, *Lives of Twelve Good Men* ; Newman, *Apologia*.

ROUTH, Martin Joseph (1755-1854), President of Magdalen College, Oxford, is interesting as representing the permanence of the Catholic tradition in the English Church and linking the theology of the Nonjurors (*q.v.*) and the Caroline Divines (*q.v.*) with the Oxford Movement (*q.v.*). He was the eldest of thirteen children of Peter Routh, Rector of South Elmham, Suffolk, was educated at Beccles, and entered Queen's College, Oxford, 1770; elected Demy at Magdalen, 1771; and Fellow, 1775. On his mother's side he was descended from a niece of Archbishop Laud (*q.v.*). He was ordained deacon, 1777, and priest, 1810, on accepting the rectory of Tilehurst, where he spent his Long Vacations. After holding various college offices he was elected President, 1791, succeeding Bishop Horne (*q.v.*). In 1783 his persuasions induced Dr. Samuel Seabury, who had come from the United States to secure episcopal consecration, to apply to the Scottish not to the titular Danish bishops, who had lost the Apostolical Succession. Dr. Routh used to say: ' I ventured to tell them, sir, that they would not find there what they wanted.' When the Oxford Movement began Routh was almost the only divine who was deeply read in the Fathers and the old theology. He appeared in Convocation in 1836 to protest against Hampden's appointment as Divinity Professor, and he was a friend to J. H. Newman (*q.v.*), whom he used to the last to call ' the great Newman.' He opposed the action of the Heads of Houses at Oxford in censuring Tract No. 90, and his cautious though real support was of some consequence to the Tractarians. He assisted W. Palmer in his efforts towards reunion with the Russian Church. [REUNION.] His great age prevented his taking much part in the Tractarian struggles. Newman dedicated to him in 1837 his volume on the *Via Media*. ' To M. J. Routh . . . who has been reserved to report to a forgetful generation what was the theology of their fathers, this volume is inscribed with a respectful sense of his eminent services to the Church, and with the prayer that what he witnesses to others may be his own support and protection in the day of account.' Routh died in his hundredth year, 22nd December 1854, leaving his splendid library to the University of Durham.   [S. L. O.]

Burgon, *Lives of Twelve Good Men*; *Magdalen College Register*, Old Series, vol. vii.; New Series, vol. v.

RURAL DEANS. From the beginning of the sixth century there appear in Gaul officers called *archipresbyteri*, or archpriests, who stand in the same relation to priests as archdeacons (*q.v.*) to deacons. On one side, the archpriest over the cathedral priests has developed into the dean; on another, the archpriest over the priests of part of a diocese has been robbed of most of his functions by the archdeacon, and has dwindled into a rural dean. The archpriest of the latter kind presided over one of the few baptismal churches within the diocese, and governed the clergy who ministered in the chapels, without right of baptism, that were scattered over the area committed to his charge. Such ancient English parishes as Leeds and Sheffield, containing a multitude of charges which have now developed into perpetual curacies, represent this state of the Church. In course of time these old baptismal churches lost their importance, many of the chapelries attaining equal rights with them, so that the archpriest no longer stood in solitary dignity. About the ninth century the new office of rural dean appears. The area often remained the same; in others the new district contained the whole or parts of the dominion of more than one original archpriest. But though the office of rural dean was new, the old title was often given to it, and at the present day the ecclesiastical provinces of France and Germany are divided into either rural deaneries or archpresbyteries, in what seems quite a capricious way. The office is the same, but the name varies. Among the provinces which have always used the title of rural dean is Rouen, from which the office was brought to England, probably by Archbishop Lanfranc (*q.v.*).

Incidentally it must be mentioned that the title ' archpriest ' was chosen (not as a survival but as a loan from abroad) for the head of each of four colleges of chantry priests, founded under Bishops Stapleton and Grandison in the diocese of Exeter early in the fourteenth century. They were at Haccombe, Beer Ferrers, and Whitchurch in Devonshire and at Penkivell in Cornwall. On the lower Rhine such collegiate churches were at that time often governed by archpriests, and the name may well have been borrowed thence. The archpriest was also incumbent of the church in which he and his colleagues ministered; and at Haccombe, though the other priests and the remainder of the endowment disappeared at the general suppression, the rector is still instituted to the benefice as archpriest. In the other instances even this trace of the past has vanished.

Norman attempts to introduce order into the English Church brought in the office of rural dean. Evidence for the name ' archpriest' in this sense in England is not to be found, yet ' archofficirial ' was sometimes used in Wales. The rural dean held the lowest court of ordinary jurisdiction, visiting in succession the churches of his deanery at which moral offenders were presented and punished. He also had matrimonial jurisdiction and probate of wills, both doubtless only in the case of humble folks. He inducted newly instituted clergy into their benefices, after the rule of institution was established, and levied the contribution of his clergy for national or ecclesiastical purposes. He had for official purposes a seal of his own. His courts were held every third or fourth week, and with greater solemnity once a quarter.

But in the thirteenth century the growing power of the archdeacon encroached upon the rural dean. The archdeacon was favoured by the new canon law, and the elaborate system of fees and fines that was developed under it made it worth his while to extend his jurisdiction as widely as possible. It was obviously inconvenient that two courts should be held at frequent intervals within the same area. Hence the archdeacons, in person or more often through their officials, ousted the rural deans from the presidency of their courts, and in time it came to be believed that the rural dean was simply a delegate of the archdeacon. In some districts where the powers of the archdeacon were strongest, as in the archdeaconries of Canterbury and Richmond, the nomination of rural deans actually passed into the hands of the archdeacon. Thus reduced to insignificance, the office seems almost to have disappeared before the Reformation, though the direction of Bishop Bentham of Lichfield at his visitation of 1565 (Dixon, *Hist. Ch. of Eng.*, vi. 80), that rural deans should receive presentations from the clergy against fornicators and adulterers at their quarterly courts, is a survival or revival of some importance.

Though the deaneries were retained within the dioceses for convenience of episcopal administration, the rural deans, when they survived, were merely honorary officers. The first effort for their effectual reinstatement was made by the Puritans, who wished under ruridecanal forms to introduce the presbytery. The restoration was vainly proposed at the Hampton Court Conference (*q.v.*) in 1604, and was promised by Charles II. in the Declaration of Breda, though this was one of the concessions to which Parliament refused its sanction; and it was advocated by Baxter (*q.v.*), as a voluntary and non-coercive office, in his letter to Clarendon declining the bishopric of Hereford. Seth Ward (*q.v.*) of Salisbury, an efficient bishop

and free from any sympathy with Presbyterianism, revived it under Charles II., without lasting effect. The same was done by one or two energetic bishops of the eighteenth century, such as Martin Benson of Gloucester. The revival of Church life which preceded the Oxford Movement (*q.v.*) was marked by a general resuscitation of the office. Where rural deans had died out they were instituted, where they survived they received a task to perform, and the old deaneries, often excessively large, were divided. Among the first to take this step were Bishops Kaye of Lincoln and Marsh of Peterborough. In London Bishop Blomfield (*q.v.*) created rural deans in 1844; he had already advocated the revival of the office while archdeacon. They are now universal, the last diocese to receive rural deans being Sodor and Man in 1880. It was thought necessary to obtain an Act of the island legislature for the purpose.

Now, as in the past, the appointment is in the bishop's hands, the canon law of the thirteenth century, which gave the archdeacon a certain share in the appointment to the office as well as a control over its occupant, having become inoperative. The bishop either nominates directly or instructs the clergy to choose one of their number, to whom he gives his commission. The tenure may either be permanent or for a term of years, and it is not clear that the commission does not expire with the death or removal of the bishop who gave it. The duties laid upon the rural dean vary according to the custom of the diocese, which means in practice the terms of the commission drawn up by the first bishop who revived the office, which may, or may not, have been modified by his successors. In practice the efficiency of the system depends entirely on the personality of the rural dean, who presides over a purely voluntary assemblage of clergy and churchwardens or lay delegates from the parishes. It appears to be entirely optional with each bishop whether he will retain the system which he inherits from his predecessor, and indeed whether or no he will have rural deans in his diocese. The provision in successive acts for legalising changes in the area of deaneries and archdeaconries does not, as in the latter case, necessarily assume that there will be an officer appointed to preside over the district so defined.

It remains to speak of certain deaneries which have, in effect, been archdeaconries. Of these the most noteworthy are those of the Canterbury Peculiars and of the Channel Islands. The archbishops of Canterbury had jurisdictions outside their diocese not only in the deaneries of Hadleigh, Bocking, and Stamford, which have a titular survival, but also in parts of Surrey and Sussex, which formed the deaneries of Croydon and Shoreham. The deans whom they appointed exercised wider powers than those of an archdeacon, and excluded the local archdeacon from all interference within their deanery. The Channel Islands, attached to the diocese of Winchester, 1499, though not included in any of its archdeaconries, were also subject to deans with very full powers, which in some measure they retain. The five deans of Jersey, Guernsey, Hadleigh, Bocking, and Stamford enjoy the title of 'Very Reverend,' which it has lately been decided that rural deans of the Roman communion in England may not assume. At least two of the greater abbeys of England, whose peculiar jurisdiction was not large enough to justify the title of archdeacon for its officer, had rural deans with the same archidiaconal authority. Evesham was one, and Battle, the dean of whose Peculiar now bears the title of 'Very Reverend,' though in fact he is now nothing more than incumbent of the place, was another. [E. W. W.]

RYLE, John Charles (1816-1900), first Bishop of Liverpool, was educated at Eton and Christ Church, Oxford, where he won the Craven Scholarship in 1836, and graduated First Class in Classics, 1837. Originally destined for the army, he was compelled to abandon this career through loss of fortune, and after some hesitation took holy orders, being ordained deacon in 1841 by Bishop Sumner of Winchester, who in 1843 collated him to the rectory of St. Thomas in that city. In 1844 he became Rector of Helmingham in Suffolk, and in 1861 the Bishop of Norwich collated

him to the vicarage of Stradbroke. He had now become a noted writer of popular tracts, about two hundred of which he issued in the course of fifty years. Some weightier writings also engaged him. In his *Christian Leaders of the Last Century* he treated rather piously than critically some of the chief men of the Evangelical Movement; he was also responsible for seven volumes of *Expository Thoughts on the Gospels* and other works, of which *Knots Untied* is perhaps the most characteristic. He was even better known as a platform speaker than as a preacher or writer, having a fine presence, a noble voice, and a singularly genial manner. He was always frankly partisan, but was not greatly addicted to controversy. In the year 1880 he was nominated to the deanery of Salisbury, but before taking possession was appointed to the new diocese of Liverpool (*q.v.*), this being one of the last official acts of Lord Beaconsfield. His administration of the diocese was from the first a surprise to those who knew him only as a popular speaker and to those who looked for little but partisan activity; some who desired this freely expressed their disappointment. He discountenanced, after some doubt, the proposal to erect a costly cathedral, preferring to devote his energies, and the offerings of the faithful, to the provision of parish churches and of a proper maintenance for the clergy. In the last respect he left his diocese the best furnished in England. The mellowing and deepening of his own religious character through the exercise of the pastoral office was marked in his later years, when he came to be interested in the Keswick Convention and similar gatherings, of which he had formerly been suspicious, and his theology would seem to have become less hard and formal. He was thrice married. [T. A. L.]

S

SACHEVERELL, Henry (1674-1724), born at Marlborough, went to Magdalen College, Oxford, where he became Demy, Fellow, and Bursar, and took the D.D. degree in 1708. He became a noted preacher and pamphleteer, writing vigorously against Whigs, latitudemen, and dissenters. He held various preferments, including that of Chaplain of St. Saviour's, Southwark, 1705. In 1709 two sermons brought him into public fame, the second, preached at St. Paul's before the Lord Mayor on 5th November, being (on its

publication) at once taken up by the House of Commons. In it 'he played particularly and expressly upon the Bishop of Sarum' (Burnet, *q.v.*), declared that the Whigs 'formerly laboured to bring the Church into the conventicle, now they labour to bring the conventicle into the Church, which will prove its inevitable ruin,' and reflected severely on the ministry, particularly on Godolphin. The sermons were declared to be seditious libels by the Commons, and the preacher's impeachment was ordered. The proceedings soon showed how thoroughly London feeling was on Sacheverell's side. It is said that forty thousand copies of the sermon were sold, and his lodgings were surrounded by enthusiastic crowds, who escorted him to Westminster Hall, and followed Queen Anne's coach, hoping her ' Majesty was for Dr. Sacheverell.' After a trial from 27th February to 20th March 1710, in which the Whig lawyers were able to set forth their reasoned theory of the constitution, he was found guilty, but sentenced only to suspension from preaching for three years. Archbishop Sharp and other bishops had voted for his acquittal, and he became a popular hero, being received with immense enthusiasm in a sort of royal progress through the Midlands. Before his suspension was over the Tories were in power with a triumphant majority, and Queen Anne had no longer a constitutional obligation to disguise her feelings, and gave him the Crown living of St. Andrew's, Holborn. His first sermon afterwards was preached at St. Saviour's, Southwark, and sold for £100. He had but two notes on which he continued to harp—the wickedness of Whiggery and the duty of passive obedience to the Crown. He was a good Tory undoubtedly and a good churchman so far as politics went, but Hearne was probably not far wrong when he described him as ' a man of much noise but little sincerity.' He left Atterbury (q.v.), then an exile in Paris, £1000 in his will. [W. H. H.]

Bloxam, *Magdalen College Register*, vol. vi. ; Hutton, *Hist. of Eng. Ch., 1625-1714.*

ST. ALBANS, Abbey of. In the year 793 Offa, King of the Mercians, desiring to expiate the murder of Ethelbert, King of the East Angles, founded an abbey at Verulam in Hertfordshire for a hundred Benedictine monks. He first discovered the bones of Alban, the proto-martyr of Britain, to whom he dedicated his foundation, and laid them in the ruins of a third-century church which had been erected on the site of the martyrdom. He then obtained the consent of Pope Adrian I. to his plan, together with the canonisation of Alban, and special privileges, among them freedom from episcopal control, for the proposed monastery. Though he appears to have intended to build a more magnificent church, he did not carry out his design, and the abbey church which now stands is mainly the work of Paul de Caen, the first Norman abbot.

St. Albans, being a royal foundation, was the premier abbey of England until the death of Abbot Thomas de la Mare in 1396, and its

abbot occupied the highest place among mitred abbots in Parliament. In the fifteenth century, however, the pre-eminence was gradually usurped by Westminster (q.v.). Throughout the Middle Ages an almost unbroken series of chroniclers were writing at St. Albans, supplying the source of much of the history of the time. The position of the abbey on Watling Street, the main north road from London, enabled the monks to hear everything of importance that occurred in the capital, and makes their evidence of exceptional value. Of this school Mathew Paris, Rishanger, and Walsingham are the most eminent. At St. Albans also a valuable library of manuscripts was collected by Abbot Symon (1167-83), and added to by many subsequent abbots. Printing was early introduced into the abbey, where in 1480 a press was set up by John of Hertford.

The abbey was richly endowed by its numerous benefactors with landed property, distributed in all parts of England. The *Valor Ecclesiasticus* in 1536 assessed the revenue at £2102, 7s. 1¾d. But the income was largely supplemented by offerings made at the shrine of St. Alban, and the gifts of distinguished visitors who passed the night at the abbey guest-house when journeying north from London.

ABBOTS OF ST. ALBANS

The list of the pre-Conquest abbots and their dates is in part legendary.

1. Willigod ; appointed 793.
2. Eadric, 796 ; perhaps mythical.
3. Wulsige, or Valsig.
4. Vulnoth, 919-30 (Searle, *Onomasticon Anglo-Saxonicum*).
5. Aedfrid, c. 930 (Searle).
6. Ulsinus.
7. Aelfric, 969 ; became Bishop of Wilton, 989 ; Archbishop of Canterbury, 994 or 995 ; d. 1002.
8. Ealdred. 9. Eadmer.
10. Leofric, c. 995 ; d. 1006
11. Aelfric, c. 1006-c. 1050.
12. Leofstan, c. 1050-66.
13. Frederic, 1066.
14. Paul de Caen, 1077 ; nephew of Archbishop Lanfranc ; rebuilt the church ; the tower, transepts, and the east side of the nave of the present cathedral are his work ; in his time the cell of Binham in Bedfordshire was given to the monastery by Petrus de Valons, and the priory of Tynemouth was also presented by its founder, Robert Mowbray, Earl of Northumberland.

15. Richard d'Aubeny, or de Albencio, 1097. The new church built by his predecessor was dedicated on Holy Innocents' Day, 1115. The priory of Wymondham and the cell of Beaulieu in Bedfordshire were given, among other benefactions, by members of the abbot's family.

16. Geoffrey de Gorham, 1119; obtained from Henry I. a charter of liberties granting him the right of holding pleas, and cognisance of crimes previously tried in the hundred and county courts; he built the hospital of St. Julien for lepers, and also founded the nunneries of Merkyate and Sopwell.

17. Ralf de Gobion, 1146.

18. Robert de Gorham, 1151; nephew of Abbot Geoffrey; it was probably in his abbacy that Nicholas Breakspear, afterwards Pope Adrian IV. (*q.v.*), was refused admittance into the abbey on the ground of insufficiency of learning; the abbot later went to Rome, and obtained extensive privileges from the English Pope.

19. Symon, 1167; left an endowment for the maintenance of one hired scribe to be employed in the abbey's literary work.

20. Warren de Cambridge, 1183; founded the hospital of St. Mary de Pratis for leprous women; he contributed two hundred marks of silver to the ransom of Richard I.

21. John de Cella, 1195. The Early English building in the church (the four arches in the north aisle and the lower portions of the west end) is his work. During his abbacy the kingdom was placed under interdict, and services at the abbey were suspended.

22. William de Trumpington, 1214; completed the work at the west end begun by his predecessor; in his time the priory of Redbourn was dedicated to St. Amphibalus, the priest whom St. Alban was supposed to have sheltered by assuming his cloak when he was in danger of persecution. This abbot attended the Fourth Lateran Council of 1215; in 1217, during his abbacy, Mathew Paris was admitted into the fraternity.

23. John de Hertford, 1235. The abbey was placed under interdict in 1256 owing to the refusal of this abbot to pay five hundred marks to the papal collectors.

24. Roger de Norton, 1260.

25. John de Berkhampsted, 1291.

26. John de Marinis, 1302.

27. Hugh de Eversden, 1308; completed the Lady Chapel in the Decorated style, and restored the south aisle, which was partially destroyed owing to some pillars giving way; his abbacy was much troubled by quarrels with the townsmen as to the rights and jurisdiction exercised by the abbey over the borough.

28. Richard de Wallingford, 1326; was learned in mathematics and astronomy, and is famous for inventing an astronomical clock.

29. Michael de Mentmore, 1335; d. 1349 of the Black Death, as did forty-seven monks.

30. Thomas de la Mare, 1349; of the same family as Peter de la Mare, first Speaker of the House of Commons. The Peasants' Revolt of 1381 gave occasion for a renewed outbreak of troubles with the town, which was suppressed with some difficulty. John Ball, the fanatical priest, was among those hanged at St. Albans as a result of the insurrection.

31. John Moote, 1396.

32. William Heyworth, 1401.

33. John Wheathampsted, 1420; previously Prior of Gloucester College, Oxford, to which he was afterwards a lavish benefactor; he spent much of the abbey's revenue in adorning and repairing the church, and instituted a new officer, 'Master of the Works,' to supervise the building operations; he resigned in 1440 in order to avoid being implicated in the disgrace of his patron, Humphrey, Duke of Gloucester.

34. John Stoke, 1440.
John Wheathampsted; re-elected, 1451. *The Register of Wheathampsted* (in R.S.), which gives an account of his second abbacy in prose and verse, is attributed to him.

35. William Alban, 1464.

36. William Wallingford, 1476; before his election held the title of *officiarius generalis*, combining the duties of archdeacon, cellarer, bursar, forester, and sub-cellarer; his notorious misdeeds called forth a letter of admonition from Archbishop Morton; d. 1492, not 1484, as has often been stated.

37. Thomas Ramryge, 1492.

38. Thomas Wolsey (*q.v.*), 1521; held the abbey *in commendam* till his death in 1530; he appears never to have taken possession; the revenues were appropriated to his foundations at Oxford

and Ipswich, for which purpose he also dissolved the priory at Wallingford and the hospital of St. Mary de Pratis in 1529.

39. Robert Catton, 1530 ; though nominated by the King was tenacious in maintaining the rights of the abbey against the royal commissioners. In the list of signatures to the Ten Articles of 1536 his name appears before that of the Abbot of Westminster. It would seem, therefore, that the premiership had returned to St. Albans.

40. Richard Boreman, *alias* Stevenache, 1538 ; surrendered the abbey and was pensioned in 1539.

The abbey was surrendered in December 1539, and part of it was granted in 1550 to Sir Richard Lee, who reconveyed it to Richard Boreman (the last abbot) in 1551. When the refounding of the abbey was contemplated Boreman reconveyed the property to Queen Mary, December 1556. It passed into private hands under Queen Elizabeth, 1564. The Crown reserved to itself the abbey church, the Lady Chapel, and some other buildings. In 1553 Edward VI. sold the church to the mayor and burgesses to be their parish church, and at the same time the Lady Chapel was cut off to be the grammar school. The exempt jurisdiction of the abbey —exercised by its archdeacon—became an archdeaconry of the diocese of Lincoln, 1542. In 1550 this archdeaconry was transferred to the diocese of London. In 1845 it was transferred to the diocese of Rochester, and in 1877, to the newly created diocese of St. Albans (*q.v.*).

Cells and hospitals subordinate to the abbey of St. Albans :—

Priories : Beaulieu (Beds), Belvoir (Lincs), Binham (Norfolk), Hatfield Peverel (Essex), Hertford (Herts), Redbourn (Herts), Tynemouth (Northumberland), Wallingford (Berks), Wymondham (Norfolk). *Nunneries*: Merkyate (Beds), Sopwell (Herts). *Hospitals*: St. Julian, St. Mary de Pratis.

[A. L. P.]

Mathew Paris, *Chronica Majora* (ed. Luard, R.S.); *Gesta abbatum monasterii S. Albani a Thoma Walsingham* (ed. Riley, R.S.); Peter Newcome, *Hist. of the Abbey of St. Albans*, 1793 ; Dugdale, *Monasticon*, vol. ii. ; *V.C.H.*, Herts, ii.

ST. ALBANS, See of, was formed to provide for the great increase of population in the districts adjoining London by means of a rearrangement of the dioceses of Rochester, Winchester, and London. The counties of Hertford and Essex were taken from Rochester to form the new diocese, and Rochester, thus relieved, took over parts of Winchester and London. A fund was formed for the endowment of the new see by taking £500 each from the incomes of the Bishops of Winchester and Rochester, by the sale, with the Bishop of Winchester's consent, of the London house of his see, and by public subscription. The see was established by Order in Council of 30th April 1877, under the Bishopric of St. Albans Act, 1875 (38-9 Vic. c. 34). The Bill had been opposed by dissenting members of the House of Commons, who objected to any State recognition of episcopacy; but the debates produced nothing of note except Sir W. Harcourt's description of the reign of Edward VI. as ' the best days of the Church of England.' An increase of the number of bishops in the House of Lords was avoided by following the precedent of the bishopric of Manchester (*q.v.*). The see consists of the counties of Hertford and Essex, together with North Woolwich. It has a population of 1,665,319, and an acreage of 1,392,573, and is divided into the archdeaconries of Essex (first mentioned, 1142), Colchester (first mentioned, 1132), and St. Albans (founded, 1542). The abbey of St. Albans (*q.v.*) was made the cathedral church. In 1900 Letters Patent were issued appointing a dean of St. Albans, but there is as yet no recognised chapter, and the bishop is therefore appointed by Letters Patent from the Crown. The income of the see is £3200. A suffragan Bishop of Colchester was appointed in 1882, and of Barking in 1901.

1. Thomas Legh Claughton, 1877 ; tr. from Rochester on the foundation of the see ; famous as a parish priest at Kidderminster ; res. 1890 ; d. 1892.
2. John Wogan Festing, 1890 ; formerly Vicar of Ch. Ch., Albany St.; a devout High Churchman ; d. 1902.
3. Edgar Jacob, 1903 ; tr. from Newcastle.

[G. C.]

ST. ASAPH, See of, may be said to owe its origin to the monastic settlement made by St. Kentigern (Cyndeyrn) in the mid-sixth century on the banks of the Elwy, where now stands the cathedral church of the diocese. The original name of the settlement was ' Llan Elwy,' *i.e.* the monastery on the Elwy. which is still the name used in Welsh for the city and the diocese, ' St. Asaph ' not being known to occur earlier than the beginning of the twelfth century. The four Welsh cathedrals were originally monasteries of the well-known Celtic type. That they were not 'diocesan' is shown by their situation. The word *llan*, which has its congeners in all the Celtic languages, means an enclosed area — thence the monastic enclosure and all within it, and to-day a parish church as well as the village about it. [ABBEYS, WELSH.]

The story of the foundation of the monastery has been told by Jocelyn of Furness in his *Life of St. Kentigern*, written c. 1180. Kentigern, owing to hostilities, had to abandon his work at Glasgow among the Cumbrian Britons, and fled to Wales. After a brief visit to St. David he settled at Llanelwy, building his monastery of timber, *more Britonum*. When peace was restored in 573 he was recalled. There were in the monastery at the time 965 monks; of these 665 left in a body with him, leaving 300 at Llanelwy, over whom he placed his favourite disciple, St. Asaph.

Pre-Norman Wales was tribal, and its Christianity likewise tribal, and monastic. Anything like the modern diocesan episcopacy was out of the question; but its beginnings were there, as the monasteries, by their great missionary zeal, managed to get large areas under their influence. Wales owes its present diocesan and parochial organisation to the master mind of the Norman. Of 'bishops' of St. Asaph before the consecration of Gilbert by the Archbishop of Canterbury in 1143 practically nothing is known, nor are there any records of the 'see.'

The diocese was originally conterminous, for the most part, with the ancient principality of Powys, within which the great monastery was Llanelwy. It now includes the entire counties of Flint and Denbigh, and portions of those of Carnarvon, Merioneth, Montgomery, and Salop, and has an area of 1,067,583 acres and a population of 288,446. The old deanery of Cyfeiliog and Mawddwy, at the extreme end of the diocese, was exchanged in 1859 for that of Dyffryn Clwyd and Cinmerch, a detached part of Bangor, within a short distance of the city of St. Asaph. An Order in Council of 1838 prospectively united the sees of St. Asaph and Bangor with a view to the foundation of the bishopric of Manchester, but happily it was repealed.

The *Taxatio* of 1291 assessed the bishop's *Temporalia*, i.e. revenues from land, at £22, 2s. 10d., and the *Spiritualia* at £166, 13s. 4d. The *Valor* of 1535 assessed the income at £131, 11s. 6d. It was rated for first-fruits at £187, 11s. 6d. (Ecton, 1711). It was fixed by Order in Council in 1846 at £4200. Down to 1844 there was but one archdeaconry, its earliest known holder (before 1115) being styled 'Archdeacon of Powys.' It was held *in commendam* by the bishop from 1573 to 1844, when it was released and divided into the two archdeaconries of St. Asaph and Montgomery. In 1890 a third archdeaconry, that of Wrexham, was constituted. The three are endowed with a residentiary canonry of £350 a year each; and there is one other residentiary canonry. St. Asaph Cathedral, like the other Welsh cathedrals, though its customs are those of the 'Old Foundation' was wrested in 1843 into 'New Foundation' (Welsh Cathedrals Act, 6-7 Vic. c. 77). The chapter consists of the dean (dating from 1210), six prebendaries, and seven cursal canons—all appointed by the bishop, as are also the four vicars-choral. There are seventeen rural deaneries.

LIST OF BISHOPS

The supposed early bishops were :—

1. St. Kentigern, c. 560. 2. St. Asaph; native of the locality; cousin to St. Deiniol of Bangor; head of monastery, 573. 3. St. Tyssilio of Meifod; son of Prince of Powys; c. 600. 4. Renchidus, c. 800. 5. Chebur, c. 928. 6. Melanus, c. 1070.

1. Gilbert, 1143; cons. at Lambeth by Archbishop Theobald; the first bishop of the see to receive his orders from England.
2. Galfrid, or Geoffrey ab Arthur, 1152; confounded with Geoffrey of Monmouth.
3. Richard, 1154; a monk.
4. Geoffrey, 1160; a nominee of Henry II.; deserted his see, 1175.
5. Adam, 1175; fellow-student with Gerald de Barri (q.v.) at Paris, with whom he had, as bishop, a controversy re Kerry; d. at Oxford, 1181.
6. John, 1183; d. 1186.
7. Reiner I., 1186; Austin Canon of Haughmond; accompanied Archbishop Baldwin in his visitation of the diocese in 1188; d. 1224.
8. Reiner II.; apparently two of the name in succession.
9. Abraham, 1225; d. 1233.
10. Hugh, 1235; a Franciscan friar; d. 1240.
11. Howel, 1240; son of Ednyfed Fychan; during his time Wales was conquered by Henry III., and the Welsh bishops and clergy had their sees and churches so

despoiled that they were forced to beg their bread ; d. 1247 at Oxford.

12. Anian or Einion ab Meredydd, 1249 ; d. 1266.

13. John, 1267 (on the authority of Wharton).

14. Anian or Einion ab Ynyr, 1268 ; known as 'The Black Friar of Nannau' ; confessor to Edward I. in the Holy Land ; best known for his bold assertion of the rights of the Church ; d. 1293.

15. Leoline Bromfield, or Llywelyn ab Llywelyn ab Ynyr of Yale, 1293 (P.) ; bore a chief part in the resettlement of the Church after the annexation ; d. 1314.

16. Dafydd ab Bleddyn, 1315 ; d. 1352.

17. John Trevor, 1346 ; cons. at Avignon ; d. 1357.

18. Llywelyn ab Madog, 1357 (P.) ; dean, 1339-57 ; cons. at Avignon ; d. 1375.

19. William Spridlington, 1376 (P.) ; dean, 1357-76 ; d. 1382.

20. Lawrence Child, 1382 (P.) ; a Benedictine monk of Battle ; d. 1389.

21. Alexander Bache, 1390 (P.) ; a Dominican Friar ; confessor to Richard II. ; d. 1395.

22. John Trevor, 1395 (P.) ; the chapter elected Gruffin Trevor, but the Pope annulled the election and provided John Trevor ; driven from his see by Henry IV. ; was tr. to St. Andrews, Scotland, but did not obtain possession ; d. 1410.

23. Robert Lancaster, 1411 (P.) ; Abbot of Valle Crucis ; cons. at Lincoln by Archbishop Arundel ; d. 1433.

24. John Lowe, 1433 (P.) ; tr. to Rochester, 1444.

25. Reginald Pecock (q.v.), 1444 (P.) ; tr. to Chichester, 1449.

26. Thomas Knight, 1449 ; depr. 1460 for his Lancastrian politics ; reinstated, 1469 ; res. and d. 1471.

27. Richard Redman, 1471 ; restored the cathedral after it had been eighty years in ruins ; tr. to Exeter, 1495.

28. Michael Deacon, 1495 (P.) ; confessor to Henry VII. ; d. 1500.

29. Dafydd ab Ieuan ab Iorwerth, 1500 ; Abbot of Valle Crucis ; d. 1503.

30. Dafydd ab Owen, 1503 (P.) ; Abbot of Aberconwy (Maenan) ; rebuilt the palace after it had been in ruins for a hundred years ; d. 1513.

31. Edmund Birkhead, 1513 (P.) ; promoted the rebuilding of Wrexham Church ; d. 1518.

32. Henry Standish (q.v.), 1518 (P.) ; d. 1535.

33. William Barlow (q.v.), 1535 ; tr. to St. David's, 1536.

34. Robert Wharton, or Parfew, 1536 ; tried to remove the see at one time to Wrexham, at another to Denbigh ; tr. to Hereford, 1554.

35. Thomas Goldwell, 1555 (P.) ; Queen Mary appointed him in October 1558 ambassador to the papal court, and nominated him for translation to the see of Oxford, but she died before it took place, and Goldwell fled to the Continent ; d. 1582 in Rome.

36. Richard Davies (q.v.), 1560 ; was depr. by Queen Mary of his preferments in Bucks, when he went into exile in Geneva, but Elizabeth on her accession promoted him to this see ; tr. to St. David's, 1561.

37. Thomas Davies, 1561 ; distinguished for his piety and charity ; d. 1573.

38. William Hughes, 1573 ; befriended and assisted Morgan (q.v.) in his translation of Welsh Bible ; d. 1600.

39. William Morgan (q.v.), 1601 ; tr. from Llandaff ; first translator of the whole Bible into Welsh, 1588 ; d. 1604, and buried in cathedral choir.

40. Richard Parry, 1604 ; Dean of Bangor, 1599 ; editor of Authorised Version of Welsh Bible, 1620 ; d. 1623 ; buried in cathedral.

41. John Hanmer, 1624 ; d. 1629 ; buried at Selattyn.

42. John Owen, 1629 ; chaplain to Charles I. ; suffered much during the Commonwealth—deprived, imprisoned in the Tower, and fined ; d. 1651 ; buried in cathedral. See vacant for nine years.

43. George Griffith, 1660 ; wrote in defence of the Church during the Commonwealth ; drew up the Form for Adult Baptism ; d. 1666 ; buried in the choir of the cathedral.

44. Henry Glemham, 1667 ; dean of Bristol ; d. 1669 ; buried at Little Glemham.

45. Isaac Barrow, 1669 ; tr. from Sodor and Man ; d. 1680 ; buried at south side of west door of the cathedral.

46. William Lloyd, 1680 ; one of the Seven Bishops (q.v.) ; a learned prelate ; tr. to Lichfield, 1692.

47. Edward Jones, 1692 ; tr. from Cloyne ; d. 1703 ; buried in St. Margaret's, Westminster.

48. George Hooper, 1703 ; Dean of Canterbury ; tr. to Bath and Wells, 1704.

49. William Beveridge, 1704 ; 'the Reviver and Restorer of Primitive Piety' ; d. 1708 ; buried in St. Paul's Cathedral.

50. William Fleetwood, 1708; tr. to Ely, 1714.
51. John Wynne, 1715; Principal of Jesus College, Oxford; tr. to Bath and Wells, 1727.
52. Francis Hare, 1727; Dean of Worcester; tr. to Chichester, 1731.
53. Thomas Tanner, 1731; a learned antiquary; friend of Bishop Gibson (*q.v.*) and Anthony à Wood; d. at Christ Church, 1735.
54. Isaac Maddox, 1736; Dean of Wells; tr. to Worcester, 1743.
55. Samuel Lisle, 1744; Dean of Peterborough; tr. to Norwich, 1748.
56. Honble. Robert Hay Drummond, 1748; Prebendary of Westminster; tr. to Salisbury, 1761.
57. Richard Newcome, 1761; tr. from Llandaff; d. 1769; buried at Hackney.
58. Jonathan Shipley, 1769; tr. from Llandaff; d. 1787.
59. Samuel Hallifax, 1787; tr. from Gloucester (the first English bishop); d. 1790, and buried at Worksop.
60. Lewis Bagot, 1790; tr. from Norwich; d. 1802, and buried at St. Asaph.
61. Samuel Horsley, 1802; tr. from Rochester; an active bishop and a powerful and learned controversialist; regarded as the greatest prelate of his day; d. 1806.
62. William Cleaver, 1806; tr. from Bangor; d. 1815, and buried at Brasenose College, Oxford.
63. John Luxmoore, 1815; tr. from Hereford; a great offender in the matter of nepotism and plurality; d. 1830, and buried at St. Asaph.
64. William Carey, 1830; tr. from Exeter; a generous benefactor to the diocese; founded the Diocesan Church Building Society; d. 1846, and buried at St. Asaph.
65. Thomas Vowler Short, 1846; tr. from Sodor and Man; res. 1870; d. 1872 at Gresford Vicarage; buried at St. Asaph; an able administrator and liberal benefactor of elementary education.
66. Joshua Hughes, 1870; first Welshman cons. to the see since Bishop Wynne in 1715; founded the Diocesan Church Extension and Board of Education Societies; d. 1889 at Crieff, N.B., and buried at St. Asaph.
67. Alfred George Edwards, 1889; Warden of Llandovery College, 1875-85.

[J. F.]

Thomas, *Hist. of the Dio. of St. Asaph*; Stubbs, *Registr. Sacr.*; Le Neve, *Fasti.*

ST. DAVID'S, See of. At the end of the fifth century the Cymry under Cunedda and his sons burst into Wales, and their coming was at once followed by the Age of the Saints, the most important being Dewi (David), grandson of Ceredig, one of Cunedda's sons. Little certain can be winnowed from the legends that have gathered round his name, but we know that he founded his house—Tyddewi—on the banks of the River Alun, and this became the mother church of Dyfed, and ultimately the ecclesiastical centre of South-West Wales. In the tenth century there were seven bishops' houses—Esgoptai—in Dyfed. Owing to the saintliness of its founder, to its reputation as a centre of education—it was from St. David's that Alfred (*q.v.*) summoned Asser—and to the connection between the bishop and the civil power, the influence and strength of St. David's grew till it became conterminous with the kingdom of Deheubarth, which as it spread brought under the control of St. David's the district between the Towy and the Tawe, modern Breconshire, and the two outlying portions of Ystradyw and Ewias. After a period of isolation following the rejection of Augustine's (*q.v.*) somewhat haughty overtures, the diocese adopted the Roman tonsure in 768, and gradually fell into line in other matters. At first its churches were dedicated to Welsh saints (in many cases their founders), but in the eighth century there were many dedications to St. Michael, as in the twelfth century to St. Mary. The visit of William the Conqueror to St. David's and the invasions of the Lords Marcher witnessed the growth of Norman power, which in ecclesiastical affairs was illustrated by the suspension of Bishop Wilfrid and his subsequent restoration by Anselm (*q.v.*). In 1115 the chapter was forced to elect Bernard, an important step in the Normanising of the Church. Yet his episcopate witnessed the canonisation of St. David. The thirteenth century saw a great increase of the power of the Welsh princes and three Welshmen as bishops of the see, while the period from the death of Llywelyn in 1282 to that of Glyndwr in 1415 was marked by ten bishops, seven of whom held high offices of state; seven, too, remained bishops of the see to the time of their death—a proof that the see was not a mere stepping-stone to promotion. Yet it was poorly endowed; the temporalities of the bishop were assessed for the *Taxatio* of 1291 at £104, and he also received £20 of the capitular income; in 1377 the temporalities were vested in the chapter at £190 during a vacancy; under Henry VI.

the spiritualities amounted to £33, 6s. 8d. The century prior to the Reformation was marked by the increased influence of the papacy and by a demoralisation that affected all classes, including clergy, monks, and friars. Translation of bishops was frequent, and there was an increasing number of absentees. The Reformation does not seem to have brought with it any sudden doctrinal or ceremonial change, but the adoption of the vernacular language created a difficulty, which did not exist in England ; the rural districts, except parts of Radnor and South Pembroke, were almost entirely Welsh, but the towns were English, and there were scattered monoglot minorities. At the time Wales suffered from a variety of dialects, a defect that was remedied by the publication of the Welsh Bible. In 1546 a Welsh manual containing the Creed, the Lord's Prayer, and the Commandments was published, probably at the expense of Sir John Price of Brecon ; in 1563 the Act for the translation of the Welsh Bible and Prayer Book was passed (5 Eliz. c. 28) ; and in 1567 the New Testament was produced by the labours at Abergwili of Bishop Richard Davies (*q.v.*) and William Salesbury (*q.v.*), assisted by Huet, the precentor of St. David's. In 1588 Bishop Morgan's Bible was published, the first Lesson having meanwhile been read in English. Financially the Reformation was most disastrous to this diocese ; the parochial incumbents do not now receive half the tithe, even allowing for that which has since been recovered. The total income of the clergy, including the bishop and chapter, was rated in the *Valor Ecclesiasticus* (*q.v.*) at £3320 ; and this had to suffice for three hundred and seventeen churches and one hundred and thirty-one chapels of ease. The bishopric was rated in the *Valor* at £457, and a little later Strype (*q.v.*) valued it at £253. Ecton (1711) gives the value as £426, 2s. 1d. The decline was probably due to alienation of estates, to the abolition of the profitable *regalia*, which accrued to the bishop as a Lord Marcher, and to a vicious system of leasing. Though attempts were made by the Tudors to set up a Welsh episcopate, the poverty of the see was fatal to the policy ; of forty bishops from 1505 to 1874 only five were Welsh, and twenty were translated to other sees. Bishop Barlow (*q.v.*), 1536, an ardent reformer, alienated Lamphey to Richard Devereux, stripped the lead off the palace roof, and tried to remove the see to Carmarthen. The suppression of the monasteries deprived the diocese of all educational institutions, and the establishment of a grammar school at Carmarthen by letters patent in 1576 was but a poor substitute. Little was heard of Nonconformity, though John Penry [MARPRELATE CONTROVERSY] was a native of the diocese. Soon after the outbreak of the Great Rebellion Puritanism was fostered by the efforts of Vavasor Powell of Radnorshire, and in 1650 the Act for the better propagation of the Gospel in Wales empowered a commission of seventy-one to eject clergy 'guilty of any delinquency, scandal, malignancy, or non-residency,' to supply ' godly and painful men,' certified by twenty-five ministers, and to appropriate the revenues of all parochial livings, rendered vacant in these or other ways. It has been calculated that some one hundred and eighty livings in this diocese were in their hands, and that at least one hundred and forty of the clergy were ejected and replaced by a few itinerant missioners or ' Gospel Postillions.' So great was the scandal that in 1654 Cromwell by ordinance appointed a new commission to inquire into the proceedings of their predecessors. Under the Act of Uniformity (*q.v.*), 1662, thirty ministers were ejected, while ten suspended ultimately conformed. In 1672 only thirty meeting-houses were licensed in the diocese. The strife of the seventeenth century was followed by reaction and torpor in the eighteenth, and quite early Bishop Bull commented on the insufficiency of the clergy, and pointed to lay impropriation of tithe as the main cause of the defect, as did Dr. Erasmus Sanders in his vivid *View of the Diocese*, 1721. As the result of a dispute the archdeacon's functions were suspended and not restored till 1837 ; but rural deans were reinstituted by Bishop Horsley (1788-94), and that there was real spiritual life is proved by the work of Griffith Jones, Rector of Llanddowror, the founder of the Circulating Schools, which in twenty-four years taught one hundred and fifty thousand people, nearly one-third of the population of Wales, to read their Welsh Bibles. His great work paved the way for the rise of Calvinistic Methodism, which can claim Howell Harris of Talgarth as its founder. though more important were Daniel Rowland, the curate of Llangeitho ; William Williams of Panty-celyn ; Peter Williams, the Bible commentator ; and Thomas Charles—all natives of this diocese, and all in holy orders except Harris. Though the first association was held at Watford in Glamorgan in 1743, the Methodists did not break away from the Church till some time after the deaths of its founders, and until the influence of the ' exhorters ' became predominant. In 1811 the congregations of one hundred and twenty-eight 'societies' in this diocese seceded; the shock to the Church was very great, and for the moment seemed fatal. But a revival of Church life followed. Since 1800 only one bishop of the see has been translated; the special requirements of the see have received greater consideration; since 1874 a Welsh-speaking episcopate has been restored, after Bishop Thirlwall (*q.v.*) prepared the way by himself learning Welsh; provision for the better education of the clergy was made by the foundation of St. David's College, Lampeter, by Bishop Burgess in 1822. Since 1831 the number of churches and mission-rooms has grown from four hundred and forty-eight to six hundred and seventy-two; the resident incumbents have more than doubled, as has the number of parsonages, while the endowment of the incumbents has been more than doubled during the last century; and with this material progress there has been a quickening of religious life. The area of the diocese was reduced by the transfer of some small portions to Llandaff in 1844 and 1846, of two parishes in the county of Montgomery to the diocese of St. Asaph in 1849, and of its territory in Hereford to that diocese in 1852. It now comprises the counties of Pembroke, Cardigan, and Carmarthen, nearly the whole of Radnor and Brecon, and part of Glamorgan. It contains 2,267,900 acres, and has a population of 509,943. In 1910 the net income from endowments amounted to £94,200 (including grants for curates to the amount of £4610), the bishop's stipend being £4500. The diocese is divided into four archdeaconries and twenty-nine rural deaneries. The archdeaconry of Brecon (first mentioned, *c.* 1135), with nine rural deaneries, corresponds roughly to the counties of Brecon and Radnor; the archdeaconry of Cardigan (*c.* 1137), with seven rural deaneries, includes the whole of Cardiganshire and portions of the counties of Carmarthen and Pembroke; the archdeaconry of Carmarthen (*c.* 1140), with seven rural deaneries, comprises the rest of Carmarthenshire, the western strip of Glamorganshire, and a very small portion of Pembrokeshire; the archdeaconry of St. David's (*c.* 1128), with six rural deaneries, includes what is left of Pembrokeshire. The cathedral chapter is composed of a dean, who was first appointed in 1840, four canons residentiary (under the Welsh Cathedrals Act, 1843, 5-6 Vic. c. 77), and twelve prebendaries, the first being the King. There are also five vicars-choral, one of whom is also vicar of the parish, and an organist. There has been a suffragan bishop of Swansea since 1890.

BISHOPS

Uncertain names are printed in italics.

1. David.
2. *Cynog*, or *Cynoc*.
3. *Teilo*.
4. *Ceneu*.
5. *Morfael*.
6. *Haerwnen*.
7. *Elwaed*.
8. *Gwrnwen*.
9. *Llunwerth*, or *Lendivord*.
10. *Gwrgwyst*.
11. *Gwgan*.
12. *Clydawg*.
13. *Eineon*.
14. *Elfod*.
15. *Ethelman*.
16. *Elanc*.
17. *Maelsgwyd*.
18. *Sadwrnfen*.
19. *Cadell*.
20. *Sulhaithnay*.
21. Novis, or Nobis, 840; d. 873.
22. *Idwal*.
23. Asser, friend of Alfred (*q.v.*); tr. to Sherborne.
24. *Arthwael*.
25. *Samson*.
26. *Ruelin*.
27. *Rhydderch*.
28. *Elvin*.
29. *Morbiw*.
30. Llunwerth, 944.
31. Enewrig, 944.
32. *Hubert*.
33. *Ivor*.
34. Morgeneu; murdered by Norsemen, 999.
35. *Nathan*.
36. *Jevan*.
37. *Arwystl*.
38. Morgeneu; d. 1025.
39. Hermin; d. 1040.
40. Trahaearn.
41. Joseph; d. 1063.
42. Bleiddud, 1063 to 1071 or 1072.
43. Sulien, Bishop, 1072 or 1073 to 1078.
44. Abraham, 1078; murdered by Norsemen, 1080.
    Sulien; recalled, 1080-5; res.; d. 1091.
45. Wilfrid, 1085-1115.
46. Bernard, 1115-47; 'the first Norman bishop of the see,' which he organised and developed; its metropolitan claims were asserted under him; d. 1147.
47. David Fitzgerald, 1147; d. 1176.
48. Peter de Leia, 1176; a foreigner; forced on the chapter in spite of Gerald de Barri (*q.v.*); he began to build the present cathedral church; Archbishop Baldwin, on a tour through Wales, celebrated Mass at the high altar; d. 1198.
49. Geoffrey de Hennelawe, 1203.
50. Gervase, 1215; d. 1229.
51. Anselm le Gros, 1230; d. 1247.
52. Thomas the Welshman, 1248; d. 1255.
53. Richard de Carrew, 1256; d. 1280.
54. Thomas Beeke, 1280; Lord High Treasurer; under him Archbishop Peckham (*q.v.*) visited St. David's; celebrated Mass at the high altar in the cathedral church; he was Chancellor of the University of Oxford; d. 1293.
55. David Martin, 1296; d. 1328.
56. Henry de Gower, 1328 (P.); d. 1347.
57. John Thoresby, 1347 (P.); Lord Chancellor, 1349-56; tr. to Worcester, 1349.

58. Reginald Brian, 1350 (P.); tr. to Worcester, 1352.
59. Thomas Falstaffe, 1353 (P.); d. 1361.
60. Adam Houghton, 1361 (P.); LL.D. Oxford; Lord Chancellor, 1377; d. 1389.
61. John Gilbert, 1389; tr. (P.) from Hereford; twice Lord Treasurer; d. 1397.
62. Guy de Mona, 1397 (P.); twice Keeper of Privy Seal; Lord High Treasurer; d. 1407.
63. Henry Chichele (*q.v.*), 1408 (P.); tr. to Canterbury.
64. John Catterick, 1414 (P.); tr. (P.) to Lichfield, 1415.
65. Stephen Patryngton, 1415 (P.); Provincial of the Carmelite order; tr. to Chichester, 1417.
66. Benedict Nicholl, 1418; tr. (P.) from Bangor; d. 1433.
67. Thomas Rodburne, 1433 (P.); d. 1442.
68. William Lyndwood (*q.v.*), 1442 (P.).
69. John Langton, 1447 (P.); d. 1447.
70. John de la Bere, 1447 (P.); res. 1460.
71. Robert Tully, 1460 (P.): d. 1481.
72. Richard Martyn, 1482 (P.); LL.D. Cambridge; Chancellor of Ireland, 1477; d. 1483.
73. Thomas Langton, 1483 (P.); Pembroke College, Cambridge; tr. to Salisbury, 1485.
74. Hugh Pavy, 1485 (P.); d. 1496.
75. John Morgan, 1496 (P.); LL.D. Oxford; d. 1504.
76. Robert Sherbourn, 1505 (P.); tr. to Chichester, 1508.
77. Edward Vaughan, 1509 (P.); LL.D. Cambridge; d. 1522.
78. Richard Rawlins, 1523 (P.); D.D.; Warden of Merton College, 1508, but deprived, 1521; d. 1536.
79. William Barlow (*q.v.*), 1536; tr. to Bath and Wells, 1548.
80. Robert Ferrar (*q.v.*), 1548; depr. 1554.
81. Henry Morgan, 1554 (P.); D.C.L.; previously Principal of St. Edmund Hall, Oxford; depr. 1559.
82. Thomas Young, 1560; Principal of Broadgates Hall, Oxford, 1542-6; tr. to York, 1561.
83. Richard Davies (*q.v.*), 1561; D.D. New Inn Hall, Oxford; tr. from St. Asaph; translator of the New Testament into Welsh; d. 1581.
84. Marmaduke Middleton, 1582; D.D. Oxon; tr. from Waterford; degraded, 1590; d. 1592.
85. Anthony Rudd, 1594; D.D. Trinity College, Cambridge; d. 1615.
86. Richard Milbourne, 1615; tr. to Carlisle, 1621.

87. William Laud (*q.v.*), 1621; tr. to Bath and Wells, 1626.
88. Theophilus Field, 1627; Fellow of Pembroke Hall, Cambridge; D.D. Oxon; tr. from Llandaff; impeached for bribery, 1621; tr. to Hereford, 1635.
89. Roger Mainwaring, 1636; D.D. All Souls College, Oxford; imprisoned for two sermons on 'Religion' and 'Allegiance,' preached before Charles I. in 1627; imprisoned by the Long Parliament: d. 1653.
90. William Lucy, 1660; Trinity College, Oxford; B.D. Cambridge; d. 1677.
91. William Thomas, 1678; D.D. St. John's College, Oxford; Dean of Worcester, 1665; tr. to Worcester, 1683.
92. Laurence Womack, 1683; D.D. Corpus Christi College, Cambridge; d. 1686.
93. John Lloyd, 1686; Merton College, Oxford; Principal of Jesus College, 1673; D.D., 1674; Vice-Chancellor, 1682-5; d. 1687.
94. Thomas Watson, 1687; D.D. St. John's College, Cambridge; dep. for simony, 1699.
95. George Bull, 1705. [CAROLINE DIVINES.]
96. Philip Bisse, 1710; D.D. New College, Oxford; tr. to Hereford, 1713.
97. Adam Otley, 1713; d. 1723.
98. Richard Smallbrooke, 1724; D.D. Magdalen College, Oxford; tr. to Lichfield, 1731.
99. Elias Sydall, 1731; tr. to Gloucester, 1731.
100. Nicholas Claggett, 1732; D.D. Cambridge; tr. to Exeter, 1742.
101. Edward Willes, 1743; tr. to Bath and Wells, 1743.
102. Honble. Richard Trevor, 1744; D.C.L. Queen's College, Oxford; tr. to Durham, 1752.
103. Anthony Ellis, 1752: D.D. Clare Hall, Cambridge; d. 1761.
104. Samuel Squire, 1761; St. John's College, Cambridge; d. 1766.
105. Robert Lowth, 1766; D.D. New College, Oxford; tr. to Oxford, 1766.
106. Charles Moss, 1766; M.A. Caius College, Cambridge; tr. to Bath and Wells, 1774.
107. Honble. James Yorke, 1774; tr. to Gloucester, 1779.
108. John Warren, 1779; D.D. Caius College, Cambridge; tr. to Bangor, 1783.
109. Edward Smallwell, 1783; tr. to Oxford, 1788.
110. Samuel Horsley, 1788; LL.B. Trinity Hall, Cambridge: a learned theologian and a High Churchman; tr. to Rochester, 1793.

111. William Stewart, 1794 ; D.D. St. John's College, Cambridge ; tr. to Armagh, 1800 ; d. 1822.
112. George Murray, 1800 ; D.D. New College, Oxford ; d. 1803.
113. Thomas Burgess, 1803 ; C.C.C., Oxford ; founder of St. David's College, Lampeter ; tr. to Salisbury, 1825.
114. John B. Jenkinson, 1825 ; Dean of Durham, 1827-40 ; d. 1840.
115. Connop Thirlwall (*q.v.*), 1840 ; d. 1875.
116. William Basil Jones, 1874 ; D.D. ; Fellow of Queen's and University Colleges, Oxford ; d. 1897.
117. John Owen, 1897 ; D.D. Jesus College, Oxford.   [F. M.]

W. Basil Jones and E. A. Freeman, *Hist. of St. David's*; W. L. Bevan, *Dio. Hist. of St. David's*; J. E. Lloyd, *A Hist. of Wales*; J. E. Newell, *Hist. of the Welsh Ch.*

SALESBURY, William (*c.* 1517 - *c.* 1600), who occupies a prominent place in the history of the translation of the Scriptures into Welsh, came of an old and distinguished Norman - Welsh family. The Salesburies came to Denbigh in the time of Edward I., and by wealthy alliances not only acquired great influence in the country, but also became thoroughly imbued with the Welsh sentiment. William, the most eminent of them all, was the son of Foulk Salesbury of the branch settled at Plâs Isa, near Llanrwst, in Denbighshire. He was born in the early part of the sixteenth century, about 1517 ; but, strange to say, nothing is known with certainty as to the date or place of his birth, or even the date of his death or the place of burial.

He received his University education at Oxford, where he entered at Broadgate Hall. Here he came into contact with the reforming movement, of which he became a strenuous supporter. In his *Baterie of the Pope's Botereulx*, which he subsequently published in 1550, he defends his change of mind ; indeed, all his publications, excepting one or two of a purely literary character, were designed to further the Reformation. The first of them was *Oll Synnwyr pen Kembero ygyd* ('The Sum of Cymric Wisdom'), a collection of proverbs, printed without date, but apparently in 1546, which is the second book published in the Welsh language, if not the first, in this year. In 1547 he published his English-Welsh dictionary, which was followed in 1551 by his *Kynniver llith a ban*, a translation of all the liturgical Epistles and Gospels of the Prayer Book. We next find him collaborating with Bishop

Richard Davies (*q.v.*) in the task of translating the New Testament and Prayer Book into Welsh, both of which appeared in 1567. The whole of the New Testament was Salesbury's work, with the exception of the five short epistles done by Davies, and the Book of Revelation, translated by Thomas Huet, Precentor of St. David's. This translation was the principal work of Salesbury's life. The expense of publishing the two translations was borne equally by Davies and Salesbury ; and the bond for the sum borrowed by Salesbury to meet his share is still in existence.

Salesbury's Welsh presents an uncouth appearance owing to the idea he had that words should be spelt according to their supposed etymology—as much like Latin as possible—and this artificiality about his translation militated much against its popularity. But the Renaissance in England also produced a great deal of spurious learning—the result of the perverted ingenuity of the so-called classicists.   [J. F.]

SALISBURY, See of. In 705 the West Saxon bishopric founded by Birinus (*q.v.*) was divided, a new bishopric, with its see at Sherborne, being created for the western portion, corresponding with the counties of Dorset, Somerset, and part of Wilts, also Devon and Cornwall, which, however, seem not to have been brought under the bishops of Sherborne till Alfred's reign. In 909 the creation of the dioceses of Wells [BATH AND WELLS] and Crediton [EXETER, SEE OF] limited Sherborne to Dorset ; and another new see was set up at Ramsbury, the counties of Berks and Wilts being taken out of Winchester (*q.v.*) as its territory. In 1058 Ramsbury and Sherborne were united under Herman, who in 1075 moved his see to Old Sarum in obedience to the decree of the Council of London. The diocese now comprised the counties of Dorset, Berks, and Wilts. In 1219 Bishop Richard le Poor, under sanction of a Bull from Honorius III., removed the see from the exposed and barren fortress of Old Sarum to New Sarum, or Salisbury, in the fertile valley of the Avon. In 1496 Alexander VI. transferred the Channel Islands from the see of Coutances to that of Sarum. In 1499 he again transferred them to Winchester. In 1542 Dorset was given to the newly formed see of Bristol (*q.v.*). But by Order in Council, 5th October 1836, it was restored to Sarum, together with the parish of Thorncomb in the Exeter diocese ; and the archdeaconry of Berks, including those parts of Wilts insulated therein, was transferred to Oxford (*q.v.*). By another Order, 19th July 1837, the deaneries of Cricklade and Malmesbury in Wilts were given to the see of Gloucester and Bristol. The diocese now consists of Dorset, Wilts (except these two deaneries), and a small part of Berks. It covers 1,309,617 acres, and is divided into the archdeaconries of Sarum (first mentioned, 1085), Wilts (first mentioned, 1157), and Dorset (first mentioned in twelfth century). The population is 372,188.

Since early in the thirteenth century the Bishop of Sarum has been precentor of the province of Canterbury. A Roman Catholic writer of 1608 says that 'in ancient tymes' he held the title of the Pope's Master of the Ceremonies, and acted as such when at Rome. The Chancellorship of the Garter, obtained by Bishop Beauchamp, 1475, was held by his successors till Henry VIII. took it from Campeggio (*q.v.*). It remained in lay hands, in spite of the efforts of Bishops Cotton and Davenant (*q.v.*) to recover it, till Seth Ward (*q.v.*) obtained its restoration in 1671. In 1836 it was transferred to Oxford with the archdeaconry of Berks. The mediæval bishops were assisted by numerous suffragans, and two were consecrated under the Act 26 Hen. VIII. c. 14, with the titles of Marlborough (1537) and Shaftesbury (1539). The *Taxatio* (*q.v.*) of 1291 assessed the *Temporalia* at £529, 19s. 5d. The *Spiritualia* amounted only to £2, which by Henry VI.'s reign had increased to £72; the *Valor Ecclesiasticus* estimated the income at £1367, 12s. 8d., and Ecton (1711) at £1385. 5s. The present income is £5000.

The secular canons of the original foundation at Sherborne were replaced in 999 by monks who were transferred to Sarum, 1075, though there remained an abbey at Sherborne. In 1091 Osmund (*q.v.*) reconstituted the cathedral body on the model of that of Bayeux [CATHEDRAL CHAPTERS], to consist of a dean, precentor, chancellor, and treasurer, four archdeacons, a sub-dean, subchanter or succentor, and thirty-two secular canons or prebendaries, each of whom nominated a vicar. The number of prebends (two of which have always been held by the bishop and dean respectively) has varied from time to time, and now stands at forty-five. One of them was annexed to the Regius Professorship of Civil Law at Oxford from 1617 to 1855. Late in the Middle Ages some of the prebendaries became canons residentiary; the number of these was fixed under Charles I. at six, and in 1840 at four (3-4 Vic. c. 113). The vicars-choral were incorporated by charter of Henry IV. in 1410. Lay vicars are first found in 1551. There are now four vicars-choral and seven lay vicars, one of whom is organist.

The cathedral church is in the Early English style; it was begun by Richard le Poor, 1220, and dedicated by Archbishop Boniface, 1258. The tower and spire were added in the fourteenth century.

BISHOPS OF SHERBORNE

1. St. Aldhelm (*q.v.*), 705; d. 709.
2. Forthere, 709; learned; a friend of Bede (*q.v.*); accompanied Queen Frithugyth of Wessex to Rome, 737.
3. Herewald, 736.   4. Aethelmod, *c.* 778.
5. Denefuth, 793.   6. Wigberht, *c.* 801.
7. Ealhstan, 824; a warrior; fought against the Mercians and the Danes; d. 867.
8. Heahmund, 868; killed in battle against the Danes, 871.
9. Ethelheah, 872.
10. Alfsige, or Wulfsige, 883.
11. Asser, *c.* 900; a Briton, and learned monk of St. David's [ST. DAVID'S, SEE OF]; friend, tutor, and biographer of Alfred; may have been coadjutor Bishop of Devon and Cornwall before his accession to Sherborne; d. *c.* 909.
12. Aethelweard, *c.* 910.
13. Waerstan; killed by the Danes *c.* 918.
14. Aethelbald, ? 918.
15. Sighelm, *c.* 926; d. 933.
16. Alfred, 933; d. 943.
17. Wulfsige, *c.* 943; d. 958.
18. Aelfwold, 958; d. 978.
19. Aethelsige, 978.
20. Wulfsige, 992; substituted monks for the secular canons of Sherborne, *c.* 999.
21. Aethelric, 1001. 22. Ethelsige, *c.* 1012.
23. Brihtwy, 1023.
24. Aelfwold, 1045; d. 1058.
25. Herman, 1058; removed the see to Old Sarum.

BISHOPS OF RAMSBURY

Aethelstan, 909.
Odo, *c.* 926; tr. to Canterbury, 942.
Aelfric.
Osulf, *c.* 952; d. 970.
Aelfstan, *c.* 974; d. 981.
Wulfgar, 981.
Sigeric, 985; tr. to Canterbury, 990.
Aelfric, 990; tr. to Canterbury, 995.
Brihtwold, 1005; d. 1045.
Herman, 1045.

BISHOPS OF SARUM

25. Herman; a Fleming; as Bishop of Ramsbury tried to get his see removed to the rich foundation of Malmesbury; chagrined by his failure he retired to the

monastery of St. Bertin in France, 1055; returned in 1058, and received the bishopric of Sherborne in addition to Ramsbury; removed the see to Old Sarum, 1075, where he laid the foundations of the cathedral; d. 1078.

26. Osmund, St. (*q.v.*), 1078; d. 1099. Vacancy of nearly three years.

27. Roger of Salisbury (*q.v.*); nominated, 1102; elected, 1103; cons. 1107; d. 1139.

28. Jocelin de Bohun, 1142; sought to reconcile Becket (*q.v.*) and Henry II., but was excommunicated for his share in the Constitutions of Clarendon (*q.v.*), and in 1170 suspended by Alexander III. for taking part in the coronation of Prince Henry; resigned, retired to a monastery, and d. 1184. See vacant five years.

29. Hubert Walter (*q.v.*), 1189; tr. to Canterbury, 1193.

30. Herbert le Poor, 1194; Archdeacon of Canterbury; remained at his post during the Interdict; prepared for the removal of the see; d. 1217.

31. Richard le Poor, 1217; tr. (P.) from Chichester; brother of his predecessor; removed the see to New Sarum; tr. to Durham, 1228.

32. Robert Bingham, 1229; a learned theologian; d. 1246.

33. William of York, 1247; a courtier; chaplain to Henry III.; Archdeacon of Stafford, *c.* 1230; d. 1256.

34. Giles Bridport, 1257; Dean of Wells; nominated, 1261, by Henry III. as one of the arbitrators between himself and the Barons; failed to assert visitatorial rights over the chapter; d. 1262.

35. Walter de la Wyle, 1263; d. 1271.

36. Robert Wickhampton, 1274; Dean of Salisbury; d. 1284.

37. Walter Scammell, 1284; Dean of Salisbury; d. 1286.

38. Henry Brandeston, 1287; held the see only eight months; d. 1288.

39. William de la Corner, 1289 (P.); chaplain to Pope Honorius IV.; the diocese now divided into rural deaneries; d. 1291.

40. Nicolas Longespée, 1292; son of William, Earl of Salisbury, natural son of Henry II.; the bishop's mother founded a nunnery at Lacock, and became its abbess; he was elderly, *annosus*, when elected; d. 1297.

41. Simon of Ghent, 1297; protested against the papal provision of foreigners to stalls in the cathedral; rebuked the clergy for non-residence and neglect of duty; d. 1315.

42. Roger Mortival, 1315; issued a code of Cathedral Statutes; d. 1330.

43. Robert Wyville, 1330 (P.); built the close wall with stones from the cathedral of Old Sarum; fortified the episcopal manors; d. 1375.

44. Ralph Erghum, 1375 (P.); tr. to Wells, 1388.

45. John Waltham, 1388 (P.); Keeper of the Rolls in Chancery, 1381; introduced the writ *sub poena*; Archdeacon of Richmond, 1385; Keeper of the Privy Seal, 1386; tried in vain to prevent Archbishop Courtenay from visiting his diocese, 1390; secured the right of visiting the chapter septennially; Treasurer, 1391; supporter of Richard II.; owing to his political preoccupations had two suffragans; d. 1395; buried in Westminster Abbey by desire of Richard II.

46. Richard Mitford, 1395; tr. (P.) from Chichester; partisan of Richard II.; d. 1407.

47. Nicholas Bubwith, 1407; tr. (P.) from London; tr. to Bath and Wells, 1407.

48. Robert Hallam, 1407 (P.); Archdeacon of Canterbury, 1400; Chancellor of Oxford, 1403; nominated to York by Pope Innocent VII., 1405, but not enthroned owing to the King's objections; attended Council of Pisa, 1409, with plenipotentiary power to bind the Church of England; made a Cardinal priest, 1411; attended Council of Constance, 1414, where he advocated reform and asserted the council was above the Pope; his death (1417) a blow to the cause of reform.

49. John Chandler, 1417; d. 1427.

50. Robert Neville, 1427 (P.); tr. to Durham, 1438.

51. William Aiscough, or Ayscough, 1438 (P.); confessor to Henry VI., whose marriage he solemnised; unpopular for non-residence and because he was thought responsible for Henry's misgovernment; murdered at Edington in a popular rising, just after saying Mass on St. Peter and St. Paul's Day, 1450.

52. Richard Beauchamp, 1450; tr. (P.) from Hereford; Chaplain of the Garter, 1452; superintended the building of the new chapel of St. George at Windsor, for which Edward IV. granted the Chancellorship of the Order to him and his successors, 1475; Dean of Windsor,

1478; procured the canonisation of St. Osmund, 1456; d. 1481.

53. Lionel Woodville, 1482 (P.); brother-in-law of Edward IV.; paid Pope Sixtus IV. 2250 golden florins for his appointment; supported Buckingham's rebellion, and fled to Henry Tudor on its failure; the temporalities of the see were then forfeited; d. 1484.

54. Thomas Langton, 1485; tr. (P.) from St. David's; guardian of the temporalities after Woodville's forfeiture; tr. to Winchester, 1493.

55. John Blyth, 1493 (P.); paid Pope Alexander VI. 4500 golden florins and other gifts; d. 1499; buried by his own desire beneath the confessional chair behind the high altar of the cathedral.

56. Henry Dean, 1500; tr. (P.) from Bangor, paying 6637 golden florins; tr. to Canterbury, 1501.

57. Edmund Audley, 1502; tr. (P.) from Hereford; d. 1524.

58. Lorenzo Campeggio (*q.v.*), 1524 (P.); depr. 1534.

59. Nicholas Shaxton, 1535; supported reformed views, and was favoured by Anne Boleyn; res. on the passing of the Act of the Six Articles, 1539; condemned to be burned for heresy, 1546; he recanted, and preached at the burning of Anne Askew (*q.v.*); under Mary he became suffragan to the Bishop of Ely, and sentenced Protestant martyrs; d. 1556.

60. John Salcot, or Capon, 1539; tr. from Bangor; Abbot of St. Benet's Hulme, 1517; made Abbot of Hyde for his services in the divorce of Henry VIII., who called him a 'great clerk'; surrendered Hyde, 1539; a zealous reformer under Edward VI.; sentenced Protestants to the stake under Mary; an unscrupulous time-server; d. 1557.

Meanwhile the popes had kept up an independent succession, nominating Gaspar Contarini on Campeggio's death, and in 1547 Cardinal Peto, who resigned from old age on Mary's accession. She nominated Francis Mallett, 1558, but before consecration he was set aside by Elizabeth.

61. John Jewel (*q.v.*), 1560; d. 1571.

62. Edmund Guest (*q.v.*), 1571; d. 1577.

63. John Piers, 1577; tr. from Rochester; tr. to York, 1589.

64. John Coldwell, 1691; compelled by Elizabeth and 'the wily intrigues of Sir Walter Raleigh' to impoverish the see; d. 1596.

65. Henry Cotton, 1598; father of nineteen children; d. 1615.

66. Robert Abbot, 1615; brother of Archbishop Abbot (*q.v.*); disowned by his brother for his second marriage; a learned anti-Roman controversialist; attacked Laud (*q.v.*) for supposed leaning towards Romanism; d. 1618.

67. Martin Fotherby, 1618; d. 1620.

68. Robert Townson, 1620; Dean of Westminster; d. 1621 of a fever contracted by unseasonable sitting up to study; left a widow and fifteen children to be provided for by Davenant, his brother-in-law and successor.

69. John Davenant (*q.v.*), 1621; d. 1641.

70. Brian Duppa, 1641; tr. from Chichester; tr. to Winchester, 1660.

71. Humfrey Henchman, 1660; tr. to London, 1663.

72. John Earle, or Earles, 1663; tr. from Worcester; Dean of Westminster; tutor to Charles II.; refused to sit in the Westminster Assembly; author of the famous *Microcosmographie* (1628); Walton praises his 'innocent wisdom,' 'sanctified learning,' and 'pious, peaceable and primitive temper'; d. 1665.

73. Alexander Hyde, 1665; first cousin to Edward Hyde, first Earl of Clarendon; Dean of Winchester, 1660; d. 1667.

74. Seth Ward (*q.v.*), 1667; tr. from Exeter; d. 1689.

75. Gilbert Burnet (*q.v.*), 1689; d. 1715.

76. William Talbot, 1715; tr. from Oxford; tr. to Durham, 1721.

77. Richard Willis, 1721; tr. from Gloucester; tr. to Winchester, 1732.

78. Benjamin Hoadly (*q.v.*), 1723; tr. from Hereford; tr. to Winchester, 1734.

79. Thomas Sherlock (*q.v.*), 1734; tr. from Bangor; tr. to London, 1748.

80. John Gilbert, 1748; tr. from Llandaff; tr. to York, 1757.

81. John Thomas I., 1757; tr. from Peterborough; tr. to Winchester, 1761.

82. Houble. Robert Hay Drummond, 1761; tr. from St. Asaph; tr. to York, 1761.

83. John Thomas II., 1761; tr. from Lincoln at the age of eighty; was four times married; d. 1766.

84. John Hume, 1766; tr. from Oxford; Canon of St. Paul's, 1748-60; Dean, 1758-66; ardent anti-Methodist; seems to have inspired the expulsion of the six students from St. Edmund Hall; said by Lady Huntingdon's biographer to hold it 'a crime to attract a great auditory and be blessed in the conversion of many' (Ollard, *Six Students*).

85. Shute Barrington, 1782 ; tr. from Llandaff ; tr. to Durham, 1791.
86. John Douglas, 1791 ; tr. from Carlisle ; as chaplain to the Guards present at Fontenoy, 1745 ; d. 1807.
87. John Fisher, 1807 ; tr. from Exeter ; friend and chaplain of George III. ; visited the Channel Islands under commission from North of Winchester, 1818 ; no bishop had been there since 1499 ; d. 1825.
88. Thomas Burgess, 1825 ; tr. from St. David's, where he had founded St. David's College, Lampeter ; energetic organiser and copious writer, publishing over a hundred works ; violently opposed Roman Catholic Emancipation ; d. 1837.
89. Edward Denison, 1837 ; brother of G. A. Denison (*q.v.*) ; consecrated at the age of thirty-six ; a wise organiser of Church life and progress ; favoured the revival of synods ; d. 1854.
90. Walter Kerr Hamilton, 1854 ; a saintly adherent of the Oxford Movement (*q.v.*) ; Fellow of Merton with Manning (*q.v.*) and Edward Denison, whom he also succeeded as Vicar of St. Peter-in-the-East, Oxford ; founded Salisbury Theological College, 1860 ; in his charges maintained the doctrines of the Eucharistic Sacrifice, Real Presence, and sacramental confession ; instituted diocesan Retreats ; d. 1869.
91. George Moberly, 1869 ; a brilliant scholar ; Fellow of Balliol College, Oxford ; Headmaster of Winchester, 1835-66 ; Canon of Chester, 1868 ; his High Churchmanship long kept him from receiving preferment ; d. 1885.
92. John Wordsworth, 1885 ; son of Bishop C. Wordsworth of Lincoln ; Fellow of Brasenose College, Oxford, 1867 ; Oriel Professor ; a scholar of European fame ; did much for reunion, and towards the close of his life was eager in the cause of the Swedish Church ; d. 1911.
93. Frederic Edward Ridgeway, 1911 ; tr. from Kensington. [G. C.]

W. Rich Jones, *Fasti Eccl. Sarisb. and Dio. Hist.* ; Cassan, *Lives of the Bishops of Salisbury.*

SANCROFT, William (1617-93). Archbishop of Canterbury, forms an interesting link between the earlier Caroline Divines (*q.v.*) and the Nonjurors (*q.v.*). He was the son of a yeoman who lived at Fressingfield, Suffolk, and nephew of a Master of Emmanuel College, Cambridge, where he himself took the ordin-

ary degrees, became Fellow, Tutor, Bursar, and Reader both in Greek and Hebrew. He was able to retain his Fellowship till 1651, in spite of Puritan dominance, but he then retired to Fressingfield, and wrote books against the party in power : *Fur praedestinatus*, 1651, against Calvinism, and *Modern Policies* (a seventh edition in 1657), against the politics and religion of the Commonwealth. He kept up relations with the banished clergy, travelled abroad from 1657, and returned to England to be chaplain to Cosin (*q.v.*) and to the King, Rector of Houghton-le-Spring, Prebendary of Durham, and in 1662 Master of Emmanuel. He took an important if not prominent part in the Savoy Conference (*q.v.*). For ten months in 1664 he was Dean of York, and Le Neve notes his remarkable generosity. Before the end of the year he was installed Dean of St. Paul's. He then set in hand the restoration which the Great Fire soon made it necessary should be undertaken from the foundations. He supported Christopher Wren most heartily throughout. Nothing was done 'without his presence, no materials bought, nor accounts passed without him.' He gave £1400 to the work, and built the present deanery at the cost of £2500. And he refused the bishopric of Chester, feeling his work lay wholly at St. Paul's. He was for two years (1668-70), however, Archdeacon of Canterbury, and in 1670 Prolocutor of the Canterbury Lower House of Convocation. On 27th January 1678 he was consecrated in Westminster Abbey Archbishop of Canterbury. He made a most active archbishop, doing his duty towards high and low. He suspended Wood, Bishop of Lichfield, for negligence. He endeavoured to bring James, Duke of York, back to the English Church. He spoke to Charles II. on his death-bed most earnestly, calling him to repentance. On the coronation of James II. he was obliged to omit the Communion, and 'under pretence of shortening the service . . . was induced by the King to ruin it'—liturgically (Wickham Legg), damage from which it never recovered. [CORONATION.] He accepted James's promises of support to the Church, but refused to sit on the Ecclesiastical Commission, and denied its legality. He was soon led into open dispute with the King, declining to allow the clergy to give up catechising, and at length, after summoning a meeting of bishops and prominent laymen, definitely refusing to obey the order to read the King's declaration of liberty of conscience in church. His further actions in this matter led to his trial and acquittal in Westminster

Hall with six other bishops. [SEVEN BISHOPS.] Sancroft calmly continued his work, and gave instruction to the clergy to have a special care against popish emissaries. As the popular mind became more and more excited, and a revolution was evidently at hand, he gave his best advice to the King, and urged the summoning of a free Parliament, and finally signed the request to William of Orange to join in procuring it. But after the King's flight he would take no part in any proceedings which recognised the legality of the new Government. He issued a commission to his suffragans, but took no part in the coronation of William and Mary. He was then (1st August 1689) suspended and (1st February 1690) deprived with the other Nonjurors. He would not leave Lambeth till the Barons of the Exchequer ordered his expulsion. He retired to Fressingfield, and lived there, performing divine service in his own house, till his death in November 1693. He was prepared to continue the succession of Nonjuring bishops, but he did not live to take part in it. On his deathbed he repeated what was really the motto of his life: 'What I have done, I have done in the integrity of my heart.'

He had never swerved from the old doctrine of divine right. He believed the hereditary succession to the throne to be the law of God and of the land; he did not think any one had power to dispense him from his oath of allegiance, but he was firm in upholding the constitutional rights of the Church and Parliament against the King. He was entirely free from self-seeking or self-interest, and was one of the most loyal, learned, generous, and pious prelates the Church of England has ever had. His theology was a reflection of that of Andrewes (*q.v.*) and Laud (*q.v.*), and he took charge of the latter's posthumous works with a view to their publication.   [W. H. H.]

D'Oyley, *Life of Sancroft.*

SARUM USE. The prevalence of the Roman rite in Western Europe during the Middle Ages did not imply 'uniformity,' which was a product, or rather an aspiration, of the sixteenth century. Neither the text, nor the ceremonial in which the text was enshrined, was everywhere identical; rather it is probable that every diocese had usages of its own. For example, when the service-books came to be printed in the second half of the fifteenth century and the first half of the sixteenth, nearly two hundred several diocesan missals — in France alone some seventy-five—were published, of which probably no two agree in

detail; while it is probable enough that some varieties were never printed at all, because the books of neighbouring dioceses were near enough for practical purposes. Such local varieties were known as 'Uses,' being each the common rite *secundum usum* of the particular church or diocese. The preface of the Book of Common Prayer of 1549—the present note 'Concerning the Service of the Church'—enumerates five English uses: those of Sarum, Hereford, York, and Lincoln. Of these five 'uses' that of the church of Salisbury, the 'Sarum Use,' was the most eminent and influential; and after the dissolution of the monasteries, which carried with it the abolition of the monastic 'use,' the breviary according to the Use of Sarum was enjoined by Convocation in 1541 on the whole province of Canterbury. The Mass-book of St. Albans, written *c.* 1095-1105, and now at Oxford (*Bodl. Rawl.*, C. 1), is considered by Dr. J. W. Legg to be the earliest known book of the Sarum group. Even before the removal of its cathedral church (*c.* 1220-5) from the fortified hill of Old Sarum to the well-watered valley of Salisbury (*q.v.*), the church of that diocese had begun to hold a commanding position on account of the excellency of its institutions, which are ascribed to St. Osmund (*q.v.*), and the care which Richard le Poor in particular was just then devoting to ritual and ceremonial. He was dean in 1197, and bishop in 1217. From the twelfth century onward the church of Salisbury 'had a very leading position in this respect.' Although York held its own, for the most part, in the northern province, the use of Salisbury gained some footing even there, as well as in Scotland and Ireland. It was Sarum, rather than York, which superseded the local use of Lincoln, and in Wales also it gained some footing, although there were two rival uses (Bangor and Hereford) to compete with it, that of Hereford having, in point of fact, sufficient importance to justify the printing of at least one edition of its mass-book (1502) and one edition of its breviary (1505).

The Sarum breviary, though not perhaps printed in this country until 1506, had been printed abroad from the time of Edward IV. (1475), within about a year of the first appearance of the Roman missal in print. The *ordinale* or 'pye of two and three commemorations of Salisbury use' was printed and advertised by Caxton at Westminster as early as 1477. The earliest known London edition of the Sarum missal was that of Julian Notary, printed by him for Caxton's successor, Wynkyn de Worde, in 1498, but it had been issued abroad in 1486 or 1487. Nearly forty editions of the Sarum breviary and fifty of the Sarum missal can be traced between the *editio princeps*, in either case, and the death of Henry VIII.

The statute of 3-4 Edw. VI. c. 10, on 25th January 1549, enacted that 'all books called antiphoners, missals, grailes, processionals, manuals, legends, pies, portuasses, primers in Latin and English, couchers, journals, ordinals, or other books or writings whatsoever. heretofore used for service of the church. written or printed in the English or Latin tongue, other than such as shall be set forth by the King's majesty, shall be . . . clearly and utterly abolished, extinguished, and forbidden for ever to be used,' etc. In addition to the principal books above enumerated, one other species of service-books, viz. hymnals. was specified among those for printing, whereof Henry VIII. had granted the monopoly to Grafton and Whitchurch and their assigns about December 1543. Some seven weeks after the accession of Queen Mary, 6th July 1553, the Latin service began to be restored, and on 21st December it became obligatory. Sarum missals, processionals, and manuals were reproduced at Rouen and elsewhere, and early in 1555 the Sarum breviary was reprinted at Paris, followed by at least half a dozen other editions in that reign. The Latin hymns of the same use reappeared, with their music, in 1555 from a London press. Of York use at least one breviary (Rouen) of that time has been traced, and one processional from the same London press, but no Marian service-book of Hereford use has come to light. The Bishop of Lincoln directed that the Sarum breviary should be adopted at Easter term, 1557, in his cathedral; and the questions of a revision of the breviary and mass-book, and the acceptance of uniform ceremonies, and of one use for the whole realm, were to have come on for debate in Convocation in November 1558 had the primate and the Queen survived.

According to Bishop Bonner's fifty-fourth article of visitation for the diocese of London in 1554, and his fifteenth injunction in 1555, the books required to be provided for each church at the cost of the parishioners were these :—

(1) A *Legend*, lectionary, or book of lessons selected (for matins) from the Bible, certain patristic treatises or sermons, lives of the saints, and homilies on the liturgical gospels. (2) An *Antiphoner* (antiphonale, antiphonarium), providing the text and music for the antiphons, invitatories, hymns, responds, verses of the canonical hours; and also the collects and the little chapters or brief readings, usually taken from the liturgical epistle, for hours other than matins. Collects and 'chapters' were sometimes written in a separate volume, the 'collectar,' and were also incorporated in the portos (see No. 10 below). (3) A *Grail* ('gradual'), containing text and music for the musical portion of the Mass (cf. No. 9 below). (4) A *Psalter*, arranged as a service-book, not simply in the Biblical order of the one hundred and fifty psalms. It had antiphons and the canticles, litany, etc., and in some cases collects and hymns. The psalter contained likewise a calendar, as did, generally speaking, Nos. 2, 3, 5, 6, 7, and 10. (5) An *Ordinal* 'to say or solemnise divine office,' not in the later sense of a form for ordaining priests, etc., but the *directorium sacerdotum*, a book containing 'the rules called the pye' (*pica*), so named because it usually had only the *magpie* colours of black ink on white paper, without such rubrication or illumination as decorated the pages of other books. The ordinal which tradition ascribed to St. Osmund, and the custom-book or consuetudinary of Bishop Poor and those who continued to adopt and develop their labours, became less and less necessary in their old form as the rubrics of the service-books were elaborated and enlarged. (6) A *Missal*, or mass-book: the altar-book containing the service of the Eucharist throughout the year, and sometimes including for convenience not only the grail (No. 3), but also portions of other books, Nos. 7 and 8. (7) A *Manual*, or book of occasional offices to be used by a priest in administering other sacraments and sacramentals; such as baptism; marriage; visitation, unction, and Communion of the sick; blessing bread, holy water and candles; burial of the dead, etc., and giving such benedictions as he might be empowered to confer on persons or things. (The manual of those occasional offices which were reserved to a bishop, such as ordination, consecration of churches, etc., was known as the *Pontifical*. It was not printed in old times for England, and was not required generally for a parish church, each bishop bringing his own MS. with him. But the confirmation service was commonly included in the printed *Manuale*.) Lastly, the parish provided (8) a *Processional*, containing the rubric, texts, and music which were used in processions in the church or churchyard, or in visiting outlying churches in the city.

These books had been named, in the same order in which Bonner enumerated them, in the English canon law (Nos. 1-7 of them) by

Archbishop Robert Winchelsey at Merton Priory in Surrey in 1305 in the text of his fourth constitution. The last (No. 8) is added in the gloss, where Lyndwood (*q.v.*) in 1433 accounts for the silence of the text of the constitution by suggesting that the processional was tacitly included with No. 7. the *manuale*—a comprehensive title for the fuller book of rites. Winchelsey in the fourteenth century had specified one more book, next in order to the Grail, viz. (9) a *Troper*, which contained the less ancient music of the Mass (and some other services), which had come into use subsequently to the time of St. Gregory the Great (*q.v.*). Music and words of this kind, composed in the tenth and following centuries, went in course of time largely out of use ; and separate Tropers, properly so called, ceased to be transcribed in the thirteenth century. Sequences, *i.e.* ' words or prose set to the prolonged notes of the repeated *Alleluia* before the gospel, and a few farsings (or interpolations of words sung) to the *Kyrie* and *Gloria in excelsis*, are still found in the Sarum books as we have them.' Thus the later MS. sequence-books. while they continued to be written, inherited or monopolised for a while the name of the more comprehensive Troper after this became an extinct species of service-book when introit, *Sanctus*, and *Agnus Dei* were no longer ' farsed.' Even the sequences of Sarum or other English uses were never printed as a separate book, except with a commentary for the use of schools; and these compositions, with such parts of the old Tropers as remained, were already incorporated in the Grail, the Missal, and, to some slight extent, even in the Breviary.

In his twenty-eighth injunction in 1555 Bonner mentioned incidentally another ' ecclesiastical book ' of great importance, namely, (10) a *Portas* (Latin. portiforium), porthors, portos, or portuesse, the usual name by which in England the *Breviary* was called. The parishioners were not legally required to provide such a book, although an archdeacon of Dorset about 1486 charged the church-wardens to see that they had in their churches ' a *portuorie*, a legend, an antiphoner, a sawter, a masse booke, a manual and a pie : whiche ye are bounde to have'; in other words. a breviary in addition to Nos. 1-7 of the list given by Winchelsey and Bonner, only omitting No. 3, possibly because in a parish church they could make shift without a Grail if they had a full Mass-book. As to the breviary, they might plead that if they provided a Legend and an Antiphoner this was all that the law required of them for the choir service, and that the parson was practically bound to have a Portos of his own in order to fulfil his daily duty of saying the divine service (matins and the other canonical hours) ; so he might as well bring it with him. However, there was in many churches a copy of the Breviary, which some former incumbent (or other benefactor) had given or bequeathed for the churchwardens to keep in the ' scob ' (*i.e.* the chest), or on the desk. for his successors' use.

The records of the diocese of Salisbury are not so well furnished with detailed church inventories of the sixteenth century as with some other documents ; nevertheless, we can give some typical indications of the manner in which the law about providing books was carried out. The Elizabethan Royal Injunctions (*q.v.*) of 1559 (No. 47) having already required that churchwardens should deliver inventories not only of vestments and ornaments but of ' books, and specially of grails, couchers,' *i.e.* large books to lie open on a desk, ' legends, processionals, hymnals, manuals, portuesses, and such like, appertaining to their church,' the Latin service-books of Sarum use were presently called in by Bishop Jewel in the spring of the year 1561, when one John Atkyns, the clerk of St. Edmund's, Salisbury, received a groat from the churchwarden ' for carrying of the Latin books to our Lady church.' They had already bought a Communion-book, and *borrowed* ' a book named the pharasyres' (*Paraphrases of Erasmus on the New Testament*), and soon afterwards procured ' a booke of the homyles.' By the parish of St. Thomas in the same city, in the first year of King Edward VI., 2d. had been paid ' for carrying of the books of the church into the Close ' after the coming of the visitors. From the inventory of a small town church in the same county (St. Peter's, Marlborough.) we know how small a number of books were owned by a church in the diocese of Sarum. 21st December 1556, viz. ' a mass-book, a procession-book. an hympner, and two portesses (new bought).' These were struck out of the list as revised on the accession of Queen Elizabeth, and ' a bybyll, a paraferis, a commenyan boke and two santers ' (psalters) were substituted. At St. Mary's, Reading, at that time belonging to Salisbury, on the accession of Queen Mary in 1553 one book was bought for 4s. It was first written down ' an antiffinar,' then corrected to ' manuell.' The ' sauter bocke ' entered earlier in the account of the year in another hand was bought by the Edwardian warden. For the fair-sized country church of St. Denys, Stanford, in the Vale of Whitehorse, the wardens bought at Oxford, and brought back, together with ' the Statute of Rebellion,' in 1555, two ' half-portusis' for 7s. 8d.: a processional in parchment, price 2s.; and an old manual in paper for 20d.

Among ' juelles' remaining in St. Edmund's Parish Church in Salisbury in April 1554, when Queen Mary had been nine months on the throne, the churchwardens had two old half-antiphoners (probably of the two-volume edition of 1519-20), three processionals, a manual, two grails, and a Mass-book. In the course of the year they purchased for 2s. 4d. two Mass-books, a manual, a portys, and a hymner. These may have been ' kept for a day' (as the saying went) by some wary well-wisher to the ' old religion' through the reign of King Edward VI. Further, they spent 30s. 4d. on an antiphoner and two grails. They also provided a new song for the *Salve*, 2d. (*Salve regina* which followed compline having been forbidden about 1547). ' Salve de Jesu' was sung on Fridays in Lent at St. Edmund's, Sarum, in 1476, 1496, 1539, 1553-9. The wardens bought also in 1554 a processional for 3s., and had two pair of psalters ' dressed.' Thus this parish church in Salisbury was refurnished with five out of the seven sorts of books required by Archbishop Winchelsey's old constitution, and with more than one copy of the processional named in Lyndwood's gloss as well. Moreover, having complied with the spirit and letter of the fifteenth-century archdeacon's charge, which has been already mentioned, by providing a (printed) portos or breviary, they could make shift without the two remaining books, the *legenda* and the *ordinale*, since the breviary included, among other things, the lessons and also a pye of two and three commemorations. The *pica* of two commemorations suited the case of Salisbury Cathedral (because the dedication there was St. Mary's, the other weekly commemoration in general use in the province being that of St. Thomas the martyr), while churches with a different dedication, such as St. Edmund's had, used to keep a commemoration of their local saint or title each week, as a rule, in addition to the two already named. Under Cromwell's (*q.v.*) influence in 1538 the commemoration of Becket had been forbidden by the Second Royal Injunctions of King Henry VIII., No. 15, and the ferial service enjoined instead.

We have in Swayne and Straton's *Churchwarden's Accounts* two copies of an inventory of books, etc., belonging to St. Edmund's parish, taken as far back as the reign of King Edward IV., before service-books began to

be printed, and belonging to the year (1472) in which the Robert Hungerford chantry was endowed with its ' ornaments.' We can therefore give here in a summary, supplemented from the church accounts of the same parish, a list of the stock of books found in a large church in the city of Salisbury before the spirit of the Reformation made itself influential.

(1) Legends, 4. one of them called ' a temporall,' *i.e.* containing lessons proper for Sundays, as distinct from other holy days, and for week days throughout the year. Another legend was bought for 40s. in 1477. (2) Antiphoners, 6. One or more of these may have been of the large size suitable for lying open on a desk or lectern for the use of two or three singers at once. Such volumes were known as ' couchers,' ' lyggars' (or ledgers), or in Latin *libri dormientes*. (3) Grails, 9. One of these in 1491 lay daily before the parish priest on the south side of the choir; two others had been specially assigned for use at Mass of the Blessed Virgin. (4) Psalter, 1. (5) Ordinal, with pye, 1. (6) Mass-books, 5. (Probably this number did not include the missals with which Reginald Tudworth's chantry, founded in 1322, and the Weavers' Gild were furnished.) (7) No Manuale is named in the inventory of 1472, but one may have been included among the processionals, and a manual is specifically included in the account for bookbinders' repairs, *c.* 1490. (At Trinity Hospital, Salisbury, there was a special book for Extreme Unction.) (8) Processionals, 13 or 14. The church in question was founded for a college consisting of the provost and twelve secular canons, of whom, however, only seven were appointed. In 1476 they had as many as fifteen chalices with their patens. William of Wykeham (*q.v.*) gave eleven antiphoners, thirteen processionals, and nineteen grails to New College, *c.* 1386. At All Saints' Church, Wycombe, Bucks, there were six processionals in 1475, and two manuals, which had increased to four in 1519. (9) No troper or sequenciar is named at St. Edmund's in 1472, but 4d. was spent in 1474-5 on writing the sequence of St. Osmund (who had been canonised in 1457), and 17d. on parchment for his *historia, i.e.* lessons, etc., for his festival; 6s. for vellum; and 5s. for engrossing the Visitation of our Lady and St. Osmund's ' stories' in 1479; and 2s. more was spent in 1495 for ' making' the new festival services for those occasions; and 20d. more in 1481 for binding the ' legends' of these and other ' new feasts'—doubtless the Transfiguration and the Name of Jesus.

The inventory and accounts also specify (10) Portesses or Breviaries of various sizes. 6 in number. One was kept in a ' scob ' or chest before the altar in the nave beneath the rood, for the use of the morrow-mass priest, who, like the rest, was bound to say on week days the services of matins, lauds, prime, terce, and sext before his Mass, and nones after it, or on fasting days before it.

There were seven or eight other books, not specifically required by the canon law, but some of them in practice usually found. viz. :—

(11-13) A Collectar, probably containing little chapters as well as orisons or collects ; an Epistolar (or ' pystol-boke ') and a Gospellar, containing respectively the liturgical epistles and gospels, used when the sub-deacon and the deacon chanted them solemnly at High Mass. There was another gospel ' text,' on vellum, to be carried ceremonially with a pax-brede or crucifixion on its cover, and to be passed round for the kiss of peace near the solemn ending of the Mass. (14) A book for the organs. In like manner Wykeham provided a *librum de cantu organico* for his college at Winchester. (15, 16) A *Dirige* book, for the dirge or matins, etc., of the dead ; and a Bead-roll, from which the names of benefactors and others, living or departed, for whom prayers were bidden, were rehearsed. (17) A Primer-book, or lay folks' prayer - book, containing the *Horae* or hours of the Blessed Virgin, etc.. litany, fifteen gradual and seven penitential psalms, and other devotions in Latin or English—a book which may have been left as a gift or offering—was sold to help the church expenses in 1479 for 3s. 4d.. probably to some parishioner. [SERVICES, CHURCH, BEFORE THE REFORMATION.] (18, etc.) There were here, as in other churches, a few miscellaneous books kept in the church for the assistance and edification of the clergy, ' A book of the Lives of the Saints,' Hugucio (probably his lexicon of grammatical derivations), chained in the Lady Chapel (as the dictionary called Catholicon was at Winchester and at Wycombe, and the little Cato for the choir boys at Lincoln) ; also ' a book called a Sentenciall, for the use of the church ' : as this last was bought for 20d. in 1475, it can hardly have been the great work of Peter Lombard, or any of the larger summaries or commentaries thereon, but possibly a collection of aphorisms from moral and ecclesiastical writers, to help meditation and sermon composition.

The All Saints', Wycombe, inventories (1475-1519) also include (19, etc.) a Psalter with the collects and the hymns, a ' martilage ' or martyrology, a book not often found in the ordinary parish churches, and one with which probably the collegiate church of St. Edmund could the better dispense, because its chaplains were bound to ' follow the choir ' of the cathedral, and so perhaps might attend the capitular service in the chapterhouse ; an invitatorie (elsewhere called *Venitare*), with the ' Alleluya ' verses of the grayles ; a responsorary with a little grail— probably both the last (twofold) items were composite books for singers ; various 'quires' or detached sheets for feasts recently introduced, viz. the Visitation of our Lady (1480) with music, the ' Transfiguration of Jhesu ' (1480), and the Jesus Mass, or the Name of Jesus (1493). Also, for study, two volumes of St. Austin and one of St. Gregory.

[c. w.]

W. H. Frere, *Sarum Use*, 2 vols. ; C. Wordsworth and H. Littlehales, *Old English Service Books* : Wilts Record Soc., *Churchwardens' Accounts . . . Sarum* (1443-1702), Swayne and Straton : Note on Mediæval Service Books in G. W. Prothero's *Memoir of H. Bradshaw*, pp. 423-6 ; J. W. Legg, *Westminster Mass-Books* (H.B.S.), iii. pp. 1408-23 ; *Burh Inventories* (Alcuin Club Collection), ix. pp. 133-9 ; *P.B. Dictionary*, Harford and Stevenson, art. ' Use.'

SAVOY CONFERENCE. In the Declaration of Breda, 16th April 1660, Charles II. proclaimed ' a liberty to tender consciences, and that no man shall be disquieted or called in question for difference of opinion in matters of religion which do not disturb the peace of the kingdom ; and that we shall be ready to consent to such an Act of Parliament as upon mature deliberation shall be offered to us, for the full granting that indulgence.' After his return to England, Charles welcomed a suggestion of Baxter's (*q.v.*), that agreement might be reached by conference between the 'episcopal' party and the 'presbyterian,' 'puritan,' or ' nonconformist' party, and promised to further such a conference. To a deputation of divines—Calamy, Reynolds, Baxter, and others—he urged that the agreement must be effected, not by the surrender of either party, but by mutual concession ; declared that it should not be his fault if the parties were not reconciled ; and invited the divines to submit proposals for reform. Accordingly an *Address* to the King was drawn up, chiefly by Calamy and Reynolds, containing proposals for the amendment of discipline, Church government, liturgy and ceremonies, praying in particular that kneeling at Communion, holidays, bowing at the Holy

Name, the sign of the cross, and the surplice should not be enforced. A reply to this was drawn up by the bishops, in which, without suggesting any concessions, they criticised the proposals in detail in a hostile sense, while expressing willingness that the Book of Common Prayer (*q.v.*) should be revised. Baxter wrote a prolix defence of the *Address*, but it was suppressed ' lest it should hinder peace.' So far little progress had been made ; and at length the King took matters into his own hands, and after consultation with both parties and after accepting Puritan amendments, issued the *Declaration* of 25th October 1660, in which he promised to promote reforms in administration and to appoint an equal number of learned divines of both persuasions to revise the Prayer Book and make such alterations as should be thought most necessary, and some additional forms, to be used as alternatives to the existing forms at the discretion of the minister ; and meanwhile he dispenses those who desire it from the use of the ceremonies which give offence, pending the determination of the questions at issue by a national synod to be held after the promised conference. Accordingly on 25th March 1661 the King issued a commission to twelve bishops and twelve Puritan divines, and nine assessors on each side, requiring and authorising them to meet together in the Master's lodgings at the Savoy or elsewhere from time to time during the next four months, to advise upon and review the Book of Common Prayer, comparing the same with the most ancient liturgies, and after consideration of the contents of the book and of the objections that should be raised against it, to make such reasonable and necessary alterations as should be agreed upon as needful for the satisfaction of tender consciences and for the restoring of peace, but avoiding all unnecessary alterations ; and when the work is done to present it to the King, that, if approved, it might be established. The Conference met first on 15th April, and Sheldon (*q.v.*) of London at once insisted that, since it was the other party that sought for the conference and desired change, it was for them first to submit in writing their objections and to propose the alterations and additions they desired. The Puritan divines objected to this procedure as not satisfying the King's commission ' to meet together, advise, and consult.' But Sheldon insisted, and Baxter supported him and persuaded his party to acquiesce, since in this way they would have better opportunity of stating their whole case before the world, and fruitless contention would be avoided. The Confer-

ence was therefore adjourned, and Baxter was entrusted with the task of compiling the additions to the Prayer Book, while the rest of the party undertook to draw up the objections to be submitted. Accordingly on 4th May the *Exceptions against the Book of Common Prayer*, which was the work of Reynolds, Wallis, Calamy, and some half-dozen others, were submitted to the conference. The *Exceptions* form a detailed criticism of the Prayer Book under two heads : first, of ' generals,' under which objections are brought against broad characteristics both of rite and of ceremony ; and secondly, of ' particulars,' under which objections are made to details throughout the book. Baxter's proposals, which were presented some days later, instead of consisting of ' some additional forms,' were, in fact, a new service-book of the Genevan type (the ' Savoy Liturgy '). Along with this Baxter presented a *Petition for Peace*, asking for the adoption of his service-book as alternative to the Prayer Book ; for the same freedom from oaths and declarations as had been granted as an *interim* measure by the King's *Declaration*; and that ministers who had not been ordained by bishops should not be required to be reordained, nor the exercise of their ministry made to depend upon conditions which they could not accept; and all this was urged with arguments and appeals of the prolixity which was customary with Baxter and seems throughout to have tried the temper of the other party. Nothing more was heard of Baxter's service-book, but to the *Exceptions* the bishops replied in writing, dealing with them point by point, and refusing all concession except in respect of seventeen points, mostly of no importance (fifteen of them were embodied in the revised book of 1662). There followed the *Rejoinder of the Ministers to the Answer of the Bishops*, composed by Baxter at greater length than ever. By this time it was July, and the conference had only ten days of life remaining. The Puritan side entreated that before it closed there might be a personal discussion between the parties. After two days' debate the proposal was agreed to, and three of each side were chosen to carry it out—Pearson (*q.v.*), Gunning, and Sparrow for the bishops; Bates, Jacomb, and Baxter for the others. There followed some stormy and fruitless debates, in which Baxter was always to the front with his ever-ready and copious eloquence. At length Cosin (*q.v.*) produced a paper as ' from a very worthy person,' proposing that the field should be narrowed by the Puritan side stating clearly what in the existing forms they held to be contrary to the Word of God and what only inexpedient ; and that, as to the former, if proved, the Puritans should be given satisfaction ; as to the latter, it should be referred to Convocation for settlement. This led to further debate and no result. The last few days of the conference were occupied in a curious discussion carried out by the champions of both sides in writing in the strict logical form of the schools, on the single issue that the Book of Common Prayer and the Canons contain what is sinful in that they require the minister to refuse Communion to any who will not receive it kneeling. In the end all that was agreed upon was ' that we give nothing in our Account to the King as charged on one another, but what is delivered in by the party in Writing ; And that all our account was to be this, that we were all agreed on the *Ends*, for the Churches Welfare. Unity, and Peace, and his Majesty's Happiness and Contentment, but after all our Debates, were disagreed of the means. And this was the End of that Assembly and Commission.'

[F. E. B.]

Documents relating to the Settlement of the Ch. of Eng. by the Act of Uniformity of 1662, 1862; Reliquiæ Baxterianæ, ed. Sylvester. 1696; Burnet. Hist. of His Own Times; Cardwell. Conferences : V. Hall, Reliquiæ liturgicæ, iv.

SCROPE, Richard (*c.* 1350-1405), Archbishop of York, member of a famous Yorkshire family, a great northern leader of popular discontent with the new royal dynasty, a martyr to his cause, and an uncanonised saint. He was son of the first Lord Scrope of Masham, a noted soldier. At first a student of law, he was ordained in 1376 in the household of Arundel, Bishop of Ely. After he had held various appointments, notably that of Chancellor of Cambridge, Pope Urban VI. consecrated him Bishop of Coventry and Lichfield in 1386. He now came much into contact with Richard II., at whose request he was translated to York in 1398. When Henry IV. assumed the crown Scrope made no demur, and aided in enthroning him. Before long disaffection set in, and Scrope, unwisely deserting the studies and offices for which he had reputation, began to confer with the great houses of the north. Northumberland and Mowbray fomented a spirit of rebellion, and Scrope joined them. They drew up articles of indictment, in which various distresses of the period were freely ascribed to the King. Scrope also boldly opposed the spoliation of the Church as proposed by the

Parliament of 1404. Henry now led an army to the north. Scrope had compromised himself by unwise profession of his determination to resist to the uttermost, and by perhaps more than one public manifesto. Yorkshiremen flocked to the rebel standard. The two forces confronted one another, and a parley followed, in which Scrope and Mowbray were persuaded to disband their followers, whilst the King, as was promised, should consider their grievances. Scrope was arrested, and a trial held at Bishopthorpe. The King was determined that he should die, and forced the tribunal to condemn him. Scrope vainly asserted that he intended reformation and not rebellion. He was sentenced to death, a sentence which was carried out on the Feast of St. William of York, whilst Scrope testified that he died for the laws and good government of England. His grave in St. Stephen's Chapel at York became a centre of pilgrimage, and the offerings made there contributed to the building of the great tower of the minster. No chapel in the building was more richly arrayed than that in which Scrope's body was laid. He was never canonised, but with Yorkshiremen was one of the most popular of saints.   [H. G.]

Annales Henrici IV. and Walsingham : D.N.B. ; Wylie. Henry IV., vol. ii.

SELWYN, George Augustus (1809-78), founder and organiser of the province of New Zealand and of the Melanesian Mission, was educated at Eton and Cambridge, where he was Second Classic. He returned to Eton as private tutor, and became Curate of Windsor. His great natural gifts, his cultivated powers of mind and body, his religious fervour, seemed already to mark him out for some great career. The call came in 1841 to be the first Bishop of New Zealand, and was at once obeyed. The bishopric was established by the Crown in the early days of the colony ; Letters Patent conveyed legal powers, and extended the diocese far into the Northern Pacific. A letter from Archbishop Howley, in terms which were never forgotten and singularly fulfilled, bade him regard his see as ' the central point of a system extending its influence in all directions, a fountain diffusing the streams of salvation over the islands and coasts of the Pacific.' New Zealand had been opened for colonisation by missions of the C.M.S. The bishop arrived to find the natives mostly Christians of the English Church. The colonists, not half so numerous as the natives, scattered, of many sects, had no Church organisation. The bishop, who learned Maori on his voyage, took the Native Church as his first care, and kept his love for it to the last. His next care was to visit the English in their widely separated towns and settlements, journeying on foot, fording and swimming rivers, sailing along uninhabited coasts. In less than a year after his arrival he had surveyed his diocese, and had formed his plans of education and of synodical constitution. He founded his College of St. John for the religious and industrial education of both races, with a view to the supply of clergy and citizens alike. This he called the 'key and pivot' of his work. His plans for synods, with admission of faithful laity, much on the American model, did not from the first lack support among the colonists. A synod of bishops and clergy met in 1844, 'the first in the Church of England since the silencing of Convocation.' A second met in 1847. In 1850 the six bishops of Australasia met in Sydney, and recommended a synodical constitution with lay representation.

Selwyn was now able to turn to the islands of the Pacific. Having ascertained that his field must be Melanesia, he began in 1849 his admirable work among those untouched islands. Persuaded that every man, however savage, was able and even likely to receive the Gospel if presented, and that every one who should receive it would be able and willing in some measure to impart it, he sought from the first to find teachers of the heathen among themselves, to 'catch men in a black net with white corks.' Risking no life but his own, landing alone on many a dangerous beach, he sought and found among crowds of savages the boys whom he would teach to be the teachers of their people, and, with a strange success, he brought them to his college.

The grant of self-government to the colony gave the opportunity to the Church. The bishop visited England, and made clear the way for the division of his diocese, the organisation of the province, the establishment of the Melanesian diocese. As a result the Church in New Zealand was soon at work with a system of trusts and co-ordinated synods. In 1859 the First General Synod was attended by five bishops, with clerical and lay representatives. But the progress of the Church, and of religion, was for ten years sadly hindered by a native war. The bishop ministered equally on both sides; the natives were in revolt against English rule and religion; the colonists were angry with the friends of the natives. But in this time of unpopularity the bishop was really making

himself better known to both races. This was shown when both bade him farewell, when, much against his will, he had become Bishop of Lichfield; it was then shown that twenty-six years of labour among them were understood and valued.

Bishop Selwyn accepted translation to Lichfield in 1867, where he laboured abundantly and fruitfully. Twice he visited the sister Church in the United States. He had to grieve for the death of Bishop Patteson (*q.v.*), to rejoice over the consecration of his own son to take the vacant place. Bishop Selwyn belongs to New Zealand; but it should be remembered that the grass of the Cathedral Close at Lichfield was long worn by the feet of the black-country people who visited his grave. [R. H. C.]

G. H. Curteis, *Life*: personal recollections.

SERVICES, Church (before the Reformation).

The services of the Church must be viewed from a twofold aspect: (1) as a dutiful offering to God, from the Bride of Christ to the King of kings, from the Body to the Head, from the recipient of grace to the Holy Ghost, the giver of life; (2) as a ministration of spiritual gifts of grace for the benefit of members of the household of faith. In their Godward aspect, the services, which are acts of worship, are (normally) confined to the consecrated house of prayer, although charity or necessity may justify their performance elsewhere (Jn. 4[22, 23]; Dan. 6[10]; Acts 8[38], 16[25, 33]), while in their function of ministering grace for the benefit of man they are sometimes ministered in private houses.

1. The Church service consisted primarily of the Sacrifice of Thanksgiving ordained by Christ Himself. This was understood to be, among other things, a daily sacrifice and a continual remembrance of Redemption. The sacring of the Mass was performed on the altar before which the bishop or priest stood, and it normally took place at 9 A.M. It was postponed on fasting days till noon.

Further, for the sake of providing opportunities for every priest to say his Mass, and in order to enable all devout lay folk, whom journeys or secular duties might otherwise preclude, to hear Mass daily, several altars were dedicated in each church, and earlier Masses, from dawn to the time of the gospel at High Mass, were provided in succession, according to the requirements of each parish or chapelry, in some cases daily, in others once or twice a week.

To take the case of St. Edmund's, Salisbury [SARUM USE], where there were parochial services in the nave as well as the collegiate services in the large choir, the latter served by the provost and six or seven secular canons, the former by the parish priest with an assistant deacon, clerk, and sexton, as well as two or more chaplains or chantry priests to say Mass for the souls of Reginald Tudworth, W. Randolph, and others. Right and left of the high altar were the Lady Chapel, and that of St. John Baptist in the choir aisles; and farther north, the chapel of St. Katherine in the churchyard, to which the Abbot of Abbotsbury presented an incumbent. The parish priest's place, when in choir, was on the south side of the church, and before him was placed a grail open upon the desk. There was a rood-loft on which the singers chanted on solemn occasions, and in this part of the church the deacon recited the gospel at Mass from the book or text brought from the altar. Beneath the rood was the parish altar, near which the confraternity of Jesus had their services, and at which the parish priest, or some chaplain appointed thereto, said the 'morrow Mass' at 6 A.M. (in some places it was said at 4 or 5 A.M.). The celebrant had first said his matins, lauds, prime, and terce from his portos (or breviary), which he took out of the 'scob' or chest, of which he kept the key. When his Mass was done he was succeeded by the chaplain of the Weavers' Gild, and he himself would say the remainder of the canonical little-hours to nones inclusive, unless he deferred them to say in choir after assisting at the High Mass in his stall. Right and left of the Jesus altar of the Holy Rood were two others: the altar of St. George's Gild, of which the aldermen and city council were members, and that of Reginald Tudworth's chantry—all three being set against the choir screen; and farther still to the south and north, where the transepts extended, or elsewhere in the nave, were other altars, with such titles and images as St. Nicholas, SS. Fabian and Sebastian, St. Lawrence, St. Julian, and St. Andrew, and lights were maintained out of endowments before some of these images, as well as before the rood or crucifix. As the worshippers came into church they each took holy water (blessed at Mass on Sunday morning) from the stoup near the south door. Some of them had primers (Hours of the Blessed Virgin with other devotions), which they read in a low voice, singly or in pairs, in their places in the nave, while service was going on at the altar or in choir; or they told their beads, reciting the rosary, or the 'psalter of our Lady,' viz. the Lord's Prayer, followed by ten Aves or Salutations of the Blessed Virgin, repeated five times in

succession, with a final Paternoster and the Creed. These forms (with the Commandments) the parish priest was charged to teach his parishioners periodically from the pulpit.

Though a considerable number of English folk heard a Mass almost every day, very few were 'houselled' (received Holy Communion) more than thrice a year at most. To prepare for these receptions they were shriven; and a chair for the priest to hear confession stood in the church (probably in sight of one of the altars). Pardons or indulgences were kept at St. Edmund's at Michaelmas and Lady Day, when the ring of St. Edmund of Canterbury (*q.v.*) and other relics were exposed, and a third part of the offerings of the faithful were sent to Rome. Hock-tide after Easter, and 'Frick-Friday' in Whitsun week, were observed, and 'king ales' and plays were held about Whitsuntide and the Translation of St. Edmund (9th June). Besides their presence at Mass and their terminal communion, the laity witnessed, and some at least followed devoutly, the processions in the church or about the 'litton' (churchyard), preparatory to High Mass, when anthems were sung, till the procession halted below the rood. Thus far, as also by kissing the pax-brede, by receiving the smoke of the censer as it was carried round, and holy bread, blessed before Sunday Mass and distributed afterwards, the laity were associated with the Sacrament ordained by Christ Himself. The forementioned services were extended beyond the walls of the church by the clerk carrying holy water round to houses, or by the cantel (or portion) of holy bread, taken perhaps by those present to friends detained at home, or received by one of the householders each week as a sign and reminder that he was to provide the next Sunday's bread and candle.

There were also the other processions of a special kind, particularly at Rogation-tide, or those in times of general supplication, ordered sometimes at the King's instance and enjoined by ecclesiastical authority, when the litany was sung. Last, but not least, there was the occasional ministration of the Communion (only in one kind) to the sick in houses, when the host was solemnly carried by the priest, preceded by the clerk with bell and light.

2. The daily service prescribed by the Church ranks in importance next to the Eucharist ordained by our Lord. The Divine Service of the Seven Canonical Hours: *matins* (originally a composite night service designed to combine a course of psalms and reading, and still retaining the term *nocturnes* as a

designation of its structure) combined with *lauds* the service of psalms of praise at the return of daylight, *prime* at 6 A.M., followed by *terce, sext,* and *nones,* each of these three consisting of recitation of a fourth portion of the long 119th (Vulgate 118th) psalm, of which the opening part had been said or sung at prime — these coming theoretically at a distance of three hours apart, the Mass or Eucharist of the day intervened at one or other of the intervals between two of these 'little' or 'lesser' hours. *Vespers,* called 'Evensong' in England, followed later in the afternoon, after the usual dinner hour, and *compline (completorium)* properly at bed-time at the ending of the day.

This form of daily service is traced to the fifth century. As adopted for the secular clergy from the Gregorian office, it provided in the first place for the recitation of the entire psalter with canticles from the Old Testament and St. Luke, to recur weekly (the Gospel canticles daily). The groups of psalms alternated with lessons from the Bible, which was intended to be read through, in a seasonable order (*e.g.* Isaiah in Advent), once a year. Of necessity the frequent occurrence of holidays and weekly commemorations, provided with certain proper psalms, interfered very often with the ferial course of the week. The systematic Bible reading also was curtailed when proper lessons from lives of the saints and from homilies on the Gospel for the day were substituted for a considerable proportion of the Biblical lessons. Each lesson at matins—and, out of Easter-tide, there were usually nine of them on Sundays and holy days—was separated from the next by the repetition of responds and versicles, which, as the lectionary was shortened, lost some of their original appropriateness. A verse or two of the Epistle of the Mass usually supplied the reading at evensong and most of the lesser hours. The psalmody preceding each set of three matins lessons, as well as the psalms assigned to other hours, had special point given by the introduction of antiphons. Canticles from the Old Testament were included in the psalmody at lauds, *Te Deum* concluded festal matins, a Gospel canticle followed the brief lesson, and a hymn at lauds, evensong, and compline.

A hymn, taken from a collection of one hundred and fifteen, was appointed for each hour, and in the case of matins, prime, terce, sext, and nones was sung early in the service. Lauds and the six services following it each culminated in the collect, with a dismissory 'Benedicamus.' This final, precatory, section of the hour services opened on week days

with the Lord's Prayer, followed by versicles and responses.

The recitation of these services was specially a clerical duty. The lay folk, however, in England usually attended evensong (work being stopped) on afternoons of Saturdays and the eves of holy days; and also matins with lauds and prime (at which *Quicumque vult* occurred), procession with High Mass, and sometimes the evensong at 2 or 3 P.M. on Sundays; and to this extent they were associated with the daily service of the Church. With the Latin words and tunes of some of the fixed psalms, hymns, and canticles they were probably familiar, as well as with the Lord's Prayer and *Ave.* recited inaudibly as preparatory to each 'hour.' Shorter services, framed on the same model, such as 'Hours' of the Blessed Virgin, of the Cross, etc., and their gild services, were known to the devout lay people, and a few of them had copies of them in their primers (*Horae*).

3. Special duties and observances marked *Shrove-*Tuesday, *Ash-*Wednesday, *Shere-* or Maundy-Thursday, and Good Friday (where there was creeping to the cross laid down upon a cushion), as well as *Candle-*mas, *Palm-*Sunday, and some other days.

4. Besides those just mentioned there were other occasional services provided for the faithful, who at some crisis in their lives were invited to seek the ministration of grace. The sacrament of baptism at the font, churching of women, espousals at the church door, wedding Mass at the altar, conferring the tonsure, and various grades of 'minor' and 'holy' orders, blessing of pilgrims, hermits, anchorites, nuns, etc., the evensong, dirge, and Masses for the dead, as well as confirmation of children, were ministered in the church itself, and (as a rule) only there. The *Manuale* contained, moreover, forms for visitation, unction, and Communion of the sick, commendation of the departing soul, and blessing the grave : as well as for the bridal chamber, a house, a boat, etc.— services and forms wherewith ministrations of the Church were carried to the home and to the work abroad. [C. W.]

For authorities see article SARUM USE.

SEVEN BISHOPS, The, who were tried for presenting to James II. a petition stating their reasons for refusing to publish in church his declaration of liberty of conscience (originally issued, 4th April 1687), which the King ordered should be read in all churches during divine service on 20th May. As soon as the King's order was issued, 4th May, Sancroft (*q.v.*), Archbishop of Canterbury, took measures to meet the danger. The declaration was illegal, as had been declared in 1672, ' being formed on such a dispensing power as at pleasure sets aside all laws, ecclesiastical and civil.' A number of important clergy and laity met at Lambeth to consult, and on 18th May six divines (Tillotson (*q.v.*), Stillingfleet (*q.v.*), Patrick (*q.v.*), Tenison, Sherlock (*q.v.*), Grove), with seven bishops, drew up resolutions explaining why a refusal to obey the King was necessary. The petition drawn up and to be presented to James said that the declaration was one ' of so much moment and consequence to the whole nation, both in Church and State, that your petitioners cannot in prudence, honour, or conscience, so far make themselves parties to it as the distribution of it all over the nation, and the solemn publication of it, once and again, even in God's house, must amount to.' The signatories were Sancroft, Lloyd of St. Asaph, Turner of Ely, Lake of Chichester, Ken (*q.v.*) of Bath and Wells, White of Peterborough, Trelawny of Bristol. James refused to receive the petition, and declared it ' a standard of rebellion.' The bishops were summoned before the Council, and finally tried on 29th June. They received a public ovation, ' the people thinking it a blessing to kiss any of these bishops' hands or garments.' After a whole night in consideration the jury, 30th June, returned a verdict of not guilty. The arguments in the case were of great constitutional importance. The Lord Chief-Justice (Sir R. Wright), when the verdict was declared, in checking the applause said : ' I am as glad as you can be that my Lords the Bishops are acquitted ; but your manner of rejoicing here in court is indecent ; you might rejoice in your chamber, or elsewhere, and not here.' The whole proceedings were published in folio, 1688, and in octavo, 1716. Sancroft designed a medal of commemoration.   [W. H. H.]

Tryal of the Seven Bishops, Lond., 1716 ; *State Trials*, xii. 183. All Sancroft's MSS. on the subject are in the Bodleian Library : Hutton, *Hist. Eng. Ch., 1625-1714.*

SHAFTESBURY ABBEY was founded by Alfred (*q.v.*) and consecrated in 888, the first abbess being his daughter, the Lady Elgiva, under whom a number of noble ladies took the veil.

Alfred endowed the abbey with a hundred hides of land, ' a nucleus much increased by his successors.' The sisterhood was of the Benedictine order. The great fame of the abbey dated from the burial there of the murdered King Eadward, 20th February 982. He had been privately buried at Warham, near Corfe, the scene of his murder, 978.

The cultus of St. Eadward the Martyr was popular and widespread, and has left its mark in the calendar of the English Prayer Book, where his ' Passion,' 18th March, and his second Translation, 20th June 1001 (when his relics were reinterred behind the high altar), are among the lesser saints' days. His shrine became one of the most popular places of pilgrimage. His name was added to the earlier dedication of the abbey to St. Mary. The town for centuries was known as Edwardstow. Aelfthryth heaped remorseful gifts on the abbey. Cnut (*q.v.*) died here, 12th November 1035. The monastery became in time so rich that Fuller (*q.v.*) records an adage that ' if the Abbess of Shaftesbury might wed the Abbot of Glastonbury their heir would have more land than the King of England.' The abbess held a whole barony of the Crown, was liable to be summoned to Parliament, and held her manorial courts in the abbey gate. Shaftesbury being a royal foundation, the King claimed to present a novice for admission and to appoint the abbess, who vowed canonical obedience to the diocesan and presented to four prebends in Salisbury Cathedral, to be held by the conventual confessors. In 1313 Elizabeth, wife of Robert Bruce, was imprisoned here. In 1218 the Pope forbade the house to admit more than a hundred nuns, but this rule appears not to have been obeyed, for in 1326 Bishop Mortival certified that there was an excessive multitude of nuns, and two years later declared the revenues equal only to the maintenance of one hundred and twenty, and ordered no more to be admitted.

The abbey appears to have maintained to the end the high reputation it bore in the time of William of Malmesbury. It was surrendered and dissolved, 23rd March 1539. Pensions were assigned to fifty-six nuns, including the abbess, the prioress, and sub-prioress. The abbess was still living in 1553. The annual revenue was assessed by the *Valor Ecclesiasticus* in 1536 at £1166, 8s. 9d. It was rated by Dugdale at the same sum at the dissolution, by Speed at £1339, 1s. 3d. The arms of the abbey were ' Azure in chief, two roses, a cross flory between four martlets or.'

On the dissolution the work of destruction seems immediately to have commenced. Leland, visiting the town a year after, says : ' The abbey stood . . .,' implying that it had already been demolished. A MS. at Wilton, 1548, shows a small drawing of the ruins, which include an arcade and tower. Soon after the last vestiges above ground disappeared. Excavations recently carried out have revealed a large part of the abbey church and cloister. The church stood on the southern edge of a rocky bluff, and must have rivalled Lincoln and Durham, Laon and Vézelay, in its magnificent situation. The great buttressed embankment wall which supports the abbey site is the only relic above ground of this wonderful pile of buildings. The choir and the north and south aisles, probably about 1120, were apsidal internally, but, like Romsey, externally their ends were rectangle. The base of the high altar was discovered, twelve and a half by four feet. On either side of the aisle ran a low stone bench, as at Salisbury. The presbytery and choir measured about seventy-five by twenty-five feet, exclusive of the aisles, which were divided from the choir by walls eight feet thick. There was a central tower at the crossing. The transepts measured internally one hundred and fourteen feet across. The eastern end of the north transept opened on an Early English crypt twenty-four by eighteen feet—a somewhat unusual arrangement. The total length of the church was probably about three hundred and fifty feet, but the western end of the nave has not yet been excavated. The chapter-house stood eight feet from the wall of the south transept. On the floor a small piece of marble was discovered, having incised on its face :—

M.
NIC
ATIO

This must be the stone spoken of in the Bodleian MS. of William of Malmesbury as to be seen in the twelfth-century chapter-house at Shaftesbury inscribed ' Anno enim Dominicae Incarnationis DCCCLXXX Alfredus Rex fecit hanc urbem Regni sui viii.' The cloister measured one hundred and eight feet six inches from east to west. Numerous fragments of fourteenth and fifteenth-century windows, also short lengths of broken Purbeck columns, bits of canopy work, and bosses richly gilt and of fine workmanship, have been found all over the site of the church and cloisters. The encaustic paving tiles are particularly interesting and varied, showing the arms of the Montacutes, Cheneys, de Bryons, Stourtons, and Cleres—families once connected with the abbey and neighbourhood.

LIST OF ABBESSES

The date when not otherwise stated is that of accession.

1. Elgiva, or Aethelgeofu, or Algiva; first abbess ; *c.* 888.
2. Aelfthrith ; occurs 918.
3. Herleva ; occurs 966 ; d. 982.
4. Alfrida ; occurs 1001 or 1009.
5. Leucua ; *temp.* Edward Confessor.
6. Eulalia, 1074.   7. Eustachia.
8. Cecilia, 1107 ; third daughter of Robert Fitzhamon.
9. Emma ; *temp.* Henry I.
10. Mary ; occurs 1189 ; d. 1216 ; natural daughter of Geoffrey, Count of Anjou ; acknowledged as half-sister by Henry II., and as aunt by John ; probably identical with Marie de France, the Anglo-Norman poetess, 'one of the most mysterious and interesting figures in the literary history of the Middle Ages '; resisted a demand of John to contribute towards repairing royal castle.
11. J., 1216.
12. Amicia Russell, 1223.
13. Agnes Lungespee, 1243 ; presumably a relation of William Longespee, Earl of Salisbury, and natural son of Henry II.
14. Agnes de Ferrers, 1247 ; summoned to attend the expedition against Llewellyn, Prince of Wales, 1250.
15. Juliana de Bauceyn ; d. 1279.
16. Laurentia de Muscegros, 1279 ; d. 1290.
17. Joan de Bridport, 1290 ; d. 1291.
18. Mabel Gifford, 1291 ; the Bishop of Sarum ordered Richard de Slykeborn, a Minorite, and Richard le Brun to be her confessors, 1302 ; her brother, Godfred Gifford, Bishop of Worcester, left her a legacy, 1301.
19. Alice de Lavyngton, 1302 ; d. 1315.
20. Margaret Aucher, 1315 ; d. 1329.
21. Dionisia le Blunde, 1329 ; d. 1345.
22. Joan Duket, 1345 ; d. 1350.
23. Margaret de Leukenore, 1350.
24. Joan Formage, 1362 ; d. 1394 ; in 1368 Bishop Wyvil granted her a dispensation ' to go out of the monastery to one of her manors to take the air and divert herself.'
25. Egelina de Counteville, 1395.
26. Cecilia Fovent ; occurs 1398 ; d. 1423.
27. Margaret Stourton, 1423 ; d. 1441.
28. Edith Bonham, 1441 ; d. 1460.
29. Margaret St. John, 1460.
30. Alice Gibbes ; d. 1496.
31. Margaret Twyneo, 1496 ; d. 1505.
32. Elizabeth Shelford, 1505 ; d. 1528.

33. Elizabeth Zouche, or Zuche, 1529; surrendered the abbey, 1539.

[W. M. W.]

V.C.H., Dorset. ii. 73-9; Hutchins, *Hist. of Dorset,* ii. : for Abbess Mary, *E.H.R.,* xxv. 303; xxvi. 317.

SHARP, John (1645-1714), Archbishop of York. His father, a wet- and dry-salter of Bradford, was Puritan in sympathy; but his mother, a Royalist, taught him to love the Prayer Book and its system. He specially admired the Litany, and it was read daily 'at the early prayers in his family as long as he lived.' He preferred, however, the Communion Office of King Edward's First Service Book (to that of 1662), 'as a more proper office for the celebration of those mysteries.' He entered Christ's, Cambridge, April 1660, holding Calvinist opinions learnt from his father. These he rejected later. He became Scholar, but failed to become Fellow. He graduated B.A., 1663; M.A., 1667, in which year he was ordained, and became tutor and domestic chaplain to Sir Heneage Finch, then Solicitor-General, afterwards Lord Nottingham. 1673 he became Archdeacon of Berkshire; 1675 Prebendary of Norwich and Rector of St. Giles-in-the-Fields. He rapidly became a famous preacher, the effect of the simplicity and directness of his sermons being aided by his beautiful voice, and he was both a scholar and a diligent parish priest. His devotion in celebrating the Holy Communion was specially remarkable. In 1681 he became Dean of Norwich, retaining his London living. In 1686, incensed by the efforts of Roman Catholic proselytisers, he preached strongly on the Roman controversy, which annoyed the King, who directed Compton, Bishop of London, to suspend him. The bishop refused, Sharp was reinstated in the royal favour, largely through Jeffreys, who was his friend. He refused to read the Declaration of 1688. [SEVEN BISHOPS.] He took the oaths to William and Mary, 1689, and was made Dean of Canterbury. He declined to accept any see vacated by a Nonjuror (*q.v.*), but in 1691 was consecrated Archbishop of York. He was a model prelate, strangely careful as to his preferment, knowing his clergy, and being specially eager about their preaching. He was scrupulous in examining ordination candidates, and his charges to them were 'very weighty and pathetical.' He was till the end of his life a frequent and diligent preacher, and was a man of spiritual life, fasting rigorously, and giving much time to prayer. He was much seen in cases of

conscience, and acted as spiritual adviser (though not actually, it would seem, as confessor) to Queen Anne. He was eager to introduce episcopacy into Prussia, cultivated relations with the orthodox Churches of the East, and was a good friend to the episcopal clergy in Scotland. He was doubtful as to the position of the foreign Protestant Churches, but helped them with money. He took little part in politics, but acted with great independence. As archbishop he exercised discipline in moral cases strictly over clergy and laity alike, and he reformed the chapter at Southwell. His interest in learning was great; he drew up an elaborate account of his see and predecessors from Paulinus (*q.v.*) to Lamplugh; and he was an authority on coins. [S. L. O.]

Life, written by his son, Archdeacon Sharp, first published 1825: Norgate in *D.N.B.*

SHELDON, Gilbert (1598-1677), Archbishop of Canterbury, was son of Roger Sheldon of Ellastone, Derbyshire, a servant to the seventh Earl of Shrewsbury. He was at Trinity College, Oxford (B.A., 1617; M.A., 1620), and Fellow of All Souls (1622), the year of his ordination. He held various benefices, and was brought into favour with the King. He became a friend of Falkland, and was often with the theological and literary coterie at Great Tew. In 1626 he became Warden of All Souls, and he was an active supporter of Laud's reforms, and anti-Roman precautions, in the University. During the war he was often in attendance on the King; he was one of the negotiators at Uxbridge, 1644; in 1646 received Charles's vow to restore all Church lands and impropriations; and in 1647 was with him at Newmarket and Carisbrooke. He was ejected from All Souls, and imprisoned for a time, in 1648, and remained in seclusion in the Midlands during the interregnum. At the Restoration he became Bishop of London (consecrated, 28th October 1660). He took but slight part, though that perhaps a controlling one, in the Savoy Conference (*q.v.*), but exercised most of the powers of the primacy while Juxon (*q.v.*) lived, and succeeded him on his death. He made the important arrangement with Clarendon, soon after he became archbishop, that the Convocations (*q.v.*) should no longer tax the clergy. He became Chancellor of the University of Oxford, 1667 (resigned, 1669), and built the Sheldon Theatre at his own cost. He was a liberal supporter of scholars. Politically he was in favour of the severe measures of Parliament against dissenters. He gave great care to the Church in England and Wales, and endeavoured to procure bishops for America. Theologically he held fast ' the true orthodox profession of the Catholic faith of Christ, being a true member of the Catholic Church within the communion of a living part thereof, the present Church of England ' (as he says in his will), and he reproved Charles II. for his wicked life, and refused him the Holy Communion, losing his favour in consequence. He died, 9th November 1677, and was buried at Croydon.

To him more than any other ecclesiastic was due the restoration of the Church under Charles II. to the position she held before the rebellion, and the establishment of Laudian principles as dominant in the Church. He was a practical, energetic, earnest man, making no show, and therefore slandered by his political and religious opponents, but the friend of good men, and so far as can be judged sincere and devoted, though reserved in his own personal religious life. His papers, in the Bodleian Library, deserve more thorough study than they have yet received, and a complete life of him would make plain many points in a critical period of the life of the English Church.

[W. H. H.]

Burrows, *Worthies of All Souls.*

SHERLOCK, William (c. 1641-1707), Dean of St. Paul's, was educated at Eton and Peterhouse, Cambridge, graduating B.A., 1660 ; M.A., 1663. He was ordained, and in 1669 was presented to the rectory of St. George's, Lower Thames Street, and became famous as a preacher. He was made Prebendary of St. Paul's, 1681, and Master of the Temple, 1685. He was an extremely clever pamphleteer. His *Case of Resistance,* 1684, was the ablest defence of the doctrine of Non-resistance in its extremest form. He refused to read the Declaration of Indulgence, and violently attacked popery under James II., but refused the oaths, 1689, and became a Nonjuror (*q.v.*), though it seems that he was not actually deprived. When he suddenly took the oaths, 1690, and published his *Case of Allegiance,* 1691, an answer to his earlier views, he was bitterly attacked by the party he deserted. He was converted, he said, by Sancroft's publication of *Overall's Convocation Book* [OVERALL], which justified obedience to a king *de facto.* June 1691 he was made Dean of St. Paul's, and a bookseller, seeing him handing his wife along St. Paul's Churchyard, said : ' There goes Dr. Sherlock, with his reasons for taking the oath at his fingers'

ends.' He became the bitter opponent of his former friends, and 1698, when White, deprived Bishop of Peterborough, was buried in the churchyard of St. Gregory's (a church under the dean's jurisdiction), Sherlock refused to allow Bishop Turner (deprived of Ely) to officiate at the grave. ' Is not this a precious mannikin of a dean ? ' Turner wrote to his brother. Sherlock embarked on the Unitarian controversy, with no great result, save that he caused two writers, W. Manning and T. Evelyn, to abandon the orthodox position. 1698 he became Rector of Therfield, Herts, and, 1704, resigned his Mastership of the Temple, where his son succeeded him. He died at Hampstead, June 1707, and is buried in St. Paul's. He was the author of forty-three works.

Sherlock, Thomas (1678-1761), Bishop of London, was his eldest son, and was educated at Eton and St. Catherine's College, Cambridge, where his lifelong rivalry with Hoadly (*q.v.*), two years his senior, began. Ordained, 1701, he became Master of the Temple, 1704, a post he held till 1753, and he was extraordinarily popular. He became Master of his college, 1714, and Dean of Chichester, 1715. He was engaged in pamphlet war with Hoadly, and was chairman of the committee of Convocation appointed to examine his notorious sermon when Convocation was prorogued, 1717. He lost his royal chaplainship a year later. He was in favour with George II., and became Bishop successively of Bangor (1728), Salisbury (1734), and London (1748). He is said to have refused both archbishoprics—York, 1743, and Canterbury, 1747. Though he supported Walpole in Parliament, some remains of his earlier High Churchmanship clung to him. He endeavoured, unsuccessfully, to get bishops consecrated for the American colonies, and pleaded nobly for the Scots episcopal clergy in the House of Lords in 1746. Even in 1716 he had not feared to say a word in a sermon on behalf of the Nonjurors.

[S. L. O.]

Lathbury, *Hist. of the Nonjurors* ; Overton, *The Nonjurors* ; *Memoirs of a Royal Chaplain, 1729-63* ; and articles in *D.N.B.*

SIBTHORP, Richard Waldo (1792-1879), priest, was educated at Eltham, Westminster, and University College, Oxford ; elected Demy of Magdalen College, 1810, and Fellow, 1818. He graduated B.A., 1813 ; M.A., 1816 ; B.D., 1823. He is remarkable, in Mr. Gladstone's phrase, as having ' thrice cleared the chasm which lies between the Roman and Anglican Churches ' (*Gleanings,*

vii. 212). As an undergraduate he fled from Oxford. October 1811, to become a Roman Catholic, but was brought back by his elder brother and a detective before his reception. He was ordained in the English Church, 1815, and became a strong Evangelical. working in Lincolnshire, Hull, and from 1825-9 at various proprietary chapels in London, and was Lecturer at St. John's, Bedford Row, under Baptist Noel, then an Evangelical leader. 1829 he returned to Oxford, where his preaching attracted Mr. Gladstone. 1830-41 he was Incumbent of St. James's, Ryde, Isle of Wight. Here, after reading the *Tracts for the Times*, his views changed about 1837 ; but he was never ' wholly what was called a " Tractarian," ' though he began more frequent and more elaborate and musical services, with surpliced choristers.

27th October 1841 he was received into the Roman Church, and was reordained priest, 21st May 1842. He worked at Birmingham, and later settled near St. Helen's, Isle of Wight. Here, after much doubt as to the devotion paid to the Blessed Virgin, he returned to the English Church, October 1843. After three years, spent chiefly at Winchester, where the dulness of the cathedral services depressed him, Bishop Sumner refused to allow him to act as a priest. He was subsequently given the required permission by Bishop Kaye of Lincoln, 1847. Having settled at Lincoln, he founded and liberally endowed a bede-house, St. Anne's, to the memory of his mother. He lived in Lincoln till 1864. January 1865 he was received again into the Roman Church, and worked in Nottingham on the staff of the Roman Catholic cathedral until 1874, when at his own request he was placed on the list of retired priests. He retained deep affection for Anglicans, and wrote (22nd November 1876) : ' After all, for sound divinity, give me the old Anglicans and the old Puritans'; and in his last letter to Dr. Bloxam : ' Whatever you do, "do not be tempted to leave your present position." is the closing advice of your old friend.' He died at Nottingham, 10th April 1879, but was buried, by his direction, with the burial service of the English Church, in Lincoln Cemetery. Mr. Gladstone described him as 'a devout, refined, attractive man,' and said : ' I can never think of him but as a simple, rare, truly elect soul.' Dean Church (*On Temper*) calls attention to his story as specially marked by ' patience. sweetness, and equity.' [S. L. O.]

MS. letters in the writer's possession : J. Fowler, *Life and Letters*; Gladstone. *Gleanings*, vii. ; *Magdalen College Register*, vii.

SIMEON, Charles (1759-1836), Evangelical divine, son of Richard Simeon of Reading, whose brother John was M.P. for Reading, and was created a baronet. He was educated at Eton, where he was a peculiarly active boy, could ' jump over half a dozen chairs in succession, and snuff a candle with his feet ' ; and he grew up to be a remarkably good horseman. In after years he said, in the self-accusing manner of the saints, that his conduct at school had been deplorable ; but no worse faults were remembered by his schoolfellows than extravagance and hot temper. In 1776 a National Fast-Day was proclaimed, as an act of self-abasement before God for national sins. Simeon was deeply moved by the call, applied it to his own case, and ' accordingly spent the day in fasting and prayer.' One of his schoolfellows recorded that he ' became peculiarly strict from that period.' In 1779 he entered King's College, Cambridge, where, as at other colleges, the rule was that every undergraduate must communicate in the chapel. ' The thought rushed into my mind that Satan himself was as fit to attend as I ; and that, if I must attend, I must *prepare* for attendance there. Without a moment's loss of time, I bought *The Whole Duty of Man*, the only religious book that I had ever heard of, and began to read it with great diligence ; at the same time calling my ways to remembrance, and crying to God for mercy ; and so earnest was I in these exercises that within the three weeks I made myself quite ill with reading, fasting, and prayer.' The appointed day arrived, and the Communion was duly made ; but it brought no peace to Simeon's troubled soul. He knew that on Easter Day he must communicate again, and he ' continued with unabated earnestness to search out and mourn over the numberless iniquities of my former life ; and so greatly was my mind oppressed with the weight of them, that I frequently looked upon the dogs with envy, wishing, if it were possible, that I could be blessed with their mortality, and they be cursed with my immortality in my stead.' These spiritual agonies went on till the beginning of Holy Week, or, as it was then called, Passion Week ; and then, when reading Bishop Wilson's *Short and Plain Instruction for the better understanding of the Lord's Supper*, Simeon came upon a passage in which the ritual of the sin-offering is interpreted as signifying the Atonement. Then, quite suddenly, ' the thought came into my mind, What, may I transfer all my guilt to another ? Has God provided an Offering for me, that I may lay my sins on His head ? Then, God willing, I will not bear them on my soul one moment longer. . . . From that hour peace flowed in rich abundance into my soul ; and at the Lord's Table in our chapel I had the sweetest access to God through my blessed Saviour.'

The practical effects of this conversion immediately became visible. Simeon had been a conspicuous dandy, and had spent a great deal on his dress ; now he ' practised the most rigid economy, consecrating a stated part of my income to the Lord, together with all that I could save out of the part reserved for my own use.' He gathered some of the college servants in his rooms for a simple service, at which he read ' a good book ' and some of the prayers of the Church. He began a life of devotional seclusion, and recorded its incidents day by day in his journal.

' Monday in Passion Week (1780). I have determined that I will neither eat nor drink all this week, except at dinner, and that sparingly.'

We know little of Simeon's intellectual progress during this period. He brought from Eton an adequate amount of Latin scholarship, but less Greek. The dubious privilege of King's prevented him from entering for any public examination, and he was elected Fellow of his college in January 1782. He was ordained deacon in Ely Cathedral on Trinity Sunday, 26th May 1782, being four months under the canonical age. He graduated B.A., January 1783. He attached himself as honorary curate to St. Edward's Church, where he preached his first sermon on the 2nd of June 1782. The effect of his preaching was immediate and remarkable. The church was filled to overflowing, and the communicants were trebled. The fame of the young preacher went abroad, and in the autumn of 1782 he was appointed to the incumbency of Trinity Church, ' which stands in the heart of Cambridge.' As the post was technically only a curacy in charge held for the bishop, the fact that Simeon was only a deacon was no bar to his appointment. He was ordained priest at Trinity, 1783. Henry Venn (*q.v.*) wrote him these words of encouragement : ' Thou art called to be a man of war from thy youth. May the Captain of our Salvation be thy guide, shield, and strength.' Simeon needed all the encouragement he could get, for his appointment was extremely unpopular with the parishioners, who had wished for another minister. But by degrees his energy and spiritual power made their mark. He gathered together the more devout members

of his congregation in a ' society,' or, as it would now be called, a ' guild,' for devotional exercises and parochial work. He was sedulous in teaching and catechising. He prepared the young most carefully for confirmation, then so often neglected or profaned. Allying himself with the illustrious Henry Venn, he often went ' itinerating ' in neglected villages, preaching the Gospel in barns and other unlicensed places. But, though he was a most zealous parish priest, it was within the University that his influence was most powerfully felt. The undergraduates gathered round him in ever-increasing numbers, and drank in from his lips the Gospel of free Redemption through the Blood of Christ. He himself thus described the threefold object of all his preaching : ' To humble the sinner, to exalt the Saviour, to promote holiness.' As the third object shows, there was nothing Antinomian in his teaching.

But, though the young men heard him gladly, he was persistently opposed by the seniors in Cambridge, and insulted, vilified, and even threatened by the godless mob, who took their tone from their superiors. One incident of that rough time must be given in his own words : ' When I was an object of much contempt and derision in the university, I strolled forth one day, buffeted and afflicted, with my little Testament in my hand. I prayed earnestly to my God that He would comfort me with some cordial from His Word, and that, on opening the book, I might find some text which should sustain me. . . . The first text which caught my eye was this: *They found a man of Cyrene, Simon by name ; him they compelled to bear His cross.* You know Simon is the same name as Simeon. What a world of instruction was here. What a blessed hint for my encouragement ! To have the cross laid upon me, that I might bear it after Jesus. What a privilege ! It was enough. Now I could leap and sing for joy as one whom Jesus was honouring with a participation of His sufferings.'

For some ten years this storm of opposition lasted, and then gradually died down. The senior part of the University became tolerant and even cordial. The undergraduates had never failed in their loyalty to him ; and he drew successive generations closer and closer to himself, not merely by his preaching, but by social intercourse. From first to last he lived in rooms in King's, and there he used to assemble his undergraduate friends. Prayer and praise and religious instruction formed the staple of the entertainment; questions on religious topics were invited, and the answers given with all possible earnestness, though flippant or foolish queries were promptly rebuked. On Friday evenings he always gave 'open tea-parties,' to which men could come without invitation, and he constantly lectured on the art of preparing sermons and the various difficulties of the ministerial office. Macaulay, whose undergraduate days coincided with those of Simeon's ascendancy, wrote : 'If you knew what his authority and influence were, and how they extended from Cambridge to the most remote corners of England, you would allow that his real sway over the Church was far greater than that of any primate.'

Simeon was fundamentally and essentially an Evangelical of the Evangelicals, but not less distinctly a loyal son of the Church of England. He exalted the Christian ministry. He taught a doctrine not distinguishable from Baptismal Regeneration. He had a pious devotion to the Holy Communion. He had a lively admiration for the Prayer Book, and found it conducive to the most exalted devotion. Mr. Gladstone (*q.v.*), reviewing the religious history of the time, said : 'There can hardly be a question that the Evangelical teaching with respect to the Church and the Sacraments fell below the standard of the Prayer Book, or the Articles, or both. Indeed, an ingenuous confession to this effect is to be found in the lectures of Mr. Simeon.' The fault which Simeon saw in some of his brother-Evangelicals he was himself most careful to avoid. Indeed, his determined churchmanship gave annoyance to some of his followers, who said that 'Mr. Simeon was more of a *Church-man* than a *Gospel-man*.' His own formula was: 'The Bible first, the Prayer Book next, and all other books and doings in subordination to both.' He may fairly be regarded as the last of the Evangelicals, as they were before what they esteemed some erroneous tendencies in the Oxford Movement converted them into Low Churchmen and controversialists.

The deep and permanent effect of Simeon's teaching was not marred, rather it was enhanced, by certain peculiarities of style and phrase. His favourite gesture in the pulpit resembled that of catching a fly between his finger and thumb. He dressed to the end as clergymen dressed in his early youth. His phraseology and pronunciation were old-fashioned. Speaking of the religious state of the country, he said : 'I see a *doo* everywhere, but a shower nowhere.' When praying extem-

pore, as a grace before breakfast, he said : 'And we pray not for ourselves alone, but also for the poor ignorant creatures who wait behind our chairs.'

He died after a short illness (contracted through his determination to pay his respects in person to the newly appointed Bishop of Ely) on the 12th November 1836. He was buried under the chapel of King's College, which had been his home for fifty-eight years.

All through life he had practised a systematic benevolence, and all that was left of his fortune—£5000—he bequeathed to the trust which he had created for buying advowsons. His published sermons—*Horæ Homileticæ*—ran to seventeen volumes.

[G. W. E. R.]

Memoirs, ed. W. Carus : Bishop Moule, Charles Simeon ; and oral tradition.

SMART, Peter (1569-1652), Puritan divine, educated at Westminster School, Student of Christ Church, Oxford; M.A., 1595. William James, Dean of Durham, appointed him Master of the Durham Grammar School in 1598. James, when Bishop of Durham, ordained Smart and gave him a prebend at Durham, 30th December 1609. When Neile was bishop (1617-27) Smart for years absented himself from the Holy Eucharist in the cathedral on account of the altar and the embroidered copes. To plain copes, such as were worn when James I. communicated there in 1617, he did not object. On Sunday, 27th July 1628, he preached, and afterwards printed, a violent sermon against the character of the services under Cosin (*q.v.*), then a prebendary. The High Commission for the province of York suspended him. In 1629 his case was transmitted to the High Commission of the province of Canterbury. He was held in custody and his book burnt. In 1631 he was at length deposed and fined £500. He refused to pay, and was imprisoned. His friends raised £400 a year to support him and his family. In 1641 the Commons resolved that his sentence was void, and directed the prosecution of Cosin. Smart's charges broke down under Cosin's replies; but he received back his preferments, took 'the League and Covenant' in 1643, and gave evidence at the trial of Laud in 1644. He died in 1652 at Baxter Wood near Durham.

His books are intemperate tirades against 'the rotten hereticall Arminian Sectaries,' as he calls the clergy who differ from him. They throw light on the ordinary Church customs of the time as well as on the changes which he disliked at Durham. He describes these changes in his *Catalogue of superstitious innovations in the change of services and ceremonial brought into Durham cathedral by Bishop Neal,* published in 1642, and *A short treatise of altars, altar furniture, altar cringing,* 1643. He objects that the people have been compelled to stand during the singing of the Nicene Creed and at the *Gloria Patri,* which suggests that they had previously sat, as is commonly done in Roman Catholic churches. Also that the preacher was no longer suffered to dismiss the congregation, and that the prayers at the altar were now concluded before the dismissal. He dislikes especially the new ' glorious high Altar ' of stone with crucifixes and tapers, and its ' precious golden Pall,' which had upon it ' the false story of the Assumption of our Lady.' He says that from 1627 to 1629 ' every day, working dayes and holy dayes, they went to the Altar (as they termed it) to say a second Service, so they call the Communion Service,' and ' they tooke for Assistants at the Communion the whole quire men and children which communicated not.' From the point of view of some modern controversies, Smart's evidence is important as proving the use of Eucharistic or Mass vestments in the Church of England after the Reformation. Owing largely to the action of Puritan bishops, who denied to their clergy the liberty of obeying the law of this Church and realm, these vestments were commonly disused. But at Durham they were certainly in use for some years early in the seventeenth century. Smart makes two distinct charges against the clergy. First, that they offend in using instead of ' decent,' that is ' plaine,' copes, ' sumptuous Copes, embroidered with Images.' Secondly, ' in using scurvie, py-bald, curtal'd, and ridiculous Vestments, falsly called Copes (being indeed very fools coats), at the Communion Table, and that dayly at the Administration of the Holy Communion.' The above statements, with no essential variation, are made in both the books mentioned above. Elsewhere he says: ' That is not a decent cope which is no cope at all, but a gay curtal'd vestment, reaching scarce down to the knee, of which our Durhamers had 2, condemned and forbidden by the Bishop in his Visitation, and some other of the præbendaries, which tearmed them jackets, tunicles, heralds' coats, etc., etc.' (Rawlinson MSS.). Cosin's entry in the Acts of Chapter relating to the above is dated 12th June 1627, and says: ' It is further agreed that the three vestments, and one white cope, now belonging to the Vestry of this Church, shall be taken and carried to London, to be

altered and changed into fair and large copes, according to the Canons and Constitutions of the Church of England.' The above passages show that at least two tunicles with another vestment, which was apparently a chasuble of the same set, were in use previous to 1627. And of the five old copes now preserved at Durham one dates from the time of Charles I., and is said to have been his gift, and one of the other four is adorned at the back with an embroidered crucifix taken from the back of a chasuble. The best is of magnificent blue cloth of gold. These five copes were in use until 1759. By a strange coincidence the ancient vestments which remain at St. John's College, Oxford, include two tunicles, a white cope of the same set, the orphreys of two chasubles (one of Mary's time), and, the finest of all, a cope of blue and gold. It is doubtful if the Marian chasuble was mutilated until late in the seventeenth century.   [L. P.]

Works; *Cosin's Correspondence*, Part I. vol. lii., Surtees Society ; *D.N.B.* ; Kitchin, *Seven Sages of Durham.*

SMITH, Sydney (1771-1845), was educated at Winchester College, where his experiences filled him with deep distaste for public schools. Of the pleasures of school-life he remembered nothing, but had a vivid memory of fagging, flogging, bullying, and gerund-grinding. In January 1789 he went up to New College, and became Fellow in 1791. Members of New College were in those days exempt from public examinations, so nothing can be known of his academical progress, but his writings show that he was a sound scholar, with a wide knowledge of English as well as of classical literature. He took his degree in 1792. He had dabbled in anatomy and chemistry at Oxford, and the Regius Professor of Medicine recommended him to be a doctor. His father wanted him to go as a supercargo to China. His own strong preference was for the bar, but necessity determined him to seek holy orders. He assumed the sacred character without enthusiasm, and looked back on its adoption with regret. He was ordained priest in Christ Church in 1796. He turned his back on Oxford, where he had never been happy, and became curate in charge of Netheravon, near Amesbury. ' Nothing.' he wrote, ' can equal the profound, the immeasurable, the awful dulness of the place.' He had worked heartily among the ignorant and degraded villagers. The squire, Mr. Hicks-Beach, took a fancy to him, and made him travelling tutor to his son. In 1798 he went with young

2 N   (561)

Beach to Edinburgh, then in the height of its intellectual fame. Here he worked hard at natural and moral philosophy ; and by often preaching at the episcopal chapel in Rose Street acquired considerable reputation for a vigorous and unconventional eloquence. He preached a sound and practical morality, but there is very little ' Gospel ' in his sermons. In July 1800 he married Amelia Pybus, and continued to reside in Edinburgh, taking private pupils.

In 1802 he joined Jeffrey, Brougham, and Murray in founding the *Edinburgh Review*. To the first number he contributed five articles, and in all he wrote close on eighty. This connection brought him into increasing prominence. In 1803 he settled in London. and was at once introduced into the brilliant society which gathered at Holland House. He obtained clerical work as ' Alternate Evening Preacher at the Foundling Hospital.' He tried to open a proprietary chapel on his own account, but was foiled by the obstinacy of the rector of the parish. He was appointed Morning Preacher at Berkeley Chapel, Mayfair, and at Fitzroy Chapel, Fitzroy Square. In 1806 the Chancellor's living at Foston - le - Clay, near York, fell vacant ; and Lord Chancellor Erskine cordially accepted ' the nominee of Lord and Lady Holland:' Foston was worth £500 a year, and the Archbishop of York allowed the rector to be non-resident ; so Smith continued in London.

The scandals of ' Non-Residence ' had now begun to disturb the minds of all who were under any serious impression of religion. In 1808 Edward Vernon (afterwards Harcourt) became Archbishop of York. He was the last of the ' Prince-Archbishops,' and ruled the northern province with zeal and splendour for forty years. He soon began to put the Clergy Residence Act of 1803 in force. One of its victims was Sydney Smith, who was now removed from the joys of London to the austerities of Foston-le-Clay, and obeyed the call with great reluctance. ' A diner-out, a wit, and a popular preacher, I was suddenly caught up by the Archbishop of York, and transported to my living in Yorkshire, where there had not been a resident clergyman for a hundred and fifty years. Fresh from London, and not knowing a turnip from a carrot, I was compelled to farm three hundred acres. I turned farmer, as I could not let my land. Added to all these domestic cares, I was village parson, village doctor, village comforter, village magistrate, and *Edinburgh Reviewer*.' He preached with such vigour

that ' the accumulated dust of a hundred and fifty years flew out of the pulpit cushion, and for some minutes made the congregation invisible.' By his constant contributions to the *Edinburgh* he was helping forward good causes, and establishing his fame as the greatest writer who ever brought humour to the service of politics and philanthropy. In 1829 he preached two splendid sermons on the principles of Christian justice before the Judges of Assize at York. He was an early, enthusiastic, and powerful advocate of Roman Catholic Emancipation. His *Letters of Peter Plymley*, published anonymously in 1807 and 1808, excited immense curiosity, and twenty thousand copies were sold.

In 1828 Lord Chancellor Lyndhurst, who though a political opponent was a private friend, appointed him to a stall in Bristol Cathedral, which carried with it the incumbency of Halberton, near Tiverton, and he exchanged the living of Foston for that of Combe Florey in Somerset, which could be held conjointly with Halberton. He instantly began to repair the parsonage, but the church he left as dilapidated as he found it. There he performed two services on Sunday, administered the Holy Communion once a month, and preached his practical sermons, transcribed from his execrable manuscript by the clerk. The common people called him a ' bould ' preacher, for he ' liked to have his arms free, and to thump the cushion.'

In November 1830, when the Whigs came in, Sydney Smith again plied pen and voice in furtherance of their policy. He had his reward —not indeed a bishopric, to which his admirers thought him entitled, but a residentiary canonry of St. Paul's : ' A snug thing, being worth full £2000 a year ' ; and a house, No. 1 Amen Court, which he let, preferring to live in the West End. He took a leading part in the business of the chapter, did much to restore and preserve the monuments, and brought the New River into the cathedral by mains.

His preaching (of which his sermon on the ' Duties of the Queen ' is a fine specimen) drew fashionable congregations. Greville said : ' Manner impressive, voice sonorous and agreeable ; rather familiar, but not offensively so.' ' Never,' said another observer, ' did anybody to my mind look more like a High Churchman, as he walked up the aisle to the altar—there was an air of so much proud dignity in his appearance.' Yet, whatever he looked, a High Churchman he certainly was not. He was not a Low Churchman, and still less an Evangelical. He was eternally poking fun at 'the patent Christianity of Clapham,' at Methodists and missionaries. He was a convinced Christian of the school of Paley, and firmly believed that the Established Church was the safeguard of national religion. The substance of his teaching was: 'Our business is to be good and happy to-day.' He detested what he saw and heard of the Oxford Movement, yet he bore significant testimony to its progress. In 1842 he wrote: 'Nothing so remarkable in England as the progress of these foolish people.'

Sydney Smith's defects as a clergyman seem to arise mainly from the tone of the time in which he grew up, and from the circumstances under which he was forced into holy orders. He was a genuinely religious man according to his light and opportunity, the happy possessor of a rich and singular talent—the talent of argumentative humour, which he used through a long life in the service of the helpless, the persecuted, and the poor.

He died on the 22nd of February 1845, and was buried at Kensal Green.

[G. W. E. R.]

Lives by Lady Holland, Stuart Reid, and G. W. E. Russell (Eng. Men of Letters).

SOCIETIES, Ecclesiastical. Under this head are grouped the voluntary organisations of churchmen which have been formed by the exigencies of the ecclesiastical controversy of the nineteenth century.

1. *The English Church Union.*—In 1844 Churchmen in the West, fearing the policy of the recently formed (1839) Committee of the Council on Education, and anxious for the safety of Church schools, formed a society known as the Bristol Church Union. This rapidly became an organ of opinion on other Church questions. In 1848 and 1849 other Unions sprang up which were affiliated to the Bristol Union, where the leading spirit was Archdeacon Denison (*q.v.*). The archdeacon's violent opposition to Mr. Gladstone (*q.v.*) when he was seeking re-election for the University of Oxford, 1853, dislocated the Bristol Union, and relations between it and its affiliated Unions were suspended. In 1859 the riots at St. George's in the East and other causes roused Churchmen to combine, and 8th February 1859 a conference of sixteen members, under the chairmanship of Sir Stephen Glynne, which met again on 12th May, founded the 'Church of England Protection Society.'

There then existed the Church Unions of Bristol, Exeter, Chester, Manchester, London, Coventry, Gloucester, Norwich, Yorkshire, and the South Church Union. The London Church Union had been most active in organising protests against the Gorham (*q.v.*) decision, and a Union (apparently dissolved by 1859), known as the 'Metropolitan Union,' had worked for the revival of Convocation. In November 1859 the Hon. Colin Lindsay, President of the Manchester Church Union, invited delegates from each Union, with the Guild of St. Alban and the recently founded Protection Society, to discuss common action. The few delegates who came resolved on 11th January 1860 that all existing Church Unions should be incorporated with the Church of England Protection Society. This was done, and on 14th March 1860 the society changed its name to the English Church Union.

The objects of the Union were those of the earlier society. They are:—

'To defend and maintain unimpaired the doctrine and discipline of the Church of England.

'To afford counsel, protection, and assistance to all persons, lay or clerical, suffering under unjust aggression or hindrance in spiritual matters.

'In general, so to promote the interests of religion as to be, by God's help, a lasting witness for the advancement of His glory and the good of His Church.'

The Hon. Colin Lindsay was elected first President. He resigned, on the ground of ill-health, in April 1868, and withdrew from the Union. Towards the end of the year he was received into the Church of Rome. His successor, Hon. C. L. Wood (afterwards second Viscount Halifax), was elected on 16th June 1868.

Membership of the English Church Union is confined to communicants of the English Church, and it has numbered in its ranks very many distinguished churchmen, as Mr. Keble (*q.v.*), Dr. Pusey (*q.v.*), and Bishop King (*q.v.*).

It has defended the clergy involved in most of the Ritual Cases (*q.v.*), and on such subjects as Church schools and the sanctity of marriage has proved itself a force to be reckoned with. On 1st January 1861 the first number of the *Church Review* appeared, 'a monthly paper, to be a medium for circulating information of the proceedings of the society,' but it was not to be called the journal of the Union, nor did it necessarily represent the opinions of the members. In 1862 it became a weekly newspaper. Difficulties occurred in 1863 as to the relations between the *Review* and the Union, and the editor of the *Review* resigned the post of secretary to the Union in 1864. The Union then began a monthly paper of its own, the *Monthly Circular*, which later changed its name to the *Church Union Gazette*. The numbers of the Union in 1911 were stated officially to be nearly 40,000, including 27 bishops.

2. *The Church Association* and kindred societies. — The Church Association was founded 6th November 1865. Its objects are : 'To uphold the doctrines, principles, and order of the Church of England, and to counteract the efforts now being made to pervert her teaching on essential points of the Christian faith, or assimilate her services to those of the Church of Rome, and, further, to encourage concerted action for the advancement and progress of spiritual religion.'

It furnished the funds for all the various ritual suits since its foundation until the Bishop of Lincoln's trial in 1888-92. It was at first supported by leading members of the Evangelical party, but its success in the law courts was fatal to its influence. Priests were imprisoned or deprived, and their goods sold to pay the costs of their prosecution, until the policy of the Association became a scandal, and Archbishop Tait (*q.v.*), at the end of his life, endeavoured, though unsuccessfully, to stop its proceedings against Mr. Mackonochie (*q.v.*). The sympathy of many Evangelicals was lost, and at the Islington Clerical Meeting of 1883 'the disastrous policy of attempting to stay error by prosecution and imprisonments' was denounced. The *Record* newspaper (the organ of Evangelical opinion in the English Church) declared in 1889 that it 'became obvious years ago that Evangelical Churchmen as a body were not in sympathy with the Church Association.' One result of the decision of Archbishop Benson in the case of the Bishop of Lincoln was that 'it caused the Church Association to abandon its policy of prosecution.' In 1870 the 'Clerical and Lay Union' was formed 'as a branch of the Church Association,' Lord Shaftesbury presiding at its first meeting. Though 'Clerical and Lay Unions' were existing in 1910, the history of the body is obscure. In 1890 the National Protestant League was founded 'to co-operate with the Church Association in maintaining the Protestant Reformation established by law, and defending it against all encroachments of Popery; also in securing the return of Protestant candidates at Parliamentary elections.' The only condition of membership appears to be the payment

of an annual subscription. The Church Association issues monthly the *Church Intelligencer*, begun in 1867, altered to another form in 1884. The Association does not publish the number of its members. In 1911 the membership of the National Protestant League was 3842.

Attempts were made to organise Evangelical Churchmen apart from the Church Association. Such were the 'Clerical and Lay Associations.' The first of these was formed for the west of England at Gloucester, 1858. Others on the same lines were the Midland Counties Association at Derby, 1859 ; Carlisle Evangelical Union, 1860 ; that for Middlesex, Hertford, and Essex, 1861 ; the Eastern District Association, 1862 ; the East Lincoln Association, 1866 ; and later Associations for the North-Western District, for Devon and Cornwall, Tunbridge Wells, Surrey, and the Northern Home Counties. Earliest and most influential was the Islington Clerical Meeting, founded in 1827 by Daniel Wilson (*q.v.*). These Associations were largely devotional, and to a great extent were intended as substitutes for the Church Congresses and Diocesan Conferences, which were regarded with suspicion by Evangelicals. Various public schools sprang from them : Trent College, Derbyshire, 1866, from the Midland Association ; the South-Eastern (now St. Lawrence) College, Ramsgate, was for a time controlled by the South-Eastern Association, founded in 1879; and the Dean Close Memorial School, Cheltenham, was founded by the Western Association in 1886. In 1880 Bishop Ryle (*q.v.*) attempted to unite the various Associations, and a central committee was formed.

In June 1889 the Protestant Churchmen's Alliance began, and in 1891 absorbed two older societies, the Protestant Association (founded 1835) and the London organisation of the Scottish Reformation Society (founded 1867), which had been amalgamated under the name of the Protestant Educational Institute in 1871. In May 1893 the Protestant Churchmen's Alliance absorbed the Union of Clerical and Lay Associations, and the united body became the National Protestant Church Union. The policy was to be one of non-litigation, and 'to educate public opinion through the press, by literature, by lectures, by schools, by the pulpit.' A 'Ladies' League,' formed in 1899, which changed its name to the Church of England League in 1904, was incorporated with the National Protestant Church Union in August 1906, and the organisation thus formed took the name of the National Church League, which has thus absorbed six different societies.

3. *Ecclesiastical Societies of Broad Church-men* have been less well known.

In 1880 was founded the 'National Church Reform Union.' It was believed that disestablishment and consequent disendowment were at hand, and the Union was formed to prevent disestablishment by Church reform. In its original paper it declared itself 'equally opposed to sectarian rigidity and to disestablishment.' It was 'identified with no theological school and, waging war on none, invites the co-operation of all.' The members of its council were, however, almost all well - known Broad Church-men, as Dean Stanley (*q.v.*), Lord Mount-Temple, Arnold Toynbee, T. H. Green, and Thomas Hughes, Q.C. The Union advocated the abolition of clerical subscription, discontinuance of the public use of the Athanasian Creed, and permission to use in the church-yards forms of burial service other than that of the Prayer Book. It supported a scheme for Church Boards to be formed in each parish to enable the laity to take a larger share in Church management, and it urged the removal of the municipal and Parliamentary disabilities for clergy. It proposed to form a Parliamentary committee, and among its most active members was the Hon. Albert Grey (later Earl Grey), who introduced Bills advocated by the Union into the House of Commons. The Union had only a brief life, but some of its aims were realised in later legislation.

A somewhat similar society, the 'Churchmen's Union,' was inaugurated on 31st October 1898 for 'the advancement of liberal religious thought.' Its first object is 'to maintain the right and duty of the Church to restate her belief from time to time as required by the progressive revelation of the Holy Spirit.' Its President was Sir Thomas Dyke - Acland, Bart. The work of the Union consists chiefly in delivering lectures and circulating pamphlets. It established a quarterly review, the *Liberal Churchman*, in November 1904, which ceased in September 1905. In April 1911 the magazine was revived under the title of the *Modern Churchman, a Mid-Monthly Magazine*. The Union in 1910 had about four hundred and fifty members.   [S. L. O.]

G. B. Roberts, *Hist. of the Eng. Ch. Union*, 1895; G. R. Balleine, *Hist. of the Evangelical Party*, 1908; information given in the official publications of the various Societies and by the courtesy of their several Secretaries.

SOCIETIES FOR THE REFORMATION OF MANNERS

were established in London during the last decade of the seventeenth century. They came into existence in order to enforce the penal statutes against vice and immorality, and may be described as an attempt to provide a private executive for these laws, the ordinary administration having failed to put them into force. The low tone of morals in England and especially in London during the century following the Restoration seemed incapable of improvement by the State, and in 1691 several private gentlemen in London attempted to remedy this by founding a society. The laws against drunkenness, profane cursing and swearing, profanation of Sunday, prostitution, and the like, largely depended for their execution upon information, and private persons were encouraged to provide information by the promise of one-third of the penalty. Among the founders of these Societies were several lawyers. In July 1691 they obtained, through Bishop Stillingfleet (*q.v.*) of Worcester, an order from Queen Mary to the justices of Middlesex urging them to put those laws into execution, and in order to provide the necessary opportunities of punishing offenders the Societies were established to provide information. Agencies were set up in London, where blank forms of warrants were kept for the conviction of offenders against whom information was laid. The members of the Societies were bidden to apply at such agencies, receive a warrant filled in with the particulars they brought, take it to the nearest magistrate, and, having sworn their information, to take the signed warrant back to the agency. These warrants, not of arrest but of conviction, were then delivered to the constables of the parishes in which the accused persons lived, and with this authority the constables could demand the statutory penalty or, in default of this, distrain on the offender's property, or, failing this, imprison him in the stocks for fixed statutory periods. A register of the warrants delivered was kept by the Society, and the constables' report to the Quarter Sessions was checked by these, as well as the accounts of the churchwardens of the parish, for the penalties levied were, by statute, given to the poor. A vigorous crusade was also carried on by the distribution of pamphlets, written against the prevailing vices, and of accounts of this new attempt to check them.

So far the original promoters had paid for printing and salaries which the movement entailed, but before long the Societies were organised upon a basis of subscriptions from members, and a constitution was defined. Weekly meetings, with a fine for absence, were held, new members were only admitted with extreme caution, and all proceedings were kept secret. Members were enjoined never to accept the one-third share of the penalty which the law allowed to informers, and the societies throughout their forty-seven years of existence always adhered to this principle. An annual meeting was held, before which a sermon was preached to the Societies at St. Mary-le-Bow. These sermons were afterwards preached quarterly. Much opposition was encountered at the outset from antagonistic magistrates, and attempts to enforce the laws were only partially successful. This antagonism was in part due to the general hatred of informing which the seventeenth century had engendered, and in part to the corruption and supineness of the justices.

The original Societies had been composed entirely of English Churchmen, but in 1693 the members, faced with the problem of securing more information, were forced to widen their basis, and the parent Society made overtures to the dissenting ministers of London to persuade their flocks to aid the movement. They did so, and henceforth the Societies cannot be called Anglican, although English Churchmen largely predominated in them. This union of churchmen and dissenters to oppose vice was held up by the Low Church bishops of the period as a hopeful sign of union, but High Churchmen did not cease to deprecate them as ' mongrel combinations ' of churchmen and dissenters. Earlier in 1693 the members of the Religious Societies (*q.v.*) in London had been persuaded to help the movement by becoming informers. Hence much confusion has been occasioned between the Religious and the Reforming Societies in both contemporary and modern writers.

The movement had influential patronage. Queen Mary, Tenison, Bishops Compton, Fowler, Trelawney, Patrick (*q.v.*), and Stillingfleet were warm supporters of it. In 1694 the Societies issued their first annual report, complaining of antagonistic and lazy magistrates. In 1695 a new Act against profane cursing and swearing (6-7 Will. III. c. 2) was passed, making conviction follow upon the oath of one witness instead of two as required by the previous statute (21 Jac. I. c. 7). By 1697 there were twenty of the Societies in London. A royal proclamation urging the executive to put the laws against vice and immorality into execution was issued in 1698 and reissued in 1699. By the foundation of the S.P.C.K. in 1698 a new

attack, and one which was to prove more profitable, was opened upon the vice of London. This Society helped the Reforming Societies by distributing their literature throughout England, and by urging its country correspondents to establish similar Societies in their several districts. More important still, it attempted to deal with the root of the evil by supplying education to the younger generation of the middle and lower classes through charity schools. In 1699 Archbishop Tenison formally commended the Societies in a circular letter to the bishops of his province, and in the next two years the official approval of the Kirk of Scotland and of the French congregation at the Savoy was secured. Some impression began to be made upon the more glaring vices, and grand juries, both in London and throughout the country, commended the efforts of the Societies.

Ever since their co-operation with the dissenters the Societies had depended mainly upon Low Churchmen for support within the Church. This tended to give them a distinctly Whig bias. In 1702 the cause received its first martyr, John Cooper, a reforming constable, being killed by some soldiers in Mayfair. In 1704 the Societies complained to Tenison of the immorality of the London stage, singling out Vanbrugh for special attack. But no result followed. In 1709 another reforming constable was killed. In this year the High Church reaction began to affect the Societies. Sacheverell (*q.v.*) preached a bitter sermon against them, which was ably answered by Josiah Woodward and John Disney (a High Churchman). The prosecutions, which numbered 3299 in 1708, had fallen by 1715 to 2571, and by 1716 to 1820. One result of this decline under Tory influence was to sever the connection begun in 1693 between the Societies and the Religious Societies.

William Nicholson, Archdeacon and afterwards Bishop of Carlisle, induced his diocesan to forbid the Carlisle churchmen to help a Society set up there in 1700. Archbishop Sharp (*q.v.*) did the same at York. The main objection was that the dissenters encouraged their congregations to attend Anglican sermons on the subject, and expected from churchmen a similar compliance. But this the high churchmen would not allow. Some of them also argued that the Societies' procedure gave the temporal magistrate authority in matters of religion, and by so doing infringed the twelfth canon. As the procedure was founded on statute law, this objection was hardly to the point. But apart from those of the High Churchmen there were other and more weighty objections to the Societies.

It was objected against them and the laws on which they were founded that they only touched the meaner criminals of the populace and allowed the influential offenders to carry on their vice unpunished. Swift and Defoe are the typical representatives of this class of objector. 'These be all cobweb laws,' writes Defoe, 'in which the small flies are catched and the greater ones break through.' And so it was. The rich drunkard was not haled before the magistrate nor the lewd young aristocrat convicted. The reason of this was to be found in the venality of the constables and the supineness and viciousness of many of the justices. What was wanted was a thorough reformation of the nation's view of vice, and this was only to be attained by striking at the root of the evil and supplying a better private and public education for the nation in general. Swift in 1709 advocated a reform of the national seminaries—the army, the navy, and the Universities, and the stage by the personal interference of the sovereign, and a stricter supervision of taverns and publishers.

Another great class of objections with which the Societies had to contend came from the frankly vicious part of the population. These were mainly levelled at the practice of laying information, and that of convicting offenders without confronting them with their accusers. Since these practices were authorised by statutes the Societies could afford to continue them, but a more serious charge from this class of objectors was that they informed for the sake of the one-third share of the penalty which the law allowed to informers. Even Lord Chief Justice Holt complained of this. In justice to the Societies it must be said that they always fearlessly stated this charge against them in their annual reports, and in denying it asked for proof, which does not seem to have been produced. On the whole, although considerable ill-feeling was aroused by their methods, yet the existence of these attacks proves that some headway against vice was made by the Societies up till 1714, though that success was mainly confined to their work in relation to the lower classes of the nation.

The Societies were not confined to London or to England. Associations were formed both on the Continent and in the American colonies, as well as in Ireland and Scotland. In England the movement spread in all directions. There was a very flourishing Society at Bristol, the minutes of which are accessible. In the north there were Societies

at Newcastle, York, Leeds, Carlisle, Chester, and Hull; in the Midlands at Nottingham, Derby, Tamworth, Warwick, Coventry, Stafford, and Leicester; in the west at Gloucester, Shrewsbury, and throughout Wales; and in the south at Canterbury, Dover, Portsmouth, Lyme Regis, and Bristol. Besides these town organisations many country Societies for Reformation existed. In Ireland several existed in Dublin and other towns. A very interesting development of the movement also occurred in Scotland.

The period 1714-38 is the period of the Societies' decline in England. Under Whig supremacy they might have been expected to revive, and though they did so for a short time they soon sank into extinction, and in 1738 published their last report. This extinction was not due to their work being completed, for the need for it was more pressing than ever, but they were being gradually superseded in their various functions by other bodies. The State began to assume its rightful responsibility of executing the laws. Commissions of magistrates were appointed to deal with various evils, and grand juries were urged to present offenders on their own account. Again, the literary crusade of the Societies was gradually assumed by the S.P.C.K., which was also, by its policy of erecting charity schools, striking at the root of the moral evils of the time—the lack of education. Besides this, the fact that the Societies had never been able to reach the upper classes had reacted on their membership. Their members were not of the same calibre as in earlier times, and were less carefully chosen. This was probably due to the fact that the general feeling of the nation was tending to be absorbed by moral rather than by theological problems. The Deistic controversy brought theological discussion into the arena of the streets, and the general philanthropic impulses if not absorbed by this were caught up by other, more distinctly charitable and less inquisitorial, societies, which were springing up all over London and the country.

The Societies could really only last until the State machinery was set to work to fulfil the State's functions. Since they awakened the State to its responsibility, however indirectly, their efforts were not wasted. The amount of their work may be judged from the fact that from 1691 to 1738 they had made no fewer than 101,638 prosecutions, and had distributed more than 444,000 books and pamphlets in support of their crusade. Later attempts to revive these organisations by the Methodists in 1707 and by William

Wilberforce (*q.v.*) and Bishop Beilby Porteous at the end of the eighteenth century were not successful, although the Wesleyan reforming societies existed for some years and caused more than 10,000 arrests. But by this time the statutes upon the operation of which the earlier Societies was based were gradually being superseded or repealed.   [G. V. P.]

G. V. Portus, *Caritas Anglicana*, 1912; Overton, *Life in the Eng. Ch., 1660-1714*; Yates, *Account of the Societies for the Reformation of Manners*, 1699; pamphlets and papers of the Societies in the Bodleian and B. Mus. and MSS. of the S.P.C.K.

SOCIETIES, Religious. The religious societies which were started in London in 1678 owe their establishment mainly to the preaching of Anthony Horneck of the Savoy Church, Beveridge (afterwards Bishop of St. Asaph), and Smythies of St. Michael's Cornhill. Several young men, powerfully attracted by the sermons of these preachers, agreed to meet together every week for religious purposes. These societies were probably in imitation of various Socinian and atheistical clubs which were then flourishing in London. Horneck became patron and director, and drew up the constitution of the first Religious Societies, which was the model for the regulation of such organisations for more than seventy years. Members were to meet every week, under pain of a fine of threepence for absence, to contribute sixpence weekly to some charitable design, and to be directed and controlled by English clergy. Stewards were elected to administer the funds, and an annual dinner, preceded by a sermon, was arranged. The Societies were cautiously co-optive, and the last chapter of the constitution forms a comprehensive rule of life, pledging them to loyalty to the Church and the cultivation of a humble Christian spirit. Soon after their foundation regular monthly Communion was enjoined on all members.

Under James II. the Societies became suspected of popery. Probably the suspicion arose from the secrecy of their meetings and the mysticism of Horneck. Many members left the Societies, but the bolder spirits proved their loyalty by establishing daily prayers at St. Clement Danes in opposition to the Mass at the Chapel Royal. This marks a new development. Henceforth it became the aim of every Society to maintain regular services in some church in London, so that by 1714 no fewer than twenty-seven of the ninety-nine London churches depended on the Religious Societies for some of their regular services. Generally the services the Societies supplied took the form of monthly lectures in preparation for the Holy Eucharist. But the meetings were still under suspicion, and in order to escape molestation the members changed the name of their 'societies' into that of 'clubs,' and by meeting at a public-house and spending an odd shilling in drink they successfully allayed suspicion, for the Societies never made total abstinence a feature of their organisation.

After the Revolution, 1688, the Societies again became active, and began deliberately to increase their numbers. No longer were they purely 'self-help' societies, for the provision of services for churches had made them distinctly philanthropic. And this character was maintained by an extension of charitable efforts on the part of individual members. This brought them more before the public, and as a result criticism of their organisations began. Thus challenged, the members laid an apology, in the form of a statement of their aims and methods, before Compton, Bishop of London. He was fully satisfied, and dismissed them with the remark: 'God forbid I should be against such excellent designs.' A little later Archbishop Tillotson (*q.v.*) also expressed himself in their favour. The chief objections to them were that they tended to schism, that they invaded the office of the parish priest, and that they engendered spiritual pride. In defence the members pointed to their rules, which enjoined loyalty, humility, and prayerfulness. The argument that they invaded the parson's office was captious at a time when the London parishes were in dire need of pastoral help. As a matter of fact, the Societies brought many dissenters, such as Quakers and Anabaptists, back to the Church. A more serious charge, that they hindered parochial Communion, was met by their declared design to extend the movement till each parish had its own Religious Society.

Meanwhile the Societies found warm supporters in Archbishop Tillotson, Bishops Compton, Beveridge of St. Asaph, Fowler of Gloucester, and Kidder of Bath and Wells, and Queen Mary. They further made provision for funeral sermons for deceased members. Their philanthropy now took another direction. In 1691 the first Societies for Reformation of Manners (*q.v.*) were started in London, and were recruited from the Religious Societies. This connection between the two has been responsible for much confusion between them in the accounts both of contemporary and modern historians of the movement. The Religious Societies were distinctly Anglican; the Reforming Societies, though originally composed of churchmen, were soon forced to abandon their denominational basis of membership.

Little more is heard of the Religious Societies until Anne's reign, when they were drawn up into the High Church reaction of 1708. Early in the Georgian period, indeed, Archbishop Wake (*q.v.*) was forced to take steps to prevent the charity schools under their control from becoming tainted with Jacobitism. During the intervening period, however, they had greatly increased. By 1701 there were no less than forty of them in London and Westminster, they had spread all over England, and had even reached Ireland, where they were warmly defended by Bonnell, the Accountant-General. In England the movement flourished more in Kent than elsewhere, perhaps because of its nearness to London. Possibly the most famous of all the English Religious Societies was that organised by Samuel Wesley in his parish at Epworth in 1701. The spread of the Societies was largely due to their connection with the S.P.C.K., which advocated the formation of Societies for Religion and for Reformation of Manners in all the districts in which they had correspondents.

The number of members in the Religious Societies appears to have varied greatly. A MS. list of some of the Societies in London in 1694 gives an average membership of seventeen, and the members appear to come mostly from the lower, and lower middle, classes. But a Religious Society at Canterbury in 1701 numbered thirty, and later one at St. Neots (Cambs) numbered seventy. Still later, in 1743, John Wesley found a Society at St. Ives in Cornwall, organised on the Horneck model, numbering one hundred and twenty.

The later history of the Religious Societies is the history of their connection with Methodism. In 1737 Whitefield's (*q.v.*) crusade among the London Societies once more brought them into prominence. They were rigidly Anglican during this period, as they had always been. Their private forms of service are almost entirely taken from the Book of Common Prayer. But the Jacobitism of the Religious Societies had tended to make them formal and lacking in the spirituality which animated the earlier members. No longer were they actively philanthropic; only the regular subscription for charity seems to have remained of all their former efforts. Orthodox divines did not hesitate to warn the Societies against White-

field, but he succeeded in reinvigorating them to some extent. In 1738 Wesley visited them frequently, and some of the members of the Fetter Lane Society were drawn from the Religious Societies. Later, after his break with the Moravians and his erection of a more purely Methodist association at the Foundry, Wesley continued to visit the Religious Societies, but there is no evidence to show the Wesleyan societies were modelled directly on the earlier Anglican organisations. The older Societies served as a recruiting ground for the Methodists, and some of the more spiritual members preferred to seek in the Methodist associations that religious communion with their fellows which their own Societies no longer supplied. In Bristol, however, the connection between the old and the new was much closer. Whitefield used the rooms of the Religious Societies there, and organised the members directly into Methodist associations. But the fact that the Methodist societies were recruited from the Religious Societies hardly justifies the assumption that they were based on the same model. The chief feature of the Methodist societies was the band system, which was an adaptation from Moravianism; and the principle of a weekly subscription for charitable purposes, which was a distinctive feature of the Religious Societies, was never utilised by the early Methodist organisations. The connection is one of *personnel* rather than of organisation. The Methodist societies, however, were indirectly the cause of the extinction of the older Societies. For they attracted the most enthusiastic of their members, and the Societies, left without their enthusiasts in an age of spiritual deadness, sank into extinction. [G. V. P.]

S.P.C.K. minutes and correspondence (published and MS.); Josiah Woodward, *Account of the Religious Societies in London and Westminster, etc.*, 1701; 'Orders of a Religious Society' (Bodleian Library); journals of J. Wesley and Whitefield; Richard Kidder, *Life of Horneck.*

SOUTH, Robert (1634-1716), divine, son of a London merchant, was at Westminster School under Busby (and recorded that on the day of Charles I.'s execution he was prayed for in the school prayers as usual), and from thence went to Christ Church, Oxford, 1651. He travelled abroad, and was ordained secretly in 1658. Before the Restoration he preached against the Independents, and after it became Public Orator at Oxford, chaplain to Clarendon, and Prebendary of Westminster (1663). D.D. Oxford, 1663; Cambridge, 1664; Canon of Christ Church, 1670; Rector of Islip, 1678.

He was chaplain to Charles II., and Sancroft (*q.v.*) recommended him to James II. for the see of Oxford. He had already become the most popular preacher of the day. His sermons were extraordinarily smart, direct, pungent, and witty. He spoke fearlessly against popular sins, but did not fear to make his audience rock with laughter. His style was florid as well as facetious, but in its later period anticipated the plainness of the age of Anne, and he remained for some thirty years unique in his success. At the Revolution it was only after long hesitation that he took the oaths. He was an old and orthodox Tory, and was not in real sympathy with the ruling powers till the reign of Anne, when he was perhaps regarded as too old for preferment. He was engaged for some years in denouncing William Sherlock (*q.v.*), Dean of St. Paul's, for unorthodoxy in his *Vindication* of the doctrine of the Trinity, 1693, and certainly succeeded in showing him to be both weak and shifty. He summed up indeed his opponent's position by saying: 'There is hardly any one subject that he has wrote upon (that of popery only excepted) but he has wrote for and against it too.' It was not till 1713 that he was offered the bishopric of Rochester and deanery of Westminster. He declined, with an irony which was perhaps justifiable. He had never sought preferment, and had always used his income to enrich the benefices he had held; and so died a poor man. 8th July 1716, and was buried in the Abbey.

[W. H. H.]

Works (pub. 1679-1711), with *Memoir* (1717).

SOUTHWARK, See of. When the diocese of Rochester (*q.v.*) was rearranged by the formation of that of St. Albans (*q.v.*) in 1875, it contained a population of 1,600,000. But, owing to the growth of South London, the population of that part of the diocese alone had, thirty years later, reached 2,000,000. In spite of the appointment of a suffragan Bishop of Southwark in 1891, it became apparent that the spiritual needs of South London could only be met by the erection of a separate see. Several attempts to secure an Act of Parliament for this purpose failed. But eventually in 1904 the Bishoprics of Southwark and Birmingham Act (4 Edw. VII. c. 30) was passed, the only opposition coming from 'a few ultra-anti-High-Church people,' as one of the supporters of the Bill termed them. Accordingly the see was established by Order in Council, 20th March 1905, to come into operation 1st May. It consists of the whole of the administrative county of London south of the Thames, together with the

Parliamentary divisions of East and Mid-Surrey. It was originally divided into the archdeaconries of Southwark and Kingston; that of Lewisham was constituted in 1906. The population is 2,068,000, and the income of the see £3000. There have been suffragan bishops of Woolwich and Kingston since 1905. The church of St. Saviour, Southwark, chiefly Early English in style, was formerly attached to the Augustinian priory of St. Mary Overy. It received its present dedication when it became a parish church in 1540. It had been a pro-cathedral since its restoration in 1897, and became the cathedral church of the see in 1905. It has a college of priests working in the diocese under the bishop as visitor and the Archdeacon of Southwark as warden, but has no legally constituted chapter, and the bishop is therefore appointed by Letters Patent from the Crown. [BISHOPS].

1. Edward Stuart Talbot, 1905; tr. from Rochester at the foundation of the see; tr. to Winchester, 1911.
2. Hubert Murray Burge, 1911; Headmaster of Winchester.   [G. C.]

SOUTHWELL, See of, was established by an Order in Council of 2nd February 1884, in accordance with the Bishoprics Act, 1878 (41-2 Vic. c. 68). It consists of the counties of Derby and Nottingham, together with small parts of those of Leicester, Lincoln, and Stafford, and was originally divided into the archdeaconries of Derby and Nottingham; the archdeaconry of Chesterfield was formed in 1910, and that of Newark in 1912. The diocese has a population of 1,287,639, and the income of the see is £3500. There has been a suffragan bishop of Derby since 1889. The counties of Derby and Nottingham had been taken from the dioceses of Lichfield (*q.v.*) and Lincoln (*q.v.*) respectively, relief which their bishops had desired for nearly twenty years. The first bishop, Dr. Ridding, had a difficult task in overcoming jealousies and bringing the two counties into one harmonious diocese. He constantly urged them to work together and to 'feel diocesan.' The collegiate church of Southwell, dedicated to the Blessed Virgin Mary, which has a Norman nave and transepts and a beautiful thirteenth-century chapter-house, was made the cathedral of the diocese, in spite of its inconvenient position. It had been the archbishop's cathedral church for the county of Nottingham before the Conquest. Its college of secular canons, after being dissolved by Henry VIII. and re-founded in 1585, was again dissolved and disendowed by the Ecclesiastical Commissioners in 1841. Dr. Ridding's attempts to have the chapter reconstituted were unsuccessful, so the bishop is appointed by Letters Patent from the Crown. Dr. Ridding lived at Thurgarton Priory, but the present episcopal residence, Bishop's Manor, Southwell, was completed in 1907.

1. George Ridding, 1884; Headmaster of Winchester; d. 1904.
2. Edwyn Hoskyns, 1904; tr. from suffragan bishopric of Burnley, to which he was cons. 1901.   [G. C.]

Lady Laura Ridding. *George Ridding, Schoolmaster and Bishop*; A. F. Leach, *Visitations and Memorials of Southwell Minster*, C.S.

SPELMAN, Sir Henry (? 1564-1641), antiquary, born of an old Norfolk family, was educated at Trinity College, Cambridge. He took some part in public affairs, and in 1597, and again in 1625, sat in Parliament. But his real tastes lay in the study of legal and ecclesiastical antiquities. In 1639 he published a volume of *Concilia, Decreta, Leges, Constitutiones* of the English Church, which formed the basis of the famous work of Wilkins (q.v.). In spite of imperfections Spelman's work (a second volume of which was published after his death) marks an epoch in the study of history, by showing for the first time how it should be based on a systematic and scientific study of original documents. He wrote with so much force and learning against the practice of turning church buildings and lands to secular uses that many who had acquired such property voluntarily restored it to the Church. To the end of his life his advice was often sought on this subject, to which his attention had originally been turned by the misfortunes which pursued him as long as he possessed the sites of two abbeys in Norfolk. His *History and Fate of Sacrilege* was not completed at his death. An attempt to publish it in 1663 was given up lest it 'should give offence to the nobility and gentry' who were in possession of the abbey lands. The type for this projected edition was destroyed in the Great Fire. Gibson (q.v.) omitted it from his edition of Spelman's works, thinking it would be taken 'as an unpardonable reflection upon' the nobility. But it was published in 1698, and edited by J. M. Neale (q.v.) and J. Haskoll in 1846, when Dr. Neale believed that the republication was hindered by the efforts of the devil.   [G. C.]

Works, with *Life* by Gibson; *History and Fate of Sacrilege*, ed. 1846.

STANDISH, Henry (d. 1535), Bishop of St. Asaph, and a consistent opponent of the changes made in the critical years of the reign of Henry VIII. Standish is a Lancashire name, and Dugdale asserts that the future bishop was a Lancashire man. He was a Franciscan friar, and studied and graduated at Oxford, if not at Cambridge also, in the reign of Henry VII. When Henry VIII. became King Standish was introduced to his favourable notice. Perhaps at this time he was willing to adapt his convictions to suit his new surroundings, for he took up a position on the question of the relation of the clergy to lay tribunals which involved him in some trouble with Convocation. The King exerted his influence in favour of Standish, and Parliament also bestirred itself to protect the bold friar who had taken up an attitude unpopular with the clergy. The controversy which took place in 1515 was of some importance, as it manifests the existence of a tendency to depress the privileges of the clergy, with which tendency Parliament and the laity generally are supposed to have sympathised. From this point, however, Standish stood forth as the patron of accepted church views. The ferment caused by Luther's doctrines soon manifested itself, whilst a recrudescence of Lollardy caused anxiety in London. Standish opposed all such ideas in sermons and in writings. When the New Testament of Erasmus was published Standish attacked it, and is said to have warned the King against what he held to be the errors of Erasmus. In 1518 he was consecrated Bishop of St. Asaph. His friendship with the King still placed him upon more than one embassy and commission. His undoubted orthodoxy recommended him to Wolsey as a commissioner to examine and punish heretics. In this way he was called upon to examine Bilney and Arthur in 1527. He took some part in the divorce proceedings, but his attitude on the question was ambiguous. He was one of the three consecrators of Cranmer, 1533. He did not take any prominent part either for or against the Submission of the Clergy, but was willing in 1535 to renounce the papal jurisdiction. That is his last recorded public act.   [H. G.]

L.P. Foreign and Domestic; Wood, *Athen. Oxon.*; Cooper, *Athen. Cant.*

STANLEY, Arthur Penrhyn (1815-81), Dean of Westminster, son of Edward Stanley, brother of the first Lord Stanley of Alderley, Rector of Alderley, and afterwards Bishop of Norwich, was educated first at Seaforth, near

Liverpool, and afterwards at Rugby under Dr. Arnold (*q.v.*), whose theological views he adopted and developed. As a boy he was extremely small and delicate, shy with strangers, but bright and gay amongst his friends, and passionately fond of books. He entered Rugby in January 1829, and quickly ran up the school, aided by cleverness and general knowledge. He won a Classical Scholarship at Balliol College in 1833, but remained at Rugby till 1834, when he went up to Oxford. He won the Ireland Scholarship and the Newdigate Prize in 1837, and a First Class in Classics, 1838, when he took his degree, and was elected Fellow at University College; and, after some boggling over the Articles and the Athanasian Creed, was ordained deacon by the Bishop of Oxford (Dr. Bagot) at Advent, 1839. He was ordained priest, 1843. He soon became tutor of his college, and, residing always in Oxford, busied himself in all University affairs, taking what was then deemed the 'Liberal' side, and specially promoting University reforms. In 1850 he was appointed secretary to the Royal Commission to inquire into the state of Oxford, and is said to have written most of the report. In recognition of his services he was made Canon of Canterbury in 1851, and chaplain to Prince Albert in 1854. In 1856 he was appointed Regius Professor of Ecclesiastical History, and in March 1858 succeeded to the stall in Christ Church vacated by the death of Dr. Bull. He was made examining chaplain to the Bishop of London (Tait) in 1856; but, violently espousing the cause of *Essays and Reviews* (*q.v.*), he wrote in the *Edinburgh Review* for April 1861 a fiery article on what he considered Tait's evasive and equivocating line. In February 1862 he was appointed to attend the Prince of Wales (afterwards King Edward VII.) on a journey to Egypt and Palestine. This circumstance, added to the fact that he had been a favourite of Prince Albert, secured his advancement in the Church, and also procured him a wife. In the autumn of 1862 he was given in marriage—no other phrase expresses the process as recorded by his biographer—to Lady Augusta Bruce, daughter of the seventh Earl of Elgin, recently lady-in-waiting to the Duchess of Kent, and a woman of surpassing prudence. At the same time he was appointed Dean of Westminster in succession to Archbishop Trench (*q.v.*), and was installed on the 9th of January 1864. He was a good administrator of the abbey, which was much improved under his rule, and he excelled in lecturing on its beauties to working men. His days were

spent in incessant activity. He preached constantly, and wrote books, and lectured on all manner of subjects, and spoke in public, and contributed articles to all imaginable journals and magazines. His style was easy and fluent, and, as Lord Beaconsfield said, he had a 'picturesque sensibility' for historic scenes and actions and persons. He was a general favourite in society, and, except when engaged in controversy, was one of the most amiable and attractive of men. Theologically, he was the untiring champion of the Latitudinarians, and the most absolute Erastian in the Church of England. He did his utmost to destroy the Athanasian Creed, he admitted a Socinian to Communion in the Abbey, and he snubbed the Pan-Anglican Conference of 1867. Whether he himself was really a Socinian or an orthodox believer in the Deity of our Lord it is impossible from his writings to discover. Dr. Liddon (*q.v.*) said of him: 'He had two intellectual defects which flourished in his mind with extraordinary vigour—he was hopelessly inaccurate, and he was more entirely destitute of the logical faculty than any highly educated man whom I have ever known. . . . His curious want of logic prevented him seeing the real drift of a great deal of his published language; but it had disastrous effects on younger men, who took him at his word.' He died on the 18th of July 1881, and was buried in the Abbey.

His best books are *The Life of Dr. Arnold*, a truly admirable biography; *Sinai and Palestine*, and *Historical Memorials of Westminster Abbey*.   [G. W. E. R.]

R. E. Prothero, *Life*.

STEERE, Edward (1828-82). Bishop of Zanzibar, was educated at Hackney and University College School, London, and London University; graduated B.A., 1847; LL.B., 1848; LL.D., with gold medal for Law, 1850. Called to the Bar by the Inner Temple, 1850, he came to be influenced by the Oxford Movement (*q.v.*), and, 1854, joined the Guild of St. Alban. May 1855 he gave up his chambers and founded a brotherhood at Tamworth. The scheme failed, and he was ordained deacon, September 1856, and priest, 1858, when he became curate-in-charge of Skegness, where the fishermen loved him as 'a downright shirt-sleeve man and a real Bible parson.'

1859 he became Rector of Little Steeping, Lines. In 1862 he went with his former vicar at Skegness, W. G. Tozer, Bishop of the Universities Mission, to Central Africa, where he mastered the Swahéli language, reduced other dialects and languages to writing, and printed part of his researches by aid of native boys. 1867-72 he worked in his Lincolnshire parish, continuing his Swaheli labours. At the Nottingham Church Congress, 1871, he made a great impression by a speech on the slave trade. He volunteered for Central Africa when Bishop Tozer's health broke down, 1872. 1873 he laid the foundation stone of a cathedral church in Zanzibar on the site of the former slave market. 1874, after several refusals, he became Bishop of Zanzibar. He insisted on the mission pressing on to Lake Nyassa. His health gave way, 1877, and he came to England, where he was deservedly honoured by Oxford (created D.D.) and Cambridge (being made Select Preacher). He returned to Africa in November. He remained there completing the New Testament and Prayer Book in Swaheli until 1882, when he again came to England for rest, but returned to Africa, arriving in Zanzibar by 24th August. He died, 28th August, and was buried in Christ Church Cathedral, Zanzibar, which he had consecrated on Christmas Day, 1879.

Steere was a consistent adherent of the Oxford Movement, a philosopher with considerable breadth of view, and of great practical ability. He was a scientific linguist of eminence. He knew nine languages besides his own, and not including the African tongues, two of which, Swaheli and Yao, he made 'practicable as written languages.' Before going to Africa he had edited Bishop Butler's *Analogy* (1857) and *Sermons* (1862), and written an essay on *The Existence and Attributes of God* (1856). His laborious studies in East African dialects first made possible the Christianisation of that part of the continent.   [S. L. O.]

R. M. Heanley, *Memoir*; article in *D.N.B.*

STEPHENS, Edward (?1633-1706), pamphleteer and priest, was a Gloucestershire squire, became a barrister, and was in some favour with Lord Chief Justice Hale, whose daughter he married. As a lawyer he wrote little. He became a political pamphleteer, supporting the Revolution of 1688, but harshly criticising the new government. His writings are, however, chiefly theological. In 1674 he began to write against Rome, though he afterwards desired reunion with her. He attacked the Quakers, and afterwards proposed plans for conciliating them. He strongly advocated frequent Communion, and early in life promoted monthly and weekly Eucharists in his district in the country. In 1691 he claims to have begun the organisations which developed into the Societies for the Reformation of Manners (q.v.), but left them later, probably on account of their collaboration with the London dissenters. In 1692 he formed a society in London for daily reception of the Eucharist, an Anglican priest whom he had 'brought off from the dissenters' being the chaplain. In 1693 he was himself ordained so that the project might not be abandoned. He obtained from Fowler, Bishop of Gloucester, the use of his church at Cripplegate for the daily Eucharists of his little society. In 1695 he wrote to the Archbishop of Canterbury, defending some liturgical interpolations he had used when celebrating. By 1698 reunion was the great work of his life, consequently he threw himself with zeal into the proposal to found a Greek college at Oxford, and for his services in that cause he was received into full communion with the Greek Church. He founded a religious society for women, c. 1697, thus reviving the idea of Religious Orders. [RELIGIOUS ORDERS, II.] He claimed in 1705 to have maintained the daily Eucharist for nearly twelve years. He embraced new projects with tremendous enthusiasm, and attempted, somewhat dictatorially, to enforce his views upon his friends. After 1698 his own theological position is not quite clear. Writing against *A Proposal for Catholic Reunion*, 1704, he said: 'The Greek Communion I take to be the only true Catholic Communion in the world.' His various changes of opinion and practice and his fondness for private organisations were typical of his age. A hint of his 'enthusiasm' is conveyed in a letter written to him by Dodwell in 1704: 'I wonder who those moderate dissenters could be who approved of your prayers for the dead and your notions of a Christian sacrifice.' His property in Gloucestershire was at Cherington and Little Sodbury.   [G. V. P.]

Union Review (1863), i. 553-79; Dr. Wickham Legg, *Trans. St. Paul's Eccl. Soc.*, vol. vi.; *Reliquiae Hearnianae*, ed. Bliss, i. 63a; pamphlets and MS. collection of works and catalogue in the Bodleian (Cherry and Rawlinson collections).

STILLINGFLEET, Edward (1635-99), Bishop of Worcester, was born at Cranborne, Dorset, of an ancient Yorkshire family. He went to St. John's College, Cambridge; took B.A., 1653; became Fellow, 1653; and M.A., 1656. He was ordained privately by Brownrigg (Bishop of Exeter), and in 1659 wrote the *Irenicum*, suggesting comprehension of Churchmen and Presbyterians. He regarded church organisation as not of divine ordering, but dissent as indefensible, and thus his book took a prominent place in the literature of the 'latitude-men,' and he was ranked by Burnet (*q.v.*) among the 'moderate episcopal-men.' He became Rector of Sutton, Beds, in 1657, and there wrote his *Origines Sacrae*, 'asserting the divine authority of the Scriptures,' and later a vindication of Laud's (*q.v.*) controversy with Fisher. He became well known in London as a preacher after the Restoration, was preacher at the Rolls Chapel, Reader of the Temple, Rector of St. Andrew's, Holborn, and Prebendary of St. Paul's. Pepys says that he was thought by bishops to be 'the ablest young man to preach the Gospel of any since the Apostles'; he was so handsome as to be called 'the beauty of holiness,' and churches were crowded whenever he preached. In 1677 he became Archdeacon of London, in 1678 Dean of St. Paul's, and continued to write theological, historical, and antiquarian books (*Works*, in 6 vols., 1710), of which perhaps the most famous is the *Origines Britannicae*, 1685. His judgment on historical and constitutional questions was considered almost beyond dispute. In the Danby case, when it was questioned whether the bishops had the right to sit, he showed much more skill 'than all the rest that had meddled in it,' and established the right beyond contradiction. He was harried by the Ecclesiastical Commission under James II., but received promotion at the Revolution, being consecrated Bishop of Worcester, 13th October 1689. His MSS. remain to show how much he was consulted by the bishops of his day, how prominent a part he played in advocating toleration and comprehension, at the same time controverting papists and Socinians. Queen Mary II. wished him to succeed Tillotson (*q.v.*) at Canterbury, but Tenison was appointed. He died, 27th March 1699, and was buried in his cathedral. He was at once the most learned and the most popular of the early Latitudinarians (*q.v.*), and had a great reputation with the second generation.   [W. H. H.]

Bentley, *Life*.

STRYPE, John (1643-1737). ecclesiastical historian and biographer, born in Houndsditch, youngest son of John van Strijp, a member of an old Brabant family who settled in London, was educated at St. Paul's School, and after entering Jesus College, Cambridge, and leaving it for being 'too superstitious' for him, at Catharine Hall.

He became perpetual curate of Theydon Bois in 1669, but resigned the appointment

the same year on being selected minister of Leyton during the vacancy of the living. This post he held until his death, receiving all the emoluments of the benefice, by virtue of a licence from the Bishop of London. He was also Lecturer of Hackney, 1689-1724, and Rector of West Tarring from 1711. He spent his last years in Hackney. For many years he devoted himself to collecting materials, and did not publish his work until he was fifty.

Most of his magnificent collection of documents came from a collection belonging to Sir William Hicks, great-grandson of Lord Burghley's secretary. Originally lent to him for purposes of transcription, he seems to have appropriated them to his own use, which was rendered possible through the owner being adjudged a lunatic in 1699. Some were sold in 1711 to Robert Harley, and are still part of the Harleian MSS. Strype's principal works are *Memorials of Cranmer*, *Annals of the Reformation*, *Ecclesiastical Memorials*, and *Lives* of Archbishops Parker, Grindal, and Whitgift, Bishop Aylmer, Sir John Cheke, and Sir Thomas Smith. His style is cumbrous, his materials are clumsily arranged and used uncritically, and his accounts are partial and biassed, but his accumulation of documents make him a storehouse of information with which no student of the sixteenth century can dispense.   [C. P. S. C.]

Works; *D.N.B.*

STUBBS, William (1825-1901), Bishop of Oxford, was the son of a lawyer at Knaresborough, showed an early taste for historical and antiquarian studies, and passed from Ripon Grammar School, by the help of Bishop Longley (afterwards Archbishop of Canterbury), to Christ Church, Oxford, 1844, as a servitor, where he attracted the attention and favour of Dean Gaisford. He took a first class *in Literis Humanioribus*, 1848, and a third in Mathematics (poverty, not lack of ability, the cause, it seems, of this latter, for he could not buy all necessary books). He was elected Fellow of Trinity, 19th June 1848. There he threw himself on to the side of the High Churchmen and Conservatives against the old irreligious and 'Liberal' parties in the University. He was Vicar of Navestock, 1850 to 1866. In 1848 he began his *Registrum Sacrum Anglicanum*, 'an attempt to exhibit the course of episcopal succession in England from the records and chronicles of the Church' (published in 1858). In 1862 Archbishop Longley made him librarian at Lambeth. From 1864 to 1889 he produced a remarkable series of editions of English Mediæval Chronicles, which showed his mastery of the manuscript sources of English history and his remarkable power of entering into mediæval life and character. The period of the Angevins became his peculiar possession ; but his wide historical and ecclesiastical knowledge spread far beyond it and was able to illuminate it at every point. In 1866 he was appointed Regius Professor of Modern History at Oxford. He held the post till 1884 ; from 1879 till 1884 he was a canon of St. Paul's. In 1870 he published *Select Charters*, the first attempt to illustrate the history of the English constitution up to Edward I. by the publication of a series of its original documents. This was followed (1873-8) by the *Constitutional History of England* (down to 1485), which placed him at the head of the English historians of the century. This great work made him famous throughout Europe, and he received many distinctions, from the German Order of Merit to degrees of foreign and American Universities. In 1881 he was appointed to sit on the Ecclesiastical Courts Commission [COMMISSIONS, ROYAL], on which he did much valuable work. One of his appendices to its Report declared that the English Church before the Reformation did not always or absolutely accept the Roman canon law as binding. This view was, later, denied by Professor F. W. Maitland, but Stubbs, though he admitted the force and learning of the contention, still believed that what he had written was true history (*Lectures on Mediæval and Modern History*, second edition). He was consecrated to the see of Chester, 25th March 1884, in York Minster. As Bishop of Chester he gave impetus to the efforts to meet the problems presented by the growth of large towns. He was translated to Oxford in 1889, where he worked as hard, struggling to meet the demands of an unwieldy and mainly agricultural diocese. In 1889 he was an assessor in the 'Lincoln case.' [BENSON.] In his episcopal charges he gave valuable sketches of early nineteenth-century church history, and criticised the 'higher criticism.' He opposed disestablishment and disendowment as fraught with disaster to the country, but was always determined in his defence of the spiritual claims and character of the Church as opposed to the views of some lawyers and politicians. He was a clear and impressive preacher and a humorous speaker and conversationalist. His chief friends were men eminent in the historical and religious circles of his time : Freeman, Green, Bryce, Liddon (*q.v.*), Church (*q.v.*). In theology he

called Pusey (*q.v.*) 'the Master.' In politics he was a strong Conservative, though opposed to the Turkish policy of Lord Beaconsfield. Since his death some of his early lectures have been published. These are of a much less finished character than the books which he himself printed. He left also some sermons and lectures which he had revised, and these, especially perhaps an important letter on Joint Sessions of Convocation, might well be given to the world.　　[W. H. H.]

W. H. Hutton, *Letters of William Stubbs* (which contains a complete bibliography).

SUDBURY, Simon of (d. 1381), Archbishop of Canterbury, was born at the Suffolk town from which he took his name, the son of middle-class parents, studied ' both laws ' at Paris, and took the degree of doctor. He was chaplain to Innocent VI., and was sent by him to England, where he became Chancellor of Salisbury. He was 'provided' to the see of London by the Pope. It is said that in 1370, on his way to Canterbury on the tercentenary of St. Thomas, he warned the pilgrims that the indulgence they would receive would not avail them without repentance, and that an aged and indignant knight warned him that he would come to a foul end. In 1375 Gregory XIII. appointed him by Bull Archbishop of Canterbury. He was engaged in much political business, and said to be lenient towards Wycliffites, but was stern in denouncing clerical abuses, particularly non-residence. He crowned Richard II. (16th July 1377), and in 1378 he tried Wyclif (*q.v.*) in Lambeth Palace Chapel, dismissing him with an injunction to silence. At his visitation the traditional resistance of St. Augustine's Abbey was met by his claim to act as *legatus natus* ; but the abbey appealed to the Pope, who gave no decision while Simon lived. Just before the rising of 1381 he imprisoned the priest, John Ball, for ' beguiling the ears of the laity by invectives, and putting about scandals concerning our own person, as also those of other prelates, and (what is far worse) using concerning our holy father the Pope himself, dreadful language, such as shocks the ears of Christians.' (He had taken the side of Urban VI. in the schism.) The Kentishmen released Ball, destroyed Simon's goods at Canterbury, sacked his palace at Lambeth, and demanded that he should be given up to them as a traitorous minister. He resigned the Chancellorship of England but remained in the Tower, said Mass before the King on 14th June, and after Richard had departed stayed behind in the chapel awaiting the end.

The mob soon afterwards came in, seized him, and beheaded him with great brutality on Tower Hill. He was buried in Canterbury Cathedral, where a monument still exists, but his head is shown in the parish church of his native place. He suffered for the part he played in politics, an inevitable result of the close connection between the State and the unreformed Church under the control of Pope and King, when, as Bishop Stubbs (*q.v.*) quotes, 'the rudder got mixed with the bowsprit sometimes'; but he seems to have been a man of liberal and tolerant mind.   [W. H. H.]

Walsingham, *Chron. Anglicæ*; Oman, *Hist. Eng.*, 1377-1485; Trevelyan, *Eng. in the Age of Wycliffe*.

SUPREMACY, Royal. This is undoubtedly a painful subject, as the doctrine was first asserted by acts of remorseless tyranny, and the very notion of a State Church, which is involved in it, seems to conflict with a pure religious ideal. Yet it does not necessarily do so, because it really involves nothing but a statement of indisputable fact, and of conditions essential in modern times to a Christian commonwealth. The King, or the Supreme Government in any country, must be supreme over all persons and over all causes, alike ecclesiastical and civil; and we have seen in our day that what are called 'free' Churches are subject, no less than other communities, to the ordinary tribunals of the land.

This, in fact, is so apparent that the difficulty in modern times is to imagine a state of matters in which the King and the law of the land were not supreme. But in the Middle Ages they were really not so. In England, as in other countries, the canon law of Rome was independent of the King's law, or the law of the land, and the final appeal in any ecclesiastical case was to the court of Rome. Every individual Christian, moreover, was quite as much a subject of the Church of Rome in spiritual as he was of the King in temporal matters. The Church was before the State, and could summon its own offenders to its own tribunals. If they were contemptuous, and after repeated admonitions would not obey the Church, they were denounced as heretics, and, being excommunicated, were handed over 'to the secular arm' for punishment by fire. [HERESY.] For it was felt to be important, even for the State, to get rid of heresy. But questions of religion and morals were entirely within the sphere of Church courts, and universal obedience to

them was expected. As to the government of the Church, moreover, even in his own kingdom, a secular prince had no right to interfere with it except through his influence with the Holy See as a devout son of the Church whom any pope would gratify in all things lawful. Such was the mediæval state of matters, and it certainly imposed some restraint upon royal tyranny, as the cases of Henry II. and John show clearly. But by the time of the Tudors kingly power had become very much stronger in England, as in other countries also. Civil law, indeed, had all along been making encroachments on the sphere of ecclesiastical law—encroachments which the canon law would never recognise as valid; but however popes might denounce Acts of Parliament like the Statute of Provisors (*q.v.*), kings could always vindicate their observance within their own sphere of action, or make some arrangement at Rome itself to suspend them for the mutual advantage of themselves and the Pope. In fact, kings generally could obtain from popes almost what favours they would; so that, powerful as secular princes were becoming, no king would probably have thought of defying papal authority altogether had it not been for Henry VIII.'s (*q.v.*) extraordinary passion for Anne Boleyn, and his still more extraordinary determination to redeem his pledge to her, even after his passion had been gratified and was beginning to burn itself out.

Henry believed, at first, that there was a flaw in the dispensation for his marriage with Katherine of Aragon by which it could be declared null, and he could thus be set free to fulfil his promises to Anne. But when he saw by the failure of the legatine court that he could not obtain his desire from Rome, he determined to obtain it otherwise, and at any cost. He laid the whole clergy of the realm under a *praemunire* for having accepted Wolsey's (*q.v.*) legatine power, and made them buy their pardon by an enormous fine (1531). But even then he would not accept them again into favour till they had recognised him as Supreme Head of the Church of England. This unheard-of title, after much debate, they conceded, but only with the qualification 'as far as the law of Christ allows.' Then he caused complaints against the clergy to be raised in the House of Commons, and affected to hear them as an impartial judge. He declared that the clergy were but half his subjects, and wrung from them on the 16th May 1532 their celebrated 'Submission,' by which they promised henceforward to enact no new canons, and to allow those already enacted to be examined by a mixed committee of thirty-two, to see how far they were compatible with the laws of the realm. The King then cut off Roman jurisdiction altogether by Act of Parliament. He also secured from his subjects generally the recognition of what he had done by oaths binding them to the succession and repudiating the Pope's jurisdiction. A few martyrs held out and submitted to the awful penalties of treason for refusing to acknowledge the King's Supremacy over the Church; but the nation generally obeyed the new decrees.

There is no doubt that the people generally were intimidated, and that foreign nations were horrified. Neither is there a doubt that the King might have been dethroned by a combination against him abroad if the two leading princes of Europe, who both disliked him, could have agreed to execute the will of the Pope against him. But the Emperor and Francis I. were suspicious of each other, and each feared to make Henry his enemy, lest he should ally himself with his rival. So royal power in an island kingdom was safe, even in defying the spiritual ruler of Christendom, whose cause no prince would avenge. Yet there was still one danger within the kingdom itself from the monasteries, which had never been accustomed to any other obedience but to that of Rome. [MONASTERIES, SUPPRESSION OF.] So these establishments had to be put down; and Henry VIII. lived out his days in fear only of danger from abroad, which at times inspired him with serious but not lasting dread. Royal Supremacy descended to his son, and what with the Smalcaldic war, the Council of Trent, and the Interim, England was still safe. Even Mary (*q.v.*) succeeded Edward as Supreme Head of the Church, and she only restored papal authority by Royal Supremacy, though she dropped the title. Under Elizabeth (*q.v.*) Supremacy was again asserted, though the title was a little changed. It was impossible to restore the old power of the papacy. All delusions on that subject were put an end to at last by the fate of the Spanish Armada, and they have never been revived.   [J. G.]

The Royal Supremacy at the present time is exercised in three ways. (1) The State has a large share in choosing the chief officers of the Church. [BISHOPS.] (2) It controls the Church's legislature, in that the royal writ is necessary for its meeting, and royal licence and assent for the civil validity of new canons. [CONVOCATION, CANON LAW.] (3) It controls the Church's courts, not so as

to usurp their functions, but to see that they act justly and do not infringe the law of the land. [COURTS.]

The Supremacy as asserted by the Tudors involved three conditions which made it acceptable to the Church. (1) It was to be exercised by a sovereign who was himself a faithful member of the Church, and would therefore accept the Church's law as binding within its sphere. Such a one would not seek to extend the temporal authority beyond its due limits. This appears from Article XXXVII., and from Canon 2 of 1604, which compares the royal authority in causes ecclesiastical to that of the godly kings of the Jews and of the Christian emperors. (2) This safeguard would have been nugatory unless the 'godly king' not only reigned but governed, and exercised the Supremacy according to his personal will. It need not be said that this was clearly understood in the sixteenth century. (3) It was not an arbitrary but a limited power, to be exercised constitutionally in certain well-defined ways; visitatory in its nature, designed to regulate and restrain the exercise of spiritual jurisdiction, but not to usurp any of its functions. This, like the preceding conditions, clearly appears in the sixteenth-century public documents, *e.g.* the Act of Supremacy, 1559 (1 Eliz. c. 1), and Article XXXVII.

The practical exercise of the Supremacy has been greatly affected by the constitutional developments of modern times. But the assumption frequently made that it has passed, together with the supreme power in the State, from the sovereign personally to Parliament and Cabinet is not a legitimate consequence of the sixteenth-century settlement, and has never been accepted by the Church. The alternative to the personal Supremacy of a godly king is not the Supremacy of the majority of a possibly godless Parliament, or of ministers who are not necessarily Churchmen or Christians; but that the Church, like the State, should enjoy a greater measure of self-government subject to its not infringing the civil law. Should the civil authority abuse its Supremacy by interfering capriciously with the Church's powers of self-government, the Church must in self-defence withdraw in its turn from the sixteenth-century settlement, and take up the position of a non-established Church, over which the State has only the authority which it must always possess over any association of its members. [CHURCH AND STATE, ESTABLISHMENT. *q.v.* also for authorities.]

     [O. C.]

SWITHUN, St., Bishop of Winchester (? 805-862). Like so many of the Anglo-Saxon saints who lived too late to have their lives recorded by Bede, and too early to get the advantage of the literary revival inaugurated by King Alfred, Swithun is very little more than a name to us. There is a life in the *Acta Sanctorum*, but it contains much more of his posthumous history—the miracles, etc., wrought long after his death—than of the actual facts of his career. He lived during a most important period of English history: his earlier years were contemporary with the conquests of Ecgbert; his later ones saw the commencement of the Danish invasion. His own city of Winchester was burnt by the Danes while he yet lived. But the compiler who wrote his life can tell us nothing of his connection with the great events of his day, which clearly must have been close and important. The Bishop of Winchester was the chief ecclesiastic in Ecgbert's West Saxon realm. The *Anglo-Saxon Chronicle* only mentions him to record his death—under the wrong year.

From the *Life* and from Florence of Worcester—both authorities too late to be safely trusted—we learn that Swithun was born of noble parents, that he early chose the clerical career, and that he was ordained in 827 by Helmstan, Bishop of Winchester, whose deacon he may have become, for there is a charter (Kemble, *C.D.*, No. 1004) in which he signs as deacon immediately after Helmstan. Unfortunately the charter is one of those whose authenticity has been doubted. But the date 827 given by Florence for Swithun's ordination must clearly be wrong, as Helmstan only obtained the bishopric of Winchester in 838. Ecgbert is said to have had a high opinion of him, and to have made him the tutor of his son Aethelwulf, whom the *Life* wrongly supposes to have been his only issue. If Aethelwulf's pious incapacity was at all the result of his instructor's lessons, Swithun bears a sad load of responsibility.

It is clear, however, that the tradition that Aethelwulf had a great respect for Swithun must be correct. Unless this had been the case, the King would not have assented to his promotion to the bishopric of Winchester, the most important see of Wessex. We may well believe, therefore, William of Malmesbury's statement that Aethelwulf made him his guide in spiritual matters, while he trusted affairs of finance and statecraft to the warlike Bishop Ealhstan of Sherborne.

Unfortunately we have no authority for stating how Swithun dealt with the great problems of his patron's reign—the second and unwise marriage with Judith, daughter of Charles the Bald, the rebellion of his son Aethelbald during his absence abroad, or the recrudescence of the Danish invasions, which had been checked for a space by Aethelwulf's victory of Aclea. Instead of history we have some petty and worthless legends. Swithun's humility was so great that when about to dedicate a church he would never ride, but always went on foot, and often under the cover of night. He built a bridge over the Itchen at the eastern end of Winchester, which was considered a fine work, and repaired many churches. His only recorded miracle during his life (after his death they abounded) was to join again by a blessing the basket of broken eggs belonging to a market woman, whom his bridge-building workmen had jostled and upset. On his death-bed he is said to have begged, in humility, that he might be buried outside his cathedral, where his grave might be trodden on by the passers-by, not within it.

A plausible guess may be made at the real significance of the saint's place of burial, which was undoubtedly where the legend places it. Winchester had been cruelly sacked by the Danes only a year before Swithun's death, and this fact (ignored by the biographer) may account for his having been laid outside the walls of a building which was probably still in a chaotic state of ruin.

That Swithun was a holy and pious prelate may be inferred from the fact that he was canonised by popular consent, and that his name and fame survived long enough to cause his successor, Bishop Aethelwold, in the reign of Edgar, a century after his death, to translate his relics into the minster with great state. The translation is said to have been caused by a vision, and to have been followed by more than two hundred miracles of healing.

The legend that Swithun objected to the moving of his coffin, and endeavoured to prevent it by causing forty days of continuous rain to fall, is pure folk-lore. It has no place in his *Life*, where it is implied that he directed his own translation in a vision, and approved it by working countless marvels when he had been laid in his new resting-place. His translation is commemorated on 15th July.

[c. w. c. o.]

The *Life* by Lanfrid, a monk of Winchester, is early eleventh century. There is also a metrical *Life* by Wolstan, equally useless. For further bibliography see W. Hunt in *D.N.B.*

SYNODALS are identical with **Cathedratica**, dues of not more than two shillings a year paid by the parochial clergy to the bishop 'in honour of the episcopal chair and in token of obedience and subjection thereto.' They were called synodals from being paid by the clergy when they came to the diocesan synod. They are stated in the legal text-books to have been reserved by the bishop on the establishment of separate parishes with independent incomes. This is merely a theory of their origin. In the Middle Ages they were a fixed item in the bishop's revenue. Their subsequent history followed the same course as that of Procurations (*q.v.*). **Synodals** is also a name for the constitutions made in provincial and diocesan synods and published in parish churches, a practice abolished under Edward VI. as tending to interrupt the service (see preface to Book of Common Prayer).

[O. C.]

Gibson, *Codex*; Phillimore, *Eccl. Law.*

T

TAIT, Archibald Campbell (1811-82), Archbishop of Canterbury, was born in Edinburgh of purely Scottish descent; and his parents were staunch adherents of the Established Kirk. In later years some doubt arose as to whether he had ever been baptized; but his biographer satisfied himself on this point. In 1821 he was admitted to the High School of Edinburgh, from which in 1824 he was transferred to the newly founded 'Edinburgh Academy'; and in 1827 to the University of Glasgow, where he gained several distinctions, and in October 1830 he won a Snell Exhibition at Balliol College, Oxford. In November 1833 he graduated B.A. with a First Class in Classics; in 1834 he was elected Fellow of Balliol. He was soon afterwards appointed to a Tutorship, and took his M.A. in 1836.

From first to last Tait was greatly influenced by his early Presbyterianism. He was a devout and orthodox Christian and no Calvinist; but on those ecclesiastical topics which distinguish Anglicanism from other systems of reformed religion his sympathies were rather with the Kirk of Scotland than with the Church of England. On all questions affecting sacramental doctrine, the structure of the Church, and the nature of the ministry he remained to the end of his life what he had been in his Presbyterian youth. It is believed that he was confirmed when an undergraduate at the instance of his Tutor, F. Oakeley, but even of this there is no certain proof. As he was a communicant, confirmation must be presumed.

As Fellow of Balliol Tait was bound by statute to be ordained within a given time from his M.A. degree. He had not the least desire to do otherwise. Indeed, he felt that the clerical character would help him in his tutorial work. But he was led to the priesthood rather by the external circumstances of his position than by inward desire or special fitness. Residing in Balliol, and actively occupied with pupils, he found time to act as curate at Marsh Baldon, near Oxford.

In 1841 Tait was one of the 'Four Tutors' who publicly protested against Tract 90. [OXFORD MOVEMENT], and thus began a policy which he pursued with unremitting ardour and varying success till the last month of his long life. In 1842 he was chosen to succeed Dr. Arnold (*q.v.*) at Rugby. His friend, Lake, afterwards Dean of Durham, warned him, with friendly candour, that his sermons would probably be dull, and his 'Latin prose, and composition generally, weak.' As a schoolmaster he was not conspicuously successful. He knew nothing about English public schools, and did not understand boys; but his resolute will and untiring energy carried him through. In the domestic part of his work he was greatly assisted by his wife, Catharine Spooner, whom he married in 1843.

In February 1848 he was suddenly stricken with rheumatic fever, and was desperately ill. Dean Bradley, then an assistant master at Rugby, described his anxious walks with a colleague up and down the Close, listening for the bell which would announce the headmaster's death. Somehow Tait pulled through; but the illness left a serious affection of the heart. It is worth recording, as characteristic of Tait's calm temper and strong will, that knowing that certain exertions, such as hurrying for a train or climbing a hill, would thenceforth be dangerous, he simply abjured them for ever. Thenceforward he would rather let the train go than run to catch it, and would wait at the bottom of a hill till he could get a conveyance to carry him up. Having been a very strong and a very active man, he quietly adopted an entirely new scheme of life; and he used to quote his own case as an encour-

agement to all young men similarly affected :
'I have done the hardest work of my life since I have had an incurable heart-disease.'

In 1849 Tait was appointed Dean of Carlisle. He was as little fitted for a dean as for a headmaster, and his life at Carlisle is memorable only for a crushing sorrow. In the spring of 1856 he lost five little daughters through an outbreak of scarlet fever strangely mismanaged. Queen Victoria heard of this desolation, and, at her instance, Lord Palmerston appointed Tait to the see of London. It was an appointment which surprised many at the time ; but as years went on Tait was found to possess great powers of statesmanship, and to be capable of exercising a strong influence on the laity.

The best result of Tait's episcopate was the establishment of the Bishop of London's Fund. This was the kind of business in which he excelled ; but in more spiritual matters his rule was disastrous. From first to last he set his face against the Catholic revival and the modest beginnings of ritualism. He persecuted Mr. Liddell of St. Paul's, Knightsbridge, for having a stone altar, and Mr. Stuart of St. Mary Magdalen, Munster Square, for having altar-lights. He revoked the licence of a curate (Mr. A. Poole) for hearing confessions. He publicly rebuked the clergy of St. Michael's, Shoreditch, for wearing coloured stoles. He voted for the Divorce Act ; he encouraged Bishop Colenso (*q.v.*). He admitted unconfirmed people to Communion. He was friendly to Evangelicals, enthusiastic for Latitudinarians and Broad Churchmen, and consistently hostile to every one who believed in the Church as a spiritual society with laws and powers of her own. And, as he was an influential speaker in the House of Lords, intimate with the Queen, and closely associated with Whig ministers, he was a most formidable foe to the Catholic cause in London. Yet his action in opening the dome of St. Paul's Cathedral to the people by bringing about the first great free popular service held there, and by preaching at it, must be counted among the causes which have led to the position which St. Paul's now fills in the religious life of London and of the country.

In 1868 he was appointed by Lord Beaconsfield to the see of Canterbury. His first important act in his new sphere was to negotiate, during the session of 1869, between Queen Victoria and Gladstone (*q.v.*) in the matter of the Irish Church ; the Church was disestablished in spite of him, and he

ruefully complained that 'a great opportunity had been poorly used.' His next attempt was to abolish the public use of the Athanasian Creed ; but in this he was frustrated by Drs. Pusey (*q.v.*) and Liddon (*q.v.*). In 1874 he introduced the Public Worship Regulation Bill (*q.v.*) in a last desperate attempt to abolish Ritualism.

Meanwhile fresh troubles fell upon Tait's home. In 1878 he lost his only son, and later in the same year his wife. He now was a stricken man, his health began to fail, and towards the end of 1882 he took to his bed, and there attempted to undo some of the mischief which he had done. He induced Mr. Mackonochie (*q.v.*) to resign the benefice of St. Alban's, Holborn, and so to avert the law-suit which had been arranged by the Church Association. This arrangement was dignified with the title of 'The Great Archbishop's Legacy of Peace' ; but it failed to secure Mr. Mackonochie from further molestation. It was, however, the act of a brave and great man, great enough to admit that he had been in the wrong ; and its indirect and moral consequences were not small.

Tait died on Advent Sunday, 1882, and was buried in the churchyard of Addington. In public life he was singularly impressive and dignified ; in private life he was a sincerely devout and affectionate man.

Davidson and Benham, *Life*; G. W. E. Russell, *Household of Faith*.

TAXATIO ECCLESIASTICA.
The word *taxatio* means a valuation by which taxes are to be levied. In 1291 Edward I. made a complete inquiry as to the amount and value of all Church property. The result is the *Taxatio Ecclesiastica Angliae et Walliae*, first printed by the Records Commission in 1802.[1] The originals have not survived ; two MSS. of Henry IV.'s reign exist in the Record Office and an older one in the British Museum. From this record the names and values of almost all thirteenth-century churches and chapelries in England and Wales can be ascertained. Each diocese is assessed under its archdeaconries, which are subdivided into rural deaneries. The record of every diocese is divided into two. The first part records the *Spiritualia*, i.e. tithes (*q.v.*) and other offerings, the second records

[1] The Record is printed in so-called facsimile type, the abbreviations of which are interpreted in *How to Write the History of a Family*, W. P. W. Phillimore, 2nd ed., 277-81. The text for the diocese of Exeter is stated by a recent editor (F. C. Hingeston-Randolph) to be 'full of inaccuracies.'

the *Temporalia, i.e.* the lands granted by laymen for spiritual purposes. The older sees in 1291, with the exception of Canterbury, have practically no *Spiritualia*, the fact being that at the outset they had been plentifully endowed with manors, from which their income was derived. The *Temporalia, i.e.* the lands, paid scutage on military fiefs and carucage on lands held by other tenure from the twelfth century, and probably in 1188 (the Saladin Tithe) the *Spiritualia* were taxed as well. No more is heard of taxing *Spiritualia* until 1207, but the Lateran Council of 1215 gave the Pope power to exact a share of the income of the clergy for a crusade, and from '1252 onwards a tenth of ecclesiastical revenue was generally taken by the Pope's authority' (Stubbs, *C.H.*, ii. 183 n.). These annual 'tenths' or 'tithes' were often granted to the King. Thus in 1288 Edward I. obtained from Nicholas IV. the grant of such an annual 'tenth' for six years, and another such grant in 1291, and it was with a view to this that the new and stringent *Taxatio* of 1291 was made under the direction of Oliver Sutton, Bishop of Lincoln, and John of Pontoise, Bishop of Winchester. It was bitterly resented by the clergy; the Canon of Barnwell, recording the three valuations of Church property (viz. those of 1219, 1256, and 1291), says: *Prima pungit, secunda vulnerat, tercia usque ad ossa excoriat.*

The *Taxatio* has been somewhat carelessly compiled. No benefices under six marks in annual value were subject to royal or papal taxation unless their rectors held another living besides, or unless appropriated to a monastery. Lists of these small livings ought to appear at the end of each diocese; in fact, if they were vicarages they are almost always omitted, though if rectories they generally appear.

This valuation was used until 1854 in the older colleges at Oxford and Cambridge, *i.e.* those founded before 1535, as the criterion of the annual value of livings for purposes of the old statutes (which forbade a living of more than a certain annual value to be held with a Fellowship). The *Taxatio* as printed in 1802 needs some explanation, and names in it appear in more than one form. The bishopric of Lichfield appears sometimes as 'Cestrensis,' and at others as 'Coventrensis.' The northern province having been devastated by the Scottish wars was reassessed in 1318. Dixon (*History of Church of England*, i. 250) sums the result revealed by the *Taxatio* at £218,802. A writer in *The Home and Foreign Review* (January 1864) reckoned it at £206,000. Bishop Stubbs (*C.H.*, ii. 581)

made it £210,644, 9s. 9d. in 1291, and under the New Taxation of 1318 £191,903, 2s. 5¼d. Reckoning the total annual income of the country at that date at £1,000,000, the Church is seen to hold some one-fifth of the whole. [S. L. O.]

Miss Rose Graham in *E.H.R.*, July 1908.

TAYLOR, Jeremy (1613-67), divine, was born at Cambridge, a descendant of Rowland Taylor (*q.v.*), the Protestant martyr. He studied at Gonville and Caius College, became a Perse Scholar and Fellow, took his degree, and was ordained. He then came to London, attracted the attention of Laud (*q.v.*) by his sermons, and was sent to Oxford, where he became M.A. from University College, and was by Laud (as visitor) made Fellow of All Souls. He became chaplain to the King and to the primate, and Juxon (*q.v.*) made him Rector of Uppingham, where he resided and worked assiduously. He preached a famous anti-Roman sermon at Oxford, 5th November 1638. He was in attendance on the King, 1642-3, and was taken prisoner in February 1645. After his release he lived at Golden Grove, Carmarthenshire, as chaplain to the Earl of Carbery. There he wrote his *Liberty of Prophesying, Holy Living*, and *Holy Dying*. He was in London at the time of the execution of Charles I., who gave him his watch, and he is said to have suggested for the book compiled in his memory the title *Eikon Basilike* (*q.v.*). During the interregnum he preached and officiated occasionally in London, and wrote his *Ductor Dubitantium*, which is practically the only systematic Anglican treatise on casuistry. In 1658 he went to Ireland, where his ministrations were interfered with by the 'Anabaptist commissioners.' At the Restoration he was appointed Bishop of Down and Connor, and he was consecrated in St. Patrick's, 27th January 1661. In the same year he was made 'administrator' of the see of Dromore. He endeavoured to make friends with the Presbyterians, and he pleaded consistently for toleration, but he failed, partly through the linguistic difficulty, to win the Roman Catholics to the national Church. He died, 24th July 1667, and was buried in the cathedral of Dromore. No description of him equals that of George Rust in his funeral sermon. 'He had the good humour of a gentleman, the eloquence of an orator, the fancy of a poet, the acuteness of a schoolman, the profoundness of a philosopher, the wisdom of a chancellor, the sagacity of a prophet, the reason of an angel, and the piety of a saint.' His *Holy Living* and *Holy Dying* are immortal, and his *Liberty* *of Prophesying* and *Ductor Dubitantium* deserve to be. There has been no greater master of rhetoric in English literature, and his style is uniquely rich, sonorous, and full of classic reminiscence. As a theologian he is consistently Anglican, anti-Roman, and anti-Puritan. On the doctrine of Holy Communion he says: 'The question is not whether the symbols be changed into Christ's body and blood or no, for it is granted on all sides' (*Works*, vol. vi. p. 20).

[W. H. H.]

Works in 'Library of Anglo-Catholic Theology,' 10 vols. ; *Life* by Heber, revised by C. P. Eden, 1854 ; by Gosse, 1904.

TAYLOR, Rowland (d. 1555), Reformer, born at Rothbury, Northumberland, was a fellow-countryman of Ridley and William Turner, Dean of Wells, who writes: 'With this man I lived for many years in great familiarity, and often and earnestly admonished him to embrace the evangelical doctrine ; and that he might the easier be brought to think as we did, I privately got him the book called *Unio Dissidentium*, by which and the sermons of Latimer he was taken and easily came over to our doctrine.' He was educated at Cambridge, was ordained in 1528, and became a Doctor in both Civil and Canon Law. In 1540 he was appointed chaplain to Cranmer (*q.v.*), and was a member of Convocation. In 1544 he was presented by Cranmer to the living of Hadleigh, Essex, where he resided, gave up his chaplaincy, and in many respects became a model parish priest. Hadleigh had already received the new doctrine through the preaching of Bilney, and Taylor carried on the same teaching with much diligence. ' No Sunday or holy-day passed nor other day when he might get the people together but he preached to them the word of God.' According to Foxe (*q.v.*), a partial witness, his life was as eloquent as his preaching. ' He was void of all pride, humble and meek as any child ; neither was his lowliness childish or fearful, but as occasion, time and place required he would be stout in rebuking the sinful and evil doers ; so that none was so rich but he would tell them plainly his fault with such earnest and grave rebuke as became a good curate and pastor.' Under Edward VI. he was put on the commission against Anabaptists, appointed Chancellor of London, one of the Six Preachers at Canterbury, and Canon of Rochester. He was a commissioner for the reformation of ecclesiastical laws, and in 1552 was appointed Archdeacon of Exeter.

His arrest was ordered six days after the accession of Mary. If Foxe's account is correct he must have been released, as he gives a lively account of his subsequent proceedings at Hadleigh. An attempt was made to say Mass in the old way at Hadleigh church. When Taylor heard the bell he found the church door barred, but got in at the chancel door, and ' saw a popish sacrificer in robes, with a broad new-shaven crown, ready to begin his popish sacrifice.' Then said Dr. Taylor: 'Thou devil! who made thee so bold to enter into this church of Christ to profane it and defile it with this abominable idolatry?' Taylor was turned out of the church, but refused to fly, and was soon afterwards arrested and imprisoned in the King's Bench. While there he signed a confession of faith with the other prisoners repudiating transubstantiation. He was tried before a commission presided over by Gardiner (*q.v.*), who urged him to be reconciled. He was obstinate in his refusal, defended the marriage of priests, rejected transubstantiation, and called the Pope's church 'the church of Antichrist.' He was condemned, and sent down to Hadleigh to be burnt. He met his end with fortitude and forbearance, saying to one of his executioners who wantonly struck him : 'O friend, I have harm enough ; what needed that ?'

[C. P. S. C.]

Foxe, *Acts and Monuments*; Strype, *Memorials.*

TEMPLE, Frederick (1821-1902), Archbishop of Canterbury, son of Major Octavius Temple, Lieutenant-Governor of Sierra Leone, was born at Santa Maura, one of the Ionian Islands, where his father was ' Resident for the Lord High Commissioner.' His early education was conducted by his mother, and on his sixth birthday he had to say the Catechism without a mistake.

His father died in 1834, leaving a widow and eight children in miserable poverty. He had bought a small farm at Axon, near Culmstock in Devon, and there Mrs. Temple brought up her family. The boys worked on the farm and the girls helped the maid-servants. By strict frugality Mrs. Temple was able to maintain her sons at Blundell's School, Tiverton, which Frederick entered in 1834. Frederick and his younger brother John lived in lodgings, and the fee for each was £4 a year. Frederick Temple was confirmed when he was twelve, and immediately became a communicant. His preparation for confirmation had been mainly conducted by his mother. He was most diligent both at books and also at games. Mathematics were his favourite study. ' I got hold of Bland's *Algebraical Problems*, and worked entirely through it in my play-time.' In 1838 he won the school-scholarship to Balliol College, Oxford, and from the early age of seventeen he made his own living. He went into residence, April 1839. He was miserably poor, and worked extraordinarily hard. 'I knew what it was to be unable to afford a fire, and consequently to be very cold, days and nights. I knew what it was, now and then, to live upon rather poor fare. I knew what it was—and I think that was the thing that pinched me most—to wear patched clothes and patched shoes.' He rose, summer and winter, at four A.M., and was busy with work, chapel, breakfast, and lectures till three. Dinner was at four, and evening chapel at five-thirty. By seven at latest he was at work again and got to bed at ten-thirty, and ' went to sleep immediately.' The result of all this labour was that, being already a first-rate mathematician, he so improved in classics that in 1842 he was *proxime accessit* for the Ireland Scholarship. In the same year he obtained a Double First, in Classics and Mathematics, and took his B.A. degree. By the then existing regulations of Balliol, a Blundell Scholar could only become a Blundell Fellow, but Temple's Lecturership in Mathematics and Logic made him the equi-valent of a modern tutorial Fellow. He made a special study of St. Thomas Aquinas. In 1845 he was ordained deacon, and in 1846 priest. On the evening before the monthly Eucharist in college, he used to invite to his rooms any of the undergraduates who chose to come, and gave them practical and devo-tional addresses.

In 1847 Temple wrote: ' It has been my dream for years to devote my full strength, as soon as I had it, to the education of the poor.' An opportunity of realising this dream, at any rate indirectly, occurred in 1848, when he became an examiner in the Education Office, with a view to becoming Principal of Kneller Hall, as soon as it should open its doors. The Hall, near Twickenham, was opened in 1850 for the training of teachers for workhouse schools. The experiment was not successful. Temple worked hard, but got on badly with the official chiefs at the Education Office, and, after a great deal of fighting and worry, resigned in May 1855. He notified the fact to a friend in an apt quotation: ' Total—all up with Squeers.'

In 1857 Dr. Goulburn, afterwards Dean of Norwich, resigned the Headmastership of Rugby; Temple was elected, and began his duties in January 1858, bringing with him to the school-house at Rugby his venerable mother, to whom he was most tenderly attached, and a sister who acted as his house-keeper. He now found himself, for the first time, in exactly the right place, and was Headmaster of Rugby for precisely twelve years. He ruled the school with splendid vigour and marked success. His sermons preached in the school-chapel were master-pieces, combining spiritual fervour with strong common-sense, and an ennobling doctrine of duty. His headmastership was blemished by only one great error, which proceeded from causes altogether outside his professional business: namely, his participation in *Essays and Reviews* (*q.v.*), 1860. His essay, the first in the volume, was a long and rather dull discourse on ' The Education of the World,' which had originally done duty as a sermon before the British Association. As one reads it now, it seems absolutely harmless, but at the time of publication it was thought to be an attack on miracles. Some of the other essays were less innocent, and some were justly chargeable with flippancy and irreverence. Temple, of course, came in for a full share of the blame. It was alleged that he was ' editor ' of the volume, which was false; and that, as head-master of a public school, he had no business to meddle with controversial matters, which was true. A determined effort was made to squeeze him out of his headmastership, and even his friend, Matthew Arnold, thought he must go: but he budged not an inch. When the Bishop of London, Tait (*q.v.*), who had been his tutor at Balliol, joined the other bishops in condemning the book, Temple, who had reason to expect quite different treatment, attacked him with remarkable vigour. ' What you did had not the in-tention, but it had all the effect of treachery.' ' You ought not to make it impossible for a friend to calculate on what you will do. I do not care for your severity. I do care for being cheated.'

Temple had been brought up a Tory. At Oxford he became a Liberal, as Liberalism was understood in the 'forties and 'fifties, and he felt a strong admiration, apart from questions of opinion, for Gladstone (*q.v.*), whose policy of Disestablishment of the Church in Ireland he supported, making several public speeches in favour of it at the General Election of 1868. To Gladstone, a man who actively supported him in the urgent controversy of the moment, whatever it might be, was always a pearl of price ; and he noted Temple for preferment.

He once said to the present writer : ' I resolved, if I ever became Prime Minister,
to recommend for the first bishopric which
fell vacant Moberly, who had been most
unjustly passed over ; and I also resolved
to offer the first good bit of preferment, not
a bishopric, which came into my hands, to
Temple.'

Gladstone became Prime Minister in
December 1868. In July 1869 he offered
the deanery of Durham, carrying with it
the Wardenship of the University, to Temple,
who declined it. In August 1869 he appointed Moberly to the see of Salisbury, and
in the autumn he had three bishoprics to fill
—Exeter, Oxford, and Bath and Wells. He
offered Temple his choice, and Temple chose
Exeter—' because of my strong affection
for the people and the place.' Gladstone
wrote to Archbishop Tait : ' I am not so
sanguine as to believe that *one* of the three
new names will pass without some noise.'
The noise soon became a tumult, High
Churchmen and Evangelicals joining in the
din. Gladstone, they said, with one accord,
was promoting to the episcopate one who,
by writing in *Essays and Reviews*, had, as Dr.
Pusey (*q.v.*) expressed it, ' participated in the
ruin of countless souls.' Temple's more timid
friends implored him to recant, or withdraw,
or explain ; but, as in 1860, he held his peace.
He was confident of his own essential orthodoxy, and confident also that as soon as he
became a bishop, that orthodoxy would become, in spite of the clamour, known to all
men. He believed that *Essays and Reviews*
had done more good than harm ; and he
could not expose himself to the obvious
reproach of recanting his opinion in order to
facilitate his advance to a great position.
The Chapter of Exeter ' elected ' him by
thirteen to six. The opposition to the
' Confirmation ' at Bow Street was overruled by the Vicar-General [BISHOPS].
December 21st was the day fixed for the
consecration in Westminster Abbey ; and
strong protests by several bishops of the
province were tendered in the Jerusalem
Chamber to the presiding bishop, Jackson of
London, but they again were overruled. On
the 29th December he was enthroned in
Exeter Cathedral, and preached a noble
sermon, of which the opening words were
these : ' Ever since I first was told that it
would be my duty to labour in this diocese
of Exeter, I have desired with an exceeding
desire for the day to come when I might
meet you face to face, and pour out before
you all that is in my heart of devotion to
you and to our common Master, our Lord

God, the Son of God, Jesus Christ.' Now
that Temple was safely established in his
seat and no power could dislodge him, he
gladly took a step which when, as Dean
Wellesley said, ' the mitre was hanging over
his head,' he regarded as dishonourable, and
he withdrew his essay from any subsequent
edition of *Essays and Reviews*. The ' Liberal '
party in the Church were bitterly disappointed. But Matthew Arnold, who was
warmly attached to the Bishop, highly
approved. ' I told him that I thought the
Essays and Reviews could not be described
throughout as " a free handling, in *a becoming spirit* " of religious matters, and he said
he quite agreed with me. . . . He is a fine
character.'

From the very outset, Temple's administration of his see was marked, not only by
strength and vigour, but by a wisdom and
tenderness which people had scarcely expected. He had a rugged exterior, a harsh
voice, and no manners. Toadies (whom no
bishop ever lacked) used to repeat his rude-
nesses as witticisms, and paraded his snubbing
speeches and ungracious ways as signs of his
invincible honesty. All this was to be
deplored, but under it there lay a truly warm
and generous heart, and a simple devotion
which compensated for some things which
were less admirable. Gradually he made his
way, and prejudices melted away as his
essential goodness became known, and his
activity pervaded the whole diocese. He
worked for diocesan organisations, Church-
restoration and extension, purity, temper-
ance, missions, foreign and domestic ; and
he secured the division of the diocese,
and the erection of Truro (*q.v.*) into a separate see. In everything which he undertook, he strove to take the line which the
Church of England takes ; and, though
he sometimes misinterpreted her intention,
no one could doubt his loyalty to her. In
his undergraduate days, he had been to some
extent affected by the Oxford Movement,
and was at one time inclined towards Rome ;
but he drew back from the movement in
some disgust when the seeming tragedy of
W. G. Ward's condemnation and degradation ended in the serio-comic episode of
his unsuspected engagement. From 1845 to
1847 his spiritual life ' passed through a
tunnel,' and we know nothing of his theological history till he emerged with his
difficulties settled, and himself ready to be
ordained. For the next thirty years he
passed as a ' Broad Churchman,' though he
never labelled himself with the nickname ;
and it was only towards the end of his

episcopate at Exeter that people began to recognise him as a kind of stiff High Churchman, on a pattern of his own. He believed in the Catholic Church as the divinely-appointed instrument for converting and saving the world. He believed in the Apostolical Succession; he believed in 'the mysterious gift' of the Holy Eucharist, and his way of accounting for it tended towards consubstantiation. He knew and cared nothing about ritual, and, as long as a priest was doing good work, Temple would not harry him. In January 1885 he was called, again by Gladstone, to the see of London; and there he ruled for eleven years, trusted and honoured even by those who disliked him, and revered by all for his transparent devotion and boundless activity. In 1896 Lord Salisbury elevated him to the see of Canterbury, and the least successful period of his career began.

In 1898 there was a sudden outbreak of Puritan fanaticism against 'ritualistic practices.' In February 1899 Temple announced that. acting on the direction in the preface to the Prayer Book, he would hear cases where doubts had arisen about the proper mode of conducting divine service, and would judge such cases with an open mind. The use of incense and portable lights were the first points submitted to his judgment, and no one could have been less qualified to decide them. He knew the Act of Uniformity and he knew the Prayer Book, and he knew nothing more about the matter. Accordingly he condemned incense and portable lights, as being ornaments not prescribed. He went on to forbid reservation of the Blessed Sacrament for the sick and dying. He frankly admitted that his decisions were merely 'opinions,' but his suffragans tried hard to enforce them. In the matter of incense they partially succeeded; as regards reservation they totally failed.

In 1897 Temple signed and promulgated the *Responsio*, which the learned Bishop John Wordsworth had written, to the Pope's Bull condemning Anglican Orders. In the same year he presided over the Fourth Lambeth Conference. He procured the sale of Addington Park, and the restoration of the old palace at Canterbury. He made over the park at Lambeth to the London County Council, and he crowned King Edward VII. He died on the 23rd December 1902, and was buried in the cloister garth of Canterbury Cathedral.

[G. W. E. R.]

Frederick Temple, by Seven Friends: personal recollections.

TERRIER. An ecclesiastical 'Terrier' is a list or description of glebe lands and tithes (*q.v.*) belonging to a benefice, which description or survey has been made by the incumbent or churchwarden. The word is sometimes spelt 'terrar.' [S. L. O.]

Thomas, *Handbook to the Public Records.*

THEODORE (c. 602-90). Archbishop of Canterbury, was born at Tarsus in Cilicia. Of his early life practically nothing is known. From a letter addressed by Pope Zacharias to St. Boniface (*q.v.*) (*M.G.H.*, *Epist.* iii.. Ep. 80) it may be inferred that Theodore received part of his education at Athens. Bede (*H.E.*, iv. 1) speaks of him as being instructed in secular and divine literature, both Greek and Latin. He must have already acquired the reputation of a scholar when in 667, at the age of sixty-six, he appeared at Rome. Here he became known to Abbot Hadrian, an African monk, who had been offered by Pope Vitalian the archbishopric of Canterbury, vacant owing to the death of Wighard before consecration. The abbot refused it, but recommended Theodore to the Pope as a man well fitted to fill the high office. Vitalian accepted him on the condition that Hadrian should accompany the new archbishop to England, to watch over him and prevent him from introducing any unorthodox tenets of the Greek Church. Theodore was immediately ordained subdeacon, but as his head was shaved bald after the Eastern practice he delayed four months in Rome to grow his hair, that he might be tonsured in the Roman fashion. On 26th March 668 he was consecrated, and two months later started with Hadrian and Benedict Biscop (*q.v.*). who was then in Rome, for England. Their journey was not accomplished without hindrance. They proceeded by sea to Marseilles, and thence by land to Arles. where they were detained by John, the archbishop, by command of Ebroin, the Mayor of the Palace. The latter suspected them of carrying on political intrigue between the Emperor Constans II. and the English King. Theodore was soon permitted to depart. though Hadrian detained longer. The winter was passed at Paris with Agilbert. formerly Bishop of Wessex. Here Raedfrith. the high reeve. who had been sent by Ecgbert. King of Kent, to conduct Theodore to England, found him, and they proceeded together on their journey. After another delay owing to sickness at Etaples. Theodore finally arrived at Canterbury on 27th May 669.

His first step was to make in company

with Hadrian a journey of inspection throughout England. He met with a good reception, and taught, says Bede (*H.E.*, iv. 2), the proper rule of life and the canonical custom of celebrating Easter, thus carrying into effect the decision of the Synod of Whitby of 664. The task of organising the English Church was not easy. The dioceses co-extensive with the kingdoms were too large for proper control, and the see of Rochester and the Mercian bishopric were vacant. He set to work at once to reform this impossible system of Church government. Chad (*q.v.*), who was ruling the Church in Northumbria while its rightful bishop, Wilfrid (*q.v.*), was administrating in Kent, had been irregularly consecrated. The modest bishop resigned his see, and Wilfrid was restored. Theodore, however, found a place for Chad in the vacant bishopric of Mercia. Chad was in some way regularised, and established at Lichfield. Theodore then appointed Putta to Rochester and Bisi to Dunwich, the centre of the East Anglian bishopric. Shortly after a bishop was found for Wessex. The late Bishop Agilbert sent over his nephew Leutherius, who was consecrated Bishop of Winchester by Theodore. After two years' work comparative order had been restored in the Church. In 673 Theodore summoned at Hertford the first important synod of the whole English Church. Theodore himself presided. Bishops Bisi, Putta, Leutherius, and Winfrith, the successor of Chad in the Mercian diocese, attended, while proxies of Wilfrid were also present. The archbishop addressed the Council, exhorting all to work for the unity of the Church, and asked their observance of the decrees of the Fathers. He then produced a book of canons, probably a collection made by Dionysius Exiguus, in which he had marked ten passages of particular importance. These dealt with the canonical observance of Easter and the sphere of a bishop's authority; they provided that monks and clergy should not leave their monasteries or dioceses without special permission; finally, that annual councils should be held at a place called Clovesho on 1st of August in each year. The ninth article, providing that the number of bishops should be increased, met with opposition, and finally had to be abandoned. It is possible that Wilfrid's representatives, who knew their master would resent a diminution of his sphere of influence, caused its rejection. The remaining articles were then subscribed by those present (Bede, *H.E.*, iv. 5).

In spite of his failure to carry the proposal for subdividing the dioceses at the Synod of Hertford, Theodore was able, on the occasion of the resignation of Bisi, to divide the bishopric of East Anglia by appointing two bishops, for Elmham in the northern, and for Dunwich in the southern, half of the kingdom. About the same time Winfrith, Bishop of Mercia, was deposed on the ground of disobedience—perhaps resistance to the proposed partition of his diocese. Saxwulf was appointed in his place, while Putta, who had retired from Rochester to Hereford, seems to have exercised episcopal authority in that district. The subdivision of Mercia was thus begun. In 678 Theodore turned his attention to the north. The Northumbrian King Egfrith was at enmity with Wilfrid, and was willing to assist Theodore to carry out the partition of the unmanageable diocese of York. Theodore knew he could not get Wilfrid to concur in his design. While therefore Wilfrid was temporarily absent he created three bishops, Bosa, Eata, and Eadhed, for Deira, Bernicia, and Lindsey. Wilfrid appealed to Rome, but though the decision was in his favour he failed to get immediate redress in England. He was even imprisoned for a short time, and afterwards was compelled to go into exile. In 679 Theodore succeeded in restoring peace between Egfrith, King of Northumbria, and Ethelred, King of Mercia. It was with the latter's consent and co-operation that Theodore now reorganised the Mercian diocese. Florence of Worcester (*M.H.B.*, 622) attributes the change to the year 679, though probably the partition of the diocese took place gradually. Under the new arrangement there were five sees in Mercia, Worcester, Dorchester (in Oxon), Leicester, Lichfield, and Sidnacester (Stow). [LICHFIELD, SEE OF.]

On 17th September 680 Theodore held his second great Church Synod at Hatfield. It was considered advisable by Pope Agatho to sound the English Church on the question of the Monothelete heresy, which had been condemned at Rome earlier in the same year. A declaration of orthodoxy was therefore drawn up and signed by those who attended, though unfortunately the names of the bishops present have not been recorded by Bede (*H.E.*, iv. 17). At the same time, John, the Archchanter of St. Peter's and Abbot of St. Martin's at Rome, who had come over to England with Benedict Biscop, laid before the synod the decrees of the Lateran Council of 649 against Monotheletism.

In 681 Theodore further subdivided the diocese of Lindisfarne by establishing a see at Hexham and consecrating a bishop for the Picts. Bishop Tunbert of Hexham was deposed in 684 for disobedience ; the see was given to Eata, and on 26th March of the next year Theodore consecrated Cuthbert at York to the see of Lindisfarne. The death of King Egfrith, however, in 686 offered an opportunity for a reconciliation between Theodore and Wilfrid. The archbishop himself wished to achieve this before his death, and no doubt the patient suffering and the missionary work of Wilfrid had won his admiration. The very partisan account of Eddius, Wilfrid's biographer, cannot be accepted in all its details, though the main facts are proved. The new King of Northumbria, Aldfrith, who did not share the animosity of his predecessor towards Wilfrid, agreed to his restoration to the see of York, though Theodore's division of the diocese remained undisturbed. The last years of Theodore's life are marked by no new achievements. He died on the 19th September 690 at the age of eighty-eight, and was buried in the church of SS. Peter and Paul at Canterbury.

Theodore, says Bede, was the first archbishop whom all the English Church obeyed (*H.E.*, iv. 2). These words indicate the importance of his work. He established something like ecclesiastical unity in a country politically divided into separate kingdoms ; the Councils of Hertford and Hatfield prove the success of his efforts in this direction. He thoroughly reorganised the Church on a permanent and workable basis, and subdivided the dioceses formerly co-extensive with the kingdoms into sees of manageable dimensions. Though he cannot be said to have founded the parochial system, as Elmham (*Hist. Mon. S. Augustini*, ed. Hardwick, p. 285) asserts, his work aided its development. Under Theodore's guidance a great advance was made in education. Assisted by Hadrian, who succeeded Benedict Biscop in the abbacy of SS. Peter and Paul at Canterbury, Theodore taught large crowds of scholars. As a testimony of their work, Bede tells us that there are many scholars in his day ' who are as well versed in the Greek and Latin tongues as in their own ' (*H.E.*, iv. 2). William of Malmesbury speaks of Theodore as the ' Philosopher ' (*De Gestis Pontificum*, p. 7).

The only work of importance which can be attributed to Theodore is the *Penitential*. It is a compilation of answers given by Theodore to questions addressed to him by one who styles himself ' Discipulus Umbrensium.' It is printed in Haddan and

Stubbs, *Councils and Ecclesiastical Documents*, iii. 173 f., from a MS. at C.C.C., Cambridge. [A. L. P.]

Bede, *H.E.* ; Eddius, *vita Wilfridi* (but for the partisan character of this source see *E.H.R.*, vi. 535 f.) ; Haddan and Stubbs, *Councils*, iii. ; Bright, *Early Eng. Ch. Hist.* ; Hook, *Lives of the Archbishops*, i.

THEOLOGICAL COLLEGES. The Council of Trent, Sess. XXIII. cap. xviii., ordered that all cathedral and metropolitan churches should maintain a college for the education of poor youths for the sacred ministry. Archbishop Cranmer (*q.v.*) in England had the same design, ' that in every Cathedral there should be provision made for Readers, of Divinity, and of Greek, and Hebrew, and a great number of Students to be both exercised in the daily worship of God, and trained up in Study and Devotion ; whom the Bishop might transplant out of this Nursery, into all parts of his Diocese. And thus every Bishop should have had a College of Clergymen under his eye ' (Burnet, *Hist. of Reformation*, Book III. vol. i. 225, fol. ed.)

Some attempt at such an institution was perhaps to be seen in the practice of the saintly Dr. Richard Sherlock (1612-89), Rector of Winwick, Lancs, who ' always entertained in his house at least three Curates for the service of his Church and chapels. So that Winwick became a very desirable place for young Divines to improve themselves in the work of the Ministry.' Such is Bishop T. Wilson's (*q.v.*) account of his uncle and rector, and upon it Mr. Keble (*q.v.*) observes: ' Winwick Rectory thus comes before us a sort of Priests' House or Parochial College.'

The first regular attempt to carry out Cranmer's ideals was made at Salisbury by Bishop Burnet (*q.v.*). He thought ' the greatest prejudice the Church was under was from the ill education of the Clergy,' and considered the Universities useless for purposes of ordinands, who there ' learned the airs of vanity and insolence ' (*Autobiog.*, 500). He determined to found a diocesan college. It was the project ' upon which his heart was most set,' to have at Salisbury ' a nursery of Students in Divinity who should follow their studies and devotions till ' the bishop ' could provide them.' He had ten students, to whom he allowed £30 a year apiece, and during the eight months of his annual residence at Salisbury the students came to him daily for an hour's lecture. The care of them was partly shared by Dr. Daniel Whitby (1638-1726), Rector of St. Edmund's,

Salisbury, and Prebendary and Precentor of the cathedral, who superintended their studies in the bishop's absence. He was a studious, unbusiness-like man, pious and unselfish, who 'used no recreation but tobacco,' a vigorous anti-Romanist controversialist, a voluminous writer, and in later life held Unitarian opinions. The experiment provoked the opposition of the University of Oxford, and after five years the bishop 'saw it was expedient to let it fall' (*Life* in *History of His Own Time.* fol. ed., ii. 708 ; *Suppl. Hist.*, ed. Foxcroft, 329, 500).

In 1698 Thomas Wilson (*q.v.*) was consecrated Bishop of Sodor and Man. His practice was to take ordination candidates to reside with him at Bishop's Court for a year before their ordination ; and here they were allowed to say the daily offices in chapel, and were thus trained in reading and speaking as well as in theology.

In 1707 Wilson proposed to the S.P.G. the training of missionary candidates at a school founded in Man by Bishop Barrow. The scheme fell through in 1711 owing to the supineness and timidity of Archbishop Tenison, the only objection being 'the lowness of the Society's funds.' For nearly a century such projects were put aside, until in 1804 Bishop Burgess of St. David's, horrified at the condition of affairs, founded 'A Society for promoting Christian Knowledge and Church Union' in his diocese, 10th October. One object of it was 'to facilitate the means of education to young men' intended for the Church's ministry, and the bishop urged that 'an establishment for their education in the diocese was very desirable.' For this object he asked the clergy to subscribe a tenth of their benefices, and though poorly paid they responded nobly. From this arose **St. David's College, Lampeter.** The bishop's projected 'Collegiate Seminary for Clerical Education' (*Life*, 292) excited interest, money came in, and in 1809 he began operations near Llandewy Brefy, but desisted since enough money was not in hand. In 1820 a Welsh landowner, Dr. Harford, offered the bishop a site at Lampeter. Building began in 1821. George IV. subscribed £1000, Oxford and Cambridge granted £200 each, and on the King's birthday, 12th August 1822, the foundation stone was laid by the bishop. In 1825 Burgess appeared to jeopardise his project by accepting translation to Salisbury; but his successor, Bishop Jenkinson, completed the work, and it was opened for the reception of students, 1st March 1827. It is by no means only a theological college, and by Royal Charters

(1852 and 1868) it is allowed to confer the degree of B.D. and B.A. and the status of Licentiate in Divinity.

St. Bees. Although a college for St. David's was projected in 1804, yet St. Bees was founded before Lampeter was built. In 1816 Bishop G. H. Law of Chester founded at St. Bees in Cumberland (then in the Chester diocese) a 'Clerical Institution' for the better instruction of those candidates for holy orders who were unable to obtain a University education. The *Gentleman's Magazine*, i. 338 (April 1817), politely patronised the new venture, and Carlisle in his *Endowed Grammar Schools* (1818), i. 169. goes out of his way to describe the new foundation and to praise 'this truly pious and benevolent design.' Bishop Law gave £200 towards building a house for the 'Superintendent.' Queen Anne's Bounty gave £300, and William, first Earl of Lonsdale (1757-1844), converted the ruined chancel of the priory church (the nave of which. disused after the Dissolution. had been restored as a parish church in 1611) into a lecture-room and library for the students. 'The young Gentlemen' from the first 'boarded themselves in private houses.' By an arrangement between the bishop and the earl, who was patron of the living of St. Bees, the principal was appointed incumbent of the parish. The college course extended over two years, and residence was indispensable. The institution seems to have flourished from the first. Wordsworth in his *Itinerary Poems of 1833* embalmed the college in his verse :—

'Oh, may that power who hushed the stormy seas,
    And cleared a way for the first Votaries,
Prosper the new-born College of St. Bees.'

In 1846-8 there were from a hundred to a hundred and twenty students in residence, 'of a somewhat mixed character.' A local guide in 1870 states that 'St. Bees supplies more candidates for orders in England and Wales than any other theological college ; the average number of students is from eighty to ninety,' and the official *College Calendar* for 1890 mentions some sixty students as in residence the previous year. A hood was invented by Dr. Parkinson and granted to the students —half red and half white silk. This was altered later to a hood of black stuff lined with puce. The principals or 'superintendents' were (1) Dr. Wm. Ainger, 1816-40 ; (2) Robert Pedder Buddicom, 1840-6 ; (3) Dr. Richard Parkinson, 1846-58 ; (4) Dr.

George Henry Ainger. 1858-71; (5) Edward Hadarezer Knowles, 1871-96.

The college ceased to exist about 1894 owing to the raising of the standard for ordinands, the institution of a Central Entrance Examination, and other tests. The fees were £10 per term, and there were four terms in the year. In 1856 the college passed from the diocese of Chester into that of Carlisle. Its existence was recognised by 3 and 4 Vic. c. 77. (*Guide to St. Bees*, 1870; *St. Bees' College Calendar*, 1890; G. Huntingdon, *Random Recollections*, 263-76.)

C.M.S. College at Islington. In 1806 the committee of the society gave ' much time and thought to the subject of a seminary in England.' Early missionaries were trained by Thomas Scott at Bledlow, Bucks, and later were distributed among various clergy. The idea of a training institution was opposed, some urging that candidates should be sent to the Universities. Later it was agreed that the society should train men of humble station free, and a house in Barnsbury was opened for the reception of students, 31st January 1825, under the secretary, Edward Bickersteth. Daniel Wilson (*q.v.*) had then become Vicar of Islington. The first stone of the present college was laid, 31st July 1826, and the first principal, J. N. Pearson (1826-38), appointed. The original 'institution' is now the principal's house. The object of the college is to train men ready to devote their lives to the missionary work of the C.M.S.

The Oxford Movement (*q.v.*) by its revival of enthusiasm led to plans for diocesan theological colleges. The first to be established was at **Chichester**, where Charles Marriott (*q.v.*) became principal, February 1839. The college was founded largely through Manning (*q.v.*), then archdeacon. Its original buildings were Cawley Priory in South Pallant (1839-44); in recent years the college has been established in West Street. In its early years it declined, and at the end of 1845 was declared non-existent. It was revived in 1846 under Philip Freeman. (Burgon, *Twelve Good Men*, 'C. Marriott.' Purcell, *Life of Manning*, confuses two projects—a diocesan college for schoolmasters and the theological college.)

Wells Theological College, opened on 1st May 1840, was founded by the bishop, G. H. Law, who had previously founded St. Bees. The first principal was J. H. Pinder, formerly Principal of Codrington College, Barbados. The college, which ever since its foundation has played a distinguished part in English Church history, is intended for graduates only.

In 1846 was founded **St. Aidan's College, Birkenhead**, originating in a private theological class held by Dr. Baylee, whose scheme for a Parochial Assistant Association was adopted, December 1846, by the Liverpool rectors. The college was opened, 24th June 1847; in 1856 large new buildings were built, but in July 1868 it closed, with a debt of £10,000. It was reopened in October 1869, since when its career has been uniformly prosperous. The founder was Dr. Baylee, with some local gentlemen.

St. Augustine's College, Canterbury, founded by Royal Charter, 1848, was a direct result of the principles of the Oxford Movement, E. Coleridge and A. J. Beresford-Hope uniting to restore the ruined buildings of the ancient abbey of St. Augustine into a college for the training of men for foreign service. The college has a Warden and Fellows, the Warden being nominated by the two Primates and the Bishop of London.

Cuddesdon Theological College, the most famous of English theological colleges, was founded by Bishop S. Wilberforce (*q.v.*), who, after interviewing his rural deans not three months after his consecration, wrote second among his *Agenda*: 'A diocesan training college for clergy to be established at Cuddesdon.' After much delay, due to the wish of the clergy to have the buildings not within the palace grounds, it was at length completed, and was opened, 15th June 1854, eight bishops being present. The first principal was Alfred Pott, the vice-principal H. P. Liddon (*q.v.*), to whom and to Bishop King (*q.v.*), the third principal, the college owed its early fame. It was more than once the object of bitter Protestant attack, especially in 1858, but notwithstanding misrepresentation its sons are among the most distinguished of modern Churchmen.

Lichfield Theological College was projected in 1852 by two clergy of the diocese (E. J. Edwards and E. T. Codd), and an address in favour of it was signed by the dean and archdeacons and presented to the bishop (Lonsdale), who in 1853 approved the suggestion in his charge. The Evangelicals of the diocese raised violent opposition, and for the sake of peace the scheme was suspended. In 1855, however, when the project was revived, the opposition was renewed. Meetings were called to oppose this attempt ' to propagate Tractarianism and force it upon the diocese in its most insidious and odious shape.' The bishop, however, stood firm. A Chancery suit to stop the college being built failed, and the college began its work in 1857. It is now one of the largest in England.

Salisbury Theological College was founded by Bishop W. K. Hamilton in 1860. He had determined on such a foundation from the time of his consecration, the idea having been suggested to him by his predecessor, Edward Denison, in 1841. At first the students lived in lodgings in the city; later the corporate life began, and buildings were acquired.

In the same year, 1860, **St. Boniface College, Warminster**, was founded in the Salisbury diocese by Canon Sir James Erasmus Philipps, Bart., a close friend of Bishop Hamilton. Its object was to take students too young to enter St. Augustine College, Canterbury, or other missionary colleges, or who from other causes were not admitted to them. It has grown to be one of the largest missionary colleges.

In 1863 the **London College of Divinity** (St. John's Hall, Highbury) was opened as an Evangelical theological college. It was founded by Alfred Peache, Incumbent of Mangotsfield, and was due to a paper read before the Western Clerical and Lay Association. [SOCIETIES, ECCLESIASTICAL.] The college is now recognised as a school of theology in the University of London.

The **Scholae Cancellarii** at **Lincoln** were founded by Bishop C. Wordsworth (*q.v.*) in January 1874, with Dr. E. W. Benson (*q.v.*) as first head. The bishop was a great benefactor to the college, spending more than £6000 on it in his life, and his successor (Bishop King) also fostered it.

In 1876 **Ely Theological College** was founded by Dr. James Russell Woodford, Bishop of Ely, 1873-85. He was the chaplain and close friend of Bishop S. Wilberforce, and the college was founded on the model of Cuddesdon, although at first, as at Salisbury, the students lived in lodgings in the city until the college was built. The college is for graduates only.

In 1876 also the **Clergy School** at **Leeds** was founded by the then vicar, Dr. John Gott, later Bishop of Truro, the object being to prepare graduates of Oxford and Cambridge for ordination, chiefly to town curacies.

St. Stephen's House, Oxford, opened in 1876, was founded mainly through Dr. King, later Bishop of Lincoln, and Dr. J. Wordsworth, later Bishop of Salisbury, and others, originally for the training of graduates as missionaries.

In 1877 **Wycliffe Hall, Oxford**, was founded from a fund raised by Evangelical Churchmen during the discussion caused by the attack on Christianity in *Supernatural Religion*. It is a college for graduates only.

In 1878, on the Conversion of St. Paul, **St. Paul's Missionary College** at **Burgh, Lincs**, was dedicated for the training of men who desire to devote their lives to the foreign service of the Church. Originally started tentatively for five years, it has flourished and extended widely. Its foundation was due to Bishop C. Wordsworth and J. H. Jowitt.

Dorchester (Oxon) Missionary College, to educate for the work of the Church abroad men unable to afford a University training, was founded in 1878 by a body of Oxford graduates presided over by Dr. King, later Bishop of Lincoln, the initiation of the scheme being due to the Vicar of Dorchester, W. C. Macfarlane.

In 1878 the **Sodor and Man Theological School** was established by Bishop Hill for training ordinands. In 1889 it was transferred by Bishop Bardsley to Bishop's Court, and renamed **Bishop Wilson's Theological School**.

In 1880 **Ridley Hall** was founded at Cambridge on the same lines as Wycliffe Hall at Oxford, and with the same objects.

In 1881 the **Clergy Training School** at Cambridge was begun. Originally it hired rooms for its lectures and meetings. In 1899 a block of buildings was built, called 'Westcott House,' and these have since been enlarged.

Manchester had three theological institutions: the **Scholae Episcopi**, founded 1890, with a lecture-room in the cathedral, ended in 1911; **St. Anselm's Hostel**, founded 1907, to give free training to carefully selected ordinands; and **Egerton Hall**, founded 1908, for graduates preparing for ordination.

Kelham Theological College, founded as the Society of the Sacred Mission in 1891 [RELIGIOUS ORDERS, MODERN], was recognised as a theological college in 1897, and marked the beginning of a new type of institution, in which the students are trained in a theological course of four years, and are expected to repay the cost of their training.

St. Michael and All Angels, Llandaff, was founded for graduates in 1892 at Aberdare by Miss Olive Talbot. It moved into new buildings at Llandaff in 1907. It also has a hostel for undergraduates in the University of Wales. From 1892-1912 three hundred men have been ordained from the college.

Ripon College, founded by Bishop W. B. Carpenter, 1897, was amalgamated in 1900 with **Lightfoot Hall, Edgbaston**, founded 1899, and represents the Midlands Clergy Training College. The **Bishop's Hostel, Farnham**, founded by Bishop H. Ryle of Winchester in 1899, and the **Bishop's Hostel**,

Newcastle-on-Tyne (since 1907 **Bishop Jacob's Hostel**), founded by Bishop Jacob, then of Newcastle, 1901, are ordinary types of diocesan theological colleges for graduates.

St. Chad's Hostel, Hooton Pagnell, founded 1902, based on the lines of Kelham, is affiliated to St. Chad's Hall at Durham; while the **College of the Resurrection, Mirfield**, founded 1902 (affiliated to the University of Leeds, 1904) is an effort of the Community of the Resurrection [RELIGIOUS ORDERS, MODERN] to train men for ordination, the course lasting five years.

Bishops' College, Cheshunt, under the direction of the Bishops of London, Southwark, and St. Albans, was founded in 1909 to train graduates on the lines of Cuddesdon, Ely, and Wells. It was founded largely by Canon Lambert, Vicar of Cheshunt, who bought the buildings of Lady Huntingdon's (*q.v.*) College at Cheshunt, formerly belonging to the Congregationalists.

St. John's Hall, Durham, founded 1909, though ranking as a theological college, is a hostel of the University of Durham.

Dr. Vaughan (*q.v.*), both as Vicar of Doncaster and Dean of Llandaff, prepared men for ordination, and was thus head of a sort of theological school. **Bishop Lightfoot** of Durham (*q.v.*) trained candidates for ordination at Auckland Castle, and this school was continued by his successor, Bishop Westcott (*q.v.*), and for a time by Bishop Moule. The diocesan theological colleges at Gloucester (founded 1868) and Truro (1877) have ceased to exist. A theological department was founded at King's College, London, in 1846, and a resident hostel in connection with it was begun in 1902. At Queen's College, Birmingham, a theological department was founded and endowed by Dr. S. W. Warneford and incorporated by 30 and 31 Vic. c. 6 in 1867.

The importance of theological colleges in the English Church is shown by a resolution of the Upper House of the Convocation of Canterbury (adopted later by the Upper House of the York province), 6th July 1909: 'That after January 1917 candidates for holy orders be required (in addition to a university degree) to have received at least one year's practical and devotional training at a recognised theological college, or under some other authorised supervision.'

[S. L. O.]

THIRLWALL, Connop (1797-1875), Bishop of St. David's, was a child of marvellous precocity, learning Latin at three years old, and at four reading Greek 'with an ease and fluency which astonished all who heard him.' In 1809 his father published Connop's *Primitiae*, 'Essays and Poems on various subjects, Religious, Moral, and Entertaining,' which annoyed the bishop so much in later life that he destroyed every copy he could find. From Charterhouse he entered Trinity College, Cambridge, 1814, becoming B.A. and Fellow of his College, 1818; M.A., 1821. He was called to the Bar, 1825, but preferred theology to law, returned to Cambridge, 1827, and was ordained. In 1834 his advocacy of the admission of dissenters to the University, and his ironical plea that it was not specially a place of religious education, caused the Master of Trinity (Wordsworth) to ask him to resign his assistant tutorship. Lord Melbourne then presented him to the living of Kirby Underdale, where he sometimes spent sixteen hours a day in his study. His *History of Greece* (1835-47) has been considered superior to that of his schoolfellow at Charterhouse, George Grote. In 1840 Melbourne offered him the bishopric of St. David's, after ascertaining his orthodoxy from Archbishop Howley (*q.v.*): 'I don't like heterodox bishops,' said the minister, and assured Thirlwall that he was interested in theology and found the Fathers 'excellent reading and very amusing.'

Thirlwall quickly learnt Welsh, and worked hard to restore church life in his diocese, but was greater as a scholar than as an administrator. In 1842 he pleaded for toleration of the Oxford Movement (*q.v.*). He recognised the value of the ritual revival, though he disliked its doctrinal tendency, and found Dr. Pusey (*q.v.*) 'a painful enigma.' He joined in the episcopal censure of *Essays and Reviews* (*q.v.*), which he thought contained opinions irreconcilable with the Church's teaching. But he considered the Judicial Committee of the Privy Council a blessing to the Church, holding that its judgments could not affect matters of faith; and feared lest the revival of synods might lead to tampering with doctrine. For the same reason he opposed the summoning of the Lambeth Conference, 1867. [COUNCILS.] Believing that Establishment was neither good nor bad in itself, but depended on the merits of each case, he supported the disestablishment of the Irish Church, and argued that Church property might, without sacrilege, be diverted to temporal uses beneficial to society. In 1870 he resigned the chairmanship of the Old Testament Revision Company, in consequence of the decision to exclude scholars who disbelieved in the Godhead of our Lord, holding that scholarship, not faith, should be the qualification. He resigned his see, 1874, died unmarried, 1875, and was buried in the same grave with Grote in Westminster Abbey.

[G. C.]

Letters, ed. J. S. Perowne and L. Stokes (with Memoir) ; *Remains*, ed. Perowne ; *Letters to a Friend*, ed. A. P. Stanley.

TILLOTSON, John (1630-94), Archbishop of Canterbury, was born at Sowerby in Yorkshire. He was a Fellow of Clare Hall, Cambridge (1651), was ordained by the Scottish Bishop Thomas Sydserff (1660 or 1661), was curate of Cheshunt (1662), Rector of Kedington (1662), Preacher at Lincoln's Inn (1664), Lecturer at St. Laurence Jewry (1664). Prebendary of Canterbury (1670), Dean of Canterbury (1672), Dean of St. Paul's (1689), Archbishop of Canterbury (1691). Though not among the members appointed by the King's warrant, he was one of two or three scholars present as watchers on the Nonconformist side at the Savoy Conference (*q.v.*) in 1661. In 1668 he took part in preparing a Bill, which the House of Commons refused to consider, by which not only might effect be given to the promises of toleration contained in Charles II.'s Declaration from Breda (1660), but also the comprehension of dissenters might be promoted by various concessions to them. In 1688 he was one of the divines who helped the 'Seven Bishops' (*q.v.*) to draw up their reasons for refusing to read James II.'s Declaration of Indulgence. In 1689 William III. appointed him Dean of St. Paul's, and proposed that he should be archbishop; but Tillotson was very reluctant to be made 'a wedge to drive out' Sancroft (*q.v.*), and succeeded in delaying his election and consecration until May 1691. In 1689 he was a member of the Commission for the revision of the Prayer Book and canons and for reforming the ecclesiastical courts ; and he drew up a paper, 'Concessions which would probably be made by the Church of England for the union of Protestants.' In November the advocates of comprehension proposed him as Prolocutor of the Lower House of Convocation, but he was defeated by fifty-five votes to twenty-eight. These events in his history indicate the main lines of his policy. He greatly dreaded Roman Catholicism, and earnestly desired to include in the Church all Protestant dissenters except Socinians by means which would not involve any sacrifice on their part of the principles which had hitherto kept them separate. He wished ' we were well rid of ' the Athanasian Creed. His apparent acceptance of Zwinglian opinions about the Eucharist, contrary to the formularies of the English Church, may have had considerable influence in promoting the growth of Zwinglianism among English Churchmen. It was his aim to raise the standard of work and life among the clergy. Though in favour at court, he died so poor that had not the King condoned his first-fruits his debts could not have been paid. His friend Burnet (*q.v.*) preached his funeral sermon, eulogising his blameless personal character as well as his learning. Tillotson's easy delivery, clearness of reasoning, and persuasive style made him famous as a preacher, and provided a pattern on which the eighteenth-century divines modelled their sermons. ' He was not only the best preacher of the age,' says Burnet, ' but seemed to have brought preaching to perfection.' He was the first married archbishop of Canterbury since Parker.   [D. S.]

Works, ed. with *Life*, by Birch, 1752 ; Beardmore, *Memorials* ; Burnet, *Hist. Own Time*.

TITHE. This article is necessarily limited to England and to the Continental antecedents of tithe in our country. The idea that Christians should pay tithe is not older than the fourth century. Before that it is only mentioned in a few rhetorical passages, with vague allusions to the Mosaic Law from which no practical inference can be drawn. In the canons of the classical councils, from Nicæa to Chalcedon, though they range over all the practical concerns of the Church, no mention of tithe can be found. But late in the fourth century St. Jerome and St. Augustine in Latin, and St. John Chrysostom in Greek, are found teaching that the tenth of the Christian's substance belongs to God, and should be distributed for His service. As a practical exemplification of this duty, Cassian tells how it was customary for the peasants of Egypt to pay tithes to the monks who dwelt near them. These monks, we must remember, were laymen, and were not in any sense ministering spiritually to those around them. But almost at once a more precise demand was made. In this same generation it became the established doctrine that the ministry of the new covenant exactly corresponds to that of the old. St. Ambrose is the first writer of importance to identify the deacon with the Levite ; he is also the first habitually to use the title *sacerdos*, which previously had meant the bishop (*e.g.* always in St. Cyprian) for the second order of the ministry. The inference was obvious ; the Christian clergy had a right to that revenue from tithe which the Jewish ministry had formerly enjoyed. In religious literature the two ideas, of charity in general and of the maintenance of the clergy, as the destination of the tithe that Christians ought to pay, are equally inculcated, and found synodical expression at the second Council of Mâcon in 585, when the bishops of Burgundy, then at the height of its power and extent, in their fifth canon command that all the people shall bring their tithes to the clergy to be spent by them, the only purposes named being the needs of the poor and the redemption of captives. Such a canon was of purely moral force; and we find that the Penitentials of the farther West, both the Irish and that of Theodore (*q.v.*) of Canterbury, which was modelled on the Irish pattern, used the same religious pressure. Tithe, as understood in such literature, is the tenth of all gains, and so includes the tithe of spoil. Such a gift, congenial to the Teutonic mind, was commended by the example of Abraham in Gen. 14²⁰.

As yet the tithe of agricultural produce had not been thought of as a specific source of ecclesiastical revenue. But under the later Roman Empire one of the chief taxes had been a tenth of the produce of land, exacted in kind. This tax was retained under the Franks, and is still levied on the Roman plan throughout the Turkish dominions. In the early Frankish period wide territories were granted to bishoprics and monasteries, subject, like all other lands, to this impost. But the kings, favouring the Church, often relieved such estates of the tax; *i.e.* the *coloni*, or half-servile tenantry, no longer paid it to the Crown but to the landlord. Lothar II. (d. 628) confirmed such grants of immunity made by himself and his predecessors (*M.G.H.*, Leges II. i. p. 19), and though this source of income was far from universal, the eyes of the Church were from that time fixed upon it. It could be collected under the owner's supervision, and being a tenth it seemed to be Scriptural. Henceforth tithe other than from land falls into the background. But as yet there was, at least in the case of the higher clergy, no urgent need. The endowments in land of the great Frankish churches, as of the English, were very large. In the eighth century, however, the Frankish State fell into distress, and Charles Martel (reigned 714-41) as his last resource seized the Church lands in order to maintain his forces. The Church was ruined; bishops could not furnish a pittance to their clerks, and ecclesiastical historians have blackened the reputation of

the aggressor. His son, Pepin the Short, made his peace with the Church. In 765 he issued what was in fact, though not in form, a capitulary, or general law, for his dominions, which made tithe compulsory, *ut unusquisque homo, aut vellet aut nollet, suam decimam donet*. The land was gone and could not be restored; tithe, and tithe from land, was to be the equivalent. An important difference between the Church history of the Frankish Empire, both in France and Germany, and that of England arose from the fact that in England the bishops and the great monasteries, retaining their lands, had no such personal interest in tithe as those on the Continent had. Later Frankish legislation only made the law of Pepin more precise; in particular, tithe was severely and even ruthlessly exacted by Pepin's son, Charles the Great, from the Saxons, whom he converted at the point of the sword.

In England, as elsewhere, the moral duty of paying tithe was inculcated, but legislation to compel obedience was later than among the Franks. The Frankish Empire was the pattern copied in many ways by English kings; and the Legatine Council of 787, whose canons were sanctioned by the Kings of Mercia, Wessex, and Northumbria, with their respective witan, was in all probability suggested by the legislation of Pepin in 765. But the English law was studiously vague. It merely enacted that tithe must be paid; neither its source nor its purpose is specified, *cum obtestatione praecipimus, ut omnes studeant de omnibus quae possident decimas dare*. We first find a definite imposition of tithe on land in the laws of Aethelstan (I. Aethelstan, *Prol.*, Liebermann, p. 146), in which it is ordered that the bishop, as well as king and ealdormen, shall pay tithe of the increase of his live stock and crops. This is repeated *verbatim* in the later laws of Eadgar and Cnut. It is important to note that the bishop is a payer and not a recipient of tithe. In fact, on episcopal estates the same system of incumbencies came to be established as on lay estates, and English bishops, anciently endowed, have never had a personal interest in the receipt or (save within narrow limits) authority as to the distribution of tithe. The recipient of the tithe was to be, according to this law, the ' old minster,' *i.e.* the church, under the control of the bishop, which was the headquarters of the priest who superintended the neighbourhood, and was the place where he administered baptism. Perhaps we may assume that there was one such church in an area as large as a modern rural deanery. If, however, there was a church with a burial ground situated on 'bocland' (land granted with full ownership and succession), the owner of such church was to give one-third of his tithe to it and two-thirds to the 'old minster.' We must bear in mind how complete was the possession which has now dwindled into patronage. [PARISH.] If, however, this private church had no burial ground, it was to claim no share of the tithe, all of which must go to the 'old minster.' This system of distribution broke down before the Norman Conquest. The private churches gradually gained fuller rights, and simultaneously the bishops obtained some control over them. On the other hand, the bishops abandoned their special interest in the 'old minsters,' constituting themselves simply patrons and collating incumbents. Thus there came to be no practical distinction between churches with cure of souls, and the special privileges of the 'old minsters' fell into oblivion, though many of them retained dignity as collegiate churches. But since the decline of the 'old minsters,' and with it the departure of their practical right to tithe, was a more rapid process than that of the establishment of parish churches, there came a time, about the Norman Conquest, when owners of land regarded themselves in some cases as free to dispose of their tithe as they would. The bishop and his cathedral were adequately endowed with land, the 'old minster' only concerned itself with its own parishioners, and the landowner either had no church or else had so complete a dominion over it that it rested with himself whether he would or would not bestow his tithe upon it. But this was a temporary phase. Such tithe soon found a permanent recipient, and all doubt was ended by Innocent III.'s assertion, *cum perceptio decimarum ad paroeciales ecclesias de iure communi pertineat* (Decretals, iii. 30, 29), which implied that unless the landowner could show that he was lawfully paying his tithe to some recipient, such as a religious house, with a claim prior to that of the parish priest, he was bound to pay it to the latter.

Before we follow the history beyond this decisive point reference must be made to the isolated appearance in the laws of Aethelred the Unready (VIII. Aethelred, c. 6, A.D. 1014, Liebermann, p. 264) of the threefold Continental division of tithe, concerning which we may doubt whether, even in the Frankish Empire, it was ever enforced. Certainly this provision of Aethelred's was never

effectual in England; it was promptly revoked by Cnut (*q.v.*), his successor, and nothing more is heard of it. In any case, it was no more than a piece of devout antiquarianism.

We now turn to the developed law concerning tithe as stated in the *Corpus Juris Canonici*. It is of divine origin and a permanent charge on land, and may not be redeemed, though a composition (or *modus*) may be made, and the recipient may lease out his rights. No lay authority can grant exemption; tithe may be exacted as a debt, and the wilful debtor is denied Christian burial. The unworthiness of the clergy does not excuse from payment. It is normally payable to the parochial or baptismal church. But if it belongs to a religious house, the bishop is to see that a portion is paid to the priest who performs the duty of the church. The tithe is to be paid according to the custom of the parish. (This might be more or less than a tenth. In England the variation was great. At Eastwood, Essex, it is said that the tithe of eggs was one in six.) Tithe of grain is not limited to old cultivation; land newly brought under the plough is liable to the payment, but tithe on it will not follow an old grant to a monastery; on the other hand, a monastery which breaks up land of its own for cultivation will not pay tithes on such additional crops. Grants of tithe by laymen are not to be accepted by a religious house without the consent of the bishop.

The Sext. iii. 13, which deals with tithes, was published in 1298, yet it assumes that such gifts by laymen are still possible. In England they were obsolete (see below). The Canon Law wavers on the point whether a layman can be a tithe-owner or not, but generally gives the impression that he cannot. It has little to say about the intangible tithe on earnings; but it allows that necessary expenses of the business may be deducted before the merchant or tradesman makes his payment.

In England we need not trouble ourselves with this last description of tithe, and the problem is simplified by the fact that the old bishoprics and religious houses were endowed with lands, and not, as in France and Germany, interested in tithes. Just as on lay estates, parish priests on theirs became what were ultimately called rectors, though there were early cases, numerous yet exceptional, in which monasteries were endowed by gift with tithe from laymen's lands. The Norman Conquest, though it led to the completion of the parochial system, led also to the impoverishment of the parish clergy. Founders of monasteries after 1066 usually endowed them not with lands, or only slightly, but with churches. We may take two examples of houses of considerable importance, the Austin Canons of Barnwell, near Cambridge, and the Benedictines of Walden (Saffron Walden) in Essex. The former received merely a site on which to build, the latter only what would be now accounted a small farm. Each monastery was endowed with all the churches in the barony of its founder. Walden received nineteen, Barnwell eight, together with two-thirds of the tithes of the demesnes of the knights holding of the barony of Bourn (*Monasticon*, iv. 133; Clark, *Liber Memorandorum de Bernewelle*). The parochial tithe had now to be turned to monastic account. The fact that many monks by the eleventh century were in the higher orders removed any objection on grounds of principle. In fact, the Popes of that age encouraged the endowment of monasteries with tithe because their inmates so frequently were priests or 'levites'; and this motive led ultimately to the command, finally given in 1311, that male religious should take such orders. At first these post-Conquest monasteries collected the whole tithe of the parish, the duty being often done by a visiting monk, if it were at hand; often—indeed always, if it were distant—by a stipendiary priest, without security of tenure. It is to the credit of the better bishops of the twelfth and thirteenth centuries that they struggled against the dependent position and inadequate remuneration of such clergy, and obtained by degrees the appointment of permanent vicars, who received a portion (perhaps a third) of the income, while the religious house, which retained the 'great' tithe, was their patron. Thus a large part of the tithe of England passed irrevocably into monastic and ultimately into lay hands. But this was not all. Districts of considerable acreage round their monasteries were often retained by monks of later creation in their own hands for spiritual purposes, which meant that where they were the landowners no tithe was levied. It was useless to go through the formality of paying it to themselves, and when the Dissolution came there was no incumbent responsible for the services, and no tithe to be paid to any one in such 'extra-parochial places.' Birkenhead was an important example, where a district now inhabited by more than a hundred thousand people was left till recent times without any of the services which the Benedictines of the priory had once rendered. A still more serious deduction from the sources

of parochial revenue was the existence of exempt orders. Till Adrian IV. (*q.v.*) the tendency was to encourage the acquisition of tithe by religious houses on the ground given above. But that Pope initiated a policy of restriction in the interest of the parish clergy, and many privileges were withdrawn by him, so that monasteries were compelled to pay tithe upon their lands, with the exception of what might be called their home farm. Adrian, however, continued the exemption in favour of the two military orders, and the existence of small parishes or townships, tithe-free and with their church unendowed, may usually be explained by former ownership on the part of Templars or Hospitallers. It was a more serious matter that Adrian's successor, Alexander III., exempted the Cistercians, his most active supporters in the great strife between Pope and Emperor. They threw themselves, soon after their foundation, into the work of agriculture, especially pastoral, in which they acquired great wealth. Whether or no the exemption from tithe on land which they owned and cultivated encouraged them in this pursuit, they certainly extended their bounds to the utmost, and not only by the legitimate method of reclaiming woods and moors. Instances are on record both in Germany and in England of their evicting the whole population of a parish which had been given them, farming the land themselves, and then refusing to pay tithe to the incumbent. For the English case see Decretals, iii. 30, 3, where Adrian IV. forbids this abuse of the exemption. But far more important were the areas which they reclaimed by the labours of their lay brothers, a class much more numerous among the early Cistercians than in other orders, though in their later days they preferred the service of hired labourers to such assistance. Thus a vast area of land, especially in the northern counties of England, came to be exempt from tithe, as owned and cultivated by these White Monks.

By the year 1200 the creation of vicarages and the exemption of the privileged orders had seriously reduced the amount of tithe available for the parochial clergy. But the process was not at an end. Living after living came to be burdened with a pension or a portion (the former fixed, the latter fluctuating with the value of produce) for the benefit of the monastery, sometimes of the bishop, who was patron. And every year, down to the Dissolution, saw further rectories reduced to vicarages. Even the wealthiest abbeys would do this. Westminster so treated Hendon in Middlesex in 1178; as late as

1517 the Cistercians of Stratford in Essex established a vicarage at West Ham in that county. Towards the end of the period papal consent had to be gained for such appropriations; previously that of the bishop of the diocese sufficed. But such transactions were not confined to the regulars. When the secular cathedrals substituted separate prebends for a share in the common fund, the estate with which the prebendary was endowed was commonly a church. He established a vicar in the place, retaining the patronage of the benefice with the larger part of the income for himself. Archbishops and bishops would do the same. Wishing to provide for the clerks who attended upon themselves, they would collate them to a rectory in their gift, which they rendered a sinecure by appointing a vicar to do the work. So Fulham provided the Bishop of London with a sinecure rectory, and Orpington, Kent, the Archbishop of Canterbury. Thus the ancient landed sees and cathedrals and monasteries copied the policy of the more modern and worse-endowed orders, and unless the Reformation had stopped the process the English Church would doubtless have reached the same state as that of France, where, at the Revolution, parochial rectories had almost ceased to exist, and the revenues of the Church were unequally divided between a few privileged clergy or corporations and a multitude of ill-paid priests.

The Suppression of the Monasteries (*q.v.*) and the consequent legislation prevented further impoverishment of the parish clergy, though, at the very time of the Dissolution, in 1536, Eton and Winchester Colleges were exempted from the payment of tithe on their estates. The few later changes in this direction have been by express Acts of Parliament, as when of late years the rectories of Somersham, Hunts, and Purleigh, Essex, which had been attached to the Regius Professorship of Divinity at Cambridge and the Provostship of Oriel at Oxford respectively, were detached from those offices, while the major part of the income of the benefices was assigned to the Professor and the Provost, now relieved from the charge, and, in the latter case, from the compulsion to holy orders. But a great amount of tithe which had been *appropriated* to religious houses and similar bodies was by the Dissolution placed at the King's disposal, and he proceeded to *impropriate* it, either retaining it for the Crown or granting it out to private persons. In neither case did any spiritual charge rest upon it, save in certain instances where an undefined condition was imposed that the grantee should make

provision for the continuance of divine service in some church or chapel. Where litigation has arisen over this, the obligation has been maintained by the courts, but has been generally interpreted with much leniency towards the impropriator. Tithe in lay hands was property of a description which English law had not contemplated, though probably in isolated instances it had existed. Its legal character therefore had to be determined, and it was assimilated in all respects to freehold, being conveyed and inherited in the same way. Transactions in regard to tithe were the easier, in that it was not subject to the law of Mortmain (*q.v.*), for a conveyance of tithe did not bring new property into permanent spiritual ownership, since it had been spiritual *ab initio*. In later times tithe had to pay its share of land-tax with other freehold property, and its subjection to local rates is a just grievance, for no other class than the clergy pays rates on a professional income. Their case, however, is complicated by the co-existence of the lay impropriator.

By the Suppression of the smaller monasteries Henry VIII. inadvertently conferred a considerable benefit on the parish clergy. Many of these houses had held land on which no tithe was levied; on the disappearance of the exempt body the common law revived, and the land under its new ownership was once more burdened with tithe. In the Act for the Dissolution of the greater monasteries (1539, 31 Hen. VIII. c. 13), it was provided that the land itself should be exempt, and to this day it is a matter of importance to ascertain whether land has, or has not, belonged to one of those greater monasteries which had exemption, for the whole or part of their estates, from tithe. To this end a list, by no means accurate, of these monasteries is given in Phillimore's *Ecclesiastical Law* (ed. 1895, vol. ii. p. 1154); certain lesser houses, whose dissolution was delayed, also confer, under the terms of this Act, the same exemption. Whether by accident or design, this provision was not repeated in Edward VI.'s Act for the Suppression of Chantries (1547, 1 Edw. VI. c. 14); but it is not probable that they held much land that had become exempt.

Tithe in England has little history from this time to the Act of 1836. Under Elizabeth a large amount of monastic tithe was forced upon bishops and chapters in exchange for lands which they had to surrender to the Crown. Under the earlier Stuarts an interesting attempt was made to recover impropriated tithes for ecclesiastical use by vesting them in trustees who should pay the income to preachers in whom the Puritans had confidence. Such trusts were dissolved and the tithe confiscated in 1633. The Commonwealth protected tithe, as it did other forms of property ; a *modus* settled at the assize of 1656 regulated the payment of certain tithes at Sutton, Beds, till the old system ceased. When, in the eighteenth century, the enclosure of parishes came into fashion, in many places land was accepted by rectors and vicars in lieu of tithe. This was especially the case in Northamptonshire, but instances may be found in all counties. It may safely be asserted that where a large glebe farm is found and no tithe is levied, the arrangement is not older than the eighteenth century. The same is true of those cases where a fixed annual payment, which must also have been established by an enclosure Act, has taken the place of tithe. The immemorial system went on, with its steady crop of litigation, without much complaint till the early years of the nineteenth century. Meanwhile, the improvement of agriculture was increasing the gross quantities of produce, and in some districts, notably in the fens, the reclamation of land was adding greatly to the tithed acreage, while special cultivation, as of orchards and hop-grounds, added a new source of income. The high prices during the Napoleonic war also compensated the clergy, with others interested in land, for the distresses of the time.

But with the depression that followed the war there came a period of difficulty, in which the clergy were often obliged to suffer illwill from the farmers whose tithe they received. When the reforming party, busily recasting English institutions, took tithe in hand, it conferred a benefit both upon recipients and payers by sweeping away the multitude of petty and complicated sources of income. By the Act of 1836 (6-7 Will. IV. c. 71) which, with some modifications, still regulates the procedure, an estimate was made of the average income from tithe of all kinds for the last seven years, and by this the future income was determined. But as the price of commodities fluctuates, an attempt was made to secure justice by adopting a plan of ' corn-rents,' already employed in some parishes under private Acts of Parliament. In these cases the payment in lieu of tithe was, and is, fixed for a term of years (usually fourteen or twenty-one), at the end of which, either party, if dissatisfied, can apply to quarter sessions for a revision, which, in its turn, establishes an unvarying payment for the next period. It seemed, however, fairer that in the general Act provision should be

made for an annual revision in accordance with the average prices of the last seven years. Unfortunately, as it has turned out, the prices taken into account were only those of wheat, barley, and oats. Had meat and wool been included, the story would have been different. However, for many years the clergy had little reason to complain. Population and prosperity increased and prices were high. As late as 1878 tithe stood at more than £112 per cent., but from that year there was a constant decline till 1901, when it fell to £66½ per cent. Since then the tendency has been upwards, and it stands at £72, 14s. 2½d. for 1912, with good prospects of further increase. Another important provision was that which made it possible to extinguish tithe by payment of a capital sum. This has been freely done where estates have been broken up for building purposes. Limitations have also been imposed in 1886 upon extraordinary tithe, charged, because of special values in the produce, upon orchards, market-gardens and hop-grounds; and by the Tithe Act of 1891 (54-5 Vic. c. 8) the collection has been made easier, and the responsibility for payment removed from the tenant to the landowner, who is compensated by a proportionate remission in cases where agricultural depression had reduced the annual value so low that the tithe was two-thirds of the rent.

In the city of London, from very early times, the clergy were paid by a small tax on each house, and this system, regulated by various Acts of Parliament, has been maintained till the present day. The payment, designed as a substitute for tithe, has borne the name since the sixteenth century, even in official documents, though its nature is quite different. The same inaccuracy has prevailed in similar instances elsewhere.

[E. W. W.]

TOLERATION. This term is commonly used to denote the absence of legal penalties for the expression of opinion of whatever kind. It will so be used in this article, and will not be taken to imply social toleration or the practical equality of all opinions—an ideal which is probably not feasible; nor will it be taken to denote tolerance, that temper of mind which is able without heat to consider the case for any and every opinion—a temper of mind which may be absent in firm believers in legal toleration.

The history of toleration is so much entangled with the history of persecution that it is hard to treat the two separately. The Church abandoned the idea of toleration so soon as, having accepted under Constantine the patronage of the Imperial Government, she surrendered the notion of herself as a society distinct from the State, with her own life inherent and independent, and accepted the antique Graeco-Roman ideal of a single omni-competent society with no real limits to its power. Henceforth the Empire is to be no more tolerant than it was under the pagan *régime*, but it is to be the *Civitas Dei* and, inspired by the Catholic religion, is to enforce uniformity. We can see the change in process in the works of St. Augustine. From the time of Theodosius, who proscribed paganism, until the religious wars of the Reformation had worked themselves out (roughly from 380-1688), toleration was neither enjoyed in practice nor was in theory the ideal of statesmen.

It must be the purpose of this article to trace the process by which a new ideal became general.

The notion of freedom of opinion began to be developed towards the close of the Middle Ages. In the course of the conflict in the fourteenth century between Pope John XXII. and Lewis of Bavaria, Marsiglio of Padua wrote in conjunction with John of Jandun the well-known tractate *Defensor Pacis*. The purport of this tractate is to deny all coercive authority to the clergy; to identify the Church with the State in the closest way and to democratise the government of it. In the course of his argument Marsiglio of Padua declares more than once that religious persecution as such is un-Christian and unreasonable. On the other hand, he declares also that the suppression of religious opinion may be for political grounds desirable. What Marsiglio disliked was the coercive power of the clergy; he had no dislike to the suppression of opinion as convenient to the State; and his importance as a pioneer has been overrated. On the principles expressed by him it would be possible to justify nearly the whole of the pagan persecutions, the Clarendon Code, and the Penal Laws of Ireland. Yet Marsiglio did make an important step by denying that religious persecution upon religious grounds is ever justifiable. Not long after this, at the close of the conciliar movement, Gregory of Heimburg, one of its last supporters, definitely laid it down that the suppression of religious opinion by force is not admissible. The Hussite wars had naturally caused on the part of many a re-examination of the problem, whether so much bloodshed was in this cause really to be approved.

Such views, however, were largely aca-demic. It was the practical results of the Reformation that forced toleration on the governments of Europe. What happened was briefly this. In the early days of his revolt Luther, with his violent individualism, wrote in a way which might lead in this direction in the *Liberty of a Christian Man*. This, however, was not his real intention; or if it were, it soon disappeared under the pressure of events. After the Peasants' Revolt Luther showed himself the strongest supporter of the princely despotism; and with the Anabaptist outbreak disappeared the last flicker of any belief in toleration on the part of the leaders of the reform. The desire to stand well with the powers that be, coupled with a real personal love of authority, drove the reformers more and more into the authoritarian camp. It is quite an error to regard them as protagonists of liberty, except in so far as they themselves set at naught the existing authority. On the contrary, as against Castellio and Brentz, who strongly developed the doctrine of toleration, they were all united. Neither Luther nor Melanchthon, nor on the other side Calvin or Beza, desired liberty of opinion. All desired a uniform State, and in process of time came to declare the rightfulness of persecuting Catholics, or idolaters as they were called. Zwingli even not only wrote against the Anabaptists, but demanded the strongest measures against them. Still, steps had been taken. The execution of Servetus awakened a thrill of resentment, and though it was hotly defended, the task was not an easy one. Orthodox Protestantism now took over from mediaeval politics the notion of the Christian State or City of God. The only difference was that in the Protestant view the real balance of power was in the hands of a layman, the 'godly prince.' This, of course, was not the case with Presbyterianism. But for Europe in general the theory that seemed to rule was that of Erastus. Brentz, however, laid down a doctrine of toleration: (a) if false beliefs lead to crime, the crimes should be punished, not the belief; (b) opinions should never be forcibly repressed, for they may turn out to be true. To persecute is to close the avenues to knowledge. In the religious peace of Augsburg (1556) the doctrine of *cujus regio ejus religio* was laid down. This, though it is often derided, is a real landmark in the history of toleration. It definitely abandoned in the Holy Roman Empire that Catholic basis on which it rested. It admitted a diversity of religions among the States of which it was composed. True, it recognised no liberty for the individual (except that of leaving the country), but in proclaiming toleration for the princes, three hundred in number, it symbolised a vast revolution.

Further results followed. In France the Huguenots had ever been an *imperium in imperio*; and partly owing to this, Presbyterianism, when it developed in Scotland, came to insist very strongly on the separateness of the two kingdoms, Church and State. Although this doctrine does not always mean toleration, nor did the Presbyterians desire it, yet by asserting the distinctness of the two societies it paves the way for it.

The Huguenots, however, were the cause of further steps in the same direction. The fever of the religious wars and the horrors of St. Bartholomew provoked a reaction. The party known as the *politiques* put the interest of the State above that of any religion, and though for the most part opposed to toleration of a new sect at the beginning were prepared to grant it rather than attempt the suppression of larger bodies of believers at the cost of civil war. This party finally triumphed with Henri IV., and the Edict of Nantes (1598) is the symbol. This grants no unlimited toleration, but recognises the existing facts, and permits the Huguenots to retain their worship undisturbed. Its principles had been early proclaimed by the chancellor, Michel de l'Hôpital, and by the philosopher, Jean Bodin. The idea that uniformity in religion is the necessary basis of the body politic is surrendered.

Somewhat the same was the view of Queen Elizabeth (*q.v.*), or was at least the position she claimed, and was the line taken by Cecil. She did not, like Philip II., prefer rather not to reign at all, than to reign over heretics. But she gave up any claim to inquire into belief, and the introduction of recusancy fines meant at least this much, that difference of religion might be endured if men were willing to pay a price for their private opinions. At the same time, the State did not give up the idea of a uniform religion, and Roman Catholics were allowed rather than tolerated. The main quarrel until the Restoration was what should be the character of the national religion. Neither Puritan nor High Churchman expected or desired toleration. Each fought for an entire dominance. To this, however, there were exceptions. Robert Browne, the founder of the 'Brownists' and the 'reputed' parent of Independency, in his tract, *Reformation without tarrying for any*, definitely proclaimed the separateness of the spheres of government and religion, and broke with the great bulk of the Puritan party,

who desired to effect their ends through the civil magistrate. But with this and other small exceptions, of which the members of the Baptist sect were an element, the ideal of a State religion homogeneous and coercive still endured. [NONCONFORMITY.] It was the true cause of the Civil War. The logic of facts, however, proved that England could not be homogeneous in this sense.

Under the first two Stuarts came the effort, ever increasing in rigour, to crush Puritanism. With the Long Parliament in 1640 this effort was seen to have failed. Then with the Civil War came the attempt of the other party. With the need of the help of Scotland, the Parliament was compelled to adopt the Solemn League and Covenant. The effect of this was to pledge the party to a further reformation in the Puritan sense, and for a time to make Presbyterianism, as defined at this moment by the Westminster Assembly, the established religion. This uniformity, however, existed only on paper. The 'Discipline' was never enforced except in London and Lancashire; the Erastian party in the Assembly and Parliament had secured the supremacy of the civil power; and the ever-increasing influence of the New Model army broke up the unity for ever. Cromwell came into power as the leader of the Independents. He has been called a believer in toleration, but in the *Humble Petition and Advice* and the *Instrument of Government* it is clear that neither popery nor prelacy is to be tolerated, *i.e.* the religion of the majority of the nation was proscribed. What Cromwell really did was to establish Independency, while he was doubtless tolerant of minor differences of opinion, and in the matter of Quakers less anxious to persecute than most of his followers. He was as tolerant as his position permitted.

The death of Cromwell provoked the Restoration. Charles II. in the Declaration of Breda made a 'liberty to tender consciences' a capital promise; but it was limited by a reference to Parliament. Parliament would have none of it. The Church party was vindictive and triumphant. There ensued the new Act of Uniformity (1662) and the famous Clarendon Code. Charles's two efforts in favour of toleration, 1662 and 1672, only raised a storm, for the danger of a Roman Catholic State was ever before men. Events, however, proved that the dissenters, as they now were, could not be suppressed by such measures as had been passed; the danger from Rome and Louis XIV. drew Churchmen and their opponents together. This was accentuated in the reign of James II., who published ineffective Declarations of Indulgence, 1687 and 1688. At the Revolution the dissenters received the natural reward for their loyalty and refusal to accept the toleration offered by James, and the Toleration Act, 1688, was passed (1 W. and M. c. 18). The toleration did not extend to the Papists or the Socinians, and was a bare toleration, not giving the rights of citizenship, which by the Test Act, 1673 (25 Car. II. c. 2), was dependent on receiving the Communion according to the rite of the Church of England. So far as the Papists were concerned, they were worse off than ever. Infamous laws were passed and enforced in Ireland, nor has England yet recovered from the resentment so caused. Scotch Presbyterianism, now triumphant and established, proceeded to a bitter persecution of episcopalians.

Locke's famous book enshrines the theory of toleration. It is not entire toleration that he enforces, for he would allow no atheists in the State, on the ground that the original compact cannot be enforced on an atheist, for he does not recognise its sanctions. It is really a toleration of indifference which Locke upholds, not the allowance of views believed to be bad.

It was not till 1829 (10 Geo. IV. c. 7) that full toleration came with Roman Catholic Emancipation; there were still disabilities for Jews. These were removed by 9-10 Vic. c. 59 and subsequent Acts. Finally, after the Bradlaugh troubles, an Act was passed which removed all difficulties from atheist members of Parliament (1888, 51-2 Vic. c. 46), and there is now no limit to the toleration enjoyed in opinion and writing, except the following :—

1. The King and the Lord Chancellor must be members of the Church of England.
2. The Blasphemy Laws.
3. The Law of Libel.

The Blasphemy Laws are commonly defended, on the ground that people ought not to have their feelings needlessly outraged, but it is doubtful if they can be upheld on principles of pure toleration. The Law of Libel, as it is at present enforced, is approved as a necessary protection to the individual against calumny.

The theory of toleration was expounded in the light of the mid-century individualism by J. S. Mill in his stirring pamphlet on *Liberty*, which provoked Sir James Fitzjames Stephen's reply, *Liberty, Equality, and Fraternity*. From the Christian point of view probably the most important book since Jeremy Taylor's *Liberty of Prophesying* is the late Bishop Creighton's Hulsean Lectures

on *Persecution and Tolerance*. Whether religious toleration will maintain itself as a principle in view of the prevailing drift against all individualism is a very doubtful question. Certainly there would be few now who would accept that distinction between acts self-regarding and social acts on which Mill's argument is based. Recent events in France and Portugal afford strong evidence that a persecution not by but of religion would be an early effort of any triumph of unbelievers. Comte, of course, asserted the right of persecution. As Creighton pointed out, toleration results in practice from a variety of contributing forces, which might very easily change.   [J. N. F.]

TOPLADY, Augustus Montague (1740-78), divine, was born at Farnham, son of a major in the British army, who died six months later at the siege of Cartagena. A precocious boy, and the only companion of a widowed mother, he was entered as a day boy at Westminster School, where he wrote sermons, essays, and hymns, and farces which he submitted to Garrick for production at Drury Lane. At fifteen he matriculated at Trinity College, Dublin, where he fell under Methodist influences, and discovered, to his dismay, what seemed to him the Calvinistic character of the Thirty-nine Articles. But at eighteen he made a complete change, and thenceforward, to his dying day, his chief aim in life seems to have been a vehement opposition to the teaching of John Wesley (*q.v.*). At nineteen he could find no preaching to suit him in Dublin but that of Mr. Rutherford, the Baptist. 'But though I heard the gospel constantly at meeting,' he wrote, 'because I could hear it nowhere else, I constantly and strictly communicated in the church only.' On 5th June 1762, when more than a year short of the canonical age, he was ordained to the curacy of Blagdon, Somerset. Another curacy at Farleigh Hungerford in the same diocese occupied him for some months, but a great part of his time was spent in London, where he became a popular preacher. In 1766 he was presented to the benefice of Harpford with Fen Offery in Devonshire, exchanging this two years later for Broad Hembury, which he retained till his death. He was still constantly in London, and in 1770 began his open controversy with John Wesley, in which every possible expression of virulent contempt was poured out without stint on both sides. Always of delicate health, he wore himself out in this fight. Hearing on his death-bed a report that he had modified some of his judgments, he had himself carried to the pulpit of Orange Street Chapel, where he poured out a savage attack on Wesley, contradicting the statement that he had expressed a wish to see him, and saying: 'I most sincerely hope my last hours will be much better employed than in conversing with such a man.' Toplady always called his own doctrine 'Calvinism,' though it had little or no dependence on the Genevan reformer. He taught an exaggerated predestinarianism, his favourite authorities being Zanchy of Heidelberg and the scholastic Thomas Bradwardine (Archbishop of Canterbury, 1349), on whom he chiefly relied in his most important work, the *Historic Proof of the doctrinal Calvinism of the Church of England.* The quality of his piety was curiously illustrated on the occasion of the burning of Harpford Vicarage just after he had exchanged with a friend. On hearing that the loss would fall on his successor, he wrote in his diary: 'Who could not trust in the Lord and wait until a cloudy dispensation is cleared up? Through grace I was enabled to do this; and the result of things has proved that it would not only have been wicked, but foolish to have done otherwise. . . . What a providential mercy was it that I resigned the living before this misfortune happened! O God, how wise and how gracious art Thou in all Thy ways!'

Toplady is gratefully remembered for the hymn 'Rock of Ages, cleft for me,' which appears to have been written in a gorge of the Mendips while he was at Blagdon. Most of his other verses are in the worst taste of the eighteenth century, and he published in the *Gospel Magazine* some scurrilous burlesque lines against Wesley; but his prose style was nervous and vivid, and he seems to have been a considerable orator.

[T. A. L.]

Works; W. Row, *Memoirs*, 1794.

TRAVERS, Walter (? 1548-1635), Puritan divine, the eldest son of a strong adherent of the Reformation, a goldsmith of Nottingham, matriculated at Christ's College, Cambridge, in 1560; graduated B.A., 1565; M.A., 1569; was elected a junior Fellow of Trinity College in 1567, and a senior Fellow two years later. Cambridge, then falling into the hands of the moderate reformers like Whitgift (*q.v.*), was distasteful to him, and he migrated to Geneva, where he became a friend and disciple of Beza. Here he wrote and published anonymously *De Disciplina Ecclesiastica* (1573), in which the true government of the Church was de-

clared to have been placed by Christ in the hands of pastors, elders, and deacons, its central government resting in a representative synod. Returning to England he proceeded B.D. at Cambridge and D.D. at Oxford (1576) without obstacle on account of his radical ideas: but, declining to subscribe the Thirty-nine Articles, he was refused a licence to preach. Early in 1578 he appeared at the English congregation in Antwerp, where he was ordained by Cartwright (*q.v.*) and others. A year or two later found him in England again as chaplain to Burghley, the Lord Treasurer, and tutor to his son, Robert Cecil, later Secretary of State. In 1581 he became afternoon lecturer at the Temple, and in 1583 would have been chosen Master had he been willing to be ordained according to the rites of the English Church. Richard Hooker (*q.v.*) became Master, and Travers, continuing as afternoon lecturer, was soon engaged in an active controversy with him, in which one answered in the afternoon what the other had preached in the morning. Travers was finally inhibited (1585?), and now gave all his time to a movement in which he and Cartwright were already engaged—an attempt actually to practise his scheme of Church discipline. He and Cartwright wrote and rewrote a Book of Discipline, now lost, but certainly based on their earlier books. In accordance with this, small classes of ministers actually met, synods were held, legislation passed, cases adjudged to which the classes submitted, and, above all, measures concerted to transform episcopacy. Travers's part is vague; he was not molested when the Government suppressed the movement; but was made by Burghley in 1595 Provost of Trinity College, Dublin. He resigned soon on the score of health (1598), and lived obscurely but comfortably in London till his death in January 1635.

[R. G. U.]

Bancroft, *Dangerous Positions* and *Survey of the Pretended Holy Discipline*; Usher, *Presbyterian Movement in the Reign of Queen Elizabeth*, C.S., 1905.

TRENCH, Richard Chenevix (1807-86), Dean of Westminster (afterwards Archbishop of Dublin), was educated at Harrow and Trinity College, Cambridge (B.A., 1829; M.A., 1833). He travelled abroad, and in 1830 joined for a short time a military expedition, under General Torrijos, for the liberation of Spain from the despotism of Ferdinand VII. At Cambridge he had come under the influence of F. D. Maurice (*q.v.*), but he sympathised with the High as well as with the Broad Church School, and on taking holy orders (deacon, 1832; priest, 1835) became curate to H. J. Rose (*q.v.*) (whom he called 'my master') at Hadleigh. He was an intimate friend of S. Wilberforce (*q.v.*), to whom he was curate at Alverstoke, and afterwards chaplain. He held the Professorship of Divinity (afterwards called that of New Testament Exegesis) at King's College, London, 1845-56; was appointed Dean of Westminster, 1856; and in 1857 began the Sunday evening services in the nave. He courageously showed his sympathy with High Churchmen during their time of fiercest persecution, lecturing and preaching for C. F. Lowder (*q.v.*) at the London Docks. In 1863 he became Archbishop of Dublin, his tenure of that office covering the disestablishment and reconstitution of the Irish Church. A divine, a scholar, and a poet, he published many works, of which his *Notes on the Parables* and *Notes on the Miracles* of our Lord are the best known. [G. C.]

Letters and Memorials.

TRURO, See of. The early history of the Cornish bishopric is obscure. It is probable that, before the Romans left Britain, Cornwall had to a large extent become Christianised. About the middle of the fifth century the Church in Cornwall seems to have been infected by Pelagianism, and was probably included in the visits of St. Germanus of Auxerre to Britain. Up to 869 there is no historical list of Cornish bishops, nor is it now known where the see was originally fixed, but it is thought that among the British bishops who met St. Augustine (*q.v.*) at Augustine's Oak two were Cornish; and at St. Chad's (*q.v.*) consecration, 664, the assisting British bishops came from Cornwall. Kenstec, bishop-elect of the Cornish people, professed obedience to the see of Canterbury, c. 865. The mission of Eadulf, Bishop of Crediton, 909, and the arms of Æthelstan finally incorporated the Cornish with the English Church during Conan's episcopate at St. Germans, 931-55. The names of Conan's successors are fairly ascertained.

BISHOPS OF CORNWALL

1. Daniel (St. Germans), 955.
2. Comoere (Bodmin), 960.
3. Wulfsige (Bodmin), 967; an Englishman.
4. Ealdred (Bodmin), 993.
5. Aethelred (uncertain).
6. Burhwold (St. Germans), 1016.

The see of Crediton, to which three towns in Cornwall were annexed, had been founded in 909. In 1027 Lyfing, Abbot of Tavistock,

became bishop, and on his uncle Burhwold's death held Cornwall with Crediton. Leofric succeeded, 1046, and in 1050, under a charter of Edward the Confessor, fixed the see of the now united diocese at Exeter (*q.v.*). Before the close of the eleventh century Cornwall was formed into an archdeaconry. For eight hundred and thirty years Devon and Cornwall were ruled as a single diocese. After prolonged efforts, 1847-76, Cornwall was reconstituted as a diocese with its see at Truro under the Act 39-40 Vic. c. 54, by Order in Council of 30th April, taking effect from 4th May 1877. The first bishop, Dr. Benson, was consecrated on St. Mark's Day, 1877, at St. Paul's Cathedral. The income is £3000 and residence.

BISHOPS OF TRURO

1. Edward White Benson (*q.v.*), 1877; tr. to Canterbury, 1883.
2. George Howard Wilkinson, 1883; Vicar of St. Peter's, Eaton Square, S.W.; founded community of the Epiphany, 1883; cons. choir and transept of cathedral, 1887; res. (through ill-health), 1891; elected to St. Andrews, 1893; Primus of Scottish Church, 1905; d. 1907.
3. John Gott, 1891; Vicar of Leeds and (1885-91) Dean of Worcester; dedicated nave of cathedral, 1903; d. 1906.
4. Charles William Stubbs, 1906; Dean of Ely; dedicated west towers and bells of cathedral, 1910; enlarged and improved the see-house, Lis Escop; d. 1912.
5. Winfrid Oldfield Burrows, 1912; Student of Christ Church, Oxford; Archdeacon of Birmingham.

Under the Truro Bishopric Act, St. Mary's, Truro, was constituted the cathedral church. In 1878 Benson inaugurated a committee for building a new cathedral. On 20th May 1880 the first stone was laid by King Edward VII., then Duke of Cornwall, the architect being J. L. Pearson, R.A. The Central (Victoria) Tower was dedicated, 22nd January 1904. In 1910 the church, which in style is Early English throughout, was completed by the erection of west towers and spires. The old south aisle of Truro Parish Church, incorporated with the cathedral, is Late Perpendicular (c. 1509). Total cost, about £220,000. Cathedral school, founded 1906 (cost £7000), in the precincts. The dean and chapter are fully constituted by the Act 50-1 Vic. c. 12, the bishop acting as dean, till the deanery is endowed. The diocese is divided into the archdeaconries of Cornwall (taken over from Exeter, 1876) and Bodmin (constituted, 1878). It comprises Cornwall, the Isles of Scilly, and five parishes in Devon, has an area of 1359 square miles, and a population of 328,131. In 1905 Dr. J. R. Cornish, Archdeacon of Cornwall, was consecrated Bishop of St. Germans.　　　　　　　　　　　　　[A. J. W.]

> Article by the late Bishop W. Stubbs on 'Ancient Bishopric in Cornwall' (*Truro Dio. Calendar*); Haddan and Stubbs, *Councils and Eccl. Documents*, i. ; Donaldson, *The Bishopric of Truro*, 1877-1902 ; *Biographies* of Archbishop Benson and Bishop Wilkinson ; Stubbs, *Registr. Sacr.*

TUNSTALL, Cuthbert (1474-1559), Bishop of London and afterwards of Durham, a famous figure in the vicissitudes of the Reformation period, siding mainly with the Old Learning, yet tolerant and gentle. He gave the impression of a strength and judgment which he did not always possess, though he caught the imagination of his contemporaries at home and abroad. A Yorkshireman by birth, he is said, without sufficient proof, to have been illegitimate. His early youth was probably troublous, but he passed to Oxford, Cambridge, and Padua. His attainments were great, and he found introduction to some of the home and foreign leaders of the Renaissance. His wander-year over, he was ordained in 1509, and was preferred to various livings. Warham (*q.v.*), recognising Tunstall's legal acumen, made him his Chancellor, and thus his introduction to public life began. More benefices came to him, and from 1515 he began the diplomatic career which took up so large a portion of his time for many years. His next step was the Mastership of the Rolls, 1516. His first ecclesiastical act which really attracted attention was his oration in 1518 on the occasion of the marriage of Princess Mary, Henry's sister, to Louis XII. of France. At this time the Lutheran movement was stirring, and Tunstall, on a lengthened embassy to the court of the new Emperor, was most unfavourably impressed by what he saw and heard in Germany. Soon after his return he became Bishop of London by papal provision, and in 1523 Keeper of the Privy Seal. He was now one of the foremost figures in the ecclesiastical world as well as in political life. He took an important part in the tortuous political negotiations of the time. He did not neglect his diocese, where a revival of Lollardy, stimulated by Lutheranism, was in progress. He was much concerned to check the movement. Hence his prohibition of various heretical books, and notably of Tyndale's

(*q.v.*) New Testament in 1526. A bitterly distasteful task now fell to him in defining his attitude towards the divorce question. Did he compromise his conscience in dissuading Queen Katherine from appealing to Rome ? His translation to Durham at this stage needs explanation. No other bishop of London has been transferred to the palatine see. It may be surmised that Henry had need of his services in the north, where family connection and previous residence would give him influence. As the proceedings of the Reformation Parliament progressed, all Tunstall's sympathies were on the conservative side. If he made no public protest, his silence is probably due to a constitutional timidity which often characterised his action. At Durham House he was near the King at Whitehall. As the Supremacy question went forward there was almost certainly conference between King and bishop. At first Tunstall made emphatic objection, but he was talked over. From this point he was a public supporter of the Supremacy, and in his diocese he ' preached the Royal Supremacy so that no part of the realm is in better order' (*L.P. Hen. VIII.*, x. 182). Tunstall's conversion in this affair (a change which Gardiner (*q.v.*) also shared) seems in no way to have injured his popularity. There was no change, however, in dogmatic conviction. Tunstall does not appear to have resisted the fall of the monasteries. It was probably to visit upon him his inaction that the rebels in the Pilgrimage of Grace (*q.v.*) rushed upon Auckland Castle, whence he had to flee at midnight. The rising synchronised with the curtailment of the palatinate regality in 1536, and gave further excuse to Henry to restrain the practical independence of the bishopric. Accordingly the Council of the North was established. It was natural and just to make Tunstall the first president. The office gave him engrossing duties, and if he found himself less of a prince palatine, he was certainly a greater royal officer than his predecessors. His correspondence as president is in the British Museum. He was not, however, too much absorbed to give attention to the wider affairs of the Church. He had a share in the *Institution of a Christian Man*, 1537 (the Bishops' Book), and in 1541 he passed in review the new translation of the Bible. He probably sympathised with the Six Articles Act of 1539. Whoever suggested the reconstitution of the dissolved Benedictine monastery of Durham as a capitular establishment, the result was probably due to Tunstall. He was in the north in the troublous years of Scottish invasion which marked the early history of the new foundation, and superintended his new buildings in Durham and Auckland. In 1545 he revived his old experiences, taking part in an important embassy to treat with France. The most humiliating part of his long career began with the accession of Edward VI. He had to take some part in Somerset's Scottish war in 1547. Coincidently with this his powers as bishop were suspended during the visitation of the diocese carried out by Royal Commissioners. Then came the direct attack upon his palatinate power which Northumberland planned with such subtlety and carried so nearly to a successful issue. It seems clear that Northumberland intended to make Durham Castle his own, to divide the diocese, to abolish the palatinate jurisdiction, and to reign in the north as Duke of Northumberland indeed. It was not, perhaps, difficult to get up a case against Tunstall, who had voted in Parliament against the abolition of chantries, the liturgical changes, and other matters. The duke succeeded in securing the imprisonment of Tunstall on a charge of treason, based probably upon north-country affairs which we cannot trace. Some mysterious words about aiding a Scottish rebellion were given as the pretext, and Tunstall remained in the Tower for ten months. The time was not wasted, for he now wrote the most famous of his works, *De Veritate Corporis et Sanguinis Domini Nostri Jesu Christi in Eucharistia.* The moment was critical. Cranmer had just published his *Defence of the true and Catholic Doctrine of the Sacrament,* and books were issuing daily on the Protestant side. Gardiner had answered Cranmer, attacking him for abandoning Catholic belief. Tunstall's intervention in the great debate was the most significant utterance of the Old Learning. The publication of the treatise was apparently delayed until Mary's reign, and this may be proof that the bishop was not anxious to prolong strife, but to make his voice heard when occasion permitted. In those dark months of imprisonment Tunstall was deprived of his see, and the bishopric of Durham was dissolved. Durham was to continue as a see; Gateshead, annexed to Newcastle, was to constitute a second see; and the palatinate jurisdiction was handed over to Northumberland. But the reign of Edward soon reached its end, and a respite came in the troubles of Bishop Tunstall. Within a month of the young King's death the bishop was restored. An Act was passed annulling the spoliation of Edward's last year (1 Mar. sess. 3, c. 3). As

to his see, it was 'now by the authority of this present Parliament fully and wholly revived, erected, and [shall] have its being in like manner and form to all intents and purposes as it was of old time used and accustomed.' Perhaps as an act of personal friendship Mary gave to Tunstall and his successors the patronage of all the prebends in the cathedral. Tunstall was growing old, and his eighty years did not sit lightly upon him. It was this fact which probably excused him from higher office in the Church. Had his years been fewer, who so fit as he to guide church politics in the new reign? He was more widely read, at least as tolerant, and far more truly in the confidence of the Old Learning than was Cardinal Pole (*q.v.*). He took part in such events as his age permitted. He went to Gravesend to meet Pole on his arrival, and to convey him to London. He conferred with various heretics when, a year later, the Commission of Inquiry had been constituted. His action was gentle, and there can be no doubt that the reputation is well deserved which credits him with having been anxious to repress the persecution. Some literary work must be attributed to Mary's reign. In 1554 he printed the short exposition of the Apocalypse attributed to St. Ambrose. He tells us how in 1546 he found the manuscript whilst searching in monastic libraries. This would probably be in France whilst he was engaged in confirming the treaty of Ardres. In 1555 he published a sermon, or more probably a charge, *Contra impios blasphematores Dei praedestinationis,* aimed apparently against the antinomian teaching, which had gained ground under the patronage of the extreme sectaries. Tunstall outlived Pole and Mary. Elizabeth dispensed him from attending Parliament in her first year, partly owing to the fact that his presence in the north was necessary to conclude peace with the Scots. At the end of June 1559 he wrote to the Queen asking for her leave to come to London in order to tell her about the peace transactions. Cecil was requested 'to further his suit for visiting the Queen.' In July he set out on his journey, and is reported to have preached on the way, exhorting the people to constancy in the faith. Arrived in London, he lodged in Southwark, as Durham House had not been restored to him. He expostulated in vain with the Queen concerning the alterations in religion. A little later he wrote a historic letter to Cecil complaining of the iconoclasm of the Visitors in London. In September the oath of allegiance was tendered to him. He refused it, and he was deprived of his see, and put under the surveillance of Archbishop Parker. Worn out with age and sorrow, the venerable bishop died in Parker's house, 18th November 1559.   [H. G.]

For Tunstall's life see the State Papers and other contemporary documents. These are indicated and summarised in Dr. Pollard's article in *D.N.B.* See also G. E. Phillip, *Extinction of the Catholic Hierarchy*; *V.C.H.*, Durham, ii. 30-5; and Ross-Lewin in *Typical English Churchmen*, series ii.

TYNDALE, or **TINDAL, William** (d. 1536), translator of the Bible, was born ' about the borders of Wales '; he belonged to a family of some standing in Gloucestershire, and was brought up from a child in the University of Oxford, where he was entered at Magdalen Hall in 1510. According to Foxe (*q.v.*), he made great progress in the knowledge of languages and of the Scriptures, and even thus early ' read privily to certain students and fellows of Magdalen College some parcel of divinity; instructing them in the knowledge and truth of the Scriptures.' From Oxford he went on to Cambridge, and afterwards became tutor to the children of Sir John Welch of Old Sodbury, in Gloucestershire. To his house ' there resorted many times sundry abbots, deans, archdeacons with divers other doctors and great beneficed men; who there together with Master Tyndale sitting at the same table did use many times to enter communication and talk of learned men, as of Luther and Erasmus; also of divers other controversies and questions upon the Scripture.' He preached principally in Bristol and its neighbourhood. Before long he was accused before the Chancellor of the diocese, who ' rated him as though he had been a dog, but let him go free.' About this time, in a dispute, he announced his intention of translating the Bible. ' If God spared his life ere many years he would cause a boy that driveth the plough to know more of the Scripture than he did.' Finding Gloucestershire too dangerous he came to London. He tried to obtain the patronage of Bishop Tunstall (*q.v.*), but Tunstall replied that his house was full. He then became preacher at St. Dunstan's-in-the-West, and lived in the house of Geoffrey Monmouth, an alderman, for six months, where, according to Monmouth, ' the said Tyndale lived like a good priest, studying both night and day. He would eat but sodden meat by his goodwill nor drink but small single beer. He was never seen in that house to wear linen.' Monmouth gave him money, and sent him

to Hamburg (1524). He visited Luther at Wittenberg, and with the help of an ex-friar, William Roy, began printing an English translation of the New Testament at Cologne. The proceedings were discovered when the work was half done, and the two fled to Worms with the unfinished sheets, and printed two editions, one in octavo and the other in quarto, of three thousand copies each, the latter with marginal glosses. [BIBLE, ENGLISH.] The English bishops were warned, and Warham (*q.v.*) ordered those who had copies to surrender them on pain of excommunication. Warham himself seems to have bought up two entire editions on the Continent, to the great profit of the translators, who lived on the proceeds of the sales and issued further editions.

In 1525 Wolsey tried to secure Tyndale's arrest at Worms, but he took refuge at Marburg. He then printed his *Parable of the Wicked Mammon*, a treatise on the parable of the unjust steward, dealing with the doctrine of Justification by Faith. In 1528 he produced also *The Obedience of a Christian Man*, a defence against the charges of lawlessness brought against the Reformers. It laid down the doctrine of passive obedience to temporal rulers and the supremacy of the Scriptures in matters of doctrine. Henry VIII. (*q.v.*) was delighted with it, ' for,' saith he, ' this book is for me and all kings to read.' His next work, *The Practyse of Prelates*, was not so acceptable, since in it he denounced the King's divorce. He entered into a bitter controversy with Sir Thomas More (*q.v.*), and translated the Pentateuch. In 1531 Henry VIII. made some overtures for his return to England, and when he declined, demanded his surrender from the Emperor, and that failing, endeavoured to kidnap him. He left Antwerp, but returned in 1533, and remained there for the rest of his life. In 1534 John Rogers (*q.v.*) arrived in Antwerp, was converted by Tyndale, and helped him in his translation of the Old Testament, of which he completed during his life only the Pentateuch and the Book of Jonah, but there is reason to think that he left a manuscript translation of the historical books down to Chronicles.

In 1535 a young Englishman, Henry Phillips, by professing zeal for the Reformation and personal regard for Tyndale, decoyed him from his house and handed him over to the Imperial officers. Great efforts were made for his release. The English merchants petitioned Henry VIII. on his behalf, and Cromwell (*q.v.*) wrote letters to the president of the council and the governor of Vilvorde asking them to use their influence in his favour. He was tried for heresy and condemned to death. His execution took place on 6th October 1536. According to Foxe, his last prayer was: 'Lord, open the King of England's eyes.'

He will always be remembered for his translation of the Bible, though he did not

live to finish it. His style was direct and forcible and his rendering substantially accurate. His version formed the model of that of 1611. [BIBLE. ENGLISH.]

[C. P. S. C.]

Foxe, *Acts and Monuments*; Gairdner, *Lollardy and the Reformation*, ii.

U

UDALL, Nicholas (1505-56), reformer and dramatist, was educated at Winchester and Corpus Christi College, Oxford, where he was much influenced by Lutheranism and the new learning. His joint authorship of the pageants which celebrated Anne Boleyn's coronation in 1533 indicates both his Protestant leanings and his literary reputation. After leaving Oxford he followed the profession of a teacher, and in 1534 was appointed Headmaster of Eton. In 1541 he was suspected of complicity in a robbery of plate from the college chapel, and in the inquiry which followed he confessed to a more heinous offence with one of his pupils. Though he lost his mastership he was soon in favour at court again, and received various minor church preferments. In 1549 he was appointed to reply to the complaints of the western rebels, who demanded the restoration of the old religion. His *Answer* is a skilful and effective piece of controversial writing. He was employed in the translation of Erasmus's *Paraphrase of the New Testament*, in which Princess Mary also took part. In spite of his Protestantism he retained her favour after her accession, probably on account of his literary talents, and he remained the recognised provider of plays and masques for the court. Shortly before his death he was made Headmaster of Westminster. His career is important as illustrating the influence of the humanist movement on the moderate reformers, and on the development of English literature. By combining the classical correctness of form, which he learnt from the Latin comedians, with the racy humour of the native English interlude, Udall produced in *Ralph Roister Doister* the first genuine English comedy.

[G. C.]

Troubles connected with the Prayer Book of 1549, C.S.; D.N.B.

UNIFORMITY, Acts of. During the Middle Ages the forms of service in use were merely matter of custom, and there was no

thought of regulating them by statute. Nor were they affected by Henry VIII.'s ecclesiastical legislation. There was some attempt at reform of the service books in his reign, and under Edward VI. the First Prayer Book was drawn up by a body of bishops and divines in 1548, and discussed at length in Parliament, which on 21st January 1549, a week before the end of Edward's second year, passed the first Act of Uniformity (2-3 Edw. VI. c. 1). It recites that 'of long time' there have been divers uses in the English Church, and of late new fashions of worship have been introduced by the 'good zeal' of innovators; the Book of Common Prayer has been drawn up 'to the intent a uniform, quiet and godly order should be had,' for which Parliament gives the King 'most hearty and lowly thanks,' and enacts that from Whitsunday (9th June), 1549, its exclusive use in the 'celebration of the Lord's Supper, commonly called the Mass,' and in all public services, shall be obligatory on all ministers on pain of six months' imprisonment and forfeiture of a year's income for the first offence, deprivation and a year's imprisonment for the second, and imprisonment for life for the third. Similar penalties are imposed for depraving or preaching against the book. Offences against the Act are to be tried by the justices of assize, with whom the bishop may sit if he pleases, or by the ecclesiastical courts. No other 'manner of Mass' than that set forth in the book is anywhere permitted, but 'for the encouraging of learning' the other services may be said publicly in the Universities in Latin, Greek, or Hebrew; and elsewhere any man may say Matins or Evensong in these 'or other strange tongue,' 'privately as they do understand.' Eight bishops and three lay peers voted against the Bill, which was supplemented by a statute (passed 22nd to 25th January 1550) ordering the destruction of all missals and service books other than the Prayer Book (3-4 Edw. VI. c. 10). This attempt to enforce uniformity was unsuccessful, for the book was a compromise which pleased neither the conservative nor the reforming party. 'It is one of the grim sarcasms of history that the first Act of Uniformity should have divided the Church of England into the two parties which have ever since contended within her.' By 1552 the reformers were in the ascendant, and the second Act of Uniformity (passed 9th March to 14th April ; 5-6 Edw. vi. c. 1) recites that, doubts having arisen as to the interpretation of the 'very godly order' authorised by the previous Act, it had been revised ; to this revision (the Second Prayer Book) the same provisions were to apply from 1st November 1552. But the Act is more stringent than its predecessor, in that it makes attendance at church on Sundays and holy days compulsory on all who are not reasonably hindered on pain of ecclesiastical censures, and attendance at any other form of service is made punishable by imprisonment for six months, a year, or life, for the first, second, and third offences respectively. Thus, whereas the former Act had applied merely to the clergy, the laity were now brought within reach of these severe penalties. The holy days to be observed, twenty-seven in number, are enumerated in 5-6 Edw. vi. c. 3. All the above-mentioned Acts were repealed in 1553 by 1 Mar. st. 2, c. 2, which enacts that from 20th December 1553 only the forms of service most commonly used in the last year of Henry viii. shall be allowed. Elizabeth's Act of Uniformity (1559, 1 Eliz. c. 2) repealed this provision, revived the Act of 1552, ordered the use of the Second Prayer Book from 24th June 1559, sanctioned certain amendments that had been made in it, increased the penalties for depraving it, and made absence from church punishable by a fine of twelve pence as well as by ecclesiastical censures. It also provided that such ornaments of the church and the minister should be retained, 'as was in the Church of England by authority of Parliament in the second year of' Edward vi., 'until other order shall be therein taken by the authority of the Queen's Majesty,' and reserves power to the Crown to ordain and publish further rites and ceremonies. This power was exercised by James i. in 1604. It has been supposed that the omission of the usual reference to the Lords Spiritual from the enacting words of the statute of 1559 is due to the fact that all the nine bishops present voted against it, but it is not impossible that it was an accident.

The Prayer Book now remained unaffected by Parliamentary action till 1645, when its use was forbidden by ordinances of the Long Parliament. [COMMONWEALTH, CHURCH UNDER.] A Bill for Uniformity passed the Commons in July 1661, but was then delayed on account of the revision which was in progress. This was completed, and adopted by Convocation in December, and in 1662 the Bill was again considered in Parliament, and also in Convocation. The revised book was not discussed by either House of Parliament, though the Commons asserted their right to discuss it if they pleased. They also threw out a clause, introduced by the Lords, giving the Crown power to dispense with the obligations of the Bill. It received the royal assent, 19th May (13-14 Car. ii. c. 4). It orders the exclusive use of the book, which is annexed to the Act, in all places of worship from St. Bartholomew's Day (24th August), 1662, before which all ministers must publicly declare their assent to it on pain of deprivation. All ministers and schoolmasters must also make a declaration of the illegality of taking arms against the King, and must abjure the Covenant. All ministers not episcopally ordained by St. Bartholomew's Day are to be deprived, and declared incapable of holding preferment. Accordingly nearly two thousand ministers withdrew, or were ejected from their livings. Further attempts were made to enforce uniformity by the persecuting laws known as the Clarendon Code. The attempts of Charles ii. and James ii. to dispense with the necessity of conforming were resisted ; and the existence of such dispensing power was denied by the Declaration of Rights, which became law in 1689 (1 W. and M. sess. 2, c. 2). The application of the Acts of Uniformity to dissenters has been relaxed by a series of statutes, the first of which, the Toleration Act, 1689 (1 W. and M. c. 18), exempts Protestant Trinitarian dissenters from their provisions, on condition of taking the oaths of allegiance and supremacy ; their ministers were also to subscribe the Thirty-Nine Articles except the 34th, 35th, 36th, and part of the 20th (and, if Baptists, part of the 27th), and their places of worship must be registered. Similarly limited relief was not extended to Roman Catholics till 1791 (31 Geo. iii. c. 32). Acts of 1779 (19 Geo. iii. c. 44) and 1812 (52 Geo. iii. c. 155) further relaxed the restrictions on Protestant dissenters, and in 1813 the relief was extended to disbelievers in the Trinity (53 Geo. iii. c. 160). Acts of 1829 and 1832 put Roman Catholics on the same level as the Protestant sects (10 Geo. iv. c. 7, 2-3 Will. iv. c. 115). The effect of the final relief Acts of 1846 and 1855 (9-10 Vic. c. 59,

18-19 Vic. c. 86), and the Universities Test Act, 1871 (34-5 Vic. c. 26), was to confine the operation of the Acts of Uniformity to members of the English Church. In this respect also they were modified in the nineteenth century. The Clerical Subscription Act, 1865, altered the oaths to be taken by the clergy, substituting Declarations of Assent to the Prayer Book and the Thirty-Nine Articles, and against Simony (28-9 Vic. c. 122). The Table of Lessons Act, 1871 (34-5 Vic. c. 37), and the Act of Uniformity Amendment Act, 1872 (35-6 Vic. c. 35), gave civil sanction to some of the recommendations of the Ritual Commission [COMMISSIONS, ROYAL]. Dissent from the form of public worship recognised by the State first became common in the sixteenth century. But the belief that it was the State's duty to enforce a common form of worship, and, as far as possible, a common doctrine on all its subjects, survived from the Middle Ages, and led to the Acts of Uniformity. Their relaxation followed as it came to be understood that dissent is not, under modern conditions, a crime against the State. This is now fully recognised, and the operation of the Acts is confined to the Church of England. They constitute the law of the State governing public worship in the Established Church, and are voluntarily accepted by the Church as an incident of its connection with the State [ESTABLISHMENT]. The forms of public worship in use derive their spiritual validity from the authority of the Church alone. The Acts of Uniformity merely give them civil sanction. The Privy Council laid down in *Westerton* v. *Liddell* and *Martin* v. *Mackonochie* that Parliament intended in these Acts to impose a rigid uniformity in the conduct of divine service, and that the slightest deviation is illegal as a breach of the Acts [COURTS, RITUAL CASES]. This rigidity is to some extent modified in practice by the *ius liturgicum* of the bishops. [AUTHORITY IN THE CHURCH; COMMON PRAYER, BOOK OF; TOLERATION.] [G. C.]

Statutes ; Procter and Frere, *Hist. of the Book of Common Prayer*; Campion, *Prayer Book Interleaved*. 1888.

USSHER, James (1581-1656), Archbishop of Armagh, was in 1594 among the first scholars of Trinity College, Dublin, where he early distinguished himself as a theologian and controversialist, was ordained by special dispensation in his twenty-first year, became Professor of Divinity, 1607, and Vice-Chancellor, 1614. His first work, *De Christianarum Ecclesiarum successione et statu* (1613), was intended as a continuation of Jewel's (*q.v.*) *Apologia*. He drafted a set of one hundred and four Articles of Religion of a Calvinistic tendency, which were accepted by the first Convocation of Irish clergy held on the English model, 1615. In 1621 he was appointed Bishop of Meath, and translated to Armagh, 1625. In 1634 he took part in imposing an amended version of the English canons on the Irish Church. He opposed the toleration of Roman Catholics, and was on good terms with Laud (*q.v.*) and Strafford, who on visiting him at Drogheda found no Holy Table in his chapel, ' which seemed to me strange ; no bowing there, I warrant you.' In 1641 he was on a Committee for Religion of the House of Lords, and drew up a scheme or 'model' of modified episcopacy, in which the bishops were to preside over synods of presbyters and to be incapable of acting without their advice. Nothing came of this plan, though it played a part in the treaty of Newport, 1648, when Charles was willing to accept it. In contrast with the advice of Williams (*q.v.*), Ussher warned the King against assenting to Strafford's execution against his conscience, and declared, after attending the earl on the scaffold, that he ' never saw so white a soul return to its Maker.'

His Irish property had been destroyed in the rebellion of 1640, and he never returned to Ireland. In 1642 Charles gave him the bishopric of Carlisle *in commendam*. He refused to attend the Westminster Assembly, and lived in Oxford till 1645 ; afterwards in London, where he preached boldly against the treatment of the King by Parliament. Cromwell, though he refused at Ussher's intercession to allow episcopal clergy increased liberty of ministering in private, treated him with deference, and on his death ordered him a public funeral in Westminster Abbey, though making Ussher's family defray three-fourths of the expense.

Ussher was much engaged in controversy, but his high character and genuine piety, as well as his wide and profound learning, made him one of the most respected men of his time. His defence of prayer for the dead was reprinted as one of the *Tracts for the Times*, 1836.   [G. C.]

Works, ed. Ebrington, with Life.

V

VALOR ECCLESIASTICUS, The, is the name given to official valuation of the ecclesiastical and monastic revenue which was made under Henry VIII. It is a survey more detailed than the *Taxatio Ecclesiastica* (*q.v.*) of 1291, which for most purposes it henceforth superseded.

The cause of the valuation was the 'unparalleled revolution in property which marked the reign of Henry VIII.,' and which was now determined. In 1532 Annates or first-fruits, *i.e.* the clear revenue and profit of a benefice for one entire year paid to the Pope, had been conditionally restrained in the case of bishops and archbishops (23 Hen. VIII. c. 20). By the Act of 1534 (25 Hen. VIII. c. 20) all payment of Annates or first-fruits was forbidden, and by a later Act of the same year (26 Hen. VIII. c. 3, the preamble of which Dr. Dixon describes as ' the most perfect example of cunning baseness to be found in the ecclesiastical laws of the reign ') all Annates or first-fruits, together with a tenth annually of the clear income of each benefice, were given to the Crown. No first-fruits were to be taken from a benefice of less than eight marks a year unless the incumbent remained in it three years. First-fruits were first claimed by the popes in England in 1256, and, at first intermittent, had become general.

To meet the requirements of the Act of 1534 a fresh valuation was necessary, and commissioners to make it were appointed, 30th January 1535. They were the usual agents of the Government at the time—the bishops, who were the only ecclesiastics on the commission, sheriffs, justices of the peace, mayors, and local gentry. The result, completed in five or six months, holds ' the pre-eminence among the ecclesiastical records of the kingdom ' (Hunter), and is comparable to the Domesday Survey of 1086. The particulars of all property of any church or monastery in England and Wales, both in *Spiritualia* and *Temporalia*, are recorded in detail. The record is complete save that the accounts of the diocese of Ely and a great part of those of London and York, and the counties of Berks, Rutland, and Northumberland, have disappeared. Fuller (*q.v.*) incorrectly states that the Welsh returns were made under Edward VI., but for these the later and briefer *Liber Valoris* (an epitome of the *Valor Ecclesiasticus*), which records all

the benefices, gives the net annual income and the tenth. Dr. Dixon concludes that the survey, though not a friendly, was probably a fair one. Speed gives the total annual value thus revealed at £320,280, 10s., which Dixon, comparing it with the total at which he arrives for the value in the *Taxatio* (£218,202), and allowing for the fact that benefices held by monasteries are not there included, shows to mean a relative decrease in the revenue of the Church as compared with that of the nation as a whole. In 1291 it was eleven-fiftieths of the whole, in 1535 it was not more than eight-seventy-fifths. When the monasteries were dissolved or surrendered their incomes were generally larger than recorded in the *Valor*, but on the whole the record is trustworthy.

These dues were renounced by the Crown in 1555 (2-3 Ph. and M. c. 4), and were resumed again by Elizabeth (1 Eliz. c. 4), who, however, discharged from first-fruits all parsonages under ten marks and all vicarages under £10. Queen Anne restored this revenue to the Church (to be administered by trustees—QUEEN ANNE'S BOUNTY). This was confirmed by statute in 1703 (2-3 An. c. 20, commonly cited as c. 11), and a later Act (6 An. c. 24) ' discharged ' from first-fruits and tenths all benefices under £50. The *Valor* is still important as determining the legal value of any Church preferment in the interpretation of rights and restrictions under any statute subsequent to 1535, and is often cited as ' The King's Books.' Editions of the epitome, the *Liber Valoris* (an abstract made from the original *Valor* in use in the First-Fruits Office) were published in the seventeenth and eighteenth centuries, the most important being that of Ecton, 1711, much enlarged as the *Thesaurus rerum Ecclesiasticarum*, 1742.

The *Valor* was first printed (by the Records Commission) in six folio volumes, with a valuable introduction, between the years 1810 and 1834. [S. L. O.]

Valor Ecclesiasticus, introd. by J. Hunter; *Oxford Studies*, i., 1909, ed. Vinogradoff, monograph by Professor Savine of Moscow; Dixon, *Hist. of Ch. of Eng.*, i. pp. 229-32, 247-50.

VAUGHAN, Charles John (1816-97), Master of the Temple and Dean of Llandaff, was son of an Evangelical vicar of St. Martin's, Leicester. He learned the Greek alphabet by his own request, on his seventh birthday. He was educated at Rugby under Dr. Arnold (*q.v.*), who considered him one of his most promising pupils, and at Trinity College, Cambridge, where, in 1838, he was bracketed with the fourth Lord Lyttelton as Senior Classic and Chancellor's Medallist, and was elected Fellow in 1839. He felt a strong inclination for the Chancery Bar, but was induced by religious considerations to seek holy orders. He was ordained in 1841, and was appointed Vicar of St. Martin's, Leicester. On the death of Dr. Arnold, he stood unsuccessfully for the Headmastership of Rugby, and in 1844 was elected Headmaster of Harrow, in succession to Dr. Christopher Wordsworth (*q.v.*). His administration of Harrow was eminently successful. His strong points were 'Greek Iambics and Tact'; the *suaviter in modo* concealed only imperfectly the *fortiter in re*; he delighted in sarcasm, and his smile was even more dreaded than his frown. In two years he raised the numbers from seventy to two hundred, and to more than four hundred before he left. He was made Chaplain in Ordinary to the Queen in 1859. He resigned unexpectedly at the end of 1859. In 1860 he became Vicar of Doncaster, and there he gathered round him a band of young graduates preparing for holy orders, whom he instructed in the Greek Testament and in *Parochialia*, and who were called 'Vaughan's Doves.' In 1869 he was appointed by Mr. Gladstone (*q.v.*) Master of the Temple; but took the title too literally, and soon found himself embroiled with the Benchers, who are the real 'masters.' His Greek scholarship was exquisite, and he served as one of the company for revising the translation of the New Testament. His sermons were always carefully written in a terse and nervous style, but his voice and manner gave the impression of unreality. He taught clearly the central truths of revelation, but denied the Apostolic Succession, ignored the Church, and held a low doctrine concerning the sacraments. His theology showed few traces of the Evangelicalism in which he had been reared; but, in its hostility to all forms of High Churchmanship, it recalled the polemical vigour of Arnold. His influence was chiefly felt by young men, whether at school, at the Universities, at the Temple, or when preparing for holy orders. To them he showed unbounded sympathy and unwearied kindness. His greatest success was in preaching before the University of Cambridge, where he was repeatedly appointed Select Preacher between the years 1860 and

1888. In 1879 he was appointed (by Bishop Ollivant) Dean of Llandaff, but continued to hold the Mastership of the Temple until February 1894, when he was taken seriously ill directly after preaching in the Temple church, and the illness necessitated the resignation of the Mastership. He retained the Deanery of Llandaff, occasionally officiated, and continued to instruct his 'Doves.' He died at the deanery on the 12th October 1897, and was buried in the cathedral. He left in his will a positive injunction that no biography of him should be attempted. He married in 1850 Catherine Stanley, daughter of the Bishop of Norwich, and sister of his friend, Arthur Penrhyn Stanley (*q.v.*).

The list of Vaughan's writings covers six pages in the Brit. Mus. Catalogue. They consist mainly of sermons, with some lectures and pamphlets, and annotated editions of the Greek text of some books of the New Testament.

[G. W. E. R.]

VENN, Henry (1725-97), Evangelical divine, was son of Richard Venn, Rector of St. Antholin's in the City, and also of Barnes, where Henry Venn was born. He was educated at St. John's College, Cambridge; B.A., 1746: became Fellow of Queens'; and was ordained deacon, 1747. Just before his ordination he played cricket for Surrey against All England. Surrey won, and when the match was finished Venn flung down his bat, exclaiming: 'Whoever wants a bat, which has done me good service, may take that, as I have no further use for it. It shall never be said of me: "Well hit, Parson!"' Henceforward his constant prayer was: 'Grant that I may live to the glory of Thy Name.' He lived a life of religious meditation. Law's (*q.v.*) *Serious Call* made a deep impression on his conscience, and he sought to frame his life after Law's precepts. With regard to fasting, he wrote: 'I have come to a compromise; which is that on Fridays I shall not breakfast, but shall eat some dinner.' In 1750 he became Curate of St. Matthew's, Friday Street, in the city, and at Horsley in Surrey. He soon began to hold gatherings for devotion in his house. He raised the number of communicants in the parish from twelve to sixty. He used to go galloping over the Surrey Downs, chanting the *Te Deum* in the fulness of his heart, and naturally incurred the reproach of being a 'Methodist' and an 'enthusiast.'

In 1754 he became curate of Clapham, already an Evangelical centre, and in 1759 he was appointed Vicar of Huddersfield. His sermons were extraordinarily long, but full of power and persuasiveness. Conversions were frequent under his ministry. A parishioner said: 'I never heard a minister like him. He was most powerful in unfolding the terrors of the Lord, and, when doing so, he had a stern look that would have made you tremble. Then he would turn off to the offers of grace, and begin to smile, and go on entreating till his eyes were filled with tears.'

To the labours of the pulpit he added those of the study, and in 1763 he published *The Complete Duty of Man*, which ran through twenty editions.

In 1771 he left Huddersfield for Gelling, a village near Cambridge. There his influence reached Charles Simeon (*q.v.*) and Thomas Robertson, afterwards Vicar of Leicester, and so became incalculably diffusive. In 1797 his failing health compelled him to resign, and he returned to Clapham, of which his son John had become rector. There he died on the 24th June.

Henry Venn's teaching was Evangelical in the best sense. He taught salvation through the Cross of Christ, and that alone. His ministry was marked by that personal devotion to the Divine Master which is the characteristic of great saints in all communions. The things of the Passion were in all his thoughts. He was keenly alive to the poison of the prevalent Socinianism. Such phrases as 'our Crucified God,' 'our Incarnate God,' 'our Adorable Redeemer' were constantly on his lips. He published a treatise on *The Deity of Christ, and the danger of denying it*. Of the Incarnation he said: 'This great mystery is the centre of all the truth, and itself a fountain of light, like the sun.' He was, like all the 'Clapham Sect,' a convinced and devoted churchman. All forms of dissent he steadily opposed. He wrote on 'The Duty of a Parish Priest, and the incomparable pleasure of a life devoted to the care of souls.' This zeal for the priesthood increased with his increasing years. He was a staunch upholder of the Prayer Book, and a resolute opponent of the schemes for revising it fashioned by semi-Socinians. He was zealous for the Means of Grace, conducted special services of preparation before Holy Communion, and dealt faithfully with lapsed communicants. He wrote that, before the Eucharist, his 'prayers had been warmly presented, that the name of the Lord Jesus might be magnified, and that many might eat the Flesh of the Son of Man, and drink His Blood to Eternal Life.' He

strenuously defended Holy Baptism against the attacks of miscalled 'Baptists,' and always tried to make a christening day a season of special devotion. He extolled worship as the object of preaching. He was careful to catechise, explaining the structure and contents of the Prayer Book, and he encouraged congregational hymn-singing in church and at the Holy Communion. 'Every one sang,' he wrote. 'It was like Heaven on earth.'

When he was nearing his latter end he was sometimes tormented by the fear of 'what is to come in the last agonies': but then he sustained his soul with a noble self-reproach: 'Who art thou that thou shouldest be afraid, when promises, and oaths, and love Divine, and Angels, and the Holy Trinity are all engaged and all united for thy help and thy salvation?' When the end came the promise was made good; and the doctor who attended him on his death-bed said: 'Sir, in this state of joyous excitement you cannot die.'

The *Life* of Henry Venn the elder was begun by his son, and published by his grandson in 1834.

His son, **John Venn** (1759-1813), was appointed Rector of Clapham in 1793. When he began his ministry there his father wrote: 'When I looked round me, after Divine Service, only the last Sunday, at Clapham, my heart bounded within me, to think how different a Sacrament, in half a year's time, there would be on that very spot.'

John Venn was one of the founders of the Church Missionary Society, of which his son Henry became secretary in 1841.

[G. W. E. R.]

VESTMENTS. By 'the vestments' is generally meant the 'ornaments' of the ministers of the altar—bishops, priests, deacons, subdeacons and acolytes—at the time of their ministration: viz. amice, alb and girdle, maniple and stole, tunicle, dalmatic, and chasuble. The basis of the whole suit is the alb with its girdle, and the chasuble, which till the eighth century were common to all five orders, and which represent and perpetuate the high-class ordinary Roman dress of the fourth century—viz. the *tunica*—a plain sleeved frock—and the *paenula*—a semicircle of woollen stuff, doubled over and sewn up along the straight edges so far as to leave only room to pass the head through, and drawn up over the arms when in use. After the fourth century the Roman dress gradually gave place to a more compact military and barbarian type, being retained only for a time by the aristocratic families, and permanently by the clergy, first as simply clerical, then as especially liturgical. The *Alb* was at first a plain linen tunic reaching to the ankles; in the Gothic period it was adorned with apparels, patches of coloured stuff or embroidery, attached to the skirts back and front, and to the ends of the sleeves. The *Chasuble* (*planeta, casula*) was at first of wool, either chestnut-coloured (*castaneus*), *i.e.* undyed, or purple, and unadorned; by the eleventh century its colour was varied, it was decorated with embroideries at the neck and round the borders, and it was made very short in front and very long behind (see Bayeux tapestry); in the Gothic period it recovered something of its old shape, but was curtailed at the sides over the arms, and was often decorated with strips of embroidery (*aurifragia*, orphreys) covering the seams back and front and over the shoulders. In the fifth century the Pope and the Roman deacons wore, over the alb, a second tunic, the *Dalmatic*, of white linen, with wide sleeves, and adorned with purple stripes (*clavi*) back and front from the shoulders to the hem and round the bottom of the sleeves, and the use of the dalmatic was later granted by the Pope as a privilege to the bishops and deacons of other churches. By the ninth century it had come into general use by bishops and deacons apart from special grant. Later its colour and material were varied, and its sleeves curtailed, and in the Gothic period it was further adorned with patches of embroidery between the stripes. In the ninth century a contracted and more unadorned form of it, the *Tunicle* (*tunicella*) was adopted by subdeacons, and worn under the dalmatic by bishops. The deacon's *Stole* (*orarium*), a narrow strip of plain white linen, later of coloured silk and adorned, worn over the left shoulder, is found in use in the East in the fourth century, in Gaul and Spain in the sixth, in Rome not till the eleventh, and then worn under, not over, the dalmatic; in origin it is probably a folded napkin or towel, such as occurs in pagan representations of religious and domestic service, which perhaps had already ceased to be of practical use, and had become conventionalised, when it was adopted as the distinctive attribute of deacons. The Roman deacons of the fifth century carried their napkin (*pallium linostinum*) in the left hand or over the left forearm; this napkin, the *Maniple* (*manipulus*), attached to the left arm, from the ninth century onwards, perhaps through confusion with the handkerchief (*mappula, sudarium*), was adopted by all the sacred orders all over the West, and underwent the same transformations as the deacon's stole. The stole of priests and bishops (sixth century in Gaul and Spain, eleventh in Rome) is probably of different origin from the deacon's, being a woollen or silk scarf for the protection of the neck. The *Amice* (*amictus*), found first in the ninth century, is of like origin, being a linen neckcloth, probably for the protection of the more important vestments from the effects of perspiration. In the Gothic period it was furnished with an apparel, which formed a decorative collar when the amice was in use.

The Book of Common Prayer, 1549, directed that the priest at the Mass, and the bishop at other ministrations also, should wear 'a white alb plain, with a vestment or cope,' and his ministers 'albs with tunicles'; where, no doubt, the amice, like the girdle, is included in 'alb,' while 'a vestment,' which in ordinary usage denoted not so much a particular garment, as a suit, may be interpreted to include stole and maniple. But two things are to be noticed: (1) 'alb plain,' *i.e.* without apparels, and 'tunicles,' without mention of dalmatics, suggest that plainness and simplicity were aimed at; and (2) the cope, hitherto only a processional and choir vestment, is allowed as an alternative to the traditional 'vestment' of the altar; and in this Lutheran precedent was followed. The Book of 1552 abolished alb, vestment, and cope, and left only the rochet for bishops, and the surplice for priests and deacons. The Act of Uniformity and the Ornaments Rubric (*q.v.*) of 1559 restored 'such ornaments as were in use by authority of Parliament in the second year of King Edward VI.,' *i.e.* probably the vestments prescribed by the Book of 1549. But, except in so far as, in accordance with the *Advertisements* (*q.v.*) of 1566 and the Canons of 1604, the cope was used in cathedral and collegiate churches, the Ornaments Rubric was probably never observed until the nineteenth century (but see SMART, PETER). The use of the chasuble was restored at Wilmcote, Warwickshire, in about 1849; by J. M. Neale at Sackville College, E. Grinstead, in 1850; at St. Ninian's Cathedral, Perth, and at Cumbrae in 1851, at Harlow in 1852, and at St. Thomas's, Oxford, in 1854. At the beginning of the present century the vestments were in use in something over 1500 churches in England and Wales. [F. E. B.]

Thomassinus, *Vetus et nova Ecclesiae Disciplina*; Marriott, *Vestiarium Christianum*; Duchesne, *Origines du culte chrétien*; Lowrie, *Christian Art and Archaeology*; Braun, *Die liturgische Gewandung*.

W

WAGSTAFFE, Thomas (1645-1712), Nonjuror, was educated at Charterhouse and New Inn Hall, Oxford, where he graduated B.A., 1664; M.A., 1667. He was ordained deacon and priest, 1669, and became Rector of Martinsthorpe. 1684 he was presented to a prebendal stall and the chancellorship at Lichfield, and to the rectory of St. Margaret Pattens, London. In 1689 he refused the oaths, and was deprived. Having, ' before his admission to holy orders,' studied physic with great diligence, he practised in London as a physician after his deprivation, ' still wearing his canonical habit.' He was with Archbishop Sancroft (*q.v.*) at his death, and wrote a touching account of his end. He was one of the two selected by James II. at St. Germans, 1693, for consecration as bishop. He was nominated by Bishop Lloyd, deprived of Norwich, as suffragan Bishop of Ipswich, and was consecrated, 24th February 1694, by Lloyd, Turner, late of Ely, and White, late of Peterborough, at the lodgings of Bishop White at the Rev. W. Giffard's house at Southgate in Middlesex. [NONJURORS.] He seems not to have performed episcopal functions; no records of ordinations by him exist; and he was practising physic in London as late as 1707. He was one of the ablest writers on the Nonjuring side. He was arrested with Bishop Ken (*q.v.*) and others for raising a fund for the poorer Nonjurors, 1696, but was soon released. In his latter years he retired to his own property at Binley, near Coventry. Before his death he desired Holy Communion from Francis Brokesby, a Nonjuring priest, who had, unknown to him, conformed and taken the oaths. On learning this fact Wagstaffe ' withdrew his request, and died without the Sacrament.'

His second son, Thomas (1692-1770), was a prominent Nonjuror, and was ordained. He lived much at Rome, where he was Anglican chaplain to Prince James Edward Stuart, and later to his son Charles Edward. He was greatly respected for his learning and piety, and is described as ' a fine, well-bred old gentleman.' At Rome his devout life caused it to be said that ' had he not been a heretic he ought to have been canonised.'

[s. l. o.]

Overton, *The Nonjurors*: J. L. Fish in *D.N.B.*

WAKE, William (1657-1737), Archbishop of Canterbury, was born at Blandford in Dorset, where his father had a considerable estate. In 1673, not yet sixteen years old, he was admitted Student of Christ Church, Oxford, graduating B.A. in 1676; M.A., 1679. He was ordained soon after, and in 1682 became chaplain to Viscount Preston, Envoy-Extraordinary at the French court. In this year the *Declaratio Cleri Gallicani* was adopted by the Assembly of the French Clergy, setting out the four Gallican propositions:—(i) that the secular power is independent of the spiritualty; (ii) that the Pope is subject to a General Council; (iii) that the ancient Gallican liberties must be respected; and (iv) that papal decrees on matters of faith are irreformable only when they have the consent of the Church. Wake interested himself in the ensuing controversies and their causes, paying special attention to the judgment of the Sorbonne (1671) on Bossuet's *Exposition de la Foi Catholique*, and the author's tacit withdrawal of the condemned passages, on which he enlarged in an *Exposition of the Doctrine of the Church of England* (1686), for the purpose of retorting on Bossuet the argument of his *Variations des Églises Protestantes*. In 1685 Wake returned to England with Preston; in 1688 became preacher at Gray's Inn; took an active part in the bitter controversies preceding the Revolution; was made Deputy-Clerk of the Closet to William and Mary; Canon of Christ Church, Oxford (1689); Rector of St. James's, Westminster (1693); and Dean of Exeter (1701). In 1705 he became Bishop of Lincoln, and in 1716 succeeded Tenison as Archbishop of Canterbury. Hitherto he had acted generally with those who were then known as Low Churchmen, supporting in the House of Lords their scheme for the comprehension of dissenters; but in 1718 he opposed the repeal of the Occasional Conformity Act, and in 1719 he succeeded in preventing the repeal of the Test and Corporation Acts. He also busied himself in the Bangorian controversy, attacking Hoadly (*q.v.*) in a Latin letter curiously addressed to the Superintendent of Zurich and published there. In 1721 he supported the Bill brought in by the Earl of Nottingham for suppressing blasphemy and profaneness, which was directed against Arianisers, and this brought him into sharp conflict with Whiston (*q.v.*), whom he had formerly defended. He was thus identified, though a steady and consistent

Whig, with the moderate High Churchmen, who were beginning to find room in that party. His last years were spent in serious mental failure. He left a considerable estate, derived from his patrimony, and bequeathed to Christ Church a library and a fine collection of coins, valued altogether at £10,000.

Wake's place in history depends chiefly on his controversy with Atterbury (*q.v.*) about Convocation, and his correspondence with Du Pin about a projected alliance of the English and French Churches. In 1697-8, when the Lower House of Convocation of Canterbury was fiercely opposing the court and the Whig bishops, he published two pamphlets in defence of the Royal Supremacy. In 1700 Atterbury attacked him with great vivacity, but weakened his case by an erroneous comparison of the Lower House with the House of Commons. Wake replied in 1703 with *The State of the Church and Clergy of England*, a work of immense erudition, tracing the history of synods in England from the beginning, and effectively disposing of this part of Atterbury's plea. In 1718 began his correspondence with Du Pin. William Beauvoir, chaplain to the English embassy at Paris, informed him of the appeal of four French bishops against the Bull *Unigenitus*, mentioning a conversation with Du Pin and other doctors of the Sorbonne, who thought that support might be found from the Church of England for their appeal to a General Council. Encouraged by the reception of this hint, Du Pin wrote to Wake definitely proposing the union of the two Churches. Wake replied cautiously, expressing a hope that the French Church would secure its independence, and that differences of practice would not hinder intercommunion between England and France. In March De Girardin spoke hopefully of such a plan in an address to the doctors of the Sorbonne, afterwards writing an account of his speech to Wake, who doubted, however, whether the Regent d'Orléans and his cardinal-minister would allow a complete breach with Rome. In the summer Du Pin wrote his *Commonitorium*, which Wake rejected, partly as demanding too much change in the Church of England, and partly because he declined to negotiate with one of inferior rank to himself. 'I do not think my character,' he wrote, 'at all inferior to that of an Archbishop of Paris; on the contrary, without lessening the authority and dignity of the Church of England, I must say it is in some respects superior.' He insisted that all dealing must be on equal terms. In August the Pope issued the Bull *Pastoralis Officio*, threatening the appellants with excommunication; and Cardinal de Noailles then sent a friendly message on his own account to Wake, who replied with long letters to Du Pin and De Girardin, urging them to accept a complete breach with Rome. Other letters passed, and information of what was going on leaked out at Paris. The Government intervened, and in February 1719 Du Pin's papers were seized. De Noailles temporised; Du Pin died in June; and the correspondence languished in the hands of De Girardin, and others less interested. In March 1720 De Noailles signed a qualified acceptance of the Bull *Unigenitus*, the internal crisis of the French Church was allayed, and Wake withdrew from the correspondence. His conduct of it was characterised throughout by a jealous regard for the independence and dignity of his see, a stiffness in rejecting even suggestions for the modification of the religious practice of the English Church, and a very large toleration of divergent practice in other Churches. The idea contemplated on both sides was that of an alliance of independent national Churches against the claims of the papacy or of the Roman Church. The Sorbonne doctors seem to have been in earnest, but De Noailles, a man of poor character, only played with the idea. Wake himself was severely attacked for the toleration which he was prepared to extend to practices commonly abused as popish. [RE-UNION, I.]   [T. A. L.]

Lupton, *Archbishop Wake and the Project of Union*, 1896. A full life of Archbishop Wake has yet to be written. His MSS. are in the Library at Christ Church, Oxford.

WAKEFIELD, See of. A South Yorkshire Bishopric Scheme had been inaugurated as early as 1875, and under the Bishoprics Act, 1878 (41-2 Vic. c. 68), the Crown was authorised to establish a bishopric of Wakefield by Order in Council. The necessary funds, however, were not raised till ten years later, and the see was established by Order in Council dated 17th May 1888. Its territory was taken from Ripon (*q.v.*), and consists of the southern part of the West Riding, amounting in all to 235,000 acres. It has a population of 750,750, and is divided into the archdeaconries of Halifax and Huddersfield, both created 1888. The income of the see is £3000. The parish church of All Saints, Wakefield, dating mainly from the fourteenth and fifteenth centuries, was made the pro-cathedral church. An enlargement in memory of Bishop Walsham How was consecrated in 1905. There is an acting but not a legal chapter, and the bishop is therefore appointed by Letters Patent from the Crown [BISHOPS]. The see-house, Bishopgarth, Wakefield, was completed 1893.

1. William Walsham How, 1888-97 (*q.v.*).
2. George Rodney Eden ; tr., 1897, from the suffragan bishopric of Dover ; cons. 1890.   [G. C.]

WALTER, Hubert (d. 1205), Archbishop of Canterbury, was a nephew of Ranulf Glanville, the great justiciar of Henry II., and began his career as a chaplain in his uncle's household. In 1184 he became a Baron of the Exchequer ; and in 1189 was sitting as a Justice of the Curia Regis. Though ill educated for the clerical profession, he was prudent and keen-witted, a born administrator, and an expert lawyer. There is reason for supposing him to be the author of the treatise *De Legibus et Consuetudinibus Regni Angliae*, commonly ascribed to Glanville, which is the first scientific and authoritative work on English law. His legal activities were rewarded with spiritual preferments—in 1186 with the deanery of York, in 1189 with the see of Salisbury. At York he took a leading part in the quarrels between the chapter and Archbishop Geoffrey, against whose election he protested (1189), though it was promoted by Richard I. Richard bore Hubert no ill-will for this opposition to his half-brother. The King mistrusted Geoffrey, and found Hubert a valuable adjutant in the Third Crusade. Hubert showed both energy and capacity in Palestine, and in 1193 was appointed to command the English contingent on the homeward voyage. But on reaching Sicily he learned of the King's capture, and went to Germany to arrange the terms of release. He was one of the commissioners who collected Richard's ransom, and his services were rewarded with the primacy, left vacant by the death of Archbishop Baldwin in the Holy Land. Immediately afterwards he was appointed Chief Justiciar, in which capacity he suppressed the rebellion of Prince John. As Richard after his release was continuously absent from England, the English administration remained entirely in Hubert's hands from 1194 to 1198. The legatine commission which he obtained in 1195 made him equally supreme over the English Church. In both his capacities he proved an energetic but high-handed ruler. As legate he humiliated Archbishop Geoffrey,

who had claimed that York was of equal rank with Canterbury, by making a careful visitation of the northern province ; and he fomented the quarrels between the King and Geoffrey which led to the latter's temporary disgrace. As justiciar he effected some useful reforms, instituting the office of coroner, reviving the hue and cry, appointing wardens of the peace in every shire, and applying the elective principle to the choice of juries, both for judicial and fiscal purposes. By this last measure, and by the liberal charters which he issued to some towns, such as Lincoln, he sensibly promoted the habit of local self-government, and schooled the nation for Parliamentary government. But the exactions necessitated by the continental wars of Richard were felt as an intolerable burden. In 1197 the Great Council, headed by St. Hugh of Lincoln (*q.v.*), were successful in resisting a demand for military aid. The financial difficulty was met next year by a new land tax, called the carucage, which was a more stringent form of the old danegeld. But Richard was dissatisfied with the results of Hubert's government, and seized the first opportunity of dismissing him. The monks of Canterbury complained of the archbishop at Rome, because he had diverted part of their revenue to maintain a college of secular priests at Lambeth ; incidentally they charged him with sacrilege, and with neglecting his sacred duties for cares of state. Innocent III. (*q.v.*) accordingly demanded and obtained the removal of Hubert from the justiciarship. But on John's accession the archbishop accepted the much inferior office of Chancellor, and became once more a political figure. He acted as a restraining influence upon John, although there are reasons for rejecting the story (told by Matthew Paris) that, in the course of the coronation service, he addressed the people, reminding them that the kingship was elective, not hereditary. Still, John rejoiced at his death, saying : 'Now at last I am King of England.' The archbishop's latter years were embittered by the Lambeth question, in which the monks were steadily supported by Innocent III. ; but he successfully resisted Gerald de Barri (*q.v.*), the bishop-elect of St. David's, who endeavoured to obtain from the Pope a recognition of the metropolitan pretensions of that see. Hubert bequeathed a large sum to Canterbury Cathedral, and was a liberal friend of religious houses. Though worldly and unlettered, he fulfilled his archiepiscopal duties with dignity and zeal, maintaining the independence of the Church against the

Crown, and defending the rights of his see against all rivals. [H. W. C. D.]

Norgate, *Eng. under the Angevin Kings* and *John Luckland* : Stubbs, *C. H.*, xii. : H. W. C. Davis, *Eng. under the Normans and Angevins*.

WARBURTON, William (1698-1779), Bishop of Gloucester, was educated at Oakham Grammar School, where his master is said to have found him 'the dullest of all dull scholars.' He was articled to an attorney, but his love of reading and of theology decided him to take holy orders (1723). His chief works are the *Alliance between Church and State*, a defence of establishment on utilitarian grounds; the *Divine Legation of Moses*, designed to prove the divine origin of the Jewish religion; and editions of Shakespeare and Pope. His writings involved him in many controversies, which he conducted with the coarse vigour that marks his style. His blustering and pretentious dogmatism brought him a reputation far beyond his deserts, and imposed even upon Johnson (*q.v.*). But in 1741 the University of Oxford refused him the degree of D.D. He was created D.D. by the Archbishop of Canterbury in 1754. He received various preferments, including a prebend at Durham, where he is said to have brought about the disuse of copes in the cathedral services because 'the stiff high collar used to ruffle his great full-bottomed wig.' In 1759 he was appointed Bishop of Gloucester. His religion, though sincere, was of the low, easy-going type of the time. He wrote against the 'enthusiasm' of the Methodists, and gave offence by his infrequent attendance at Holy Communion, but he required a stricter preparation of candidates for confirmation than was then usual. His works show wide reading and much ingenuity but little real ability. As a critic he is prolific in tasteless and unnecessary explanations and emendations, and his writings generally are remarkable for the ferocious arrogance with which he treats other writers, a quality which was sometimes accompanied by dishonourable conduct towards them in private.

[G. C.]

Works (with biographical preface by Hurd), J. S. Watson, *Life* ; Nichols, *Literary Anecdotes and Illustrations*.

WARD, Seth (1617-89), Bishop of Salisbury, son of an attorney at Aspenden, Herts, where the bishop in 1684 founded a small hospital or alms-house. He was educated at the local grammar school and Sidney Sussex College, Cambridge, where he was 'servitor' (sizar) to the master, Dr. Samuel Ward.

When Dr. Ward (1643) was imprisoned in St. John's College with others who refused to take the Solemn League and Covenant, Seth Ward, now Fellow of their college and Mathematical Lecturer, though no blood relation, attended him faithfully. Though Seth was deprived of his Fellowship by the Puritan visitors in 1644, in 1649, through the good offices of Scarburg and others, he was appointed Savilian Professor of Mathematics at Oxford, where he made the lectures a reality. He also acquired celebrity as a preacher, though the conditions of his professorship exempted him from obligation to preach. In later years Charles II. said that Ward and Croft of Hereford were the only prelates whom he 'could not have bad sermons from.' After the Restoration Ward's public policy towards papists and other dissidents was more rigorous than King James approved, and Colonel Blood was sent to reprimand him. He was, however, kind in individual cases privately. A mathematician and astronomer of no mean order, he was intimate with Barrow, Oughtred, Scarburg, and Wilkins, and being incorporated at Oxford as 'fellow-commoner' of Wadham in 1650, he was one of the first members of the Philosophical Society of Oxford with Boyle (*q.v.*), Evelyn (*q.v.*), and others; and in 1662 he was one of the original members of the Royal Society.

In 1656 he had been collated to the precentorship of Exeter by the deprived bishop, Ralph Brownrigg, and, fully believing that Church and King would be one day restored, he paid the secretary's fees, and in due time received the emoluments, which helped him to repair the palace at Exeter when he was promoted to the bishopric in 1662, after half a year's tenure of the deanery, in which time he carried out an extensive restoration of the cathedral church. In September 1667 he was translated to Sarum. As at Exeter, so here he compiled in a large pocket-book, with a map at either end, a thorough diocesan calendar, *Liber Notitiae generalis Sethi episcopi Sar.*, in which the clergy and principal residents, the value of benefices, etc. (which in time he helped to augment), as in the King's Books, and also as estimated before and after the Civil War, are entered, with references to episcopal and capitular muniments, and other memoranda made at various times from 1667 to 1685. He regained for his see the Chancellorship of the Order of the Garter in 1671. He became a valetudinarian, and the prey to an imaginary malady in one of his toes, which he bathed in sherry, etc., and shod in fox fur. His mental powers failed about four years before his death, one of his latest conscious acts being a reconciliation with Dr. T. Pierce, the dean of the cathedral, who with some acrimony had disputed the bishop's right to collate to one of the prebends, but after the award of a commission was required to apologise. Ward never married. He contributed largely to a scheme to make the Avon navigable from Christ Church, and founded in 1682 the 'Matrons' College' in the Close, containing forty-two rooms for widows of clergy.

[c. w.]

W. Pope, *Life* (1697): reprinted in Cassan's *Bishops of Salisbury.*

WARHAM, William (c. 1450-1532), Archbishop of Canterbury, patron of Erasmus and the Renaissance. A Hampshire man and a Wykehamist, Warham passed from Winchester to New College, Oxford. His particular study was law, and after leaving Oxford he practised in the ecclesiastical courts. More than one embassy or commission reckoned him as member. In 1493 he was sent to Flanders to nullify the negotiations of Perkin Warbeck with Margaret of Burgundy. On his return he was ordained, and held various benefices. He was also made Master of the Rolls. His most important task at this time was the part he played as ambassador in arranging the marriage of Prince Arthur with Katherine of Aragon. A good deal of other political work fell to his lot, as Henry VII. trusted him completely in many negotiations. This stage of his life ended in 1502, when he was appointed Bishop of London. Two years later he became Archbishop of Canterbury, and almost coincidently Lord Chancellor. In 1506 he became Chancellor of Oxford, and in this way was conversant with the change of educational methods and of religious feeling which soon became apparent in the University. One of the crying abuses of the time which was ventilated again and again was the condition of the ecclesiastical courts. Alive to this, Warham in 1508 regulated the procedure of the Court of Audience. When Henry VIII. became king Warham succeeded to his confidence, and as Chancellor spoke at the opening of Parliament. He crowned Henry and Katherine in 1509, and next year presented the golden rose from the Pope. Erasmus had long since been brought to his notice, and in Henry's early years the archbishop helped him with gifts of money. But the gradual eclipse of the primate was in progress. Wolsey's (*q.v.*) star was in the ascendant, and Warham had the mortifica-

tion of playing an entirely secondary part when the cardinal's hat arrived for Wolsey in 1515. The older statesmen of Henry VII. were deeply suspicious of the new men and the new political methods. Warham consequently resigned his chancellorship, which was bestowed upon Wolsey. Warham's eclipse was still further manifest when Campeggio (*q.v.*) arrived as legate in 1518. The position was repeated something like a century later, when Abbot was thrown into the shade by the rise of Laud. Warham, however, was not entirely left out of sight, for he was present at various functions, and notably at the Field of the Cloth of Gold in 1520. The views of Luther were at this time influencing students at the Universities, and were permeating the city of London. Warham, as Chancellor of Oxford and primate, rather underrated the importance of the crisis, and evidently thought with Tunstall (*q.v.*) and Fisher (*q.v.*) that the public burning of Lutheran literature at Paul's Cross in 1521 would prove effective. Men's minds were drawn off for a time to the political situation. Warham took some part as archbishop in preparing Kent for the expected invasion by the Emperor. His demands of money from his clergy in order to meet the expected foe were not at all popular. Claim after claim was made upon men who were reluctant to contribute. When the King's divorce was mooted Warham was naturally associated with Wolsey in the inquiry. His one desire was to have the matter tried in strictest form of law. When the legatine court was constituted he was too ill to be present. The process was carried out in the issue with little reference to him, and in this he considered himself happy, for he had no wish to meddle with the affair. The Reformation Parliament began to sit in November 1529. Warham was probably much stung by the attack which at once began on the very church courts that had been the special object of his reforming skill. But he took no effective measures to prevent the legislation passed as regards fees in the courts. Possibly he thought that the anti-clerical spirit of the new Parliament would spend itself with such action. The drama developed rapidly, and Warham witnessed in surprised consternation Henry's proceedings, which presently culminated in the events leading to the Submission of the Clergy. His anxiety is manifested by his action in proposing to modify the assertion of the King's supremacy by the insertion of the words *quantum per Christi legem licet.* At this juncture the divorce question again came to the front, and the aged primate was selected by the King to pronounce the decision. Warham would not consent to this, and made a solemn protest against all the attacks delivered by Parliament upon the position of clergy or of Pope. It was now that the King inspired the petition of the Commons against the clergy, and this in order to justify the anti-clerical policy of the time. Warham directed or drew up an answer, in which he justified the position of affairs, and laboured to prove that reforms had taken place. How greatly the anxiety of such proceedings told upon him was increasingly manifest. He lived to see the attack upon the clergy almost complete, dying soon after the Submission of the Clergy in 1532. He was buried in Canterbury Cathedral.

[H. G.]

Contemporary chronicles, the documents in the State Papers, and Dr. Gairdner in *D.N.B.*

WATERLAND, Daniel (1683-1740), divine, was born in Walesby in Lincolnshire. He was a Fellow of Magdalene College, Cambridge (1704), Master of Magdalene College and Rector of Ellingham in Norfolk (1713), Vice-Chancellor of the University of Cambridge (1715), Chaplain in Ordinary to the King (1717), Rector of St. Austin and St. Faith, London (1721), Chancellor of the diocese of York (about 1723), Canon of Windsor (1727), Vicar of Twickenham and Archdeacon of Middlesex (1730). In 1734 he declined the Prolocutorship of the Lower House of Canterbury Convocation, and either in 1738 or 1740 the bishopric of Llandaff. He is said to have been industrious in the performance of the duties connected with the offices which he held, and he was a most voluminous writer. During the years from 1713 to his death in 1740 there are only nine in which he is not known to have published some work, and in several years there were more than one, in one year so many as six. The most important of his writings are: *A Vindication of Christ's Divinity* (1719), *The Case of Arian Subscription Considered* (1721), *A Supplement to the Case of Arian Subscription Considered* (1722), *A Critical History of the Athanasian Creed* (1723), *Scripture Vindicated* (three parts, 1730, 1731, 1732), *The Nature, Obligation, and Efficacy of the Christian Sacraments Considered* (1730), *The Importance of the Doctrine of the Holy Trinity Asserted* (1734), *A Review of the Doctrine of the Eucharist* (1737), *The Christian Sacrifice Explained* (1738), and *The Sacramental Part of the Eucharist Explained* (1739). His works indicate the four chief matters with which as a theologian he was concerned.

(1) He actively resisted the Latitudinarian attempt to make room within the Church of England for various forms of denying the divinity of Christ, and in opposition to this attempt he did valuable work in regard to the doctrines of the Holy Trinity and the Incarnation. [LATITUDINARIANS.] (2) His historical treatment of the Athanasian Creed is for his time of a very high order, and it is interesting to compare his conclusions with those of the best modern authorities. He was of opinion that the Creed was written between A.D. 420 and 430 in Gaul, and that the probable author was St. Hilary of Arles. (3) He was strongly opposed to the Deism widely prevalent in the eighteenth century. [DEISTS.] (4) His Eucharistic teaching was that those who communicate worthily receive the virtue and grace of Christ's body and blood; and that the Eucharist is 'a true and proper sacrifice' consisting in a 'sacrifice of alms,' a 'sacrifice of prayer,' a 'sacrifice of praise and thanksgiving,' a 'sacrifice of a penitent and contrite heart,' a 'sacrifice of ourselves,' an 'offering up the mystical body of Christ'—'His Church,' an 'offering up of true converts or sincere penitents to God by their pastors,' and a 'sacrifice of faith and hope and self-humiliation in commemorating the grand sacrifice and resting finally upon it.' His writings on this subject were directed against the Zwinglianism of Hoadly (q.v.), as well as against the views on the Eucharistic sacrifice of the Nonjurors (q.v.).   [D. S.]

Works, with *Life*, by Van Mildert.

WATSON, Joshua (1771-1855), born on Tower Hill, where his father was a wine merchant. In 1786 he entered this business, retiring in 1814 in order to give himself to work for the Church. He married a sister of Thomas Sikes, Vicar of Guilsborough, one of the old High Church party, and soon became the leader of that school. From 1811-22 he lived at Clapton, close to his only brother, J. J. Watson (Archdeacon of St. Albans and Rector of Hackney), and the 'Clapton Sect' or 'Hackney Phalanx,' became a recognised contrast to the Evangelicals of the 'Clapham Sect.'

Watson was a devout layman of the best Anglican type, cultivated and widely read, especially in theology, and of unbounded munificence. He was one of the three originators (in 1811) of the National Society (for the education of the poor), and he was chiefly responsible for the Church Building Society, begun in 1817. He gave much time to the S.P.G. and the S.P.C.K. In 1837 he formed the constitution of the Additional

Curates Society, and became its first treasurer. He was a trusted friend of successive Archbishops of Canterbury: Manners Sutton and Howley; of Bishops Van Mildert (of Durham), Lloyd (of Oxford), and C. J. Blomfield (*q.v.*).

The official atmosphere in which he had thus come to move, advancing age, and the caution and even timidity with which formerly High Church views had been expressed, caused him to regard the Oxford Movement with some alarm, which deepened when Froude's *Remains* and Tract No. 90 appeared. But he had helped to draft the clerical Address to Archbishop Howley in 1833, and composed the lay Declaration which followed in 1834, and these were an outcome of the meeting at Hadleigh. [ROSE, H. J.] Newman (*q.v.*) in 1840 dedicated the fifth volume of his famous *Sermons* 'To Joshua Watson, Esq., D.C.L., the Benefactor of all his brethren, by his long and dutiful ministry, and patient service, to his and their common Mother,' as 'an unsanctioned offering of respect and gratitude.' Dr. Pusey (*q.v.*) wrote to him: 'I cannot say how cheering it was to be recognised by you as carrying on the same torch which we had received from yourself and from those of your generation who had remained faithful to the old teaching.'

[S. L. O.]

E. Churton. *Memoir*, 2 vols.

WAYNFLETE, William (1395-1486), Bishop of Winchester, Lord Chancellor, and school and college founder, is perhaps the first Englishman who owed a bishopric to his success as a schoolmaster. He was the son of Richard Patyn, *alias* Barbour, of Wainfleet, Lincolnshire. He was educated at Oxford, but the assertion often made that he was at Winchester and New College is not supported by documents. He may, however, have been a commoner at Winchester living out of college. Waynflete is possibly the William Waynflete ordained subdeacon, deacon, and priest by Bishop Fleming of Lincoln, with title from Spalding Priory, December 21, 1426. He is perhaps the William Waynflete admitted Scholar (*i.e.* Fellow) of King's Hall, Cambridge, 6th March 1428 (*Exch. Q.R.*, Bdle. 346, No. 31), who, as LL.B., with the warden received letters of protection for an embassy to Rome, 15th July 1429 (*Proc. P.C.*, iii. 347). He is the Master William Wannflete who was paid fifty shillings as *Magister Informator*, or headmaster, of Winchester College for the term beginning 24th June 1430. While there he was made by

Beaufort, Bishop of Winchester, Master of St. Mary Magdalen Hospital.

King Henry VI., having founded Eton College in imitation of Winchester on 11th October 1440, on 31st January 1441 visited Winchester to see its working. In the result, Waynflete left the headmastership at Michaelmas, 1441. Whether he went to Eton as Headmaster, as often stated, there is no evidence to show. He certainly was not named a Fellow in the foundation charter of Eton, as often alleged. He received a royal livery as provost at Christmas, 1442. Eton School was not opened before May 1442, perhaps not before 1443. Waynflete was at one time said to have taken half Winchester to Eton. In fact, five scholars and one commoner left Winchester for Eton in 1443, the full number of seventy scholars not being completed till 1446. On the death of Cardinal Beaufort (*q.v.*), 1447, Henry secured the election of Waynflete as his successor in the see of Winchester, and on 13th July Waynflete was consecrated at Eton. That year Henry began to rebuild Eton on a larger scale, and Waynflete was made chief 'executor' of his 'will' for that purpose. Waynflete took a prominent part in politics. In 1454 he was the chief of a commission to treat with the King, then insane. In 1456 he was made Lord Chancellor, as apparently a *persona grata* to both Yorkists and Lancastrians. He resigned after the Yorkist victory at Northampton on 7th July 1460. He took a leading part in obtaining the restitution of Eton after its annexation to St. George's, Windsor, by Edward IV., and from 1467 to 1469 he was busy completing the chapel, and built the ante-chapel. Waynflete was prominent in receiving Henry on his restoration in 1470, which cost him a new pardon from Edward IV. in 1471 and a loan of two thousand marks (some £40,000).

From this time he took no further part in politics, and devoted himself to his educational foundations. On 6th May 1448 he had obtained licence to found, and on 20th August founded 'Seint Marie Maudeleyn Halle' at Oxford for a president and fifty graduate scholars. St. Mary Magdalen College was founded by deed of 12th June 1458, the hall surrendering its possessions, including St. John the Baptist Hospital, acquired two years before, in which the new college was placed. Political troubles stopped further progress till 5th May 1474, when the foundation stone of the present building was laid. On 23rd August 1480 new statutes, often misinterpreted as the foundation of the college, copied from those of New College, with few exceptions, were made, and a new president, Richard Mayhew, Fellow of New College, was installed with seventy scholars, divided into forty Fellows and thirty scholars, called demies from their commons being half those of the fellows. The free grammar school, known as Magdalen College School, was established at its gates. The Headmaster's (boarding) house has lately been removed across the Cherwell. In 1484 Waynflete endowed, and placed under the college, another free grammar school, the building of which remains almost untouched, at his native place, Wainfleet in Lincolnshire. In 1471 and 1485 he set a precedent, destined to far-reaching imitation under the Lady Margaret Tudor, Wolsey (q.v.), and Henry VIII. (q.v.), in the suppression of the priories of Sele, Sussex, and Selborne, Hants, and the annexation of their endowments to his college. On 27th April 1486 he made his will, giving great gifts to Winchester, New, and Magdalen Colleges, the latter being residuary devisee. On 11th May he died, and was buried in a chantry chapel behind the high altar of Winchester Cathedral, the effigy on which is probably a portrait.

[A. F. L.]

WESLEY, John (1703-91), and **Charles** (1707-88), evangelists and founders of Methodism, were respectively fifteenth and eighteenth children of Samuel Wesley (1662-1735), whose father, John, and grandfather, Bartholomew Westley (so he spelt the name), were both ministers ejected in 1662 under the Act of Uniformity (q.v.). Samuel, however, was ordained in the English Church, and attained some distinction as man of letters and High Church divine. In 1695 he became Rector of Epworth, Lincs, where he remained the rest of his life, bringing up a large family (he had nineteen children, of whom nine died in infancy), and struggling against pecuniary difficulties. His wife was Susannah, daughter of Dr. Samuel Annesley, also an ejected minister. A disciple in some respects of the Caroline Divines (q.v.) and the Nonjurors (q.v.), 'a zealous churchwoman yet rich in a dowry of nonconforming virtues,' 'the mother of Methodism' exercised a powerful influence in the religious development of her famous sons.

John Benjamin Wesley, to give him the full name he never used, developed early. At eight years old his father admitted him to Communion. His love of reasoning and argument in childhood were remarkable. In 1714 he entered the Charterhouse, and in 1720 went up to Christ Church, Oxford,

where he began ' to set in earnest upon a new life.' He graduated B.A., 1724, was ordained deacon, 1725 ; elected Smithsonian Fellow of Lincoln, 1726 ; and in 1727 became M.A., and went to be curate to his father. Recalled to Oxford by the duties of his Fellowship in 1729, he found his brother Charles, who had come up to Christ Church from Westminster in 1726, one of a little group of 'Methodists,' which had arisen from Charles Wesley's attending the weekly Eucharist in the cathedral and inducing two or three friends to do the same. The nickname was not new, but was applied in general to any who affected to be methodical ; and Charles and his friends had agreed ' to observe with strict formality the method of study and practice set down in the statutes of the University.' John Wesley held strongly that idleness and neglect of study were sinful, and quickly became acknowledged leader of the group. The practice of the Oxford Methodists included not only regular habits and earnest study, but social service, chiefly in visiting prisons, almsgiving, systematic prayer, and regular Communion. They observed the Church's fasts, and some at least laid stress upon private confession. At this time John Wesley believed in prayer for the departed, the use of the mixed chalice, and similar practices which he derived from primitive antiquity. He was much under the influence of William Law (q.v.), and so the ancestry of Oxford Methodism may be traced in part to the Nonjurors. The membership of the group rose to twenty-seven (including some ladies), and during the absence of the Wesleys from Oxford sank as low as five. They were ridiculed as 'the Holy Club,' but Bishop Potter of Oxford declared that, though 'irregular,' they had done good.

In April 1735 the Rector of Epworth died, and John, going to London to present his father's last work, *Dissertations on Job*, to Queen Caroline, fell in with the founders of the new colony of Georgia, who were looking out for men to preach the Gospel there. He was persuaded to undertake the task, with a stipend of £50 from the S.P.G. Charles, after some hesitation, gave up work at Oxford, was ordained, and became secretary to General Oglethorpe, with whom the brothers sailed for America late in the year. John was much impressed with the piety of some Moravians on the ship, and to further his intercourse with them learnt German and adopted a vegetarian diet. The work in Georgia proved a disappointment, lying not, as the Wesleys had hoped, among the heathen, but among rough colonists, for whom their precise application of the letter of the Church's law in worship and discipline was utterly unsuited. In 1736 John proposed marriage to Sophia Hopkey, niece of a leading colonist, but after consulting the Moravian elders decided 'to proceed no further in the matter.' After her marriage he injudiciously refused to admit her to Communion for faults the nature of which does not appear. Legal proceedings followed, and eventually (December 1737) he returned to England, whither Charles had preceded him.

While still depressed by a sense of failure, and under the influence of Moravian Evangelicalism, John Wesley met Peter Böhler, a famous Moravian preacher, who wrote of him: 'He knew he did not properly believe in the Saviour and was willing to be taught. His brother . . . is . . . in much distress in his mind, but does not know how he shall begin to be acquainted with the Saviour.' On 24th May 1738 John experienced a conversion at a devotional meeting in Aldersgate Street. 'I felt I did trust in Christ, Christ alone, for salvation; and an assurance was given me that He had taken away *my* sins, even *mine*, and saved *me* from the law of sin and death.' Charles had undergone a similar experience a few days earlier. After forcing a quarrel on William Law for declining to follow him, John visited the Moravian headquarters at Herrnhut, and returned determined to preach the Gospel to others. His teaching attracted the notice of Bishop Gibson (*q.v.*), who was reassured by an interview with the brothers, warning them against the enthusiasm of Whitefield (*q.v.*). In March 1739 John Wesley joined Whitefield at Bristol, where he preached in the open for the first time on 3rd April. His dislike of the practice was overcome by its evident results. 'The devil does not love field-preaching. Neither do I; I love a commodious room, a soft cushion, a handsome pulpit.' His preaching, like Whitefield's, was accompanied by strong excitement and convulsions among his hearers, which Charles thought 'no sign of grace.' The unfamiliar enthusiasm of the preachers and their followers roused opposition and even persecution. The hostility of the clergy forced them to preach in the open or at private meetings, *e.g.* those of the Religious Societies (*q.v.*). The United Society, as it was called, rose out of a little group who near the end of 1740 began to meet every Thursday evening at an old 'Foundery' in Moorfields for prayer and preaching. In 1740 the Wesleys finally broke with the Moravians on account of their quietism. The split between Wesley and the Arminian,

and Whitefield and the Calvinist, section followed in 1741. From this time United Societies of Methodists appeared all over the country, and John Wesley devoted himself to organising the movement and to itinerant preaching. Between 1738 and his death he is said to have travelled two hundred and fifty thousand miles and preached forty thousand sermons. Forty-two times he crossed the Irish Channel. He held the inactivity of the clergy and the prevailing spiritual destitution a sufficient reason for disregarding Church order, and declared: 'I look upon the whole world as my parish.'

Charles Wesley was not, like his brother, a great organiser and ruler of men, nor had he, like him, a vigorous intellect of the first order. But as an itinerant preacher determined to carry the Gospel to the lowest and most neglected classes he was scarcely less energetic. Both realised that religious truth could not be apprehended by the intellect alone, and that the use of the emotions had been neglected. Both also continued to maintain their High Church views, and it is clear they intended a Church revival, not a separation. Their elder brother Samuel, however, quickly detected the real tendency of their movement. In October 1739 he wrote: 'They design separation. They are already forbidden all the pulpits in London; and to preach in that diocese is actual schism. In all likelihood, it will come to the same all over England, if the bishops have courage enough. They leave off the liturgy in the fields; and though Mr. Whitefield expresses his value for it, he never once read it to his tatterdemalions on a common. . . . As I told Jack I am not afraid the Church should excommunicate him (discipline is at too low an ebb), but that he should excommunicate the Church.'

The story of the movement is told elsewhere. [NONCONFORMITY. v.] Its separatist tendency caused Charles to take alarm as early as 1755. From 1761 he gave up active work, chiefly owing to bad health; but there was no cessation of confidence and affection between the brothers. Charles continued to preach, and to urge his hearers to 'live and die in the Church of England.' His fame rests chiefly on his hymns. He is said to have written over six thousand. They form, as his brother said, 'a body of . . . practical divinity,' and bear ample witness to his high sacramental views as well as to his poetical gifts. His son and grandson were famous musicians. [MUSICIANS OF THE CHURCH.]

The Calvinistic controversy broke out again

in 1769, Toplady (*q.v.*) being John Wesley's principal antagonist. One of its results was the *Arminian Magazine*, founded by Wesley in 1778 to controvert the doctrine that, as he put it, 'God is not loving unto every man, that His Mercy is not over all His works.' It occupied much of his time and energy during the rest of his life. In 1778, also, the 'New Chapel,' City Road, was opened, as the headquarters of Methodism, Wesley insisting that it should be 'free and open,' and that the sexes should be separated.

In 1784, though still protesting his dislike to separation, he took the decisive step by 'ordaining presbyters,' and 'setting apart,' with imposition of hands, Thomas Coke, who was in priest's orders, as 'superintendent' for the Methodists in America. Other ordinations followed, chiefly for Scotland and America. He also executed a 'Deed of Declaration' defining the constitution of the Methodist body. Its organisation was the principal work of his latter years. He travelled about seeking to regulate the personal habits of his followers, and prescribing their physic, diet, and dress no less than their doctrines and worship. He had now lived down opposition, and was universally respected. Many of the clergy invited him to preach in their churches. He maintained wonderful health and strength. At seventy-one he thought preaching at five in the morning 'one of the most healthy exercises in the world.' In 1789 he reiterated his determination to 'live and die a member of the Church of England.' His last open-air sermon was preached at Winchelsea in October 1790, and he died in the following February.

His incomparable energy and industry combined with his strong personality and great powers of organisation to give him an almost unparalleled influence. He had a cheerful temper and considerable wit. His intellectual powers were not inconsistent with a remarkable simplicity. Charles declared his brother was born 'for the benefit of knaves.' This side of his character appears strongly in his relations with women. Both the brothers were said in their early days to be 'a dangerous snare to many young women.' And John's susceptibility drew him into several innocent and pious flirtations. In early life he believed in clerical celibacy, but at the Bristol Conference of 1748 was persuaded that 'a believer might marry without suffering loss in his soul.' In 1749 he proposed marriage to Grace Murray, a young widow of lowly birth, who had attended him during an illness; and imprudently

allowed her to accompany him on his missionary journeys. The lady, though lost in joyous amazement at his proposal, apparently did not know her own mind, and for some months wavered between Wesley and John Bennett, a preacher of the society, whom she eventually married, owing to the prompt and somewhat unscrupulous action of Charles Wesley, who feared lest the match should destroy his brother's work. This did not permanently save John from unsuitable marriage. In 1751 he married Mary Vazeille, who had been a domestic servant and was now widow of a London merchant. She was a woman of violent temper, jealous of her husband's absorption in his work, and of the female converts to whom he wrote his 'devotional endearments.' With characteristic imprudence he appointed as his housekeeper Sarah Ryan, a woman of thirty-three, who had three husbands living. Yet such blunders cannot excuse Mrs. Wesley's behaviour. She tampered with her husband's papers, disseminated slanders against him, and set him at loggerheads with his brother. Once a friend found her 'foaming with fury.' Her husband was on the floor, where she had been trailing him by the hair of his head; and she herself was still holding in her hands venerable locks which she had plucked up by the roots.' She finally left him in 1776. Charles, on the other hand, was happily married (1749) to Sarah Gwynne, who proved a faithful companion to him, though John Berridge, Vicar of Everton, declared matrimony had 'maimed' him, 'and might have spoiled John and [Whitefield] if a wise Master had not graciously sent them a brace of ferrets.'   [G. C.]

Journal of John Wesley, ed. Curnock; *Journal of Charles Wesley*, ed. Jackson; *Lives* of J. Wesley by Southey, Tyerman, and Urlin; of C. Wesley by Jackson; Townsend and Workman, *Hist. of Methodism*; Abbey and Overton, *Eng. Ch. in Eighteenth Century*; Leger, *John Wesley's Last Love*.

WESTCOTT, Brooke Foss (1825-1901), Bishop of Durham, was born at Birmingham, and educated at King Edward's School under Prince Lee, who later, as Bishop of Manchester, ordained him deacon and priest (1851), and at Trinity College, Cambridge (Senior Classic and Twenty-fourth Wrangler, 1848; Fellow, 1849). From 1852-69 he was a master at Harrow under Vaughan (*q.v.*) and Butler, subsequently becoming Canon of Peterborough (1869-83) and of Westminster (1883-90), and Regius Professor of Divinity at Cambridge (*vice* Jeremie) for twenty years (1870-90). He was a member of the New Testament Revision Company (1870-81) and of the Ecclesiastical Courts Commission (1881-3), and was consecrated Bishop of Durham in succession to his school-fellow, Lightfoot, on 1st May 1890.

The senior of the three men [HORT, LIGHT-FOOT] who gave the Cambridge school of theology world-wide fame, Dr. Westcott achieved a greater general reputation than any of his pupils, save Archbishop Benson (*q.v.*). As it came unsought, so it left him unchanged. Outwardly a man of small, fragile frame, with a leonine head and a silver voice, he left upon his hearers the impress—to many of them an enduring stimulus—of a personality aflame with intense spiritual earnestness and deeply stirred by social questions. This influence made itself felt in his sermons at Harrow and elsewhere; in his addresses to the Christian Social Union, which he helped to found in 1887; in his intercourse with his pupils, and in a wider field in the settlement of the great Durham Coal Strike on 1st June 1892. It was expressed also in his efforts for the advancement of clerical education, which resulted in the establishment of the Universities Preliminary Examination (1872), the Cambridge Theological Tripos (1874), and the Clergy Training School (1881-7).

The permanence of the influence of his writings is more difficult to estimate. Apart from *The New Testament in Greek* (with Dr. Hort, 1881), on which his fame chiefly rests; the articles in *Dict. Chris. Biog.* ('Clement,' 'Origen,' etc.) and *Dict. Bible*; and *The Gospel of Life* (1892)—a valuable essay towards distinguishing Christianity in the light of other modes of faith—his works fall perhaps into two classes. The first includes the *History of the Canon* (1855), *The Study of the Gospels* (1860), and commentaries on St. John (reprinted from *Speaker's Comm.*, 1882, 2nd edit. with Greek text, 1908). Epistles of St. John (1883), Hebrews (1889), and Ephesians (1906). Though most are superseded in some points by modern scholarship, from all the student may still learn much, *e.g.* the section of the introduction to St. John, which contains the argument from internal evidence as to the authorship of the Fourth Gospel, though not in itself conclusive, is permanently valuable as an element in any discussion of the subject, and many again will feel that they have learnt more from Westcott of 'the mind of St. John' than from any other. The second class comprises (*a*) popular works tending to foster the religious study of the Bible, *e.g.* *The Bible in the Church* (1864), *History of the*

English Bible (1868), *The Paragraph Psalter* (1879); (*b*) works dealing with the relation of Theology to Christian life. Among these the most valuable perhaps are *The Religious Office of the Universities* (1891) and *Religious Thought in the West* (1891). The others include the *Gospel of the Resurrection* (1866), *Christian Life* (1869), *Revelation of the Risen Lord* (1881), *Historic Faith* (1883), *Revelation of the Father* (1884), *Christus Consummator* (1886), *Social Aspects of Christianity* (1887), *The Victory of the Cross* (1888), *The Incarnation and Common Life* (1893), *Christian Aspects of Life* (1897), and *Lessons from Work* (1901). These (many originally sermons) have enjoyed an enormous popularity among readers rather conscious of difficulties and desirous of finding them discussed than anxious for definitive solutions, which the author would have distrusted had he given them.   [C. J.]

A. Westcott, *Life and Letters*, 1903, abridged edit., 1905; J. Clayton, *Life*, 1906; H. S. Holland, *Personal Studies*, 1905; A. C. Benson, *Leaves of the Tree*, 1911.

WESTMINSTER ABBEY.

In the days of Aethelberht, king of Kent (d. 616), a rich citizen of London built a church to St. Peter at Westminster, then an island in the marshes of the Thames, and called Thorney. Mellitus (*q.v.*), Bishop of London, came to consecrate the building, and pitched his tent in the neighbourhood. But that same evening the Apostle Peter appeared on the farther bank of the river to a fisherman, who ferried him across; then the apostle with the aid of a celestial choir consecrated the church. The fisherman, rewarded with an ample haul of salmon, was sent to inform Mellitus, who, when he had seen the signs of consecration, departed. Such was the story told by Westminster monks in the eleventh century. In the next century the rich citizen was identified with Sebert, king of Essex. Unfortunately, Bede never mentions a church at Westminster, and all that we can safely assert comes to this: Westminster was not the desolate place that has been pictured: traces of Roman buildings have been found; and it is likely that there was a Christian church here in early times. A charter of Offa, exhibited in the chapter-house, shows (if genuine) that there was a monastery here, *c.* 785. Dunstan (*q.v.*) was not abbot here, as Flete claimed; but he may have reformed this among other monasteries, and a genuine charter of King Edgar is extant. In any case, the monastery remained a small one until the days of Edward the Confessor.

Flete, the mediæval historian of the abbey, gives these names and dates of abbots : Siward, Ordbritht (mentioned in Offa's charter), Alfwy, Alfgar, Adymer, Alfnod, Alfric St. Dunstan, St. Wulsin (958-1005, Bishop of Sherborne), Alfwy (1005-25), Wulfnoth (1025-49). [For the abbots which follow, the dates down to Litlyngton are taken from Robinson's *Flete*; the tombstones or monuments of those marked with a * are still to be seen in the abbey.]

With Edwin (1049-71) we get on to firm historical ground. For his king, Edward the Confessor, was the real founder of Westminster Abbey and its greatness. The story is that the king was required to found a monastery for having failed to keep a vow to make a pilgrimage to Rome, and that the vision of a hermit pointed out the site ; but a simpler reason for the choice of Westminster lay in the vicinity of the royal palace. Here, then, Edward built a great stone church, on the model of Jumièges. This was the first specimen seen in England of the great ' Norman churches ' which were hereafter to stud the land, and a few fragments of it remain to-day. The king was unable to be present at its consecration on 28th December 1065 ; he died on 4th January 1066, and by the gift of his body contributed a surer source of greatness. For William the Conqueror chose to be crowned in the church where King Edward lay ; and consequently the church of St. Peter has ever since been the place of coronation of the kings and queens of England.

The Saxon abbot ruled till 1071. Then came three Norman abbots : Geoffrey (1071, sent back to Jumièges in 1075); Vitalis (1076-85), Abbot of Bernay ; Gilbert Crispin * (1085-1117), under whom was completed the building of the new monastery, of which much remains to-day, *e.g.* the ' Norman undercroft ' and so-called ' chapel of the Pyx.' Gilbert was a monk of Bec, a disciple and friend of St. Anselm (*q.v.*), a writer and a theologian. His endowment of the *camera* to enable it to clothe eighty monks is a witness to the rapid development of the monastery under its new régime. Herbert (1121-?36) was a monk of the place. Gervase (?1137-?56), a natural son of King Stephen, dissipated both its property and its morals until he was expelled by Henry II., *c.* 1156. Laurence * (?1158-73), monk of St. Albans and a preacher, reintroduced order. He also succeeded in obtaining the canonisation of Edward the Confessor, whose body was accordingly translated to a new tomb on 13th October 1163. With Laurence's name

is associated St. Katharine's chapel in the infirmary, the scene of several councils and consecrations of bishops. He was followed by Walter (1175-90), Prior of Winchester ; William Postard (1191-1200); Ralph Arundel (1200-14), who was deposed by a papal legate ; and William Humez * (1214-22) of Caen, the last abbot from Normandy.

Abbot Laurence had obtained from the Pope the privilege of wearing the mitre. In 1220 the convent secured its complete exemption from the jurisdiction of the bishops of London; and its new position of independence made the abbey still more suitable for a national centre. Being, as it were, the royal chapel, the monastery which had been so insignificant in Anglo-Saxon times now began to challenge with St. Albans (*q.v.*) and Canterbury the primacy of the Benedictine abbeys in England. Living so near to court, the abbots were brought into close contact with the king, who tended to use them more and more in matters of state. Thus they became great magnates of the realm, as is notably seen in the case of the abbots of the thirteenth century : Richard Berking (1222-46), Richard Crokesley (1246-58), Philip Lewisham (August to October 1258), Richard Ware * (1258-83), who brought the famous pavement of the presbytery from Rome, and Walter Wenlok (1283-1307)—all of whom (except Lewisham) were much occupied in state business and offices. The exaltation of the abbots was not established without internal conflict. There was a vigorous life in the convent, and the monks with their officers (obedientiaries) struggled hard against the arbitrary rule of the abbots. The chief subject of quarrel was the division of the property of the convent between abbot and monks, which only received its settlement under Wenlok. The aggrandisement of the abbey called for a corresponding adornment of its buildings, and in 1220 a new lady chapel was begun. But the matter of building was soon to be taken out of their hands by Henry III.

Henry III. was as devoted to St. Edward as St. Edward had been to St. Peter, and he determined to rebuild Edward's church at an expense which proved to be enormous. He began in 1245 by pulling down the whole eastern part of the building, and then built the magnificent church which still stands to-day and justly claims to be one of the most beautiful buildings in Christendom. On 13th October 1269 he translated the body of St. Edward to the shrine where it now rests ; and in his death, like St. Edward, he conferred yet another benefit upon the church. For he elected to be buried by the Confessor's shrine, and so the church became the place of royal sepulture as well as coronation, and to-day it holds the remains of sixteen sovereigns of England (besides the Confessor), viz. Henry III., Edward I., Edward III., Richard II., Henry V., Edward V., Henry VII., Edward VI., Mary, Elizabeth, James I., Charles II., William III., Mary II., Anne, George II. Further, the bodies of the kings have gathered round them the dust of many of the best and greatest of Englishmen.

Another cause of the identification of the abbey with the national history was the sitting of Parliament within its precincts. There has been some exaggeration in this matter. The latest authority can find no evidence of a session here in Henry III.'s time or indeed before 1351. The Commons sat at intervals in the chapter-house from 1351 to 1395, and in the refectory from 1397 to 1416. After that it is thought that they returned to their original place of meeting, the palace.[1]

On 31st March 1298 a fire which began in the palace destroyed all the buildings of the monastery except the church and chapter-house. [Other fires occurred in 1447, when the dormitory was burnt; in 1694, when all the MSS. in the library were burnt; in 1731 in Ashburnham House, when the Cotton library was greatly injured; and in 1803 in the lantern.] This trouble was aggravated by the great scandal of the robbery in 1303 of the royal treasures kept in the chapel of the Pyx. The rebuilding after the fire was carried on with difficulty under Richard Kedyngton (1308-15) and William Curtlyngton (1315-33). In Thomas Henley's days (1333-44) the old nave of the Confessor's church had to be restored, and then Simon Byrcheston (1344-9) began to rebuild the cloister. But another disaster was at hand, for the great plague of 1348-9 carried off the abbot and twenty-six of the monks. So closed a half-century in which the instability of society at large had been reflected in the life of the convent.

A new era began with Simon Langham * (1349-62), who restored order both to the finances and the morals of the exhausted convent, and won the title of second founder. Quickly promoted, because of his abilities, to high offices of state and to the sees of Ely and Canterbury, and then leaving Canterbury to become a cardinal at the papal court at Avignon, he always retained his affection for Westminster; he conceived and pressed on the design of rebuilding the nave to match

Henry's choir, and at his death at Avignon on 22nd July 1376 he left his great wealth to the convent.

Nicholas Litlyngton (1362-86) has left on the abbey the mark of a great builder. He finished the cloister in 1365, added Jerusalem Chamber and the 'College Hall' to the Abbot's House, and built a new set of cellarer's buildings, which still stand on the east side of Dean's Yard; his initials are still to be seen in glass and stone. The old nave was now pulled down, and on 3rd March 1376 he laid the foundation stone of the 'new work.' On 11th August 1378 Hawley, a knight who had taken refuge in the abbey, was murdered in the choir at the time of High Mass. This scandal led to a great attack upon the church's privilege of sanctuary, but the right was maintained, though limited under the Tudors, till the reign of James I. Almost necessary in ages of violence, the privilege led to abuses; but whether it was the cause of the crowding (especially towards the end of the fourteenth century) of the precincts of the abbey with houses, the parents of slums which were only cleared away in the nineteenth century, is uncertain: the normal development of property in view of the vicinity of the court was quite sufficient to account for this. The close of the fourteenth century also witnessed the settlement of the struggle of the convent for jurisdiction over St. Stephen's chapel in the palace. Founded by Edward III., this chapel had been the constant object of the abbey's jealousy. Similar struggles, characteristic of the litigious spirit of the churchmen of that age, had marked the last century and a half, viz. contests with the Bishop of Worcester over Malvern (Ware), with Archbishop Peckham (q.v.) concerning the friars (Wenlok), and with the Royal Treasurer over St. James's Hospital (Henley).

Richard II. was almost as devoted to the abbey as Henry III., and his contemporary portrait still hangs in the presbytery. His friendship led to the indifference of Henry IV., though the abbot, William Colchester * (1386-1420), was not the traitor that Shakespeare represents. Henry IV. actually died in the abbot's house, in Jerusalem Chamber; and Henry V. determined to carry out the building of the nave, which had come to a standstill. For this he promised one thousand marks a year, and put in charge of the work the well-known Richard Whitington, and Richard Harweden, a monk, afterwards abbot (1420-40). Henry V. had a magnificent funeral in the church; and his chantry, which was completed in 1441, forms a con-

[1] Mr. A. I. Dasent in *Speakers of the House of Commons,* 1911, pp. 41-9.

spicuous feature of the building. Little progress was made under Abbot Edmund Kyrton * (1440-62); but at this time John Flete wrote his history of the monastery. The abbey was not much affected by the Wars of the Roses, unless the abdication of George Norwych (1463-69) was due to political causes. His successor, Thomas Millyng (1469-74), an able man and a strong Yorkist, gave shelter to Queen Elizabeth Wydville, who took sanctuary for six months in 1470-1, in which time her son Edward V. was born. The grateful Queen founded the chapel of St. Erasmus. The story how she fled again to the abbey in 1483 for fear of Richard III. is told by Shakespeare.

Millyng pressed on the building of the nave, but was soon promoted to the see of Hereford. John Esteney * (1474-98) did the substantial work of roofing and vaulting, and finished the great west window. George Fasset * (1498-1500) contributed £600 (= £6000) to the work, and John Islip * (1500-32) completed it. Islip also built the Jesus chapel as a chantry for himself, and added the Jericho parlour and other rooms to the Abbot's House. At the same time Henry VII., the last royal benefactor, rebuilt the Lady Chapel. The sumptuous edifice, erected between the years 1503-12, was meant to contain, besides the king's own tomb, a shrine of Henry VI.; but as the king failed to obtain the canonisation of the latter, he left his body at Windsor.

Islip was the last great abbot; his successor, William Boston (1532-40), who won his appointment by bribery, made no resistance to the surrender of the monastery, which was signed by him and twenty-four monks on 16th January 1540. This number must not be taken to indicate the real strength of the convent. Up to the great plague (1348) there had generally been about sixty monks; after that the number averaged about fifty; in the sixteenth century it sank to forty. The decline in numbers was accompanied by a decay in the independent life of the convent. The abbots had become the *de facto* rulers of the convent, its officers being practically their deputies; in fact, Esteney and his successors united in themselves the offices of sacrist, cellarer, and warden of the new work. So when Henry VIII. refounded Westminster as a cathedral church with a dean and twelve prebendaries (17th December 1540) the change was not very great. The abbot became dean, taking his personal name of Benson (1540-9), six monks became prebendaries, six others petty canons, and two others students at the Universities.

Thomas Thirlby was made bishop of Westminster and given the abbot's house. His jurisdiction included the whole county of Middlesex (save the vill of Fulham), taken out of the diocese of London.

The contribution of the monastery to literature had not been great. Gilbert Crispin was its greatest writer. Sulcard and Prior Osbert of Clare also wrote in Norman times, and sermons of Abbot Laurence are extant. In the thirteenth and fourteenth centuries there were chroniclers such as John of London, John Redyng, and others—not of the first rank. Other literary names are Richard of Cirencester, William of Sudbury (fourteenth), John Wilton and John Flete (fifteenth century).

Under Edward VI. the bishopric was surrendered and suppressed, March 1550, and the county of Middlesex restored to the see of London, and by an Act of 1552 (5-6 Edw. VI. c. 11) the abbey church, with its dean and chapter, was united to the bishopric of London. Richard Cox was the dean (1549-53). The fabric of the church seems to have suffered little damage from the Reformation. The refectory and the chapel of St. Katharine were dismantled, and the other buildings made into prebendaries' houses, etc., and so for the most part preserved. But the church suffered the spoliation of its goods; the wealth of vestments, furniture, and ornaments used for divine worship disappeared, the kings taking the best treasures and the prebendaries destroying the rest. The chapter also suffered much from the greed of Somerset, but were saved from further perils by the accession of Queen Mary, when Cox made way for Hugh Weston (1553-6). In 1556 the Queen re-established the monastery by licence from Cardinal Pole (*q.v.*), 15th September 1556, under John Feckenham (*q.v.*), Dean of St. Paul's, and a man of very high character, as abbot (1556-9).

The death of Mary was followed by the suppression of the monastery, 12th July 1559, and on 21st May 1560 Queen Elizabeth refounded the collegiate church, consisting of a dean and twelve prebendaries; and her foundation, as somewhat modified in the nineteenth century, remains to-day. William Bill * (1560-1), Master of Trinity and Provost of Eton, made the first draft of the new statutes, and Gabriel Goodman * (1561-1601) organised the church on its new footing. Lancelot Andrewes (*q.v.*) (1601-5) adorned the church with his piety, but was soon raised to the episcopate. Richard Neile (1605-10), a chandler's son of Westminster, did much for the furnishing of the church, but was promoted to higher offices, dying Archbishop of York. George Montaigne (1610-17) likewise became Archbishop of York. Robert Townson (1617-20) went to Salisbury. And then we come to a name which revived the glories of a past when abbots held great offices of state. For John Williams (*q.v.*) (1620-44) was also Bishop of Lincoln and Lord Keeper of the Great Seal. He distinguished himself by spending £4500 on the repair of the outside of the church, and £2000 in founding the present library.

In 1644 Williams gave up the deanery on being made Archbishop of York, and Richard Steward (1644-51), who had been made Dean of St. Paul's in 1641, was appointed. But since 1643 the abbey had been in the hands of the Parliament. The regalia were dispersed, the church purged of superstition by the destruction of windows, pictures, organs, and Torrigiano's altar - piece in Henry VII.'s chapel; and the Westminster Assembly (1643-52) held its sittings in Jerusalem Chamber. On 18th November 1645 a committee of Parliament was appointed to govern the church, school, and almshouses of Westminster. They administered the estates with efficiency; and the deanery was let to 'Lord Bradshaw,' who died there in 1659.

The Restoration brought back the old régime and some sober piety[1] under John Earle(s) (1660-2), promoted to Worcester; John Dolben (1662-83), translated to York; and Thomas Sprat * (1683-1713). Dolben had been made Bishop of Rochester in 1666, and the deans of Westminster held the same bishopric all through the eighteenth century until Horsley, the last of the episcopal deans. Under Sprat, through the influence of the great preacher, Robert South (*q.v.*) (prebendary, 1663-1716), Sir Christopher Wren was put in charge of the restoration of the exterior of the church (1693-1723), towards which Parliament in 1697 made a grant of a part of the coal duties. South declined the deanery in 1713; then Francis Atterbury * (*q.v.*) (1713-23) infused new vigour into the life of the abbey. From his time date the school dormitory in the garden, the remodelling of the Little Cloisters, and the glass of the North Transept Rose. But Atterbury's militant spirit soon brought him into collision with the prebendaries; and becoming entangled in Jacobite intrigues, he was in 1723 found guilty of high treason by the House of Lords, deprived, and banished. Samuel Bradford * (1723-31), an opponent in the chapter,

[1] Herbert Thorndike (1661-72); Simon Patrick (1672-89); Anthony Horneck (1693-6), were prebendaries.

took his place. He witnessed the revival of the Order of the Bath, and its association with Henry VII.'s chapel in 1725. Under Joseph Wilcocks * (1731-56) the building of the church was at last brought to an end by the addition of the western towers in 1735-45. At the same time Richard Widmore, the librarian, was cataloguing the muniments of the abbey and preparing the way for the study of the history of the abbey by his *Enquiry into the Foundation* (1743) and *History of Westminster Abbey* (1751). History has little to tell of the abbey under Zachary Pearce * (1756-68), John Thomas * (1768-93), and Samuel Horsley (1793-1802), a vigorous personality, who gave up Westminster and Rochester for St. Asaph.

At the beginning of the nineteenth century the abbey had reached its lowest point—in the slovenliness of the services, in its unpopularity (a large fee being charged for admission into the church), and in the disfigurement of the fabric by monstrous memorials. But the century was to be one of gradual reform in all points. William Vincent * (1802-15), who had been headmaster of the school, enclosed Tothill Fields (Vincent Square), restored the exterior of Henry VII.'s chapel, and cleared away the monuments from the nave arches. Under John Ireland * (1815-42) the classic reredos put up in 1706 was removed (1822), and the choir screen brought to its present form (1831). In Ireland's latter years, as in those of Buckland, because of the dean's infirmities, the abbey was ruled by Lord John Thynne, subdean from 1834 to 1880, and he began the improvement of the divine worship; he introduced, *e.g.*, a weekly Eucharist and early services. In 1840 the Cathedral Act (3-4 Vic. c. 113) reduced the twelve prebendaries to six; and later Acts in 1868 (31-2 Vic. c. 114) and 1888 (51-2 Vic. c. 11) made the school independent of the abbey, and handed over the valuable estates of the church to the Ecclesiastical Commissioners in return for a fixed annual payment of £20,000.

Under Thomas Turton (1842-5) occurred the first consecration of bishops in the church in modern times. Samuel Wilberforce (*q.v.*) (1845) was dean but a few months. William Buckland * (1845-56), the geologist, devoted his attention to the pressing needs of sanitation. In 1848 the choir was rearranged and fitted with its present stalls by Blore, while the partitions which shut off the transepts were removed. In 1852 Convocation, which had sat in the abbey since the Reformation until its suppression in 1717, once more began to sit in Jerusalem Chamber. Richard Chenevix

Trench * (*q.v.*) (1856-64) initiated Sunday evening services in the nave and the custom of inviting preachers from outside the chapter.

Arthur Penrhyn Stanley * (*q.v.*) (1864-81) was fascinated by the historical interest of the abbey, and to his enthusiasm and his *Memorials of Westminster Abbey* is largely due the great hold which the abbey has upon the patriotic feelings of Englishmen and the sometimes extravagant devotion with which it is regarded by those beyond the sea. In 1867 the screen behind the altar was brought to its present condition by G. G. Scott ; but Stanley's great work on the fabric was the restoration (by Scott) of the chapter-house, which since the dissolution had been the storehouse of the national records.

George Granville Bradley * (1881-1902) carried on Stanley's traditions. He placed the finances of the abbey on a firmer footing and pressed forward the work on the fabric ; the exterior of the south side of the nave was renewed and the great north front erected by Pearson.

Joseph Armitage Robinson (1902-11) gave up the deanery for that of Wells in 1911, and was succeeded by the then Bishop of Winchester, Herbert Edward Ryle.

In 1222 the Precinct of the Abbey and the whole parish of St. Margaret, Westminster, were declared exempt from the jurisdiction of the Bishop of London, and became a Peculiar, the jurisdiction being exercised by an archdeacon (Glastonbury and St. Albans had also their archdeacons). This exempt archdeaconry continued down to the Dissolution, and when the see of Westminster was founded, 1540, the archdeacon of the abbey became, it may be assumed, the archdeacon of the diocese. When the diocese was suppressed the archdeacon continued, becoming again an archdeacon of the Peculiar jurisdiction of the abbey, and the office continued after the foundation of the collegiate church by Queen Elizabeth. Under the statutes of this fresh foundation, 1560, the archdeacon was to be elected annually by the dean and chapter, and this arrangement continues. The archdeaconry of Westminster is thus the only exempt archdeaconry surviving in the English Church.   [R. B. R.]

R. Widmore, *Enquiry*, 1713, and *Hist. of Westminster Abbey*, 1751 ; J. P. Neale and E. W. Brayley, *Westminster Abbey*, 1818-23 ; G. G. Scott. *Gleanings from Westminster Abbey*, 1863, and W. R. Lethaby, *Westminster Abbey*, 1906, for the architecture ; A. P. Stanley, *Memorials*, 1869 ; Francis Bond, *Westminster Abbey*, 1909 ; V.C.H. *London*, vol. i., contains a good history of the monastery ; J. A. Robinson, *Notes*

and Documents relating to Westminster Abbey, Nos. 1-4. 1909-11, and articles in *Archæologia*, *Proc. of Brit. Acad.*, and *Ch. Quart. Rev.*, contain a detailed and critical account of several important epochs.

WHARTON, Henry (1664-95), was son of the Vicar of Worstead, and born there, 9th November 1664. He went to a local school, but was mostly taught by his father, and so thoroughly that when he went to Caius College, Cambridge, he was soon known as 'an extraordinary young man.' He held a scholarship at Caius till 1687, and studied almost every branch of human knowledge. From 1686 he helped William Cave, the Church historian, as secretary, was ordained in 1687, assisted Tenison (afterwards archbishop) in controversy, and wrote four remarkable works of his own. In 1688 he became chaplain to Sancroft (*q.v.*), with whom he remained on affectionate terms till his death, though he did not hesitate to accept the Revolution. On 19th September 1689 he became Rector of Chartham ; he resided there from 1694, died 5th March 1695, and was buried in Westminster Abbey, with special anthems by Purcell. No English scholar of the seventeenth, and few of any, century surpassed him in industry and ability. His *Anglia Sacra* (1691), 'a collection of the lives, partly by early writers, partly compiled by himself, of the English archbishops and bishops down to 1540' (*D.N.B.*), was indeed ' a work of incredible pains,' and it was but one fruit of his incessant labours in the Lambeth Library. He left vast collections in MS., catalogues, materials for editions of mediæval writers, criticisms of other writers, etc. Sixteen volumes of these are still in the Lambeth Library. He prepared for publication the remains of Archbishop Laud (*q.v.*), by the direction of Sancroft, and many of his own books are of permanent value. Under the pseudonym of Anthony Harmer in 1693 he exposed many of the errors of Burnet's (*q.v.*) *History of the Reformation*. The service which he rendered to students of English Church history is unrivalled, for he came at a critical time, to preserve and classify manuscript materials, and to inspire a generation of antiquaries and scholars. No account of him would be complete which does not quote the eulogy of Bishop Stubbs (*q.v.*) (*Registrum Sacrum Anglicanum*, second edition, p. 6): ' This wonderful man died in 1695, at the age of thirty, having done for the elucidation of English Church history (itself but one of the branches of study in which he was the most eminent scholar of his time) more than any one before or since.' [W. H. H.]

D'Oyley, *Life of Sancroft.*

WHATELY, Richard (1787-1863), Archbishop of Dublin, was educated at Oriel College, Oxford, graduating in 1808 with a double second class. In 1811 he was elected Fellow with his close friend, John Keble (*q.v.*), and found himself associated with some of the most brilliant men of his time, the *Noetics* or Intellectuals, as they were called. Blanco White, the Anglo-Spaniard, who had passed from Romanism to the most extreme Liberal Protestantism of his day, became a member of the Common Room, and exercised a great influence over the younger men. He introduced Whately in particular to the method of the scholastic philosophy, critically treated. The Oxford Liberals of that date were acutely described by Church (*q.v.*) as 'intellectually aristocratic, dissecting the inaccuracies or showing up the paralogisms of the current orthodoxy.' In 1822 Whately delivered the Bampton Lectures on *The Use and Abuse of Party Feeling in Religion.* About the same time he published anonymously the curious skit on the critical method, *Historic Doubts relative to Napoleon Buonaparte.* After three years as Rector of Halesworth he returned to Oxford in 1825 as Principal of St. Alban Hall, where he made Newman (*q.v.*) vice-principal. With some help from Newman he wrote his *Elements of Logic* (1826). In 1828 he warmly supported, against the general opinion of Oxford, the removal of the political disabilities laid on papists, and supported the re-election of Sir Robert Peel, who had resigned his seat as burgess for the University on that question. This caused an estrangement from Newman, who was rapidly passing away from his temporary connection with Liberalism, while Whately's bent in that direction became more marked. In 1830 he was made Professor of Political Economy, and published some lectures of small value. In 1831 he was appointed Archbishop of Dublin, where he added to himself the reputation of a wit, and poured out for many years a constant stream of sermons, pamphlets, and other publications dealing with many religious and political questions, also doing admirable work as a Commissioner of National Education. In 1836 he persuaded the Prime Minister, against the advice of the Archbishop of Canterbury, to nominate his friend Hampden (*q.v.*) Regius Professor of Divinity, being thus the chief author of the confusing controversies which followed. Apart from this incident he retained his own decided Liberalism without challenging the more orthodox, and indeed made a pungent attack upon *Essays and Reviews* (*q.v.*). He died after an uneventful and most unpopular episcopate in 1863. He was a man of hard and brilliant intellect, without any touch of originality.

[T. A. L.]

E. J. Whately, *Life of Richard Whately*; Tuckwell, *Pre-Tractarian Oxford.*

WHISTON, William (1667-1752), a divine 'of very uncommon parts and more uncommon learning,' was educated at Clare Hall, Cambridge. After taking holy orders he continued to apply himself to mathematics and science. In 1703 he succeeded Sir Isaac Newton as Lucasian Professor of Mathematics, but in 1710 was deprived of his post for heresy, and banished from the University. His principal work, *Primitive Christianity Revived,* was published in 1711 to show that the accepted doctrines concerning the Persons of the Blessed Trinity were not in accordance with Scripture nor with the faith of the primitive Church, which he thought was Arianism, or, as he preferred to call it, Eusebianism. For this Convocation (*q.v.*) 'fell pretty vehemently upon him,' and the question whether it could act as a court to try him for heresy was referred to the judges, eight of whom, with the law officers, replied that Convocation had such jurisdiction, and that no Act of Parliament had taken it away. The other four maintained that since the Reformation statutes it had no such jurisdiction, but could only examine and condemn heretical tenets without convening their maintainers. On consideration Convocation followed this course with Whiston, and condemned his book, but the censure was never confirmed by the Queen. Proceedings were also taken against him in the ecclesiastical courts, but after a time were allowed to drop.

He spent the rest of his life in writing and lecturing on scientific subjects and on his theological speculations, discovering, for instance, that some prophecies in the Apocalypse had been fulfilled by Prince Eugene's campaigns. The Prince said 'he did not know he had the honour of being known to St. John,' but sent Whiston fifteen guineas. He made the acquaintance of the leading Latitudinarian divines of the time, who, however, fought shy of his 'Society for promoting Primitive Christianity.' He remained a communicant of the Church of England till 1747, when he finally left it 'as utterly incorrigible,' and joined the Baptists. He lived a simple, ascetic life, fasting till three in the afternoon on Wednesdays and Fridays. His simple, plain-spoken honesty appears in such incidents as his rebuking Queen Caroline for talking in church, and in his conduct of the many controversies into which he was led by his fanciful, ill-balanced intellect, ' much set on hunting for paradoxes,' which, however, was combined with genuine learning. It has been thought that he was in some respects the original of Goldsmith's Dr. Primrose. [G. C.]

Memoir, Historical Preface to Primitive Christianity Revived, both by Whiston himself: Burnet, *History of My Own Time*; Nichols, *Literary Anecdotes*.

WHITEFIELD, George (1714-70), evangelist, was born at the Bell Inn, Gloucester, then kept by his father (afterwards by the father of Bishop Phillpotts, *q.v.*). He describes himself as from infancy ' so brutish as to hate instruction '; and could see nothing in his early life but ' fitness to be damned.' At fifteen he became drawer at the Bell, but afterwards went back to school, and in 1732 entered Pembroke College, Oxford, as a servitor. He was attracted by the Oxford Methodists, and ordered his life after their pattern. ' I now began to pray and sing psalms thrice every day, besides morning and evening, and to fast every Friday, and to receive the Sacrament.' He did not openly join them till 1735, in which year he experienced a conversion. In 1736 he graduated B.A., and became leader of the few Methodists remaining in Oxford after the departure of the Wesleys (*q.v.*) for Georgia. He was ordained deacon by Bishop Benson of Gloucester, who hearing that Whitefield's first sermon had driven fifteen persons mad, expressed a hope that the affliction would be lasting. The story shows that his exceptional powers as a preacher were quickly recognised. Both in England and America, which he visited in 1738, crowds flocked to hear him on Sundays and week days alike. Bishop Gibson (*q.v.*) at this time described him as ' pious and well meaning but too enthusiastic.' On Christmas Day, 1738, he used extempore prayer for the first time. In January 1739 he was ordained priest. Finding the Bristol churches closed against him, he preached in the open air to two hundred colliers at Kingswood on 17th February. The daring irregularity of the act made a great impression. Within two months he was preaching to crowds of several thousands. At Moorfields and Kennington his audiences

are said to have reached fifty thousand. At these services he made collections for his proposed orphanage in Georgia, whither he returned and founded the institution in 1740. He now habitually gave up the surplice, and exchanged pulpits with dissenters, disregarding the sentence of suspension passed on him by the Church court at Charleston (said to be the first exercise of jurisdiction by a Church court in the colonies). Returning to England, 1741, he championed the cause of predestination against J. Wesley, whose provocative assumption of superiority partially excuses Whitefield's unseemly violence and use of such expressions as ' Infidels of all sorts are on your side.' The two men were soon reconciled, and were close friends till death, but the breach between Calvinists (*q.v.*) and Arminians (*q.v.*) remained unhealed. [NONCONFORMITY, V.] In 1743 the Calvinistic Methodists chose Whitefield as their moderator. Though he declared he would never leave the Church of England unless thrust out, he was not so essentially orthodox as the Wesleys.

In 1741 he married Elizabeth James, a widow ten years older than himself, whom he describes as ' neither rich in fortune nor beautiful as to her person.' But she proved a helpful wife till her death in 1768. In 1744 he came into contact with Lady Huntingdon (*q.v.*). His relations with her were marred by fulsome servility. He had not the force of character which enabled Wesley to maintain a sturdy independence of what Whitefield called ' tip-top gentility.'

Whitefield was first and foremost a preacher. His natural advantages of voice and manner were supported by wonderful eloquence, unsurpassed dramatic power, and most of all by his great sincerity and love of souls. The effect of his preaching was extraordinary, not only in producing faintings, convulsions, and ' violent agonies ' among his hearers, but in its lasting results. He visited America seven times, and effected a great revival of religion, though he justified slavery and was himself a slave-owner. For many years he is said to have preached from forty to sixty hours a week, and Toplady (*q.v.*) credits him with the delivery of eighteen thousand sermons. By 1770 he was utterly worn out. ' Lord Jesus,' he exclaimed on 29th September, ' I am weary in Thy work, but not of it'; and during a two hours' sermon preached that day to an immense multitude at Exeter, New Hampshire, he cried: ' I go to rest prepared.' At night a crowd assembled at the house where he was staying at Newbury Port, and on his way to bed he spoke to them from the stairs till his candle burnt out. At six next morning he died. He is buried at Newbury Port. [G. C.]

Journals, etc., ed. Wale ; Tyerman, *Life* ; authorities cited for Wesley.

WHITGIFT, John (1530-1604). Archbishop of Canterbury, succeeded Grindal in 1583. He thus embodied the ecclesiastical policy of the second half of Elizabeth's reign. Throughout he had her favour, and to an unprecedented extent her support. He was able therefore to bring the condition of the Church to a stability which it had not had for a long time, and which it was speedily to lose again, through its alliance with the political incompetency of the Stuarts.

Whitgift, the son of a wealthy merchant of Grimsby, was sent to school in London, and passed thence to Cambridge, where he came under the influence of Ridley (*q.v.*) as Master of Pembroke, and Bradford, the Marian martyr, as his tutor. The University claimed him in various capacities until 1577, as Professor, Master of Trinity, and Vice-Chancellor. He distinguished himself as the opponent of Cartwright (*q.v.*), the learned Puritan leader, and he showed to Parker (*q.v.*) and Burghley good evidence of his powers as a disciplinarian and an able champion of the Church platform against the growing Presbyterianism. During the last five years of his Cambridge career he was being drawn into wider spheres of activity as Prolocutor in Convocation, and the chosen advocate of the Church in the controversy that arose from the publication of the *Admonition to the Parliament*, 1572. He gave up his academic position in 1577 to become Bishop of Worcester ; and after six years of vigorous rule in that diocese, and in other capacities in the west of England, he was called to Canterbury. The same qualities distinguished his rule as archbishop, though as time went on he realised increasingly the largeness and complexity of the problems with which he had to deal ; and he tempered his executive zeal with generosity and even gentleness towards those who came into collision with him. In the early years the controversy with Puritanism was sharp ; and the malcontents, baffled in their high hopes of transforming the English Church into a novel Presbyterian organisation, spent themselves in bitter slander against Whitgift even more than against other bishops, though he stood out above a crowd of far less worthy prelates, conspicuous for fearlessness, incorruptibility, reforming zeal, and personal piety. As a bachelor and a rich

man he was spared many of the temptations of an avaricious and self-seeking age ; and his greatness is best shown in the fact that he was severest against courtiers and others in high positions who posed as Church defenders, and gentlest towards smaller and less successful men, who, honestly though perversely, were hostile to the Church polity.

As a result of the consistent and evenhanded pressure of the early years there ensued an unexampled time of quiet. The Puritans and sectaries indeed never ceased their denunciations ; they merely kept their activity in abeyance, so that in many respects it broke out again in the following century, after Whitgift was gone. But the ten years of comparative peace which comprised the second half of his rule as archbishop were of priceless value to the Church. In them there sprang into being the maturer work of the English Reformation, which in turn made possible the constructive basis laid by the Jacobean and Caroline divines : and on this the Church was to find a solid and lasting resting-place. The archbishop's own *Apologia*, in his *Answer to the Admonition*, was to make way for the far nobler work of Hooker (*q.v.*) in the *Ecclesiastical Polity*, while his purely disciplinary view of Church orders and sacraments was to make way for the more theological, spiritual, and catholic conceptions of Andrewes (*q.v.*) and his followers. It is no small part of Whitgift's glory that he encouraged all this, and enabled the younger men to make progress which he himself could hardly follow. Doctrinally he remained very Calvinistic ; the famous Lambeth Articles of 1595 showed both how fully he clung to that point of view, and also how much less narrowly he held it than most of its advocates. But he saw clearly the wide gulf that lay between the adoption of the predestinarian theology and the acceptance of the revolutionary theories of Church polity, which were equally disseminated from Geneva. The Puritans saw no such distinction ; and probably they were for that reason honestly convinced that the archbishop was dishonest and time-serving, because he held so closely to the former and so vehemently suppressed the latter. This is the best excuse that can be made for the caricature of Whitgift which they at one time almost persuaded posterity to accept as the true portrait. But in Whitgift's case, as in Laud's (*q.v.*), modern research and historical criticism have recovered the genuine picture.

With Roman Catholics the archbishop had much less to do. Politics had already

taken the decided turn which made recusancy a political rather than an ecclesiastical
question. It was only in that form that he
was to any large extent concerned with it ;
and he dealt with it, much as any other
patriot did, as though it was merely a menace
to the welfare, or even the existence, of the
Queen and her realm.

At James's accession the archbishop was
almost at the end of his tether. He took
part in the Hampton Court Conference (*q.v.*)
in 1604, but the chief conduct of it was in
the hands of Bancroft (*q.v.*), the Bishop of
London. Six weeks later Whitgift died at
Lambeth (29th February 1604), paralysed,
and only able to ejaculate at intervals *Pro
Ecclesia Dei* 'on behalf of the Church of
God.' He thus pronounced the best verdict
on his own career. Whitgift, who never
married, was buried at Croydon, where he
had lately erected and endowed the Trinity
Hospital—a combined almshouse and school,
which still, in a developed form, is the best
monument to his memory.   [W. H. F.]

Strype. *Life of Grindal*, 1718, etc : Paule,
Life, 1612, reprinted in Wordsworth's *Eccl.
Biography*, vol. iv.: Clayton, *Archbishop
Whitgift*, 1911.

WHITTINGHAM, William (? 1524-79)
Dean of Durham, was born at Chester and
educated at Brasenose College, Oxford,
becoming B.A. and Fellow of All Souls, 1545.
He became Student of Ch. Ch., 1548, but
having adopted extreme Protestant opinions
left England soon after Mary's accession,
1553. He went to reside at Frankfort
[MARIAN EXILES], June 1554, and soon
became violent on the Calvinist side, with
Knox urging the disuse of the Prayer Book.
After the defeat of his party he followed
Knox to Geneva, September 1554. Whittingham is generally believed to have been the
historian of these events in *A Brief Discourse,
etc.*, published 1575. At Geneva he was twice
elected a 'senior' or elder of the Church
(December 1555 and December 1556). In
December 1558 he was appointed deacon,
and in 1559 succeeded Knox as minister.
Whittingham was eager in the work of translating the Bible. He produced a version of
the New Testament at Geneva, June 1557,
which differs from the later well-known
Genevan version. In this last, the Genevan
Bible (the well-known 'Breeches' Bible),
Whittingham claimed the most important
share, and he remained at Geneva to complete it. It was issued in 1560, and was
in a way a manifesto of the Calvinists. It
was the first version to omit the Apocrypha.

Even after the Authorised Version of 1611
the Genevan 'Breeches' Bible was the ordinary Bible in English households. [BIBLE,
ENGLISH.] At Geneva, Whittingham turned
into metre many of the Psalms, the Ten
Commandments, and the Lord's Prayer.

Returning to England he attached himself
to the Dudleys, becoming chaplain to
Ambrose Dudley, Earl of Warwick, owing to
whose efforts, and those of his brother, Lord
Leicester, Whittingham was made Dean of
Durham, 19th July 1563. On his way north
he preached before Elizabeth at Windsor.
At Durham he remained till death, though
in 1572 Leicester wished him made Secretary
in succession to Burleigh (become Treasurer).
His career at Durham is notable for extreme
iconoclasm, various scandalous charges
against him, and the question of the validity
of his ordination. In Durham Cathedral
he removed the marble and freestone slabs
that covered the graves of the priors, and
had some used for troughs for horses and hogs,
others to build a wash-house. A holy-water
stoup he put in his kitchen, and used it for
steeping beef. His wife 'did most injuriously burn in her fire' the famous banner
of St. Cuthbert. He further protested against
' the old popish apparel ' without apparently
much success. [SMART, PETER.]

In 1578 a commission was appointed to
inquire into charges against him. Apart
from questions of his orders, these included
such things as his being defamed as an
adulterer and a drunkard, which in a document in the Record Office are endorsed
respectively as 'partly proved' and 'proved'
(*C.S. Misc.*, vi. p. 47). Professor Pollard
regards them, however, as 'too vague
to deserve acceptance.' The chief point
against Whittingham was doubtless the
question of his orders. Deaneries were not
beneficia curata, i.e. they had not the cure
of souls, and throughout the later Middle
Ages and in the sixteenth and seventeenth
centuries were held occasionally by laymen.
Such cases exist after as well as before the
breach with Rome ; less frequently after,
since they were recognised as a mediæval
abuse. In 1547, however, Sir John Mason,
Kt., was made Dean of Winchester; and the
deanery of Durham seems to have been a
favourite post for laymen, since two held it after
Whittingham—his successor, Thomas Wilson
(1580), and Sir Adam Newton, a Scot (1606-20).
Such men either did not reside, or if they did
acted merely as does the lay head of an Oxford
or Cambridge college; but Whittingham took
his position more seriously, devoted some
time and care to the school and to the music

of his Church, and occasionally celebrated the Holy Communion. The Archbishop of York (Sandys) took up the case against him, and it was alleged that even his Genevan ordination was not proved. This charge does not seem to have been made good, but the charge that he had never received episcopal ordination was not denied, and it was sought to deprive him as *mere laicus.* Lord Leicester and Whittingham's powerful friends procured a delay, but the matter was proceeding when Whittingham's death at Durham in 1579 ' rendered further proceedings unnecessary.' When his case was alleged by Travers (*q.v.*) as a reason against his own inhibition, Archbishop Whitgift replied that ' altho' his case and Mr. Travers are nothing like,' yet ' if Mr. Whittingham had lived he had been deprived without special grace and dispensation ' (Strype, *Whitgift,* Bk. III. App. No. xxx., ed. 1718). Whittingham's tomb at Durham was destroyed by the Scots, 1640— a tragic return for his destruction of the graves of his predecessors.

His wife is described in an inscription on his grave as ' sister of John Calvin,' but ' chronology makes the supposition almost impossible,' and she seems to have been a French heiress. She shared the violent disposition of her husband, for in 1583 she was charged with criminally libelling the wife of a Durham schoolmaster (*Surtees Soc.,* vol. xxi. p. 314).   [S. L. O.]

A. F. Pollard in *D.N.B.*; Life in *C.N. Misc.,* vi. (1871), reprinted, with introd., in *A Brief Discourse of the Troubles at Frankfort,* ed. Arber, 1908; Denny, *The Eng. Ch. and the Ministry of the Reformed Churches,* Ch. Hist. Soc., 1900.

WILBERFORCE, Robert Isaac (1802-57), Archdeacon of the East Riding, second son of William Wilberforce (*q.v.*), entered Oriel College, Oxford, 1820, and graduated B.A. (First Class both in Classics and Mathematics), 1824; elected Fellow (with R. H. Froude. *q.v.*) in 1826. He was ordained and became Tutor (with Froude and Newman. *q.v.*), 1828. The moral and religious guardianship exercised by the tutors over their pupils caused friction with the Provost (Hawkins). Ultimately the tutors resigned. Wilberforce became Vicar of East Farleigh, Kent, 1832; Vicar of Burton Agnes, Yorkshire, 1840; and in 1841 Archdeacon of the East Riding. He married a second time (his first wife died 1834) in 1837. He early threw in his lot with the Oxford Movement (*q.v.*), and wrote in the *Lyra Apostolica* over the signature ε, though not in the *Tracts for the Times.* He was one of the deepest theologians of his

day, and his *Doctrine of the Incarnation* (1848), *Doctrine of Holy Baptism* (1849), and *Doctrine of the Holy Eucharist* (1853) are monuments of sound learning. About 1843 he became the close friend of Archdeacon Manning (*q.v.*), who confided to him his difficulties as to the English Church. The Gorham judgment [GORHAM, G. C.] in 1851 and consequent secession of Manning caused him grave doubts, but he was reassured and helped by Keble, Pusey, Gladstone, and Bishop S. Wilberforce (*q.v.*). Doubts as to the Royal Supremacy grew upon him, and Manning was constantly urging the claims of Rome. His *Principles of Church Authority* (1854) was a sign of the step he contemplated, and he resigned his preferments, proposing to live in lay communion. He did not resign until he was assured that he would not be prosecuted for his book on the Holy Eucharist, as he was ready to stay to justify the holding of the doctrine of the Real Presence in the English Church. He entered the Roman Church in Paris, 1st November 1854, seeking to call as little attention to the step as possible for the sake of his brother the bishop and other Anglican friends. He hesitated to enter the Roman priesthood but, urged by Manning, entered the Accademia Ecclesiastica at Rome in 1855, and died while still in minor orders. His photograph to the end of the Cardinal's life hung close to the altar in Newman's private oratory at Edgbaston. R. I. Wilberforce was, in the judgment of Bishop A. T. Lyttelton. ' the greatest philosophical theologian of the Tractarians.'   [S. L. O.]

Life of Bishop S. Wilberforce; Purcell, *Life of Cardinal Manning;* Dr. Overton, *D.N.B.*

WILBERFORCE, Samuel (1805-73). Bishop, was son of William Wilberforce (*q.v.*), who, like most of the Evangelicals of that time, disapproved of Public Schools, and Samuel was educated by private tutors; but he owed less to them than to his affectionate intimacy with his father. Amid all the press of political and philanthropic work the emancipator found, or made, time to write constantly to ' my dear lamb,' as he called young Samuel. His letters display, as might be expected from their writer, both fervent piety and excellent common-sense. There is no note of Samuel's confirmation, but he seems to have made his first Communion at Easter, 1822. In addition to his spiritual counsels, Mr. Wilberforce took great pains to cultivate his son's faculty of public speech, ' causing him to make himself well acquainted with a given subject, and then speak on it, without notes, and trusting to the inspiration of the moment for suitable words.'

Samuel Wilberforce went up to Oriel College, Oxford, in 1823. He immediately joined the 'United Debating Society,' which had just been founded, and which soon afterwards developed into 'The Union.' From the first he took a prominent part in the debates, arguing on the Liberal side. He was an active and not particularly studious undergraduate, much addicted to hunting; yet he obtained a First Class in Mathematics and a Second in Classics, 1826. He had thought of going to the bar, for which his peculiar talents obviously qualified him. When he abandoned this idea he seems to have decided to seek holy orders, for Hurrell Froude (*q.v.*) wrote to him in March 1827: 'From what you said . . . I thought you seemed more reconciled to the idea of taking orders early if at all.' The cause of these uncertainties was probably the fact that he had long been in love with Emily Sargent, daughter of the Vicar of Lavington, whom in 1828 he married. In after-years he said: 'When I saw her first, she was thirteen and I was fifteen, and we never changed our minds.' Through this alliance he became eventually possessor of the Lavington estate, which belonged to Mr. Sargent's mother. He was ordained deacon by Bishop Lloyd of Oxford in Christ Church Cathedral, Advent, 1828, and was licensed to the sole charge of Checkendon, near Henley-on-Thames. He was ordained priest in 1829, and in June 1830 was appointed to the rectory of Brightstone in the Isle of Wight. As illustrating the manners and customs of the island at that date the following extract from Wilberforce's diary, describing his first Tithe Audit Dinner, is worth preserving:—'18th Jan. 1831. A good Audit Dinner; 23 people drank 11 bottles of wine, 28 quarts of beer, 2½ of spirits, and 12 bowls of punch; and would have drunk twice as much if not restrained. None, we hope, drunk.'

Even while at Checkendon he had made it clear that he held (as his father is said to have held) the doctrine of Baptismal Regeneration; and in 1833 he preached, at Bishop Sumner's Visitation, a sermon which boldly asserted 'that unbroken succession whereby those who ordained us are joined unto Christ's own Apostles.' In 1839 this friend and patron, Charles Richard Sumner, the last Prince-Bishop of Winchester, made him Archdeacon of Surrey—a preferment which carried with it a canonry of Winchester; and

in 1840 gave him the important living of Alverstoke. In 1840 also he was chosen Bampton Lecturer for 1841; and Prince Albert, who had heard him speak at an Anti-Slavery meeting at Exeter Hall, made him one of his chaplains. In 1841 he was suddenly called to undergo the great and abiding sorrow of his life. His wife died on the 10th of March. On the following day he wrote in his diary: 'May yᵉ utter darkening of my life, which never can be dispelled, kill in time all my ambitions, desires, and earthly purposes, my love of money and power and place, and make me bow meekly to Christ's yoke.'

This heavy blow fell on Wilberforce at a critical moment of his life. He was just rising into fame as an indefatigable parish priest, as a popular orator on religious platforms, as an eloquent preacher, and as a favourite at court, whither his duties as chaplain to Prince Albert often took him. He was talked of as tutor to the infant Prince of Wales, and dreaded the prospect of being called from congenial work to an office for which he felt himself unfitted. But this trial was averted, for in March 1845 he was appointed by Sir Robert Peel to the deanery of Westminster, which he accepted with misgiving. He was installed on the 9th of May, retaining the benefice of Alverstoke, and thereby drawing down on himself from the *Morning Post* the reproach of avarice. On the 14th of October Sir Robert Peel offered him 'the Bishoprick of Oxford.' There was no nonsense of *Nolo Episcopari*, asking for time to consider, consulting friends, and the like. The diary simply says: 'I had wished for this, and now that it comes, it seems *awful*. Wrote to Sir R., whose letter was remarkably cordial, and accepted.' He was consecrated on the 30th November, and enthroned in Christ Church Cathedral on the 13th December. So began the most memorable episcopate of modern times. From 1845 to 1873 the life of Bishop Wilberforce is indeed the life of the English Church, and, to no small extent, the life also of the English State.

Wilberforce had been born and brought up an Evangelical of the older, *i.e.* the more Churchman-like, school. Through his membership of Oriel he had been brought into rather close relations with both Newman (*q.v.*) and Pusey (*q.v.*), but he was never an adherent of the Oxford Movement (*q.v.*). From first to last he had an even passionate hatred of Rome, 'that great *Cloaca* into which all abominations naturally run.' Burgon (*q.v.*) wrote: 'From the phraseology and many of the conventionalities of "evangelicalism," he never, to the last hour of his life, was able to shake himself entirely free,' and probably he had not the slightest wish to do so.

From the very beginning of his episcopate to 1852 Wilberforce was engaged in almost incessant controversy with Pusey on such subjects as the Intermediate State, vows for sisters, and adaptations of Roman Catholic manuals. In all such discussions Pusey's theological and patristic learning gave him an immense advantage, while the bishop's common-sense and knowledge of the world laid bare the extreme unwisdom of some of Pusey's actions.

Meanwhile the bishop, who, though not a particularly strong man, had untiring activity of mind and body, pervaded every corner of his large and somnolent diocese. Everywhere he laboured to quicken the zeal of the clergy, to develop all the resources of the Church, to bring men of discordant views into harmony, and to raise the spiritual tone of the whole diocese. The modern conception of a bishop as a man who should be incessantly moving about, seeing with his own eyes and hearing with his own ears, grew out of the example of Bishop Wilberforce. The solemnity and pathetic earnestness of his addresses at confirmations produced a deep effect, and, together with his impressive manner in conferring holy orders, set a new standard for the public ministrations of the episcopate. He did much to promote Communities for women at Clewer and at Wantage [RELIGIOUS ORDERS, MODERN]; and, with a view to providing more adequate training for the clergy, he established, close to the palace at Cuddesdon, the theological college which afterwards became famous. [THEOLOGICAL COLLEGES.]

1847 was a decisive year in Wilberforce's life. The nomination of Dr. Hampden (*q.v.*) to the see of Hereford excited lively and widespread indignation. Thirteen of the bishops, including Wilberforce, addressed a formal remonstrance to the Prime Minister, and were well snubbed for their pains, and there the matter might have been left. Unfortunately some well-meaning busybodies resolved to impede Hampden's elevation to the bench by commencing a suit against him, in the Court of Arches, on a charge of false doctrine. As a professor in the University Hampden was exempt from episcopal control, but as Rector of Ewelme he was subject to the jurisdiction of the Bishop of Oxford. When approached by the clergy who were promoting the suit, Wilberforce declined to institute the

proceedings, but did not discourage them. The promoters then asked him to sign 'Letters of Request' to the Court of Arches, which he did, giving thereby his sanction to the commencement of the suit. He had been advised that, if he did not grant the 'Letters of Request,' a *mandamus* compelling him to sign would most certainly have been granted. In fact, he was advised that in signing the 'Letters of Request' he was merely acting ministerially, and that he had no option but to sign. But, later on, he was advised that he had the power and duty of examining into the charges contained in the letters, so as to assure himself that a *prima facie* case was made out *to his satisfaction*; or, in other words, that he could and should act judicially. Thereupon he set himself to do what he obviously had better have done before, and applied himself, 'with all the study he was master of,' to Hampden's incriminated writings, with the result that he satisfied himself of Hampden's essential soundness, and on the 24th of December he withdrew the 'Letters of Request' which he had signed on the 16th, thereby bringing the suit to an abrupt close. This lame and impotent conclusion pleased no one. Hampden declined further communications with the bishop except through his solicitor. Every one, High and Low alike, who had wished to bring Hampden to trial was furious with Wilberforce for stopping the proceedings, and the Bishop of Exeter (Phillpotts) wrote him such a rebuke as prelates seldom receive. At the same time the court and the Government, naturally incensed by Wilberforce's attempt to interfere with the appointment, were not the least placated by his sudden submission. As Lord High Almoner and as Chancellor of the Order of the Garter he was still brought into official relations with the Queen and the Prince Consort, but he was no longer the familiar friend and spiritual adviser. In 1880 Dr. Liddon (*q.v.*) wrote : 'The Hampden affair, by making him unpopular at court, was probably the greatest blessing of his life. . . . He was in a fair way to be spiritually ruined outright, and was saved by the consequences of the Hampden matter. It cut him off from the court, and from ambitious visions which had overclouded his soul; and it sent him back to his conscience and his diocese.'

In 1849 Wilberforce, reviewing the events of the year, numbers among them ' Evident withdrawal of Royal favour.' As years went on this ' favour ' was further withdrawn, and one reason, at least, for the withdrawal came to the knowledge of the present writer.

In the days of his intimacy at court Wilberforce was always urging the fitness of H. E. Manning (who had married his sister-in-law, Caroline Sargent) for a bishopric. In 1851, when Manning seceded to Rome, Prince Albert said to Wilberforce : ' You see we were right in not attending to your advice about Manning. It would have been a great scandal if an English bishop had gone over to Rome.' ' But, sir,' said Wilberforce, ' if Manning had been made a bishop he never would have gone.' There was a certain savour of worldliness and calculation in this remark which tended to shake the royal confidence, just as the affair of Hampden had roused the royal ire.

' Sent back,' as Liddon said, ' to his conscience and his diocese,' Wilberforce worked with an incredible vigour. He was the first to introduce Parochial ' Missions ' in his diocese, and the first Bishop of Oxford to make special attempts to reach the undergraduates. He did more than any other prelate to restore Convocation (*q.v.*). In the House of Lords he was a constant and effective debater whenever any measure affecting the Church came up. He played a brilliant part on the platform and in society, and as years went on he contrived to acquire a kind of primacy among English bishops. His reputation for humour was exaggerated, and he was the centre of countless anecdotes, mostly false ; but his powers of unpremeditated speech could scarcely be exaggerated. Gladstone (*q.v.*) said he was one of the three men whom he had ever known who had the greatest faculty of public speaking. His theology developed, though very slightly, in the Catholic direction, though now and then he courted popularity by rebuking the despised ritualists. None of the ' Three Schools ' trusted him very completely ; but there was a fourth school, formed chiefly of those who fell under his personal influence, and this school adored him. The Radicalism of his early youth had made way for Toryism, and Toryism again for a kind of Liberal Conservatism, in which he was a close follower of Gladstone. Unfortunately for his chances of promotion, he had offended equally the court, Lord Palmerston, and Disraeli. Accordingly he was passed over for the sees of Canterbury, York, London, and Durham. Had Gladstone become Prime Minister six weeks sooner than he did he would inevitably have sent Wilberforce to Canterbury ; but Tait was appointed by Disraeli on the 12th of November 1868, and Gladstone did not kiss hands till the 3rd of December. The first act of Gladstone's ministry was to disestablish and disendow the Irish Church. Archbishops Tait and Thomson and Bishop Wilberforce abstained from voting on the Second Reading, and in the following September Gladstone translated Wilberforce to the see of Winchester, amid disagreeable innuendoes from those who had reckoned the Bishop of Oxford as a staunch supporter of the Irish establishment. After a brief but energetic occupancy of his new diocese, Wilberforce was killed by a fall from his horse on the 19th of July 1873. He was buried by the side of his wife in Lavington Churchyard. The sincerity of his personal devotion is unquestionable, and he was, as Burgon called him, the Remodeller of the Episcopate.   [G. W. E. R.]

Lives by Ashwell and R. G. Wilberforce (3 vols.) ; by R. G. Wilberforce (1905) ; J. W. Burgon ; and oral tradition.

WILBERFORCE, William, politician and philanthropist (1759-1833). The Wilberforces spring from a place called Wilberforce, or Wilberfoss, in the East Riding. In the eighteenth century they were established in business at Hull, and there William Wilberforce, famous as the emancipator, was born. Having inherited ample wealth, he parted with his father's business as soon as he was twenty-one, and made his choice for politics. As an undergraduate at Cambridge he had been renowned for the beauty of his singing voice, and the same organ stood him in good stead when he abandoned singing for speech-making. In 1780 he was elected M.P. for Hull ; and, though his body was so small and frail that ' he looked as if a breath could blow him away,' he was at once recognised as a power in politics. His melodious tones, his grace of gesture, and his expressive play of features made him a most attractive speaker, whether on the hustings or in the House ; and these qualifications, added to the fact that he was the intimate friend of Pitt, seemed to mark him out for a great political career. In 1784 he was returned for Yorkshire as a staunch supporter of his friend the Prime Minister, and his political advancement seemed more than ever a certainty ; but there was a change at hand which altered his whole career. Let it be told in his own words. Down to this time his life had been ' not licentious, but gay,' and yet something was amiss. ' Often while in the full enjoyment of all that the world could bestow, my conscience told me that in the true sense of the word I was not a Christian. I laughed, I sang, I was apparently gay and happy, but the thought would steal across me: "What madness is all this, to continue easy in a state in which a sudden call out of the world would consign me to everlasting misery, and that when eternal happiness was within my grasp!"' In brief, he underwent an old-fashioned conversion; and, as a result of it, he 'devoted himself, for whatever might be the term of his future life, to the service of his God and Saviour.'

His conversion showed itself in very practical forms. He gave up card-playing, of which he had been very fond. He took to early rising, and did his best to fast, but found it difficult on account of his physical frailty. He stripped himself of luxuries, spent a great deal of his time in prayer and in the study of his Bible, and was a regular and most devout communicant. For a brief space he thought of abandoning politics and seeking holy orders, but was dissuaded from that course by the famous Evangelical, John Newton, who insisted that Parliament was the appointed sphere of action for a man so conspicuously endowed with Parliamentary gifts and opportunities. He therefore returned to his work in the House of Commons with greater zeal and a more determined purpose than before; and, fore-seeing the offers which his intimacy with Pitt made almost inevitable, he resolved within himself never to accept either office or a peerage. Henceforward his life was dedicated to the unrewarded service of humanity.

In 1797 he published a book which at once became famous, *A Practical View of the Prevailing Religious System of Professed Christians in the Higher and Middle Classes in the Country, contrasted with real Christianity.* It is a grave and tender appeal to consciences deadened by conventionality. It reminds them of the great realities of life and death, sin and repentance; it insists that 'faith, when genuine, always supposes repentance and abhorrence of sin'; and it calls on them 'gratefully to adore that undeserved goodness which has awakened them from the sleep of death, and to prostrate themselves before the Cross of Christ with humble penitence and deep self-abhorrence.' The book from first to last is eloquent of personal experience. It won the warm admiration of Edmund Burke; it ran through fifty editions, and it established its writer as the lay-leader of Evangelical religion. Wilberforce was Evangelical in the best and highest sense. He was no Calvinist, but proclaimed Universal Redemption. He appealed throughout to 'the Holy Scriptures, and, with them, the Church of England.'

He believed in Baptismal Regeneration, and loved a cheerful Sunday. He worked for all the causes which were then most un-fashionable—Christian Missions, the circulation of the Bible, the suppression of vice, the mitigation of the criminal code, and popular education; above all—and on this achievement his fame eternally rests—for the Abolition of the Slave Trade.

The horrors of the 'Middle Passage' had already been brought before public notice by Granville Sharp; and in 1787 a group of men whose hearts were touched by divine indignation formed the first Committee for the Suppression of the Slave Trade. Wilberforce became the Parliamentary leader of the movement, and in 1788 he induced Pitt to espouse the cause—a notable triumph of persuasive power. In 1789 Pitt moved his Resolution in favour of Abolition; but the moment was not propitious for humanitarian reform. France was in the throes of revolution; men's minds were fixed on the dangers which impended over England; and all the energy of the Prime Minister's majestic mind was absorbed in the task of safeguarding the kingdom against foreign and domestic foes. At such times of crisis moral causes fare badly, but Wilberforce and his friends were men not easily daunted. In 1792, in 1796, and again in 1804 they carried a Bill for Abolition through the House of Commons, and in each year it was defeated in the Lords. But no disappointments and no delays could damp the ardour or slacken the efforts of the abolitionists. Throughout all those dark years Wilberforce's motto was: 'This one thing I do.' He worked for the cause nine hours a day, scarcely stopping for his meals. Sometimes he was writing all night. He roused a spirit of intercessory prayer for his object among all his Evangelical connection, and at the same time conducted a public agitation up and down the country. Almost the last written words of the great John Wesley (*q.v.*) were addressed to him.

'MY DEAR SIR,—Unless the Divine Power has raised you up to be an *Athanasius contra mundum*, I see not how you can go through your glorious enterprise, in opposing that execrable villainy which is the scandal of religion, of England, and of human nature. Unless God has raised you up for this very thing, you will be worn out by the opposition of men and devils; but, if God be for you, who can be against you? Oh, be not weary of well-doing. Go on, in the name of God and in the power of His might, till even American slavery, the vilest that ever saw the sun, shall vanish away before you. That He, who has guided you from your youth up, may continue to strengthen you in this and all things, is the prayer of, dear sir, your affectionate servant, JOHN WESLEY.'

These words were written in 1791, but sixteen years of arduous fighting and diligent labour and uncomplaining endurance had to pass before the consummation of Wesley's hopes. The Act abolishing the Slave Trade passed into law in 1807, and 'the whole House of Commons rose to cheer the Member for Yorkshire, by whose devoted toil this great triumph of mercy had been achieved.' Pitt said that of all the men he knew Wilberforce had the greatest power of natural eloquence. Burke said the same, though he had only known him in the early stages of his career. Lord Brougham testified to 'the inspiration which deep feeling alone can breathe into spoken thought.' In Wilberforce the gift of persuasion was blended with a turn for sarcasm, which, as a rule, was sedulously controlled; but those who heard it long remembered his reply to a scoffing opponent who had taunted him with a facetiousness not in keeping with his religious profession. 'I submit that a religious man may sometimes be facetious; and I would remind the Hon. Member that the irreligious do not necessarily escape being dull.' To these gifts he added another not less valuable to a Parliamentarian. 'If there is any one,' said Canning, 'who thoroughly understands the tactics of debate, and knows exactly what will carry the House along with him, it is certainly my Hon. friend.' His high character and absolute freedom from self-seeking gave his words a moral weight more impressive than even eloquence; and, in his later years, Sydney Smith (q.v.) declared roundly that he 'could do anything he liked with the House.' Such as he was in public life, such also he was in private. Madame de Staël, after making his acquaintance, said that she had always heard that Mr. Wilberforce was the 'most religious man in England,' but she had never before known that he was also the most agreeable. 'No one,' said another admirer, 'touched life at so many points.' 'He always,' said a third, 'had the charm of youth.' When once the Slave Trade was abolished, the friends of humanity determined to abolish Slavery itself. After moving in 1824 for total abolition, Wilberforce said: 'I have delivered my soul.' Age and infirmity were increasing on him, and he retired from Parliament, leaving what remained of the fight to younger

and stronger men. At a public meeting of his supporters in 1830 he said: 'The object is bright before us; the light of heaven beams on it, and is an earnest of success.' The anticipation was justified. In the session of 1833 the first Reformed Parliament passed the Act which abolished Slavery, and 'the Father of the movement lived just long enough to bless God that the object of his life had been attained.' He died on the 29th of July 1833, and the two Houses of Parliament followed his body to its resting-place in the Abbey. [G. W. E. R.]

WILFRID (634-709), Bishop of York, son of a Northumbrian thegn, had an unkind stepmother, and when about fourteen left his home and went to Oswy's (q.v.) court, where Queen Eanflaed befriended him. He studied at Lindisfarne, without receiving the tonsure, and in 653 set out for Rome in company with Benedict Biscop (q.v.). There he studied the Gospels and the rules of the Catholic Church. Returning, he stayed three years at Lyons with the archbishop, who gave him the Roman tonsure. In 658 (?) the archbishop was slain, and Wilfrid well-nigh shared his fate. He returned to Northumbria convinced of the excellence of the Roman usages. Alchfrid, the under-king of Deira, was of like mind; he gave him land for a monastery at Stamford, and later, having expelled the Scotic monks from Ripon, made him abbot there. He was ordained priest by Agilbert, the dispossessed Bishop of Dorchester, probably early in 664, and at that time was prominent in the Roman party in Northumbria. Oswy in 664 held a conference at Whitby on the questions in dispute between the Roman and Scotic parties, at which Wilfrid, on behalf of Agilbert, upheld the Roman calculation of Easter against the Scotic Bishop Colman. Oswy decided in favour of the Roman usage, and Colman and those of his party who refused to accept his decision left Northumbria. Wilfrid was chosen Bishop of the Northumbrians, with his see at York, and as he held bishops ordained by the Scots to be uncanonical, he received consecration from Gaulish bishops at Compiègne. He lingered in Gaul, and Oswy in 666 gave his bishopric to Chad (q.v.). On his way home his ship was stranded on the Sussex coast, and he incurred some danger from the heathen people. Finding his see filled he retired to Ripon, and did work as a bishop both in Mercia and Kent. When Chad (q.v.) vacated York in 669 he regained his bishopric. He restored his cathedral church and built noble churches at Ripon and Hexham, worked diligently, was widely popular, and though wealthy and magnificent was personally abstemious.

In 678 Archbishop Theodore (*q.v.*), in pursuance of his system of subdividing dioceses, and in conjunction with Egfrid, the Northumbrian King, divided Wilfrid's vast diocese without his consent, leaving him only the greater part of Deira. He could obtain no redress, for Egfrid was his enemy, and he therefore appealed to the Pope, and set out for Rome. Theodore consecrated bishops for Bernicia, Lindsey, and the whole of Deira, and thus deprived Wilfrid of York. On his way to Rome Wilfrid preached the Gospel in Frisia and baptized many. His journey was dangerous, for Egfrid sought to have him slain, or delivered up to him, in Gaul, in Frisia, and in Lombardy. At Rome Pope Agatho and his council decreed in 679 that the whole of his former bishopric should be restored to him. On his return Egfrid put him in prison, and finally confined him straitly at Dunbar, until in 681 the King's aunt, Ebbe, procured his release. Egfrid caused other Christian kings to refuse him refuge, and he went to the heathen South Saxons and evangelised them, founding a monastery at Selsey, which became the seat of the South Saxon bishopric. [CHICHESTER, SEE OF.] Thence he sent a mission, which converted the Isle of Wight. After the death of Egfrid, Theodore was reconciled to him, and in 686-7 he was restored, though only to York, Hexham, and the abbacy of Ripon.

In 691 Aldfrith, Egfrid's successor, demanded his assent to Theodore's partition of his original diocese, and contemplated taking Ripon from him. He resisted, was banished, and took refuge in Mercia, where he administered the diocese of Leicester. He appeared before a council of the whole Church at Estrefeld, probably Austerfield, in 702, could get no redress, was excommunicated, and appealed to the Pope. He journeyed to Rome on foot, though nearly seventy, visiting Willibrord (*q.v.*) on his way, and in 704 John VI. urged the King and Archbishop Bertwald to come to an agreement with him; English resistance made John take a less peremptory course than Agatho. After Aldfrith's death a reconciliation was effected at a council of the Northumbrian Church held on the Nidd in 705, and Wilfrid was adjudged the bishopric of Hexham and the monastery of Ripon. He was ill in 708; he died at Oundle on 3rd October 709, and was buried at Ripon. He was a man of holy life and signal ability, and was full of missionary zeal; if he loved

power and wealth he used them for the good of the Church. [w. h.]

Bede: *Life* by Eddius, one of Wilfrid's clergy, in *Historians of York*, R.S., which Bede evidently used, but as to its value see *E.H.R.*, vi. 535.

WILKINS, David (1685-1745), scholar, was born of German parents, whose name of Wilke he anglicised as Wilkins. After studying in many countries he was ordained in the English Church, and was appointed by Archbishop Wake (*q.v.*) librarian at Lambeth. He also received various minor preferments. He was an orientalist and antiquary of great learning. His best known work is the *Concilia Magnae Britanniae*, a collection of documents bearing on the constitutional history of the English Church from the earliest times to 1717. It was based on the earlier and much smaller work of Spelman (*q.v.*). Published in 1737, this 'magnificent monument of learning and industry' still remains a standard work of reference. [G. C.]

Nichols, *Literary Anecdotes* and *Illustrations*.

WILLIAM, St., of Norwich (1132-44). Apart from a few meagre notices in chronicles (one in the *A.-S. Chronicle* being the earliest in date), our source of information about this St. William is confined to his *Life and Miracles*, in seven books, written before 1175 by Thomas of Monmouth, a monk of Norwich Cathedral Priory. It is preserved in a single manuscript coeval with the author, now in the University Library, Cambridge.

It has a special importance as being the starting point of the long and disastrous series of legends of 'ritual murders' of Christian children by Jews.

St. William was the child of Wenstan, a Norfolk farmer, and Elviva. The usual premonitory vision of his future greatness and the usual marks of early sanctity are related. In 1140 or 1141 he was apprenticed to a skinner, and went to live in Norwich. Here he attracted the notice of the Jews. On the Monday before Easter of 1144 (20th March) a man who professed to be the cook of the Archdeacon of Norwich appeared at his mother's door, and asked to be allowed William's services as kitchen-helper. Permission was extorted from the reluctant mother by the help of three shillings. William went off with the man, was traced to a Jew's house, and never seen again alive. Thomas proceeds to relate what was done to him, but it rests upon the most shadowy evidence. The boy was kindly treated by the Jews until after the synagogue service on the Wednesday

(22nd March). Then they gagged and bound
him, tormented him with thorn pricks, bound
and nailed him by way of crucifixion to
timbers in the house, and finally pierced his
side, and poured boiling water over the body
to stanch the bleeding. Maundy Thursday
was spent in deliberating how to dispose of
the body, and on Good Friday it was carried
to Thorpe Wood.

The body was discovered—owing to a
miraculous light which shone over Thorpe
Wood—on Easter Eve, and was buried where
it was found. Then came a delay of some
weeks, until the synod of the clergy of the
district met. There Godwin Sturt, the boy's
uncle, made a formal accusation of the Jews.
Popular feeling was excited against them,
and they took refuge in the castle precincts,
under the protection of the sheriff. On
24th April the body was translated to the
monks' cemetery, adjoining the cathedral.
Miracles began to take place, and William's
career as a saint was inaugurated There
was, however, a strong party, even within the
monastery, which refused to acknowledge his
claims. At first it seems to have been headed
by the prior, Elias (d. 1150). As time went
on resistance died away. St. William was
successively translated to the chapter-house
(1150), to a place near the high altar (1151),
and to the chapel of the martyrs (1154).
At the period of the Dissolution he had a
chapel under the choir-screen.

A considerable portion of Thomas's
narrative deals with the disturbances to
which the supposed martyrdom of William
gave rise.

He dwells at great length also upon the
evidence of the martyrdom. This, as has
been said, is of the weakest kind. The one
fact which is probably to be relied upon is
that the boy William's body was found in
Thorpe Wood, and that he had been murdered.
But one of Thomas's 'arguments' is of extreme interest and importance in its bearing
on the belief in Jewish 'ritual murders.' He
was informed by a Cambridge Jew, Theobald,
who subsequently became a monk in Norwich
Priory, that it was written that the Jews
could never obtain their freedom or return to
their fatherland without the shedding of
human blood. The chiefs of the Spanish
Jews therefore assembled annually at Narbonne, and cast lots to determine what country
should furnish the victim for the year. Lots
were cast again in the capital town of the
selected country, and the city thus chosen
had to provide the sacrifice.

The church historian Socrates (vii. 16) is
the first to record anything resembling the

mediæval legends of child murder. His
instance took place at Inmestar in Syria
about A.D. 415, and was apparently an
accidental occurrence. The next instance is
that of St. William, which is speedily followed
by others from Gloucester (1160?), Orleans
and Blois (1171), Pontoise (1179), Bury St.
Edmunds (1181), Huntingdon (1181), Winchester (1192). Of the many subsequent
cases the most famous in England was that
of little St. Hugh of Lincoln in the thirteenth
century. Among the Continental child
martyrs St. Werner of Bacharach, St. Simon
of Trent, and St. Andrew of Rinn in the Tyrol
may be named. The belief in ritual murders
is by no means extinct at the present day in
Eastern Europe. In the very large majority
of cases the accusation has been made with the
object of stirring up the 'Judenhetze,' or of
gratifying private grudges. No practice even
distantly countenancing the belief has ever
been sanctioned by the Jews. There may be
a small residue of cases in which superstition
or insanity has actually prompted the murder
of a Christian child by a Jew ; but we know
of none for which good evidence can be
produced.   [M. R. J.]

M. R. James and A. Jessopp, *St. William of
Norwich.*

WILLIAMS, Isaac (1802-65), divine and
poet, was educated at Harrow and Trinity
College, Oxford. He came up a finished
Latin scholar and first-rate cricketer, with no
care for religion. 1822 he became Scholar,
and 1823 won the Latin verse prize, and came
to know J. Keble (*q.v.*), with whom he went
to read at his curacy at Southrop, near
Fairford, and to Keble he felt he owed his
soul. R. I. Wilberforce (*q.v.*) and R. H.
Froude (*q.v.*) were with him at Southrop.
He took no honours owing to overwork. He
became Fellow, 1831, and Tutor, 1832, having been ordained deacon, 1829, and worked
as curate to T. Keble at Windrush. On
returning to Oxford he became Newman's
friend and curate at St. Mary's through
R. H. Froude, who brought them together.
He threw himself heartily into the Oxford
Movement (*q.v.*), wrote in the *Lyra Apostolica*
(where his poems are signed ζ) and in the
Tracts for the Times. The title of one of his
tracts, No. 80, *On Reserve in Communicating
Religious Knowledge*, published 1839, caused
a disturbance 'like the explosion of a mine.'
Bishops denounced it (sometimes without
reading it). Its object was to prevent sacred
words and phrases (especially concerning the
Atonement) being used at random; but its
title suggested ' a love of secret and crooked

ways.' In 1841 Williams was a candidate for the Poetry Professorship, vacated by J. Keble. There was much bitterness, and Williams withdrew, his supporters' promises being six hundred and twenty-three against nine hundred and twenty-one for his opponent. In 1842 Williams, distrustful of a new party in the Movement, retired to Bisley, married, and devoted himself to preparing his well-known *Devotional Commentaries.* Almost alone of the Tractarians he corresponded with Newman after 1845. Newman stayed with him in 1865, and Williams insisted on driving him to the station, which caused an attack of illness from which he died. 'He has really been a victim,' Newman wrote, 'of his old love for me.' Williams began a series of *Plain Sermons* in 1839, and represented the more moderate and old-fashioned churchmanship. All his life he remained in close touch with Dr. Pusey (*q.v.*) and Mr. Keble. It was tragic that so gentle and saintly a scholar should have been the centre of two of the heaviest storms (1839 and 1841) which overtook the Movement in which he shared. His poems are still read, and his hymns are in common use.　　　　　　　　　　　[S. L. O.]

Autobiography ; Church, *Oxford Movement.*

WILLIAMS, John (1582-1650), Archbishop of York, born at Conway, and educated at St. John's College, Cambridge, was an ecclesiastical statesman of the seventeenth century. Ordained in 1605, he was speedily advanced through royal favour, held many benefices, and became Dean of Westminster in 1620. His learning, caution, and ability to see both sides of a question fitted him to be an adviser of James I., whom he accompanied to Scotland when the Church was being slowly restored to its former position. He was made Lord Keeper in place of Bacon in 1621, being advanced at the same time to the see of Lincoln, as the profits of the secular office were much diminished.

On the accession of Charles I. the Great Seal was taken from him, and he retired to his diocese. In 1627 he took part in a controversy of the greatest importance. The Vicar of Grantham and some of his parishioners differed about the position of the Holy Table. Williams settled the question against the vicar, and decided, according to injunction and canon, that it should not be placed 'altarwise' at the east end. He gave a similar decision at Leicester, and wrote a book, *Holy Table, Name and Thing,* in 1636, which was answered by Heylin (*q.v.*), Laud's chaplain. The

archbishop offered him another bishopric, and wished to make peace on the withdrawal of the book and acknowledgment of other charges which had been laid against him. The bishop had experienced the usual fate of fallen ministers, had been heavily fined, in 1637 was imprisoned in the Tower, and in 1639 was in further trouble, being again fined for libel against Laud. He recovered his influence and power for a short period after his release at the beginning of the Long Parliament. He was the chairman of the committee appointed to inquire into innovations and to reform the Church. Their deliberations are of value upon one controversial question of to-day, for they considered 'whether the Rubrique should not bee mended when all Vestments in them of Divine Service are now commanded which were used 2 Edw. VI.' In the debates upon episcopacy he also tried to play the part of moderator, proposing that assistants should be appointed to help the bishop in exercise of jurisdiction and ordination.

In 1642 the King appointed him Archbishop of York, but he was unable to do more than visit York for his enthronement. He joined the King in 1644 at Oxford, and at the close of the war made the best terms he could, and lived in retirement in North Wales until his death. He was a generous benefactor to his college. He was a friend to N. Ferrar (*q.v.*) at Little Gidding, which was in his diocese, and restrained Ferrar's nieces from taking life vows; but he is specially remembered for his disingenuous advice to Charles I. hesitating to sign the Attainder of Strafford, to remember that he had two consciences —public and private.　　　　　　　[B. B.]

WILLIBRORD (658 ?-739), Archbishop of Utrecht, son of Wilgils, a Northumbrian, who became an anchorite, was educated in Wilfrid's monastery at Ripon. When twenty he went to Ireland for the sake of learning, and abode twelve years with Egbert, the organiser of missions. Egbert sent him in 690, in his thirty-third year, with eleven companions on a mission to Frisia. Finding that Radbod and his people would not be converted, they went to the Frank, Pippin of Heristal, who had subdued part of the country, and at his invitation preached to his new subjects in 'Hither Frisia,' the Meuse district. Willibrord went to Rome, obtained the approval of Pope Sergius I. for his work, and returned with many relics. Though successful with the conquered people, he could do little with the independent Frisians, who were constantly at war with the Franks; he visited the Danes,

and took off with him thirty youths to educate, and in Heligoland he violated the sacred
places of the deity of the island. For this
act he was brought before Radbod ; one of
his companions was martyred, but Willibrord's undaunted courage excited the
admiration of Radbod, and he spared his life.
In 695 he again visited Rome, and on 22nd
November Sergius consecrated him as archbishop of the Frisians. Pippin assigned him
Utrecht as the place of his see ; he consecrated
bishops, founded monasteries, built churches,
and ordained priests for them with separate
cures. In 703 or 704 he received a visit from
Wilfrid (*q.v.*), who had preached in Frisia before him. Pippin's son and successor, Charles
Martel, held him in honour, and he baptized Charles's son Pippin, afterwards King.
When his strength failed he consecrated a
bishop as his coadjutor. He died at Epter-
nach, one of the monasteries he had founded,
on 6th or 7th November, probably in 739.

[w. h.]

Bede, *H.E.* ; two *Lives*, prose and verse, by
Alcuin. See *Mon. Alcuin.*, ed. Jaffé.

WILSON, Daniel (1778-1858), fifth Bishop
of Calcutta, eldest son of Stephen Wilson, a
prosperous silk manufacturer. He left school
at fourteen to enter an uncle's office in London,
and though trained in a strictly Evangelical
home led a careless life until 1796, when he
was converted. He desired ordination ; his
father refused consent, but finally gave way,
and Wilson entered St. Edmund Hall, Oxford
(then the Evangelical centre), 1798. He
graduated B.A., 1802 ; won the English
Essay (May 1803) on Common-Sense, which
provoked a Head to say to his Vice-Principal :
' So common-sense has come to Edmund Hall
at last.' ' Yes,' he replied, ' but not yet to the
other colleges.' Wilson was examined formally
for his M.A. degree, 1802, and took it, 1804.
He was ordained as curate to Richard Cecil at
Chobham, Surrey. 1801 he returned to Oxford
as assistant Tutor (1804-7) and Vice-Principal
(1807-12) of St. Edmund Hall, but was also
curate, and after 1811 minister, of St. John's,
Bedford Row. At Oxford he was very stiff
in enforcing University regulations (as the
wearing of bands), but was an excellent
tutor, and the Hall flourished under him.
His chapel in London soon became the headquarters of the Evangelicals. As Vicar of
Islington (1824) he introduced morning
prayers on Wednesdays and Fridays, and
saints' days and early Eucharists. He was one
of the earliest Evangelicals to be made bishop,
being consecrated to Calcutta, 1832. Arriving in India, 5th November 1832, he soon

made himself felt, was indefatigable in
visitations, built a new cathedral (1839-47),
improved the palace, and was a firm if masterful ruler. He regarded the ' mild and, I hope,
firm Churchmanship, which I have maintained
all my life at home,' as ' of infinite importance.' During his twenty-five years in India
Wilson only returned to England once. He
violently opposed the Oxford Movement,
which he regarded as the work of ' the great
spiritual adversary.' Despite narrowness of
view he was a devoted bishop. He died at
Calcutta, and was buried beneath the altar
of his cathedral.   [s. l. o.]

Life, 2 vols., by Bateman ; *Family Letters*,
ed. by his son ; Gladstone, *Gleanings*, vii.

WILSON, Thomas (1663-1755), Bishop of
Sodor and Man, of a middle-class family of
Burton, Cheshire, was educated at Trinity
College, Dublin, ' whither most of the young
gentlemen of Lancashire and Cheshire were
at that time sent.' He was intended for the
medical profession, and throughout life
delighted to act as a physician to the poor ;
but was persuaded to seek holy orders, and
in 1687 became curate to his uncle, Richard
Sherlock, at Newchurch Kenyon (Lancs).
In 1692 he became chaplain to the ninth
Earl of Derby, and, his income being now
£50, he devoted a fifth of it to pious uses
instead of a tenth as before, a proportion
which in later life he increased, ultimately to
more than a half. In 1697 Lord Derby
' forced ' on him the bishopric of Sodor and
Man. He was consecrated, 16th January
1698, and installed in St. German's Cathedral, 11th April. The income of the see
being only about £300, Lord Derby offered
him the living of Baddesworth, Yorkshire, *in
commendam*, which he refused, having made
resolutions against plurality and non-residence.

The Church in the Isle of Man (*q.v.*) not being
bound by English Acts of Parliament, Wilson
was free to rule it according to ecclesiastical
law. He held an annual synod of his clergy,
in which in 1704 he promulgated ten constitutions dealing with the duties of the
clergy, church discipline, and education.
They were approved by the civil power, and
it was said of them that ' the ancient discipline
of the Church' might be found ' in all its
purity in the Isle of Man.' Wilson was
active in the exercise of discipline (*q.v.*),
inflicting public penance for immorality,
slander, perjury, profanity, witchcraft, and
other offences. Accused persons were allowed
to clear themselves, if they could, by compurgation, and penitents were publicly

absolved and reconciled to the Church. His jurisdiction was supported by the civil power with fine and imprisonment. His excommunication involved practical outlawry. Slanderers were made to wear ' the bridle,' and prostitutes dragged through the sea after a boat. In 1716 an excommunicated woman appealed to the Lord of the Isle, and Wilson, refusing to appear in answer, was fined £10, which was remitted in 1719, for as Man belonged to the province of York by 33 Hen. VIII. c. 31, the appeal should have been to the archbishop. Further conflicts with the civil jurisdiction followed, Wilson being opposed by Horne, governor of the island, whose wife he sentenced to do penance for slander in 1721; and by his archdeacon, Horrobin, whom in 1722 he suspended for preaching false doctrine. Horrobin appealed to the governor, who fined Wilson and his vicars-general and imprisoned them in Castle Rushen on St. Peter's Day, 1722, to the great distress of the people, who assembled in crowds beneath the prison window, whence the bishop blessed and exhorted them. He petitioned the King in Council, on whose order he was released, 31st August. The dampness of the prison had crippled his fingers, ' so that he was constrained to write ever after with the whole hand grasping the pen.' The case was eventually decided in his favour in 1724, when he refused to accept the bishopric of Exeter as compensation. The repression of church discipline by the civil authority continued, and though some offenders voluntarily submitted to penance, and ecclesiastical censures on the clergy were frequent, the discipline as a whole decayed in Wilson's later years.

During his episcopate of fifty-seven years Wilson watched ever the material as well as the spiritual interests of his people with patriarchal care. His *Principles and Duties of Christianity* (1699) was the first book printed in Manx. He favoured the principles of the Revolution, but was a High Churchman in doctrine as well as in his views of Church authority. He broke down what he called ' the bad custom of having the Lord's Supper administered in country parishes only three times a year.' He allowed dissenters (presumably visitors to the island, as all its inhabitants were Church people) to sit or stand at Communion. His views on marriage were usually strict, and he abhorred the union with a deceased wife's sister as incest ; but in 1698 he allowed a man who petitioned him for leave to remarry, on the ground that his wife had been transported, ' to make such a choice as shall be most for your support

and comfort.' He was an early supporter of the S.P.C.K. and S.P.G., wrote in support of missions, and drew up a scheme for the training of missionaries. He kept up ' the old custom of the island of approaching the bishop on one knee'; and at Kirk Michael the congregation used to wait kneeling outside the church for his blessing. The veneration with which his humility, sweetness of temper, and devout piety were regarded spread far beyond the island. Cardinal Fleury sent him a message that ' they were the two oldest, and, as he believed, the two poorest bishops in Europe.' In 1749 he accepted a dignity offered him by the Moravian Church. Even in the streets of London he was surrounded by crowds crying: ' Bless me too, my lord.' Queen Caroline said at his approach : ' Here is a bishop who does not come for a translation ' ; and George II. specially asked his prayers. Ninety-nine of his sermons were published, and his *Instruction for the Lord's Supper* and *Sacra Privata* have remained popular devotional works. [G. C.]

Lives by Cruttwell, 1781 ; Stowell, 1819; and Keble (prefixed to *Works* in Lib. Anglo-Cath. Theol., 1863) ; Moore, *Hist. Isle of Man.*

WINCHESTER, See of. The kingdom of Wessex was one of the last of the Old English states to embrace Christianity. In 635 its aged King Cynegils was baptized by Birinus (*q.v.*) at the persuasion of his suzerain, Oswald (*q.v.*) of Northumbria. At this time it contained not only the regions south of Thames from the border of Kent as far as the Mendips, but the land of the ' Chilternsaetas ' beyond Thames, the modern counties of Oxfordshire and Buckinghamshire. Cynegils at his baptism conferred on Birinus (*q.v.*) the town of Dorchester-on-Thames, which was the residence of the first three bishops of the West Saxons. Coenwalch (643-71), the son and successor of Cynegils, remained for some years a heathen, till he learnt Christianity, in a moment of defeat and exile, at the court of the pious Anna, King of the East Angles (645). On his restoration he took Birinus as his teacher, and brought over his whole kingdom to the faith (648). At the death of Birinus (650) he invited from the Continent, and placed in his stead at Dorchester, Agilberct, a Frankish bishop. A few years later Coenwalch, not agreeing well with Agilberct, proceeded to cut up the bishopric of the West Saxons into two parts, leaving the Frank at Dorchester, and installing a subject of his own, Wini, as bishop at Winchester.

But this division, which seemed to foreshadow the later see of Winchester, was not to continue. Agilbert resigned his see and departed. Wini was expelled from Winchester by his master after three years, and Wessex was actually destitute of a bishop when Theodore (*q.v.*) became archbishop in 669. One of the new primate's first acts was to persuade Coenwalch to restore Agilbert to his place; but when the King besought him to return, the expelled bishop (who had meanwhile been elected to the important see of Paris) refused to recross the Channel, but sent in his stead his nephew Lothere (Eleutherius), whom Theodore and Coenwalch consented to receive.

After the death of Coenwalch (672) Wessex fell into decay and disunion for some years, and Wulfhere of Mercia seized on the lands north of Thames, and perhaps on Surrey also. Bishop Hedde, since Dorchester had become Mercian soil, retired to Winchester, which remained from this time onward the permanent residence of the bishops of Wessex. The lost lands became for a short time a new Mercian bishopric of Dorchester, which only lasted, however, for some twenty-five years. The rest of the Wessex country was ruled as a single see by Hedde till his death in 704. King Ine, at the counsel of Archbishop Bertwald, divided it into two dioceses— Winchester retaining the parts east of the forest of Selwood (Hants, Surrey, Berks, and part of Wilts), while the new bishopric of Sherborne [SALISBURY, SEE OF] took over the western regions. In 931 King Edward the Elder and Archbishop Plegmund took up the old policy of Archbishop Theodore, and began to subdivide the unwieldy sees. Berkshire and Wiltshire were taken from Winchester and formed into a new diocese, that of Ramsbury. This left Frithstan, the twenty-third Bishop, in charge of a see whose limits were not to be varied for nearly six hundred years.

All through Norman and Plantagenet times the great and wealthy see of Winchester, held by a long series of great prelates, of whom a vast number became chancellors of the realm, preserved the exact limits left to it in 931. In 1480 Bishop Rotherham of Lincoln transferred the precincts of Magdalen College, Oxford, to the diocese of Winchester. This transference was confirmed by a Bull of Sixtus IV., 1481. The arrangement still subsists. In 1499 the Channel Islands were transferred to Winchester from Salisbury, but the authority of the Bishop of Winchester in them does not seem to have been fully established till the time of Elizabeth.

In 1845 the Ecclesiastical Commissioners by Order in Council of 8th August 1845 transferred to Canterbury the Surrey parishes of Addington, Croydon, and the district of Lambeth Palace, so as to give the archbishop territorial jurisdiction in his own two palaces. By the same Order the populous regions of South London were to be transferred to London on the next avoidance of the see of Winchester. But before this order took effect it was repealed by Act of Parliament (1863, 26-7 Vic. c. 36). In 1877, in consequence of the establishment of the new see of St. Albans (*q.v.*), Rochester was compensated for its loss of Essex by being given the parts of Surrey which lay near to its border. Instead of using old ecclesiastical boundaries, the Act which made the change took a line derived from political divisions, giving Rochester the land comprised in the Parliamentary constituencies of East and Mid-Surrey, a line by no means coinciding with the old boundary between the two great old Surrey rural deaneries of Ewell and Stoke, but comprising practically the whole of South London.

Winchester, however, still remains one of the largest English dioceses, consisting of Hants, West Surrey, and the Channel Islands, a total area of 1,386,381 acres, with a population of 1,124,603, and containing 571 benefices served by 1021 clergy.

In the Middle Ages Winchester was not only one of the largest but also the wealthiest of the English bishoprics. According to an old saying attributed to Bishop Edington, 'Canterbury had the higher rack, but Winchester had the fuller manger.' In the *Taxatio Ecclesiastica* (*q.v.*) of 1291 the bishop is credited with an income from spiritualities and temporalities combined of £2977, 19s. 10d. In the *Valor Ecclesiasticus* of Henry VIII. the total has grown by about a third—being, spiritualities £154, 5s. 3½d., and temporalities £4037, 19s. 11d., a total of £4192, 5s. 2½d. It is stated by Ecton (1711) to be rated for first-fruits at £3193, 4s. 7¼d. The see lost much at the Reformation, but by the appreciation of landed property in the seventeenth and eighteenth centuries was considered to be worth about £10,000 annually in 1836. The Ecclesiastical Commissioners in 1851 fixed its revenue at £7000, but deductions having been made for the benefit of other sees, when East Surrey was taken out of it, the annual value is now £6500.

The bishop is Prelate of the Order of the

Garter and Provincial Chancellor of Canterbury. The first complete map of England divided into rural deaneries is that which can be compiled from the *Taxatio* of Pope Nicholas IV. (1291). In this we find Winchester with two archdeaconries, those of Winchester (first mentioned, 1142) and Surrey (first mentioned, c. 1120), and twelve deaneries — nine in the archdeaconry of Winchester, viz. Andover, Basingstoke, Alton, Droxford, Winchester, Fordingbridge, Somborne, Southampton, and Wight, and only three in Surrey, those of Guildford (or Stoke), Ewell, and Southwark. These divisions have been little altered. In 1878 the old rural deanery of Stoke, of unwieldy size, was cut up into more handy units, Farnham, Dorking, and Godalming. A new archdeaconry of the Isle of Wight was created in 1874. Guernsey and Jersey are peculiars under their respective deans, and are not in any archdeaconry. Bishops suffragan have been appointed of Guildford, 1874; Southampton, 1895; and Dorking, 1905.

The early chapter of the minster consisted of secular canons. They were expelled by Bishop Aethelwold in 964, who substituted forty Benedictine monks under a prior, the diocesan himself being the titular abbot. In 1539 the last prior, William Kingsmill, surrendered the monastic lands to Henry VIII., and was made the first dean under the Reformation settlement. The new foundation consisted of the dean and twelve prebendaries. Seven prebends were suspended by the Cathedrals Act, 1840 (3-4 Vic. c. 113).

BISHOPS OF THE WEST SAXONS

1. Birinus (*q.v.*), A.D. 634-50.
2. Agilberct, 650-62; a Frank by birth; resided at Dorchester; quarrelled with King Coenwalch, and retired to France.
3. Wini, 662-5; set up by Coenwalch at Winchester; expelled by him three years later, and retired to London, where he became bishop. The see vacant five years.
4. Lothere (Eleutherius), 670-6; a Frank, and nephew of Agilberct.
5. Hedde, 676-705; permanently made Winchester the see-town of the West Saxon diocese.

BISHOPS OF WINCHESTER

6. Daniel, 705-44; the West Saxon diocese was divided on his consecration.
7. Hunfrith, 744.
8. Kineheard, 754.
9. Aethelheard, 759.
10. Ecgbald, 778.
11. Dudda, 781.
12. Kinebert, 785.

13. Ealhmund, 803.
14. Wigthegn, 814-25.
15. Herefrith, 825.
16. Eadmund, 833.
17. Eadhun, 836.
18. Helmstan, 836.

The dates from Dudda to Helmstan are not quite certain.

19. St. Swithun (*q.v.*), 852.
20. Ealfrith, 862; tr. to Canterbury, 872.
21. Tunberht, 872; d. 879.
22. Denewulf, 879; a protégé and councillor of King Alfred; d. 909.
23. Frithstan, 909.
24. Beornstan, 931.
25. Aelfheah 'the Bald,' 934; uncle of St. Dunstan (*q.v.*), of whom he was the early patron.
26. Elfsige, 951; tr. to Canterbury, and perished in the Alps while on a journey to Rome, 959.
27. Brithelm, 960.
28. Aethelwold, 963; Abbot of Abingdon; a great friend and ally of St. Dunstan; substituted monks for secular canons in the chapter; d. 984; was canonised.
29. Aelfheah II. (*q.v.*), 985; tr. to Canterbury, 1005 ('St. Alphege').
30. Kenulf, 1005.
31. Aethelwold II., 1006.
32. Elfsige II., 1014.
33. Alwin, 1032.
34. Stigand, 1047; tr. from Elmham; a great supporter of Earl Godwin and Harold; intruded uncanonically on the archbishopric of Canterbury in 1052, during the exile of Robert, and held Winchester in plurality with it, 1052-70; dep. by William I., 1070; d. 1072.
35. Walkelin, 1070; rebuilt the cathedral; the transepts are the sole remainder of his work; d. 1098. See vacant two years.
36. William Giffard, 1100; not consecrated till 1107 owing to Investitures Controversy (*q.v.*); introduced the Cistercians into England; d. 1129.
37. Henry of Blois (*q.v.*), 1128-71. See vacant three years.
38. Richard Toclive, 1174; Chief Justice of England; had been a bitter opponent of Becket (*q.v.*); d. 1128.
39. Godfrey de Lucy, 1189; built the present east end of the cathedral; d. 1204.
40. Peter des Roches, 1204 (P.); one of the foreign favourites of John and Henry III.; a self-seeking intriguer; held the justiciarship; was driven into exile by Hubert Walter and Stephen Langton; introduced the Dominicans into England; d. 1238. See vacant five years, King Henry III. trying to intrude his relative, William de Valence.
41. William de Rayleigh, 1244; tr. (P.) from Norwich; d. 1250.

42. Aymer de Valence, 1249 ; half-brother of Henry III. ; imposed by the King's violence on the chapter ; driven out of England by de Montfort ; d. at Paris, 1260.
43. John Gervaise, 1260 (P.) ; Chancellor of York ; a warm partisan of de Montfort ; suspended by the legate Ottobon after Evesham ; d. in exile at Viterbo, 1268.
44. Nicholas Ely, 1268 ; tr. (P.) from Worcester : twice Chancellor of Henry III. ; d. 1280.
45. John Sawbridge, 1282 (P.) ; Archdeacon of Exeter ; d. 1304.
46. Henry Woodlock, 1305 ; supported Archbishop Winchelsey in his quarrel with Edward I.; crowned Edward II.; d. 1316.
47. John Sandall, 1316 ; Chancellor of Edward II ; d. 1319.
48. Reginald Asser, 1320 (P.) ; d. 1323.
49. John Stratford, 1323 (P.) ; tr. to Canterbury, 1333.
50. Adam de Orleton, 1333 ; tr. (P.) from Worcester ; a bitter enemy of Edward II. and supporter of Queen Isabella and Mortimer ; Chancellor of England ; d. 1345.
51. William of Edington, 1345 (P.) ; built the present nave of the cathedral ; first Prelate of the Garter in 1346 ; was Chancellor of England ; d. 1366.
52. William of Wykeham (q.v.), 1367 ; d. 1404.
53. Henry Beaufort (q.v.), 1404 ; tr. (P.) from Lincoln ; d. 1447.
54. William of Waynflete (q.v.), 1447 (P.) ; d. 1486.
55. Peter Courtenay, 1487 ; tr. (P.) from Exeter ; d. 1492.
56. Thomas Langton, 1493 ; tr. (P.) from Salisbury ; a friend of the ' new learning ' ; d. 1501, just after he had been elected Archbishop of Canterbury.
57. Richard Fox (q.v.), 1500 ; tr. (P.) from Durham ; d. 1528.
58. Thomas Wolsey (q.v.), 1529 (P.) ; d. 1530.
59. Stephen Gardiner (q.v.), 1531-50 and 1553-5 (P.) ; d. 1555.
60. John Poynet (q.v.), 1551 ; dep. 1553.
61. John White, 1556-9 ; tr. from Lincoln ; a scholar and supporter of Queen Mary and a persecutor of Protestants ; deprived by Elizabeth whom he insulted at Mary's funeral sermon ; d. 1560.
62. Robert Horne, 1561 ; a fanatical Puritan ; Dean of Durham, 1551 ; an exile under Mary ; well known for his controversies with Feckenham (q.v.) and Bonner (q.v.); administered the diocese harshly on puritanical lines ; d. 1580.

63. John Watson, 1580; d. 1584.
64. Thomas Cooper, 1583 ; tr. from Lincoln ; scurrilously attacked in the Martin Marprelate tracts ; a scholar of merit; d. 1594.
65. William Wickham, 1594; tr. from Lincoln; d. ten weeks after enthronement.
66. William Day, 1596; d. 1596.
67. Thomas Bilson, 1597 ; tr. from Worcester ; a controversialist, who took a large part in the Hampton Court Conference under James I. ; d. 1616.
68. James Montagu, 1616 ; tr. from Bath and Wells; d. 1618.
69. Lancelot Andrewes (q.v.), 1619 ; tr. from Ely ; d. 1626.
70. Richard Neile, 1628 ; tr. from Ely ; tr. to York, 1632.
71. Walter Curle, 1632-47 ; tr. from Bath and Wells ; a zealous supporter of Laud (q.v.) ; evicted by the Parliament, and d. in retirement, 1647. The see vacant thirteen years.
72. Brian Duppa, 1660 ; tr. from Salisbury ; a strong Royalist ; wrote many devotional books ; d. 1662.
73. George Morley, 1662 ; tr. from Worcester ; a great benefactor to the diocese ; rebuilt Wolvesey Palace ; patron of Ken (q.v.); d. 1684.
74. Peter Mews, 1684 ; tr. from Bath and Wells ; had been a military officer under Charles I. ; supported James II., but quarrelled with him over the Magdalen College case, and became a Whig; d. 1706.
75. Sir Jonathan Trelawney, 1706 ; tr. from Exeter ; one of the Seven Bishops (q.v.) (' and shall Trelawney die ? ') ; an active supporter of William III. ; d. 1721.
76. Charles Trimnell, 1721 ; tr. from Norwich ; d. 1723.
77. Richard Willis, 1723 ; tr. from Salisbury ; a Whig, and a founder of the S.P.C.K.; d. 1734.
78. Benjamin Hoadly (q.v.), 1734 ; tr. from Salisbury; d. 1761.
79. John Thomas, 1761 ; tr. from Salisbury ; tutor to George III. ; d. 1781.
80. Honble. Brownlow North, 1781 ; tr. from Worcester ; brother of the Prime Minister. Lord North ; a nepotist who much dilapidated the revenues of the see ; d. 1820.
81. George Pretyman Tomline, 1820 ; tr. from Lincoln ; tutor to William Pitt the younger ; d. 1827.
82. Charles Richard Sumner, 1827 ; tr. from Llandaff ; a prominent Evangelical ; a hard-working organiser for a diocese

which he found in a sad condition of neglect ; d. 1874.

83. Samuel Wilberforce (*q.v.*), 1869 ; tr. from Oxford ; d. 1873.

84. Edward Harold Browne, 1873 ; tr. from Ely ; res. 1890 ; d. 1891.

85. Anthony Wilson Thorold, 1890 ; tr. from Rochester; d. 1895.

86. Randall Thomas Davidson, 1895; tr. from Rochester ; tr. to Canterbury, 1903.

87. Herbert Edward Ryle, 1903 ; tr. from Exeter; res. and became Dean of Westminster, 1911.

88. Edward Stuart Talbot, 1911 ; tr. from Southwark.   [C. W. C. O.]

Benham, *Dio. Hist* ; *V.C.H.*, Hants, Surrey.

WOLSEY, Thomas (1471-1530), Cardinal, was born at Ipswich, his father probably a grazier and well-to-do. At eleven he went to Oxford, where he became Fellow and Bursar of Magdalen, then Master of the Grammar School attached to it ; Rector of Lymington (Somerset). But the bent of his mind was towards the public service, and he entered (1503) the service of Sir R. Nanfan, the Governor of Calais. Here he gained experience not only in government and public life, but also in foreign politics. On Nanfan's retirement he entered the royal service (1508), being employed on missions to Scotland and to the Netherlands (to negotiate a marriage for Henry VII. with Margaret). Under Henry VIII. he soon made himself the most trusted of the King's servants—as almoner, then on the Council (1511)—being unwearied in business. He was rewarded with the deanery of Lincoln, and he was made Lord Chancellor (1515). He was also Bishop of Bath and Wells (1518-23), Abbot of St. Albans (1521), Bishop of Lincoln, which he gave up for York (1514), Bishop of Durham (1523-30), of Winchester (1529), and Archbishop of York. On his disgrace he surrendered Winchester and St. Albans. He was also Bishop of Tournai, but this instance of pluralism did not stand alone at the time. In September 1515 he was created Cardinal. In 1518 he was made *legatus a latere*, with special powers of visitation. For these two honours both he and the King had asked. This legateship was renewed and even confirmed for life. Wolsey's power thus exceeded that of the archbishop. He obtained authority to visit monasteries, but authority to visit secular clergy was refused in the interests of regular organisation. He impressed people at home and abroad by his magnificence and style ; his hospitality and expenses were equally great. His

growth in royal favour he seemed to settle and do everything - led people to think his power over Henry great ; in reality, although Henry left much to him, he never controlled the King. By the nobility he was hated-partly perhaps as an ecclesiastic, partly as an upstart, but possibly more because he was independent, and fearless in rebuking them for ill-doings. To the poor he was charitable and just ; in the matter of enclosures his commission of 1517 inquired not only into the conversion of arable to pasture, but also into the 'imparking' for sport, and this was unpopular with the nobles and gentry. For the poor he made justice cheap and speedy, so that he was—except when his foreign policy closed channels of popular trade—dear to the multitude ; his interference with freedom of debate in Parliament is well known. He was thus a really great minister, as important in Europe as in England. He was a type of the great mediæval ecclesiastics, given up more to statecraft than to religion, and he was a foreign minister just when the rivalry of France and Spain under Charles V. (also Emperor) gave England, growing in power, the position of an arbiter. But Wolsey's skill made England a real power upon the Continent, and although the acquisition of the papacy for himself may have been a minor object of his policy, ambition for his country outweighed ambition for himself. Opinions differ as to the wisdom of his foreign policy, which partook of both the cleverness and the lack of scruple common to the day. But out of the skill with which he carried out his policy, and of his knowledge of the world, there can be no question. He incited, it was said, the French war of 1512, and it was he who made the peace with France in 1514. The alliance with France was never popular, and after the Field of the Cloth of Gold (1520) Wolsey returned to an alliance with Charles V. The general aim of his policy was to prevent any power becoming too strong, and to make England powerful. But these ends were dearly bought by the wars and the taxation needed for them. In the conduct of war, as in peace, Wolsey had shown unequalled diligence and mastery of detail. Just before the divorce the peace with France in April 1527 was again his work. When the King's divorce came up Wolsey for a time worked to help the King, in ignorance of his real intention, and hoping to replace his Spanish by a French wife. The King kept him in the dark, and his agents and the King's did not work together. After he discovered the King's wishes he still helped him, for he depended upon the King's favour, and he strove to secure for himself and his colleague, Campeggio (*q.v.*), by a decretal commission the right to decide the case in England upon issues chosen. But the evocation of the case to Rome (13th June 1529) meant ruin for Wolsey, and this soon appeared. A writ of *Praemunire* (*q.v.*) was issued against him (9th October 1529), and the Great Seal was taken from him and given to Sir Thomas More (*q.v.*). He submitted without a struggle. He surrendered his property, and of all his offices he was only allowed to keep the archbishopric of York. After some little time at Esher and Richmond he went to York, keeping Easter at Peterborough, and Whitsuntide at his manor of Southwell. Then he reached Cawood, near York, and preparations were made for his enthronement on 7th November, so neglectful had he been hitherto of his office. But although he had lost all his property his enemies had not yet forgiven him. His physician (De Augustinis) gave evidence upon which he was accused of treason; negotiations of his with the King of France were twisted to mean this. He was arrested (4th November) and moved southwards. His health was already broken, and he was now seized with dysentery. At Sheffield Park the Constable of the Tower came for him, and it was plain what his end would be. He only got as far as Leicester (26th November) when he took to his bed. He died on St. Andrew's Eve (1530). During these last months he had devoted himself to his episcopal work and to devotion, and had life and strength been spared him might have made himself a religious force in the north. His issue of Constitutions (mainly enforcing older rules) for the diocese, and his design of visiting all monasteries, had showed his wish for efficiency. Towards the end he showed a spirituality which had been wanting in his earlier life. He left a son and daughter.

He narrowly escaped election as Pope, and when Clement VII. was thought to be dying (February 1529), success seemed near. During Clement's captivity Wolsey had plans of a government by the Cardinals, and in his efforts to gain the divorce he did not fear to speak of a possible breach with Rome and the organisation of a purely national Church. The wishes of Henry, the captivity of the Pope, the position of affairs abroad and at home, made it impossible for him to keep his position. A policy based on expediency and craft breaks down, where one built on principles succeeds. Wolsey had unmatched ability but little principle. As his legatine commission had been given him at the King's request (instigated by Wolsey himself), the proceedings against him were shameless and vindictive. He had sacrificed interests, national and personal, spiritual and temporal, for the King who now crushed him.

In general character Wolsey belongs to the great ecclesiastical statesmen of the Renaissance and of the new political age; splendid, a patron of architecture, in touch with the literary and political thought of the day as a statesman should be. It is significant that he wished the pupils at his school of Ipswich to learn Italian. In spiritual and religious issues he had less interest. His attitude towards (*a*) the Renaissance, (*b*) the new religious movements, may be sketched. (*a*) He was a faithful son of Oxford; the University (1518) placed all its statutes in his hands to be dealt with at his pleasure, as did Cambridge also (1524). He began at Oxford by founding seven lectureships filled by men of talent, and a professorship of Greek. His new college (Cardinal College, Christ Church) was meant to prepare some five hundred youths for the secular priesthood, and it was to be fed by a great school at his birthplace, Ipswich, as King's College was by Eton, and New College by Winchester. The college was to have an income of £2000, obtained from twenty-two suppressed monasteries, a Bull being procured from the Pope empowering Wolsey to suppress small houses. One such was St. Frideswide at Oxford. He attended to all the details himself. His plans may be compared with those of Bishop Fisher (*q.v.*) at Cambridge, and of Bishop Richard Fox (*q.v.*) at Oxford. For the staff of the college he drew mainly upon Cambridge and upon the younger party of reform. As yet (1527) Wolsey had shown no fear of Lutheranism or of new tendencies in religion. (*b*) The disturbance at Cambridge—Christmas, 1524, caused by a sermon of Barnes—brought Barnes, Latimer (*q.v.*), and others under Wolsey's notice. He dealt leniently with them, and gave Latimer, who had been inhibited by the Bishop of Ely, a general licence to preach. But the growth of the movement led to a change, brought some students at Cambridge (Joye, Bilney, and others) before Wolsey, and the Cambridge group was broken up (1527). At Oxford a rigorous inquiry purified Cardinal College, and some of the Cambridge scholars there were imprisoned. Wolsey thus showed that while he had been willing to patronise anything likely to prove useful—and a busy statesman had to depend upon experts for guidance as to such usefulness—he had no sympathy with any new departures in religion or worship. He represented the political and intellectual sides of the last generation at its best, but he stood aloof from the newer movements of the younger generation. Had he become Pope instead of Adrian VI. he would have worked for efficiency and large control, learning, education, and activity. But spiritual earnestness was another matter; that he only learnt by hard adversity too late to teach the world he had influenced and aspired to guide. How he had defended the Church is shown by the events which followed his fall, and its subjection by Henry VIII.

[J. P. W.]

Cavendish, *Life of Wolsey*; Mandell Creighton, *Cardinal Wolsey*; Taunton, *Wolsey, Legate and Reformer*; Brewer, *Reign of Henry VIII.*; Fisher, *Pol. Hist. Eng.*, 1485-1547; Gairdner, *Hist. Eng. Ch.*, 1509-58.

WOODARD, Nathaniel (1810-91), born at Basildon Hall, Essex, the fifth son of John Woodard, was educated privately, and in due course went to Magdalen Hall, Oxford; B.A., 1840; M.A., 1866. In 1841 he was ordained deacon (priest 1842), and worked as a curate in East London, where he realised, in his own words, 'that the greatest possible good that a nation can enjoy is unity among the several classes of society, and certain it is that nothing can promote this so effectually as all classes being brought up together, learning from their childhood the same religion, and the same rudiments of secular learning.'

He therefore determined to attempt a remedy by providing public-school education on definite Church lines for all save the lowest classes. In 1847 he became curate at New Shoreham, and almost immediately devoted part of the vicarage to the purpose of a day school, placing his own family in lodgings. In 1848 he published his famous pamphlet, *A Plea for the Middle Classes*, maintaining that they were neglected in the matter of education, which attracted bitterly hostile criticism and strong support.

In this same year, 1848, a society, called by the name of St. Nicolas, was founded to extend education among the middle classes, and especially their poorer members, in the doctrines and principles of the Church. For this purpose stately buildings arose at Lancing, Hurstpierpoint, and Ardingly. The idea underlying the scheme was that the parent society was to govern a federation of similar societies. The country was mapped out into five divisions, in each of which the founder hoped to plant a society, and in each of the

divisions there were to be schools for three social grades within the middle class.

This idea has made its mark in the north in the form of girls' schools at Scarborough and Harrogate—the beginning of a northern group; in the Midlands, Denstone, Ellesmere, Worksop, and Abbots Bromley have established a reputation as successful educational centres. In addition to Lancing, Hurstpierpoint, and Ardingly, schools at Bloxham and Bognor complete the southern group. At Bangor in North Wales there is a school for girls, founded in 1887; and in 1880 King Alfred's School, Taunton, was opened.

In 1870 Mr. Woodard's work was recognised. He became Canon of Manchester (on the nomination of Mr. Gladstone) and Rector of St. Philip's, Salford. In the same year he was created D.C.L. at Oxford by Lord Salisbury at his installation as Chancellor. In 1873 the first of the Midland schools, Denstone, was begun, through the energy and munificence of Sir Percival Heywood. An important point in the development of Woodard's scheme was marked by the consecration in July 1911 of the splendid chapel at Lancing, designed to serve as a common centre for all his societies.   [A. L. W.]

WORCESTER, See of, dates from 679 or 680, when the diocese of Lichfield (*q.v.*) was divided, and a separate diocese formed for the Hwiccas, which ultimately became that of Worcester. Worcester had already a small religious house of St. Peter, founded by Saxulph, and it was adopted as the see. Tatfrith, who came from Whitby, was selected as bishop, but died before his consecration, and Bosel, another Whitby monk, became the first Bishop of Worcester.

In 693 a great bishop arose, St. Egwine, a native Hwiccian of noble birth. He found that his diocese was only nominally Christian, the effect of the sudden conversion of a whole tribe by the example or even order of the prince. To convert the converted therefore became Egwine's ambition, and he devoted himself to mission-preaching up and down his diocese, sometimes faring ill, as once at Alcester. Among other methods for keeping alive real Christianity was founding centres of devout living and teaching. In 702, therefore, he created what became one of the greatest of English monasteries, the religious house of Evesham, and there he himself retired twelve years later as abbot, and died, 717.

In the days of his successor, Wilfrid, King Aethelbald added largely to the estates of the Church. Offa did the same in Tilhere's time. Meanwhile the importance of the church of Worcester was rising. St. Peter's monastery was a mixed community of seculars and regulars under the rule of the bishop, all having one purse; but in 747, owing to the Council of Clovesho, the monastic rule became more precise, and two religious houses, the old St. Peter's and the newer St. Mary's, grew side by side until St. Oswald's day.

At this time religious houses appeared all over the diocese. At the end of the seventh century Pershore had been founded by King Ethelred. Gloucester (then in the diocese) by Osric. Early in the eighth century Deerhurst, Winchcombe, Bredon, Tewkesbury, and Kidderminster appeared. Others followed, so that in the end nearly half of the whole county of Worcester was in the hands of the Church. It is a remarkable testimony in favour of the monks there, and contrary to the usual allegation that they had become generally unworthy and unpopular, that at the time of the Reformation the older form of religion kept strong hold of the country. This would not have been the case after the suppression of the religious houses, and the alienation of their lands and the withdrawal of their influence, if their teaching and life had been vicious.

In 850 King Burhed granted Hartlebury to the bishop, possibly with a view of establishing a strong spiritual and temporal position against the usual inroads from across the Severn.

In the tenth century a connection between the archbishopric of York and the bishopric of Worcester, which is not altogether easy to account for, grew up, four of the Bishops of Worcester holding York in plurality.

Dunstan (*q.v.*) was succeeded by Oswald, who at first appeared to be his understudy; but presently this man of noble blood, fine presence, and great capacity in affairs proved almost as strong a person as his patron. His influence also went in the direction of fortifying the stricter monastic rule, and he finally absorbed the old secular cathedral of St. Peter in the renewed Benedictine church of St Mary, which by inheritance is now the cathedral. In 983 the new cathedral, all of stone, with twenty-seven altars, was completed. Yet so rapid were the changes in those days that in a century this building, which was a marvel in the diocese, had given place to a new church built by Wulfstan II. (*q.v.*). This bishop brought the diocese into order when disorder reigned elsewhere, and among other works built a new cathedral, on a somewhat different site from Oswald's,

the crypt of which, a fine example of Norman architecture, still exists.

After the foundation of the Court of the Welsh Marches by Edward IV., the duty of keeping peace on the Welsh border passed from the bishop to that body, and the see was used openly for non-resident Italians, who were employed as emissaries between Pope and King. Two of these held the deanery of Lucca as well, and two were Cardinals.

Until 1541 the diocese included all Worcestershire except a few parishes in that of Hereford; Gloucestershire east of the Severn, and the southern part of Warwickshire. It was divided into the archdeaconries of Worcester (first mentioned, 1089) and Gloucester (first mentioned, 1122). It lost its territory in Gloucestershire at the foundation of the sees of Gloucester (*q.v.*), 1541, and Bristol (*q.v.*), 1542, and consisted of only one archdeaconry until that of Coventry (first mentioned, 1135) was transferred from Lichfield to Worcester by Order in Council, 22nd December 1836. An Order in Council of 19th July 1837 readjusted the boundaries of Worcester and Gloucester. The archdeaconry of Birmingham was founded, 1892, and the see of Birmingham (*q.v.*) in 1905. An Order in Council of 11th July 1905 sanctioned a scheme agreed to by the bishops of Birmingham, Hereford, Lichfield, and Worcester for the rearrangement of their common boundaries. The archdeaconry of Warwick was founded in 1909. The diocese now consists of the county of Worcester, nearly all the county of Warwick, and small portions of Oxfordshire, Gloucestershire, and Staffordshire. There are 27 rural deaneries and 386 benefices.

The temporalities of the see were assessed by the *Taxatio* of 1291 at £485, 12s. 8d., and the spiritualities at £8, 13s. 4d., which by Henry VI.'s reign had increased to £66, 13s. 4d.; and the *Valor* of 1535 assessed its total income at £1049, 17s. 3d. The value for first-fruits as given by Ecton (1711) is £944, 17s. 9d. The Ecclesiastical Commissioners fixed the revenue of the see at £5000, but £800 was transferred to the see of Birmingham, leaving it £4200. The bishop is Provincial Chaplain of Canterbury.

During the episcopates of the non-resident Italians the work of the diocese was done by suffragans, with titles taken from Oriental sees, such as Sidon and Ascalon. In 1538 Henry Holbeach, Prior of St. Mary's, Worcester, was consecrated bishop suffragan to Worcester, with the title of Bishop of Bristol. From 1891 to 1903 there were suffragan bishops of Coventry. The present Bishop of Worcester advocates the reconstitution of the old see of Coventry, and in preparation he has created a collegiate chapter in the fine church of St. Michael, with the bishop as dean. The intention is that St. Michael's should become the Warwickshire cathedral.

The priory of St. Mary of Worcester was suppressed, January 1540, and the secular chapter founded by charter of 24th January 1542. Holbeach, the last prior, became first dean. The chapter included ten major canonries, of which six were suspended by the Cathedrals Act, 1840 (3-4 Vic. c. 113). These canonries are in the gift of the Crown. In 1627 Charles I. annexed a prebend at Worcester to the Margaret Professorship of Divinity at Oxford. This was exchanged in 1840 for a canonry in Christ Church. There are also twenty-four honorary canons appointed by the bishop.

BISHOPS OF WORCESTER

1. Bosel, 680 ; a monk of Whitby ; res. from infirmity, 691.
2. Oftfor, or Ostfor, 692 ; a monk of Whitby ; d. 693.
3. Aecgwine (St. Egwine), 693 ; d. 717.
4. Wilfrid, 717 ; d. 743.
5. Milred, 743 ; d. 775.
6. Waeremund, 775.
7. Tilhere, 777 ; Abbot of Berkeley ; entertained Offa at a feast at Fladbury, when the King gave the church of Worcester 'a very choice Bible with two clasps of pure gold ' ; d. 781.
8. Heathored, 781 ; d. 798.
9. Deneberht, 798 ; d. 822.
10. Eadberht, 822 ; d. 848.
11. Aelhun, 848 ; Hartlebury given to the see by Burhed, King of the Mercians, 850 ; d. 872.
12. Werefrith, 873 ; d. 915.
13. Aethelhun, 915 ; Abbot of Berkeley ; d. 922.
14. Wilferth, 922 ; d. 929.
15. Cynewold, 929 ; d. 957.
16. St. Dunstan (*q.v.*), 957 ; held Worcester with London, 959-60 ; tr. to Canterbury, 960.
17. St. Oswald, 961 ; held York in addition ; d. 992.
18. Aldulf, 992 ; succeeded to both sees ; d. 1002.
19. Wulfstan I., 1003 ; succeeded to both sees ; res. Worcester, 1016 ; d. 1023.
20. Leofsin, 1016 ; Abbot of Thorney ; d. 1033.
21. Brihteah, 1033 ; Abbot of Pershore ; d. 1038.
22. Lyfing, 1038 ; cons. to Crediton, 1027 [EXETER, SEE OF] ; afterwards also Bishop of Cornwall, and appears to have held both sees with Worcester ; d. 1046.
23. Ealdred (*q.v.*), 1046 ; tr. to York, 1061 ; res. Worcester, 1062.
24. St. Wulfstan II. (*q.v.*), 1062 ; d. 1095.
25. Samson, 1096 ; a Norman ; Canon of Bayeux ; d. 1112.
26. Theulf, 1115 ; Canon of Bayeux ; chaplain to Henry I. ; cons. the Great Church at Tewkesbury, 1121 ; d. 1123.
27. Simon, 1125 ; chancellor to Queen Adeliza ; d. 1150.
28. John of Pageham, 1151 ; d. at Rome, 1158.
29. Alfred, 1158 ; chaplain to Henry II. ; d. 1160.
30. Roger, 1164 ; son of Robert, Earl of Gloucester ; d. and was buried at Tours, 1179.
31. Baldwin, 1180 ; tr. to Canterbury, 1184.
32. William Northall, 1186 ; Archdeacon of Gloucester ; d. 1190.
33. Robert Fitz-Ralph, 1191 ; Canon of Lincoln ; Archdeacon of Nottingham ; d. 1193.
34. Henry de Soilli, 1193 ; Abbot of Glastonbury ; d. 1195.
35. John of Coutances, 1196 ; Dean of Rouen ; Archdeacon of Oxford ; d. 1198.
36. Mauger, 1200 ; his election annulled on the ground of illegitimacy by Innocent III., who reversed his decision after hearing Mauger in person ; replaced the bones of Wulfstan, which had been disturbed by his predecessor, and secured Wulfstan's canonisation, 1203 ; fled from England on account of the Interdict, 1208, and refused to pronounce the Pope's excommunication of John ; became a monk, and d. at Pontigny, 1212.
37. Walter Gray, 1214 ; tr. to York, 1215.
38. Silvester of Evesham, 1216 ; Prior of Worcester ; dedicated the cathedral in presence of Henry III., 1218 ; d. 1218.
39. William of Blois, 1218 ; Archdeacon of Buckingham ; d. 1236.
40. Walter Cantelupe, 1237 ; enthroned in the presence of Henry III., his Queen, the archbishop, and a legate ; fortified Hartlebury ; espoused the cause of the Barons against Henry, and blessed their troops before Evesham ; fled after their defeat, and was excommunicated by the Pope ; an able and saintly bishop, who might have been canonised but for his championship of the Barons' cause ; d. 1266.

41. Nicolas of Ely, 1266; tr. to Winchester, 1268.

42. Godfrey Giffard, 1268; brother of Walter Giffard, Archbishop of York; Archdeacon of Wells; Chancellor of England, 1266; had disputes with his chapter and with the Abbot of Westminster; said to have been attended on his progresses by one hundred knights; completed Hartlebury Castle and beautified the cathedral church; became a Franciscan; d. 1302.

43. William Gainsborough, 1302 (P.); Franciscan friar of Oxford; John of St. Germans, a Worcester monk, was elected, but the archbishop refused to confirm him, and on appeal the Pope quashed the election and provided Gainsborough, who d. 1307.

44. Walter Reynolds, 1308 (P.); tr. to Canterbury, 1313.

45. Walter Maidstone, 1313 (P.); Canon of St. Paul's; d. 1317.

46. Thomas Cobham, 1317 (P.); Chancellor of Cambridge University; d. 1327.

47. Adam de Orleton, 1327; tr. (P.) from Hereford; the chapter had elected Wulstan Bransford, Prior of Worcester, to whom the King restored the temporalities, and recommended him to the Pope, but Orleton was provided; tr. to Winchester, 1333.

48. Simon Montacute, 1334 (P.); Archdeacon of Canterbury; tr. to Ely, 1337.

49. Thomas Hemenhale, 1337 (P.); a monk of Norwich; d. 1338.

50. Wulstan Bransford, 1339; again elected, this time successfully; d. 1349.

51. John Thoresby, 1350; tr. (P.) from St. David's, the Pope setting aside the election of the Prior of Worcester, John de Evesham; tr. to York, 1352.

52. Reginald Brian, 1352; tr. (P.) from St. David's; d. of the plague, 1361.

53. John Barnet, 1362 (P.); Archdeacon of London; tr. to Bath and Wells, 1363.

54. William Whittlesey, 1364; tr. (P.) from Rochester; tr. to Canterbury, 1368.

55. William de Lynn, 1368; tr. (P.) from Chichester; d. 1373.

56. Henry Wakefield, 1375 (P.); Archdeacon of Canterbury; the election of Walter de Legh, the prior, set aside by the Pope; d. 1395.

57. Tideman of Winchcomb, 1395; tr. (P.) from Llandaff; physician and adherent of Richard II.; d. 1401.

58. Richard Clifford, 1401 (P.); Archdeacon of Canterbury and Dean of York; tr. to London, 1407.

59. Thomas Peverell, 1407; tr. (P.) from Llandaff; a Carmelite; d. 1419.

60. Philip Morgan, 1419 (P.); tr. to Ely, 1426.

61. Thomas Polton, 1426; tr. (P.) from Chichester; one of the English representatives at the Council of Constance; d. at the Council of Basle, 1433.

62. Thomas Bourchier, 1435 (P.); tr. to Ely, 1443.

63. John Carpenter, 1444 (P.); Provost of Oriel and Chancellor of Oxford; built the gatehouse at Hartlebury, and refounded the college at Westbury, near Bristol, for which place he had so great an affection as to wish to be styled Bishop of Worcester and Westbury; res. 1476; d. 1476; buried at Westbury.

64. John Alcock, 1476; tr. (P.) from Rochester; tr. to Ely, 1486.

65. Robert Morton, 1487 (P.); Archdeacon of Gloucester, Winchester, and York; Master of the Rolls; d. 1497.

66. John de Gigliis, 1497 (P.); an Italian scholar and diplomatist; Archdeacon of Gloucester and Dean of Wells; d. at Rome, 1498.

67. Silvester de Gigliis, 1498 (P.); nephew of his predecessor; suspected of poisoning Bainbridge, Archbishop of York; d. at Rome, 1521.

68. Julius de Medicis; Cardinal; Archbishop of Florence and of Narbonne; appointed administrator of the see by a papal Bull, 1521; res. 1522; became Pope Clement VII., 1523, and refused to annul Henry VIII.'s marriage with Katherine of Aragon: d. 1534.

69. Jerome Ghinucci, 1522 (P.); Italian Cardinal; served Wolsey and Henry VIII. as diplomatist; dep. for nonresidence by Act of Parliament, 1534, and pensioned; d. at Rome, 1541.

70. Hugh Latimer (*q.v.*), 1535; res. 1539.

71. John Bell, 1539; Archdeacon of Gloucester; Chancellor of Worcester, 1518; served Henry VIII. as a diplomatist, and in the matter of the divorce, in which he appeared as one of the King's counsel; one of the composers of the *Bishops' Book*, 1537, and one of the revisers of the New Testament, 1542; res. 1543; d. 1556.

72. Nicholas Heath (*q.v.*), 1543; tr. from Rochester; dep. 1551.

73. John Hooper (*q.v.*), 1552; held the see in conjunction with that of Gloucester; dep. 1553.

Nicholas Heath; restored, 1553; tr. to York, 1555.

74. Richard Pates, 1555 (P.); papally provided on death of Ghinucci, 1541; attended Council of Trent as Bishop of Worcester, 1547; obtained possession of the see from Mary, 1555; dep. by Elizabeth, 1559; d. at Louvain, 1565.
75. Edwin Sandys, 1559; tr. to London, 1570.
76. Nicholas Bullingham, 1571; tr. from Lincoln; impoverished the see; d. 1576.
77. John Whitgift (q.v.), 1577; tr. to Canterbury, 1583.
78. Edmund Freke, 1584; tr. from Norwich; formerly a monk of Waltham; Dean of Rochester and Salisbury; Great Almoner to Queen Elizabeth; d. 1591.
79. Richard Fletcher, 1593; tr. from Bristol; tr. to London, 1594.
80. Thomas Bilson, 1596; tr. to Winchester, 1597.
81. Gervase Babington, 1597; tr. from Exeter; d. 1610.
82. Henry Parry, 1610; tr. from Gloucester; d. 1616.
83. John Thornborough, 1616; tr. from Bristol; an alchemist; d. 1641.
84. John Prideaux, 1641; Rector of Exeter College and Regius Professor of Divinity at Oxford; an able controversialist; died at Baden in great poverty, 1650. Ten years' vacancy.
85. George Morley, 1660; tr. to Winchester, 1662.
86. John Gauden (q.v.), 1662; tr. from Exeter; d. 1662.
87. John Earle, 1662; tr. to Salisbury, 1663.
88. Robert Skinner, 1663; tr. from Oxford; d. 1670.
89. Walter Blandford, 1671; tr. from Oxford; d. 1675.
90. James Fleetwood, 1675; Provost of King's College, Cambridge; present at battle of Edgehill, 1642, whence he carried Prince Charles to a place of safety; d. 1683.
91. William Thomas, 1683; tr. from St. David's; suspended for refusing oath to William and Mary; told his dean, Hickes (q.v.), 'I think I would burn at a stake before I took this oath'; d. 1689.
92. Edward Stillingfleet (q.v.), 1689; d. 1699.
93. William Lloyd, 1699; tr. from Lichfield; one of the Seven Bishops (q.v.); d. 1717.
94. John Hough, 1717; tr. from Lichfield; elected President of Magdalen College, Oxford, in preference to James II.'s nominee, 1687, and ejected, but restored, 1688; d. 1743 at the age of

ninety-three, having been a bishop fifty-three years.
95. Isaac Maddox, 1743; tr. from St. Asaph; d. 1759.
96. James Johnson, 1759; tr. from Gloucester; chaplain to George III.; killed by a fall from his horse, 1774.
97. Honble. Brownlow North, 1774; tr. from Lichfield; tr. to Winchester, 1781.
98. Richard Hurd, 1781; tr. from Lichfield; scholar; friend of Warburton (q.v.) and of George III.; declined the primacy, 1783; enriched Hartlebury Castle; preached against enthusiasm; d. unmarried, 1808.
99. Ffolliot, Herbert Walker Cornewall, 1808; tr. from Hereford; d. 1831.
100. Robert James Carr, 1831; tr. from Chichester; favourite of George IV.; d. 1841.
101. Henry Pepys, 1841; tr. from Sodor and Man; d. 1860.
102. Henry Philpot, 1861; distinguished scholar; Master of St. Catherine's College, Cambridge; res. 1890; d. 1892.
103. John James Stewart Perowne, 1891; Dean of Peterborough; res. 1901; d. 1904.
104. Charles Gore, 1902; Canon of Westminster; tr. to Birmingham, 1905.
105. Huyshe Wolcott Yeatman-Biggs, 1905; tr. from Southwark; cons. 1891.

[H. W.]

V.C.H., Worcester and Norwich; Smith and Onslow, *Dio. Hist.*; Creighton, *The Italian Bishops of Worcester* (*Hist. Essays and Reviews*).

WORDSWORTH, Christopher (1807-85), Bishop of Lincoln, was son of Christopher Wordsworth, Master of Trinity College, Cambridge, and nephew of the poet. He was educated at Winchester College, where he had a brilliant career, in athletics as well as in scholarship. He played cricket for Winchester against Harrow, and caught out H. E. Manning (q.v.). He was renowned for just severity as a prefect, wrote priggish and pedantic letters, and 'prayed most sincerely every day for the good estate of the Catholic Church.' In October 1826 he entered Trinity College, Cambridge, where he swept the board of all classical prizes and distinctions. In 1830 he came out Senior Classic and first Chancellor's Medallist, took his B.A. degree, and was elected Fellow of Trinity. In the winter of 1832-3 he made a prolonged tour in the Ionian Islands and Greece, which supplied him with the material for two excellent books on *Greece* and *Athens and Attica*, both abounding not only in scholarship but in literary and artistic beauty. At Athens he had a severe illness, during which his thoughts seem to have taken a more solemn turn than had before been usual with him.

Returning to England, he was ordained deacon in 1833; priest, 1835. On the elevation of C. T. Longley to the see of Ripon in 1836, Wordsworth was chosen to succeed him as Headmaster of Harrow.

Under the easy-going rule of ' good-natured Longley ' Harrow had sunk into a condition of absolute lawlessness. Wordsworth resolved to restore order, and set about his task with tactless vigour. Eventually he reduced the numbers to seventy, and those seventy were so far from satisfactory that his successor, Dr. Vaughan (*q.v.*), was recommended to expel them all and start with a clean slate. In one point Wordsworth was a benefactor to Harrow. He endeavoured to arouse a spirit of definite Churchmanship; and to do so when the Tractarian party were becoming every day more unpopular required uncommon courage. His *Theophilus Anglicanus* and *Preces Selectae* were written for the use of Harrow boys; and he suggested and secured the erection of the first school-chapel. In 1844 he left Harrow on his appointment as Canon of Westminster, where he preached long and learned sermons in the abbey. He found opportunity for the exercise of the pastoral charge at Stanford in the Vale of White Horse, of which he became vicar in 1850. He studied and wrote and published incessantly; and plunged vigorously into all ecclesiastical controversies.

From first to last, in Church and in State, Wordsworth was a convinced and dogged Tory. He was a zealous champion of the Church of Ireland, and insisted that she derived her succession from St. Patrick, and that to disestablish her would be a national sin.

In March 1868 Gladstone (*q.v.*) proclaimed the policy of Irish Disestablishment, which he carried to a successful issue in July 1869. In October 1868 Archbishop Longley died; and as a result of the changes which followed Wordsworth was informed by Disraeli that he had recommended the Queen to raise him to the episcopate, ' because I have confidence in your abilities, your learning, and the shining example which you have set, that a Protestant may be a good Churchman.' His administration of the see of Lincoln was marked by single-minded devotion, by untiring activity, by an intensely practical belief in the value of ecclesiastical institutions, and by a morbid horror of Rome and Romanism.

He revived the office of suffragan bishop, and he created a diocesan synod. He promoted the division of the diocese and the creation of the see of Southwell. He zealously promoted church-building and church-restoration. He bestowed the utmost pains on his confirmations and ordinations. In matters of ritual he was eclectic; pertinaciously adhered to the north end in celebrating the Holy Communion, and declined to don a mitre; but he wore the cope and pectoral cross, and carried his pastoral staff. He studied and wrote as intently, if not so continuously, as of old, and was as vigorous as ever in ecclesiastical controversy. He protested against the appointment of Temple to the see of Exeter; and against the exclusion of Anglican bishops from the Vatican Council. He denounced the New Lectionary and the Revised Version of the New Testament. He opposed the Burials Act with all his power; he objected to calling a Wesleyan minister ' Reverend '; he publicly rebuked a horse-racing vicar; he refused to institute a clergyman who had obtained his living by simony (and had to pay heavy damages for his conscientiousness). In the debates on the Public Worship Regulation Act he withstood Archbishop Tait (*q.v.*) to his face. Yet through all these storms of controversy he maintained the most friendly relations even with those whose conduct he denounced, and from those who knew him most intimately he elicited a singular degree of affection as well as respect. He made E. W. Benson (*q.v.*) Chancellor of Lincoln, and with his aid founded the *Scholae Cancellarii*. [THEOLOGICAL COLLEGES.] Benson wrote on the 16th May 1883: ' The Bishop still rises at six; still reads and writes as much as ever; still quotes Fathers and Classics aptly and abundantly, and still reasons as ill, and is as beautifully courteous as ever.' On 9th February 1885 Wordsworth resigned his see. On hearing that his successor was to be Edward King (*q.v.*), he telegraphed to Gladstone, who had made the appointment, *Deo gratias*. He died on the 21st March 1885, and was buried on Lady Day in the churchyard of Riseholme, then the episcopal residence of the see.

The list of his books covers thirteen pages in the Brit. Mus. Catalogue. The most remarkable were his annotated edition of the Greek Testament and his Commentary on the Holy Bible—works of extraordinary labour, of solid learning and quaint interpretation.

[G. W. E. R.]

Overton and Wordsworth, *Life*; A. C. Benson, *Leaves of the Tree*.

WREN, Matthew (1585-1667), Bishop of Ely, born in London, 1585, eldest son of Francis, mercer; admitted scholar of Pembroke Hall, Cambridge, 1601, by influence of L. Andrewes (*q.v.*), then Master; Fellow, 1605; M.A., 1608; D.D., 1634; ordained deacon and priest, 1611; chaplain to Andrewes, now Bishop of Ely, and rector of Teversham, Cambs, 1615; became chaplain to Charles Prince of Wales, 1622, and accompanied him on his visit to Spain in 1623; Canon of Winchester, 1623; rector of Bingham, Notts, 1624; in 1625 he was elected Master of Peterhouse, Cambridge, and exerted himself to collect money for the building of the chapel, which was dedicated in 1633; Dean of Windsor and Wolverhampton, and Registrar of the Garter, and Vice-Chancellor at Cambridge, 1628; accompanied Charles I. on his journey to Scotland, and became Clerk of the Closet in 1633. He was elected Bishop of Hereford, 5th December 1634, and consecrated, 8th March 1635, and drew up new statutes for his cathedral chapter. Translated to Norwich, 10th November 1635, he set himself to enforce the Laudian discipline, and was denounced by Prynne in *News from Ipswich*, 1636. He was translated to Ely, 24th April 1638. On 19th December 1640, the morrow of Laud's impeachment, J. Hampden was sent by the Commons to the Lords with the message that they had received information against Wren 'for setting up idolatry and superstition in divers places, and acting some things of that nature in his own person,' and to ask that security be required of him 'to be forthcoming and abide the judgment of Parliament,' since they hear he is endeavouring to escape from England. Consequently he was bound, with three other bishops, in £10,000 each, for his daily appearance; 5th July 1641 his impeachment was determined upon, and 20th July Sir T. Widdrington made a violent speech against him before the Lords, and twenty-four articles of impeachment were laid against him. In August, along with the archbishop and twelve other bishops, he was impeached for making canons in 1640, and was imprisoned in the Tower from December 1641 to May 1642. Meanwhile the original charges were maintained, and on 1st September he was again thrown into the Tower. An able and effective defence which he drew up on all the twenty-four charges was betrayed; the impeachment was dropped, but his continued imprisonment was decreed. In 1644, in the terms of the Treaty of Uxbridge, he was expressly excluded from hope of pardon; and in 1648 the Commons voted that he should not be tried for his life, but should be imprisoned till further order; and he remained in the Tower till 1660, for part of the time (1644-6) having, by connivance of his guardians, free intercourse with George Monk. He might more than once have gained his freedom had he been willing to ask it from Cromwell. He was released, 17th March 1660. He devoted £5000 of the income of his recovered see to the rebuilding of the chapel of Pembroke Hall. He was on the committee of the Upper House of the Convocation of Canterbury for the revision of the Book of Common Prayer, and read the Gospel at Charles II.'s coronation. He died at Ely House, 24th April 1667, and was solemnly buried in Pembroke Chapel, Rougedragon carrying the crozier and Norroy the mitre (both of which are preserved at Pembroke College), and Pearson (*q.v.*) preaching his funeral sermon. Clarendon describes him as 'of a severe and sour nature,' but this seems to have reference to his character as a disciplinarian, and his insistence on the rights of his see, rather than to his personal temper; and it is further illustrated by his reply to an expostulation of Charles II., 'Sir, I know my way to the Tower.' Clarendon also describes him as 'particularly versed in the old liturgies of the Greek and Latin churches'; accordingly, he was associated with Laud and Juxon to form a committee for supervising the Scottish Canons and Book of Common Prayer of 1636-37; while Bishop of Hereford he drew up the order for the consecration of Abbey Dore, and after the Restoration that for the consecration of Pembroke Chapel; and his suggestions largely influenced the revision of the Book of Common Prayer (*q.v.*) in 1661. He was a 'ritualist' of the type of Andrewes and Laud, and along with the latter was the butt of Puritan satire.

> The after that, unto this jolly fair,
> A little *Wren* came flying through the air,
> And on his back, betwixt his wings he bore
> A minster, stuffed with *crosses, altars'* store,
> With sacred Fonts, with rare gilt cherubims,
> And bellowing *organs*, chanting curious
>   hymns . . .
> 'Buy my high altars,' he lifts up his voice,
> 'All sorts of *mass-books*, here you may have
>   choice.'
>   *Lambeth Fair.*

The only works of Wren were *Meditationes sacrae in S. Paginam, de genuino sensu atque exacta nostra versione divinorum textuum; Epistolae variae ad viros doctissimos*, from which his son Matthew compiled *Increpatio Barjesu*, 1660; a sermon on Prov. 24²¹, printed in *Parentalia*, p. 115; and *The Abandoning of the Scotch Covenant: a brief theological treatise touching that unlawful Scottish Covenant,* 1662. There is an engraved portrait of Wren in *Parentalia.*   [F. E. B.]

C. and S. Wren, *Parentalia*; Clarendon, *Rebellion*; Staley, *Hierurgia Anglicana*; J. W. Legg, *English Orders for Consecrating Churches* (H.B.S.), 1911.

WULFSTAN, St. (*c.* 1007-95), Bishop of Worcester, was a native of Warwickshire, the son of wealthy and well-connected parents. Educated in the monastic schools of Evesham and Peterborough, he developed a retiring and studious disposition, although in youth he was handsome and athletic. His parents having embraced the monastic profession at Worcester, Wulfstan attached himself to the household of Bishop Brihteah (who held that see from 1033 to 1038). Brihteah induced him to become a priest, and gave him the parish of Hawkesbury (co. Gloucester); but shortly afterwards Wulfstan entered the cathedral monastery, to devote himself more completely to God's service. At Worcester he held in succession the offices of schoolmaster, precentor, sacristan, and prior. As prior he earned distinction, in the time of Bishop Ealdred (*q.v.*) (1046-62), by preaching regularly to the people of the diocese, for whose instruction Ealdred had made no adequate provision. Wulfstan's detractors argued that this activity was reprehensible, inconsistent with the monastic profession, and injurious to the bishop, who alone had the right of preaching. But Wulfstan made powerful friends by the charm of his personality; among these are mentioned the Countess Godiva of Mercia, her son, Earl Aelfgar, and Harold, son of Godwin. In 1062, Ealdred having vacated the see of Worcester, Wulfstan was proposed for the vacancy by two papal legates who had made his acquaintance at Worcester. Edward the Confessor accepted the suggestion, and Wulfstan was appointed with general approbation. He was consecrated on 8th September 1062 by Archbishop Ealdred at York, because Stigand of Canterbury had been branded by Pope Alexander as a schismatic and usurper. Wulfstan, however, acknowledged Stigand as his superior. He also espoused the cause of Harold on the death of the Confessor. But a prompt submission and his saintly character saved him from deposition after the Norman Conquest. Lanfranc (*q.v.*) meditated his removal, on the ground that he was too ignorant for a bishop, but William I. stood his friend. Wulfstan and Lanfranc subsequently co-operated in resisting the claims of York to jurisdiction over the diocese of Worcester. Wulfstan was deputed by Lanfranc to visit the diocese of Lichfield, and distinguished himself by compelling his own clergy to observe the legislation of 1076 against clerical marriages. To the new dynasty he rendered good service in 1075, and again in 1088, by making head with his own knights and retainers against local rebellions. In 1085 he helped the Domesday commissioners to make their survey of Worcestershire. In his diocese he was active in visitations, in preaching and confirming, in the building and restoration of churches. Between 1084 and 1089 he rebuilt his own cathedral; his crypt may still be seen, but the main fabric was destroyed by fire in 1113. He shares with Lanfranc the credit of suppressing the export trade in slaves, of which Bristol was the centre. He visited Bristol frequently to preach against this abuse, and finally shamed the slave merchants out of their evil practices. He died of old age on 18th January 1095, and was buried at Worcester. Locally he was at once venerated as a saint, but his formal canonisation was delayed till 1203.

[H. W. C. D.]

Freeman, *Norman Conquest* and *William Rufus*; H. W. C. Davis, *Eng. under the Normans and Angevins*; Dean Church, *St. Wulfstan,* 'Lives of the Eng. Saints,' 1844; reprinted 1901.

WYCLIF, or WICLIF, John (*c.* 1320-84), reformer, was born probably at Hipswell, near Richmond, Yorks; went to Balliol College, Oxford, and became Master of the college (1360-1). After a petition by the university to the Pope in his favour he was provided to the prebend of Aust in the church of Westbury-on-Trym (24th November 1352). He was given dispensation to hold this along with a promised canonry in Lichfield (26th December 1373), which he lost, as on his refusal to pay first-fruits it was given by Gregory XI. to a young foreigner. Up to this date, therefore, he was in favour at Rome. He proceeded D.D. about 1372, and we are told that this date was a turning-point in his teaching. His preferments were Fillingham (1361), Ludgershall (November 1368), Lutterworth (by the Crown, April 1374), but he was probably mostly non-resident in these parishes. There was another John Wyclif or Whitclif, a Fellow of Merton (1356), who (probably) was the Vicar of Mayfield (1361) by Archbishop Islip's appointment. There was also a John Wyclif, Warden of Canterbury Hall (now part of Christ Church), who may be identified with one of these. This Hall was founded for monks and seculars jointly; later the monks were expelled, and John Wyclif was made Warden. Archbishop Langham (March 1369) restored the monks (1371), a measure confirmed two years later by Edward III. It was said soon afterwards that his hostility to the papacy was caused by this judgment, but it has also been doubted if the reformer were the Warden who may have been Wyclif of Mayfield. Wyclif mentions the incident himself quite calmly, and although it is probable that he was the Warden, any ordinary suit such as this could have given rise to no anger. The beginning of his public life must now be placed not in 1366 but about 1375, when a demand was made by the Pope (1374) for the tribute promised by King John. Wyclif, who had been one of the commissioners at Bruges to discuss the non-observance of the statute of Provisors (*q.v.*), disputed on the justice of this claim. The King, he urged, held his kingdom directly from Christ; the Pope, who like all lords lost his power by deadly sin, had no claim. Wyclif here appears as an advocate of the State against the Church, and as a critic of the Church's claim to endowments or revenues. His assertion of regal sovereignty, his feeling of nationality, and his dislike of endowments were fixed principles—almost his only fixed principles—throughout his life. This was the beginning of his public career. Before 1374-5 his activity had been academic and philosophic. From 1360 to 1370 or so he wrote much, chiefly on philosophy, as a follower of St. Augustine, with a belief in predestination and in the doom of some to damnation. He was a strong Realist, attributing to general ideas a real existence, and he denied the possibility of anything being annihilated. His academic discussions on these points shaped his later views. Like some of the Friars (with whom he long kept friendly) he held endowments to be wrong, and with his strong views of the power of the State he held that the civil power and lay lords were bound to enforce reformation of Church abuses. After 1375 he preached these views to a larger public.

He was much indebted for his views to Grosseteste (*q.v.*) and Richard Fitz-Ralph, Archbishop of Armagh (1347-60). From Fitz-Ralph he took his theory of dominion or lordship: true worship was derived from God, and is lost by deadly sin ('dominion is founded in grace'). This doctrine was meant to enforce responsibility, but was open to abuse, and might be dangerous. To William of Ockham (*q.v.*) (although a Nominal-

ist) Wyclif owed much of his doctrine of sovereignty and national power, and of his criticism of the papacy. Upon the Eucharist his views went through three stages. Up to 1370 he accepted Transubstantiation, although it implied an exception to his theory of the indestructibility of 'substance.' About 1372 (at his doctorate) he was more doubtful, and inclined to leave the question aside. About 1380 he became convinced that the permanence of substance held good here too, and therefore that Transubstantiation, which implied the annihilation of the substance of the elements, was untrue. His denial of Transubstantiation was thus based on scientific or philosophic grounds, and did not affect his belief in the reality of Christ's Presence. About 1382 the controversies into which his views of endowments led him became more bitter, and the monks especially opposed him. In September 1376 he was asked by John of Gaunt, the leader of the lay party who opposed the interference of ecclesiastics like William of Wykeham (*q.v.*) in politics and administration, to preach in London. This led to a summons to appear (February 1379) before Convocation. The presence with him of John of Gaunt and Percy saved him, but a riot of the citizens against the insolent duke followed. Bulls from Rome to Archbishop Sudbury (*q.v.*), the King, and the University were now procured by the monks along with some bishops. The eighteen errors charged by them against him mainly concerned endowments and the submission of ecclesiastics to civil courts. At the end of 1377 the University was urged to inquire into his doctrines, and although disliking the tone of the Bull, they obeyed. His views were decided to be dangerous, but not heterodox. In the spring of 1378 he was summoned before the archbishop and Courtenay of London, whom the Pope had named as commissioners. This time the Londoners were on his side, and the Princess of Wales protected him. But he was charged to keep silent on his errors. The schism of 1378, leading to the crusade in Flanders by Bishop Despenser (*q.v.*) of Norwich (1382), intensified Wyclif's dislike of the existing abuses; it showed churchmen striving for power and forgetting the law of Christ. Henceforth he became more antipapal. But, strongly as he spoke against the existing papacy and its methods, he was not opposed to a Pope who should resemble Christ, although the seat of his power need not be at Rome. In the idea of the papacy he saw nothing wrong, much as he hated existing popes and the abuses of their power. The events of the time and its abuses, joined to his strong sense of national life, intensified his anger and its expression. His scholastic love of speculation, and the freedom of thought common in mediæval Universities, made his criticism of the general Church system very thorough. Holy orders, and all sacraments, were questioned or even denied. Such teaching spread broadcast had a deeper effect than when confined to the University. His Latin works are mainly his Oxford lectures, some recast and edited; they give us his views, often violent and sometimes changeable.

Wyclif's devotion to St. Augustine led to his being called 'Joannes Augustini'; his love and knowledge of the Scriptures gained him the name of *Doctor Evangelicus*. His *de Veritate Sacrae Scripturae* (1378) appeals to the Bible against the abuses of the day, and advocates a translation of it into English; and incidentally the work shows that there was no interference at that time with the Scriptures in the vernacular; it was only unlicensed preaching which was checked. There were already many partial translations (such as Rolle of Hampole's (*q.v.*) Psalms), but none complete. We have statements by Hus, Archbishop Arundel (1411), and Knighton (anti-Wycliffite) that Wyclif translated the whole Bible, but there are many difficulties as to the two Wyclif versions (one rough and early, the other more polished and later, but both from the Vulgate). The prologue to the second version—strongly Lollard in tone—is certainly not Wyclif's work, it is possibly Purvey's. The best conclusion is that an impulse towards the translation came from Wyclif, but (although statements on both sides are often too positive) he did not do much of the work (which was completed after his death) himself. Gasquet's theory that the translation known as Wyclif's was really an orthodox version recognised by the Church has little support. It is true, however, that the version, apart from the prologues, was not prohibited, could be possessed with episcopal licence, and was widely read. [BIBLE, ENGLISH.]

Another controversy has arisen as to Wyclif's 'Poor Priests or preachers.' Doubts have been expressed whether they ever existed, but the numerous mentions of them in Wyclif's Latin and English works, and the irritation expressed at the prohibition of certain priests (poor and by choice unbeneficed) are strong evidence of their existence. Their foundation, tentative and not very formal, dates from Wyclif's Oxford days (1377). At first they were priests, then laymen, as he came to make less of learning, more

of personal piety. They resembled the Friars (*q.v.*), with whom Wyclif was then friendly. After his death they were laymen, and Wyclif's own expressed contempt for orders favoured the change. His English sermons were probably intended for their use. By this means Wyclifitism was spread, especially in certain districts, such as Leicestershire, and later on Norfolk.

The outbreak of 1381, its popular excitement, the murder of Archbishop Sudbury, and the succession of Courtenay, changed things. John of Gaunt fell from power. Wyclif's teaching as to endowments (based on the fable of Constantine's donation to Pope Sylvester, when ' poison was poured into the veins of the Church ') and upon Transubstantiation was blamed as causing the trouble. Wyclif's own sympathy was with the peasants; both his teachings and the Poor Priests favoured communism, and (1380) his attack upon Transubstantiation had intensified controversies. In 1381 his teaching was condemned at Oxford; the ' earthquake ' council at Blackfriars (May 1382) condemned ten of his doctrines as heresies, fourteen as errors. Arundel then attacked Wyclif at Oxford, where his supporters (Nicholas Hereford, Repyngdon, Aston, and others) were busy. A strife of some months, in which the King's council and the archbishop were opposed by Wyclifites and the party of academic independence, ended in the complete silencing of Wyclifites at Oxford. He was shut out from the schools, and probably promised not to use some terms —substance, etc.—outside. There is no evidence for his recantation. His boldness, in his appeal to the King and the nation, circulated now and in his later writings, tells against it. He was cited to Rome, but refused to go, and (probably paralysed) remained at Lutterworth (having left Oxford) until his death (St. Sylvester's Day, 31st December 1384). The struggle (1382-4) had been primarily academic, and its effect upon Oxford was very great. The popular side of the movement remained. But the catalogue of Wyclif's heresies had given an easy means of measuring heresy, hitherto almost unknown in England. The bishops—impelled by the party of order in England, and by the papacy outside, faced, moreover, by popular disturbance of all kinds (preaching, Lollard schools, teaching, circulating of Lollard tracts and of prologues, added to orthodox works and Scriptures)—made the most of their authority for investigating and suppressing heresy until later Acts devised fresh means of dealing with it. Wyclifitism ceased to be academic; it lingered on as a popular movement. [LOLLARDS.] Wyclif's chief importance lies in his being the last of the great English scholastics; in his expression of strong nationalism, roused to vigour against papal claims and ecclesiastical privileges which worked against the State; in his dislike of endowments, his democratic tendencies, and his suggestion of a reform carried out by the State and by laymen. His own name falls into the background in England until the condemnation of his heresies at Constance brought it forward again. In Bohemia, whither his works were carried by students from Oxford, his influence was great, and was one element in the Hussite movement. The exact connection between Wyclif as a teacher and the later Lollards is obscure, and so is that between Wyclif and the Reformation. There is no exact proof of direct connection in either case. But in any case, Wyclif is the product of mediæval thought and of its break up, of national and political tendencies which later on issued in the Reformation. But he has, apart from his bold revolutionary speculations, more links with mediæval than with Reformation thought. [J. P. W.]

See *Camb. Hist. of Eng. Lit.*, II. ii., for full bibliography; Workman, *Dawn of the Reformation*; Trevelyan, *Age of Wycliffe*; Rashdall in *D.N.B.*; Figgis in *Typical Eng. Churchmen*, series ii. (S.P.C.K.); R. L. Poole, *Movements of Reform*, also *Illustrations of Mediæval Thought*; *Select Eng. Works*, ed. T. Arnold; and Latin *Works* in publications of Wyclif Society.

WYKEHAM, William of (1323-1404), Bishop of Winchester, Lord Chancellor, and founder of colleges, according to the only contemporary authority, the life written by Robert Heete about 1430, was born at Wickham, Hants, in 1323 or 1324, the son of John, nicknamed Long, of whom all we know is that he was 'endowed with the freedom of his ancestors,' and Sybil, who is described as 'of gentle birth,' daughter of William Bowate and granddaughter of Sir William Stratton of Stratton, near Micheldever, Hants. Some patrons, unnamed, paid for his education at Winchester in the primitive sciences, beyond which he never passed. The primitive sciences are defined in a papal Bull of 1335 (Leach, *Educational Charters*, 290) as grammar, logic, and philosophy.

On leaving school Wykeham became 'under-notary (vice-tabellio) to a certain squire, constable of Winchester Castle,' viz. Robert of Popham, who became con-

stable, 25th April 1340. On 10th May 1356 he was made clerk of the King's works in the manors of Henley and Easthampstead, his duty being to pay for all wages and purchases of materials, subject to the supervision of three controllers. In June he was a commissioner for the Statute of Labourers in the liberty of St. George's, Windsor, and in October surveyor of the works of Windsor Castle, with the same duties as at Henley.

This appointment has been supposed to mark his becoming architect to Windsor Castle. A well-known story, traceable to Archbishop Parker (*q.v.*), imputes to Wykeham the Round Tower and the inscription on it: *Hoc fecit Wykeham*, which, when brought to the King's notice, would have cost him his place had he not explained that it meant, not 'Wykeham made this,' but 'This made Wykeham.' The Round Tower was, however, a Norman work. Wykeham was paymaster and manager, not architect. The architect was William of Wynford, the chief mason, whom Wykeham employed afterwards as chief mason at Winchester College and Winchester Cathedral. At first under Wykeham there was a great reduction in expenditure. During the years 1356 to 1361 of Wykeham's office the chief work was some new royal apartments to the east of the Round Tower, and some gateways leading to them. Whatever were Wykeham's duties, his performance of them brought him greatly into favour. On 14th November 1357 his name first occurs in an ecclesiastical connection. The grant of the living of Irstead, Norfolk, in 1349 to William of Wykeham, chaplain, at one time attributed to our Wykeham, has been proved to refer to another man of the same name. In 1357 Wykeham, the King's clerk, was given one shilling a day extra wages—his wages as surveyor were also one shilling a day—'until peacefully advanced to some benefice.' On 30th November he was presented to the rectory of Pulham, worth £53 a year—one of the richest livings in Norfolk. This was the subject of a contest in the papal court, and though Wykeham obtained a papal grant of it on 8th July 1358, on 16th April 1359 he was given a pension of £20 a year by the King until he could get peaceful possession. It was not till 10th July 1361 when he got a new grant from the King that he obtained possession.

On 16th April 1359 the King gave Wykeham the canonry or prebend of Flixton in Lichfield Cathedral, but he only obtained induction 29th January 1361. In June 1359 after a French fleet had sacked Winchelsea, Wykeham was made surveyor of Dover and other southern castles, and next year held an inquiry with a jury as to the defects of the walls and towers at Dover. In 1360 he was employed in negotiating the Peace of Bretigny, to which he was one of the witnesses, on 24th October. Meanwhile he had been given on 21st May 1360 the deanery of St. Martin's-le-Grand, London. On 13th February 1361, at the joint petition of the Kings of France and England, the Pope ' provided ' him to a canonry at Lincoln. In 1361, after the second visitation of the plague, the *secunda pestis*, a large number of canonries fell to the King through the deaths of bishops and canons, and preferments were heaped on Wykeham. Thus he became a prebendary of Hereford, 12th July; of the collegiate churches of Abergwilly and Llandewybrewi, 16th July; of Bromyard, 24th July; of Auckland (by papal provision), 11th August; of Beverley, 1st October; of the cathedral churches of Salisbury, 16th August; of St. Paul's, 1st October; of St. David's, 22nd November; and of Wherwell Monastery, Hants, on 20th December. Yet it was not till 5th December that this many-beneficed clerk was ordained acolyte, and it was only next year that he took holy orders by becoming sub-deacon in March and priest in June. He then added to his possessions several more prebends at Shaftesbury Abbey and Lincoln Cathedral, and early in 1363 at Hastings and St. Stephen's, Westminster, with the archdeaconries first of Northampton, then of Lincoln, the provostry of the fourteen prebends of Combe in Wells, and prebends at Bridgnorth and St. Patrick's, Dublin, and the rectory at Menheniot, Cornwall. It is not to be supposed that he ever saw the rectory or any of his prebends outside London. He was still a civil servant, Clerk of the Exchequer, and Keeper of all the Forests south of Trent. On 5th May 1364 he was made Keeper of the Privy Seal, and as such was practically Prime Minister, figuring in Froissart's *Chronicle* (i. 249) as ' a priest called Sir William de Wican who reigned in England . . . by him everything was done and without him they did nothing.' William of Edyngdon, Bishop of Winchester, died in 1366, and Wykeham was recommended for bishop by the King. The delay of six months before the issue of Bull of 4th July 1367, providing him to the see, has been attributed (Moberly, *Life of Wykeham*) to papal opposition to Wykeham as the leader of a nationalist antipapal party. But many of Wykeham's previous preferments were conferred by the

Pope. The delay is sufficiently accounted for by the fact that the papal court was at this time engaged in moving to Rome after its long exile at Avignon.

Wykeham was made Chancellor on 17th September, and consecrated bishop, 10th October 1367. As Chancellor he was responsible for the disastrous war with France which began in June 1368. When Parliament met in 1371 the blame for the disasters was laid on him and his clerical colleagues ; a lay ministry was demanded, and he resigned. In 1373 John of Gaunt and his lay ministers, having been equally unsuccessful against France, Wykeham was made one of a council of advice. In the Good Parliament of February 1376 he was leader in the impeachment of Lord Latimer and the dismissal of Alice Perrers, the King's mistress. But on the Black Prince's death on 8th June Alice Perrers returned, and Wykeham in his turn was impeached. He was convicted (wrongfully) on a charge of remitting half of a fine for licence to alienate land and altering the rolls of Chancery accordingly, and was declared liable to a fine of nine hundred and sixty thousand marks (£640,000). He was banished the court, and his episcopal revenues were seized.

Wykeham had almost immediately after becoming bishop begun to act as the ' pious founder.' On 6th January 1368 he bought the manor of Boarhunt in Southwick, with which he endowed a chantry for his parents' souls in Southwick Priory. On 1st September 1373 he contracted with Master Richard of Herton, grammarian, to instruct in the art of grammar for ten years the poor scholars whom he maintained—showing that he had already started the school which became Winchester College. When his revenues were sequestrated in 1376 and he ' brake up household,' he also sent home the seventy scholars whom he was maintaining at Oxford—showing that he had already maintained the house which became New College.

On 18th June 1377 his episcopal revenues were restored through, it was said, a bribe to Alice Perrers. He certainly bought part of the endowment of Winchester College from her husband three years later. But his restoration was probably due to the Princess of Wales, since after the accession of her son, Richard II., he was granted a full pardon. Winchester College was soon after begun with a Bull from Pope Urban VI., 1st June 1378, enabling Wykeham to appropriate Downton Rectory, Wilts, ' for seventy poor scholars clerks to live college-wise and study in grammaticals near the city of Winchester.'

Under papal Bull and royal licence, the foundation charter of 'Seinte Marie College of Wynchestre in Oxenford' for a Warden and seventy scholars to study theology, canon and civil law and arts was granted by Wykeham, 26th November 1379; and on 5th March 1380 the first stone was laid of the New College, as it is still called, and the college entered on the completed buildings 14th April 1386. On 6th October 1382 the charter of 'Seinte Marie College of Winchestre by Wynchestre' was issued. But the first stone of the present buildings was not laid till 26th March 1388, nor were they inhabited till 28th March 1394, the college meanwhile living in the parish of St. John the Baptist.

The cause of the long delays in the erection of the colleges is to be found in the disturbed state of politics, the Papal Schism in 1379, the Peasants' Revolt in 1381, the wars with France, Scotland, and Spain, and the constitutional struggles in 1388, followed by Wykeham's second chancellorship from 3rd May 1389 to 27th September 1391. He ceased to attend the Council and Parliament during Richard II.'s unconstitutional attempts at arbitrary power. He probably favoured Henry IV.'s revolution, attending the Council again four times in Henry's first year, and making him great loans. When Winchester College was finished in September 1394 Wykeham began rebuilding Winchester Cathedral. He made his will, 24th July 1403, and died on 27th September 1404, at the age of eighty, and was buried in the beautiful chantry chapel he had built and endowed in the nave of the cathedral, where as a boy he used to attend the early 'Morrow Mass' at the Virgin's altar, called 'Pek's Mass.'

His rapid rise from a mere clerk in 1357 to the highest places in Church and State in 1359 was apparently due to his business capacity as steward and lawyer. As a war minister he was not successful. His churchmanship was Erastian, and to some extent reactionary and opposed to Wycliffism. His fame rests on his two great foundations, by far the largest and richest educational establishments in England of that age, which eclipsed even the great Navarre College of Paris University, the foundation of the Queen of France and Navarre in 1304. By placing his grammar boys in a separate college at his native place, he originated a new and wider view of a great school as an independent institution instead of a mere appanage to a church. By recognising paying commoners, 'sons of noblemen,' as an integral part of the school college, and transferring the institution of prefects from the grown students to boys, incidentally, and almost by accident, he founded the English Public School system as it now exists.   [A. F. L.]

Y

YONGE, Charlotte Mary (1823-1901), writer, came of an old Devonshire family. She was born, lived, and died in Otterbourne, a hamlet of Hursley, Hants. Her father was an intimate friend of John Keble (*q.v.*), and Miss Yonge was brought into close contact with the Oxford Movement (*q.v.*). Mr. Keble prepared her for confirmation, and was always her intimate friend and guide. She began to write in early youth, and never ceased to work until her death. Her writings have influenced at least two generations. She made the idea of the Church as a great living force really a working principle in the lives of many of her readers. Throughout her quiet, almost uneventful, life she worked incessantly for the glory of God and the good of His Church. She showed in every book how intimately creed and character are intertwined; she tried to inculcate always, not by direct words but by implication, that the one thing needful 'is to find out what God requires me to do.' She had an extraordinary skill in the portraiture of characters within the bounds she fixed. The people live, they reveal themselves; and she has almost a dramatic power in the development of character, a skill in making her characters consistent with themselves. This power is shown very early in some of the simpler stories. Marian in the *Two Guardians* is a remarkable character study. She exalted the domestic virtues, and invested 'the trivial round, the common task' with an atmosphere of romance; and she had a passion for goodness, and a desire that people should use their circumstances as opportunities for the development and training of character. But she never lost sight of the possibility of calls to other than the purely domestic career. She recognised the 'religious life' as a normal development of home life, and herself became in 1868 an Exterior Sister of the Community of St.

Mary's, Wantage. She was ever alive to the claims of foreign missions. She was the biographer of the martyr bishop, John Coleridge Patteson (*q.v.*). For forty years she edited the *Monthly Packet*, a magazine which exercised a great influence in its day, and which nothing has replaced. It was redolent with the atmosphere of Hursley and the earlier Tractarians. She was an ardent lover of nature, history, astronomy, botany, and many excellent papers appeared in the *Packet* on these subjects, historical and literary, and papers on education, on ethical training, and endless tales.

Miss Yonge's work may be divided into village tales (excellent studies of village life in the 'sixties); short stories, of which the best is the *Castle Builders*; novels and family chronicles, *The Heir of Redclyffe*, *The Daisy Chain*, etc.; historical stories, *The Chaplet of Pearls*, etc.; biographies, *Life of Bishop Patteson*, etc.; religious studies, *Conversations on the Catechism*, *Bible Readings*; *Musings on 'The Christian Year*,' etc. [E. R.]

C. Coleridge, *Life and Letters*: E. Romanes, *C. M. Yonge*.

YORK, See of. That Christianity was established in the Roman city of York is proved by the presence of a bishop of York at the Council of Arles in 314. The Romano-British Church was overthrown by the English invaders, to whom Christianity came through the ministrations of Paulinus (*q.v.*). After the famous witan which met at York in 627 and declared for Christianity, Paulinus established his see at York, and extended his influence north and south. Then came the overthrow of his work. Its roots probably penetrated deeper than many think, so that King Oswald (*q.v.*) only revived and spread what had already been planted. St. Aidan (*q.v.*), his missionary bishop from Iona, worked from Lindisfarne as a base. Oswald restored the church at York, and built it of stone. In 664 York again became the seat of a bishop, first of St. Chad (*q.v.*) and then St. Wilfrid (*q.v.*). In 678 Theodore (*q.v.*) subdivided a diocese which had encroached upon Lindisfarne, Hexham, and Lindsey. In the issue the diocese of York seems to have been conterminous with Deira, a district extending from Humber to Tees. In 735 the Bishop of York became Archbishop and Primate of the Northern Province. During the Danish invasions the Church, sorely depressed, was never uprooted. About 854 the diocese of Hexham was divided between Lindisfarne and York, which now extended its boundaries beyond Tees to the Tyne (*Sim. Durh.*, ii. 101). The Archbishop of York greatly increased in prestige during the Danish occupation. With the establishment of the Lindisfarne see at Durham (*q.v.*) in 995, any authority exerted by the archbishop over the country north of Tees disappeared. At the Norman Conquest the Humber was recognised by Lanfranc as the boundary between the two provinces, saving that Nottinghamshire was included in the York diocese. Thomas, the first Norman archbishop, claimed jurisdiction over Lincoln, Lichfield, and Worcester; the claim was rejected by a national council at Windsor in 1072, but was revived during the twelfth century, Roger of Pont l'Évêque in 1175 adding a claim to Hereford. The Council of Windsor also asserted the supremacy of Canterbury over the whole of Britain, but the strife for precedence between the two archbishops continued until the fourteenth century. The Archbishop of York is from 1353 styled Primate of England. Archbishop Thomas also reorganised the cathedral and the diocese. There were probably two archdeaconries then instituted, York and Richmond. In the twelfth century archdeaconries of the East Riding (c. 1130), of Cleveland (c. 1170), and of Nottingham (c. 1174) were added. The formation of the diocese of Carlisle (*q.v.*) defined the north-western boundary of the diocese in the twelfth century. Abbeys and other religious houses now sprang up rapidly. In no other part of England did more noble buildings exist than at York, Beverley, and Ripon. From the end of the twelfth century a new strife began as the palatinate power of Durham increased, and the archbishop was often thrown into the shade. Parishes had sprung up irregularly, and often with very wide boundaries. Bede had drawn attention to this in the eighth century. In the thirteenth Archbishop Gray took vigorously in hand the subdivision of parishes. The friars and hospitals now tried to cope with the increase of population in cities. The same century saw a great increase of building and adaptation of older buildings. The *Taxatio* (*q.v.*) of Nicholas, drawn up in 1291, the year of the foundation of the new nave at York, shows the existence of the five archdeaconries mentioned above, and gives their included deaneries as follows:—(1) York 5; (2) Cleveland 3, besides Beverley and the parcels of Durham in the county; (3) East Riding 4; (4) Richmond 6; (5) Nottingham 7. The diocese suffered severely from the Scottish invasions and Black Death of the fourteenth century. Archbishop Thoresby's measures for the religious instruction of his diocese are noteworthy. In the fifteenth century the minster was completed, and in 1472 the re-dedication took place. In 1472 also St. Andrews became an archiepiscopal see, and the archbishops in consequence lost the shadowy jurisdiction which they had exer-cised in the south of Scotland. The end of the fifteenth century is marked by a series of presentments made at visitations, which exhibit 'a manifest decay of piety, of rever-ence, even of common decency in the cele-bration of divine offices.' In the parish churches there is evidence of neglect, decay, and desolation. The New Learning did not make its way in the north as in London, for instance, although some northern names can be given of those who were in sympathy with it. There was, however, no general sym-pathy with the action of the Reformation Parliament, as the Pilgrimage of Grace (q.v.) testifies, in which much simmering discontent found a vent. The rebellion in some of its stages was largely identified with the diocese of York. It led to the surrender of many large monastic houses. Their desolation marked the whole of Yorkshire, where monasteries abounded. No further rising was attempted until the Durham rising of 1569, in which the diocese of York took an emphatic share. Archbishop Holgate (q.v.) was invested by Cranmer with the pallium in evidence of the abolition of Roman jurisdiction. Next came the suppression of chantries and colleges, which left a deep mark on the diocese when Ripon, Beverley, and innumerable smaller houses came to an end or lived on in dimin-ished magnificence. In 1542 the diocese of Man (q.v.) was added to the northern province. York tolerated the Edwardine changes and gladly welcomed those of Mary. Holgate was deprived, and Heath (q.v.) was substi-tuted—a prelate of much tolerance and wise feeling. The discontent with which the Elizabethan system was regarded broke into rebellion in 1569. The last of the Elizabethan Homilies shows what was thought of it. Grindal (q.v.) helped on the reformation process, but the dislike of the papal party soon took shape in Jesuit and Seminarist missions. The new penal statutes were in-voked, and recusancy put down. The seventeenth century brought in a period of restoration. Ripon was set up again as a collegiate church. Neile led and extended a widespread reformation as he had done in Durham. Notwithstanding this, Puritanism was a great force in the cities, and when Archbishop Williams (q.v.) fled in 1643, the Parliamentary and Presbyterian cause went

forward. At York Presbyterian discipline was organised. The clergy were persecuted. Quakerism and other sectarianism flourished. The Restoration restored everything, and outwardly the monarchy and the Church were popular. Much effort was made to suppress recusancy. Archbishop Sharp (q.v.) (d. 1714) inaugurated a new epoch of diocesan energy and improvement, but no prelate of like mind arose after him for many years. A return entitled *Notitia parochialis* shows the condition of the parishes in his day. A good deal of church building went forward in the eighteenth century. Methodism laid strong hold upon the diocese after the first appearance of Wesley (q.v.) in 1742. Venn (q.v.) and Romaine were beneficed in Yorkshire, and being sympathetic with the new movement had some influence upon those of the clergy who were like-minded. The spiritual stirring of the period was con-siderable. Its effects had not died out when the great reconstruction scheme of 1836 made the over-populous diocese more manageable by the formation of the sees of Ripon (q.v.) and Manchester (q.v.). The Tractarian movement presently found many supporters in Yorkshire, two archdeacons (E. Churton and R. I. Wilberforce) being strong in their sympathy with it. Dr. Hook (q.v.), though beneficed in the diocese of Ripon, was a great force in the county generally. At Ripon, Dean Goode and Dean M'Neile opposed the spread of Tractarianism, and were looked to as leaders in the northern province. One more division of the older diocese took place in 1888, when Wakefield (q.v.) was taken out of Ripon.

In the Middle Ages the archbishops were frequently assisted by suffragan bishops, with titles taken from foreign and Irish sees. Under the Act 26 Hen. VIII. c. 14 a suffragan bishop of Berwick was consecrated in 1537, of Hull in 1538, and of Nottingham in 1567. There are now suffragan bishops of Beverley (since 1889), Hull (since 1891), and Sheffield (since 1901). The income of the see was estimated by the *Taxatio* of 1291 at £1333, 6s. 8d.; by the *Valor* of 1534 at £1609, 19s. 2d. Ecton (1711) gives the value as £1610. The present income is £10,000.

The boundaries of the mediaeval diocese of York, as defined in the eleventh and twelfth centuries, were unaltered until 1541, when the diocese of Chester (q.v.) was instituted. The large archdeaconry of Richmond, with its great extension outside Richmondshire into Lancashire, Westmorland, and South Cumberland, was then subtracted from York. In 1836 and 1847 the two new sees of Ripon and Manchester took away two fresh slices of the diocese. By Order in Council of 21st August 1837 Nottinghamshire was given to the diocese of Lincoln, and in 1878 to Southwell (*q.v.*). By an Order of 22nd December 1836 Hexhamshire was added to Durham. In 1888 the diocese of Wakefield (*q.v.*) was instituted, and York diocese was restricted in consequence to the centre and east of the county. From the mouth of the Tees a line drawn loosely to Northallerton, Wetherby, Sheffield, and the Humber will roughly contain the existing diocese, which has an acreage of 1,730,704 and a population of 1,507,383.

The four Yorkshire archdeaconries corresponded more or less to the three Ridings and Richmondshire. That of the West Riding. or York, is first mentioned 1093. that of the East Riding 1130, Cleveland 1170, Richmond 1088. The rural deaneries within them appear to have been coeval with the archdeaconries in which they were situated, and in general corresponded to the ancient wapentakes. The archdeaconry of Richmond was transferred to Chester in 1542. That of Nottingham, first mentioned 1174, was originally in York diocese, but was transferred to Lincoln 1837, and to Southwell 1884. In 1884 the archdeaconry of Sheffield was formed, four deaneries in the extreme south-west of the diocese being assigned to it. At the present time there are six hundred and sixty benefices situate within the four existing archdeaconries, and these are comprised within thirty-two deaneries.

York Minster, dedicated under the name of St. Peter (minster north of the Trent is often applied to secular churches), is a cathedral of the old foundation. It is governed by customary usage as limited by Acts of Henry VIII., William III., and George III. The great officers of the chapter are, besides the dean, the precentor, the chancellor, the sub-dean, and the succentor —all mediæval dignities, now usually attached to the four residentiary canonries. There are also twenty-eight prebendaries. The vicars-choral are an ancient corporation dating from the thirteenth century. The canonries are in the gift of the archbishop. The dean and chapter are patrons of twenty-three benefices, of which five are situate within the city of York.

BISHOPS OF YORK

1. Paulinus (*q.v.*), 627 ; fled before the pagan invasion, 633 ; the see collapsed until

2. Ceadda, or St. Chad (*q.v.*), 664.
3. St. Wilfrid (*q.v.*), 664, who had been chosen to reconstitute the fallen see ; he went to Gaul for consecration, and found St. Chad in occupation on his return, 667 ; St. Chad retired, and St. Wilfrid held the see until 678.
4. Bosa, 678 ; cons. by Theodore over the contracted see of York ; d. 705.
5. John of Beverley, 705 ; Bishop of Hexham ; res. 718.
6. Wilfrid II., 718 ; res. 732.
7. Egbert. 734 ; of royal lineage ; correspondent of Bede.

ARCHBISHOPS OF YORK

7. Egbert, 735 ; received the pall, and became Archbishop of York and Primate of the Northern Province ; founded the school of York ; d. 766.
8. Aethelberht, or Coena, 767 ; rebuilt the cathedral ; d. 780.
9. Eanbald, 780 ; d. 796.
10. Eanbald II., 796.
11. Wulfsige, 812 ? The invasions of the Danes obscure the history.
12. Wigmund, c. 837.
13. Wulfhere, 854 ; d. 900.
14. Aethelbald, 900.
15. Rodewald, c. 928.
16. Wulfstan, c. 931 ; appointed by Athelstan ; sided with the Danes ; tr. to Dorchester.
17. Oskytel, 956 ; tr. from Dorchester ; a Dane contemporary with the Danish Odo of Canterbury ; d. 971.
18. Oswald, 972 ; Bishop of Worcester ; retained his former see ; introduced Benedictine reformation ; d. 992.
19. Adulf, 992 ; Abbot of Peterborough ; also held the see of Worcester ; d. 1002.
20. Wulfstan II., 1003 ; also held the see of Worcester ; d. 1023.
21. Aelfric, 1023 ; d. 1051.
22. Kinsige, 1051 ; chaplain of Edward the Confessor ; d. 1060.
23. Ealdred (*q.v.*), 1061 ; also held the see of Worcester, but compelled by Pope Nicholas II. to resign it ; d. 1069.
24. Thomas, 1070 ; a Canon of Bayeux ; controversy with Canterbury, Worcester, Lincoln ; reconstructed York Minster.
25. Gerard, 1101 ; tr. from Hereford ; strife with Canterbury renewed.
26. Thomas II., 1109.
27. Thurstan, 1119 ; Canon of St. Paul's ; great patron of the Cistercian revival ; leader at the Battle of the Standard ; res. 1140.

28. William Fitz-Herbert, 1143; Treasurer of York; appointed after a dispute; Henry de Coilli, Stephen's nephew, was first elected, but the Pope refused to confirm; d. 1154. Canonised as St. William of York in thirteenth century. In 1147 Fitz-Herbert was superseded by

29. Henry Murdac, 1147 (P.); Abbot of Fountains; cons. by Pope, and superseded William, who was restored, 1153.

30. Roger of Pont l'Evêque, 1154; took the King's side against Becket; the Canterbury dispute settled; built Ripon Minster: d. 1181. See vacant ten years.

31. Geoffrey Plantagenet, 1191; natural son of Henry II.; had held the see of Lincoln without consecration, 1173-82; cons. to York, 1191; feuds with Puiset of Durham and with his own chapter; retired to Normandy, 1207; d. 1212. More than four years' vacancy.

32. Walter Gray, 1216; tr. (P.) from Worcester; appointed by Pope to supersede the chapter's nominee; a prelate of great distinction; translated St. Wilfrid at Ripon; great patron of York Minster; d. 1255.

33. Sewall de Bovill, 1256; Dean of York; d. 1258.

34. Godfrey de Ludham, 1258; Dean of York; d. 1265.

35. Walter Giffard, 1266 (P.); reformed monasteries; d. 1279.

36. William Wickwane, 1279; Chancellor of York; a builder of churches; res. 1285.

37. John Romanus, 1286; Canon of York; began new nave of York Minster and chapter-house; d. 1296.

38. Henry Newark, 1298; Dean of York; d. 1299.

39. Thomas Corbridge, 1300; Canon of York; d. 1304.

40. William Greenfield, 1306; Dean of Chichester and Chancellor of England; d. 1315.

41. William de Melton, 1317; Prebendary of Lincoln; Canon of York; Provost of Beverley; an important prelate; much occupied in Scottish politics; completed the nave at York; d. 1340.

42. William de la Zouche, 1340 (P.); cons. by Clement VI. at Avignon, 1342; Dean of York; leader in the battle of Neville's Cross, 1346; began the Zouche Chapel at York; d. 1352.

43. John Thoresby, 1352; tr. (P.) from Worcester; cardinal; a prelate of great zeal and munificence; final settlement of the Canterbury dispute; built the Lady Chapel; d. 1373.

44. Alexander Neville, 1374 (P.); Canon of York and Archdeacon of Durham; an adherent of Richard II.; hence his exile and translation (P.) to St. Andrews; retired to Louvain; d. 1392.

45. Thomas Arundel, 1388; tr. (P.) from Ely; tr. to Canterbury, 1396; the first northern primate so translated.

46. Robert Waldby, 1396; tr. (P.) from Chichester; an opponent of the Wycliffites; d. 1398.

47. Richard Scrope (q.v.), 1397; tr. (P.) from Coventry and Lichfield; d. 1405.

48. Henry Bowet, 1407; tr. (P.) from Bath and Wells after two disputed elections; d. 1423.

49. John Kemp, 1426; tr. (P.) from London after chapter election of Philip Morgan, Bishop of Worcester, rejected by the Pope, and papal provision of Fleming, Bishop of Lincoln, rejected by the council; Cardinal; tr. to Canterbury, 1452.

50. William Booth, 1452; tr. (P.) from Coventry and Lichfield; d. 1464.

51. George Neville, 1465; tr. (P.) from Exeter; brother of Warwick the Kingmaker; resisted erection of St. Andrews as an archiepiscopal see; d. 1476.

52. Laurence Booth, 1476; tr. (P.) from Durham; brother of William; d. 1480.

53. Thomas Rotherham, 1480; tr. (P.) from Lincoln; Chancellor of England; d. 1500.

54. Thomas Savage, 1501; tr. (P.) from London; d. 1507.

55. Christopher Bainbridge, 1508; tr. (P.) from Durham; Cardinal, 1511; poisoned at Rome, 1514.

56. Thomas Wolsey (q.v.), 1514; tr. (P.) from Lincoln; did not enter the diocese until after his fall; held Durham, and then Winchester, with York; d. 1530.

57. Edward Lee, 1531 (P.); Canon of York; Chancellor of Salisbury; the King's Almoner; a man of learning, but opposed to the New Learning; d. 1544.

58. Robert Holdegate, or Holgate (q.v.), 1545; tr. from Llandaff; depr. 1554.

59. Nicholas Heath (q.v.), 1555; tr. from Worcester; depr. 1559.
William May (q.v.), elected August 8, 1560; died same day.

60. Thomas Young, 1561; tr. from St. David's; President of the Council of the North; d. 1568.

61. Edmund Grindal (q.v.), 1571; tr. from London; tr. to Canterbury, 1576.

62. Edwin Sandys, 1577; tr. from London;

less Puritan than Grindal ; proposed a college for Ripon ; d. 1588.

63. John Piers, 1589 ; tr. from Salisbury ; a prelate of great learning ; d. 1594.

64. Matthew Hutton, 1595 ; tr. from Durham ; President of the Council of the North ; d. 1606.

65. Tobias Matthew, 1606 ; tr. from Durham ; a great preacher ; d. 1628.

66. George Monteigne, 1628 ; tr. from Durham ; d. 1628.

67. Samuel Harsnett, 1628 ; tr. from Norwich ; friend of Laud and upholder of ' Arminian ' reformation ; d. 1631.

68. Richard Neile, 1632 ; tr. from Winchester ; carried out Laud's policy ; d. 1640.

69. John Williams (*q.v.*), 1641 ; tr. from Lincoln ; d. 1650.

70. Accepted Frewen, 1660 ; tr. from Coventry and Lichfield ; d. 1664.

71. Richard Sterne, 1664 ; tr. from Carlisle ; d. 1683.

72. John Dolben, 1683 ; tr. from Rochester ; d. 1686. A vacancy followed.

73. Thomas Lamplugh, 1688 ; tr. from Exeter ; d. 1691.

74. John Sharpe, 1691 (*q.v.*) ; d. 1714.

75. Sir William Dawes, Bart., 1714 ; tr. from Chester ; scholar and preacher ; chaplain to William III. and Anne ; as Rector of Bocking established monthly celebrations of Holy Communion ; an active and able bishop ; d. 1724.

76. Launcelot Blackburn, 1724 ; tr. from Exeter ; a moderate and quiet prelate ; d. 1743.

77. Thomas Herring, 1743 ; tr. from Bangor ; Latitudinarian ; tr. to Canterbury, 1747.

78. Matthew Hutton II., 1747 ; tr. from Bangor ; lineal descendant of his namesake ; of the same school as Herring ; tr. to Canterbury, 1757.

79. John Gilbert, 1757 ; tr. from Salisbury ; an infirm archbishop ; d. 1761.

80. Honble. Robert Hay Drummond, 1761 ; tr. from Salisbury ; a man of parts and of aristocratic connection ; built extensively at Bishopthorpe ; d. 1776.

81. William Markham, 1777 ; tr. from Chester ; a considerable Latin scholar and Dean of Christ Church, Oxford ; a man of magnificent presence ; d. 1807.

82. Edward Venables Vernon, 1807 ; tr. from Carlisle ; an eloquent speaker ; took the name of Harcourt, 1831 ; d. 1847.

83. Thomas Musgrave, 1847 ; tr. from Hereford ; a prelate of much practical ability ; a strong Evangelical ; opposed revival of Convocation ; d. 1860.

84. Charles Thomas Longley, 1860 ; tr. from Durham ; tr. to Canterbury, 1862.

85. William Thomson, 1862 ; tr. from Gloucester and Bristol ; Provost of Queen's College, Oxford ; gained the interest of the industrial population of the north ; d. 1890.

86. William Connor Magee (*q.v.*), 1891 ; tr. from Peterborough ; d. 1891.

87. William Dalrymple Maclagan, 1891 ; tr. from Lichfield ; officer in Madras Cavalry, 1846-9 ; ordained, 1856 ; Vicar of Kensington, 1875-8 ; res. 1908 ; d. 1910.

88. Cosmo Gordon Lang, 1909 ; tr. from Stepney, to which he was consecrated 1901. [H. G.]

V.C.H., Yorkshire, ii. ; Ornsby, *Dio. Hist.*

INDEX

Bridges, John .	*see* Oxford, See of.
Briefs	Bulls, Papal.
British and Foreign Bible Society . . .	Evangelicals ; Nonconformity, v.
Broad Church .	Church, High, Low, Broad.
Brotherhoods .	Religious Orders.
Browne, Robert	Nonconformity, 111. ; Toleration.
Burghersh, Henry . . .	Lincoln.
Bush, Paul . .	Bristol.
Byrd, William .	Music : Musicians ; Plainsong.
Byrom, John. .	Nonjurors ; Poetry.
Caedmon . . .	Aldhelm : Bible ; Hilda.
Calamy . . .	Savoy Conference.
Canons (of Cathedral Churches) . .	Abbeys : Chapters ; Religious Orders.
Cantilupe, St. Thomas . .	Hereford.
Cantilupe, Walter . .	Worcester.
Carey, William .	Nonconformity, iv.
Carmelites . .	Friars.
Carte, Thomas .	Nonjurors.
Carthusians . .	Abbeys ; Hugh ; Religious Orders.
Cartwright, William . .	Nonjurors.
Cassock . . .	Dress of the Clergy.
Catechism, Church . . .	Common Prayer, Book of : Hampton Court Conference ; Nowell.
Cathedral Chapters	Chapters.
Cathedrals Commission . .	Commissions, Royal.
Cathedratica . .	Synodals.
Celibacy . . .	Marriage of the Clergy.
Chancellor . .	Chapters, Cathedral ; Courts.
Channel Isles .	Rural Deans : Salisbury ; Winchester.
Charitable Trusts . . .	Mortmain.
Charity Schools	Education ; Jones, Griffith ; Societies for Reformation of Manners.
Charles II. . .	Evelyn ; Juxon ; Ken : Popish Plot ; Reunion (1).
Charles, Thomas	Llandaff ; Nonconformity. v.
Chasuble . . .	Ornaments Rubric : Smart ; Vestments.
Cherry, Francis	Nonjurors.
Cheyney, Richard . . .	Bristol.
Chimere . . .	Dress of the Clergy.
Chubb, Thomas	Deists.
Church Association	Evangelicals : Societies, Ecclesiastical.
Church Congress . . .	Councils.

Church Discipline Act . . .	*see* Courts.
Churchmen's Union . . .	Societies, Ecclesiastical.
Church Missionary Society .	Evangelicals ; Missions, Foreign ; Venn, John.
Church Pastoral Aid Society .	Evangelicals.
Churchwardens .	Discipline : Parish.
Cistercians . .	Abbeys ; Architecture : Religious Orders ; Tithe.
Clapham Sect .	Evangelicals ; Venn, Henry ; Wilberforce, W.
Clapton Sect .	Watson, Joshua.
Clarendon Code .	Puritanism ; Toleration.
Clarke, Samuel .	Butler ; Latitudinarians ; Nonconformity, ii.
Clerical and Lay Union . . .	Societies, Ecclesiastical.
Clerical Disabilities Act . . .	Parliament, Clergy in.
Clerical Dress .	Dress of the Clergy.
Clerical Subscription . .	Commissions, Royal.
Clergy Discipline Act	Courts (Church Courts in modern times).
Clerks, Parish .	Archdeacon.
Cluniacs . . .	Abbeys ; Religious Orders.
Coke, Sir Edward	Bancroft ; High Commission.
Coke, Thomas .	Nonconformity, v ; Wesley, J. and C.
Collectar . .	Sarum Use.
Collins, Anthony	Deists.
Colman . .	Durham.
Colonial and Continental Church Society . . .	Evangelicals ; Missions, Foreign.
Colonies, Church in	Bray, Dr. ; Missions, Foreign.
Columba, St. .	Missions, Foreign ; Oswald.
Compton, Henry	London : Societies, Religious.
Communities .	Religious Orders, Modern.
Concilia Magnae Britanniae . .	Wilkins, David.
Confession of Sin	Discipline.
Congregationalists . . .	Nonconformity, iii.
Constantinople, Chaplains at .	Reunion (2).
Cope	Ornaments Rubric : Ritual Cases ; Smart ; Vestments.
Cornwallis, Frederick	Canterbury : Latitudinarians.
Corpus Iuris Canonici . .	Canon Law to 1534.
Courtenay, W. .	Canterbury.
Coventry, See of	Lichfield.
Courayer, P. F. le	Ordinations, Anglican : Reunion (1).
Cowley. Society of St. John the Evangelist . .	Religious Orders, Modern.
Cowper, William	Evangelicals ; Hymns.
Cox, Richard .	Ely ; Marian Exiles : Westminster.

Losinga, Herbert . . .	*see* Norwich.	
Low Church . .	Church, High, Low, Broad ; Evangelicals.	
Lucar, Cyril . .	Reunion (2).	
Lucius, King	British Church.	
Lupus, St. .	British Church.	
Lutheranism . .	Articles of Religion ; Bucer ; Reformation ; Reunion (3).	
Lux Mundi . .	Convocation ; Denison ; Liddon.	
Lyra Apostolica	Poetry.	
Magdalen College, Oxford .	Waynflete, William.	
Malmesbury .	Aldhelm ; Salisbury.	
Maniple . .	Vestments.	
Manual . . .	Sarum Use.	
Marvell, Andrew	Parker, S. ; Poetry.	
Mass	Common Prayer, Book of ; Holy Eucharist ; Services, Church.	
Matthew, Thos.	Rogers, John.	
Mawman, Timothy	Nonjurors.	
Mennonites . .	Nonconformity, IV.	
Merbecke, John	Music ; Musicians ; Plainsong.	
Methodism . .	Nonconformity, V.	
Mildmay Deaconesses .	Evangelicals ; Religious Orders, Modern.	
Millenary, Petition . . .	Cartwright, T. (?1535-1603) ; Common Prayer, Book of ; Puritanism.	
Milner, Isaac .	Evangelicals.	
Miracle Plays .	Drama.	
Missal	Common Prayer, Book of ; Sarum Use.	
Moberly, George	Keble ; Salisbury.	
Monk, W. H. .	Musicians.	
Monks	Religious Orders.	
Moral Plays . .	Drama.	
Moravian Church . .	Nonconformity, V. ; Reunion (3) ; Wesley, J. and C. ; Wilson, T.	
More, Henry .	Cambridge Platonists.	
Mountague, Rich.	Arminianism ; Caroline Divines ; Charles I. ; Norwich ; Reunion (1).	
Nag's Head Fable . .	Ordinations, Anglican ; Parker, Matthew.	
National Society	Education.	
Nayler, James .	Nonconformity, VI.	
Necessary Doctrine, etc. . .	Cranmer.	
New Learning .	Colet ; Fisher ; More, Sir T. ; Reformation.	
Newmarsh, Timothy	Nonjurors.	
Newton, John .	Evangelicals ; Hymns ; More, Hannah ; Poetry.	
Nigel of Ely . .	Ely ; Roger le Poer.	
Non-Usagers .	Nonjurors.	
Norris, John . .	Cambridge Platonists.	

Nun of Kent . .	*see* Cranmer ; Fisher ; More, Sir T.	
Nunneries . .	Religious Orders.	
Oates, Titus . .	Popish Plot.	
O'Bryan, Wm. . .	Nonconformity, V.	
Observants . .	Friars ; Henry VIII.	
Offa	Lichfield ; St. Albans, Abbey of.	
Oldcastle, Sir John . . .	Heresy ; Holy Eucharist ; Lollards.	
Old Catholics .	Reunion (3).	
Olney Hymns .	Evangelicals ; Hymns.	
Order of Corporate Reunion .	Reunion (1).	
Otho (Otto) and Othobon (Ottobuoni) . . .	Canon Law to 1534 ; Legates ; Papacy.	
Pan-Anglican Conference .	Councils.	
Paris, Matthew	St. Albans, Abbey of.	
Parish Clerks .	Archdeacon.	
Pelagius . . .	British Church.	
Penal Laws . .	Nonconformity ; Roman Catholics ; Toleration.	
Penance . . .	Discipline.	
Penn, William .	Mystics ; Nonconformity, VI.	
Penry, John . .	Marprelate Controversy ; Nonconformity, III. ; St. David's.	
Peto, William .	Pole.	
Philadelphian Society . . .	Mystics.	
Playford, John .	Music.	
Pontifical . . .	Sarum Use.	
Poor, Richard le	Salisbury ; Sarum Use.	
Portos	Sarum Use.	
Porteous, Beilby	London ; More, Hannah ; Societies for Reformation of Manners.	
Præmunientes, Clause . . .	Parliament, Clergy in.	
Prayer Book . .	Common Prayer, Book of.	
Prebendaries .	Chapters, Cathedral.	
Precentor . . .	Chapters, Cathedral ; Religious Orders.	
Predestination .	Calvinism ; Evangelicals ; Nonconformity, IV. ; Toplady.	
Premonstratensians . .	Abbeys ; Peculiars ; Religious Orders.	
Presbyterianism	Bancroft ; Cartwright, T. (?1535-1603) ; Nonconformity, I.	
Price, Kenrick .	Nonjurors.	
Primitive Methodists . . .	Nonconformity, V.	
Privy Council .	Courts ; Ritual Cases.	
Processional . .	Common Prayer, Book of ; Sarum Use ; Services, Church.	
Prohibition . .	Courts.	
Protectorate, Church under .	Commonwealth ; Ussher.	
Prophesyings .	Elizabeth ; Grindal.	

Printed by T. and A. Constable, Printers to His Majesty
at the Edinburgh University Press

ImTheStory.com

Personalized Classic Books in many genre's

Unique gift for kids, partners, friends, colleagues

Customize:

- Character Names
- Upload your own front/back cover images (optional)
- Inscribe a personal message/dedication on the
  inside page (optional)

Customize many titles Including
- Alice in Wonderland
- Romeo and Juliet
- The Wizard of Oz
- A Christmas Carol
- Dracula
- Dr. Jekyll & Mr. Hyde
- And more...

Emily's Adventures in Wonderland

Ryan & Julia

CPSIA information can be obtained at www.ICGtesting.com
Printed in the USA
LVOW08s1536291014

411074LV00002B/345/P

9 781407 675152